SSC CHSL

COMBINED HIGHER SECONDARY LEVEL (10+2)

2025 (TIER I)

Coverage of All 36 Sets
*Exam Held From **1 to 11 July 2024***

HIGHER SCORE GUARANTEED

36 SOLVED PAPERS

3600 TCS MCQs

Authors
Sushil Singh, Sanjeev Dixit
Deepali, Pradeep Srivastava

SSC CHSL

COMBINED HIGHER SECONDARY LEVEL (10+2)

2025 (TIER I)

36 SOLVED PAPERS

3600 TCS MCQs

With 100% Detailed Explanation/ Solution

ISBN 978-93-6437-716-4

Arihant Publications (India) Limited

Published by Arihant Publications (India) Ltd.
For further information about the books published by Arihant, log on to www.arihantbooks.com or e-mail at info@arihantbooks.com

Follow us on...   

Administrative Offices

Regd. Office
'Ramchhaya' 4577/15,
Agarwal Road, Darya Ganj,
New Delhi -110002
Tele: 011- 47630600, 43518550

Head Office
Kalindi, TP Nagar, Meerut (UP)
250002, Tel: 0121-7156203, 7156204

Sales & Support Offices

Agra, Ahmedabad, Bengaluru, Bareilly, Chennai, Delhi, Guwahati, Hyderabad, Jaipur, Jhansi, Kolkata, Lucknow, Nagpur & Pune.

PO No : TXT-59-T065735-06-25

PRICE ₹ 415.00

Search Index

Coverage of All 36 Sets Exam
Held on 1st July to 11th July, 2024

SSC Cutoff 2023-24 Exams

Exam	Tier	Year	SC	ST	EWS	OBC	UR	ESM
SSC CGL	TIER I	2024	126.45554	111.8893	142.01963	146.26291	153.18981	69.92674
		2023	126.68201	118.16655	143.44441	145.93743	150.04936	100.29326
	TIER II	2024	285.45	266.49	300.03	306.27	322.77	202.28
		2023	252	241	265	271	287	223
SSC CHSL	TIER I	2024	139.68408	129.44568	150.51731	156.61665	157.36168	78.23008
		2023	136.41166	124.52592	151.09782	152.26953	153.91142	102.47651
	TIER II	2024	89.8581	82.6568	111.4352	113.50911	119.80335	40.07024
		2023	79.3189	78.13852	103.97465	102.9603	115.04762	40
SSC CPO	Grade C	2024	-	-	-	-	-	-
		2023	136.08122	128.04746	-	145.03097	147.45086	147.45086
SSC STENO	Grade D	2024	-	-	-	-	-	-
		2023	109.41004	88.71217	40.15035	125.02167	131.32184	126.29805
SSC GD	Tier I	2024	148.21914	143.65896	151.15627	152.28771	153.56851	94.65261
		2023	129.75	126.45	139.16	140.75	142.03	75.01

SSC CHSL Tier I
Exam Pattern & Strategy

01

Know About Exam Pattern

In order to crack any exam, you must know the pattern and syllabus of the exam. You must go through the SSC CHSL previous year papers to analyze the complete syllabus, pattern and to know the weightage of each topic.

Make a Study Plan

In order to get success in SSC CHSL exam, you need to make a proper study plan which should be based on latest syllabus as well as pattern. Plan to go through each and every topic of the SSC CHSL syllabus but make sure that you don't waste time in reading futile preparation material.

03

Time Management

Time management is a key to success in any exam. You may come across many students who have been preparing for many exams for a long time but they are unable to achieve positive results. One of the reasons can be the lack of proper time management. You should allot time subject as well as topic wise and implement it pin–pointedly.

04

Command on Your Basics

While starting your preparation, don't look for shortcuts, instead try to know the basics of all subjects and grab the knowledge in depth. Once you have command over these topics, you can switch to shortcuts or tricks for quick calculations.

05

Take Online Mock Test Series

To get an idea about the online exam, mock tests are the best. They will help you boost your speed. This applies to both categories of aspirants who have just started their preparation and also those who have been preparing since long time. Speed and accuracy are the key points that all competitive exams seek for. Allot your last 20 to 25 days to take as many mock tests as you can.

06

Prepare Study Notes

While preparing for the exam, preparing study notes is very important. Good notes will help the candidates to develop understanding and also identifying the important content and topics. Making study notes increases the chances of success.

Some benefits of making study notes are given below

- It improves your focus and attention.
- It helps in comprehension and retention of the topic.
- It promotes active learning.
- It improves your organisational skills.

07

Revision

Revision is an essential part of exam preparation. It helps you understand the key points of a subject and also test your memory. It is almost hard to memorise everything after one reading. Candidates should develop the habit of revising the study materials to review essential facts. It will help in preparation during study hours. The review enhances accuracy and speed, resulting in improved results.

08

Priorization of the Topics

This is the one leading cause that sets your performance apart from others. e.g. there are at least one or two topics that don't bother an aspirant at all. Judging providently, concentrate more on the topics you are not so good at or which bag your attention the most. The rest of the story ends up with consistency in solving maximum questions, revising the topics and repeating the practice with Daily Quizzes, Mock Tests, Online Test Series and Practice Sets.

09

Refer Only one Source for Study

Many of you think that if you follow more than one book or study material, then you can cover the topics in depth. This is all myth. If you use more than one book, you are more likely to get confused. So you should refer only one source for study. It makes your chances high to clear SSC CHSL Exam.

10

Trust Yourself

Never give up hope or feel defeated and trust yourself. Always be determined that you have to crack SSC CHSL this time. This will make you stay motivated as well as energized and you will definitely crack SSC CHSL exam by practicing all above ideas in your study routine.

SSC CHSL Tier I & II
Exam Pattern & Syllabus

- Tier-I will consist of Objective Type, Multiple choice questions. The questions will be set both in English & Hindi except for English Comprehension.
- There will be negative marking of 0.50 for each wrong answer.

Scheme of Tier-I Examination

Tier	Subject	Number of Ques.	Maximum Marks	Time allowed
I.	A. General Intelligence and Reasoning	25	50	1 hour (1 hour and 20 minutes for the candidates eligible for scribe as per Para 7.1, 7.2 and 7.3)
	B. General Awareness	25	50	
	C. Quantitative Aptitude	25	50	
	D. English Comprehension	25	50	

Scheme of Tier-II Examination

Tier	Paper	Session	Subject	Number of Questions	Maximum Marks	Time allowed
II	Paper-I	**Session-I :** **(2 hours and 15 minutes)**	**Section-I :** **Module-I :** Mathematical Abilities **Module-II :** Reasoning and General Intelligence.	30 30 Total = 60	60*3 = 180	1 hour (for each section)
			Section-II : **Module-I :** English Language and Comprehension **Module-II :** General Awareness	40 20 Total = 60	60*3 = 280	(1 hours and 20 minutes for the candidates eligible for scribe as per Para-8.1 and 8.2)
			Section-III : **Module-I :** Computer Knowledge Test	15	15*3 = 45	15 Minutes (20 minutes for the candidates eligible for scribe as per Para-8.1 and 8.2)
		Session-II : (15 minutes)	**Section-III :** Module-II : Skill test/Typing	Part A : Skill test for DEOs	-	15 Minutes (20 minutes for the candidates eligible for scribe as per Para-8.1 and 8.2)
				Part B : Typing Test for LDC/ JSA.		10 Minutes (15 minutes for the candidates eligible for scribe as per Para-8.1 and 8.2)

Syllabus (Tier I)

1. English Language

Spot the Error, Fill in the Blanks, Synonyms/ Homonyms, Antonyms, Spellings/ Detecting mis-spelt words, Idioms & Phrases, One word substitution, Improvement of Sentences, Active/ Passive Voice of Verbs, Conversion into Direct/ Indirect narration, Shuffling of Sentence parts, Shuffling of Sentences in a passage, Cloze Passage, Comprehension Passage.

2. General Intelligence

It would include questions of both verbal and non-verbal type. The test will include questions on Semantic Analogy, Symbolic operations, Symbolic/ Number Analogy, Trends, Figural Analogy, Space Orientation, Semantic Classification, Venn Diagrams, Symbolic/ Number Classification, Drawing inferences, Figural Classification, Punched hole/ pattern-folding & unfolding, Semantic Series, Figural Pattern-folding and completion, Number Series, Embedded figures, Figural Series, Critical Thinking, Problem Solving, Emotional Intelligence, Word Building, Social Intelligence, Coding and de-coding, Numerical operations, Other sub-topics, if any.

3. Quantitative Aptitude

Number Systems: Computation of Whole Number, Decimal and Fractions, Relationship between numbers.

Fundamental arithmetical operations: Percentages, Ratio and Proportion, Square roots, Averages, Interest (Simple and Compound), Profit and Loss, Discount, Partnership Business, Mixture and Allegation, Time and distance, Time and work.

Algebra: Basic algebraic identities of School Algebra and Elementary surds (simple problems) and Graphs of Linear Equations.

Geometry: Familiarity with elementary geometric figures and facts: Triangle and its various kinds of centres, Congruence and similarity of triangles, Circle and its chords, tangents, angles subtended by chords of a circle, common tangents to two or more circles.

Mensuration: Triangle, Quadrilaterals, Regular Polygons, Circle, Right Prism, Right Circular Cone, Right Circular Cylinder, Sphere, Hemispheres, Rectangular Parallelepiped, Regular Right Pyramid with triangular or square Base.

Trigonometry: Trigonometry, Trigonometric ratios, Complementary angles, Height and distances (simple problems only) Standard Identities like sin2q + cos 2q =1 etc.

Statistical Charts: Use of Tables and Graphs: Histogram, Frequency polygon, Bar diagram, Pie-chart.

General Awareness

Questions are designed to test the candidate's general awareness of the environment around him and its application to society. Questions are also designed to test knowledge of current events and of such matters of everyday observation and experience in their scientific aspect as may be expected of an educated person.

The test will also include questions relating to India and its neighboring countries especially pertaining to History, Culture, Geography, Economic Scene, General policy and scientific research.

Syllabus (Tier II)

Module-I of Section-I (Mathematical Abilities)

Number Systems: Computation of Whole Number, Decimal and Fractions, Relationship between numbers.

Fundamental arithmetical operations: Percentage, Ratio and Proportion, Square roots, Averages, Interest (Simple and Compound), Profit and Loss, Discount, Partnership Business, Mixture and Alligation, Time and distance, Time and work.

Algebra: Basic algebraic identities of School Algebra and Elementary surds (simple problems) and Graphs of Linear Equations.

Geometry: Familiarity with elementary geometric figures and facts: Triangle and its various kinds of centres, Congruence and similarity of triangles, Circle and its chords, tangents, angles subtended by chords of a circle, common tangents to two or more circles.

Mensuration: Triangle, Quadrilaterals, Regular Polygons, Circle, Right Prism, Right Circular Cone, Right Circular Cylinder, Sphere, Hemispheres, Rectangular Parallelepiped, Regular Right Pyramid with triangular or square Base.

Trigonometry: Trigonometry, Trigonometric ratios, Complementary angles, Height and distances (simple problems only) Standard Identities like sin2q + Cos2q = 1 etc.

Statistics and probability: Use of Tables and Graphs: Histogram, Frequency polygon, Bar-diagram, Pie-chart; Measures of central tendency: mean, median, mode, standard deviation; calculation of simple probabilities.

Module-II of Section-I (Reasoning and General Intelligence)

Questions of both verbal and non-verbal type. These will include questions on Semantic Analogy, Symbolic operations, Symbolic/Number Analogy, Trends, Figural Analogy, Space Orientation, Semantic Classification, Venn Diagrams, Symbolic/Number Classification, Drawing inferences, Figural Classification, Punched hole/pattern-folding & unfolding, Semantic Series. Figural Pattern-folding and completion, Number Series, Embedded Figures, Figural Series, Critical Thinking, Problem Solving, Emotional Intelligence, Word Building, Social Intelligence, Coding and de-coding, Numerical operations, Other sub - topics, if any.

Module-I of Section-II (English Language and Comprehension)

Vocabulary, grammar, sentence structure, synonyms, antonyms and their correct usage; Spot the Error, Fill in the Blanks, Synonyms/ Homonyms, Antonyms, Spellings/ Detecting mis-spelt words, Idioms & Phrases, One word substitution, Improvement of Sentences, Active/ Passive Voice of Verbs, Conversion into Direct/Indirect narration, Shuffling of Sentence parts, Shuffling of Sentences in a passage, Cloze Passage, Comprehension Passage. To test comprehension, two or more paragraphs will be given and questions based on those will be asked. Atleast one paragraph should be a simple one based on a book or a story and the other paragraph should be based on current affairs editorial or a report.

Module-II of Section-II (General Awareness)

Questions are designed to test the candidates' general awareness of the environment around them and its application to society. Questions are also designed to test knowledge of current events and of such matters of everyday observation and experience in their scientific aspect as may be expected of an educated person. The test will also include questions relating to India and its neighboring countries especially pertaining to History, Culture, Geography, Economic Scene, General policy and scientific research.

Module-I of Section-III of Paper-I (Computer Proficiency)

Computer Basics: Organization of a computer, Central Processing Unit (CPU), input/ output devices, computer memory, memory organization, back-up devices PORTs, Windows Explorer, Keyboard shortcuts.

Software: Windows Operating system including basics of Microsoft Office like MS word, MS Excel and Power Point etc.

Working with Internet and E-mails: Web Browsing & Searching. Downloading & Uploading, Managing an E-mail Account, E-Banking.

Basics of Networking and Cyber security: Network devices and protocols, Network and Information Security threats (like hacking, virus, worms, Trojan etc.) and preventive measures.

The Indispensable Role of PYQs *in SSC Exam Success*

The Previous Year Question Papers (PYQs) hold immense importance for candidates preparing for the Staff Selection Commission (SSC) exams. Here's a breakdown of their significance:

01 Understanding Exam Pattern and Syllabus

- **Familiarisation:** PYQs provide a clear understanding of the exam pattern, including the number of sections, types of questions asked, marking scheme and time duration.
- **Syllabus Insights:** By analysing PYQs, candidates can identify frequently asked topics and the weightage given to different sections of the syllabus. This helps in prioritising their studies.

02 Assessing Difficulty Level

- **Gauge Preparation:** Solving PYQs helps candidates assess the difficulty level of the actual exam. This allows them to understand the level of preparation required to crack the exam.
- **Identify Trends:** Regular practice with PYQs helps in identifying any changes in the difficulty level over the years.

03 Identifying Important Topics

- **Focus on Repetition:** SSC often repeats concepts and question patterns. By solving PYQs, candidates can identify frequently asked topics and focus more on them.
- **Strategic Study:** This knowledge enables candidates to channel their efforts in the right direction, maximising their chances of scoring well.

04 Improving Time Management and Accuracy

- **Simulate Exam Conditions:** Solving PYQs within the stipulated time frame helps candidates develop effective time management skills.
- **Enhance Speed and Accuracy:** Regular practice improves both speed and accuracy in solving questions, which is crucial for competitive exams like SSC.

05 Boosting Confidence and Reducing Exam Anxiety

- **Familiarity Breeds Confidence:** Solving PYQs creates a sense of familiarity with the actual exam, reducing anxiety and boosting confidence.
- **Performance Evaluation:** It allows candidates to track their progress and identify their strengths and weaknesses.

06 Understanding Question Framing

- **SSC's Perspective:** PYQs provide insights into how the SSC frames questions, the language used and the common tricks employed.
- **Effective Problem-Solving:** This understanding helps candidates approach questions more strategically and avoid common pitfalls.

In conclusion, Previous Year Question Papers are not just practice material; they are a crucial tool for strategic preparation, offering insights into the exam pattern, syllabus, difficulty level and question trends. Consistent practice with PYQs is indispensable for success in SSC exams like CGL and CHSL.

Ranker's Tips for
SSC CHSL Exam

Time-Saving Techniques for SSC MTS

1. **Prioritize High-Weightage Topics** Focus on topics that frequently appear in exams. For Quantitative Aptitude, concentrate on:
   - **Arithmetic:** Simplification, Percentages, Profit & Loss, Time & Work
   - **Algebra:** Quadratic Equations, Linear Equations
   - **Data Interpretation:** Bar Graphs, Pie Charts, Tables

   For General Awareness, emphasize:
   - **Current Affairs:** Last 6 months
   - **Static GK:** Important dates, events, and facts
2. **Practice Mock Tests and Previous Year Papers**
   Regularly solve mock tests and previous year papers to familiarize yourself with the exam pattern and improve speed. This practice helps in time management and identifying frequently asked questions.
3. **Use the "Skip & Return" Strategy**
   If a question seems time-consuming or difficult, skip it and move on to the next. Return to it later if time permits. This ensures you don't waste time on a single question.
4. **Master Mental Math**
   Enhance your mental calculation skills to solve arithmetic problems quickly without relying on a calculator. Practice basic operations like addition, subtraction, multiplication and division to improve speed.

Last-Minute Tricks and Shortcuts

1. **Quantitative Aptitude Shortcuts**
   - **Simplification:** Use approximation techniques to quickly estimate answers.
   - **Percentages:** Convert percentages to fractions for easier calculations.
   - **Speed, Time & Distance:** Memorize key formulas and units to quickly solve related problems.
2. **Reasoning Shortcuts**
   - **Blood Relations:** Use symbols to represent family relations for quicker analysis.
   - **Coding-Decoding:** Identify patterns in letter sequences to decode messages faster.
   - **Series Completion:** Recognize common patterns like arithmetic or geometric sequences.
3. **English Language Tips**
   - **Reading Comprehension:** Skim through the passage first, then read the questions to know what information to look for.
   - **Error Spotting:** Familiarize yourself with common grammatical errors to quickly identify mistakes.
   - **Vocabulary:** Learn synonyms and antonyms to enhance understanding and speed.
4. **General Awareness Hacks**
   - **Mnemonics:** Create memory aids for historical dates, scientific facts and other important information.
   - **Mind Maps:** Visualize connections between concepts to improve recall.
   - **Current Affairs:** Focus on major events and developments from the last 6 months.

Expert Tips and Shortcuts

General Intelligence & Reasoning

Key Topics
- **Verbal Reasoning:** Analogy, Classification, Series, Coding-Decoding, Blood Relations, Direction Sense, Syllogism
- **Non-Verbal Reasoning:** Mirror Images, Embedded Figures, Paper Folding, Figure Matrix
- Time Allocation: Aim to solve 25 questions in 25 minutes.

Approach
- Start with easier questions to build confidence.
- Use elimination techniques for tricky questions.
- Practice regularly to improve speed and accuracy.

Resources
- Books like Arihant Master Reasoning.
- Examwitharihant online platform offering practice sets and mock tests.

General Awareness

Key Topics
- **Static GK:** History, Geography, Polity, Economy, Science
- **Current Affairs:** Last 6 months

Strategy
- **Time Allocation:** Aim to attempt 20 questions in 18–20 minutes.

Approach

- Focus more on Static GK as it has a higher weightage.
- Stay updated with current affairs through daily news and monthly magazines.
- Use mind maps and notes for quick revision.

Resources

- Current Affairs apps and websites.
- Arihant Static GK and General Knowledge by Manohar Pandey.

Quantitative Aptitude

Key Topics

- **Arithmetic:** Percentages, Profit & Loss, Time & Work, Speed & Distance
- **Algebra:** Linear Equations, Quadratic Equations
- **Geometry & Mensuration:** Area, Volume, Surface Area
- **Data Interpretation:** Bar Graphs, Pie Charts, TablesTestbook

Strategy

- **Time Allocation:** Aim to solve 25 questions in 30 minutes.

Approach

- Start with easier arithmetic questions to gain confidence.
- Use shortcuts and tricks for faster calculations.
- Practice regularly to improve speed and accuracy.

Resources

- Books like Fast Track Objective Arithmetic.
- Examwitharihant online platform offering practice sets and mock tests.

English Language

Key Topics

- **Grammar:** Error Spotting, Fill in the Blanks, Phrase Replacement
- **Vocabulary:** Synonyms, Antonyms, One Word Substitution
- **Comprehension:** Reading Comprehension, Cloze Test.

Strategy

- **Time Allocation:** Aim to solve 25 questions in 25 minutes.

Approach

- Start with vocabulary-based questions as they are less time-consuming.
- For comprehension, read the questions first, then the passage.
- Practice regularly to improve speed and accuracy.

Resources

- Books like Objective General English by S.P. Bakshi.
- Apps or websites offering daily vocabulary quizzes.

Overall Exam Strategy

- **Sequence of Attempt:** Start with Reasoning, followed by General Awareness, English Language, and Quantitative Aptitude.
- **Time Management:**
  - Allocate approximately 25 minutes to each section.
  - Keep track of time to ensure all sections are attempted.
- **Accuracy Over Speed:** Focus on solving questions correctly rather than rushing through them.
- **Revision:** Allocate the last 5 minutes to review your answers.

Strategies to Tackle Tricky Questions

1. **Read the Question Thoroughly**
   Carefully read each question to understand what is being asked. Pay attention to keywords such as "except," "not," or "only," as they can significantly change the meaning of the question. Misinterpreting these can lead to incorrect answers.
2. **Break Down Complex Questions**
   For multi-part or complex questions, break them down into smaller, manageable parts. This approach makes it easier to identify the core issue and find the correct solution.
3. **Eliminate Clearly Incorrect Options**
   In multiple-choice questions, use the process of elimination to discard obviously incorrect answers. This increases the probability of selecting the correct answer from the remaining options.
4. **Look for Clues in Other Questions**
   Sometimes, other questions in the exam can provide hints or information that can help answer a tricky question. Keep an eye out for such connections.
5. **Trust Your First Instincts**
   Often, your initial answer choice is correct. Avoid overthinking, as second-guessing can lead to mistakes.
6. **Manage Your Time Wisely**
   Allocate a specific amount of time to each question. If you find a question particularly challenging, move on and return to it later if time permits. This ensures you don't spend too much time on a single question at the expense of others.

Set 01 01 July, 2024 (Shift I)

SSC CHSL Tier-I SOLVED PAPER

Instructions

1. This paper contains 100 questions.
2. It has 4 Parts, **Part I** General English, **Part II** General Intelligence & Reasoning, **Part III** Quantitative Aptitude and **Part IV** General Awareness.
3. Each question carries **2 marks**.

Part I General English

1. The following sentence has been divided into four segments. Identify the segment that contains a grammatical error.
Passengers started behaving / violent when / they were asked / to leave the bus station.
(a) to leave the bus station
(b) Passengers started behaving
(c) violent when
(d) they were asked

2. The following sentence has been split into four segments. Identify the segment that contains a grammatical error.
The couple / preferred to walk / until the last house / of the town.
(a) The couple
(b) preferred to walk
(c) of the town
(d) until the last house

3. Select the sentence in the future tense.
(a) I will be twenty five next Sunday.
(b) I have been twenty five next Sunday.
(c) I should be twenty five next Sunday.
(d) I could be twenty five next Sunday.

4. The underlined phrase in the given sentence has been used incorrectly. Select the option that can correctly replace the underlined segment.
I am <u>down with</u> her complaints.
(a) passed out with
(b) fed up with
(c) held down with
(d) looked down with

Directions (Q. Nos. 5-9) *In the following passage, some words have been deleted. Read the passage carefully and select the most appropriate option to fill in each blank.*

As Paul was (1) ……… his supper, Aunt Jenny (2) ……… him questions that have been full of deceit , and had a very deep meaning, for she wanted to trap him. It seemed as if she was endowed with a (3) ……… which could hunt for dark and mysterious tact.

She asked, "Did you now not want to swim, Paul?"

Paul felt an uncomfortable (4) ……… .

He (5) ……… Aunt Jenny's face; however it informed him nothing. So, he said, "No, ma'am."

5. Select the most appropriate option to fill in blank no. (1).
(a) eating
(b) churning
(c) feeding
(d) grazing

6. Select the most appropriate option to fill in blank no. (2).
(a) demanded
(b) allowed
(c) submitted
(d) asked

7. Select the most appropriate option to fill in blank no. (3).
(a) technique (b) purpose
(c) talent (d) weakness

8. Select the most appropriate option to fill in blank no. (4).
(a) drop (b) suspicion
(c) view (d) guess

9. Select the most appropriate option to fill in blank no. (5).
(a) chased (b) ruffled
(c) searched (d) pursued

10. Select the most appropriate option that can substitute the underlined segment in the given sentence.
<u>This is best book</u> for children to read.
(a) This is the best book
(b) This is good book
(c) This is very good book
(d) This is very best book

11. Select the most appropriate meaning of the underlined idiom.
The realtors of the new venture <u>sold plots like hot cakes.</u>
(a) Sold innovatively
(b) Sold quickly and in large numbers
(c) Sold illegally
(d) Sold with great difficulty

12. Select the most appropriate meaning of the given idiom.
Black and white
(a) In dispute
(b) A false invention
(c) In writing
(d) Doubtful

13. Select the most appropriate antonym of the given word.
Glory
(a) Shame (b) Honour
(c) Delight (d) Gluttony

14. Select the most appropriate option that can substitute the underlined segment in the given sentence.
The skunk had a <u>conspicuous</u> spinal stripe.
(a) obscure (b) charming
(c) noticeable (d) faint

15. Select the most appropriate antonym of the underlined word.
Would you please <u>support</u> me for once in your life?
(a) establish
(b) refute
(c) document
(d) disclaim

16. Select the most appropriate antonym of the given word .

Trivial

(a) Vain (b) Essential
(c) Liable (d) Lavish

17. Select the incorrectly spelt word.

(a) Encraoch
(b) Delegate
(c) Illusion
(d) Obtain

18. Select the most appropriate option that can substitute the underlined segment in the given sentence.

Rahul had strong pain in his stomach.

(a) severe (b) high
(c) deep (d) strict

19. Select the most appropriate antonym of the underlined word in the given sentence.

How can you be so joyless on hearing the news?

(a) beaming
(b) rapt
(c) blissful
(d) dubious

20. Select the most appropriate option to fill in the blank.

In both countries we have leaders of .... ability.

(a) powerful
(b) almighty
(c) compelling
(d) exceptional

21. The following sentence has been split into four segments. Identify the segment that contains a spelling error.

I begged him/to reconcider/the decision but / he refused to yield.

(a) the decision but
(b) I begged him
(c) he refused to yield
(d) to reconcider

22. Select the most appropriate option that can substitute the underlined words in the given sentence.

It is a general belief that the female ostrich guard the nest at night.

(a) guarded the nest at night
(b) guards the nest at night
(c) does guard the nest in night
(d) is guarding the nest at night

23. Select the most appropriate option to fill in the blank.

Yesterday, I ate only a .... of apples for my dinner.

(a) pair (b) pier (c) pare (d) pear

24. Select the most appropriate synonym of the bracketed word in the following sentence to fill in the blank.

The documentary explored the historical and cultural significance of the ....(antique) ruins in the region.

(a) obsolete (b) contemporary
(c) modern (d) ancient

25. Select the most appropriate option that can substitute the underlined segment in the given sentence. If there is no need to substitute it, select 'No substitution required'.

The little boy cried with pain when he burnt his fingers.

(a) No substitution required
(b) when he burns his fingers
(c) while he burn his fingers
(d) as he burning his fingers

Part II
General Intelligence

26. Select the set in which the numbers are related in the same way as are the numbers of the following sets.

(**Note** Operations should be performed on the whole numbers, without breaking down the numbers into its constituent digits. E.g., 13 – Operations on 13 such as adding/deleting/multiplying etc. to 13 can be performed. Breaking down 13 into 1 and 3 and then performing mathematical operations on 1 and 3 is not allowed.)

(10, 5, 20)
(14, 7, 28)

(a) (48, 24, 58)
(b) (33, 11, 44)
(c) (22, 11, 44)
(d) (54, 18, 72)

27. Identify the figure given in the options that when put in place of the question mark (?) will logically complete the series.

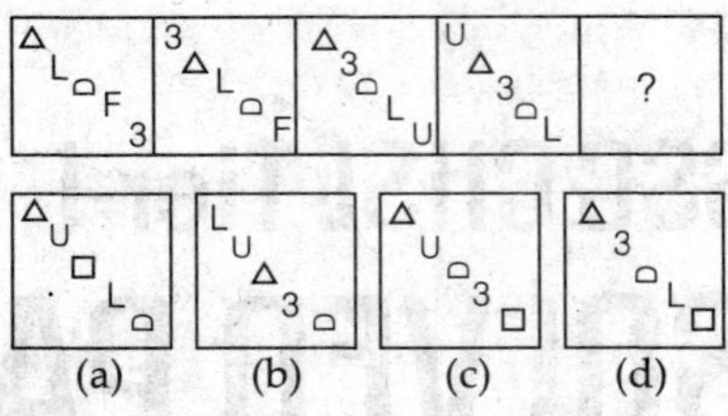

28. Select the correct mirror image of the given figure, when the mirror is placed at MN as shown below.

(a) Ƨuϱʌǝɔ (b) ƨu9ʌ6ɔ
(c) c9v6n2 (d) ɔǝʌϱuƧ

29. Select the combination of letters that when sequentially placed in the blanks of the given series will logically complete the series.

A_A_CAB_B_A__BCABA_C

(a) BBACABB
(b) BBABBCB
(c) BBACBAB
(d) BABACBA

30. LBXF is related to SYCM in a certain way based on the English alphabetical order. In the same way, TGFY is related to AGHF. To which of the following is ZDMK related, following the same logic?

(a) GRNE (b) GREN
(c) GNER (d) GNRE

31. If 'U' stands for '÷', 'D' stands for '×', 'B' stands for '+' and 'T' stands for '–', what will come in place of the question mark (?) in the following equation?

13 T 26 U 13 D 24 B 7 = ?

(a) –56 (b) –87 (c) –43 (d) –28

32. What should come in place of the question mark (?) in the given series?

129, 128, 124, 115, 99, ?

(a) 73 (b) 71
(c) 74 (d) 72

33. The position of how many letters will remain unchanged, if each of the letters in the word 'VIRTUAL' is arranged in English alphabetical order?

(a) None (b) One
(c) Three (d) More than three

34. Which two numbers should be interchanged to make the given equation correct?

$74 - 52 + (39 \div 13) \times 16 + (14 \div 2) = 106$

(**Note** Numbers must be interchanged and not the constituent digits e.g., if 2 and 3 are to be interchanged in the equation $43 \times 3 + 4 \div 2$, then interchanged equation is $43 \times 2 + 4 \div 3$)

(a) 52 and 39 (b) 74 and 52
(c) 14 and 52 (d) 14 and 16

35. If the year is not a leap year, then how is the last day of the year and first day of the same year related?

(a) First day is Sunday, last day is Friday
(b) First day is Sunday, last day is Saturday
(c) First day is Tuesday, last day is Saturday
(d) They are the same

36. What should come in place of question mark (?) in the given series based on the English alphabetical order?

FNV, LUE, ?, XIW, DPF

(a) GQZ (b) UWZ
(c) HRY (d) RBN

37. What would be the letter on the opposite side of 'Y', if the given sheet is folded to form a cube?

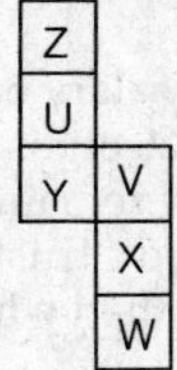

(a) Z (b) V (c) W (d) X

38. Six numbers 1, 3, 5, 6, 7 and 8 are written on different faces of a dice. Two positions of this dice are shown in the figure. Which is the number on the face opposite to the face containing 6?

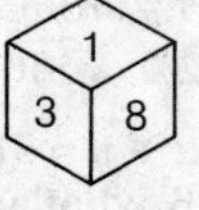

(a) 5 (b) 7
(c) 3 (d) 8

39. 96 is related to 16 following a certain logic. Following the same logic, 156 is related to 26. To which of the following is 228 related following the same logic?

(**Note** Operations should be performed on the whole numbers, without breaking down the numbers into its constituent digits. E.g. 13 – Operations on 13 such as adding /deleting /multiplying etc., to 13 can be performed. Breaking down 13 into 1 and 3 and then performing mathematical operations on 1 and 3 is not allowed.)

(a) 42 (b) 34
(c) 38 (d) 36

40. What should come in place of the question mark (?) in the given series?

40, ?, 18, 10, 4, 0

(a) 22 (b) 25
(c) 30 (d) 28

41. 'A + B' means 'A is the brother of B'.
'A – B' means 'A is the wife of B'.
'A × B' means 'A is the father of B'.
'A ÷ B' means 'A is the sister of B'.

In 'T × X ÷ Y + Z', how is T related to Z using the same meaning of the mathematical operators as given above?

(a) Father (b) Daughter
(c) Father-in-law (d) Brother

42. What will come in the place of the question mark (?) in the following equation, if '+' and '–' are interchanged and '×' and '÷' are interchanged?

$162 \times 9 - 452 + 7 \div 9 = ?$

(a) 707 (b) 407 (c) 507 (d) 607

43. Select the pair which follows the same pattern as that followed by the two set of pairs given below. Both pairs follow the same pattern.

DFG : IKL
MOP : RTU

(a) WYZ : GIJ (b) FHI : EGH
(c) TVW : YAB (d) PST : KHG

44. Read the given statements and conclusions carefully. Assuming that the information given in the statements is true, even if it appears to be at variance with commonly known facts, decide which of the given conclusions logically follow(s) from the statements.

Statements

Some keys are chains.
All chains are locks.
No lock is a rock.

Conclusions

I. No rock is a key.
II. At least some keys are locks.

(a) None of the conclusion follow
(b) Both Conclusions I and II follow
(c) Only Conclusion II follows
(d) Only Conclusion I follows

45. Three of the following four are alike in a certain way and thus form a group. Which is the one that does not belong to that group?

(**Note** The odd one out is not based on the number of consonants/vowels or their position in the letter-cluster.)

(a) AJQ (b) MVC
(c) OXC (d) ENU

46. How many triangles are there in the given figure?

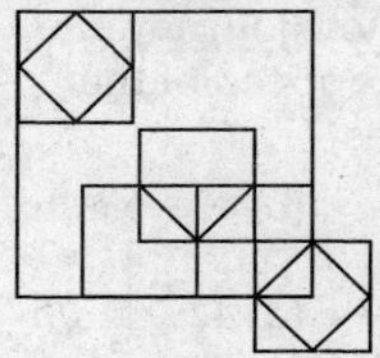

(a) 15 (b) 13 (c) 14 (d) 11

47. Select the correct mirror image of the given figure when the mirror is placed at MN as shown below.

RTYZXC57
M ——————— N

(a) ꓤTʎZXC5ㄥ
(b) ꓤ⊥ʎZXCꙄㄥ
(c) ꓤ⊥ZʎXCꙄㄥ
(d) ㄥϛƆXZʎ⊥ꓤ

48. In a certain code language, BEAM is coded as 2349 and MEAN is coded as 4327. What is the code for N in that language?

(a) 3 (b) 7 (c) 4 (d) 2

49. In a certain code language, 'strong and mighty' is written as 'ui yv tk' and 'soft yet strong' is written as 'hd tk bw'. How is 'strong' written in the given language?

(a) hd (b) bw (c) ui (d) tk

50. What would be the symbol on the opposite side of '≠', if the given sheet is folded to form a cube?

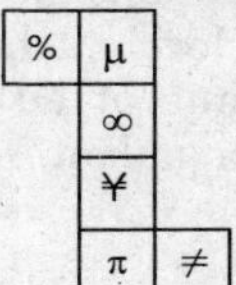

(a) ¥ (b) ∞ (c) % (d) μ

Part III
Quantitative Aptitude

51. If Arun's salary was decreased by 50% and subsequently increased by 50%, then how much per cent did he lose?
(a) 25% (b) 40%
(c) 10% (d) 36%

52. Simplify the following expression.
$3 + 28 \div 35 \times 15 + 4 - 3 \times 4$
(a) 10 (b) 26
(c) 64 (d) 7

53. A motorcycle covered the first 60 km of its journey at an average speed of 40 km/h. The speed of the motorcycle for covering the rest of the journey, i.e. 90 km was 45 km/h. During the whole journey, the overall average speed of the motorcycle was
(a) 42 km/h (b) $42\frac{1}{2}$ km/h
(c) $42\frac{1}{7}$ km/h (d) $42\frac{6}{7}$ km/h

54. A shopkeeper decides to raise the marked price of an article by 40%. How much percentage discount should he allow to be able to sell the article at the original marked price?
(a) $26\frac{3}{7}\%$ (b) $24\frac{3}{7}\%$
(c) $31\frac{2}{7}\%$ (d) $28\frac{4}{7}\%$

55. A largest possible sphere is carved from a cube of side 14 cm. What is its volume in cm^3?
(a) $1600\frac{1}{3}$ (b) $1437\frac{1}{3}$
(c) $205\frac{1}{3}$ (d) $1707\frac{1}{3}$

56. A and B can do a work in 10 days and 40 days, respectively. How long will it take together to complete the work?
(a) 12 days (b) 8 days
(c) 15 days (d) 20 days

57. A company has five plants for manufacturing spare parts. Each plant manufactures local quality and export quality. What is the ratio of the production of local quality and export quality units of the highest manufacturing plant?

Manufacturing capacity of different plants

Plant	A	B	C	D	E
Local Quality	420	350	360	80	440
Export Quality	140	150	120	440	110

(a) 2 : 11 (b) 4 : 1
(c) 3 : 1 (d) 7 : 3

58. Which of the following is a correct statement?
(a) The sum of the angles of a cyclic quadrilateral is always 180°
(b) Equal chords are equidistant from the centre of the circle but not always subtend equal angle at centre of the circle
(c) If two circles touch each other, the point of contact lies on the line joining the two centres
(d) Angles subtended by the arc in the same segment of the circle are in ratio of 2 : 1

59. Radhika requested the cashier of a bank to get her coins in lieu of her cheque worth ₹1845. Cashier gave her a packet containing ₹5, ₹10 and ₹20 coins in the ratio of 3 : 5 : 7. What is the total worth of the smallest coin received by her?
(a) ₹125 (b) ₹105
(c) ₹145 (d) ₹135

60. The percentage of students enrolled in different activities in a school, which are displayed in the first pie-chart. The total number of students is 5000.
In the second pie-chart, the total number of girls is 1550 and their percentage breakup enrolled in these activities.

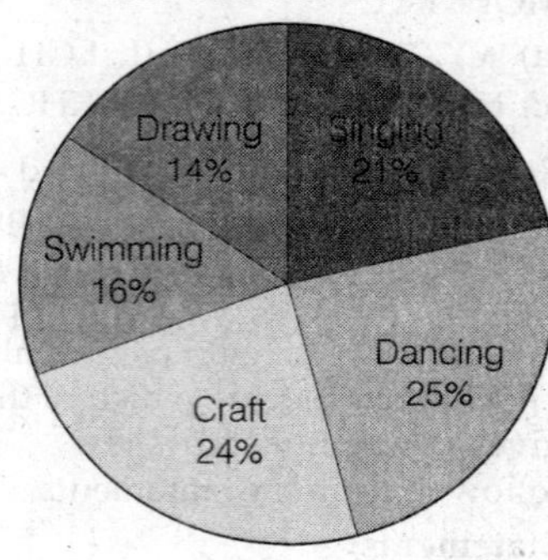

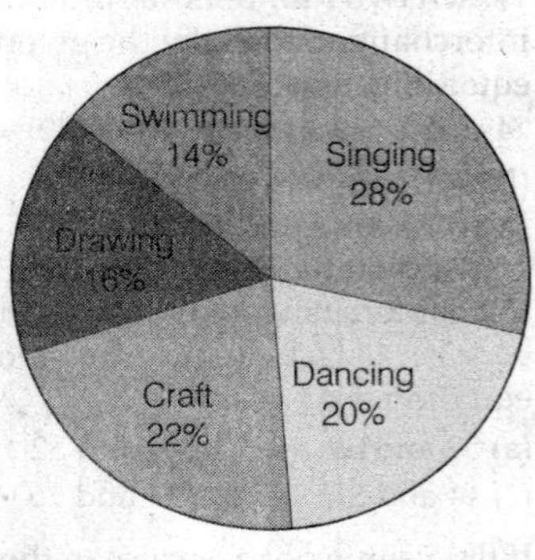

The number of girls enrolled in Craft forms what per cent of the total number of students in the school?
(a) 6.82% (b) 5.81%
(c) 5.82% (d) 7.11%

61. In how many years will the simple interest on a sum of money be equal to the principle at the rate of $2\frac{6}{7}\%$ per annum?
(a) 35 yr (b) 34 yr (c) 33 yr (d) 37 yr

62. Given that the perimeters of two similar triangles, ΔABC and ΔDEF, are 24 cm and 9 cm, respectively, and $DE = 3$ cm, what is the ratio between the area of ΔABC and that of ΔDEF?
(a) 64 : 9 (b) 54 : 9
(c) 64 : 7 (d) 54 : 7

63. A man spent 60% of his salary on household expenses, 20% of his salary on rent and out of remaining salary, he donated 80% to a trust. If he is left with ₹20000, then what is his salary?
(a) ₹400000 (b) ₹500000
(c) ₹550000 (d) ₹50000

64. A shopkeeper marks up the price of oil by 40% and uses a faulty machine, which measures 15% less. If the shopkeeper gives a discount of 32%, the profit/loss percentage is
(a) 15% Loss (b) 25% Profit
(c) 18% Loss (d) 12% Profit

65. If equation of line p is $x + y = 5$ and that of line q is $x - y = 3$, what are the co-ordinates of the point common to both the lines?
(a) (2, 1) (b) (2, 3)
(c) (4, 1) (d) (1, 4)

66. Study the given pie-charts and answer the question that follows. The pie-charts show the 'data of students' progress after graduation.

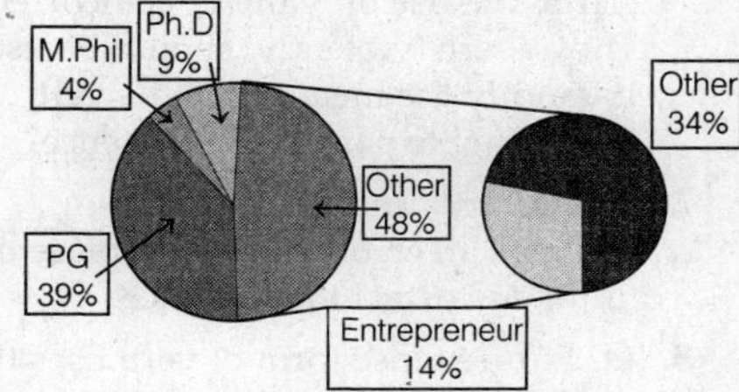

Which two combined have the same number of students as the other?
(a) PG + M. Phil.
(b) Entrepreneur + Ph.D.
(c) Entrepreneur + PG
(d) PG + Ph.D.

67. What will be the least value of x, so that the 5-digits number $627x5$ becomes divisible by 9?
(a) 7 (b) 4 (c) 3 (d) 9

68. The ratio of the diameters of two spheres is given as 1 : 4. The larger sphere is melted and 125 identical spheres are made out of the molten material. The smaller sphere is melted and 27 identical spheres are made out of the molten material. If the ratio of the volume of each of the 125 identical spheres to the volume of each of the 27 identical spheres is given as $1 : m$, what is the value of m?
(a) $\frac{1728}{125}$ (b) $\frac{27}{8000}$ (c) $\frac{125}{1728}$ (d) $\frac{64}{3375}$

69. If PQ and PR are the two tangents to a circle with centre O, and $\angle QOR = 150°$, then $\angle QPR$ is equal to
(a) 60° (b) 30°
(c) 90° (d) 45°

70. A man walking at the speed of 5 km/h covers a certain distance in 3 h 45 min. If he covers the same distance by a cycle in 2 h 10 min, then the speed of the cycle (in km/h) is
(a) $7\frac{16}{26}$ (b) $9\frac{11}{26}$
(c) $8\frac{17}{26}$ (d) $5\frac{11}{26}$

71. Two parallel chords on the same side of the centre of a circle are 12 cm and 20 cm long and the radius of the circle is $5\sqrt{13}$ cm. What is the distance between the chords?
(a) 3 cm (b) 5 cm (c) 2 cm (d) 4 cm

72. The surface area of a cube is 486 cm^2. Find the volume.
(a) 486 cm^3 (b) 729 cm^3
(c) 625 cm^3 (d) 512 cm^3

73. In right-angled triangle ABC, $\angle B = 90°$ and $\angle A$ and $\angle C$ are acute angles.
If $\text{cosec } A = 2\sqrt{2}$, then find the value of $\sin A \cdot \cos C + \cos A \cdot \sin C$.
(a) 0 (b) $2\sqrt{2}$ (c) 1 (d) $\sqrt{2}$

74. Mohan gets 12% increase in his sale amount in the first year and 15% increase in the second year, with that his present sale is ₹128800. What was his sale two years ago?
(a) ₹125000 (b) ₹150000
(c) ₹175000 (d) ₹100000

75. The given table shows the percentage of marks obtained by 5 students in different subjects. Study the table and answer the question that follows. (Maximum marks are given beside subject)

Subjects →	Physics	Maths	Music	Hindi	Botany
Students ↓	300	300	100	100	200
Ram	60	80	90	60	95
Shyam	90	70	80	70	40
Sohan	70	90	95	80	75
Mohan	80	60	70	95	80
Karn	90	50	85	85	80

What is the marks (in percentage) obtained by Mohan?
(a) 77.5% (b) 76.5%
(c) 74.5% (d) 75.5%

Part IV
General Awareness

76. Average function is listed in the drop-down menu of which of the following tools?
(a) Financial function
(b) Auto Sum function
(c) Move function
(d) Insert function

77. Where can you find the emoticons in an instant messaging conversation window?
(a) At the middle of the chat window
(b) Any where in the chat window
(c) At the bottom of the chat window
(d) At the top of the chat window

78. Who has the power to regulate the right of citizenship in India?
(a) Supreme Cour (b) President
(c) Governor (d) Parliament

79. In which year has India hosted the Asian Games for the first time?
(a) 1948 (b) 1951 (c) 1950 (d) 1949

80. Who among the following was the author of 'Brihat Katha Kosh'?
(a) Dandin (b) Harisena
(c) Kshemendra (d) Bhavabhuti

81. Langvir Nritya is a folk dance from the state of ....
(a) Haryana (b) Gujarat
(c) Uttar Pradesh (d) Uttarakhand

82. Geoid is the .... of Earth.
(a) shape (b) axis
(c) colour (d) orbit

83. In the context of DNA, which of the following principles governs the process of transcription?
(a) The transforming principle
(b) The principle of complementarity
(c) Semiconservative nature of DNA
(d) The principle of inheritance

84. With which of the following states is the Bhatiali folk music, which is mostly sung by the fishermen, associated?
(a) West Bengal (b) Odisha
(c) Andhra Pradesh
(d) Kerala

85. Who was the founder of Arya Samaj?
(a) Rabindranath Tagore
(b) Dayanand Saraswati
(c) Keshub Chandra Sen
(d) Swami Vivekananda

86. Daler Mehndi is primarily a famous singer of pop songs in which Indian language?
(a) English (b) Punjabi
(c) Hindi (d) Bengali

87. The Five-Year Plans for India with their duration are given below. Which of the following is correctly matched?

A.	Second Five-Year Plan	1956-57 to 1960-61
B.	Third Five-Year Plan	1961-62 to 1965-66
C.	Fourth Five-Year Plan	1966-67 to 1970-71

Codes
(a) Both A and C (b) Both B and C
(c) Only A (d) Both A and B

88. Which of the following states/UTs has the first 100% fully digital literate Panchayat in India?
(a) Delhi (b) Puducherry
(c) Maharashtra (d) Kerala

89. Former minister of the state and former president of BJP alliance partner IPFT .... received the Padma Shri award (posthumously) in 2023.
(a) Prabhat Choudhury
(b) Narendra Chandra Debbarma
(c) Rebati Mohan Das
(d) Pinaki Das Choudhury

90. Sakewa is a religious festival celebrated by the Kirat Khambu Rai community of ....
(a) Arunachal Pradesh
(b) Sikkim
(c) Himachal Pradesh
(d) Goa

91. The growth rate of India's population has been declining since ....
(a) 1971 (b) 1991 (c) 1951 (d) 1981

92. As of March 2024, who among the following is the Chairperson of the National Green Tribunal?
(a) Lokeshwar Singh Panta
(b) Prakash Shrivastava
(c) Ajay Narayan Jha
(d) Swatanter Kumar

93. According to the Census of India 2011, most people had out-migrated from .... to other states in India.
(a) Uttar Pradesh and Bihar
(b) Rajasthan and Gujarat
(c) Uttar Pradesh and Madhya Pradesh
(d) Maharashtra and Gujarat

94. National Institute of Mountaineering and Adventure Sports (NIMAS) is located at ....
(a) Mizoram
(b) Nagaland
(c) Himachal Pradesh
(d) Arunachal Pradesh

95. How many squares are there on a chessboard?
(a) 69 (b) 67 (c) 68 (d) 64

96. In which part of the Constitution will you find the six broad categories of Fundamental Rights?
(a) Part II (b) Part III
(c) Part IV (d) Part I

97. The financial year in India starts from 1st April and ends on ....
(a) 30th June (b) 31st March
(c) 31st July (d) 31st May

98. What is the Balance of Trade (BOT) of a country?
(a) Ratio of international trade
(b) Number of exports
(c) Difference between imports and exports
(d) Number of imports

99. The peninsular plateau of India was a part of which continent earlier?
(a) South America
(b) Europe
(c) Africa
(d) North America

100. In which year did Johannes Nicolaus Bronsted and Thomas Martin Lowry propose the fundamental concept of acids and bases?
(a) 1928 (b) 1921
(c) 1925 (d) 1923

Answers

1. (c)	2. (d)	3. (a)	4. (b)
5. (a)	6. (d)	7. (c)	8. (b)
9. (c)	10. (a)	11. (b)	12. (c)
13. (a)	14 (c)	15. (b)	16. (b)
17. (a)	18. (a)	19. (c)	20. (d)
21. (d)	22. (b)	23. (a)	24. (d)
25. (a)	26. (c)	27. (c)	28. (a)
29. (c)	30. (c)	31. (d)	32. (c)
33. (b)	34. (a)	35. (d)	36. (d)
37. (a)	38. (c)	39. (c)	40. (d)
41. (a)	42. (b)	43. (c)	44. (c)
45. (c)	46. (c)	47. (b)	48. (b)
49. (d)	50. (c)	51. (a)	52. (d)
53. (d)	54. (d)	55. (b)	56. (b)
57. (c)	58. (c)	59. (d)	60. (a)
61. (a)	62. (a)	63. (b)	64. (d)
65. (c)	66. (d)	67. (a)	68. (c)
69. (b)	70. (c)	71. (c)	72. (b)
73. (c)	74. (d)	75. (c)	76. (b)
77. (c)	78. (d)	79. (b)	80. (b)
81. (d)	82. (a)	83. (b)	84. (a)
85. (b)	86. (b)	87. (d)	88. (d)
89. (b)	90. (b)	91. (d)	92. (b)
93. (a)	94. (d)	95. (d)	96. (b)
97. (b)	98. (c)	99. (c)	100. (d)

Explanations

1. *(c)* Part (c) 'violent when' contains an error. The use of 'violent' is incorrect. The adverb 'violently' should be used to modify the meaning of the verb 'behaving' to correct the sentence.

2. *(d)* Part (d) 'until the last house' contains an error. Use 'to' in place of 'until' to correct the sentence.

3. *(a)* Future tense form of verb uses the modal verb 'will/shall' in all forms. Hence, the sentence in future tense is– I will be twenty five next Sunday.

4. *(b)* The underlined part of the given sentence contains an error. The phrasal verb 'down with' means suffering from which does not fit the context of the sentence.
Hence, replace it with 'fed up with' to correct the sentence.

5. *(a)* The correct filler for the given blank is 'eating'.

6. *(d)* The correct filler for the given blank is 'asked'.

7. *(c)* The correct filler for the given blank is 'talent'.

8. *(b)* The correct filler for the given blank is 'suspicion' which means 'doubt'.

9. *(c)* The correct filler for the given blank is 'searched'.

10. *(a)* The underlined part of the given sentence contains an error. The superlative degree of adjective takes article 'the'. Hence, add 'the' before 'best'.

11. *(b)* 'Sold plots like hot cakes' means to be sold very quickly and effortlessly.

12. *(c)* 'Black and white' means in writing.

13. *(a)* 'Glory' means high renown or honour won by notable achievements. Hence, its antonym is 'shame'.
- 'Delight' means joy.
- 'Gluttony' means habitual greed or excess in eating.

14. *(c)* 'Conspicuous' means attracting notice or attention.
- 'Obscure' means not discovered or known about; uncertain.
- 'Faint' means not visible.

15. *(b)* The antonym of 'Support' is to refute which means prove that (someone) is wrong.

- 'Document' means to keep track of something.
- 'Disclaim' means to refuse to acknowledge; deny.

16. *(b)* 'Trivial' means insignificant and small. Hence, its antonym is 'essential'.
- 'Vain' means useless.
- 'Liable' means responsible.
- 'Lavish' means wealthy.

17. *(a)* The incorrectly spelt word is 'encraoch'. The correct spelling is 'encroach'.

18. *(a)* From the given options, 'severe' can be replaced by 'strong'.

19. *(c)* The antonym of 'joyless' is 'blissful' which means 'happiness'.
- Beaming means smiling broadly; grinning.
- 'Rapt' means completely fascinated or absorbed by what one is seeing or hearing.
- 'Dubious' means hesitating or doubting.

20. *(d)* The given sentence points out that the leaders have great quality. Hence, the correct filler is 'exceptional' which means unusual; not typical.

21. *(d)* Part (d) 'to reconcider' contains a spelling error. The correct spelling is 'reconsider'.

22. *(b)* The underlined part of the sentence contains an error. As the subject of the sentence 'It is a general belief that the female ostrich' is singular, singular verb 'guards' should be used to correct the sentence.

23. *(a)* As the given sentence refers to the number of apples, the correct filler for the given blank is 'pair'.

24. *(d)* 'Antique' means old and ancient. Hence, the correct filler is 'ancient'.

25. *(a)* The underlined segment is grammatically and contextually correct.

26. *(c)* As, (10, 5, 20)

$\Rightarrow \quad 5 \times 2 = 10$

$\Rightarrow \quad 5 \times 4 = 20$

and (14, 7, 28)

$\Rightarrow \quad 7 \times 2 = 14$

$\Rightarrow \quad 7 \times 4 = 28$

Similarly, (22, 11, 44)

$\Rightarrow \quad 11 \times 2 = 22$

$\Rightarrow \quad 11 \times 4 = 44$

27. *(c)* The given series follows the two following alternate patterns.

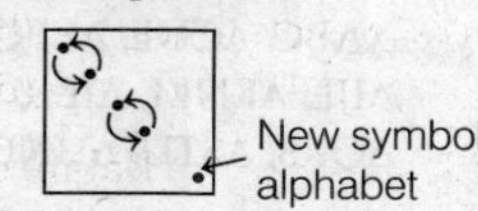

From fig. 1 to fig 2 and from fig 3 to fig 4

From fig. 2 to fig 3 and from fig 4 to fig 5

Hence, figure given in option (c) will complete the given series.

28. *(a)* The correct mirror image of the given figure, when the mirror is placed at MN is option (a).

M

c9v6n2 | Snəvɘɔ

N

29. *(c)* The correct combination of the letters is as follows,

$A\,\underline{B}\,A\,\underline{B}\,C\,/\,A\,B\,\underline{A}\,B\,\underline{C}\,/\,A\,\underline{B}\,\underline{A}\,B\,C\,/\,A\,B\,A\,\underline{B}\,C$

$\Rightarrow$ BBACBAB

30. *(c)* As, and

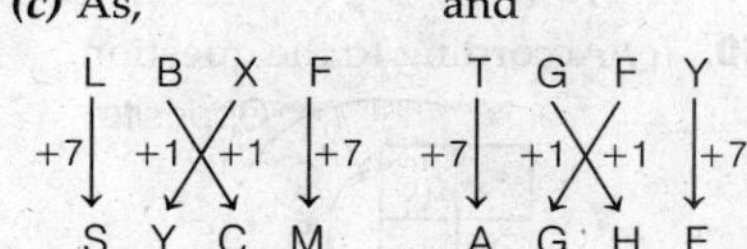

Similarly,

Z D M K

+7 +1 +1 +7

G N E R

31. *(d)* Given expression,

13 T 26 U 13 D 24 B 7 = ?

After interchanging the signs, we get

$? = 13 - 26 \div 13 \times 24 + 7$

$= 13 - 2 \times 24 + 7$

$= 20 - 48$

$= -28$

32. *(c)* The pattern of the series is as follows,

129 128 124 115 99 74

$-(1^2)$ $-(2^2)$ $-(3^2)$ $-(4^2)$ $-(5^2)$

33. *(b)* According to the question,

Given word	V I R T U A L
Alphabetically arranged word	A I L R T U V

One letter i.e. I will remain unchanged.

34. *(a)* According to the question,

$74 - 52 + (39 \div 13) \times 16 + (14 \div 2) = 106$

After replacing the two numbers 52 and 39 by option (a), we get

$74 - 39 + (52 \div 13) \times 16 + (14 \div 2) = 106$

$\Rightarrow \quad 74 - 39 + 64 + 7 = 106$

$\Rightarrow \quad 74 - 39 + 71 = 106$

$\Rightarrow \quad 145 - 39 = 106$

$\Rightarrow \quad 106 = 106$

35. *(d)* When the year is not a leap year. The first day of the year is same as the last day of the same year.

36. *(d)* The pattern of the series is as follows,

F $\xrightarrow{+6}$ L $\xrightarrow{+6}$ R $\xrightarrow{+6}$ X $\xrightarrow{+6}$ D

N $\xrightarrow{+7}$ U $\xrightarrow{+7}$ B $\xrightarrow{+7}$ I $\xrightarrow{+7}$ P

V $\xrightarrow{+9}$ E $\xrightarrow{+9}$ N $\xrightarrow{+9}$ W $\xrightarrow{+9}$ F

37. *(a)* According to the question,

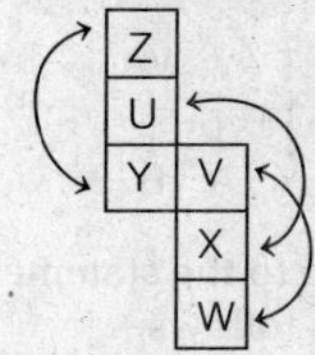

W is the opposite side of V and *vice-versa.*

U is the opposite side of X and *vice-versa.*

$\therefore$ Z is the opposite side of Y and *vice-versa.*

38. *(c)* According to the question,

From the common position of both the dice moving in clockwise direction

3	7	5
3	1	8

Number 1, 8, 7 and 5 are adjacent to face containing number 3.

Clearly, 3 is the number on the face opposite to the 6.

39. *(c)* As,

$\Rightarrow \quad 96 \div 6 = 16$

and

$\Rightarrow \quad 156 \div 6 = 26$

Similarly,

$\Rightarrow \quad 228 \div 6 = 38$

40. *(d)* The pattern of the series is as follows,

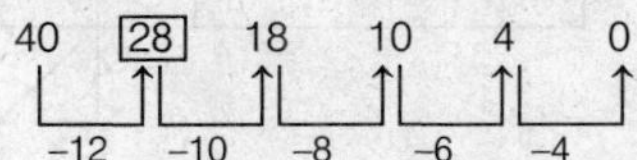

41. *(a)* Given, $T \times X \div Y + Z$

According to the question, relation diagram is as follows,

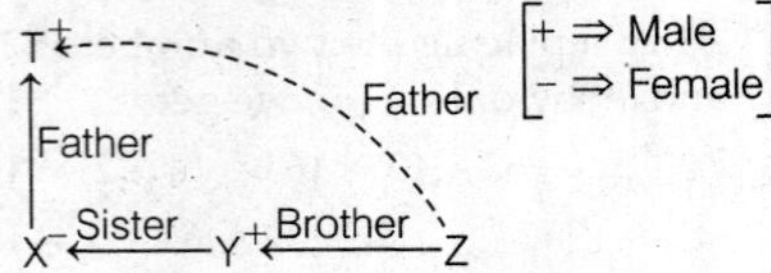

Clearly, T is the father of Z.

42. *(b)* Given expression,

$162 \times 9 - 452 + 7 \div 9 = ?$

According to the question, after interchanging the signs, we get

$162 \div 9 + 452 - 7 \times 9$

$= 18 + 452 - 63$

$= 470 - 63 = 407$

43. *(c)* As,

D F G → (+5, +5, +5) → I K L

and

M O P → (+5, +5, +5) → R T U

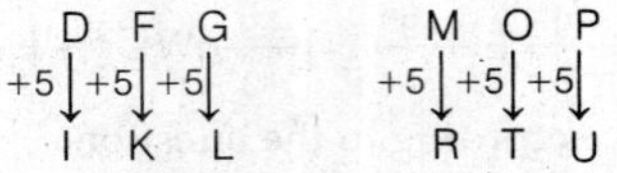

Similarly,

T V W → (+5, +5, +5) → Y A B

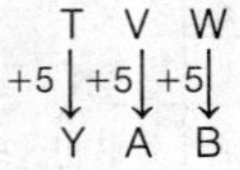

44. *(c)* According to the statements, venn diagram is as follows,

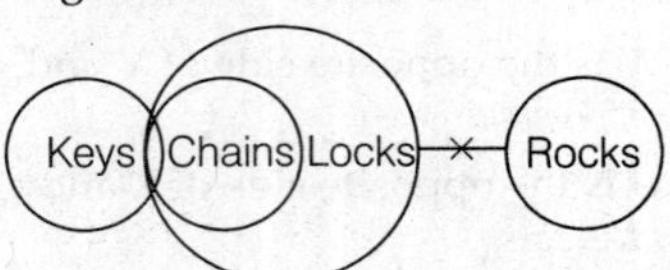

Conclusions I. (✗) II. (✓)

Only Conclusion II follows.

45. *(c)* As, A J Q (+9, +7); M V C (+9, +7); E N U (+9, +7); But, O X C (+9, +5)

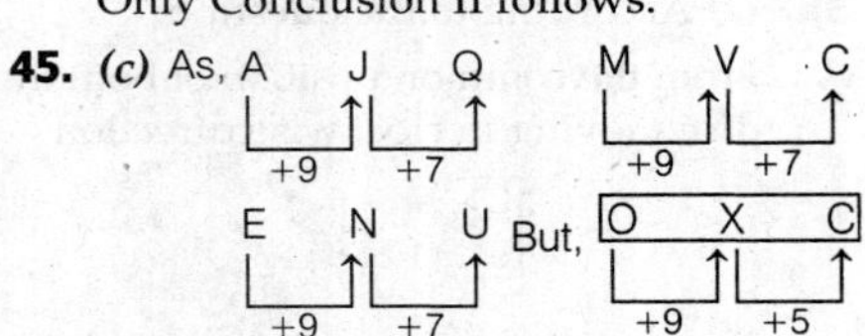

Clearly, option (c) does not belong to that group.

46. *(c)* According to the question,

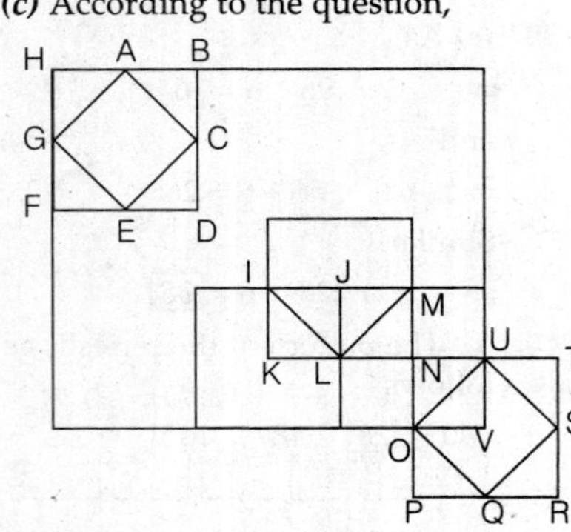

⇒ There are 14 triangles in the given figure and these are

ΔABC, ΔCDE, ΔEFG, ΔGHA, ΔIKL, ΔIJL, ΔLNM, ΔJLM, ΔILM, ΔOPQ, ΔQRS, ΔSTU, ΔUNO, ΔUVO

47. *(b)* The correct mirror image of the given figure, when the mirror is placed at MN is figure in option (b)

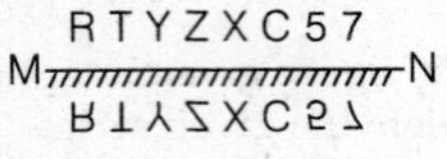

R T Y Z X C 5 7

M————————N

(mirror image of R T Y Z X C 5 7)

48. *(b)* According to the question,

B E A M → 2 3 4 9

M E A N → 4 3 2 7

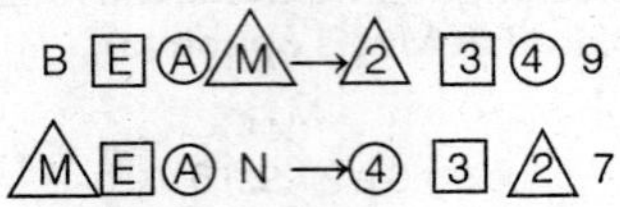

Clearly, code for N is 7.

49. *(d)* According to the question,

strong and mighty = ui yv tk

soft yet strong = hd tk bw

∴ 'strong' is written as 'tk' in the code language.

50. *(c)* According to the question,

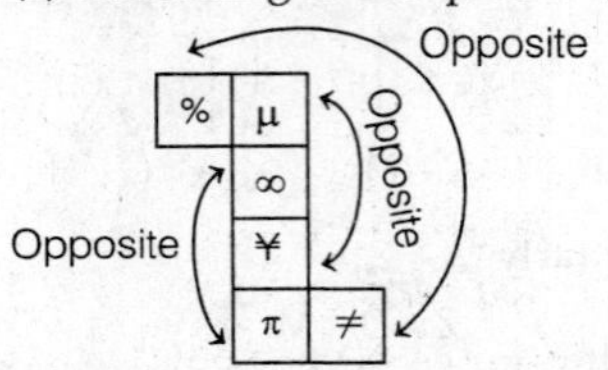

- μ is the opposite side of ¥ and *vice-versa.*.
- ∞ is the opposite side of π and *vice-versa.*

∴ % is the opposite side of ≠ and *vice-versa.*

51. *(a)* Let the salary of Arun be ₹ 100.

Arun's salary after subsequent decrease and increase of 50%

$= 100 \times \frac{(100 - 50)}{100} \times \frac{(100 + 50)}{100}$

$= 100 \times \frac{50}{100} \times \frac{150}{100} = ₹\ 75$

Arun's loss in salary

$= (100 - 75) = ₹\ 25$

∴ Arun lost 25% in salary.

52. *(d)* Given expression,

$3 + 28 \div 35 \times 15 + 4 - 3 \times 4$

Applying BODMAS rule, we get

$= 3 + \frac{28}{35} \times 15 + 4 - 3 \times 4$

$= 3 + 12 + 4 - 12$

$= 3 + 12 - 8 = 15 - 8 = 7$

53. *(d)* We know that,

$\text{Average speed} = \frac{\text{Total distance}}{\text{Total time}}$

$= \frac{60 + 90}{\left(\frac{60}{40} + \frac{90}{45}\right)} \quad \left[\because \text{Time} = \frac{\text{Distance}}{\text{Speed}}\right]$

$= \frac{150}{\frac{3}{2} + \frac{2}{1}} = \frac{150}{\left(\frac{3 + 4}{2}\right)}$

$= \frac{300}{7} = 42\frac{6}{7}$ km/h

54. *(d)* Let the marked price (MP) of an article be ₹ 100.

New marked price (MP) of an article

$= 100 \times \left(\frac{140}{100}\right)$

$= ₹\ 140$

To sell the article at same price, the discount required

$= (140 - 100)$

$= ₹\ 40$

∴ Required discount percentage

$= \frac{40}{140} \times 100$

$= 28\frac{4}{7}\%$

55. *(b)* Side of cube $(a) = 14$ cm

Radius of largest sphere carved out of the cube $(r) = \frac{a}{2} = \frac{14}{2} = 7$ cm

We know that,

$\text{Volume of sphere} = \frac{4}{3}\pi r^3$

$= \frac{4}{3} \times \frac{22}{7} \times (7)^3$

$= 1437\frac{1}{3}\text{cm}^3$

56. *(b)* *A*'s one day's work $= \frac{1}{10}$

B's one day's work $= \frac{1}{40}$

(*A* and *B*)'s one day's work $= \frac{1}{10} + \frac{1}{40}$

$= \frac{4 + 1}{40}$

$= \frac{5}{40} = \frac{1}{8}$

∴ *A* and *B* together will take 8 days to complete the work.

57. *(c)* Total production of all following manufacturing plants

A = 420 + 140 = 560 (Highest)

B = 350 + 150 = 500

C = 360 + 120 = 480

D = 440 + 80 = 520

E = 440 + 110 = 550

Highest manufacturing plant is A.

Ratio of production of local quality and export quality units in plant A

$= \frac{420}{140}$

$= \frac{3}{1} = 3:1$

58. *(c)* According to the question,

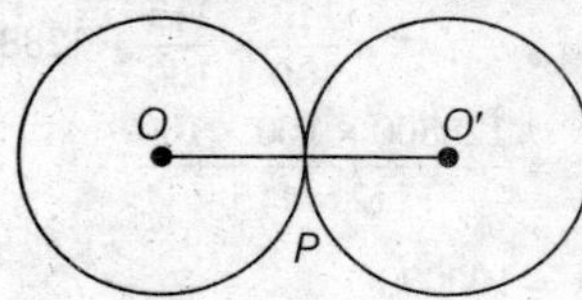

Statement given in option (c) is true, that if two circles touch each other, the point of contact (*P*) lies on the line joining the two centres *O* and *O'*.

59. *(d)* Let the number of ₹ 5, ₹ 10 and ₹ 20 coins be 3*x*, 5*x* and 7*x*, respectively.

Value of the all coins = ₹ 1845

$3x \times 5 + 5x \times 10 + 7x \times 20 = 1845$

$\Rightarrow \quad 15x + 50x + 140x = 1845$

$\Rightarrow \quad 205x = 1845$

$\Rightarrow \quad x = \frac{1845}{205}$

$\therefore \quad x = 9$

Worth of smallest coin = $5 \times 3x$

$= 5 \times 3 \times 9$

= ₹ 135

60. *(a)* Total number of girls = 1550

Number of girls enrolled in Craft forms $= \frac{22}{100} \times 1550 = 341$

Required percentage $= \frac{341}{5000} \times 100$

= 6.82%

61. *(a)* Let the principle be ₹ *P*.

then, simple interest (SI) = ₹ *P*

Rate of interest $(r) = 2\frac{6}{7}\%$ p.a.

$= \frac{20}{7}\%$ p.a.

Let the required time be '*t*' yr.

We know that,

Simple interest (SI) $= \frac{P \times r \times t}{100}$

$\Rightarrow \quad P = \frac{P \times \frac{20}{7} \times t}{100}$

$\therefore \quad t = 35$ yr

62. *(a)* We know that,

$\Delta ABC \sim \Delta DEF$

We know that, the ratio of perimeters of two similar triangles is equal to the ratio of their corresponding sides.

$\frac{\text{Perimeter of } \Delta ABC}{\text{Perimeter of } \Delta DEF} = \frac{AB}{DE}$

$\frac{24}{9} = \frac{AB}{3}$

$\Rightarrow \quad AB = 8$ cm

Now, by Area similarity theorem,

$\frac{\text{Area } (\Delta ABC)}{\text{Area } (\Delta DEF)} = \frac{AB^2}{DE^2}$

$\frac{8^2}{3^2} = \frac{64}{9}$

$\therefore$ Required ratio = 64 : 9

63. *(b)* Let the salary of man be ₹ *x*.

Part of salary spent on household expenses = ₹ $\frac{60}{100}x$

Part of salary spent on rent = ₹ $\frac{20}{100}x$

Remaining salary $= x - \frac{60}{100}x - \frac{20}{100}x$

= ₹ $\frac{20}{100}x$

Part of salary donated to trust

$= \frac{80}{100} \times \frac{20}{100}x =$ ₹$\frac{16}{100}x$

According to the question,

$\frac{20}{100}x - \frac{16}{100}x = 20000$

$\Rightarrow \quad \frac{4}{100}x = 20000$

$\therefore \quad x =$ ₹ 500000

64. *(d)* Let the cost price (CP) of oil be ₹ 100.

$\therefore$ Marked price (MP) of oil

$= \frac{100 \times 140}{100}$

= ₹ 140

Selling price (SP) of oil

$= \frac{140 \times 68}{100}$

= ₹ 95.2

CP after using faulty machine

$= 100 \times \left(\frac{100 - 15}{100}\right)$

= ₹ 85

$\therefore$ Required profit percentage

$= \frac{95.2 - 85}{85} \times 100$

= 12%

65. *(c)* Equation of line *p* is $x + y = 5$ ...(i)

Equation of line *q* is $x - y = 3$ ...(ii)

Adding Eqs. (i) and (ii), we get

$2x = 8$

$x = 4$

Putting $x = 4$ in Eq. (i), we get

$4 + y = 5$

$y = 1$

$\therefore$ Co-ordinates of points common to both are is (4, 1).

66. *(d)* Combining PG and Ph.D

= 39 + 9 = 48%

Percentage of others is 48%.

Hence, PG and Ph.D combined have the same number of students as the other.

67. *(a)* Given number = 627*x*5

We know that, if the sum of digits of a number is divisible by 9, then the number is also divisible by 9.

Sum of digits = $6 + 2 + 7 + x + 5$

$= 20 + x$

If we put $x = 7$, then $20 + 7 = 27$, which is divisible by 9.

$\therefore$ The required least value of *x* is 7.

68. *(c)* Ratio of diameters = Ratio of radius = 1 : 4

Let the radius of larger sphere be 4*x* cm and radius of smaller sphere be *x* cm.

Let the radius of each of the 125 identical spheres be *y* cm.

We know that,

Volume of sphere $= \frac{4}{3}\pi\,(\text{radius})^3$

Now, according to the question,

$\frac{4}{3}\pi(4x)^3 = 125 \times \frac{4}{3}\pi y^3$

$\Rightarrow \quad 64x^3 = 125y^3$

$\Rightarrow \quad y^3 = \frac{64x^3}{125}$

$\Rightarrow \quad y = \frac{4x}{5}$ cm

Let the radius of each of the 27 identical spheres be *z* cm, then

$\frac{4}{3}\pi x^3 = 27 \times \frac{4}{3}\pi z^3$

$\Rightarrow \quad x^3 = 27z^3$

$z^3 = \frac{x^3}{27} \Rightarrow z = \frac{x}{3}$ cm

Now, $\frac{\frac{4}{3}\pi y^3}{\frac{4}{3}\pi z^3} = \frac{1}{m}$

$$\Rightarrow \frac{\left(\frac{4x}{5}\right)^3}{\left(\frac{x}{3}\right)^3} = \frac{1}{m}$$

$$\Rightarrow \frac{64}{125} \times 27 = \frac{1}{m}$$

$$\Rightarrow \frac{1728}{125} = \frac{1}{m}$$

$$\therefore \quad m = \frac{125}{1728}$$

69. *(b)* Given,

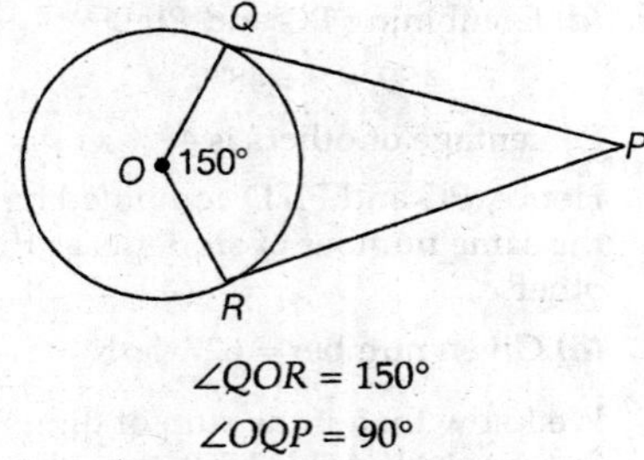

$\angle QOR = 150°$

$\angle OQP = 90°$

$\angle ORP = 90°$

(lines joining the centre of the circle to the point of contact of tangent is always perpendicular to the tangent)

Now, in quadrilateral $OQPR$

$\angle QOR + \angle OQP + \angle ORP + \angle QPR = 360°$

($\because$ angles sum property of quadrilateral)

$150° + 90° + 90° + \angle QPR = 360°$

$\Rightarrow \quad 330° + \angle QPR = 360°$

$\therefore \quad \angle QPR = 360° - 330° = 30°$

70. *(c)* Speed of man = 5 km/h

Time taken = 3 h 45 min = $3\frac{3}{4}$ h

Distance covered = Speed × Time

$= 5 \times 3\frac{3}{4} = 5 \times \frac{15}{4}$

$= \frac{75}{4}$ km

Now, time taken by cycle = 2 h 10 min

$= 2\frac{1}{6}$ h

$= \frac{13}{6}$ h

Speed of the cycle

$$= \frac{\text{Total distance}}{\text{Time taken by cycle}}$$

$$= \frac{\left(\frac{75}{4}\right)}{\left(\frac{13}{6}\right)} = \frac{450}{52}$$

$= 8\frac{17}{26}$ km/h

71. *(c)* Chord, $AB = 20$ cm

and $CD = 12$ cm,

Radius, $OA = OC = 5\sqrt{13}$ cm

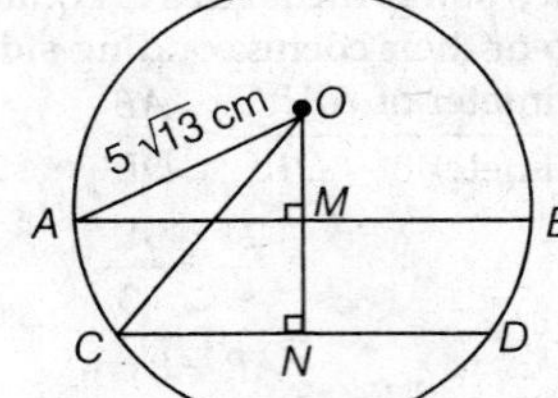

We know that, perpendicular from the centre of the circle to the chord bisects the chord.

$\therefore AM = MB$ and $CN = ND$

In right ΔOMA,

$OA^2 = OM^2 + AM^2$

$(5\sqrt{13})^2 = OM^2 + \left(\frac{20}{2}\right)^2$ $\left(\because AM = \frac{1}{2}AB\right)$

$\Rightarrow \quad 325 = OM^2 + 100$

$\Rightarrow \quad OM^2 = 225$

$\therefore \quad OM = \sqrt{225} = 15$ cm

Similarly, in right ΔONC,

$OC^2 = ON^2 + CN^2$

$(5\sqrt{13})^2 = ON^2 + \left(\frac{12}{2}\right)^2$ $\left(\because CN = \frac{1}{2} \times CD\right)$

$\Rightarrow \quad 325 = ON^2 + 36$

$\Rightarrow \quad ON^2 = 289$

$\Rightarrow \quad ON = \sqrt{289} = 17$ cm

$\therefore$ Distance between two chords = MN

$= ON - OM$

$= 17 - 15 = 2$ cm

72. *(b)* Let the edge of cube be a cm.

Surface area of cube = $6a^2$

$\Rightarrow \quad 6a^2 = 486$

$\Rightarrow \quad a^2 = \frac{486}{6}$

$\Rightarrow \quad a^2 = 81$

$\therefore \quad a = \sqrt{81} = 9$ cm

$\therefore$ Volume of cube = $a^3 = 9^3$

$= 729$ cm^3

73. *(c)* In right ΔABC,

$\angle B = 90°$

$\angle A + \angle B + \angle C = 180°$

($\because$ angles sum property of triangle)

$\angle A + \angle C = 180° - \angle B$

$\Rightarrow \quad \angle A + \angle C = 180° - 90°$

$\Rightarrow \quad \angle A + \angle C = 90°$

Now, $\sin A \cos C + \cos A \sin C$

$= \sin(A + C)$

$[\because \sin x.\cos y + \cos x.\sin y = \sin(x + y)]$

$= \sin 90° = 1 \quad (\because \angle A + \angle C = 90°)$

74. *(d)* Let the sale two years ago be ₹ x.

Then, according to the question,

$$x \times \left(\frac{100 + 12}{100}\right) \times \left(\frac{100 + 15}{100}\right) = 128800$$

$$\Rightarrow \quad x \times \frac{112}{100} \times \frac{115}{100} = 128800$$

$$\Rightarrow \quad x = \frac{128800 \times 100 \times 100}{112 \times 115}$$

$\therefore \quad x = 100000$

75. *(c)* Marks scored by Mohan in following subjects are

Physics = $\frac{80}{100} \times 300 = 240$

Maths = $\frac{60}{100} \times 300 = 180$

Music = $\frac{70}{100} \times 100 = 70$

Hindi = $\frac{95}{100} \times 100 = 95$

Botany = $\frac{80}{100} \times 200$

$= 160$

Total marks obtained in all the subjects = 745

Total maximum marks in all the subjects = 300 + 300 + 100 + 100 + 200

= 1000

$\therefore$ Required percentage = $\frac{745}{1000} \times 100$

= 74.5%

76. *(b)* Average function is listed in the drop-down menu of Auto Sum function.

This menu provides quick access to common calculation functions, including sum, average, count, max, min.

77. *(c)* At the bottom of the chat window, you can find the emoticons in an instant messaging conversation window.

This allows users to easily access and insert emoticons into their messages. Examples of popular messaging apps with emoticons i.e. Whatsapp, Facebook Messenger, Skype, Google Hangouts, Telegram etc.

78. *(d)* The Parliament has the right to make any provision concerning the acquisition and termination of citizenship and any other matter relating to citizenship.

- Article 11 Parliament to regulate the right of citizenship by law.
- Right of Citizen Right to freedom of speech and expression, assembly, association or union, movement, residence and right to practice any profession or occupation.

79. *(b)* In 1951, India has hosted the Asian Games for the first time.

- The 1951 Asian Games, officially known as the First Asian Games, was a multi-sport event celebrated in New Delhi, India from 4th to 11th March, 1951.
- The games received names like First Asiad and 1951 Asiad.
- India was ranked second with 15 gold medals, 16 silver medals and 20 bronze medals in the overall medal table, only behind Japan.

80. *(b)* The author of 'Brihat Katha Kosh' is Harisena.

- Harisena was a Sanskrit scholar and poet who lived in the 4th century CE.
- 'Brihat Katha Kosh' is a collection of ancient Indian folk tales and legends.
- Harisena was a court poet of King Samudragupta of the Gupta dynasty.

81. *(d)* Langvir Nritya is a folk dance from the state of Uttarakhand, India. It originated in the Chamoli district of Uttarakhand.

- This dance is performed by only men, who wear traditional clothing and marks.
- The dance is known for its acrobatic mones that require a high level of physical agility.

82. *(a)* Geoid is the shape of Earth.

- The geoid is a model of global mean sea level that is used to measure precise surface elevations.
- The geoid shape is not perfectly spherical. The Geoid shape of the Earth is due to the centrifugal force of its rotation.

83. *(b)* The principle of complementarity governs the process of both transcription and DNA replication due to the fact that when two DNA or RNA sequences are aligned anti parallel to each other, the nucleotides bases at each position in the sequences will be complementary or like mirror image.

84. *(a)* Bhatiali is the traditional folk music of West Bengal.

- Bhatiali is a river song mostly sung by boatmen while going down streams of the river.
- It is mostly sung in several parts of greater riparian Bengal delta.
- Notable collectors, composers and writers in the genre are Miraz Ali, Ukil Munshi, Rashid Uddin, Jala Khan, Jang Bahadur, Shah Abdul Karim and Umed Ali.

85. *(b)* Arya Samaj was founded by Swami Dayanand Saraswati in 1875.

- He was the first to give the call for Swaraj as 'India for Indian' in 1876.
- He wrote three books namely: 'Satyartha Prakash', 'Veda Bhashya Bhumika' and 'Veda Bhashya'.
- The organisation voiced for causes like widow remarriage and education of girl children.

86. *(b)* Daler Mehndi, the renowned Indian singer, is primarily associated with Punjabi pop songs.

- In 1998, Mehndi launched the 'Daler Mehndi Green Drive', inducted in the Special Task Force of the Delhi Government.
- In 1994, he was awarded the Voice of Asia International Ethnic and Pop Music Contest in 1994 in Almaty, Kazakhstan.

87. *(d)* Both pairs (A and B) are correctly matched about the duration of Five Year Plans.

- The Second Five-year Plan (1956-1961) focused on the development of the public sector and 'rapid Industrialisation'. It was drafted and planned under the leadership of PC Mahalanobis.
- The Third Five Year Plan (1961-1966) of the Economic Development of India is also popularly called 'Gadgil Yojna'.
- Pair (C) is incorrect because the duration of fourth Five-Year Plan was 1969-1974. During the implementation of the fourth Five-Year Plan 'Garibi Hatao' slogan was given by the late Prime Minister Indira Gandhi of that time.

88. *(d)* Pullampara, Kerala has the first 100% fully digital literate Panchayat in India.

- The 'Digi Pullampara' project was launched on 15th August, 2021 to import digital education to the most unprevileged section of society in the Panchayat.
- Digital literacy was imperative for the public to get government services as well as connect with the global knowledge network.
- Pullampara Gram Panchayat finished 'Digi Pullampara', a campaign to ensure total digital literacy among the people of the Panchayat.

89. *(b)* Former minister of the state and former president of BJP alliance partner IPFT Narendra Chandra Debbarma received the Padma Shri Award (posthumously) in 2023.

- Debbarma allied his party with the BJP in the 2018 Tripura Legislative Assembly election and won 8 seats out of 9 which constituted 7.5% of the total votes polled.
- Debbarma died at Agartala Hospital on 1st January, 2023, at the age of 80 after he suffered a massive cerebral stroke.

90. *(b)* Sakewa is a religious festival celebrated by the Kirat Khambu Rai community of Sikkim.

- It is also known as the Bhoomi Puja or Chandi Puja (worship of mother Earth).
- The festival begins on the full Moon day of the Hindu month of Baisakh, which usually falls in April/May.

91. *(d)* Since 1981, the birth rate has declined sharply.

- India has improved women's education, improved their quality of life, and raised the mean age of marriage. Due to this, the birth rate was declined.
- The declining growth rate is a positive indicator of the efforts to control birth rates.

92. *(b)* The Chairperson of the National Green Tribunal is Justice Prakash Shrivastava since August 2023.

- The National Green Tribunal (NGT) is a statutory body in India that deals with expeditious disposal of cases related to environmental protection and other natural resources.

- India is the third country in the world, after Australia and New Zealand, to set up a statutory body for environmental protection.

93. *(a)* According to the 2011 census, Uttar Pradesh and Bihar are responsible for the most number of migrants as 20.9 million people migrated outside the state from the two states.
- This is 37% of the total number of people who were inter-state migrants according to that enumeration.
- Uttar Pradesh has the highest share of out-migrants while Maharashtra has the highest share of in-migrants.

94. *(d)* National Institute of Mountaineering and Adventure Sports (NIMAS) is located at Arunachal Pradesh.
- NIMAS is the first National Institute of India mandated to conduct adventure courses in the field of land, air and aqua.
- The National Institute of Mountaineering and Allied Sports is an autonomous institute under Ministry of Defence.

95. *(d)* Chess is played on a board of 64 squares arranged in eight vertical rows called files and eight horizontal rows called ranks.
- These squares alternate between two colours: one light, such as white, beige, or yellow; and the other dark, such as black or green.
- Rameshbabu Praggnanandhaa is an Indian chess prodigy and Chess Grandmaster.
- As of 20th June, 2024 Praggnanandhaa is ranked No. 8 in the world by the International Chess Federation.

96. *(b)* Articles 12 to 35 contained in Part III of the Constitution deal with Fundamental Rights.
- Fundamental Rights are those rights that are important for the moral and intellectual development of all people.
- Fundamental Rights are Right to Equality, Right to Freedom, Right against Exploitation, Right to Freedom of Religion, Cultural and Educational Rights, Right to Constitutional Remedies.

97. *(b)* In India, the financial year starts on 1st April and ends on 31st March.
- The sowing of crops begins in April, and the harvest takes place between October and March.
- Therefore, the fiscal year from April to March allows the government to align its budget with the country's agricultural cycle.

98. *(c)* Balance of Trade (BOT) is the difference between the value of a country's exports and the value of a country's imports for a given period.
- It is also known as the trade balance.
- A positive trade balance indicates a trade surplus while a negative trade balance indicates a trade deficit.

99. *(c)* The peninsular plateau of India was a part of Africa (Gondwana land) earlier.
- The peninsular plateau is the oldest landmass as it was formed due to the breaking and drifting of the Gondwana land.
- The plateau consists of two broad divisions:
  The Central Highlands and The Deccan Plateau.
- The peninsular plateau is a tableland composed of the old crystalline, igneous and metamorphic rocks.

100. *(d)* In 1923, Johannes Nicolaus Bronsted and Thomas Martin Lowry proposed the fundamental concept of acids and bases.
- In this theory, acids are defined as proton donors, whereas bases are defined as proton acceptors.
- Bronsted-Lowry theory of acids and bases took the Arrhenius definition one step further, as a substance no longer needed to be composed of hydrogen (H^+) or hydroxide (OH^-) ions in order to be classified as an acid or base.

Set 02 01 July, 2024 (Shift II)

SSC CHSL Tier-I SOLVED PAPER

Instructions

1. This paper contains 100 questions.
2. It has 4 Parts, **Part I** General English, **Part II** General Intelligence & Reasoning, **Part III** Quantitative Aptitude and **Part IV** General Awareness.
3. Each question carries **2 marks**.

Part I General English

1. The given sentence is divided into four segments. Select the option that has the segment with a grammatical error.

She always/likes to/show on/her wealth.

(a) show on (b) she always
(c) likes to (d) her wealth

2. Parts of the following sentence have been underlined and given as options. Select the option that contains an error.

If it will rain tomorrow, I will stay at home.

(a) I will (b) at home
(c) will rain (d) If it

3. The following sentence has been split into four segments. Identify the segment that contains a grammatical error.

Hard had she / thrown the basketball / when it fell / on the ground.

(a) when it fell
(b) on the ground
(c) thrown the basketball
(d) Hard had she

4. Parts of the following sentence have been given as options. Select the option that contains an error.

'Ramayana' is an ancient Sanskrit epic; it is believed to be written around 500 BC to 100 BC.

(a) 'Ramayana' is an ancient
(b) Sanskrit epic; it is
(c) believed to be written
(d) around 500 BC to 100 BC

Directions (Q.Nos. 5-9) *In the following passage, some words have been deleted. Read the passage carefully and select the most appropriate option to fill in each blank.*

The period from 1858-1905 was the seed time of Indian nationalism; and the early nationalists (1) .... the seeds well and deep. Instead of basing their nationalism or appeals to (2) .... sentiments and passing emotions, or abstract rights of freedom and liberty, or on obscurantist appeals to the past, they (3) .... it in a hard-headed and penetrating analysis of the complex mechanism of modern imperialism and the chief contradiction between the interests of the Indian people and British rule. The result was that they (4) .... a common political and economic programme which (5) .... rather than divided the different sections of the people. Later on, the Indian people could gather around this programme and wage powerful struggles.

5. Select the most appropriate option to fill in blank number 1.

(a) buried (b) scattered
(c) threw (d) sowed

6. Select the most appropriate option to fill in blank number 2.

(a) shallow (b) grounded
(c) profound (d) deep

7. Select the most appropriate option to fill in blank number 3.

(a) controlled (b) rooted
(c) drove (d) minded

8. Select the most appropriate option to fill in blank number 4.

(a) evolved (b) banished
(c) uprooted (d) collapsed

9. Select the most appropriate option to fill in blank number 5.

(a) united
(b) dissolved
(c) classified
(d) complicated

10. Select the most appropriate option to fill in the blank.

It took 4 hours straight to .... the deal with the regional company.

(a) stop (b) get
(c) perform (d) close

11. Select the most appropriate option that can substitute the underlined segment in the given sentence.

As I have no time to discuss the points, so I wrote a email to her.

(a) so I wrote an e-mail for her
(b) so I wrote a e-mail to her
(c) I write an email to her
(d) I wrote an email to her

12. Select the most appropriate meaning of the given idiom.

At one's fingertips

(a) To be unaware of something
(b) To take revenge
(c) Out of reach
(d) To have complete knowledge

13. Select the most appropriate antonym of the given word.

Resistance

(a) Awareness (b) Tolerance
(c) Tenderness (d) Reliance

14. Select the most appropriate option that can replace the bracketed word segment in the following sentence.

Children should avoid giving out personal details online (which will) identify them or their location.

(a) what will
(b) that could
(c) whichever can
(d) which might lead

15. Select the most appropriate antonym of the underlined word.
The rocky terrain made the hike difficult and <u>strenuous</u>.
(a) demanding
(b) lively
(c) intense
(d) easy

16. Select the most appropriate option that can substitute the underlined segment in the given sentence.
The road which <u>connecting</u> the two states is overcrowded.
(a) connected
(b) connects
(c) has connecting
(d) have connected

17. Select the most appropriate antonym of the underlined word in the given sentence.
Ria is liked by everyone as she is very <u>amicable</u>.
(a) hateful
(b) unfriendly
(c) stupid
(d) dangerous

18. Select the option that can be used as a one-word substitute for the given group of words.
Hospital for people with mental illnesses
(a) Hangar (b) Druggist
(c) Asylum (d) Shelter

19. Select the incorrectly spelt word in the given sentence.
A distinguished academecian, Amartya Sen has taught in India, Britain and the United States.
(a) academecian
(b) taught
(c) britain
(d) distinguished

20. Select the most appropriate meaning of the underlined idiom.
Teja followed his friend's advice so now he is <u>in deep water</u>.
(a) in deep thoughts
(b) in dilemma
(c) in trouble
(d) in good position

21. Select the most appropriate antonym of the underlined word in the given sentence.
The committee <u>deposed</u> him from his office.
(a) interacted (b) demolished
(c) promoted (d) segregated

22. Select the most appropriate antonym of the underlined word.
Language <u>interacts</u> with all aspects of human life and society.
(a) co-operates (b) interrelates
(c) disconnects (d) intermingles

23. Select the incorrectly spelt word.
(a) Category (b) Hygiene
(c) Congratulate (d) Aquire

24. Select the most appropriate antonym of the given word.
Beautiful
(a) Pungent (b) Stingy
(c) Slimy (d) Ugly

25. Select the most appropriate antonym of the word 'Defeat' in the given sentence.
The first battle of Panipat was fought on 21st April, 1526 where Babur introduced canon warfare and was able to gain victory on Delhi and subjugated sultanate ruler Ibrahim Lodi.
(a) Gain (b) Subjugated
(c) Warfare (d) Victory

Part II
General Intelligence

26. Select the combination of letters that when sequentially placed in the blanks of the given series will complete the series.
KJ_HIJKI_JM_EJ_K
(a) GIJO (b) IGJO
(c) IMKR (d) KJOM

27. 'Q + R' means 'Q is the father of R'
'Q – R' means 'Q is the wife of R'
'Q × R' means 'Q is the brother of R'
'Q ÷ R' means 'Q is the daughter of R'.
What does ' M – N + O' mean?
(a) M is the brother of O
(b) M is the daughter of O
(c) M is the mother of O
(d) M is the father of O

28. What would be the word on the opposite side of 'Blue', if the given sheet is folded to form a cube?

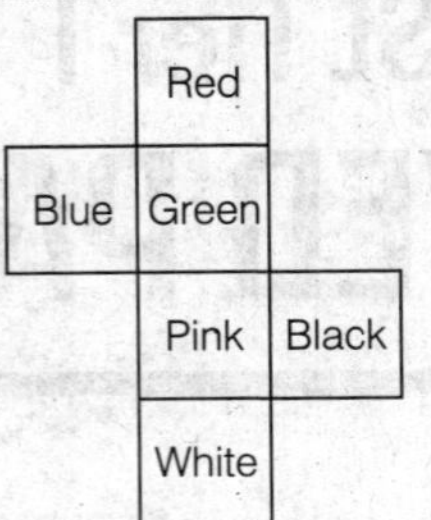

(a) Black (b) Red
(c) Pink (d) White

29. Select the correct mirror image of the given combination, when the mirror is placed at MN as shown below.

H 4 L 7 d e R (mirror MN)

(a) Я ɘ b Ꞁ ⅃ 4 H
(b) ꓤ ɘ p ∠ ⅂ 4 H
(c) d e R Ꞁ ⅃ 4 H
(d) Я ɘ b ∠ ⅂ 4 H

30. In this question, three statements are given, followed by three conclusions numbered I, II and III. Assuming the statements to be true, even if they seem to be at variance with commonly known facts, decide which of the conclusion(s) logically follow(s) from the statements.
Statements
All rings are earrings.
Some rings are chains.
All chains are bangles.
Conclusions
I. Some rings are bangles.
II. Some earrings are bangles.
III. Some chains are earrings.
(a) Both Conclusions II and III follow
(b) All Conclusions I, II and III follow
(c) Both Conclusions I and III follow
(d) Both Conclusions I and II follow

31. Select the word-pair that best represents a similar relationship to the one expressed in the pair of words given below.
(The words must be considered as meaningful English words and must not be related to each other based on the number of letters/number of consonants/vowels in the word)

Hand : Wrist
(a) Skull : Stomach
(b) Muscle : Bone
(c) Ear : Hair
(d) Foot : Ankle

32. Based on the alphabetical order, three of the following four letter-clusters are alike in a certain way and thus form a group. Which letter-cluster does not belong to that group?
(**Note** The odd one out is not based on the number of consonants/ vowels or their position in the letter-cluster.)
(a) QNL (b) ROL
(c) WTQ (d) LIF

33. Select the set in which the numbers are related in the same way as are the numbers of the following sets.
(**Note** Operations should be performed on the whole numbers, without breaking down the numbers into its constituent digits. E.g. 13 – Operations on 13 such as adding /subtracting /multiplying etc. to 13 can be performed. Breaking down 13 into 1 and 3 and then performing mathematical operations on 1 and 3 is not allowed.)
(21, 34, 76)
(39, 26, 104)
(a) (34, 25, 102) (b) (37, 43, 127)
(c) (25, 31, 108) (d) (28, 23, 79)

34. Which figure should replace the question mark(?), if the following series were to be continued?

△ ♡ S A R C O 9	♡ C 9 R A △ S O	C S △ 9 R A O ♡	S A ♡ R 9 C △ O	?

△ O S 9 R A ♡ C	A △ C ♡ R 9 O S	O S R 9 C ♡ A △	O S C ♡ R 9 A △
(a)	(b)	(c)	(d)

35. How many squares are there in the given figure?

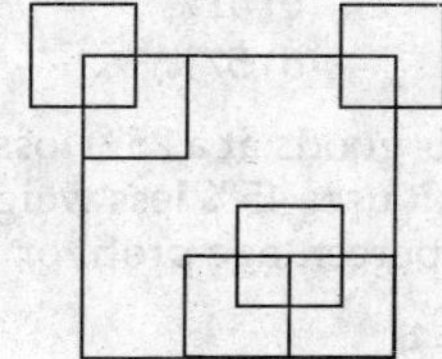

(a) 9 (b) 11
(c) 12 (d) 10

36. If 'T' stands for '×', 'M' stands for '+', 'K' stands for '÷' and 'G' stands for '–', what will come in place of the question mark(?) in the following equation?
100K5M73T48M56G23 = ?
(a) 3500 (b) 3560
(c) 3557 (d) 3575

37. In a certain code language, 'KIOSK' is coded as 'LJRTL' and 'FLAME' is coded as 'GMDNF'. What is the code for 'ENJOY' in the given code language?
(a) EMOQY (b) FOMPZ
(c) ENOQZ (d) GNMRY

38. 11 is related to 55 following a certain logic. Following the same logic, 22 is related to 110. To which of the following is 44 related following the same logic?
(**Note** Operations should be performed on the whole numbers, without breaking down the numbers into its constituent digits. E.g. 13— Operations on 13 such as adding /deleting/multiplying etc. to 13 can be performed. Breaking down 13 into 1 and 3 and then performing mathematical operations on 1 and 3 is not allowed.)
(a) 230 (b) 200
(c) 220 (d) 210

39. What would be the letter on the opposite side of 'K', if the given sheet is folded to form a cube?

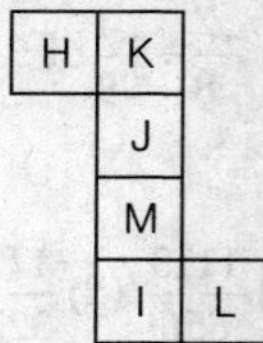

(a) L (b) M
(c) H (d) I

40. What will come in the place of '?' in the following equation, if '+' and '÷' are interchanged and '×' and '–' are interchanged?
$21 + 3 - 7 \div 11 \times 4 = ?$
(a) 63 (b) 48
(c) 51 (d) 56

41. Select the option figure in which the given figure (X) is embedded as its part (rotation is not allowed).

(X)

(a) 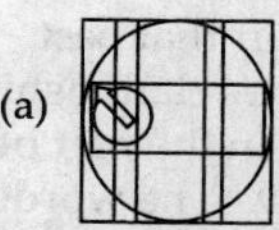 (b) 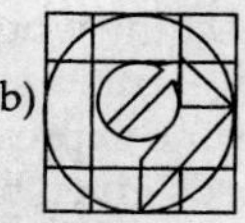

(c) 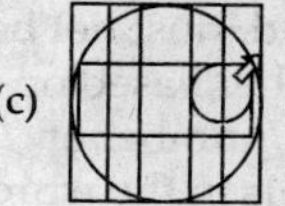 (d) 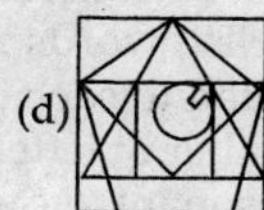

42. What should come in place of question mark (?) in the given series based on the English alphabetical order?
ZRJ, EUK, JXL, ?, TDN
(a) OAM (b) HST (c) WNE (d) QHR

43. What should come in place of the question mark(?) in the given series?
162, 167, 172, 177, 182,?
(a) 187 (b) 186 (c) 188 (d) 185

44. In a certain code language, 'messages are encrypted' is written as 'tg gc mz' and 'are you coming' is written as 'ze fp mz'. How is 'are' written in the given language?
(a) mz (b) fp (c) ze (d) gc

45. Select the correct mirror image of the given figure, when the mirror is placed at MN as shown below.

D U P E 5 2 S H
M————————N

(a) D ∩ ᑲ E Ƨ Ƨ Ƨ H
(b) H Ƨ Ƨ Ƨ Ǝ ᑫ U ᗡ
(c) D ᑯ ∩ E Ƨ Ƨ Ƨ H
(d) H Ƨ 2 Ƨ Ǝ ᑫ ∩ ᗡ

46. If 15th December, 2006 is a Friday, then what will the day of the week on 13th October, 2009?
(a) Monday (b) Friday
(c) Saturday (d) Tuesday

47. Which of the following numbers will replace the question mark (?) in the given series?
54, 58.7, 64.4, 71.1, 78.8, ?
(a) 86.8 (b) 87.5
(c) 84.4 (d) 85.1

48. If 'Z' stands for '÷', 'Q' stands for '×', 'H' stands for '+' and 'E' stands for '−', what will come in place of the question mark (?) in the following equation?
17 H 23 Q 42 Z 7 E 13 = ?
(a) 975 (b) 785 (c) 142 (d) 688

49. Select the word-pair that best represents a similar relationship to the one expressed in the pair of words given below. (The words must be considered as meaningful English words and must not be related to each other based on the number of letters/number of consonants/vowels in the word.)
Continue- Interrupt
(a) Connect– Join
(b) Safe – Secure
(c) Cow– Buffalo
(d) Attic – Common

50. If 6th May, 2005 is a Friday, then what will the day of the week on 25th September, 2018?
(a) Tuesday
(b) Thursday
(c) Sunday
(d) Friday

Part III
Quantitative Aptitude

51. The age of the older of two boys is thrice that of the younger. 9 yr ago, it was five times that of the younger. Find the present age of each.
(a) 15 yr, 45 yr (b) 12 yr, 36 yr
(c) 17 yr, 51 yr (d) 18 yr, 54 yr

52. The price of an electric bike was ₹ 125000 last year. This year, its price got decreased by 30%. What is the price (in ₹) of the electric bike this year?
(a) 86000 (b) 87500
(c) 86500 (d) 87000

53. The respective ratio between numerical values of the curved surface area and the volume of a right circular cylinder is 2 : 3. If the respective ratio between the radius and the height of the cylinder is 3 : 7, what is the total surface area of the cylinder?
(a) $62\pi \text{ cm}^2$
(b) $60\pi \text{ cm}^2$
(c) $45\pi \text{ cm}^2$
(d) $65\pi \text{ cm}^2$

54. Find the number when successively divided by 3,5 and 7 leaves remainder 2,1and 3, respectively, and the last quotient is 3.
(a) 360 (b) 362
(c) 365 (d) 367

55. In a circle, $ABCD$ is a cyclic quadrilateral in which AE is drawn parallel to CD, and BA is produced to F. If $\angle ABC = 85°$ and $\angle FAE = 24°$, find the value of $\angle BCD$.
(a) 125° (b) 115°
(c) 124° (d) 119°

56. If 18 toys out of 75 toys are for boys and the rest are for girls, what is the percentage of girls toys?
(a) 18% (b) 57%
(c) 67% (d) 76%

57. A person drives 110 miles at 55 miles per hour, he drives the next 120 miles at 60 miles per hour, and then he drives the next 60 miles in an hour. What is his average speed for the entire journey in miles per hour ?
(a) 58
(b) 55
(c) 63
(d) 60

58. In a ΔABC, two medians AD and BE intersect at G at right angles. If $AD = 18$ cm and $BE = 12$ cm, then the length of BD is equal to
(a) 10 cm (b) 15 cm
(c) 8 cm (d) 20 cm

59. What is the value of the following expression?
$$\frac{4}{7}\times4\frac{1}{2}\div5\frac{1}{3}\text{ of }2\frac{1}{2}-\left(7\frac{7}{8}\div5\frac{1}{9}\text{ of }9\frac{9}{20}\right)+\frac{1}{2}$$
(a) $\frac{853}{1610}$ (b) $\frac{1093}{111}$ (c) $\frac{1113}{856}$ (d) $\frac{1759}{3250}$

60. The surface areas of two spheres are in the ratio 25 : 36. What is the ratio of their volumes?
(a) $\frac{25}{36}$ (b) $\frac{36}{115}$
(c) $\frac{125}{216}$ (d) $\frac{36}{125}$

61. The following bar-graph shows the sales (in thousands) of magazines from six branches (A, B, C,D,E and F) of a publishing company during two consecutive years 2021 and 2022.

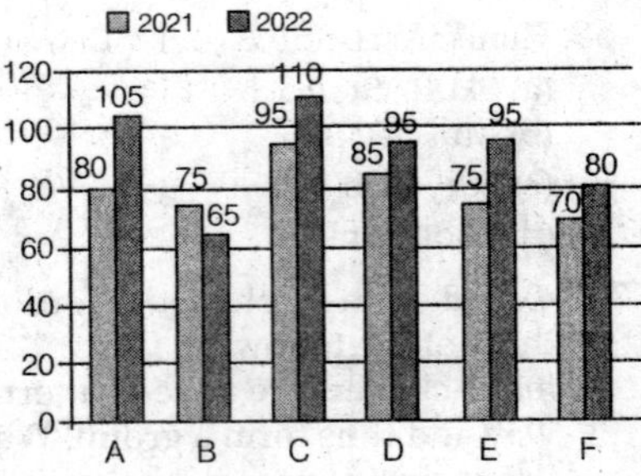

What per cent of the average sales of branches A, B and C in 2022 is the average sales of branches A, C and F in 2021?
(a) 86.2% (b) 88.4%
(c) 87.5% (d) 82.3%

62. A and B can do a piece of work in eight days and B alone can do it in 16 days. In how many days, can A do it alone?
(a) 24 days (b) 10 days
(c) 18 days (d) 16 days

63. If $\sin\theta = \frac{2xy}{x^2+y^2}$, then the value of $\tan\theta$ is
(a) $\frac{x^2+y^2}{x^2-y^2}$ (b) $\frac{2xy}{x^2-y^2}$
(c) $\frac{x^2-y^2}{2xy}$ (d) $\frac{x^2-y^2}{x^2+y^2}$

64. PQ is a diameter of a circle with centre O. The tangents at R meets PQ produced at A. If $\angle RPQ = 27°$, then measure of $\angle RQP$ is
(a) 63° (b) 54° (c) 153° (d) 27°

65. Ram travelled an equal distance with the speed of 40 km/h, 45 km/h and 60 km/h. What is the average speed of Ram during the whole journey? Correct to two decimal places.
(a) 66.94 km/h (b) 94.66 km/h
(c) 64.96 km/h (d) 46.96 km/h

66. Three persons ran for office and got, 1136, 7636 and 11628 votes, respectively. What was the winning candidate's percentage of the total votes?
(a) 52% (b) 61%
(c) 59% (d) 57%

67. Ravi sells his goods at a 25% loss on cost price but uses 45% less weight. What is his percentage profit or loss?
(a) Profit, $47\frac{9}{10}$% (b) Loss, $36\frac{4}{11}$%
(c) Loss, $47\frac{9}{10}$% (d) Profit, $36\frac{4}{11}$%

68. Two circles touch each other at a point O. AB is a simple common tangent to both the circles touching at point A and point B. If radii of the circles are 9 cm and 4 cm, then find AB.
(a) 72 cm (b) 144 cm
(c) 12 cm (d) 24 cm

69. If $2^3 : 8^{5.06} :: 8^{-4.06} : x$, find the value of x.
(a) $\frac{1}{2^3}$ (b) 1
(c) 2^3 (d) 0

70. The following graph shows the production (in thousands) of two types (A and B) of cars by a company over the years 2016 to 2021.

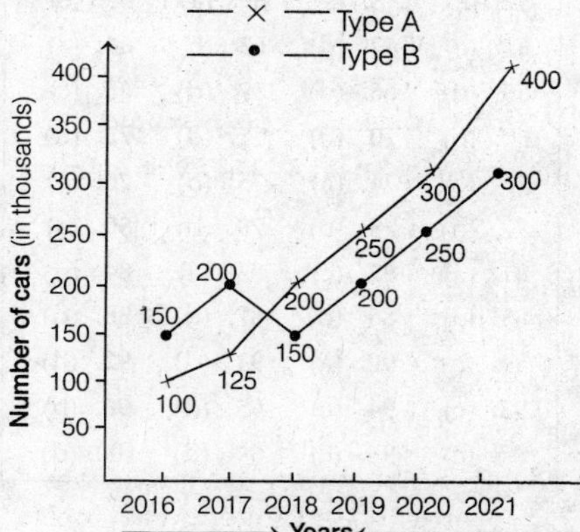

In how many of the given years was the production of type A cars more than the average production of this type car in the given years?
(a) 2 (b) 3
(c) 1 (d) 4

71. The given table shows the marks obtained by 100 students out of 50 marks in Mathematics and Physics in an examination.

Marks/ Subjects	40 or above	30 or above	20 or above	10 or above	0 or above
Mathem -atics	9	32	80	92	100
Physics	4	21	66	81	100
Average	7	27	73	87	100

If atleast 60% marks in Physics are required for pursuing higher studies in Physics, how many students will be eligible to pursue higher studies in Physics?
(a) 27 (b) 81
(c) 66 (d) 21

72. Reshma took a loan of ₹1200000 with simple interest for as many years as the rate of interest. If she paid ₹ 972000 as interest at the end of the loan period, what was the rate of interest per annum ?
(a) 7.5% (b) 8% (c) 8.7% (d) 9%

73. The value of $\left(\frac{7+8\times7\div8+7\div7\div7}{3+3\times3\div3+5\div5\div5}\right)$ is
(a) $3\frac{27}{217}$ (b) $1\frac{81}{217}$
(c) $2\frac{61}{217}$ (d) $1\frac{31}{217}$

74. The sides of a cuboid are in the ratio 3 : 4 : 5 and its surface area is equal to the surface area of the cube with side 6 units. What is the approximate volume of the cuboid?
(a) 210 (b) 150
(c) 240 (d) 180

75. Study the given three-dimensional chart and answer the question that follows. The chart details the sale of fruits in different months.

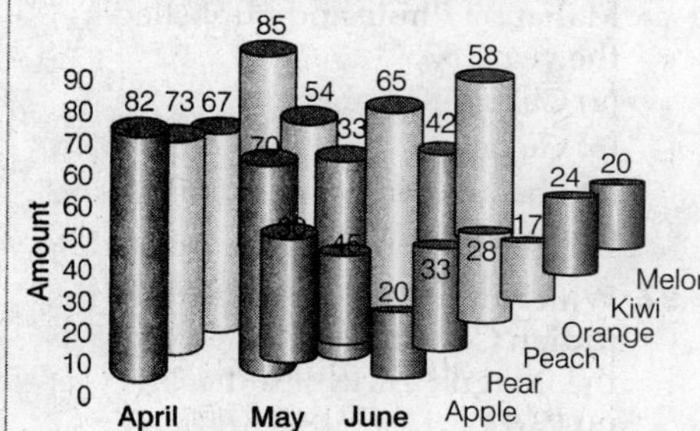

In which month was the sale of Melons the lowest and by how much was it more than the sale of Oranges in that month?
(a) June, 4 (b) June, 3
(c) April, 3 (d) May, 3

Part IV
General Awareness

76. Which of the following is not a stringed instrument?
(a) Flute (b) Violin
(c) Mandolin (d) Guitar

77. Which power were the Badami (or Vatapi) Chalukyas originally subjects of?
(a) Hoysalas (b) Pallavas
(c) Pandyas (d) Kadambas

78. According to the National Crime Records Bureau data, from 2016 to 2019, suicide cases due to unemployment have increased by ....
(a) 21%
(b) 24%
(c) 18%
(d) 20%

79. When was the Swarnajayanti Gram Swarozgar Yojana (SGSY) launched by the Government of India?
(a) 1995 (b) 1999
(c) 2000 (d) 1991

80. In the given main characteristics of farming which is not a characteristic of the Indian commercial farming?
(a) Slash and burn
(b) Chemical fertilisers
(c) Insecticides and pesticides
(d) High yielding variety seeds

81. ICC Word Cup (cricket) 2023 was hosted by ....
(a) India
(b) India and Bangladesh
(c) India, Sri Lanka and Bangladesh
(d) India and Sri Lanka

82. Who was the chief coordinator for the G20 summit which held in India in 2023?
(a) S.Jaishankar
(b) Vinay Kwatra
(c) Harsh Vardhan Shringla
(d) Vijay Gokhale

83. On 26th January, 1950 India became
(a) a sovereign, democratic, republic state
(b) a socialist and secular state
(c) an independent state
(d) a unitary state

84. Which of the following is not one of the main pillars of the 'Namami Gange Programme', launched by the Government of India in 2014?
(a) Sewerage Treatment Infrastructure
(b) River-Front Development
(c) Industrial Effluent Monitoring
(d) River Linkage Development

85. The song 'Teri mitti' is from which of the following movies?
(a) Kesari
(b) Rajniti
(c) Satya Mev Jayte
(d) Jai Ho

86. Which of the following statements about eutrophication is correct?
(a) It happens when too much carbon enriches the water, causing excessive growth of bacteria and reduced growth of plants.
(b) It happens when too less nitrogen is present in the water, causing reduced growth of plants and algae.
(c) It is a beneficial process for environment restoration.
(d) It happens when too much nitrogen enriches the water, causing excessive growth of plants and algae.

87. Mohammad Yunus established which of the following banks in 1983?
(a) Indian Bank (b) Union Bank
(c) State Bank (d) Grameen Bank

88. In which year did Robert Brown observe the Zigzag Movement of colloidal particles in solution?
(a) 1829 (b) 1826 (c) 1828 (d) 1827

89. Which of the following are needed for Skype to function on a computer?
1. A web cam
2. A microphone
3. A speaker

Codes
(a) 1 and 3 (b) 1, 2 and 3
(c) 2 and 3 (d) 1 and 2

90. In year 2023, the Government of India launched which of the following schemes to bring Indian-origin researchers to higher educational institutional in the country?
(a) VAIBHAV
(b) Amantran
(c) Vapsi
(d) Seekho

91. Which is, by far, the closest dwarf planet orbiting at only 2.8 times Earth's distance from the Sun?
(a) Makemake (b) Pluto
(c) Eris (d) Ceres

92. According to Global Multidimensional Poverty Index (2022), which of the following groups of states is included in top 10 poorest states of India?
(a) Punjab and Gujarat
(b) Manipur and Nagaland
(c) Karnataka and Tamil Nadu
(d) Meghalaya and Madhya Pradesh

93. The default width of a column in MS Excel is
(a) 7 characters (b) 9 characters
(c) 8 characters (d) 6 characters

94. Which of the following statements is correct about the Five-Year Plan?
(a) All Five-Year Plans have equal rates of growth.
(b) The Planning Commission was constituted in 1951.
(c) The first Five-Year Plan was started in 1951.
(d) The President was the ex-officio chairperson of the Planning Commission.

95. Who among the followings won gold at the International Shooting Sport Federation (ISSF) Junior World Cup 2023?
(a) Mahesh Pasupathy Anandakumar
(b) Rajkanwar Singh Sandhu
(c) Umamahesh Maddineni
(d) Dhanush Srikanth

96. .... is one of the first criticism of the caste system written by Mahatma Phule and published in the year 1873.
(a) Gulami Ki Kahani
(b) Gulamgiri
(c) Bharat Mein Jaati Evam Prajaati
(d) Jati ka Unmoolan

97. Which of the following parts of the Indian Constitution is described as the 'Magna Carta of India'?
(a) Part IV (b) Part II
(c) Part III (d) Part I

98. 'Hampi Utsava,' which is celebrated in Karnataka, is also called .... The festival that captures the pomp, splendour and glory of the historical period of Karnataka is celebrated over a week.
(a) Sarhul Mahotsava
(b) Rajasi Utsava
(c) Vijaya Utsava
(d) Nritya Mahotsav

99. Nehru Institute of Mountaineering is located at ....
(a) Leh
(b) Jammu and Kashmir
(c) Himachal Pradesh
(d) Uttarakhand

100. Which of the following dances developed in the monasteries of Assam?
(a) Kuchipudi (b) Kathak
(c) Bharatanatyam (d) Sattriya

Answers

1. (a)	2. (c)	3. (d)	4. (a)
5. (d)	6. (a)	7. (b)	8. (a)
9. (a)	10. (d)	11. (d)	12. (d)
13. (b)	14 (b)	15. (d)	16. (b)
17. (b)	18. (c)	19. (a)	20. (c)
21. (c)	22. (c)	23. (d)	24. (d)
25. (d)	26. (b)	27. (c)	28. (a)
29. (a)	30. (b)	31. (d)	32. (a)
33. (d)	34. (b)	35. (b)	36. (c)
37. (b)	38. (c)	39. (b)	40. (d)
41. (d)	42. (a)	43. (a)	44. (a)
45. (a)	46. (d)	47. (b)	48. (c)
49. (d)	50. (a)	51. (d)	52. (b)
53. (b)	54. (c)	55. (d)	56. (d)
57. (a)	58. (a)	59. (a)	60. (c)
61. (c)	62. (d)	63. (b)	64. (a)
65. (d)	66. (d)	67. (d)	68. (c)
69. (b)	70. (b)	71. (d)	72. (d)
73. (c)	74. (a)	75. (b)	76. (a)
77. (d)	78. (b)	79. (b)	80. (a)
81. (a)	82. (c)	83. (a)	84. (d)
85. (a)	86. (d)	87. (d)	88. (d)
89. (b)	90. (a)	91. (d)	92. (d)
93. (c)	94. (c)	95. (d)	96. (b)
97. (c)	98. (c)	99. (d)	100. (d)

Explanations

1. *(a)* Part (a) 'show on' contains an error. The phrasal verb 'show on' is incorrect for the sentence. The correct phrasal verb is 'show off' which means display someone or something that is a source of pride.'

2. *(c)* Part (c) 'will rain' contains an error. The sentence is a future hypothetical conditional wherein the 'if' clause is in present tense. Hence, 'rains' should be used to correct the sentence.

3. *(d)* Part (d) 'Hard had she' contains an error. Use 'Hardly' in place of 'Hard' to correct the sentence.

4. *(a)* Part (a) 'Ramayana is an ancient' contains an error. Definite article 'the' is used with the name of holy books. Hence, add 'The' before 'Ramayana' to correct the sentence.

5. *(d)* The correct filler for the given blank is 'sowed'.

6. *(a)* The correct filler for the given blank is 'shallow' which means 'not deep'.

7. *(b)* The correct filler for the given blank is 'rooted'.

8. *(a)* The correct filler for the given blank is 'evolved'.

9. *(a)* The correct filler for the given blank is 'united'.

10. *(d)* The correct filler for the given blank is 'close'. The phrase 'close the deal' means to complete or to get a deal successfully.

11. *(d)* The underlined part of the sentence contains an error. The conjunction 'as' does not take 'so'. Hence, remove 'so' to correct the sentence.

12. *(d)* 'At ones fingertips' means to have complete knowledge.

13. *(b)* 'Resistance' means the refusal to accept or comply with something. Hence, its antonym is 'tolerance' which means the ability or willingness to tolerate the existence of opinions or behaviour that one dislikes or disagrees with.

- 'Tenderness' means with love and affection.
- 'Reliance' means to depend on.

14. *(b)* The bracketed part of the sentence contains an error. Use 'that could' to correct the sentence.

15. *(d)* 'Strenuous' means complex and difficult. Hence, its antonym is 'easy'. 'Intense' means of extreme force, degree, or strength.

16. *(b)* The underlined part of the sentence contains an error. Use 'connects' to correct the sentence.

17. *(b)* 'Amicable' means warm and friendly. Hence, its antonym is unfriendly.

18. *(c)* An asylum is a place where people with mental illness are kept and treated.

- 'Hangar' means a large building with an extensive floor area, typically for housing aircraft.
- 'Druggist' means a person who sells or dispenses drugs and medicines.
- 'Shelter' means a place where one is kept safe and secure.

19. *(a)* The incorrectly spelt word is 'academecian'. The correctly spelt word is 'academician'.

20. *(c)* 'In deep water' means to be in a difficult situation or trouble.

21. *(c)* 'Deposed' means remove from office suddenly and forcefully. Hence, its antonym is 'promoted' which means raise (someone) to a higher position or rank.

- 'Interacted' means to communicate.
- 'Demolished' means to be destroyed.
- 'Segregated' means separated.

22. *(c)* 'Interacts' means to communicate. Hence, its antonym is 'disconnects'.

- 'Co-operates' means assist someone or comply with their requests.
- 'Interrelates' means relate or connect to one another.
- 'Intermingles' means mix or mingle together.

23. *(d)* The incorrectly spelt word is 'aquire'. The correct spelling is 'acquire'.

24. *(d)* The antonym of 'beautiful is ugly'.

- 'Pungent' means having a sharply strong taste or smell.
- 'Stingy' means mean; ungenerous.
- 'Slimy' means slippery.

25. *(d)* 'Defeat' means loss. Hence, its antonym is 'victory' which means 'to win'.
'Subjugated' means to bring under domination or control, especially by conquest.

26. *(b)* The pattern of the series is as follows,

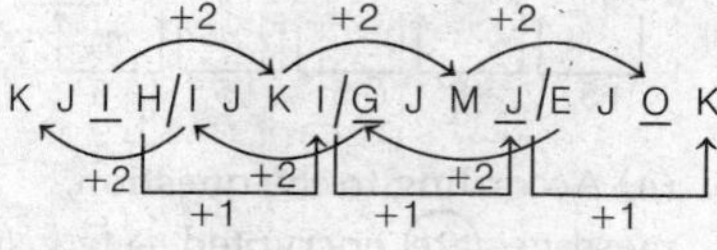

⇒ IGJO

27. *(c)* Given,
M − N + O
According to the question,

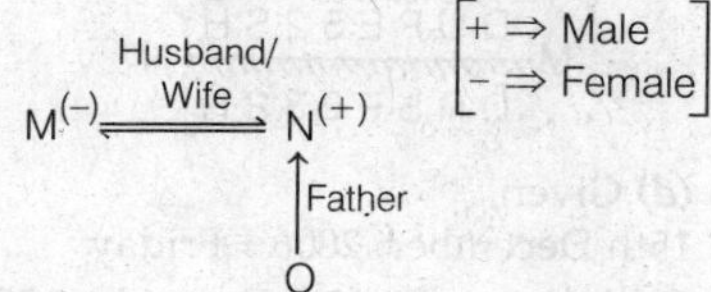

So, it is clear from the diagram that 'M is the mother of O' is the correct option.

28. *(a)* According to the question,

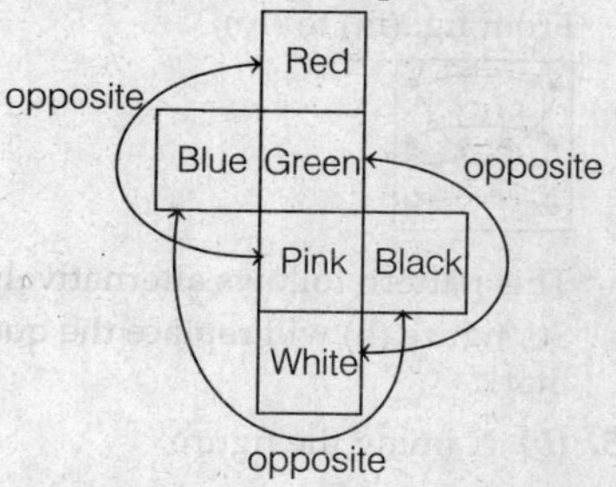

After folded the sheet to the cube, it is clear that the opposite side of 'blue' is 'black'.

29. *(a)* Option (a) is the correct mirror image of the given question figure.

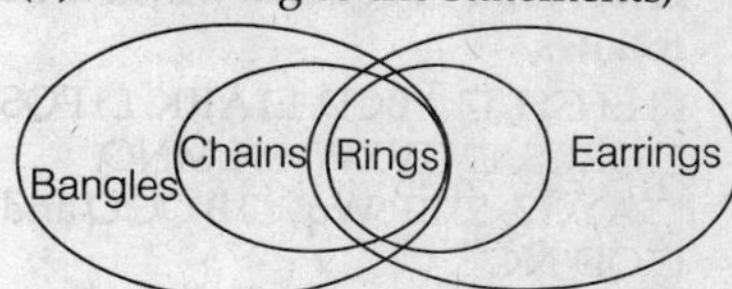

30. *(b)* According to the statements,

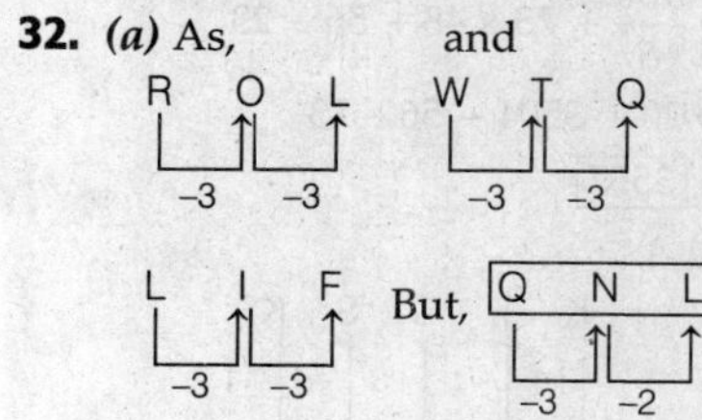

Conclusions

I. (✓) II. (✓) III. (✓)

Hence, all Conclusions I, II and III follow.

31. *(d)* As, 'wrist' is the part of hand. Similarly, 'ankle' is the part of foot.

32. *(a)* As, and

R O L: −3, −3 W T Q: −3, −3

L I F: −3, −3 But, Q N L: −3, −2

Hence, QNL is the odd one.

33. *(d)* As, (21, 34, 76)
⇒ 21 + 34 ⇒ 55 + 21 = 76
and (39, 26, 104)
⇒ 39 + 26 ⇒ 65 + 39 = 104
Similarly, (28, 23, 79)
⇒ 28 + 23 = 51 + 28 = 79

34. *(b)* The figure series is as follows,
From fig. (i) to (ii),
From fig. (iii) to (iv),

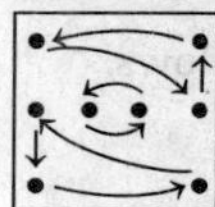

From fig. (ii) to (iii),
From fig. (iii) to (iv)

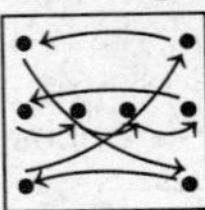

This pattern follows alternatively.
So, figure (b) will replace the question mark.

35. *(b)* Naming the figure,

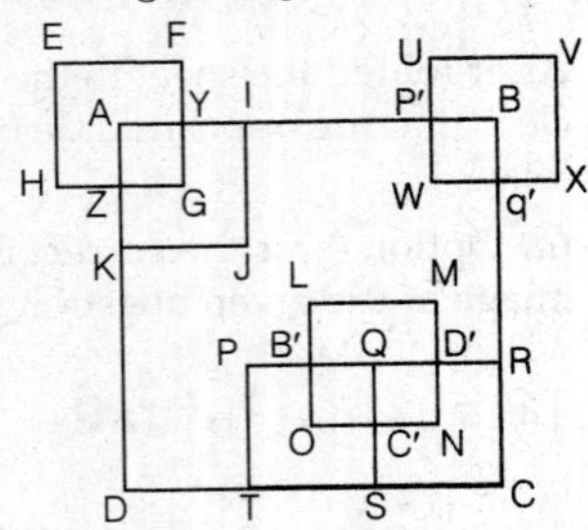

Here, total 11 squares which are as follows,
□ EFGH, □ ABCD, □ AIJK, □ PQST, □QRCS, □ UVXW, □ LMNO, □ AYGZ, □ BP'Wq', □ B'QC'O and □QD'NC'

36. *(c)* Given equation,
? = 100 K 5 M 73 T 48 M 56 G 23 = ?
After replacing the letters with signs, we get
? = 100 ÷ 5 + 73 × 48 + 56 − 23
Applying BODMAS,

$$= \frac{100}{5} + 73 \times 48 + 56 - 23$$
$$= 20 + 3504 + 56 - 23$$
$$= \boxed{3557}$$

37. *(b)* As,

K I O S K
+1 +1 +3 +1 +1
L J R T L

and

F L A M E
+1 +1 +3 +1 +1
G M D N F

Similarly,

E N J O Y
+1 +1 +3 +1 +1
F O M P Z

38. *(c)* The pattern is as follows,
As, 11 × 5 = 55
and 22 × 5 = 110
Similarly, 44 × 5 = $\boxed{220}$

39. *(b)* According to the question,

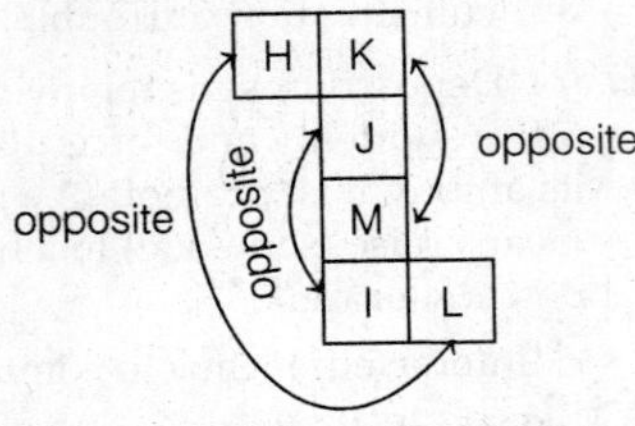

It is clear that after folded sheet to form a cube, the opposite side of K will be M.

40. *(d)* Given equation,
21 + 3 − 7 ÷ 11 × 4 = ?
After interchanging the signs, we get
? = 21 ÷ 3 × 7 + 11 − 4
Applying BODMAS,

$$= \frac{21}{3} \times 7 + 11 - 4$$
$$= 49 + 11 - 4 = 56$$

41. *(d)* Option (d) consist the embedded figure.

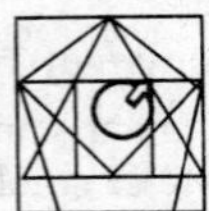

42. *(a)* The pattern of the series is as follows,

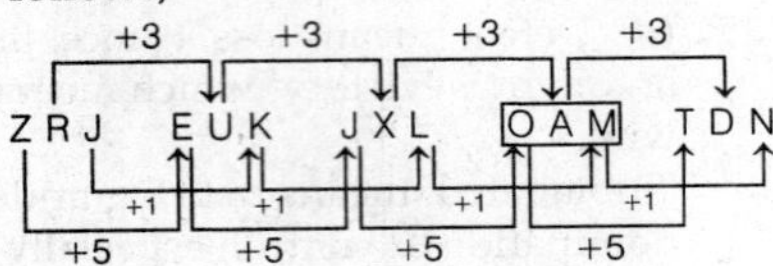

43. *(a)* The pattern of the series is as follows,

162, 167, 172, 177, 182, $\boxed{187}$
+5 +5 +5 +5 +5

44. *(a)* According to the question,
messages (are) encrypted → tg gc (mz)
(are) you coming → ze fp (mz)
So, 'mz' is the code of are.

45. *(a)* Option (a) is the correct mirror image of the given question figure.

DUPE52SH
M————N
ᗡՈᑫƎ5ƧSH

46. *(d)* Given,
15th December, 2006 = Friday
Odd days from 15th December, 2006 to 15th December, 2008
= 1 + 2 = 3
It means on 15th December, 2008, it is Friday + 3 ⇒ Monday

Now, from 15th December, 2008 to 13th October, 2009
Number of odd days
⇒ 16 + 31 + 28 + 31 + 30 + 31 + 30 + 31 + 31 + 30 + 13

$$= \frac{302}{7}$$
= 1 odd day
∴ On 13th October, 2009, it is Monday + 1odd day ⇒ Tuesday

47. *(b)* The pattern of the series is as follows,

54 58.7 64.4 71.1 78.8 $\boxed{87.5}$
+4.7 +5.7 +6.7 +7.7 +8.7

48. *(c)* Given equation,
17 H 23 Q 42 Z 7 E 13 = ?
After substituting the letters with signs, we get,
? = 17 + 23 × 42 ÷ 7 − 13
Applying BODMAS rule,

$$= 17 + 23 \times \frac{42}{7} - 13$$
$$= 17 + 23 \times 6 - 13$$
$$= 17 + 138 - 13 = 142$$

49. *(d)* As, 'Interrupt' is the antonym of 'Continue'. So, it is the pair of antonyms of word.
Hence, 'Attic - Common' is a correct answer.

50. *(a)* Given, 6th May, 2005 = Friday
We know that,
Every ordinary year has 1 odd day.
Every leap year has 2 odd days.
From 6th May, 2005 to 6th May, 2018, number of odd days
= 1 + 1 + 2 + 1 + 1 + 1 + 2 + 1 + 1 + 1 + 2 + 1 + 1

$$= \frac{16}{7} = \text{remaining odd days} = 2$$

It means 6th May, 2018 = Friday + 2 = Sunday
Now, from 6th May, 2018 to 25th September, 2018 number of odd days
= 25 + 30 + 31 + 31 + 25

$$= \frac{142}{7} \Rightarrow 2 \text{ odd days}$$

∴ On 25th September, 2018, the day = Sunday + 2 odd days
⇒ Tuesday

51. *(d)* According to the question,
Present age of younger boy = x yr
Present age of older boy = $3x$ yr

$$\frac{3x - 9}{x - 9} = \frac{5}{1}$$

9 yr ago,

$\Rightarrow 3x - 9 = 5x - 45$

$\Rightarrow \quad 2x = 36 \Rightarrow \quad x = 18$

So, their present ages are 18 yr and 54 yr, respectively.

52. *(b)* According to the question,

Last year bike price = ₹ 125000

Decrease percentage in price

$= 30\% = \frac{3}{10}$

10 → 7 (× 12500)

125000 → ₹ 87500

∴ This year electric car price

= ₹ 87500

53. *(b)* According to the question,

$\frac{2\pi rh}{\pi r^2 h} = \frac{2}{3}$

$r = 3$ unit

and ratio of radius to height = 3 : 7

So, height = 7 unit

Total surface area $= 2\pi r(r + h)$

$= 2\pi \times 3(3 + 7)$

$= 6\pi(10) = 60\pi \text{ cm}^2$

54. *(c)* Given, last quotient = 3

Remainder when divided by 7 is 3.

∴ Dividend = Divisor × Quotient + Remainder

Dividend = 7 × 3 + 3 = 24

∵ 24 is the result of division by 5 leaving a remainder of 1.

∴ The number before division

$\Rightarrow \quad 5 \times 24 + 1 = 121$

∵ 121 is the result of division by 3 leaving a remainder of 2.

∴ $\quad 121 \times 3 + 2 = 363 + 2$

$= 365$

Hence, the original number = 365

55. *(d)* ∵ *ABCD* is a cyclic quadrilateral.

$\therefore \angle ABC + \angle ADC = 180°$

$85° + \angle ADC = 180°$

$\Rightarrow \quad \angle ADC = 95°$

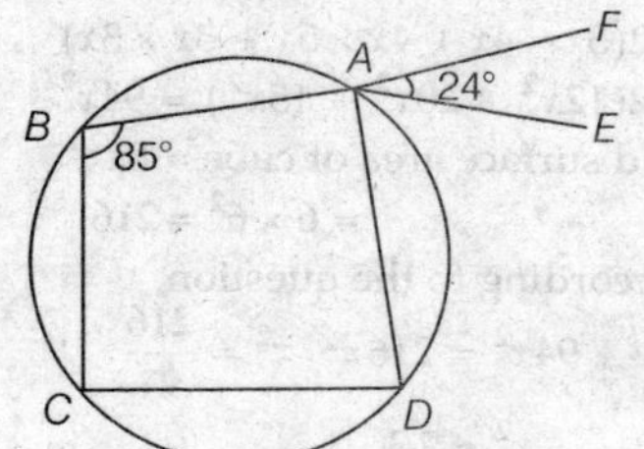

According to the question,

AE || *CD*

$\therefore \quad \angle EAD = \angle ADC = 95°$

(∵ Alternate angles)

We know that, the exterior angle of a cyclic quadrilateral is equal to the interior opposite angle.

$\therefore \quad \angle BCD = \angle DAF$

$\angle BCD = \angle EAD + \angle EAF$

$\Rightarrow \angle BCD = 95° + 24°$

$\Rightarrow \angle BCD = 119°$

Hence, $\angle BCD = 119°$

56. *(d)* Given, total toys = 75

Toys for boys = 18

∴ Toys for girls = 75 − 18 = 57

Required percentage $= \frac{57}{75} \times 100$

$= \frac{57 \times 4}{3} = 76\%$

57. *(a)* According to the question,

For 110 miles he takes 2 h

For next 120 miles, he takes 2 h

For last 60 miles, he takes 1 h

So, average speed

$= \frac{\text{Total distance covered}}{\text{Total time taken}}$

$= \frac{110 + 120 + 60}{2 + 2 + 1} = \frac{290}{5} = 58$

58. *(a)* Given, *AD* and *BE* are medians of ΔABC and they intersect at *G* at right angles.

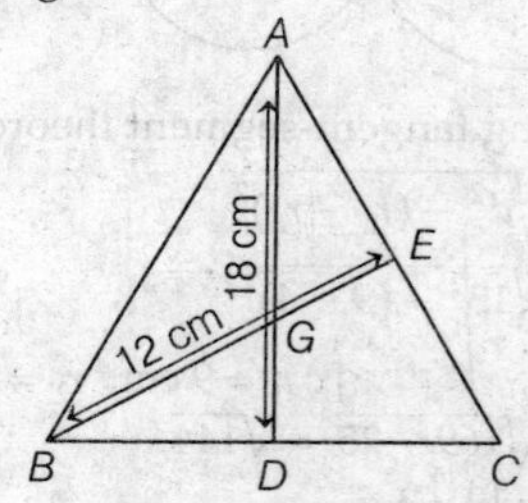

∵ In any triangle, the centroid divides each median into a ratio of 2 : 1 with the longer segment being closer to the vertex.

$\Rightarrow AG = \frac{2}{3} \times 18 = 12 \text{ cm}$

$GD = \frac{1}{3} \times 18 = 6 \text{ cm}$

$BG = \frac{2}{3} \times 12 = 8 \text{ cm}$

$GE = \frac{1}{3} \times 12 = 4 \text{ cm}$

By using Pythagoras theorem,

$BD^2 = BG^2 + GD^2$

$\Rightarrow \quad BD^2 = 8^2 + 6^2$

$\therefore \quad BD = 10 \text{ cm}$

Hence, length of $BD = 10$ cm

59. *(a)* $\frac{4}{7} \times 4\frac{1}{2} \div 5\frac{1}{3} \text{ of } 2\frac{1}{2} - \left(7\frac{7}{8} \div 5\frac{1}{9} \text{ of } 9\frac{9}{20}\right) + \frac{1}{2}$

$= \frac{4}{7} \times \frac{9}{2} \div \frac{16}{3} \times \frac{5}{2} - \left(\frac{63}{8} \div \frac{46}{9} \times \frac{189}{20}\right) + \frac{1}{2}$

$= \frac{4}{7} \times \frac{9}{2} \div \frac{40}{3} - \left(\frac{60}{3} \div \frac{483}{10}\right) + \frac{1}{2}$

$= \frac{4}{7} \times \frac{9}{2} \div \frac{40}{3} - \frac{105}{644} + \frac{1}{2}$

$= \frac{4}{7} \times \frac{27}{80} - \frac{105}{644} + \frac{1}{2} = \frac{27}{140} - \frac{105}{644} + \frac{1}{2}$

$= \frac{97}{140} - \frac{105}{644} = \frac{1706}{3220} = \frac{853}{1610}$

60. *(c)* ∵ Surface area of sphere $= 4\pi r^2$

According to the question,

$\frac{4\pi r_1^2}{4\pi r_2^2} = \frac{25}{36} \Rightarrow \frac{r_1}{r_2} = \frac{5}{6}$

$\therefore$ Ratio of volumes $= \frac{\frac{4}{3}\pi r_1^3}{\frac{4}{3}\pi r_2^3}$

$= \left(\frac{r_1}{r_2}\right)^3 = \left(\frac{5}{6}\right)^3 \quad \left[\because \text{given, } \frac{r_1}{r_2} = \frac{5}{6}\right]$

$= \frac{125}{216}$

61. *(c)* According to the graph,

Branches	2021	2022
A	80	105
B	75	65
C	95	110
D	85	95
E	75	95
F	70	80

Average sales of branches A, B and C in 2022

$= \frac{105 + 65 + 110}{3} = \frac{280}{3}$

Average sales of branches A, C and F in 2021

$= \frac{80 + 95 + 70}{3} = \frac{245}{3}$

∴ Required percentage

$= 100\% - \frac{\frac{35}{3}}{\frac{280}{3}} \times 100\%$

$= 100\% - \frac{35}{280} \times 100\%$

$= 100\% - 12.5\% = 87.5\%$

62. *(d)* According to the question,

A + *B* — 8 days ⟩ LCM 16 — 2 [Efficiency of *A* and *B*]

B — 16 days ⟩ — 1 [Efficiency of *B*]

Let total work = 16

So, *A* alone can do it in $= \frac{16}{1}$

= 16 days

63. *(b)* Given, $\sin\theta = \frac{2xy}{x^2+y^2}$

We know that,

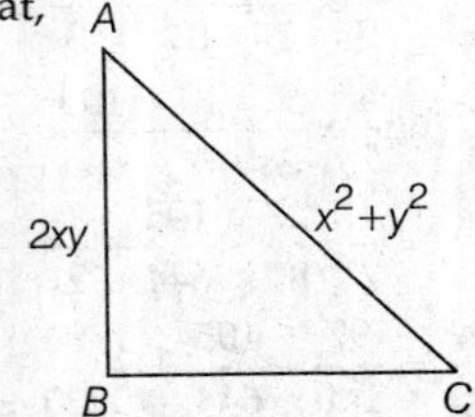

$\sin\theta = \frac{\text{Perpendicular}}{\text{Hypotenuse}}$

and $\tan\theta = \frac{\text{Perpendicular}}{\text{Base}}$

So, by using Pythagoras theorem,

$AC^2 = AB^2 + BC^2$

$(x^2+y^2)^2 = (2xy)^2 + BC^2$

$\Rightarrow BC = \sqrt{(x^2+y^2)^2 - (2xy)^2}$

$= \sqrt{x^4 + 2x^2y^2 + y^4 - 4x^2y^2}$

$= \sqrt{x^4 - 2x^2y^2 + y^4} = \sqrt{(x^2-y^2)^2}$

$BC = |x^2 - y^2|$

$\therefore \tan\theta = \frac{AB}{BC} = \frac{2xy}{x^2-y^2}$

64. *(a)* Given, $\angle RPQ = 27°$

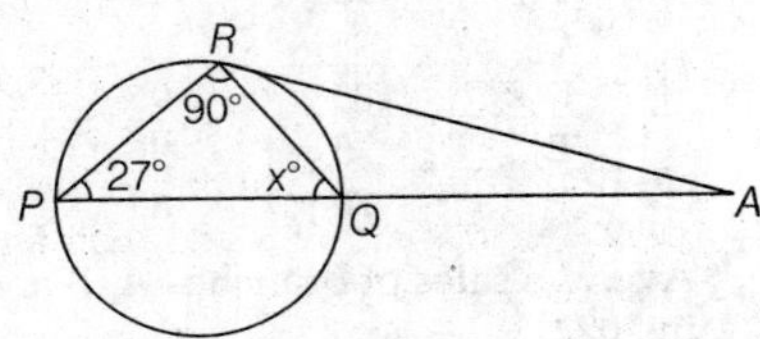

Since, PQ is a diameter.

$\therefore \angle PRQ$ is 90° because it is subtended by a diameter in semi-circle.

By applying angle sum property,

$\angle PRQ + \angle RPQ + \angle RQP = 180°$

$\Rightarrow 90° + 27° + \angle RQP = 180°$

$\Rightarrow \angle RQP = 180° - 117° = 63°$

65. *(d)* Let distance = d

According to the question,

$t_1 = \frac{d}{40}, t_2 = \frac{d}{45}, t_3 = \frac{d}{60}$

$\therefore$ Average speed $= \frac{\text{Total distance}}{\text{Total time}}$

$= \frac{d+d+d}{\frac{d}{40}+\frac{d}{45}+\frac{d}{60}} = \frac{3d}{\frac{90d+80d+60d}{3600}}$

$= \frac{3d \times 3600}{230d} = \frac{1080}{23} = 46.96$ km/h

66. *(d)* According to the question,

Winner gets = 11628 votes

Total votes = 20400

So, required percentage $= \frac{11628}{20400} \times 100$

$= 57\%$

67. *(d)* Let cost price = 100 units

Selling price = 75 units

$\because$ He uses 45% less weight means, he uses 55% of original weight and sells 55% of the weight for 75% of the cost price.

$\therefore \frac{75\% \text{ CP}}{55\% \text{ Weight}} = \frac{75}{55} \times \text{CP}$

$= 1.36 \times \text{CP}$

$\because$ SP/unit is more than CP.

$\therefore$ Ravi makes profit

$\therefore$ Profit per cent $= \frac{1.3636 - 1}{1} \times 100$

$= 36.36\%$

$\approx 36\frac{4}{11}\%$

68. *(c)* We know that,

When two circles touch each other externally, the distance between their centres is equal to the sum of their radii.

$\because AB$ is common external tangent to both circles.

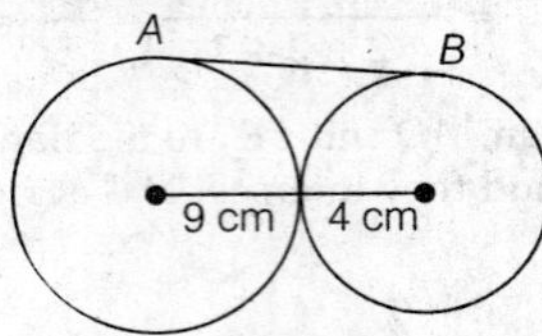

By using tangent-segment theorem,

$AB = \sqrt{d^2 - (r_1 - r_2)^2}$

$AB = \sqrt{13^2 - (9-4)^2}$

$[\because r_1 = 9 \text{ cm}, r_2 = 4 \text{ cm}]$

$= \sqrt{169 - 25} = \sqrt{144}$

$\therefore AB = 12$

Hence, length of AB = 12 cm

69. *(b)* $2^3 : 8^{5.06} :: 8^{-4.06} : x$

$\Rightarrow \frac{2^3}{2^{3(5.06)}} = \frac{(2^3)^{-4.06}}{x}$

$\Rightarrow \frac{2^3}{2^{15.18}} = \frac{2^{-12.18}}{x}$

$\Rightarrow 2^{3-15.18} = \frac{2^{-12.18}}{x}$

$\Rightarrow 2^{-12.18} = \frac{2^{-12.18}}{x} \Rightarrow x = 1$

70. *(b)* According to the graph,

Years	Type A	Type B
2016	100	150
2017	125	200
2018	200	150
2019	250	200
2020	300	250
2021	400	300

Average production of type A car

$= \frac{100 + 125 + 200 + 250 + 300 + 400}{6}$

$\simeq 229$

Hence, in 3 yr, 2019, 2020 and 2021 type A car production more than the average of type A car production.

71. *(d)* From the given table, it is clear that only 21 students obtained 30 or above marks in Physics.

$\because 60\% \times 50 = 30$

$\therefore$ Required marks = 30

Hence, 21 students will be eligible.

72. *(d)* Loan amount = ₹ 1200000

Interest = ₹ 972000

$\text{SI} = \frac{P \times R \times T}{100}$

$\Rightarrow 972000 = \frac{1200000 \times x \times x}{100}$

[$\because$ time and rate are same]

$\Rightarrow x^2 = 81 \Rightarrow x = 9$

Hence, rate (R) = 9%

73. *(c)* Given expresseion,

$\left(\frac{7 + 8 \times 7 \div 8 + 7 \div 7 \div 7}{3 + 3 \times 3 \div 3 + 5 \div 5 \div 5}\right)$

$= \left(\frac{7 + 8 \times \frac{7}{8} + \frac{7}{7} \times \frac{1}{7}}{3 + 3 \times \frac{3}{3} + \frac{5}{5} \times \frac{1}{5}}\right)$

$= \left(\frac{7 + 7 + \frac{1}{7}}{3 + 3 + \frac{1}{5}}\right)$

$= \left(\frac{14 + \frac{1}{7}}{6 + \frac{1}{5}}\right) = \frac{\frac{99}{7}}{\frac{31}{5}} = \frac{99}{7} \times \frac{5}{31}$

$= \frac{495}{217} = 2\frac{61}{217}$

74. *(a)* Let the sides of cuboid be $3x$, $4x$ and $5x$.

Surface area of cuboid

$= 2(lb + bh + hl)$

$= 2(3x \times 4x + 4x \times 5x + 5x \times 3x)$

$= 2(12x^2 + 20x^2 + 15x^2) = 94x^2$

and surface area of cube $= 6a^2$

$= 6 \times 6^2 = 216$

According to the question,

$\Rightarrow 94x^2 = 216 \Rightarrow x^2 = \frac{216}{94}$

$\Rightarrow x^2 \approx 2.3$

$\therefore x \simeq 1.52$

$\therefore$ Volume of cuboid

$= 3x \times 4x \times 5x = 60x^3$

$= 60 \times (1.52)^3$

≈ 210.6

Hence, option (a) is correct.

75. *(b)* It is clear from the 3D chart that lowest sale of melons in month June = 20

Sale of oranges in June = 17

So, it is clear that, Sales of melon is 3 more than the sales of oranges in the month June.

Hence, option (b) is correct.

76. *(a)* The flute is a woodwind instrument, not a stringed instrument.

- **Mandolin** A small, eight-stringed instrument played with a pick or fingers, commonly used in folk and classical music.
- **Guitar** A fretted, stringed instrument played by plucking or strumming, popular in various genres like rock, pop, and classical music.
- **Violin** A bowed, four-stringed instrument played with the fingers or a bow, known for its expressive and melodic sound in classical and folk music.

77. *(d)* The Badami (or Vatapi) Chalukyas were originally subjects of the Kadambas.

- The Chalukyas were feudatories of the Kadambas and later overthrew them to establish their own empire in the 6th century CE.
- The Chalukya dynasty was established by Pulakeshin I in 543 AD.

78. *(b)* According to the NCRB, suicides due to unemployment went up by 24% from 2016 to 2019.

- As per NCRB, 2,851 people commited suicide due to unemployment in 2019.
- Karnataka registered the greatest number (553) of suicides due to unemployment in 2019.
- NCRB is an Indian Government agency to collect and analyse crime data in accordance with the Indian Penal Code (IPC) and Special and Local Laws (SLL).

79. *(b)* The Swarnajayanti Gram Swarozgar Yojana (SGSY) was launched by the Government of India in 1999.

- It was a self-employment program aimed at providing financial assistance to rural poor people, particularly those below the poverty line, to help them start their own businesses and become self-employed.
- The SGSY was replaced by the National Rural Livelihoods Mission (NRLM) in 2011.

80. *(a)* Slash and burn is a characteristic of shifting cultivation, not a characteristic of the Indian commercial farming.

It is also known as jhumming. It involves clearing land by burning vegetation and farming on it for a fewy ears before moving to a new area.

Indian commercial farming is characterised by

- Use of insecticides and pesticides to control pests and diseases.
- Use of chemical fertilisers to enhance soil fertility and crop yields.
- Use of High-Yielding Variety (HYV) seeds to increase crop productivity.

81. *(a)* The 2023 ICC Men's Cricket World Cup was hosted by India from 5th October to 19th November, 2023.

- The tournament took place in ten different stadiums across India, with the final match held at Narendra Modi Stadium in Ahmedabad.
- Australia won the tournament by defeating India in the final match.
- Virat Kohli was named the player of the tournament, scoring the most runs in the tournament.

82. *(c)* The chief coordinator for the G20 summit held in India in 2023 was Harsh Vardhan Shringla.

- The G20 summit was held in Bharat Mandapam, Delhi on 9th-10th September, 2023. It was the first G20 summit held in India.
- The chief coordinator is responsible for organising the summit, which includes ensuring the smooth execution of the event, coordinating with various stakeholders, and overseeing the overall preparations.
- Amitabh Kant was sherpa Under the presidency of India in 2023.

83. *(a)* 26th January, 1950, India adopted its Constitution and became a sovereign, democratic, republic state.

- The Constitution replaced the Government of India Act 1935 as the country's fundamental governing document, and the Dominion of India became the Republic of India.
- January 26th is celebrated as Republic Day in India to commemorate the adoption of the Constitution.

84. *(d)* River Linkage Development is not a main pillar of the program.

The program focuses on cleaning and rejuvenating the Ganges river, but it does not involve linking rivers.

- The 'Namami Ganga Programme' launched by the Government of India in 2014 has several pillars, including
- **Sewerage Treatment Infrastructure** Upgrading and creating new sewage treatment infrastructure to reduce pollution.
- **Industrial Effluent Monitoring** Regulating and monitoring industrial effluents to prevent pollution.
- **River-Front Development** Developing and restoring riverfronts to promote tourism and cultural heritage.

85. *(a)* 'Teri Mitti' is a popular patriotic song from the Bollywood film 'Kesari' in 2019.

- The song was composed by Arko Pravo Mukherjee and sung by B. Praak, pays tribute to the bravery and sacrifice of the Indian soldiers who fought in the Battle of Saragarhi.
- 'Kesari' is a historical action-war film based on the true story of the Battle of Saragarhi, where 21 Sikh soldiers fought against 10,000 Afghan invaders in 1897.

86. *(d)* Statement (d) is correct about eutrophication.

- Eutrophication is process that occurs when too much nitrogen and other nutrients build zip in water, causing algae and plants to grow rapidly.
- This causes a number of environment issues such as oxygen depletion, algal blooms, ocean acidification etc.

87. *(d)* Muhammad Yunus founded Grameen Bank in 1983.

- Grameen Bank is a microfinance bank that provides small loans to rural and impoverished people, particularly women, without requiring collateral.
- Muhammad Yunus was awarded the Nobel Peace Prize in 2006 for

his pioneering work in microfinance and poverty reduction through Grameen Bank.

88. *(d)* Robert Brown, a Scottish botanist, observed the Zigzag Movement of colloidal particles in solution in 1827.

- This phenomenon is known as Brownian motion.
- This observation led to a deeper understanding of the behaviour of particles at the microscopic level and laid the foundation for the development of modern particle theory.
- In 1828, Brown published a pamphlet, 'A Brief Account of Microscopical Observations', about his observations of the 'rapid oscillatory motion' of a variety of microscopic particles.

89. *(b)* All three (1,2 and 3) are necessary for a fully functional Skype experience, including video and audio calls.

Skype requires the following to function on a computer

- A webcam (or camera) to capture and transmit video.
- A microphone to capture and transmit audio.
- A speaker (or headphones) to play received audio.

90. *(a)* In 2023, the Government of India launched the VAIBHAV schemes to bring Indian-Origin researchers to higher educational institutions in the country.

- It is implemented by the Department of Science and Technology (DST), Ministry of Science and Technology.
- VAIBHAV fellows will receive a monthly fellowship grant of INR 4,00,000, which will support their research activities during the collaboration period.

91. *(d)* Ceres is the closest dwarf planet to the Sun, orbiting at an average distance of 2.88 Astronomical Units (AU), which is approximately 2.8 times Earth's distance from the Sun.

- Ceres is located in the asteroid belt between Mars and Jupiter and is the largest object in the asteroid belt.
- Astronomical Unit (AU) is a unit of length used to measure the distances between objects in our solar system.

92. *(d)* According to Global Multidimensional Poverty Index (2022), Meghalaya and Madhya Pradesh were included in top 10 poorest states of India.

- The Global Multidimensional Poverty Index (MPI) 2022 was released by the United Nations Development Programme (UNDP) and the Oxford Poverty and Human Development Initiative (OPHI).
- Bihar, Jharkhand and Uttar Pradesh have emerged as the poorest states in India, according to NITI Aayog's Multidimensional Poverty Index (MPI).

93. *(c)* The default width of a column in MS Excel is 8 characters. This is based on the default font calibri, and font size 11 points.

94. *(c)* Statement (c) is correct about the Five-Year Plan; the first Five-Year Plan was started in 1951.

- Various Industrialists came together in 1944 and drafted a joint proposal for setting up a planned economy in India. It is famously known as the Bombay Plan.
- The Five-Year Plans were formulated, implemented and regulated by a body known as the Planning Commission.
- The Planning Commission was replaced by a think tank called NITI Aayog in 2015.

95. *(d)* Dhanush Srikant won gold at the International Shooting Sport Federation (ISSF) Junior World Cup 2023 in the men's 10m air rifle event.

- The 2023 ISSF Junior World Championships will be a third edition of the best junior shooters to be held in Changwon, South Korea for Rifle, Pistol and Shotgun from 14th July to 25th July.
- Indian shooters bagged a total of 17 medals with six gold, six silver and five bronze medals at the ISSF Junior World Championships 2023.

96. *(b)* 'Gulamgiri' (Slavery) is a book written by Mahatma Jyotirao Phule and published in 1873.

- It is one of the first criticisms of the caste system and is considered a seminal work in the history of social reform in India.
- Mahatma Jyotirao Phule was a pioneering social reformer and activist who fought against the caste system and for the rights of lower-caste people, women, and other marginalisd communities in India.

97. *(c)* Part III of the Indian Constitution is described as the 'Magna Carta of India'.

The term 'Magna Carta' refers to the medieval charter signed by King John of England in 1215, which established certain rights and limitations on the power of the monarch.

- Part I (Articles 1-4) deals with the Union and its territories.
- Part II (Articles 5-11) deals with citizenship.
- Part IV (Articles 36-51) deals with the Directive Principles of State Policy, which are guidelines for the government to follow while making laws and policies.

98. *(c)* Hampi Utsava is also known as Vijaya Utsava, a cultural festival celebrated in Karnataka, India.

- The festival features music, dance, theatre, and art performances, as well as processions, exhibitions, and food festivals.
- Hampi, a UNESCO World Heritage Site, was the capital of the Vijayanagara empire, and the festival is a tribute to the region's rich history and cultural legacy.

99. *(d)* The Nehru Institute of Mountaineering (NIM) is located in Uttarkashi, Uttarakhand, India.

- It was established in 1965 to honour the memory of Jawaharlal Nehru, the first Prime Minister of India, who was a keen mountaineer and adventurer.
- It provides training in mountaineering, rock climbing and adventure sports.

100. *(d)* Sattriya is a classical dance form that originated in the monasteries (Satras) of Assam, India.

It was developed in the 15th century by the Vaishnavite saints, particularly Mahapurush Srimanta Sankardev.

- Bharatanatyam is a classical dance form from Tamil Nadu, South India.
- Kathak is a classical dance form from Uttar Pradesh.
- Kuchipudi is a classical dance form from Andhra Pradesh, South India.

Set 03 01 July, 2024 (Shift III)

SSC CHSL Tier-I SOLVED PAPER

Instructions

1. This paper contains 100 questions.
2. It has 4 Parts, **Part I** General English, **Part II** General Intelligence & Reasoning, **Part III** Quantitative Aptitude and **Part IV** General Awareness.
3. Each question carries **2 marks**.

Part I

General English

1. The following sentence has an error in its tense. Identify the error and select the correct sentence from the options.

If you had apprised me about your problem earlier, I would have allow you to go.

(a) If you had apprised me about your problem earlier, I would have allowed you to go.
(b) If you apprised me about your problem earlier, I would have allowed you to go.
(c) If you had apprised me about your problem earlier, I would allow you to go.
(d) If you can apprise me about your problem earlier, I would have allowed you to go.

2. Select the option with the correct use of article(s).

(a) She kept lot of rules in her life due to which she is flourishing today
(b) She kept an lot of rules in her life due to which she is flourishing today
(c) She kept a lot of rules in her life due to which she is flourishing today.
(d) She kept the lot of rules in her life due to which she is flourishing today.

3. The following sentence has been divided into parts. One of them may contain an error. Select the part that contains the error from the given options. If you don't find any error, mark 'No error' as your answer.

The project was completed / more quicker / than expected.

(a) No error
(b) more quicker
(c) The project was completed
(d) than expected

4. There is an error in the given sentence. From the options given, identify the sentence that corrects the error to make it a grammatically accurate sentence.

Harmit is not innocent such as Uday.

(a) Harmit is not as innocent more than Uday.
(b) Harmit is not as much as innocent as Uday.
(c) Harmit is not as innocent as Uday.
(d) Harmit is not innocent than Uday.

Directions (Q. Nos. 5-9) *In the following passage, some words have been deleted. Read the passage carefully and select the most appropriate option to fill in each blank.*

Many parents think of overweight children as 'cute' and cuddly. However, obesity must not be (1) .... as a healthy sign. (2) .... obese children grow up, they will be more prone (3) .... health problems like high blood pressure (4) .... diabetes. Today, overweight children are becoming a common (5) .... in many countries.

5. Select the most appropriate option to fill in blank no. (1).

(a) saw (b) seen
(c) see (d) seeing

6. Select the most appropriate option to fill in blank no. (2).

(a) When (b) Who
(c) What (d) Wwhere

7. Select the most appropriate option to fill in blank no. (3).

(a) to (b) in
(c) at (d) on

8. Select the most appropriate option to fill in blank no. (4).

(a) neither (b) or
(c) nor (d) never

9. Select the most appropriate option to fill in blank no. (5).

(a) sight (b) might
(c) light (d) tight

10. Select the most appropriate option that can substitute the underlined segment in the given sentence.

Riding a horse was <u>a piece of cake</u> for him.

(a) an everyday affair
(b) a very easy task
(c) confusing work
(d) a very difficult task

11. Select the most appropriate meaning of the given idiom.

Blowing smoke

(a) To tease someone relentlessly
(b) To hide something
(c) To burn something important
(d) To lie to perplex others

12. Select the most appropriate antonym of the underlined word in the given sentence.

It is no exaggeration to say the Hussain Sagar Lake is an <u>integral</u> element of Hyderabad and Hyderabad's history.

(a) essential (b) total
(c) extra (d) inherent

13. Select the most appropriate antonym of the underlined word in the given sentence.

His opponents viewed him as stubborn, <u>dogmatic</u>, and inflexible.

(a) Dishonest
(b) Biased
(c) Careless
(d) Amenable

14. Select the incorrectly spelt word.
(a) Foresee (b) Rebuke
(c) Seize (d) Dissappoint

15. Select the option that will most suitably substitute the underlined part of the given sentence.
He was not happy until he gave up his job and live as a fakir in the forests.
(a) unless he gave up his job and lives
(b) until he gave up his job and lived
(c) until he gave up his job and lives
(d) until he gives up his job and lived

16. Select the most appropriate antonym of the word 'bold' in the given sentence.
A person can be friendly, timid, clever, or fearless based on the context of the situation.
(a) friendly (b) clever
(c) timid (d) fearless

17. Select the incorrectly spelt word in the given sentence.
'Vande Mataram', a poignant poem, is obviously and indisputebly the premier national song of India.
(a) Obviously (b) Premier
(c) Indisputebly (d) Poignant

18. Select the most appropriate homonyms from the given alternatives to fill in the blanks.
He .... imitate the playful movement of the ....
Alternatives
A. does (female deer)
B. does C. dose
(a) C, B (b) B, A (c) A, B (d) A, C

19. Select the most appropriate option that can substitute the underlined segment in the given sentence.
Dhruv's anger blazed of uncontrollably.
(a) anger blazed onwards
(b) anger blazed after
(c) anger blazed up
(d) anger blazed into

20. Select the most appropriate option to substitute the underlined segment in the following sentence.
The company do not broke the law at any time.
(a) do not brakes
(b) did not breaking
(c) did not broken
(d) does not break

21. Select the most appropriate homonym to fill in the blank.
Sonu eats .... like a rabbit.
(a) karat
(b) carrot
(c) carat
(d) caret

22. Select the most appropriate option that can best replace the bracketed word to fill in the blank
His...........stature was not a measure of his overall personality. (scrawny)
(a) muscular (b) thin
(c) keen (d) sickly

23. Select the most appropriate option that can substitute the underlined word in the given sentence.
The family was saved from the burning building by the brave firefighter.
(a) fearless (b) unafraid
(c) timid (d) cowardly

24. Select the most appropriate synonym of the given word.
Respect
(a) Honour
(b) Disrespect
(c) Attend
(d) Invalidate

25. Select the most appropriate antonym of the given word.
Shame
(a) Disgrace
(b) Defamation
(c) Pride
(d) Fear

Part II
General Intelligence

26. Select the word-pair that best represents a similar relationship to the one expressed in the pair of words given below.
(The words must be considered as meaningful English words and must not be related to each other based on the number of letters/number of consonants/vowels in the word)
Modest : Humble
(a) Obvious : Evident
(b) Knowledge : Ignorance
(c) Brave : Fearful
(d) Success : Failure

27. What will come in the place of the question mark (?) in the following equation, if '+' and '×' are interchanged and '–' and '÷' are interchanged?
$46 \times 17 + 4 \div 98 - 7 = ?$
(a) 80 (b) 90
(c) 85 (d) 100

28. Select the correct mirror image of the given figure, when the mirror is placed at MN as shown below.

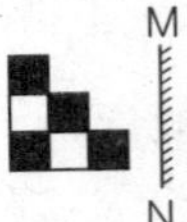

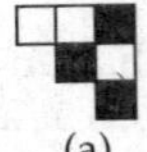
(a)
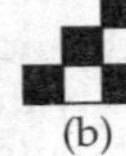
(b)

(c)
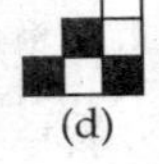
(d)

29. Which of the following numbers will replace the question mark(?) in the given series?
119, 171, 223, 275, 327, ?
(a) 386
(b) 379
(c) 357
(d) 369

30. What should come in place of question mark (?) in the given series?
4, 13, ?, 58, 94, 139, 193
(a) 36 (b) 27
(c) 26 (d) 31

31. How many triangles are there in the given figure?

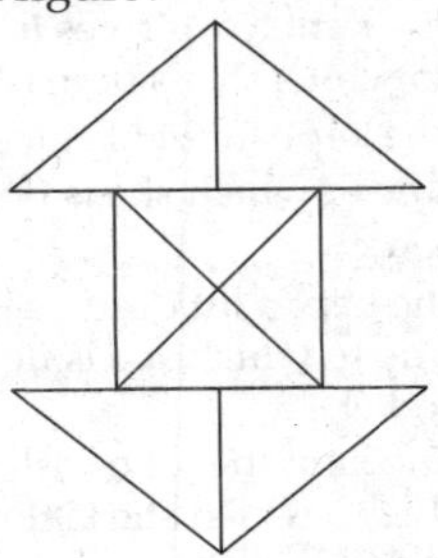

(a) 14 (b) 16
(c) 15 (d) 12

32. What will come in the place of question mark (?) in the following equation, if '+' and '–' are interchanged and '×' and '÷' are interchanged?
$14 + 6 \times 3 \div 7 - 2 = ?$
(a) 8 (b) 3
(c) 10 (d) 2

33. Read the given statements and conclusions carefully. Assuming that the information given in the statements is true, even if it appears to be at variance with commonly known facts, decide which of the given conclusions logically follow(s) from the statements.

Statements

Some handles are bars.

All bars are rods.

No rod is a stick.

Conclusions

I. Some handles are rods.

II. No bar is a stick.

(a) None of the conclusions follow
(b) Only Conclusion II follows
(c) Both Conclusions I and II follow
(d) Only Conclusion I follows

34. Identify the figure given in the options that when put in place of the question mark (?) will logically complete the series.

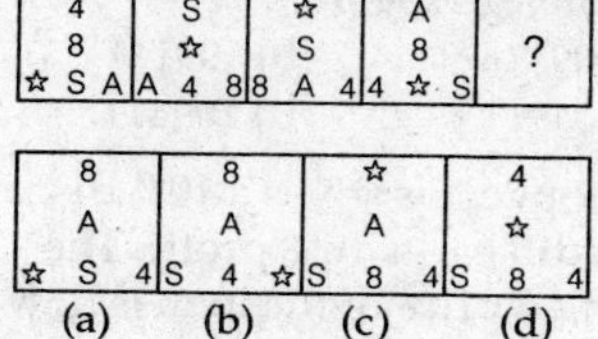

35. Select the pair which follows the same pattern as that followed by the two set of pairs given below. Both pairs follow the same pattern.
CJM : FMP
AHL : DKO
(a) LTV : TVL
(b) KOQ : PLJ
(c) NRS : QUV
(d) GHA : AHG

36. If 15th August, 2006 is a Tuesday, then what will the day of the week on 19th February, 2012?
(a) Friday
(b) Sunday
(c) Saturday
(d) Tuesday

37. In a certain code language, 'CERTAIN' is coded as '9643821' and 'UNCERTAIN' is coded as '964382117'. What is the code for 'U' in that language?
(a) 7 (b) 1
(c) 6 (d) 4

38. What would be the number on the opposite side of '20', if the given sheet is folded to form a cube?

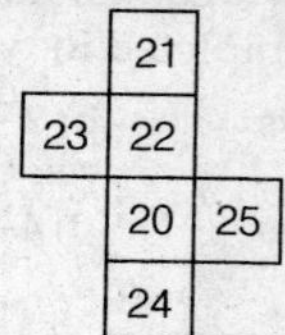

(a) 21 (b) 22
(c) 23 (d) 25

39. Select the set in which the numbers are related in the same way as are the numbers of the given sets.
(**Note** Operations should be performed on the whole numbers, without breaking down the numbers into its constituent digits. E.g. 13-Operations on 13 such as adding/subtracting/multiplying etc. to 13 can be performed. Breaking down 13 into 1 and 3 and then performing mathematical operations on 1 and 3 is not allowed.)
(111, 16, 7)
(167, 14, 12)
(a) (190, 21, 9) (b) (140, 8, 17)
(c) (131, 12, 11) (d) (108, 9, 12)

40. Three of the following four letter-clusters are alike in a certain way and thus form a group. Which letter-cluster does not belong to that group?
(**Note** The odd one out is not based on the number of consonants/ vowels or their position in the letter-cluster)
(a) VWZU
(b) EFHD
(c) MNQL
(d) OPSN

41. What would be the symbol on the opposite side of '@', if the given sheet is folded to form a cube?

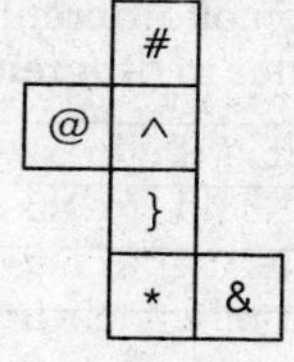

(a) } (b) &
(c) # (d) *

42. How many meaningful English words can be formed with letters CKIK, using each letter only once in each word?
(a) 1 (b) 4
(c) 2 (d) 3

43. In a certain code language,
A + B means 'A is the son of B'
A – B means 'A is the brother of B'
A × B means 'A is the wife of B'
A ÷ B means 'A is the father of B'
Based on the above, how is P related to T, if 'P × Q – R + S ÷ T'?
(a) Mother
(b) Sister
(c) Brother's wife
(d) Brother's wife's mother

44. What will come in the place of the question mark(?) in the following equation, if '+' and '–' are interchanged and '×' and '÷' are interchanged?
$91 \times 7 + 27 - 7 \div 13 = ?$
(a) 66 (b) 88
(c) 99 (d) 77

45. Select the correct mirror image of the given combination, when the mirror is placed at MN as shown below.

M
U4b2weR
N

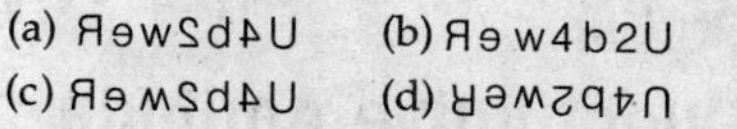

(a) ꓤɘwƧdᔭU (b) ꓤɘ w4 b2U
(c) ꓤɘ ʍƧdᔭU (d) ꓤɘʍƨqᔭ∩

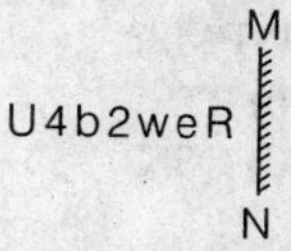

46. Select the correct mirror image of the given combination, when the mirror is placed at MN as shown below.

M
h57Pc2m
N

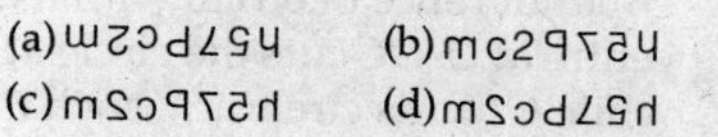

(a) ɯƨɔd⅃ƨμ (b) mc2ꟼ⅂ƨμ
(c) mƧɔꟼ⅂ƨh (d) mƧɔd⅃ƨh

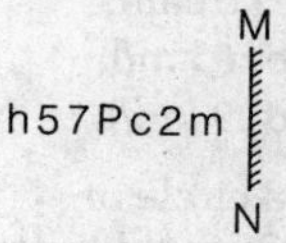

47. 105 is related to 15 following a certain logic. Following the same logic, 154 is related to 22. To which of the following is 189 related following the same logic?

(Note Operations should be performed on the whole numbers, without breaking down the numbers into its constituent digits. e.g. 13-Operations on 13 such as adding /deleting /multiplying etc., to 13 can be performed. Breaking down 13 into 1 and 3 and then performing mathematical operations on 1 and 3 is not allowed.)

(a) 21 (b) 23
(c) 27 (d) 29

48. In a certain language, 'this is music' is written as 'Ta Bu Ka' and 'who touched this' is written as 'Pi Ka Bi'. How is 'this' written in the given language?

(a) Bi (b) Bu
(c) Ka (d) Ta

49. What should come in place of the question mark (?) in the given series based on the English alphabetical order?

CKS, LRC, ?, DFW, MMG

(a) YAM (b) UYM
(c) VMO (d) HGO

50. What should come in place of the question mark (?) in the given series based on the English alphabetical order?

LDP, GHO, BLN, WPM, ?

(a) QSM (b) RTL
(c) RSN (d) QSN

Part III
Quantitative Aptitude

51. A man can row 18 km/h in still water. It takes him two times as long to row up as to row down the river. Find the rate of the stream.

(a) 12 km/h (b) 6 km/h
(c) 24 km/h (d) 9 km/h

52. CD is a tangent to a circle of circumference of 88 cm with its centre at O. OC cuts the circle at P, while OD cuts circle at V such that $\angle COD = 90°$. Length of PC is 6 cm. What is half of CD (in cm), if OD exceeds OC by 1 cm?

(a) 15.5 (b) 14.5
(c) 31 (d) 16.5

53. If $1234567y$ is divisible by 11, then what is the value of y?

(a) 3 (b) 1 (c) 4 (d) 2

54. A and B can do a piece of work in 9 days and 15 days, respectively. If they work together, then the work will be completed in

(a) $3\frac{3}{8}$ days (b) $2\frac{1}{8}$ days
(c) $5\frac{5}{8}$ days (d) $4\frac{5}{8}$ days

55. If the selling price of 100 pens is equal to the cost price of 140 pens, find the profit percentage.

(a) 30% (b) 45%
(c) 40% (d) 36%

56. If $A : B = 3 : 7$ and $B : C = 2 : 5$, find $A : B : C$.

(a) 10 : 3 : 4 (b) 4 : 10 : 3
(c) 4 : 3 : 10 (d) 6 : 14 : 35

57. The curved surface area of a cone is 2200 cm^2 and its radius is 28 cm, what is the slant height (in cm) of the cone? $\left(\text{use } \pi = \frac{22}{7}\right)$

(a) 25 (b) 24
(c) 22 (d) 23

58. P pays Q a sum of ₹ 150 using coins of ₹ 2, ₹ 5 and ₹ 10. He uses a total of 50 coins. If the ratio of ₹ 2 and ₹ 5 coins used is 5 : 2, then how many coins of ₹ 10 are used in the payment?

(a) 1 (b) 4
(c) 5 (d) 2

59. An amount becomes double in 7 yr on simple interest. The amount would be four times in .... yr on the same rate of simple interest.

(a) 14 (b) 28
(c) 21 (d) 18

60. If $\cot A = 7$, then the value of $\frac{5\cos A + 4\sin A}{\cos^3 A + 7\sin^3 A + 6\sin A}$ is

(a) 3 (b) 2
(c) 0 (d) 1

61. The bar-graph represents the production of different spare parts of computer in different months.

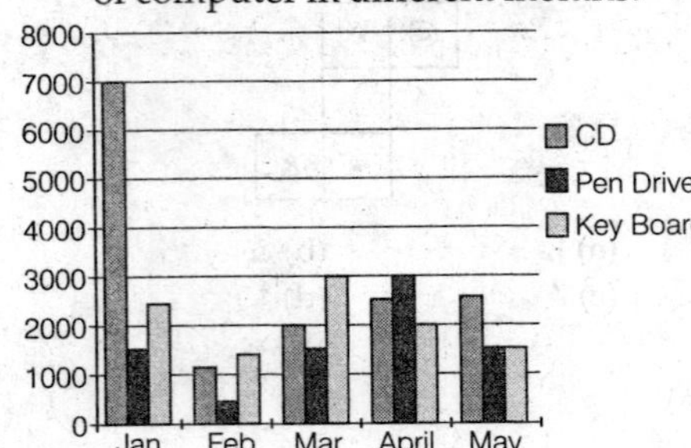

The ratio between the number of pen drives produced in the month of January, March and April is

(a) 1 : 1 : 2 (b) 1 : 1 : 1
(c) 1 : 1 : 3 (d) 3 : 1 : 2

62. The radius of a roller is 49 cm and its length is 200 cm. It takes 700 complete revolutions to move once over to level a playground. Find the area of the playground. $\left(\text{use } \pi = \frac{22}{7}\right)$

(a) 4312×10^3 cm^2 (b) 4312×10^2 cm^2
(c) 4322×10^4 cm^2 (d) 4312×10^4 cm^2

63. Simplify : $(36 \div 6) \div 3 + (18 \div 9) \times 4 - (12 \div 6) \times (5 \div 2)$

(a) 10 (b) 5
(c) 21 (d) 15

64. In an election between two candidates A and B, A got 33% of total votes casted and still lost by 55522 votes. Find the total number of votes got by B.

(a) 109114 (b) 109141
(c) 104911 (d) 109411

65. A shopkeeper gives a 10% discount and still earns 10% profit. The marked price of the item is how many times (correct to 2 decimal places) the cost price?

(a) 1.28 (b) 1.24
(c) 1.22 (d) 1.20

66. The given pie-charts show the distribution of Graduate and Post-Graduate level students in five different colleges A, B, C, D and E.

Total number of Graduate level students = 18900

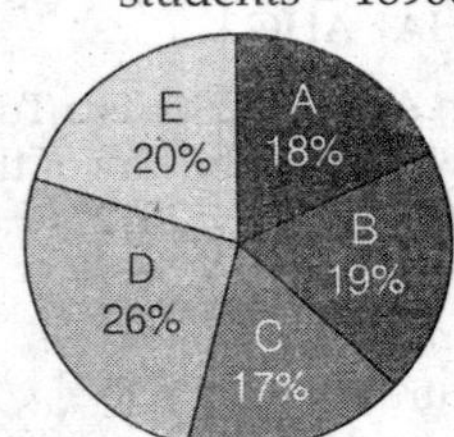

Total number of Post-Graduate level students = 16800

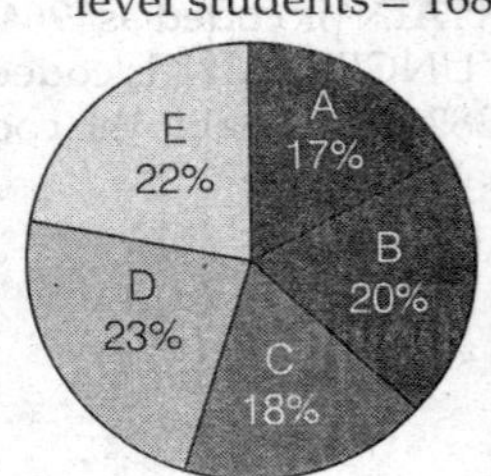

What is the ratio between the number of students studying at Post-Graduate and Graduate levels, respectively, from college E?
(a) 32 : 43 (b) 16 : 17
(c) 44 : 45 (d) 48 : 37

67. Following pie-chart presents monthly expenditure by Sushma and Preeti in different heads. Sushma and Preeti make equal expenditure every month.

Sushma's Expenditure (in ₹)

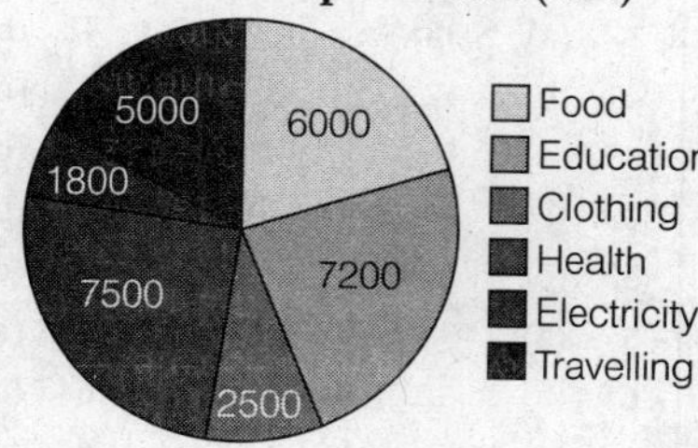

Preeti's Expenditure (in %)

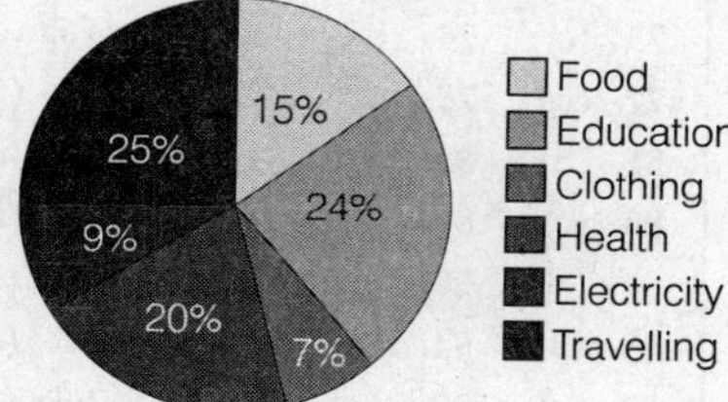

What is the difference between the expenditure (in ₹) done on Food by Sushma and Preeti?
(a) 1500 (b) 500
(c) 750 (d) 1000

68. Given below is the observed data of the ages of various children.

Ages (in year)	Number of children
6	8
7	3
8	7
9	2
10	20

What is the difference between the mean and mode of the ages?
(a) 4.425 yr
(b) 2.425 yr
(c) 1.425 yr
(d) 3.425 yr

69. In a ΔABC, $AB = 6$ units, $BC = 8$ units and $AC = 10$ units. Let M be a point on AC such that $BM = 5$ units. With a point D, a ΔBMD is formed and the ΔBMD is similar to the triangle ABC with $\frac{BM}{AB} = \frac{BD}{AC}$. What is the length of BD in units?
(a) $\frac{35}{3}$ (b) $\frac{40}{3}$
(c) $\frac{25}{3}$ (d) $\frac{10}{3}$

70. If the radii of two circles are 6 cm and 3 cm and the length of the transverse common tangent is 8 cm, then the distance between the two circles is
(a) $\sqrt{145}$ cm (b) $\sqrt{141}$ cm
(c) $\sqrt{147}$ cm (d) $\sqrt{143}$ cm

71. In what ratio must a grocer mix two varieties of pulses costing ₹ 60 and ₹ 75 per kg, respectively, so as to get a mixture worth ₹ 65 per kg?
(a) 3 : 4 (b) 2 : 1
(c) 2 : 3 (d) 1 : 2

72. In an isosceles triangle, the angle between equal sides is 40°. The bisectors of the other two angles will intersect each other at an angle of
(a) 100° (b) 105°
(c) 120° (d) 110°

73. If the price of an article is raised by 35%, by how much per cent must a householder reduce his consumption of that article, so as not to increase his expenditure?
(a) $25\frac{22}{27}$% (b) $25\frac{23}{27}$%
(c) $25\frac{25}{27}$% (d) $25\frac{24}{27}$%

74. The cost price of an item increased from ₹ 2500 to ₹ 3000. Find the increase percentage.
(a) 25% (b) 20%
(c) 30% (d) 15%

75. Find the circumference of a circle, whose area is 154 m^2.
(a) 44 m (b) 29.5 m
(c) 39 m (d) 52 m

Part IV
General Awareness

76. Which country do the 'Veddas' traditional forest dwellers who foraged, hunted and lived in close-knit groups in caves in the dense jungles?
(a) Myanmar (b) Nepal
(c) Bhutan (d) Sri Lanka

77. Which folk music is based on the Mahabharata with Bhima portrayed as hero?
(a) Mando
(b) Alha
(c) Pandavani
(d) Dandiya

78. Which amongst the following terms was used for the land given to Brahmins during the Chola empire?
(a) Tirunmatukkani
(b) Shalabhoga
(c) Vellanvagai
(d) Brahmadeya

79. How might ICT enhance the openness of e-land records?
(a) Enabling quick search and retrieval of land records.
(b) Enforcing strict regulations on land transactions.
(c) Facilitating manual record updates and amendments.
(d) Reducing the need for land surveys and assessments.

80. Which of the following Articles of the Constitution of India cannot be amended with simple majority?
(a) 21 (b) 3
(c) 2 (d) 169

81. In his 'Drain of Wealth' argument, who among the following stated that Britain was completely draining India?
(a) Lala Lajpat Rai
(b) Dadabhai Naoroji
(c) Bal Gangadhar Tilak
(d) Badruddin Tyabji

82. How is the structure of health infrastructure and health care system in India?
(a) Three-tier system
(b) Four-tier system
(c) Five-tier system
(d) Two-tier system

83. In which year did Indian archers participate in the Olympics for the first time?
(a) 1988 (b) 1973
(c) 1980 (d) 1975

84. Which language is known as 'Italian of the East'?
(a) Malayalam
(b) Kannada
(c) Marathi
(d) Telugu

85. Which of the following states launched the first Migration Monitoring System in the year 2022?
(a) Karnataka (b) Goa
(c) Maharashtra (d) Kerala

86. As compared to monopolistic competition, the demand curve in a monopoly is:
(a) infinitely elastic
(b) equally elastic
(c) more elastic
(d) less elastic

87. Which group of animals has a segmented spinal column together with a few primitive forms in which the backbone is represented by a notochord?
(a) Arthropoda (b) Echinodermata
(c) Mollusca (d) Vertebrata

88. The Indian festival of Holi comes every year in the season of.
(a) spring
(b) autumn
(c) summer
(d) winter

89. Who is the author of Natyashastra?
(a) Bharatmuni (b) Patanjali
(c) Prabhupada (d) Panini

90. What is the circumference of the International Football Association Board (IFAB) approved football?
(a) 80-82 cms
(b) 78-80 cms
(c) 68-70 cms
(d) 70-72 cms

91. In field hockey, ... occurs when a player pushes the ball and raises it off the ground.
(a) flick (b) centre pass
(c) slap (d) bully

92. What is the name of the highest peak of the Eastern Ghats?
(a) Khasi
(b) Anamudi
(c) Mahendragiri
(d) Kangchenjunga

93. In MS Word, which option allows you to align text in a way that it appears vertically at the bottom of a cell or text box?
(a) Distributed Alignment
(b) Justify Alignment
(c) Center Alignment
(d) Bottom Alignment

94. Which of the following is not associated with the Industrial Policy Resolution, 1956?
(a) Regional equality was promoted.
(b) It formed the basis of the Third-Five Year Plan.
(c) A system of licenses for the private sector was introduced.
(d) It classified industries into three categories.

95. Which of the following planets does not have a ring around it?
(a) Jupiter (b) Saturn
(c) Uranus (d) Mercury

96. Writ of Mandamus is a Fundamental Right classifiable under
(a) the right to equality
(b) cultural and educational rights
(c) constitutional remedies
(d) the right to freedom of religion

97. In 2022, the National Green Tribunal advised which of the following Ministries to form a three-member panel to formulate safeguards and guidelines to be followed by the State Environment Impact Assessment Authorities?
(a) Ministry of Environment, Forest and Climate Change
(b) Ministry of Health and Family Welfare
(c) Ministry of Law and Justice
(d) Ministry of Home Affairs

98. .... was sworn in as Central Vigilance Commissioner on 29th May, 2023.
(a) Uday Veer Singh
(b) Praveen Kumar Srivastava
(c) Arti C. Srivastava
(d) Sarvan Kumar

99. Who is known as the 'Father of Carnatic Music'?
(a) Thirunal Rama Varma
(b) Vishwanath Iyer
(c) Vidyaranya
(d) Purandara Dasa

100. The method of separating a mixture of soluble solids by dissolving them in a suitable hot solvent and then lowering the temperature slowly is called
(a) fractional crystallisation
(b) dephlegmation
(c) azeotropic distillation
(d) sublimation

Answers

1. (a)	2. (c)	3. (b)	4. (c)
5. (b)	6. (a)	7. (a)	8. (b)
9. (a)	10. (b)	11. (d)	12. (c)
13. (d)	14 (d)	15. (b)	16. (c)
17. (c)	18. (b)	19. (c)	20. (d)
21. (b)	22. (b)	23. (a)	24. (a)
25. (c)	26. (a)	27. (d)	28. (b)
29. (b)	30. (d)	31. (a)	32. (d)
33. (c)	34. (b)	35. (c)	36. (b)
37. (a)	38. (a)	39. (c)	40. (b)
41. (b)	42. (a)	43. (c)	44. (d)
45. (a)	46. (c)	47. (c)	48. (c)
49. (b)	50. (b)	51. (b)	52. (b)
53. (c)	54. (c)	55. (c)	56. (d)
57. (a)	58. (a)	59. (c)	60. (a)
61. (a)	62. (d)	63. (b)	64. (d)
65. (c)	66. (c)	67. (a)	68. (c)
69. (c)	70. (a)	71. (b)	72. (d)
73. (c)	74. (b)	75. (a)	76. (d)
77. (d)	78. (d)	79. (a)	80. (a)
81. (b)	82. (a)	83. (a)	84. (d)
85. (c)	86. (c)	87. (d)	88. (a)
89. (a)	90. (c)	91. (a)	92. (c)
93. (d)	94. (b)	95. (d)	96. (c)
97. (a)	98. (b)	99. (d)	100. (a)

Explanations

1. *(a)* The given sentence contains an error. The verb 'has/have' takes the second form of the verb. Hence, the correct sentence is- If you had apprised me about your problem earlier, I would have allowed you to go.

2. *(c)* The sentence that correctly uses the articles is- She kept a lot of rules in her life due to which she is flourishing today.

3. *(b)* Part (b) 'more quicker' contains an error. The use of 'quicker' is incorrect. Use 'quickly' to correct the sentence.

4. *(c)* The given sentence contains an error. As there is a comparison between Harmit and Uday, 'as ... as' will be used. Hence, the correct sentence is- Harmit is not as innocent as Uday.

5. *(b)* The correct filler for the given blank is 'seen'.

6. *(a)* The correct filler for the given blank is 'when'.

7. *(a)* The correct filler for the given blank is 'to'.

8. *(b)* The correct filler for the given blank is 'or'.

9. *(a)* The correct filler for the given blank is 'sight'.

10. *(b)* A piece of cake means a very easy task.

11. *(d)* Blowing smoke means to lie to perplex others.

12. *(c)* 'Integral' means central and important. Hence, its antonym is 'extra'.

'Inherent' means natural or existing in something as a permanent, essential, or characteristic attribute.

13. *(d)* 'Dogmatic' means characterised by or given to the expression of opinions very strongly or positively as if they were facts. Hence, its antonym is 'amenable' which means open and responsive to suggestion; easily persuaded or controlled.

'Biased' means showing an unreasonable like or dislike for someone or something based on personal opinions.

14. *(d)* The incorrectly spelt word is 'dissappoint'. The correct spelling is 'disappoint'.

15. *(b)* The underlined part of the given sentence contains an error. As the given sentence is in past tense, 'lived' should be used to correct the sentence.

16. *(c)* The antonym of 'bold' is 'timid' which means 'showing a lack of courage or confidence; easily frightened.'

17. *(c)* The incorrectly spelt word is 'indisputebly'. The correct spelling is 'indisputably'.

18. *(b)* The correct fillers for the given blanks are 'does' and 'does'. The first 'does' is a verb and the second 'does' refers to female deer.

19. *(c)* The underlined part of the given sentence contains an error. Use 'anger blazed up' to correct the sentence.

20. *(d)* The underlined part of the given sentence contains an error. The use of 'do' is incorrect as the subject is singular, so singular verb is used. Hence, use 'does' to correct the sentence.

21. *(b)* The correct filler for the given blank is 'carrot'.

22. *(b)* The word 'scrawny' means unattractively thin and bony. Hence, 'thin' is the correct filler for the given blank.

23. *(a)* The word 'brave' means 'fearless'.

'Timid' means cowardly.

24. *(a)* The synonym of 'respect' is 'honour'.

'Invalidate' means to state to be false.

25. *(c)* The antonym of 'shame' is 'pride'.

- 'Disgrace' means loss of reputation or respect as the result of a dishonourable action.
- 'Defamation' means the act of harming someone's reputation by saying or writing bad things about them.

26. *(a)* As, 'modest' and 'humble' are synonyms of each other.

Similarly, 'obvious' and 'evident' are synonyms of each other.

27. *(d)* Given expression,

$46 \times 17 + 4 \div 98 - 7 = ?$

Now, on interchanging + and ×, – and ÷, we get

$\Rightarrow \quad 46 + 17 \times 4 - 98 \div 7 = ?$

$\Rightarrow \quad 46 + 68 - 14 = ?$

$\Rightarrow \quad 114 - 14 = ?$

$\therefore \quad ? = \boxed{100}$

28. *(b)* Figure given in option (b) will be correct mirror image.

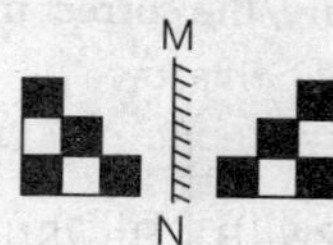

29. *(b)* The pattern of the series is as follows,

119 171 223 275 327 [379]
+52 +52 +52 +52 +52

30. *(d)* The pattern of the series is as follows,

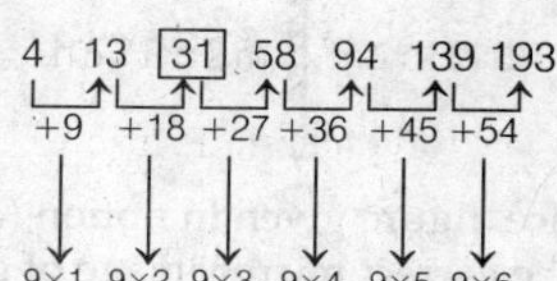

31. *(a)* Naming the figure,

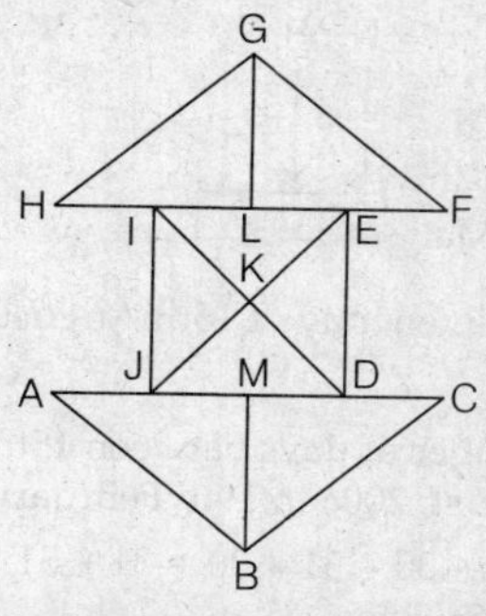

Total number of triangles are given as, ΔABM, ΔBMC, ΔABC, ΔHLG, ΔGLF, ΔHGF, ΔJKD, ΔDKE, ΔIKE, ΔIKJ, ΔJED, ΔDIJ, ΔIED, ΔJIE

Hence, total 14 triangles are present in the given figure.

32. *(d)* Given expression,

$14 + 6 \times 3 \div 7 - 2 = ?$

Now, on interchanging '+' and '–' and '×' and '÷', we get

$\Rightarrow 14 - 6 \div 3 \times 7 + 2 = ?$

$\Rightarrow \quad 14 - 14 + 2 = ?$

$\therefore \quad ? = \boxed{2}$

33. *(c)* According to the statements,

Conclusions I. (✓) II. (✓)

Hence, both Conclusions I and II follow.

34. *(b)* Here, the series follows two alternative pattern which are as follows,

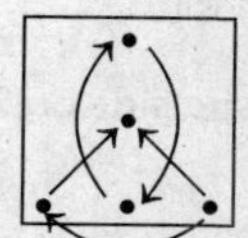
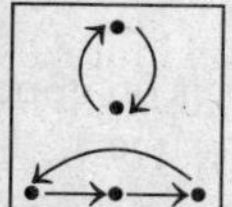

Figure 1 to 2 Figure 2 to 3
Figure 3 to 4 Figure 4 to 5

Hence, option figure (b) will come in place of question mark (?).

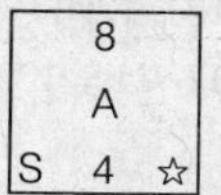

35. *(c)* As,

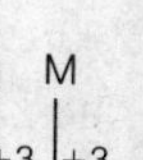

and

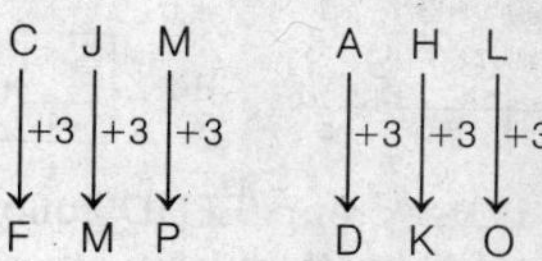

Similarly,

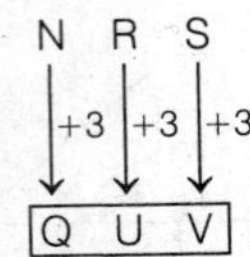

36. *(b)* Given, day of 15th August, 2006 → Tuesday

Number of days between 15th August, 2006 to 19th February, 2007

$= 16 + 30 + 31 + 30 + 31 + 31 + 19$

$= \frac{188}{7} = 26$ weeks + 6 odd days

∴ Day on 19th February, 2007

= Tuesday + 6 = Monday

Now, number of odd days between years 2007 to 2012

⇒ 2008 + 2009 + 2010 + 2011 + 2012

= 1 + 2 + 1 + 1 + 1 = 6

∴ Required day = Monday + 6

= Sunday

37. *(a)* As, C E R T A I N → 9 6 4 3 8 2 1

and U N C E R T A I N → 9 6 4 3 8 2 1 1 7

∴ The code for 'U' in that language is 7.

38. *(a)* According to the question,

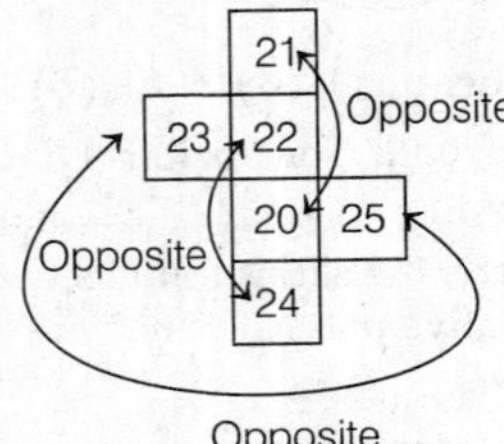

∴ '21' is on opposite side of '20' in given cube.

39. *(c)* As, (111, 16, 7)

⇒ $16 \times 7 - 1 = 112 - 1 = 111$

and (167, 14, 12)

⇒ $14 \times 12 - 1 = 168 - 1 = 167$

Similarly, (131, 12, 11)

⇒ $12 \times 11 - 1 = 132 - 1 = 131$

40. *(b)* As,

V W Z U (+1, +3, −5), M N Q L (+1, +3, −5)

O P S N (+1, +3, −5), But, E F H D (+1, +2, −4)

∴ Letter group 'EFHD' follows different pattern from others.

41. *(b)* According to the question,

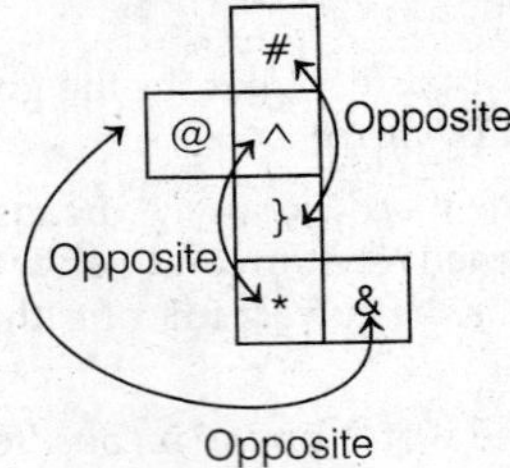

∴ Symbol '&' is on opposite side of '@' in the given cube.

42. *(a)* Given letters are C, K, I, K.

Meaningful words can be formed using the letters is 'KICK'.

∴ Only 1 meaningful word can be made using each letter only once in each word.

43. *(c)* Given expression, $P \times Q - R + S \div T$

According to the question,

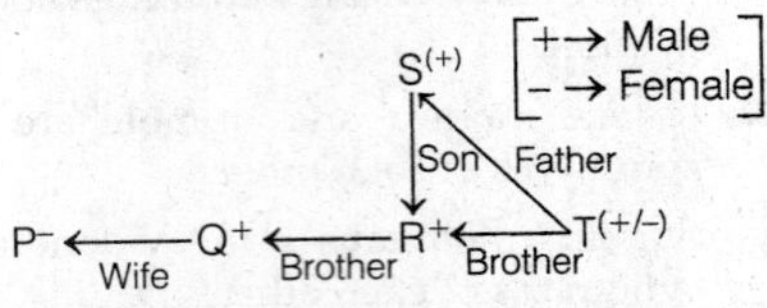

Hence, P is 'brother's wife' of T.

44. *(d)* Given expression,

$91 \times 7 + 27 - 7 \div 13 = ?$

On interchanging '+' and '−', '×' and '÷,' we get

⇒ $91 \div 7 - 27 + 7 \times 13 = ?$

⇒ $13 - 27 + 91 = ?$

⇒ $104 - 27 = ?$

∴ ? = 77

45. *(a)* When mirror is placed at MN in given figure, the correct mirror image is given as,

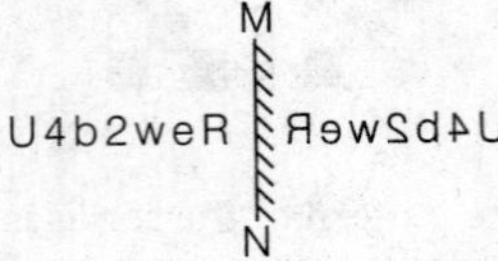

Hence, figure given in option (a) will be the correct mirror image.

46. *(c)* When mirror is placed at MN, the correct mirror image is as follows,

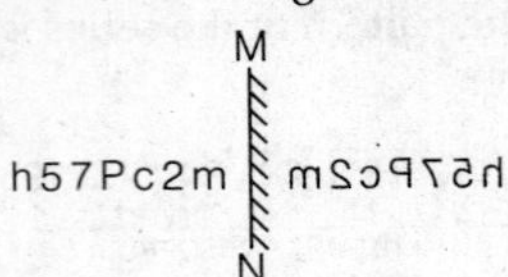

Hence, figure given in option (c) will be the correct mirror image of given figure.

47. *(c)* As, $\frac{105}{7} = 15$

and $\frac{154}{7} = 22$

Similarly, $\frac{189}{7} = 27$

48. *(c)* According to the question,

this is music — Ta Bu Ka

who touched this — Pi Ka Bi

∴ The code for this is 'Ka'.

49. *(b)* The pattern of the series is as follows,

C →(+9) L →(+9) U →(+9) D →(+9) M

K →(+7) R →(+7) Y →(+7) F →(+7) M

S →(+10) C →(+10) M →(+10) W →(+10) G

50. *(b)* The pattern of the series is as follows,

L →(−5) G →(−5) B →(−5) W →(−5) R

D →(+4) H →(+4) L →(+4) P →(+4) T

P →(−1) O →(−1) N →(−1) M →(−1) L

51. *(b)* Let rate of stream = a km/h

and distance travelled = y km

Given, rate of man in still water = 18 km/h

∴ Rate of downstream = $(18 + a)$ km/h

Rate of upstream = $(18 - a)$ km/h

According to the question,

$$\frac{18 + a}{y} = 2\frac{(18 - a)}{y}$$

⇒ $18 + a = 36 - 2a \Rightarrow 3a = 18$

⇒ $a = 6$ km/h

Hence, the rate of stream is 6 km/h.

52. *(b)* Given, circumference = 88 cm

⇒ $2\pi r = 88$ cm

⇒ $2 \times \frac{22}{7} \times r = 88$

∴ $r = 14$ cm

According to the question,

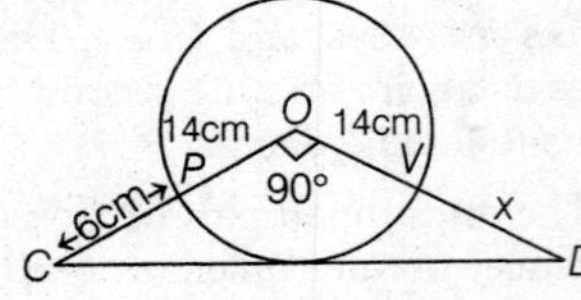

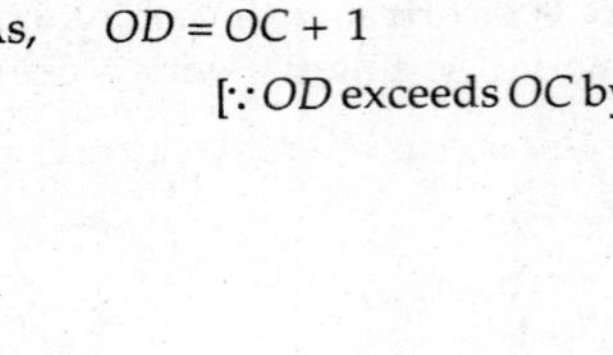

$PC = 6$ cm (given)

$OV = OP =$ radius = 14 cm

Let $DV = x$ cm

As, $OD = OC + 1$

[∵ OD exceeds OC by 1 cm]

$\therefore \quad x + 14 = 20 + 1$

$x + 14 = 21$

$\therefore \quad x = 7$ cm

Hence, $OD = 14 + 7 = 21$ cm

In ΔCOD, by Pythagoras, we get

$CD = \sqrt{(OC)^2 + (OD)^2}$

$\Rightarrow CD = \sqrt{(20)^2 + (21)^2}$

$\Rightarrow CD = \sqrt{400 + 441} = \sqrt{841}$

$\therefore CD = 29$ cm

Now, half of $CD = \frac{29}{2} = 14.5$ cm

53. *(c)* According to the divisibility rule, to divide any number with 11, the sum of even place digit – sum of odd place digit = 0 or 11

$\therefore$ In number $1234567y$

$1 + 3 + 5 + 7 - (2 + 4 + 6 + y) = 0$

$\Rightarrow 16 - 12 - y = 0$

$\therefore y = 4$

54. *(c)* A's 1 day's work $= \frac{1}{9}$

B's 1 day's work $= \frac{1}{15}$

$(A + B)$'s 1 day's work

$= \frac{1}{9} + \frac{1}{15} = \frac{5+3}{45} = \frac{8}{45}$

$\therefore (A + B)$ complete the whole work in

$= \frac{45}{8}$

$= 5\frac{5}{8}$ days

55. *(c)* According to the question,

Selling price × 100 pens = Cost price × 140 pens

$\frac{\text{Selling price}}{\text{Cost price}} = \frac{140}{100} = \frac{7}{5}$

$\therefore$ Profit percentage

$= \frac{\text{Selling price} - \text{Cost price}}{\text{Cost price}} \times 100$

$= \frac{(7-5)}{5} \times 100$

$= \frac{2}{5} \times 100$

$= 40\%$

56. *(d)* Given, $A:B = 3:7$ and $B:C = 2:5$

$3 : 7$
$2 : 5$

$A:B:C = (3 \times 2):(7 \times 2):(5 \times 7)$

$= 6:14:35$

57. *(a)* Given, curved surface area of cone $= 2200 \text{ cm}^2$

Radius $(r) = 28$ cm

We know that, curved surface area of cone $= \pi rl$

$\therefore \frac{22}{7} \times 28 \times l = 2200$

$\therefore l = \frac{2200 \times 7}{22 \times 28} = 25$ cm

58. *(a)* Let ratio of number of ₹ 2 and ₹ 5 coins $= 5x : 2x$

Let number of ₹ 10 coins $= y$

Then, $5x + 2x + y = 50$

$7x + y = 50 \quad \ldots(i)$

$\therefore$ Total amount = 150

$\Rightarrow 2 \times 5x + 5 \times 2x + y \times 10 = 150$

$\Rightarrow 10x + 10x + 10y = 150$

$\Rightarrow 2x + y = 15 \quad \ldots(ii)$

Subtracting Eq. (ii) from (i),

$5x = 35$

$\therefore x = 7$

From Eq. (ii),

$2 \times 7 + y = 15$

$\therefore y = 1$

$\therefore$ Number of ₹ 10 coins = 1

59. *(c)* Given, time $(T) = 7$ yr

Let sum = ₹ P

An amount becomes double *i.e.*, $2P$ in 7 yr,

$SI = 2P - P = P$

$\therefore SI = \frac{P \times R \times T}{100} \Rightarrow P = \frac{P \times R \times 7}{100}$

$R = \frac{100}{7}\%$

Again, the amount becomes 4 times in T yr.

$SI = 4P - P = 3P$

$\therefore SI = \frac{P \times R \times T}{100} \Rightarrow 3P = \frac{P \times 100 \times T}{7 \times 100}$

$\therefore T = 21$ yr

60. *(a)* According to the question,

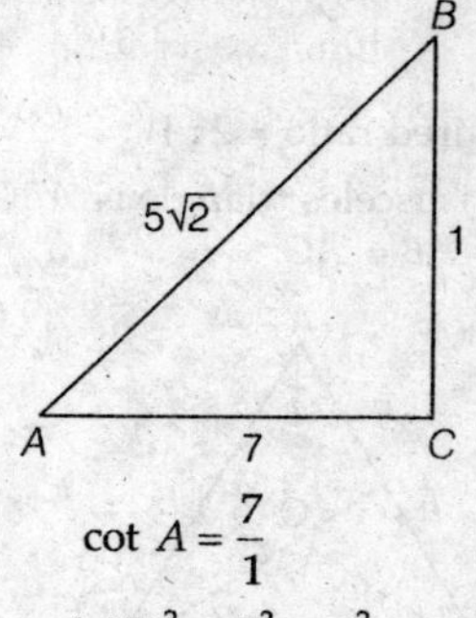

$\cot A = \frac{7}{1}$

Now, $(AB)^2 = 7^2 + 1^2$

$= 49 + 1$

$\therefore AB = \sqrt{50} = 5\sqrt{2}$

Now,

$5\cos A + 4\sin A = 5 \times \frac{7}{5\sqrt{2}} + 4 \times \frac{1}{5\sqrt{2}}$

$= \frac{35 + 4}{5\sqrt{2}} = \frac{39}{5\sqrt{2}}$

and $\cos^3 A + 7\sin^3 A + 6\sin A$

$= \left(\frac{7}{5\sqrt{2}}\right)^3 + 7 \times \left(\frac{1}{5\sqrt{2}}\right)^3 + 6 \times \frac{1}{5\sqrt{2}}$

$= \frac{343 + 7 + 300}{250\sqrt{2}} = \frac{650}{250\sqrt{2}}$

Now,

$\frac{5\cos A + 4\sin A}{\cos^3 A + 7\sin^3 A + 6\sin A} = \frac{\frac{39}{5\sqrt{2}}}{\frac{650}{250\sqrt{2}}}$

$= \frac{39}{5\sqrt{2}} \times \frac{250\sqrt{2}}{650} = 3$

61. *(a)* Pen-drives produced in month of January = 1500

Pen-drives produced in month of March = 1500

Pen-drives produced in month of April = 3000

$\therefore$ Required ratio = 1500 : 1500 : 3000

= 1 : 1 : 2

62. *(d)* Given, radius = 49 cm,

length = 200 cm

We know that,

Area of playground

= Curved surface area of roller × 700

$\Rightarrow 2\pi rh = 2 \times \frac{22}{7} \times 49 \times 200$

$= 61600$ sq. cm

In 700 revolutions, area covered

$= 61600 \times 700$

$= 4312 \times 10^4 \text{ cm}^2$

63. *(b)* Given statement,

$(36 \div 6) \div 3 + (18 \div 9) \times 4 - (12 \div 6) \times (5 \div 2)$

[using BODMAS]

$= 6 \div 3 + 2 \times 4 - 2 \times 5 \div 2$

$= 2 + 8 - 5 = 5$

64. *(d)* Let the total votes casted = 100%

Given, A got 33% of total votes.

$\therefore$ Votes got by $B = 100 - 33 = 67\%$

According to the question,

$67\% - 33\% = 55522$

$\Rightarrow 34\% = 55522$

$\Rightarrow 100\% = \frac{55522}{34} \times 100$

$= 163300$

The votes got by $B = \frac{67}{100} \times 163300$

$= 109411$

65. *(c)* Let marked price (MP) = ₹ 100

After 10% discount on (MP), the selling price will be

$= \frac{100 - 10}{100} \times 100 = \frac{90}{100} \times 100$

= ₹ 90

The shopkeeper earns profit of 10%, the cost price will be

$\frac{SP}{(100 + \text{profit } \%)} \times 100$

$= \frac{90}{110} \times 100 = \frac{900}{11}$

Now, x times of CP = MP

$\therefore \quad x \times \frac{900}{11} = 100$

$x = \frac{11 \times 100}{900} = \frac{11}{9}$

= 1.22 times

66. *(c)* The number of students studying in post graduate in college E

$= \frac{22}{100} \times 16800 = 3696$

The number of students studying in graduate level in college E

$= \frac{20}{100} \times 18900 = 3780$

∴ Required ratio = 3696 : 3780
= 44 : 45

67. *(a)* Expenditure on food by Sushma
= ₹ 6000

According to the question, total expenditure of Sushma and Preeti is equal.

∴ Total expenditure of Preeti

= (6000 + 7200 + 2500 + 7500 + 1800 + 5000)

= ₹ 30000

Now, expenditure on food by Preeti

$= \frac{15}{100} \times 30000 =$ ₹ 4500

∴ Required difference

= (6000 – 4500) = ₹ 1500

68. *(c)* According to the question,

Mean

$= \frac{6 \times 8 + 7 \times 3 + 8 \times 7 + 9 \times 2 + 10 \times 20}{8 + 3 + 7 + 2 + 20}$

$= \frac{48 + 21 + 56 + 18 + 200}{40}$

$= \frac{343}{40} = 8.575$

Mode = 10

∴ Required difference = 10 – 8.575
= 1.425 yr

69. *(c)* According to the question,

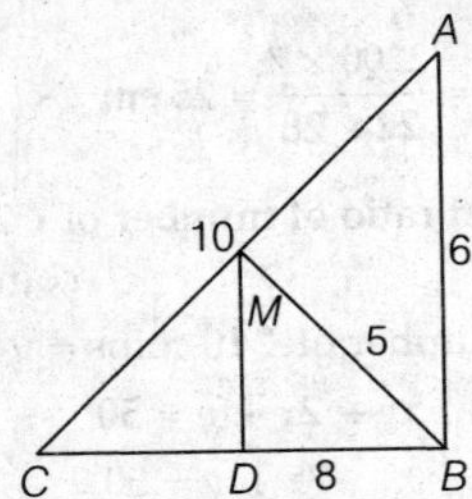

$AB = 6$ units, $BC = 8$ units

$AC = 10$ units, $BM = 5$ units.

$\Delta BMD \sim \Delta ABC$

$\therefore \quad \frac{BD}{AC} = \frac{BM}{AB}$

$\Rightarrow \quad \frac{BD}{10} = \frac{5}{6}$

$\Rightarrow \quad BD = \frac{5 \times 10}{6}$

$\therefore \quad BD = \frac{25}{3}$ units

70. *(a)* Given, $r_1 = 6$ cm, $r_2 = 3$ cm,

Transverse common tangent = 8 cm

Let the distance between the two circles = d cm

∴ (Transverse common tangent)^2

$= (d)^2 - (r_1 + r_2)^2$

$\Rightarrow \quad 8^2 = d^2 - (6 + 3)^2$

$\Rightarrow \quad 64 = d^2 - 81$

$\therefore \quad d^2 = 81 + 64$

$d = \sqrt{145}$

∴ Distance betweeen two circles

$= \sqrt{145}$ cm

71. *(b)* According to the rule of alligation,

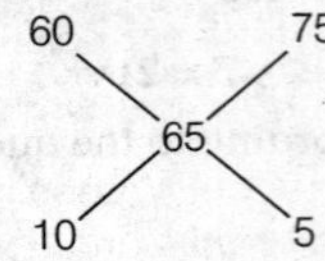

∴ Required ratio = 2 : 1

72. *(d)* Let isosceles triangle is ABC, where $AB = AC$

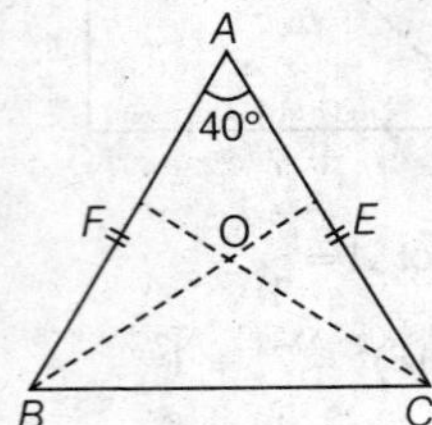

According to the question,

$\angle BAC = 40°$

$\therefore \quad \angle BOC = 90° + \frac{\angle A}{2}$

[from angle bisector theorem]

$\Rightarrow \quad \angle BOC = 90° + \frac{40°}{2}$

$\therefore \quad \angle BOC = 110°$

73. *(c)* Let the price of an article = ₹ 100

Now, the price of article is raised by ₹ 35.

∴ New price of article $= 100 \times \frac{135}{100}$

= ₹ 135

∴ Required reduction

$= \frac{(135 - 100)}{135} \times 100$

$= \frac{35}{135} \times 100$

$= \frac{700}{27}\% = 25\frac{25}{27}\%$

74. *(b)* According to the question,

Cost price$_1$ = ₹ 2500

Cost price$_2$ = ₹ 3000

Percentage increased

$= \frac{3000 - 2500}{2500} \times 100$

$= \frac{500}{2500} \times 100 = 20\%$

75. *(a)* Given, area of circle = 154 m^2

$\Rightarrow \quad \pi r^2 = 154$

$\Rightarrow \quad \frac{22}{7} \times r^2 = 154$

$\Rightarrow \quad r^2 = 154 \times \frac{7}{22} = 49$

$\therefore \quad r = 7$ m

Now, circumference of circle = $2\pi r$

$= 2 \times \frac{22}{7} \times 7 = 44$ m

76. *(d)* Sri Lanka do perform the 'Veddas' traditional forest dwellers who foraged, hunted and lived in close-knit groups in caves in the dense jungles.

- The Veddas have their own unique inheritance and call themselves as 'Wanniyala-Aetto'.
- The term 'Vedda' bestowed by the Sinhalese neighbours to the aboriginal community.

77. *(d)* Pandavani folk music is based on the Mahabharata with Bhima portrayed as hero.

- Pandavani folk theatre is popular in the state of Chhattisgarh and in the neighbouring tribal areas of Orissa and Andhra Pradesh.

78. *(d)* Brahmadeya used for the land given to Brahmins during the chola empire.

- Brahmadeya was tax free land gift either in form of single plot or whole village donated to Brahmanas in the early medieval India.
- Brahmadeya was also known as Agrahara.
- Agrahra in Sanskrit refers to 'land exempt from leasing rights'.

79. *(a)* Information and Communication Technology (ICT) can enhance the openness of e-land records by enabling quick search and retrieval of land records in several ways.

- **Online Accessibility** Land records can be made available online, allowing citizens to access and view records from anywhere anytime.
- **Transparency** ICT can facilitate real time updates and tracking of land transactions, reducing the risk of fraud and manipulation.
- **Automated Workflows** ICT can automate/and registration processes, reducing manual errors and increasing efficiency.
- **Data Analytics** ICT can provide insights and analytics on land use, ownership and transactions, supporting informed decision-making.

80. *(a)* Article 21 of the Constitution of India cannot be amended with simple majority.

- Changes to the Fundamental Reights require a constitutional amendment.
- It has to be passed by a special majority of both Houses of Parliament.
- It means that an amendment requires the approval of two-thirds of the members present and voting.

81. *(b)* Dadabhai Naoroji, in his Drain of Wealth theory, argumented that Britain was completely draining India's wealth.

- His book 'Poverty and Un-British Rule in India' brought attention to this theory.
- The Drain of Wealth was the portion of India's wealth that Britishers transferred to Britain.
- Dadabhai Naoroji, was also known as the 'Grand old Man of India' and 'Official Ambassador of India'.

82. *(a)* The Three-tier system of health infrastructure and health care system in India.

These three-tier are Primary, Secondary and Tertiary.

- **Primary** They treat only basic health issues.
- **Secondary** They provide primary health care facilities + additional facilities like ECG, X-Ray.
- **Tertiary** They provide specialised health care as well as quality medical knowledge.

83. *(a)* In 1988, Indian archers participated in the Olympics for the first time.

- Indian Round event (playing with bamboo bow and arrow) was introduced in 1993 by Archery Association of India (AAI) for enhancing he popularity of this game.
- In Paris 2014, India send an archery team to the Olympics.

84. *(d)* Telugu language is known as 'Italian' of the East.

- It is because the words in the Telugu language end with vowels, just like these in Italian.
- Telugu language ranks Aisa's 7th and world's 14th in the number of native speakers who speak it as their mother tongue.

85. *(c)* Maharashtra State launched the first migration monitoring system in the year 2022.

- The system provides information about migrant pregnant women, lactating women and children in a single system.
- Maharashtra Women and Children Development Minister Aditi Sunil Tatkare Launched the 'Migration Monitoring Systems'.
- The State department has created website-based Migration Tracking System (MTS).

86. *(c)* As compared to monopolistic competition, the demand curve in a monopoly is more elastic.

- It is because the monopolistically competitive firm has less column over the price that it can charge for its output.

87. *(d)* Vertebrata group of animals has a segmented spinal column together with a few primitive forms in which the backbone is represented by a notochord.

- Vertebrates are advanced chordates.
- The notochord is present only in the embryonic stage and afterwards is incorporated invertebral column, i.e. the backbone.
- Some examples are fishes, amphibians, reptiles, birds and mammals.

88. *(a)* The Indian festival of Holi comes every year in the season of spring.

- Holi is celebrated at the end of winter, on the last full Moon day of the Hindu luni-solar calender month.
- The date falls typically in March, but sometimes in February of the Gregorian calendar.

89. *(a)* Bharatmuni is the author the 'Natyashastra'.

- Natyashastra is a detailed treatise and handbook on dramatic art that deals with all aspects of classical Sanskrit theatre. It is believed to be written by Brahman saga Bharata.
- It has largely influenced dance, music and literary tradition in India.

90. *(c)* 68-70 cms is the circumference of International Football Association Board (IFAB) approved football.

The qualities and measurements of all balls must be

- Spherical in shape.
- Made up of suitable material.
- Must be between 410 g (140 z) and 450 g (160 z) in weight at the start of the match.
- The pressure must be equal to 0.6-1.1 atmosphere (600-1,100 g/cm^2) at sea level.

91. *(a)* In field hockey, flick occurs when a player pushes the ball and raises it off the ground.

- Sandeep Singh earned the nickname 'Flicker Singh' as his drag-flick speed was measured at speeds above 145 km per hour.
- In 2010, 145 km/h became the world record for the fastest drag flick.

92. *(c)* Mahendragiri is the highest peak of the Eastern Ghats.

- Mahendragiri is a mountain in Rayagada block of the district of Gajapati, Odisha.
- It is situated amongst the Eastern Ghats at an elevation of 1501 metres.
- Mahendragiri had proposed as a Biodiversity Hotspot area by the State Government of Odisha in 1986.

93. *(d)* In MS Word, Bottom Alignment allows you to align text in a way that it appears vertically at the bottom of a cell or text box.

This option is useful when you want to position text at the bottom of a table cell, text box or other container.

94. *(b)* The Industrial Policy Resolution, 1956 is not associated with Third-Five.

Hence, it was associated with Second Five-Year Plan.

- The policy emphasised the need to promote regional equality by establishing industries in backward regions of the country.
- It introduced a system of licenses for the private sector.
- It classified industries into three categories.

95. *(d)* Mercury does not have a ring around it.

- The inner planets (Mercury, Venus, Earth, Mars) couldn't have likely that large rings.
- It is because the rings are made of frozen icy dust, and the Sun is too hot, this is close to inner plants and does not allow rings to form properly.

96. *(c)* Writ of Mandamus is a Fundamental Right classifed under the constitutional remedies.

- Article 32 is constitutional remedies issued by Supreme Court for enforcement of Fundamental Rights.
- Under Article 266 Issued by High Court for the enforcement of fundamental as well as statutory rights.
- All writs are given below
  1. Habeas Corpus
  2. Mandamus
  3. Certiorari
  4. Quo warranto
  5. Prohibition

97. *(a)* In 2022, The NGT advised Ministry of Environment, Forest and Climate Change to from a three-member panel.

- To formulate safeguards and guidelines to be followed by the State environment Impact Assessment Authorities.
- The National Green Tribunal (NGT) is a statutory body in India that deals with expeditious disposal of cases related to environmental protection and other natural resources.

98. *(b)* Praveen Kumar Srivastava was sworn in as Central Vigilance Commissioner on 29th May, 2023.

- Central Vigilance Commission is an apex Indian Government body created in 1964.
- CVC has the status of an autonomous body, free fo control from any executive authority.
- It is charged with monitoring all vigilance activity under the Central Government of India.

99. *(d)* Purandara Dasa is known as the 'Father of Carnatic Music'.

- He was also known as Srinivasa Nayaka.
- He was a composer, singer and a Haridasa philsopher.
- In honour of his contributions to Carnatic music, he is referred as the Pitamaha of Carnatic music.

100. *(a)* The method of separating a mixture of soluble solids by dissolving them in a suitable hot solvent and then lowering the temperature slowly is called fractional crystallisation.

Set 04 01 July, 2024 (Shift IV)

SSC CHSL Tier-I SOLVED PAPER

Instructions

1. This paper contains 100 questions.
2. It has 4 Parts, **Part I** General English, **Part II** General Intelligence & Reasoning, **Part III** Quantitative Aptitude and **Part IV** General Awareness.
3. Each question carries **2 marks**.

Part I
General English

1. Select the option with the correct use of present tense.
(a) She spended all her money on make-up in order to look beautiful.
(b) She had spend all her money on make-up in order to look beautiful.
(c) She spends all her money on make-up in order to look beautiful.
(d) She has spend all her money on make-up in order to look beautiful.

2. The given sentence is divided into four segments. Identify the segment that contains a grammatical error.
When it / come to football, / my brother is / an addict.
(a) come to football,
(b) an addict
(c) my brother is
(d) When it

3. The following sentence has been divided into four segments. Identify the segment that contains an error.
Throw of / the old shoes; / nobody will wear / them now.
(a) them now
(b) nobody will wear
(c) the old shoes;
(d) Throw of

4. Select the option with the correct use of article(s).
(a) I was rude to him when I was in an fit of rage.
(b) I was rude to him when I was in fit of rage.
(c) I was rude to him when I was in the fit of rage.
(d) I was rude to him when I was in a fit of rage.

Directions (Q. Nos. 5-9) *In the following passage, some words have been deleted. Read the passage carefully and select the most appropriate option to fill in each blank.*

During the days of slavery, there lived (1) ……… very hard-working slave. One day, (2) ……… freedom, he ran away from his masters house. As he passed a forest, he saw a lion (3) ……… with pain, for a huge thorn had pierced its paw. The slave felt sorry for the lion and took out the thorn gently. The grateful lion licked the slaves hand. But just then, both of (4) ……… were captured by the soldiers.

The king ordered, "Let the runaway slave (5) ……… thrown in front of a hungry lion." But, when the slave was thrown in front of the lion, the lion licked him and quietly sat beside him. The amazed king asked the reason. The slave told the king everything. The king pardoned the slave. The lion was also freed and sent to the forest.

5. Select the most appropriate option to fill in blank number (1).
(a) the (b) a
(c) an (d) two

6. Select the most appropriate option to fill in blank number (2).
(a) gain (b) gains
(c) to gain (d) gained

7. Select the most appropriate option to fill in blank number (3).
(a) roars (b) roared
(c) roar (d) roaring

8. Select the most appropriate option to fill in blank number (4).
(a) her (b) him
(c) us (d) them

9. Select the most appropriate option to fill in blank number (5).
(a) been (b) being
(c) be (d) is

10. Identify the most appropriate antonym of the underlined word in the following sentence.
A boisterous horse must have a rough bridle.
(a) rowdy (b) loud
(c) bouncy (d) calm

11. Select the most appropriate option that can substitute the underlined segment in the given sentence. If there is no need to substitute it, select 'No improvement required'.
I am so glad that I ran into you on the way.
(a) ran over
(b) No improvement required
(c) ran away
(d) ran out of

12. Select the most appropriate antonym of the given word.
Stingy
(a) Generous (b) Humorous
(c) Lascivious (d) Deceitful

13. Select the most appropriate idiom for the underlined segment in the following sentence.
The arrival of Pragati in the house brought disharmony among the family members.
(a) tenterhooks
(b) a cry in the wilderness
(c) rift in the lute
(d) hair breadth

14. Select the most appropriate synonym of the given word.
Titanic
(a) Deep (b) Huge
(c) Attractive (d) Disastrous

15. Select the most appropriate antonym of the underlined word in the given sentence.
Prajakta is a very vain girl.
(a) honourable (b) humble
(c) honest (d) hopeful

16. Select the most appropriate antonym of the underlined word in the given sentence.
Ralph's condition worsened in the hospital.
(a) improved (b) scaled
(c) changed (d) traversed

17. Select the option that will improve the underlined part of the given sentence.
This win could enhance to be a historic turning point in the fortunes of the team.
(a) prove (b) demonstrate
(c) accomplish (d) confirm

18. Select the most appropriate synonym of the given word.
Fasten
(a) Loosen (b) Bolt
(c) Undo (d) Detach

19. There is a spelling error in the given sentence. Select the option that contains the incorrectly spelt word.
The precious bookshelf was carefully decorated with religiuos books.
(a) precious (b) decorated
(c) carefully (d) religiuos

20. Identify the incorrectly spelt word in the following sentence and select its correct spelling from the given options.
The committee heard that he had been negliegent in his duty.
(a) negligent (b) dutie
(c) comittee (d) hurd

21. Select the option that will improve the underlined part of the given sentence.
Mothers have great animosity for their children.
(a) affection (b) absurdity
(c) affectation (d) abasement

22. Select the most appropriate option to fill in the blank.
The CEO's decision to cut benefits was a ……… move.
(a) harsh (b) humorous
(c) rigorous (d) laborious

23. Select the most appropriate option that can substitute the underlined segment in the given sentence.
Sonam's cat used to chase the mouse into the kitchen and knock through a tower of pots and pans.
(a) knock inside a tower of pots
(b) knock over a tower of pots
(c) knock away a tower of pots
(d) knock out a tower of pots

24. Select the most appropriate antonym of the underlined word in the given sentence.
The organisation's furtive actions must be taken into notice and dealt with accordingly.
(a) futuristic (b) truthful
(c) shady (d) foxy

25. Select the most appropriate meaning of the given idiom.
Cost an arm and a leg
(a) To be moderately priced
(b) To be inexpensive
(c) To be very expensive
(d) To be affordable

Part II
General Intelligence

26. Select the correct mirror image of the given combination when the mirror is placed at MN as shown below.

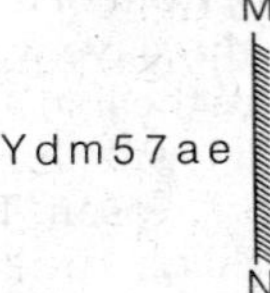

(a) ɘɒ7ƨmbY (b) ɘɒ57mbY
(c) ɘɒ7ƨdmY (d) ɘɒ75ɯdʎ

27. What should come in place of question mark (?) in the given series based on the English alphabetical order?
DLT, ZHP, VDL, ?, NVD
(a) DNX (b) RZH
(c) CMW (d) BLV

28. What would be the symbol on the opposite side of '@', if the given sheet is folded to form a cube?

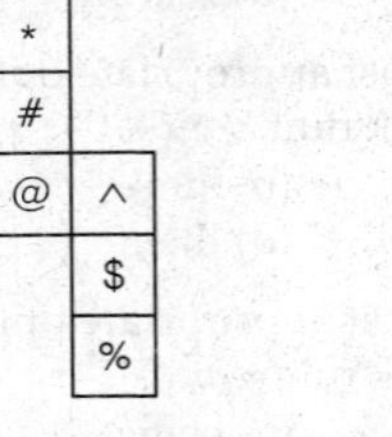

(a) $ (b) * (c) % (d) ^

29. In a certain code language, 'I am boy' is coded as 'it sit pit' and 'I am girl' is coded as 'sit nit it'. What is the code for 'girl' in that language?
(a) it (b) nit
(c) pit (d) sit

30. What should come in place of the question mark (?) in the given series?
4, 20, 100, 500, 2500, ?
(a) 12200 (b) 12700
(c) 12600 (d) 12500

31. Select the correct mirror image of the given combination, when the mirror is placed at MN as shown below.

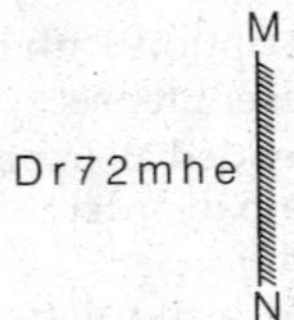

(a) ɘdmƧ7ɿD (b) ɘɥmƧ7ɿD
(c) ɘdm72ɿD (d) ɘɥmƧ⅂ɿD

32. What will come in the place of the question mark (?) in the following equation, if '+' and '−' are interchanged and '×' and '÷' are interchanged?
$209 \div 2 + 14 - 120 \times 3 = ?$
(a) 412 (b) 454
(c) 434 (d) 444

33. Select the option figure in which the given figure (X) is embedded as its part (rotation is not allowed).

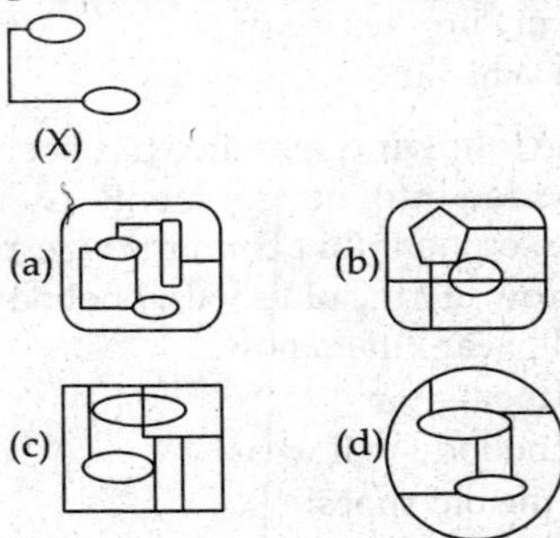

34. Select the option that is related to the third number in the same way as the second number is related to the first number and the sixth number is related to the fifth number.
64 : 512 :: 169 : ? :: 225 : 3375
(a) 2197
(b) 872
(c) 1852
(d) 1026

35. Identify the figure given in the options that, when put in place of the question mark (?) will logically complete the series.

D 2 K V O X	X O V K 2 D	V X O 2 D K	K D 2 O X V	?

D 2 K X V O	2 K D V O X	2 K D X V O	D 2 K V O X
(a)	(b)	(c)	(d)

36. Read the given statements and conclusions carefully. Assuming that the information given in the statements is true, even if it appears to be at variance with commonly known facts, decide which of the given conclusions logically follow(s) from the statements.

Statements

All watches are dials.

All dials are phones.

Some phones are mobiles.

Conclusions

I. No watch is a phone.

II. Some dials are mobiles.

(a) None of the Conclusions follow
(b) Only Conclusion II follows
(c) Only Conclusion I follows
(d) Both Conclusions I and II follow

37. In a certain code language,
'M & N' means 'M is the father of N',
'M@N' means 'M is the daughter of N',
'M#N' means 'M is the brother of N',
'M % N' means 'M is the mother of N'.
Based on the above, how is A related to E, if 'A & B # C @ D % E'?
(a) Father's brother
(b) Father
(c) Son
(d) Brother

38. Select the combination of letters that, when sequentially placed in the blanks of the given series will complete the series.
_ n p _ r r _ p _ m m _ p q _ r q _ n m _ n p _ r r q _ n m
(a) mqqrnrpmqp
(b) mrqnnrmpqp
(c) mqqnnrpmqp
(d) mqqrnnpmqp

39. If 1st January, 2020 was a Wednesday, then what day of the week was it on 1st January, 2021?
(a) Thursday (b) Wednesday
(c) Tuesday (d) Friday

40. What should come in place of question mark (?) in the given series?
21, 60, 177, 528, 1581, ?
(a) 4636 (b) 4740
(c) 4892 (d) 4570

41. FHGE is related to IKJH in a certain way based on the English alphabetical order. In the same way, HJIG is related to KMLJ. To which of the following is RTSQ related, following the same logic?
(a) UVWT (b) VWUT
(c) UWVT (d) TVUS

42. CZ22 is related to HE33 in a certain way. In the same way, QN47 is related to VS58. To which of the following is WT7 related following the same logic?
(a) GA21
(b) BY21
(c) BY18
(d) GA18

43. In a certain language, 'make someone happy' is written as 'Ab Te Dp' and 'someone robbed him' is written as 'Te Ko Vi'. How is 'someone' written in the given language?
(a) Vi (b) Te
(c) Ab (d) Ko

44. If 'A' stands for '÷', 'B' stands for '×', 'C' stands for '+' and 'D' stands for '–', then the resultant of which of the following will be 217?
(a) 32 B 5 D 10 A 2 C 62
(b) 32 A 5 D 10 B 2 C 62
(c) 32 B 5 D 10 C 2 A 62
(d) 32 D 5 B 10 A 2 C 62

45. Three of the following four are alike in a certain way and thus form a group. Which is the one that does not belong to that group?
(**Note** The odd one out is not based on the number of consonants/vowels or their position in the letter-cluster.)
(a) JMP (b) SVZ
(c) BEI (d) KNR

46. Select the correct mirror image of the given figure, when the mirror is placed at MN as shown below.

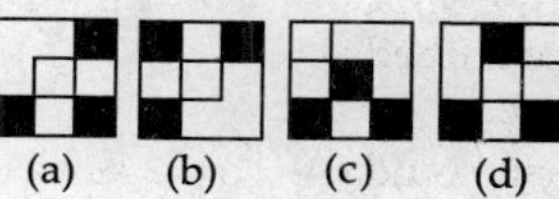

47. The position of how many letters will change, if each of the letters in the word TROUBLEMAKING is arranged from left to right in alphabetical order?
(a) Twelve (b) All
(c) Ten (d) Eleven

48. Select the set in which the numbers are related in the same way as are the numbers of the following sets.
(**Note** Operations should be performed on the whole numbers, without breaking down the numbers into its constituent digits. E.g. 13 – Operations on 13 such as adding /subtracting /multiplying etc. to 13 can be performed. Breaking down 13 into 1 and 3 and then performing mathematical operations on 1 and 3 is not allowed.)
(59, 83, 97)
(63, 87, 101)
(a) (67, 91, 115) (b) (71, 95, 109)
(c) (51, 65, 89) (d) (48, 82, 96)

49. What will come in the place of question mark (?) in the following equation, if '×' and '÷' are interchanged?
18 – 2 + 12 × 4 ÷ 7 = ?
(a) 30 (b) 37 (c) 49 (d) 45

50. How many triangles are there in the given figure?

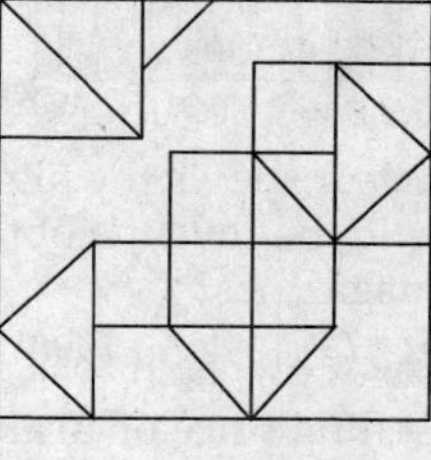

(a) 11 (b) 15
(c) 12 (d) 13

Part III
Quantitative Aptitude

51. Given is a circle with centre at C. A, B and D are the points on the circumference. Find $\angle ABC$.

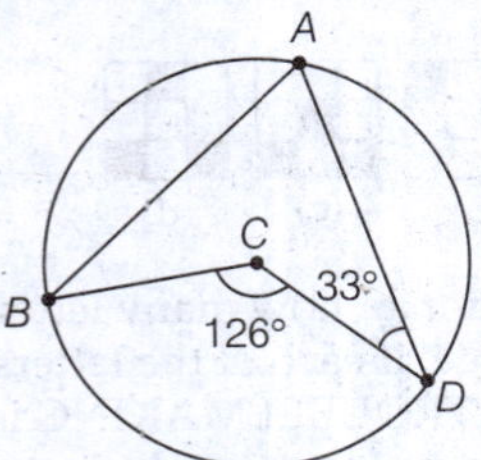

(a) 30° (b) 37°
(c) 35° (d) 33°

52. A robber steals a bag from a man at 5 pm and starts running at 10 km/h. A policeman is informed about the robber at 5 :12 pm and he chases him on a cycle at 15 km/h. At what time is the robber caught by the policeman?
(a) 5:48 pm (b) 5:36 pm
(c) 5:12 pm (d) 5:40 pm

53. Fifteen persons working 12 h a day earn ₹18000 per week. How many rupees will 18 persons working 9 h a day earn per week?
(a) ₹16020 (b) ₹12600
(c) ₹12060 (d) ₹16200

54. Answer the following question on the basis of the bar-graph given.
Revenue obtained by a publisher on journals, magazines and books

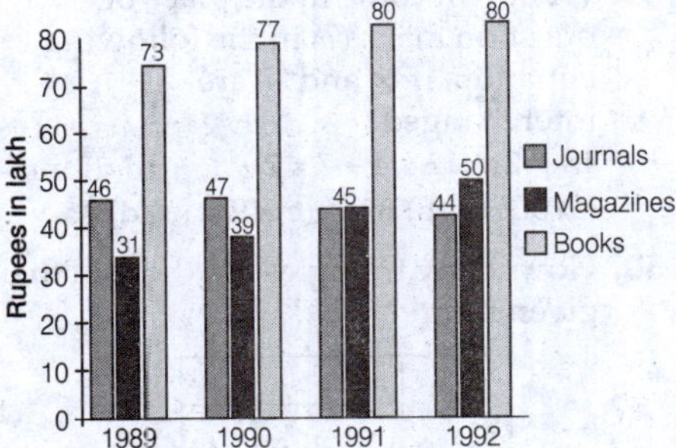

Which year shows the highest change in the revenue obtained from magazines?
(a) 1991 (b) 1992 (c) 1990 (d) 1989

55. If the selling price of 40 articles is equal to the cost price of 50 articles, then the percentage gain is
(a) 25% (b) 20%
(c) 30% (d) 35%

56. The surface area of a sphere is 2464 cm^2. Find its volume.
(a) $13121\frac{1}{3}\text{cm}^3$ (b) $11892\frac{2}{3}\text{cm}^3$
(c) $11498\frac{2}{3}\text{cm}^3$ (d) $11621\frac{1}{3}\text{cm}^3$

57. The following graph shows the production of milk in 4 states in 2010 and 2011.

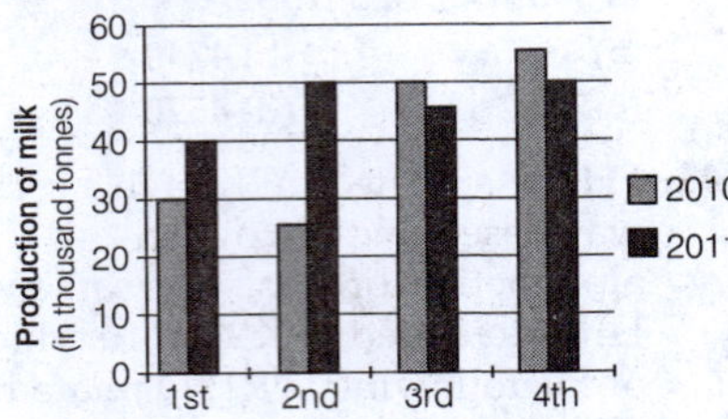

The difference between the average production (in thousand tonnes) for all states in both years is
(a) 6.25 (b) 6.75
(c) 7.75 (d) 7.25

58. The difference between two numbers is 48. The ratio of these two numbers is 7 : 3. What is the sum of the two numbers?
(a) 110 (b) 90 (c) 100 (d) 120

59. Study the given table and answer the question that follows.
The table shows the results of half-yearly and annual examinations of three sections A, B, C of Class X students in a school.

Result	Number of students		
	Section A	Section B	Section C
Students failed in both exams	39	20	12
Students failed in half-yearly but passed in annual exams	16	14	6
Students passed in half-yearly but failed in annual exams	10	12	8
Students passed in both exams	65	45	35

Find the failed percentage of section C in at lest one of the two examinations.
(a) 30.81% (b) 10.42%
(c) 38.23% (d) 42.62%

60. The population of a city was 5000000 in 2020. The population grows 7.5% annually. The population in 2022 is
(a) 5778125 (b) 5875215
(c) 5558875 (d) 5887125

61. In an election, a candidate secured 41% of the votes polled and lost the election by 97632. What is the number of votes obtained by the winning candidate?
(a) 320016 (b) 542400
(c) 222384 (d) 360072

62. There are 12 workers in an office and the average age of all the workers is $35\frac{1}{2}$ yr. A new worker joins the office, the average becomes 37 yr. The current age of the newly joined worker is
(a) $55\frac{1}{2}$ yr (b) $57\frac{1}{2}$ yr
(c) $47\frac{1}{2}$ yr (d) 55 yr

63. If the side of a cube is 3 units,which of the following options is equal to the ratio between the surface area and the volume of the cube?
(a) 2 : 5 (b) 2 : 7
(c) 2 : 1 (d) 2 : 3

64. M varies inversely as $(N^2 + 3)$. If $M = 3$ when $N = 3$, then what will be the value of M, when $N^2 = 69$?
(a) $\frac{1}{2}$ (b) 1
(c) $\sqrt{69}$ (d) $\frac{1}{4}$

65. $12\sin^2 A + 2\cos^2 A = 7$, where $0 < A < 180°$. Then, $\cot A$ is
(a) ± 1 (b) $\pm\frac{1}{2}$
(c) $\pm\frac{1}{\sqrt{2}}$ (d) $\pm\frac{1}{\sqrt{3}}$

66. Diagonals of a trapezium $ABCD$ with $AB \parallel DC$, intersect each other at the point 'O'. If $AB = 2.5CD$, find the ratio of the area of triangle AOB to the area of triangle COD.
(a) 25:4 (b) 16:1
(c) 5:2 (d) 9:2

67. Which of the following are the sides of a right-angled triangle?
(a) 6 cm, 7 cm, 10 cm
(b) 5 cm, 11 cm, 13 cm
(c) 12 cm, 16 cm, 20 cm
(d) 16 cm, 31 cm, 34 cm

68. One company is offering a 25% discount on a particular product. Anurag visited a store. He was trying to find a deal that would allow him to save at least ₹390. How many minimum items should he purchase, if each item costs ₹340?

(a) 7 (b) 4
(c) 6 (d) 5

69. Find the lowest positive value of $(c-b)$ such that the 7-digits number $1738b9c$ is divisible by 12.

(a) 4 (b) 2
(c) 1 (d) 7

70. The simple interest on the sum for 12 yr is three-fifth of the sum. The rate of interest per annum is

(a) 4% (b) 6%
(c) 5% (d) 3%

71. Sumit's income in 2020 was ₹ 21000. He gets an increment of 10% every year. What was his income in 2022?

(a) ₹ 23100 (b) ₹ 25410
(c) ₹ 29100 (d) ₹ 26530

72. Successive division of a number by 2, 3, 5 and 7 gives remainders 1,4,0 and 5, respectively. What will be the sum of the remainders, if the same number is divided by 7, 5,3 and 2 successively?

(a) 8 (b) 9
(c) 10 (d) 17

73. The following graph shows the production (in thousands) of two types (A and B) of cars by a company over the years 2016 to 2021.

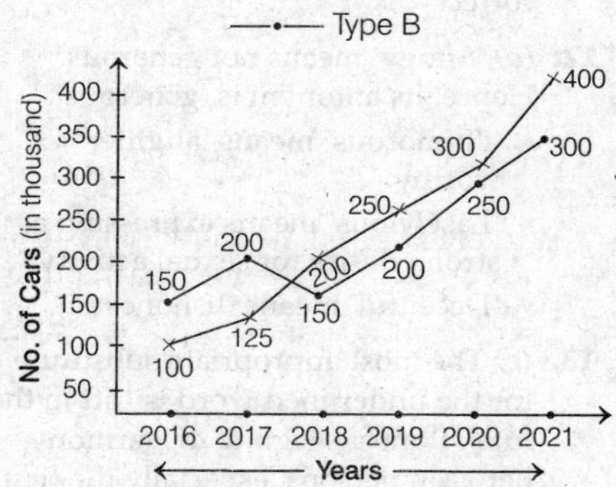

The ratio of the total production of type A cars to type B cars over the years is

(a) 11 : 10
(b) 21 : 10
(c) 10 : 21
(d) 10 : 11

74. Two circles of radius 7 units each, intersect in such a way that the common chord is of length 7 units. What is the common area in square units of the intersection?

(a) $98\left(\frac{\pi}{6}-\frac{\sqrt{3}}{3}\right)$ (b) $98\left(\frac{\pi}{3}-\frac{\sqrt{3}}{4}\right)$
(c) $98\left(\frac{\pi}{6}-\frac{\sqrt{3}}{6}\right)$ (d) $98\left(\frac{\pi}{6}-\frac{\sqrt{3}}{4}\right)$

75. Find the diameter of a spherical ball, whose volume is 38.808 cm^3. $\left(\text{use } \pi=\frac{22}{7}\right)$

(a) 4.2 cm (b) 4.8 cm
(c) 4.6 cm (d) 4.4 cm

Part IV

General Awareness

76. Folk songs in .... are called Raganis.

(a) Uttar Pradesh
(b) Madhya Pradesh
(c) Haryana
(d) Bihar

77. Mayadhar Raut is an exponent of the Indian classical dance form ....

(a) Kuchipudi
(b) Odissi
(c) Bharatanatyam
(d) Kathak

78. Symmetric encryption is also known as

(a) hybrid encryption
(b) public-key encryption
(c) asymmetric encryption
(d) conventional encryption

79. Mewar festival is celebrated during the .... festival at Udaipur.

(a) Gangaur (b) Teej
(c) Dusshera (d) Holi

80. Which of the following Articles prohibits traffic in human beings and forced labour?

(a) Article 25 (b) Article 28
(c) Article 23 (d) Article 22

81. If there is a fall in the demand of a good, the equilibrium price is expected to

(a) fall
(b) neither fall nor rise
(c) rise
(d) first rise, and then fall sharply

82. In which event at the 2023 U-20 Asian Athletics Championships did Siddharth Choudhary win a gold medal for India?

(a) Discus throw
(b) Hammer throw
(c) Triple jump
(d) Shot put

83. The zone separating the troposphere from the stratosphere is called the ....

(a) Stratomerge
(b) Tropopause
(c) Tropomerge
(d) Stratospause

84. Which technology is associated with providing high-speed wireless data transmission for mobile devices?

(a) GPRS (b) GPS
(c) Wi-Max (d) LTE

85. Of the football clubs listed below, which is the oldest in India?

(a) Calcutta FC (b) Bombay FC
(c) Madras FC (d) FC Kochin

86. In January 2023, Captain Shiva Chouhan was in the news for being the first women officer to be deployed at which battlefield?

(a) Leh (b) Kargil
(c) Dras (d) Siachen

87. Mendel proposed the law of independent assortment on the basis of ....

(a) genes
(b) dihybrid crosses
(c) alleles
(d) monohybrid crosses

88. Which sub-division of Himalayas are famous for Karewa formations?

(a) Uttarakhand Himalayas
(b) Kashmir Himalayas
(c) Arunachal Himalayas
(d) Sikkim Himalayas

89. After independence, the Census Act was enacted in India in the year ....

(a) 1960 (b) 1955
(c) 1962 (d) 1948

90. Who wrote the Indian patriotic song, 'Sare Jahan Se Acchha, Hindustan Hamara'?

(a) Rabindranath Tagore
(b) Ishwar Chandra Vidyasagar
(c) Mohammad Iqbal
(d) Mahatma Gandhi

91. Which of the following is not a domestic cricket tournament organised by the Board of Control for Cricket in India (BCCI) in India?
(a) Vizzy Trophy
(b) Super Fours
(c) Ranji Trophy
(d) ZR Irani Cup

92. Which of the following articles of the Constitution of India deal with citizenship?
(a) Articles 10 – 17 (b) Articles 8 – 15
(c) Articles 5 – 11 (d) Articles 12 – 18

93. Who discovered the atomic number based on X-ray wavelength in 1913?
(a) AEB de Chancourtois
(b) Dmitri Mendeleev
(c) Henry Moseley
(d) RA Millikan

94. In which country is the 'Kachin Manaw Festival' celebrated?
(a) Sri Lanka (b) Myanmar
(c) Nepal (d) Maldives

95. Which of the following is more important to promote modernisation and overall prosperity of a country?
(a) Stable export
(b) Stable employment
(c) Stable import
(d) Stable unemployment

96. Which organisation launched the Indian customs Compliance Information Portal (CIP) for providing free access to information on all customs procedures and regulatory compliance for nearly 12,000 Customs Tariff items in the year 2021?
(a) Central Board for Indirect Taxes and Customs
(b) Income Tax Settlement Commission
(c) Central Board for Direct Taxes
(d) Directorate of Enforcement

97. On 31st October 1940, who among the following was arrested for offering individual Satyagraha to protest against India's forced participation in Second World War?
(a) Saifuddin Kitchlew
(b) Subhas Chandra Bose
(c) Jawaharlal Nehru
(d) Sardar Vallabhbhai Patel

98. Match the following.

	Type of Industries		Name of Company
A.	Public sector	1.	Tata Iron and Steel Company
B.	Private Sector	2.	Bharat Heavy Electricals Limited
C.	Joint sector	3.	Oil India Ltd.

Codes

	A	B	C		A	B	C
(a)	2	3	1	(b)	1	2	3
(c)	3	2	1	(d)	2	1	3

99. In April 2023, the Maharashtra Government has approved how much percentage of reservation for Divyang employees in promotions?
(a) 5% (b) 2%
(c) 3% (d) 4%

100. Who among the following was the founder of 'Vikramshila Vishwavidyalaya'?
(a) Dharmapala (b) Mahipala I
(c) Govindapala (d) Ramapala

Answers

1. (c)	2. (a)	3. (d)	4. (d)
5. (b)	6. (c)	7. (d)	8. (d)
9. (c)	10. (d)	11. (b)	12. (a)
13. (c)	14 (b)	15. (b)	16. (a)
17. (a)	18. (b)	19. (d)	20. (a)
21. (a)	22. (a)	23. (b)	24. (b)
25. (c)	26. (a)	27. (b)	28. (b)
29. (b)	30. (d)	31. (a)	32. (d)
33. (a)	34. (a)	35. (c)	36. (a)
37. (b)	38. (c)	39. (d)	40. (b)
41. (c)	42. (c)	43. (b)	44. (a)
45. (a)	46. (a)	47. (a)	48. (b)
49. (b)	50. (d)	51. (a)	52. (b)
53. (d)	54. (c)	55. (a)	56. (c)
57. (a)	58. (d)	59. (d)	60. (a)
61. (a)	62. (d)	63. (c)	64. (a)
65. (a)	66. (a)	67. (c)	68. (d)
69. (c)	70. (c)	71. (b)	72. (b)
73. (a)	74. (d)	75. (a)	76. (c)
77. (b)	78. (d)	79. (a)	80. (c)
81. (a)	82. (d)	83. (b)	84. (d)
85. (a)	86. (d)	87. (b)	88. (b)
89. (d)	90. (c)	91. (b)	92. (c)
93. (c)	94. (b)	95. (b)	96. (a)
97. (c)	98. (d)	99. (d)	100. (a)

Explanations

1. *(c)* The sentence in present tense is- She spends all her money on make-up in order to look beautiful.

2. *(a)* Part (a) 'come to football' contains an error. As the subject of the sentence is singular, singular verb 'comes' should be used to correct the sentence.

3. *(d)* Part (d) 'throw of' contains an error. Use 'dispose of' or throw off to correct the sentence.

4. *(d)* The sentence with correct use of articles is- I was rude to him when I was in a fit of rage.

5. *(b)* The correct filler for the given blank is 'a'.

6. *(c)* The correct filler for the given blank is 'to gain'.

7. *(d)* The correct filler for the given blank is 'roaring'.

8. *(d)* The correct filler for the given blank is 'them'.

9. *(c)* The correct filler for the given blank is 'be'.

10. *(d)* 'Boisterous' means noisy, energetic, and cheerful. Hence, its antonym is 'calm'.
- 'Rowdy' means noisy and disorderly.
- 'Bouncy' means bouncing or causing things to bounce.

11. *(b)* The underlined part is grammatically and contextually correct.

12. *(a)* 'Stingy' means not generous. Hence, its antonym is 'generous'.
- 'Humorous' means laughter worthy.
- 'Lascivious' means expressing a strong desire for sexual activity.
- 'Deceitful' means dishonest.

13. *(c)* The most appropriate substitute for the underlined word is 'rift in the lute'. It means sign of disharmony between persons, especially the first evidence of a quarrel that may become worse.

14. *(b)* 'Titanic' means of exceptional strength, size, or power; huge.

15. *(b)* 'Vain' means proud and arrogant. Hence, its antonym is 'humble' which means kind and polite.

16. *(a)* The antonym of 'worsened' is 'improved'.

- 'Scaled' means covered with or made up of scales.
- 'Traversed' means travel across or through.

17. *(a)* The underlined part of the sentence contains an error. Use 'prove' to correct the sentence.

18. *(b)* The word 'Fasten' means close or do up securely. Hence, its synonym is 'Bolt' which means a bar that slides into a socket to fasten a door or window.

'Detach' means disengage (something or part of something) and remove it.

19. *(d)* The incorrectly spelt word is 'religiuos'. The correct spelling is 'religious'.

20. *(a)* The incorrectly spelt word is 'negliegent'. The correct spelling is 'negligent'.

21. *(a)* The underlined part of the sentence contains an error. The use of word 'animosity' is incorrect in the context of the sentence. Use 'affection' to correct the sentence.

22. *(a)* The correct filler for the given blank is 'harsh'.

23. *(b)* The underlined part of the sentence contains an error. Use 'over' in place of 'through' to correct the sentence.

24. *(b)* 'Furtive' means attempting to avoid notice or attention, typically because of guilt or a belief that discovery would lead to trouble; secretive. Hence, its antonym is 'truthful'.

- 'Futuristic' means relating to the future.
- 'Shady' means situated in or full of shade.
- 'Foxy' means resembling or likened to a fox.

25. *(c)* Cost an arm and a leg means to be very expensive.

26. *(a)* The figure given in option (a) is the correct mirror image of the given question figure.

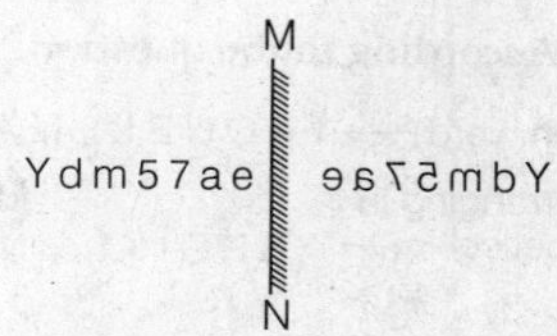

27. *(b)* The pattern of the series is as follows,

D $\xrightarrow{-4}$ Z $\xrightarrow{-4}$ V $\xrightarrow{-4}$ **R** $\xrightarrow{-4}$ N

L $\xrightarrow{-4}$ H $\xrightarrow{-4}$ D $\xrightarrow{-4}$ **Z** $\xrightarrow{-4}$ V

T $\xrightarrow{-4}$ P $\xrightarrow{-4}$ L $\xrightarrow{-4}$ **H** $\xrightarrow{-4}$ D

∴ ? = RZH

28. *(b)* According to the question,

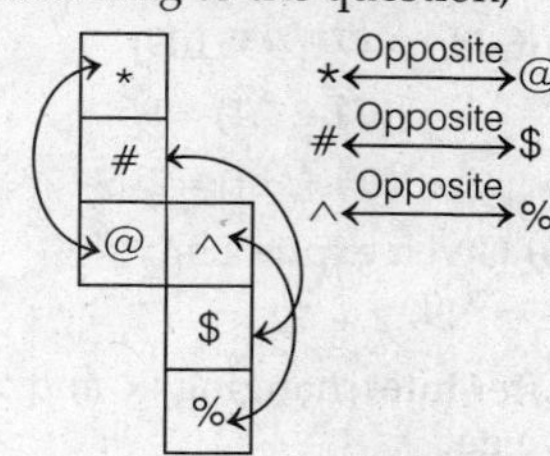

Hence, '*' is opposite to face '@'.

29. *(b)* According to the question,

I am boy ⟶ it sit pit

I am girl ⟶ sit nit it

Hence, the code for 'girl' is 'nit'.

30. *(d)* The pattern of the series is as follows,

4 → 20 → 100 → 500 → 2500 → **12500** (each ×5)

31. *(a)* The figure given in option (a) is the correct mirror image of the given question figure.

M
Dr72mhe
N

32. *(d)* Given expression,

$209 \div 2 + 14 - 120 \times 3 = ?$

After interchanging '+' and '−' and '×' and '÷' signs, we get

$? = 209 \times 2 - 14 + 120 \div 3$

$= 418 - 14 + 40$

$= 458 - 14 = 444$

33. *(a)* The figure (X) is embedded in option figure (a).

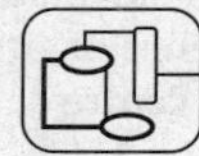

34. *(a)* As, 64 : 512 → $(8)^2$ $(8)^3$

and 225 : 3375 → $(15)^2$ $(15)^3$

Similarly, **169 : 2197** → $(13)^2$ $(13)^3$

∴ ? = 2197

35. *(c)* There are two alternate series in the given question, which are as follows,

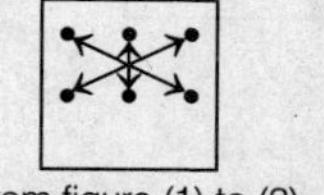

From figure (1) to (2) and figure (3) to (4)

From figure (2) to (3) and figure (4) to (5)

Hence, option figure (c) will replace the question mark.

36. *(a)* According to the given statements,

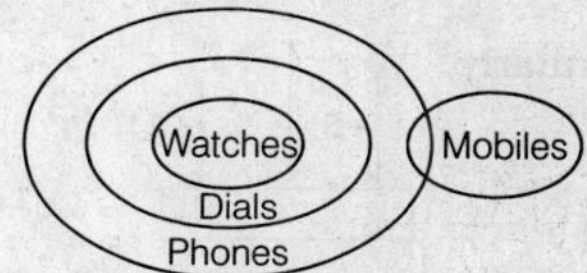

Conclusions I. (✗) II. (✗)

Hence, none of the conclusions follows.

37. *(b)* Given, A&B#C@D%E

According to the question,

(+)A ←Couple→ D(−); A Father ↑ B; D Daughter ↓ C; (+)B ←Brother→ C(−) ←Sibling→ E

[+ → Male, − → Female]

Hence, A is the father of E.

38. *(c)* The pattern of the series is as follows,

m n p q r r q p n m / m n p q r r q p n m/ m n p q r r q p n m.

⇒ m q q n n r p m q p

39. *(d)* It was Wednesday on 1st January, 2020.

As, 2020 is a leap year.

So, number of odd days in leap year is 2 days.

∴ Day on 1st January, 2021

= Wednesday + 2 = Friday

40. (b) The pattern of the series is as follows,

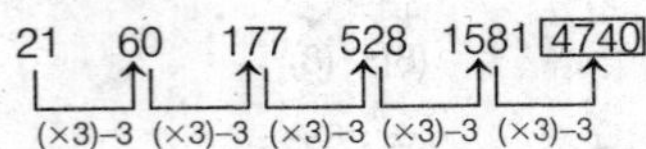

41. (c) As, F H G E → (+3 each) → I K J H

and H J I G → (+3 each) → K M L J

Similarly, R T S Q → (+3 each) → U W V T

42. (c) As, C Z 22 → (+5, +5, +11) → H E 33

and Q N 47 → (+5, +5, +11) → V S 58

Similarly, W T 7 → (+5, +5, +11) → B Y 18

43. (b) According to the question,

make someone happy ⟶ Ab Te Dp

someone robbed him ⟶ Te Ko Vi

Hence, the code for someone is 'Te'.

44. (a) From option (a),

32 B 5 D 10 A 2 C 62

After substituting the letters with signs, we get

32 × 5 – 10 ÷ 2 + 62

= 160 – 5 + 62

= 222 – 5= 217

45. (a) As, S $\xrightarrow{+3}$ V $\xrightarrow{+4}$ Z

B $\xrightarrow{+3}$ E $\xrightarrow{+4}$ I

K $\xrightarrow{+3}$ N $\xrightarrow{+4}$ R

But, J $\xrightarrow{+3}$ M $\xrightarrow{+3}$ P

46. (a) The figure given in option (a) is the correct mirror image of the given figure.

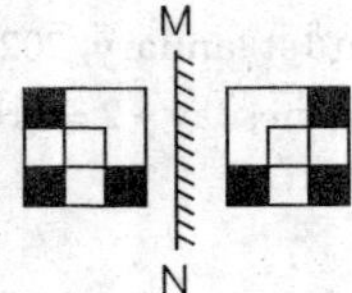

47. (a) According to the question,

Given word ⟶ TROUBLEMAKING

After arranging in alphabetical order ⟶ ABEGIKLMNORTU

Hence, the position of 12 letters will change.

48. (b) As, (59, 83, 97)

⇒ (59 + 24) = 83

⇒ (83 + 14) = 97

and (63, 87, 101)

⇒ (63 + 24) = 87

⇒ (87 + 14) = 101

Similarly, (71, 95, 109)

(71 + 24) = 95

⇒ (95 + 14) = 109

49. (b) Given expression,

18 – 2 + 12 × 4 ÷ 7 = ?

After interchanging '×' and '÷' signs, we get

? = 18 – 2 + 12 ÷ 4 × 7

= 16 + 3 × 7

= 16 + 21= 37

50. (d) Naming the figure,

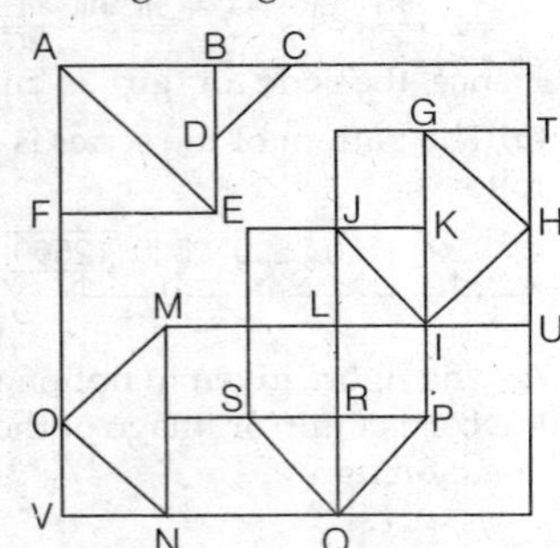

Δ ABE, Δ AEF, Δ BCD, Δ MNO, ΔGTH, Δ HUI, ΔGHI, Δ JKI, Δ JIL, ΔSRQ, Δ RPQ, ΔSPQ and ΔOVN.

∴ There are 13 triangles in the given figure.

51. (a)

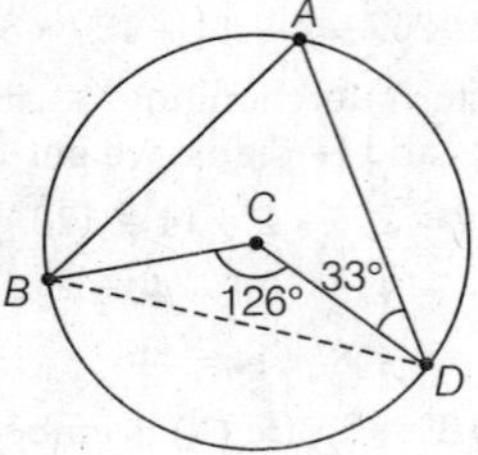

∵ The angle formed at the circumference of circle is the half of that of the centre of the circle.

$\therefore \quad \angle BAD = \frac{126}{2} = 63°$

In Δ BCD,

$\angle CBD = \angle CDB = \frac{180° - 126°}{2} = 27°$

$\therefore \quad \angle ADB = \angle ADC + \angle CDB$

$= 33° + 27° = 60°$

In Δ ABD,

$\angle ABD + \angle BAD + \angle ADB = 180°$

$\angle ABD + 63° + 60° = 180°$

$\therefore \quad \angle ABD = 180° - 123° = 57°$

Hence, $\angle ABC = \angle ABD - \angle CBD$

$= 57° - 27° = 30°$

52. (b) Distance travelled by robber in 12 min

= Speed × Time

$= 10 \times \frac{12}{60} = 2$ km

∴ Time taken to chase a robber

$= \frac{\text{Distance between both}}{\text{Relative speed}}$

$= \frac{2}{15 - 10} = \frac{2}{5}$ h

$= \frac{2}{5} \times 60$ min = 24 min

Hence, required time

= 5 : 12 pm + 24 min

= 5 : 36 pm

53. (d) $\because \frac{M_1 T_1}{W_1} = \frac{M_2 T_2}{W_2}$

$\Rightarrow \frac{15 \times 12}{18000} = \frac{18 \times 9}{W_2}$

$\Rightarrow W_2 = \frac{18 \times 9 \times 18000}{15 \times 12}$

= ₹ 16200

Hence, 18 persons working 9 h a day earn ₹ 16200 per week.

54. (c) Increase in revenue obtained by magazine in year 1990

= (39 – 31) = ₹ 8 lakh

Increase in revenue obtained by magazine in year 1991

= (45 – 39) = ₹ 6 lakh

Therefore, increase in revenue obtained by magazine in year 1992

= (50 – 45) = ₹ 5 lakh

Hence, the highest change in the revenue obtained from magazines is in the year 1990.

55. (a) If SP of 40 articles = CP of 50 articles

So, 40 SP = 50 CP

$\frac{CP}{SP} = \frac{40}{50}$

Hence, the required gain percentage

$= \frac{(50-40)}{40} \times 100$

$= \frac{10}{40} \times 100 = 25\%$

56. *(c)* ∵ Surface area of sphere $= 4\pi r^2$

$\therefore \quad 4\pi r^2 = 2464$

$4 \times \frac{22}{7} \times r^2 = 2464$

$r^2 = \frac{2464 \times 7}{88} = 196$

$r = 14$ cm

So, volume of sphere $= \frac{4}{3}\pi r^3$

$= \frac{4}{3} \times \frac{22}{7} \times 14 \times 14 \times 14$

$= \frac{34496}{3}$

$= 11498\frac{2}{3}$ cm^3

57. *(a)* Average production of milk in all states in year 2010

$= \frac{30+25+50+55}{4} = \frac{160}{4}$

= 40 thousand tonnes

Average production of milk in all states in year 2011

$= \frac{40+50+45+50}{4} = \frac{185}{4}$

= 46.25 thousand tonnes

Hence, the difference between the average production of milk for all states in both year

= (46.25 – 40) thousand tonnes

= 6.25 thousand tonnes

58. *(d)* Let the two numbers be $7x$ and $3x$.

According to the question,

$7x - 3x = 48$

$\Rightarrow \quad 4x = 48$

$\therefore \quad x = 12$

Hence, the sum of two numbers is $(7x + 3x) = 10 \times 12 = 120$

59. *(d)* According to the question,

Number of students failed in Section C in atleast one of the two examinations = 12 + 6 + 8 = 26

Total number of students in Section C = 12 + 6 + 8 + 35 = 61

Hence, the required failed percentage

$= \frac{26}{61} \times 100 = 42.62\%$

60. *(a)* The population of a city in 2020 = 5000000

Population grows 7.5% annually.

Hence, the population in 2022

$= \frac{5000000 \times 107.5 \times 107.5}{100 \times 100}$

= 5778125

61. *(a)* Let the total number of votes $= x$

According to the question,

$\frac{x \times 59}{100} - \frac{x \times 41}{100} = 97632$

$\Rightarrow \quad \frac{x \times 18}{100} = 97632$

$\therefore \quad x = \frac{97632 \times 100}{18} = 542400$

Hence, the number of votes obtained by the winning candidate

$= \frac{542400 \times 59}{100} = 320016$

62. *(d)* Total age of 12 workers in an office

$= 12 \times \frac{71}{2}$

= 426 yr

After joining the new worker, the total age of all the workers in an office = 37 × 13 = 481 yr

∴ The current age of newly joined worker

= (481 – 426) = 55 yr

63. *(c)* Given, side of a cube = 3 units

∵ Surface area of cube $= 6a^2$

Volume of cube $= a^3$

Hence, the required ratio between the surface area and the volume of the cube

$= \frac{6a^2}{a^3} = \frac{6}{a}$

$= \frac{6}{3} = 2:1$

64. *(a)* Given,

$M \propto \frac{1}{N^2+3}$

$M = \frac{K}{N^2+3}$

Putting the value of M and N

$3 = \frac{K}{3^2+3}$

$\Rightarrow \quad K = 36$

Now, $\quad M = \frac{K}{N^2+3}$

$= \frac{36}{69+3} = \frac{36}{72} = \frac{1}{2}$

Hence, the value of $M = \frac{1}{2}$

65. *(a)* $\quad 12\sin^2 A + 2\cos^2 A = 7$

$12\sin^2 A + 2(1 - \sin^2 A) = 7$

$12\sin^2 A + 2 - 2\sin^2 A = 7$

$10\sin^2 A = 5 \Rightarrow \sin^2 A = \frac{1}{2}$

$\therefore \quad \cos^2 A = 1 - \sin^2 A = 1 - \frac{1}{2} = \frac{1}{2}$

$\therefore \quad \cot^2 A = \frac{\cos^2 A}{\sin^2 A} = \frac{1}{2} \times \frac{2}{1} = 1$

$\therefore \quad \cot A = \pm 1$

66. *(a)*

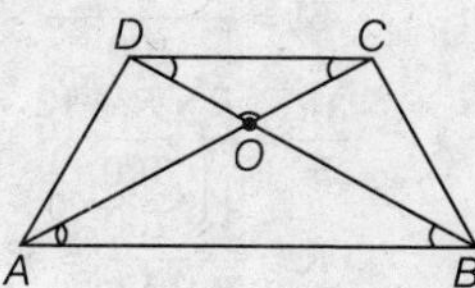

In ΔOCD and ΔOAB,

$\angle BAO = \angle DCO$ [alternate angles]

$\angle ABO = \angle CDO$ [alternate angles]

and $\angle COD = \angle AOB$

[vertical opposite angle]

$\therefore \quad \Delta AOB \sim \Delta COD$ [Rule of AAA]

$\frac{\text{Area of } \Delta AOB}{\text{Area of } \Delta COD} = \frac{AB^2}{CD^2}$

$= \frac{(2.5\,CD)^2}{CD^2}$

$= \frac{6.25}{1} = \frac{625}{100}$

$= \frac{25}{4} = 25:4$

67. *(c)* From option (d),

$(12)^2 + (16)^2 = (20)^2$

$\Rightarrow \quad 144 + 256 = 400$

$\Rightarrow \quad 400 = 400$

So, 12, 16, 20 will be side of right-angled triangle.

68. *(d)* Let the minimum cost on minimum number of items = ₹ x

According to the question,

$x \times \frac{25}{100} \geq 390$

$\therefore \quad x \geq 390 \times 4$

$\geq$ ₹ 1560

Given, cost of one product = ₹ 340

Hence, the number of minimum items

$\geq \frac{1560}{340}$ i.e., 5

69. *(c)* Given number, $1738b9c$

By divisibility rule of 4,

$\frac{9c}{4}$ = completely divisible

$\therefore \quad c = 6$ [For maximum value]

So, the sum of digits of number

$= 1 + 7 + 3 + 8 + b + 9 + 6$

$= 34 + b$

$\therefore \quad b = 5$

So, the value of $(c - b)$

$= 6 - 5 = 1$

70. *(c)* Let the principal be ₹ P.

∴ Simple interest = ₹ $\frac{3P}{5}$

Given, time = 12 yr

∵ $SI = \frac{P \times R \times T}{100}$

$\frac{3P}{5} = \frac{P \times R \times 12}{100}$

$R = \frac{3 \times 100}{5 \times 12} = 5\%$

Hence, the rate of interest = 5%

71. *(b)* Given, Sumit's income in 2020

= ₹ 21000

According to the question,

Sumit gets an increment of 10% every year.

Hence, the income of Sumit in 2022

$= 21000 \times \frac{110}{100} \times \frac{110}{100}$

= ₹ 25410

72. *(b)* According to the question,

$[\{(7 \times 1 + 5) \times 5 + 0\} \times 3 + 4] \times 2 + 1$

$= (60 \times 3 + 4) \times 2 + 1$

$= (184 \times 2) + 1 = 369$

Now, on dividing 369 by 7,

quotient = 52 and remainder = 5

On dividing 52 by 5, quotient = 10 and remainder = 2

On dividing 10 by 3, quotient = 3 and remainder = 1

On dividing 3 by 2, quotient = 1 and remainder = 1

∴ Required remainder = 5 + 2 + 1 + 1

= 9

Alternate Method

		Remainder
2	369	1
3	184	4
5	60	0
7	12	5
	1	

The number is 369.

No.		Remainder
7	369	5
5	52	2
3	10	1
2	3	1

∴ Sum of remainder

$= 5 + 2 + 1 + 1 = 9$

73. *(a)* Production of type A car by a company over the years 2016 to 2021

= 100 + 125 + 200 + 250 + 300 + 400

= 1375 thousand

Production of type B car by a company over the years 2016 to 2021

= 150 + 200 + 150 + 200 + 250 + 300

= 1250 thousand

Hence, the ratio of the total production of type A cars to type B cars

$= \frac{1375}{1250} = \frac{11}{10}$

74. *(d)*

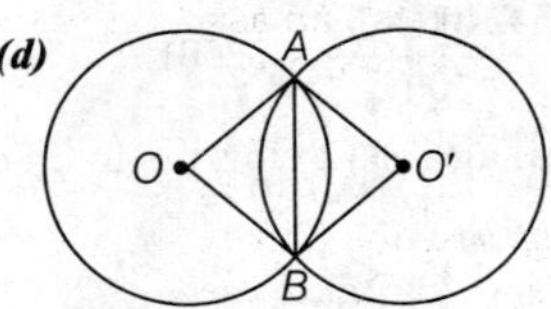

Given, radius of circle = 7 units

∴ $OA = OB = 7$ units

and $AB = 7$ units [chord of circle]

∴ ΔAOB is an equilateral triangle.

and $\angle AOB = 60°$

Hence, required area

$= 2 \times \left[\frac{\pi r^2 \theta}{360} - \frac{\sqrt{3}a^2}{4}\right]$

$= 2 \times \left[\frac{\pi \times 7^2 \times 60}{360} - \frac{\sqrt{3} \times 7^2}{4}\right]$

$= 2 \times \left[\frac{49\pi}{6} - \frac{49\sqrt{3}}{4}\right]$

$= 98 \left[\frac{\pi}{6} - \frac{\sqrt{3}}{4}\right]$ sq. unit

75. *(a)* ∵ Volume of sphere $= \frac{4}{3}\pi r^3$

(r = radius)

$\Rightarrow 38.808 = \frac{4}{3} \times \frac{22}{7} \times r^3$

$\Rightarrow r^3 = \frac{38.808 \times 21}{88} = 9.261$

∴ $r = 2.1$ cm

So, diameter of sphere = 2 × radius

$= 2 \times 2.1 = 4.2$ cm

76. *(c)* Folk songs in Haryana are called Raginis.

- Haryanvi has a very rich culture in terms of folk songs that are called Raginis.
- Rigorous and lively performance, full of colour and rhythm, tone and expressions, the songs are sung in the local dialect.
- Raginis are performed on special occasions to mark the cycle of birth and death, harvest, weddings, etc.
- It is supplemented by folk dramas, known by the name of Saang.

77. *(b)* Mayadhar Raut is an exponent of the Indian classical dance form Odissi.

- He was born in 6th July, 1930 Kantepenhara, near Cuttack, Orissa, India.
- As a child, Rout was Gotipua, a boy designated to learn a style of temple dance previously performed by female temple dances.

78. *(d)* Symmetric encryption is also known as conventional encryption.

- Symmetric encryption is a form of cryptosystem in which encryption and decryption are performed using the same key.
- Symmetric encryption transforms plain text into cipher text using a secret key and an encryption algorithm.

79. *(a)* Mewar festival is celebrated during the Gangaur festival at Udaipur.

- Gangaur is a colourful festival which celebrates by the people of Rajasthan.
- It is observed throughout the state with great devotion by women folk who worship the Goddess Gauri (Parvati) during the Hindu month of Chaitra (March-April).

80. *(c)* Article 23 deals with Prohibition of traffic in human beings and forced labour.

- Violation of this provision shall be an offence punishable in accordance with law.
- It recognises the inherent dignity and rights of individuals.
- It ensures protection against such practices.

81. *(a)* If there is a fall in the demand of a good, the equilibrium price is expected to fall.

- A decrease in demand and an increase in supply will cause a fall in equilibrium price. But the effect on equilibrium quantity cannot be determined.
- Consumers place a lower value on the good, and producers are willing to accept a lower price therefore, price will fall.

82. *(d)* In shot put event at the 2023 U-20 Asian Athletics Championships, Siddharth Choudhary won a gold medal for India.

- Siddharth Choudhary, a talented shot putter, secured India's third gold medal at the Asian U-20 Athletics Championship with an outstanding performance in Yecheon, South Korea in 2023.
- The 17-year-old athlete achieved a personal best shot-put throw.

83. *(b)* The zone separating the troposphere from the stratosphere is called the Tropopause.

- A small layer called tropopause separates the stratosphere from the troposphere.
- It is the point where air ceases to cool with height, and becomes almost completely dry.

84. *(d)* LTE technology is associated with providing high speed wireless data transmission for mobile devices.

- LTE (Long-Term Evolution) is a fourth-generation (4G) wireless standard that provides increased network capacity and speed for cell phones and other cellular devices compared with third-generation (3G) technology.
- LTE offers higher peak data transfer rates than 3G, up to 100 Mbps downstream and 30 Mbps upstream.
- LTE eventually became universally available as a standard that is still commonly available in areas that don't yet have 5G.

85. *(a)* Calcutta FC was the first and oldest club to be established in 1872.

- This was the first club to be under the rule of the army. Both Hindus and Muslims players played in it. Several football clubs like Calcutta FC, Sovabazar and Aryan Club were established in Calcutta during the 1890s.
- Other early clubs are Dalhousie Club, Traders Club and Naval Volunteers Club.
- In 1889, India's oldest current team, Mohun Bagan AC, was founded as 'Mohun Bagan Sporting Club'.

86. *(d)* In January 2023, Captain Shiva Chouhan was the first women officer to deployed at the highest battlefield of the Siachen.

- Captain Shiva Chouhan of Fire and Fury Sappers became the first woman officer to be operationally deployed in Kumar post, completion of arduous training, at the highest battlefield of the world, Shiachen.
- The officer was posted at the Kumar post, located at an altitude of around 15,600 feet in Siachen in January 2023, for a three month stint.

87. *(b)* Mendel proposed the law of independent assortment on the basis of dihybrid crosses.

- The Law of Independent Assortment states that during a dihybrid cross (crossing of two pairs of traits), an assortment of each pair of traits is independent of the other.
- In other words, during gamete formation, one pair of traits segregates from another pair of traits independently.

88. *(b)* Kashmir Himalayas are famous for Karewa formations and it is divided into two stages, lower and upper.

A succession of plateaus in the Kashmir Himalayas like terraces is called Karewas.

89. *(d)* The Census Act was enacted in 1948, just after Independence.

- It aim to provide a plan for conducting population censuses and to define the duties and responsibilities of census officers.
- The first census under this act was conducted in 1951.
- The Census Act was amended in 1994.

90. *(c)* Allama Muhammad Iqbal composed the famous song 'Sare Jahan Se Acchha'.

- The song is also referred to as 'Taranah-e-Hindi'.
- This song was originally a poem at first written by Muhammad Iqbal.
- The poem was published in the weekly journal 'Ittehad' on 16th August, 1904.

91. *(b)* Super Fours is not a domestic cricket tournament organised by the Board of Control for Cricket in India (BCCI) in India.

- The Super Fours was administered by England and Wales Cricket Board.
- The Super Fours was a women's limited overs cricket competition which was played annually in England between 2002 and 2013.

92. *(c)* Part II of the Constitution of India (Articles 5-11) deals with the Citizenship of India.

- The term 'citizenship' entails the enjoyment of full membership of any state in which a citizen has civil and political rights.
- Article 5 speaks about the citizenship of India at the commencement of the Constitution (26th November, 1949).
- Article 11 gave powers to the Parliament of India to regulate the right of citizenship by law.

93. *(c)* The atomic number based on X-ray wavelength discovered and published by the English physicist Henry Moseley in 1913-1914.

- Henry Moseley collected the X-ray spectra of a variety of elements and found that the frequency of X-ray radiation has a precise mathematical relationship to an element's atomic number.
- This relationship is now called Moseley's Law and allowed scientists a new, more accurate way to organise elements.

94. *(b)* In Myanmar, the 'Kachin Manaw Festival' is celebrated.

- The festival is held at Myitkyina, the capital of Kachin State.
- In this festival, the Kachins perform the Manaw dance-a dance that was part of the Nat (spirit worship) many years ago.

95. *(b)* Stable employment is more important to promote modernisation and overall prosperity of a country.

- Industry provides employment which is more stable than the employment in agriculture.
- It is for this reason that the Five-Year Plans place a lot of emphasis on industrial development.

96. *(a)* Central Board for Indirect Taxes and Customs launched the Indian Customs Compliance Information Portal (CIP) in 2021 to provide free access to information on all customs procedures and regulatory compliance for nearly 12,000 Customs Tariff items.

- The CIP helps people stay updated on the rules for importing and exporting in India, including requirements from customs and

other government agencies like FSSAI, AQIS, PQIS, and the Drug Controller.
- The portal will provide complete knowledge of all import and export-related requirements for all items covered under the Customs Tariff, thereby improving the ease of doing cross border trade.

97. *(c)* On 31st October , 1940 Pt. Jawahar Lal Nehru was arrested for offering individual Satyagraha to protest against India's forced participation in 2nd World War.
- He was released along with the other leaders in December 1941.
- 7th On August 1942, Pt. Nehru moved the historic 'Quit India' resolution at the AICC session in Bombay.
- On 8th August, 1942 he was arrested along with other leaders and taken to Ahmednagar Fort.

98. *(d)* The correct matching is A-2, B-1, C-3.
- Bharat Heavy Electricals Limited (BHEL) is an Indian central public sector undertaking and the largest government-owned power generation equipment manufacturer.
- TISCO (Tata Iron and Steel Company) is a private sector industry. It is multinational steelmaking Indian company, with their headquarters in Maharashtra, founded by Jamshedji Tata.
- Oil India Private Limited was incorporated on 18th February, 1959. It became a joint venture company of Government of India and Burmah Oil Company Limited, UK.

99. *(d)* In April 2023, the Maharashtra Government has approved 4% of reservation for Divyang employees in promotions.
- The Maharashtra Government has introduced a 4% quota for employees with disabilities in promotions.
- In December 2022, Maharashtra became the first state to establish a Divyang department for the differently-abled people in the country.
- As per Census 2011, there are 59,392 persons with disabilities in Maharashtra and which is 2.63% of the total population of the state.

100. *(a)* Dharmapala was the founder of 'Vikramshila Vishwavidyalaya'.
- 'Vikramshila Vishwavidyalaya' was founded by the Pala emperor Dharmapala (783 to 820 AD) in response to decline in the quality of scholarship at Nalanda.
- The Pala King Dharmapala, son of Gopala, reigned from the late 8th century CE to early 9th century CE.
- Vikramshila University is located in Bhagalpur district of Bihar.

Set 05 02 July, 2024 (Shift I)

SSC CHSL Tier-I SOLVED PAPER

Instructions

1. This paper contains 100 questions.
2. It has 4 Parts, **Part I** General English, **Part II** General Intelligence & Reasoning, **Part III** Quantitative Aptitude and **Part IV** General Awareness.
3. Each question carries **2 marks**.

Part I General English

1. The following sentence has been divided into four segments. Identify the segment that contains an error.

They have decided / to wind out / their business / without delay.

(a) They have decided
(b) their business
(c) to wind out
(d) without delay

2. Select the option that corrects the following sentence.

All the workers have called of the strike.

(a) All the workers have called at the strike.
(b) All the workers have called through the strike.
(c) All the workers have called between the strike.
(d) All the workers have called off the strike.

3. The given sentence is divided into four segments. Select the option that has the segment with a grammatical error.

He organises / a children's fair every year / and his friends comes / to attend it.

(a) He organises
(b) a children's fair every year
(c) to attend it
(d) and his friends comes

4. The underlined phrase in the given sentence has been used incorrectly. Select the option that can correctly replace the underlined segment.

Samita <u>asked out</u> a favour of going early today.

(a) asked for (b) asked over
(c) asked around (d) asked after

Directions (Q. Nos. 5 to 9) *In the following passage some words have been deleted. Read the passage carefully and select the most appropriate option to fill in each blank.*

(1) .... health benefits, including protection from cardiovascular disease and cancer, have been (2) .... to antioxidants; however, according to dietitian Vinson, these benefits depend on how well antioxidants are absorbed and (3) .... by the body.

According to the study, coffee has more antioxidant power than other well-known foods and drinks, like tea, milk, chocolate, and cranberries. Dates had the highest antioxidants per serving out of all the foods and drinks (4) ...., but because dates are not consumed to the same extent as coffee, the latter comes out on (5) ...., according to Vinson.

5. Select the most appropriate option to fill in blank number (1).

(a) numerous (b) countable
(c) limited (d) few

6. Select the most appropriate option to fill in blank number (2).

(a) attributed (b) negative
(c) similar (d) parallel

7. Select the most appropriate option to fill in blank number (3).

(a) utilised (b) impede
(c) rejected (d) hinder

8. Select the most appropriate option to fill in blank number (4).

(a) assimilated
(b) analysed
(c) synthesised
(d) consumed

9. Select the most appropriate option to fill in blank number (5).

(a) bottom (b) lowest
(c) below (d) top

10. Select the most appropriate synonym of the given word.

Competent

(a) Qualified (b) Chatty
(c) Unskilled (d) Dumb

11. Select the most appropriate antonym of the underlined word.

My parents have a <u>fertile</u> land in the backyard.

(a) barren (b) timid
(c) scanty (d) potent

12. Select the most appropriate meaning of the given idiom.

Dog eat dog

(a) Ruthlessly competitive
(b) Tit for tat
(c) Being calculative
(d) Like-minded people connect better

13. Select the most appropriate connotation to fill in the blank.

I always love the .... of my mother's cooking.

(a) aroma (b) stench
(c) perfume (d) scent

14. Select the most appropriate antonym of the given word.

Enemy

(a) Combatant (b) Colleague
(c) Friend (d) Attacker

15. Select the correctly spelt word.

(a) Illuseon (b) Illusion
(c) Illuzion (d) Ilusion

16. Read the given sentence carefully. Change the meaning of the sentence by replacing the underlined word with its antonym from the following options.

The <u>equivocal</u> tone of the Prime Minister in his speech caused uproar in the chamber.

(a) conflicting (b) iffy
(c) explicit (d) irresolute

17. Select the most appropriate option that can substitute the underlined segment in the given sentence. If there is no need to substitute it, select 'No substitution required'.

The plum tree in our garden <u>is cover in</u> blossoms, as are the trees outside my office window.

(a) is covering at
(b) are cover at
(c) is covered in
(d) No substitution required

18. Select the most appropriate option that can substitute the underlined segment in the given sentence. If there is no need to substitute it, select 'No substitution required'.

A soldier of the tenth legion leaped into the water as soon as <u>the ship touches the shore</u>.

(a) No substitution required
(b) the ship touched the shore
(c) the ship was touch the shore
(d) the ship touch the shore

19. Select the most appropriate option that can substitute the underlined segment in the given sentence.

We feel <u>warm on</u> the subject

(a) warmly about
(b) warming about
(c) warmer on
(d) warmed on

20. Select the most appropriate meaning of the given idiom.

Put in mind

(a) To calculate (b) To remind
(c) To forget (d) To understand

21. Select the most appropriate option that can substitute the underlined segment in the given sentence.

The dictator ordered the traitor <u>were</u> jailed.

(a) is (b) to be
(c) might (d) was

22. Select the incorrectly spelt word.

(a) marijuena (b) stationery
(c) dictator (c) lascivious

23. Select the most appropriate antonym of the underlined word in the sentence.

He laboured very hard but could not yield anything from the <u>barren</u> piece of land.

(a) Fertile (b) Fruitless
(c) Vile (d) Sterile

24. Select the most appropriate antonym of the underlined word in the given sentence.

The <u>dearth</u> of governmental policies on the basic rights and comforts of the impaired population leads to low standard of public life in a country.

(a) Brevity
(b) Lacunae
(c) Abundance
(d) Paucity

25. Select the most appropriate synonym of the given word.

Wonderful

(a) Upright
(b) Synthetic
(c) Amazing
(d) Awful

Part II
General Intelligence

26. 5 is related to 27 by certain logic. Following the same logic, 7 is related to 51. To which of the following is 4 related, following the same logic?

(**Note** Operations should be performed on the whole numbers, without breaking down the numbers into its constituent digits. E.g. 13 – Operations on 13 such as adding/subtracting/multiplying etc. to 13 can be performed. Breaking down 13 into 1 and 3 and then performing mathematical operations on 1 and 3 is not allowed.)

(a) 15 (b) 64
(c) 18 (d) 37

27. A paper is folded and cut as shown below. How will it appear when unfolded?

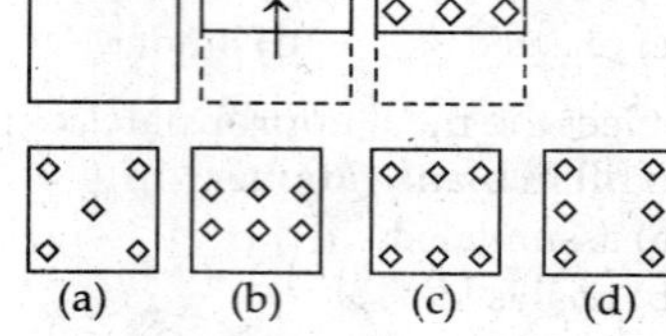

(a) (b) (c) (d)

28. Which of the following numbers will replace the question mark (?) in the given series?

6, 16, 36, 76, ? , 316

(a) 152 (b) 146 (c) 156 (d) 168

29. Select the correct mirror image of the given figure, when the mirror is placed at AB as shown below.

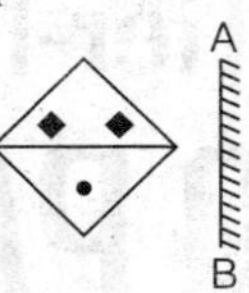

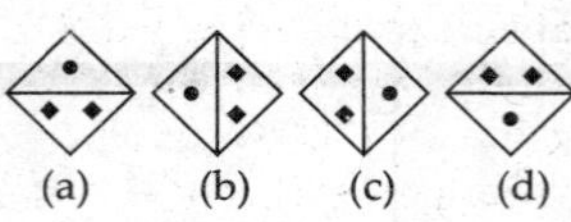

(a) (b) (c) (d)

30. Select the option figure in which the given figure (X) is embedded as its part (rotation is not allowed).

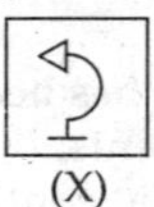

(X)

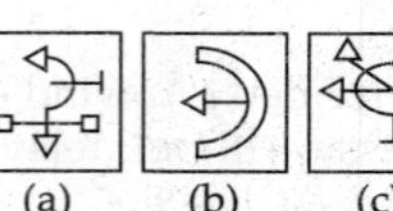

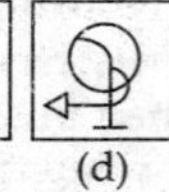

(a) (b) (c) (d)

31. Three statements are followed by conclusions numbered I, II. You have to consider these statements to be true, even if they seem to be at variance with commonly known facts. Decide which of the given conclusions logically follow(s) from the given statements.

Statements

All journals are books.

Some books are fans.

All fans are wood.

Conclusions

I. Some journals are wood.

II. Some fans are books.

(a) Neither Conclusion I nor II follows
(b) Both Conclusions I and II follow
(c) Only Conclusion II follows
(d) Only Conclusion I follows

32. The position of how many letters will remain unchanged, if each of the letters in the word 'ABDUCTS' is arranged in English alphabetical order?

(a) More than four
(b) Three
(c) Four
(d) Two

33. What should come in place of the question mark (?) in the given series?

131, 263, 527, 1055, ?

(a) 1121 (b) 2121 (c) 1211 (d) 2111

34. What will come in the place of the question mark (?) in the following equation, if '+' and '×' are interchanged and '–' and '÷' are interchanged?

$132 - 12 \times 17 + 3 \div 27 = ?$

(a) 30 (b) 36
(c) 32 (d) 35

35. What will come in the place of the question mark (?) in the following equation, if '+' and '–' are interchanged and '×' and '÷' are interchanged?

$80 + 18 \times 3 \div 5 - 23 = ?$

(a) 73 (b) 85
(c) 88 (d) 80

36. Select the set in which the numbers are related in the same way as are the numbers of the following sets.

(**Note** Operations should be performed on the whole numbers, without breaking down the numbers into their constituent digits. E.g. 13 – Operations on 13 such as adding/ subtracting/ multiplying etc. to 13 can be performed. Breaking down 13 into 1 and 3 and then performing mathematical operations on 1 and 3 is not allowed.)

(6, 12, 3)
(10, 20, 5)

(a) (21, 28, 7) (b) (14, 28, 7)
(c) (14, 21, 7) (d) (14, 28, 9)

37. What would be the letter on the opposite side of 'R', if the given sheet is folded to form a cube?

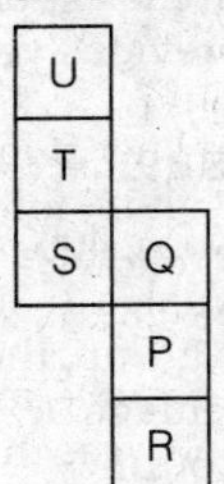

(a) T (b) S (c) U (d) Q

38. Identify the figure given in the options that when put in place of the question mark (?) will logically complete the series.

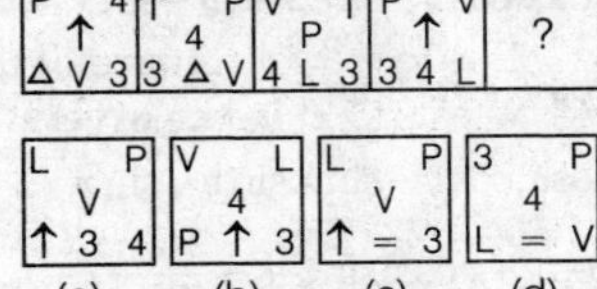

39. 'A × B' means 'A is B's brother'.
'A ÷ B' means 'A is B's sister'.
'A + B' means 'A is B's father'.
'A – B' means 'A is B's mother'.

Using the same meaning of the mathematical operators as given above, which of the following means 'X is Z's mother's father'?

(a) $X + Y - Z$ (b) $X - Y + Z$
(c) $X + Y \times Z$ (d) $X \times Y + Z$

40. Four letter-clusters have been given, out of which three are alike in some manner and one is different. Select the one that is different.

(**Note** The odd one out is not based on the number of consonants/ vowels or their position in the letter cluster.)

(a) PTV (b) EJH
(c) XCA (d) LQO

41. What is the maximum number of rectangles in the given figure?

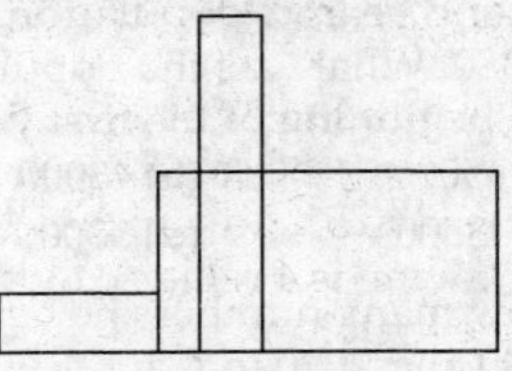

(a) 12 (b) 8 (c) 10 (d) 9

42. What should come in place of the question mark (?) to complete the following letter-cluster series?

BDC, EGF, HJI, ?

(a) KLN (b) LMN (c) KML (d) KLM

43. Select the option in which the given figure is embedded (rotation is not allowed).

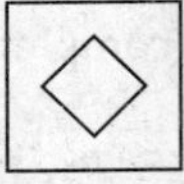

(a) 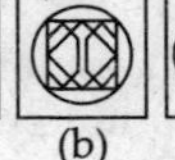 (b) 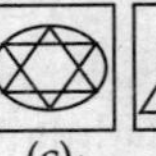 (c)  (d)

44. What should come in place of the question mark (?) in the given series?

8, 21, 34, 47, 60, ?

(a) 71 (b) 72 (c) 73 (d) 70

45. In a certain code language, 'art of war' is coded as 'gb pr ml' and 'the lost art' is coded as 'ml sj ak'. How is 'art' coded in the given language?

(a) gb (b) ml (c) pr (d) ak

46. If 9th March, 2007 was Friday, then what was the day of the week on 13th March, 2012?

(a) Tuesday (b) Thursday
(c) Monday (d) Wednesday

47. In a certain code language, 'MONEY' is coded as '64381' and 'HONEY' is coded as '54381'. What is the code for 'H' in that language?

(a) 5 (b) 6
(c) 4 (d) 8

48. Select the pair which follows the same pattern as that followed by the two set of pairs given below. Both pairs follow the same pattern.

PTL : NRJ
AEX : YCV

(a) GIF : FIG (b) BTM : DVO
(c) TVN : RTL (d) ABC : ZTS

49. Which two numbers should be interchanged to make the given equation correct?

$45 \div 3 + 12 \times 9 - 15 + 2 \times 5 = 36$

(**Note** Numbers must be interchanged and not the constituent digits e.g. if 2 and 3 are to be interchanged in the equation $43 \times 3 + 4 \div 2$, then interchanged equation is $43 \times 2 + 4 \div 3$)

(a) 3 and 9 (b) 2 and 9
(c) 5 and 3 (d) 12 and 5

50. Select the word-pair that best represents a similar relationship to the one expressed in the pair of words given below.

(The words must be considered as meaningful English words and must not be related to each other based on the number of letters/number of consonants/vowels in the word.)

Plain : Austere

(a) Clean : Sterile
(b) Lonely : Gloomy
(c) Neutral : Detached
(d) Abandon : Barren

Part III
Quantitative Aptitude

51. The ratio of a father's age to his son's age is 7 : 4. The product of the numbers representing their ages is 1372. The ratio of their ages after 8 yr will be

(a) 19 : 11 (b) 19 : 12
(c) 19 : 13 (d) 19 : 14

52. The following table shows the production of cars in a company from 2016 to 2020.

Cars \ Years	2016	2017	2018	2019	2020
A	30	23	39	25	18
B	16	10	14	12	8
C	15	18	19	25	30
D	31	12	21	19	20

There was a continuous decrease in the production of cars of which types during the period 2018 to 2020?

(a) A, B (b) C, D
(c) B, C (d) B, D

53. In $\Delta ABC, XY$ is drawn parallel to BC, cutting sides at X and Y, where $AB = 5.4$ cm, $BC = 7.2$ cm and $BX = 3$ cm. What is the length of XY (in cm)?

(a) 4.3 (b) 3.0 (c) 3.2 (d) 2.8

54. Simplify :
$18 \div (7 \times 2 - 5) \times 5 \times 24 \div 30$

(a) 8 (b) 0.5 (c) 10 (d) 6

55. If the diameter of a hemisphere is 21 cm, then the curved surface area (in cm^2) of the hemisphere is $\left(\text{Take } \pi = \frac{22}{7}\right)$

(a) 693 (b) 963 (c) 939 (d) 639

56. Study the given graph and select the most appropriate option to fill in the blanks.

Consider the percentage of workers in three categories, Skilled, Semi-skilled and Un-skilled in four companies, A, B, C and D in the graph below.

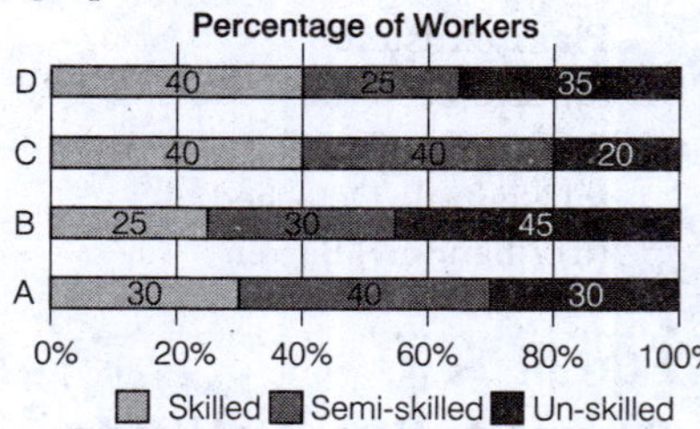

If all the companies have same number of total workers, then the company ……… has the highest number of Un-skilled workers and the company ……… has the lowest number of Skilled workers.

(a) B; C (b) B; B
(c) C; C (d) C; B

57. A boat can travel 60 km downstream in 4 h. If the speed of the boat in still water is 13 km/h, then in what time will it cover 30 km upstream?

(a) $2\frac{8}{11}$ h
(b) $3\frac{4}{7}$ h
(c) $2\frac{4}{7}$ h
(d) $3\frac{5}{7}$ h

58. A dozen pairs of gloves of ₹ 180 are available at a discount of 10%. How many pairs of gloves can be bought for ₹ 54?

(a) 2 (b) 8
(c) 4 (d) 6

59. During the first year, the population of a village increased by 5% and during the second year it diminished by 5%. At the end of the second year its population was 47880. What was the population at the beginning of the first year?

(a) 45000 (b) 48000
(c) 43500 (d) 53000

60. How many numbers lie between 2000 and 2020 that are divisible by 8?

(a) 2 (b) 5 (c) 3 (d) 4

61. Mahesh's annual salary increased from ₹ 200000 to ₹ 240000. Find the percentage increase in the salary.

(a) 22% (b) 18%
(c) 24% (d) 20%

62. Twelve men working for 9 h a day complete a piece of work in 24 days. In how many days can 8 men working for 12 h a day complete the same piece of work?

(a) 27 days (b) 28 days
(c) 21 days (d) 24 days

63. The perimeter of a minor sector of a circle of radius 4 units subtending an angle of 45° is

(a) $4-\pi$ units (b) $8-\pi$ units
(c) $8+\pi$ units (d) $4+\pi$ units

64. The areas of two similar triangles ΔPQR and ΔXYZ are 12.96 cm^2 and 635.04 cm^2, respectively. If $QR = 2.9$ cm, then the length (in cm) of YZ equals

(a) 30.4 (b) 20.3
(c) 23.2 (d) 25.2

65. Study the following line graph carefully and answer the question below.

Given graph represents marks obtained by Riya and Rida in six subjects of 12th exam of CBSE. Maximum marks in Maths, Physics and Chemistry is 140, whereas maximum marks in English, IP and Biology is 180.

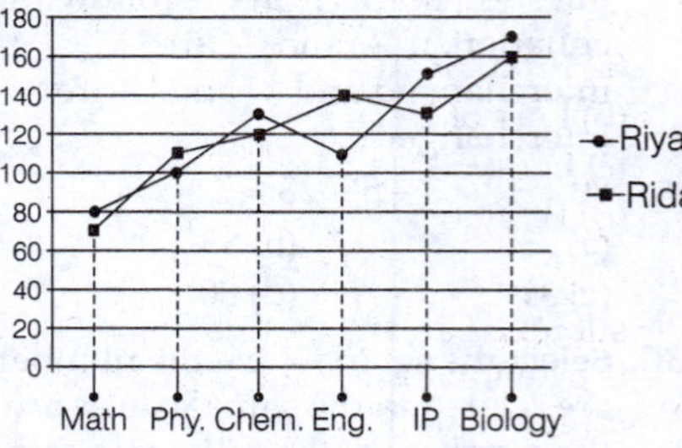

What is percentage marks obtained by Rida in PCM (Maths, Physics and Chemistry)?

(a) 81.32% (b) 50%
(c) 71.43% (d) 78.57%

66. Study the given bar-graph carefully and answer the question that follows.

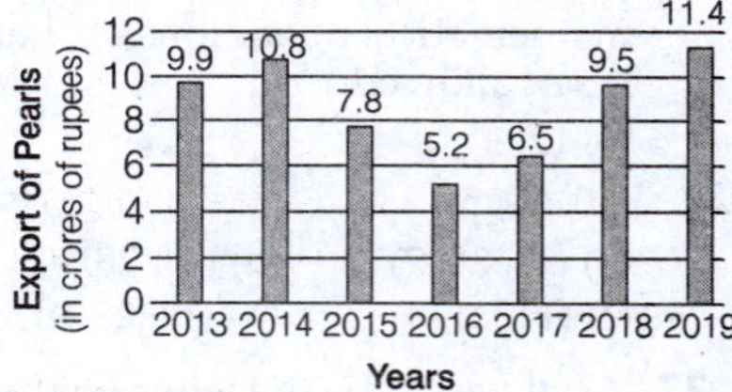

In which year was there maximum percentage increase in the export of pearls to that in the previous year?

(a) 2018 (b) 2014
(c) 2017 (d) 2019

67. In a group of 250 persons, 40% are males and 60% are females. If 30 more females join the group, then what will be the percentage of females in the new group? (Correct to 2 decimal places)

(a) 62.58% (b) 72.25%
(c) 64.29% (d) 90.25%

68. What is the value of $\cos(x+y) - \sin(x-y) + \tan(2z)$?

(a) $\cos x.\cos y - \sin x.\sin y - \sin x.$
$\cos y - \cos x.\sin y + \frac{2\tan z}{1-\tan^2 z}$

(b) $\cos x.\cos y - \sin x.\sin y - \sin x.$
$\cos y + \cos x.\sin y + \frac{2\tan z}{1-\tan^2 z}$

(c) $\cos x \cdot \cos y - \sin x \cdot \sin y - \cos x \cdot \sin y + \frac{\tan z}{1-\tan^2 z}$

(d) $\sin x . \sin y + \frac{2\tan z}{1-\tan^2 z}$

69. A merchant sold two refrigerators for ₹ 10000 each. On one refrigerator, he incurred a 20% loss and on the other, he gained 20%. What was his profit/loss percentage on the whole transaction?
(a) Profit of 4%
(b) Loss of 2%
(c) Loss of 4%
(d) Profit of 2%

70. O is the centre and the arc PQR subtends an angle of 240° at O. PQ is extended to A. Then, $\angle AQR$ is
(a) 180° (b) 60°
(c) 240° (d) 120°

71. A bank charges simple interest for ₹ K at the rate of $r^{\frac{1}{2}}$ for n^2 yr. Another bank charges simple interest for ₹ L at the rate of $r^{\frac{3}{2}}$ for n^3 yr and gives the same interest. The ratio between K and L is
(a) $\frac{1}{r}:\frac{1}{n}$ (b) $r\,n:1$
(c) $r^2:n^2$ (d) $r^{\frac{1}{2}}:n^{\frac{1}{2}}$

72. The graphs of two linear equations, $x + 2y = 15$ and $4x + 8y = 13$ will be
(a) parallel
(b) coincident
(c) intersecting at one point
(d) intersecting at two points

73. The capacity of a cylinder tank is 8316 cm^3. If the radius of its base is 21 cm, then find the depth of the tank.
(a) 4 cm (b) 8 cm
(c) 10 cm (d) 6 cm

74. How much water should be added to 60 L of milk at $1\frac{1}{2}$ L a rupee, so as to have a mixture worth $1\frac{7}{8}$ L a rupee?
(a) 15 L (b) 12 L
(c) 27 L (d) 20 L

75.

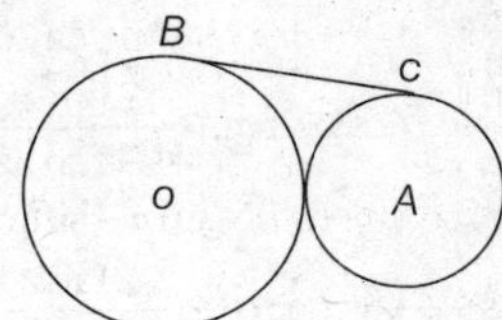

Two circles touch each other externally as shown in the figure above. The radius of the circle with centre O is 49 cm. The radius of the circle with centre A is 16 cm. Find the length (in cm) of their common tangent BC.
(a) 56 (b) 55
(c) 58 (d) 57

Part IV
General Awareness

76. On which river in India was the Somasila dam built?
(a) Krishna river
(b) Pennar river
(c) Sabarmati river
(d) Tapti river

77. Which theory describes the collective effects of changes in Earth's movements on its climate over thousands of years?
(a) Plate tectonics theory
(b) Copernicus' heliocentric theory
(c) Milankovitch theory
(d) Continental drift theory

78. How many times has India won the South Asian Football Federation (SAFF) Championship as of December 2023?
(a) 5 times (b) 7 times
(c) 6 times (d) 9 times

79. Which of the following types of crops are sown after the end of the monsoon season?
(a) Zaid crops
(b) Kharif crops
(c) Rabi crops
(d) Vital crops

80. By which ministry of Government of India was the Deendayal Antyodaya Yojana started?
(a) Ministry of Rural Development
(b) Ministry of Home affairs
(c) Ministry of Labour and Employment
(d) Ministry of Corporate affairs

81. How many types of writs can be issued by the Supreme Court to protect the Fundamental Rights of Indian citizens?
(a) Six
(b) Four
(c) Five
(d) Seven

82. What is the name of the centrally sponsored scheme related with literacy that was launched by the Government of India in March 2023?
(a) National Literacy Programme
(b) New India Literacy Programme
(c) India Literacy Programme
(d) Bharat Padhega

83. Match the following musical instruments with the maestros who play them.

List I	List II
A. Santoor	1. Bismillah Khan
B. Sitar	2. Ustad Binda Khan
C. Shehnai	3. Pt Shiv Kumar Sharma
D. Sarangi	4. Anushka Shankar

Codes

	A	B	C	D		A	B	C	D
(a)	4	3	2	1	(b)	1	2	3	4
(c)	2	3	1	4	(d)	3	4	1	2

84. In 2023, Gulab Chand Kataria become the Governor of which of the following states?
(a) Himachal Pradesh
(b) Tamil Nadu
(c) Odisha
(d) Assam

85. Match List-I (Name of the composition) with List-II (Writer).

List-I (Name of the Composition)	List-II (Writer)
A. Vande Mataram	1. Pradeep
B. Jana Gana Mana	2. Bankim Chandra Chattopadhyay
C. Ae Mere Watan Ke Logon	3. Rabindranath Tagore

Codes

	A	B	C
(a)	3	2	1
(b)	3	1	2
(c)	1	2	3
(d)	2	3	1

86. As per Olympic rules, in the third game, badminton players change ends when a side scores .... points.
(a) 11 (b) 13 (c) 15 (d) 12

87. The loss of water in the form of water droplets from leaves of plants is called ....
(a) Pressure gradient
(b) Guttation
(c) Translocation
(d) Plasmolysis

88. A .... is a cloud of dust and gas inside a galaxy.
(a) photosphere
(b) black hole
(c) chromosphere
(d) nebula

89. Who among the following was appointed, to the UN tax committee in July 2021, as a member for the 2021 to 2025 term?
(a) Vivek Singh
(b) Vipul Bansal
(c) Rasmi Ranjan Das
(d) TV Somanathan

90. Who is the founder of modern micro finance ?
(a) VKV Rao
(b) Rangarajan
(c) YV Reddy
(d) Muhammad Yunus

91. PC Mahalanobis is remembered as a major contributor of India's developmental path because he ....
A. set up Indian Institutes of Management located in different parts of India
B. formulated the Second Five-Year Plan
C. was the first Minister of Statistics and Programme Implementation

Codes
(a) (A) and (C) are true
(b) (A) and (B) are true
(c) (A) is true
(d) (B) is true

92. Who among the following was primarily an integral part of the Indian National Army (INA)?
(a) Rabindranath Tagore
(b) Chittaranjan Das
(c) Abanindranath Tagore
(d) Subhas Chandra Bose

93. Which Clause of Article 20 incorporates the doctrine of double jeopardy?
(a) 1 (b) 4 (c) 3 (d) 2

94. According to the Census of India-2011, which state has the largest gap between male and female literacy rates?
(a) Assam
(b) Rajasthan
(c) Karnataka
(d) Andhra Pradesh

95. Which of the following was the last dynasty of the Vijayanagara Empire?
(a) Aravidu dynasty
(b) Sangam dynasty
(c) Saluva dynasty
(d) Tuluva dynasty

96. In MS Word, which feature allows you to create different headers and footers for odd and even pages in a document?
(a) Different First Page
(b) Page Breaks
(c) Different Odd and Even Pages
(d) Section Breaks

97. .... is a significant festival of the Parsi people who practice Zoroastrianism as it marks the birth anniversary of Zoroaster.
(a) Jamshed-e-Navroz
(b) Pateti
(c) Khordad Sal
(d) Gahambars

98. Who among the following is a famous classical dancer?
(a) Sonal Mansingh (b) Asha Bhosle
(c) Pratibha Ray (d) S Janaki

99. In which year was tennis included in the Olympic games?
(a) 1948 (b) 1935 (c) 1896 (d) 1927

100. Which kind of computer security requires verifying the genuineness of the individuals or organisations that want to access a system?
(a) Non-repudiation
(b) Availability
(c) Authentication
(d) Confidentiality

Answers

1. (c)	2. (d)	3. (d)	4. (a)
5. (a)	6. (a)	7. (a)	8. (b)
9. (d)	10. (a)	11. (a)	12. (a)
13. (a)	14 (c)	15. (b)	16. (c)
17. (c)	18. (b)	19. (a)	20. (b)
21. (b)	22. (a)	23. (a)	24. (c)
25. (c)	26. (c)	27. (b)	28. (c)
29. (d)	30. (a)	31. (c)	32. (b)
33. (d)	34. (d)	35. (a)	36. (b)
37. (d)	38. (c)	39. (a)	40. (a)
41. (d)	42. (c)	43. (b)	44. (c)
45. (b)	46. (a)	47. (a)	48. (c)
49. (a)	50. (a)	51. (b)	52. (a)
53. (c)	54. (a)	55. (a)	56. (b)
57. (a)	58. (c)	59. (b)	60. (a)
61. (d)	62. (a)	63. (c)	64. (b)
65. (c)	66. (a)	67. (c)	68. (b)
69. (c)	70. (d)	71. (b)	72. (a)
73. (d)	74. (a)	75. (a)	76. (b)
77. (c)	78. (d)	79. (c)	80. (a)
81. (c)	82. (b)	83. (d)	84. (d)
85. (d)	86. (a)	87. (b)	88. (d)
89. (c)	90. (d)	91. (d)	92. (d)
93. (d)	94. (b)	95. (a)	96. (c)
97. (c)	98. (a)	99. (c)	100. (c)

Explanations

1. *(c)* Part (c) 'to wind out' contains an error. Use 'to wind up' which means to shut down to correct the sentence.

2. *(d)* The given sentence is grammatically correct. The use of preposition 'of' is incorrect. Use 'off' to correct the sentence.

3. *(d)* Part (d) 'and his friends comes' contains an error. As the subject 'friends'. is singular, the singular verb should be used. Hence, 'come' should be used to correct the sentence.

4. *(a)* The underlined part of the sentence contains an error. The phrasal verb 'asked out' is incorrect. Use 'asked for' which means 'to request' to correct the sentence.

5. *(a)* The correct filler for the given blank is 'numerous'.

6. *(a)* The correct filler for the given blank is 'attributed'.

7. *(a)* The correct filler for the given blank is 'utilised'.

8. *(b)* The correct filler for the given blank is 'analysed'.

9. *(d)* The correct filler for the given blank is 'top'.

10. *(a)* The word 'competent' means 'skilled and Qualified'.

'Chatty' means talkative.

11. *(a)* The antonym of 'fertile' is 'barren' which means too poor to produce much or any vegetation.
- 'Timid' means cowardly.
- 'Scanty' means not enough.
- 'Potent' means having great power, influence, or effect.

12. *(a)* Dog eat dog means ruthlessly competitive.

13. *(a)* The correct filler for the given blank is 'aroma' which fits well with the smell of mother's cooking.

14. *(c)* The antonym of 'enemy' is 'friend'.

'Combatant' means a person or nation engaged in fighting during a war.

15. *(b)* The correctly spelt word is 'Illusion', which means a false idea or belief.

16. *(c)* 'Equivocal' means open to more than one interpretation; ambiguous. Hence, its antonym is 'explicit' is fully revealed or expressed without vagueness, implication, or ambiguity.
- 'Conflicting' means contradictory.
- 'Iffy' means full of uncertainty; doubtful.
- 'Irresolute' means showing or feeling hesitancy; uncertain.

17. *(c)* The underlined part of the sentence contains an error. Use 'is covered in' to correct the sentence.

18. *(b)* The underlined part of the sentence contains an error. As the sentence is in past tense, 'the ship touched the shore' should be used to correct the sentence.

19. *(a)* The underlined part of the sentence contains an error. Use 'warmly about' to correct the sentence.

20. *(b)* Put in mind means to remind.

21. *(b)* The underlined part of the sentence contains an error. Use 'to be' to correct the sentence.

22. *(a)* The incorrectly spelt word is 'marijuena'. The correct spelling is 'marijuana' which is a drug that is smoked illegally in many countries.

23. *(a)* The antonym of 'barren' meaning 'unproductive' is fertile.
- 'Vile' means extremely unpleasant.
- 'Sterile' means not able to produce children or young.

24. *(c)* 'Dearth' means lack of something. Hence, its antonym is 'Abundance' which means in large quantities.
- 'Brevity' means concise and exact use of words in writing or speech.
- 'Lacunae' means an unfilled space; a gap.
- 'Paucity' means lack.

25. *(c)* The synonym of 'Wonderful' is 'Amazing'.

26. *(c)* As, $5 : 27 = (5)^2 + 2 = 25 + 2 = 27$

and $7 : 51 = (7)^2 + 2 = 49 + 2 = 51$

Similarly, 4 : ?

$= (4)^2 + 2 = 16 + 2 = \boxed{18}$

27. *(b)* When we unfold the paper given in the question, it will look like as option figure (b).

28. *(c)* The pattern of the series is as shown below,

6 → 16 → 36 → 76 → [156] → 316
(×2+4 at each step)

∴ ? = 156

29. *(d)* The correct mirror image of the given question figure is option figure (d).

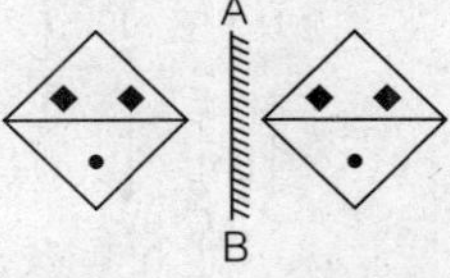

30. *(a)* The problem figure is embedded in option figure (a).

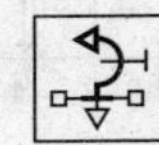

31. *(c)* According to the statements,

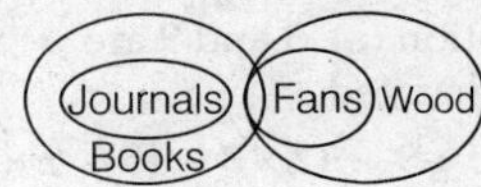

Conclusions I. (✗) II. (✓)

Hence, only Conclusion II follows.

32. *(b)*

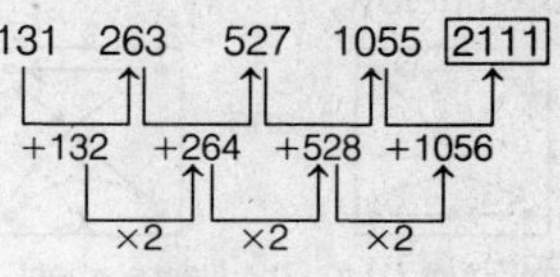

Hence, three letters i.e., 'A', 'B' and 'T' will remain unchanged.

33. *(d)* The pattern of the series is as shown below,

131 → 263 → 527 → 1055 → [2111]
+132, +264, +528, +1056 (each ×2)

∴ ? = 2111

34. *(d)* Given expression,

$132 - 12 \times 17 + 3 \div 27 = ?$

After interchanging the signs, '+' and '×' and '−' and '÷', we get

$? = 132 \div 12 + 17 \times 3 - 27$
$= 11 + 17 \times 3 - 27$
$= 11 + 51 - 27$
$= 62 - 27$
$= 35$

35. *(a)* Given expression,

$80 + 18 \times 3 \div 5 - 23 = ?$

After interchanging the signs, '+' and '−' and '×' and '÷', we get

$? = 80 - 18 \div 3 \times 5 + 23$
$= 80 - 6 \times 5 + 23$
$= 80 - 30 + 23$
$= 103 - 30 = 73$

36. *(b)* As, (6, 12, 3)

$= 6 + (3 \times 2)$
$= 6 + 6 = 12$

and (10, 20, 5)

$= 10 + (5 \times 2)$
$= 10 + 10 = 20$

Similarly, by option (b),

(14, 28, 7)
$= 14 + (7 \times 2)$
$= 14 + 14 = 28$

37. *(d)* According to the question,

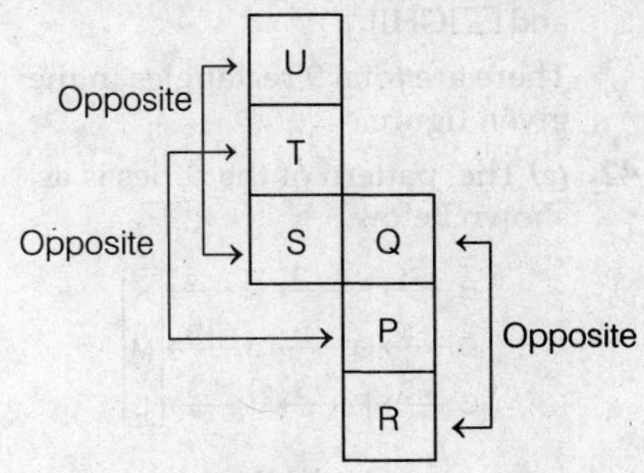

Opposite letters are

U T [Q]
↕ ↕ ↕
S P [R]

Hence, letter 'Q' is opposite side of letter 'R'.

38. *(c)* Pattern of the given series is as shown below,

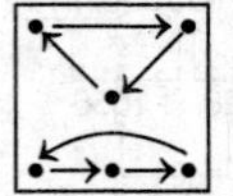 and 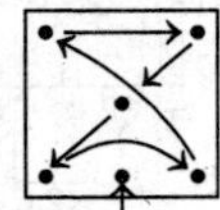

From Figure (1) to (2) and Figure (3) to (4)

New element From Figure (2) to (3) and Figure (4) to (5)

Hence, option (c) figure will replace the question figure.

39. *(a)* According to the question,

By option (a), X + Y – Z

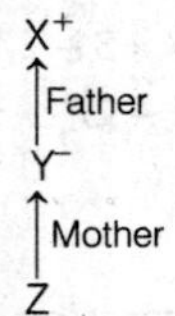

Here, 'X' is the Z's mother's father.

40. *(a)* Here,

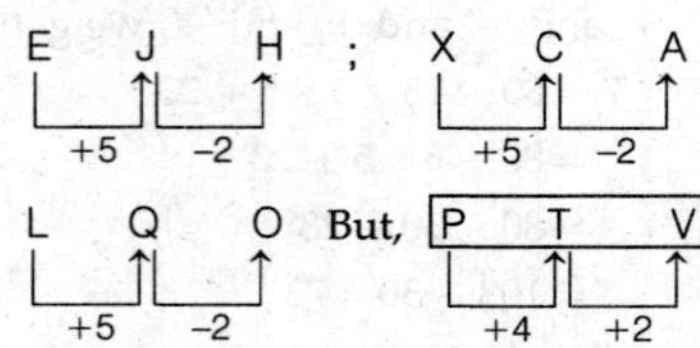

Hence, 'PTV' is the odd one.

41. *(d)* Naming the figure,

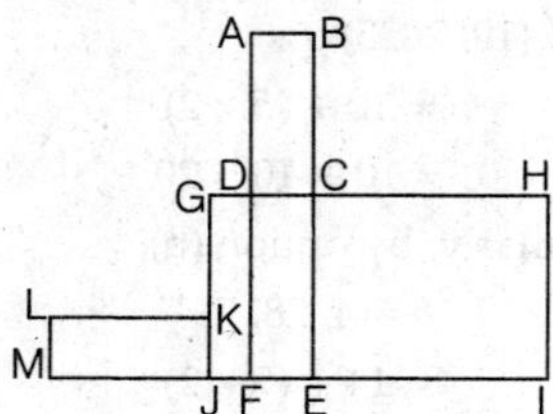

□LKJM, □GDFJ, □DCEF, □ABCD, □ABEF, □CHIE, □DHIF, □GCEJ and □GHIJ.

There are total 9 rectangles in the given figure.

42. *(c)* The pattern of the series is as shown below,

B $\xrightarrow{+3}$ E $\xrightarrow{+3}$ H $\xrightarrow{+3}$ [K]

D $\xrightarrow{+3}$ G $\xrightarrow{+3}$ J $\xrightarrow{+3}$ [M]

C $\xrightarrow{+3}$ F $\xrightarrow{+3}$ I $\xrightarrow{+3}$ [L]

∴ ? = KML

43. *(b)* The problem figure is embedded in option figure (b).

44. *(c)* The pattern of the series is as shown below,

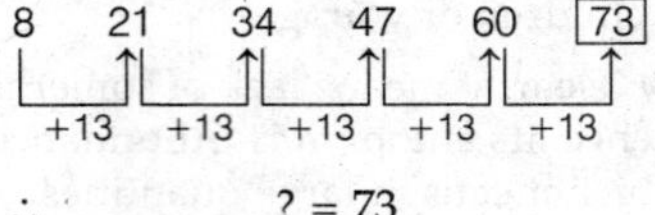

∴ ? = 73

45. *(b)* According to the question,

[art] of war ⟶ gb pr [ml]

the lost [art] ⟶ [ml] sj ak

Hence, 'art' is coded as 'ml'.

46. *(a)* Given, 9th March, 2007 was Friday.

[∵ Ordinary year = 1 odd day; leap year = 2 odd days]

= 2008 (2) + 2009 (1) + 2010 (1) + 2011 (1) + 2012 (2)

= 2 + 1 + 1 + 1 + 2 = 7 ÷ 7 = 0 odd day

Day on 9th March, 2012 = Friday.

Now, number of days between 9th March, 2012 to 13th March, 2012 is 4.

⇒ Day on 13th March, 2012 = Friday + 4 = Tuesday

47. *(a)* According to the question,

M [O N E Y] ⟶ 6 [4 3 8 1]

(H) [O N E Y] ⟶ (5) [4 3 8 1]

Hence, 'H' is coded as '5'.

48. *(c)* As,

P T L → (−2) → N R J

and

A E X → (−2) → Y C V

Similarly, by option (c),

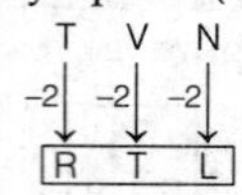

49. *(a)* Given expression,

$$45 \div 3 + 12 \times 9 - 15 + 2 \times 5 = 36$$

By option (a), 3 and 9 are interchanged,

$$45 \div 9 + 12 \times 3 - 15 + 2 \times 5 = 36$$

$$\Rightarrow 5 + 36 - 15 + 10 = 36$$

$$\Rightarrow 51 - 15 = 36$$

$$\Rightarrow 36 = 36$$

50. *(a)* As, 'Plain – Austere' is the synonyms of each other. Similarly, Clean-Sterile is the synonyms of each other.

51. *(b)* Let the age of father is $7x$ yr and the age of son is $4x$ yr.

According to the question,

$$7x \times 4x = 1372$$

$$\Rightarrow 28x^2 = 1372$$

$$\Rightarrow x^2 = 49$$

$$\therefore x = 7$$

Present age of father and son are

$= (7 \times 7)$ and (7×4)

$= 49$ and 28

∴ Ratio of their ages after 8 yr

$= (49 + 8) : (28 + 8)$

$= 57 : 36 = 19 : 12$

52. *(a)* We can easily see,

From 2018 to 2019 to 2020, the production of cars of A and B type decreases continuously and production of car C increases and production of car D first decreases then increased.

53. *(c)* According to the question,

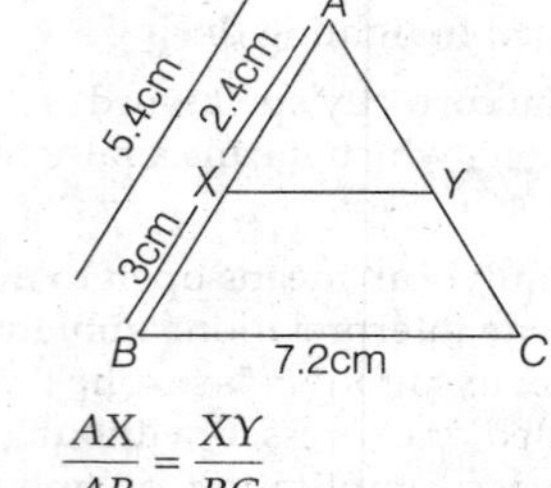

$$\frac{AX}{AB} = \frac{XY}{BC}$$

$$\Rightarrow \frac{24}{5.4} = \frac{XY}{7.2}$$

$$\Rightarrow XY = \frac{2.4 \times 7.2}{5.4} = 3.2 \text{ cm}$$

54. *(a)* Given, $18 \div (7 \times 2 - 5) \times 5 \times 24 \div 30$

$= 18 \div (14 - 5) \times 5 \times 24 \div 30$

$= 18 \div 9 \times 5 \times 24 \div 30$

$= 18 \div 9 \times 5 \times \frac{24}{30}$

$= 18 \div 9 \times 4$

$= 2 \times 4 = 8$

55. *(a)* Given, Diameter = 21 cm

$$\text{Radius} = \frac{21}{2} = 10.5 \text{ cm}$$

∴ Curved surface area = $2\pi r^2$ $\left[\because \pi = \frac{22}{7}\right]$

$$= 2 \times \frac{22}{7} \times 10.5 \times 10.5 = \frac{4851}{7} = 693$$

56. *(b)* According to the given graph, if total number of workers is same then, the company 'B' has the highest number of un-skilled workers and company 'B' has the lowest number of skilled workers.

57. *(a)* Speed of the boat in still water

$= 13$ km/h

Let the speed of water is y km/h.
According to the question,

$\Rightarrow \quad \dfrac{60}{13+y} = 4$

$\Rightarrow \quad 15 = 13 + y \Rightarrow y = 2$ km/h

$\therefore$ Time taken to cover 30 km upstream

$= \dfrac{30}{(13-2)} = \dfrac{30}{11} = 2\dfrac{8}{11}$ h

58. *(c)* According to the question,

Price of 1 dozen pairs of gloves

$= 180 \times \left(\dfrac{100-10}{100}\right)$

$= 180 \times \dfrac{90}{100} =$ ₹ 162

$\therefore$1 dozen of gloves can be buy in ₹ 162, then number of gloves which can buy in ₹ 54

$= \dfrac{54 \times 12}{162} = 4$

59. *(b)* According to the question,

Population of village in first year

$= 47880 \times \dfrac{100}{(100+5)} \times \dfrac{100}{(100-5)}$

$= 47880 \times \dfrac{100}{105} \times \dfrac{100}{95} = 48000$

60. *(a)* Divisibility rule of 8 is its last three digits is divisible by 8.

Now, numbers between 2000 to 2020, which is divisible by 8 is *i.e.*, 2008 and 2016.

Hence, only two number is divisible by 8.

61. *(d)* Percentage increase in Mahesh's annual salary

$= \dfrac{(240000 - 200000)}{200000} \times 100$

$= \dfrac{40000}{200000} \times 100$

$\therefore$ Required answer is 20%.

62. *(a)* According to the question,

$M_1 = 12, D_1 = 24, H_1 = 9$

$M_2 = 8, D_2 = x, H_2 = 12$

$\therefore \quad M_1 \times D_1 \times H_1 = M_2 \times D_2 \times H_2$

$\Rightarrow \quad 12 \times 24 \times 9 = 8 \times x \times 12$

$\Rightarrow \quad x = \dfrac{12 \times 24 \times 9}{8 \times 12} = 27$ days

63. *(c)* Given,

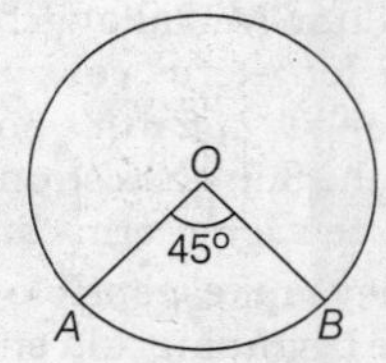

Given, $\theta = 45°$

We know that,

Perimeter of a sector $= 2\pi r \dfrac{\theta}{360} + 2r$

$= 2\pi \times 4 \times \dfrac{45}{360} + 2 \times 4$

$= (\pi + 8)$ units

64. *(b)* Given, area of two triangles ΔPQR and ΔXYZ are 12.96 cm^2 and 635.04 cm^2.

If $\quad QR = 2.9$ cm

$\therefore \quad \left(\dfrac{PQ}{XY}\right)^2 = \left(\dfrac{QR}{YZ}\right)^2$

$= \dfrac{\text{Area of } \Delta PQR}{\text{Area of } \Delta XYZ}$

$\Rightarrow \quad \left(\dfrac{2.9}{YZ}\right)^2 = \dfrac{12.96}{635.04}$

$\Rightarrow \quad \dfrac{8.41}{(YZ)^2} = \dfrac{12.96}{635.04}$

$\Rightarrow \quad (YZ)^2 = \dfrac{8.41 \times 635.04}{12.96} = 412.09$

$\Rightarrow \quad YZ = \sqrt{412.09} = 20.3$ cm

65. *(c)* Marks of Rida in Physics, Math and Chemistry

$= 70 + 110 + 120 = 300$

Total marks $= 140 \times 3 = 420$

$\therefore$Percentage of marks obtained by

Rida $= \dfrac{300}{420} \times 100\%$

$= 71.43\%$

66. *(a)* According to the given bar-graph,

Percentage increase in 2018

$= \dfrac{(9.5 - 6.5)}{6.5} \times 100 = 46.15\%$

Percentage increase in 2014

$= \dfrac{(10.8 - 9.9)}{9.9} \times 100 = 9.09\%$

Percentage increase in 2017

$= \dfrac{(6.5 - 5.2)}{5.2} \times 100 = 25\%$

Percentage increase in 2019

$= \dfrac{(11.4 - 9.5)}{9.5} \times 100 = 20\%$

$\therefore$ Required answer is the maximum percentage increase in the year 2018.

67. *(c)* Total number of persons in a group = 250

Number of males $= 250 \times \dfrac{40}{100} = 100$

Number of females $= 250 \times \dfrac{60}{100} = 150$

Now, 30 more females join the group

$= 150 + 30$

$= 180$

$\therefore$ Percentage of females in the group now

$= \dfrac{180}{(250+30)} \times 100 = \dfrac{180}{280} \times 100 = 64.29\%$

68. *(b)* Trigonometric expression,

$\cos(x+y) - \sin(x-y) + \tan(2z)$

$= (\cos x . \cos y - \sin x . \sin y)$

$- (\sin x . \cos y - \sin y . \cos x)$

$+ \dfrac{2 \tan z}{1 - \tan^2 z}$

$= \cos x . \cos y - \sin x . \sin y$

$- \sin x . \cos y + \sin y . \cos x + \dfrac{2 \tan z}{1 - \tan^2 z}$

69. *(c)* According to the question,

Merchant receive loss per cent in whole transaction,

$= \left(-20 + 20 - \dfrac{20 \times 20}{100}\right)\% = -4\%$

Hence, loss of 4%.

70. *(d)* Given, O is the centre and the arc PQR subtends an angle of 240° at O and PQ is extended to A.

$\because \quad \angle PQR = \dfrac{120°}{2} = 60°$

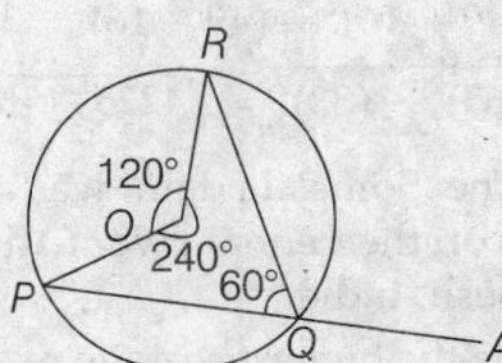

$\therefore \quad \angle RQA = 180° - 60° = 120°$

71. *(b)* Given that, the simple interest in both the bank is same.

$\dfrac{K \times n^2 \times r^{1/2}}{100} = \dfrac{L \times n^3 \times r^{3/2}}{100}$

$\Rightarrow \quad \dfrac{K}{L} = \dfrac{r^{3/2} \times n^3}{r^{1/2} \times n^2} = \dfrac{r \times n}{1}$

So, ratio between K and L is $rn : 1$.

72. *(a)* Two linear equation are

$x + 2y = 15 \Rightarrow x + 2y - 15 = 0$

and $\quad 4x + 8y = 13$

$\Rightarrow \quad 4x + 8y - 13 = 0$

Here, $\frac{a_1}{a_2} = \frac{1}{4}, \frac{b_1}{b_2} = \frac{2}{8} = \frac{1}{4}$

and $\frac{c_1}{c_2} = \frac{-15}{-13} = \frac{15}{13}$

$\therefore \quad \frac{a_1}{a_2} = \frac{b_1}{b_2} \neq \frac{c_1}{c_2}$

Hence, lines are parallel.

73. *(d)* As, we know that,

Capacity of a cylinder $= \pi r^2 h$

$\pi \times 21 \times 21 \times h = 8316$

$\Rightarrow \frac{22}{7} \times 21 \times 21 \times h = 8316 \Rightarrow h = 6$ cm

So, the depth of tank is 6 cm.

74. *(a)* In ₹ 1 value $1\frac{1}{2}$ L of milk.

$\Rightarrow$ 60 L milk $= \frac{60}{3/2} =$ ₹ 40

$\Rightarrow$ In a mixture value of $1\frac{7}{8}$ L milk in ₹ 1.

$\therefore$ Value of milk and water in

₹ 40 $= 40 \times \frac{15}{8} = 75$ L

$\therefore$ Value of water

$= (75 - 60)$ L $= 15$ L

75. *(a)* According to the question,

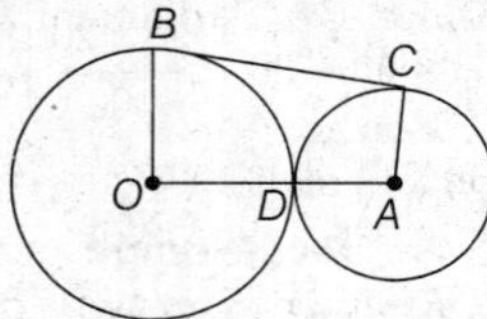

Length of the common tangent (BC)

$= \sqrt{(OA)^2 - (OB - AC)^2}$

$= \sqrt{(49 + 16)^2 - (49 - 16)^2}$

$= \sqrt{(65)^2 - (33)^2} = \sqrt{4225 - 1089} = 56$

76. *(b)* The 'Somasila dam' was a dam built on the Pennar river, Andhra Pradesh, India.

- It is the biggest storage reservoir in Penna river basin and can store all the inflows from its catchment area in a normal ear.
- The reservoir can get water by gravity from the Srisailam reservoir located in Krishna basin.
- Under Indian Rivers Inter-link projects, it is planned to connect the reservoir with the Nagarjunasagar reservoir to augment its water inflows.

77. *(c)* Milankovitch theory describes the collective effects of changes in Earth's movements on its climate over thousands of years.

- A century ago, Serbian scientist Milutin Milankovitch hypothesised the long-term, collective effects of changes in Earth's position relative to the Sun are a strong driver of Earth's long-term climate.
- They are responsible for triggering the beginning and end of glaciation periods (Ice Ages).

78. *(d)* India won 9 times the South Asian Football Federation (SAFF) Championship as of December 2023.

- India marked a remarkable victory in the (SAFF) Championship 2023 held in Bengaluru, Karnataka, securing their ninth title by defeating Kuwait in a thrilling football match.
- SAFF was found in 1997 by founding member association from Bangladesh, India, Maldives, Nepal, Pakistan and Sri Lanka.
- Its headquarters is located and operated from Dhaka, Bangladesh.

79. *(c)* Rabi crops are sown after the end of the monsoon season.

- Also known as Winter crops are grown in October or November.
- The crops are then harvested in spring.
- These crops are grown in dry areas. Wheat, gram, and barley are some of the rabi crops grown in India.

80. *(a)* Deendayal Antyodaya Yojana-National Rural Livelihoods Mission (DAY-NRLM) was launched by the Ministry of Rural Development (MoRD).

- The mission aims at creating efficient and effective institutional platforms of the rural poor.
- It enables them to increase household income through sustainable livelihoods enhancements and improved access to financial services.

81. *(c)* The Supreme Court or the High Court can issue five different types of writs/orders to enforce the Fundamental Rights of Indian citizens.

- They are called Habeas Corpus. Mandamus, Quo-Warranto, Prohibition, and Certiorari.
- Habeas corpus is 'you should have the body'.
- Mandamus is 'we command'.
- Certiorari is 'to be certified'.
- Prohibition is 'to forbid'.
- Quo-Warranto is 'by what authority or warrant'.

82. *(b)* New India Literacy Programme is the centrally sponsored scheme related with literacy that was launched by the Government of India in March 2023.

- The NILP aims to provide functional literacy and numeracy to over 60 million non-literate and low-literate adults in the age group of 15-45 years.
- The programme has five objectives
  (i) Foundational Literacy and Numeracy,
  (ii) Critical Life Skills
  (iii) Vocational Skills Development
  (iv) Basic Education
  (v) Continuing Education

83. *(d)* The correct matching is A-3, B-4, C-1 and D-2.

- Pandit Shiv Kumar Sharma (born 13th January, 1938) is an Indian music composer and santoor player from the state of Jammu and Kashmir.
- Anushka Hemangini Shankar born 9th June, 1981 is a British-American sitar player and musician of Indian descent, as well as occasional writer.
- Ustad Bismillah Khan (born Qamaruddin Khan, 21st March 1916 - 21th August, 2006), often referred to by the title Ustad, was an Indian musician credited with popularising the shehnai, a reeded woodwind instrument.
- Ustad Sultan Khan (15th April, 1940 - 27th November 2011) was an Indian sarangi player and classical vocalist belonging to Sikar Gharana.

84. *(d)* In 2023 Gulab Chand Kataria became the 31 st Governor of Assam.

- Chief Justice Guwahati High Court Justice Sandeep Mehta administered the oath of office to the new Governor.
- Shri Gulab Chand Kataria hails from Udaipur, Rajasthan.

85. *(d)* The correct matching is A-2, B-3, C-1.

- 'Vande Mataram' was written by Bankim Chandra Chattopadhyay in Bengali and was first sung by Rabindranath Tagore.
- Rabindranath Tagore originally composed 'Jana Gana Mana' in

Bengali by India's first Nobel Laureate. Kavi Pradeep,written the song 'Aye Mere Watan Ke Logo' and sung by Lata Mangeshkar.

86. *(a)* As per Olympic rules, in the third game, badminton players change ends when a side scores 11 points.
- Breaks-are given when the leading scorer reaches 11 points (60-second break) and when a game is completed (two-minute break).
- Sides are switched after each game and during the third game once 11 points is reached for the first time by one side.

87. *(b)* Guttation is called the loss of water in the form of water droplets from hydathodes (small pores) on the leaf margin of a plant.
- Translocation is the movement of materials in plants from the leaves to other parts of the plant.
- Plasmolysis is defined as the process of contraction or shrinkage of the protoplasm of a plant cell and is caused due to the loss of water in the cell.
- Pressure gradient is when the pressure change is due to depth it is known as hydrostatic pressure gradient. It is seen in plants as they have a large amount of food stored in the leaves in the form of sugar.

88. *(d)* A nebula is a cloud of dust and gas inside a galaxy.
- A nebula is a giant cloud of dust and gas in space. Some nebulae (more than one nebula) come from the gas and dust thrown out by the explosion of a dying star, such as a supernova.
- Other nebulae are regions where new stars are beginning to form.

89. *(c)* Rasmi Ranjan Das (India) was appointed, to the UN tax committee in July 2021, as a member for the 2021 to 2025 term.
- The UN Tax Committee has been impressive, technically unpacking salient tax matters and new areas, such as taxation of the digitalised economy.
- The Committee gives special focus to developing countries and their policy environment.
- The majority of the newly appointed members come from developing countries, and for the first time since its inception, the Committee has a majority of women experts.

90. *(d)* The founder of modern micro finance Muhammad Yunus.
- In 2006, he won the Nobel Prize for his "efforts through microcredit to create economic and social development from below."
- Muhammad Yunus won Nobel Peace Prize in (2006).

91. *(d)* Only (B) is true He formulated the Second Five-Year Plan.
- PC Mahalanobis is remembered as a major contributor of India's developmental path because he formulated the second Five-Year Plan.
- He made pioneering studies in anthropometry in India.
- He founded the Indian Statistical Institute, and contributed to the design of large-scale sample surveys.

92. *(d)* Subhas Chandra Bose was primarily an integral part of INA.
- It was revived under the leadership of Subhas Chandra Bose after his arrival in South East Asia in 1943.
- The army was declared to be the army of Bose's Arzi Hukumat-e-Azad Hind (the Provisional Government of Free India)

93. *(d)* Article 20 clause (2) incorporates the doctrine of double jeopardy.
- Article 20 (2) of the Constitution stales that no person shall be prosecuted and punished for the same offence more than once.
- Moreover, this provision is not only applicable to citizens but to every person within the country.

94. *(b)* According to the Census of India-2011 Rajasthan has the largest gap between male and female literacy rates.

According to census 2011
- Kerela has the highest total literacy rate and female literacy rate.
- Where as Lakshadweep has the highest male literacy rate.
- Bihar has the lowest total literacy rate and male literacy rate.

95. *(a)* Aravidu dynasty, fourth and last dynasty of the Hindu empire of Vijayanagar in Southern India.
- Its founder was Tirumala, whose brother Rama Raya had been the masterful regent of the Sadasiva Raya of the Tuluva dynasty.
- Rama Raya's death at the Battle of Rakasa-Tangadi (also known as Talikota) in 1565.

96. *(c)* In MS Word, the feature allows you to create different headers and footers for odd and even pages called 'Different Odd and Even Pages'. This will allow you to set seperate headers and footers for odd and even pages in a document.

97. *(c)* Khordad Sal is a significant festival of people who believe in the Parsi religion as it marks the birth anniversary of Zoroaster.
- The festival is celebrated by Parsi all over the world, especially in India, as more than half of the population of Parsi community is residing in India.
- Khordad Sal is observed with great happiness and devotion on the 6th day of the Parsi month, which comes around August to September.

98. *(a)* Sonal Mansingh is a famous classical dancer.
- Sonal Mansingh (born 30th April, 1944) is an Indian classical dancer and Guru in Bharatanatyam and Odissi dancing style.
- She has been nominated by the President of India to become a Member of Parliament, Rajya Sabha.
- She is the recipient of Padma Bhushan in 1992 and Padrna Yibhushan in 2003.

99. *(c)* In 1896 tennis was included in the Olympic Games.
- Tennis was part of the Summer Olympic Games program from the inaugural 1896 Summer Olympics officially known as the Games of the I Olympiad.
- It was the first international Olympic Games held in modern history, organised by the International Olympic Committee (IOC).

100. *(c)* Authentication is the computer security requires verifying the genuineness of the individuals or organisations that want to access a system.
- Authentication is the process that companies use to confirm that only the right people, services, and apps with the right permissions can get organisational resources.
- It's an important part of cybersecurity because a bad actor's number one priority is to gain unauthorised access to systems.

Set 06 02 July, 2024 (Shift II)

SSC CHSL Tier-I
SOLVED PAPER

Instructions

1. This paper contains 100 questions.
2. It has 4 Parts, **Part I** General English, **Part II** General Intelligence & Reasoning, **Part III** Quantitative Aptitude and **Part IV** General Awareness.
3. Each question carries **2 marks**.

Part I
General English

1. The following sentence has been split into segments. Identify the segment that contains a grammatical error. If you don't find any error, mark 'No error' as your answer.

I goes to / attend dance classes at / the National Dance Academy.

(a) No error
(b) attend dance classes at
(c) the National Dance Academy
(d) I goes to

2. Select the option that corrects the following sentence.

He has broken his leg yesterday.

(a) He broke his leg yesterday.
(b) He had broke his leg yesterday.
(c) He have broken his leg yesterday.
(d) He has broke his leg yesterday.

3. The following sentence has been split into four segments. Identify the segment that contains a grammatical error.

I noticed that they/did not went to / the museum but entered / a shopping complex.

(a) the museum but entered
(b) did not went to
(c) a shopping complex
(d) I noticed that they

4. The given sentence is divided into three segments. Select the option that has the segment with a grammatical error. If there is no error, select 'No error'.

The meeting was called off / due to a medical emergency of / the manager of the company.

(a) No error
(b) the manager of the company
(c) The meeting was called off
(d) due to a medical emergency of

Directions (Q.Nos. 5-9) *In the following passage, some words have been deleted. Read the passage carefully and select the most appropriate option to fill in each blank.*

If we look at the global population, out of every six persons living in this world, one is an Indian and (1) .... a Chinese. The population of Pakistan is very (2).......... and accounts for roughly about one-tenth of China or India. Though China is the largest nation and geographically (3).......... the largest area among the three nations, its density is the lowest. Scholars point out the one child (4).......... in China in the late 1970s as the major reason for low population growth. They also state that this measure led to a (5).......... in the sex ratio, the proportion of females per 1000 males.

5. Select the most appropriate option to fill in blank number (1).

(a) many (b) another
(c) either (d) second

6. Select the most appropriate option to fill in blank number (2).

(a) small (b) obscure
(c) much (d) a little

7. Select the most appropriate option to fill in blank number (3).

(a) grasps (b) occupies
(c) rents (d) lodges

8. Select the most appropriate option to fill in blank number (4).

(a) average
(b) statute
(c) ordeal
(d) standard

9. Select the most appropriate option to fill in blank number (5).

(a) decline (b) suspension
(c) diminish (d) failure

10. Select the most appropriate Antonym of the given word.

Lethargic

(a) Exhausted (b) Intelligent
(c) Active (d) Cute

11. Select the most appropriate option that can substitute the underlined segment in the given sentence.

Please take <u>many</u> as you want.

(a) so much (b) as much
(c) too much (d) much of

12. Select the most appropriate synonym of the bracketed word in the following sentence to fill in the blank.

The city's infrastructure was ill-equipped to handle the influx of .... (visitors) during the peak season.

(a) tourists (b) citizens
(c) natives (d) residents

13. Select the most appropriate option to fill in the blank.

Both the criminals were cruel and ....

(a) sympathetic (b) warm
(c) brutal (d) diligent

14. Select the most appropriate option that can substitute the underlined segment in the following sentence.

Rimjhim received <u>a children's very illustrated colourful atlas</u> on her 10th birthday.

(a) a very illustrated colourful atlas children
(b) a very colourful illustrated children's atlas

(c) an very illustrated colourful children's atlas
(d) a colourful very illustrated children's atlas

15. Identify the incorrectly spelt word and select its correct spelling.
Wether we want to admit it or not, we all wish everyone would like us.
(a) addmit (b) whether
(c) admitt (d) whither

16. Select the most appropriate meaning of the given idiom.
Slip your mind
(a) Forget about something
(b) Think about something for a short time
(c) Immediately think of something
(d) Can't think of anything to say

17. Select the most appropriate option to fill in the blank.
I was in the .... of a meeting when somebody called me.
(a) centre (b) corner
(c) round (d) middle

18. Select the most appropriate spelling of the underlined word in the given sentence.
The prison is euphemistically called a '<u>rehabillitation</u> centre'.
(a) rehabilition (b) rehabilitation
(c) rehbilitation (d) rehabilation

19. Identify the most appropriate synonym of the following word.
Implicate
(a) Complain (b) Confuse
(c) Accuse (d) Interrogate

20. Select the most appropriate Antonym of the word given in bracket to fill in the blank.
The firefighter summoned all her .... (cowardice) and rushed into the burning building.
(a) skills (b) erudition
(c) courage (d) expertise

21. Select the most appropriate homonym to fill in the blank.
.... is a red-coloured root vegetable.
(a) beet (b) beat
(c) bead (d) bit

22. Select the most appropriate synonym of the given word.
Pliable
(a) Severe (b) Probable
(c) Malleable (d) Rigid

23. Select the most appropriate meaning of the given idiom.
Lose heart
(a) To be suspicious of your success
(b) To get success by believing in yourself
(c) To stop believing that you can succeed
(d) To believe in your success

24. Select the most appropriate option that can substitute the underlined words in the following sentence.
I hope you <u>have enjoying yourselves</u> at the party tonight!
(a) enjoys yourselves
(b) will be enjoy himself
(c) are enjoying themselves
(d) enjoy yourselves

25. Select the most appropriate option that can substitute the underlined segment in the given sentence.
<u>Their was a large snake</u> found in the garden last evening.
(a) There was a large snake
(b) There was the larger snake
(c) There was not a large snake
(d) Their was the larger snake

Part II
General Intelligence

26. In a certain code language,
'M & N' means 'M is the wife of N',
'M @ N' means 'M is the brother of N',
'M $ N' means 'M is the father of N',
'M # N' means 'M is the sister of N'.
Based on this, how is D related to H, if 'D & E $ F # G @ H'?
(a) Father's sister
(b) Sister
(c) Father's mother
(d) Mother

27. Select the set in which the numbers are related in the same way as are the numbers of the following sets.
(**Note** Operations should be performed on the whole numbers, without breaking down the numbers into its constituent digits. E.g. 13 – Operations on 13 such as adding /subtracting /multiplying etc., to 13 can be performed. Breaking down 13 into 1 and 3 and then performing mathematical operations on 1 and 3 is not allowed.)
(5, 7, 74)
(6, 4, 52)
(a) (11, 5, 146) (b) (6, 2, 52)
(c) (9, 5, 206) (d) (9, 5, 405)

28. If 'A' stands for '÷', 'B' stands for '×', 'C' stands for '+' and 'D' stands for '–', what will come in place of the question mark (?) in the following equation?
44 B 5 C 68 D 144 A 4 = ?
(a) 252 (b) 250
(c) 254 (d) 256

29. What should come in place of the question mark (?) in the given series?
3977, 3877, 3777, 3677, 3577, ?
(a) 3333 (b) 3477
(c) 3277 (d) 3377

30. Three statements are followed by conclusions numbered I and II. You have to consider these statements to be true, even if they seem to be at variance with commonly known facts. Decide which of the given conclusions logically follow(s) from the given statements.
Statements
All shirts are pants.
Some dresses are pants.
Some pants are ties.
Conclusions
I. Some dresses are ties.
II. Some ties are shirts.
(a) Only Conclusion I follows
(b) Both Conclusions I and II follow
(c) Only Conclusion II follows
(d) Neither Conclusion I nor II follows

31. How many triangles are there in the following figure?

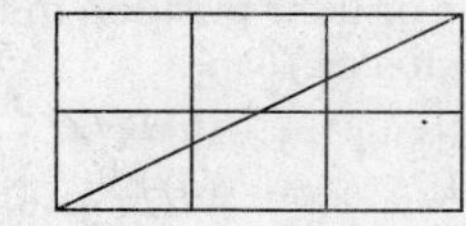

(a) 8 (b) 5 (c) 7 (d) 6

32. A paper is folded and cut as shown below. How will it appear when unfolded?

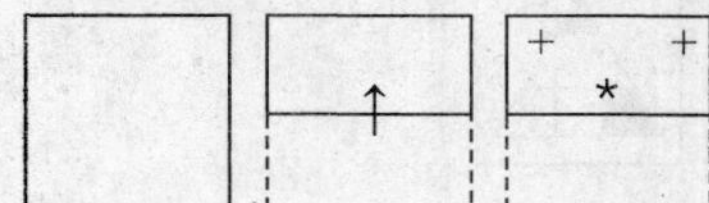

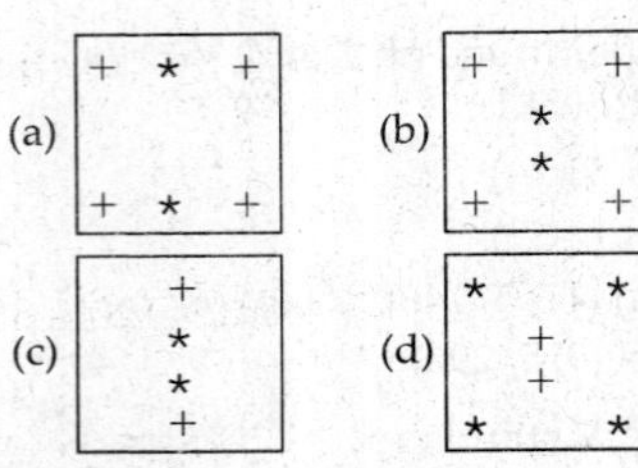

33. What should come in place of the question mark (?) in the given series based on the English alphabetical order?

YAU, DFZ, IKE, NPJ, ?

(a) SUO (b) RUS (c) SOU (d) SRU

34. Select the correct mirror image of the given combination when the mirror is placed at MN as shown below.

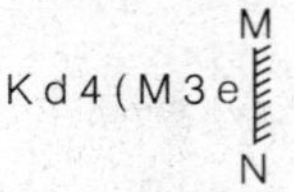

Kd4(M3e | M N

(a) ɘM3)4bK

(b) ɘƐM)d4K

(c) ɘƐM)4bK

(d) ɘƐM)4bK

35. If the seventh day of a month is three days earlier than Friday, then what day will it be on the 20th day of the month?

(a) Thursday (b) Tuesday
(c) Monday (d) Wednesday

36. Which of the following numbers will replace the question mark (?) in the given series?

67, 100, 146, 179, 225, 258, ?

(a) 325 (b) 318 (c) 292 (d) 304

37. Three of the following four are alike in a certain way and thus form a group. Which is the one that does not belong to that group?

(**Note** The odd one out is not based on the number of consonants/vowels or their position in the letter-cluster.)

(a) GJN (b) RVZ
(c) LPT (d) BFJ

38. Select the correct mirror image of the given figure, when the mirror is placed at MN, as shown below.

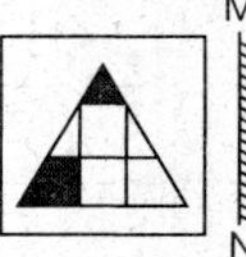

(a) 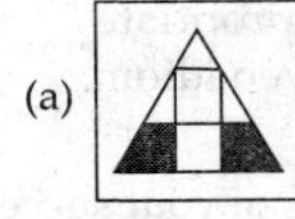 (b) 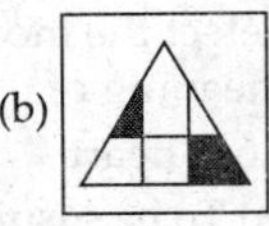

(c) 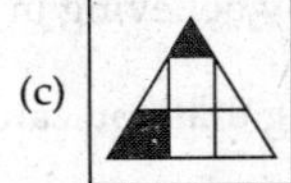 (d) 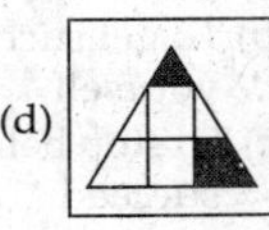

39. What would be the number on the opposite side of '30', if the given sheet is folded to form a cube?

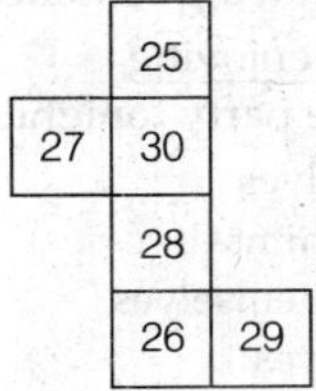

(a) 27 (b) 29
(c) 28 (d) 26

40. 99 is related to 77.3 following a certain logic. Following the same logic, 84.4 is related to 62.7. To which of the following is 72.6 related, following the same logic?

(a) 52.7 (b) 50.9
(c) 57.3 (d) 54.2

41. Select the word-pair that best represents a similar relationship to the one expressed in the pair of words given below.

(The words must be considered as meaningful English words and must not be related to each other based on the number of letters/consonants/vowels in the word).

Problem : Solution

(a) Lost : Found (b) Time : Money
(c) Success : Fame (d) Talk : Speak

42. If 'E' stands for '×', 'O' stands for '+', 'U' stands for '–' and 'V' stands for '÷', what will come in place of the question mark (?) in the following equation?

12 V 2 O 36 E 48 U 53 = ?

(a) 3142 (b) 1650
(c) 6234 (d) 1681

43. What will come in the place of question mark (?) in the following equation, if '+' and '–' are interchanged and '×' and '÷' are interchanged?

$21 + 23 - 46 \times 23 \div 21 = ?$

(a) 90 (b) 65
(c) 78 (d) 40

44. Select the option in which the given figure is embedded (rotation is not allowed).

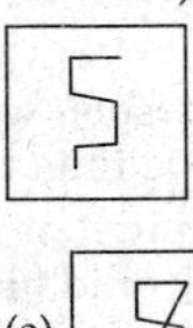

(a) 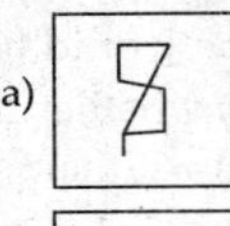 (b) 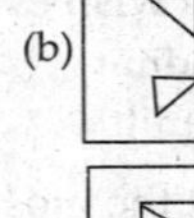

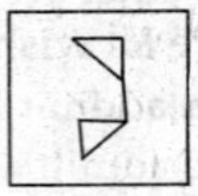

(c) 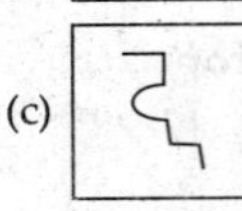 (d)

45. Identify the figure given in the options that when put in place of the question mark (?) will logically complete the series.

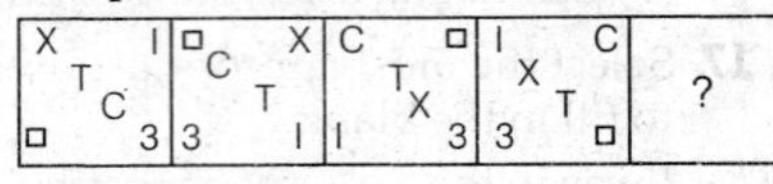

(a) 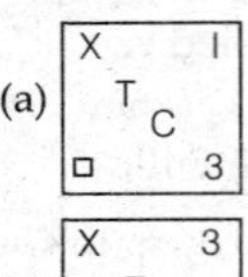 (b) 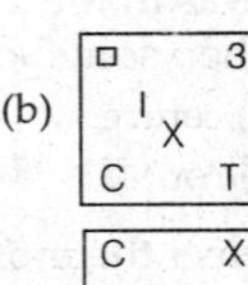

(c) 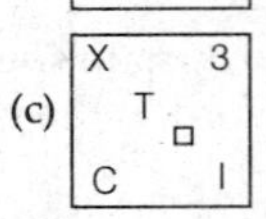 (d)

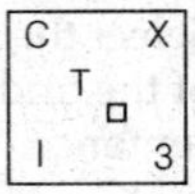

46. In a certain code language, 'no way out' is written as 'rp ab lm' and 'out of house' is written as 'mr rp bd'. How is 'out' written in the given language?

(a) ab (b) rp
(c) lm (d) mr

47. Select the word-pair that best represents a similar relationship to the one expressed in the pair of words given below.

(The words must be considered as meaningful English words and must not be related to each other based on the number of letters/number of consonants/vowels in the word.)

Honest : Corrupt

(a) Observe : Watch
(b) Strong : Fragile
(c) Admire : Respect
(d) Scarce : Rare

48. HF 16 is related to KI 8 in a certain way. In the same way, RP 10 is related to US 5. To which of the following is NL 6 related, following the same logic?

(a) QS 2 (b) OQ 2
(c) LJ 3 (d) QO 3

49. In a certain code language, 'love to god' is coded as 'xr od yk' and 'god bless you' is coded as 'tc ap od'. How is 'god' coded in the given language?
(a) od (b) yk (c) tc (d) ap

50. Which of the following letter-clusters can replace the question mark (?) in the given series to make it logically complete?
PQR, RTV, TWZ, VZD, ?
(a) YCZ (b) WXT
(c) OPS (d) XCH

Part III

Quantitative Aptitude

51. On dividing a certain number by 304, we get 43 as the remainder. If the same number is divided by 16, what will be the remainder?
(a) 8 (b) 11 (c) 15 (d) 12

52. The sum of the five consecutive even numbers is 2720. The sum of the third and fifth numbers is
(a) 1192 (b) 1292
(c) 1092 (d) 1392

53. An electric vehicle company produces three different car models: A, B and C. The production of three different models over a period of four years has been shown in the bar-graph below.
Productions of three different electric car models- A, B, C by a company over the year (in lakhs).

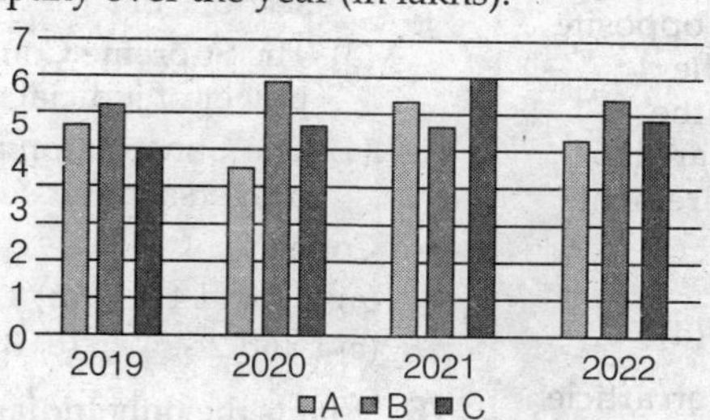

What is the difference between the average production of Model A in 2019, 2021 and 2022 and the average production of Model B in 2020, 2021 and 2022?
(a) 95000 cars (b) 80000 cars
(c) 45000 cars (d) 50000 cars

54. A hemisphere has a radius of 6.2 cm. Find its total surface area (use $\pi = 3.14$) (round off to two decimal places).
(a) 282.25 cm^2 (b) 358.52 cm^2
(c) 276.35 cm^2 (d) 362.10 cm^2

55. Consider two concentric circles having radii 17 cm and 15 cm. What is the length (in cm) of the chord, of the bigger circle, which is a tangent to the smaller circle?
(a) 16 (b) 10 (c) 12 (d) 8

56. The volume of a cube is reduced to 72.9%. By how much is the side of the cube reduced?
(a) 9.5% (b) 10%
(c) 8.5% (d) 9%

57. When a number is increased by 8, it becomes 120% of itself. The number is
(a) 30 (b) 40
(c) 60 (d) 50

58. What is the effective discount percentage, if a shopkeeper offers a scheme discount 'buy five and get one free'?
(a) 15.67% (b) 16.67%
(c) 16.33% (d) 15.33%

59. Simplify the following expression.
$(3 - 3 \times 3 + 3 \div 3 + 3 \times 5) \times 2 \text{ of } 5 + (2 + 2 \div 2 + 2 \times 2 - 2)$
(a) 102 (b) 100
(c) 106 (d) 105

60. Read the given information and answer the question that follows.
The following table gives the percentage of marks obtained by seven students in six different subjects in an examination.
The number in the brackets gives the maximum marks in each subject.

Student	Subjects (Max. Marks)					
	Maths	Chemistry	Physics	Geography	History	Computer Science
	(150)	(130)	(120)	(100)	(60)	(40)
Ayush	90	50	90	60	70	80
Aman	100	80	80	40	80	70
Sajal	90	60	70	70	90	70
Rohit	80	65	80	80	60	60
Muskan	80	65	85	95	50	90
Tanvi	70	75	65	85	40	60
Tarun	65	35	50	77	80	80

What is the total raw score obtained by Rohit?
(a) 425
(b) 444.5
(c) 430.5
(d) 440.5

61. 47 masons can dig a 35 m long trench in one day. How many masons should be employed for digging a 105 m long trench of the same type in one day?
(a) 94 (b) 141
(c) 128 (d) 70

62. The simple interest on a sum of money for $1\frac{1}{2}$ yr at 10% per annum is ₹30 more than the simple interest on the same sum for 1 yr at 12% per annum. Find the sum.
(a) ₹ 1000 (b) ₹ 1050
(c) ₹ 1250 (d) ₹ 1200

63. Moving at $\frac{6}{7}$ of its usual speed, a bus is 20 min late. What is its usual time to cover the journey?
(a) 2 h (b) 4 h (c) 1.5 h (d) 3 h

64. The average monthly expenditure of a family was ₹ 2500 during the first 4 months, ₹ 2750 during the next 5 months and ₹ 3550 during the last 3 months of a year. If the total saving during the year was ₹ 5500, what was the average monthly income of the family?
(a) ₹ 3325
(b) ₹ 4375
(c) ₹ 5790
(d) ₹ 7355

65. The distance between the centres of two circles of radii 4 cm and 2 cm is 10 cm. The length (in cm) of a transverse common tangent is
(a) 13 (b) 11
(c) 6 (d) 8

66. If the brick size is 25 cm × 12 cm × 9 cm, then how many bricks are required to construct a wall of length 10 m, breadth 22.5 cm and height 6 m?
(a) 6000 (b) 4500
(c) 5000 (d) 8000

67. Study the given bar-graph and answer the question that follows.

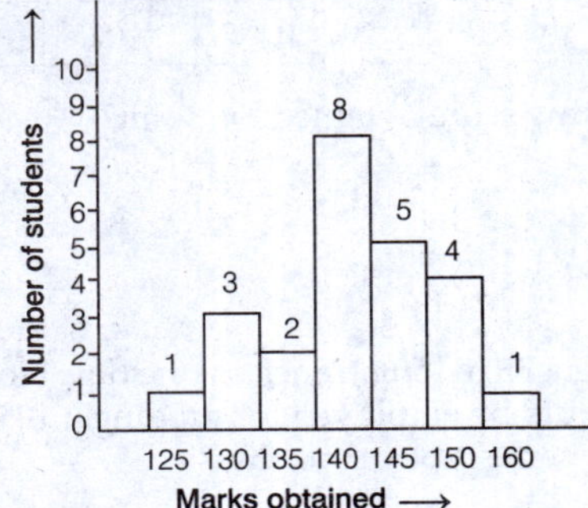

How many students obtained less than the average marks of the class?
(a) 14 (b) 6
(c) 11 (d) 10

68. Given that, $\sin\theta = \frac{15}{17}$. Evaluate $\frac{15\cot\theta + 17\sin\theta}{8\tan\theta + 16\sec\theta}$, where $0° < \theta < 90°$.
(a) $\frac{23}{49}$ (b) $\frac{49}{23}$
(c) $\frac{49}{26}$ (d) $\frac{26}{23}$

69. Study the given pie-chart and answer the question that follows.
The pie-chart shows the monthly expenditure incurred by a family on various items and their savings.

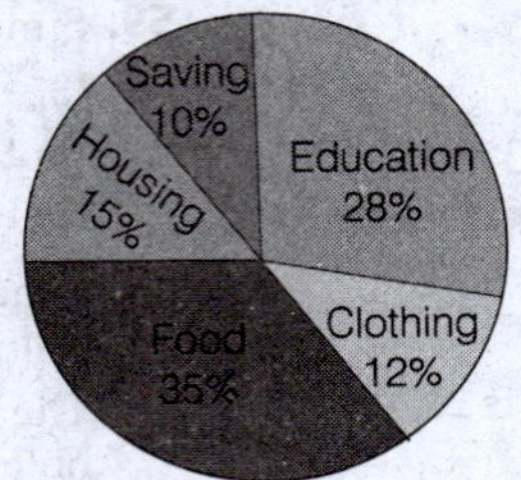

If the total expenditure is ₹84000, then what is the expenditure on food (in ₹)?
(a) 29400 (b) 23500
(c) 19400 (d) 27400

70. Two equal circles are drawn on a square in such a way that opposite side of the square forms the diameter of each circle. If the remaining area of the square is 42 cm^2, what is the measurement (in cm) of the diameter of each circle?
(a) 3.5 (b) 2.5 (c) 14 (d) 7

71. If 70% of the cost price of an article is equal to 40% of its selling price, what is the profit percentage?
(a) 75% (b) 45% (c) 85% (d) 20%

72. From the salary of a software engineer, if 15% is used as house rent, 25% of the remaining is spent on household items, 25% of the remaining as income tax and 15% of the remaining on clothing, then he is left with ₹10404. Find his total salary.
(a) ₹ 22600 (b) ₹ 24600
(c) ₹ 25600 (d) ₹ 23600

73. If the side of a square is increased by 5%, then the percentage increase in its area will be
(a) 10% (b) 11%
(c) 10.5% (d) 10.25%

74. If 35 is the mean proportional of 25 and x, then what is value of x?
(a) 46 (b) 47
(c) 49 (d) 48

75. If ΔABC and ΔPQR are similar. $AB = 8$ cm, $PQ = 12$ cm, $QR = 18$ cm and $RP = 24$ cm, then the perimeter of ΔABC is
(a) 27 cm (b) 36 cm
(c) 42 cm (d) 54 cm

Part IV
General Awareness

76. The Industrial Policy Resolution, 1948 mainly categorised the large-scale industries into .... fragments.
(a) three (b) four
(c) two (d) five

77. Which of the following statements are Incorrect *vis-à-vis* features of the Indian Constitution?
(1) The Constitution empowers the Prime Minister to proclaim three types of emergencies.
(2) A Reservation Policy is there to uplift the disadvantaged sections of society.
(3) The Supreme Court has no power of judicial review.
(4) The Constitution provides for universal adult suffrage.

Codes
(a) 1, 2 and 4 (b) 1 and 3
(c) 1 and 2 (d) 3 and 4

78. Who is the only Indian woman who has been ranked world's no.1 for badminton?
(a) P V Sindhu (b) Rituparna Das
(c) Jwala Gutta (d) Saina Nehwal

79. Which famous book was written by 'Haripala'?
(a) Sangeeta Sudhakara
(b) Sangeet Darpan
(c) Sangeet Ratnakara
(d) Gita Govinda

80. Which of the following is an example of a 'solid in a liquid' type of solution?
(a) Tincture of iodine
(b) Vinegar
(c) Brass
(d) Bronze

81. In September 2022, the book 'Ambedkar and Modi: Reformer's Ideas, Performer's Implementation' has been written by which of the following personalities?
(a) Sarvepalli Radhakrishnan
(b) APJ Abdul Kalam
(c) Ram Nath Kovind
(d) Pratibha Patil

82. According to Census of India 2011, how many districts are there in India?
(a) 620 (b) 640 (c) 630 (d) 610

83. Mahabalipuram temple was built under the reign of which of the following dynasties?
(a) Rashtrakuta (b) Pratihara
(c) Chola (d) Pallava

84. Which folk music does not belong to Nagaland?
(a) Nyioga (b) Hereileu
(c) Heliamleu (d) Neuleu

85. Article 20 of the Constitution of India is related to ....
(a) protection in respect of conviction for offences
(b) abolition of titles
(c) equality of opportunities in matters of public employment
(d) freedom to manage religious affairs

86. Which of the following is not a poverty alleviation programme in India?
(a) Swarna Jayanti Shahari Rozgar Yojana
(b) Rashtriya Ucchatar Shiksha Abhiyan
(c) Integrated Rural Development Program
(d) Prime Minister Rozgar Yojana

87. On what type of data can MS Excel functions operate?
(a) External data sources only
(b) Range of cells or groups of cells
(c) Entire worksheets only
(d) Individual cells only

88. Which of the following was not a venue for the 66th National School Games 2022-23?
(a) Delhi (b) Gwalior
(c) Bhopal (d) Ludhiana

89. Which of the following groups of places in India has little differences in day and night temperatures?
(a) Bhopal and Indore
(b) Chennai and Thiruvananthapuram
(c) Jammu and Kashmir
(d) Jaipur and Jaisalmer

90. Which of the following is the festival of Kerala that heralds the harvest season, lasts for 10 days, and has snake boat races etc.
(a) Thiruvathira
(b) Onam
(c) Thrissur Pooram
(d) Vishu

91. When was the Bharat Nirman Programme launched by the Government of India?
(a) 2010 (b) 2014
(c) 2005 (d) 2000

92. 'Chhau' is a popular dance of which of the following state?
(a) Gujarat (b) Kerala
(c) Haryana (d) Jharkhand

93. What is the main objective of Fiscal Responsibility and Budget Management Act (FRBMA), 2003?
(a) To reduce subsidies
(b) To increase exports
(c) To reduce fiscal deficit
(d) To increase excise duty

94. How do the muscle cells help in movement?
(a) The lining of the vessels inside helps in movement.
(b) The contraction and relaxation of these cells result in movement.
(c) The blood flow of the cells helps in movement.
(d) The thickness of the cell layer helps in movement.

95. What will happen when you select the cell contents of a particular row in MS-Excel and then click the Delete button?
(a) Entries in all the selected cells will be deleted.
(b) Only first three cells will be deleted.
(c) Entire row will be deleted.
(d) First five cell entries will be deleted.

96. The Reserve Bank of India was fully nationalised and owned by the Government of India in which of the following years?
(a) 1949 (b) 1950 (c) 1947 (d) 1948

97. Orographic rainfall occurs when ....
(a) a cyclone makes a landfall
(b) the air masses collide at Intertropical Conversion Zone
(c) saturated air mass comes across a mountain
(d) hot air rises up in conventional currents

98. The fifth edition of the Khelo India Youth Games were organised in Bhopal city in which year?
(a) 2022 (b) 2020
(c) 2021 (d) 2023

99. In April 2023, Government of India launched Vibrant Village Programme from Kibithoo village which is located in ....
(a) Meghalaya
(b) Bihar
(c) Arunachal Pradesh
(d) Assam

100. In July 2021, which State Government passed a resolution supporting an ad hoc committee report that favoured the creation of a Legislative Council?
(a) West Bengal
(b) Bihar
(c) Telangana
(d) Odisha

Answers

1. (d)	2. (a)	3. (b)	4. (a)
5. (b)	6. (a)	7. (b)	8. (b)
9. (a)	10. (c)	11. (b)	12. (a)
13. (c)	14 (b)	15. (b)	16. (a)
17. (d)	18. (b)	19. (c)	20. (c)
21. (a)	22. (c)	23. (c)	24. (d)
25. (a)	26. (d)	27. (a)	28. (a)
29. (b)	30. (d)	31. (a)	32. (b)
33. (a)	34. (d)	35. (c)	36. (d)
37. (a)	38. (d)	39. (d)	40. (b)
41. (a)	42. (d)	43. (d)	44. (a)
45. (a)	46. (b)	47. (b)	48. (d)
49. (a)	50. (d)	51. (b)	52. (c)
53. (d)	54. (d)	55. (a)	56. (b)
57. (b)	58. (b)	59. (d)	60. (d)
61. (b)	62. (a)	63. (a)	64. (a)
65. (d)	66. (c)	67. (a)	68. (a)
69. (a)	70. (c)	71. (a)	72. (c)
73. (d)	74. (c)	75. (b)	76. (b)
77. (b)	78. (d)	79. (d)	80. (a)
81. (c)	82. (b)	83. (d)	84. (a)
85. (a)	86. (b)	87. (c)	88. (d)
89. (b)	90. (b)	91. (c)	92. (d)
93. (c)	94. (b)	95. (a)	96. (a)
97. (c)	98. (a)	99. (c)	100. (a)

Explanations

1. *(d)* Part (d) 'I goes to' contains an error. The pronoun 'I' takes the plural form of verb. Hence, use 'go' to correct the sentence.
2. *(a)* The given sentence contains an error. As the sentence is in past tense, use 'broke' in place of 'has broken' to correct the sentence.
3. *(b)* Part (b) 'did not went to' contains an error. The verb 'do/does/did' takes the base form of verb. Hence, use 'go' to correct the sentence.
4. *(a)* The given sentence is grammatically correct and contextually meaningful.
5. *(b)* The correct filler for the given blank is 'another'.
6. *(a)* The correct filler for the given blank is 'small'.
7. *(b)* The correct filler for the given blank is 'occupies'.
8. *(b)* The correct filler for the given blank is 'statute'.
9. *(a)* The correct filler for the given blank is 'decline'.
10. *(c)* Lethargic means lazy. Hence, its antonym is 'active'.
11. *(b)* The underlined part of the sentence contains an error. Use 'as much' to correct the sentence.
12. *(a)* The word 'visitors' means 'tourists' which is appropriate to fill in the blank.
13. *(c)* The correct filler for the given blank is 'brutal' which fits well with the words 'criminal' and 'cruel'.
14. *(b)* The underlined part of the sentence contains an error. Use 'a very colourful illustrated children's atlas' to correct the sentence.
15. *(b)* The incorrectly spelt word is 'wether'. The correct spelling is 'whether'.
16. *(a)* Slip your mind means to forget about something.
17. *(d)* The correct filler for the given blank is 'middle'.
18. *(b)* The correct spelling is 'rehabilitation'.
19. *(c)* The word 'implicate' means 'show (someone) to be involved in a crime/ accuse'.
20. *(c)* The antonym of 'cowardice' is 'courage', which is the correct filler for the given blank.
21. *(a)* The correct filler for the given blank is 'beet'.
22. *(c)* 'Pliable' means easily bent; flexible. Hence, its synonym is 'malleable' which means (of a metal or other material) able to be hammered or pressed into shape without breaking or cracking.

    'Rigid' means stiff.
23. *(c)* Lose heart means to stop believing that you can succeed.
24. *(d)* The underlined part of the sentence contains an error. Use 'enjoy yourselves' to correct the sentence.
25. *(a)* The underlined part of the sentence contains an error. Use 'there was a large snake' to correct the sentence.
26. *(d)* Given expression,

    D & E $ F # G @ H

    According to the question,

    [+ → Male; – → Female]

    D(–) ←Wife— E(+)
    E(+) —Father→ F(–)
    F(–) ←Sister— G(+) ←Brother— H

    Hence, D is the mother of H.
27. *(a)* As, (5, 7, 74)

    $\Rightarrow (5)^2 + (7)^2 = 25 + 49 \Rightarrow 74$

    and (6, 4, 52)

    $\Rightarrow (6)^2 + (4)^2 = 36 + 16 \Rightarrow 52$

    Similarly, (11, 5, 146)

    $\Rightarrow (11)^2 + (5)^2 = 121 + 25 \Rightarrow 146$
28. *(a)* Given expression,

    44 B 5 C 68 D 144 A 4 = ?

    According to the question, replacing the symbols with their respective signs, we get

    $44 \times 5 + 68 - 144 \div 4 = ?$

    $\Rightarrow 220 + 68 - 36 = ?$

    $\Rightarrow 288 - 36 = ?$

    $\therefore ? = \boxed{252}$
29. *(b)* The pattern of the given series is as follows,

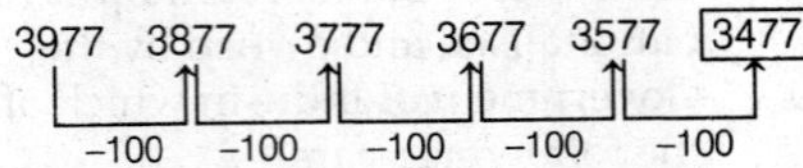

30. *(d)* According to the statements,

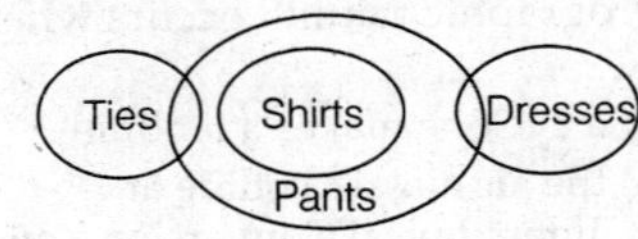

Conclusions

I. (✗) II. (✗)

Hence, neither Conclusion I nor II follows.

31. *(a)* Naming the figure,

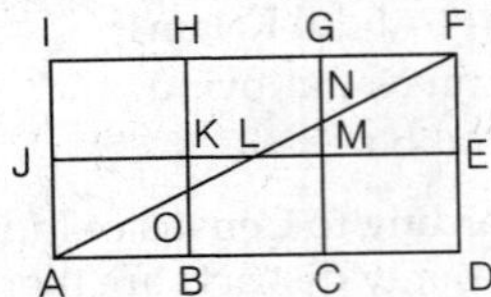

Total number of triangles are ΔAOB, ΔANC, ΔAFD, ΔFNG, ΔFOH, ΔFAI, ΔKOL and ΔLNM.

∴ Total triangles = 8

32. *(b)* When the paper is unfolded, it will look like option figure (b).

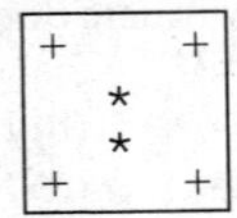

33. *(a)* The pattern of the given series is as follows,

    Y —+5→ D —+5→ I —+5→ N —+5→ S

    A —+5→ F —+5→ K —+5→ P —+5→ U

    U —+5→ Z —+5→ E —+5→ J —+5→ O
34. *(d)* The correct mirror image of given combination is as shown below,

    M

    Kd4(M3e | e3M)4bK

    N
35. *(c)* 7th day = Friday – 3 = Tuesday

    Now,

    7th, 14th and 21th of the month = Tuesday

    ∴ 20th of that month = Tuesday – 1 = Monday
36. *(d)* The pattern of the given series is as follows,

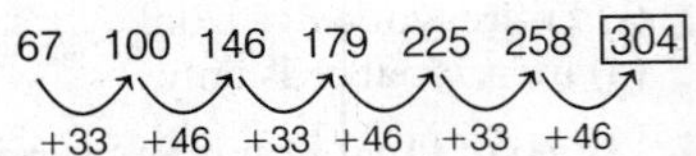

37. *(a)* As,

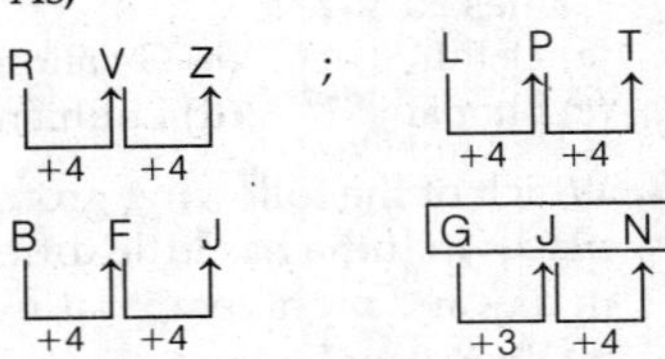

Hence, 'GJN' is the odd one.

38. *(d)* The correct mirror image of given figure is as shown below,

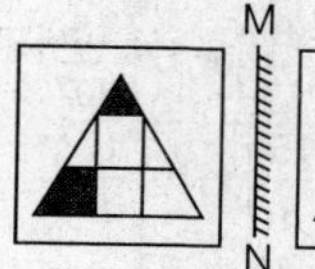
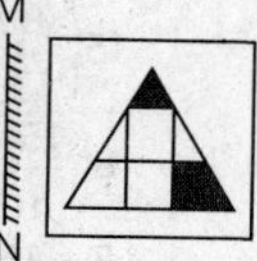

39. *(d)* According to the question,

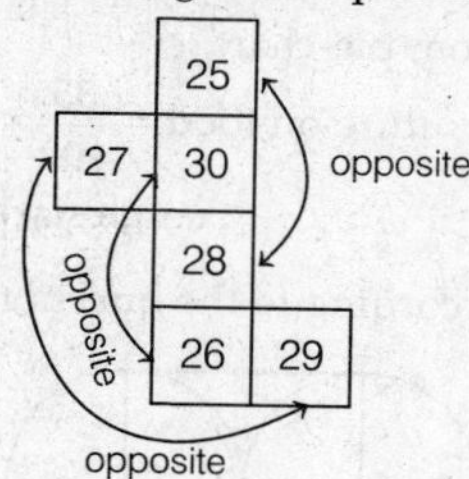

∴ Number '26' will be opposite side of '30' in given sheet of cube.

40. *(b)* As, $99 - 77.3 = 21.7$

and $84.4 - 62.7 = 21.7$

Similarly, $72.6 - x = 21.7$

$$x = 72.6 - 21.7 = 50.9$$

41. *(a)* As, the words 'Problem' and 'Solution' are antonyms to each other.

Similarly, 'Lost' and 'Found' are antonyms to each other.

42. *(d)* Given expression,
12 V 2 O 36 E 48 U 53

According to the question, after replacing the letters with their respective signs, we get

$12 \div 2 + 36 \times 48 - 53 = ?$

$\Rightarrow \quad 6 + 1728 - 53 = ?$

$\Rightarrow \quad 1734 - 53 = ? \Rightarrow ? = 1681$

43. *(d)* Given expression,

$$21 + 23 - 46 \times 23 \div 21 = ?$$

Replacing '+' and '–', '×' and '÷', we get

$21 - 23 + 46 \div 23 \times 21 = ?$

$\Rightarrow \quad 21 - 23 + 2 \times 21 = ?$

$\Rightarrow \quad 21 - 23 + 42 = ?$

$\Rightarrow \quad 63 - 23 = ? \Rightarrow ? = \boxed{40}$

44. *(a)* The given figure is embedded in option figure (a).

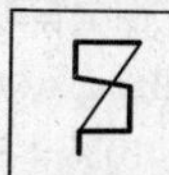

45. *(a)* The elements in series are moving as shown below,

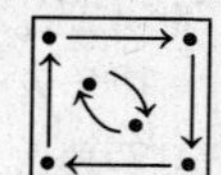
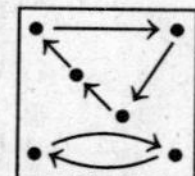

Figure 1 to 2 Figure 2 to 3
Figure 3 to 4 Figure 4 to 5

Hence, option figure (a) will come in place of question mark in given series.

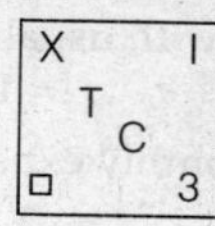

46. *(b)* According to the question,

no way (out) ⟶ (rp) ab lm

(out) of house ⟶ mr (rp) bd

The word 'out' and code 'rp' is common in both the given sentences.

∴ Code for 'out' is 'rp'.

47. *(b)* As, 'Honest' is a antonym of 'Corrupt'. Similarly, 'Strong' is a antonym of 'Fragile'.

48. *(d)* As,

H F 16 → (+3, +3, ÷2) → K I 8

and

R P 10 → (+3, +3, ÷2) → U S 5

Similarly,

N L 6 → (+3, +3, ÷2) → Q O 3

49. *(a)* According to the question,

love to [god] ⟶ xr [od] yk

[god] bless you ⟶ tc ap [od]

∴ Code for 'god' is 'od'.

50. *(d)* The pattern of the given series is as follows,

P →(+2) R →(+2) T →(+2) V →(+2) [X]

Q →(+3) T →(+3) W →(+3) Z →(+3) [C]

R →(+4) V →(+4) Z →(+4) D →(+4) [H]

51. *(b)* Let the number is N.

Then, $N = 304K + 43$

when, $K = 1$, then $N = 347$

$\therefore \quad \frac{N}{16} = \frac{347}{16} = 11$ (remainder)

∴ When N is divided by 16, then remainder is 11.

52. *(c)* Let the five consecutive even numbers are $a - 4$, $a - 2$, a, $a + 2$, $a + 4$

According to the question,

$a - 4 + a - 2 + a + a + 2 + a + 4 = 2720$

$\Rightarrow \quad 5a = 2720$

$\Rightarrow \quad a = 544$

The sum of third and fifth numbers

$= a + a + 4$

$= 2a + 4 = 2 \times 544 + 4 = 1092$

53. *(d)* Average product of Model A in 2019, 2021 and 2022

$= \left(\frac{5 + 5.5 + 4.5}{3}\right)$ lakhs cars

$= \frac{15}{3} = 5$ lakhs cars

Average product of Model B in 2020, 2021 and 2022

$= \frac{6 + 5 + 5.5}{3}$ lakhs cars

$= \frac{16.5}{3} = 5.5$ lakhs cars

∴ Required difference

$= (5.5 - 5)$ lakhs cars

$= 0.5$ lakhs $= 50000$ cars

54. *(d)* Given, radius $(r) = 6.2$ cm

Total surface area $= 3\pi r^2$

$= 3 \times 3.14 \times (6.2)^2$

$= 9.42 \times 38.44$

$= 362.10 \text{ cm}^2$

55. *(a)* Given,

$r = 15$ cm, $R = 17$ cm

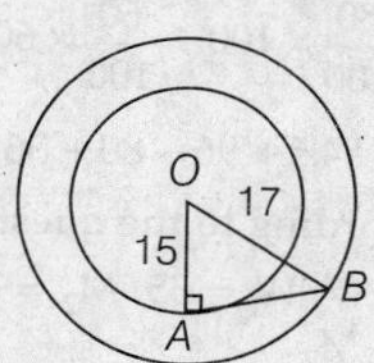

In ΔAOB,

$(AB)^2 = (OB)^2 - (OA)^2$

$(AB)^2 = (17)^2 - (15)^2 = 289 - 225$

$AB = \sqrt{64} = 8$ cm

∴ The length of tangent to smaller circle $= 8 \times 2$

$= 16$ cm

56. *(b)* Let volume of cube $= 1000a^3$

∴ Side of cube $= \sqrt[3]{1000a^3} = 10a$

According to the question,

Volume of new cube $= 1000a^3 \times \frac{72.9}{100}$

$= 729a^3$

∴ New side $= \sqrt[3]{729a^3} = 9a$

∴ Percentage decrease in side of cube

$= \left(\frac{10a - 9a}{10a}\right) \times 100$

$= \frac{1}{10} \times 100 = 10\%$

57. *(b)* Let the number be x.

According to the question,

$$x + 8 = x \times \frac{120}{100}$$

$\Rightarrow \quad x+8 = x \times \frac{6}{5}$

$\Rightarrow \quad 5x + 40 = 6x$

$\Rightarrow \quad x = 40$

$\therefore$ The number is 40.

58. *(b)* The effective discount percentage

$= \frac{1}{1+5} \times 100$

$= \frac{1}{6} \times 100$

$= 16.67\%$

59. *(d)* Given equation,

$(3 - 3 \times 3 + 3 \div 3 + 3 \times 5) \times 2 \text{ of } 5 + (2 + 2 \div 2 + 2 \times 2 - 2)$

(using BODMAS rule)

$= (3 - 9 + 1 + 15) \times 10 + (2 + 1 + 4 - 2)$

$= (19 - 9) \times 10 + (7 - 2)$

$= 10 \times 10 + 5$

$= 105$

60. *(d)* Total row score obtained by Rohit

$= \left[\frac{80}{100} \times 150 + \frac{65}{100} \times 130 + \frac{80}{100} \times 120 + \frac{80}{100} \times 100 + \frac{60}{100} \times 60 + \frac{60}{100} \times 40\right]$

$= [120 + 84.5 + 96 + 80 + 36 + 24] = 440.5$

61. *(b)* According to the question,

$M_1 = 47, W_1 = 35, M_2 = ?, W_2 = 105$

$\therefore \frac{M_1}{W_1} = \frac{M_2}{W_2}$

$\frac{47}{35} = \frac{M_2}{105} \Rightarrow M_2 = 141$

$\therefore$ The 141 masons on should be employed for digging 105 m long trench.

62. *(a)* Let principal = ₹ P

According to the question,

$\frac{P \times 3 \times 10}{2 \times 100} - \frac{P \times 1 \times 12}{100} = 30$

$\frac{15P}{100} - \frac{12P}{100} = 30$

$\Rightarrow \quad \frac{3P}{100} = 30$

$\therefore \quad P = ₹ 1000$

63. *(a)* New speed $= \frac{6}{7}$ of usual speed

$\left[\because \text{Speed} \propto \frac{1}{\text{Time}}\right]$

Now, time taken $\frac{7}{6}$ of usual speed

time taken with

$\left[\frac{7}{6} \text{of usual speed} - \text{usual speed}\right]$

$= 20 \text{ min}$

$\Rightarrow \frac{1}{6}$ of the usual speed = 20 min

Time taken with usual speed

$= 120 \text{ min} = 2 \text{ h}$

64. *(a)* Total monthly expenditure of a family

$= (2500 \times 4 + 2750 \times 5 + 3550 \times 3 + 5500)$

$= (10000 + 13750 + 10650 + 5500)$

$= 39900$

$\therefore$ Average monthly income $= \frac{39900}{12}$

$= ₹ 3325$

65. *(d)* Given, $r_1 = 4$ cm, $r_2 = 2$ cm,

Distance between the centres

$(d) = 10$ cm

Length of transverse common tangent

$= \sqrt{(d)^2 - (r_1 + r_2)^2}$

$= \sqrt{(10)^2 - (4+2)^2}$

$= \sqrt{100 - 36}$

$= \sqrt{64}$

$= 8$ cm

66. *(c)* Required bricks

$= \frac{10 \text{ m} \times 22.5 \text{ cm} \times 6 \text{ m}}{25 \text{ cm} \times 12 \text{ cm} \times 9 \text{ cm}}$

$= \frac{10 \times 100 \times 22.5 \times 6 \times 100}{25 \times 12 \times 9}$

$= 5000$

67. *(a)* From bar-graph,

Average marks of the class

$= \frac{(125 \times 1) + (130 \times 3) + (135 \times 2) + (140 \times 8) + (145 \times 5) + (150 \times 4) + (160 \times 1)}{(1 + 3 + 2 + 8 + 5 + 4 + 1)}$

$= \frac{125 + 390 + 270 + 1120 + 725 + 600 + 160}{24}$

$= \frac{3390}{24} = 141.25$

Now, students who obtained marks less than average marks

$= 1 + 3 + 2 + 8 = 14$

68. *(a)* Given, $\sin\theta = \frac{P}{H} = \frac{15}{17}$

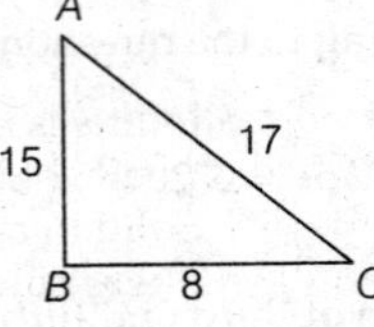

From triplets, 8, 15, 17, $BC = 8$

Now, $\frac{15\cot\theta + 17\sin\theta}{8\tan\theta + 16\sec\theta}$

$= \frac{15\left(\frac{8}{15}\right) + 17\left(\frac{15}{17}\right)}{8\left(\frac{15}{8}\right) + 16\left(\frac{17}{8}\right)}$

$= \frac{8 + 15}{15 + 34} = \frac{23}{49}$

69. *(a)* From pie-chart,

Expenditure on food $= \frac{35}{100} \times 84000$

$= ₹ 29400$

70. *(c)* According to the question,

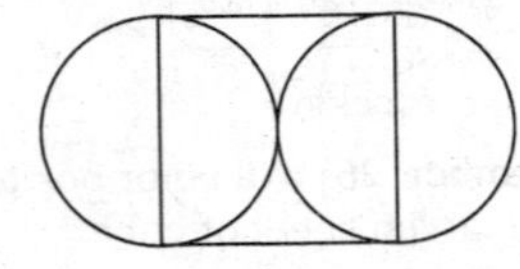

$\pi r^2 + 42 = a^2$

$\pi\left(\frac{a}{2}\right)^2 + 42 = a^2$

$\Rightarrow \quad \frac{\pi a^2}{4} + 42 = a^2$

$\Rightarrow \quad a^2\left(1 - \frac{\pi}{4}\right) = 42$

$\Rightarrow \quad a^2\left(1 - \frac{22}{7 \times 4}\right) = 42$

$\Rightarrow \quad a^2 \times \frac{6}{28} = 42$

$\Rightarrow \quad a^2 = \frac{42 \times 28}{6}$

$\Rightarrow \quad a^2 = 49 \times 4$

$\therefore \quad a = 14$ cm

71. *(a)* According to the question,

$\frac{70}{100} \times \text{cost price} = \frac{40}{100} \times \text{selling price}$

$\frac{\text{Selling price}}{\text{Cost price}} = \frac{70}{40} = \frac{7}{4}$

Profit per cent $= \frac{(7-4)}{4} \times 100$

$= \frac{3}{4} \times 100 = 75\%$

72. *(c)* Let total salary = 100%

House rent = 15%

Remaining salary

$= (100 - 15)\% = 85\%$

Remaining salary after expenditure on household items

$= \left(85 - \frac{85 \times 25}{100}\right)\%$

$= (85 - 21.25)\%$

$= 63.75\%$

Remaining salary after income tax

payment $= \left(63.75 - \frac{63.75 \times 25}{100}\right)$

$= 63.75 - 15.93$

$= 47.81\%$

Remaining salary after expenditure on clothing

$= \left(47.81 - \frac{15}{100} \times 47.81\right)$

$= (47.81 - 7.17)$

$= 40.63\%$

According to the question,

$40.63\% = 10404$

$100\% = \frac{10404}{40.63} \times 100$

$= ₹25606 \approx ₹25600$

73. *(d)* Let side of square is 10.

$\therefore$ Area $= (10)^2 = 100$

Now, side is increase by 5%.

$\therefore$ New side $= 10 \times \frac{105}{100} = 10.5$

New area $= (10.5)^2 = 110.25$

$\therefore$ Required increase

$= \frac{110.25 - 100}{100} \times 100 = 10.25\%$

74. *(c)* Given, $a = 25$, $b = x$

Mean proportion $= \sqrt{a \times b}$

According to the question,

$\sqrt{25 \times x} = 35$

Squaring both sides, we get

$25 \times x = 1225$

$\Rightarrow \quad x = \frac{1225}{25}$

$\therefore \quad x = 49$

75. *(b)* Given, $\Delta ABC \sim \Delta PQR$

$\therefore \frac{AB}{PQ} = \frac{BC}{QR} = \frac{AC}{PR}$

$= \frac{\text{Perimeter of } \Delta ABC}{\text{Perimeter of } \Delta PQR}$

Now, $\frac{AB}{PQ} = \frac{BC}{QR} \Rightarrow \frac{8}{12} = \frac{BC}{18}$

$\Rightarrow \quad BC = 12$ cm

and $\frac{AB}{PQ} = \frac{AC}{PR} \Rightarrow \frac{8}{12} = \frac{AC}{24}$

$\Rightarrow \quad AC = 16$ cm

Perimeter of $\Delta ABC = AB + BC + AC$

$= 8 + 12 + 16$

$= 36$ cm

76. *(b)* The Industrial Policy Resolution of 1948 categorised large-scale industries into four fragments.

- Exclusive monopoly of Central Government (arms and ammunitions, production of atomic energy and management of railways).
- New undertaking undertaken only by state (coal, iron and steel, aircraft manufacturing, ship building, telegraph, telephone etc).
- Industries to be regulated by the government (Industries of basic importance).
- Open to private enterprise, individuals and cooperatives (remaining).

77. *(b)* Statements (1) and (3) are incorrect.

- The Constitution empowers the President to proclaim three types of Constitution.
- The Supreme Court has power of Judicial review.

Statements (2) and (4) are correct.

- A Reservation Policy is there to uplift the people belonging to backward groups.
- The Constitution provides for universal adult suffrage in Article 326.

78. *(d)* Saina Nehwal is the only one Indian woman who has been ranked world's no.1 for badminton.

- Sania Nehwal is the first female player from India to achieve the world no. 1 spot, which she did in April 2015.
- The first Indian badminton player to win a medal at the Olympic Games.
- Award received by Saina Nehwal are
  (i) Most Promising Player of the Year (2008) Award by Badminton World Federation
  (ii) Arjuna Award (2009)
  (iii) Padma Shri (2010)
  (iv) Major Dhyan Chand Khel Ratna (2009-2010)
  (v) Padma Bhushan (2016)

79. *(d)* Sangeeta Sudhakara was famous book written by 'Haripala'.

- Sangeeta Sudhakara was written in the 14th Century CE.
- The term 'Carnatic' and 'Hindustani' to classify musical styles first appeared in it.

80. *(a)* A tincture of iodine is a solution of iodine dissolved in alcohol, making it an example of a 'Solid in a liquid' type of solution. Sugar solution and salt solution are the solutions of solids in liquids.

81. *(c)* The book 'Ambedkar and Modi: Reformer's Ideas', Performer's Implementation' was written by Ram Nath Kovind.

- The book was released in September 2022.
- The book explores the connection between the ideas of B.R. Ambedkar, the architect of the Indian Constitution, and the policies implemented by Prime Minister Narendra Modi.

82. *(b)* According to the census of India 2011 there are 640 districts in India.

- The census also covered 5,924 sub-districts, 7,935 towns and more than 600,000 villages.
- The census is conducted by the Ministry of Home Affairs under the provisions of the Census Act of 1948.
- India's first census was conducted in 1872 under British Viceroy Lord Mayo however, first synchronous census held in 1881 under Viceroy Lord Rippon.

83. *(d)* The Mahabalipuram temple, also known as the Shore Temple, was built during the reign of the Pallava dynasty in the 8th century AD.

- Specifically, it is believed to have been built during the reign of King Narasimhavarman II (also known as Rajasimha) in the 8th century AD.
- The Pallava dynasty was a powerful South Indian kingdom and Mahabalipuram was one of their major ports and cultural centres.

84. *(a)* Nyioga music does not belong to Nagaland.

- Nyioga music is belonged to Arunachal Pradesh.
- It is sung when a marriage ceremony is concluded and the bride's family returns leaving the bride in her home.
- It contains pieces of advice to the bride for her future life.

85. *(a)* Article 20 of the Constitution of India is related to protection in respect of conviction for offences.

- It means that no one can be convicted for an act that was not an offence at the time of its commission.
- And no one can be given punishment greater than what was provided in the law prevalent at the time of its commission.

86. *(b)* Rashtriya Ucchatar Shiksha Abhiyan was not a poverty alleviation programme in India.

- Rashtriya Ucchatar Shiksha Abhiyan (RUSA) is a Centrally Sponsored Scheme (CSS), launched in 2013.
- It aims is to improve the overall quality of state institutions.
- It ensures reforms in the affiliation, academic and examination system.

87. *(c)* MS Excel functions can operate on a range of cells or groups of cells, which allows you to perform calculations, data analysis, and other operations on specific sets of data. This includes

- A single cell
- A range of adjacent cells (e.g. Al:Al0)
- A range of non-adjacent cells (e.g. A1, C3, E5)
- An entire row or column
- A group of cells that meet certain criteria (e.g. using the IF function)

88. *(d)* Ludhiana was not a venue for the 66th National School Games 2022-23.

- The 66th National School Games 2022-23 was announced at Bhopal from 6th to 9th June and l0th to 13th June, 2023.
- The 66th National School Games 2022-23 was also announced at NCT of Delhi from 6th to 12th, June 2023. This is due to their coastal locations and proximity to the equator.

89. *(b)* Chennai and Thiruvananthapuram are the places in India has little differences in day and night temperatures.

90. *(b)* Onam is festival of Kerala that heralds the harvest season, lasts for 10 days, and has snake boat races etc.

- Onam is an annual harvest and cultural festival related to Hinduism that is celebrated mostly by the people of Kerala.
- It marks the beginning of the Malayalam calendar month of Chingam, which usually falls between August and September.
- The festival is celebrated by boat races, dance forms, Rangoli, food and traditional clothing. Women draw floral designs called Pookkalam, while men perform the Pulikali art.
- Onam Sadya, a grand feast, is prepared with 13 dishes served on banana leaves.

91. *(c)* The Bharat Nirman Programme was launched by the Government of India in 2005.

- The program aimed at improving rural infrastructure, including roads, bridges, irrigation, water supply and housing.
- It provides a better life to the people in rural areas.

92. *(d)* Chhau is a popular dance of the states of Odisha (formerly known as Orissa), Jharkhand, West Bengal.

- Chhau is a traditional folk dance that originated in the eastern part of India, and is popular in these three states.
- It is known for its energetic and athletic movements, and is often performed during festivals and celebrations.

93. *(c)* The main objective of the Fiscal Responsibility and Budget Management Act (FRBMA), 2003 is to reduce fiscal deficits and debts and to promote fiscal discipline and transparency.

94. *(b)* The contraction and relaxation of these cells result in movement.

- Muscle contraction is initiated by the signal sent by the CNS to the muscle fibres.
- During contraction, the muscles fibres shorter, the muscle pulls on the ligaments that connect the bones and the movable body parts.

95. *(a)* Entries in all the selected cells will be deleted, when select the cell contents of a particular row in MS Excel and then click the delete button.

96. *(a)* The Reserve Bank of India was fully nationalised and owned by the Government of India in 1949.

- The RBI was established in 1935 as a private entity, but it became a state-owned entity on 1st January, 1949 under the Reserve Bank of India. (Transfer of Public Ownership Act, 1948).
- The RBI headquarter is located in Mumbai.

97. *(c)* Orographic rainfall occurs when a saturated air mass is forced to rise over a mountain or hill, resulting in cooling and condensation, leading to precipitation.

- This type of rainfall is also known as relief rainfall.
- The mountain acts as a barrier, causing the air to rise and cool, resulting in the formation of clouds and precipitation.

98. *(a)* The 5th edition of the Khelo India Youth Games was organised in Bhopal, Madhya Pradesh from 21st to 30th March, 2022.

- The Khelo India Youth Games (KIYG) is a multi-disciplinary sports competition for school and college students in India.
- The games are held annually in January or February and are part of the government's Khelo India initiative.
- The games began as the Khelo India School Games in New Delhi in 2018 and were renamed the Khelo India Youth Games in 2019.
- Tamil Nadu hosted the Khelo India Youth Games 2024.

99. *(c)* In April 2023, Government of India launched Vibrant Village Programme from Kibithoo village located in Arunachal Pradesh.

- The program aims to develop and transform villages along the India-China border.
- Transformation into 'Vibrant and sustainable' hubs of economic activity, with a focus on infrastructure development, tourism promotion and livelihood generation.

100. *(a)* On 6th July 2021, West Bengal Government passed a resolution supporting and Hoc Committee report that favoured the creation of a Legislative Council.

- Six states that have a Legislative Council are Maharashtra, Telangana, Uttar Pradesh, Andhra Pradesh, Karnataka and Bihar.
- Before bifurcation in 2019, Jammu and Kashmir also had Legislative Council.
- Article 169 of the Constitution grants every state the right to create or abolish the Legislative Council.

Set 07 02 July, 2024 (Shift III)

SSC CHSL Tier-I
SOLVED PAPER

Instructions

1. This paper contains 100 questions.
2. It has 4 Parts, **Part I** General English, **Part II** General Intelligence & Reasoning, **Part III** Quantitative Aptitude and **Part IV** General Awareness.
3. Each question carries **2 marks**.

Part I
General English

1. Select the option that corrects the following sentence.

What are you looking around?

(a) What are you looking among?
(b) What are you looking for?
(c) What are you looking across?
(d) What are you looking through?

2. The following sentence has been divided into four segments. Identify the segment that contains an error in the usage of indefinite articles.

We took / an ice / and applied it on / the wound.

(a) an ice
(b) We took
(c) and applied it on
(d) the wound

3. The following sentence has been split into four segments. Identify the segment that contains a grammatical error.

Since the little girl answers / a few simple questions, / her parents say that / she is too intelligent.

(a) Since the little girl answers
(b) her parents say that
(c) she is too intelligent
(d) a few simple questions

4. The following sentence has been split into four segments (A), (B), (C) and (D). Identify the segment that contains a grammatical error.

It is difficult to live in (A) / the societal expectations (B) / when one has (C) / fewer resources (D).

(a) B (b) A
(c) D (d) C

Directions (Q. Nos. 5-9) *In the following passage, some words have been deleted. Read the passage carefully and select the most appropriate option to fill in each blank.*

Cities are the great havens for knowledge, culture and social life. Vibrant cultures are found in cities because it takes a (1)............... population to support museums, concert halls, sports teams, and night-life districts. Cities also offer rich social opportunities. People in rural areas enjoy only limited social opportunities because (2)............ the small local population. City dwellers can choose their friends and mates from among a large number of people of (3)............ interests and inclinations. We are not likely to abandon the city as a (4)............ institution, but we need to make sure that our transport arrangements do not (5)........... the city's other functions.

5. Select the most appropriate option to fill in blank no. 1.

(a) large (b) small
(c) lazy (d) dumb

6. Select the most appropriate option to fill in blank no. 2.

(a) off (b) with
(c) of (d) for

7. Select the most appropriate option to fill in blank no. 3.

(a) wasteful (b) declining
(c) similar (d) feigning

8. Select the most appropriate option to fill in blank no. 4.

(a) psychological (b) educational
(c) cultural (d) religious

9. Select the most appropriate option to fill in blank no. 5.

(a) boost (b) help
(c) damage (d) support

10. Select the most appropriate option that can substitute the underlined segment in the given sentence. If there is no need to substitute it, select 'No substitution required'.

Then I unfurled the Indian tri-colour and <u>keep</u> it aloft at the roof of the world.

(a) keeping
(b) held
(c) No substitution required
(d) hold

11. Select the most appropriate antonym of the underlined word.

She was known for her <u>refined</u> manners.

(a) crude (b) elegant
(c) shrewd (d) brood

12. Select the most appropriate homonym to fill in the blank.

Ravi is ....

(a) bawled (b) balled
(c) baled (d) bald

13. Select the most appropriate idiom to fill in the blank.

After a day long trek, we were so tired that we were ready to ....

(a) face the music
(b) get into deep water
(c) go from rags to riches
(d) hit the sack

14. Select the most appropriate synonym of the word 'intuitive' to fill in the blank.

In a split second, her .... reaction kicked in as she swiftly reached out to catch the falling glass.

(a) shrewd
(b) instinctive
(c) voluntary
(d) insightful

15. Select the most appropriate synonym of the word 'Abandon' from the given sentence.

Ramita has decided to forsake her participation in college activities until she improved her scores.

(a) Forsake
(b) Improved
(c) Decided
(d) Participation

16. Select the most appropriate idiom to fill in the blank.

The two brothers .... when their father died.

(a) fell down
(b) fell out
(c) got the sack
(d) look down upon

17. Select the most appropriate option that can substitute the underlined segment in the given sentence.

One of my best friends are here.

(a) better friends are here
(b) best friends is here
(c) better friends is here
(d) best friend is here

18. Select the most appropriate synonym of the underlined word in the given sentence.

We should not discriminate against people who are different from us.

(a) differentiate (b) divide
(c) part (d) sever

19. Select the most appropriate option to fill in the blank.

The teacher asked the students to .... electricity by switching off lights when they left the room.

(a) save (b) deposit
(c) rescue (d) retain

20. Select the option that will improve the underlined part of the given sentence.

This book provides an unrestrained account of the natural resources in India.

(a) exhausting (b) limlited
(c) exhaustive (d) excessive

21. Select the most appropriate antonym of the underlined word in the given sentence.

The truth was revealed in the interrogation.

(a) evident (b) found
(c) declared (d) concealed

22. Select the most appropriate antonym of the underlined word.

We should desecrate our national flag.

(a) integrate (b) sanctify
(c) violate (d) damage

23. Select the option that will improve the underlined part of the given sentence. In case no improvement is needed, select 'No improvement'.

The Privacy Shield establishes a process to allow companies to transfer consumer data from European Union countries to the United States in compliance in EU law.

(a) No improvement
(b) in compliance for the
(c) in compliance under the
(d) in compliance with

24. Identify the incorrectly spelt word and select its correct spelling.

This will sound weired, but bear with me.

(a) wired (b) beer
(c) weird (d) bier

25. Select the incorrectly spelt word.

(a) Betrey (b) Destroy
(c) Develop (d) Demolish

Part II
General Intelligence

26. How many semi-circles are there in the given figure?

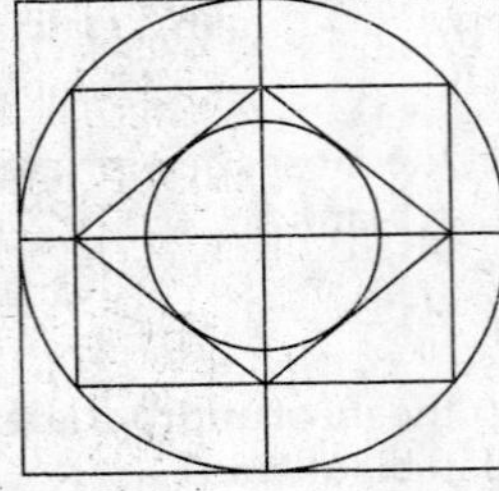

(a) 8 (b) 12 (c) 10 (d) 9

27. 'ETHICS' is related to 'AVDKYU' in a certain way based on the English alphabetical order. In the same way, 'CUSTOM' is related to 'YWOVKO'. To which of the following is 'PRINCIPLES' related, following the same logic?

(a) LSEPYKLNAU
(b) LTEPYKLNAU
(c) LTFPYKLNAU
(d) LTEPYKLMAU

28. 45 is related to 100 following a certain logic. Following the same logic, 65 is related to 140. To which of the following is 105 related, following the same logic?

(**Note** Operations should be performed on the whole numbers, without breaking down the numbers into their constituent digits. E.g. 13 – Operations on 13 such as adding /subtracting /multiplying to 13 can be performed. Breaking down 13 into 1 and 3 and then performing mathematical operations on 1 and 3 is not allowed.)

(a) 210 (b) 215 (c) 220 (d) 230

29. Three of the following letter-clusters are alike in some manner and hence form a group. Which letter-cluster does not belong to that group?

(**Note** The odd one out is not based on the number of consonants/ vowels or their position in the letter-cluster.)

(a) TBG (b) CKP (c) LTY (d) EMS

30. Identify the figure in the options that, when put in place of the question mark (?) will logically complete the series?

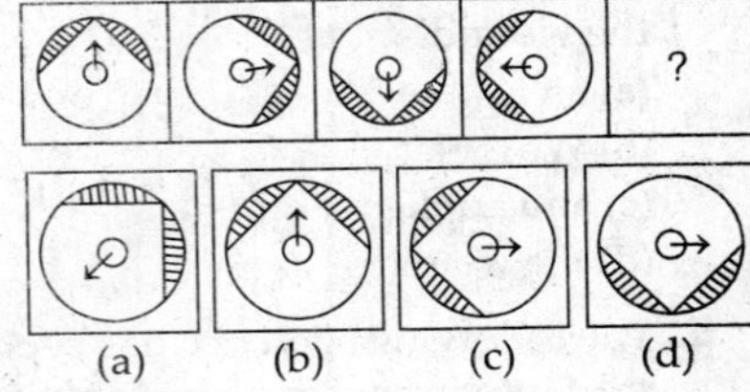

31. What should come in place of question mark (?) in the given series based on the English alphabetical order?

YQI, CZQ, GIY, KRG, ?

(a) DMX (b) EOZ (c) OAO (d) CNY

32. Select the option in which the given figure is embedded (Rotation is not allowed).

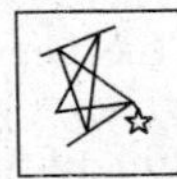

(a) 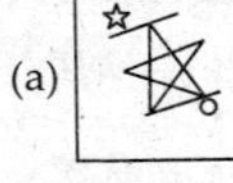 (b) 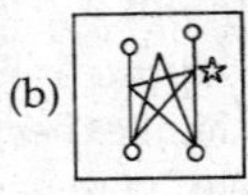

(c) 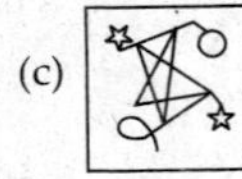 (d) 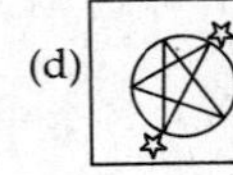

33. Which two numbers should be interchanged to make the given equation correct ?

$8 \times (7+5-3)+(46 \div 23) \times 6-69=44$

(**Note** Numbers must be interchanged and not the constituent digits e.g., if 2 and 3 are to be interchanged in the equation $43 \times 3 + 4 \div 2$, then interchanged equation is $43 \times 2 + 4 \div 3$)

(a) 6 and 7 (b) 3 and 5
(c) 46 and 69 (d) 8 and 6

34. The position of how many letters will remain unchanged, if each of the letters in the word DICTIONARY is arranged in alphabetical order?

(a) 4 (b) 1 (c) 3 (d) 2

35. In a certain code language, 'tiffin is heavy' is written as 'ct qm lb' and 'heavy weight gain' is written as 'rx yb ct'. How is 'heavy' written in the given language?

(a) ct (b) qm (c) lb (d) rx

36. Three statements are followed by conclusions numbered I and II. You have to consider these statements to be true, even if they seem to be at variance with commonly known facts. Decide which of the given conclusions logically follow(s) from the given statements.

Statements

Some bottles are pens.

All pens are tables.

All tables are glasses.

Conclusions

I. Some glasses are bottles.

II. Some pens are glasses.

(a) Only Conclusion I follows
(b) Only Conclusion II follows
(c) Both Conclusions I and II follow
(d) Neither Conclusion I nor II follows

37. In a certain code language,

'A + B' means 'A is the mother of B',

'A – B' means 'A is the brother of B',

'A × B' means 'A is the father of B',

'A ÷ B' means 'A is the daughter of B'.

Based on the above, how is E related to A, if 'A × B – C + D ÷ E'?

(a) Brother
(b) Daughter's husband
(c) Son
(d) Wife's brother

38. What should come in place of the question mark (?) in the given series?

27, 32, 42, 47, 57, ?

(a) 62 (b) 60
(c) 61 (d) 63

39. Select the option figure in which the given figure (X) is embedded as its part (rotation is not allowed).

(a)  (b) 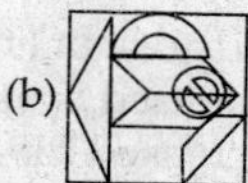

(c) 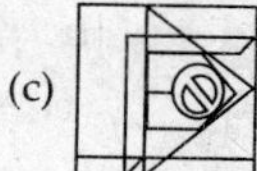 (d) 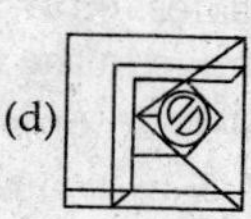

40. If 'A' stands for '÷', 'B' stands for '×', 'C' stands for '+' and 'D' stands for '–', then the resultant of which of the following will be 233?

(a) 21 C 11 D 33 A 11 B 5
(b) 21 A 11 D 33 B 11 C 5
(c) 21 B 11 D 33 A 11 C 5
(d) 21 B 11 A 33 D 11 C 5

41. Which of the following numbers will replace the question mark (?) in the given series?

12, 26, 54, ?, 222, 446

(a) 98 (b) 94
(c) 88 (d) 110

42. In a certain code language, 'INDULGE' is coded as '48' and 'PURGE' is coded as '24'. How will 'PUNY' be coded in that language?

(a) 25 (b) 20
(c) 18 (d) 15

43. The sequence of folding a piece of paper and the manner in which the folded paper is punched is shown in the following figures. How would this paper look when unfolded?

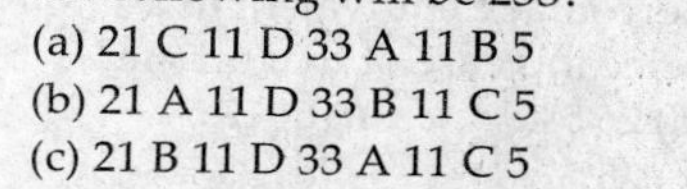

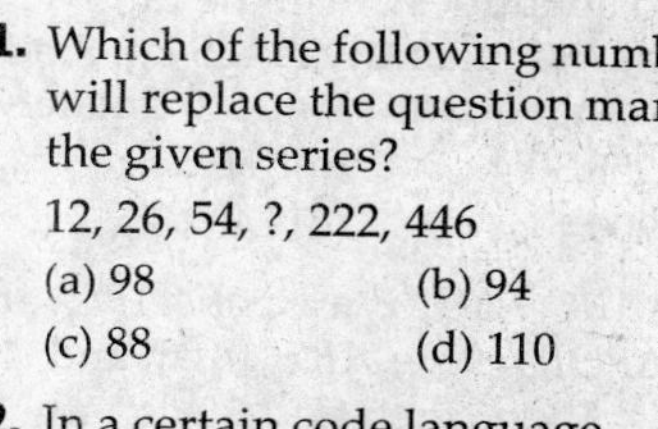

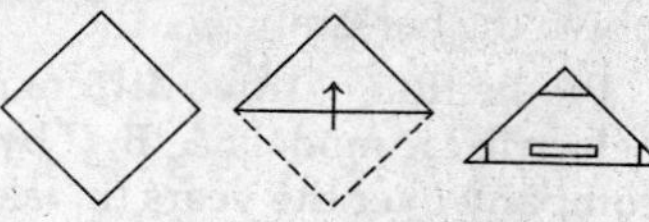

(a) 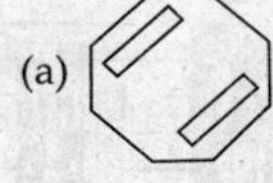 (b) 

(c) 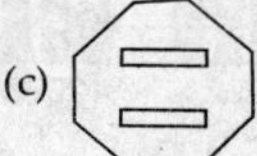 (d)

44. If 24th August, 1932 was a Wednesday, then what was the day of the week on 11th September, 1943?

(a) Monday (b) Saturday
(c) Wednesday (d) Sunday

45. Select the correct mirror image of the given figure, when the mirror is placed at MN as shown below.

K B V S Y X P C

M ―――――――― N

(a) K B V S Y X ь C
(b) Ɔ ᑫ X Y Ƨ V ᗺ ꓘ
(c) ꓘ B Λ Ƨ ⅄ X ь C
(d) K B Λ Ƨ ⅄ X ь C

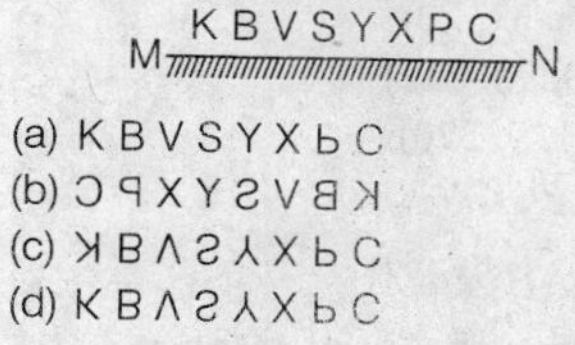

46. LH3 is related to RN21 in a certain way. In the same way, JF5 is related to PL35. To which of the following is ZV6 related following the same logic?

(a) FB45 (b) EA45
(c) FB42 (d) EA24

47. Select the correct mirror image of the given figure, when the mirror is placed at MN as shown below.

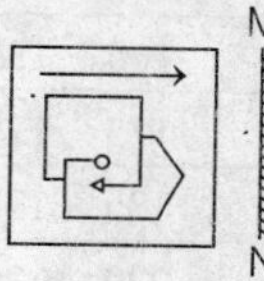

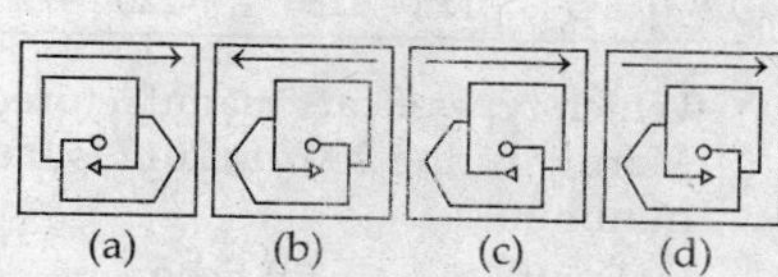

48. What will come in the place of question mark (?) in the following equation, if '+' and '–' are interchanged and '×' and '÷' are interchanged?

$90 \times 2 - 43 + 7 \div 7 = ?$

(a) 39 (b) 49 (c) 29 (d) 19

49. Which letter-cluster will replace the question mark (?) to complete the given series?

NDGB, OFJF, ?, TMSQ, XRYX

(a) QINK (b) QJNK
(c) RHNK (d) RINJ

50. Select the set in which the numbers are related in the same way as are the numbers of the following sets.

(**Note** Operations should be performed on the whole numbers, without breaking down the numbers into its constituent digits. E.g. 13 – Operations on 13 such as adding /subtracting /multiplying etc., to 13 can be performed. Breaking down 13 into 1 and 3 and then performing mathematical operations on 1 and 3 is not allowed.)

(26, 38, 128)
(42, 19, 122)

(a) (25, 36, 183)
(b) (18, 52, 70)
(c) (33, 23, 112)
(d) (71, 9, 320)

Part III
Quantitative Aptitude

51. The given table shows the number of 5 types of cars (Swift, Sx4, Ertiga, Zen, Echo) manufactured (in thousand) by Maruti over the years.

Years	Type of Cars				
	Swift	Sx4	Ertiga	Zen	Echo
2007	250	200	128	140	115
2008	200	230	150	155	120
2009	230	225	142	160	135
2010	245	210	170	175	125
2011	260	135	180	185	130
2012	275	155	230	220	120

Which type of cars manufactured by Maruti during 2007 to 2012 is the minimum?
(a) Swift (b) Echo
(c) Zen (d) Sx4

52. What is the number which needs to be added to 20% of 460 to have the sum as 70% of 920 ?
(a) 926 (b) 762
(c) 552 (d) 335

53. Simplify the following expression.
$[40 - 48 \div 4 \text{ of } 3] \div \{(6+4) - 4 \text{ of } 4 + 4 + (6-4) + (4 \times 4) \div 4\} \times 3$
(a) 25 (b) 27
(c) 30 (d) 26

54. Simplify
$$\left\{(3^3 + 2^3) \times \frac{22}{7}\right\} \times \left\{(6^2 + 3^2 - 4^2) \div \left(14\frac{1}{2}\right)\right\}$$
(a) 220 (b) 198
(c) 110 (d) 145

55. The shortest length of the intercept between the X-axis and Y-axis of the equation $6x + 8y - 48 = 0$ is
(a) 10 units (b) 6 units
(c) 14 units (d) 12 units

56. A and B, working together, take 15 days to complete a piece of work. If A alone can do this work in 18 days, then how long would B take to complete the same work?
(a) 33 days (b) 90 days
(c) 8 days (d) 15 days

57. The price of an article is first increased by 40% and then decreased by 45%, due to reduction in sales. Find the net percentage change in the final price of the article.
(a) –23% (b) 23%
(c) 13% (d) –13%

58. If price of an article increases successively by 15% and 10%, respectively, then what is the percentage equivalent to a single price increase of that article?
(a) 26.5% (b) 12.5%
(c) 25% (d) 23.5%

59. Two quantities are in the ratio 3 : 5. If the first quantity is 155 kg. Find the other quantity (approximately).
(a) 258.3 kg (b) 150.5 kg
(c) 200.4 kg (d) 240.6 kg

60. If $\Delta ABC \sim \Delta QRP$; area of ΔABC : area of $\Delta PQR = 9:4$; $AB = 18$ cm and $BC = 15$ cm, then find the length of PR.
(a) 15 cm (b) 10 cm
(c) 12 cm (d) 14 cm

61. Study the given bar-graph and answer the question that follows.
An electric vehicle company produces three different car models – A, B and C. The production of three different models over a period of four years (in lakhs) has been shown the bar-graph.

Production of three different electric car models A, B, C by a company over the years (in lakhs)

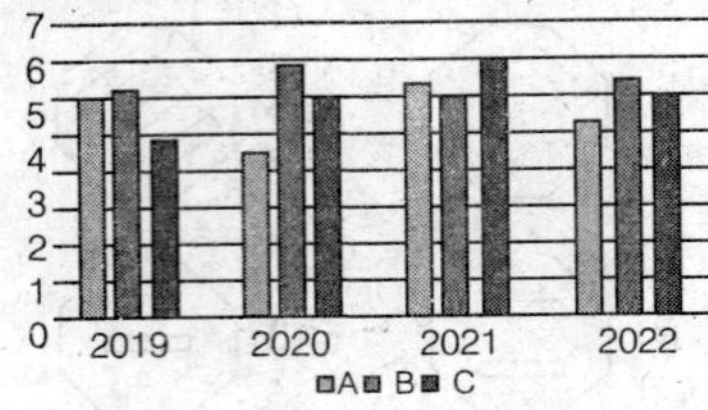

The total production of model C in 2021 and 2022 is what percentage of the total production of model A in 2019 and 2020 ?
(a) 102.26% (b) 105.22%
(c) 115.57% (d) 122.22%

62. Let C be a circle with Centre O and P be an external point to C. Let PQ and PR be the tangents to C, such that Q and R be the points of tangency, respectively.
If $\angle ROQ = 110°$, find $\angle RPQ$.
(a) 90° (b) 70° (c) 80° (d) 110°

63. An iron box with external dimensions 60 cm, 40 cm and 20 cm is made of 1 cm thick sheet. If 1 cm^3 of iron weighs 50 gm, the weight of the empty box is
(a) 214.05 kg (b) 240 kg
(c) 400 kg (d) 416.40 kg

64. Two circles of diameters 16 cm and 20 cm are such that the distance between their centres is 13 cm. What is the length (in cm) of a common tangent to these circles that does not intersect the line joining the centres?
(a) $\sqrt{165}$ (b) $\sqrt{173}$
(c) $\sqrt{167}$ (d) $\sqrt{163}$

65. Find the difference between the curved surface area and total surface area of a right circular cylinder having a length of 68 cm and base diameter of 28 cm.
(a) 1432 cm^2 (b) 1132 cm^2
(c) 1332 cm^2 (d) 1232 cm^2

66. If the diameter of a hemisphere is 42 cm, then the volume of hemisphere (in cm^3) is $\left(\text{Take } \pi = \frac{22}{7}\right)$
(a) 19404 (b) 19254
(c) 19154 (d) 19444

67. Study the given bar-graphs and answer the question that follows.

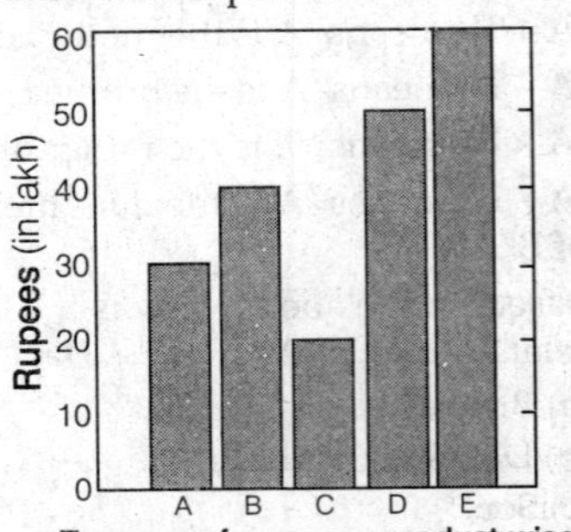

Turnover of company product-wise

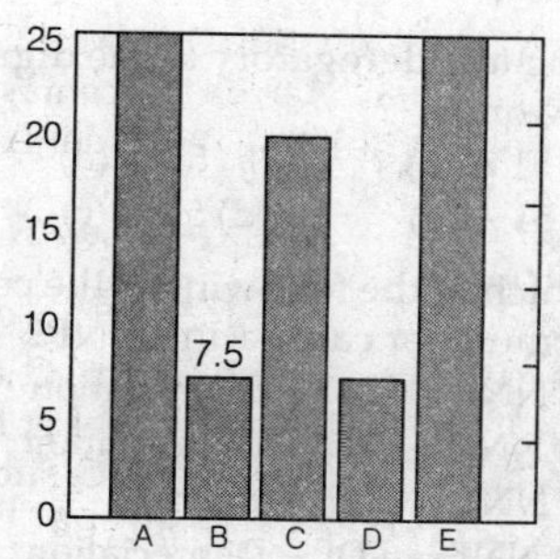

Profitability percentage of product

Turnover of Company X
(Product-wise: A, B, C, D and E)

Approximately what is the share in the total profit enjoyed by A and E together?

(a) 70% (b) 80%
(c) 60% (d) 50%

68. The perimeter of a triangle is 36 units. Its area cannot be more than

(a) $36\sqrt{2}$ (b) $36\sqrt{3}$
(c) $12\sqrt{7}$ (d) $18\sqrt{5}$

69. A shopkeeper marks an article at ₹150 and sells it at a discount of 25%. He also gives a gift worth ₹ 2.5. If he still makes a 10% profit, then the cost price (in ₹) of the article is

(a) 100 (b) 175
(c) 112 (d) 125

70. If θ is an acute angle and $\tan\theta + \cos\theta = 2$, then find the value of $\tan^3\theta + \cot^3\theta + 6\tan^3\theta\cot^2\theta$.

(a) 6 (b) 10 (c) 12 (d) 8

71. A policeman received information that a thief is at a distance of 1.5 km from him. The thief starts moving by car and the policeman chases him by car. The thief and the policeman are moving at the speeds of 90 km/h and 120 km/h, respectively.

At what distance (in km) will the police catch the thief?

(a) 45 km (b) 5 km
(c) 6 km (d) 4.5 km

72. A shopkeeper bought 288 oranges for ₹ 115.20. He sold 50 of them at 70 paise each and the remaining at ₹ 46.20. Find his profit or loss

(a) Profit, ₹ 25 (b) Loss, ₹ 34
(c) Profit, ₹ 37 (d) Loss, ₹ 36

73. Mithila covers 50 km by bus in 90 min. After deboarding the bus, she takes rest for 15 min and covers another 30 km by a taxi in 35 min. Find the average speed (in km/h) for the whole journey.

(a) $31\frac{2}{7}$ (b) $32\frac{2}{7}$ (c) $34\frac{2}{7}$ (d) $33\frac{2}{7}$

74. Find the total amount of debt that will be discharged by 5 equal instalments of ₹ 200 each, if the debt is due in 5 yr at 5% p.a. at simple interest.

(a) ₹ 1400 (b) ₹ 1100
(c) ₹ 1200 (d) ₹ 1255

75. Study the given bar-graph and answer the question that follows.

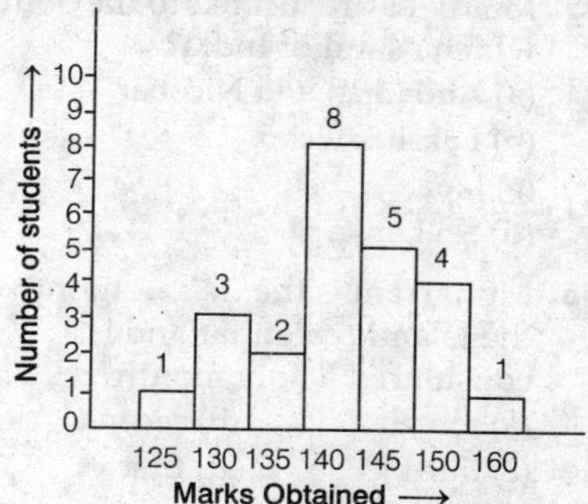

How many students obtained more than the average marks of the class?

(a) 11 (b) 6 (c) 10 (d) 8

Part IV

General Awareness

76. The Citizenship Act, 1955 does not deal with ....

(a) termination (b) election
(c) determination (d) acquisition

77. Which of the following animals can change their gender during their life span?

(a) Ascaris (b) Humans
(c) Nereis (d) Snail

78. Match the following renewable sources of energy with their producing regions in India correctly.

Renewable source of energy	Regions in India
A. Tidal energy	1. Gulf of Khambhat
B. Wind energy	2. Nagercoil
C. Geo Thermal energy	3. Puga valley

Codes

	A	B	C		A	B	C
(a)	2	3	1	(b)	1	2	3
(c)	2	1	3	(d)	3	2	1

79. Khubakeshei is a kind of song accompanied by clapping, sung in the state of ....

(a) Manipur (b) Bihar
(c) Karnataka (d) Odisha

80. Which of the following methods measures poverty on the basis of income and consumption levels?

(a) Poverty limit (b) Poverty line
(c) Poverty bar (d) Poverty band

81. The Lushai Hills are also known as ....

(a) Mizo Hills (b) Khasi Hills
(c) Patkai Hills (d) Naga Hills

82. Where is Birsa Munda International Hockey Stadium located?

(a) Bhubaneswar (b) Jamshedpur
(c) Ranchi (d) Rourkela

83. To enhance the interoperability between the Indian and Russian Armies, a joint training exercise called ...., commenced at Prudboy Ranges, Volgograd in the year 2021.

(a) SHAKTI 2021
(b) INDRA 2021
(c) SURYA KIRAN 2021
(d) VARUNA 2021

84. Which of the following is not one of the consequences of the Green Revolution?

(a) Rising prices and a shift in the mode of payment of agricultural workers from payment in cash to payment in kind (grain)
(b) The rich grew richer and many of the poor stagnated or grew poorer
(c) Wages of agricultural workers increased
(d) Employment of agricultural workers increased

85. Which of the following is the maximum file size that can be attached to an email message in Gmail?

(a) 100 MB (b) 200 MB
(c) 50 MB (d) 25 MB

86. The famous folk music 'Hekialeu' has its origin in which state?

(a) Tami Nadu (b) Nagaland
(c) Goa (d) Assam

87. The British Government passed a law in the year 1856. It was meant for which among the following social reforms?

(a) Abolition of the Practice of Sati
(b) Widow Remarriage

(c) Abolition of Practice of Child Marriage
(d) Law against Murdering of Female Child

88. A circular coil having 'n' turns produces a field .... times large as that produced by a single turn.
(a) 2n (b) n
(c) 4n (d) 3n

89. Which of the following statements is incorrect regarding the Coriolis force?
(a) It is absent at the equator.
(b) Deflection is less when the wind is high.
(c) It deflects the wind to the right in the North and left in the South.
(d) It is directly proportional to the angle of altitude.

90. Which of the following states is the best governed state in the large states category as per the Public Affairs Index, 2020, which was released by the Public Affairs Centre, a non-profit organisation?
(a) Odisha (b) Bihar
(c) Kerala (d) Uttar Pradesh

91. In April 2023, Wing Commander Deepika Misra received which of the following awards?
(a) Vayu Sena Medal
(b) Uttam Yudh Seva Medal
(c) Vir Chakra
(d) Shaurya Chakra

92. Gugga is the famous ritualistic dance of ...., which is performed in the procession taken out in memory of Gugga Pir.
(a) Puducherry
(b) Uttar Pradesh
(c) Haryana
(d) Jammu and Kashmir

93. What takes place when you click the Save button or press Ctrl + S in Microsoft Word?
(a) The document is copied to the clipboard.
(b) The document is printed.
(c) The document is closed.
(d) The document is saved in a disk file.

94. What is the colour of the sending off card in football?
(a) Black (b) Red
(c) Blue (d) Yellow

95. Maldives are located to the South of which island of India?
(a) Andaman and Nicobar
(b) Lakshadweep
(c) Japan
(d) Sri Lanka

96. Muharram is the .... month of the Islamic calendar and is considered a holy month.
(a) fourth (b) second
(c) third (d) first

97. Fighting in the upright position in judo is called ....
(a) Tachi-waza (b) Ne-waza
(c) Ashi-waza (d) Koshi-waza

98. At which place was the magnificent temple of Saiva constructed by the great Rashtrakuta king 'Krishna I'?
(a) Kanchi (b) Badami
(c) Kannauj (d) Ellora

99. Which of the following articles of the Constitution states that "It shall be the duty of every citizen of India to promote harmony and the spirit of common brotherhood amongst all the people of India transcending religious, linguistic and regional or sectional diversities; to renounce practices derogatory to the dignity of women"?
(a) 51 A (b) (b) 51 A (d)
(c) 51 A (e) (d) 51 A (c)

100. Which of the following is the correct formula for calculating NNP?
(a) NNP = GNP – Depreciation
(b) NNP = GNP + Depreciation
(c) NNP = GDP – Income
(d) NNP = GDP – Depreciation

Answers

1. (b)	2. (a)	3. (c)	4. (b)
5. (a)	6. (c)	7. (c)	8. (c)
9. (c)	10. (b)	11. (a)	12. (d)
13. (d)	14 (b)	15. (a)	16. (b)
17. (b)	18. (a)	19. (a)	20. (c)
21. (d)	22. (b)	23. (d)	24. (c)
25. (a)	26. (a)	27. (b)	28. (c)
29. (d)	30. (b)	31. (c)	32. (c)
33. (c)	34. (d)	35. (a)	36. (c)
37. (b)	38. (a)	39. (c)	40. (c)
41. (d)	42. (d)	43. (c)	44. (b)
45. (d)	46. (c)	47. (b)	48. (a)
49. (a)	50. (c)	51. (b)	52. (c)
53. (b)	54. (a)	55. (a)	56. (b)
57. (a)	58. (a)	59. (a)	60. (b)
61. (d)	62. (b)	63. (d)	64. (a)
65. (d)	66. (a)	67. (a)	68. (b)
69. (a)	70. (d)	71. (c)	72. (b)
73. (c)	74. (b)	75. (c)	76. (b)
77. (d)	78. (b)	79. (a)	80. (b)
81. (a)	82. (d)	83. (b)	84. (a)
85. (d)	86. (b)	87. (b)	88. (b)
89. (a)	90. (c)	91. (a)	92. (c)
93. (d)	94. (b)	95. (b)	96. (d)
97. (a)	98. (d)	99. (c)	100. (a)

Explanations

1. *(b)* The given sentence contains an error. The use of phrasal verb 'looking around' is incorrect. The correct phrasal verb is 'looking for' which means 'to search for' to correct the sentence.
2. *(a)* Part (a) 'an ice' contains an error. Remove 'an' to correct the sentence as ice is an uncountable noun.
3. *(c)* Part (c) 'she is too intelligent' contains an error. The use of 'too' is incorrect. Use 'very' to correct the sentence.
4. *(b)* Part (A) 'It is difficult to live in' contains an error. Use 'under' in place of 'in' to correct the sentence.
5. *(a)* The correct filler for the given blank is 'large'.
6. *(c)* The correct filler for the given blank is 'of'.
7. *(c)* The correct filler for the given blank is 'similar'.
8. *(c)* The correct filler for the given blank is 'cultural'.
9. *(c)* The correct filler for the given blank is 'damage'.
10. *(b)* The underlined part of the sentence contains an error.
    - The use of the word 'keep' is incorrect in the context as well as the past tense of the sentence.
    - Use 'held' to correct the sentence.
11. *(a)* 'Refined' means made pure by removing unwanted material. Hence, its antonym is 'crude' which means simple and not skilfully done or made.
    - 'Elegant' means beautiful and graceful.
    - 'Shrewd' means evil.
    - 'Brood' means a group.
12. *(d)* The correct filler for the given blank is 'bald', which means to not have any hair on the head.
13. *(d)* The correct idiom to fill in the blank is 'hit the sack', which means to go to sleep.
    - 'To face the music' means to get punished for your action.
    - 'To get into deep water' means to be in a difficult or awkward situation.
    - 'To go from rags to riches' means to become rich suddenly.
14. *(b)* The word 'intuitive' means using or based on what one feels to be true even without conscious reasoning; instinctive.
    - 'Shrewd' means clever.
    - 'Voluntary' means willing.
    - 'Insightful' means to give information.
15. *(a)* The word 'forsake' means to abandon or leave.
16. *(b)* The correct phrasal verb for the given blank is 'fell out', which means to argue with someone and stop being friendly with them.
    - 'Fell down' means to fall.
    - 'Got the sack' means to be removed from a job.
    - 'Look down upon' means to treat someone as unworthy.
17. *(b)* The underlined part of the sentence contains an error. Use 'best friends is here' to correct the sentence as the phrase 'one of...' takes a singular verb.
18. *(a)* The word 'discriminate' means to differentiate on the basis of race, gender, etc.
19. *(a)* The given sentence states the teacher's advice to save electricity. Hence, the correct filler for the given blank is 'save'.
20. *(c)* The underlined part of the sentence contains an error. The word 'unrestrained', which means 'not controlled', is not correct in the sentence. Use 'exhaustive' meaning that which can finish, to correct the sentence.
21. *(d)* The antonym of 'revealed' is 'concealed', which means 'hidden'.
22. *(b)* 'Desecrate' means to treat (a sacred place or thing) with violent disrespect. Hence, its antonym is 'sanctity' which means the state or quality of being holy, sacred, or saintly.

    'Integrate' means 'to join'.
23. *(d)* The underlined part of the sentence contains an error. Use 'in compliance with' to correct the sentence.
24. *(c)* The incorrectly spelt word is 'weired'. The correct spelling is 'weird'.
25. *(a)* The incorrectly spelt word is 'betrey'. The correct spelling is 'betray'.
26. *(a)* Naming the figure,

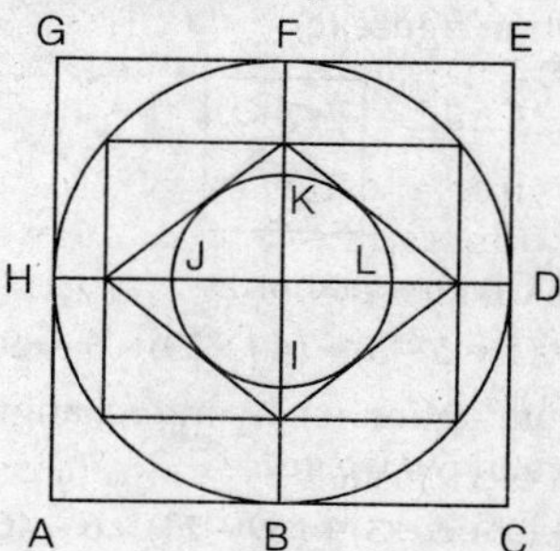

The number of semi-circles are given below,

HBD, BDF, DFH, FHB, JIK, ILK, LKJ, JIL = 8

∴ Total 8 semi-circles are present in the figure.

27. *(b)* As,

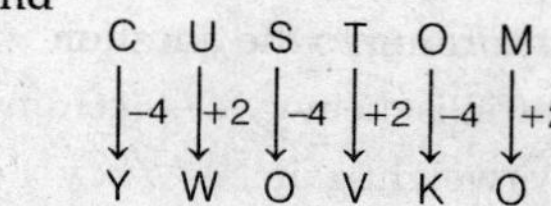

and

C U S T O M
−4 +2 −4 +2 −4 +2
Y W O V K O

Similarly,

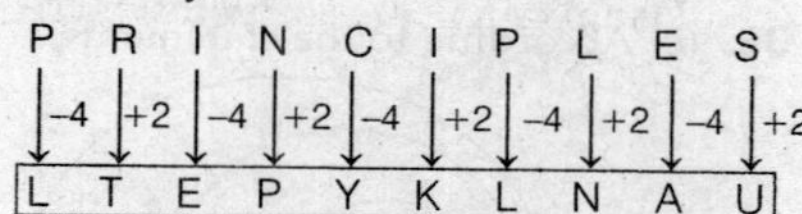

28. *(c)* As, $45 \rightarrow 45 \times 2 + 10 = 100$

and $65 \rightarrow 65 \times 2 + 10 = 140$

Similarly, $105 \rightarrow 105 \times 2 + 10 = \boxed{220}$

29. *(d)* As,

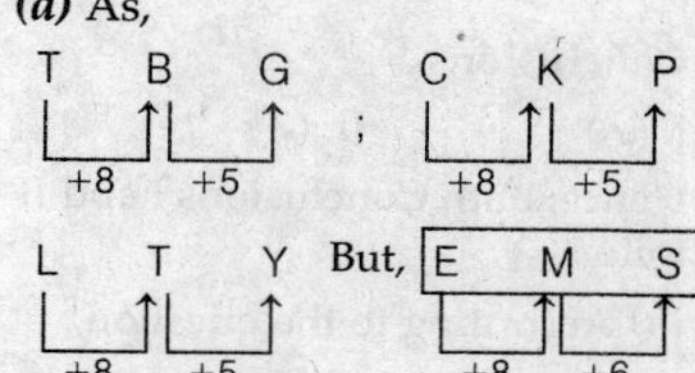

30. *(b)* The figure is moving 90° in clockwise direction.

Hence, figure given in option (b) will complete the series.

31. *(c)* The pattern followed by the series is given as follows,

$Y \xrightarrow{+4} C \xrightarrow{+4} G \xrightarrow{+4} K \xrightarrow{+4} \boxed{O}$

$Q \xrightarrow{+9} Z \xrightarrow{+9} I \xrightarrow{+9} R \xrightarrow{+9} \boxed{A}$

$I \xrightarrow{+8} Q \xrightarrow{+8} Y \xrightarrow{+8} G \xrightarrow{+8} \boxed{O}$

32. *(c)* The given figure is embedded in option figure (c).

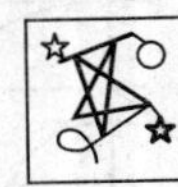

33. *(c)* Given equation,

$8\times(7+5-3)+(46\div 23)\times 6-69=44$

From option (c), by interchanging 46 and 69, we get

$8\times(7+5-3)+(69\div 23)\times 6-46=44$

$\Rightarrow \quad 8\times(9)+3\times 6-46=44$

$\Rightarrow \quad 72+18-46=44$

$\Rightarrow \quad 90-46=44$

$\Rightarrow \quad 44=44$

34. *(d)*

Given word →	D	I	C	T	I	O	N	A	R	Y
Alphabetical order of letters →	A	C	D	I	I	N	O	R	T	Y

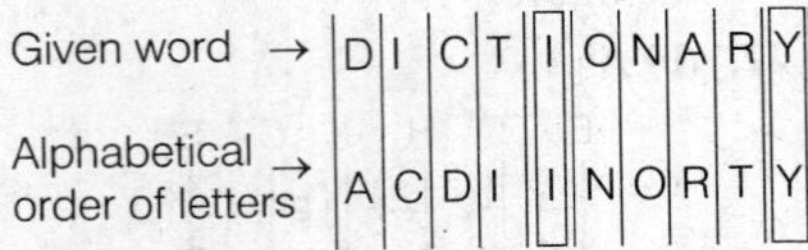

∴ Only 2 letters will remain unchanged.

35. *(a)* According to the question,

tiffin is heavy ⟶ ct qm lb

heavy weight gain ⟶ rx yb ct

∴ Code for heavy is 'ct'.

36. *(c)* According to the statements,

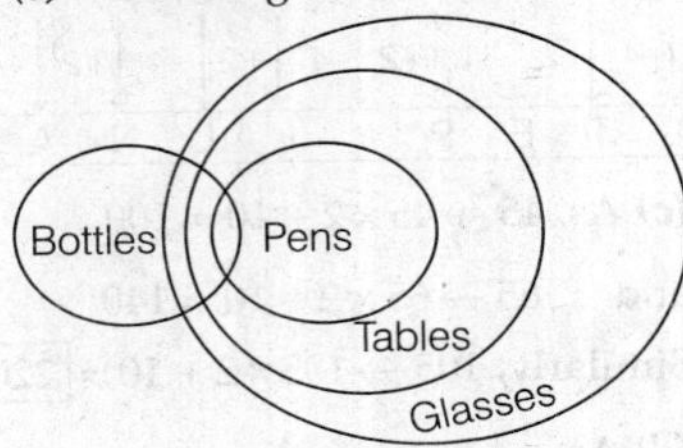

Conclusions

I. (✓) II. (✓)

Hence, both Conclusions I and II follow.

37. *(b)* According to the question,

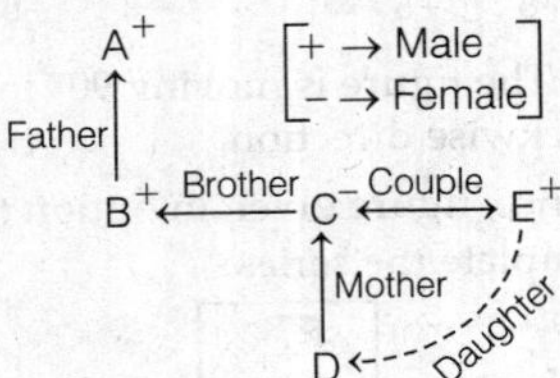

Hence, E is A's daughter's husband.

38. *(a)* The pattern of the series is as follows,

27 →(+5) 32 →(+10) 42 →(+5) 47 →(+10) 57 →(+5) [62]

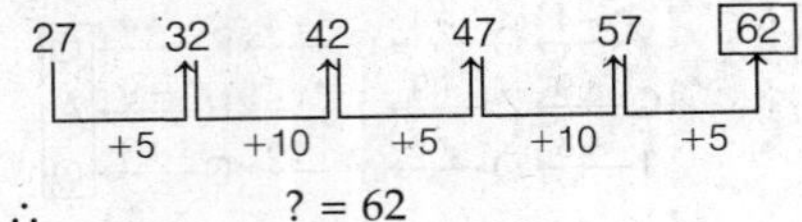

∴ ? = 62

39. *(c)* The given figure is embedded in option figure (c).

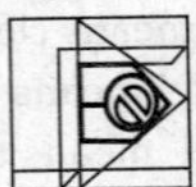

40. *(c)* According to the question,

A → ÷, B → ×, C → +, D → –

From option (c), replacing the letters with symbols

$=21\times 11-33\div 11+5$

$=231-3+5=236-3=233$

41. *(d)* The pattern of the series is as follows,

12 →(×2+2) 26 →(×2+2) 54 →(×2+2) [110] →(×2+2) 222 →(×2+2) 446

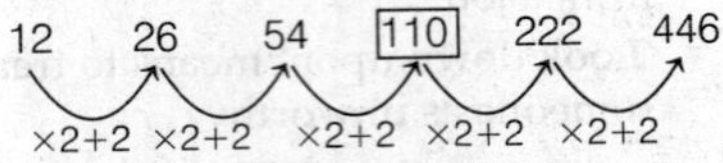

42. *(d)* As, INDULGE → (Total number of letters)^2 – 1

$=7^2-1=48$

and PURGE → (Total number of letters)^2 – 1

$=5^2-1=24$

Similarly, PUNY → $(4)^2-1=$ [15]

43. *(c)* When piece of paper is unfolded, it will look like option figure (c).

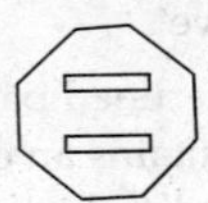

44. *(b)* Given, 24th August, 1932 → Wednesday

Number of odd days between 1932 to 1943

1933	1934	1935	1936	1937	1938	1939	1940	1941	1942	1943
1	+ 1	+ 1	+ 2	+ 1	+ 1	1	+ 2	+ 1	+ 1	+ 1

= 13 odd days

Number of odd days between 24th August, 1943 to 11th September, 1943

= 7 + 11 = 18 odd days

Total odd days $=\frac{13+18}{7}=\frac{31}{7}\Rightarrow 3$

∴ Day on 11th September, 1943

= Wednesday +3 = Saturday

45. *(d)* The figure given in option (d) is the correct mirror image of the given figure.

M K B V S Y X P C N

K B Λ S ⅄ X Ь C

46. *(c)* As,

L →(+6) R, H →(+6) N, 3 →(×7) 21

and

J →(+6) P, F →(+6) L, 5 →(×7) 35

Similarly, Z →(+6) F, V →(+6) B, 6 →(×7) 42

[F B 42]

47. *(b)* The mirror image of given figure is given below.

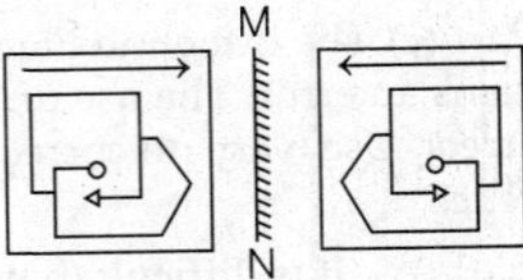

48. *(a)* Given expression,

$90\times 2-43+7\div 7=?$

After interchanging '+' and '–' and '×' and '÷', we get

$90\div 2+43-7\times 7=?$

$\Rightarrow \quad 45+43-49=?$

$\Rightarrow \quad ?=88-49$

$\therefore \quad ?=$ [39]

49. *(a)* The pattern of the series is as follows,

N →(+1) O →(+2) [Q] →(+3) T →(+4) X

D →(+2) F →(+3) [I] →(+4) M →(+5) R

G →(+3) J →(+4) [N] →(+5) S →(+6) Y

B →(+4) F →(+5) [K] →(+6) Q →(+7) X

50. *(c)* As,

(26, 38, 128) →

$(26+38)\times 2=64\times 2\Rightarrow 128$

and (42, 19, 122) →

$(42+19)\times 2=61\times 2\Rightarrow 122$

Similarly,

(33, 23, 112) →

$(33+23)\times 2=56\times 2=112$

51. *(b)* Total swift cars manufactured over the years

= 250 + 200 + 230 + 245 + 260 + 275

= 1460000

Total Sx4 cars manufactured over the years

= 200 + 230 + 225 + 210 + 135 + 155

= 1155000

Total Ertiga cars manufactured over the years

= 128 + 150 + 142 + 170 + 180 + 230

= 1000000

Total Zen cars manufactured over the years

= 140 + 155 + 160 + 175 + 185 + 220

= 1035000

Total Echo cars manufactured over the years

$= 115 + 120 + 135 + 125 + 130 + 120$

$= 745000$

∴ The manufacturing of car 'Echo' was minimum.

52. *(c)* Let the number added be x.

According to the question,

$$\frac{20}{100} \times 460 + x = \frac{70}{100} \times 920$$

$$\Rightarrow \quad 92 + x = 644 \Rightarrow x = 644 - 92$$

$$\therefore \quad x = 552$$

53. *(b)* Given equation,

$[40 - 48 \div 4 \text{ of } 3] \div [(6+4) - 4 \text{ of } 4 + 4 + (6-4) + (4 \times 4) \div 4] \times 3$

$= [40 - 48 \div 12] \div [10 - 16 + 4 + (6-4) + 16 \div 4] \times 3$

$= \left(40 - \frac{48}{12}\right) \div (10 - 16 + 4 + 2 + 4) \times 3$

$= \left(\frac{36}{4}\right) \times 3 = 27$

54. *(a)* Given equation,

$\left\{(3^3 + 2^3) \times \frac{22}{7}\right\} \times \left\{(6^2 + 3^2 - 4^2) \div \left(14\frac{1}{2}\right)\right\}$

$= \left\{(27+8) \times \frac{22}{7}\right\} \times \left\{(36 + 9 - 16) \div \frac{29}{2}\right\}$

$= \{5 \times 22\} \times \left\{(29) \div \frac{29}{2}\right\}$

$= 110 \times 2 = 220$

55. *(a)* Given equation, $6x + 8y - 48 = 0$

Length of intercept at X-axis, when $y = 0$

$$6x + 0 = 48$$

$$\Rightarrow \quad 6x = 48 \Rightarrow x = 8$$

$$\Rightarrow \quad x = (8, 0)$$

Length of intercept at Y-axis, when $x = 0$

$$0 + 8y = 48$$

$$\Rightarrow \quad 8y = 48 \Rightarrow y = 6 \Rightarrow y = (0, 6)$$

$\therefore$ Shortest length $= \sqrt{8^2 + 6^2}$

$= \sqrt{100} = 10$ units

56. *(b)* $(A + B)$'s 1 day's work $= \frac{1}{15}$

A's 1 day's work $= \frac{1}{18}$

$\therefore B$'s 1 day's work $= \left[\frac{1}{15} - \frac{1}{18}\right]$

$= \left[\frac{18 - 15}{18 \times 15}\right]$

$= \frac{3}{18 \times 15} = \frac{1}{90}$

Hence, total days taken by B to complete the work is 90 days.

57. *(a)* Net change

$$= \left[(40 - 45) + \frac{40 \times (-45)}{100}\right]\%$$

$$= [-5 + (-18)]\% = -23\%$$

58. *(a)* Single increased price

$$= \left[15 + 10 + \frac{15 \times 10}{100}\right]\%$$

$$= (25 + 1.5)\% = 26.5\%$$

59. *(a)* Given, ratio of two quantity = 3 : 5

First quantity = 155 kg

$\therefore$ Other quantity $= \frac{5}{3} \times 155$ kg

$= 258.3$ kg

60. *(b)* Given, $\Delta ABC \sim \Delta QRP$, $AB = 18$ cm

$BC = 15$ cm

We know that,

$$\frac{\text{Area } \Delta ABC}{\text{Area } \Delta QRP} = \frac{AB^2}{QR^2} = \frac{BC^2}{PR^2}$$

$$\frac{9}{4} = \frac{15^2}{PR^2} \Rightarrow PR^2 = \frac{225 \times 4}{9}$$

$$\Rightarrow \quad PR^2 = 100 \Rightarrow PR = 10 \text{ cm}$$

61. *(d)* Total production of model C in 2021 and 2022 = 6 + 5 = 11 lakhs

Total production of model A in 2019 and 2020 = 5 + 4 = 9 lakhs

$\therefore$ Required percentage $= \frac{11}{9} \times 100$

$= 122.22\%$

62. *(b)* According to the question,

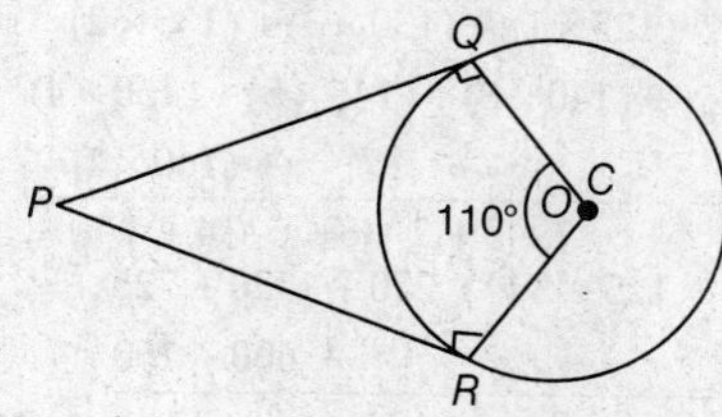

$$\angle P + \angle Q + \angle C + \angle R = 360°$$

$$\Rightarrow \angle P + 90° + 110° + 90° = 360°$$

$$\angle P = 360° - 290° = 70°$$

63. *(d)* Weight of empty box = [External volume of box – Internal volume of box] $\times \frac{50}{1000}$

$= [60 \times 40 \times 20 - 58 \times 38 \times 18] \times \frac{50}{1000}$

$= [48000 - 39672] \times \frac{1}{20}$

$= 8328 \times \frac{1}{20} = 416.40$ kg

64. *(a)* Here, $r_1 = \frac{16}{2} = 8$ cm

$r_2 = \frac{20}{2} = 10$ cm

$OO' = 13$ cm

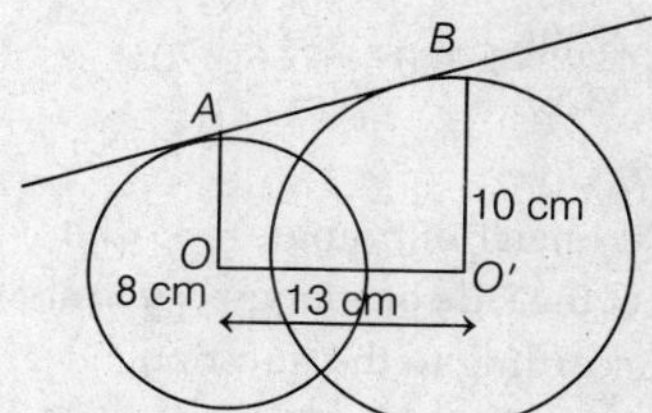

Length of common tangent

$= \sqrt{(13)^2 - (10-8)^2}$

$= \sqrt{169 - 4}$

$= \sqrt{165}$

65. *(d)* Given, length = height (h) of cylinder = 68 cm

Base diameter (d) = 28 cm

$\therefore$ Radius $(r) = \frac{d}{2} = \frac{28}{2} = 14$ cm

Curved surface area $= 2\pi rh$

$= 2 \times \frac{22}{7} \times 14 \times 68$

$= 5984 \text{ cm}^2$

Total surface area $= 2\pi r(h + r)$

$= 2 \times \frac{22}{7} \times 14(68 + 14)$

$= 2 \times 22 \times 2 \times 82$

$= 7216 \text{ cm}^2$

$\therefore$ Required difference

$= (7216 - 5984)$

$= 1232 \text{ cm}^2$

66. *(a)* Given, diameter of hemisphere = 42 cm

$\therefore \quad$ Radius $(r) = \frac{42}{2} = 21$ cm

Volume of hemisphere $= \frac{2}{3}\pi r^3$

$= \frac{2}{3} \times \frac{22}{7} \times 21 \times 21 \times 21$

$= 19404 \text{ cm}^3$

67. *(a)* From bar-graphs,

$\therefore$ Total profit

$$= \frac{\left(30L \times \frac{25}{100}\right) + \left(60L \times \frac{25}{100}\right)}{\left(30L \times \frac{25}{100}\right) + \left(40L \times \frac{7.5}{100}\right) + \left(20L \times \frac{20}{100}\right) + \left(50L \times \frac{7.5}{100}\right) + \left(60L \times \frac{25}{100}\right)} \times 100$$

$$= \frac{\frac{750L}{100} + \frac{1500L}{100}}{\frac{750L}{100} + \frac{300L}{100} + \frac{400L}{100} + \frac{375L}{100} + \frac{1500L}{100}} \times 100$$

$$= \frac{2250L}{3325L} \times 100 = 67.66 \sim 70\%$$

68. *(b)* Given,

Perimeter of triangle = 36 units

Let the side of triangle = a units

According to the question,

$\therefore \quad 3a = 36$ units

$a = 12$ units

$\therefore$ As, all 3 sides of triangle are equal. Hence, it is an equilateral triangle.

$\therefore$ Area of equilateral triangle

$= \frac{\sqrt{3}}{4} \times \text{side}^2 = \frac{\sqrt{3}}{4} \times 12 \times 12$ units

$= 36\sqrt{3}$ units

Hence, area of triangle cannot be more than $36\sqrt{3}$ units.

69. *(a)* Marked price of article = ₹ 150

$\therefore$ Discount $= \left(150 \times \frac{25}{100}\right) + 2.5$

$= (37.5 + 2.5) =$ ₹ 40

$\therefore$ Selling price = 150 − 40 = ₹ 110

Cost price $= 110 \times \frac{100}{110} =$ ₹ 100

70. *(d)* $\tan\theta + \cot\theta = 2$

$\Rightarrow \tan\theta + \frac{1}{\tan\theta} = 2 \Rightarrow \frac{\tan^2\theta + 1}{\tan\theta} = 2$

$\Rightarrow \tan^2\theta - 2\tan\theta + 1 = 0$

$\Rightarrow \quad (\tan^2\theta - 1)^2 = 0$

$\tan\theta = 1 \Rightarrow \theta = 45°$

Now,

$\tan^3 45° + \cot^3 45° + 6\tan^3 45° \cot^2 45°$

$= (1)^3 + (1)^3 + 6(1)^3 \cdot (1)^2 = 8$

71. *(c)* Given,

Speed of police = 120 km/h

Speed of thief = 90 km/h

Distance between them = 1.5 km

Time when police catch the thief

$= \frac{3}{2(120 - 90)} \quad \left[\because \text{Time} = \frac{\text{Distance}}{\text{Speed}}\right]$

$= \frac{3}{2 \times 30} = \frac{1}{20}$

Distance covered by police in $\frac{1}{20}$ h

$= \frac{1}{20} \times 120$

$[\because \text{Distance} = \text{Speed} \times \text{Time}]$

$= 6$ km

72. *(b)* Cost price of 288 oranges

= 11520 paisa

Selling price of 50 oranges = 50×70

= 3500 paisa

Remaining 238 he sold for ₹ 46.20

= 4620 paisa

Total selling price = 3500 + 4620

= 8120 paisa

Loss = 11520 − 8120 = 3400 paisa

= ₹ 34

73. *(c)* Total distance covered by Mithila

= 50 + 30 = 80 km

Total time taken by Mithila

= (90 + 15 + 35) min = 140 min

$\therefore$ Average speed $= \frac{80}{\frac{140}{60}}$

$= 34.28 \sim 34\frac{2}{7}$ km/h

74. *(b)* Let principal = ₹ P

According to the question,

$P = (200 \times 5) + \left(200 \times \frac{5}{100} \times 4\right) + \left(200 \times \frac{5}{100} \times 3\right) + \left(200 \times \frac{5}{100} \times 2\right) + \left(200 \times \frac{5}{100} \times 1\right)$

$\Rightarrow \quad P = [1000 + 40 + 30 + 20 + 10]$

$\therefore \quad P =$ ₹ 1100

75. *(c)* From bar-graph,

Average marks of class

$$= \frac{(125 \times 1) + (130 \times 3) + (135 \times 2) + (140 \times 8) + (145 \times 5) + (150 \times 4) + (160 \times 1)}{1 + 3 + 2 + 8 + 5 + 4 + 1}$$

$$= \frac{125 + 390 + 270 + 1120 + 725 + 600 + 160}{24}$$

$$= \frac{3390}{24} = 141.25$$

Students who obtained more than average marks = 5 + 4 + 1 = 10

76. *(b)* The Citizenship Act, 1955 does not deal with election.

- The Citizenship Act, 1955 deals with acquisition, determination and termination of citizenship.
- The acquisition of citizenship is acquired by birth, descent, registration, naturalisation and incorporation of territory.

77. *(d)* Snail can change their gender during life span.

- Snails are hermaphradites, meaning they possess both male and female reproductive organs and can switch genders depending on the situation.
- When the two snails detach, each snail has egg fertilised by the sperm of the snail.

78. *(b)* The correct matching is A-1, B-2 and C-3.

- Tidal energy is produced in Gulf of Khambhat, Gujarat State.
- Wind energy is produced in Nagercoil, Tamil Nadu.
- Geothermal energy is produced in Puga Valley, Ladakh.

79. *(a)* Khubakeshei is a kind of song accompanied by clapping, sung in the state of Manipur.

- Domkach is folk dance of Bihar and Jharkhand performed in marriage ceremonies.
- Ban-Vara is song usually sung by Hindus during cremation.
- Gha-To-Kito dance is folk dance of Sikkim.

80. *(b)* Poverty line measures poverty on basis of income and consumption levels.

- It categorises people as above and below poverty line.
- It depends on income of the household and their expenditure level.
- Tendulkar Committe (2009), Lakdawal Committee (1993), Alagh Committee are some committees for poverty estimation.

81. *(a)* Lushai Hills are also known as Mizo Hills.

- The Mizo Hills are part of the larger Patkai range located in Mizoram.
- The Mizo Hills are also home to number of endangered and endemic species of fauna.
- The average elevation of the hills are 400 metre, but height is Phawngpui (Blue mountain).

82. *(d)* Birsa Munda International Hockey Stadium is located in Rourkela.

- It became the venues for 15th Men's Hockey World Cup.
- Kalinga Stadium is located in Bhubaneswar.

83. *(b)* To enhance the interoperability between Indian and Russian Armies, a joint training exercise called INDRA

2021 commenced at Prudboy Ranges, Volgarad in the year 2021.

- SURYA-KIRAN 2021 was joint-military exercise between Indian and Nepalese Armies.
- VARUNA 2021 was bilateral naval exercise between Indian and French Armies.
- SHAKTI 2021 was joint military exercise between Indian and French Armies.

84. *(a)* "Rising prices and a shift in mode of payment of agricultural workers from payment in cash to payment in kind (grain)" is not the consequence of Green Revolution.

- Worldwide, father of Green Revolution is Norman Borlaug and MS Swaminathan is regarded as father of Green Revolution in India.
- The Green Revolution increased the production of food grains using the High-Yielding Varieties of seeds.

85. *(d)* Maximum file size that can be attached to email message in Gmail is 25 MB.

- It includes message, headers, encoded attachments.
- If it exceeds 25 MB limit, it automatically added to Google drive.

86. *(b)* 'Hekialeu' folk music belongs to North-Eastern state of Nagaland.

- The young and old of Nagaland involve them in making of Hekialeu song.
- Romatic themes are selected for this song.

87. *(b)* Widow Remarriage Law was passed by British Government in 1856, allowing Hindu widows to remarry.

- This act was enacted by the tireless efforts of social reformer Ishwar Chandra Vidyasagar.
- Lord Canning was Governor-
- Lord Canning was Governor-General during enactment of this act.

88. *(b)* A circular coil with '*n*' turns produces a magnetic field that is '*n*' times stronger that the field produced by a single turn. This is based on the principle of magnetic fields, where the field strength increases proportionally with the number of turns.

89. *(a)* The incorrect statement regarding coriolis force is (a) because coriolis force is not absent at the equator. Coriolis force is maximum at equator and zero at the pole.

90. *(c)* Kerala is the best governed state in large states category as per the Public Affairs Index, 2020, released by Public Affairs Centre, a non-profit organisation.

- In small states, Goa ranked first, followed by Meghalaya and Himachal Pradesh.
- Among union territories, Chandigarh emerged at top, followed by Puducherry and Lakshadweep.

91. *(a)* In April 2023, Wing Commander Deepika Misra received Vayu Sena Medal.

- The Vir Chakra is India's third highest military award for gallantry in wartime.
- Uttam Seva Medal is one of the India's military decoration for wartime.
- The Shaurya Chakra is Indian military decoration awarded for valour, courageous action or self-sacrifice, while not engaged in direct action with enemy.

92. *(c)* 'Gugga' is famous ritualistic dance of Haryana, which is performed in the procession taken out in memory of Gugga Pir.

- This dance is typically performed during the Bhadon month (August-September) on occasion of Gugga Navami.
- This dance is performed by male dancers in group with colourful attires and musical instrument.

93. *(d)* The document is saved in a disk when click the save button or press Ctrl+S is Microsoft wrod.

94. *(b)* Red card is the colour of the sending off card in football.

- A yellow card is shown by the referee to indicate that a player has been officially cautioned or warned.
- Blue card is shown when players temporarily suspended from play for 2 minutes.
- Black card is shown to remove a player from competition when he breaks code of honour.

95. *(b)* Maldives are located to South of Lakshadweep Island.

- Maldives is a chain of 1192 islands located South-West of Sri Lanka and India in Indian Ocean.
- It consists of approximately 1192 coral islands, 26 atolls, distributed over approximately 90,000 square kilometres. It along with the Chagos and the Lakshadweep, froms a terrestrial ecoregion.

96. *(d)* Muharram is the first month of Islamic calender and is considered holy month.

- The word 'Muharram' means 'forbidden' in Arabic.
- Ashura, the tenth day of Muharram, is most significant day of this month.
- It is observed by both Sunni and Shia Muslims.

97. *(a)* Fighting in the upright position in judo is called Tachi - waza.

- Ne-waza is technique to hold down an opponent and limit his movement.
- Koshi-waza is technique that uses hips and waist as the main focus.
- Ashi-waza is technique including sweeping, reaping and hooking.

98. *(d)* At Ellora, magnificent temple of Saiva constructed by the great Rastrakuta king 'Krishna I'.

- He was a great patron of art and architecture. The Kailasha temple at Ellora, Cave 16, is the largest of 34 Buddhist, Jain and Hindu cave temples.

99. *(c)* According to 51A (e), it shall be the duty of the every citizen of India to promote harmony and the spirit of common brotherhood amongst all the people of India transcending religious, linguistic and regional or sectional diversities to renounce practices derogatory to the dignity of women.

100. *(a)* NNP = GNP – Depreciation

- Net National Product (NNP) is calculated by subtracting the depreciation from Gross National Product (GNP).
- NNP is the total market value of the goods and services produced by a nation during specified period with depreciation subtracted from it.

Set 08 02 July, 2024 (Shift IV)

SSC CHSL Tier-I SOLVED PAPER

Instructions

1. This paper contains 100 questions.
2. It has 4 Parts, **Part I** General English, **Part II** General Intelligence & Reasoning, **Part III** Quantitative Aptitude and **Part IV** General Awareness.
3. Each question carries **2 marks**.

Part I

General English

1. Identify the grammatical error in the following sentence and select the correct tense from the options given below.

I have met my friend yesterday.

(a) had been meeting
(b) was meeting
(c) met my friend
(d) have been meeting

2. The following sentence has been split into four segments. Identify the segment that contains a grammatical error.

The teacher was / taken back by/ the audacity of (c)/ the new student.
A B C D

(a) D (b) C
(c) A (d) B

3. Select the most appropriate article to fill in the blank.

.... bed you sleep in is broken.

(a) A (b) On
(c) The (d) An

4. Select the option that will improve the given sentence by using the most appropriate verb.

That Macbook belong to Xavier.

(a) That Macbook is belonged to Xavier.
(b) That Macbook belongs to Xavier.
(c) That Macbook belonging to Xavier.
(d) That Macbook is belong to Xavier.

Directions (Q. Nos. 5-9) *In the following passage, some words have been deleted. Read the passage carefully and select the most appropriate option to fill in each blank.*

It is generally (1) .... that the methodology of teaching-learning is the concern of teachers only. Learners have (2) .... or nothing to do with it. But this is not true. The teaching-learning (3) .... are concerns of learners as well. Knowing and understanding that how different subjects are taught are important for the learners of all subjects, but it has more (4) .... for the learners of physical education. When we talk about you as learners of physical education, we mean that you have actually participated in the subject area, rather than (5) ...... studied it.

5. Select the most appropriate option to fill in blank no. (1).

(a) hoped
(b) wished
(c) planned
(d) believed

6. Select the most appropriate option to fill in blank no. (2).

(a) light (b) minute
(c) little (d) sparse

7. Select the most appropriate option to fill in blank no. (3).

(a) forms (b) breaks
(c) customs (d) methods

8. Select the most appropriate option to fill in blank no. (4).

(a) reference
(b) recurrence
(c) relevance
(d) consistency

9. Select the most appropriate option to fill in blank no. (5).

(a) merely
(b) hardly
(c) purely
(d) entirely

10. Select the most appropriate meaning of the given idiom.

On its last legs

(a) Creeping on legs
(b) Last choice
(c) Slow movement
(d) In a bad condition

11. Select the most appropriate antonym of the underlined word in the following sentence.

The upshot of the consultation with the doctor was an operation scheduled for the next week.

(a) blame (b) cause
(c) result (d) estimate

12. Select the most appropriate idiomatic expression that can substitute the underlined segment in the given sentence.

It feels like I made a promise of more than my ability when I promised to complete this worksheet in one day.

(a) beat my brain out
(b) beat the drum
(c) bit off more than I could chew
(d) burnt a hole in my pocket

13. Select the most appropriate option that can substitute the underlined segment in the given sentence.

It will take two hours to walk across the forest.

(a) through
(b) over
(c) away
(d) between

14. Select the most appropriate option that can substitute the underlined segment in the given sentence.

The wizard, while performing an item, accidentally set his own hat on fire and prompted the fire alarm to go on.

(a) the fire alarm to go away
(b) the fire alarm to go under
(c) the fire alarm to go off
(d) the fire alarm to go above

15. Identify the incorrectly spelt word and select its correct spelling.
Maybe he wanted to make sure he didn't embarrese her.
(a) sware (b) shure
(c) embarrass (d) emberess

16. Select the most appropriate antonym of the underlined word in the given sentence.
The plot of the novel is very dull.
(a) diverting (b) riveting
(c) plodding (d) charming

17. Select the most appropriate option that collocates with 'wish' to fill in the blank.
The genie asked Aladdin to .... a wish.
(a) make (b) take (c) ask (d) tell

18. Select the most appropriate synonym of the given word.
Remission
(a) Pardon (b) Retribution
(c) Punishment (d) Overlook

19. Read the sentence carefully and select the most appropriate option to substitute the underlined part.
You can be sentenced for trespassing on someone else's property.
(a) conspiring against others
(b) entering without permission
(c) leaving without permission
(d) showing unselfish devotion

20. Select the most appropriate synonym of the underlined word.
Let us assume that we will do the job honestly.
(a) allow (b) think
(c) take (d) give

21. Select the most appropriate option to fill in the blank.
She could easily eat the .... biryani by herself.
(a) whole (b) haul
(c) hall (d) hole

22. Select the option that rectifies the spelling of the underlined word in the given sentence.
It has been a usual ocurrence for a few days now.
(a) occerrence (b) occurrance
(c) occurence (d) occurrence

23. Select the most appropriate option that can substitute the underlined segment in the given sentence. If there is no need to substitute it, select 'No improvement required'.
We set up on the journey early in the morning.
(a) set off
(b) set in
(c) No improvement required
(d) set about

24. Select the most appropriate antonym of the word given in the bracket to fill in the blank.
The State media houses present .... (vociferous) views compared to private media.
(a) political (b) biased
(c) mild (d) assertive

25. Select the most appropriate antonym of the underlined word in the given sentence.
Few people turned up to attend the tawdry promo of the new movie.
(a) elegant (b) showy
(c) inferior (d) gawdy

Part II

General Intelligence

26. What should come in place of question mark (?) in the given series based on the English alphabetical order?
SLE, CXS, ?, WVU, GHI
(a) COR (b) HAP
(c) OWG (d) MJG

27. Select the correct mirror image of the given figure when the mirror is placed at MN.

M
Rf6y7e
N

(a) ɘ7y∂fЯ
(b) e7λ∂fЯ
(c) ɵ7y9fR
(d) ɵ7y97Я

28. Three of the following four are alike in a certain way and thus form a group. Which is the one that does not belong to that group?
(**Note** The odd one out is not based on the number of consonants/vowels or their position in the letter cluster.)
(a) MPR (b) TWY
(c) BEG (d) JMN

29. Select the letter-cluster pair that best represents a similar relationship to the one expressed in the pairs of letter-clusters given below.
GKI : MQO
CGE : IMK
(a) HLJ : NRO (b) LPN : RVT
(c) RUT : VZX (d) JOM : PUR

30. Select the correct mirror image of the given combination when the mirror is placed at MN as shown below.

M
5@hRp7
N

(a) 7qЯh@5
(b) 7qЯh@ꙅ
(c) 7qRh@ꙅ
(d) 7dRh@5

31. 9 is related to 47 following a certain logic. Following the same logic, 12 is related to 62. To which of the following is 17 related, following the same logic?
(**Note** Operations should be performed on the whole numbers, without breaking down the numbers into their constituent digits. E.g. 13 – Operations on 13 such as adding/ subtracting /multiplying to 13 can be performed. Breaking down 13 into 1 and 3 and then performing mathematical operations on 1 and 3 is not allowed.)
(a) 97 (b) 87
(c) 85 (d) 75

32. Select the word-pair that best represents a similar relationship to the one expressed in the pair of words given below.
(The words must be considered as meaningful English words and must not be related to each other based on the number of letters/number of consonants/vowels in the word)
Happy : Ecstatic
(a) Loyal : Betray
(b) Honest : Deceptive
(c) Polite : Courteous
(d) Progress : Stagnation

33. What should come in place of the question mark (?) in the given series?

3, 10, 24, ?, 73, 108, 150, 199

(a) 40 (b) 30
(c) 35 (d) 45

34. 'A + B' means 'A is the brother of B'.
'A – B' means 'A is the sister of B'.
'A × B' means 'A is the father of B'.
'A ÷ B' means 'A is the mother of B'.
Using the same meaning of the mathematical operators as given above, which of the following shows 'P is the father's father of S'?

(a) P – Q + R ÷ S (b) P × Q × R + S
(c) P + Q – R ÷ S (d) P + Q ÷ R × S

35. If 'A' stands for '÷', 'B' stands for '×', 'C' stands for '+' and 'D' stands for '–', what will come in place of the question mark (?) in the following equation?

95 B 8 D 12 A 2 C 16 = ?

(a) 710 (b) 750
(c) 730 (d) 770

36. Each of the letters in the word FRAMED is arranged in alphabetical order. How many letters are there in the English alphabetical series between the letter which is second from the left and the one which is second from the right in the new letter-cluster thus formed?

(a) Nine (b) Eight
(c) Six (d) Seven

37. If 'A' stands for '÷', 'B' stands for '×', 'C' stands for '+' and 'D' stands for '–', what will come in place of the question mark (?) in the following equation?

11 B 11 D 68 A 4 C 4 = ?

(a) 106 (b) 102
(c) 108 (d) 104

38. A square sheet of paper is folded along the dotted line successively along the directions shown and is then punched in the last. How would the paper look when unfolded?

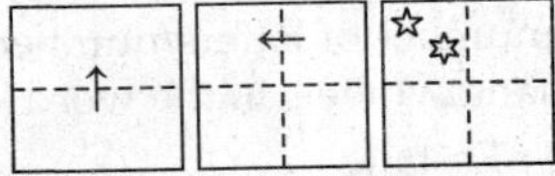

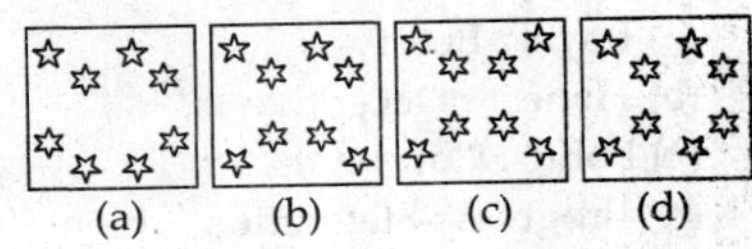

39. In a certain code language, 'BROW' is coded as '7542' and 'WORM' is coded as '7295'. What is the code for 'B' in the given code language?

(a) 2 (b) 9 (c) 4 (d) 7

40. How many triangles are there in the following figure?

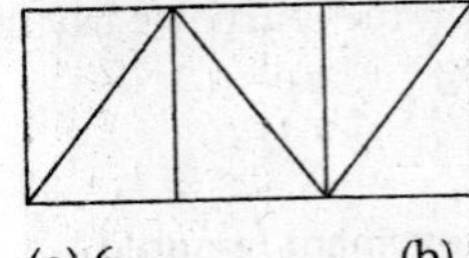

(a) 6 (b) 5
(c) 7 (d) 8

41. What will come in the place of '?' in the following equation, if '+' and '×' are interchanged and '–' and '÷' are interchanged?

90 – 10 × 36 + 52 ÷ 49 = ?

(a) 654 (b) 1832
(c) 879 (d) 567

42. Each of the letters in the word JUSTICE are arranged in alphabetical order. How many letters are there in the English alphabetical series between the letter that is second from the left and the one that is fourth from the right in the new letter-cluster thus formed ?

(a) 6 (b) 4
(c) 7 (d) 5

43. Which of the following numbers will replace the question mark (?) in the given series?

12, 60, 20, 100, 60, 300, 260, ?

(a) 1300 (b) 1160
(c) 1240 (d) 1280

44. What should come in place of the question mark (?) in the given series based on the English alphabetical order?

ECF, JHK, OMP, TRU, ?

(a) YWZ (b) XVZ
(c) XYZ (d) YVZ

45. Three statements are followed by conclusions numbered I and II. You have to consider these statements to be true, even if they seem to be at variance with commonly known facts. Decide which of the given conclusions logically follow(s) from the given statements.

Statements

All fire is water.
Some water is earth.
No earth is air.

Conclusions

I. Some fire is earth.
II. Some fire is air.

(a) Neither Conclusion I nor II follows
(b) Only Conclusion II follows
(c) Both Conclusions I and II follow
(d) Only Conclusion I follows

46. Select the correct mirror image of the given combination, when the mirror is placed at MN as shown below.

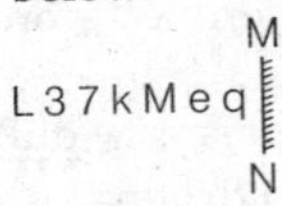

(a) Meqʞ٢Ɛ⅃
(b) pɘMʞ٢Ɛ⅃
(c) bɘMʞLƐ⅂
(d) pɘMʞLƐL

47. Select the option in which the given figure (X) is embedded (rotation is not allowed).

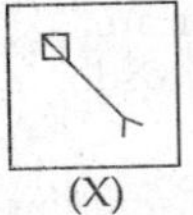

(X)

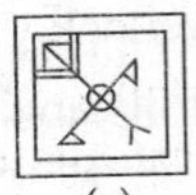
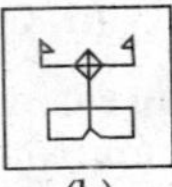

(a) (b) (c) (d)

48. Which figure should replace the question mark (?), if the following figure series were to be continued?

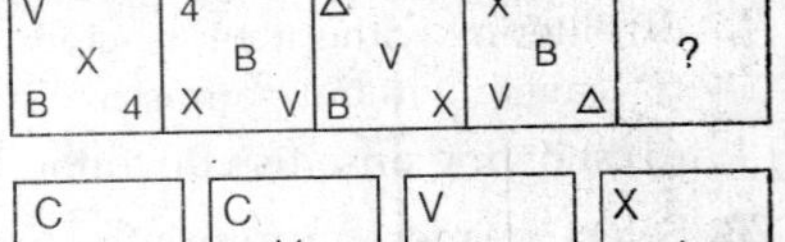

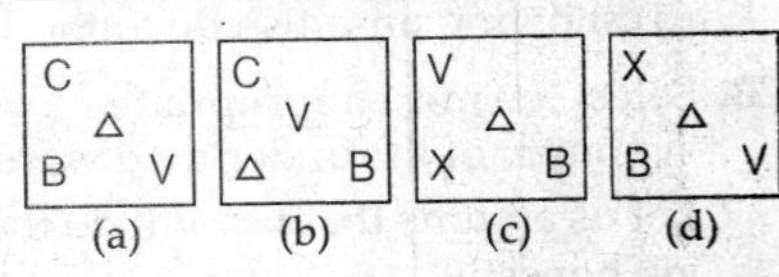

(a) (b) (c) (d)

49. In a certain code language, 'SORT' is coded as '4698' and 'RUST' is coded as '6429'. How is 'O' coded in the given language?

(a) 6 (b) 9 (c) 4 (d) 8

50. Select the set in which the numbers are related in the same way as are the numbers of the following sets.

(**Note** Operations should be performed on the whole numbers, without breaking down the numbers into its constituent digits. E.g. 13 – Operations on 13 such as adding/subtracting/multiplying etc.

to 13 can be performed. Breaking down 13 into 1 and 3 and then performing mathematical operations on 1 and 3 is not allowed.)

(18, 7, 119)

(11, 9, 90)

(a) (13, 5, 58) (b) (16, 5, 65)
(c) (12, 4, 44) (d) (17, 6, 102)

Part III

Quantitative Aptitude

51. If $\sqrt{13}\sin\theta = 2$, then the value of $\dfrac{3\tan\theta + \sqrt{13}\sin\theta}{\sqrt{13}\cos\theta - 3\tan\theta}$ is

(a) 4 (b) 3
(c) 2 (d) 0

52. In ΔABC the straight line parallel to the side BC meets AB and AC at the points P and Q, respectively. If $AP = QC$, the length of AB is 12 cm and the length of AQ is 2 cm, then the length (in cm) of CQ is

(a) 6 (b) 4
(c) 3 (d) 2

53. Simplify the following:

$$\frac{3}{2} \times \frac{11}{5} \div \left(\frac{25}{44} \times \frac{11}{5}\right) \div \frac{33}{15} = ?$$

(a) $\frac{6}{5}$ (b) $\frac{1}{2}$
(c) $\frac{2}{3}$ (d) $\frac{5}{6}$

54. At the beginning of day 1 of a month, Rajesh has 500 eggs. He sells 20% of the eggs by the end of the day and added b% of the eggs at the beginning of the next day and sold 20% of the eggs at the end of the next day. This pattern continued up to the end of the third day of the month when he is left with 1024 eggs. The value of b is equal to

(a) 20 (b) 10
(c) 500 (d) 100

55. The outer surface of a sphere having diameter 10 m is painted at the rate of ₹ $\frac{80}{\pi}$ per m^2. What is the cost of painting?

(a) ₹ 4000 (b) ₹ 6000
(c) ₹ 8000 (d) ₹ 9000

56. The given pie-charts show the distribution of Graduate and Post-Graduate level students in five different colleges A, B, C, D and E.

Total number of Graduate level students = 18900

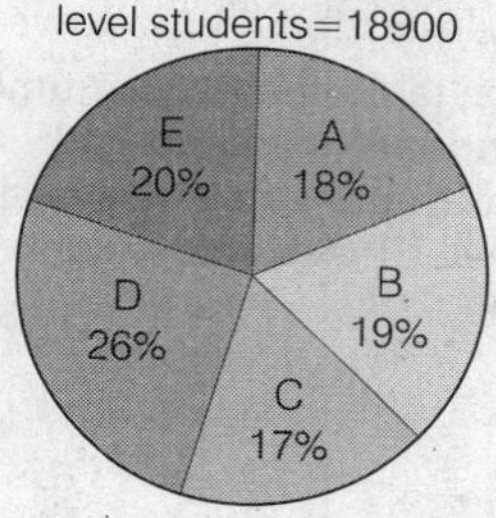

Total number of Post-Graduate level students = 16800

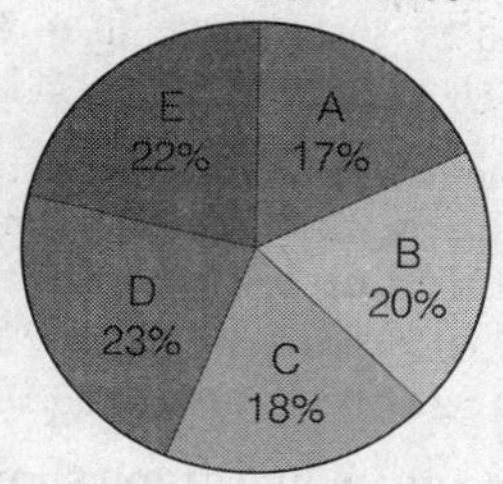

How many students of colleges A and B are studying at Graduate level?

(a) 5987 (b) 4520
(c) 6993 (d) 7052

57. L and M are the mid points of sides AB and AC of a triangle ABC, respectively and $BC = 18$ cm. If $LM \parallel BC$, then find the length of LM (in cm).

(a) 6 (b) 3
(c) 9 (d) 12

58. Study the given bargraph and answer the question that follows.

The bar-graph shows the production (in lakh) of kitchen appliances manufactured by three companies A, B and C over a period of six years from 2012 to 2017.

Production (in lakh) of kitchen appliances manufactured by three Companies A, B and C over a period of six years from 2012 to 2017

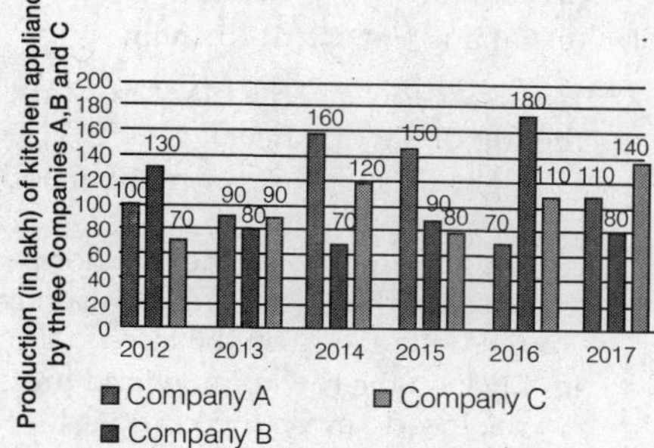

80% of the combined average production of companies B and C is what percentage (to the nearest integer) more/less than 90% of the average production of company A, for the given period of 2012 to 2017?

(a) 21% more (b) 21% less
(c) 19% less (d) 19% more

59. In an election between two candidates, one got 65% of the total valid votes. 20% of the votes were invalid. If the total number of votes was 7500, the number of valid votes that the other candidate got was

(a) 1700 (b) 2100
(c) 4300 (d) 1900

60. In ΔPQR, $PR = 10$ cm. Find the length of PT, where $ST \parallel QR$. Given that $PS = 6$ cm and $QS = 14$ cm.

(a) 2 cm (b) 4 cm
(c) 1.5 cm (d) 3 cm

61. The radius and height of a cylinder are in the ratio 6 : 7 and its volume is 792 cm^3. Calculate its curved surface area in cm^2.

(a) 490 (b) 226 (c) 264 (d) 262

62. Two trains of lengths 310 m and 330 m, respectively, are 160 m apart. They start moving towards each other on parallel tracks, at speeds 130 km/h and 158 km/h, respectively. In how much time (in seconds) will the trains cross each other?

(a) 10 (b) 8 (c) 12 (d) 18

63. A sum becomes ₹ 6600 in 4 yr at simple interest at a yearly interest rate of 5% per annum. What is the sum?

(a) ₹ 4400 (b) ₹ 3300
(c) ₹ 5500 (d) ₹ 6000

64. Divide some money in the ratio Ravi, Reeta and Rahul that 5 (Part of Ravi) = 3 (Part of Reeta) = 11 (Part of Rahul). The money ratio of Ravi : Reeta : Rahul is equal to

(a) 5 : 11 : 3 (b) 33 : 55 : 15
(c) 11 : 33 : 15 (d) 11 : 5 : 3

65. What is the number of digits required for numbering a book with 428 pages?

(a) 1176 (b) 1500 (c) 2000 (d) 988

66. In June, Rohit's bank account balance is ₹ 5000 for 25 days, ₹ 20000 for 2 days and ₹ 1500 for 3 days. What is the average balance (in ₹) in Rohit's bank account in June?

(a) 5575 (b) 5650
(c) 5200 (d) 6000

67. Two offers were being made to Swaroop for a watch with a marked price of ₹ 1600. Either two successive discounts of 20%, or two discounts of 30% and 10% after each other is offered. If Swaroop opted for the better plan over the other, how much more must he have saved?

(a) ₹ 35 (b) ₹ 30
(c) ₹ 16 (d) ₹ 22

68. A man spends 35% of his monthly income on food and four-thirteenths of the remaining income on transport. He incurs some other expenses, but also saves ₹ 6300 per month, the latter being equal to 20% of the balance remaining just after spending on food and transport. What is his monthly income (₹ in)?

(a) 67500 (b) 72000
(c) 70000 (d) 63000

69. *A*, *B* and *C* can complete a work in 12, 15 and 20 days, respectively. How many days are required to finish the work if they work together?

(a) 5 days (b) 3 days
(c) 6 days (d) 4 days

70. In ΔEFG, $XY \parallel FG$, area of the quadrilateral $XFGY = 44\ \text{m}^2$. If $EX : XF = 2 : 3$, then find the area of ΔEXY (in m^2).

(a) 8.38 (b) 9.46
(c) 7.28 (d) 8.10

71. If the point of intersection of lines $x + y = 2$ and $2x - y = 1$ lies on $y = Kx + 5$, what is the value of K?

(a) 3 (b) −4
(c) 4 (d) −3

72. The difference between the cost price and the selling price of an article is ₹ 1800. If there is a profit of 20%, then the cost price of the article is

(a) ₹ 9000 (b) ₹ 11000
(c) ₹ 8000 (d) ₹ 7000

73. The triangle has sides 3 cm, 4 cm and 5 cm. What is the length of the perpendicular from the opposite vertex to the side whose length is 5 cm?

(a) 2.4 cm
(b) 3.5 cm
(c) 1.4 cm
(d) 2.2 cm

74. Study the given table and answer the question that follows.

The table shows the number of students appeared and qualified (in thousands) district-wise in the EMCET examination in a state.

Years	A	B	C	D	E	F
	App/Qual	App/Qual	App/Qual	App/Qual	App/Qual	App/Qual
2014	40/21	50/35	60/29	50/37	45/22	48/32
2015	50/26	60/38	60/42	40/26	35/22	45/19
2016	55/42	35/22	48/26	50/30	55/27	60/19

The total percentage of students who qualified in the year 2016 (correct up to two decimals) is

(a) 54.78% (b) 44.72%
(c) 52.82% (d) 55.18%

75. The given line graph shows the number of scooters manufactured (in thousands) by companies X and Z, over the years.

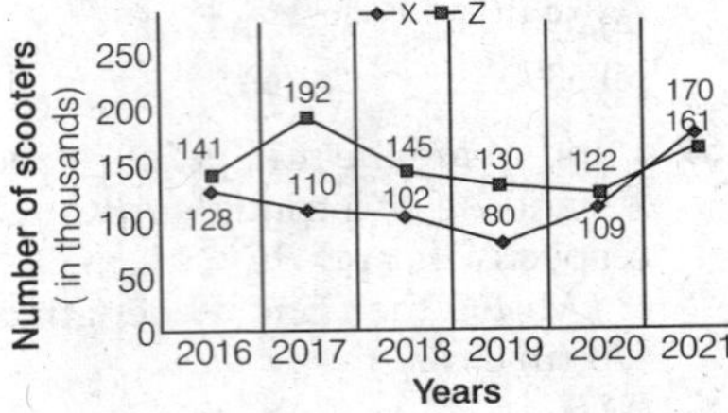

What is the average number of scooters manufactured by company X over the given period?

(a) 126500 (b) 213000
(c) 256000 (d) 115000

Part IV
General Awareness

76. Which of the following musical forms in Carnatic Classical is the simplest composition of Raga?

(a) Varnam (b) Pada
(c) Gitam (d) Kirtnam

77. How can you insert a blank row at the top of a worksheet?

(a) Right click on the row number and select Insert.
(b) Drag the mouse on the row border to select the row and click Insert in the Cells group on the Home tab.
(c) Click on the row number and press the Insert key on the keyboard.
(d) Click on the row number and press the Delete key on the keyboard.

78. In Microsoft PowerPoint, what is the shortcut key combination to insert a new slide in a presentation?

(a) Ctrl + N
(b) Ctrl + D
(c) Ctrl + I
(d) Ctrl + M

79. Which of the following was a feature of the Indian economy before the British rule?

(a) Prosperous economy
(b) Self-reliant economy
(c) Dependent economy
(d) Independent economy

80. A distinctive cross-shaped constellation best seen in the Northern hemisphere during the summer and fall months around September is

(a) Pegasus
(b) Ursa Major
(c) Cassiopeia
(d) Cygnus

81. Which of the following dynasties' genealogy was found in the Bijolia inscription?

(a) Gahadavala
(b) Parmara
(c) Chahamana
(d) Chandela

82. In Kabaddi, a super tackle is when a raider is caught/self out/declared out with or less than how many defenders defending?

(a) Four (b) Three
(c) Six (d) Five

83. Bali Yatra is a traditional cultural festival of which state?

(a) Odisha (b) Bihar
(c) West Bengal (d) Assam

84. In April 2023, India's External Affairs Minister S. Jaishankar launched the project for restoration of which of the following Ghats?

(a) Manikarnika Ghat
(b) Assi Ghat
(c) Cheer Ghat
(d) Tulsi Ghat

85. In which year did Eric A. Cornell, Wolfgang Ketterle and Carl E. Wieman receive the Nobel Prize in Physics for the achieving 'Bose-Einstein condensation in dilute gases of alkali atoms'?

(a) 2002 (b) 2000
(c) 2001 (d) 2003

86. In which judgement did the Supreme Court extend the scope of Article 21 and observed that 'the Right to education flows directly from the Right to life'?
(a) Kharak Singh v/s State of UP
(b) Malak Singh v/s State of Punjab
(c) Mohini Jain v/s State of Karnataka
(d) Neerja Choudhari v/s State of MP

87. When did the first War of Indian Independence (Sepoy Mutiny) start?
(a) 1819 (b) 1887
(c) 1857 (d) 1839

88. In a dihybrid cross between two heterozygous fruit flies with brown bodies and red eyes (BbEe X BbEe), what will be the probability of getting BBEE genotype?
(a) 1/16 (b) 1/4 (c) 1/8 (d) 1/2

89. Which of the following Articles was amended by The Constitution Fiftieth Amendment Act, 1984?
(a) Article 56
(b) Article 33
(c) Article 78
(d) Article 99

90. .... has called the Right to Constitutional Remedy as the 'Soul of the Constitution'.
(a) Dr. BR Ambedkar
(b) Lal Lajpat Rai
(c) Jawaharlal Nehru
(d) Bal Gangadhar Tilak

91. Which type of soil is found on about 40% of the total area of India?
(a) Black soil
(b) Red and Yellow soil
(c) Laterite soil
(d) Alluvial soil

92. ...... at Market Price refers to the sum total of factor incomes earned by residents of a country during an accounting year including net indirect taxes.
(a) Net Domestic Product (NDP)
(b) Gross Domestic Product (GDP)
(c) Gross National Product (GNP)
(d) Net National Product (NNP)

93. According the Census of India 2011, which group of states has the least urban population?
(a) Himachal Pradesh and Meghalaya
(b) Himachal Pradesh and Bihar
(c) Uttar Pradesh and Bihar
(d) Madhya Pradesh and Bihar

94. .... was an Indian dancer and choreographer best known for creating a fusion style of dance adapting European theatrical techniques to Indian classical and folk-dance forms.
(a) Smita Nagdev
(b) Ravi Shankar
(c) Shovana Narayan
(d) Uday Shankar

95. Who among the following wrote the popular Telugu patriotic song 'Desamunu Preminchumanna, manchi annadi Penchumanna' meaning 'Love the nation, Grow the goodness'?
(a) Goparaju Ramachandra Rao
(b) Gurajada Apparao
(c) Sri Krishnadevaraya
(d) Bammera Potana

96. Lakshmibai National Institute of Physical Education (LNIPE) is located at ....
(a) Madhya Pradesh
(b) Haryana
(c) Punjab
(d) Uttar Pradesh

97. Which of the following districts of India has the highest literacy rate as per Census 2011?
(a) Champhai
(b) Serchhip
(c) Idukki
(d) Ernakulam

98. How many countries participated in the first Asian Games held in 1951?
(a) 24 (b) 11
(c) 16 (d) 20

99. The Bist Doab Canal System and Makhu Canal System are associated with which state of India?
(a) Punjab
(b) Assam
(c) Uttar Pradesh
(d) Gujarat

100. On 9th August, 2021, the Parliament had passed the Limited Liability Partnership (Amendment) Bill, 2021. It amended the
(a) Limited Liability Partnership Act, 2012
(b) Limited Liability Partnership Act, 2008
(c) Limited Liability Partnership Act, 2004
(d) Limited Liability Partnership Act, 2016

Answers

1. (c)	2. (d)	3. (c)	4. (b)
5. (d)	6. (c)	7. (d)	8. (c)
9. (a)	10. (d)	11. (b)	12. (c)
13. (a)	14 (c)	15. (c)	16. (b)
17. (a)	18. (a)	19. (b)	20. (b)
21. (a)	22. (d)	23. (a)	24. (c)
25. (a)	26. (d)	27. (a)	28. (d)
29. (b)	30. (b)	31. (b)	32. (c)
33. (d)	34. (b)	35. (d)	36. (b)
37. (c)	38. (c)	39. (c)	40. (d)
41. (b)	42. (b)	43. (a)	44. (a)
45. (a)	46. (b)	47. (a)	48. (a)
49. (d)	50. (c)	51. (a)	52. (b)
53. (a)	54. (d)	55. (c)	56. (c)
57. (c)	58. (c)	59. (b)	60. (d)
61. (c)	62. (a)	63. (c)	64. (b)
65. (a)	66. (b)	67. (c)	68. (c)
69. (a)	70. (a)	71. (b)	72. (a)
73. (a)	74. (a)	75. (d)	76. (c)
77. (a)	78. (d)	79. (d)	80. (d)
81. (c)	82. (b)	83. (a)	84. (d)
85. (c)	86. (c)	87. (c)	88. (a)
89. (b)	90. (a)	91. (d)	92. (d)
93. (b)	94. (d)	95. (b)	96. (a)
97. (b)	98. (b)	99. (a)	100. (b)

Explanations

1. *(c)* The given sentence contains an error of tense. The sentence is in simple past tense. So, use 'met my friend' to correct the sentence.

2. *(d)* Part (B) 'taken back by' contains an error. Use 'taken aback by' which means 'surprised by' to correct the sentence.

3. *(c)* The correct filler for the given problem is 'the'.

4. *(b)* The given sentence contains an error of verb. As the subject of the sentence is singular, a singular verb should be used. So, the correct sentence is- That Macbook belongs to Xavier.

5. *(d)* The correct filler for the given blank is 'believed'.

6. *(c)* The correct filler for the given blank is 'little'.

7. *(d)* The correct filler for the given blank is 'methods'.

8. *(c)* The correct filler for the given blank is 'relevance'.

9. *(a)* The correct filler for the given blank is 'merely'.

10. *(d)* On its last legs means in a bad condition.

11. *(b)* Upshot means result. Hence, its antonym is 'cause'.

12. *(c)* The most appropriate substitution for the underlined word is- bit off more than I could chew. It means to try to do something that is too difficult for you.

- 'Beat my brain out' means to hit someone repeatedly.
- 'Beat the drum' means to speak with enthusiasm.
- 'Burnt a hole in my pocket' means to cost a lot of money.

13. *(a)* The underlined part of the given sentence contains an error. Use 'through' to correct the sentence.

14. *(c)* The underlined part of the given sentence contains an error. Use 'off' in place of 'on' to correct the sentence.

15. *(c)* The incorrectly spelt word is 'embarrese'. The correct spelling is 'embarrass'.

16. *(b)* The antonym of 'dull' is riveting which means having the power to fix the attention. 'Diverting' means to shift attention to other things. 'Plodding' means to move slowly.

17. *(a)* The correct filler for the given blank is 'make' to make the phrase 'make a wish'.

18. *(a)* The word 'remission' means the cancellation of a debt, charge, or penalty; pardon. 'Retribution' means punishment.

19. *(b)* Trespassing means to enter any area without permission.

20. *(b)* The word 'assume' indicates 'to think that something may be true or false'.

21. *(a)* The correct filler for the given blank is 'whole'.

22. *(d)* The correct spelling is 'occurrence'.

23. *(a)* The underlined part of the given sentence contains an error. Use 'off' in place of 'up' to correct the sentence.

24. *(c)* Vociferous means expressing or characterised by strong opinions; loud and forceful. Hence, its antonym is mild.

- 'Biased' means to show like or dislike towards something or someone due to personal opinion.
- 'Assertive' means confident and forceful.

25. *(a)* Tawdry means showy but cheap and of poor quality. Hence, its antonym is 'elegant'. 'Gawdy' means showy.

26. *(d)* The pattern of the series is as shown below,

S $\xrightarrow{+10}$ C $\xrightarrow{+10}$ [M] $\xrightarrow{+10}$ W $\xrightarrow{+10}$ G

L $\xrightarrow{+12}$ X $\xrightarrow{+12}$ [J] $\xrightarrow{+12}$ V $\xrightarrow{+12}$ H

E $\xrightarrow{+14}$ S $\xrightarrow{+14}$ [G] $\xrightarrow{+14}$ U $\xrightarrow{+14}$ I

27. *(a)* Given, option (a) figure is the correct mirror image of the question figure.

M

Rf6y7e | e7y6fR

N

28. *(d)* As,

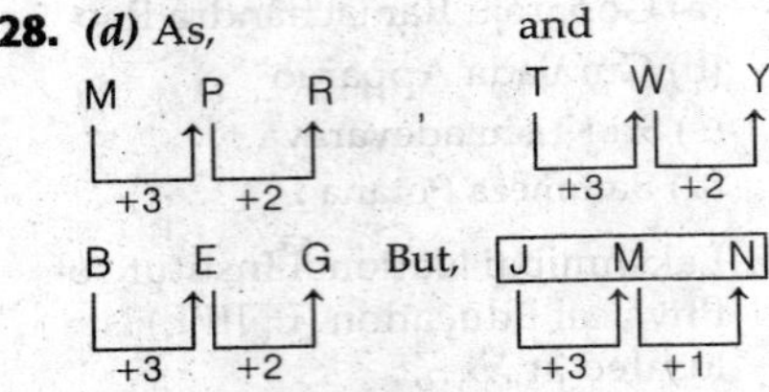

Hence, 'JMN' is the odd one.

29. *(b)* As,

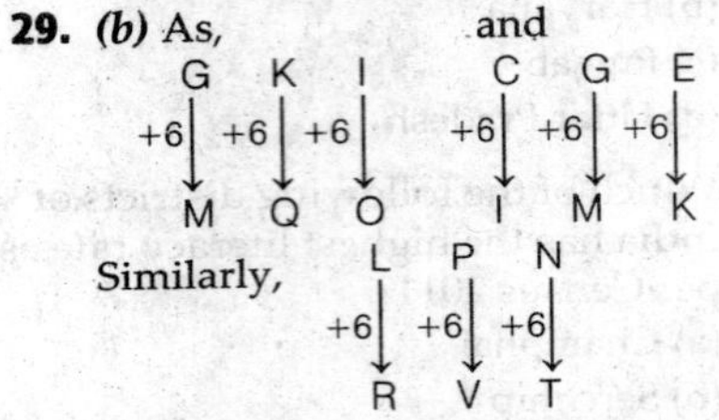

30. *(b)* Given, option (b) is the correct mirror image of the given question figure.

M

5@hRp7 | 7pRh@5

N

31. *(b)* As, 9 is related to 47

$= (9 \times 5) + 2 = 45 + 2 = 47$

and 12 is related to 62

$= (12 \times 5) + 2 = 60 + 2 = 62$

Similarly,

17 is related to '?'

$= (17 \times 5) + 2 = 85 + 2 = \boxed{87}$

32. *(c)* As, 'Happy' and 'Ecstatic' are synonym to each other. Similarly, 'Polite' and 'Courteous' are synonym to each other.

33. *(d)* The pattern of the series is as shown below,

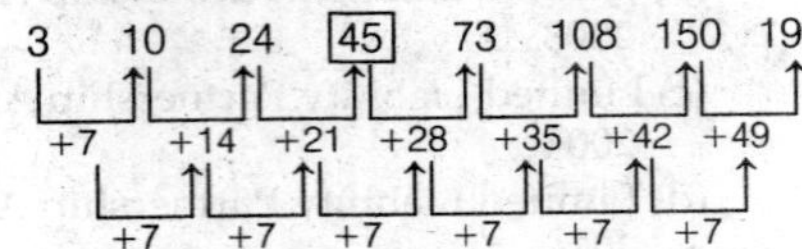

34. *(b)* According to the question,

By option (b), $P \times Q \times R + S$

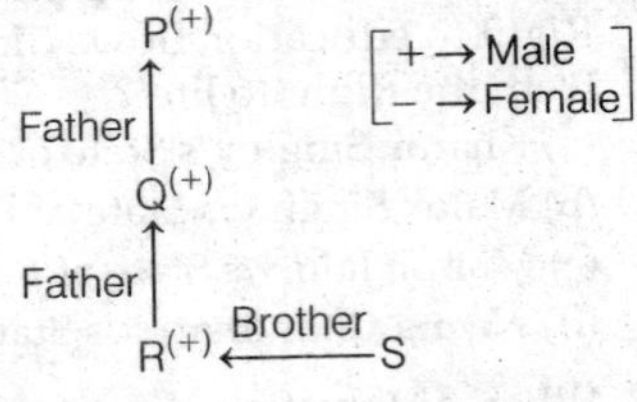

Hence, 'P' is father's father of 'S'.

35. *(d)* Given expression,

95 B 8 D 12 A 2 C 16 = ?

After replacing alphabets with signs, we get

$95 \times 8 - 12 \div 2 + 16 = 95 \times 8 - 6 + 16$

$= 760 - 6 + 16 = 770$

36. *(b)* Given word : F R A M E D

After arranging alphabetically order

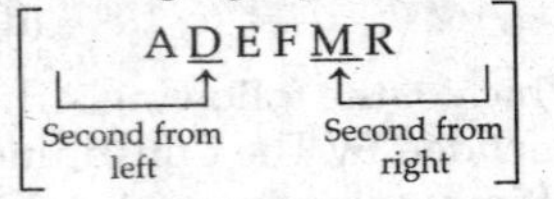

There are eight letters between D and M, i.e., E, F, G, H, I, J, K and L.

37. *(c)* According to the question,

$A \rightarrow \div$, $B \rightarrow \times$, $C \rightarrow +$, $D \rightarrow -$

Given expression,

11 B 11 D 68 A 4 C 4 = ?

After interchanging the signs, we get

$? = 11 \times 11 - 68 \div 4 + 4$

$= 11 \times 11 - 17 + 4$

$= 121 - 17 + 4 = 125 - 17 = 108$

38. *(c)* The paper when opened will appear as the figure given in option (c).

39. *(c)* According to the question,

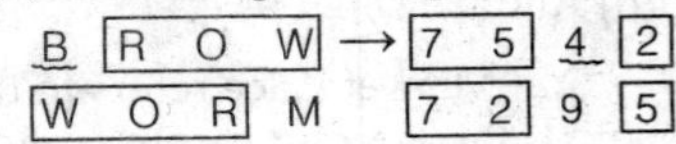

Hence, 'B' is coded as '4'.

40. *(d)* Naming of the figure,

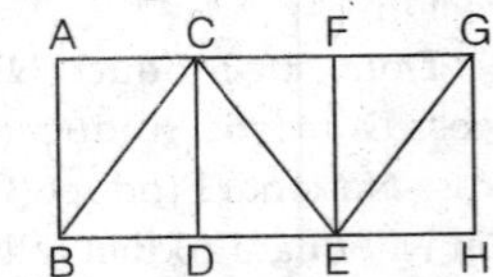

There are total 8 triangles, ΔABC, ΔBCD, ΔDCE, ΔBCE, ΔCEF, ΔFEG, ΔCEG and ΔGEH.

41. *(b)* Given expression,

$90 - 10 \times 36 + 52 \div 49$

After interchanging the signs, we get

$= 90 \div 10 + 36 \times 52 - 49$

$= 9 + 36 \times 52 - 49 = 9 + 1872 - 49$
$= 1881 - 49 = 1832$

42. *(b)* Given word : J U S T I C E

After arranging in alphabetical order :

C E I J S T U

There are four letters between E and J. i.e. F, G, H and I.

43. *(a)* The pattern of the series is as follows,

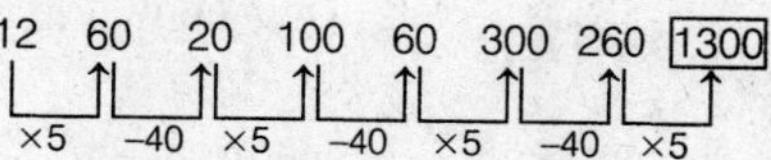

44. *(a)* The pattern of the series is as follows,

E $\xrightarrow{+5}$ J $\xrightarrow{+5}$ O $\xrightarrow{+5}$ T $\xrightarrow{+5}$ Y
C $\xrightarrow{+5}$ H $\xrightarrow{+5}$ M $\xrightarrow{+5}$ R $\xrightarrow{+5}$ W
F $\xrightarrow{+5}$ K $\xrightarrow{+5}$ P $\xrightarrow{+5}$ U $\xrightarrow{+5}$ Z

45. *(a)* According to the statements,

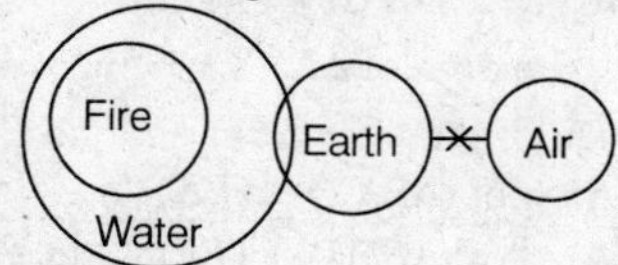

Conclusions

I. (✗) II. (✗)

Hence, neither Conclusion I nor II follows.

46. *(b)* Given, option figure (b) is the correct mirror image of the given option figure.

M

L 3 7 k M e q | p e M k 7 E J

N

47. *(a)* The problem figure is embedded in option figure (a).

48. *(a)* The pattern of the series is as follows,

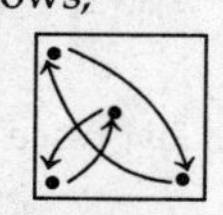

From figure (1) to (2) and (3) to (4)

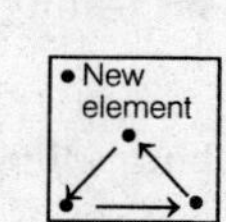

From figure (2) to (3) and (4) to (5)

Hence, from this pattern option figure (a) is complete the series.

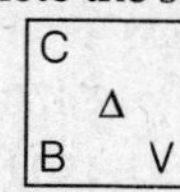

49. *(d)* According to the question,

S O R T → 4 6 9 8

R U S T → 6 4 2 9

Hence, letter 'O' is coded as '8'.

50. *(c)* As, $(18, 7, 119) = (18 \times 7) - 7 = 119$

and $(11, 9, 90) = (11 \times 9) - 9 = 90$

Similarly, by option (c),

$(12, 4, 44) = (12 \times 4) - 4 = 44$

51. *(a)* According to the question,

$\sqrt{13} \sin\theta = 2$

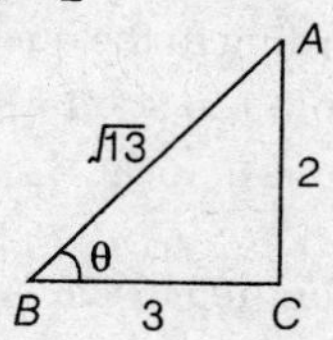

In ΔACB,

$(BC)^2 = (AB)^2 - (AC)^2$
$= (\sqrt{13})^2 - (2)^2 = 9$

$\therefore \quad BC = 3$

$\therefore \dfrac{3\tan\theta + \sqrt{13}\sin\theta}{\sqrt{13}\cos\theta - 3\tan\theta}$

$= \dfrac{3 \times \frac{2}{3} + \sqrt{13} \times \frac{2}{\sqrt{13}}}{\sqrt{13} \times \frac{3}{\sqrt{13}} - 3 \times \frac{2}{3}} = \dfrac{2+2}{3-2} = 4$

52. *(b)* $AP = QC = x$ cm (let)

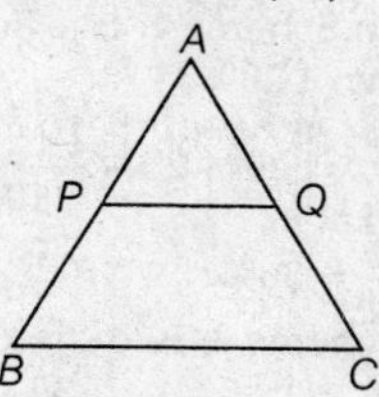

Given, $AB = 12 \text{ cm} \Rightarrow AQ = 2 \text{ cm}$

$\Delta APQ \sim \Delta ABC$

$\therefore \quad \dfrac{AP}{AB} = \dfrac{AQ}{AC} \Rightarrow \dfrac{x}{12} = \dfrac{2}{x+2}$

$x(x+2) = 4 \times 6$

On comparing, $x = 4$ cm

$\therefore$ Length of $CQ = 4$ cm

53. *(a)* Given,

$\dfrac{3}{2} \times \dfrac{11}{5} \div \left(\dfrac{25}{44} \times \dfrac{11}{5}\right) \div \dfrac{33}{15} = ?$

$= \dfrac{3}{2} \times \dfrac{11}{5} \div \dfrac{5}{4} \div \dfrac{33}{15}$

$= \dfrac{3}{2} \times \dfrac{11}{5} \times \dfrac{4}{5} \times \dfrac{15}{33} = \dfrac{6}{5}$

54. *(d)* According to the question,

$500 \times \dfrac{80}{100} \times \dfrac{(100+b)}{100} \times \dfrac{80}{100} \times \dfrac{(100+b)}{100} \times \dfrac{80}{100} = 1024$

$(100+b)^2 = \dfrac{1024 \times 100 \times 100 \times 100 \times 100 \times 100}{500 \times 80 \times 80 \times 80}$

$(100+b)^2 = 40000$

$\therefore \quad 100 + b = 200 \Rightarrow b = 100$

55. *(c)* Radius of sphere $(r) = \dfrac{10}{2} = 5$ cm

Total surface area of sphere $= 4\pi r^2$
$= 4 \times \pi \times 5 \times 5 = 100\pi$

Cost of paint $= \dfrac{80}{\pi} \times 100 \times \pi =$ ₹ 8000

56. *(c)* Total number of students graduate from College A = 18%

Total number of students graduate from College B = 19%

Total from College (A + B)
$= (18 + 19)\% = 37\%$
$= 18900 \times 37\% = 6993$

57. *(c)* According to the question,

$LM \parallel BC$

L and M are the mid-point of AB and AC.

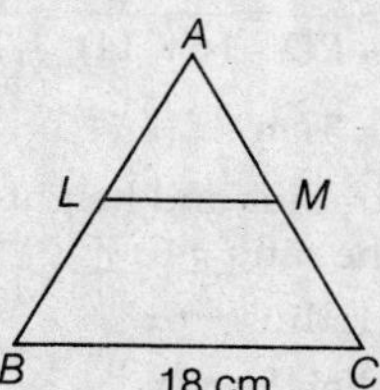

As, we know that in triangle the line joining the mid-point of two sides is parallel and half of the third side.

$\therefore$ Length of $LM = \dfrac{1}{2} \times BC$

$= \dfrac{1}{2} \times 18 = 9$ cm

58. *(c)* Average production from 2012 to 2017 of Company B and C

$= \dfrac{(130 + 70 + 80 + 90 + 70 + 120 + 90 + 80 + 180 + 110 + 80 + 140)}{12}$

$= \dfrac{1240}{12}$

Average production of Company A from 2012 to 2017 is

$= \dfrac{(100 + 90 + 160 + 150 + 70 + 110)}{6}$

$= \dfrac{680}{6}$

According to the question,

Company B and C average production ×80% : Company A average production ×90%

$= \dfrac{1240}{12} \times 80\% : \dfrac{680}{6} \times 90\% = 124 : 153$

$\therefore \dfrac{29}{153} \times 100\% = 18.95\% \approx 19\%$ less

59. *(b)* Total number of votes = 7500

Invalid votes $= 7500 \times \dfrac{20}{100} = 1500$

$\therefore$ Valid votes $= 7500 - 1500 = 6000$

Valid votes getting by first candidate

$= 6000 \times \frac{65}{100} = 3900$

$\therefore$ Valid vote getting by second candidate $= 6000 - 3900 = 2100$

60. *(d)* According to the question,

$ST \parallel QR$

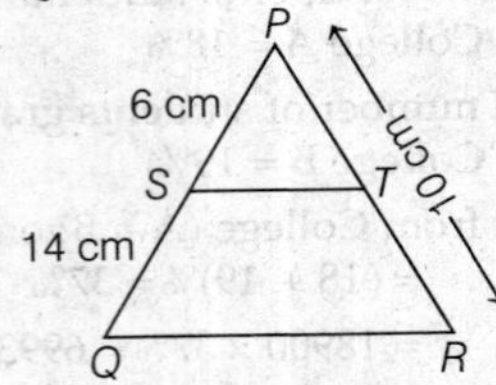

Given, $PR = 10$ cm, $PS = 6$ cm

and $QS = 14$ cm

$\because \Delta PST \sim \Delta PQR$

$\therefore \frac{PT}{PR} = \frac{PS}{PQ} = \frac{6}{(6+14)} = \frac{PT}{10}$

$\therefore PT = 3$ cm

61. *(c)* The radius and height of cylinder are in the ratio $= 6:7$

Let the radius $= 6x$

Let the height $= 7x$

$\therefore$ Volume of cylinder $= \pi r^2 h = 792$ cm^3

$\Rightarrow \frac{22}{7} \times 6x \times 6x \times 7x = 792$

$x^3 = \frac{792 \times 7}{22 \times 6 \times 6 \times 7} = 1 \Rightarrow x = 1$

$\therefore$ Radius of cylinder $= 6 \times 1 = 6$

$\therefore$ Height of cylinder $= 7 \times 1 = 7$

Now, curved surface area $= 2\pi rh$

$= 2 \times \frac{22}{7} \times 6 \times 7 = 264$ cm

62. *(a)* Time taken by both the train to cross each other =

$$\frac{\text{Length of both trains + Distance between both trains}}{\text{Sum of speed of both trains}}$$

$= \frac{(310 + 330 + 160)}{(130 + 158) \times \frac{5}{18}} = \frac{800 \times 18}{288 \times 5} = 10$ sec

Hence, train will cross each other in 10 sec.

63. *(c)* Let the principal = ₹ P

$\therefore P + \frac{P \times 5 \times 4}{100} = 6600$

$\frac{P(100+20)}{100} = 6600$

$P = \frac{6600 \times 100}{120} =$ ₹ 5500

64. *(b)* Let $5 \times$ Part of Ravi $= 3 \times$ Part of Reeta $= 11 \times$ Part of Rahul $= K$

$\therefore$ Part of Ravi $= \frac{K}{5}$

Part of Reeta $= \frac{K}{3}$

and part of Rahul $= \frac{K}{11}$

Ratio of Ravi : Reeta : Rahul $= \frac{K}{5} : \frac{K}{3} : \frac{K}{11}$

$= 33 : 55 : 15$

65. *(a)* According to the question,

Digits from 1 to 9 $\rightarrow 1 \times 9 = 9$ digits

Digits from 10 to 99 $\rightarrow 2 \times 90 = 180$ digits

Digits from 100 to 428 $\rightarrow 3 \times 329 = 987$ digit

$\therefore$ Total number of digits from 1 to 428

$= 9 + 180 + 987 = 1176$

66. *(b)* According to the question,

Average

$= \left[\frac{25 \times 5000 + 2 \times 20000 + 3 \times 1500}{30}\right]$

$= \left[\frac{125000 + 40000 + 4500}{30}\right]$

$= \left[\frac{169500}{30}\right] =$ ₹ 5650

67. *(c)* From Scheme 1, two successive discount of 20%

$= \left(20 + 20 - \frac{20 \times 20}{100}\right)\%$

$= 36\%$

From Scheme 2, two discount 30% and 10% $= \left(30 + 10 - \frac{30 \times 10}{100}\right)\%$

$= 37\%$

If Swaroop choose the second offer, then he saved,

$= 1600 \times (37\% - 36\%)$

$= 1600 \times 1\% =$ ₹ 16

68. *(c)* Let the monthly income = ₹ x

Expenses on food = 35% of x.

$\therefore$ Remaining income after food expenses $= x \times 65\%$

Expenses on transport

$= (x \times 65\%) \times \frac{4}{13}$

$\therefore$ Remaining income after transport expenses $= (x \times 65\%) \times \frac{9}{13}$

Now, $(x \times 65\%) \times \frac{9}{13} \times \frac{20}{100} =$ ₹ 6300

$x = \frac{6300 \times 100 \times 100 \times 13}{65 \times 9 \times 20} =$ ₹ 70000

69. *(a)* A's one day's work $= \frac{1}{12}$

B's one day's work $= \frac{1}{15}$

C's one day's work $= \frac{1}{20}$

Together they can A, B and C can complete in 1 day $= \frac{1}{12} + \frac{1}{15} + \frac{1}{20}$

$= \frac{5+4+3}{60} = \frac{12}{60} = \frac{1}{5}$

$\therefore$ They all together can complete the work in 5 days.

70. *(a)* According to the question,

$XY \parallel FG$

$EX : XF = 2 : 3$

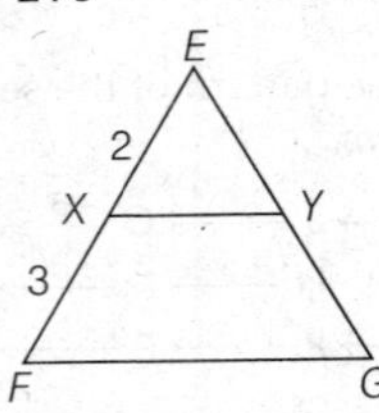

Area of ($\square XYGF$) = 44 cm^2

Let the area of $\Delta EXY = x$ cm^2

Then, $\Delta EXY \sim \Delta EFG$

$\therefore \frac{\text{Area of }(\Delta EXY)}{\text{Area of }(\Delta EFG)} = \frac{(EX)^2}{(EF)^2} = \frac{x}{(x+44)}$

$\frac{(2)^2}{(5)^2} = \frac{x}{x+44}$

$25x = 4x + 176$

$x = \frac{176}{21} = 8.38$

$\therefore$ Area of $\Delta EXY = 8.38$ cm^2

71. *(b)* According to the question,

$x + y = 2$ ...(i)

$2x - y = 1$ ...(ii)

From Eqs. (i) and (ii),

$x = 1$

$\therefore y = 1$ [From Eq. (i)]

$\because (x, y) = (1, 1)$, Point $y = kx + 5$

This is satisfied the situation,

$\therefore 1 = k \times 1 + 5 \Rightarrow k = -4$

72. *(a)* Selling price = Cost price $\times \frac{120}{100}$ ...(i)

and Selling price − Cost price = ₹ 1800 ...(ii)

$\therefore$ Cost price $\times \frac{120}{100}$ − Cost price = ₹ 1800

[From Eqs. (i) and (ii)]

$120 \times$ Cost price $- 100 \times$ Cost price

= ₹ 1800×100

$20 \times$ Cost price $= 1800 \times 100$

Cost price $= \frac{1800 \times 100}{20} =$ ₹ 9000

73. *(a)* Given,

Let BE is the height of ΔABC.

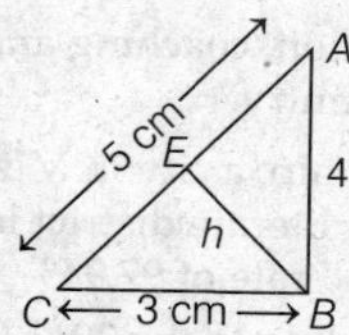

∴ Area of $\Delta ABC = \frac{1}{2} \times \text{Base} \times \text{Height}$

$$\frac{1}{2} \times 5 \times h = \frac{1}{2} \times 3 \times 4$$

$$h = \frac{12}{5} = 2.4 \text{ cm}$$

∴ Length of perpendicular vertex

= 2.4 cm

74. *(a)* Total number of present students in EMCET in the year 2016
= 55+ 35 + 48 + 50 + 55 + 66 = 303

Passing students in the year 2016 from EMCET
= 42 + 22 + 26 + 30 + 27 + 19 = 166

$$\text{Required per cent} = \frac{166}{303} \times 100\%$$
$$= 54.78\%$$

75. *(d)* Average number of scooters produce by company X from 2016 to 2021

$$= \frac{(128+110+102+80+109+161) \times 1000}{6}$$
$$= \frac{690 \times 1000}{6} = 115 \times 1000$$
$$= 115000$$

76. *(c)* Gitam musical forms in Carnatic Classical is the simplest composition of raga.

- It is sung without repetition from the beginning to the end.
- The theme of the song is usually devotional, though there are a few gitas in praise of musical luminaries and Acharyas.
- Gitas have been composed in Sanskrit, Kannada and Bhandira Bhasha.

77. *(a)* Right click on the row number and select Insert, you can insert a blank row at the top of a worksheet.

78. *(d)* In Microsoft PowerPoint, Ctrl + M is the shortcut key combination to insert a new slide in a presentation.

79. *(d)* Before the British rule India was independent economy.

- India was known for its handicraft industry in cotton and silk textiles, metal and precious stone production, and other sectors.
- A significant shift in the Indian economy is that it became a net supplier of raw materials and a net consumer of completed industrial products from the United Kingdom.

80. *(d)* A distinctive cross-shaped constellation best seen in the Northern hemisphere during the summer and fall months around September is Cygnus.

- It is a beautiful constellation that is fairly easy to spot in the night sky, especially if you are far from light pollution.
- It is a Northern constellation on the plane of the Milky Way, deriving its name from the Latinized Greek word for swan.

81. *(c)* Chahamana dynasty genealogy was found in Bijolia inscription dated 1170 A.D.

- Bijolia inscription is engraved on a large rock to the north of a water reservoir attached to the Parshvanath temple at the Bijolia temple.
- According to the 1170 CE Bijolia rock inscription of Someshvara, the early Chahamana king Samantaraia was born at Ahichchhatrapura in the gotra of sage Vatsa.

82. *(b)* In Kabaddi, a super tackle is when a raider is caught/self out/declared out with or less than three defenders.

- A kabaddi match typically runs for 40 minutes (two halves of 20 minutes each). Its ground measurement and the playing surface measures 13 * 10 meters.
- Every team has a total of seven players and both teams lodge opposite halves of the field.

83. *(a)* Bali Yatra, is traditional cultural festival of Odisha.

- In the city of Cuttack, a week-long event is organised starting from the day of Kartika Purnima (full moon day in the month of Kartik i.e October-November).
- It is considered to be one of Asia's largest open trade fair.
- The term Bali Yatra literally means 'Voyage to Bali'.

84. *(d)* In April 2023, India's External Affairs Minister S Jaishankar launched the project for restoration of Tulsi ghat in Varanasi.

- During his three-day visit to Uganda's Kampala, External Affairs Minister S. Jaishankar launched the 'Tulsi Ghat Restoration Project' in Varanasi. Uganda has been selected to chair the Non-Aligned Movement (NAM) for the period of 2022 to 2025 on behalf of Africa.

85. *(c)* Eric A. Cornell, Wolfgang Ketterle, and Carl E. Wieman received the nobel prize in Physics in 2001 for achieving Bose-Einstein condensation in dilute gases of alkali atoms. This recognition was culmination of their groundbreaking work, which began with Cornell and Wieman's successful creation of the World's first Bose-Einstein Condensate (BEC) in June at JILA.

86. *(c)* In Mohini Jain vs State of Karnataka judgement, the Supreme Court extend the scope of Article 21 and observed that 'the Right to education flows directly from the Right to life'.

- In the Kharak Singh vs State of UP, Supreme Court of India, granted relief the Right to Privacy although the Court did not acknowledge it.
- The Neeraja Chaudhary vs. State of Madhya Pradesh case in 1984 is a significant judgement that addressed the issue of bonded labour and the enforcement of the Bonded Labour System (Abolition) Act, 1976.

87. *(c)* First War of Indian Independence start in 1857.

- The revolt began on 10th May 1857, at Meerut as a sepoy mutiny.
- It was initiated by sepoys in the Bengal Presidency against the British.
- This War of Independence marked the end of rule by the British East India Company.

88. *(a)* In a dihybrid cross between two heterozygous fruit flies with brown bodies and red eyes (BbEe X BbEe), the probability of getting BBEE genotype will be 1/16. BBEE is pure (homozygous for both characters) dominant genotype of F2 - generation of dihybrid cross of Mendel, which has 16 progenies, of which only one has this type of genotype.

BbEe X BbEe

	BE	Be	bE	be
BE	BBEE	BBEe	BbEE	BbEe
Be	BBEe	BBee	BbEe	Bbee
bE	BbEE	BbEe	bbEE	bbEe
be	BbEe	Bbee	bbEe	bbee

89. *(b)* The 50th Amendment dealt with the modification of Article 33 majorly in year 1984.

- The Act has been amended to include employees working for the State for purposes of intelligence and counter intelligence bureaus.
- The 52nd Amendment Act has made defection to another party, after elections illegal.
- The Constitution (54th Amendment) Act, 1986 enhances the salaries of Judges of the High Courts and Supreme Court of India.

90. *(a)* BR Ambedkar has called the Right to Constitutional Remedy (Art 32) as the 'Soul of the Constitution'.

- Article 32 also empowers
- Parliament to authorise any other court to issue these writs.
- Before 1950, only the High Courts of Calcutta, Bombay, and Madras had the power to issue the writs.
- Article 226 empowers all the High Courts of India to issue the writs.
- Writs of India are borrowed from English law where they are known as 'Prerogative writs'.

91. *(d)* Alluvial soil type of soil is found on about 40% of the total area of India.

- It is one of the best soils, requiring the least water due to its high porosity.
- It is also known as riverine soil because they are found in river basins and are formed when streams and rivers slow their velocity.
- These soils are deposited by surface water along rivers, in floodplains and deltas, stream terraces, and areas called alluvial fans.

92. *(d)* Net National Product at Market Price refers to the sum total of factor incomes earned by residents of a country during an accounting year including net indirect taxes.

- It is a term that is often used to represent the difference between gross national product and depreciation.
- Gross National Product (GNP) includes what is produced domestically national product and depreciation and what is produced by domestic labour and business abroad in a year.
- **Gross Domestic Product** (GDP) is the total monetary or market value of all the finished goods and services produced within a country's borders in a specific time.

93. *(b)* According the Census of India 2011, Himachal Pradesh and Bihar has the least urban population.

- The state with the lowest urban population in India is Sikkim.
- Goa is the most urbanized state with 62.17% population living in cities.
- State with the highest population density is Bihar.
- State with the lowest population density is Arunachal Pradesh.

94. *(d)* Uday Shankar was an Indian dancer and choreographer best known for creating a fusion style of dance adapting European theatrical techniques to indian classical and folk dance.

- Smita Nagdev is an Indian sitarist, Passed M.A. in Ancient Indian History in 1995 and Master of Music from Khairagarh Music University, Madhya Pradesh in 1996.
- Ravi Shankar was an Indian sitarist and composer, who became the world's best-known expert of North Indian classical music in the second half of the 20th century.
- Shovana Narayan is a recognised Indian Kathak dancer and a career officer with Indian Audit and Accounts Service.

95. *(b)* Gurajada Apparao wrote the Telugu patriotic song 'Desamunu preminchumanna, manchi annadi penchumanna' meaning 'Love the nation, grow the goodness'.

- He was an Indian playwright. dramatist. poet, and writer known for his works in Telugu theatre.
- Rao wrote the play Kanyasulkam in 1892. which is considered as the greatest play in the Telugu language.
- Bammera Pothana was a Telugu poet best known for his translation of the Srimad Bhaagavatam from Sanskrit to Telugu.

96. *(a)* Lakshmibai National Institute of Physical Education (LNIPE) is located at Madhya Pradesh.

- It is under the aegis of Ministry of Youth Affairs and Sports and committed for excellence in physical education, coaching and sports in the country.

97. *(b)* Serchhip, a city in Mizoram, was the most literate district in India with a literacy' rate of 97.91%.

- According to the 2011 Census of India, the literacy rate in India was 74.04%, with 82.14% for males and 65.46% for females.

Top five literate states are

1. Kerala - 94.00 %
2. Lakshadweep- 91.85 %
3. Mizoram -91.33%
4. Goa - 88.70 %
5. Tripura - 87.22 %

98. *(b)* 11 countries participated in the first Asian Games held in 1951.

- The 1951 Asian Games, officially known as the First Asian Games, was a multi-sport event celebrated in New Delhi. India from 4th to 11th March, 1951.
- Motto of the game was Play the game in the spirit of the game.
- Total 11 nations 489 Athletes, 57 Events took place.
- It was opened by first President Dr. Rajendra Prasad.

99. *(a)* The Bist Doab Canal System and Makhu Canal System are associated with Punjab.

- The Bist Doab Canal system, constructed in 1954-55, is spread over a length of 805 km.
- The Makhu Canal system spreads over a length of 92.8 km and has a culturable command area of 20600 hectares.
- Indira Gandhi Canal is the longest canal in India. It is approximately 650 km long and flows across Punjab, Haryana and Rajasthan.

100. *(b)* On 9th August 2021, the Parliament had passed the Limited Liability Partnership (LLP) Bill, 2021 by amending the Limited Liability Partnership Act, 2008.

- Under LLP, a partner's liabilities are limited to their investment in the business.
- The Bill converts certain offences into civil defaults and changes the nature of punishment for these offences.
- It also defines small LLP, provides for appointment of certain adjudicating officers, and establishment of special courts.

Set 09 03 July, 2024 (Shift I)

SSC CHSL Tier-I SOLVED PAPER

Instructions

1. This paper contains 100 questions.
2. It has 4 Parts, **Part I** General English, **Part II** General Intelligence & Reasoning, **Part III** Quantitative Aptitude and **Part IV** General Awareness.
3. Each question carries **2 marks**.

Part I

General English

1. The following sentence has been divided into parts. One of them may contain an error. Select the part that contains the error from the given options. If you don't find any error, mark 'No error' as your answer.

Ramya is working / hardly / to get good marks.

(a) hardly
(b) Ramya is working
(c) No error
(d) to get good marks

2. Identify the error in the given sentence and select the correct sentence from the given options.

Petrified wood is type of fossilised wood that exhibits the original details of the wood.

(a) Petrified wood is the type of fossilised wood that exhibits a original details of the wood.
(b) A petrified wood is type of fossilised wood that exhibits an original details of the wood.
(c) The petrified wood is the type of fossilised wood that exhibits a original details of the wood.
(d) Petrified wood is a type of fossilised wood that exhibits the original details of the wood.

3. Parts of the following sentence have been given as options. Select the option that contains an error.

His mother's transfer from a small town to Delhi brought up a huge change in his schooling.

(a) from a small town to Delhi
(b) His mother's transfer
(c) in his schooling
(d) brought up a huge change

4. The following sentence has been divided into parts. One of them may contain an error. Select the part that contains the error from the given options. If you don't find any error, mark 'No error' as your answer.

Mrs. Meera and family / received his letter / a week ago.

(a) No error
(b) Mrs. Meera and family
(c) received his letter
(d) a week ago

Directions (Q.Nos. 5-9) *In the following passage, some words have been deleted. Read the passage carefully and select the most appropriate option to fill in each blank.*

On the afternoon of 30th March, 1981, many Americans experienced a (1) .... of déjà-vu. Déjà-vu is a name given to the feeling that a person has seen or experienced an event before. Many Americans could not help having that feeling on this day.

The (2) .... hit TVs and radios immediately. President Ronald Raegan had been shot. He was leaving a hotel in Washington DC, turned to wave at some of the people gathered to see him, and fell towards the ground. Before he could hit the ground, his Secret Service Agents (3) .... him into the car and rushed to the nearest hospital. This same story had been heard before. On 22nd November, 1963, President John F. Kennedy was riding in a motorcade through Dallas, Texas. He smiled and waved to the crowd that had gathered to see him. (4) .... rang out from a nearby building. The President collapsed into the backseat of the car and was immediately taken to the nearest hospital. He was (5) .... dead at the hospital. Now, just seventeen years later, the news sounded eerily the same.

5. Select the most appropriate option to fill in blank no. (1).

(a) feeling
(b) dealing
(c) blinking
(d) recalling

6. Select the most appropriate option to fill in blank no. (2).

(a) arrow (b) sceptre
(c) news (d) ball

7. Select the most appropriate option to fill in blank no. (3).

(a) whisked (b) pulled
(c) called (d) pushed

8. Select the most appropriate option to fill in blank no. (4).

(a) Shots (b) Alarm
(c) Music (d) Prayers

9. Select the most appropriate option to fill in blank no. (5).

(a) acting (b) shot
(c) pronounced (d) almost

10. Identify the most appropriate antonym of the given word.

Lenient

(a) Strict
(b) Rude
(c) Kind
(d) Rowdy

11. Read the sentence carefully and select the synonym of the underlined word from the given alternatives.

The Television show was hosted by a young and <u>vivacious</u> woman called Laura.

(a) legendary (b) atrocious
(c) liberal (d) energetic

12. Select the most appropriate option that can substitute the underlined segment in the given sentence.
The woman lost much <u>to her body weight due to</u> diabetes.
(a) from her body weight due to
(b) for her body weight due to
(c) off her body weight due to
(d) of her body weight due to

13. Select the most appropriate synonym of the given word.
Abscond
(a) Flee (b) Avoid (c) Annoy (d) Stay

14. Select the most appropriate option that can substitute the underlined segment in the given sentence.
In every country of the world, <u>primary caregivers are the women of</u> children and elders.
(a) women are the caregivers primary of
(b) the women primary caregivers are of
(c) primary caregivers women are of the
(d) women are the primary caregivers of

15. Select the appropriate meaning of the given idiom.
Last resort
(a) Last hotel on the way
(b) Last ride
(c) Last friend remaining
(d) Last course of action

16. Select the most appropriate synonym of the given word.
Confidential
(a) Public (b) Limited
(c) Secret (d) Open source

17. Select the most appropriate antonym of the given word.
Adverse
(a) Listless (b) Striking
(c) Propitious (d) Critical

18. Select the most appropriate option to fill in the blank.
She .... gracefully and greeted the interview committee with respect.
(a) grinned
(b) leered
(c) smiled
(d) smirked

19. Select the most appropriate spelling of the underlined word in the given sentence.
Nobody could move on after such a <u>scandlous</u> allegation is made on them.
(a) skandelous
(b) scandalous
(c) scandelous
(d) scendolous

20. Select the most appropriate synonym of the given word.
Interpret
(a) Clarify
(b) Cleanse
(c) Celebrate
(d) Complicate

21. Select the most appropriate option that can substitute the underlined segment in the given sentence.
I will require a quiet room to work <u>at</u>.
(a) on (b) about
(c) with (d) in

22. Choose the most appropriate meaning of the given idiom.
Ace in the hole
(a) A lot to do
(b) On the point of
(c) A second chance to do something
(d) A hidden advantage

23. Select the most appropriate synonym of the bracketed word in the following sentence to fill in the blank.
Lead paint is an environmental .... (danger) and can harm children.
(a) conflict (b) empathy
(c) toil (d) hazard

24. Select the most appropriate option that can substitute the underlined segment in the given sentence.
Gulliver <u>hear his watch ticking</u> in his pocket.
(a) heard his watch tickling
(b) watch ticking
(c) could hear his watch ticking
(d) could hear his watch ticked

25. Select the incorrectly spelt word.
(a) Aspirant (b) License
(c) Autonomous (d) Ommision

Part II
General Intelligence

26. 'Z + Y' means 'Z is the father of Y'
'Z − Y' means 'Z is the mother of Y'
'Z × Y' means 'Z is the brother of Y'
'Z ÷ Y' means 'Z is the sister of Y'.
What does '$A \times B - C$' mean?
(a) A is the father's father of C
(b) A is the father of C
(c) A is the mother's brother of C
(d) A is the father's brother of C

27. Three statements are followed by conclusions numbered I and II. You have to consider these statements to be true, even if they seem to be at variance with commonly known facts. Decide which of the given conclusions logically follow(s) from the given statements.
Statements
All paints are houses.
All houses are wood.
Some streets are wood.
Conclusions
I. Some streets are houses.
II. All paints are wood.
(a) Both Conclusions I and II follow
(b) Only Conclusion II follows
(c) Only Conclusion I follows
(d) Neither Conclusion I nor II follows

28. Select the correct option that, when filled in the blanks in the same sequence will make the series logically complete.
TRIC_TRI_KT_IWK_R_TK
(a) KIRTA (b) KATIR
(c) KBTIR (d) KZRTI

29. Identify the figure in the options that, when put in place of the question mark (?) will logically complete the series?

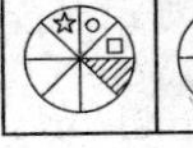  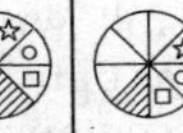  ?

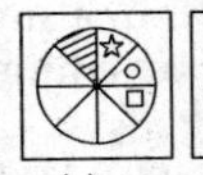 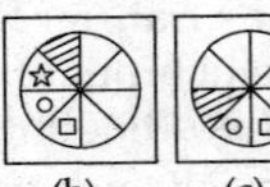  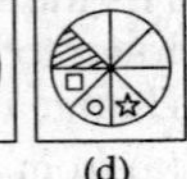 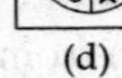

(a) (b) (c) (d)

30. Select the correct mirror image of the given figure, when the mirror is placed at MN as shown below.

M

V 2 0 9 G 5

N

(a) V 2 0 9 G 5 (b) 5 G 9 0 2 V (mirrored)
(c) 5 G 9 0 2 V (inverted) (d) V 2 0 9 G 5 (inverted)

31. What is opposite to 'V', when the given figure is folded to form a cube?

X
Z
W V
U
Y

(a) W (b) Y
(c) Z (d) X

32. What will come in the place of question mark (?) in the following equation, if '+' and '–' are interchanged and '×' and '÷' are interchanged?

$66 \times 11 - 26 + 3 \div 9 = ?$

(a) 5 (b) 15 (c) 8 (d) 11

33. If 3rd April, 1996 was Wednesday, then what was the day of the week on 7th April, 2001?

(a) Sunday (b) Monday
(c) Friday (d) Saturday

34. If 15th January, 2019 was a Tuesday, then what day of the week was it on 29th January, 2020 ?

(a) Wednesday (b) Tuesday
(c) Thursday (d) Friday

35. In a certain code language, 'MENIAL' is coded as 'NIEAML' and 'INCOME' is coded as 'CONMIE'. What is the code for 'FOREGO' in the given code language?

(a) OFOREG (b) FOGERO
(c) OGEROF (d) REOGFO

36. What should come in place of the question mark (?) in the given series based on the English alphabetical order?

ECZ, HFC, KIF, NLI, ?

(a) OLQ (b) QOL
(c) OQL (d) QLO

37. What should come in place of the question mark (?) in the given series?

499, 498, 490, 463, 399, ?

(a) 273 (b) 275 (c) 274 (d) 276

38. HJKN is related to EGHK in a certain way based on the English alphabetical order. In the same way, QSTW is related to NPQT. To which of the following is IKLO related, following the same logic?

(a) FHIL (b) FHJL
(c) FGIL (d) FHIK

39. Which of the following numbers will replace the question mark (?) in the given series?

549, 482, 439, 372, 329, 262, 219, ?

(a) 152 (b) 149 (c) 132 (d) 162

40. How many triangles are there in the given figure?

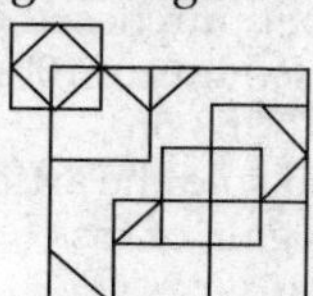

(a) 14 (b) 11 (c) 13 (d) 12

41. Select the correct mirror image of the given combination, when the mirror is placed at MN as shown below.

M

5 F m 3 9 d

N

(a) d 9 3 m F 5 (mirrored) (b) b 3 9 m F 5 (mirrored)
(c) d 9 3 m F 5 (inverted) (d) b 9 3 m F 5 (mirrored)

42. Four letter-clusters have been given, out of which three are alike in some manner and one is different. Select the letter-cluster that is different.

(**Note** The odd one out is not based on the number of consonants/vowels or their position in the letter-cluster.)

(a) RWVU (b) IMNL
(c) PUTS (d) AFED

43. Which of the following letter numeric-clusters will replace the question mark (?) in the given series to make it logically complete?

JX 26, KY 31, ?, PD 47, TH 58

(a) NB 37 (b) MA 38
(c) NA 38 (d) MB 37

44. In a certain code language, 'mobile switched off' is written as 'rq mg cr' and 'turn off light' is written as 'my cp rq'.

How is 'off' written in the given language?

(a) cr (b) mg (c) rq (d) cp

45. What will come in the place of the question mark (?) in the following equation, if '+' and '–' are interchanged and '×' and '÷' are interchanged?

$333 \times 3 + 11 - 5 \div 5 = ?$

(a) 192 (b) 125
(c) 175 (d) 152

46. Select the set in which the numbers are related in the same way as are the numbers of the following sets.

(**Note** Operations should be performed on the whole numbers, without breaking down the numbers into its constituent digits. E.g. 13 – Operations on 13 such as adding/deleting/multiplying etc. to 13 can be performed. Breaking down 13 into 1 and 3 and then performing mathematical operations on 1 and 3 is not allowed.)

(10, 20, 4)

(15, 30, 6)

(a) (20, 30, 8) (b) (20, 40, 8)
(c) (10, 40, 8) (d) (20, 40, 6)

47. Select the correct mirror image of the given figure, when the mirror is placed at MN as shown below.

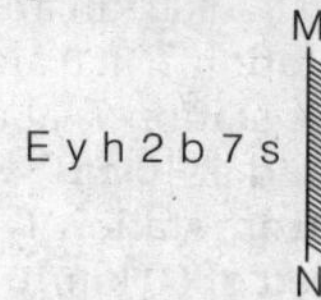

(a) s 7 b 2 h y E (inverted) (b) s 7 d 2 h y E (mirrored)
(c) s 7 d 2 h y E (inverted) (d) s 7 d 2 h y E (mirrored)

48. Six numbers 1, 2, 5, 6, 8 and 9 are written on different faces of a dice. Two positions of this dice are shown in the figure. Which is the number on the face opposite to the face containing 8?

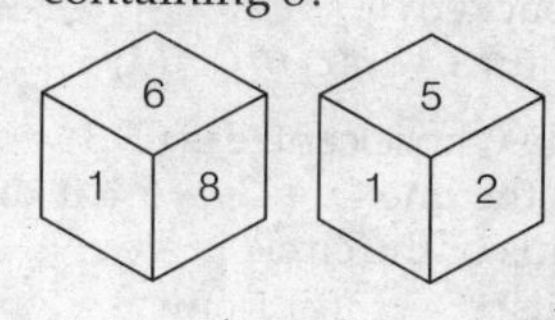

(a) 2 (b) 5
(c) 1 (d) 9

49. 72 is related to 96 following a certain logic. Following the same logic, 66 is related to 88. Which of the following numbers is related to 104 using the same logic?
(**Note** Operations should be performed on the whole numbers, without breaking down the numbers into its constituent digits. E.g. 13 – Operations on 13 such as adding / subtracting/multiplying etc. to 13 can be performed. Breaking down 13 into 1 and 3 and then performing mathematical operations on 1 and 3 is not allowed.)
(a) 75 (b) 77
(c) 78 (d) 80

50. What will come in the place of the question mark (?) in the following equation, if '+' and '÷' are interchanged and '×' and '–' are interchanged?
$16 - 33 + 11 \div 22 \times 5 = ?$
(a) 60 (b) 62
(c) 65 (d) 69

Part III
Quantitative Aptitude

51. When a number is divided by 512 it leaves a remainder 67. If the same number is divided by 32, then what will be the remainder?
(a) 4 (b) 0 (c) 5 (d) 3

52. Two stations T_1 and T_2 300 km apart. A car starts from station T_1 at 8 am and moves towards station T_2 at a speed of 45 km/h and at 10 am another car starts from station T_2 towards T_1 at a speed of 60 km/h. Then the cars will meet at
(a) 11 : 00 am (b) 1 : 00 pm
(c) 12 : 00 pm (d) 10 : 00 am

53. The internal length, breadth and height of a cardboard box are 6 cm, 10 cm and 12 cm, respectively. How many boxes are needed in which cubes, whose volume is 2160 cm^3 can be packed?
(a) 4 (b) 3 (c) 6 (d) 5

54. If a circle whose centre is (2, 3) touches the line $4x + 3y - 7 = 0$, then the radius of the circle is
(a) 4 units (b) 1 unit
(c) 2 units (d) 3 units

55. If the radius of a sphere is doubled, then the volume of the sphere becomes _____ times the previous volume.
(a) eight (b) two
(c) four (d) one

56. Monthly expenditure of Ritvik decreases from ₹ 12800 to ₹ 11712. Find the percentage decrease in his expenditure.
(a) 7.7% (b) 6.25%
(c) 8.5% (d) 9.25%

57. In ΔPQR, S and T are points on PQ and PR, respectively, such that $ST \parallel QR$ and ST divides the ΔPQR into two parts of equal areas. Then the ratio of PS and QS is
(a) $1 : \sqrt{2} - 1$ (b) 1 : 1
(c) $1 : \sqrt{2} + 1$ (d) $1 : \sqrt{2}$

58. The marked price of an article is ₹ 600. A shopkeeper purchased it on two successive discounts of 10% and 20%. He spent ₹ 68 on transportation and sold the article for ₹ 600. Find his gain or loss percentage.
(a) 25% loss
(b) 15% profit
(c) 20% profit
(d)0 18% loss

59. Joey completed the school project in 15 days. How many days will Tim take to complete the same work, if he is 25% more efficient than Joey?
(a) 8 days (b) 10 days
(c) 12 days (d) 16 days

60. A retail fruit vendor buys a score of apples for ₹ 400 and retails them for ₹ 264 at a dozen. What was his loss/gain per cent?
(a score = 20 no's)
(a) 20% profit
(b) 10% loss
(c) 10% profit
(d) 5% loss

61. In an election between two candidates, the defeated candidate secured 42% of the valid votes polled and lost the election by 2545800 votes. If 365500 votes were declared invalid and 30% people did not cast their vote, what was the approximate number of people (in millions) in the electorate who did not cast their votes?
(a) 5 (b) 6
(c) 8 (d) 7

62. In a circle with centre O, ABC is a secant intersecting the circle at A and B and DC is a tangent to the circle at D. If $DC = 12$ cm and $BC = 6$ cm, then the length of AB is equal to
(a) 20 cm (b) 18 cm
(c) 22 cm (d) 16 cm

63. The 8-digits number is divisible by 99. If the digits are shuffled, then the number is always divisible by ....
(a) 6 (b) 9 (c) 5 (d) 11

64. A and B are centres of two circles of radii 32 cm and 8 cm, respectively. CD is a direct common tangent to the circles. If the length of AB = 30 cm, then the length of CD will be
(a) 10 cm (b) 20 cm
(c) 9 cm (d) 18 cm

65. The given line graph shows the number of scooters manufactured (in thousands) by companies X and Z, over the years.

Number of scooters manufactured (in thousands) **by companies X and Z, over the years**
X Z
Number of scooters (in thousands)
250 200 150 100 50 0
2016 2017 2018 2019 2020 2021
Years
141 128 192 110 145 102 130 80 122 109 170 161

What is the approximate difference between the total production by companies X and Z in the given years?
(a) 205000
(b) 292000
(c) 192000
(d) 210000

66. A bus driver must complete a 240 km trip in 4 h. If his average speed 70 km/h for the first 3 h of his trip. How fast must he travel (in km/h) in the last/final hour?
(a) 60 (b) 50
(c) 30 (d) 35

67. In an election between two candidates, a candidate who gets 78% of the votes is elected by a majority of 448 votes. What is the total number of votes polled?
(a) 700 (b) 850
(c) 800 (d) 750

68. Among the ratios 3 : 4, 5 : 8, 1 : 2, 6 : 9, which is the greatest?
(a) 5 : 8 (b) 3 : 4 (c) 6 : 9 (d) 1 : 2

69. Study the given chart based on the population using different types of transport in the given cities. Assuming that no person uses more than one type of transport, answer the question that follows.

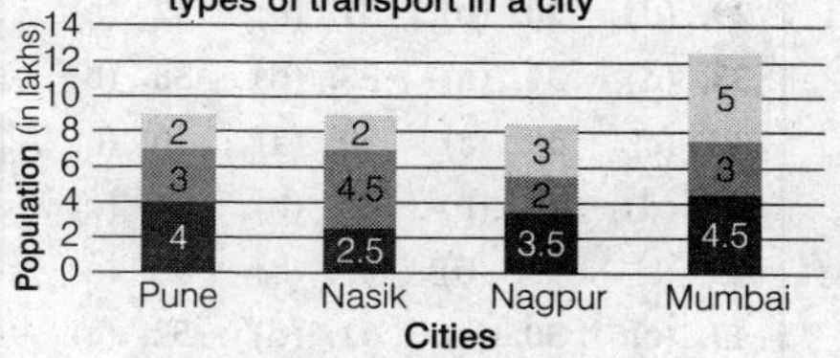

What is the percentage of people using all types of transportation in pune to the total number of people using all types of transportation in all cities ?
(a) 23.08% (b) 22.08%
(c) 33.08% (d) 28.08%

70. The heights of two cones are in the ratio of 5 : 3 and their radii are in the ratio 6 : 5. Find the ratio of their volumes.
(a) 11 : 5 (b) 10 : 5 (c) 12 : 5 (d) 13 : 5

71. The following table shows the production of cars in a company from 2016 to 2020.

Years	2016	2017	2018	2019	2020
A	30	23	39	25	18
B	16	10	14	12	8
C	15	18	19	25	30
D	31	12	21	19	20

There was a continuous increase in the production of cars of which type during the period 2016 to 2020 ?
(a) D (b) C (c) A (d) B

72. What is the present worth of ₹ 2400 due in 4 yr at a rate of 5% simple interest per annum?
(a) ₹ 2240 (b) ₹ 2000
(c) ₹ 2456 (d) ₹ 2200

73. $(\cot\theta + \tan\theta)(\operatorname{cosec}\theta - \sin\theta)(\cos\theta - \sec\theta) =$ ....
(a) 0 (b) 1
(c) 2 (d) –1

74. Study the given pie-chart and answer the question that follows.

The pie-chart represents the total number of valid votes obtained by four students, who contested for school leadership. The total number of valid votes polled was 720.

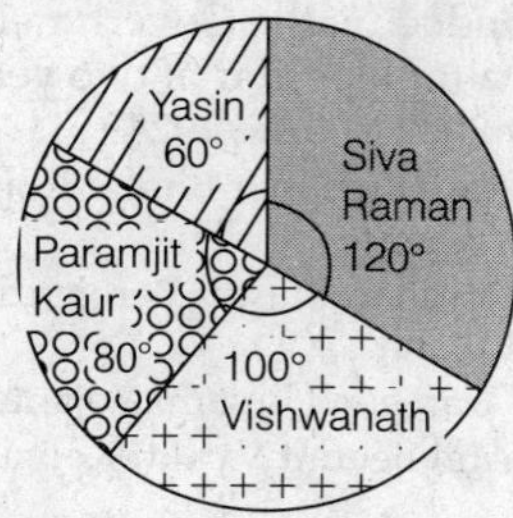

What is the minimum number of votes obtained by any candidate?
(a) 240 (b) 120 (c) 160 (d) 200

75. The length of the portion of the straight line $5x + 12y = 60$ intercepted between the axis is
(a) 5 (b) 13 (c) 17 (d) 12

Part IV
General Awareness

76. Which of the following statements about climate is incorrect?
(a) Coastal areas of India experience less contrasts in temperature conditions as compared to the interior of the country.
(b) India experiences comparatively stronger winters as compared to Central Asia.
(c) India's climate has characteristics of tropical as well as subtropical climates.
(d) 'Monsoon' type of climate is found mainly in South and Southeast Asia.

77. What kind of technology is most frequently used to manage and digitise e-land records?
(a) Blockchain
(b) Augmented Reality (AR)
(c) Geographic Information System (GIS)
(d) Virtual Reality (VR)

78. What is the main sense organ that Virtual Reality displays are aiming for?
(a) Smell (b) Taste
(c) Vision (d) Touch

79. According to Census of India 2011, which of the following states recorded the least population?
(a) Tamil Nadu
(b) Gujarat
(c) Sikkim
(d) Punjab

80. Which state is introduced India's first 'Right to Health Care Act, 2022'?
(a) Kerala
(b) Rajasthan
(c) Assam
(d) Chhattisgarh

81. In May 2023, the Supreme Court of India issued a set of directions to strengthen the POSH Act. To which of the following is this Act related?
(a) Food security
(b) Sexual harassment of women at workplace
(c) Amenities in jails
(d) Child trafficking

82. Which is the largest part of the northern plains and is formed of older alluvium?
(a) Terai (b) Bhangar
(c) Khadar (d) Bhabar

83. According to the Census of India, who are considered to be literates?
(a) Person aged eighteen and above, who can both read and write with understanding in any language
(b) Person aged seven and above, who can both read and write with understanding in any language
(c) Person aged five and above, who can both read and write with understanding in any language
(d) Person aged fifteen and above, who can both read and write with understanding in any language

84. Which of the following enzymes are essential of DNA replication in an animal cell?
(a) Reverse transcriptase, DNA polymerase, DNA primase
(b) Topoisomerase, DNA ligase, DNA polymerase, DNA primase
(c) Reverse transcriptase, RNA polymerase, Ligase
(d) Reverse transcriptase, DNA polymerase, Ligase

85. Certiorari comes under the
(a) Right against Exploitation
(b) Right to Constitutional Remedies
(c) Right to Equality
(d) Right to Religious Freedom

86. Balban followed the tradition of 'Sijda and Pabos' from which of the following traditions?
(a) Persian
(b) Chinese
(c) Mangol
(d) Roman

87. Which of the following statements is correct with respect to the Badminton game and match length?
(a) A match consists of the best of five games of 21 points.
(b) A match consists of the best of two games of 21 points.
(c) A match consists of the best of four games of 21 points.
(d) A match consists of the best of three games of 21 points.

88. Which of the following statements are true?
1. The First Five-Year Plan was based on the PC Mahalanobis Model.
2. The First Five-Year Plan laid emphasis on agriculture development.
3. The Five-Year Planning Model in India was borrowed from Russia.

Codes
(a) 2 and 3 (b) 1 and 3
(c) 1 and 2 (d) 1, 2 and 3

89. Match the following names of primitive forms of cultivation in different states correctly.

States	Name of Primitive form of cultivation
A. Madhya Pradesh	1. Penda
B. Andhra Pradesh	2. Bewar
C. Odisha	3. Kuruwa
D. Jharkhand	4. Bringa

Codes

	A	B	C	D		A	B	C	D
(a)	2	1	4	3	(b)	1	2	3	4
(c)	1	2	4	3	(d)	2	1	3	4

90. Jamshedi Navroz is a festival of .... community.
(a) Hindu (b) Jain
(c) Parsi (d) Christian

91. Indian athlete Shaili Singh won bronze medal in women's long jump at the Golden Grand Prix 2023 athletics meet held at ....
(a) South Korea (b) Japan
(c) Singapore (d) Malaysia

92. Which of the following Indian classical dances has originated from Andhra Pradesh?
(a) Odissi
(b) Mohiniyattam
(c) Kathakali
(d) Kuchipudi

93. Which from following unemployment schemes was extended by the Government of India for a period of two years from July 2022 to June 2024?
(a) Aatmanirbhar Bharat Rojgar Yojana
(b) Pradhan Mantri Berojgari Bhatta Yojana
(c) Grameen Udyami Yojana
(d) Atal Beemit Vyakti Kalyan Yojana

94. The Ghadar Party was founded in .... by Sohan Singh Bhakna, Kanshi Ram, Harnam Singh Tundilat, Lala Har Dayal and others.
(a) 1901 (b) 1913
(c) 1905 (d) 1910

95. Which folk music of Jammu and Kashmir is sung in wedding ceremonies?
(a) Baul (b) Alha
(c) Panihari (d) Wanawun

96. Who was the first female Indian wrestler to win gold at the Commonwealth Games?
(a) Geeta Phogat (b) Babita Phogat
(c) Sakshi Malik (d) Alka Tomar

97. .... Fundamental Duties were added in Part IV of the Constitution under Article 51 A in the year 1976 through the 42nd Constitutional Amendment.
(a) Eight (b) Ten
(c) Twelve (d) Nine

98. In 2000-01, NABARD instituted Micro Finance Development Fund with a corpus of ....
(a) ₹ 245 crores (b) ₹ 100 crores
(c) ₹ 150 crores (d) ₹ 189 crores

99. The Yakshagana is the dance-drama primarily associated with which of the following states?
(a) Himachal Pradesh
(b) Karnataka
(c) Bihar
(d) Odisha

100. In which year did Hans Christian Oersted discover that a compass needle gets deflected when an electric current passes through a metallic wire placed nearby?
(a) 1826
(b) 1824
(c) 1820
(d) 1822

Answers

1. (a)	2. (d)	3. (d)	4. (a)
5. (a)	6. (c)	7. (a)	8. (a)
9. (c)	10. (a)	11. (d)	12. (d)
13. (a)	14 (d)	15. (d)	16. (c)
17. (c)	18. (c)	19. (b)	20. (a)
21. (d)	22. (d)	23. (d)	24. (c)
25. (d)	26. (c)	27. (b)	28. (d)
29. (d)	30. (b)	31. (b)	32. (a)
33. (d)	34. (a)	35. (d)	36. (b)
37. (c)	38. (a)	39. (a)	40. (c)
41. (d)	42. (b)	43. (b)	44. (c)
45. (b)	46. (b)	47. (b)	48. (a)
49. (c)	50. (c)	51. (d)	52. (c)
53. (b)	54. (c)	55. (a)	56. (c)
57. (a)	58. (c)	59. (c)	60. (c)
61. (d)	62. (b)	63. (b)	64. (d)
65. (c)	66. (c)	67. (c)	68. (b)
69. (a)	70. (c)	71. (b)	72. (b)
73. (d)	74. (b)	75. (b)	76. (b)
77. (c)	78. (c)	79. (c)	80. (b)
81. (b)	82. (b)	83. (b)	84. (b)
85. (b)	86. (a)	87. (d)	88. (a)
89. (a)	90. (c)	91. (b)	92. (d)
93. (d)	94. (b)	95. (d)	96. (a)
97. (b)	98. (b)	99. (b)	100. (c)

Explanations

1. ***(a)*** Part 'hardly' contains an error. The correct adverb form for the sentence is 'hard'.

2. ***(d)*** The given sentence is missing an article. Hence, the correct sentence is- Petrified wood is a type of fossilised wood that exhibits the original details of the wood.

3. ***(d)*** Part 'brought up a huge change' contains an error. The phrasal verb 'brought up' means to nurture which is incorrect for the sentence. The correct phrasal verb would be 'brought about'.

4. ***(a)*** The given sentence is grammatically correct and contextually meaningful.

5. ***(a)*** The correct filler for the given blank is 'feeling'.

6. ***(c)*** The correct filler for the given blank is 'news'.

7. *(a)* The correct filler for the given blank is 'whisked'.

8. *(a)* The correct filler for the given blank is 'Shots'.

9. *(c)* The correct filler for the given blank is 'pronounced'.

10. *(a)* 'Lenient' means not harsh, severe, or strict. Hence, its antonym is 'strict'. 'Rowdy' means wild and uncrontrolled.

11. *(d)* The word 'vivacious' means attractively energetic and enthusiastic.

- 'Legendary' means very famous and admired or spoken about.
- 'Atrocious' means horrifying.
- 'Liberal' means free and open to new ideas.

12. *(d)* The underlined part of the given sentence contains an error. Use 'of' in place of 'to' to correct the sentence.

13. *(a)* The word 'abscond' means to leave hurriedly and secretly, typically to escape from custody or avoid arrest. Hence, its synonym is 'flee' which means the same.

14. *(d)* The underlined part of the given sentence contains an error. Use 'women are the primary caregivers of' to correct the sentence.

15. *(d)* Last resort means the only choice that remains after all others have been tried/ last course of action.

16. *(c)* The word 'confidential' means a secret not to be discussed openly.

17. *(c)* 'Adverse' means unfavourable. Hence, its antonym is 'propitious' which means giving or indicating a good chance of success; favourable.

- 'Listless' means nervous and anxious.
- 'Striking' means gaining attention.
- 'Critical' means having negative views about something.

18. *(c)* The correct filler for the given blank is 'smiled'.

19. *(b)* The correct spelling is 'scandalous'.

20. *(a)* 'Interpret' means explain the meaning of (information or actions) for clarity.

21. *(d)* The underlined part of the given sentence contains an error. Use 'in' to correct the sentence.

22. *(d)* Ace in the hole means a hidden advantage or resource kept in reserve until needed.

23. *(d)* The word 'hazard' means danger and thus, can be used to fill in the blank.

24. *(c)* The underlined part of the given sentence contains an error. Add 'could' before 'hear' to correct the sentence.

25. *(d)* The incorrectly spelt word is 'Ommision'. The correct spelling is 'Ommission'.

26. *(c)* According to the question,

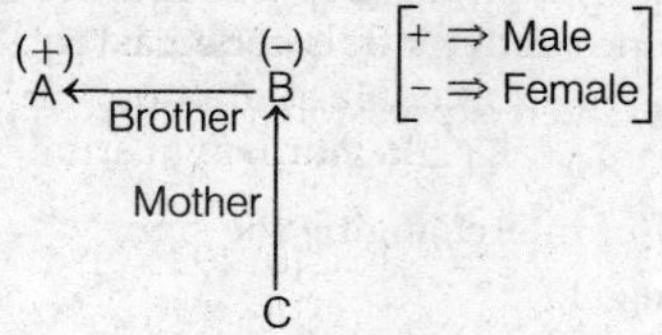

Hence, A is the mother's brother of C.

27. *(b)* According to the statements,

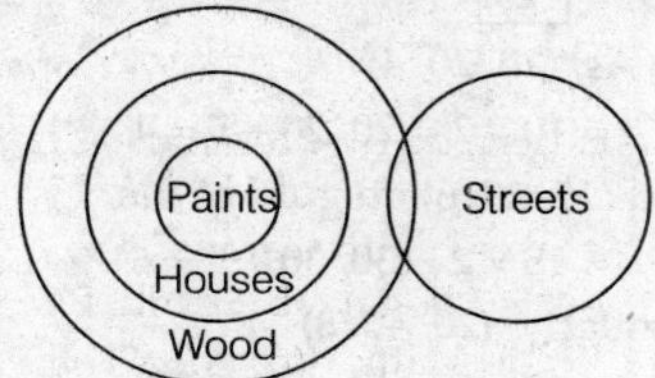

Conclusions I. (✗) II. (✓)

Hence, only Conclusion II follows.

28. *(d)* The pattern of the series is as follows,

TRICK/TRIZK/TRIWK/TRITK

−3 −3 −3

⇒ KZRTI

29. *(d)* In the given series each symbol is shifted one place in the clockwise direction. Hence, option figure (d) is the correct answer.

30. *(b)* In the given question, option figure (d) is the correct mirror image of question figure.

M

V 2 0 9 G 5 | ꓨ 9 Ɛ 0 2 V

N

31. *(b)* Given,

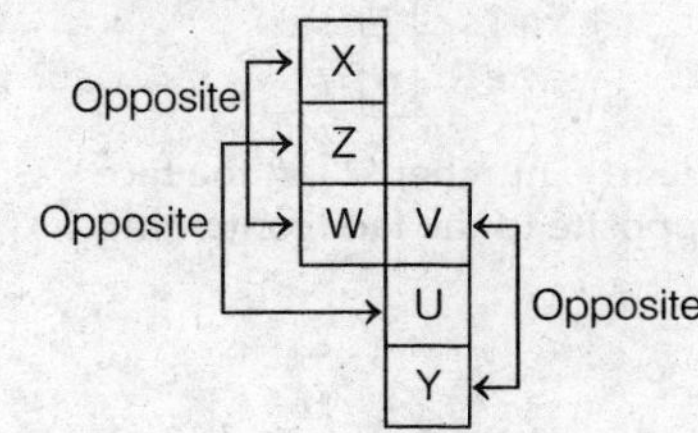

Opposite Pairs

X ↕ W, Z ↕ U, V ↕ Y

Hence, letter 'Y' is the opposite of 'V'.

32. *(a)* Given expression,

$66 \times 11 - 26 + 3 \div 9 = ?$

After interchanging the signs according to the question,

we get,

$? = 66 \div 11 + 26 - 3 \times 9$

$= 6 + 26 - 27$

$= 32 - 27$

$= 5$

33. *(d)* Given, 3rd April, 1996 was Wednesday.

Day on the week of 3rd April, 2001 is

$\Rightarrow 1997\,(1) + 1998\,(1) + 1999\,(1) + 2000\,(2) + 2001\,(1)$

[∵ Ordinary year → 1 odd day
Leap year → 2 odd days]

$\Rightarrow 1 + 1 + 1 + 2 + 1 = 6$

$\Rightarrow$ Wednesday + 6 = Tuesday

Now, day on 7th April, 2001

= Tuesday + 4 = Saturday

34. *(a)* Given, 15th January, 2019 was a Tuesday.

Day on 15th January, 2020 was

= Tuesday + 1

= Wednesday

∴ Now, number of days between 15th January, 2020 to 29th January, 2020

$= 14 \div 7 = 0$ odd day

So, the day of the week on 29th January, 2020 = Wednesday

35. *(d)* As,

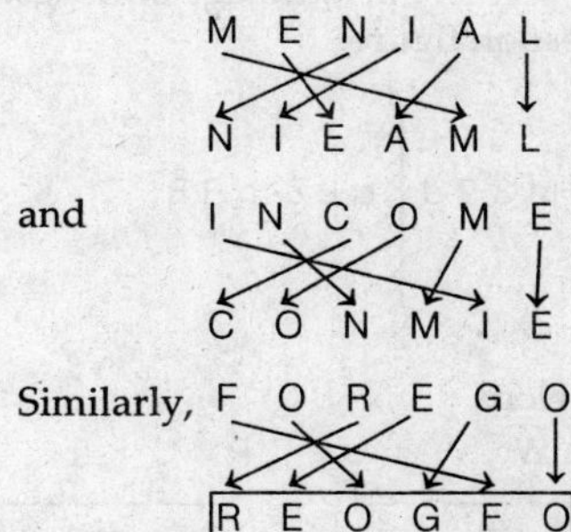

36. *(b)* The pattern of the series is as shown below,

E →(+3) H →(+3) K →(+3) N →(+3) Q

C →(+3) F →(+3) I →(+3) L →(+3) O

Z →(+3) C →(+3) F →(+3) I →(+3) L

37. *(c)* The pattern of the series is as shown below,

499 498 490 463 399 [274]

$(-1)^3$ $(-2)^3$ $(-3)^3$ $(-4)^3$ $(-5)^3$

38. *(a)* As,

H J K N
–3 –3 –3 –3
E G H K

and

Q S T W
–3 –3 –3 –3
N P Q T

Similarly,

I K L O
–3 –3 –3 –3
[F H I L]

39. *(a)* The pattern of the series is as shown below,

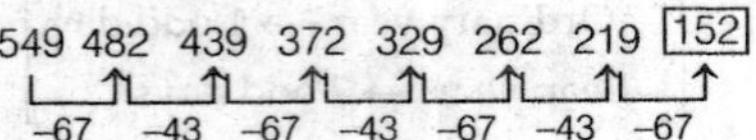

40. *(c)* Naming of the figure,

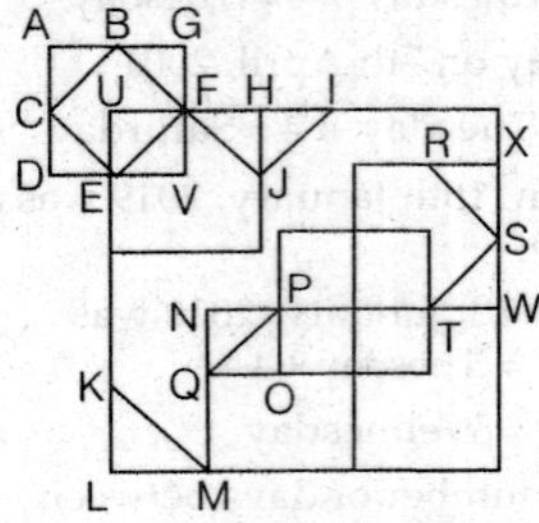

There are total 13 number of triangles ΔACB, ΔBGF, ΔCDE, ΔFVE, ΔUFE, Δ FHJ, ΔHIJ, ΔFIJ, ΔKLM, ΔNQP, ΔQOP, ΔRXS and ΔSWT

41. *(d)* In the given question option (d) is the correct mirror image of the given question figure.

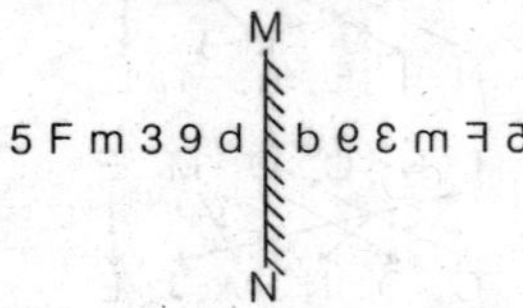

42. *(b)* Here,

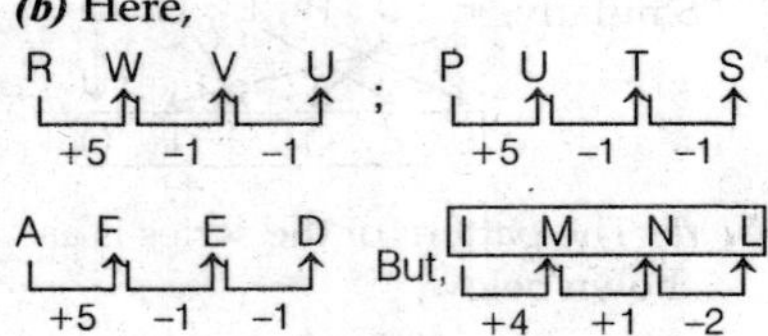

43. *(b)* The pattern of the series is as shown below,

J $\xrightarrow{+1}$ K $\xrightarrow{+2}$ [M] $\xrightarrow{+3}$ P $\xrightarrow{+4}$ T

X $\xrightarrow{+1}$ Y $\xrightarrow{+2}$ [A] $\xrightarrow{+3}$ D $\xrightarrow{+4}$ H

26 $\xrightarrow{+5}$ 31 $\xrightarrow{+7}$ [38] $\xrightarrow{+9}$ 47 $\xrightarrow{+11}$ 58

44. *(c)* According to the question,

mobile switched (off) → (rq) mg cr

turn (off) light → my cp (rq)

Hence, letter 'off' is coded as 'rq'.

45. *(b)* Given expression,
333 × 3 + 11 – 5 ÷ 5 = ?
After interchanging the sign, we get,

$? = 333 \div 3 - 11 + 5 \times 5$
$= 111 - 11 + 25$
$= 136 - 11$
$= \boxed{125}$

46. *(b)* As, (10, 20, 4)
$= 10 \times 2 = 20,\ 20 \div 5 = 4$
and (15, 30, 6)
$= 15 \times 2 = 30,\ 30 \div 5 = 6$
Similarly, (20, 40, 8)
$= 20 \times 2 = 40,\ 40 \div 5 = 8$

47. *(b)* In the given question, option (b) figure is the correct mirror image of the given question.

M

E y h 2 b 7 s | s 7 b 2 h y E (mirror)

N

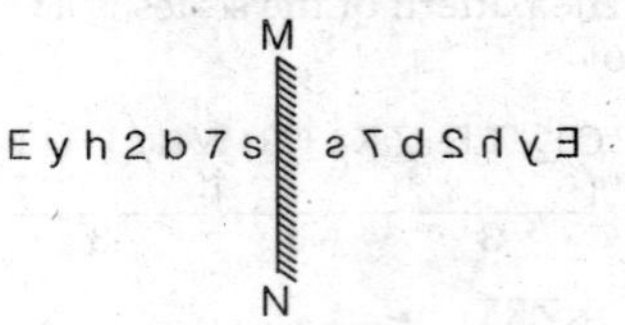

48. *(a)* Given,

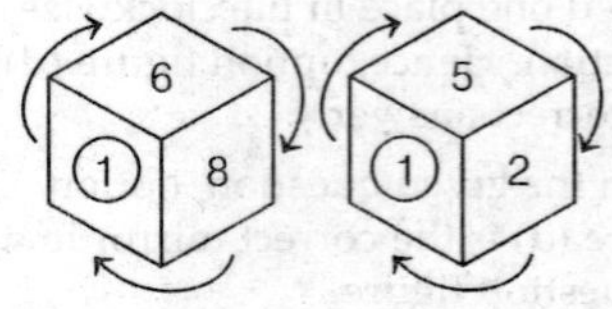

In the given dice number '1' is common and dice is rotate in clockwise from common number.

Opposite pairs

1	6	[8]
↕	↕	↕
1	5	[2]

Clearly, number '2' on the face opposite to the face containing 8.

49. *(c)* As, 72 related to 96
$= 12 \times 6 = 72$ and $12 \times 8 = 96$
and 66 related to 88
$= 11 \times 6 = 66$ and $11 \times 8 = 88$
Similarly, 104 related to
$= 13 \times 6 = \boxed{78}$ and $13 \times 8 = 104$

50. *(c)* Given expression,
16 – 33 + 11 ÷ 22 × 5 = ?
After interchanging the signs, we get,
$= 16 \times 33 \div 11 + 22 - 5$
$= 16 \times 3 + 22 - 5$
$= 48 + 22 - 5$
$= 70 - 5$
$= 65$

51. *(d)* Let the number be N and the quotient be x, the number
$N = 512x + 67$

Now, $\frac{512x + 67}{32} = \frac{512x + 32 + 35}{32}$

$= (16x + 1) + \frac{35}{32}$

Hence, the required remainder = 3

52. *(c)* Distance covered by T_1 till 10 am
$= 45 \times 2 = 90$ km
Remaining distance
$= 300 - 90 = 210$ km
Relative speed = 45 + 60 = 105 km/h

Time to cover 210 km $= \frac{210}{105} = 2$ h

So, they meet 2 h after 10 am *i.e.*, 12 : 00 pm.

53. *(b)* Volume of cardboard box
$= l \times b \times h = 6 \times 10 \times 12$
$= 720\ \text{cm}^3$
According to the question,

Required boxes $= \frac{2160}{720} = 3$

Hence, 3 boxes are needed to pack 2160 cm^3.

54. *(c)* We need to determine the perpendicular distance from the centre of the circle to the line. The distance will be equal to the radius of the circle.

∴ Perpendicular distance d from a point (x_1, y_1) to line $Ax + By + C = 0$

$\Rightarrow \quad d = \frac{|Ax_1 + By_1 + C|}{\sqrt{A^2 + B^2}}$

$[\because (x_1, y_1) = (2, 3)]$

$A = 4, B = 3$ and $C = -7$

$$d = \frac{|4(2) + 3(3) - 7|}{\sqrt{4^2 + 3^2}} = \frac{|8 + 9 - 7|}{\sqrt{16 + 9}}$$

$$= \frac{10}{\sqrt{25}} = \frac{10}{5} = 2 \text{ units}$$

$\therefore$ Radius of the circle is 2 units.

55. *(a)* Volume of sphere $= \frac{4}{3}\pi r^3$

Let the initial radius $= r$

Let the final radius $= 2r$

Initial volume of sphere $= \frac{4}{3}\pi r^3$

Final volume of sphere $= \frac{4}{3}\pi(2r)^3$

$\therefore$ Then ratio of new and old sphere

$$= \frac{\frac{4}{3}\pi(2r)^3}{\frac{4}{3}\pi r^3} = \frac{8}{1}$$

$\therefore$ Required volume of sphere become 8 times the previous volume.

56. *(c)* According to the question,

Initial expenditure = ₹ 12800

After decrease in expenditure = ₹ 11712

Percentage decrease in his expenditure

$$= \frac{12800 - 11712}{12800} \times 100$$

$$= \frac{1088}{12800} \times 100 = 8.5\%$$

57. *(a)* Given,

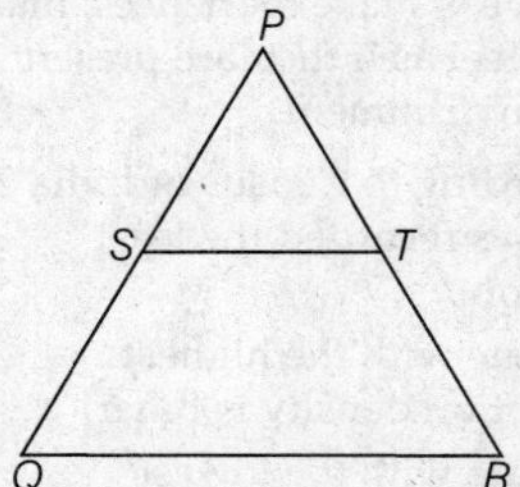

In ΔPQR and ΔPST,

$\angle QPR = \angle SPT$

$\angle PQR = \angle PST$ [$\because ST \parallel QR$]

$\therefore$ $\Delta PQR \sim \Delta PST$

Let the area of ΔPQR and ΔPST be 2 : 1

[$\because ST$, ΔPQR is divided into two equal area]

$$= \frac{\text{area of } \Delta PQR}{\text{area of } \Delta PST} = \frac{PQ^2}{PS^2}$$

$$\therefore \quad \frac{PQ^2}{PS^2} = \frac{2}{1} \Rightarrow \frac{PQ}{PS} = \frac{\sqrt{2}}{1}$$

$$QS = PQ - PS = \sqrt{2} - 1$$

Hence, $PS : QS = (1 : \sqrt{2} - 1)$

58. *(c)* Given,

Marked price of an article = ₹ 600

$\therefore$ Successive discount $= x + y - \frac{xy}{100}$

$$= 10 + 20 - \frac{(10 \times 20)}{100} = 28\%$$

Cost price of the article

$$= 600 \times \frac{(100 - 28)}{100} = ₹\ 432$$

Spent on the transportation

$= 432 + 68 = ₹\ 500$

Then, they sold again at the rate $= ₹\ 600$

$$\therefore \text{Gain percentage} = \frac{600 - 500}{500} \times 100$$

$$= \frac{100}{500} \times 100$$

$= 20\%$ profit

59. *(c)* Let the day taken by Joey be $= x$.

The ratio of the time taken by Joey and Tim $= 125 : 100$

$= 5 : 4$

$$\therefore \quad 5 : 4 :: 15 : x \Rightarrow x = \frac{4 \times 15}{5}$$

$\therefore \quad x = 12$

Hence, Tim will takes 12 days.

60. *(c)* Fruit vendor buys a score of apples = ₹ 400

(a score = 20 no's)

$$\text{Price of one apple} = \frac{400}{20} = ₹\ 20$$

$\therefore$ Sale dozen of apple = ₹ 264

Selling price of one apple is

$$= \frac{264}{12} = ₹\ 22$$

$$\therefore \text{ Profit percentage} = \frac{22 - 20}{20} \times 100$$

$$= \frac{2}{20} \times 100 = 10\% \text{ profit}$$

61. *(d)* Percentage of total valid votes that winning candidate secured

$= (100 - 42) = 58\%$

Difference between the winning and defeated candidate $= (58 - 42) = 16\%$

Total number of valid votes

$= 2545800 \div 16\% = 15911250$

Total number of voters (both valid and invalid)

$= 15911250 + 365500 = 16276750$

Total number of voters

$= 16276750 \div (100 - 30)\% = 23252500$

Number of people who did not cast their vote

$= 23252500 \times 30\% = 6975750$

Approx = 7 millions.

62. *(b)* Given,

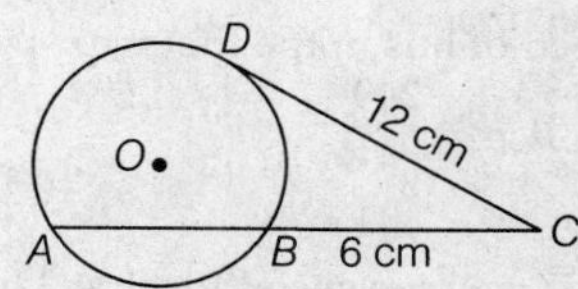

$CD^2 = BC \times AC$

$12^2 = 6 \times AC$

$\Rightarrow \quad AC = \frac{144}{6}$

$= 24$ cm

$\therefore \quad AB = AC - BC$

$= 24 - 6$

$= 18$ cm

63. *(b)* **Divisibility by 9** A number is divisible by 9, if the sum of its digits is divisible by 9.

Divisibility by 11 A number is divisible by 11 if the difference between the sum of the digits in the odd position and the sum of the digits in the even position is divisible by 11.

$\therefore$ Now that the shuffled number will always be divisible by 9, but not necessarily by 11.

Hence, the shuffled number is always divisible by 9.

64. *(d)* Given,

Distance between the centres (d) = 30 cm

and $r_1 = 32$ cm

$r_2 = 8$ cm

$$\therefore \quad CD = \sqrt{d^2 - (r_1 - r_2)^2}$$

$$= \sqrt{(30)^2 - (32 - 8)^2}$$

$$= \sqrt{30^2 - 24^2}$$

$$= \sqrt{(30 + 24)(30 - 24)}$$

$$= \sqrt{54 \times 6}$$

$$= \sqrt{3 \times 18 \times 6}$$

$$= \sqrt{18 \times 18} = 18$$

$\therefore \quad CD = 18$ cm

65. *(c)* Total production by company Z in all the year

$= (141 + 192 + 145 + 130 + 122 + 161) = 891$

Total production by company X in all the year

$= (128 + 110 + 102 + 80 + 109 + 170) = 699$

$\therefore$ Difference between total production by companies X and Z

$= 891 - 699$ (thousand)

$= 192000$

66. *(c)* Given,

Speed of bus in the first trip

$= \frac{240}{4}$

$= 60$ km/h

If his average speed for first 3 h at 70 km/h then distance = 210 km

∴ He travel fast in the last hour.

∴ Required speed = (240 – 210) ÷ 1

= 30 km/h

67. *(c)* Let the total number of vote polled be 100.

Winning candidate got = 78%

Lossing candidate got = 22%

∴ Difference between winning or lossed candidate

= 78% – 22% = 56%

Now, the total number of vote polled

$= \frac{100 \times 448}{56}$

= 800

68. *(b)* Given, ratios convert into fraction

$= \frac{3}{4}, \frac{5}{8}, \frac{2}{6}, \frac{6}{9}$

LCM of denominators of (4, 8, 6, 9)

= 216

Now converting the fraction

$= \frac{3 \times 54}{4 \times 54} = \frac{162}{216}$

$= \frac{5 \times 27}{8 \times 27} = \frac{135}{216}$

$= \frac{2 \times 36}{6 \times 36} = \frac{72}{216}$

$= \frac{6 \times 24}{9 \times 24} = \frac{144}{216}$

Denominator of all the fraction will same, fraction with the greatest numerator will be the greatest.

∴ Required ratio 3 : 4 is the greatest.

69. *(a)* Total number of people using all types of transportation in all cities

= Pune + Nasik + Nagpur + Mumbai

= 9 + 9 + 8.5 + 12.5 = 39

Total number of person use transportation in Pune = 9

∴ Percentage of people $= \frac{9}{39} \times 100$

= 23.08%

70. *(c)* Given, height of two cone in ratio $= h_1 = 5$ and $h_2 = 3$

Radius of two cone in ratio $R_1 = 6$ and $R_2 = 5$

As we know,

∴ Volume of cone $= \pi r^2 h$

$$\Rightarrow \frac{\pi r_1^2 h_1}{\pi r_2^2 h_2} = \frac{\pi \times (6)^2 \times 5}{\pi \times (5)^2 \times 3} = \frac{\pi \times 36 \times 5}{\pi \times 25 \times 3} = \frac{12}{5}$$

Hence, ratio of their volumes is 12 : 5.

71. *(b)* From the given table, we can see that company *C* shows the continuous increase in the production of cars.

72. *(b)* Given, amount = ₹ 2400

Present value = ₹ x

∴ SI = ₹ (2400 – x)

∴ $SI = \frac{P \times R \times T}{100}$

$\Rightarrow 2400 - x = \frac{x \times 5 \times 4}{100}$

$\Rightarrow 240000 - 100x = 20x$

$\Rightarrow x = \frac{240000}{120} =$ ₹ 2000

Hence, the present value is ₹ 2000.

73. *(d)* $(\cot\theta + \tan\theta)(\operatorname{cosec}\theta - \sin\theta) \times (\cos\theta - \sec\theta)$

$$= \left(\frac{\cos\theta}{\sin\theta} + \frac{\sin\theta}{\cos\theta}\right)\left(\frac{1}{\sin\theta} - \sin\theta\right) \times \left(\cos\theta - \frac{1}{\cos\theta}\right)$$

$$= \left(\frac{\sin^2\theta + \cos^2\theta}{\sin\theta\cos\theta}\right)\left(\frac{1 - \sin^2\theta}{\sin\theta}\right) \times \left(\frac{\cos^2\theta - 1}{\cos\theta}\right)$$

$$= \left(\frac{1}{\sin\theta \cdot \cos\theta}\right)\left(\frac{\cos^2\theta}{\sin\theta}\right)\left(\frac{-\sin^2\theta}{\cos\theta}\right) = -1$$

74. *(b)* As per given pie-chart, Yasin obtained the minimum number of votes

$= 720 \times \frac{60}{360} = 120$

75. *(b)* Given, $5x + 12y = 60$

$\therefore \frac{5x}{60} + \frac{12y}{60} = \frac{60}{60}$

$\frac{x}{12} + \frac{y}{5} = 1$

So, the length of portion straight line

$= \sqrt{12^2 + 5^2}$

$= \sqrt{144 + 25} = \sqrt{169} = 13$

76. *(b)* India experiences comparatively lesser winters as compared to Central Asia.

- India's climate has characteristics of tropical as well as subtropical climates.
- Coastal areas of India experience less contrasts in temperature conditions as compared to the interior of the country.
- 'Monsoon' type of climate is found mainly in South and Southeast Asia.

77. *(c)* Geographic Information System (GIS) technology is most frequently used to manage and digitise e-land records.

- Blockchain Technology is an advanced database mechanism that allows transparent information sharing within a business network.
- Augmented Reality (AR) is an interactive experience that enhances the real world with computer-generated perceptual information.
- Virtual Reality (VR) is a technology that simulates a computer-generated environment and makes it possible to interact with it in a very realistic way.

78. *(c)* Vision is the primary sense organ targeted by Virtual Reality (VR) displays.

VR displays are designed to create immersive visual experiences, making the user feel as if they are present in a virtual environment.

79. *(c)* According to Census of India 2011, Sikkim has recorded the least population.

- The state with the highest population density is Bihar.
- The state with the lowest population density is Arunachal Pradesh.
- The union territory with least population is Lakshadweep.
- The state with the highest population is Uttar Pradesh.

80. *(b)* On 21st March, 2023, Rajasthan became the first state in the country to pass an act implementing the right to health.

- It is titled as 'Rajasthan Right to Heath 2022'.

- The act aims to provide every citizen with access to quality healthcare services and facilities.
- It also includes provisions for free medical treatment and medicines for certain categories of people.

81. *(b)* In May 2023, the Supreme Court of India issued a set of directions to strengthen the POSH Act which related to sexual harassment of women at workplace.

- Under the POSH Act, limitation period for filing the sexual harassment complaint is 3 months from the date of the incident/last incident.
- Section 75 deals with sexual harassment and the punishment for it, the limitation period is 3 years from the date of the incident.

82. *(b)* Bhangar is the largest part of the northern plains and is formed of older alluvium.

- Bhabar is a hilly area that is composed of loose rocks and boulders.
- Khadar is an alluvial soil that can be found all throughout the floodplains.
- Terai is a belt of marshy land at the foot of mountains, especially at the foot of the Himalayas in India.

83. *(b)* According to the Census of India, any person aged seven and above, who can both read and write with understanding in any language is called literate.

For literacy rate

- Best Performer states: Kerala > Delhi > Uttarakhand > Himachal Pradesh > Assam
- Worst Performer states: Andhra Pradesh < Rajasthan < Bihar < Telangana < Uttar Pradesh

84. *(b)* DNA replication in animal cells requires Topoisomerase, DNA ligase, DNA polymerase, DNA primase.

- **DNA polymerase** Binds to a DNA strand and uses it as a template to assemble a new strand of nucleotides.
- **DNA ligase** Joins Okazaki fragments together to complete the DNA strands.
- **DNA primase** Add an RNA primer to the leading and lagging strands to DNA.
- **Topoisomerase** Relieves the supercoiling that occurs as the DNA replication fork progresses.

85. *(b)* Certiorari comes under the Right to Constitutional Remedies.

- Article 32 of the Indian Constitution of India confers the Right to Constitutional Remedies.
- The Parliament can empower any other court to issue directions, orders, and writs of all kinds, without prejudicing the same powers of the Supreme Court.
- Its significance made Dr. BR. Ambedkar hail this right as the 'heart and soul' of the Constitution.

86. *(a)* Balban followed the tradition of 'Sijda and Pabos' from Persia.

- The first Sultan of Delhi, Ghiyasuddin Balban, introduced the practice of Sijda and Pabos.
- Sijda and Pabos mean prostration and kissing the monarch's feet.
- Balban belonged to the Slave dynasty.

87. *(d)* The correct statement is "A match consists of the best of three games of 21 points".

- Badminton is a racquet sport played using racquets to hit a shuttlecock across a net.
- Important terminologies associated with badminton are

Alley A 1/2-foot extension of the court on both sides for doubles play.

Back Alley The area between the back boundary line and the long double service line.

88. *(a)* Statements (1) and (3) are true.

- The First Five-Year Plan was launched in 1951 which mainly focused in the development of the primary sector.
- First Five-Year Plan in India was borrowed from Russia.
- First Five-Year Plan was based on Harrod-Domar Model.
- The Second Plan was based on Mahalanobis Model which focuses on development of the public sector and rapid industrialisation'.

89. *(a)* The correct matching is A-2, B-1, C-4 and D-3.

Primitive forms of cultivation in different states are

Madhya Pradesh	Bewar • Bewar, also known as Dahiya, is a traditional method of agriculture. • It involves cutting down and burning forests to create fertile fields for cultivation.
Andhra Pradesh	Penda • It is a shifting cultivation or slash-and-burn agriculture performed in northern hill of Andhra Pradesh.
Odisha	Bringa • A primitive farming technique in Odisha where a farmer cultivates on a plot of land temporarily, and the then moves on to another plot when the soil becomes infertile.
Jhar-khand	Kuruwa • It is the name of the slash-and burn agriculture practiced in Jharkhand.

90. *(c)* Jamshedi Navroz is a festival of Parsi community.

- 'Navroz' comes from the Persian words 'nav' and 'roz,' meaning new and day, respectively.
- While the festival traditionally falls on the Spring Equinox around 21st March.
- The Parsi community in India follows the Shahenshahi calendar and celebrates their new year in July or August.

91. *(b)* Indian athlete Shaili Singh won bronze medal in women's long jump at the Golden Grand Prix 2023 athletics in Japan.

- The 19-year-old Shaili Singh registered a jump of 6.65 m to finish third on the podium.
- Shaili Singh had burst onto the scene back in 2021 after winning a silver medal at the World Athletics U-20 Championships in Nairobi.

92. *(d)* Indian classical dance Kuchipudi has originated in Andhra Pradesh.

- Odissi (Odisha) is a dance of love and passion touching on the divine and the human, the sublime and the mundane.
- Kathakali (Kerala) is basically a dance drama and is famous for its huge elaborate costumes, amazing make-up style, face masks and ornaments.

- Mohiniyattam (Kerala) is a dance form with soft, calm and gentle movements and is usually done by women.

93. *(d)* Atal Beemit Vyakti Kalyan Yojana is an unemployment scheme was extended by the Government of India for a period of two years from July 2022 to June 2024.

- It is a welfare measure being implemented by the Employee's State Insurance (ESI) Corporation.
- It offers cash compensation to insured persons when they are rendered unemployed.
- The scheme is implemented on pilot basis for a period of two years initially, later on extended upto 20th June, 2021.

94. *(b)* The Ghadar Party was founded in 1913 by Sohan Singh Bhakna, Kanshi Ram, Harnam Singh Tundilat, Lala Har Dayal and others.

- The Ghadar Party leaders wanted to free India from colonial rule through armed revolution.
- The literal meaning of 'Ghadar' is 'revolution' in Urdu. The Ghadar Party started the Ghadar Movement.
- The headquarters of the Ghadar Party was established at Yugantar Ashram in San Francisco, USA.

95. *(d)* Wanawun, a folk music of Jammu and Kashmir, is sung in wedding ceremonies.

- Wanawun, with its fluid dance steps, beautiful music and festive atmosphere, perfectly captures the essence of Kashmiri weddings.
- Kashmir's traditional folk music, 'Wanawun' (sometimes spelt 'Rouf'), has a long and storied history and is an integral part of the region's rich cultural legacy.
- In this beautiful musical form, women produce a wave-like motion to the accompaniment of traditional Kashmiri music, making it a highlight of Kashmiri wedding festivities.

96. *(a)* Geeta Phogat is the first female Indian wrestler to win gold at the Commonwealth Games.

- At the 2016 Summer Olympics, Sakshi Malik won the bronze medal in the 58 kg category, becoming the first Indian female wrestler to win a medal at Olympics.
- Alka Tomar became the National Women wrestling Champion of India, and received the bronze medal in Wrestling at the Doha Asian Games in 2006.
- Babita Kumari Phogat is an Indian wrestler, who won the gold medal in 2014 Commonwealth Games.

97. *(b)* Ten Fundamental Duties were added in Part IV of the Constitution under Article 51 A in the year 1976 through the 42nd Constitutional Amendment.

- There are 11 fundamental duties in the Indian Constitution.
- The 42nd Amendment Act is also known as the 'Mini-Constitution' because of the enormous number of amendments it has made to the Indian Constitution.

98. *(b)* In 2001-2002 NABARD instituted Micro Finance Development Fund with a corpus of 100 crores.

- National Bank for Agriculture and Rural Development (NABARD) is a development bank focusing on rural sector of country.
- Its headquarter is in Mumbai.
- It is a statutory body established in 1982.

99. *(b)* Yakshagana is the dance-drama primarily associated with state of Karnataka.

- It is a rare combination of dance, music, song, scholarly dialogues and colourful costumes.
- Nati Nati is a traditional folk dance of Himachal Pradesh.

Jhumar is a traditional folk dance of Bihar, which is performed by the rural women.

100. *(c)* Hans Christian Oersted, a Danish physicist, discovered the relationship between electricity and magnetism on 21st April, 1820. He observed that a compass needle was deflected when an electric current passed through a nearby metallic wire.

Set 10 03 July, 2024 (Shift II)

SSC CHSL Tier-I SOLVED PAPER

Instructions

1. This paper contains 100 questions.
2. It has 4 Parts, **Part I** General English, **Part II** General Intelligence & Reasoning, **Part III** Quantitative Aptitude and **Part IV** General Awareness.
3. Each question carries **2 marks.**

Part I
General English

1. The following sentence has been divided into four segments. Identify the segment that contains a grammatical error.

The meeting / will taking / place next / Wednesday.

(a) place next (b) will taking
(c) The meeting (d) Wednesday.

2. The following sentence has been split into four segments. Identify the segment that contains a grammatical error.

Urgent activities are those things / that you must do immediately, / as they require quick action / and cannot be put on.

(a) and cannot be put on
(b) that you must do immediately
(c) Urgent activities are those things
(d) as they require quick action

3. The following sentence has been split into four segments. Identify the segment that contains a grammatical error.

(A) When Christy (B) grew out, (C) he turned out (D) to be a gentleman.

(a) D (b) C
(c) B (d) A

4. The following sentence has been split into four segments. Identify the segment that contains a grammatical error.

Rashmi was / quite amusing when / she heard about / what had happened.

(a) Rashmi was
(b) quite amusing when
(c) she heard about
(d) what had happened

Directions (Q.Nos. 5-9) *In the following passage, some words have been deleted. Read the passage carefully and select the most appropriate option to fill in each blank.*

There is nothing more (1) .... than when you sit down at your table to study with the most sincere of intentions and instead of being able to finish the task at hand you find your thoughts (2) .... However, there are certain techniques that you can use to (3) .... your concentration. To begin with, one should (4) .... to create the physical environment that is conducive to (5) .... thought.

5. Select the most appropriate option to fill in blank no. (1).

(a) exciting (b) frustrating
(c) surprising (d) interesting

6. Select the most appropriate option to fill in blank no. (2).

(a) worrying (b) tiring
(c) interesting (d) wandering

7. Select the most appropriate option to fill in blank no. (3).

(a) enhance (b) convince
(c) commit (d) discover

8. Select the most appropriate option to fill in blank no. (4).

(a) attempt (b) announce
(c) imagine (d) lead

9. Select the most appropriate option to fill in blank no. (5).

(a) dazzling (b) focussed
(c) cautious (d) joyful

10. Select the most appropriate option to fill in the blank.

My sister's paintings were .... at the national museum.

(a) in display (b) on display
(c) upon display (d) into display

11. Select the most appropriate meaning of the given idiom.

Stick to one's guns

(a) To become a rebel
(b) To shoot at
(c) To become unfaithful to
(d) To remain faithful to

12. Select the incorrectly spelt word.

(a) Litrature
(b) Reformation
(c) Schedule
(d) Miserable

13. Select the most appropriate option that can replace the bracketed word segment in the following sentence.

An (imperfect positioning) of the Sun, Earth and Moon results in the Moon passing through only part of Earth's umbra, resulting in a partial lunar eclipse.

(a) imperfect alliance
(b) imperfect revolution
(c) imperfect allegiance
(d) imperfect alignment

14. Select the option that can substitute the bracketed word segment meaningfully.

The city of Hyderabad is located (on the heart from Telangana).

(a) with the heart in Telangana
(b) in the heart with Telangana
(c) of the heart in Telangana
(d) in the heart of Telangana

15. Select the most appropriate antonym of the underlined word in the given sentence.

Anthony Trollope was an <u>industrious</u> and disciplined writer.

(a) exhausting
(b) skittish
(c) dizzy
(d) lazy

16. Select the most appropriate antonym of the word 'Contaminate' from the given sentence.

She spent the entire night working non-stop to clean the blood stains from the rug.

(a) Rug (b) Spent
(c) Working (d) Clean

17. Select the most appropriate synonym of the given word.

Frivolity

(a) Consequence (b) Substantial
(c) Meaningful (d) Insignificance

18. Select the most appropriate meaning of the given idiom.

Have a bee in your bonnet

(a) Be preoccupied or obsessed with something
(b) Unable to stay at a place for long
(c) To keep worrying about yourself
(d) Having a cruel intention or grudge against someone

19. Select the most appropriate option that can substitute the underlined segment in the given sentence.

There is no way I can swallow the <u>ghastly</u> medicine.

(a) horrible (b) comforting
(c) agreeable (d) pleasant

20. Select the most appropriate option that can substitute the underlined word in the given sentence.

The recent cloudburst completely <u>dismantled</u> the village and its people.

(a) took back (b) took apart
(c) took after (d) took up

21. Select the most appropriate antonym of the underlined word in the given sentence.

Please don't touch that, it's <u>flammable</u>.

(a) non-combustible
(b) nonexplosive
(c) incendiary (d) fire-resistant

22. Select the incorrectly spelt word.

(a) Immigrete (b) Combat
(c) Relevant (d) Professional

23. Select the most appropriate option that can substitute the underlined segment in the given sentence.

The new chief is <u>gifted at</u> the power of eloquence.

(a) gifted with (b) gifted for
(c) gifted among (d) gifted of

24. Select the most appropriate antonym of the given word.

Fastidious

(a) Scrupulous (b) Lax
(c) Late (d) Speedy

25. Select the option that will improve the underlined part of the given sentence.

I was looking for a <u>barren seat</u> in the bus but could not find one.

(a) hollow seat (b) deserted seat
(c) vacant seat (d) vacuous seat

Part II
General Intelligence

26. If 17th August, 2003 was a Sunday, then what was the day of the week on 12th September, 2014 ?

(a) Sunday (b) Friday
(c) Monday (d) Wednesday

27. Select the option that is embedded in the given figure (rotation is not allowed).

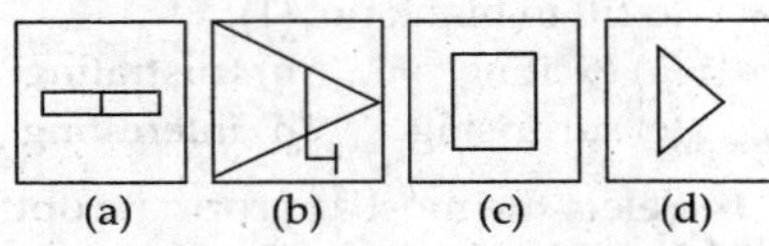

28. In this question, three statements are given, followed by three conclusions numbered I, II and III. Assuming the statements to be true, even if they seem to be at variance with commonly known facts, decide which of the conclusion(s) logically follows/follow from the statements.

Statements

No pen is a scale.
All scales are erasers.
All pens are calculators.

Conclusions

I. Some erasers are calculators.
II. No pen is an eraser.
III. No scale is a calculator.

(a) Both Conclusions II and III follow
(b) Neither Conclusion I, II nor III follows
(c) All Conclusions I, II and III follow
(d) Both Conclusions I and II follow

29. Select the correct mirror image of the given figure, when the mirror is placed at MN.

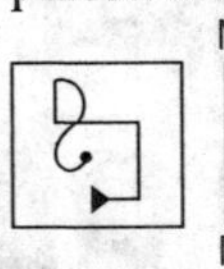

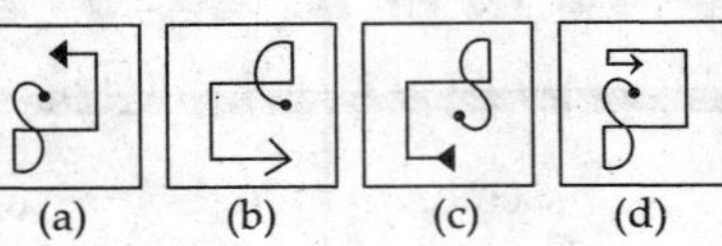

30. Identify the figure in the options that, when put in place of the question mark (?) will logically complete the series ?

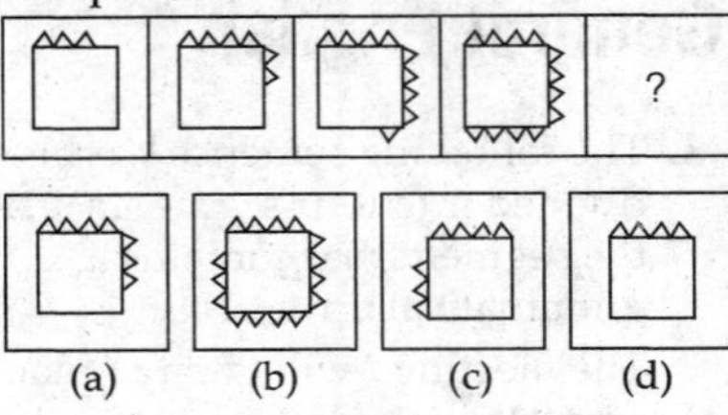

31. In a certain code language, 'COVER' is coded as '9-45-66-15-54' and 'BOAST' is coded as '6-45-3-57-60'. What is the code for 'APRON' in the given code language ?

(a) 2-46-52-40-41 (b) 3-48-54-45-42
(c) 2-46-52-44-40 (d) 4-47-53-42-40

32. In a certain code language, COMB is coded as 2681 and MOBE is coded as 8163. What is the code of E in that language?

(a) 6 (b) 3 (c) 1 (d) 8

33. Select the correct mirror image of the given combination, when the mirror is placed at MN as shown below.

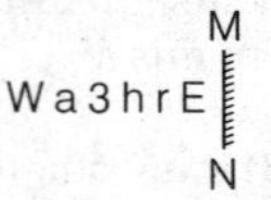

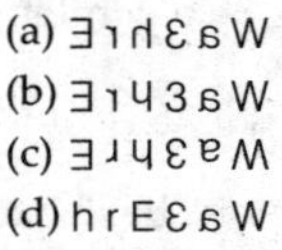

Wa3hrE

(a) ∃ɿɦƐɒW
(b) ∃ɿԿ3ɒW
(c) ∃ɹɥƐɐM
(d) hrEƐɒW

34. Select the word-pair that best represents a similar relationship to the one expressed in the pair of words given below.

(The words must be considered as meaningful English words and must not be related to each other based on the number of letters/number of consonants/vowels in the word).

Proud : Arrogant
(a) Wise : Ignorant
(b) Authentic : Genuine
(c) Trust : Doubt
(d) Offend : Praise

35. In a certain code language, 'A @ B' means 'A is the husband of B' and 'A # B' means 'A is the mother of B' and 'A & B' means 'A is the sister of B'.
Based on the above, how is T related to P, if 'P @ Q # R & S @ T' ?
(a) Son's wife (b) Daughter
(c) Sister (d) Wife's sister

36. Which of the following numbers will replace the question mark (?) in the given series?
7, 28, 84, 336, 1008, ?
(a) 3902 (b) 4128 (c) 3036 (d) 4032

37. Select the combination of letters that, when sequentially placed in the blanks of the given series will logically complete the series.
AB_Z DEF_ G_IX JKL_ M_OV
(a) CYHWN (b) YGHVN
(c) CYGWN (d) CYHVN

38. The position of how many letters will remain unchanged, if each of the letters in the word MENTOR is arranged in the alphabetical order ?
(a) Two (b) None
(c) One (d) Three

39. 'D + E' means 'D is the father of E'.
'D − E' means 'D is the sister of E'.
'D × E' means 'D is the mother of E'.
'D ÷ E' means 'D is the brother of E'.
Which of the following represents 'K is the brother's daughter of L'?
(a) L − F + K − P (b) K − L × X ÷ U
(c) U + F + X ÷ P (d) L ÷ Z × X − K

40. If 'Z' stands for '÷', 'H' stands for '×', 'M' stands for '+' and 'T' stands for '−', what will come in place of the question mark (?) in the following equation?
52 M 36 Z 18 T 46 H 19 = ?
(a) −754 (b) −820
(c) −654 (d) −898

41. A paper is folded and cut as shown below. How will it appear, when unfolded?

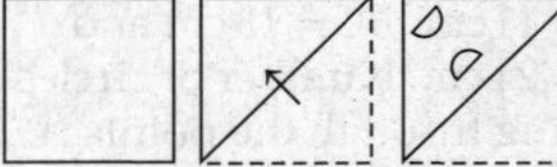

(a) (b) (c) (d)

42. What will come in the place of the question mark (?) in the following equation, if '+' and '−' are interchanged and '×' and '÷' are interchanged ?
198 × 9 + 29 − 7 ÷ 10 = ?
(a) 61 (b) 60 (c) 62 (d) 63

43. Select the set in which the numbers are related in the same way as are the numbers of the following sets.
(**Note** Operations should be performed on the whole numbers, without breaking down the numbers into its constituent digits. E.g. 13 – Operations on 13 such as adding/subtracting/multiplying etc. to 13 can be performed. Breaking down 13 into 1 and 3 and then performing mathematical operations on 1 and 3 is not allowed.)
(245, 49, 5)
(144, 9, 16)
(a) (246, 9, 28) (b) (200, 8, 25)
(c) (312, 24, 9) (d) (186, 21, 8)

44. How many triangles are there in the given figure?

(a) 15 (b) 20 (c) 18 (d) 16

45. What should come in place of question mark (?) in the given series based on the English alphabetical order ?
PHO, SRP, VBQ, ?, BVS
(a) UMO (b) CFE
(c) YLR (d) VXY

46. Six numbers 2, 3, 5, 7, 8 and 9 are written on different faces of a dice. Two positions of this dice are shown in the figure. Which is the number on the face opposite to the face containing 5 ?

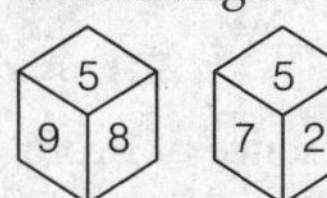

(a) 9 (b) 2
(c) 3 (d) 8

47. Select the word-pair that best represents a similar relationship to the one expressed in the pair of words given below.
(The words must be considered as meaningful English words and must not be related to each other based on the number of letters/ consonants/vowels in the word.)
Pleasure : Delight
(a) Silly : Serious
(b) Rain : Sky
(c) Knowledge : Book
(d) Demolish : Destroy

48. 100 is related to 20 following a certain logic. Following the same logic, 250 is related to 50. To which of the following is 550 related, following the same logic?
(**Note** Operations should be performed on the whole numbers, without breaking down the numbers into its constituent digits. e.g. 13 – Operations on 13 such as adding /deleting /multiplying etc. to 13 can be performed. Breaking down 13 into 1 and 3 and then performing mathematical operations on 1 and 3 is not allowed).
(a) 105 (b) 110
(c) 115 (d) 100

49. If 'H' stands for '÷', 'A' stands for '+', 'B' stands for '−' and 'L' stands for '×', what will come in place of the question mark (?) in the following equation?
84 H 42 A 63 L 46 B 23 = ?
(a) 2877 (b) 2482
(c) 2864 (d) 4632

50. What should come in place of the question mark (?) in the given series?
91, 100, 109, 118, 127, ?
(a) 135 (b) 136
(c) 138 (d) 137

Part III
Quantitative Aptitude

51. Find the value of the following expression.
$\sin(30° + \theta°) - \cos(60° - \theta)$
(a) $2\sin(30 + \theta)$ (b) 1
(c) $\frac{\sqrt{3}}{2}$ (d) 0

52. A man invested a sum of ₹ 5000 on simple interest for 5 yr such that the rate of interest for the first 2 yr is 10% per annum, for the next 3 yr it is 12% per annum. How much interest (in ₹), will he earn at the end of 5 yr?
(a) 3180 (b) 2800
(c) 3000 (d) 2450

53. In a right-angled triangle ABC such that $\angle BAC = 90°$ and AD is perpendicular to BC. If the area of ΔABC is $63\,cm^2$, area of $\Delta ACD = 7\,cm^2$ and $AC = 5\,cm$, then the length of BC is equal to
(a) 10 cm (b) 15 cm
(c) 18 cm (d) 12 cm

54. A sells a bike to B at 45% profit. Then, B, sells it to C at 30% profit. If C pays ₹ 43355, then what is the cost price of the bike for A?
(a) ₹ 23000 (b) ₹ 27000
(c) ₹ 29000 (d) ₹ 21000

55. What is the area of the region created by the two linear equations $2x + y = 6$ and $2x - y = -2$ bounded by these lines and the X-axis?
(a) 5 sq. units (b) 8 sq. units
(c) 3 sq. units (d) 6 sq. units

56. The following table shows admitted students in an institute during the academic years 2015 to 2020 in different courses.

Academic years	Engineering	Science	Arts	Management
2015	1200	850	450	240
2016	1362	821	525	275
2017	1351	870	624	286
2018	1409	921	615	293
2019	1421	931	795	300
2020	1400	950	750	320

Which course had the highest growth rate (in percentage) during the period from 2015 to 2020 ?
(a) Arts (b) Management
(c) Engineering (d) Science

57. A circle of diameter 26 cm has two equal parallel chords of length 10 cm each, then the distance between the two chords is
(a) 23 cm (b) 26 cm
(c) 21 cm (d) 24 cm

58. Following pie-chart presents monthly expenditure by Sushma and Preeti in different heads. Sushma and Preeti make equal expenditure every month.

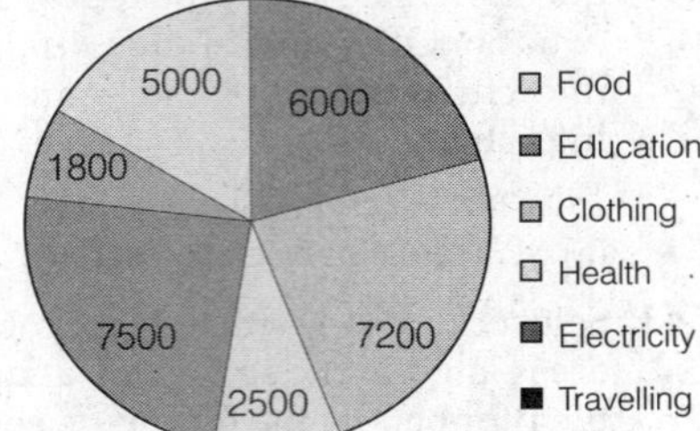

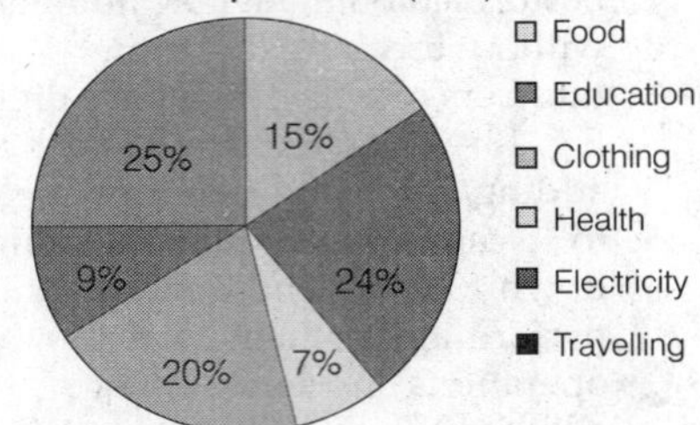

What is the ratio of central angles of expenditure on Education incurred by Sushma and Preeti ?
(a) 2 : 3 (b) 1 : 2
(c) 1 : 1 (d) 2 : 1

59. Two circles touch each other externally at M. PQ is a direct common tangent to the two circles, P and Q are points of contact and $\angle MPQ = 38°$. $\angle MQP$ is
(a) 38° (b) 52° (c) 42° (d) 48°

60. A fraction $\frac{3}{5}$ is decreased by $\frac{2}{5}$. The resulting fraction is then increased by 20%. What is the percentage decrease/increase in the value of the original fraction ?
(a) Increase, 60% (b) Decrease, 50%
(c) Increase, 50% (d) Decrease, 60%

61. Study the following bar chart, which represents the income and expenditure of a company.

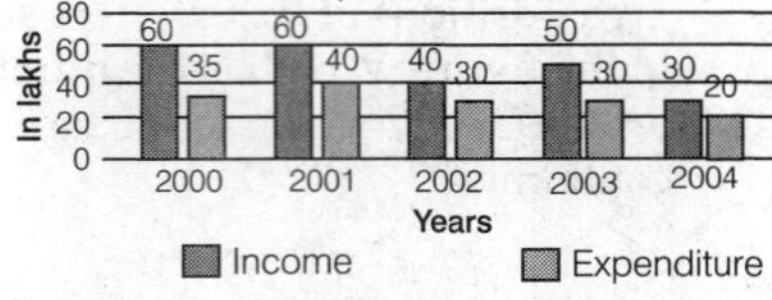

What is the difference of profit between the years 2001 and 2002 ?
(a) 10 lakhs (b) 2 lakhs
(c) 5 lakhs (d) 15 lakhs

62. A policeman starts chasing a thief, who is 500 m ahead of him. The speed of the thief is 18 km/h and the speed of the policeman is 36 km/h. Find the time taken by the policeman to catch the thief.
(a) 300 sec
(b) 100 sec
(c) 150 sec
(d) 250 sec

63. Find the remainder, when $179 \times 172 \times 173$ is divided by 17.
(a) 3 (b) 6
(c) 9 (d) 2

64. By selling an article at 66% of its marked price, a merchant makes a profit of 10%. If he sells the article at 80% of its marked price, then the profit percentage will be
(a) 20% (b) $33\frac{1}{3}$%
(c) 25% (d) $33\frac{2}{3}$%

65. The value of $(17 + 15) \div 2 - 11 + 16 \times 4 - 28 + 13(-16 + 13)$ is
(a) 3 (b) 1
(c) 0 (d) 2

66. The salaries of T in twelve months of a year are ₹ 12000, ₹ 12000, ₹ 12000, ₹ 15000, ₹ 15000, ₹ 15000, ₹ 21000, ₹ 21000, ₹ 21000, ₹ 30000, ₹ 30000, ₹ 30000. The average salary of T per month in ₹ is
(a) 19500 (b) 18500
(c) 18000 (d) 19000

67. The curved surface area, of a right circular cylinder of height 14 cm, is $88\,cm^2$. Find the total surface area of the cylinder.
(a) $\frac{560}{7}\,cm^2$
(b) $\frac{360}{7}\,cm^2$
(c) $\frac{660}{7}\,cm^2$
(d) $\frac{460}{7}\,cm^2$

68. If $a : b = 3 : 7$ and $b : c = 4 : 9$, then find $a : b : c$.
(a) 12 : 28 : 63 (b) 3 : 28 : 63
(c) 12 : 28 : 9 (d) 3 : 28 : 9

69. A, B, C are three points such that $AB = 11\,cm$, $BC = 13\,cm$ and $AC = 24\,cm$. Number of circles passing through the points A, B, C is
(a) 0 (b) 3 (c) 1 (d) 2

70. A person wants to buy 10 chairs. The total cost of 10 chairs is ₹ 4500. After bargaining, the shopkeeper agrees to decrease the cost of each chair by 20%. Then, the person purchased 10% more chairs. What will be the cost of the chairs that he purchased ?
(a) ₹ 4100 (b) ₹ 3960
(c) ₹ 3260 (d) ₹ 3900

71. 18 men can complete $\frac{1}{5}$ of a work in 10 days. How many people are required to complete $\frac{2}{5}$ of the same work in 5 days ?
(a) 36 (b) 90
(c) 72 (d) 54

72. Ramana spends 75% of his income. His income is increased by 25% and he increases his expenditure by 10%. By what percentage are his savings increased ?
(a) 60% (b) 50%
(c) 70% (d) 40%

73. Study the given bar-graph and answer the question that follows.
The bar-graph show the production (in lakh) of kitchen appliances manufactured by three companies A, B and C over a period of six years from 2012 to 2017.

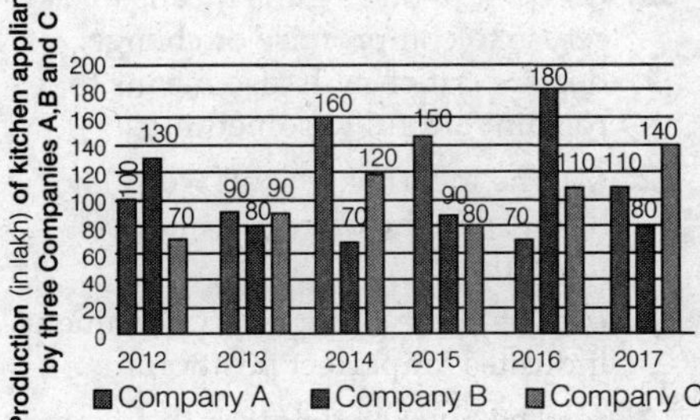

What is the difference (in lakh) between the average production of company B during the period 2012 to 2017 and the company average of the production of company A in 2012, 2014, 2015 and the production of company C in 2014, 2016 and 2017, respectively?
(a) 25 (b) 40
(c) 30 (d) 50

74. The area of a rectangular field is 3600 m^2. If the field is 45 m long, what is its perimeter ?
(a) 260 m (b) 255 m
(c) 265 m (d) 250 m

75. If the surface area of cuboid is 108 m^2, then find the height of the cuboid, whose length is 6 m and breadth is 3 m.
(a) 4.5 m (b) 4 m
(c) 5 m (d) 5.5 m

Part IV
General Awareness

76. We can add a table in an MS Word document from which of the following tabs?
(a) View Tab (b) Home Tab
(c) Design Tab (d) Insert Tab

77. In which year was the first underground section (Vishwavidyalaya- Kashmere Gate) of the Golden Route opened in New Delhi?
(a) 2004 (b) 2000
(c) 1997 (d) 1998

78. Name the digital payment platform launched in 2021 by the National Payments Corporation of India (NPCI) in association with Department of Financial Services (DFS), National Health Authority (NHA) and Ministry of Health and Family Welfare (MoHFW).
(a) MobiKwik (b) e-RUPI
(c) Dhani (d) YONO

79. Which article of the Constitution mentions that "the Parliament consists of the President and two Houses known as the Council of States (Rajya Sabha) and the House of the People (Lok Sabha)"?
(a) 82 (b) 79 (c) 70 (d) 73

80. Which of the following statements best describes the Hardy Schulze rule?
(a) The ions are removed from the solution by the phenomenon of diffusion through a permeable membrane.
(b) The partial pressure of a component in a liquid mixture is proportional to its mole fraction in that mixture.
(c) This is applied to obtain a colloidal solution of metals such as gold, silver or platinum.
(d) The amount of electrolyte required for the coagulation of a definite amount of a colloidal solution is dependent on the valency of the coagulating ion.

81. What was the name of Swami Vivekananda's Guru?
(a) Swami Ram Singh
(b) Swami Dayananda
(c) Aadi Shankaracharya
(d) Ramakrishna Paramhansa

82. The Green Revolution was due to the introduction of
(a) irrigation
(b) fertilisers
(c) High Yielding Varieties of seeds
(d) fisheries

83. Guru Vempati Chinna Satyam is a famous dancer of .... dance form of India.
(a) Bharatanatyam (b) Manipuri
(c) Odissi (d) Kuchipudi

84. The famous book 'Sangraha Choodamani', which deals with the current system of Carnatic music was written by
(a) Damodara Misra
(b) Matanga
(c) Haripala
(d) Govindacharya

85. Kiran Nadar was conferred with the highest civilian award of which country in April 2023?
(a) France (b) Poland
(c) Egypt (d) Germany

86. What do you mean by semiconservative DNA replication?
(a) After the completion of replication, each DNA molecule would have two parental and two newly synthesised strand.
(b) RNA is dependent on DNA for the synthesis of proteins.
(c) DNA is dependent on RNA for the synthesis of proteins.
(d) After the completion of replication, each DNA molecule would have one parental and one newly synthesised strand.

87. The colour of the surface of Mars is red because of the presence of large amounts of chemical compounds in it. What is the name of that compound?
(a) Tin oxide
(b) Iron oxide
(c) Magnesium oxide
(d) Nitrogen oxide

88. In MS Word, a number printed above the base line is called ....
(a) superscript (b) strikethrough
(c) above BL (d) subscript

89. How many censuses had been completed in India as of year 2011?
(a) 12 (b) 7
(c) 15 (d) 16

90. Which of the following statements is/are Incorrect *vis-à-vis* features of the Indian Constitution?
(1) Though India has a federal system, the Constitution does not mention the word 'federation'.
(2) Article 5 of the Constitution says that the Parliament by law can create a new state.
(3) On the subjects in the Union List, each State Legislature can enact laws for the state.
(4) Both the Parliament and State Legislature can pass laws on subjects in Concurrent List.

Codes
(a) 1 and 4 (b) 1 and 3
(c) Only 1 (d) 2 and 3

91. Under which Gharana do the composition of blend of Khayal and Dhrupad-Dhamar styles come?
(a) Indore Gharana
(b) Agra Gharana
(c) Gwalior Gharana
(d) Patiala Gharana

92. The number of Indian athletes who participated in the Tokyo Paralympics 2020 was ....
(a) 57 (b) 56
(c) 54 (d) 55

93. Which Pala ruler temporarily occupied Kanauj?
(a) Gopala (b) Dharmapala
(c) Devapala (d) Harapala

94. According to Census of India 2011, what was the sex ratio recorded in the Union Territory of Puducherry?
(a) 980 females/1000 males
(b) 1095 females/1000 males
(c) 1037 females/1000 males
(d) 890 females/1000 males

95. The Ultimate Kho-Kho League was started in which year?
(a) 2020 (b) 2021
(c) 2022 (d) 2023

96. Indian Constitution came into force on .... and is celebrated as Republic Day.
(a) 26th Jan, 1951
(b) 26th Jan, 1950
(c) 26th Jan, 1948
(d) 26th Feb, 1950

97. Who among the following launched the digital platform 'FASTER'?
(a) Chief Justice of India
(b) Prime Minister
(c) Finance Minister
(d) President

98. In field hockey, in a penalty stroke, an attacker shoots at goal from .... yards away in a one-on-one confrontation with the goalkeeper.
(a) 10 (b) 8
(c) 7 (d) 9

99. Who was appointed as the Chief Economic Advisor to the Government of India in the year 2022?
(a) S. Somanath
(b) Krishnamurthy Subramanian
(c) V. Anantha Nageswaran
(d) R. Rangarajan

100. Which river is known as the sorrow of Bihar?
(a) Mahi (b) Betwa
(c) Son (d) Kosi

Answers

1. (b)	2. (a)	3. (c)	4. (b)
5. (b)	6. (d)	7. (a)	8. (a)
9. (b)	10. (b)	11. (d)	12. (a)
13. (d)	14 (d)	15. (d)	16. (d)
17. (d)	18. (a)	19. (a)	20. (b)
21. (a)	22. (a)	23. (a)	24. (b)
25. (c)	26. (b)	27. (d)	28. (b)
29. (c)	30. (b)	31. (b)	32. (b)
33. (a)	34. (b)	35. (a)	36. (d)
37. (a)	38. (c)	39. (a)	40. (b)
41. (c)	42. (d)	43. (b)	44. (c)
45. (c)	46. (c)	47. (d)	48. (b)
49. (a)	50. (b)	51. (d)	52. (b)
53. (b)	54. (a)	55. (b)	56. (a)
57. (d)	58. (c)	59. (b)	60. (d)
61. (a)	62. (b)	63. (a)	64. (b)
65. (d)	66. (a)	67. (c)	68. (a)
69. (a)	70. (b)	71. (c)	72. (c)
73. (a)	74. (d)	75. (b)	76. (d)
77. (a)	78. (b)	79. (b)	80. (d)
81. (d)	82. (c)	83. (d)	84. (d)
85. (a)	86. (d)	87. (b)	88. (a)
89. (c)	90. (d)	91. (b)	92. (c)
93. (b)	94. (c)	95. (c)	96. (b)
97. (a)	98. (c)	99. (c)	100. (d)

Explanations

1. *(b)* Part (b) 'will taking' contains an error. Use 'take' in place of 'taking' to correct the sentence.

2. *(a)* Part (a) 'and cannot be put on' contains an error. Add 'hold' after 'on' to complete the meaning of the sentence.

3. *(c)* Part (B) 'grew out', contains an error. Use 'up' in place of 'out' to correct the sentence.

4. *(b)* Part (b) 'quite amusing when' contains an error. The use of present participle adjective is incorrect in the sentence. Use past participle 'amused' to correct the sentence.

5. *(b)* The correct filler for the given blank is 'frustrating'.

6. *(d)* The correct filler for the given blank is 'wandering'.

7. *(a)* The correct filler for the given blank is 'enhanced'.

8. *(a)* The correct filler for the given blank is 'attempt'.

9. *(b)* The correct filler for the given blank is 'focused'.

10. *(b)* The correct filler for the given blank is 'on display' as it indicates that the paintings were put for public viewing.

11. *(d)* Stick to one's guns means to refuse to compromise or change, despite criticism. It also means to remain faithful to something.

12. *(a)* The incorrectly spelt word is 'litrature'. The correct spelling is 'literature'.

13. *(d)* The phrase 'imperfect alignment' indicates 'imperfect positioning'.

14. *(d)* The bracketed part of the given sentence contains an error. Use 'in the heart of Telangana' to correct the sentence.

15. *(d)* Industrious means hard working and dedicated. Hence, its antonym is 'lazy'.
- 'Skittish' means nervous or excitable; easily scared.
- 'Dizzy' means feeling faint, woozy, weak or unsteady.

16. *(d)* Contaminate means to make impure or dirty. Hence, its antonym is 'clean'.

17. *(d)* The word 'frivolity' means 'insignificance or non-importance'.

18. *(a)* To have a bee in your bonnet means to be preoccupied or obsessed with something.

19. *(a)* The word 'ghastly' means 'horrible and scary'.

20. *(b)* The word 'dismantled' means 'to take something apart'.

21. *(a)* 'Flammable' means easily set on fire. Hence, its antonym is 'non-combustible' which means not capable of igniting and burning.

- 'Non-explosive' means something that will not burst open
- 'Incendiary' means designed to cause fires.

22. *(a)* The incorrectly spelt word is 'immigrete'. The correct spelling is 'immigrate'.

23. *(a)* The underlined part of the given sentence contains an error. Use 'gifted with' to correct the sentence.

24. *(b)* Fastidious means very attentive to and concerned about accuracy and detail. Hence, its antonym is 'lax' which means not sufficiently strict, severe, or careful.

'Scrupulous' means careful, thorough, and extremely attentive to details.

25. *(c)* The underlined part of the given sentence contains an error. Use 'vacant seat' to correct the sentence.

26. *(b)* Odd day in ordinary year = 1

Odd days in leap year = 2

Day on 17th August, 2003 → Sunday

Number of odd days from 17th August, 2003 to 17th August, 2014

$= 2 + 1 + 1 + 1 + 2 + 1 + 1 + 1 + 2 + 1 + 1$

$= \frac{14}{7} = 2$ weeks

Number of days between 17th August, 2014 to 12th September, 2014

$= 14 + 12 = \frac{26}{7}$

= 3 week and 5 days (odd)

∴ The day of the week on 12th September, 2014 = Sunday + 5 = Friday

27. *(d)* The option figure (d) is embedded in the given figure.

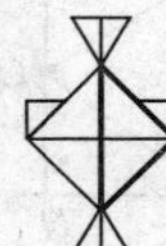

28. *(b)* According to the statements,

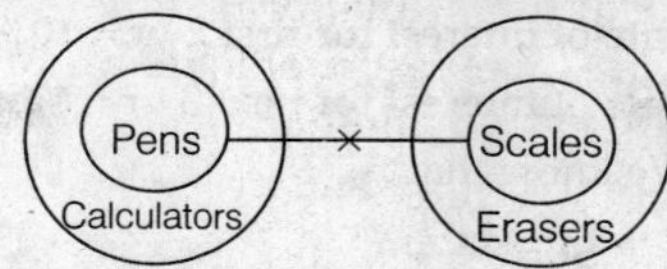

Conclusions I. (✗) II. (✗) III. (✗)

Hence, neither Conclusions I, II nor III follows.

29. *(c)* The figure given in option (c) is the correct mirror image of the given figure.

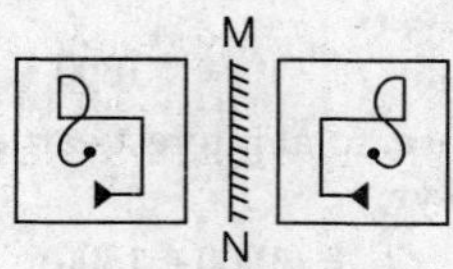

30. *(b)* The number of triangles is increasing by 3 outside the square in every next figure.

So, option (b) will replace the question mark.

31. *(b)* As, C O V E R → 9 45 66 15 54

[Number of positional value of letter × 3]

and B O A S T → 6 45 3 57 60

Similarly, A P R O N

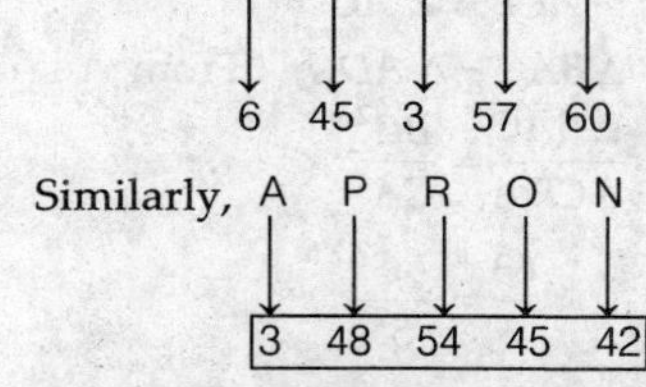

32. *(b)* As, C OMB → 2 681

and MOB E → 816 3

Hence, the code for E = 3.

33. *(a)* The figure given in option (a) is the correct mirror image of the given figure.

Wa3hrE | M/N | mirror image

34. *(b)* As, Proud and Arrogant are synonyms to each other. Similarly, Authentic and Genuine are synonyms to each other.

35. *(a)* According to the question,

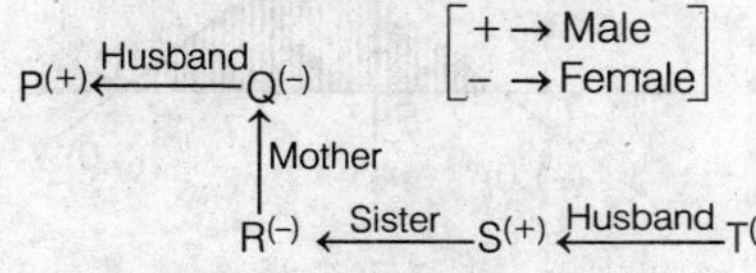

Hence, T is son's wife of P.

36. *(d)* The pattern of the series is as follows,

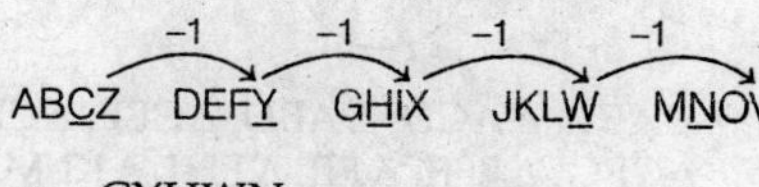

37. *(a)* The pattern of the series is as follows,

ABCZ DEFY GHIX JKLW MNOV (–1 each)

⇒ CYHWN

38. *(c)* Given word → M E N T O R

After arranging the letters in alphabetical order → E M N O R T

Hence, one letter will remain unchanged.

39. *(a)* According to the question,

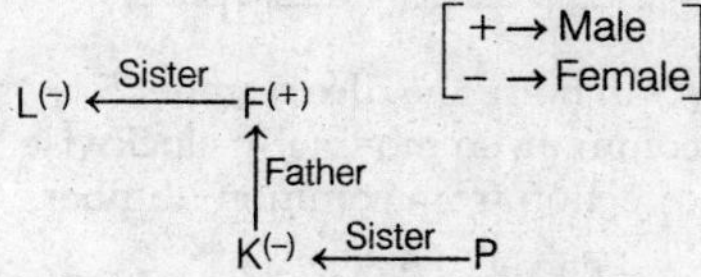

Hence, 'K is the brother's daughter of L'.

40. *(b)* Given expression,

52 M 36 Z 18 T 46 H 19 = ?

After substituting the letters with signs, we get

$52 + 36 \div 18 - 46 \times 19 = ?$

$? = 52 + 2 - 874$

$? = 54 - 874 = -820$

41. *(c)* When we unfold the paper, then it will appear as the figure given in option (c).

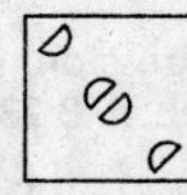

42. *(d)* Given expression,

$198 \times 9 + 29 - 7 \div 10 = ?$

After interchanging the sign '+' and '–' and '×' and '÷', we get

$= 198 \div 9 - 29 + 7 \times 10$

$= 22 - 29 + 70$

$= 92 - 29 = 63$

43. *(b)* As, (245, 49, 5)

⇒ $245 \div 5 = 49$

and (144, 9, 16)

⇒ $144 \div 16 = 9$

Similarly, (200, 8, 25)

⇒ $200 \div 25 = 8$

44. *(c)* Naming the figure,

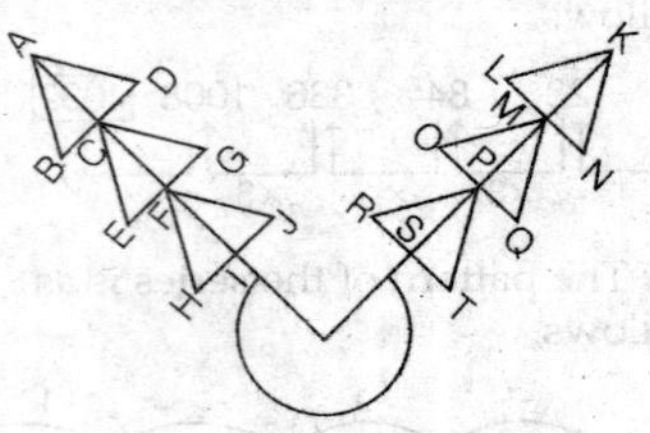

Δ ABC, Δ ACD, Δ ABD, ΔCEF, ΔCFG, ΔCEG, ΔFHI, ΔFIJ, ΔFHJ, ΔKLM, ΔKMN, ΔKLN, ΔMOP, ΔMPQ, ΔMOQ, ΔPRS, ΔPST and ΔPRT.

Hence, there are 18 triangles in the given figure.

45. *(c)* The pattern of the series is as follows,

$P \xrightarrow{+3} S \xrightarrow{+3} V \xrightarrow{+3} \boxed{Y} \xrightarrow{+3} B$

$H \xrightarrow{+10} R \xrightarrow{+10} B \xrightarrow{+10} \boxed{L} \xrightarrow{+10} V$

$O \xrightarrow{+1} P \xrightarrow{+1} Q \xrightarrow{+1} \boxed{R} \xrightarrow{+1} S$

46. *(c)* In both, the dice number 5 is common, so moving in clockwise direction from common number.

Dice I $\rightarrow$ 5 8 9

Dice II $\rightarrow$ 5 2 7

$\therefore$ Number 3 is opposite to the face containing 5.

47. *(d)* As, Pleasure and Delight are synonyms to each other.

Similarly, Demolish and Destroy are the synonyms to each other.

48. *(b)* As, $\frac{100}{5} = 20$

and $\frac{250}{5} = 50$

Similarly, $\frac{550}{5} = \boxed{110}$

49. *(a)* Given expression,
84 H 42 A 63 L 46 B 23 = ?

After substituting the letters with signs, we get

$84 \div 42 + 63 \times 46 - 23$
$= 2 + 2898 - 23$
$= 2900 - 23$
$= 2877$

50. *(b)* The pattern of the series is as follows,

91 100 109 118 127 $\boxed{136}$
+9 +9 +9 +9 +9

51. *(d)* $\sin(30° + \theta) - \cos(60° - \theta)$
$= \sin(30° + \theta) - \sin[90° - (60° - \theta)]$
$= \sin(30° + \theta) - \sin(30° + \theta)$
$= 0$

52. *(b)* Given, Principal = ₹ 5000

Rate of interest for first 2 yr = 10%

Rate of interest for next 3 yr = 12%

We know that,

$$SI = \frac{PRT}{100}$$

$\because$ Interest for first 2 yr

$$= 5000 \times \frac{10}{100} \times 2$$
$$= ₹\ 1000$$

Interest for next 3 yr $= 5000 \times \frac{12}{100} \times 3$

$$= ₹\ 1800$$

Hence, total interest earned at the end of 5 yr

$$= (1000 + 1800)$$
$$= ₹\ 2800$$

53. *(b)* According to the question,

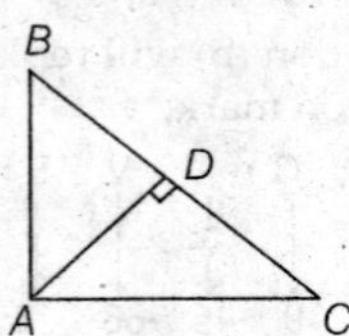

In Δ ACB and Δ ACD,

$\angle BAC = \angle ADC = 90°$

$\angle ACB = \angle ACD$

$\therefore$ $\Delta BAC \sim \Delta ADC$ [From AA rule]

$$\frac{\Delta BAC}{\Delta CDA} = \frac{BC^2}{CA^2}$$

$$\frac{63}{7} = \frac{BC^2}{5^2}$$

$BC^2 = 9 \times 25 = 225$

$\therefore$ $BC = 15$ cm

54. *(a)* Let A bought the article at ₹ x.

According to the question,

$(100 + 30)\%$ of $(100 + 45)\%$ of x
$= 43355$

$$\frac{130}{100} \times \frac{145}{100} \times x = 43355$$

$$\Rightarrow \quad x = \frac{43355 \times 100 \times 100}{130 \times 145} = ₹\ 23000$$

55. *(b)* Given equation,

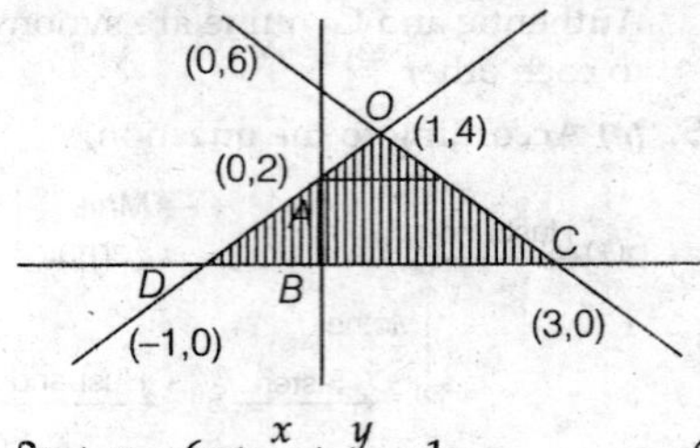

$2x + y = 6 \Rightarrow \frac{x}{3} + \frac{y}{6} = 1$ ...(i)

and $2x - y = -2 \Rightarrow \frac{x}{-1} + \frac{y}{2} = 1$ ...(ii)

From Eqs. (i) and (ii),

$4x = 4$

$\Rightarrow \quad x = 1$

and $y = 4$

$OD = \sqrt{(4-0)^2 + (1+1)^2}$
$= \sqrt{16+4} = 2\sqrt{5}$

$OC = \sqrt{(4-0)^2 + (1-3)^2}$
$= \sqrt{16+4} = 2\sqrt{5}$

or $CD = \sqrt{(3+1)^2 + (0-0)^2} = 4$

Angle between OD and OC is

$$\tan\theta = \frac{4-0}{1+1} = 2$$

$$\Rightarrow \sin\theta = \frac{2}{\sqrt{5}}$$

$\therefore$ Area of ΔODC

$$= \frac{1}{2} \times OD \times DC \times \sin\theta$$
$$= \frac{1}{2} \times 2\sqrt{5} \times 4 \times \frac{2}{\sqrt{5}}$$
$$= 8 \text{ sq. units}$$

56. *(a)* Percentage increase in growth rate from year 2015 to 2020 in Engineering

$$= \frac{1400 - 1200}{1200} \times 100 = 16.67\%$$

Percentage increase in growth rate from year 2015 to 2020 in Science

$$= \frac{950 - 850}{850} \times 100$$
$$= 11.76\%$$

Percentage increase in growth rate from year 2015 to 2020 in Arts

$$= \frac{750 - 450}{450} \times 100 = 66.67\%$$

Percentage increase in growth rate from year 2015 to 2020 in Management

$$= \frac{320 - 240}{240} \times 100$$
$$= 33.33\%$$

Hence, Arts has the highest growth rate (in percentage) during the period from 2015 to 2020.

57. *(d)* According to the question,

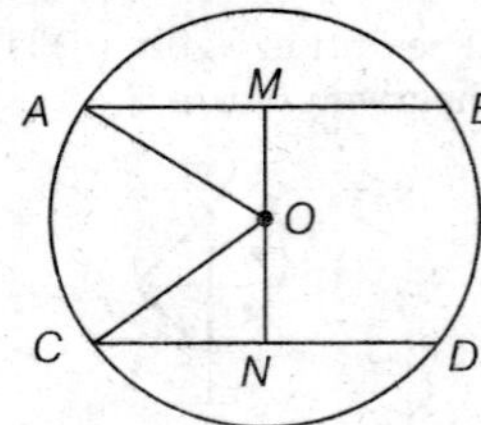

Given, diameter of circle = 26 cm

$\therefore$ Radius of circle $= \frac{26}{2} = 13$ cm

$AM = CN = \frac{AB}{2} = \frac{10}{2} = 5$ cm

In ΔAMO,

$MO = \sqrt{AO^2 - AM^2} = \sqrt{(13)^2 - 5^2}$

$= 12$ cm

Hence, the distance between the two chords $(MN) = 2 \times MO$

$= 2 \times 12$

$= 24$ cm

58. *(c)* Total expenditure

$= 1800 + 5000 + 6000 + 7200 + 2500 + 7500$

$= ₹30000$

Central angles of expenditure on education incurred by Sushma

$= \frac{360}{30000} \times 7200$

$= 86.4°$

Central angles of expenditure on education incurred by Preeti

$= \frac{360}{100} \times 24$

$= 86.4°$

Hence, the required ratio

$= 86.4° : 86.4° = 1:1$

59. *(b)* Given,

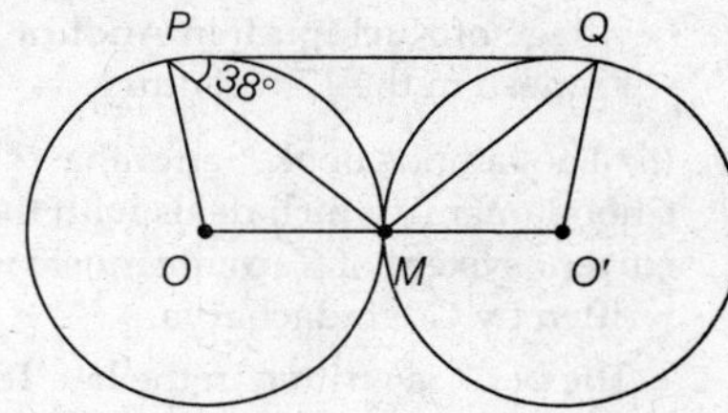

$\because \quad \angle OPQ = 90°$

and $\angle O'QP = 90°$

$\therefore \quad \angle OPM = 90° - 38° = 52° = \angle PMO$

$[OP = OM]$

In ΔOPM,

$\angle POM = 180° - (52° + 52°)$

$= 76°$

In quadrilateral $POO'Q$,

$90° + 76° + 90° + \angle QO'O = 360°$

$\angle QO'O = 360° - 256°$

$[\angle QO'O = \angle QO'M]$

$= 104°$

In $\Delta MQO'$,

$\angle O'MQ = \angle MQO' = \frac{180° - 104°}{2} = 38°$

$\therefore \quad \angle MQP = 90 - 38° = 52°$

60. *(d)* Given, fraction $= \frac{3}{5}$

After decreasing, fraction $= \frac{3}{5} - \frac{2}{5}$

$= \frac{1}{5}$

After 20% increase in fraction

$= \frac{1}{5} \times \frac{120}{100} = \frac{6}{25}$

Hence, the required decrease in percentage

$= \frac{\frac{3}{5} - \frac{6}{25}}{3/5} \times 100 = \frac{9}{25} \times \frac{5}{3} \times 100$

$= 60\%$ decrease

61. *(a)* Profit in year 2001 = Income – Expenditure

$= 60 - 40 = 20$ lakh

Profit in year 2002 = 40 – 30 = 10 lakh

Hence, the required profit = 20 – 10 = 10 lakh

62. *(b)* Time taken by policeman to catch the thief

$= \frac{\text{Distance}}{\text{Relative speed}} = \frac{500 \times 18}{(36 - 18) \times 5}$

$= \frac{500 \times 18}{18 \times 5} = 100$ sec

63. *(a)* Remainder of $\frac{179 \times 172 \times 173}{17}$

$=$ Remainder of $\frac{9 \times 2 \times 3}{17}$

$=$ Remainder of $\frac{54}{17} = 3$

64. *(b)* Let the cost price of article = 100 units

$\therefore$ Selling price of an article

$= \frac{100 \times 110}{100} = 110$ units

Marked price of an article

$= \frac{110 \times 100}{66} = \frac{500}{3}$ units

New selling price

$= \frac{500 \times 80}{3 \times 100} = \frac{400}{3}$ units

Hence, required profit per cent

$= \frac{\frac{400}{3} - 100}{100} \times 100$

$= \frac{100}{3} = 33\frac{1}{3}\%$

65. *(d)* According to the question,

$(17 + 15) \div 2 - 11 + 16 \times 4 - 28 + 13(-16 + 13)$

$= 32 \div 2 - 11 + 64 - 28 + 13 \times (-3)$

$= 16 - 11 + 64 - 28 - 39$

$= 80 - 78 = 2$

66. *(a)* The average salary of T per month is

$= \frac{12000 \times 3 + 15000 \times 3 + 21000 \times 3 + 30000 \times 3}{12}$

$= \frac{36000 + 45000 + 63000 + 90000}{12}$

$= \frac{234000}{12} = ₹ 19500$

67. *(c)* The curved surface area of a cylinder $= 2\pi rh$

$\therefore \quad 2 \times \frac{22}{7} \times r \times 14 = 88$

$r = \frac{88 \times 7}{44 \times 14} = 1$ cm

Hence, the total surface area of cylinder $= 2\pi r(r + h)$

$= 2 \times \frac{22}{7} \times 1(1 + 14)$

$= \frac{2 \times 22 \times 15}{7} = \frac{660}{7}$ cm^2

68. *(a)* $a : b = 3 : 7$

$b : c = 4 : 9$

$a : b : c = 12 : 28 : 63$

69. *(a)* $\because AC = AB + BC$

$24 = 11 + 13$

$24 = 24$

$\therefore A, B, C$ are collinear.

So, there do not exist any circle, which is passed to the colinear points.

70. *(b)* Total cost price of 10 chairs

$= ₹ 4500$

After decrease by 20% in cost price, Cost price of 10 chairs

$= \frac{4500 \times 80}{100} = ₹ 3600$

$\therefore$ Cost price of 1 chair

$= \frac{3600}{10} = ₹ 360$

Person purchase 10% more chairs

New number of chairs

$= \frac{10 \times 110}{100} = 11$

Hence, cost price of 11 chairs

$= ₹ 3960$

71. *(c)* Here, $M_1 = 18, D_1 = 10$ days, $W_1 = \frac{1}{5}$

$M_2 = ?, D_2 = 5$ days, $W_2 = \frac{2}{5}$

$\because \quad \frac{M_1 D_1}{W_1} = \frac{M_2 D_2}{W_2}$

$$\frac{18 \times 10 \times 5}{1} = \frac{M_2 \times 5 \times 5}{2}$$

$$M_2 = 18 \times 2 \times 2$$

$= 72$ people are required.

72. *(c)* Let income of Ramana = ₹100

Expenditure of Ramana = ₹75

$\therefore$ Savings of Ramana = 100 − 75 = ₹25

New income of Ramana

$$= \frac{100 \times 125}{100} = ₹125$$

and new expenditure of Ramana

$$= \frac{75 \times 110}{100} = ₹\ 82.5$$

$\therefore$ New savings of Ramana = 125 − 82.5 = ₹42.5

Hence, percentage increase in savings

$$= \frac{42.5 - 25}{25} \times 100 = \frac{17.5}{25} \times 100$$

$= 70\%$

73. *(a)* The average production of Company B during the period 2012 to 2017

Production

$$= \frac{130 + 80 + 70 + 90 + 180 + 80}{6}$$

$$= \frac{630}{6} = 105 \text{ lakh}$$

Combined average production of Company A in 2012, 2014, 2015 and Company C in 2014, 2016 and 2017

$$= \frac{100 + 160 + 150 + 120 + 110 + 140}{6}$$

$$= \frac{780}{6} = 130 \text{ lakh}$$

Hence, required difference

$= (130 - 105)$ lakh $= 25$ lakh

74. *(d)* Given, area of a rectangular field

$= 3600 \text{ m}^2$

$l \times b = 3600$

$45 \times b = 3600 \Rightarrow b = \frac{3600}{45} = 80$ m

Hence, the perimeter $= 2(l + b)$

$= 2(45 + 80)$

$= 2 \times 125 = 250$ m

75. *(b)* $\because$ Surface area of cuboid

$= 2(lb + bh + hl)$

$[\because l = 6 \text{ m}, b = 3 \text{ m}]$

$\therefore \quad 2(6 \times 3 + 3 \times h + 6 \times h) = 108$

$\Rightarrow \quad 9h + 18 = 54$

$\Rightarrow \quad 9h = 54 - 18 \Rightarrow 9h = 36$

$\Rightarrow \quad h = \frac{36}{9} = 4$ m

Hence, the height of cuboid is 4 m.

76. *(d)* We can add a table in an MS Word document from Insert Tab. Alternatively, use the shortcut key Ctrl+T to insert a table.

77. *(a)* In 2004, the first underground section (Vishwavidyalaya- Kashmere Gate) of the Golden Route opened in New Delhi.

- Vishwavidyalaya-Kashmere Gate metro is also known as Yellow Line metro.
- The first underground metro was started in 1984 in Kolkata.
- The Delhi Metro Rail is the largest and busiest metro network in India.

78. *(b)* e-RUPI is the digital payment platform launched in 2021 by the National Payments Corporation of India (NPCI) in association with Department of Financial Services (DFS), National Health Authority (NHA) and Ministry of Health and Family Welfare (MoHFW).

- e-Rupee is a digital currency that acts as a legal tender for digital transactions.
- It allows people to make digital payments and purchases securely whereas UPI is a platform that enables digital transactions to take place.

79. *(b)* Article 79 of the Constitution mentions that "the Parliament consists of the President and two Houses known as the Council of States (Rajya Sabha) and the House of the People (Lok Sabha)".

- The Indian Constitution gives Parliament the power to create laws for the country.
- The Lok Sabha, or Lower House of the Indian Parliament, has a sanctioned strength of 550 members.
- The Rajya Sabha, or Upper House of the Indian Parliament, has a sanctioned strength of 250 members.
- The President is the nominal head of the executive, the first citizen of the country and the supreme commander of the Indian Armed Forces.

80. *(d)* Statement (d) best describes the Hardly Schulze rule. The amount of electrolyte required for the coagulation of a definite amount of a colloidal solution is dependent on the valency of the coagulating ion.

81. *(d)* The name of Swami Vivekanand's guru is Ramakrishna Paramhansa.

- Swami Vivekananda's real name is Narendranath Datta, born in 1863 at Kolkata.
- He was an Indian Hindu monk, philosopher, author and religious teacher. He is the founder of Ramakrishna Mission.

82. *(c)* The Green Revolution was due to the introduction of High Yielding Varieties of seeds.

- The Green Revolution is the term given to the use of High-Yielding Varieties (HYVs) of wheat and rice to increase food crop production.
- In India, the Green Revolution began in the 1960s in Third Five-Year Plane and converted agriculture into a modern industrial system.
- MS Swaminathan is known as the Father of India's Green Revolution.

83. *(d)* Guru Vempati Chinna Satyam is a famous dancer of Kuchipudi dance form of India.

- He was born in a Brahmin family at Kuchipudi, Andhra Pradesh in 1929.
- He started the Kuchipudi Artwork Academy at Madras in 1963.
- Kuchipudi is a classical Indian dance form that originated in the village of Kuchipudi in Andhra Pradesh in the 17th century.

84. *(d)* The famous book 'Sangraha Choodamani', which deals with the current system of Carnatic music was written by Govindacharya.

- The book is written in the late 18th century.
- It is a collection of Lakshana Geetas in various Melakarthanadjanya Ragas.

85. *(a)* Kiran Nadar was conferred with the highest civilian award of France in Apri1 2023.

- Kiran Shiv Nadar is an Indian art collector and philanthropist.
- She is the founder of the Kiran Nadar Museum of Art.
- The highest civilian award of France is 'Chevalier de la Legion d'Honneur' (Knight of the Legion of Honour).

86. *(d)* In semiconservative DNA replication, after the completion of replication, each DNA molecule would have one parental and one newly synthesised strand.

Semi-conservative replication of DNA is the process of duplicating the original DNA such that the finished products are two double DNA strands, each with one original and one new strand, to be distributed to the daughter cells.

87. *(b)* The colour of the surface of Mars is red because of the presence of large amounts of iron oxide in it.

- Mars is the fourth planet from the Sun.
- Mars has 2 Moons called Deimos and Phobos.

88. *(a)* In MS Word, a number printed above the base line is called superscript.

89. *(c)* 15 censuses had been completed in India as of year 2011.

- First Census in India was conducted by Governor-General Lord Mayo in 1872.
- The first synchronous census in India was conducted in 1881 by WC Plowden.

90. *(d)* Statements (2) and (3) are incorrect regarding the feature of Indian Constitution because

- Article 5 is about Citizenship for people at the commencement of the Indian Constitution, i.e. 26th January 1950.
- The Parliament enacts laws on subjects that are listed in Union List.
- The state enacts laws on subjects that are listed in State List.
- Both Central and State Government can enact laws on subject that are in the Concurrent List.

91. *(b)* Agra Gharana is the composition of blend of Khayal and Dhrupad-Dhamar styles.

- The Agra Gharana is a tradition of Hindustani classical vocal music. It was founded by Hajisujan Khan.
- Gharana is a system of social organisation linking musicians or dancers adherence to a particular musical style.
- Indore Gharana is one of the vocal Gharanas of Indian classical music. It was founded by Amir Khan.
- Patiala Gharana is one of the vocal Gharanas of Hindustani classical music, named after the city of Patiala in Punjab. It was originally founded by Mian Kallu.
- Gwalior Gharana is a style of Hindustani classical music that is considered to be one of the oldest and most influential. It was founded by Ustad Nathan Pir Baksh and Ustad Nathu Khan.

92. *(c)* The number of Indian athletes participated in Tokyo Paralympic 2020 was 54.

- India finishes 24th in medal tally with 19 medals, which includes five gold, eight silver, and six bronze medals.
- China was ranked first in medal tally followed by Great Britain.
- France hosted the 2024 Summer Paralympics.

93. *(b)* Dharmapala was the Pala king who temporarily occupied Kanauj.

- By the end of the 8th century, Dharmapala occupied Kanauj and placed Chakrayudha, one of his ministers in thrown.
- Dharmapala was the second ruler of the Pala empire of Bengal region in the Indian subcontinent.
- He was the son and successor of Gopala, the founder of Pala Empire.
- The famous universities Nalanda and Vikramshila were founded by Dharmapala.

94. *(c)* According to the 2011 Census, the sex ratio of Puducherry was 1037 females per 1,000 males.

- It has higher sex ratio than the national average of 943 females per 1,000 males in India in 2011.
- Kerala has the highest sex ratio (1084) followed by Puducherry.
- Haryana has the lowest sex ratio (877) in Indian states while in union territory Daman and Diu has lowest sex ratio of 618.

95. *(c)* The Ultimate Kho-Kho League was started in 2022.

- Ultimate Kho Kho (UKK) is an Indian franchise-based Kho-Kho league.
- The first ever rules and regulations of modern day Kho Kho were written by Lokmanya Bal Gangadhar Tilak.
- Each Kho-Kho team consists of 12 players, but during a contest only 9 players from each team take the field.

96. *(b)* Indian Constitution came into force on 26th January, 1950 and is celebrated as Republic Day.

- The Constitution was adopted by the Constituent Assembly of India on 26th November, 1949.
- It came into effect on 26th January, 1950.
- The date was chosen because the Indian National Congress had proclaimed Purna Swaraj (complete independence) on 26th January in, 1930.

97. *(a)* Chief Justice of India NV Ramana launched the digital platform 'FASTER' (Fast and Secured Transmission of Electronic Records).

- FASTER is a digital platform to communicate interim orders, stay orders, bail orders etc., of the Supreme Court to authorities concerned through a secured electronic communication channel.
- The Supreme Court has also introduced 'SUPACE' AI based portal which aims to assist judges in legal search.

98. *(c)* In field hockey, in a penalty stroke, an attacker shoots at goal from 7 yards away in a one-on-one confrontation with the goalkeeper.

- It is also known as penalty flick.
- It is predominantly awarded when a foul has prevented a certain goal from being scored or for a deliberate infringement by a defender in the penalty circle.

99. *(c)* V. Anantha Nageswaran was appointed as the Chief Economic Advisor to the Government of India in the year 2022.

- The Chief Economic Adviser (CEA) to the Government of India advises the government on economic matters. He is responsible for the preparation of the Economic Survey of India.
- It is tabled in Parliament before the Union Budget of India.
- He holds the rank of a Secretary to the Government of India.

100. *(d)* Kosi river is known as the 'Sorrow of Bihar'.

- The Kosi is a transboundary river which flows through China, Nepal and India.
- The Kosi river is also known as the 'Saptakoshi' for its seven upper tributaries.
- The Kosi is the third-largest tributary of the Ganges after the Ghaghara and the Yamuna.

Set 11 03 July, 2024 (Shift III)

SSC CHSL Tier-I
SOLVED PAPER

Instructions

1. This paper contains 100 questions.
2. It has 4 Parts, **Part I** General English, **Part II** General Intelligence & Reasoning, **Part III** Quantitative Aptitude and **Part IV** General Awareness.
3. Each question carries **2 marks.**

Part I
General English

1. Parts of the following sentence have been given as options. Select the option that contains an error.

Today she said to her friend, "You're the sweetest person I have met ever".

(a) I have met ever".
(b) her friend, "You're
(c) Today she said to
(d) the sweetest person

2. The following sentence has been split into four segments. Identify the segment that contains an incorrect preposition.

Please remember to take / your notice to the reception area / if you want it to be displayed / upon the bulletin board.

(a) Please remember to take
(b) upon the bulletin board
(c) if you want it to be displayed
(d) your notice to the reception area

3. The given sentence is divided into four segments. Select the option that has the segment with a grammatical error.

The class / teacher was / wounded in / a leg.

(a) a leg (b) teacher was
(c) wounded in (d) The class

4. The following sentence has been divided into four segments. Identify the segment that contains a grammatical error.

Don't go / outside / because it is / raining heavy.

(a) Don't go
(b) outside
(c) raining heavy
(d) because it is

Directions (Q. Nos. 5-9) *In the following passage, some words have been deleted. Read the passage carefully and select the most appropriate option to fill in each blank.*

The tuatara, which lives on New Zealand's islands, is affectionately known as Living fossil. It is called that because it is the only (1)......... reptile in a group of reptiles that dates back about 220 million years to the time of the dinosaurs. The colour of the tuatara is grey or olive green. It (2)......... to a length of around 60 cm. The fact that this lizard has three eyes is its most (3)......... feature.

The pineal eye is the name given to the cone-shaped third eye. This eye is in a space between the brain and head. It has an eyelid

over the third eye, which closes on a horizontal level. The tuatara has teeth that are (4)......... from those of other reptiles. The lower jaw has only one row of teeth, while the upper jaw has two rows.

The tuatara is most active at night. It eats the eggs of birds, frogs, rats and insects. A tuatara's average lifespan is less than 77 years, but some species can live up to 100 years. In the spring, the female tuatara lays 8 to 15 eggs. These eggs are (5)......... during summer.

5. Select the most appropriate option to fill in blank number (1).

(a) living (b) being
(c) entity (d) life

6. Select the most appropriate option to fill in blank number (2).

(a) creates (b) develops
(c) links (d) nourishes

7. Select the most appropriate option to fill in blank number (3).

(a) intriguing (b) absorbing
(c) diverting (d) escalating

8. Select the most appropriate option to fill in blank number (4).

(a) separate (b) distinct
(c) discrete (d) sharp

9. Select the most appropriate option to fill in blank number (5).

(a) pollinated (b) fertilised
(c) germinated (d) fructified

10. Select the most appropriate meaning of the given idiom.

Around the clock

(a) Something that is done at night
(b) Something that is done within one hour
(c) Something that is time bound
(d) Something that goes on day and night

11. Select the most appropriate meaning of the given idiom.

Best thing since sliced bread

(a) Breaking news
(b) Something to be cautious about
(c) Extremely good, interesting
(d) Rated well amongst cooks

12. Select the most appropriate synonym of the given word.

Ablaze

(a) Extinguished (b) Burning
(c) Brazen (d) Sharp

13. Select the most appropriate antonym of the underlined word in the given sentence.

Mr. Stein is a very cold and <u>hard</u> man.

(a) clement (b) relaxed
(c) charitable (d) tolerant

14. Select the most appropriate option to fill in the blank.

Many developing nations are having a .... economy these days.

(a) boosting (b) resounding
(c) ringing (d) booming

15. Read the sentence carefully and select the synonym of the underlined word from the given alternatives.

Everyone revered my austere father who was the high priest of the famous Shiva temple.

(a) stern (b) composed
(c) morose (d) aged

16. Select the most appropriate option that can substitute the underlined segment in the given sentence.

Little that I knew of the English language was not sufficient to make me an English teacher.

(a) So little (b) A little
(c) The little (d) Very little

17. Select the most appropriate antonym of the underlined word in the following sentence.

My most vivid recollection of that summer is the ocean.

(a) vague (b) eloquent
(c) pictorial (d) lucid

18. Select the most appropriate option that can substitute the underlined segment in the given sentence. If there is no need to substitute it, select 'No improvement required'.

The annual seed festival hosted in Auroville promote sharing of traditional knowledge and sustainable farming practices.

(a) promotes sharing of traditional
(b) promotes sharing of traditionally
(c) promotes sharing of tradition
(d) No improvement required

19. Select the incorrectly spelt word.

(a) Magnanimos (b) Accompanied
(c) Fascination (d) Psychology

20. Select the most appropriate antonym of the given word.

Sacred

(a) Grave (b) Narrow
(c) Holy (d) Profane

21. Select the incorrectly spelt word.

(a) Chief (b) Relevant
(c) Colleague (d) Judgment

22. Select the most appropriate antonym of the given word.

Alive

(a) Wise (b) Animated
(c) Spry (d) Dead

23. Select the most appropriate antonym of the underlined word in the following sentence.

You should never visit her without her consent.

(a) approval (b) permission
(c) knowledge (d) refusal

24. Select the most appropriate option that can substitute the underlined segment in the given sentence. If there is no need to substitute it, select 'No substitution'.

He was the fastest between all the contestants.

(a) No substitution
(b) since
(c) amongst
(d) from

25. Select the most appropriate option that can substitute the underlined segment in the given sentence.

There is no place on the bench.

(a) more space (b) no life
(c) more place (d) no room

Part II

General Intelligence

26. If 29th December, 1956 was a Saturday, then what was the day of the week on 16th January, 1967?

(a) Friday (b) Saturday
(c) Monday (d) Sunday

27. Select the option figure in which the given figure is embedded as its part (rotation is not allowed).

(a)  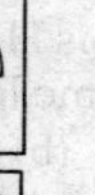 (b) 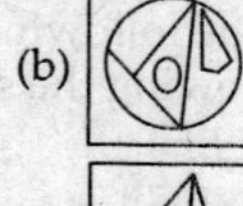

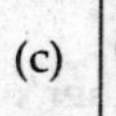 (c)  (d) 

28. In a certain code language, 'GCJL' is coded as '14-6-20-24' and 'WTRO' is coded as '46-40-36-30'. What is the code for 'BZKQ' in the given code language?

(a) 4-52-22-34
(b) 2-52-22-34
(c) 4-52-21-32
(d) 3-51-20-33

29. What will come in the place of the question mark (?) in the following equation, if '+' and '−' are interchanged and '×' and '÷' are interchanged?

$800 \times 16 - 8 \div 12 + 18 = ?$

(a) 128 (b) 126 (c) 129 (d) 127

30. What should come in place of question mark (?) in the given series?

8, 15, 29, 57, 113, ?

(a) 222 (b) 225
(c) 223 (d) 224

31. 'MANGO' is related to '35' in a certain way based on the English alphabetical order. In the same way, 'CHERRIES' is related to '56'. To which of the following is 'ADMINISTRATION' related, following the same logic?

(a) 112 (b) 98 (c) 102 (d) 96

32. What should come in place of the question mark (?) in the given series based on the English alphabetical order?

FQN, CLL, ZGJ, WBH, ?

(a) SVF (b) TVE (c) SVE (d) TWF

33. Select the correct mirror image of the given figure, when the mirror is placed at MN as shown below.

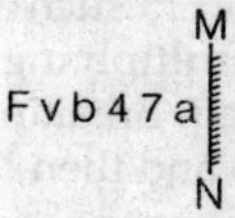

M
Fvb47a
N

(a)  ɒ ᒥ 4 d v Ⅎ
(b) ɒ ᒥ ᔭ d v ꟻ
(c) ɒ ᒥ 4 d v ꟻ
(d) ɒ ㄥ ㄣ d v ꟻ

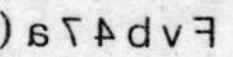

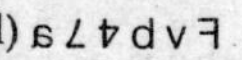

34. In this question, three statements are given, followed by three conclusions numbered I, II and III. Assuming the statements to be true, even if they seem to be at variance with commonly known facts, decide which of the conclusion(s) logically follow(s) from the statements.

Statements

All chairs are sofas.
Some chairs are beds.
No sofa is a table.

Conclusions

I. Some tables are beds.
II. No table is a chair.

III. Some sofas are beds.
(a) Both Conclusions I and II follow
(b) All Conclusions I, II and III follow
(c) Both Conclusions II and III follow
(d) Both Conclusions I and III follow

35. How many rectangles are there in the following figure?

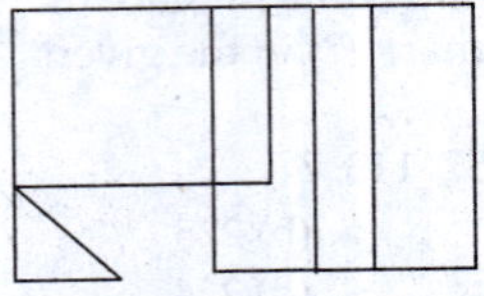

(a) 8 (b) 9 (c) 10 (d) 11

36. If 'A' stands for '÷', 'B' stands for '×', 'C' stands for '+' and 'D' stands for '–', what will come in place of the question mark (?) in the following equation?

93 A 3 C 15 B 5 D 12 = ?

(a) 93 (b) 94 (c) 91 (d) 92

37. 765 is related to 876 following a certain logic. Following the same logic, 682 is related to 793.

To which of the following is 587 related, following the same logic?

(**Note** Operations should be performed on the whole numbers, without breaking down the numbers into its constituent digits. E.g. 13– Operations on 13 such as adding/subtracting/multiplying etc. to 13 can be performed. Breaking down 13 into 1 and 3 and then performing mathematical operations on 1 and 3 is not allowed.)

(a) 543 (b) 798 (c) 675 (d) 698

38. What will come in the place of the question mark (?) in the following equation, if '+' and '–' are interchanged and '×' and '÷' are interchanged?

$73 - 27 \times 9 + 5 \div 13 = ?$

(a) 23 (b) 17 (c) 11 (d) 9

39. What would be the word on the opposite side of 'Run', if the given sheet is folded to form a cube?

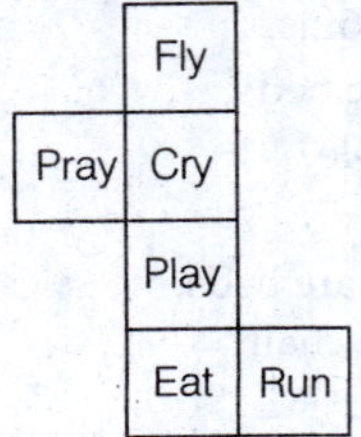

(a) Cry (b) Play (c) Fly (d) Pray

40. What should come in place of question mark (?) in the given series based on the English alphabetical order?

QJC, ATM, KDW, UNG, ?

(a) SBA
(b) BAA
(c) CWO
(d) EXQ

41. Identify the figure given in the options which when put in place of question mark (?) will logically complete the series.

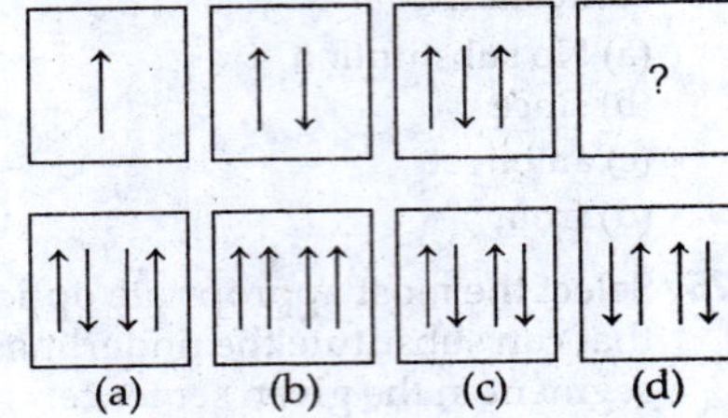

42. In a certain code language, 'time and money' is coded as 'zoo zee zig' and 'time and tide' is coded as 'zee zoo zaa'.

Which word is coded as 'zaa' in that language?

(a) and (b) time
(c) money (d) tide

43. What should come in place of question mark (?) in the given series?

34, 58, 106, 202, 394 ?

(a) 778 (b) 792
(c) 798 (d) 774

44. PCNZ is related to ALWQ in a certain way based on the English alphabetical order. In the same way, RYLD is related to EHUS. To which of the following is HAXM related, following the same logic?

(a) NJGI (b) NIGJ
(c) NIJG (d) NJIG

45. 'A + B' means 'A is B's brother'.
'A – B' means 'A is B's wife'.
'A × B' means 'A is B's father'.
'A ÷ B' means 'A is B's daughter'.

Using operations with the same meaning as given above, which of the following options shows 'M is the mother of O'?

(a) M – N × O
(b) M ÷ N × O
(c) M ÷ N + O
(d) M – N + O

46. What would be the word on the opposite side of 'Pear', if the given sheet is folded to form a cube?

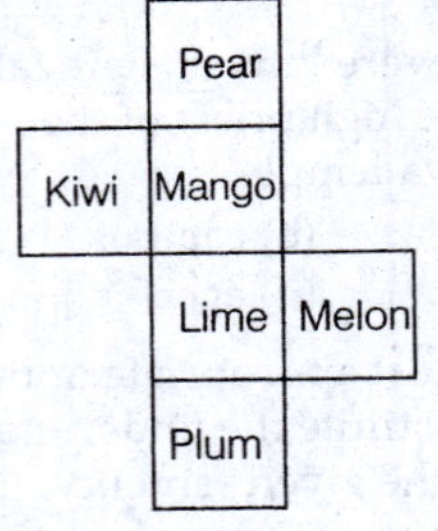

(a) Melon
(b) Kiwi
(c) Lime
(d) Mango

47. Select the set in which the numbers are related in the same way as are the numbers of the following sets.

(**Note** Operations should be performed on the whole numbers, without breaking down the numbers into their constituent digits. E.g. 13 – Operations on 13 such as adding/subtracting/multiplying etc. to 13 can be performed. Breaking down 13 into 1 and 3 and then performing mathematical operations on 1 and 3 is not allowed.)

(45, 15, 3)
(120, 40, 8)

(a) (175, 55, 11)
(b) (165, 55, 9)
(c) (165, 55, 11)
(d) (165, 54, 11)

48. Three of the following four are alike in a certain way and thus form a group. Which is the one that does not belong to that group?

(**Note** The odd one out is not based on the number of consonants/vowels or their position in the letter-cluster.)

(a) QWD (b) EKR
(c) RXE (d) TZD

49. A paper is folded and cut as shown below. How will it appear when unfolded?

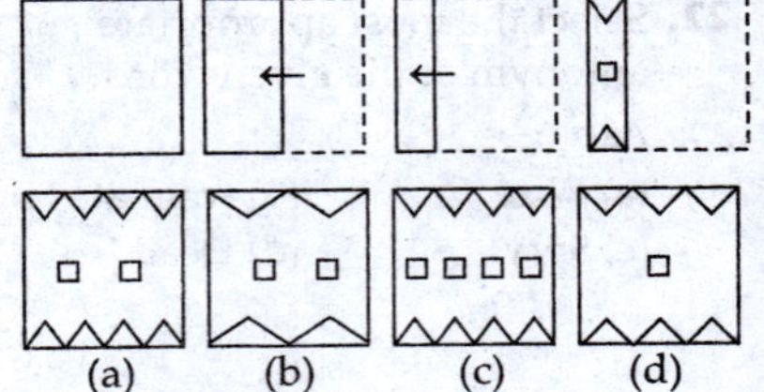

50. If 26th September, 2005 was Monday, then what was the day of the week on 26th September, 2017?
(a) Saturday (b) Wednesday
(c) Sunday (d) Tuesday

Part III
Quantitative Aptitude

51. Simplify the given expression.
$8 - 5 \div 2^3 \times 3 + (7 \div 7 \times 7) \div 7 + \left(3 \times 6 \div \frac{1}{3}\right) \times \frac{1}{3^3}$
(a) $\frac{73}{9}$ (b) $\frac{73}{21}$
(c) $\frac{73}{27}$ (d) $\frac{73}{8}$

52. The following table represents the number of computers (in thousands) manufactured by four companies during the period 2010 to 2014.

Years	A	B	C	D
2010	240	120	270	280
2011	300	530	490	650
2012	1250	650	430	710
2013	470	320	1180	890
2014	320	1070	550	480

Which company has the minimum average (in thousands) of manufacturing the computers from 2010 to 2014?
(a) B (b) A (c) C (d) D

53. For a given circle of radius 4 cm, the angle of its sector is 45°. Find the area (in cm^2) of the sector.
(Use $\pi = 3.14$)
(a) 6.18 (b) 7.28 (c) 6.28 (d) 7.18

54. In an election between two candidates, 10% of the registered voters did not cast their vote. The winning candidate got 60% of the total votes cast and defeated the other candidate by 1242 votes. Find the total number of registered voters.
(a) 9600 (b) 6200
(c) 8640 (d) 6900

55. If the average of 50 numbers $N_1, N_2, \ldots\ldots\ldots N_{50}$ is M. Then, the average of the numbers $N_1 - 100, N_2 - 100, \ldots\ldots\ldots N_{50} - 100$ will be
(a) 100 M (b) $M - 50$
(c) 50 M (d) $M - 100$

56. In 800 m race, the ratio of the speeds of two contestants Ankur and Neha is 5 : 6. If Ankur has a head-start of 200 m, then Ankur will win by ……… .
(a) 89 m (b) 80 m
(c) 76 m (d) 69 m

57. Solve the following system of linear equations.
$x + y + z = 15, 2x - y + z = 12$ and $x - y - z = -1$
(a) $x = 7, y = 5, z = 3$
(b) $x = 2, y = 5, z = 3$
(c) $x = 7, y = 2, z = 3$
(d) $x = 7, y = 5, z = 1$

58. A seven digit number $489y5z6$ is divisible by 72. Which of the options gives the highest possible product of y and z?
(a) 21 (b) 30
(c) 42 (d) 3

59. If the income of P is 40% less than Q, then the combined income of P and Q is how much per cent more than the income of P?
(a) $164\frac{1}{3}$ (b) $166\frac{1}{3}$
(c) $166\frac{2}{3}$ (d) $164\frac{2}{3}$

60. The following graph shows the sale of few items of a garment company for three months.

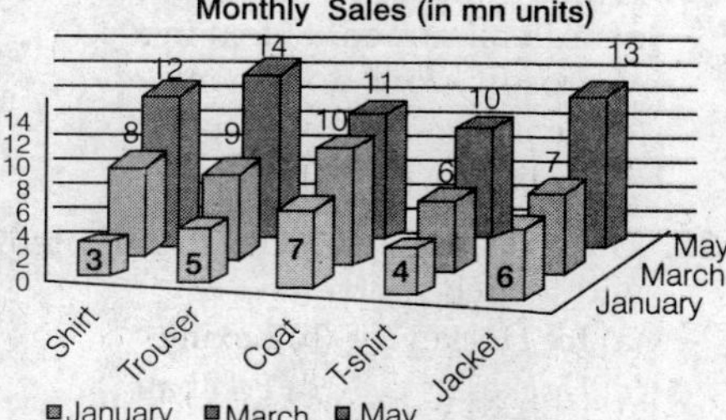

What is the percentage of the sale of the least selling item in the three months over the total sale of the company?
(a) 16% (b) 25% (c) 20% (d) 28%

61. If the height of a right circular cone is 24 cm and radius of its base is 10.5 cm, then the volume of right circular cone (in cm^3) is
$\left(\text{Take } \pi = \frac{22}{7}\right)$
(a) 2772
(b) 2727
(c) 2237
(d) 2277

62. The given pie-diagram shows the expenditure incurred on the preparation of a book by a publisher, under various heads. Study the pie-diagram and answer the question that follows.

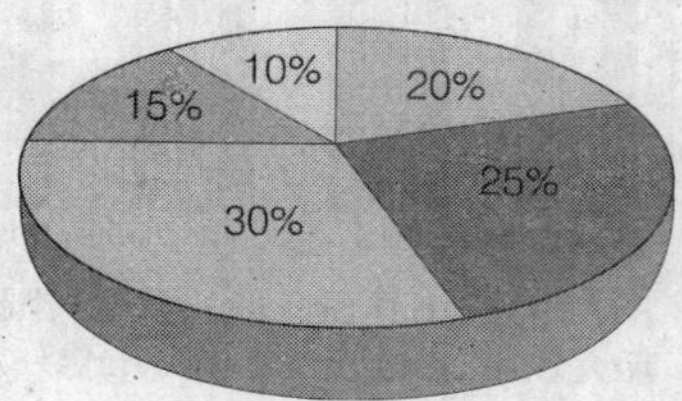

Various Expenditures (in percentage) incurred in Publishing a Book

What is the angle of the pie-diagram showing the expenditure incurred on paying royalty?
(a) 15° (b) 48° (c) 54° (d) 24°

63. By selling 30 m of cloth a shopkeeper makes a profit equivalent to the selling price of 10 m of cloth. Find the selling price of 1 m of cloth, when the cost price of 1 m of cloth is ₹ 480.
(a) ₹ 520 (b) ₹ 720 (c) ₹ 960 (d) ₹ 820

64. If 6,18, x are sides of a triangle and x is an integer, then the number of possible values of x is
(a) 11 (b) 15 (c) 13 (d) 14

65. An amount of ₹ 50000 becomes ₹ 72000 in 4 yr on a simple rate of interest. The rate of interest is ………. per annum.
(a) 9% (b) 10% (c) 11% (d) 12%

66. A dealer buys an article listed at ₹ 100 and get successive discounts of 10% and 20%. He spends 10% of the cost price on transportation. At what price should he sell the article to earn a profit of 15%?
(a) ₹ 76.07 (b) ₹ 81.07
(c) ₹ 89.08 (d) ₹ 91.08

67. A and B can complete a piece of work in 12 days. B and C can complete the same work in 15 days and C and A in 10 days. How many days will A take to complete the work by himself ?
(a) $16\frac{1}{7}$ (b) $17\frac{1}{7}$
(c) $13\frac{3}{7}$ (d) $9\frac{1}{8}$

68. Answer the following question on the basis of the bar-graph given.

Revenue obtained by publisher on the journals, magazines and books.

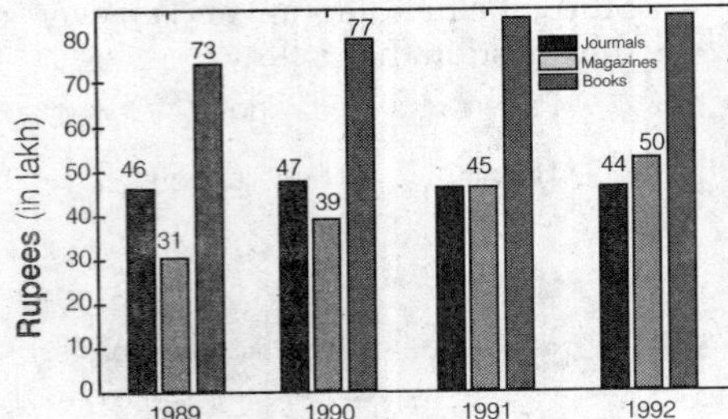

In 1991, what percentage of the total revenue came from journals? (Correct up to one decimal place)

(a) 24.73% (b) 25.8%
(c) 22.9% (d) 26.5%

69. If the perimeter of a square is 64 cm, what would be its area?

(a) 256 cm^2 (b) 206 cm^2
(c) 216 cm^2 (d) 266 cm^2

70. Which is the greatest ratio among the following?

$\frac{8}{11}, \frac{4}{5}, \frac{1}{2}$ and $\frac{1}{11}$

(a) $\frac{4}{5}$ (b) $\frac{1}{2}$
(c) $\frac{1}{11}$ (d) $\frac{8}{11}$

71. 12.75% is equivalent to ....

(a) $\frac{37}{400}$ (b) $\frac{51}{400}$
(c) $\frac{41}{400}$ (d) $\frac{17}{200}$

72. AB and AC are two tangents to a circle having centres at the point X. What will be the measure of $\angle BAC$, if $\angle BXC = 125°$?

(a) 50° (b) 48°
(c) 55° (d) 52°

73. PQ is parallel to SR in a trapezium $PQRS$. It is given that $PQ > SR$ and the diagonals PR and QS intersect at O. If $PO = 3x - 15$, $OQ = x + 9$, $OR = x - 5$ and $OS = 5$ and x has two values x_1 and x_2, then the value of $(x_1^2 - x_2^2)$ is

(a) 15 (b) 11
(c) 19 (d) 13

74. If the radius of a sphere is increased by 12 per cent, then the volume will be increased by approximately

(a) 42.5% (b) 45.49%
(c) 40.49% (d) 41.49%

75. $\frac{3\cos^3\theta - 2\cos\theta}{\sin\theta - 3\sin^3\theta}$ is equal to

(a) $\tan\theta$ (b) $\cot^2\theta$
(c) $\cot\theta$ (d) $\tan^2\theta$

Part IV

General Awareness

76. The Maritime Anti-Piracy Act, 2022, received the assent of the President on ....

(a) 31st March, 2023
(b) 30th April, 2023
(c) 31st December, 2022
(d) 31st January, 2023

77. Where was India's first hockey club founded?

(a) Madras (b) Delhi
(c) Calcutta (d) Shimla

78. For which discovery did Henri Becquerel receive the Nobel Prize in Physics in 1903?

(a) Spontaneous Radioactivity
(b) Radioactive Elements
(c) Radium Emanation
(d) Diagnostic Radiography

79. As per the Census 2011, the population growth during the decade remained ....

(a) 15.30% (b) 14.25%
(c) 17.64% (d) 18.30%

80. Which of the following is the default alignment of text in a Microsoft Word document?

(a) Center (b) Left
(c) Justified (d) Right

81. The term 'banana kick' is associated with which sport?

(a) Ice Hockey (b) Boxing
(c) Hockey (d) Football

82. Ursa Major is a/an

(a) comet (b) asteroid
(c) constellation (d) satellite

83. The Deccan Plateau is a .... landmass that lies to the South of the River Narmada.

(a) quadrilateral
(b) rectangular
(c) hexagonal
(d) triangular

84. In which state is the Raika tribe found?

(a) West Bengal (b) Rajasthan
(c) Kerala (d) Manipur

85. Where did the indigenous sport 'Kalaripayattu' originate from?

(a) Kerala (b) Karnataka
(c) Goa (d) Tamil Nadu

86. .... is a form of Sikh festival.

(a) Khamaj
(b) Hola Mohalla
(c) Bhairav
(d) Kalyan

87. 'Which of the following statements about the pala dynasty of eastern India is incorrect?

(a) The Pala dynasty was founded by Gopala.
(b) Dharmapala founded the Valabhi University.
(c) The Pala kings were the followers of Buddhism.
(d) Devapala was the grandson of Gopala.

88. In January 2022, which evacuation mission did the Government of India launch to evacuate the Indians stranded in Ukraine?

(a) Operation Ganga
(b) Operation Safe Homecoming
(c) Operation Vande Bharat
(d) Operation Raahat

89. Who developed the technique of preserving the quality of food by raising its temperature to prevent microbial growth in the food?

(a) Robert Koch
(b) Antonie van Leeuwenhoek
(c) Louis Pasteur
(d) Joseph Lister

90. Which section of the Representation of People's Act (RPA), 1951 deprives the prisoners of their right to vote?

(a) Section 62 (5)
(b) Section 15 (3)
(c) Section 72 (5)
(d) Section 10 (4)

91. The government of which state started the Tansen Samman?

(a) Himachal Pradesh
(b) Uttar Pradesh
(c) Madhya Pradesh
(d) Arunachal Pradesh

92. Which city is referred to as the 'Manchester of India'?

(a) Ahmedabad
(b) Kanpur
(c) Kolkata
(d) Mumbai

93. Which article of the Constitution mentions about establishing and maintaining institutions for religious and charitable purposes?
(a) Article 28 (b) Article 26
(c) Article 29 (d) Article 30

94. Good Friday is related to
(a) Christianity (b) Hinduism
(c) Sikhism (d) Jainism

95. The proclamation of which act by the King of England in 1773 paved the way for the establishment of the Supreme Court at Calcutta?
(a) Pitt's India Act
(b) Indian Councils Act
(c) Charter Act
(d) Regulating Act

96. Which of the following folk musics of Chhattisgarh is based on the epic 'Mahabharata'?
(a) Paani Haari (b) Ghumar
(c) Pandavani (d) Maand

97. Which of the following is issued by commercial banks at a discount on face value?
(a) Commercial papers
(b) Certificates of deposits
(c) Treasury bills
(d) Promissory notes

98. In a situation wherein A (female) and B (male) are working in same office, same designation, same nature of work but unequal payment, which of the following articles of the Constitution will be applicable?
(a) Article 21
(b) Article 39 (d)
(c) Article 18
(d) Article 48A

99. Which of the following is an example of application software?
(a) A web browser
(b) A programming language
(c) An operating system
(d) A word processor

100. The Green Revolution led to an increase in the agricultural output primarily due to the use of HYV seeds. Here, HYV refers to
(a) High Yielding Variance
(b) Heat Yielding Variant
(c) High Yielding Variety
(d) High Yield Variant

Answers

1. (a)	2. (b)	3. (a)	4. (c)
5. (a)	6. (b)	7. (a)	8. (b)
9. (b)	10. (d)	11. (c)	12. (b)
13. (c)	14 (d)	15. (a)	16. (c)
17. (a)	18. (a)	19. (a)	20. (d)
21. (d)	22. (d)	23. (d)	24. (c)
25. (d)	26. (c)	27. (c)	28. (a)
29. (a)	30. (b)	31. (b)	32. (d)
33. (b)	34. (c)	35. (b)	36. (b)
37. (d)	38. (c)	39. (d)	40. (d)
41. (c)	42. (d)	43. (a)	44. (a)
45. (a)	46. (c)	47. (c)	48. (d)
49. (c)	50. (d)	51. (d)	52. (b)
53. (c)	54. (d)	55. (d)	56. (b)
57. (a)	58. (c)	59. (c)	60. (a)
61. (a)	62. (c)	63. (b)	64. (a)
65. (c)	66. (d)	67. (b)	68. (d)
69. (a)	70. (a)	71. (b)	72. (c)
73. (b)	74. (c)	75. (c)	76. (c)
77. (c)	78. (a)	79. (c)	80. (b)
81. (d)	82. (c)	83. (d)	84. (b)
85. (a)	86. (b)	87. (b)	88. (a)
89. (c)	90. (a)	91. (c)	92. (a)
93. (b)	94. (a)	95. (d)	96. (c)
97. (b)	98. (b)	99. (d)	100. (c)

Explanations

1. *(a)* Part 'I have met ever' contains an error. Place 'ever' before 'met' to correct the sentence.

2. *(b)* Part 'upon the bulletin board' contains an error. Use 'on' in place of 'upon' to correct the sentence.

3. *(a)* Part 'a leg' contains an error. Use article 'the' to correct the sentence.

4. *(c)* Part 'raining heavy' contains an error. The verb requires an adverb and not an adjective. Hence, use 'heavily' to correct the sentence.

5. *(a)* The correct filler for the given blank is 'living'.

6. *(b)* The correct filler for the given blank is 'develops'.

7. *(a)* The correct filler for the given blank is 'intriguing'.

8. *(b)* The correct filler for the given blank is 'distinct'.

9. *(b)* The correct filler for the given blank is 'fertilised'.

10. *(d)* Around the clock means all day and all night.

11. *(c)* Best thing since sliced bread is used to emphasise one's enthusiasm about a new idea, person, or thing. It means extremely good, interesting.

12. *(b)* The word 'Ablaze' means 'to set on fire or burning.

'Brazen' means bold and unashamed.

13. *(c)* The nearest antonym of 'hard' is 'charitable'. 'Clement' means inclined to be merciful.

14. *(d)* The given sentence presents that economies of many countries are growing. Hence, the correct filler for the given blank is 'booming'.

15. *(a)* The word 'austere' means severe or strict in manner or attitude. Hence, the synonym of 'austere' is 'stern'.

'Morose' means sullen and ill-tempered.

16. *(c)* The underlined part of the given sentence contains an error. Use 'The little' to correct the sentence.

17. *(a)* 'Vivid' means clear and descriptive. Hence, its antonym is 'vague' which means no clearly defined.

- 'Eloquent' means fluent or persuasive in speaking or writing.
- 'Pictorial' means of or expressed in pictures; illustrated.
- 'Lucid' means clear.

18. *(a)* The underlined part of the given sentence contains an error. Use 'promotes sharing of traditional' to correct the sentence as the subject of the sentence is singular.

19. *(a)* The incorrectly spelt word is 'Magnanimos'. The correct spelling is 'Magnanimous'.

20. *(d)* 'Sacred' means holy or related to God. Hence, its antonym is 'Profane' which means not relating to that which is sacred or religious; secular.

21. *(d)* The incorrectly spelt word is 'Judgment'. The correct spelling is 'Judgement'.

22. *(d)* The antonym of 'Alive' is 'Dead'.

23. *(d)* 'Consent' means to agree to something. Hence, its antonym is 'Refusal'.

24. *(c)* The underlined part of the given sentence contains an error. Use 'amongst' to correct the sentence as we are referring to more than two contestants.

25. *(d)* The underlined part of the given sentence contains an error. Use 'no room' to correct the sentence.

26. *(c)* Given,

29th December, 1956 → Saturday

Odd days in ordinary year = 1

Odd days in leap year = 2

Number of odd days from 29th December, 1956 to 29th December, 1966

$= 1 + 1 + 1 + 2 + 1 + 1 + 1 + 2 + 1 + 1 = 12$

(12 + 18) odd days from 29th, December, 1966 to 16th January, 1967.

$= \frac{30}{7} =$ 4 weeks 2 odd days

∴ The day of the week on 16th January, 1967

= Saturday + 2 = Monday

27. *(c)* The given question figure is embedded in the option figure (c).

28. *(a)* As,

7	3	10	12
G	C	J	L
×2	×2	×2	×2
14	6	20	24

and

23	20	18	15
W	T	R	O
×2	×2	×2	×2
46	40	36	30

Similarly,

2	26	11	17
B	Z	K	Q
×2	×2	×2	×2
4	52	22	34

29. *(a)* Given expression,

$800 \times 16 - 8 \div 12 + 18 = ?$

After interchanging, '+' and '–' and '×' and '÷', we get

$800 \div 16 + 8 \times 12 - 18$

$= 50 + 96 - 18 = 146 - 18 = 128$

30. *(b)* The pattern of the series is as follows,

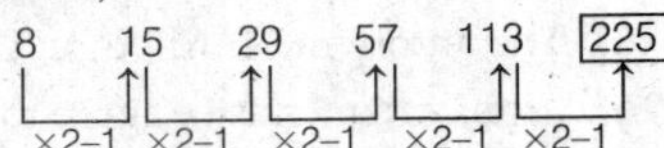

31. *(b)* As, M A N G O → 35

[Number of letters in word × 7]

$= 5 \times 7 = 35$

and C H E R R I E S → 56

$= 8 \times 7 = 56$

Similarly, A D M I N I S T R A T I O N → ?

$= 14 \times 7 =$ **98**

32. *(d)* The pattern of the series is

F →(–3) C →(–3) Z →(–3) W →(–3) **T**

Q →(–5) L →(–5) G →(–5) B →(–5) **W**

N →(–2) L →(–2) J →(–2) H →(–2) **F**

33. *(b)* The option (b) is the correct mirror image of the given figure.

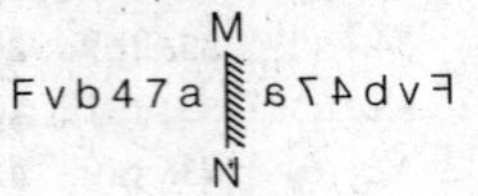

M

Fvb47a | ꓭ7ꓯdvꟻ

N

34. *(c)* According to the statements,

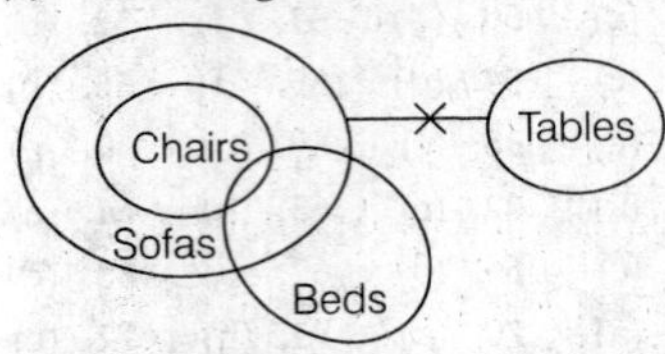

Conclusions I. (✗) II. (✓) III. (✓)

Hence, both Conclusions II and III follow.

35. *(b)* Naming the figure,

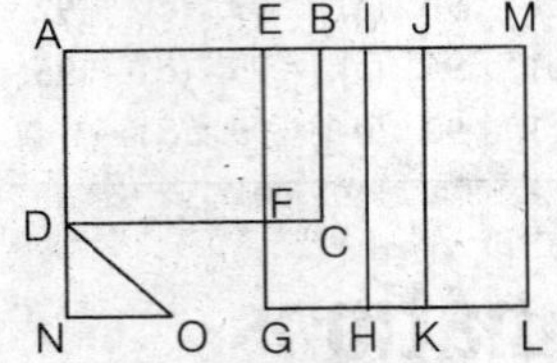

☐ ABCD, ☐ AEFD, ☐ EBCF, ☐ IJKH, ☐ JMLK, ☐ EMLG, ☐ IMLH, ☐ EIHG, ☐ EJKG

Hence, there are total 9 rectangles in the given figure.

36. *(b)* Given expression,

93 A 3 C 15 B 5 D 12 = ?

After substituting the letters with signs, we get

A → ÷	B → ×
C → +	D → –

$= 93 \div 3 + 15 \times 5 - 12$

$= 31 + 75 - 12 = 106 - 12 = 94$

37. *(d)* As, 765 + 111 = 876

and 682 + 111 = 793

Similarly, 587 + 111 = 698

38. *(c)* Given expression,

$73 - 27 \times 9 + 5 \div 13 = ?$

After interchanging '+' and '–' and '×' and '÷' signs, we get

$73 + 27 \div 9 - 5 \times 13$

$= 73 + 3 - 65 = 11$

39. *(d)* According to the question,

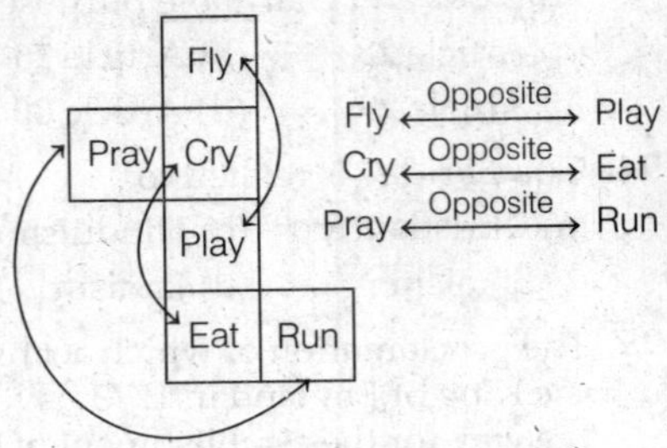

Hence, 'Pray' is opposite to 'Run'.

40. *(d)* The pattern of the series is

Q →(+10) A →(+10) K →(+10) U →(+10) **E**

J →(+10) T →(+10) D →(+10) N →(+10) **X**

C →(+10) M →(+10) W →(+10) G →(+10) **Q**

41. *(c)* In the given figure series, the number of arrows is increasing by 1 in every next series and the arrow is getting up and down alternatively.

Hence, option (c) is the correct figure.

42. *(d)* According to the question,

time and money → zoo zee zig

time and tide → zee zoo zaa

Hence, tide is coded as zaa.

43. *(a)* The pattern of the series is as follows,

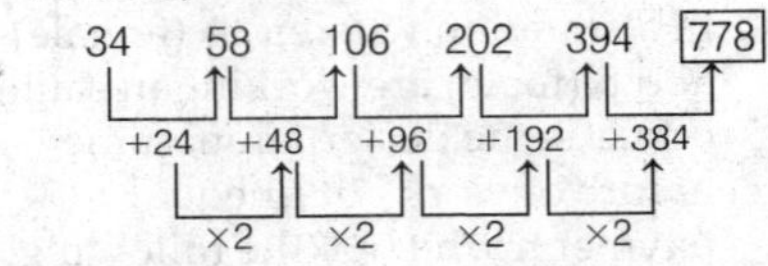

44. *(a)* As,

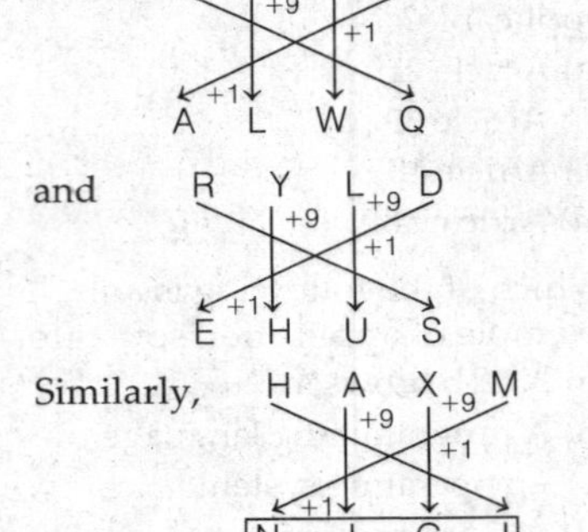

45. *(a)* According to the question,

From option (a),

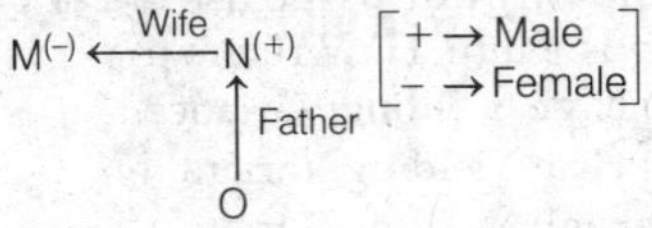

M(–) ←Wife→ N(+) [+ → Male, – → Female]

N(+) ↑ Father — O

Hence, M is the mother of O.

46. *(c)* According to the question,

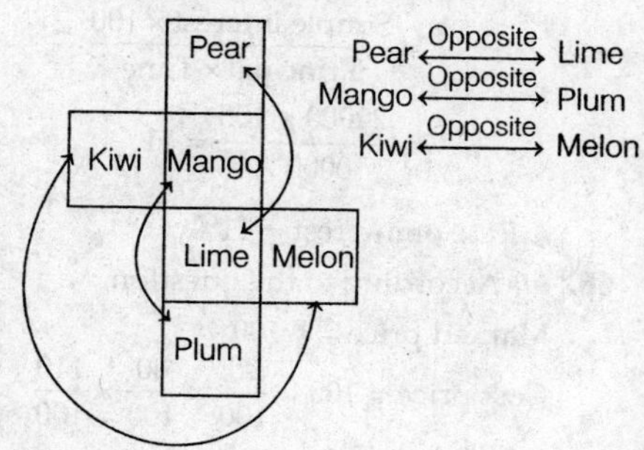

Hence, Lime is opposite to Pear.

47. *(c)* As, $(45, 15, 3) \Rightarrow \frac{45}{3} = 15$

$\Rightarrow \frac{15}{5} = 3$

and $(120, 40, 8) \Rightarrow \frac{120}{3} = 40$

$\Rightarrow \frac{40}{5} = 8$

Similarly, $(165, 55, 11) \Rightarrow \frac{165}{3} = 55$

$\Rightarrow \frac{55}{5} = 11$

48. *(d)* As, Q W D (+6, +7)

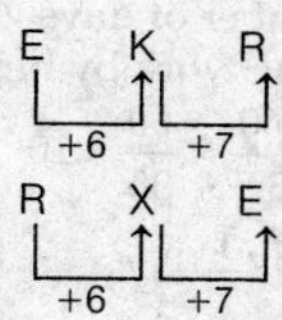

But,

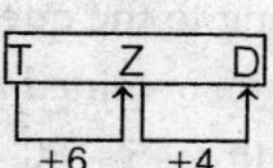

Hence, 'TZD' is the odd one.

49. *(c)* After unfolding, the paper will look like as option figure (c).

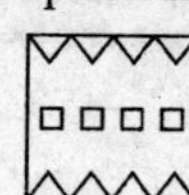

50. *(d)* Odd day in ordinary year = 1

Odd days in leap year = 2

Day on 26th September, 2005 → Monday

Number of odd days from 26th September, 2005 to 26th September, 2017.

$= 1 + 1 + 2 + 1 + 1 + 1 + 2 + 1 + 1 + 1 + 2 + 1 = 15$

$= \frac{15}{7} = 2$ weeks 1 odd day

∴ The day of the week on 26th September, 2017

= Monday + 1 = Tuesday

51. *(d)* According to the question,

Given expression,

$$8 - 5 \div 2^3 \times 3 + (7 \div 7 \times 7) \div 7 + \left(3 \times 6 \div \frac{1}{3}\right) \times \frac{1}{3^3}$$

$$= 8 - 5 \div 2^3 \times 3 + \frac{7}{7} \times 7 \div 7 + 3 \times 6 \times 3 \times \frac{1}{3^3}$$

$$= 8 - \frac{5}{8} \times 3 + 1 \times \frac{7}{7} + 2$$

$$= 8 - \frac{15}{8} + 3$$

$$= 11 - \frac{15}{8} = \frac{73}{8}$$

52. *(b)* According to the question,

Average number of computers (in thousands) manufactured by four companies during the period 2010 to 2014.

Company A

$$= \frac{240 + 300 + 1250 + 470 + 320}{5}$$

$$= \frac{2580}{5} = 516$$

Company B

$$= \frac{120 + 530 + 650 + 320 + 1070}{5}$$

$$= \frac{2690}{5} = 538$$

Company C

$$= \frac{270 + 490 + 430 + 1180 + 550}{5}$$

$$= \frac{2920}{5} = 584$$

Company D

$$= \frac{280 + 650 + 710 + 890 + 480}{5}$$

$$= \frac{3010}{5} = 602$$

Hence, Company A has the minimum average (in thousands) of manufacturing the computers from 2010 to 2014.

53. *(c)* According to the question,

Radius of circle = 4 cm

Angle of its sector (θ) = 45°

$\therefore$ Area of the sector $= \frac{\theta}{360°} \times \pi r^2$

$$= \frac{45°}{360°} \times 3.14 \times 4 \times 4 \quad [\pi = 3.14]$$

$$= 6.28 \text{ cm}^2$$

54. *(d)* According to the question,

Let the total number of registered voters = $100x$

Percentage of registered voters did not cast their vote = 10%

∴ Total voters cast their vote

$= 100x \times 90\% = 90x$

Winning candidate got number of votes

$= 90x \times 60\% = 54x$

∴ Losing candidate got number of votes $= (90 - 54)x = 36x$

$\therefore \quad 54x - 36x = 1242$

$\Rightarrow \quad 18x = 1242$

$\Rightarrow \quad 100x = \frac{1242 \times 100}{18} = 6900$

∴ Total number of registered voters

= 6900

55. *(d)* Average of 50 numbers $(N_1, N_2, ..., N_{50}) = M$

Sum of 50 numbers = $50M$

Sum of 50 numbers

$(N_1 - 100, N_2 - 100, ..., N_{50} - 100)$

$= (N_1 + N_2 + N_3 \dots N_{50}) -$

$(100 + 100 + 100 \dots +$ up to 50 terms$)$

$= 50M - 50 \times 100$

$= 50M - 5000$

∴ Required average $= \frac{50M - 5000}{50}$

$= M - 100$

56. *(b)* According to the question,

Speed of Ankur : Speed of Neha

= 5 : 6

P ←200 m→ Q ←(600–x) m→ R ←x m→ S

Neha Ankur Neha Ankur

Let Ankur will win by x m.

∴ Time taken by Neha from P to R and Q to S is same.

∴ Time of Neha = Time of Ankur

$$\frac{800 - x}{6} = \frac{600}{5} \quad \left[\because \text{Time} = \frac{\text{Distance}}{\text{Speed}}\right]$$

$\Rightarrow \quad 4000 - 5x = 3600$

$\Rightarrow \quad 5x = 400$

$\therefore \quad x = 80$ m

∴ Ankur will win by 80 m.

57. *(a)* According to the question,

$x + y + z = 15 \quad \dots(i)$

$2x - y + z = 12 \quad \dots(ii)$

and $x - y - z = -1$ ...(iii)

On combining Eqs. (i) and (iii), we get

$x + y + z = 15$

$x - y - z = -1 \Rightarrow 2x = 14$

$x = 7$ ...(iv)

From Eq. (i),

$7 + y + z = 15$

$\Rightarrow y + z = 8$ ...(v)

From Eq. (ii),

$2x - y + z = 12$

$\Rightarrow 2 \times 7 - y + z = 12$

$\Rightarrow z - y = -2$ ...(vi)

On combining Eqs (v) and (vi), we get

$y + z = 8$

$\Rightarrow z - y = -2$

$\Rightarrow 2z = 6$

$\therefore z = 3$

From Eq. (v),

$y + z = 8$

$\Rightarrow y + 3 = 8 \Rightarrow y = 5$

$\therefore \left.\begin{array}{l} x = 7 \\ y = 5 \\ z = 3 \end{array}\right\}$

58. *(c)* According to the question,

Given number = $489y5z6$

This number is divisible by 72.

(and $72 = 9 \times 8$)

$\therefore$ Last three digits of the given number $5z6$, to be divided by 8

$\frac{5z6}{8}$,

Putting $z = 7$ is divisible by 8.

[By taking the maximum value of z]

$\therefore$ Number = $489y576$.

Now, inorder to divide the number by 9, sum of digits of number will be divided by 9.

$\therefore 4 + 8 + 9 + y + 5 + 7 + 6 = y + 39$

Putting $y = 6$ is divisible by 9.

$\therefore y \times z = 7 \times 6 = 42$

59. *(c)* According to the question,

Income of $P : Q = 60 : 100 = 3 : 5$

$\therefore$ Required per cent

$= \frac{(8-3)}{3} \times 100 = \frac{500}{3} = 166\frac{2}{3}$

60. *(a)* According to the question,

Total sales of items of a garment company for three months is

Total sales of shirt = 3 + 8 + 12 = 23

Total sales of trouser = 5 + 9 + 14 = 28

Total sales of coat = 7 + 10 + 11 = 28

Total sales of T-shirt = 4 + 6 + 10 = 20

Total sales of Jacket = 6 + 7 + 13 = 26

Hence, total sales of company

= 23 + 28 + 28 + 20 + 26

= 125

$\therefore$ Percentage of the sale of the least selling item in the three months over the total sale of the company

$= \frac{20}{125} \times 100\% = 16\%$

61. *(a)* Given,

Height of right circular cone (h) = 24 cm

Radius of its base (r) = 10.5 cm

$\therefore$ Volume of right circular cone

$= \frac{1}{3} \times \pi r^2 h$

$= \frac{1}{3} \times \frac{22}{7} \times 10.5 \times 10.5 \times 24$

$= 2772 \text{ cm}^3$

62. *(c)* According to the question,

Required angle of expenditure incurred on paying royalty is

$= \frac{360° \times 15}{100} = 54°$

63. *(b)* According to the question,

30 × (Selling price – Cost price)

= 10 × Selling price

20 × Selling price = 30 × Cost price

$\therefore$ Selling price = Cost price $\times \frac{3}{2}$

$= 480 \times \frac{3}{2} =$ ₹ 720

64. *(a)* According to the question,

Let the third side = x

We know that, the sum of two sides in each triangle is greater than third side of the triangle and the difference of two sides in each triangle is less than third side of the triangle.

$\therefore (18 + 6) > x > (18 - 6)$

$\Rightarrow 24 > x > 12$

$\therefore$ Possible value of x = 13, 14, 15, 16, 17, 18, 19, 20, 21, 22, 23

$\therefore$ Total possible value of x = 11

65. *(c)* Given,

Principal = ₹ 50000

Amount = ₹ 72000

Simple interest

= 72000 – 50000

= ₹ 22000

Time = 4 yr

$\therefore$ Rate of interest

$= \frac{\text{Simple interest} \times 100}{\text{Principal} \times \text{Time}}$

$= \frac{22000 \times 100}{50000 \times 4} = 11$

$\therefore$ Rate of interest = 11%

66. *(d)* According to the question,

Marked price = ₹ 100

Cost price $= 100 \times \frac{90}{100} \times \frac{80}{100} \times \frac{110}{100}$

= ₹ 79.2

$\because$ The article should be sold in order to earn a profit of 15%.

Selling price $= 79.2 \times \frac{115}{100}$

= ₹ 91.08

67. *(b)* According to the question,

A + B = 12 days — 5

B + C = 15 days — 4 → Total work 60

C + A = 10 days — 6

$2(A + B + C) = 15$

$A + B + C = \frac{15}{2} = 7.5$

$\therefore A = 7.5 - (B + C) = 7.5 - 4 = 3.5$

So, $A = 3.5$

Hence, number of days A will take to complete the work by himself

$= \frac{60}{3.5} = \frac{60}{35} \times 10$

$= 17\frac{1}{7}$ days

68. *(d)* According to the question,

Total revenue obtained in 1991

= 45 + 45 + 80

= 170

So, in 1991 percentage of the total revenue came from journals

$\therefore$ Required per cent $= \frac{45}{170} \times 100$

$= 26.47\% \approx 26.5\%$

69. *(a)* According to the question,

Let area of square = a cm^2

$\therefore$ Perimeter of square, $4a = 64$ cm

$\Rightarrow a = 16$ cm

$\therefore$ Area of square = a^2

$= 16 \times 16$

$= 256 \text{ cm}^2$

70. *(a)* According to the question,

$\frac{8}{11} = 0.72, \quad \frac{4}{5} = 0.8$

$\frac{1}{2} = 0.5, \quad \frac{1}{11} = 0.09$

Clearly, $0.8 > 0.72 > 0.5 > 0.09$

$\therefore$ Greatest ratio $= \left(\frac{4}{5}\right)$

71. *(b)* According to the question,

$$12.75\% = \frac{12.75}{100} = \frac{1275}{100 \times 100} = \frac{51}{400}$$

72. *(c)* According to the question,

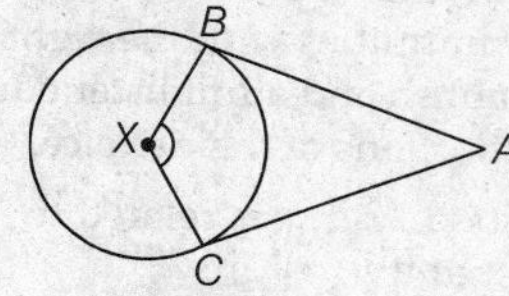

$\angle BXC = 125°$

$\therefore \angle BXC + \angle BAC = 180°$

$\therefore \angle BAC = 180° - \angle BXC$

[$\because$ $ABXC$ is cyclic quadrilateral]

$= 180° - 125° = 55°$

73. *(b)* According to the question,

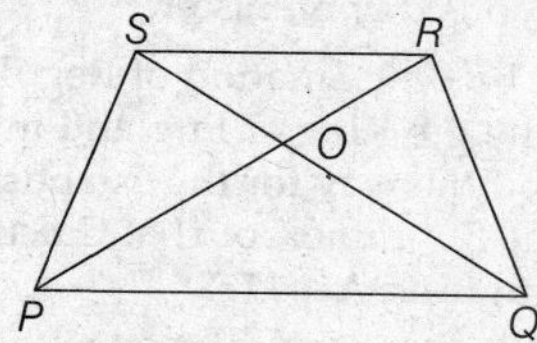

In equilateral trapezium $PQRS$,

$PO = 3x - 15$

$OQ = x + 9$

$OR = x - 5$

$OS = 5$

Now, $\Delta SRO \sim \Delta QPO$

$$\therefore \frac{SO}{QO} = \frac{RO}{PO}$$

$$\frac{5}{(x+9)} = \frac{(x-5)}{(3x-15)}$$

$\Rightarrow 15x - 75 = x^2 + 9x - 5x - 45$

$\Rightarrow x^2 - 11x + 30 = 0$

$\Rightarrow (x-6)(x-5) = 0$

$\Rightarrow x = 6, 5$

$\therefore x_1 = 6, x_2 = 5$

[$\because$ There are two values of x, x_1 and x_2]

Now,
$(x_1^2 - x_2^2) = 6^2 - 5^2 = 36 - 25 = 11$

74. *(c)* According to the question,

Let radius of sphere = 100 units

$\therefore$ Volume $= \frac{4}{3}\pi \times (100)^3$

New radius of sphere = 112 units

$\therefore$ New volume $= \frac{4}{3}\pi \times (112)^3$

$\therefore$ Percentage increase in volume

$$= \frac{4}{3}\pi (112)^3 - \frac{4}{3}\pi \times (100)^3$$

$$= \frac{4}{3}\pi ((112)^3 - (100)^3)$$

$$= \frac{4}{3}\pi \times (112 - 100)(112^2 + 100^2 + 112 \times 100)$$

$$= \frac{4}{3}\pi \times 12 \times (12544 + 10000 + 11200)$$

$$= \frac{4}{3}\pi \times 404928$$

$\therefore$ Required increase in percentage

$$= \frac{\frac{4}{3}\pi \times 404928}{\frac{4}{3}\pi \times 100 \times 100 \times 100} \times 100\%$$

$= 40.49\%$

75. *(c)* According to the question,

$$\frac{3\cos^3\theta - 2\cos\theta}{\sin\theta - 3\sin^3\theta} = \frac{\cos\theta\,(3\cos^2\theta - 2)}{\sin\theta\,(1 - 3\sin^2\theta)}$$

$$= \frac{\cos\theta\,\{3(1 - \sin^2\theta) - 2\}}{\sin\theta\,(1 - 3\sin^2\theta)}$$

$$= \cot\theta \frac{(3 - 3\sin^2\theta - 2)}{(1 - 3\sin^2\theta)}$$

$$= \cot\theta \frac{(1 - 3\sin^2\theta)}{(1 - 3\sin^2\theta)}$$

$= \cot\theta$

76. *(c)* The Maritime Anti-Piracy Act, 2022 received the assent of the President on 31st December, 2022.

- The Maritime Anti-Piracy Act, 2022 is related to repression of piracy on high seas and for matters connected therewith or incidental place.
- This legislation is designed to align with the United Nations Convention on the Law of the Sea.

77. *(c)* India's first hockey club was founded in Calcutta in 1885-86.

- The club hosted the country's first hockey tournament, the Beighton Cup.
- The 2023 Men's FIH Hockey World Cup was hosted by Bhubaneswar -Rourkela, India.

78. *(a)* Henri Becquerel received the Nobel Prize in Physics in 1903 for Spontaneous Radioactivity.

- Becquerel was awarded half of the Nobel Prize for Physics in 1903, the other half being given to Pierre and Marie Curie for their study of the Becquerel radiation.
- The SI unit of radioactivity is Becquerel (Bq) the term is named after Henri Becquerel.

79. *(c)* As per the Census 2011, the population growth during the decade remained 17.64%.

- As per Census 2011, Uttar Pradesh is the populous state and Sikkim is least populated state in India.
- In 1961-1971 census, the decadal population growth of India was recorded highest.
- The first census in India was done in 1872 under Lord Mayo.

80. *(b)* Left is the default alignment of text in a Microsoft Word document.

81. *(d)* The term 'banana kick' is associated with Football.

- Banana kick is a football kick that causes the ball to curve or change direction in the air.
- Some famous kicks associated with football are
  - Bicycle kick also known as an overhead kick, this shot involves jumping and kicking the ball over the player's head.
  - Volley also known as a full volley, this kick involves directly kicking the ball while it's in the air, before it hits the ground.
  - Free kick is a method of restarting play in football. It is awarded after an infringement of the laws by the opposing team.

82. *(c)* Ursa Major is a constellation.

- A constellation is a group of stars that appears to form a pattern or picture that are easily recognisable by people.
- There are 88 official constellations.
- The Latin name 'Ursa Major' means 'greater (or larger) bear'.
- This is the third-largest constellation in the sky after Hydra and Virgo.
- It is the largest constellation in the Northern Hemisphere and most recognisable constellation in the Northern Hemisphere.

83. *(d)* The Deccan Plateau is a triangular landmass that lies to the South of the River Narmada.

- The Deccan is the largest plateau of the Indian subcontinent.
- The Deccan Plateau is bounded by the Satpura and Vindhya mountain ranges to the North, the Western Ghats to the West, and the Bay of Bengal to the East.
- The average elevation of the plateau is 600 metres above sea level.

84. *(b)* Raika tribe is found in Rajasthan.

- Raika tribe is a nomadic pastoralist community in the deserts of Western Rajasthan, India.
- They are known for their animal husbandry practices, including raising camels, goats, sheep and cattle.
- They are also called Rabari in Gujarat.

85. *(a)* The indigenous sport 'Kalaripayattu' originated in Kerala.

- Kalaripayattu is a combination of two Malayalam words-Kalari (training ground or battleground) and Payattu (training of martial arts), which is roughly translated as 'practice in the arts of the battlefield'.
- Kalaripayattu is a martial art which developed out of combat-techniques of the 11th-12th century.

86. *(b)* Hola Mohalla is a form of Sikh festival.

- Hola Mohalla is a three-day Sikh festival that takes place in Anandpur Sahib, Punjab.
- It takes place on the next day of Holi, usually in March.
- The festival celebrates brotherhood, fraternity, valour and Sikh martial traditions.

87. *(b)* Statement (b) is incorrect regarding the Pala Dynasty of Eastern India.

- Valabhi University was founded by Bhattarka,the Maitrak King in Gujarat.
- Dharmapla founded Nalanda and Vikramshila University.
- Pala dynasty,was spreaded over Bihar and Bengal, India, from the 8th to the 12th century.
- The Pala dynasty was founded by Gopala.

88. *(a)* In January 2022, the Government of India launches Mission Ganga to evacuate the Indians stranded in Ukraine.

- **Operation Safe Homecoming** It was an air-sea evacuation operation launched by the Indian government on 26th, February 2011 to bring back Indian citizens fleeing the Libyan Civil War.
- **Operation Vande Bharat** It was a repatriation operation launched by the Indian Government on 7th May, 2020 to bring back Indian citizens stranded abroad during the COVID-19 pandemic.
- **Operation Raahat** It was an operation of the Indian Armed Forces to evacuate Indian citizens and foreign nationals from Yemen during the 2015 Yemen crises.

89. *(c)* Louis Pasteur, a French chemist, in 1862 developed the technique of preserving the quality of food by raising its temperature to prevent microbial growth in the food.

Louis Pasteur is best known for inventing the process that bears his name, Pasteurisation.

90. *(a)* Section 62(5) of the Representation of People's Act (RPA), 1951 deprives the prisoners for their right to vote.

- The Indian Parliament passed the Representation of the People Act, 1951, to regulate elections for the Houses of Parliament and Houses of the Legislature of each state.
- It was introduced in Parliament by **Dr. B.R. Ambedkar**.
- The Act was enacted by the provisional parliament under Article 327 of Indian Constitution.

91. *(c)* Madhya Pradesh state government started the Tansen Samman in 1980.

- Tansen award is presented every year for excellence in Hindustani classical music.
- It is presented during the Tansen Samaroh at Gwalior.
- Pt Ganpati Bhatt Hasanagi was awarded the Tansen Samman Award 2023.

92. *(a)* Ahmedabad is referred as the "Manchester of India" because of its thriving textile industry.

- This name was given due to the similarities between the textile industries in Manchester and Ahmedabad.
- Kanpur : Leather City of the World
- Kolkata : City of Joy
- Mumbai : City of Dreams

93. *(b)* Under Article 26 of the Indian Constitution it is mentioned about establishing and maintaining institutions for religious and charitable purposes.

- **Article 28** It protects the freedom of religion in educational institutions.
- **Article 29** It protects the cultural and educational rights of minorities.
- **Article 30** It provides minority communities with the right to establish and administer educational institutions of their choice.

94. *(a)* Good Friday is related to Christianity.

- Good Friday is one of remembrance, marking the crucifixion of Jesus Christ at the hands of the Romans.
- It is believed that Jesus rose from the dead the following Sunday of Good Friday, which is commemorated in the form of the joyous day of Easter.

95. *(d)* The proclamation of Regulating Act by the King of England in 1773 paved the way for the establishment of the Supreme Court at Calcutta.

Regulating Act 1773

- The act was the first step taken by the British Government to control and regulate the affairs of East India company in India.
- It changed the post of Governor of Bengal to "Governor-General of Bengal".
- The first Governor-General of Bengal was Warren Hastings.
- Under this act, in the year 1774, Supreme Court was established at Calcutta with one Chief Justice and three other judges.
- The first Chief Justice of Supreme Court was Sir Elijah Impey.

96. *(c)* Pandavani is a folk music of Chhattisgarh which is based on the epic Mahabharata.

- It depicts the story of the Pandavas, the leading characters in the epic Mahabharata.
- Bhima, the second of the Pandava is the hero of the story.
- Panihari, Ghumar and Maand are the folk music and dance of Rajasthan.

97. *(b)* Certificates of deposits are issued by commercial banks at a discount on face value. Certificate of deposites is basically a fixed-income financial tools issued in dematerialised form and administered by the RBI.

- Commercial paper is an unsecured form of promissory note that pays a fixed rate of interest.
- Treasury bill are money market instruments issued by the Government of India as a promissory note with guaranteed repayment at a later date.
- Promissory notes is a legally binding document that establishes a promise to pay a specified a amount to a designated individual or entity at a predetermined time.

98. *(b)* Article 39 (d) of the Indian Constitution will be applicable

- **Article 39 (d)** It states about equal pay for equal work for both men and women.
- **Article 21** It protects the Fundamental Right to life and liberty.
- **Article 18** It abolisbes all titles and prohibits the state from conferring them on anyone.
- **Article 48 A** It protects and improves the environment and wildlife.

99. *(d)* A word processor is an example of application software.

100. *(c)* HYV refers to High Yielding Variety.

- The Green Revolution in India started in 1960's during which agriculture in India was converted into a modern industrial system.
- It was led by the adoption of technology such as the use of HYV seeds, mechanised farm tools, irrigation facilities, pesticides and fertilisers.
- MS Swaminathan is known as the Father of the Indian Green Revolution.
- MS Swaminathan received Bharat Ratna in 2024.

Set 12 03 July, 2024 (Shift IV)

SSC CHSL Tier-I SOLVED PAPER

Instructions

1. This paper contains 100 questions.
2. It has 4 Parts, **Part I** General English, **Part II** General Intelligence & Reasoning, **Part III** Quantitative Aptitude and **Part IV** General Awareness.
3. Each questions carries **2 mark**.

Part I
General English

1. The following sentence has been split into four segments. Identify the segment that contains an error.

I had seen / her with her mother / in the cinema hall / yesterday.

(a) in the cinema hall
(b) her with her mother
(c) yesterday
(d) I had seen

2. Select the option to replace the incorrect word in the following sentence.

Chotu is a bright young child, who yearn to go to school but works in his uncle's dhaba.

(a) worked
(b) working
(c) yearns
(d) yearned

3. Select the most appropriate option to fill in the blank.

He ....a long distance.

(a) runned (b) running
(c) ran (d) run

4. The following sentence has been divided into three segments. One of them may contain an adverbial usage error. Select the option that has the segment with the error. If you don't find any error, select 'No error' as your answer.

Mr. Narayanan / is a rather / lazy man.

(a) No error
(b) Mr. Narayanan
(c) is a rather
(d) lazy man.

Directions (Q. Nos. 5-9) *In the following passage, some words have been deleted. Read the passage carefully and select the most appropriate option to fill in each blank.*

Trees are (1)......... best gift of nature for us. They make the environment beautiful and clean. Water and sunlight are very important to helping trees grow. Human beings get food from trees. Trees also give us wood and shade. Houses, chairs and toys (2) .... from wood we receive from trees. Trees can be called the best friends of mankind. Many animals get their food from leaves, vegetables and fruits grown (3) .... trees. They also live in the shadows of trees. We (4) .... cutting trees to save nature. Children and adults need to plant more trees and teach each other to stop causing harm to (5) .... One tree can save many lives.

5. Select the most appropriate option to fill in blank number (1).

(a) the (b) a
(c) an (d) No article

6. Select the most appropriate option to fill in blank number (2).

(a) are made (b) had make
(c) was make (d) will made

7. Select the most appropriate option to fill in blank number (3).

(a) on (b) out
(c) of (d) for

8. Select the most appropriate option to fill in blank number (4).

(a) can stopped (b) may stopped
(c) should stop (d) have stop

9. Select the most appropriate option to fill in blank number (5).

(a) nurturing (b) nature
(c) nurture (d) natural

10. Select the most appropriate to fill in the blank.

The boxer was knocked out cold by a powerful .... punch to the jaw.

(a) write
(b) wright
(c) rite
(d) right

11. Select the option that can substitute the bracketed word segment meaningfully.

If you behave well and exhibit good manners, then (people will be likely to remember you) in a positive way.

(a) people likely you remember
(b) people are like remember you
(c) people will like in remember
(d) people are likely to remember you

12. Select the most appropriate idiom that can substitute the underlined word segment in the given sentence.

Delivering that furniture to the tenth floor without the lift and an incline is <u>incredibly foolish and next to impossible</u> .

(a) like a tree known by its fruits
(b) like nailing jelly to the tree
(c) as tight as the bark of the tree
(d) like going between the bark and the tree

13. Select the most appropriate antonym of the underlined word in the given sentence.

This makes readers <u>contemplate</u> the motives people have for performing acts of charity.

(a) understate
(b) follow up
(c) overlook
(d) deviate

14. The following sentence has been split into four segments. Identify the segment that contains a spelling error.

In all instances of frustrasion, / you will always find / the anger directed towards / a single person only.

(a) the anger directed towards
(b) In all instances of frustrasion
(c) you will always find
(d) a single person only

15. Select the most appropriate option to fill in the blank.

The movie 'Desperate Ghosts' was watched by my younger brother and he was .... horror.

(a) filled with (b) filled of
(c) filled on (d) filled off

16. Read the sentence carefully and select the most appropriate option to substitute the underlined part.

The sudden declaration of war between two countries led to a <u>disarray.</u>

(a) peaceful treaty
(b) disorderly situation
(c) refined argument
(d) elusive situation

17. Select the incorrectly spelt word.

(a) Acknowledgment
(b) Apparent
(c) Fulfil
(d) Conscientous

18. Select the most appropriate idiom to fill in the blank.

This gun should be handled with care and ....

(a) nip in the bud
(b) shot for safety
(c) mince the matters
(d) kept at arm's length

19. Select the most appropriate synonym of the word 'echoed' to fill in the blank.

The thunderous applause .... through the stadium.

(a) reverberated
(b) recoiled
(c) bounced
(d) pulsed

20. Select the most appropriate synonym of the given word.

Chaste

(a) Flashy (b) Corrupt
(c) Sullied (d) Pure

21. Select the most appropriate antonym of the given word.

Cheerful

(a) Sunny (b) Hilarious
(c) Gloomy (d) Joyful

22. Select the most appropriate antonym of the underlined word in the sentence.

He tried to <u>improve</u> the working conditions in his office.

(a) spatter (b) sprinkle
(c) specify (d) spoil

23. Select the most appropriate option that can substitute the underlined segment in the given sentence.

It was <u>her</u> who first saw the criminal.

(a) she (b) them (c) hers (d) him

24. Select the most appropriate synonym of the underlined word in the given sentence. Can I please <u>request</u> you all to stand up?

(a) require (b) plead
(c) claim (d) petition

25. Read the sentence carefully and select the most appropriate option to substitute the underlined part.

Greta Thunberg's <u>tirade</u> against environmental degeneration shocked the world leaders.

(a) minute observation
(b) debatable account
(c) long and angry speech
(d) innate liberal opinion

Part II
General Intelligence

26. What should come in place of the question mark (?) in the given series based on the English alphabetical order?

BOJ, FQO, JST, NUY, ?

(a) RVB (b) QWD (c) QVC (d) RWD

27. 'P + F' means 'P is the son of F'
'P − F' means 'P is the wife of F'
'P × F' means 'P is the brother of F'
'P ÷ F' means 'P is the mother of F'
'P = F' means 'P is the sister of F'.
What does ' K = R ÷ M ' mean?

(a) K is the daughter of M
(b) K is the aunt (mother's sister) of M
(c) K is the sister of M
(d) K is the niece of M

28. A paper is folded and cut as shown below. How will it appear when unfolded?

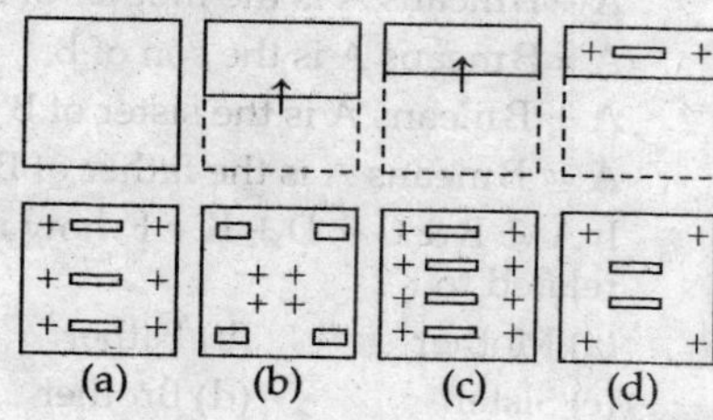

29. In a certain code language, 'BABE' is coded as '20' and 'EACH' is coded as '34'. What is the code for 'FACT' in the given code language?

(a) 63 (b) 62
(c) 64 (d) 60

30. 129 is related to 387 following a certain logic. Following the same logic, 164 is related to 492. To which of the following is 148 related, following the same logic?

(a) 444 (b) 468
(c) 352 (d) 362

31. If 'R' stands for '÷', 'K' stands for '×', 'G' stands for '+' and 'D' stands for '−', what will come in place of the question mark (?) in the following equation?

32 G 15 R 15 D 17 K 18 = ?

(a) −456 (b) −273
(c) −879 (d) −235

32. Which of the following numbers will replace the question mark (?) in the given series?

244, 232.1, 220.2, 208.3, 196.4, ?

(a) 176.5 (b) 172.5
(c) 180.5 (d) 184.5

33. What will come in the place of the question mark (?) in the following equation, if '+' and '−' are interchanged and '×' and '÷' are interchanged?

59 + 39 − 63 × 21 ÷ 26 = ?

(a) 98 (b) 96 (c) 90 (d) 93

34. Identify the figure given in the options that when put in place of the question mark (?) will logically complete the series.

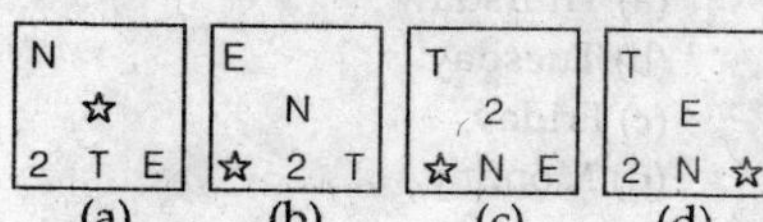

35. In a certain language,
A & B means A is the wife of B,
A ÷ B means A is the mother of B,
A × B means A is the son of B,
A + B means A is the sister of B and
A @ B means A is the father of B.
If A @ B & C @ D + K ÷ F, how is C related to K?
(a) Mother (b) Father
(c) Sister (d) Brother

36. In this question, three statements are given, followed by three conclusions numbered I, II and III. Assuming the statements to be true, even if they seem to be at variance with commonly known facts, decide which of the conclusion(s) logically follows from the statements.

Statements

Some carrots are onions.
All onions are potatoes.
All potatoes are radish.

Conclusions

I. Some carrots are radish.
II. All onions are radish.
III. No carrot is a potato.
(a) Only Conclusion II follows
(b) Only Conclusion I follows
(c) Both Conclusions I and II follow
(d) Only Conclusion III follows

37. Select the correct mirror image of the given figure, when the mirror is placed at MN as shown below.

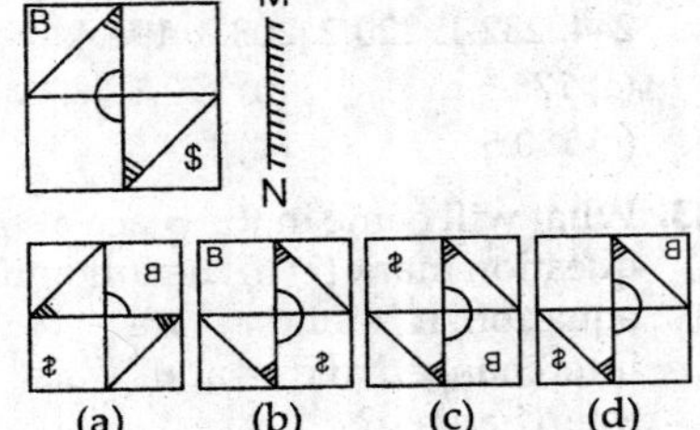

38. In a certain code language, 'RISK' is coded as '3921' and 'KIRT' is coded as '1693'. How is 'S' coded in the given language?
(a) 2 (b) 3 (c) 1 (d) 6

39. If 10th October, 2003 was a Friday, then what was the day of the week on 8th October, 2015?
(a) Thursday
(b) Tuesday
(c) Friday
(d) Monday

40. What will come in the place of the question mark (?) in the following equation, if '+' and '–' are interchanged and '×' and '÷' are interchanged?
$105 \div 2 + 4 - 120 \times 6 = ?$
(a) 266 (b) 126 (c) 216 (d) 226

41. Select the correct mirror image of the given combination, when the mirror is placed at MN as shown below.

M
We63BF
N

(a) ℲᗺƐ9əM
(b) BFƐ∂ɘW
(c) ꟻᗺƐ∂ɘM
(d) ꟻᗺƐ∂ɘW

42. Select the option figure in which the given figure is embedded as its part (rotation is not allowed).

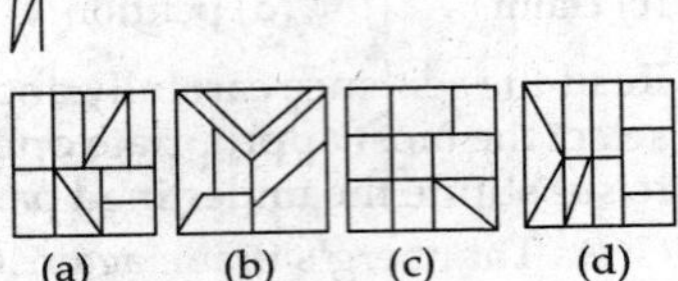

43. Select the correct mirror image of the given combination, when the mirror is placed at MN as shown below.

M
Zar27hF
N

(a) ꟻᖹ27ɿɒZ
(b) ꟻᖹ7Ƨɿɒ Z
(c) Ⅎᖹ7ƧɿɒZ
(d) ꟻᖹ7ƧɿɒZ

44. Select the set in which the numbers are related in the same way as are the numbers of the following sets.
(**Note** Operations should be performed on the whole numbers, without breaking down the numbers into its constituent digits. E.g. 13 – Operations on 13 such as adding /subtracting /multiplying etc. to 13 can be performed. Breaking down 13 into 1 and 3 and then performing mathematical operations on 1 and 3 is not allowed.)
(4, 16, 32)
(7, 49, 98)
(a) (12, 144, 288)
(b) (12, 144, 278)
(c) (12, 134, 288)
(d) (14, 144, 288)

45. This question consists of a pair of words, which have a certain relationship to each other. Select the pair which does not have the same relationship.
Allure : Repulse
(1) Creation : Destruction
(2) Fluctuate : Stabilize
(3) Immense : Huge
(4) Notion : Reality
(a) 4 (b) 3
(c) 1 (d) 2

46. What should come in place of the question mark (?) in the given series based on the English alphabetical order?
WYS, BDX, GIC, LNH, ?
(a) QSM (b) QMS
(c) SMQ (d) PSM

47. What should come in place of X in the given series?
3, 9, 21, 41, 71, X
(a) 110 (b) 117
(c) 113 (d) 120

48. How many triangles are there in the given figure?

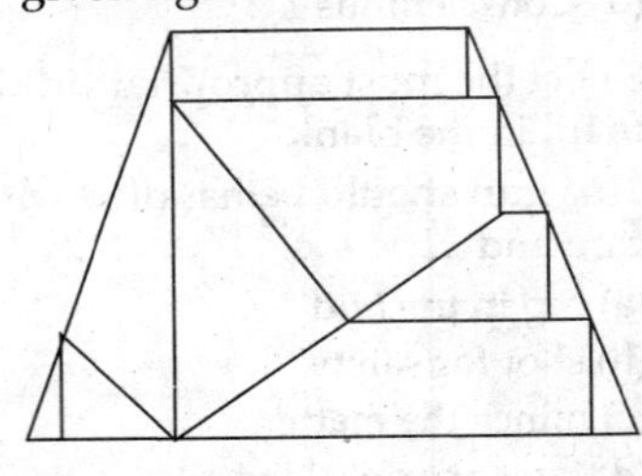

(a) 10 (b) 11 (c) 9 (d) 12

49. 'ADFI' is related to 'CFHK' in a certain way based on the English alphabetical order. In the same way, 'EHJM' is related to GJLO. To which of the following is ILNQ related to, following the same logic?
(a) KMPS (b) KNQT
(c) KNQS (d) KNPS

50. If 19th July, 2000 is Wednesday, then what will be the day of the week on 17th March, 2015?
(a) Wednesday (b) Friday
(c) Tuesday (d) Sunday

Part III
Quantitative Aptitude

51. In an engineering college, there are four branches namely Computer Science (CS), Electronics (EC), Civil Engineering (CE), and Mechanical Engineering (ME). The respective ratio of the number of students in these branches is 11 : 5 : 6 : 7. What is the percentage of students belonging to CS and ME branches in the college (correct up to two decimal places)?
(a) 61.07% (b) 61.37% (c) 62.07% (d) 62.37%

52. If the perimeters of two similar triangles are in the ratio of 4 : 7 and the sum of the areas is 195 cm^2, then what is $\frac{1}{3}$rd of the difference between the areas (in cm^2) of the two triangles?
(a) 33 (b) 54 (c) 99 (d) 63

53. Riya and Sangeeta can finish a work in 6 days and 8 days, respectively. Riya started the work alone and then after 3 days, Sangeeta joined Riya. They both finish the remaining work. How long did the total work last?
(a) $4\frac{3}{7}$ days (b) $4\frac{5}{7}$ days (c) $4\frac{2}{7}$ days (d) $4\frac{4}{7}$ days

54. Four cubes each of volume 216 cubic cm are joined end to end to form a new solid. The surface area of the new solid is
(a) 1296 sq cm (b) 648 sq cm (c) 672 sq cm (d) 324 sq cm

55. If the area of a triangle, whose base measures 6 cm is 18 cm^2, then its height is
(a) 6 cm (b) 3.1 cm (c) 2.2 cm (d) 9 cm

56. There are 160 multiple choice questions in a test. 4 marks are allotted for a correct answer and 1 mark is deducted for a wrong answer or un-attempted question from the total score of correct answers. If a candidate scored 400 marks in the test, how many questions did he answer correctly?
(a) 110 (b) 115 (c) 112 (d) 120

57. In an election between two candidates, one got 60% of the total valid votes and 15% of the votes were invalid. If the total number of votes were 8400, the number of valid votes that the other candidate got were
(a) 2856 (b) 2998 (c) 3117 (d) 3213

58. When x is added to each of the numbers 7, 11, 18 and 23, then the number so obtained are in proportion. What is the mean proportional between the $(x-1)$ and $(2x-10)$?
(a) 68 (b) 78 (c) 98 (d) 48

59. Read the given information and answer the question that follows.

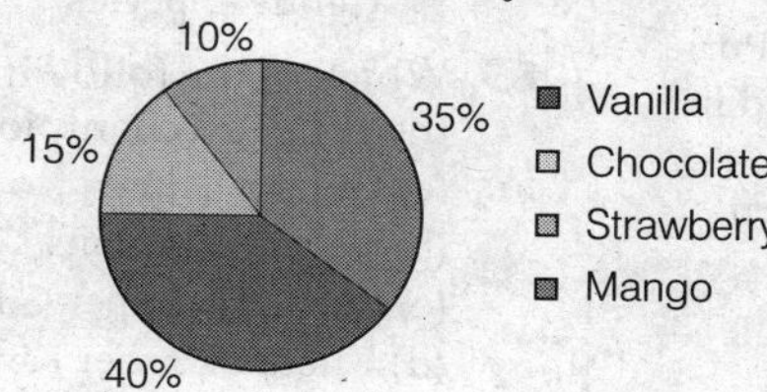

If 400 chocolate ice-creams are sold in a day, how many vanilla ice-creams are sold?
(a) 100 (b) 350 (c) 300 (d) 400

60. The distribution of total 1500 students in a school for different games is shown in the following figure. Study the given figure carefully and answer the question that follows.

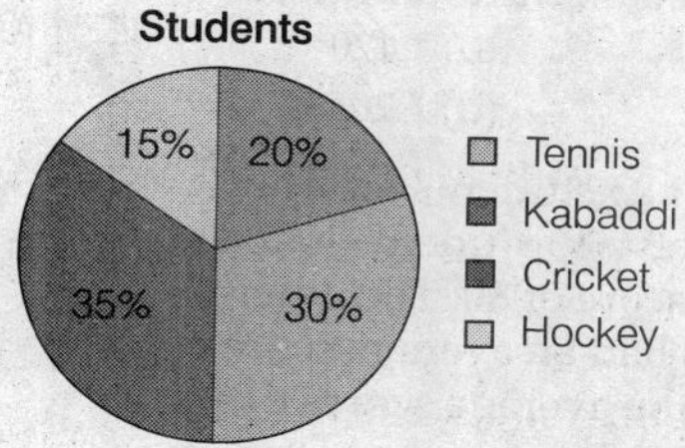

Find the total number of students selected for Cricket and Tennis.
(a) 825 (b) 525 (c) 415 (d) 625

61. Simplify the following expression.
$$2\frac{1}{4}\times3\frac{1}{5}+5\frac{1}{6}\text{ of }2\frac{4}{31}\div3\frac{2}{3}+4\frac{1}{7}\text{ of }1\frac{6}{29}$$
(a) $13\frac{1}{5}$ (b) $16\frac{1}{5}$ (c) $14\frac{1}{5}$ (d) $15\frac{1}{5}$

62. $\Delta ABC \sim \Delta EDF$ and area (ΔABC) : area $(\Delta EDF) = 9 : 4$. If $AB = 5$ cm, $BC = 8$ cm and $CA = 10$ cm, then DF is equal to
(a) $3\frac{2}{3}$ cm (b) $3\frac{1}{4}$ cm (c) $5\frac{1}{3}$ cm (d) $4\frac{2}{3}$ cm

63. If $\alpha + \beta = 45°$ and $(\tan\alpha + 1)(\tan\beta + 1) = 2x$, then x is
(a) 2 (b) −1 (c) 0 (d) 1

64. Study the given bar-graph and answer the question that follows.
The bar-graph shows the production (in lakh) of kitchen appliances manufactured by three companies A, B, and C over a period of six years from 2012 to 2017.

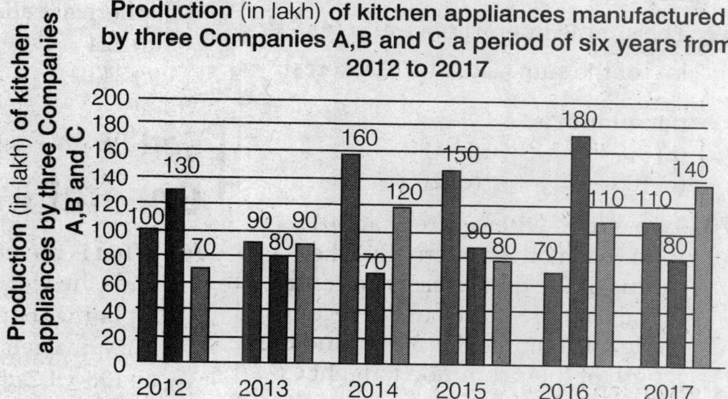

In which year was the percentage of rise/fall in production from the previous year the maximum for company C?
(a) 2013 (b) 2017 (c) 2016 (d) 2015

65. A seller decreased the selling price of each item from ₹ 5000 to ₹ 4680, by which his loss percentage increased by 4%. If he has to get 4% profit, then the selling price of the item should be
(a) ₹ 7280 (b) ₹ 8320
(c) ₹ 8840 (d) ₹ 7800

66. What is the discount that Rohan should offer on the remaining ₹ 8000 of a laptop priced at ₹ 48000, given that, he has already given a 12% discount on the first ₹ 28000 and 8% discount on the next ₹ 12000 to match the discount amount of 9.5% given on the total price?
(a) ₹ 402 (b) ₹ 420
(c) ₹ 240 (d) ₹ 204

67. A class of 25 students took an English test. 15 students had an average score of 80. The other students had an average score of 60. What is the average score of the whole class?
(a) 80 (b) 76
(c) 74 (d) 72

68. Study the given graph and answer the question that follows.
The graph shows the exports from three companies (A, B and C) over the years (in ₹ crore).

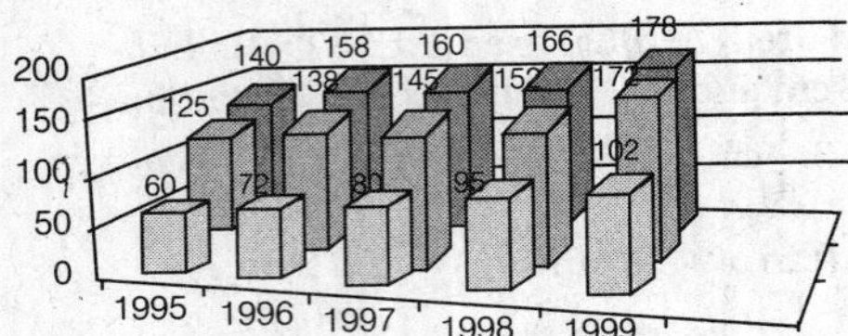

In which year was the difference between the exports from Companies A and B the minimum?
(a) 1997 (b) 1998
(c) 1995 (d) 1994

69. The simple interest on a sum for 8 yr is $\frac{4}{5}$ of the sum. The rate of interest per annum is
(a) 5% (b) 15%
(c) 10% (d) 20%

70. Two circles with centre O and A touch each other externally. The radius of the first circle with centre O is 6 cm. The radius of the second circle with centre A is 3 cm. Find the length of their common tangent CB (in cm).
(a) $3\sqrt{2}$ (b) $4\sqrt{3}$
(c) $4\sqrt{2}$ (d) $6\sqrt{2}$

71. Two parallel chords of length 8 units each are 6 units away from each other in a circle. What is the radius of the circle in units?
(a) 3 (b) 6
(c) 5 (d) 4

72. When the integer n is divided by 18, the quotient is x and the remainder is 6. When the integer n is divided by 25, the quotient is y and the remainder is 15. Which of the following is true?
(a) $25y + 18x = 9$
(b) $25y - 18x = 9$
(c) $18x + 25y = 9$
(d) $18x - 25y = 9$

73. Rakesh is the owner of a rectangular field. Because of the construction of an expressway near his field, the length and breadth of his field are reduced by 30% and 10%, respectively. What is the percentage decrease in the area of his field?
(a) 40% (b) 35%
(c) 37% (d) 33%

74. Ram and Shyam start walking from the same place in the opposite direction. If Shyam walks at a speed of $5\frac{1}{4}$ km/h and Ram at a speed of 3 km/h, then after how much time will they be 44 km apart?
(a) 3 h 20 min
(b) 5 h 20 min
(c) 6 h 20 min
(d) 4 h 20 min

75. A cylindrical rod of iron, whose height is 12 times its radius, is melted and cast into spherical balls, each of one-third the radius of the cylinder. Find the number of spherical balls.
(a) 224 (b) 212
(c) 243 (d) 198

Part IV
General Awareness

76. What is the name of the festival that ends the Holy Ramzan month?
(a) Eid-Ul-Fitr
(b) Muharram
(c) Eid-Ul-Zuha
(d) Bakrid

77. The Palas were
(a) a dynasty that appeared in Puri
(b) a dynasty that first appeared in Cambodia
(c) a dynasty that united Eastern India and Burma
(d) a dynasty that appeared in Eastern India

78. The largest inland salt lake 'Sambhar' is located in the ....of India.
(a) North-East (b) South-East
(c) South-West (d) North-West

79. In India, the musical instrument 'Flute' is also known as ....
(a) Tabla (b) Manjira
(c) Bansuri (d) Veena

80. According to Global Multidimensional Poverty Index (2022), on the basis of four indicators- nutrition, cooking fuel, sanitation and housing, how much poor people live in India?
(a) 24.4 million
(b) 54.4 million
(c) 44.4 million
(d) 34.4 million

81. In Microsoft Excel, which chart type is best suited for comparing proportions or percentages of a whole?
(a) Pie Chart
(b) Bar Chart
(c) Scatter Chart
(d) Line Chart

82. Who wrote the book 'Gulamgiri'?
(a) Jyotiba Phule
(b) Dwarkanath Tagore
(c) Swami Shraddhanand
(d) BR Ambedkar

83. In cost theory, the usual shape of the .... curve is a rectangular hyperbola.
(a) total cost
(b) fixed cost
(c) average fixed cost
(d) variable cost

84. Which of the following sequences is correct, according to taxonomy?
(a) Class - Phylum - Family - Order-Genus - Species
(b) Family - Phylum - Class - Order - Genus - Species
(c) Phylum - Class - Order - Family - Genus - Species
(d) Class - Phylum - Order - Family - Genus - Species

85. Which of the following teams won the IPL 2023 championship?
(a) Gujarat Titans
(b) Mumbai Indians
(c) Lucknow Super Giants
(d) Chennai Super Kings

86. Norman Ernest Borlaug was awarded the ……… in 1970 for his contributions to the Green Revolution.
(a) Nobel Peace Prize
(b) Nobel Prize in Physiology
(c) Nobel Prize in Chemistry
(d) Nobel Prize in Physics

87. Who among the following discovered that a wire carrying electric current can attract or repel another wire next to it that's also carrying electric current?
(a) Michael Faraday
(b) Andre-Marie Ampere
(c) Guglielmo Marconi
(d) James Maxwell

88. Which articles of the Constitution deal with citizenship?
(a) Articles 5 to 11
(b) Articles 5 to 10
(c) Articles 5 to 8
(d) Articles 5 to 9

89. The establishment of Union Public Service Commission, State Public Service Commissions and Joint Public Service Commission falls under which of the following features of the Constitution of India?
(a) Federalism
(b) Parliamentary Government
(c) Directive Principles of State Policy
(d) Fundamental Rights

90. Chhannulal Mishra is related to which Musical Lineage?
(a) Agara Musical Family
(b) Delhi Musical Family
(c) Kirana Musical Family
(d) Jaipur Musical Family

91. According to the Census of India 2011, which of the following states is the most urbanised?
(a) Goa (b) Kerala
(c) Himachal Pradesh
(d) Punjab

92. On 7th November, 2022, the Supreme Court of India upheld the reservations for the weaker sections (EWS). Which of the following amendments brought this reservation in the first place?
(a) 103rd Amendment of the Constitution
(b) 102nd Amendment of the Constitution
(c) 104th Amendment of the Constitution
(d) 101st Amendment of the Constitution

93. The moderate margin of a page in MS Word can be applied to the page from which of the following?
(a) Page Layout Tab
(b) Design Tab
(c) Review tab
(d) View Tab

94. Who was the first Indian woman wrestler to win a medal at the Olympics?
(a) Alka Tomar
(b) Babita Phogat
(c) Geeta Phogat
(d) Sakshi Malik

95. 'Chang dance' is popular in the state of
(a) Goa (b) Tripura
(c) Rajasthan (d) Bihar

96. Who among the following Cabinet Ministers was appointed as the Governor of Karnataka in July 2021?
(a) Arjun Munda
(b) Rajendra Vishwanath
(c) Thawarchand Gehlot
(d) Hari Babu Kambhampati

97. Which dwarf planet orbits the Sun in 310 years at a distance between 38.5 to 53 AU?
(a) Ceres
(b) Eris
(c) Makemake
(d) Pluto

98. Which country hosted the first FIFA Word Cup?
(a) Brazil (b) Italy
(c) Uruguay (d) France

99. Dinesh K. Tripathi was appointed as ……… in January, 2024.
(a) Vice Chief of Naval Staff
(b) Chief of Naval Staff
(c) Rear Admiral
(d) Chief of Personnel

100. According to Ministry of Agriculture and Farmers Welfare, what was the total food grain production of India in the year 2022-23?
(a) 2266.23 lakh tonnes
(b) 2876.17 lakh tonnes
(c) 2491.58 lakh tonnes
(d) 3296.87 lakh tonnes

Answers

1. (d)	2. (c)	3. (c)	4. (a)
5. (a)	6. (a)	7. (a)	8. (c)
9. (b)	10. (d)	11. (d)	12. (b)
13. (c)	14 (b)	15. (a)	16. (b)
17. (d)	18. (d)	19. (a)	20. (d)
21. (c)	22. (d)	23. (a)	24. (b)
25. (c)	26. (d)	27. (b)	28. (c)
29. (d)	30. (a)	31. (b)	32. (d)
33. (a)	34. (d)	35. (b)	36. (c)
37. (d)	38. (a)	39. (a)	40. (d)
41. (d)	42. (d)	43. (b)	44. (a)
45. (b)	46. (a)	47. (c)	48. (a)
49. (d)	50. (c)	51. (c)	52. (a)
53. (b)	54. (b)	55. (a)	56. (c)
57. (a)	58. (d)	59. (b)	60. (a)
61. (d)	62. (c)	63. (d)	64. (c)
65. (b)	66. (c)	67. (d)	68. (b)
69. (c)	70. (d)	71. (c)	72. (d)
73. (c)	74. (b)	75. (c)	76. (a)
77. (d)	78. (d)	79. (c)	80. (d)
81. (c)	82. (a)	83. (c)	84. (c)
85. (d)	86. (a)	87. (b)	88. (a)
89. (a)	90. (c)	91. (a)	92. (a)
93. (a)	94. (d)	95. (c)	96. (c)
97. (c)	98. (c)	99. (a)	100. (d)

Explanations

1. *(d)* Part (d) 'I had seen' contains an error. As the sentence is in past tense, use 'saw' to correct the sentence.

2. *(c)* The given sentence contains an error of subject verb agreement. Use 'yearns' as the subject is singular to correct the sentence.

3. *(c)* The correct filler for the given blank is 'ran'.

4. *(a)* The given sentence is grammatically correct and contextually meaningful.

5. *(a)* The correct filler for the given blank is 'the'.

6. *(a)* The correct filler for the given blank is 'are made'.

7. *(a)* The correct filler for the given blank is 'on'.

8. *(c)* The correct filler for the given blank is 'should stop'.

9. *(b)* The correct filler for the given blank is 'nature'.

10. *(d)* The correct filler for the given blank is 'right'.

11. *(d)* The bracketed part of the given sentence contains an error. Use 'people are likely to remember you' to correct the sentence.

12. *(b)* The most appropriate substitute for the underlined words is 'like nailing jelly to the tree'. It means incredibly difficult or impossible.

13. *(c)* Contemplate means to think about something. Hence, its antonym is 'overlook'.

14. *(b)* Part (b) 'In all instances of frustrasion,' contains a spelling error. The correct spelling is 'frustration'.

15. *(a)* The correct filler for the given blank is 'filled with'.

16. *(b)* The word 'disarray' means disorderly situation.

17. *(d)* The incorrectly spelt word is 'Conscientous'. The correct spelling is 'Conscientious'.

18. *(d)* The correct idiom to fill in the blank is - kept at arm's length. It means to keep someone at distance.

19. *(a)* The correct filler for the given blank is 'reverberated' which means (of a loud noise) be repeated several times as an echo.

20. *(d)* The word 'Chaste' means 'pure'. Sullied means dirty or made impure.

21. *(c)* The antonym of 'Cheerful' is 'gloomy'.

22. *(d)* Here, 'improve' means to enhance the quality of something. Hence, 'spoil' (which means of make something bad) will be its antonym.

23. *(a)* The underlined part of the given sentence contains an error. Use 'she' to correct the sentence.

24. *(b)* The underlined part of the given sentence contains an error. Use 'plead' to correct the sentence.

25. *(c)* A tirade is a long and angry speech.

26. *(d)* The pattern of the series is as follows,

B $\xrightarrow{+4}$ F $\xrightarrow{+4}$ J $\xrightarrow{+4}$ N $\xrightarrow{+4}$ [R]

O $\xrightarrow{+2}$ Q $\xrightarrow{+2}$ S $\xrightarrow{+2}$ U $\xrightarrow{+2}$ [W]

J $\xrightarrow{+5}$ O $\xrightarrow{+5}$ T $\xrightarrow{+5}$ Y $\xrightarrow{+5}$ [D]

27. *(b)* According to the question,

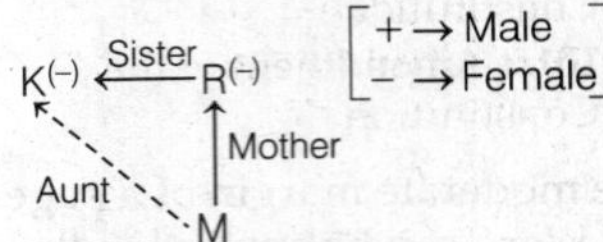

∴ 'K is the aunt of M' is true.

28. *(c)* The paper when unfolded, will appear as the figure given in option (c).

29. *(d)* As,

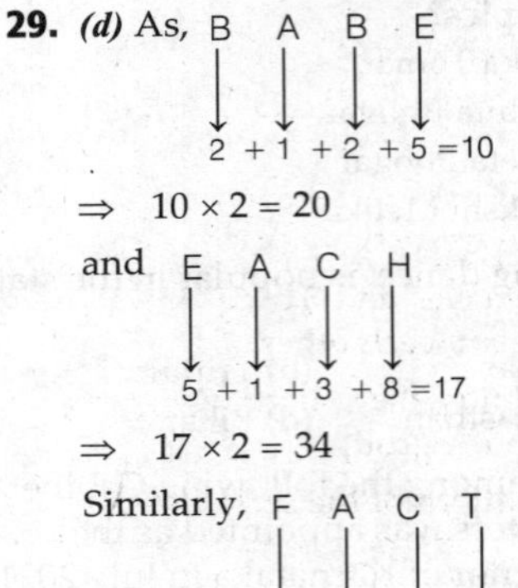

B A B E → 2 + 1 + 2 + 5 = 10

⇒ $10 \times 2 = 20$

and E A C H → 5 + 1 + 3 + 8 = 17

⇒ $17 \times 2 = 34$

Similarly, F A C T → 6 + 1 + 3 + 20 = 30

⇒ $30 \times 2 = 60$

30. *(a)* As, $129 \times 3 = 387$

and $164 \times 3 = 492$

Similarly, $148 \times 3 = \boxed{444}$

31. *(b)* Given expression,

32 G 15 R 15 D 17 K 18

After interchanging letters with signs, we get

R → ÷	K → ×
G → +	D → −

$32 + 15 \div 15 - 17 \times 18$

By applying BODMAS, we get

$32 + 1 - 306$

$= 33 - 306 = -273$

32. *(d)* The pattern of the series is as follows,

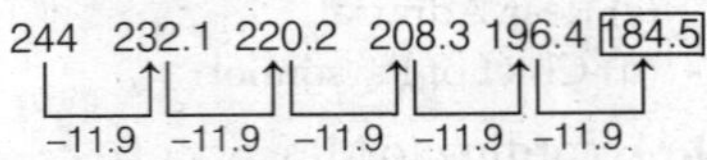

33. *(a)* Given expression,

$59 + 39 - 63 \times 21 \div 26 = ?$

After interchanging '+' and '−' and '×' and '÷', we get

$59 - 39 + 63 \div 21 \times 26$

By applying BODMAS,

$20 + 3 \times 26$

$= 20 + 78 = 98$

34. *(d)* The given figure series follows following two alternate patterns.

I. From figure (i) to (ii), From figure (iii) to (iv),

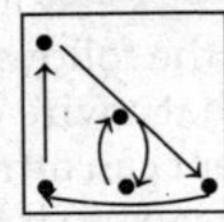

II. From figure (ii) to (iii), From figure (iv) to (v),

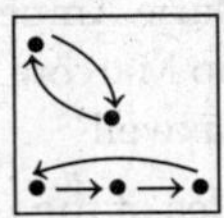

∴ Figure given in option (d) will complete the series.

35. *(b)* According to the question,

Given expression,

A @ B & C @ D + K ÷ F

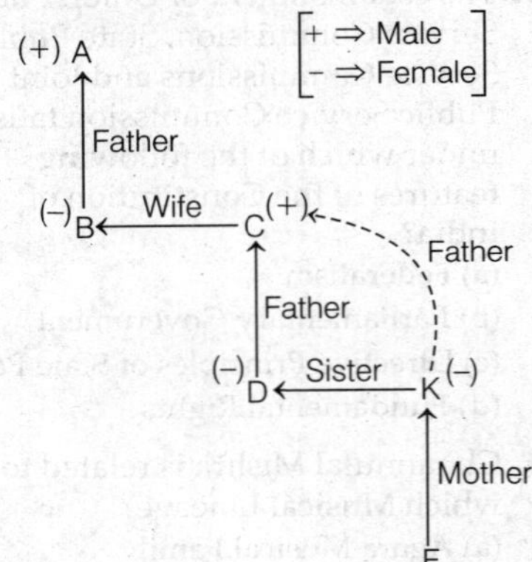

∴ C is the father to K.

36. *(c)* According to the statements,

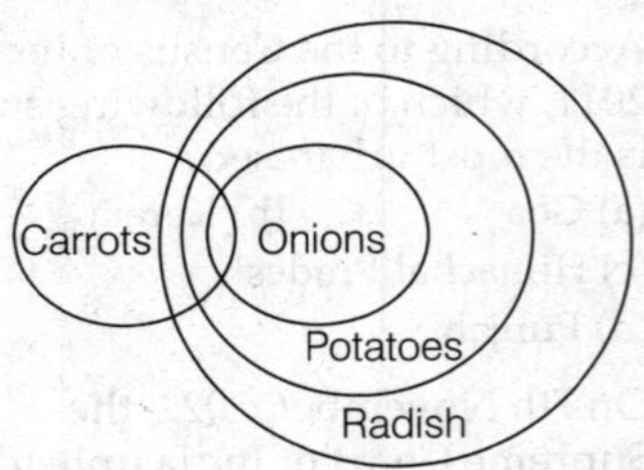

Conclusions I. (✓) II. (✓) III. (✗)

∴ Both Conclusions I and II follow.

37. *(d)* Figure given in option (d) is the correct mirror image of the given figure.

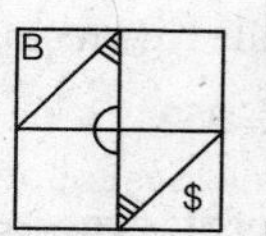

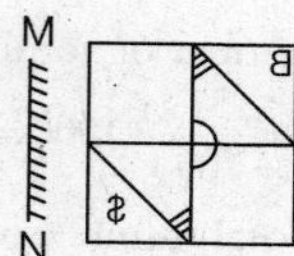

38. *(a)* According to the question,

R I (S) K → 3 9 (2) 1

K I R T → 1 6 9 3

∴ Code for S is '2'.

39. *(a)* Given,

10th October, 2003 = Friday

Number of odd days from 10th October, 2003 to 10th October, 2014

$$= \frac{2+1+1+1+2+1+1+1+2+1+1}{7}$$

$$= \frac{14}{7} = 0 \text{ odd days}$$

(∵ 2004, 2008 and 2012 are leap years)

Number of odd days from 11th October, 2014 to 8th October, 2015

$$= \frac{(21+30+31+31+28+31+30+31+30+31+31+30+8)}{7}$$

$$= \frac{363}{7} = 6 \text{ odd days}$$

∴ 8th October, 2015 = Friday + 6 days

= Thursday

40. *(d)* Given expression,

105 ÷ 2 + 4 − 120 × 6

After interchanging '+' and '−' and '×' and '÷', we get

105 × 2 − 4 + 120 ÷ 6

After applying BODMAS, we get

210 − 4 + 20

= 230 − 4

= 226

41. *(d)* The figure given in option (d) will be the correct mirror image of the question figure.

We63BF | M/N | (mirror image of We63BF)

42. *(d)* The given figure is embedded in the option figure (d).

43. *(b)* The figure given in option (d) is the correct mirror image of the given question figure.

Zar27hF | M/N | (mirror image of Zar27hF)

44. *(a)* As, 4 → (×4) → 16 → (×2) → 32

and 7 → (×7) → 49 → (×2) → 98

Similarly, 12 → (×12) → 144 → (×2) → 288

45. *(b)* As, 'Allure' and 'Repulse' are antonyms to each other.

But, 'Immense' and 'Huge' are synonyms to each other.

Hence, 'Immense : Huge' does not belong to the group.

46. *(a)* The pattern of the series is as follows,

W →(+5) B →(+5) G →(+5) L →(+5) Q

Y →(+5) D →(+5) I →(+5) N →(+5) S

S →(+5) X →(+5) C →(+5) H →(+5) M

47. *(c)* The pattern of the series is as follows,

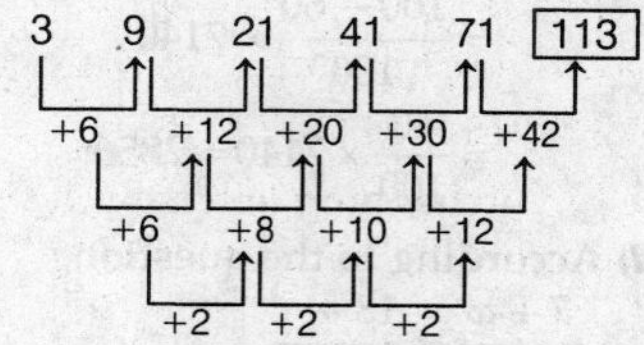

48. *(a)* Naming the figure,

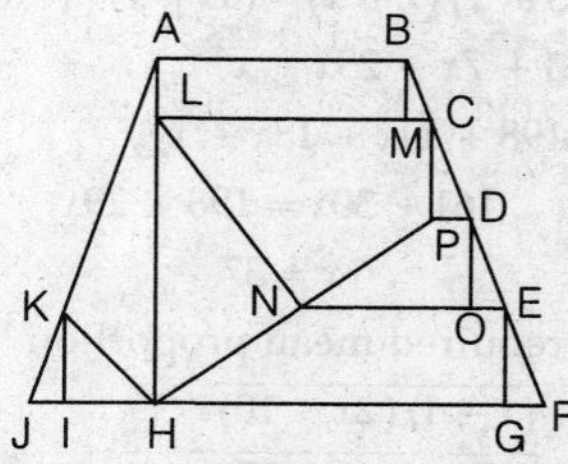

There are total 10 triangles in the figure, which are

Δ JKI, Δ KIH, Δ JKH, Δ AKH, Δ JAH, Δ LNH, Δ BMC, Δ CPD, Δ DOE and Δ EGF.

49 *(d)* As, A →(+2) C, D →(+2) F, F →(+2) H, I →(+2) K

and E →(+2) G, H →(+2) J, J →(+2) L, M →(+2) O

Similarly, I →(+2) K, L →(+2) N, N →(+2) P, Q →(+2) S

50. *(c)* Given, 19th July, 2000 → Wednesday

Number of odd days from 19th July, 2000 to 19th July, 2014

$$= \frac{1+1+1+2+1+1+1+2+1+1+1+2+1+1}{7}$$

$$= \frac{17}{7} = 3 \text{ odd days}$$

(∵ 2004, 2008 and 2012 are leap years)

Number of odd days from 20th July, 2014 to 17th March, 2015

$$= \frac{12+31+30+31+30+31+31+28+17}{7}$$

$$= \frac{241}{7} = 3 \text{ odd days}$$

Total odd days = 3 + 3 = 6

∴ 17th March, 2015 = Wednesday + 6

= Tuesday

51. *(c)* Let the number of students in Computer Science (CS), Electronics (EC), Civil Engineering (CE) and Mechanical Engineering (ME) be $11x$, $5x$, $6x$ and $7x$, respectively.

Percentage of students belonging to CS and ME branches

$$= \frac{11x + 7x}{11x + 5x + 6x + 7x} \times 100$$

$$= \frac{18x}{29x} \times 100 = 62.07\%$$

52. *(a)* Let the area of first triangle be x cm^2, then the area of second triangle will be $(195 - x)$ cm^2.

We know that,

Ratio of perimeters of two similar triangles = Ratio of their corresponding sides

⇒ Ratio of their corresponding sides $= \frac{4}{7}$

Now, by Area similarity theorem, Ratio of areas of two similar triangles = Square of ratio of corresponding sides

$$\frac{x}{195 - x} = \left(\frac{4}{7}\right)^2$$

$49x = 3120 - 16x$

$\Rightarrow 65x = 3120$

$\Rightarrow x = \frac{3120}{65}$

$x = 48 \text{ cm}^2$

Area of second triangle $= 195 - x$

$= 195 - 48 = 147 \text{ cm}^2$

$\frac{1}{3}$ rd of the difference between areas

$= \frac{1}{3}(147 - 48)$

$= \frac{99}{3} = 33 \text{ cm}^2$

53. *(b)* Riya's one day's work $= \frac{1}{6}$ units

Sangeeta's one day's work $= \frac{1}{8}$ units

Part of work completed by Riya in 3 days $= 3 \times \frac{1}{6} = \frac{1}{2}$ units

Remaining work $= 1 - \frac{1}{2}$

$= \frac{1}{2}$ units

Number of days taken by Riya and Sangeeta to complete the remaining work $= \frac{\left(\frac{1}{2}\right)}{\left(\frac{1}{6} + \frac{1}{8}\right)}$

$= \frac{\left(\frac{1}{2}\right)}{\left(\frac{4+3}{24}\right)} = \frac{12}{7}$ days

Time taken to complete the total work

$= 3 + \frac{12}{7}$

$= \frac{21 + 12}{7}$

$= \frac{33}{7} = 4\frac{5}{7}$ days

54. *(b)* Let the edge of each cube be a cm. then, volume of cube $= 216 \text{ cm}^3$

$a^3 = 216$

$\Rightarrow a = \sqrt{216} = 6 \text{ cm}$

Length of new solid (cuboid) $= 4a$

$l = 4 \times 6 = 24 \text{ cm}$

Width of new solid $(b) = a = 6$ cm

Height of new solid $(h) = a = 6$ cm

Total surface area of new solid

$= 2(lb + bh + hl)$

$= 2(24 \times 6 + 6 \times 6 + 6 \times 24)$

$= 2(144 + 36 + 144)$

$= 2 \times 324 = 648 \text{ cm}^2$

55. *(a)* We know that,

Area of triangle $= \frac{1}{2} \times \text{base} \times \text{height}$

$18 = \frac{1}{2} \times 6 \times \text{height}$

$\Rightarrow \text{height} = \frac{18 \times 2}{6}$

$\therefore \text{height} = 6 \text{ cm}$

56. *(c)* Let the candidates answered x number of questions correctly, then, number of questions, which are either incorrect or unattempted are $(160 - x)$.

According to the question,

$4x - 1(160 - x) = 400$

$\Rightarrow 4x - 160 + x = 400$

$\Rightarrow 5x = 560$

$x = \frac{560}{5} = 112$

$\therefore$ He attempted 112 questions correctly.

57. *(a)* Total number of votes = 8400

Number of valid votes

$= \frac{100 - 15}{100} \times 8400$

$= 85 \times 84 = 7140$

Number of votes got by other candidate

$= \frac{100 - 60}{100} \times 7140$

$= \frac{40}{100} \times 7140 = 2856$

58. *(d)* According to the question,

$\frac{7 + x}{11 + x} = \frac{18 + x}{23 + x}$

$(23 + x)(7 + x) = (11 + x)(18 + x)$

$\Rightarrow 161 + 7x + 23x + x^2$

$= 198 + 11x + 18x + x^2$

$\Rightarrow 161 + 30x = 198 + 29x$

$\Rightarrow x = 37$

Now, required mean proportion

$= \sqrt{(x-1)(2x-10)}$

$= \sqrt{(37-1)(2 \times 37 - 10)}$

$= \sqrt{36 \times 64}$

$= 6 \times 8 = 48$

59. *(b)* Let the total number of ice-creams sold be x. Then,

Number of chocolate ice-creams

$= \frac{40}{100} \times x$

$400 = \frac{40}{100} x$

$x = 1000$

$\therefore$ Number of vanilla ice-creams

$= \frac{35}{100} \times 1000 = 350$

60. *(a)* Total number of students selected for Cricket and Tennis

$= \frac{(20 + 35)}{100} \times 1500$

$= \frac{55}{100} \times 1500 = 825$

61. *(d)* $2\frac{1}{4} \times 3\frac{1}{5} + 5\frac{1}{6}$ of $2\frac{4}{31} \div 3\frac{2}{3} + 4\frac{1}{7}$ of $1\frac{6}{29}$

$= \frac{9}{4} \times \frac{16}{5} + \frac{31}{6}$ of $\frac{66}{31} \div \frac{11}{3} + \frac{29}{7}$ of $\frac{35}{29}$

[by applying BODMAS]

$= \frac{36}{5} + 11 \div \frac{11}{3} + 5$

$= \frac{36}{5} + 11 \times \frac{3}{11} + 5$

$= \frac{36}{5} + 3 + 5 = \frac{36}{5} + \frac{8}{1} = \frac{36 + 40}{5}$

$= \frac{76}{5} = 15\frac{1}{5}$

62. *(c)* Given, $\Delta ABC \sim \Delta DEF$

By Area similarity theorem,

$\frac{\text{ar}(\Delta ABC)}{\text{ar}(\Delta EDF)} = \frac{BC^2}{DF^2}$

$\frac{9}{4} = \frac{8^2}{DF^2}$

$\Rightarrow \frac{9}{4} = \frac{64}{DF^2}$

$\Rightarrow DF^2 = \frac{64 \times 4}{9}$

$\Rightarrow DF = \sqrt{\frac{64 \times 4}{9}} = \frac{16}{3} = 5\frac{1}{3}$

63. *(d)* $(\tan\alpha + 1)(\tan\beta + 1) = 2x$

$\Rightarrow \tan\alpha \tan\beta + \tan\alpha + \tan\beta + 1 = 2x$ ...(i)

We know that,

$\tan(\alpha + \beta) = \frac{\tan\alpha + \tan\beta}{1 - \tan\alpha \tan\beta}$

$\tan 45° = \frac{\tan\alpha + \tan\beta}{1 - \tan\alpha \tan\beta}$

$\Rightarrow 1 = \frac{\tan\alpha + \tan\beta}{1 - \tan\alpha \tan\beta}$

$\Rightarrow 1 - \tan\alpha \tan\beta = \tan\alpha + \tan\beta$

Now, putting the value of $\tan\alpha + \tan\beta$ in Eq. (i), we get

$\tan\alpha \tan\beta + 1 - \tan\alpha \tan\beta + 1 = 2x$

$2x = 2$

$\therefore x = \frac{2}{2} = 1$

64. *(c)* Percentage rise and fall in production of company C for years,

$2013 = \frac{70-90}{70} \times 100 = -2.85\%$ (Fall)

$2015 = \frac{80-120}{120} \times 100 = -33.33\%$ (Fall)

$2016 = \frac{110-80}{80} \times 100 = 37.5\%$ (Rise)

$2017 = \frac{140-110}{110} \times 100 = 27.27\%$ (Rise)

Hence, percentage rise/fall is maximum in the year 2016.

65. *(b)* Reduction in selling price

(SP) = (5000 − 4680)

= ₹ 320

Now, loss percentage = 4%

$\frac{4}{100} \times$ Cost Price (CP) = 320

$CP = \frac{320 \times 100}{4}$

CP = ₹ 8000

Profit = 4%

Now, SP = CP × $\left(\frac{100 + \text{Profit}\%}{100}\right)$

$= 8000 \times \frac{104}{100}$

= ₹ 8320

66. *(c)* Total discount to be given on total price

$= \frac{9.5}{100} \times 48000 =$ ₹ 4560

Discount of first ₹ 28000 = $\frac{12}{100} \times 28000$

= ₹ 3360

Discount on next ₹ 12000

$= \frac{8}{100} \times 12000$

= ₹ 960

Remaining discount

= [4560 − (3360 + 960)]

= 4560 − 4320

= ₹ 240

∴ Rohan should offer a discount of ₹ 240 on remaining ₹ 8000.

67. *(d)* Average score of whole class

$= \frac{15 \times 80 + 10 \times 60}{25}$

$= \frac{1200 + 600}{25}$

$= \frac{1800}{25}$

= 72

68. *(b)* Difference between the exports of Companies A and B in the year

1995 = 125 − 60 = ₹ 65 crores

1994 = Data insufficient

1997 = 145 − 80 = ₹ 65 crores

1998 = 152 − 95 = ₹ 57 crores

∴ The difference between the exports is minimum in year 1998.

69. *(c)* Let the principal be ₹ *P*.

Then, Simple Interest (SI) = ₹ $\frac{4}{5}P$

Let the rate of interest be r% p.a.

Time (t) = 8 yr

We know that,

$SI = \frac{P \times r \times t}{100}$

$\frac{4}{5}P = \frac{P \times r \times 8}{100}$

$\Rightarrow \quad r = \frac{4 \times 100}{5 \times 8}$

$\therefore \quad r = 10\%$ p.a.

70. *(d)* Given,

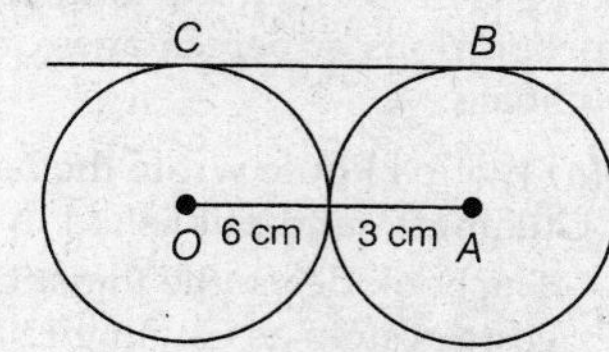

Radius of first circle (R) = 6 cm

Radius of second circle (r) = 3 cm

Length of their common tangent

$(CB) = 2 \times \sqrt{R \times r}$

$= 2 \times \sqrt{6 \times 3}$

$= 2 \times \sqrt{18}$

$= 6\sqrt{2}$ cm

71. *(c)* Given, two parallel chords *AB* and *CD*.

AB = *CD* = 8 units,

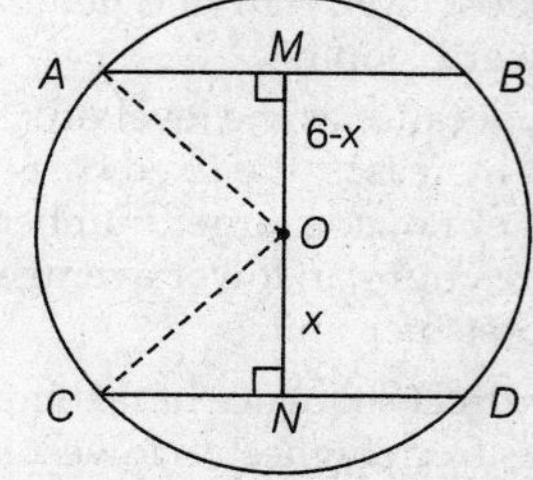

Let radius *ON* = x units,

then, *OM* = $(6 - x)$ units

Now, $AM = \frac{1}{2} \times AB = \frac{1}{2} \times 8 = 4$ units

$CN = \frac{1}{2} \times CD = \frac{1}{2} \times 8 = 4$ units

[∵ Perpendicular from the centre bisects the chord]

In right Δ*ONC*,

$OC^2 = ON^2 + CN^2$

$\Rightarrow \quad OC^2 = x^2 + 4^2$

$\Rightarrow \quad OC^2 = x^2 + 16$

In right Δ*OMA*,

$OA^2 = 4^2 + (6 - x)^2$

$OA^2 = 16 + 36 + x^2 - 12x$

Now, $\quad OA^2 = OC^2$

$16 + 36 + x^2 - 12x = x^2 + 16$

$\Rightarrow \quad 52 - 12x = 16$

$\Rightarrow \quad 36 = 12x$

$x = 3$

Now, radius $OC = \sqrt{x^2 + 16}$

[from Eq. (i)]

$= \sqrt{3^2 + 16}$

$= \sqrt{25} = 5$ units

72. *(d)* When n is divided by 18, the quotient is x and the remainder is 6.

$\Rightarrow \quad n = 18x + 6 \quad$ ...(i)

When n is divided by 25, the quotient is y and remainder is 15

$n = 25y + 15 \quad$ ...(ii)

From Eqs. (i) and (ii),

$18x + 6 = 25y + 15$

$\Rightarrow \quad 18x - 25y = 9$

73. *(c)* Percentage decrease in length

$(x) = -30\%$

Percentage decrease in breadth

$(y) = -10\%$

∴ Percentage decrease in area

$= + x + y + \frac{xy}{100}$

$= -30 - 10 + \frac{30 \times 10}{100}$

$= -40 + \frac{300}{100}$

$= -40 + 3$

$= -37\%$

Here, (−) sign indicates decrease in area.

74. *(b)* Relative speed of Ram and Shyam

$= \left(3 + 5\frac{1}{4}\right)$

$= 3 + \frac{21}{4}$

$= \frac{12 + 21}{4}$

$= \frac{33}{4}$ km/h

$\therefore$ Required time $= \frac{\text{Distance}}{\text{Speed}}$

$= \frac{44}{\left(\frac{33}{4}\right)}$

$= \frac{16}{3}$ h

$= 5$ h 20 min

75. *(c)* Let the radius of cylinder be r cm.

Then, radius of spherical ball will be $\frac{r}{3}$ cm.

Height of cylinder $(h) = 12r$

Let the number of spherical balls be x.

Then, Volume of cylinder = x × volume of each spherical ball

$$\pi r^2 \times h = x \times \frac{4}{3}\pi\left(\frac{r}{3}\right)^3$$

$$\Rightarrow \pi r^2 \times (12r) = x \times \frac{4}{3}\pi \times \frac{r^3}{27}$$

$$\Rightarrow 12r^3 = x \times \frac{4}{3} \times \frac{r^3}{27}$$

$$\Rightarrow x = \frac{12 \times 27 \times 3}{4}$$

$$\therefore x = 243$$

76. *(a)* Eid-Ul-Fitr is a religious festival celebrated by Muslims at the end of the holy month Ramzan.

It is celebrated on the first day of Shawwal, the tenth month of the Islamic calendar.

77. *(d)* The Palas were a dynasty that appeared in Eastern India.

- The Pala empire was founded by Gopala, probably in AD 750.
- The Pala Dynasty ruled over Bengal and Bihar from the 8th to the 12th century.
- The Pala Empire was dethroned by the Hindu Sena dynasty.

78. *(d)* The largest inland salt lake 'Sambhar' is located in the North-West of India.

- It is located in Rajasthan.
- Sambhar lake is famous for harbouring flamingos.
- The largest saltwater lake in India is Chilika lake, Odisha.

79. *(c)* In India, the musical instrument 'Flute' is also known as Bansuri.

- The flute is a member of a family of musical instruments in the woodwind group.
- Flutes are aerophones, producing sound with a vibrating column of air.

80. *(d)* According to the Global Multidimensional Poverty Index (2022), 34.4 million poor people live in India.

- The Global Multidimensional Poverty Index (MPI) is an internationally comparable index that measures poverty in over 100 developing countries.
- It's a joint publication by the United Nations Development Programe (UNDP) and the Oxford Poverty and Human Development Initiative (OPHI).
- The MPI measures deprivations in education, health and living standards, such as housing, drinking water, sanitation and electricity.
- According to the 2023 Global Multidimensional Poverty Index (MPI), India's MPI value decreased from 29.17% in 2013-14 to 11.28% in 2022-23.

81. *(c)* In Microsoft Excel, scatter chart type is best suited for comparing proportions or percentages of a whole.

82. *(a)* Jyotiba Phule wrote the book 'Gulamgiri' and published in 1873.

- The book deals, the injustice of the caste system as Gulamgiri (Slavery).
- Jyotirao Govindrao Phule was an Indian social activist, businessman, anticaste social reformer and writer from Maharashtra.
- He founded the first school for girls in Pune in 1848 and also established the Satyashodhak Samaj.

83. *(c)* In cost theory, the usual shape of the average fixed cost curve is a rectangular hyperbola.

- The typical shape of the Average Fixed Cost (AFC) curve is generally downward-sloping.
- This is because as the level of output increases, the fixed costs are spread out over a larger number of units, resulting in lower average fixed costs per unit.

84. *(c)* The correct sequence of taxonomic categories from highest to lowest is Phylum/Division - Class - Order - Family - Genus - Species.

This sequence is also known as the taxonomic hierarchy. It's a system that classifies organisms in a systematic way, making it easier to study them.

85. *(d)* Chennai Super Kings won 2023 IPL championship.

- In the final, Chennai Super Kings defeated Gujarat Titans.
- In 2024, Kolkata Knight Riders defeated Sunrisers Hyderabad in the final match.

86. *(a)* Norman Ernest Borlaug was awarded the Nobel Peace Prize in 1970 for his contributions to the Green Revolution.

- The Nobel Prize is given in six categories only Physics, Chemistry, Medicine or Physiology, Economics, Literature and Peace.
- Norman Ernest Borlaug is known as Father of Green Revolution in world.
- The Borlaug Award is an award recognition for outstanding Indian scientists for their research and contributions in the field of agriculture and the environment.

87. *(b)* Andre - Marie Ampere discovered that a wire carrying electric current can attract or repel another wire next to it that's also carrying electric current. Also he was the first scientist to attempt to theoretically explain and mathematically describe this phenomenon.

88. *(a)* Articles 5 to 11 of Indian Constitution deals with citizenship of India.India adopted the concept of single citizenship from the British Constitution.

- **Article 5** Citizenship at the commencement of the Constitution, on 26th January, 1950.
- **Article 6** Citizenship rights of certain people who have migrated to India from Pakistan
- **Article 7** Citizenship rights of certain migrants to Pakistan.
- **Article 8** Citizenship rights of certain people of Indian origin residing outside India.
- **Article 9** People who voluntarily acquire citizenship of another country are not citizens of those countries.
- **Article 10** Continuation of citizenship privileges.
- **Article 11** Parliament regulates the right of citizenship by law.

89. *(a)* The establishment of Union Public Service Commission, State Public Service Commissions and Joint Public Service Commission falls under

Federalism features of the Constitution of India.

- Federalism is a system of government in which the power is divided between a Central Government and State Government.
- Parliamentary government is a democratic system where the head of government is accountable to the legislature (Parliament).
- Directive Principles of State Policy (DPSP) set of guidelines or principles contained in the Indian Constitution.
- Fundamental Rights are universal legal guarantces that protect human dignity and fundamental freedoms for all people, regardless of status.

90. *(c)* Chhannulal Mishra is related to Musical Lineage of Kirana Musical Family.

- Pandit Chhannulal Mishra born on 3rd August, 1936 and a Hindustani classical singer from Banaras.
- He was awarded the Padma Vibhushan India's second highest civilian award in 2020.

91. *(a)* According to the Census of India 2011, Goa is the most urbanised state in India followed by Mizoram.

Uttar Pradesh has the highest rural population in India according to Census of India 2011.

In respect to geographical area and total population Tamil Nadu is most urbanised according to census of India 2011.

92. *(a)* On 7th November, 2022 the Supreme Court of India upheld the Reservations for the Weaker Sections (EWS) under 103rd Amendment Act of Indian Constitution.

- The 103rd Constitution Amendment Act in India came into existence to offer 10% reservation to Economically Weaker Sections (EWS) of society for admission to the center of government and private educational institutions along with recruitment in government jobs.
- The Constitution of India can be amended under Article 368.
- As of August 2024 , the Constitution of India has been amended 106 times since it was enacted in 1950.

93. *(a)* The moderate margin of a page in MS Word can be applied to the page from Page Layout Tab.

94. *(d)* Sakshi Malik is the first Indian woman wrestler to win an Olympic medal.

- She won a bronze medal in the 58 kg freestyle wrestling event at the 2016 Summer Olympics in Rio, Brazil.
- Geeta Phogat is (1 freestyle wrestler who won India's first ever gold medal in wrestling at the Commonwealth Games in 2010.
- Alka Tomar is an Indian wrestler,she received the bronze medal in Wrestling at the Doha Asian Games in 2006.
- Babita Phogat is an Indian wrestler, who won the gold medal in 2014 Commonwealth Games, silver medals at 2010 and 2018 Commonwealth Games.

95. *(c)* 'Chang dance' is popular in the state of Rajasthan.

- It is performed during the Hindu festival Holi to celebrate the defeat of evil.
- It is also referred as Dhamal, dhuff dance,and as Holi dance.
- It is a group dance performed by men, carousing and singing riotously to the rhythmic beat of the chang instrument.

96. *(c)* Cabinet Minister Thawarchand Gehlot was appointed as the Governor of Karnataka in July 2021.

- He is the current (as of July 2024) and 13th Governor of Karnataka.
- As of July 2024 Shri Siddaramaiah is the Chief Minister of Karnataka.

97. *(c)* Makemake dwarf planet orbits the Sun in 310 years at a distance between 38.5 to 53 AU.

- Makemake is the third largest and second brightest dwarf planet.
- Dwarf planets are heavenly bodies that are too small to be considered a planet but too large to fall under smaller categories.
- As of July 2024, the International Astronomical Union (IAU) has recognised five dwari planets in our solar system Ceres, Pluto, Eris, Haumea, and Makemake.

98. *(c)* Uruguay hosted the First FIFA World Cup in 1930.

- Uruguay became the first champion by defeating Argentina in the final.
- Football International Federation of Association (FIFA) was founded in 1904.
- It is the international self-regulatory governing body of association football, beach soccer, and futsal.
- In 2026 FIFA World Cup will be jointly hosted by three North American countries: Canada, Mexico, and the United States.

99. *(a)* In January, 2024 Dinesh K Tripathi was appointed as Vice Chief of Naval Staff,

- On 30th April, 2024 he was appointed as Chief of the Naval Staff (CNS) of the Indian Navy.
- As of July 2024, Air Chief Marshal Vivek Ram Chaudhari is the Chief of the Air Staff (CAS) of the Indian Air Force.
- As of July 2024, General Upendra Dwivedi is the Chief of the Indian Army Staff (COAS).
- As of July 2024 General Anil, Chauhan is the Chief of Defence Staff.

100. *(d)* According to Ministry of Agriculture and Farmers Welfare, the total food grain production of 2023 was 3296.87 lakh tonnes .

As of July 2024 Shivraj Singh Chouhan is the Agriculture Minister of India.

Set 13 04 July, 2024 (Shift I)

SSC CHSL Tier-I SOLVED PAPER

Instructions

1. This paper contains 100 questions.
2. It has 4 Parts, **Part I** General English, **Part II** General Intelligence & Reasoning, **Part III** Quantitative Aptitude and **Part IV** General Awareness.
3. Each question carries **2 marks**.

Part I
General English

1. The given sentence is divided into four segments. Select the option that has the segment with a grammatical error.

I am sure / that he will praying / for a good crop / this year.

(a) that he will praying
(b) I am sure
(c) this year
(d) for a good crop

2. The following sentence has been divided into four segments. Identify the segment that contains a grammatical error.

My students are / waiting for / their flights / at the gate no. 6.

(a) at the gate no. 6
(b) waiting for
(c) their flights
(d) My students are

3. The following sentence has been split into four segments. Identify the segment that contains a grammatical error.

I am very much / obliged of my friend / for the help / he rendered to me.

(a) I am very much
(b) he rendered to me
(c) for the help
(d) obliged of my friend

4. Parts of the following sentence have been underlined and given as options. Select the option that contains an error.

She will being studying for her exams tomorrow.

(a) studying (b) tomorrow
(c) will being (d) exams

Directions (Q.Nos. 5-9) *In the following passage, some words have been deleted. Read the passage carefully and select the most appropriate option to fill in each blank.*

Oil is almost certainly one of the ocean's greatest resources. 33% of the world's oil comes from seaward fields in seas. Oils are liquids that easily burn and do not (1)……… in water. Most of the time, they are made of chains of carbon and hydrogen atoms. There are three (2)……… types of oils: mineral, essential and fixed oils. From plants, essential oils are thin, scented oils. Because they frequently have an odour, essential oils are (3)……… in perfumery and food flavouring. Aromatic extraction processes like cold pressing, distillation and extraction are typically used to prepare essential oils. Fatty acids are used by animals and plants to make fixed oils.

They are especially non-volatile oils that are found in the seeds of cotton, corn, flax, sunflowers, peanuts, coconuts and olives, as well as in fatty animal tissues. Mineral oils are (4)……… from petroleum which has been underground for millions of years from sea organism skeletons. Mineral oils are one of the petroleum by-products with the lowest prices. Mineral oils are colourless and transparent. They are made up of a (5)……… of hydrocarbons.

5. Select the most appropriate option to fill in blank number (1).

(a) dissolve (b) diffuse
(c) melt (d) evaporate

6. Select the most appropriate option to fill in blank number (2).

(a) initial
(b) original
(c) early
(d) primary

7. Select the most appropriate option to fill in blank number (3).

(a) applied
(b) utilised
(c) operated
(d) employed

8. Select the most appropriate option to fill in blank number (4).

(a) produced (b) invented
(c) renewed (d) fabricated

9. Select the most appropriate option to fill in blank number (5).

(a) collaboration
(b) cooperation
(c) combination
(d) association

10. Select the most appropriate antonym of the given word.

Merit

(a) Result (b) Tumult
(c) Fault (d) Occult

11. Select the correct spelling of the underlined word in the following sentence.

I am contant with my day's work.

(a) contint (b) contante
(c) content (d) cuntent

12. Select the most appropriate option to fill in the blank.

The ……… in my shoelace created a lot of trouble.

(a) not (b) naught
(c) nought (d) knot

13. Select the most appropriate option that can substitute the underlined segment in the given sentence.

If you are thinking about investing in share markets, isn't it make sense to find an expert?

(a) did it (b) is it
(c) doesn't it (d) do it

14. Select the most appropriate antonym of the given word.
Important
(a) Recurring
(b) Productive
(c) Trivial
(d) Significant

15. Select the most appropriate meaning of the underlined idiom in the following sentence.
Independence Day is considered as a red-letter day in the history of India.
(a) regular day
(b) uneventful day
(c) memorable day
(d) unimportant day

16. Select the most appropriate option that can substitute the underlined segment in the given sentence.
He lived on the bank of a mighty river, broad and deep, that have always silently rolling on to a vast undiscovered ocean.
(a) which were always silently rolling
(b) which was always silently rolling
(c) that were always silently rolling
(d) what has always silently rolling

17. Select the most appropriate homophone to fill in the blank.
Namita still cannot .... the pain of her cat's untimely demise.
(a) bier (b) bear
(c) beer (d) bare

18. Select the most appropriate option to fill in the blank.
A sailor was .... through the high tides.
(a) ceiling (b) sailing
(c) swelling (d) selling

19. Select the most appropriate meaning of the underlined idiom.
Vishnu and Vignesh are always like two peas in a pod.
(a) Very similar to each other
(b) Smart and intelligent
(c) Happy and compassionate
(d) Good in every way

20. Select the most appropriate option to fill in the blank.
The crowd gave them a .... of applause.
(a) yell (b) load
(c) laugh (d) round

21. Select the most appropriate option that can substitute the underlined segment in the given sentence. If there is no need to substitute it, select 'No substitution required'.
Applications are to be sent to the school's e-mail ID before 30th June.
(a) will be send to
(b) is sending
(c) No substitution required
(d) would be send to

22. Select the incorrectly spelt word.
(a) Adulterous (b) Amendment
(c) Advertisment (d) Astounding

23. Select the most appropriate option that can substitute the underlined segment in the given sentence.
The painting look good in this room.
(a) have looking (b) looking
(c) had look (d) looks

24. Replace the underlined word in the given sentence with an appropriate synonym from the options listed below.
They gave us the impression that Clara was a cold and calculating woman, who was only after power.
(a) callous (b) unscrupulous
(c) unsympathetic (d) manipulative

25. Fill in the blank with the most appropriate antonym of the underlined word.
Gentlemen always go for a lawful approach, but rouges choose .... ways to solve problems.
(a) legal (b) legitimate
(c) sophisticated (d) illicit

Part II
General Intelligence

26. In a certain code language,
'M & N' means 'M is the wife of N',
'M @ N' means 'M is the brother of N',
'M $ N' means 'M is the father of N',
'M # N' means 'M is the son of N'.
Based on the above, how is T related to G, if 'T @ S # M & N $ G'?
(a) Brother
(b) Father
(c) Son
(d) Father's brother

27. Select the combination of letters that when sequentially placed in the blanks of the given series will logically complete the series.
_ F _ G E E _ E _ E E F _ G E E _ E G _
(a) EEFGEFE
(b) EFGFEEF
(c) EFFGFEF
(d) FEFGFFE

28. What should come in place of the question mark (?) in the given series?
22, 24, 28, 30, 34, ?
(a) 36 (b) 35
(c) 37 (d) 38

29. Based on the alphabetical order, three of the following four letter-clusters are alike in a certain way and thus form a group. Which letter-cluster does not belong to that group?
(**Note** The odd one out is not based on the number of consonants/vowels or their position in the letter-cluster.)
(a) PRV (b) HJN
(c) GIM (d) EGJ

30. The position of how many letters will remain unchanged if each of the letters in the word, SOUNDBAR is arranged in alphabetical order?
(a) Three (b) Four (c) One (d) Two

31. How many rectangles are there in the given figure?

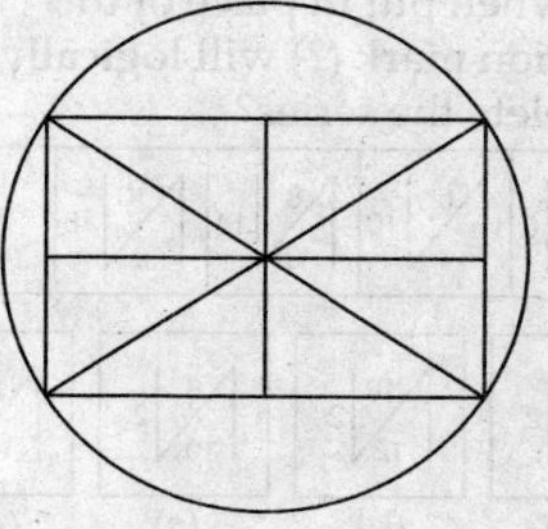

(a) 9 (b) 7 (c) 8 (d) 6

32. What should come in place of question mark (?) in the given series based on the English alphabetical order?
RST, VZW, ZGZ, DNC, ?
(a) ALF
(b) HUF
(c) COD
(d) MOC

33. Select the word-pair that best represents a similar relationship to the one expressed in the pair of words given below.
(The words must be considered as meaningful English words and must not be related to each other based on the number of letters/number of consonants/vowels in the word.)
Palate : Mouth
(a) Hill : Range (b) Rivulet : Dam
(c) Ceiling : Room (d) Rainbow : Sky

34. What would be the symbol on the opposite side of '*', if the given sheet is folded to form a cube?

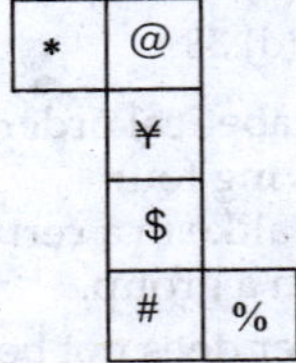

(a) ¥ (b) #
(c) $ (d) %

35. If 16th July, 2001 is Monday, then what will be the day of the week on 23rd December, 2006?
(a) Wednesday (b) Monday
(c) Thursday (d) Saturday

36. What should come in place of the question mark (?) in the given series?
13, 22, 33, 46, ?, 78, 97
(a) 60 (b) 65 (c) 61 (d) 56

37. Identify the figure in the options that when put in place of the question mark (?) will logically complete the series?

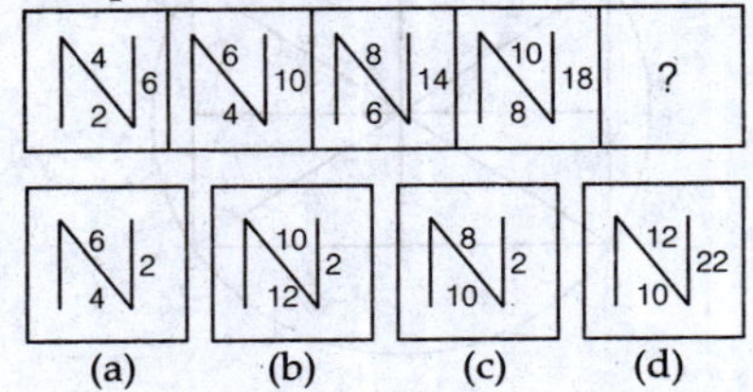

38. What will come in the place of the question mark (?) in the following equation, if '+' and '×' are interchanged and '–' and '÷' are interchanged?
$35 \times 96 - 8 + 3 \div 11 = ?$
(a) 55
(b) 60
(c) 40
(d) 42

39. Select the correct mirror image of the given combination, when the mirror is placed at 'MN' as shown below.

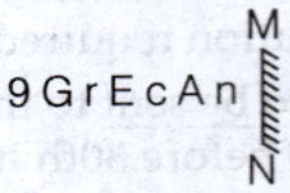

9GrEcAn (mirror MN)

(a) ∩AↄƎ1Ə9
(b) ∩AↄƎ1G9
(c) A∩ↄƎ1Ə9
(d) ∩AↄE1Ə9

40. What would be the word on the opposite side of 'Eat', if the given sheet is folded to form a cube?

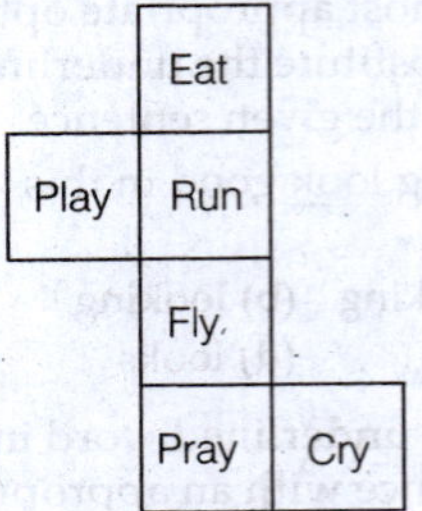

(a) Cry (b) Play
(c) Fly (d) Pray

41. In a certain code language, 'I missed breakfast' is written as 'nl zn kq' and 'train is missed' is written as 'zm kg nl'.
How is 'missed' written in the given language?
(a) zn (b) kq
(c) nl (d) zm

42. Select the option figure in which the given figure (X) is embedded as its part (rotation is not allowed).

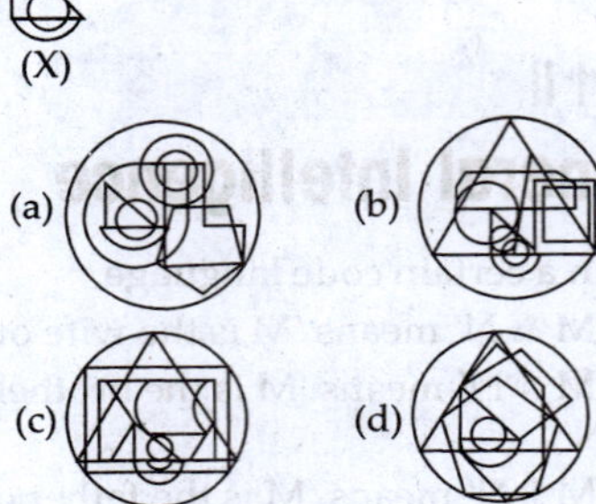

43. If 'A' stands for '÷', 'B' stands for '×', 'C' stands for '+' and 'D' stands for '–', what will come in place of the question mark (?) in the following equation?
32 B 4 D 116 A 2 C 13 = ?
(a) 83 (b) 84 (c) 81 (d) 82

44. In a certain code language, 'MOAT' is coded as '8652' and 'TRAM' is coded as '4256'. What is the code for 'R' in the given code language?
(a) 8 (b) 6
(c) 4 (d) 2

45. 529 is related to 23 following a certain logic. Following the same logic, 324 is related to 18. To which of the following is 625 related following the same logic?
(**Note** Operations should be performed on the whole numbers, without breaking down the numbers into its constituent digits. E.g. 13 – Operations on 13 such as adding /subtracting /multiplying etc. to 13 can be performed. Breaking down 13 into 1 and 3 and then performing mathematical operations on 1 and 3 is not allowed.)
(a) 23 (b) 35
(c) 27 (d) 25

46. Select the correct mirror image of the given figure when the mirror is placed at MN as shown below.

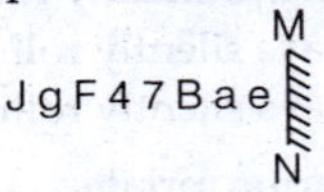

JgF47Bae (mirror MN)

(a) ɘɒBΓ4ꟻϱႱ
(b) ɘɒBL4ꟻ6Γ
(c) ɘɒBΓ4ꟻϱႱ
(d) ɘɒBΓ4ꟻϱႱ

47. Read the given statements and conclusions carefully. Assuming that the information given in the statements is true, even if it appears to be at variance with commonly known facts, decide which of the given conclusions logically follow(s) from the statements.

Statements
All rings are bangles.
Some bangles are anklets.
No anklet is a pendant.

Conclusions
I. All rings being anklets is a possibility.
II. All bangles can never be pendants.

(a) Only Conclusion II follows
(b) Both Conclusions I and II follow
(c) Only Conclusion I follows
(d) None of the conclusions follow

48. Select the word-pair that best represents a similar relationship to the one expressed in the pair of words given below.

(The words must be considered as meaningful English words and must not be related to each other based on the number of letters/number of consonants/vowels in the word)

India : Mango

(a) Greece : Banana
(b) New Zealand : Kiwi
(c) Australia : Grapes
(d) France : Apple

49. If 'J' stands for '÷', 'V' stands for '×', 'K' stands for '+' and 'A' stands for '−', what will come in place of the question mark (?) in the following equation?

12 J 2 K 17 A 15 V 19 = ?

(a) −262 (b) −75
(c) −76 (d) −776

50. Select the set in which the numbers are related in the same way as are the numbers of the following sets.
(**Note** Operations should be performed on the whole numbers, without breaking down the numbers into its constituent digits. E.g. 13 – Operations on 13 such as adding/subtracting/multiplying etc. to 13 can be performed. Breaking down 13 into 1 and 3 and then performing mathematical operations on 1 and 3 is not allowed.)

(5, 25, 50)
(8, 64, 128)

(a) (12, 144, 278) (b) (12, 144, 288)
(c) (12, 134, 288) (d) (12, 144, 298)

Part III
Quantitative Aptitude

51. What is the value of tan 570°?

(a) $-\frac{1}{\sqrt{3}}$ (b) $-\sqrt{3}$
(c) $\frac{1}{\sqrt{3}}$ (d) $\sqrt{3}$

52. A clock is sold for ₹ 550 cash or in the instalment scheme, for ₹ 250 cash down payment and ₹ 310 after one month. Find the rate of interest charged in the instalment scheme.

(a) 40% (b) 20%
(c) 35% (d) 45%

53. A person spends 10% of his income on groceries, 10% on medicines, 20% on children's education, 15% on house rent, and he saves the remaining amount. If his monthly income is ₹ 30000, find his savings.

(a) ₹ 15500 (b) ₹ 16500
(c) ₹ 13500 (d) ₹ 12500

54. In a state election between two parties, 83% of the voters cast their votes, out of which 4% of the votes were declared invalid. Party A got 156611 votes which were 83% of the total valid votes. Find the total number of votes enrolled in that election. (Consider integer part only)

(a) 258233 (b) 234888
(c) 236807 (d) 2346807

55. A man looks at the reflection of the top of the lamp-post on the mirror that is 6.6 m away from the foot of the lamppost. The man's height is 1.25 m and he is standing 2 m away from the mirror. Assuming that the mirror is placed on the ground, facing the sky and the man, and that the mirror and the lamppost are in a same line, find the height of the lamp-post (in m).

(a) 4.28 (b) 4.45
(c) 3.97 (d) 4.13

56. Given below is the observed data of the ages of various children.

Age in years	Number of children
6	8
7	3
8	7
9	2
10	20

What is the mean of the ages of the children?

(a) 6.575 yr (b) 8.575 yr
(c) 7.575 yr (d) 5.575 yr

57. The number nearest to 7658 and exactly divisible by 45 is

(a) 7645 (b) 7660
(c) 7650 (d) 7640

58. There is a circle with a centre T and a radius of 8 cm. Two tangents KE and KI are drawn from point K, which is 17 cm from the centre. The area of the quadrilateral $TEKI$ is

(a) 130 sq.cm (b) 136 sq.cm
(c) 120 sq.cm (d) 127.5 sq.cm

59. ΔABC is a right-angles triangle where $m\angle ABC = 90°$. If $m(\overline{AB}) = 15$ cm, $m(\overline{BC}) = 20$ cm, and $\overline{BD} \perp \overline{AC}$, intersecting $\overline{AC}$ at the point D, find $m(\overline{BD})$ (in cm).

(a) 12.5 (b) 12 (c) 10 (d) 9

60. In the year 2000, Monu was 3 times his sister's age. In 2010, he was 24 yr older than her. Find Monu's age in 2010.

(a) 46 yr (b) 52 yr
(c) 38 yr (d) 62 yr

61. The given bar-graph shows the number of accidents in a city during the first 6 months of a year. Examine the bar-graph and answer the question.

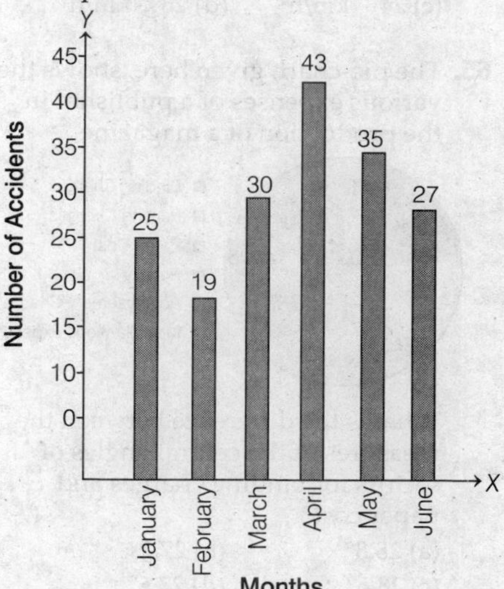

What is the percentage of accidents in the month of April with respect to the total accidents in the city during six months? (Correct to nearest integer)

(a) 15% (b) 24%
(c) 20% (d) 22%

62. The following bar-graph represents the population of a city (in lakhs) as per the census across different years.

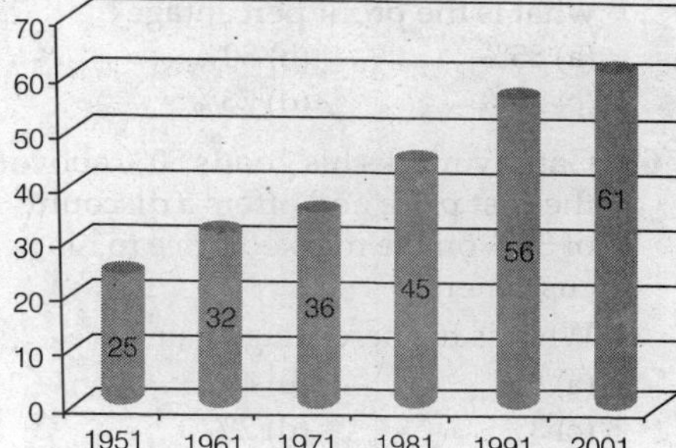

What is the per cent increase in population from 1951 to 2001?
(a) 144% (b) 22%
(c) 35% (d) 120%

63. Which of the following numbers is divisible by 22?
(a) 893002 (b) 645372
(c) 602351 (d) 654320

64. Shankar covers a certain distance by a car driving at 40 km/h and he returns to the starting point riding on a scooter with a speed of 20 km/h. Find the average speed of the whole journey.
(a) $22\frac{2}{3}$ km/h (b) $29\frac{2}{3}$ km/h
(c) $24\frac{2}{3}$ km/h (d) $26\frac{2}{3}$ km/h

65. The pie-chart, given here, shows the various expenses of a publisher in the production of a magazine.

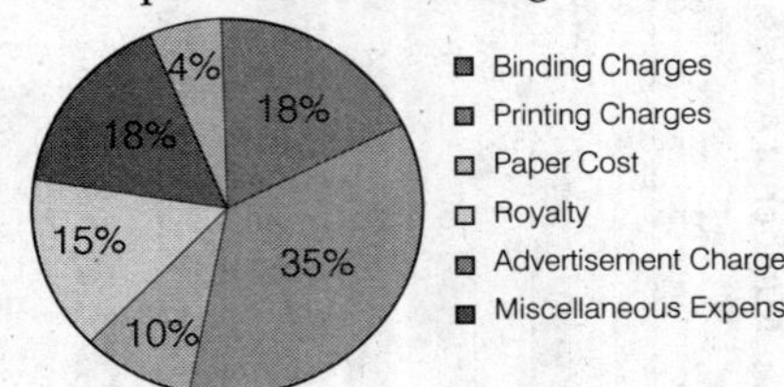

What is the difference between the measures of the central angles of sectors for binding charges and paper cost?
(a) 28.8° (b) 27.2°
(c) 28.6° (d) 27.6°

66. Three solid cubes of metal have sides 6 cm, 8 cm and 10 cm, respectively. They are melted to form a new cube. What is the surface area of this new cube?
(a) 915 cm^2
(b) 864 cm^2
(c) 950 cm^2
(d) 812 cm^2

67. If 70% of the cost price of an article is equal to 40% of its selling price, what is the profit percentage?
(a) 85% (b) 80%
(c) 70% (d) 75%

68. Gaurav marks his goods 50% above the cost price and offers a discount of 30% on the marked price to his customers.
What is his percentage gain?
(a) 5% (b) 4%
(c) 3% (d) 2%

69. The edges of a rectangular box are in the ratio of 3 : 5 : 8, and its surface area is 632 cm^2. What will be the volume of the box?
(a) 801 cm^3
(b) 990 cm^3
(c) 510 cm^3
(d) 960 cm^3

70. Convert 28% into the form of ratio.
(a) 25 : 7 (b) 18 : 7
(c) 7 : 25 (d) 7 : 18

71. A box filled with gift articles weighs 25 kg. If the weight of the box and the gift articles, respectively, are in the ratio 1 : 9, then the weight of the articles (in grams) is
(a) 21500 (b) 22500
(c) 24500 (d) 23500

72. If the diameter of the base and curved surfaced area of a cylinder are 14cm and 352 cm^2, respectively, then the total surface area of the cylinder is equal to
(a) 660 cm^2 (b) 760 cm^2
(c) 754 cm^2 (d) 654 cm^2

73. Find the average of natural numbers from 1 to 69. (both included)
(a) 37 (b) 31
(c) 35 (d) 33

74. In the given figure, O is the centre of the circle, AE is the diameter and $\angle AOC = 100°$.

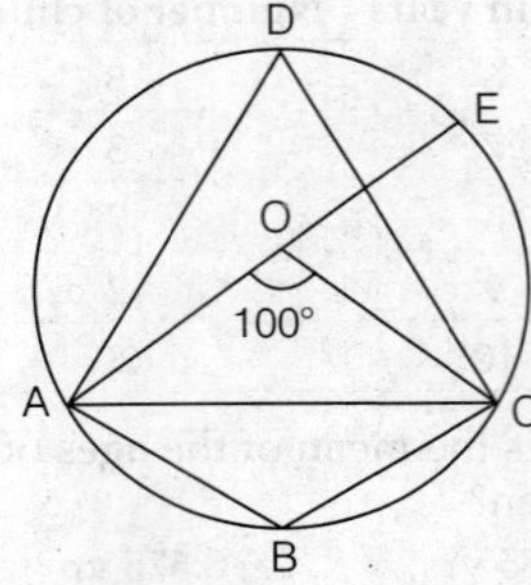

The value of $\angle CDE + \angle CEA$ is
(a) 90° (b) 80°
(c) 60° (d) 100°

75. A and B can complete a piece of work in 15 days, B and C in 30 days and C and A in 45 days. In how many days will they complete the work, if they start working together?
(a) $8\frac{3}{11}$ (b) $11\frac{1}{3}$
(c) $11\frac{2}{3}$ (d) $16\frac{4}{11}$

Part IV
General Awareness

76. Which of the following statement(s) is/are incorrect *vis-à-vis* Fundamental Duties?
1. The 44th Amendment Act introduced Fundamental duties in the Constitution.
2. Fundamental Duties were expanded by the 86th Amendment Act.
3. Article 51A (a) entails respect its ideals and institutions, national flag and the national anthem.
4. Fundamental Duty obliges parents to provide opportunities for education to their child between 6-14 years of age.

Codes
(a) Only 3 (b) 2 and 4
(c) 2 and 3 (d) Only 1

77. Who among the following Delhi Sultanate rulers took the policy of 'Blood and Iron' to deal with the Mewati community?
(a) Balban
(b) Qutubuddin Aibak
(c) Rajiya
(d) Iltutmish

78. Which of the following is the second nearest star to Earth?
(a) Delta Velorum
(b) Polaris
(c) Sirius
(d) Proxima Centauri

79. Where is the Save button in Microsoft Word?
(a) Top left corner of a Word window
(b) Bottom right corner of a Word window
(c) Bottom left corner of a Word window
(d) Top right corner of a Word window

80. In which year was the Konkan Railway constructed?
(a) 2008 (b) 1988
(c) 1998 (d) 1978

81. What is the minimum over rate per hour in a test match?
(a) 15 overs per hour
(b) 13 overs per hour
(c) 10 overs per hour
(d) 17 overs per hour

82. Which of the following occupies less memory when saving an MS Word file?
(a) .docm (b) .docc
(c) .doc (d) .docx

83. Hemis festival is associated with which of the following religions?
(a) Hinduism (b) Buddhism
(c) Sikhism (d) Jainism

84. According to the International Football Association Board (IFAB), which colour must the football goal post be?
(a) Black (b) White
(c) Red (d) Blue

85. Where is the ITC Sangeet Research Academy located?
(a) Indore (b) Kolkata
(c) Delhi (d) Bengaluru

86. The Office of the Registrar General and Census Commissioner, India comes under the
(a) Ministry of Finance
(b) Ministry of Home Affairs
(c) Ministry of Corporate Affairs
(d) Ministry of Rural Development

87. Identify the incorrect statement regarding invertebrates from the options given below.
(a) They have open circulatory system as there is no organisation in the distribution.
(b) They have radial or bilateral body symmetry.
(c) They have a pair of solid nerve cords, situated ventrally and bearing segmentally arranged ganglia.
(d) They possess a backbone and an internal skeleton.

88. What is the name of the scheme aimed at conservation of wetlands, which was announced in the Union Budget 2023-24?
(a) Amrit Dharohar
(b) Dharohar
(c) Paryavaran Prahari
(d) Paryavaran Suraksha

89. In February 2023, Shiv Pratap Shukla was appointed Governor of which state?
(a) Haryana
(b) Himachal Pradesh
(c) Tamil Nadu
(d) Bihar

90. Which is the natural habitat of the Asiatic Lion in India?
(a) Kaziranga National Park
(b) Sundarbans
(c) Gir Forest
(d) Dudhwa National Park

91. Which of the following contains small droplets of liquid or particles of solid dispersed in a gas?
(a) Gel (b) Vapour
(c) Aerosol (d) Foam

92. Ajit Kumar Mohanty took over the charge of Chairman, ..., in May 2023.
(a) Bhabha Atomic Research Centre
(b) National Human Rights Commission of India
(c) National Commission for Backward Classes
(d) Atomic Energy Commission

93. Bharat Muni, in his 'Natya Shastra', categorises musical instruments into four different parts. What is the categorisation of musical instruments by Bharat Muni based on?
(a) Different sounds of the musical instruments
(b) The uses of the musical instruments in different occasions, such as wedding, festivals and public gathering
(c) Different materials used in the musical instruments
(d) The Shape of the musical instruments

94. Secularism is a feature of the Indian Constitution, which means
(a) the state can promote any religion
(b) the state does not promote any religion
(c) the state promotes the religion of the minority community
(d) the state promotes the religion of the majority community

95. Who introduced the concept of virtual water?
(a) MS Swaminathan
(b) Glubler Triplets
(c) Norman Borlaug
(d) John Anthony Allan

96. Which Governor General of India issued the famous Regulation XVII in 1829, which declared the practice of Sati illegal and punishable by the courts?
(a) Lord Ellenborough
(b) Lord William Bentinck
(c) Lord Minto
(d) Lord Napier

97. Who is the Indian batsman after whom the Ranji Trophy is named?
(a) Ranjit Patel
(b) Ranjit Singh Bedi
(c) Ranjit Wadekar
(d) Ranjit Sinhji

98. Which of the following is the official language of Tripura?
(a) Khasi (b) Garo
(c) Kokborak (d) Mizo

99. Which of the following currency notes was discarded by the Government of India in November 2016?
(a) ₹ 100 (b) ₹ 200
(c) ₹ 500 (d) ₹ 2000

100. Giddha dance is a folk dance of which of the following states?
(a) Manipur (b) Nagaland
(c) Punjab (d) Odisha

Answers

1. (a)	2. (a)	3. (d)	4. (c)
5. (a)	6. (d)	7. (b)	8. (a)
9. (c)	10. (c)	11. (c)	12. (d)
13. (c)	14 (c)	15. (c)	16. (b)
17. (b)	18. (b)	19. (a)	20. (d)
21. (c)	22. (c)	23. (d)	24. (d)
25. (d)	26. (a)	27. (a)	28. (a)
29. (d)	30. (c)	31. (a)	32. (b)
33. (c)	34. (d)	35. (d)	36. (c)
37. (d)	38. (b)	39. (a)	40. (c)
41. (c)	42. (d)	43. (a)	44. (c)
45. (d)	46. (a)	47. (b)	48. (b)
49. (a)	50. (b)	51. (c)	52. (a)
53. (c)	54. (c)	55. (d)	56. (b)
57. (c)	58. (c)	59. (b)	60. (a)
61. (b)	62. (a)	63. (a)	64. (d)
65. (a)	66. (b)	67. (d)	68. (a)
69. (d)	70. (c)	71. (b)	72. (a)
73. (c)	74. (a)	75. (d)	76. (d)
77. (a)	78. (d)	79. (a)	80. (c)
81. (a)	82. (d)	83. (b)	84. (b)
85. (b)	86. (b)	87. (d)	88. (a)
89. (b)	90. (c)	91. (c)	92. (d)
93. (a)	94. (b)	95. (d)	96. (b)
97. (d)	98. (c)	99. (c)	100. (c)

Explanations

1. *(a)* Part (a) 'that he will praying' contains an error. Add 'be' before 'praying' to correct the sentence.

2. *(a)* Part (a) 'at the gate no. 6' contains an error. Remove 'the' to correct the sentence.

3. *(d)* Part (d) 'obliged of my friend' contains an error. Use 'obliged to' to correct the sentence.

4. *(c)* Part (c) 'will being' contains an error. Use 'be' in place of 'being' to correct the sentence.

5. *(a)* The correct filler for the given blank is 'dissolve'.

6. *(d)* The correct filler for the given blank is 'primary'.

7. *(b)* The correct filler for the given blank is 'utilised'.

8. *(a)* The correct filler for the given blank is 'produced'.

9. *(c)* The correct filler for the given blank is 'combination'.

10. *(c)* Merit means skill or talent. Hence, its antonym is 'fault'.
'Tumult' means a loud and confused noise. 'Occult' means supernatural.

11. *(c)* The correct spelling is 'content'.

12. *(d)* The correct filler for the given blank is 'knot'.

13. *(c)* The underlined part of the given sentence contains an error. Use 'doesn't it' to correct the sentence.

14. *(c)* The antonym of 'Important' is 'trivial' as it means insignificant.

15. *(c)* A Red letter day means a day that is pleasantly noteworthy or memorable.

16. *(b)* The underlined part of the given sentence contains an error. Use 'which was always silently rolling' to correct the sentence.

17. *(b)* The correct filler for the given blank is 'bear' which means 'to suffer from something'.

18. *(b)* The correct filler for the given blank is 'sailing'.

19. *(a)* Two peas in a pod means very similar to each other.

20. *(d)* The correct filler for the given blank is 'round'.

21. *(c)* The underlined part is grammatically correct and contextually meaningful.

22. *(c)* The incorrectly spelt word is 'Advertisment'. The correct spelling is 'Advertisement'.

23. *(d)* The underlined part of the given sentence contains an error. Use 'looks' to correct the sentence as the subject of the sentence is singular.

24. *(d)* The word 'manipulative' means 'scheming and calculative'.

25. *(d)* The antonym of lawful is illicit which means not legal.

26. *(a)* Given, T @ S # M & N $ G

According to the question,

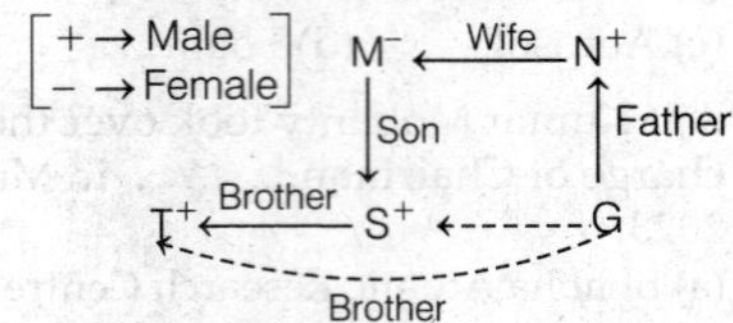

Hence, T is 'brother' of G.

27. *(a)* The pattern of the series is as follows,

E F E G E / E F E G E / E F E G E / E F E G E

∴ Required combination = EEFGEFE

28. *(a)* The pattern of the series is as follows,

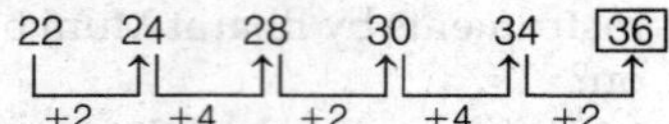

29. *(d)* Here,

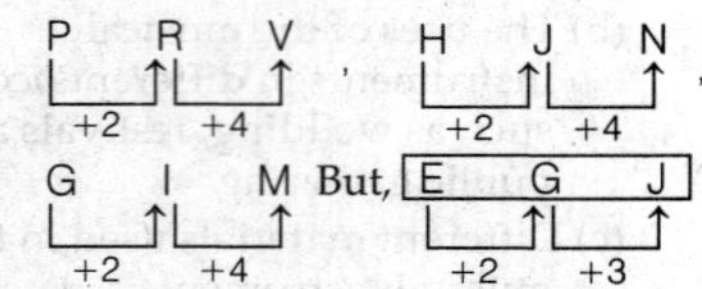

∴ EGJ is odd one out.

30. *(c)*

Given word → S O U N D B A R

Alphabetical order of letters → A B D N O R S U

∴ Position of only 1 letter remain unchanged.

31. *(a)* Naming the figure,

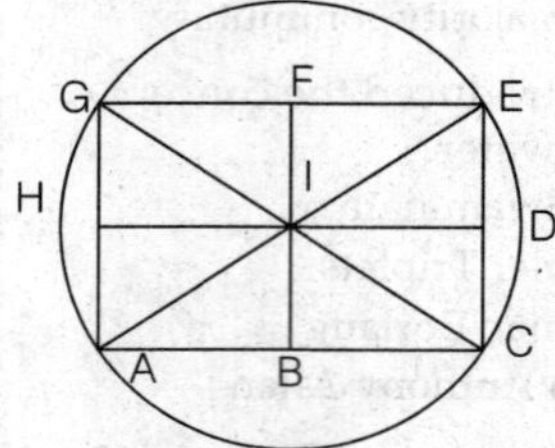

Rectangles can be represented as

□AHIB, □BIDC, □FEDI, □GFIH, □AGFB, □BFEC, □GEDH, □AHDC and □ACEG

∴ Total rectangles = 9

32. *(b)* The pattern of the series is as follows,

R $\xrightarrow{+4}$ V $\xrightarrow{+4}$ Z $\xrightarrow{+4}$ D $\xrightarrow{+4}$ H

S $\xrightarrow{+7}$ Z $\xrightarrow{+7}$ G $\xrightarrow{+7}$ N $\xrightarrow{+7}$ U

T $\xrightarrow{+3}$ W $\xrightarrow{+3}$ Z $\xrightarrow{+3}$ C $\xrightarrow{+3}$ F

33. *(c)* As, 'Palate' is roof of the 'Mouth'. Similarly, 'Ceiling' is roof of the 'Room'.

34. *(d)* According to the question,

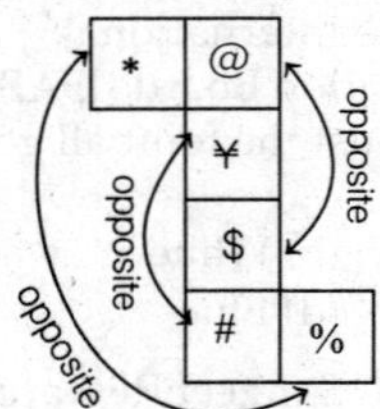

∴ '%' is on opposite side of '*'.

35. *(d)* 16th July, 2001 → Monday

Number of odd days between year 16th July, 2001 to year 16th July, 2006

⇒ 2002 + 2003 + 2004 + 2005 + 2006

↓ 1 + 1 + 2 + 1 + 1

$= \frac{6}{7} = 6$ odd days

Now, number of odd days from 16th July, 2006 to 23rd December, 2006.

= July + August + September + October + November + December

= 15 + 31 + 30 + 31 + 30 + 23

$= \frac{160}{7} = 6$ odd days

∴ Total odd days

$= \frac{6+6}{7} = \frac{12}{7} \Rightarrow 5$ odd days

∴ Required day = Monday + 5 = Saturday

36. *(c)* The pattern of the series is as follows,

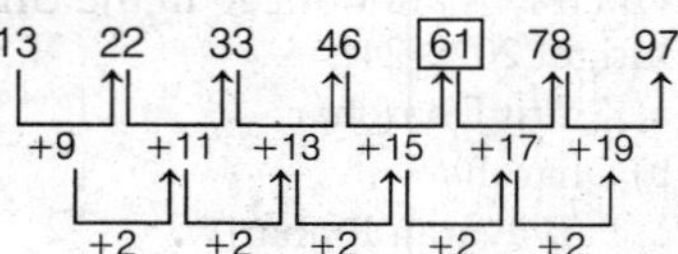

37. *(d)* The pattern in the digits in given series is as follows,

4 $\xrightarrow{+2}$ 6 $\xrightarrow{+2}$ 8 $\xrightarrow{+2}$ 10 $\xrightarrow{+2}$ 12

2 $\xrightarrow{+2}$ 4 $\xrightarrow{+2}$ 6 $\xrightarrow{+2}$ 8 $\xrightarrow{+2}$ 10

6 $\xrightarrow{+4}$ 10 $\xrightarrow{+4}$ 14 $\xrightarrow{+4}$ 18 $\xrightarrow{+4}$ 22

∴ ? = 12, 22, 10 (figure)

38. *(b)* Given equation,

$35 \times 96 - 8 + 3 \div 11 = ?$

Interchanging '+' and '×', '–' and '÷', we get

$35 + 96 \div 8 \times 3 - 11 = ?$

$\Rightarrow \quad 35 + 12 \times 3 - 11 = ?$

$\Rightarrow \quad 35 + 36 - 11 = ?$

$\Rightarrow \quad 71 - 11 = ?$

$\therefore \quad ? = 60$

39. *(a)* The correct mirror image of the given combination is as below,

9GrEcAn | nAcErG9 (mirror line MN)

40. *(c)* According to the question,

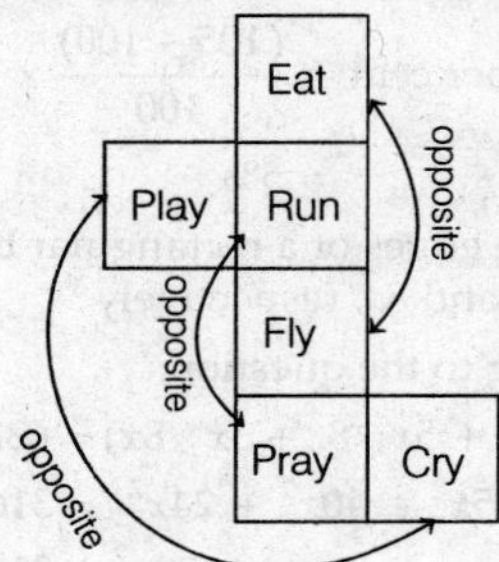

$\because$ 'Fly' is opposite to 'Eat'.

41. *(c)* According to the question,

I missed breakfast — nl zn kq

train is missed — zm Kg nl

$\therefore$ Code for missed in 'nl'.

42. *(d)* The option figure (d) is embedded the figure (X) as its part.

43. *(a)* Given equation,

32 B 4 D 116 A 2 C 13 = ?

According to the question,

$A \rightarrow \div, B \rightarrow \times, C \rightarrow +, D \rightarrow -$

After changing the letters with signs, we get

$32 \times 4 - 116 \div 2 + 13 = ?$

$\Rightarrow \quad 128 - 58 + 13 = ?$

$\Rightarrow \quad 141 - 58 = ?$

$\therefore \quad ? = 83$

44. *(c)* According to the question,

M O A T → 8 6 5 2

T R A M → 4 2 5 6

$\therefore$ code for 'R' is '4'.

45. *(d)* As, $\sqrt{529} = 23$

and $\sqrt{324} = 18$

Similarly, $\sqrt{625} = 25$

46. *(a)* The correct mirror image of given combination is as follows,

JgF47Bae | eaB74FgJ (mirror line MN)

47. *(b)* According to the statements,

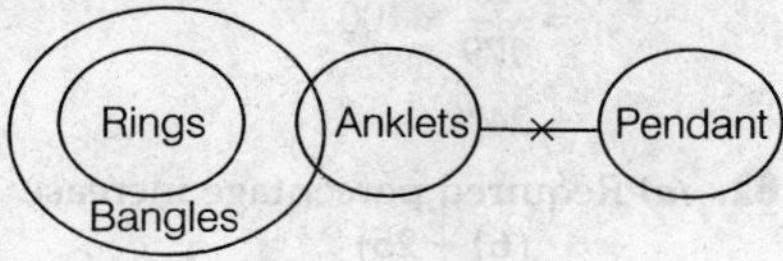

Conclusions I. (✓) II. (✓)

Hence, both Conclusions I and II follow.

48. *(b)* As, 'Mango' is the national fruit of 'India'.

Similarly, 'Kiwi' is the national fruit of 'New Zealand'.

49. *(a)* Given equation,

12 J 2 K 17 A 15 V 19

According to the question,

$J \rightarrow \div, V \rightarrow \times, K \rightarrow +, A \rightarrow -$

After inter changing the letters with signs, we get

$\therefore \quad 12 \div 2 + 17 - 15 \times 19 = ?$

$\Rightarrow \quad 6 + 17 - 285 = ?$

$\Rightarrow \quad 23 - 285 = ?$

$\therefore \quad ? = -262$

50. *(b)* As, $5 \xrightarrow{\times 5} 25 \xrightarrow{\times 2} 50$

$8 \xrightarrow{\times 8} 64 \xrightarrow{\times 2} 128$

Similarly, $12 \xrightarrow{\times 12} 144 \xrightarrow{\times 2} \boxed{288}$

51. *(c)* Given, tan 570°

$= \tan(540° + 30°) = \tan 30°$

$= \frac{1}{\sqrt{3}}$

52. *(a)* Given, total amount = ₹ 550

Down payment = ₹ 250

Amount paid = ₹ 310

Time = 1 month

$\therefore$ The remaining amount after down payment

= 550 – 250 = ₹ 300

Interest = 310 – 300 = ₹ 10

Now, $SI = \frac{P \times R \times T}{100}$

$10 = \frac{300 \times R}{100} \times \frac{1}{12} \Rightarrow R = 40\%$

53. *(c)* Let the total income = 100%

According to the question,

Savings

= [100% – (10% + 10% + 20% + 15%)]

= (100% – 55%)

= 45%

$\therefore$ Savings $= \frac{45}{100} \times 30000$

= ₹ 13500

54. *(c)* Let the total voters are 100%.

Total casted votes $= 100 \times \frac{83}{100} = 83\%$

Total valid votes $= 83 \times \frac{96}{100} = 79.68\%$

According to the question,

Total valid votes by Party

$A = 79.68 \times \frac{83}{100} = 156611$

$\Rightarrow \quad 66.1344\% = 156611$

$\Rightarrow \quad 100\% = \frac{156611 \times 100}{66.13}$

$\Rightarrow \quad = 236807$

55. *(d)* According to the question,

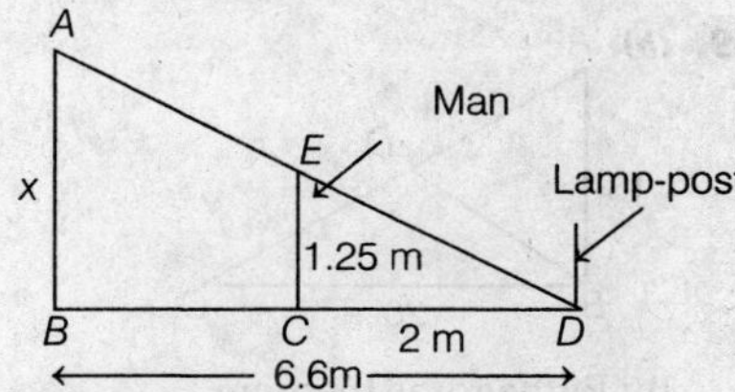

In ΔABD and ΔECD

$\angle ABD = \angle ECD$

$\angle ADB = \angle EDC$

From the rule of similarity,

$\frac{AB}{EC} = \frac{BD}{CD}$

$\Rightarrow \quad \frac{x}{1.25} = \frac{6.6}{2}$

$\Rightarrow \quad x = \frac{6.6 \times 1.25}{2}$

$\Rightarrow \quad x = 4.125 \sim 4.13$ m

Hence, the height of lamp-post is 4.13 m.

56. *(b)* The mean ages of the children

$= \frac{(6 \times 8) + (7 \times 3) + (8 \times 7) + (9 \times 2) + (10 \times 20)}{8 + 3 + 7 + 2 + 20}$

$= \frac{48 + 21 + 56 + 18 + 200}{40}$

$= \frac{343}{40}$

= 8.575 yr

57. *(c)* On dividing 7658 by 45, we get remainder

$= \frac{7658}{45} = 8$ (remainder)

$\therefore$ Required number $= 7658 - 8$

$= 7650$

58. *(c)* According to the question,

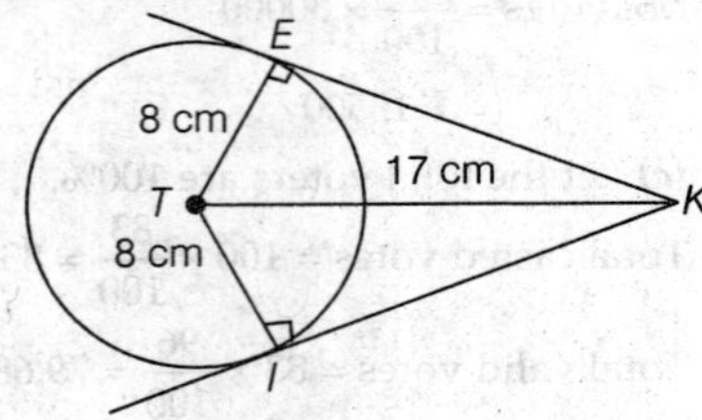

In ΔETK,

$TK^2 = ET^2 + EK^2$

$(17)^2 = (8)^2 + EK^2$

$EK^2 = 289 - 64 = 225$

$EK = 15$

Now, area of quadrilateral *TEKI*

$= \frac{1}{2} \times 15 \times 8 \times 2$

$= 120$ sq. cm.

59. *(b)*

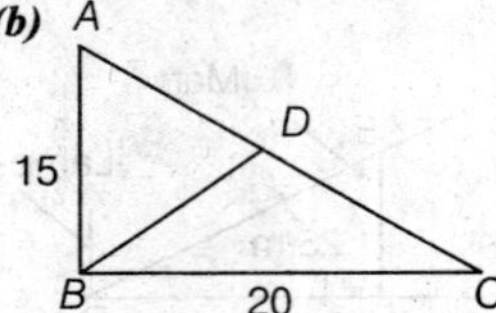

By Pythagoras theorem,

$AC^2 = AB^2 + BC^2$

$AC^2 = (15)^2 + (20)^2$

$AC^2 = 225 + 400$

$AC^2 = 625$

$AC = 25$

Now, area of triangle

$= \frac{1}{2} \times AB \times BC = \frac{1}{2} \times AC \times BD$

$\Rightarrow \frac{1}{2} \times 15 \times 20 = \frac{1}{2} \times 25 \times BD$

$\Rightarrow BD = \frac{15 \times 20}{25}$

$\therefore BD = 12$

60. *(a)* Let the Monu's age $= 3x$ and his sister's age $= x$

Total years from 2000 to 2010

$= 2010 - 2000$

$= 10$ yr

According to the question,

$3x + 10 - (x + 10) = 24$

$\Rightarrow 2x = 24$

$x = 12$

$\therefore$ Monu's age in 2010 $= 3x + 10$

$= 3 \times 12 + 10$

$= 46$ yr

61. *(b)* Total accidents in month of April = 43

Total accidents during six months

$= 25 + 19 + 30 + 43 + 35 + 27$

$= 179$

$\therefore$ Required percentage

$= \frac{43}{179} \times 100$

$= 24\%$

62. *(a)* Required percentage increase

$= \frac{(61 - 25)}{25} \times 100$

$= \frac{36}{25} \times 100 = 144\%$

63. *(a)* A number which is divisible by 22, it must be divisible by 11 and 2 both.

From option (a),

Number 893002 is an even number.

Hence, it is divisible by 2.

Now, the check the divisibility with 11

$\Rightarrow 8 + 3 + 0 - 9 + 0 + 2 = 0$ or 11

$\Rightarrow 11 - 11 = 0$

Hence, it is also divisible by 11.

$\therefore$ Required number is 893002.

64. *(d)* Given, $S_1 = 40$, $S_2 = 20$

Average speed $= \frac{2(S_1 \times S_2)}{S_1 + S_2}$

$= \frac{2 \times 40 \times 20}{60}$

$= \frac{1600}{60}$

$= 26\frac{2}{3}$ km/h

65. *(a)* From pie-chart,

Required difference

$= \left[\frac{(18 - 10)}{100} \times 360\right]^\circ$

$= \left[\frac{8}{100} \times 360\right]^\circ$

$= 28.8°$

66. *(b)* Given, sides 6 cm, 8 cm and 10 cm.

According to the question,

$a^3 = 6^3 + 8^3 + 10^3$

$a^3 = 1728$

$a = 12$

Now, surface area of cube $= 6a^2$

$= 6 \times 12 \times 12$

$= 864$ cm^2

67. *(d)* According to the question,

$\frac{70}{100} \times$ Cost price $= \frac{40}{100} \times$ Selling price

$\therefore \frac{\text{Selling price}}{\text{Cost price}} = \frac{70}{40} = \frac{7}{4}$

Gain per cent $= \frac{(7 - 4)}{4} \times 100$

$= \frac{3}{4} \times 100$

$= 75\%$

68. *(a)* Let the cost price be ₹ 100.

$\therefore$ Marked price $= 100 \times \frac{150}{100} =$ ₹ 150

Selling price $= 150 \times \frac{(100 - 30)}{100}$

$= 150 \times \frac{70}{100} =$ ₹ 105

$\therefore$ Gain per cent $= \frac{(105 - 100)}{100} \times 100$

$= 5\%$

69. *(d)* Let the edges of a rectangular box are $3x$, $5x$ and $8x$, respectively.

According to the question,

$2(3x \times 5x + 5x \times 8x + 3x \times 8x) = 632$

$\Rightarrow (15x^2 + 40x^2 + 24x^2) = 316$

$\Rightarrow 79x^2 = 316$

$\Rightarrow x^2 = 4$

$\Rightarrow x = 2$

$\therefore$ Edges of rectangular box are 3×2, 5×2, 8×2 = 6, 10 and 16

Now, volume of the box $= 6 \times 10 \times 16$

$= 960$ cm^3

70. *(c)* $28\% = \frac{28}{100} = \frac{7}{25}$

$= 7 : 25$

71. *(b)* Let the weight of box and gift articles are $x : 9x$.

According to the question,

$x + 9x = 25 \times 1000$

$10x = 25 \times 1000$

$x = 2500$ gm

$\therefore$ The weight of articles $= 9x$

$= 9 \times 2500$

$= 22500$ gm

72. *(a)* Given, diameter $(d) = 14$ cm

Curved surface area $= 352$ cm^2

Radius $= \frac{d}{2} = \frac{14}{2} = 7$ cm

According to the question,

$2\pi rh = 352$ cm^2 [C.S.A. $= 2\pi rh$]

$2 \times \frac{22}{7} \times 7 \times h = 352$ [$\because r = 7$ cm]

$\Rightarrow h = 8$ cm

Now, total surface area = $2\pi r (h + r)$

$= 2 \times \frac{22}{7} \times 7 [8 + 7]$

$= 44 \times 15$

$= 660 \text{ cm}^2$

73. *(c)* Required average

$= \frac{\text{First number + Last number}}{2}$

$= \frac{1 + 69}{2}$

$= 35$

74. *(a)* According to the question,

In ΔADC,

$\angle ADC = \frac{1}{2} \times \angle ACC = \frac{1}{2} \times 100° = 50°$

[$\because$ *AC* is a chord]

Now, $\angle ADE = \angle ADC + \angle CDE$

$90° = 50° + \angle CDE$

[$\because$ *AE* is a diameter]

$\angle CDE = 90° - 50° = 40°$

Again, in ΔOEC,

$\angle CEA + \angle ECO + \angle COE = 180°$

$2 \angle CEA + \angle COE = 180°$

[$\angle CEA = \angle ECO$]

$\Rightarrow \; 2 \angle CEA + 80° = 180°$

$\angle CEA = \frac{100}{2} = 50°$

Hence, the value of $\angle CDE + \angle CEA$

$= 40° + 50°$

$= 90°$

75. *(d)* Here, $(A + B)$'s 1 day's work $= \frac{1}{15}$

$(B + C)$'s 1 day's work $= \frac{1}{30}$

$(C + A)$'s 1 day's work $= \frac{1}{45}$

Now, $2(A + B + C)$'s 1 day's work

$= \frac{1}{15} + \frac{1}{30} + \frac{1}{45}$

$= \frac{6 + 3 + 2}{90}$

$= \frac{11}{90}$

$\therefore (A + B + C)$'s 1 day work

$= \frac{11}{90 \times 2} = \frac{11}{180}$

Hence, $(A + B + C)$ complete the work in $\frac{180}{11}$ days $= 16\frac{4}{11}$ days

76. *(d)* The statement "The 44th Amendment Act introduced Fundamental Duties in the Constitution" is incorrect.

- The Fundamental duties were added to the Constitution through the 42nd Amendment Act of 1976.
- Part IV A of the Constitution deals with Fundamental Duties.
- The Fundamental Duties were recommended by the Swaran Singh Committee. There are 11 Fundamental Duties mentioned in the Constitution of India.

77. *(a)* Balban took the policy of 'Blood and iron' to deal with the Mewati community.

- Balban was the Sultan of the Mamluk or Slave dynasty.
- The 'Blood and Iron' policy was a violent and harsh policy adopted to deal with internal revolts and foreign invaders.
- The policy involved using ruthless methods, such as the sword, to suppress enemies, maintain strict discipline in the court, and create terror in the minds of the people.
- The policy also included maintaining a strong army and ruthlessly punishing any threats.

78. *(d)* Proxima Centauri is the second nearest star to Earth.

- It is also known as Alpha Centauri.
- It's located in the constellation Centaurus and is about 4.24 light years away, or about 25 trillion miles.
- It is three times closer than the next nearest star that's similar to the Sun.

79. *(a)* Top left corner of a Word window is the save button in Microsoft Word.

80. *(c)* Konkan Railways was constructed in the year 1998.

- Konkan railway is a 760 km route.
- It connects Roha in Maharashtra to Mangalore in Karnataka.
- It is known as an engineering marvel.
- This rail route crosses 146 river streams, nearly 2000 bridges and 91 tunnels.

81. *(a)* There are a minimum of 15 over per hour in a test match.

In a Test match, maximum 90 overs usually are there in a single day but it is not fixed.

82. *(d)* .docx occupies less memory when saving an MS Word file.

83. *(b)* The Hemis festival is associated with Buddhism.

- It is celebrated in the Ladakh region mainly.
- It is celebrated during June and July.
- Hemis festival is the celebration of the Guru Padmasambhava's Birth.
- People from different parts of the world visit Ladakh to witness this colourful celebration.

84. *(b)* According to the International Football Association Board (IFAB), the football goalpost must be white.

- The International Football Association Board (IFAB) was founded in 1886 by the four British football associations (The FA, the Scottish FA, the FA of Wales and the Irish FA).
- The sole responsibility of IFAB is developing and preserving the Laws of the Game.

85. *(b)* The ITC Sangeet Research Academy is located in Kolkata.

- ITC Sangeet Research Academy is a Hindustani classical music academy run by the corporate house, ITC Ltd.
- Prominent musicians associated with the academy include Ulhas Kashalkar, Falguni Mitra, Ajoy Chakrabarty, Ustad Rashid Khan, Mashkoor Ali Khan, Girija Devi, and Subhra Guha.

86. *(b)* The office of the Registrar General and Census Commissioner, India comes under the Ministry of Home Affairs.

- The Registrar General and Census Commissioner of India (RGCCI) is responsible for conducting the country's decadal census.
- Shri Mritunjay Kumar Narayan assumed the charge as Registrar General and Census Commissioner of India w.e.f. 1st November , 2022.
- Henry Walter is known as the Father of the Indian Census.
- The first census of Independent India was conducted in 1951, which was the seventh census in its continuous series.

87. *(d)* Option (d) is incorrect statement regarding invertebrates because vertebrates possess a backbone and an internal skeleton.

- The backbone, also called the vertebral column, is a key characteristic of vertebrates, providing support and structure for the body.

- Vertebrates have an internal skeleton, meaning their bones are located inside their body, unlike invertebrates which may have external skeleton.

88. *(a)* The scheme 'Amrit Dharohar' announced in the Union budget 2023-24 was aimed at the conservation of wetlands.
- The Amrit Dharohar scheme is an initiative launched by the Ministry of Environment, Forest, and Climate Change (MoEF&CC) in June 2023 to promote the conservation values of Ramsar sites in India. The scheme aims to generate employment opportunities and support local livelihoods.
- It also aims to identify the importance of wetlands and promote their optimal use.

89. *(b)* In February 2023, Shiv Pratap Shukla was appointed as Governor of Himachal Pradesh.
- The Governor of a State is appointed by the President for a term of five years and holds office at his pleasure.
- Only Indian citizens above 35 years of age are eligible for appointment to this office. The executive power of the State is vested in the Governor.

90. *(c)* The Gir Forests are the natural habitat of the Asiatic Lion in India.
- The lion is the second largest cat species in the world. It is divided into two subspecies: the African lion and the Asiatic lion (Persian or Indian Lion).
- The Gir forest is home to nearly 700 Asiatic lions, which are found only in this region and are a vital species for conservation.
- Conservationists have raised concerns about the vulnerability of having the entire lion population concentrated in one area.
- Epidemics and natural disasters like the 2018 outbreak of Babesiosis and Cyclone Tauktae in 2019 pose significant risks to the survival of the lions.

91. *(c)* Aerosol contains small droplets of liquid or particles of solid dispersed in a gas.

92. *(d)* Ajit Kumar Mohanty took over the charge of Chairman, of Atomic Energy Commission, in May 2023.
- The Atomic Energy Commission (AEC) was established in the Department of Atomic Energy.
- The commission was created on 10th August 1948 by the Department of Scientific Research.
- The objectives of the commission are to produce electricity from atomic energy, increase the yield of food grains and make them last longer, set up the technology for achieving this and develop nanotechnology.

93. *(a)* Bharat Muni categorised musical instruments based on the different sounds of the musical instruments.
- Bharat Muni composed Natya Shastra between 200 BC and 200 AD.
- He classified musical instruments into four groups:
- Avanaddha Vadya (membranophones or percussion instruments),
- Ghan Vadya (idiophones or solid instruments),
- Sushir Vadya (aerophones or wind instruments),
- Tat Vadya (chordophones or stringed instruments).

94. *(b)* Secularism means that the state does not promote any religion.
- The term 'secularism' was introduced in the year 1976 by the 42nd Amendment of the Constitution.
- Articles 25 to 28 establish that the state will not discriminate, patronise, or interfere with the practice of any religion.
- These articles also guarantee individuals the right to practice, profess, and propagate any religion, as well as the freedom to change their religion or beliefs.

95. *(d)* The concept of virtual water was introduced by John Anthony Allan.
- Virtual water, also known as 'embedded water' or 'indirect water', is the amount of water used to produce a product or service from start to finish.
- It includes water used for feed crops, animal drinking water, and the final product itself.
- Virtual water is often hidden from the end user of a product or service.

96. *(b)* Lord William Bentinck issued the famous regulation XVII in 1829, which declared the practice of Sati illegal and punishable by the courts.
- He made other important administrative reforms in the Indian government and society.
- He reformed the finances, opened up judicial posts to Indians, and suppressed such practices as thuggee, or ritual murder by robber gangs.
- Lord William Bentinck made significant reforms to India's judicial system between 1828 and 1835 as Governor-General.
- He established a second Sadar Adalat in Allahabad to improve access to justice. In criminal law, he replaced Circuit Courts with Commissioners and created District and Sessions Judges.

97. *(d)* Ranji Trophy is named after the Indian Batsman Ranjit Sinhji.
- The Ranji Trophy is a premier domestic first-class cricket championship played in India and organised annually by the Board of Control for Cricket in India.
- The teams representing regional and state cricket associations participate in the series.
- The 1934-35 Ranji Trophy was the inaugural edition of India's first-class cricket championship.

98. *(c)* Kokborak is the official language of Tripura.

Khasi, Mizo and Garo are the official languages of Meghalaya.

99. *(c)* ₹ 500 currency notes were discarded by the Government of India in November 2016.

In the process of demonitisation in November 2016 the currency notes of ₹ 1000 were also discarded.

100. *(c)* Giddha is a folk dance of Punjab.
- Jagoi, Cholom, Thang-Ta and Raas Leela are the folk dance from Manipur.
- The major folk dances of Nagaland include Modse, Bamboo Dance, Agurshikukula, Butterfly Dance, Aaluyattu, Sadal Kekai, Changai Dance, Kuki Dance, etc.
- The folk dances of Odisha include Ghumura, Sambalpuri and Chhau.

Set 14 04 July, 2024 (Shift II)

SSC CHSL Tier-I SOLVED PAPER

Instructions

1. This paper contains 100 questions.
2. It has 4 Parts, **Part I** General English, **Part II** General Intelligence & Reasoning, **Part III** Quantitative Aptitude and **Part IV** General Awareness.
3. Each question carries **2 marks.**

Part I

General English

1. The following sentence has been split into four segments. Identify the segment that contains an incorrect preposition.

I am writing to invite you / to give a presentation / for our Jobs and Careers Conference / for engineering graduates.

(a) for engineering graduates
(b) I am writing to invite you
(c) for our Jobs and Careers Conference
(d) to give a presentation

2. Select the grammatically correct sentence.

(a) Ragini plays the guitar melodiously.
(b) Ragini plays the guitar melodious.
(c) Ragini plays the guitar with a melody.
(d) Ragini plays the guitar with melodiousness.

3. The following sentence has been divided into four parts. Identify the part that contains an error.

(A) I am hearing / (B) that the heat wave / (C) is going to be / (D) worse this year.

(a) B (b) D
(c) C (d) A

4. Select the option with the correct use of future tense.

(a) I hope your health is getting better by next week.
(b) I hope your health will get better by next week.
(c) I hope your health have been getting better by next week.
(d) I hope your health is get better by next week.

Directions (Q. Nos. 5-9) *In the following passage, some words have been deleted. Read the passage carefully and select the most appropriate option to fill in each blank.*

Once upon a time, there was a man (1) .... used to tell the fortunes of people. One day, he was telling the fortune as usual when a man came to him and said, "Somebody (2) .... broken the door of your house and has stolen many valuables. Go home at once!"

The fortune teller was (3) .... shocked to hear the news. He could not utter a word out of shock. He just ran to his house as fast as he could. He was in such a hurry that he left all his things behind. Now, one of his customers saw him rushing and (4) .... "Every day he (5) .... the fortunes of so many people but today he could not see his own future!" The fortune teller felt very embarrassed.

5. Select the most appropriate option to fill in blank number (1).

(a) whose (b) whom
(c) by whom (d) who

6. Select the most appropriate option to fill in blank number (2).

(a) shall have (b) had
(c) have (d) has

7. Select the most appropriate option to fill in blank number (3).

(a) so less (b) so more
(c) many (d) quite

8. Select the most appropriate option to fill in blank number (4).

(a) comments (b) commented
(c) commenting (d) comment

9. Select the most appropriate option to fill in blank number (5).

(a) tell (b) tells
(c) telling (d) told

10. Select the most appropriate synonym of the given word.

Lousy

(a) Praiseworthy (b) Moral
(c) Funny (d) Pitiful

11. Select the most appropriate antonym of the given word.

Agile

(a) Active (b) Apathetic
(c) Energetic (d) Sluggish

12. Select the incorrectly spelt word in the given sentence.

The West Africans have a heritage of produsing sculpture using wax and bronze.

(a) sculpture (b) bronze
(c) heritage (d) produsing

13. Select the most appropriate option that can substitute the underlined word in the following sentence.

His flight departs <u>in</u> 5:00 pm.

(a) of (b) for
(c) at (d) from

14. Select the option that will most suitably substitute the underlined part of the given sentence.

I gave my best dress to her <u>on condition that she return it</u> the very next day in a clean condition.

(a) on the condition that she would return
(b) on the condition that she return
(c) on condition that she returned
(d) on the conditions that she had return

15. Select the most appropriate option that can substitute the underlined segment in the given sentence.

The novel highlights the <u>place</u> of the endangered species in the rainforest.

(a) prowess (b) position
(c) plight (d) perspective

16. Select the most appropriate option that can substitute the underlined segment in the given sentence.
The boy watched a sci-fi movie in the lieu of playing in the game zone.
(a) in lieu of play
(b) in lieu off playing
(c) in lieu of playing
(d) on lieu of playing

17. Identify the incorrectly spelt word in the following sentence and select its correct spelling from the given options.
The boy found the project to be a peice of cake because it was incredibly easy.
(a) piece (b) incrediblly
(c) foaund (d) praject

18. Select the most appropriate antonym of the underlined word in the following sentence.
There is also an increase in juvenile delinquency.
(a) Teenage (b) Adult
(c) Puerile (d) Minor

19. Fill in the blank using the correct collocation.
We need to ……… a decision on the housing project tomorrow morning.
(a) make (b) draw
(c) build (d) frame

20. Select the most appropriate antonym of the given word.
Alluring
(a) Enticing (b) Glamourous
(c) Repulsive (d) Fascinating

21. Select the most appropriate synonym that can replace the underlined word in the given sentence.
It did not take her very long to ascend to power.
(a) grab (b) climb
(c) reach (d) arise

22. Select the most appropriate option that can substitute the underlined part in the following sentence.
My entire family left me in the lurch when I went to them after I divorced my husband.
(a) refused to help me in my distress
(b) blamed only me for my failure
(c) scorned me for committing mistakes
(d) attempted to harass me

23. Select the most appropriate meaning of the underlined idiom.
Prakash could not make up his mind about what to do with the project.
(a) Abandon (b) Think
(c) Abide (d) Decide

24. Select the most appropriate antonym of the given word.
Resourceful
(a) Incompetent (b) Ingenious
(c) Immaculate (d) Impeccable

25. Select the most appropriate synonym of the given word.
Peculiar
(a) Revolutionary (b) Strange
(c) Frequent (d) Usual

Part II
General Intelligence

26. Select the set in which the numbers are related in the same way as are the numbers of the following sets.
(**Note** Operations should be performed on the whole numbers, without breaking down the numbers into its constituent digits. E.g. 13–Operations on 13 such as adding/subtracting/multiplying etc. to 13 can be performed. Breaking down 13 into 1 and 3 and then performing mathematical operations on 1 and 3 is not allowed.)
(3, 12, 26)
(7, 9, 53)
(a) (7, 5, 25) (b) (4, 9, 16)
(c) (12, 4, 114) (d) (5, 15, 45)

27. A paper is folded and cut as shown below. How will it appear when unfolded?

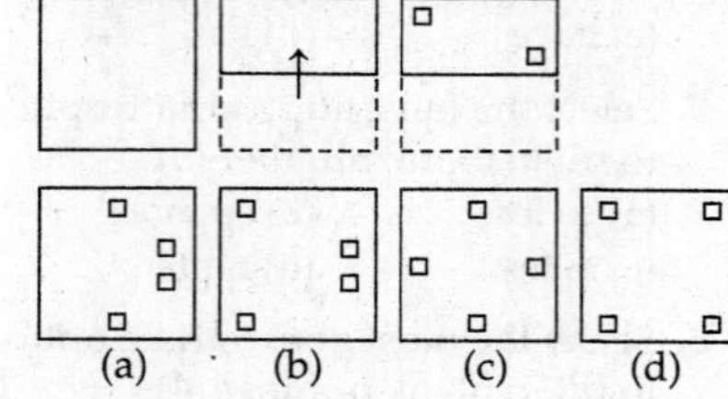

28. Select the option figure in which the given figure is embedded as its part (rotation is not allowed).

(a) 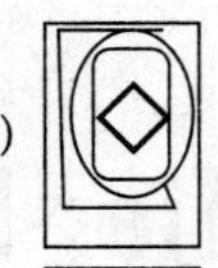 (b) 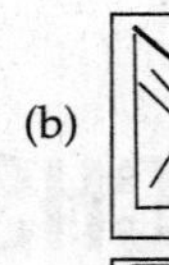

(c) 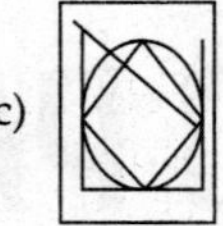 (d) 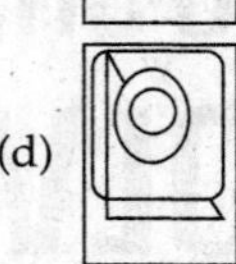

29. Which two numbers should be interchanged to make the given equation correct?
$17 \times 7 + (21 \div 3) \times 5 - 28 + 34 = 72$
(**Note** Numbers must be interchanged and not the constituent digits e.g. if 2 and 3 are to be interchanged in the equation $43 \times 3 + 4 \div 2$, then interchanged equation is $43 \times 2 + 4 \div 3$)
(a) 7 and 3 (b) 17 and 28
(c) 21 and 28 (d) 5 and 7

30. How many triangles are there in the given figure?

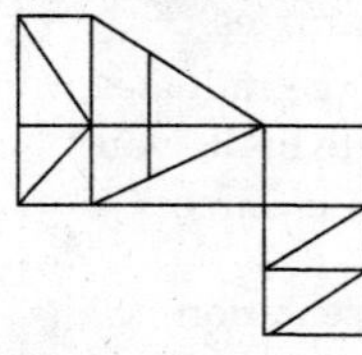

(a) 12 (b) 9
(c) 16 (d) 14

31. If 'A' stands for '÷', 'B' stands for '×', 'C' stands for '+' and 'D' stands for '–', what will come in place of the question mark (?) in the following equation?
16 B 8 D 51 A 3 C 57 = ?
(a) 188 (b) 168
(c) 128 (d) 148

32. Select the option in which the given figure is embedded. (Rotation is not allowed).

(a) 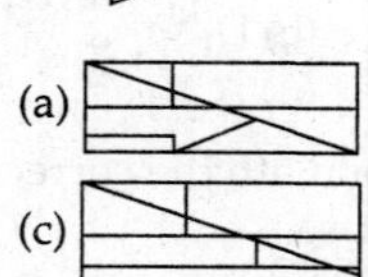 (b) 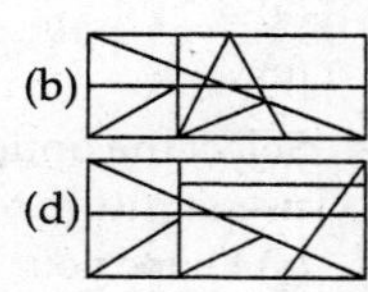

(c) (d)

33. Which of the following numbers will replace the question mark (?) in the given series?
93, 111, 139, 157, 185, 203, ?
(a) 227 (b) 211
(c) 215 (d) 231

34. In a certain code language, 'hands are dirty' is written as 'ca bx vp' and 'dirty things flies' is written as 'by vp cb'. How is 'dirty' written in the given language?
(a) by (b) cb (c) bx (d) vp

35. 11 is related to 121 by certain logic. Following the same logic, 21 is related to 441. To which of the following is 31 related, following the same logic?
(**Note** Operations should be performed on the whole numbers, without breaking down the numbers into its constituent digits. E.g. 13 – Operations on 13 such as adding/subtracting/multiplying etc. to 13 can be performed. Breaking down 13 into 1 and 3 and then performing mathematical operations on 1 and 3 is not allowed.)
(a) 356 (b) 960 (c) 961 (d) 428

36. Select the option figure in which the given figure is embedded as its part (rotation is not allowed).

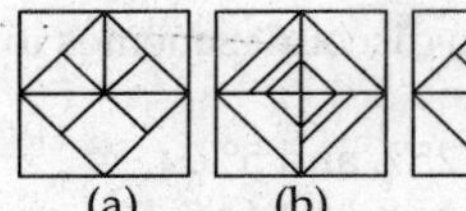

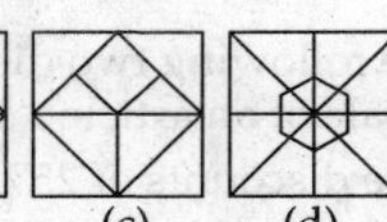

37. In a certain code language,
A + B means 'A is the mother of B'
A – B means 'A is the sister of B'
A × B means 'A is the wife of B'
A ÷ B means 'A is the son of B'
Based on the above, how is Z related to W, if 'Z × Y ÷ X – V + W'?
(a) Mother's sister's son's wife
(b) Mother's sister's son's daughter
(c) Mother's brother's son's wife
(d) Mother's sister's daughter

38. Select the option in which the given figure is embedded (rotation is not allowed).

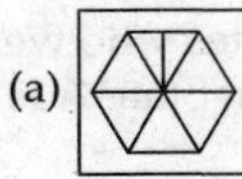

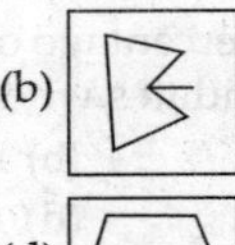

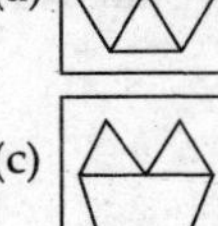

39. Which figure should replace the question mark (?), if the following figure series were to be continued?

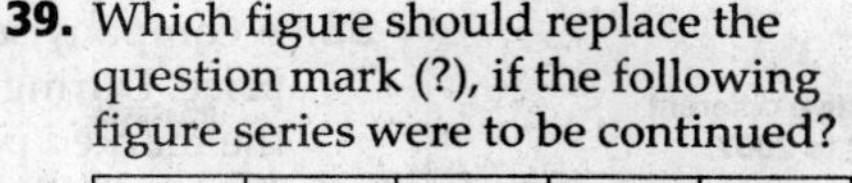

(a)	(b)	(c)	(d)
3 Z A / T / 6 =	3 T 6 / Z / A =	Z = T / T / A 3	3 Z T / 6 / A =

40. Three of the following four are alike in a certain way and thus form a group. Which is the one that does not belong to that group?
(**Note** The odd one out is not based on the number of consonants/vowels or their position in the letter-cluster.)
(a) BEH (b) NQT
(c) KMP (d) RUX

41. If 'E' stands for '÷', 'U' stands for '×', 'A' stands for '+' and 'C' stands for '–', what will come in place of the question mark (?) in the following equation?
16 A 24 C 30 E 15 U 9 = ?
(a) 22 (b) 32
(c) 66 (d) 78

42. AQLZ is related to SIDR in a certain way based on the English alphabetical order. In the same way, CPDV is related to UHVN. To which of the following is EBRY related, following the same logic?
(a) WQJT (b) WQTJ
(c) WTJQ (d) WTQJ

43. If 23rd January, 2002 was Wednesday, then what was the day of the week on 26th January, 2007?
(a) Friday (b) Sunday
(c) Saturday (d) Monday

44. What should come in place of the question mark (?) in the given series based on the English alphabetical order?
MKH, PNK, SQN, VTQ, ?
(a) YWT (b) WTY
(c) WYT (d) YTW

45. If 26th November, 2013 was Tuesday, then what was the day of the week on 29th November, 2018?
(a) Wednesday
(b) Friday
(c) Saturday
(d) Thursday

46. Which letter-cluster will replace the question mark (?) to complete the given series?
UTHS, VRKO, ?, XNQG, YLTC
(a) WPNK (b) WONJ
(c) WPMN (d) TONK

47. What should come in place of the question mark (?) in the given series?
77, 79, 83, 89, 97, ?
(a) 106 (b) 107
(c) 105 (d) 108

48. Select the pair which follows the same pattern as that followed by the two set of pairs given below. Both pairs follow the same pattern.
FJK : KOP
MQR : RVW
(a) GMN : FLM (b) ADE : ZWV
(c) PRS : SRP (d) JMP : ORU

49. Three statements are followed by conclusions numbered I, II. You have to consider these statements to be true, even if they seem to be at variance with commonly known facts. Decide which of the given conclusions logically follow(s) from the given statements.

Statements
All space is wind.
Some wind is earth.
Some fire is earth.

Conclusions
I. All earth is space.
II. Some wind is fire.
(a) Neither Conclusion I nor II follows
(b) Only Conclusion I follows
(c) Only Conclusion II follows
(d) Both Conclusions I and II follow

50. What should come in place of the question mark (?) in the given series?
77, 88, 101, 116, ?
(a) 331 (b) 133
(c) 313 (d) 131

Part III
Quantitative Aptitude

51. Study the given bar-graph and answer the question that follows.
The bar-graph shows the production of refrigerators (in thousand) by five different companies A, B, C, D and E during 2004 to 2007.

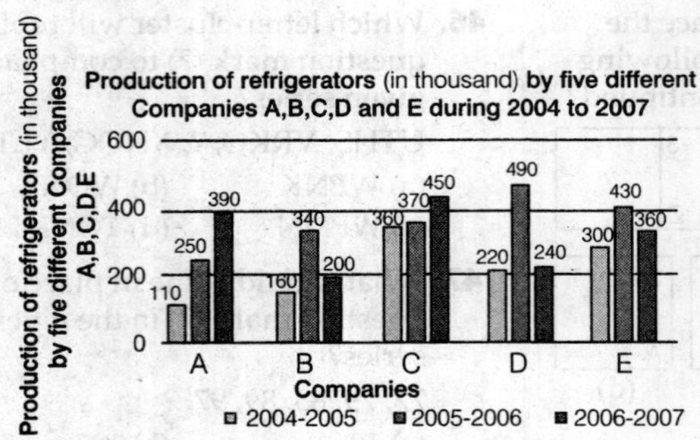

What is the ratio of the average production of the refrigerators by companies A, B and E taken together for the year 2004-2005 to the average production of the refrigerators by companies C and D taken together for the year 2005-2006?

(a) 41 : 19 (b) 19 : 41
(c) 19 : 43 (d) 43 : 19

52. Arun and Bhaskar run a race of 3 km. First, Arun gives Bhaskar a head start of 400 m and beats him by 30 sec. While coming back, Arun gives Bhaskar a lead of 2.5 min and gets beaten by 500 m. What is the difference between the times in minutes in which Arun and Bhaskar can run the race for one side separately?

(a) 3 min (b) 1.5 min
(c) 2.5 min (d) 2 min

53. The value of

$$10 + 3\frac{3}{5} \div \left[2\frac{2}{3} \div \left\{7\frac{1}{6} - \left(2\frac{1}{2} + \frac{2}{3}\right)\right\}\right] \text{ is equal to}$$

(a) $\frac{77}{5}$ (b) $\frac{5}{77}$
(c) $\frac{55}{27}$ (d) $\frac{27}{55}$

54. *A* can complete a piece of work in 20 days and *B* can complete the same work in 10 days. With the help of *C*, working together they completed the work in 5 days. The number of days in which *C* alone can complete the work is

(a) 25 (b) 10
(c) 15 (d) 20

55. The radius of a sphere is increased by 25%. What is the increase per cent in surface area?

(a) 56.25% (b) 36.45%
(c) 25.25% (d) 15.55%

56. In ΔABC, P and Q are the middle points of the sides AB and AC, respectively. R is a point on the segment PQ such that $PR : RQ = 1 : 5$. If $PR = 6$ cm, then $BC = \ldots\ldots$

(a) 70 cm (b) 66 cm
(c) 68 cm (d) 72 cm

57. What is the value of

$$\frac{1}{\sin^4(90° - 2\alpha)} + \frac{1}{\cos^2(90° - 2\alpha) - 1}?$$

(a) $\sin^2 2\alpha + \tan^2 2\alpha$ (b) $\sec^2 2\alpha \tan^2 2\alpha$
(c) $\sec^2 2\alpha + \cot^2 2\alpha$ (d) $\cos^2 2\alpha \cot^2 2\alpha$

58. A company sells goods at a markup of 25% above the cost price. During a sale, the company offers a 10% discount on the marked price. If the customer pays ₹ 540 after the discount, then what was the original cost price of the goods?

(a) ₹ 460 (b) ₹ 470
(c) ₹ 480 (d) ₹ 450

59. Study the given table and select the most appropriate option to fill in the blanks.

Consider the data of sales of products, A, B and C, by three Companies, X, Y and Z in the table given below.

Product → / Company ↓	A	B	C
X	2750	3250	2250
Y	2500	3000	1750
Z	3500	3150	2400

The highest average sale per company is for the product ……… and the lowest average sale per product is for the company ……… .

(a) B; Z (b) A; Y
(c) A; X (d) B; Y

60. Rahul spends 70% of his income. His income increased by 15% and his expenditure increased by 7.5%. What is the percentage increase in his savings?

(a) 25.5% (b) 30.5%
(c) 50% (d) 32.5%

61. Kamlesh offers the following two discount schemes to his customers on the sale of an article

(i) Two successive discounts of 25% and 5%.

(ii) Two successive discounts of 20% and 10%.

What is the difference between the selling price (in ₹) of the article under these two discount schemes if its marked price is ₹ 1000 ?

(a) 7.0 (b) 7.5
(c) 6.5 (d) 8.0

62. The given table shows the number of candidates who have appeared, qualified and been selected in an examination from two states A and B over the years 2001 to 2005.

Years	State A			State B		
	Applied	Qualified	Selected	Applied	Qualified	Selected
2001	8000	850	94	8200	680	85
2002	4800	500	48	6800	600	70
2003	7500	640	82	6500	525	65
2004	9500	850	90	7800	720	84
2005	9000	800	70	5700	485	60

In the year 2001, the percentage of candidates who were selected over the candidates who applied in State A is

(a) 1.165% (b) 1.175%
(c) 1.155% (d) 1.185%

63. What is the curved surface area of cylinder, whose radius is 3 cm and height is 14 cm? $\left(\text{Take } \pi = \frac{22}{7}\right)$
(a) 262 cm^2 (b) 264 cm^2
(c) 263 cm^2 (d) 261 cm^2

64. If two numbers are each divided by the same divisor, then the remainders are 6 and 7, respectively. If the sum of the two numbers be divided by the same divisor, then the remainder is 5. The divisor is
(a) 6 (b) 8
(c) 13 (d) 4

65. Last year, Ranjan's monthly salary was ₹ 34500 and this year his monthly salary is ₹ 38640. What is the percentage increase in Ranjan's monthly salary this year over his monthly salary last year?
(a) 15% (b) 12%
(c) 20% (d) 13%

66. Find the fourth proportional to 2, 6, 8.
(a) 12 (b) 48
(c) 36 (d) 24

67. 10 yr ago, a man's age was 5 times of his son's age. 2 yr hence, twice his age will be equal to 4 times the age of his son. What is the present age (in years) of the son?
(a) 20 (b) 16
(c) 18 (d) 14

68.

Completed
Implemented
Approval
Proposals
0 2 4 6 8 10
2015
2016
2017
2018

A company starts constructing buildings for a college. The constructions have 4 stages.
1. Buildings proposals
2. Proposals approval
3. Constructions implemented
4. Buildings completed
The above 3D-bar graph indicates the status of constructions for 4 yr 2015 to 2018.
The X-axis scale 0, 2, 4, 6, 8, 10 indicates 0, 20%, 40%, 60%, 80%, 100%.
Study the bar-graph carefully and answer the following question.
Find the total percentage of buildings completed during the total period, 2015 to 2018.
(a) 40% (b) 50%
(c) 30% (d) 60%

69. Find the area of a rhombus, whose diagonals are of lengths 10 cm and 8.2 cm.
(a) 43 cm^2 (b) 41 cm^2
(c) 40 cm^2 (d) 42 cm^2

70. The centers of two circles of radii 25 cm and 35 cm are 80 cm apart. What is the ratio of the lengths of the transverse common tangent to the direct common tangent to these circles?
(a) $2:3$ (b) $\sqrt{7}:3$
(c) $3\sqrt{7}:2$ (d) $2:\sqrt{7}$

71. In right triangle ABC with right angle at C, M is the mid-point of hypotenuse AB. C is joined to M and produced to a point D, such that $DM = CM$. Point D is joined to B. If $CD = 10$ cm and $BD = 6$ cm, find the value of CM.
(a) 8 cm (b) 5 cm
(c) 9.5 cm (d) 11.4 cm

72. The measures of the three angles of a triangle are such that the smallest angle measures 42° less than the greatest angle, while the measure of the remaining angle is 24° more than the measure of the smallest angle. Find the measure of the smallest angle of the triangle.
(a) 42° (b) 40°
(c) 38° (d) 36°

73. In a college, the average weight of 40 boys in a section among 72 students is 33 kg and that of the remaining students is 15 kg. What is the average weight of all the students in the section?
(a) 18 kg (b) 25 kg
(c) 24 kg (d) 22 kg

74. How much time (in years) will it take for an amount of ₹ 450000 to yield ₹ 45000 as simple interest at a 5% per annum rate of interest?
(a) 5 (b) 4
(c) 2 (d) 3

75. The cost of rice is increased by 25% but its consumption is decreased by 30%. Find the percentage increase or decrease in the expenditure of money.
(a) Increase $12\frac{1}{2}\%$
(b) Increase $13\frac{1}{3}\%$
(c) Decrease $12\frac{1}{2}\%$
(d) Decrease $13\frac{1}{3}\%$

Part IV
General Awareness

76. How many fundamental duties were recommended to be inserted in the Indian Constitution by the Swaran Singh Committee?
(a) 7 (b) 6 (c) 8 (d) 9

77. Parkash Singh Badal passed away in April 2023. He served as Chief Minister of .... for five times.
(a) Bihar
(b) Punjab
(c) Himachal Pradesh
(d) Haryana

78. Dussehra festival is celebrated in which of the following Hindu months?
(a) Chaitra (b) Ashwin
(c) Vaisakha (d) Ashadha

79. Which feature in MS Word allows you to see a document's layout and formatting as it will appear when printed?
(a) Draft View (b) Screen View
(c) Print Preview (d) Reading View

80. In whose ashram did the Beatles compose rock music in 1968 influenced by classical music?
(a) Maharshi Mahesh Yogi Ashram
(b) Osho Rajnish Ashram
(c) Pandit Ravishankar Ashram
(d) Maharshi Aurobindo Ashram

81. What is the standard weight of hammer for women in the hammer throw event?
(a) 6 kg (b) 8 kg
(c) 4 kg (d) 5 kg

82. Brihadiswara Temple of Tanjore was built by which of the following Chola emperors?
(a) Rajendra I
(b) Raja Raja Chola
(c) Vijayalaya
(d) Chamunda Raya

83. In which of the following years did the Constitution (One Hundredth Amendment) Act come into force?
(a) 2001 (b) 2020
(c) 2015 (d) 2009

84. On 12th September, 2002, ISRO launched the Kalpana-1 satellite using the Polar Satellite Launch Vehicle. What is the application of this satellite?
(a) Disaster Management System
(b) Climate and Environment Communication
(c) Earth Observation
(d) Planetary Observation

85. Which of the following writs in Latin means 'we command'?
(a) Prohibition (b) Habeas corpus
(c) Quo-warranto (d) Mandamus

86. What is the primary aim of Regional Rural Banks in India?
(a) Development of rural economy
(b) Development of urban economy
(c) Development of semi-urban economy
(d) Development of metropolitan economy

87. In which state is the Nanda Devi Biosphere Reserve located?
(a) Uttarakhand
(b) Himachal Pradesh
(c) Assam
(d) Odisha

88. Which was the first programmable general purpose computer in the world?
(a) Pascaline (b) Napier's bones
(c) ENIAC (d) Mark I

89. Which country's national game is Chinlone (Caneball)?
(a) Afghanistan (b) Bhutan
(c) China (d) Myanmar

90. Which Act was enacted by the British which regulated the manufacture, sale, possession and transport of firearms?
(a) Indian Arms Act, 1878
(b) The Arm Rules, 1839
(c) The Arms Act,1857
(d) The Firearms Act, 1871

91. Which classical dance was introduced by the great Vaishnava saint and reformer of Assam?
(a) Kuchipudi (b) Odissi
(c) Kathak (d) Sattriya

92. India hosted Men's Hockey World Cup in 2023 at
(a) Bhubaneshwar and Rourkela
(b) Patna and Gaya
(c) Nashik and Nagpur
(d) Amritsar and Bathinda

93. What does SAARC stand for?
(a) South Asian Association of Regional Cartography
(b) South Asian Association of Regional Cooperation
(c) South Asian Association of Regional Climate change
(d) South Asian Association of Regional Corporation

94. The Atal Tunnel has been built by Border Road Organisation at an altitude of 3000 metres. Which places are connected by this tunnel?
(a) Shimla to Ladakh
(b) Shimla to Srinagar
(c) Manali to Shimla
(d) Manali to Lahaul-Spiti

95. Which type of system did the leaders of independent India decide to adopt?
(a) A system that would promote the welfare of the government.
(b) A system that would promote the welfare of few rather than all.
(c) A system that would promote the welfare of all rather than a few.
(d) A system that would promote the welfare of private enterprises.

96. The 9th Men's ICC T20 World Cup Cricket 2024 will be hosted by which of the following countries?
(a) Canada and USA
(b) India and Sri Lanka
(c) West Indies and USA
(d) India and Bangladesh

97. In February 2023, PARAKH became the First National Assessment Regulator. What does 'R' stand for in PARAKH?
(a) Related
(b) Report
(c) Review
(d) Recall

98. In which year did Wilhelm Johannsen coin the term 'gene' to describe the Mendelian units of heredity?
(a) 1909 (b) 1900
(c) 1920 (d) 1910

99. Electrochemical cell is a device which converts chemical energy into electrical energy in a/an ....
(a) oxidation reaction
(b) reduction reaction
(c) direct redox reaction
(d) indirect redox reaction

100. In classical Carnatic music, tempo is called as ....
(a) Gita (b) Laya
(c) Achala (d) Padam

Answers

1. (c)	2. (a)	3. (d)	4. (b)
5. (d)	6. (d)	7. (d)	8. (b)
9. (b)	10. (d)	11. (d)	12. (d)
13. (c)	14 (a)	15. (c)	16. (c)
17. (a)	18. (b)	19. (a)	20. (c)
21. (b)	22. (a)	23. (d)	24. (a)
25. (b)	26. (a)	27. (b)	28. (d)
29. (a)	30. (c)	31. (b)	32. (a)
33. (d)	34. (d)	35. (c)	36. (b)
37. (a)	38. (a)	39. (d)	40. (c)
41. (a)	42. (c)	43. (a)	44. (a)
45. (d)	46. (a)	47. (b)	48. (d)
49. (a)	50. (b)	51. (c)	52. (b)
53. (a)	54. (d)	55. (a)	56. (d)
57. (b)	58. (c)	59. (d)	60. (d)
61. (b)	62. (b)	63. (b)	64. (b)
65. (b)	66. (d)	67. (d)	68. (b)
69. (b)	70. (a)	71. (b)	72. (c)
73. (b)	74. (c)	75. (c)	76. (c)
77. (b)	78. (b)	79. (c)	80. (a)
81. (c)	82. (b)	83. (c)	84. (b)
85. (d)	86. (a)	87. (a)	88. (c)
89. (d)	90. (a)	91. (d)	92. (a)
93. (b)	94. (d)	95. (c)	96. (c)
97. (c)	98. (a)	99. (c)	100. (b)

Explanations

1. *(c)* Part (c) 'for our Jobs and Careers Conference' contains an error. Use 'in' in place of 'for' to correct the sentence.

2. *(a)* The grammatically correct sentence is- Ragini plays the guitar melodiously.

3. *(d)* Part (A) 'I am hearing' contains an error. Use 'hear' to correct the sentence as the verbs of sense do not take the -ing form of the verb.

4. *(b)* The sentence in future tense is- I hope your health will get better by next week.

5. *(d)* The correct filler for the given blank is 'who'.

6. *(d)* The correct filler for the given blank is 'has'.

7. *(d)* The correct filler for the given blank is 'quite'.

8. *(b)* The correct filler for the given blank is 'commented'.

9. *(b)* The correct filler for the given blank is 'tells'.

10. *(d)* The word 'Lousy' means very poor or bad. Hence, its synonym is 'pitiful' which means the same.

11. *(d)* 'Agile' means active and energetic. Hence, its antonym is 'sluggish' which means lazy and slow.

'Apathetic' means uncaring and indifferent.

12. *(d)* The incorrectly spelt word is 'produsing'. The correct spelling is 'producing'.

13. *(c)* The underlined part of the given sentence contains an error. Use 'at' to mention the exact time and to correct the sentence.

14. *(a)* The underlined part of the given sentence contains an error. Use 'on the condition that she would return' to correct the sentence.

15. *(c)* The underlined part of the given sentence contains an error. Use 'plight' to correct the sentence.

16. *(c)* The underlined part of the given sentence contains an error. Use 'in lieu of playing' to correct the sentence.

17. *(a)* The incorrectly spelt word is 'peice'. The correct spelling is 'piece'.

18. *(b)* 'Juvenile' means for or relating to young people. Hence, its antonym is 'adult'.

'Puerile' means childishly silly and immature.

19. *(a)* The correct filler for the given blank is 'make'.

20. *(c)* 'Alluring' means attractive. Hence, its antonym is 'repulsive' which means to make someone dislike.

- 'Enticing' and 'Glamourous' mean attractive or appealing in an exotic or exciting way.
- 'Fascinating' means interesting.

21. *(b)* The word 'ascend' means to rise and climb.

22. *(a)* Left me in the lurch means to leave (someone) without help or protection when it is needed.

23. *(d)* Make up his mind to decide something.

24. *(a)* The antonym of 'Resourceful' means 'Incompetent' which means not useful.

- 'Ingenious' means (of a person) clever, original, and inventive.
- 'Immaculate' means clean and tidy.
- 'Impeccable' means flawless.

25. *(b)* The word 'Peculiar' means 'unusual and strange'.

26. *(a)* As, (3, 12, 26)

$\Rightarrow \quad 12 \times 3 - 10 = 36 - 10 = 26$

and (7, 9, 53)

$\Rightarrow \quad 7 \times 9 - 10 = 63 - 10 = 53$

Similarly, (7, 5, 25)

$\Rightarrow \quad 7 \times 5 - 10 = 35 - 10 = 25$

27. *(b)* When we unfolded the paper, then it will appear as the figure given in option (b).

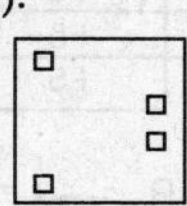

28. *(d)* The option figure (d) is embedded in the given question figure.

29. *(a)* Given expression,

$17 \times 7 + (21 \div 3) \times 5 - 28 + 34 = 72$

From option (a),

After interchanging number 7 and 3, we get,

$17 \times 3 + (21 \div 7) \times 5 - 28 + 34 = 72$

$\Rightarrow \quad 51 + 3 \times 5 - 28 + 34 = 72$

$\Rightarrow \quad 51 + 15 - 28 + 34 = 72$

$\Rightarrow \quad 100 - 28 = 72$

$\Rightarrow \quad 72 = 72$

30. *(c)* Naming the figure,

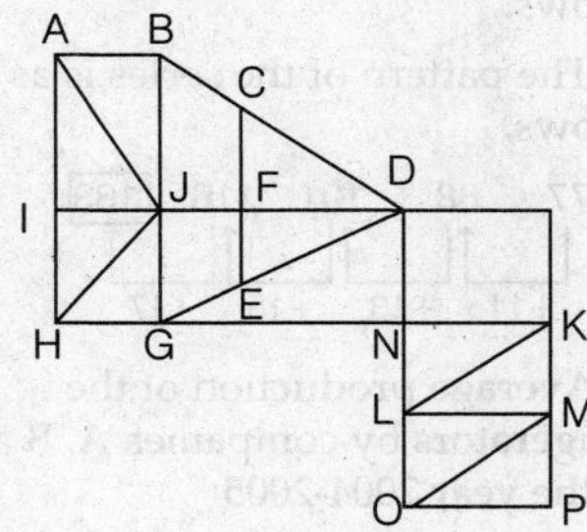

ΔAJB, ΔAJI, ΔIJH, ΔJGH, ΔAJH, ΔCDF, ΔFDE, ΔCDE, ΔBDJ, ΔJDG, ΔBDG, ΔNKL, ΔKLM, ΔLMO, ΔMPO and ΔDNG.

Hence, there are 16 triangles in the given figure.

31. *(b)* Given expression,

16 B 8 D 51 A 3 C 57

After substituting letters with signs, we get

A → ÷	B → ×
C → +	D → −

$= 16 \times 8 - 51 \div 3 + 57$

$= 128 - 17 + 57 = 185 - 17 = 168$

32. *(a)* The given question figure is embedded in option figure (a).

33. *(d)* The pattern of the series is as follows,

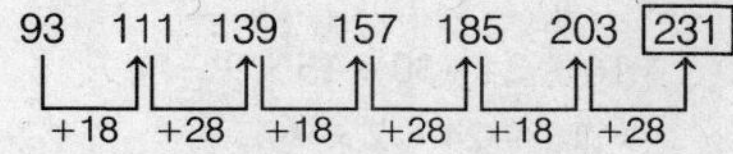

34. *(d)* According to the question,

hands are dirty ⟶ ca bx vp

dirty things flies ⟶ by vp cb

Hence, the code for dirty is vp.

35. *(c)* As, $11 \xrightarrow{(11)^2} 121$

and $21 \xrightarrow{(21)^2} 441$

Similarly, $31 \xrightarrow{(31)^2} \boxed{961}$

36. *(b)* The given question figure is embedded in option figure (b).

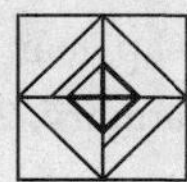

37. *(a)* According to the question,

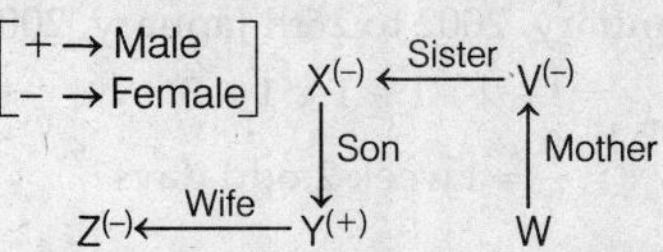

Hence, Z is mother's sister's son's wife to W.

38. *(a)* The given question figure is embedded in the option figure (a).

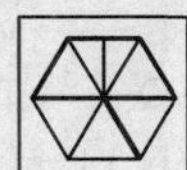

39. *(d)* There are two alternate series in the given question, which are as follows,

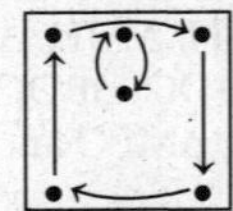
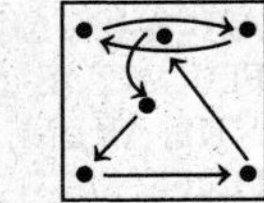

From figure (1) to (2) (3) to (4) From figure (2) to (3) (4) to (5)

Hence, option figure (d) will replace the question mark.

40. *(c)* As,

B $\xrightarrow{+3}$ E $\xrightarrow{+3}$ H

N $\xrightarrow{+3}$ Q $\xrightarrow{+3}$ T

R $\xrightarrow{+3}$ U $\xrightarrow{+3}$ X

But, K $\xrightarrow{+2}$ M $\xrightarrow{+3}$ P

Hence, 'KMP' is the odd one.

41. *(a)* Given expression,
16 A 24 C 30 E 15 U 9

After substituting letters with signs, we get

E → ÷	U → ×
A → +	C → −

$16 + 24 - 30 \div 15 \times 9$

$= 16 + 24 - 2 \times 9$

$= 16 + 24 - 18$

$= 40 - 18 = 22$

42. *(c)* As, and

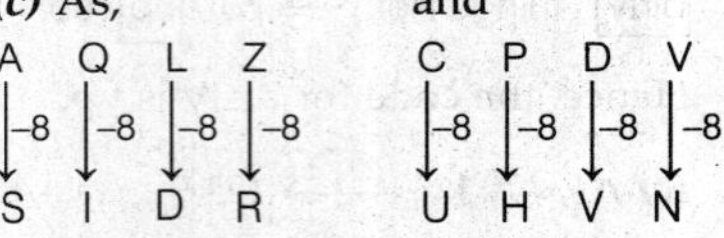

Similarly, E B R Y
−8 −8 −8 −8
W T J Q

43. *(a)* Odd days in ordinary year = 1

Odd days in leap year = 2

Day on 23rd January, 2002
= Wednesday

Number of odd days from 23rd January, 2002 to 26th January, 2007.

$= 1 + 2 + 1 + 1 + 1 + 3$

$= \frac{9}{7} = 1$ week 2 odd days

∴ The day of the week on 26th January, 2007 = Wednesday + 2 = Friday

44. *(a)* The pattern of the series is as follows,

M $\xrightarrow{+3}$ P $\xrightarrow{+3}$ S $\xrightarrow{+3}$ V $\xrightarrow{+3}$ Y

K $\xrightarrow{+3}$ N $\xrightarrow{+3}$ Q $\xrightarrow{+3}$ T $\xrightarrow{+3}$ W

H $\xrightarrow{+3}$ K $\xrightarrow{+3}$ N $\xrightarrow{+3}$ Q $\xrightarrow{+3}$ T

45. *(d)* Odd days in ordinary year = 1

Odd days in leap year = 2

Day on 26th November, 2013
= Tuesday

Number of odd days from 26th November, 2013 to 29th November, 2018

$= 1 + 1 + 2 + 1 + 1 + 3$

$= \frac{9}{7} = 1$ week 2 odd days

∴ The day of the week on 29th November, 2018 = Tuesday + 2
= Thursday

46. *(a)* The pattern of the series is as follows,

U $\xrightarrow{+1}$ V $\xrightarrow{+1}$ W $\xrightarrow{+1}$ X $\xrightarrow{+1}$ Y

T $\xrightarrow{-2}$ R $\xrightarrow{-2}$ P $\xrightarrow{-2}$ N $\xrightarrow{-2}$ L

H $\xrightarrow{+3}$ K $\xrightarrow{+3}$ N $\xrightarrow{+3}$ Q $\xrightarrow{+3}$ T

S $\xrightarrow{-4}$ O $\xrightarrow{-4}$ K $\xrightarrow{-4}$ G $\xrightarrow{-4}$ C

47. *(b)* The pattern of the series is as follows,

77 79 83 89 97 107

+2 +4 +6 +8 +10

48. *(d)* As, F J K ⟶ K O P
+5 +5 +5

and M Q R ⟶ R V W
+5 +5 +5

Similarly,

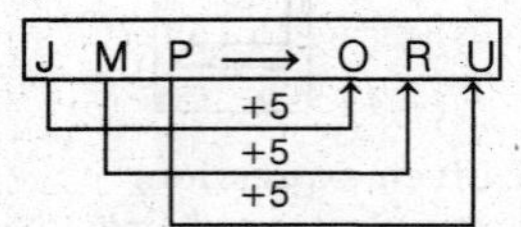

49. *(a)* According to the statements,

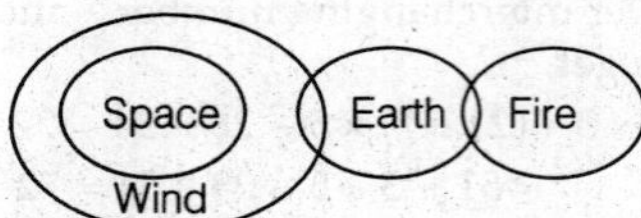

Conclusions

I. (✗) II. (✗)

Hence, neither Conclusion I nor II follows.

50. *(b)* The pattern of the series is as follows,

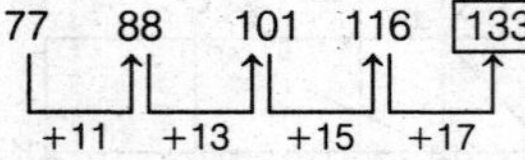

51. *(c)* Average production of the refrigerators by companies A, B and E for the year 2004-2005

$= \frac{110 + 160 + 300}{3}$

$= \frac{570}{3} = 190$

Average production of the refrigerators by Companies C and D for the year 2005-2006

$= \frac{370 + 490}{2} = \frac{860}{2}$

$= 430$

∴ Required ratio = 190 : 430 = 19 : 43

52. *(b)* Let the speed of Arun = S_A

Speed of Bhaskar = S_B

According to the question,

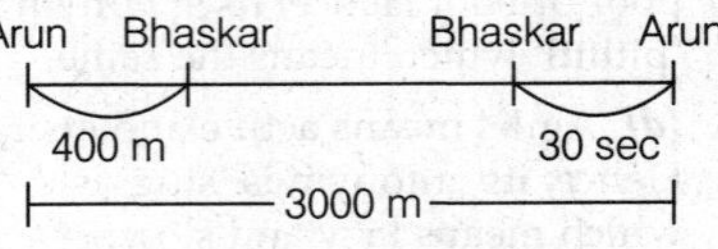

By first condition,

$\frac{3000}{S_A} = \frac{2600}{S_B} - 30$

$\frac{3000}{S_A} = \frac{2600 - 30S_B}{S_B}$ ...(i)

By second condition,

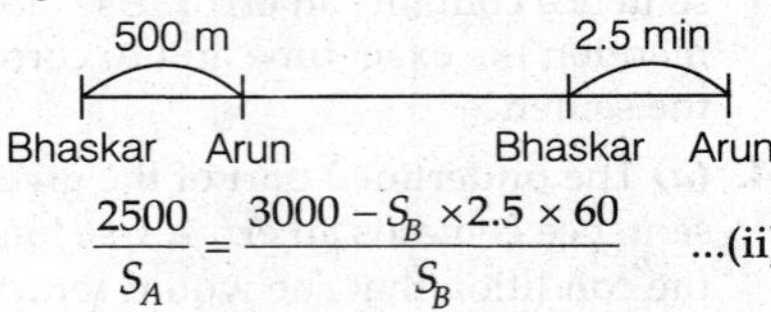

$\frac{2500}{S_A} = \frac{3000 - S_B \times 2.5 \times 60}{S_B}$ ...(ii)

By Eqs. (i) and (ii),

$\frac{6}{5} = \frac{2600 - 30S_B}{3000 - 150S_B} = \frac{260 - 3S_B}{300 - 15S_B}$

$\Rightarrow 1800 - 90S_B = 1300 - 15S_B$

$\Rightarrow S_B = \frac{500}{75} = \frac{20}{3}$

By Eq. (i), $S_A = \frac{25}{3}$

$\therefore \quad t_A = \frac{3000}{\frac{25}{3}} = \frac{3000 \times 3}{25} = 360$ sec

$t_B = \frac{3000}{\frac{20}{3}} = \frac{3000 \times 3}{20} = 450$ sec

∴ Required difference = 450 − 360
= 90 sec = 1.5 min

53. *(a)* According to the question,

$10 + 3\frac{3}{5} \div \left[2\frac{2}{3} \div \left\{7\frac{1}{6} - \left(2\frac{1}{2} + \frac{2}{3}\right)\right\}\right]$

$= 10 + \frac{18}{5} \div \left[\frac{8}{3} \div \left\{\frac{43}{6} - \left(\frac{5}{2} + \frac{2}{3}\right)\right\}\right]$

$= 10 + \frac{18}{5} \div \left[\frac{8}{3} \div \left\{\frac{43}{6} - \left(\frac{15 + 4}{6}\right)\right\}\right]$

$= 10 + \frac{18}{5} \div \left[\frac{8}{3} \div \left\{\frac{43}{6} - \frac{19}{6}\right\}\right]$

$= 10 + \frac{18}{5} \div \left[\frac{8}{3} \div \left\{\frac{24}{6}\right\}\right]$

$= 10 + \frac{18}{5} \div \left[\frac{8}{3} \times \frac{6}{24}\right]$

$= 10 + \frac{18}{5} \div \frac{2}{3} = 10 + \frac{18}{5} \times \frac{3}{2}$

$= 10 + \frac{27}{5} = \frac{77}{5}$

54. **(d)** According to the question,

A completes work in 20 days.

B completes work in 10 days.

$A + B + C$ completes work in 5 days

Total number of work

$= 40$ [LCM of 20, 10, 5]

Efficiency of 1 day work

$A \rightarrow 20 \rightarrow 2$

$B \rightarrow 10 \rightarrow 4$

$A + B + C \rightarrow 5 \rightarrow 8$

$\therefore \quad (A + B + C) = 8$

$\Rightarrow \quad 2 + 4 + C = 8$

$\Rightarrow \quad C = 8 - 6$

$\Rightarrow \quad C = 2$

$\therefore$ C alone can complete the work in

$= \frac{40}{2} = 20$ days

55. **(a)** Let radius of sphere $= x$

Radius of sphere is increased by 25%.

$\therefore$ Required per cent

$= \left(x + x + \frac{x \times x}{100}\right)$

$= \left(25 + 25 + \frac{25 \times 25}{100}\right) = 56.25\%$

56. **(d)** According to the question,

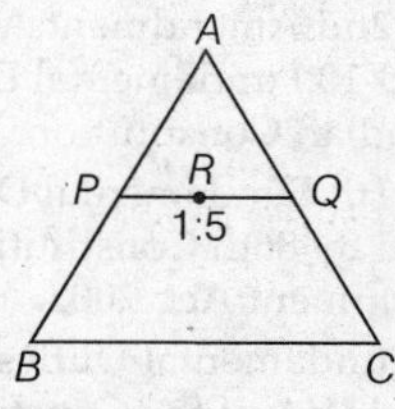

$PR : RQ = 1 : 5 = x : 5x$

and $\quad x = 6$ cm

$\therefore \quad 6x = 6 \times 6 = 36$ cm

$\therefore \quad PQ = 36$ cm

Now, $\quad BC = 2 \times PQ$

$= 2 \times 36 = 72$ cm

$\left[PQ = \frac{BC}{2}\right]$

57. **(b)** $\frac{1}{\sin^4(90° - 2\alpha)} + \frac{1}{\cos^2(90° - 2\alpha) - 1}$

$= \frac{1}{\cos^4 2\alpha} + \frac{1}{\sin^2 2\alpha - 1}$

$= \frac{1}{\cos^4 2\alpha} - \frac{1}{1 - \sin^2 2\alpha}$

$= \frac{1}{\cos^4 2\alpha} - \frac{1}{\cos^2 2\alpha}$

$= \frac{1}{\cos^2 2\alpha}\left(\frac{1}{\cos^2 2\alpha} - 1\right)$

$= \frac{1}{\cos^2 2\alpha} \frac{(1 - \cos^2 2\alpha)}{\cos^2 2\alpha}$

$= \frac{1}{\cos^2 \alpha} \times \frac{\sin^2 2\alpha}{\cos^2 2\alpha}$

$= \sec^2 2\alpha \times \tan^2 2\alpha$

58. **(c)** Let cost price = ₹ x

According to the question,

$x \times \frac{(100 + 25)}{100} \times \frac{(100 - 10)}{100} = 540$

$\Rightarrow x \times \frac{125}{100} \times \frac{90}{100} = 540$

$\Rightarrow x = \frac{540 \times 100 \times 100}{125 \times 90}$

$\therefore x = 480$

$\therefore$ Cost price = ₹ 480

59. **(d)** According to the question,

Average sale of Product A

$= \frac{2750 + 2500 + 3500}{3}$

= ₹ 2916.6

Average sale of Product B

$= \frac{3250 + 3000 + 3150}{3} =$ ₹ 3133.33

Average sale of Product C

$= \frac{2250 + 1750 + 2400}{3} =$ ₹ 2133.33

$\therefore$ Clearly, Product B has the highest average sale per company.

Average sale per product by Company

$X = \frac{2750 + 3250 + 2250}{3}$

$= \frac{8250}{3} =$ ₹ 2750

Average sale per product by Company

$Y = \frac{2500 + 3000 + 1750}{3}$

$= \frac{7250}{3} =$ ₹ 2416.66

Average sale per product by Company

$Z = \frac{3500 + 3150 + 2400}{3}$

$= \frac{9050}{3} =$ ₹ 3016.66

$\therefore$ Clearly, Company Y has the lowest average sale per product.

60. **(d)** Let income be ₹ 100.

$\therefore$ Expenditure = ₹ 70

Savings = ₹ 30

New income = ₹ 115

New expenditure

$= 70 \times \frac{107.5}{100} =$ ₹ 75.25

$\therefore$ Savings = ₹ 39.75

$\therefore$ Increase percentage in savings

$= \frac{(39.75 - 30)}{30} \times 100$

$= \frac{9.75 \times 100}{30} = 32.5\%$

61. **(b)** According to the question,

(i) Successive discount

$= \left(25 + 5 + \frac{25 \times 5}{100}\right) = 31.25\%$

(ii) Successive discount

$= \left(20 + 10 + \frac{20 \times 10}{100}\right) = 32\%$

Difference $= (32 - 31.25)\% = 0.75\%$

$\therefore$ Required difference

$= 1000 \times \frac{0.75}{100} =$ ₹ 7.5

62. **(b)** According to the question,

Percentage of candidates, who were selected over the candidates who applied in State A.

$= \frac{94}{8000} \times 100 = 1.175\%$

63. **(b)** According to the question,

Radius of cylinder = 3 cm

Height = 14 cm

$\therefore$ Curved surface area of cylinder

$= 2 \times \frac{22}{7} \times 3 \times 14 = 264$ cm^2

64. **(b)** Let divisor be x and numbers are y and z.

Then, $\quad y = x \times n + 6 \quad$ ...(i)

$z = x \times m + 7 \quad$ ...(ii)

$\therefore (y + z) = (x \times n + x \times m + 6 + 7)$

Now, $\frac{(y + z)}{x} = \frac{(x \times n + x \times m + 13)}{x}$

$= \frac{13}{x}$

$\therefore$ Remainder = 5

$\therefore$ Divisor = 8

65. **(b)** According to the question,

Last year, Ranjan's monthly salary

= ₹ 34500

This year Ranjan's monthly salary

$= ₹ 38640$

Hence, required increase percentage

$= \frac{(38640 - 34500)}{34500} \times 100$

$= \frac{4140}{34500} \times 100$

$= 12\%$

66. *(d)* Let 2, 6, 8, *a* are in proportion.

$\therefore \frac{2}{6} = \frac{8}{a}$

$a = \frac{8 \times 6}{2} = 24$

67. *(d)* Let the present age of man = *y* yr and the present age of son = *x* yr

According to the question,

10 yr ago,

$y - 10 = 5(x - 10)$

$y - 10 = 5x - 50$

$y - 5x + 40 = 0$

$5x - y = 40$ ...(i)

2 yr hence,

$2(y + 2) = 4(x + 2)$

$y + 2 = 2x + 4$

$y - 2x = 2$ ...(ii)

From Eqs. (i) and (ii),

$5x - y = 40$

$-2x + y = 2$

$3x = 42$

$x = 14$

Hence, present age of the son = 14 yr

68. *(b)* From the bar-graph,

The total percentage of buildings completed during the total period of 2015 to 2018 is 50%.

69. *(b)* Diagonals of rhombus,

$AC = 10$ cm

$BD = 8.2$ cm

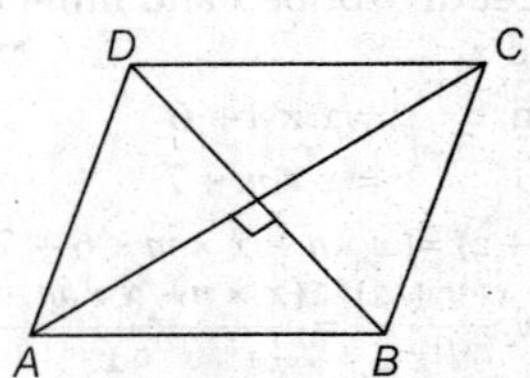

Now, area of rhombus

$= \frac{1}{2} \times AC \times BD$

$= \frac{1}{2} \times 10 \times 8.2 \text{ cm}^2$

$= 41 \text{ cm}^2$

70. *(a)* According to the question,

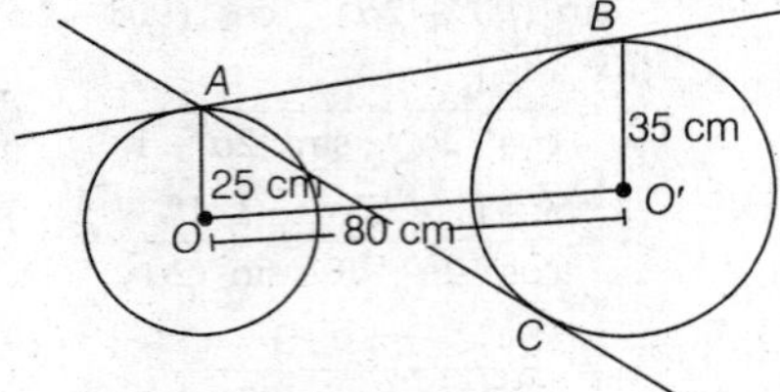

Length of $AB = \sqrt{(OO')^2 - (OB - OA)^2}$

$= \sqrt{(80)^2 - (35 - 25)^2}$

$= \sqrt{6400 - 100}$

$= \sqrt{6300}$ cm ...(i)

Length of $AC = \sqrt{(OO')^2 - (OB + OA)^2}$

$= \sqrt{(80)^2 - (35 + 25)^2}$

$= \sqrt{6400 - 3600}$

$= \sqrt{2800}$

Now, $\frac{AC}{AB} = \frac{\sqrt{2800}}{\sqrt{6300}} = \frac{10 \times 2\sqrt{7}}{10 \times 3\sqrt{7}} = \frac{2}{3}$

$\therefore \frac{\text{Transverse common tangent}}{\text{Direct common tangent}} = \frac{2}{3}$

$= 2 : 3$

71. *(b)* According to the question,

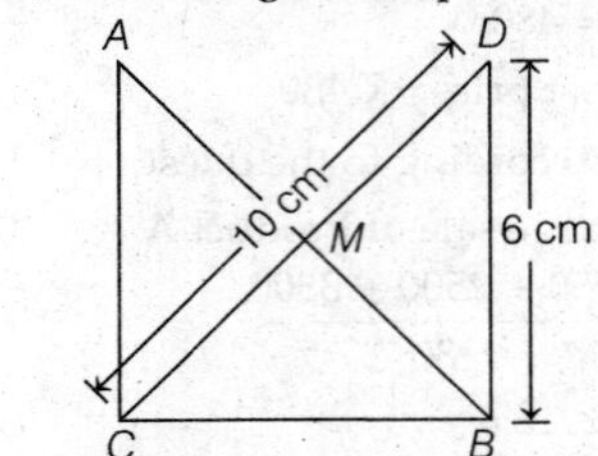

$\because CD = 10$ cm

$\therefore CM + MD = 10$ cm

$CM + CM = 10$ cm $[\because CM = MD]$

$\Rightarrow 2CM = 10$ cm

$CM = 5$ cm

72. *(c)* Let the smallest angle $= x°$

$\therefore$ The greatest angle $= x° + 42°$

Third angle $= x° + 24°$

Now, sum of all angles in triangle $= 180°$

$x + x + 42° + x + 24° = 180°$

$\Rightarrow 3x = 180° - 66° = 114$

$x = 38°$

$\therefore$ The smallest angle $= 38°$

73. *(b)* Average weight of 40 boys = 33 kg

Total weight of 40 boys = 40×33 kg = 1320 kg

$\therefore$ Average weight of 32 boys = 15 kg

Total weight of 32 boys = 15×32 kg = 480 kg

$\therefore$ Average age of all students

$= \frac{(1320 + 480)}{72}$ kg

$= \frac{1800}{72}$ kg $= 25$ kg

74. *(c)* According to the question,

Principal = ₹ 450000

$R = 5\%$

SI = ₹ 45000

$T = ?$

$\therefore \text{Time} = \frac{\text{SI} \times 100}{P \times R}$

$= \frac{45000 \times 100}{450000 \times 5}$

$= 2$ yr

75. *(c)* According to the question,

Cost of rice increase by 25%.

Consumption is decreased by 30%.

$x = 25\%$ increase

$y = 30\%$ decrease

$\therefore$ Required per cent $= \left(x + y + \frac{x \times y}{100}\right)$

$= \left(25 - 30 + \frac{25 \times (-30)}{100}\right)$

$= (-5 - 7.5)\%$

$= -12.5\% = -12\frac{1}{2}\%$

Hence, there is an decrease of $12\frac{1}{2}\%$ in the expenditure of money.

76. *(c)* The Swaran Singh Committee recommended of adding about eight Fundamental Duties in the Indian Constitution, however later on at the time of addition, ten duties were added.

- The 42nd Amendment Act of 1976 added 10 Fundamental Duties to the Indian Constitution.
- The 11th Fundamental Duty was added by 86th Constitutional Amendment Act, 2002.
- The Fundamental Duties are listed in Part IVA of the Constitution.

77. *(b)* Parkash Singh Badal served as Chief Minister of Punjab for five times.

- He was chief of political party Shiromani Akali Dal.
- Badal first became Chief Minister of Punjab in March 1970.
- Bhagwant Singh Mann (AAP) is Chief Minister of Punjab since 2022.

78. *(b)* Dussehra festival is celebrated in Hindu month Ashwin.

- It's also called Kunwaar month in Eastern Uttar Pradesh and Western Bihar state.
- It is the seventh month of Hindu calender which falls in September and October.
- The other important festivals in Ashwin month are Indira Ekadashi, Saraswati puja, Durga Ashtami, Maha Navami, Sharad Purnima, Upang Lalita Vrat, and Kojagara Puja.

79. *(c)* Print Preview in MS Word allows you to see the document's layout and formatting as it will appear when printed.

Check margins, page breaks and formatting before printing.

80. *(a)* In Maharshi Mahesh Yogi Ashram the Beatles compose rock music in 1968 influenced by classical music.

- Maharshi Mahesh Yogi was the creator of Transcendental Meditation.
- He was well known for his association with the rock band 'The Beach Boys and The Beatles'.
- He was a disciple of Swami Brahmananda Saraswati.

81. *(c)* The standard weight of hammer for women in the hammer throw event is 4 kg.

- The hammer throw is a track and field event where athletes compete by throwing a hammer, which is a metal ball that's attached to a grip by a steel wire.
- The first women's hammer throw event took place in 2000 at the Sydney Games.

82. *(b)* Brihadiswara Temple of Tanjore was built by Raja Raja Chola.

- It is dedicated to the Lord Shiva.
- It is the largest temple in the Southern India.
- It is in the list of UNESCO World Heritage Site.

83. *(c)* In year 2015, the One Hundredth Constitutional Amendment Act came into force.

- It gave effect to the acquiring of 51 territories by India and transfer of 3 territories to Bangladesh.
- This act amended the First Schedule of Indian Constitution.

84. *(b)* The application of Kalpana-1 satellite was Climate and Environment Communication.

- This was the first satellite launched by the PSLV (Polar Satellite Launch Vehicle) into the Geo-stationary orbit.
- The satellite was originally known as MetSat-1 but it was renamed to Kalpana-1 by the Indian Prime Minister Atal Bihari Vajpayee in memory of Kalpana Chawla.

85. *(d)* The word 'Mandamus' means 'We command' in Latin.

- Article 32 of Indian constitution provides five types of writs to Supreme Court. These are
- **Habeas Corpus** The Latin meaning of the word 'Habeas Corpus' is 'To have the body of '.
- **Mandamus** The literal meaning of this writ is 'We command.'
- **Prohibition** The meaning of 'Prohibition' is 'To forbid.'
- **Certiorari** The meaning of the writ of 'Certiorari' is 'To be certified' or 'To be informed.'
- **Quo-Warranto** The meaning of the writ of 'Quo-Warranto' is 'By what authority or warrant.'

86. *(a)* The primary aim of Regional Rural Banks in India is development of rural economy.

- The Regional Rural Banks (RRBs) were established in 1975 under the Regional Rural Banks Act, 1976.
- Regional Rural Banks (RRBS) are government-owned scheduled commercial banks of India.
- RRBS are financial institutions which ensure adequate credit for agriculture and other rural sectors.

87. *(a)* Nanda Devi Biosphere Reserve is located in Uttarakhand.

- Nanda Devi Biosphere Reserve is a UNESCO recognised biosphere reserve under Man and Biosphere Programme.
- Nanda Devi Biosphere Reserve is spread across three districts of Uttarakhand *viz.* Chamoli, Pithoragarh and Bageshwar.
- The biosphere reserve has significant populations of globally threatened species like the snow leopard, the Himalayan musk deer.

88. *(c)* ENIAC was the first programmable general purpose computer in the world.

89. *(d)* Chinlone (Caneball) is national game of Myanmar.

- It is a non-competitive sport played typically in six people team.
- The ball used in the sport is made from handwoven rattan that sounds like a basket when hit.

90. *(a)* The Indian Arms Act, 1878 was enacted by the British which regulated the manufacture, sale, possession and transport of firearms.

- According to the act, an Indian carrying arms without a license would be declared a 'criminal offender'.
- The penalty was a monetary fine or three years in prison up to a maximum of 7 years, or both.
- The Arms Act mandated that for any Indian wishing to own a gun, a license was essential.

91. *(d)* Sattriya dance was introduced by the great Vaishnava saint and reformer of Assam Mahapurusha Sankaradeva.

- Sattriya dance tradition is governed by strictly laid down principles in respect of hasta mudras, footwork, aharyas, music, etc.
- Sattriya dance is traditionally performed by male monks.
- Sattriya dance was known by many names such as Nadu Bhangi, Jhumura Naach, Chali-Nach, Behar Nach, Sutradhari, Gosain Pravesh, Gopi Pravesh, Ojapali Nach.

92. *(a)* India hosted Men's Hockey World Cup in 2023 at Bhubaneshwar and Rourkela.

- India hosted the Hockey world cup fourth time in history.
- The Hockey World Cup conducted once every four years.
- India won the Hockey World Cup only once in 1975.

93. *(b)* SAARC stands for South Asian Association for Regional Cooperation.

- SAARC comprises of eight member states: Afghanistan, Bangladesh, Bhutan, India, Maldives, Nepal, Pakistan and Sri Lanka.
- The Secretariat of the association was set-up in Kathmandu, Nepal.

- Afghanistan became the newest member of SAARC at the 13th annual summit in 2005.

94. *(d)* The Atal Tunnel connects Manali to Lahaul-Spiti valley.
- It is the longest highway tunnel in the world above the height of 3,000 metres.
- It was built by the Border roads Organisation (BRO).
- It is present on the Pir Panjal Range of Himalayas.

95. *(c)* The leaders of independent India decide to adopt system that would promote the welfare of all rather than a few.
- The Directive Principles of State Policy enshrined in Part IV of the Indian Constitution reflects that India is a welfare state.

The Welfare State
- It provides basic minimum services to its citizens like law and order.
- It has a multi-party democratic system.
- It has a mixed economy.

96. *(c)* The 9th Men's ICC T20 World Cup Cricket 2024 was held in West Indies and USA.
- India became the world champion after defeating South Africa in the final.
- India and Sri Lanka will jointly host the 10th edition of the T20 World Cup in 2026.

97. *(c)* In PARAKH, 'R' stands for 'Review'. The full form of PARAKH is Performance Assessment, Review, and Analysis of Knowledge for Holistic Development.
- It is launched as part of the implementation of the National Education Policy (NEP) 2020.
- It will act as a constituent unit of the NCERT.
- It is tasked with holding periodic learning outcome tests like the National Achievement Survey (NAS) and State Achievement Surveys.

98. *(a)* Wilhelm Johannsen coined the term 'gene' in 1909 to describe the Mendelian units of heredity. Johannsen was a Danish botanist and pharmacologist who investigated plant seed size.

99. *(c)* Electrochemical cell is a device which converts chemical energy into electrical energy in direct redox reaction.

100. *(b)* In classical Carnatic music, tempo is called as Laya.
- It owes its name to the Sanskrit term Karnâtaka Sangitam which denotes 'traditional' or 'codified' music.
- It has developed in the South Indian states of Tamil Nadu, Kerala, Andhra Pradesh and Karnataka. It is composed of a system of Ragam (Raga) and Thalam (Tala).

Set 15 04 July, 2024 (Shift III)

SSC CHSL Tier-I SOLVED PAPER

Instructions

1. This paper contains 100 questions.
2. It has 4 Parts, **Part I** General English, **Part II** General Intelligence & Reasoning, **Part III** Quantitative Aptitude and **Part IV** General Awareness.
3. Each question carries **2 marks.**

Part I
General English

1. The following sentence has been split into four segments. Identify the segment that contains a grammatical error.
This artwork / are a wonderful example / of the period's vogue / for realistic style.
(a) This artwork
(b) of the period's vogue
(c) for realistic style
(d) are a wonderful example

2. The following sentence has been divided into four parts. Identify the part that contains an error.
Pratigya arrived / to the / railway station / five hours early.
(a) railway station
(b) Pratigya arrived
(c) to the
(d) five hours early

3. Identify the error in the following sentence and select the option with the correct use of the phrasal verb.
Prateek was planning to ask Shreya for a favour. But he could not muster up the courage. So, he blacked out.
(a) Prateek was planning to ask Shreya for a favour. But he could not muster up the courage. So, he broke in.
(b) Prateek was planning to ask Shreya for a favour. But he could not muster up the courage. So, he chickened out.
(c) Prateek was planning to ask Shreya for a favour. But he could not muster up the courage. So, he checked out.
(d) Prateek was planning to ask Shreya for a favour. But he could not muster up the courage. So, he turned down.

4. The following sentence has been split into four segments. Identify the segment that contains a grammatical error.
The companies were / giving in the prizes / to attract customers / during the festive season.
(a) The companies were
(b) giving in the prizes
(c) during the festive season
(d) to attract customers

Directions (Q. Nos. 5-9) *In the following passage, some words have been deleted. Read the passage carefully and select the most appropriate option to fill in each blank.*

Famines were (1) ……… during the period of British rule due to many reasons (2) ……… unemployment following import of machine-made goods from Britain, overexploitation of farmers and (3) ……… access to food. India suffered two very severe droughts in 1965 and 1966. India achieved (4) ……… in food grains by the year 1976 through the implementation of the seedwater- fertiliser-led (5) ……… . The country is no longer exposed to real famines. However, lack of purchasing power continues to haunt people in some parts of the country.

5. Select the most appropriate option to fill in blank number (1).
(a) caused (b) excruciated
(c) paused (d) discouraged

6. Select the most appropriate option to fill in blank number (2).
(a) excluding large-scale
(b) excluding small-scale
(c) including small-scale
(d) including large-scale

7. Select the most appropriate option to fill in blank number (3).
(a) basic (b) restricted
(c) unlimited (d) inflated

8. Select the most appropriate option to fill in blank number (4).
(a) goal (b) incompetency
(c) success (d) self-sufficiency

9. Select the most appropriate option to fill in blank number (5).
(a) Blue Revolution
(b) Pink Revolution
(c) Green Revolution
(d) White Revolution

10. Read the sentence carefully and select the most appropriate option to substitute the underlined part.
The revolt of the labourers will be considered as an <u>epoch</u> in the world history.
(a) unpopular measure
(b) hostile event
(c) important period
(d) commendable act

11. Read the given sentence carefully. Change the meaning of the sentence by replacing the underlined word with its antonym from the following options.
I have keen interest in reading the mind of those students who are <u>boisterous</u> at home but on their best behaviour at school.
(a) clamorous
(b) frothing
(c) placid
(d) raucous

12. Choose the option that best describes the meaning of the idiom and phrase underlined in the given sentence.
You can best identify the <u>fair weather friends</u> at the time of adversity.
(a) Friends who come in good weather conditions
(b) Best friends
(c) Friends who bring good rain
(d) Friend only at the time of prosperity

13. Select the most appropriate meaning of the underlined idiom in the following sentence.
I can't begin to talk on this situation right now; I am still wrapping my head around it.
(a) Ignoring something completely
(b) Understanding something complicated
(c) Comparing two things that can't be compared
(d) Revealing a secret nobody knows

14. There is a spelling error in the given sentence. Select the option that contains the incorrectly spelt word.
The mighty gaint brought a marigold for the princess.
(a) gaint (b) princess
(c) marigold (d) mighty

15. Identify the incorrectly spelt word and select its correct spelling.
The calandar was reformed during the time of Julius Caesar.
(a) reeformed
(b) celender
(c) riformed
(d) calendar

16. Select the most appropriate synonym of the given word.
Fertile
(a) Productive (b) Destructive
(c) Hectic (d) Amusing

17. Select the most appropriate option that can substitute the underlined segment in the given sentence.
Many a women work for the betterment of their family.
(a) Many a woman worked for
(b) Many a women working for
(c) Many a woman works for
(d) Many a women works for

18. Select the most appropriate antonym of the underlined word in the sentence.
He purchased very cheap dresses.
(a) expensive (b) doltish
(c) lively (d) paltry

19. Select the most appropriate option that can substitute the underlined segment in the given sentence.
He is almost quiet well.
(a) almost quietly
(b) quiet
(c) very quite
(d) quite

20. Complete the given sentence with an appropriate homophone from the given options.
It is better to focus on your .... than to wander aimlessly.
(a) carrier (b) courier
(c) career (d) carreer

21. Select the most appropriate option to correct the sentence by using meaning of the undelined word.
In the winter season, the poor woman needed a refuge where she could live freely and independently.
(a) school (b) shelter
(c) inn (d) tent

22. The balloon started to deflate after being pricked with a needle. What is the antonym of 'deflate'?
(a) flatten (b) compress
(c) inflate (d) shrink

23. Select the most appropriate synonym of the given word.
Affirm
(a) Confirm (b) Convey
(c) Correlate (d) Deliver

24. Select the most appropriate homophone to fill in the blank.
The mechanics tried a lot to get that car .... from the accident spot.
(a) told (b) towed
(c) toed (d) toad

25. Select the most appropriate option that can substitute the underlined word segment in the following sentence.
It is a high-pay job.
(a) high-paying (b) low-paid
(c) high-paid (d) low-pay

Part II
General Intelligence

26. What would be the symbol on the opposite side of '≤', if the given sheet is folded to form a cube?

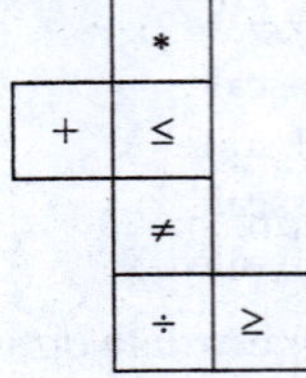

(a) ÷ (b) ≥
(c) + (d) *

27. What should come in place of the question mark (?) in the given series?
15, 30, 90, 360, 1800, ?
(a) 11000 (b) 12000
(c) 14000 (d) 10800

28. Select the option figure in which the given figure is embedded as its part (rotation is not allowed).

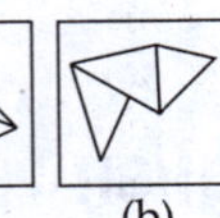
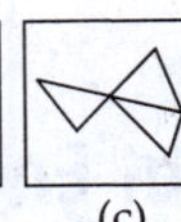
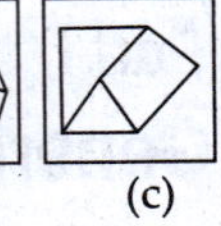

(a) (b) (c) (c)

29. Identify the figure given in the options which when put in place of (?) will logically complete the pattern.

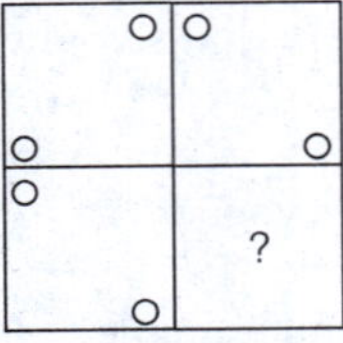

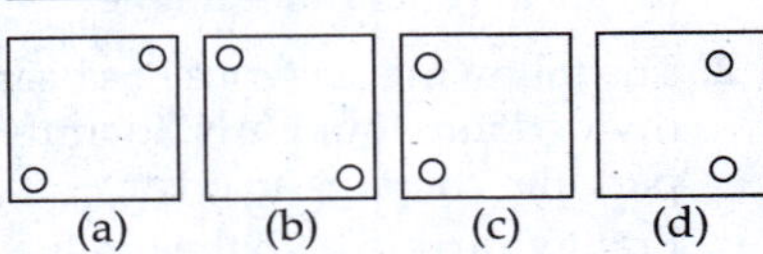

(a) (b) (c) (d)

30. If 'W' stands for '÷', 'Y' stands for '×' 'Z' stands for '+' and 'A' stands for '–', what will come in place of the question mark (?) in the following equation?
11 W 11 Y 11 Z 11 A 11 = ?
(a) 21 (b) 42
(c) 11 (d) 22

31. In a certain code language, 'cold summers day' is written as 'kl bn ix' and 'day and night' is written as 'kj ed bn'. How is 'day' written in the given language?
(a) bn (b) kj
(c) ix (d) kl

32. How many triangles are there in the following figure?

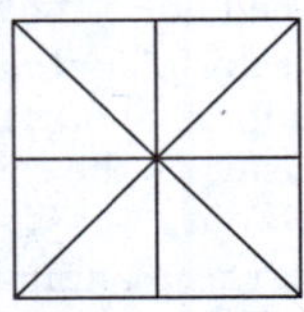

(a) 17 (b) 16
(c) 15 (d) 14

33. In a certain code language,
A + B means 'A is the son of B'
A – B means 'A is the brother of B'
A × B means 'A is the wife of B'
A ÷ B means 'A is the father of B'
Based on the above, how is P related to T, if 'P × Q – R ÷ S + T' ?
(a) Husband's mother
(b) Husband's brother's daughter
(c) Husband's brother's wife
(d) Husband's sister

34. In a certain code language, 'bottle is blue' is coded as 'see mo tu' and 'sky is blue' is coded as 'mo tu lo'. What is the code for 'bottle ' in that language?
(a) see (b) tu (c) mo (d) lo

35. What should come in place of question mark (?) in the given series based on the English alphabetical order?
GOW, NIB, UCG, BWL, ?
(a) ZQH (b) XOF (c) VLB (d) IQQ

36. If 'A' stands for '÷', 'B' stands for '×', 'C' stands for '+' and 'D' stands for '–', then the resultant of which of the following will be 59?
(a) 22 B 6 D 190 C 2 A 22
(b) 22 A 6 D 190 B 2 C 22
(c) 22 B 6 C 190 A 2 D 22
(d) 22 B 6 D 190 A 2 C 22

37. Select the word-pair that best represents a similar relationship to the one expressed in the pair of words given below.
(The words must be considered as meaningful English words and must not be related to each other based on the number of letters/number of consonants/vowels in the word.)
Antibiotic : Infection
(a) Purgative : Eating
(b) Antidote : Poisoning
(c) Antibody : Braise
(d) Anticlimax : Episode

38. Select the option in which the given figure (X) is embedded (i.e. contains figure (X) in the same form).

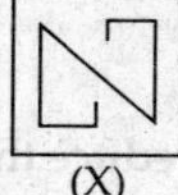
(X)

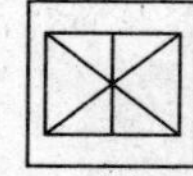 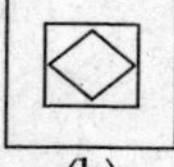  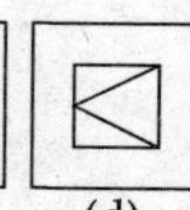
(a) (b) (c) (d)

39. What would be the symbol on the opposite side of '÷', if the given sheet is folded to form a cube?

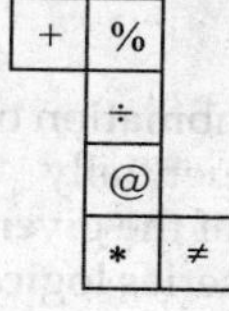

(a) % (b) +
(c) * (d) ≠

40. Select the set in which the numbers are related in the same way as are the numbers of the following sets.
(**Note** Operations should be performed on the whole numbers, without breaking down the numbers into its constituent digits. E.g. 13 – Operations on 13 such as adding/subtracting/multiplying etc. to 13 can be performed. Breaking down 13 into 1 and 3 and then performing mathematical operations on 1and 3 is not allowed.)
(3, 34, 5)
(10, 136, 6)
(a) (7, 113, 8) (b) (9, 115, 6)
(c) (5, 60, 6) (d) (11, 125, 4)

41. If 'A' stands for '÷', 'B' stands for '×', 'C' stands for '+' and 'D' stands for '–', what will come in place of the question mark (?) in the following equation?
96 B 3 D 285 A 5 C 11 = ?
(a) 252 (b) 262
(c) 242 (d) 272

42. Read the given statements and conclusions carefully. Assuming that the information given in the statements is true, even if it appears to be at variance with commonly known facts, decide which of the given conclusions logically follow(s) from the statements.
Statements
No pillow is a cushion.
All cushions are sheets.
No sheet is a blanket.
Conclusions
I. No cushion is a blanket.
II. Some pillows are sheets.
(a) Only Conclusion I follows
(b) None of the conclusions follow
(c) Both Conclusions I and II follow
(d) Only Conclusion II follows

43. Which of the following numbers will replace the question mark (?) in the given series?
291, 256, 310, 275, 329, 294, ?
(a) 356 (b) 375
(c) 331 (d) 348

44. Three of the following four letter-clusters are alike in a certain way and thus form a group. Which is the one that does not belong to that group?
(**Note** The odd one out is not based on the number of consonants/ vowels or their position in the letter-cluster.)
1. ADBC 2. JMKL
3. FJHI 4. VYWX
(a) FJHI (b) VYWX
(c) JMKL (d) ADBC

45. 30 is related to 216 by certain logic. Following the same logic, 40 is related to 226. To which of the following is 50 related, following the same logic?
(**Note** Operations should be performed on the whole numbers, without breaking down the numbers into its constituent digits. E.g. 13 – Operations on 13 such as adding/subtracting/multiplying etc. to 13 can be performed. Breaking down 13 into 1 and 3 and then performing mathematical operations on 1 and 3 is not allowed.)
(a) 236 (b) 238
(c) 250 (d) 248

46. A paper is folded and cut as shown below. How will it appear when unfolded?

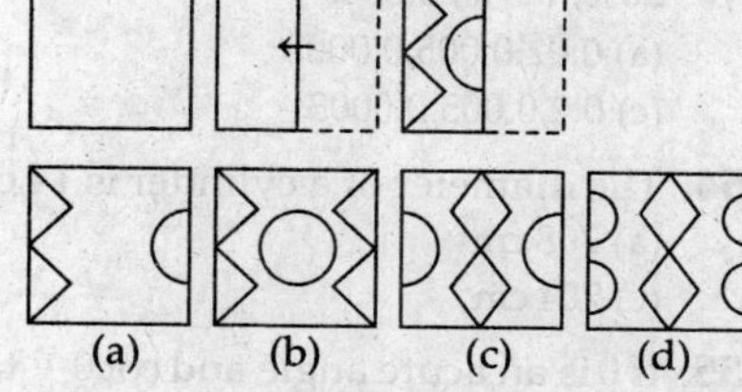
(a) (b) (c) (d)

47. The position of how many letters will remain unchanged, if each of the letters in the word FLAMINGOES is arranged from left to right in alphabetical order?
(a) None (b) Three
(c) One (d) Two

48. Select the word-pair that best represents a similar relationship to the one expressed in the pair of words given below.
(The words must be considered as meaningful English words and must not be related to each other based on the number of letters/number of consonants/vowels in the word)
Carpenter : Furniture

(a) Cook : Soup
(b) Dam : Engineer
(c) Book : Author
(d) Magazine : Editor

49. Select the correct combination of letters that when sequentially placed in the blanks of the given series will make the series logically complete.
_WSVR_QTPS_RNQM_ LOK_

(a) XUQPM (b) XVQLM
(c) TVOLN (d) TUOPN

50. If 16th September, 2010 is Thursday, then what will be the day of the week on 17th August, 2017?
(a) Wednesday
(b) Monday
(c) Sunday
(d) Thursday

Part III
Quantitative Aptitude

51. Read the given information and answer the question that follows.
The following table gives the percentage of marks obtained by seven students in six different subjects in ..n examination.
The number in the brackets gives the maximum marks in each subject.

	Subject (Max. Marks)					
Students	**Maths (150)**	**Chemistry (130)**	**Physics (120)**	**Geography (100)**	**History (60)**	**Computer Science (40)**
Ayush	90	50	90	60	70	80
Aman	100	80	80	40	80	70
Sajal	90	60	70	70	90	70
Rohit	80	65	80	80	60	60
Muskan	80	65	85	95	50	90
Tanvi	70	75	65	85	40	60
Tarun	65	35	50	77	80	80

How many students secured a raw score of at least 30 in Computer Science?
(a) 3 (b) 5
(c) 4 (d) 2

52. The perimeter of a semi-circle is 56.54 cm. What is its diameter (in cm)? (use $\pi = 3.14$)
(a) 11 (b) 22
(c) 10 (d) 20

53. Express the following as decimals, respectively.
20%, 0.5%, 0.03%
(a) 0.02,0.005,0.0003 (b) 0.02,0.005,0.003
(c) 0.2,0.005,0.0003 (d) 0.2,0.0005,0.0003

54. The diameter of a cylinder is 14 cm and its height is 9 cm. Find the total surface area of the cylinder.
(a) 708 cm^2 (b) 714 cm^2
(c) 704 cm^2 (d) 700 cm^2

55. If θ is an acute angle and $\cot\theta + \tan\theta = 2$, then find the value of $\tan^{12}\theta + \cot^{12}\theta + 2\tan^5\theta\cot^7\theta$.
(a) 4 (b) 3
(c) 1 (d) 2

56. A car covers a certain distance in 85 min, if it runs at a speed of 36 km/h. The speed at which the car must run to reduce the time of journey to 51 min will be
(a) 70 km/h (b) 80 km/h
(c) 60 km/h (d) 50 km/h

57. The profit (in ₹) earned by four companies in the different quarters of the year 2020 are shown in the chart. The data shown is in crores.

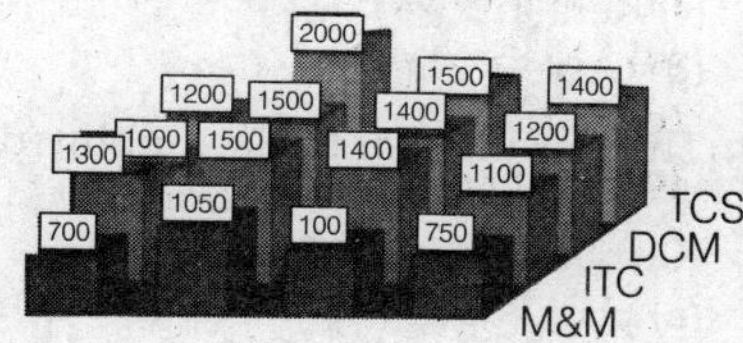

How much is the average profit earned by ITC in the year 2020?

(a) ₹ 1400 crore (b) ₹ 1325 crore
(c) ₹ 1350 crore (d) ₹ 1225 crore

58. Two circles with centres M and N have radii 5 cm and 8 cm, respectively. The circles touch each other externally at point T. A line PR is drawn such that the points M, T and N lie on PR, P being closer to M. From P, a tangent $PQ = 12$ cm is drawn to the circle with centre M touching at Q and from R, another tangent $RS = 15$ cm is drawn to the circle with centre N touching at S. What is the length (in cm) of PR?

(a) 37 (b) 43
(c) 53 (d) 26

59. Find the remainder, when we divide $2x^3 - 3x^2 + 6x - 4$ by $2x - 3$.

(a) 5 (b) 6
(c) –5 (d) –6

60. Find the third proportion to 36 and 48.

(a) 36 (b) 54
(c) 64 (d) 48

61. A retailer purchased a batch of goods for ₹ 5000. Due to a manufacturing defect, 5% of the goods were damaged. If the retailer wants to make a profit of 20% on the remaining goods, at what price should the undamaged goods be sold?

(a) ₹ 5700 (b) ₹ 5800
(c) ₹ 6000 (d) ₹ 5900

62. Find the capacity of an overhead cylindrical water tank, in litres, whose radius is 2.1 m and height is 6.3 m.

(a) 61802 (b) 87318
(c) 611726 (d) 65622

63. The total surface area of a solid hemisphere of diameter 28 cm is

(a) 1784 cm^2 (b) 1488 cm^2
(c) 1648 cm^2 (d) 1848 cm^2

64. Last year, Geeta's monthly salary was ₹ 12000 and Seeta's monthly salary was ₹ 10000. This year, Geeta's monthly salary is ₹ 14400, while Seeta's monthly salary is ₹ 12500. If the percentage increase in Seeta's monthly salary this year over her monthly salary last year is denoted by x% and the percentage increase in Geeta's monthly salary this year over her monthly salary last year is denoted by y%, then what is the value of $\left(\frac{x-y}{y} \times 100\right)$% ?

(a) 24 (b) 20
(c) 22 (d) 25

65. ΔDEF and ΔGHI are two similar triangles. If $DE = 64$ cm, $GH = 24$ cm and the perimeter of ΔGHI is 72 cm, then what is the sum of the lengths (in cm) of the sides EF and FD of the ΔDEF?

(a) 192 (b) 96
(c) 128 (d) 82

66. If the average of a number and its reciprocal is 2, then the average of its cube and its reciprocal is equal to

(a) 28 (b) 26
(c) 48 (d) 36

67. Simplify

$$3\frac{4}{7} - \left[16\frac{1}{2} \div \left\{6^2 - \left(7 - 2\frac{1}{2}\right)\right\}\right]$$

(a) $\frac{64}{21}$ (b) $\frac{25}{21}$
(c) $\frac{64}{11}$ (d) $\frac{25}{11}$

68. The price of pulses has increased by 45%. By what percentage (rounded off to the nearest integer) the increased price of the pulses should be reduced, so that the price of the pulses remains unaltered?

(a) 45 (b) 31
(c) 41 (d) 35

69. To finish a work in 12 days, 8 workers are engaged. After 2 days, due to some urgency, the work is to be finished in next 2 days. How many more workers are to be engaged now to finish it on time?

(a) 30 (b) 32
(c) 36 (d) 40

70. Study the given graph and answer the question that follows.

Ratio of imports to exports from two companies over the years.

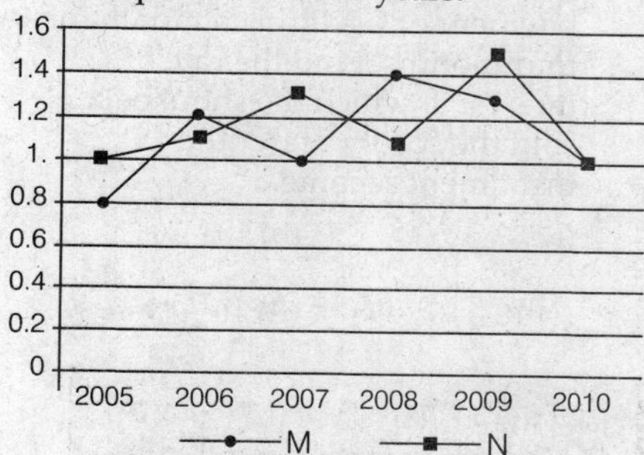

In how many of the given years were the imports more than the exports of Company N ?

(a) 2 (b) 1 (c) 3 (d) 4

71. The marked price of an article is 25% more than its cost price. If a scheme discount of 40% is given, then the loss percentage is

(a) 20% (b) 25%
(c) 30% (d) 15%

72. A circle of diameter 26 cm has two equal chords of length 10 cm each, separated by a distance h cm. What is the value of h?

(a) 18 cm (b) 12 cm
(c) 24 cm (d) 16 cm

73. The age of a father will be double the age of his son ten years later. 10 yr ago, the father's age was six times the age of the son. How many years from now, the ratio of their ages will be 3 : 2?

(a) 35 (b) 30
(c) 20 (d) 25

74. The given line graph shows the number of scooters manufactured (in thousands) by Companies X and Z, over the years.

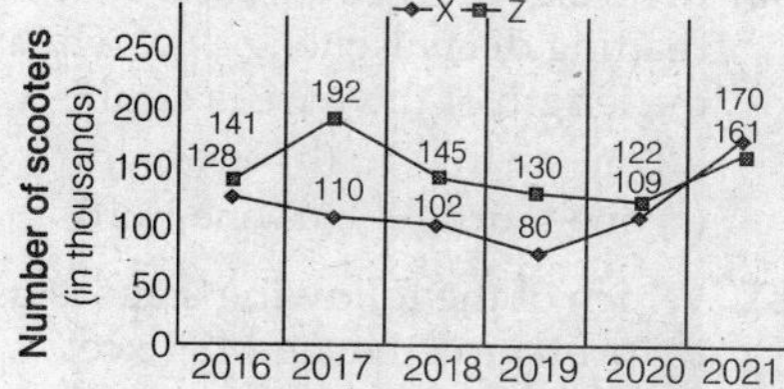

In which of the following years was the difference between the production by Companies X and Z the maximum among the given years?

(a) 2018 (b) 2017
(c) 2020 (d) 2019

75. Rahna decided to buy a scooty that costs ₹ 40000. The shopkeeper agreed to sell the scooty under the condition of ₹ 25000 cash down payment of ₹ 4000 each month for four months. Find the rate of interest at which the shopkeeper sold the scooty under the instalment scheme.

(a) 33% (b) $10\frac{1}{3}\%$

(c) $18\frac{1}{2}\%$ (d) $16\frac{1}{2}\%$

Part IV

General Awareness

76. The 5th edition of the Khelo India Youth Games 2023 was hosted in January-February, 2023 by ....

(a) Uttar Pradesh

(b) Delhi

(c) Rajasthan

(d) Madhya Pradesh

77. In a spreadsheet, page orientation is changed through ....

(a) page setup dialog box

(b) format dialogue box

(c) print dialog box

(d) paper dialog box

78. Which of the following is a part of apical meristem found in roots?

(a) Protoderm

(b) Leaf primordium

(c) Differentiating vascular tissue

(d) Axillary bud

79. The institute established by Kaka Hathrasi in 1932 is

(a) Music Art Centre

(b) Swar Sangam Kendra

(c) Sangeet Karyalaya

(d) Music Art Kendra

80. In an electrical circuit, the ammeter reading decrease to .... when the length of the wire is doubled.

(a) one-sixth (b) one-half

(c) one-fourth (d) one-third

81. Which of the following steps is used to format a cell in an MS Excel Spreadsheet?

(a) Menu → Select cell → Format

(b) Select cell → Right click → Format cell

(c) Select cell → View → Format cell

(d) View → Select cell → Format

82. Match the following ports with their related states correctly.

List I (Ports)	List I (States)
A. Mormugao Port	1. West Bengal
B. Paradip Port	2. Odisha
C. Haldia Port	3. Tamil Nadu
D. Tuticorin Port	4. Goa

Codes

	A	B	C	D		A	B	C	D
(a)	2	4	3	1	(b)	1	2	4	3
(c)	4	2	1	3	(d)	2	4	1	3

83. Which is the first state to receive rain from the monsoon in India?

(a) Kerala (b) Goa

(c) Andhra Pradesh

(d) Karnataka

84. In which of the following cities was the Asian Wrestling Championship 2023 held?

(a) Mumbai (b) Astana

(c) Tokyo (d) Karachi

85. Federalism in the Indian constitutional context means

(a) the existence only one level of government in the country

(b) the existence of one nation, one government in the country

(c) the existence of states in the country

(d) the existence of more than one level of government in the country

86. Which of the following schemes is related to minimising the use of chemical fertilisers, given in the Union Budget 2023-24?

(a) PM PRANAM (b) PM DevINE

(c) SEED (d) PM Shri

87. Jagoi and Cholom are two divisions in the Indian classical dance form of ....

(a) Kathak

(b) Manipuri

(c) Kathakali

(d) Bharatanatyam

88. Which of the following is not any position in the Basketball sport?

(a) Point guard

(b) Shooting guard

(c) Small forward

(d) All rounder

89. As of August 2023, which of the following states has India's first fully functionally literate district?

(a) Madhya Pradesh

(b) Maharashtra

(c) Kerala

(d) Goa

90. The President of India appointed .... as the Governor of Karnataka in July 2021.

(a) Hari Babu Kambhampati

(b) Thaawar Chand Gehlot

(c) Rajendra Vishwanath Arlekar

(d) Mangubhai Chhaganbhai Patel

91. In Hindustani classical music, according to Vishnu Narayana Bhatkhande, how many thaats are the origins of Ragas?

(a) 52 (b) 72 (c) 10 (d) 20

92. The Prarthana Samaj was established in .... by Dr. Atmaram Pandurang.

(a) Bombay (b) Calcutta

(c) Adyar (d) Delhi

93. Where is the oldest centre of lace work located in Gujarat?

(a) Ahmedabad (b) Rajkot

(c) Jamnagar (d) Kutch

94. The Chhau dancers of .... organise a festival named Chhau-Jhumur Utsav, where an open stage is designed for the performance by Chhau groups.

(a) West Bengal

(b) Chhattisgarh

(c) Jharkhand

(d) Madhya Pradesh

95. In which year was the 'Aatmanirbhar Bharat Rojgar Yojana' launched by the Government of India?

(a) 2020 (b) 2022 (c) 2015 (d) 2010

96. Which of the following years were considered plan holidays in Independent India?

(a) 1964-1967 (b) 1990-1992

(c) 1969-1972 (d) 1966-1969

97. .... is defined as excess of total expenditure over total receipts excluding borrowings during a fiscal year.

(a) Fiscal deficit

(b) Income deficit

(c) Structural deficit

(d) Gross Primary deficit

98. Part IV A of the Indian Constitution is related to ....
(a) Directive Principles of State Policy
(b) Fundamental Duties
(c) Fundamental Rights
(d) Citizenship

99. Which of the following statements most accurately describes the planet Saturn?
(a) Its surface is reddish in colour.
(b) It is a gas giant made up mostly of hydrogen and helium and the density is less than that of water.
(c) It was the seventh planet discovered in the solar system.
(d) Its cloud-like outer regions consist of methane in the gaseous form and ammonia in crystalline form.

100. Who defeated Mohammad Ghori in the First Battle of Tarain fought in the year 1191?
(a) Prithviraj Chauhan
(b) Vasudev
(c) Yashovarman
(d) Vidyadhar

Answers

1. (d)	2. (c)	3. (b)	4. (b)
5. (a)	6. (d)	7. (b)	8. (d)
9. (c)	10. (c)	11. (c)	12. (d)
13. (b)	14 (a)	15. (d)	16. (a)
17. (c)	18. (a)	19. (d)	20. (c)
21. (b)	22. (c)	23. (a)	24. (b)
25. (a)	26. (a)	27. (d)	28. (a)
29. (a)	30. (c)	31. (a)	32. (b)
33. (c)	34. (a)	35. (d)	36. (d)
37. (b)	38. (a)	39. (c)	40. (a)
41. (c)	42. (a)	43. (d)	44. (a)
45. (a)	46. (b)	47. (d)	48. (a)
49. (d)	50. (d)	51. (a)	52. (b)
53. (c)	54. (c)	55. (a)	56. (c)
57. (b)	58. (b)	59. (a)	60. (c)
61. (a)	62. (b)	63. (d)	64. (d)
65. (c)	66. (b)	67. (a)	68. (b)
69. (b)	70. (d)	71. (b)	72. (c)
73. (a)	74. (b)	75. (a)	76. (d)
77. (a)	78. (a)	79. (c)	80. (b)
81. (b)	82. (c)	83. (a)	84. (b)
85. (d)	86. (a)	87. (b)	88. (d)
89. (a)	90. (b)	91. (c)	92. (a)
93. (c)	94. (a)	95. (a)	96. (d)
97. (a)	98. (b)	99. (b)	100. (a)

Explanations

1. *(d)* Part (d) 'are a wonderful example' contains an error. Use 'is' in place of 'are' to correct the sentence. As the subject of the sentence is singular, singular verb should be used.

2. *(c)* Part (c) 'to the' contains an error. Use 'at' as preposition of in place of 'to' to correct the sentence.

3. *(b)* The phrasal verb 'blacked out' in the given sentence is incorrect as it means to get unconscious. The correct phrasal verb for the sentence would be 'chickened out' which means to get scared.

4. *(b)* Part (b) 'giving in the prizes' contains an error. Use 'out' to make the phrasal verb 'giving out' which means to distribute.

5. *(a)* The correct filler for the given blank is 'caused'.

6. *(d)* The correct filler for the given blank is 'including large-scale'.

7. *(b)* The correct filler for the given blank is 'restricted'.

8. *(d)* The correct filler for the given blank is 'self-sufficiency'.

9. *(c)* The correct filler for the given blank is 'Green Revolution'.

10. *(c)* The word 'epoch' means 'an important period'.

11. *(c)* 'Boisterous' means noisy, energetic, and cheerful. Hence, its antonym is 'placid' which means 'calm'.
- 'Clamorous' means making a loud and confused noise.
- 'Frothing' means bubbles formed in or on a liquid.
- 'Raucous' means making or constituting a disturbingly harsh and loud noise.

12. *(d)* Fair weather friends are people who become good friends when it is easy to be one and who stops being one when you are having problems.

13. *(b)* 'Wrapping my head around it' means to understand something, especially something strange or out of the ordinary.

14. *(a)* The incorrectly spelt word is 'gaint'. The correct spelling is 'giant'.

15. *(d)* The incorrectly spelt word is 'calandar'. The correct spelling is 'calendar'.

16. *(a)* The word 'Fertile' means able to produce something or productive.
'Hectic' means busy.

17. *(c)* The underlined part of the given sentence contains an error. Use 'Many a woman works for' to correct the sentence. The expression 'Many a' takes the singular form of noun.

18. *(a)* The antonym of 'cheap' is 'expensive'.
- 'Doltish' means (of a person) stupid; idiotic.
- 'Paltry' means very small or meagre.

19. *(d)* The underlined part of the given sentence contains an error. Use 'quite' to correct the sentence.

20. *(c)* The correct filler for the given blank is 'career'.

21. *(b)* The word 'refuge' means a place or situation providing safety or shelter.

22. *(c)* 'Deflate' means let air or gas out of (a tyre, balloon, or similar object). Hence, its antonym is 'inflate' which means to swell with air or gas.
- 'Flatten' means to be made flat.
- 'Compress' and 'Shrink' means to reduce in size.

23. *(a)* The word 'affirm' means 'to accept; to confirm'.

24. *(b)* The correct filler for the given blank is 'towed' which means (of a motor vehicle or boat) pull (another vehicle or boat) along with a rope, chain, or tow bar.

25. *(a)* The underlined part of the given sentence contains an error. Use 'high-paying' to correct the sentence.

26. *(a)* According to the question,

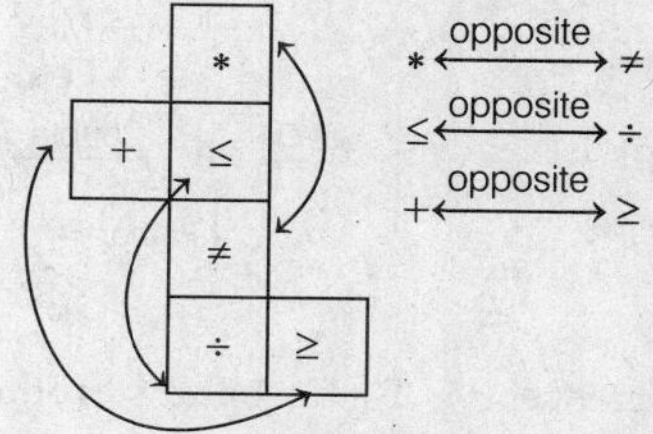

Hence, '÷' will be opposite to '≤' side.

27. *(d)* The pattern of the series is as follows,

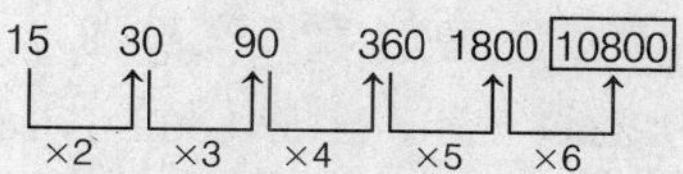

28. *(a)* The given figure is embedded in the option figure (a).

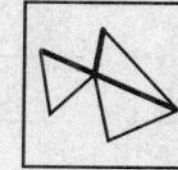

29. *(a)* The option figure (a) will complete the pattern in the given figure.

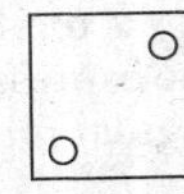

30. *(c)* Given expression,
11 W 11 Y 11 Z 11 A 11

After substituting letters with signs, we get

W → ÷	Y → ×
Z → +	A → –

$11 \div 11 \times 11 + 11 - 11$
$= 1 \times 11 + 11 - 11$
$= 11 + 11 - 11 = \boxed{11}$

31. *(a)* According to the question,

cold summers [day] → kl [bn] ix

[day] and night → kj ed [bn]

Hence, code for 'day' is 'bn'.

32. *(b)* Naming the figure,

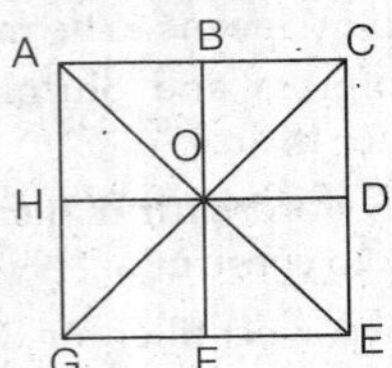

ΔOAB, ΔOBC, ΔOCD, ΔODE, ΔOEF, ΔOFG, ΔOGH, ΔOHA, ΔAOG, ΔOAC, ΔOCE, ΔOEG, ΔAEG, ΔACG, ΔACE and ΔCEG.

Hence, there are 16 triangles in the given figure.

33. *(c)* According to the question,

[+ → Male, – → Female]

P(–) ←Wife→ Q(+) ←Brother→ R(+) ←Couple→ T(–)
R(+) ↑ Father — S(+)
T(–) — Son → S(+)

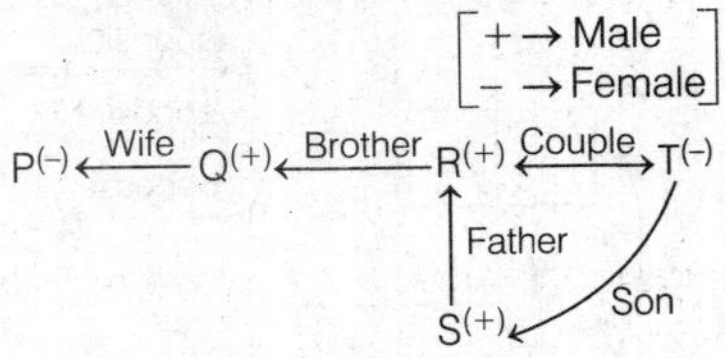

Hence, P is T's husband's brother's wife.

34. *(a)* According to the question,

[bottle] is blue → [see] mo tu

sky is blue → mo tu lo

Hence, the code for 'bottle' is 'see'.

35. *(d)* The pattern of the series is as follows,

G —+7→ N —+7→ U —+7→ B —+7→ [I]
O —–6→ I —–6→ C —–6→ W —–6→ [Q]
W —+5→ B —+5→ G —+5→ L —+5→ [Q]

36. *(d)* After substituting letters with signs in option (d), we get

$= 22 \times 6 - 190 \div 2 + 22$
$= 132 - 95 + 22 = 154 - 95 = 59$

37. *(b)* As, Antibiotic is used to prevent infection. Similarly, Antidote is used to prevent any type of poison.

38. *(a)* The figure (X) is embedded in the option figure (a).

39. *(c)* According to the question,

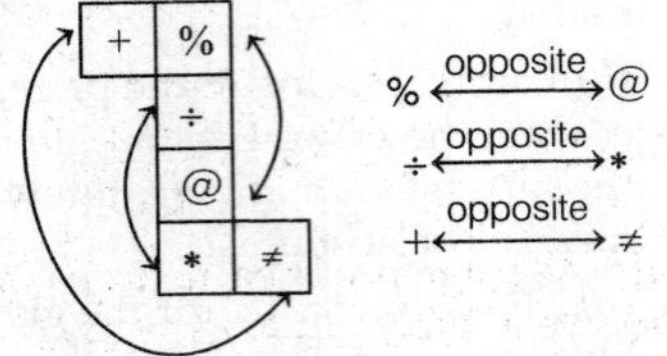

Hence, '*' is opposite to '÷'.

40. *(a)* As,
$(3, 34, 5) \rightarrow (3)^2 + (5)^2 = 9 + 25 = 34$
and (10, 136, 6)
$\rightarrow (6)^2 + (10)^2 = 36 + 100 = 136$
Similarly, (7, 113, 8)
$\rightarrow (8)^2 + (7)^2 = 64 + 49 = 113$

41. *(c)* Given expression,
96 B 3 D 285 A 5 C 11 = ?

After substituting letters with signs, we get

A → ÷	B → ×
C → +	D → –

$96 \times 3 - 285 \div 5 + 11$
$= 288 - 57 + 11$
$= 299 - 57 = \boxed{242}$

42. *(a)* According to the statements,

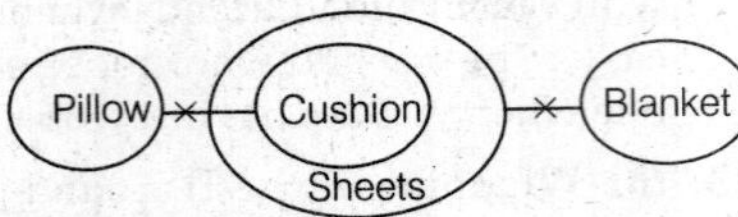

Conclusions

I. (✓) II. (✗)

Hence, only Conclusion I follows.

43. *(d)* The pattern of the series is as follows,

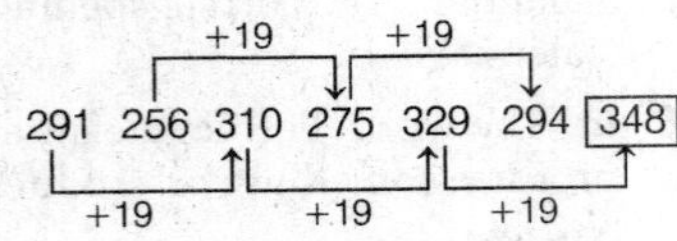

44. *(a)* As,

A —+3→ D —–2→ B —+1→ C
J —+3→ M —–2→ K —+1→ L
V —+3→ Y —–2→ W —+1→ X

But, [F —+4→ J —–2→ H —+1→ I]

45. *(a)* As, 30 + 186 = 216
and 40 + 186 = 226
Similarly, 50 + 186 = [236]

46. *(b)* When we unfolded the paper, then it will appear as the figure given in option (b).

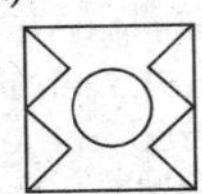

47. *(d)*

Given word → F L A M [I] N G O E [S]

After arranging in alphabetical order → A E F G [I] L M N O [S]

Hence, position of letters I and S remain unchanged.

48. *(a)* As, Carpenter makes furniture. Similarly, Cook make soup.

49. *(d)* The pattern of the series is as follows,

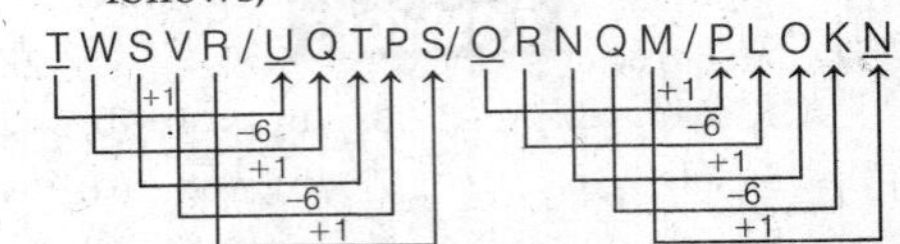

Hence, the correct order is TUOPN.

50. *(d)* Odd days in ordinary year = 1

Odd days in leap year = 2

Day on 16th September, 2010
= Thursday

Number of odd days from 16th September, 2010 to 31st December, 2010
= 14 (Sept.) + 31 (Oct.) + 30 (Nov.) + 31 (Dec.) + 1 + 2 + 1 + 1 + 1 + 2
$= \frac{114}{7} = 16$ weeks 2 odd days.

Now, number of odd days from 1st January, 2017 to 17th August, 2017
= 31 (Jan) + 28 (Feb) + 31 (March) + 30 (April) + 31 (May) + 30 (June) + 31 (July) + 17 (Aug)
$= \frac{229}{7} = 32$ weeks and 5 odd days

Total number of odd days
$= 2 + 5 = 7$ odd days $= \frac{7}{7} = 0$

∴ The day of the week on 17th August, 2017 = Thursday + 0
= Thursday

51. *(a)* In Computer Science,

Marks obtained by Ayush

$= 40 \times \frac{80}{100} = 32$

Marks obtained by Aman

$= 40 \times \frac{70}{100} = 28$

Marks obtained by Sajal

$= 40 \times \frac{70}{100} = 28$

Marks obtained by Rohit

$= 40 \times \frac{60}{100} = 24$

Marks obtained by Muskan

$= 40 \times \frac{90}{100}$

$= 36$

Marks obtained by Tanvi

$= 40 \times \frac{60}{100} = 24$

Marks obtained by Tarun

$= 40 \times \frac{80}{100} = 32$

Hence, 3 students secured a raw score of at least 30 in Computer Science.

52. *(b)* Perimeter of a semi-circle $= \pi r + 2r$

$56.54 = 3.14r + 2r$

$\Rightarrow \quad 5.14r = 56.54$

$\Rightarrow \quad r = 11\text{ cm}$

Hence, diameter of a circle

$= 11 \times 2 = 22$ cm

53. *(c)* According to the question,

$20\% = \frac{20}{100} = 0.2$

$0.5\% = \frac{0.5}{100} = 0.005$

and $0.03\% = \frac{0.03}{100} = 0.0003$

54. *(c)* Given, diameter of cylinder $= 14$ cm

Radius $(r) = \frac{14}{2} = 7$ cm

and height $(h) = 9$ cm

Total surface area of the cylinder

$= 2\pi rh + 2\pi r^2$

$= 2\pi r(r + h)$

$= 2 \times \frac{22}{7} \times 7(7 + 9)$

$= 2 \times 22 \times 16 = 704\text{ cm}^2$

55. *(a)* Given, $\cot\theta + \tan\theta = 2$

Let $\theta = 45°$

$\Rightarrow \cot 45° + \tan 45° = 2$

$1 + 1 = 2 \Rightarrow 2 = 2$

$\therefore \tan^{12}\theta + \cot^{12}\theta + 2\tan^5\theta\cot^7\theta$

$= \tan^{12} 45° + \cot^{12} 45° + 2\tan^5 45° \times \cot^7 45°$

$= (1)^{12} + (1)^{12} + 2 \times (1)^5 \times (1)^7$

$= 1 + 1 + 2 = 4$

56. *(c)* According to the question,

Distance travelled by car in 85 min

$= 36 \times \frac{85}{60}$ [$\because$ 1 h = 60 min]

$= 51$ km

$\therefore$ Required speed $= \frac{51}{\frac{51}{60}}$

$= \frac{51}{51} \times 60$

$= 60$ km/h

57. *(b)* Average profit earned by ITC in the year 2020

$= \frac{1300 + 1500 + 1400 + 1100}{4}$

$= \frac{5300}{4} =$ ₹ 1325 crore

58. *(b)* Given, $MQ = 5$ cm, $NS = 8$ cm

$PQ = 12$ cm and $RS = 15$ cm

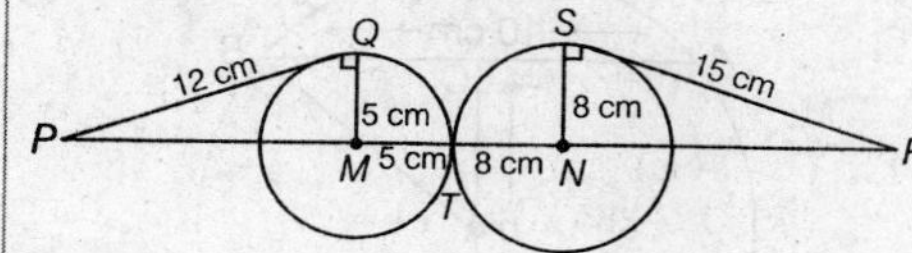

$\therefore$ In ΔPMQ, by Pythagoras theorem,

$PM^2 = PQ^2 + MQ^2$

$\Rightarrow \quad PM^2 = 12^2 + 5^2$

$\Rightarrow \quad PM = \sqrt{144 + 25}$

$\Rightarrow \quad PM = \sqrt{169} = 13$ cm

In ΔRNS, by Pythagoras theorem,

$RN^2 = NS^2 + SR^2$

$\Rightarrow \quad RN^2 = 8^2 + 15^2$

$\Rightarrow \quad RN = \sqrt{64 + 225}$

$\therefore \quad RN = \sqrt{289} = 17$ cm

$\therefore \quad PR = PM + MT + TN + RN$

$= 13 + 5 + 8 + 17 = 43$ cm

59. *(a)* $f(x) = 2x^3 - 3x^2 + 6x - 4$

To find the remainder,

$2x - 3 = 0$

$x = \frac{3}{2}$

$\therefore f\left(\frac{3}{2}\right) = 2 \times \left(\frac{3}{2}\right)^3 - 3\left(\frac{3}{2}\right)^2 + 6 \times \frac{3}{2} - 4$

$= 2 \times \frac{27}{8} - 3 \times \frac{9}{4} + 9 - 4$

$= \frac{27}{4} - \frac{27}{4} + 9 - 4 = 5$

Hence, required remainder = 5

60. *(c)* Let the third proportion to 36 and 48 is x.

$\therefore \quad 36 : 48 :: 48 : x$

$\Rightarrow \quad \frac{36}{48} = \frac{48}{x}$

$\Rightarrow \quad x = \frac{48 \times 48}{36}$

$\therefore \quad x = 64$

61. *(a)* Let the number of goods = 100

Remaining goods $= 100 \times \frac{95}{100} = 95$

According to the question,

Price of remaining goods

$= \frac{5000}{100} \times 95$

$=$ ₹ 4750

Hence, the required selling price

$= 4750 \times \frac{120}{100} =$ ₹ 5700

62. *(b)* Given, radius = 2.1 m = 210 cm

and height = 6.3 m = 630 cm

$\therefore$ Volume of tank/ capacity $= \pi r^2 h$

$= \frac{22}{7} \times 210 \times 210 \times 630\text{ cm}^3$

$= 87318000\text{ cm}^3$

$= 87318$ L $\left[\because 1\text{ L} = \frac{1}{1000}\text{ cm}^3\right]$

63. *(d)* Total surface area of a hemisphere

$= 3\pi r^2$

$= 3 \times \frac{22}{7} \times \left(\frac{28}{2}\right)^2$

$= 3 \times \frac{22}{7} \times 14 \times 14$

$= 1848\text{ cm}^2$

64. *(d)* Given, last year Geeta's monthly salary = ₹ 12000

Last year Seeta's monthly salary = ₹ 10000

This year Geeta's monthly salary = ₹ 14400

This year Seeta's monthly salary = ₹ 12500

According to the question,

$y\% = \left(\frac{14400 - 12000}{12000}\right) \times 100$

$= \frac{2400}{12000} \times 100 = 20\%$

Also, $x\% = \left(\frac{12500 - 10000}{10000}\right) \times 100$

$= \frac{250000}{10000} = 25\%$

$\therefore \left(\frac{x-y}{y} \times 100\right)\% = \left(\frac{25-20}{20} \times 100\right)\%$

$= 25\%$

65. *(c)* Given, $\Delta DEF \sim \Delta GHI$

$DE = 64$ cm, $GH = 24$ cm

Also, perimeter of $\Delta GHI = 72$ cm

$\because \Delta DEF \sim \Delta GHI$

$\therefore \frac{DE}{GH} = \frac{\text{Perimeter of } \Delta DEF}{\text{Perimeter of } \Delta GHI}$

$\frac{64}{24} = \frac{\text{Perimeter of } \Delta DEF}{72}$

Perimeter of $\Delta DEF = 192$ cm

Hence, $EF + FD = 192 - 64$

$= 128$ cm

66. *(b)* Let number $= x$

According to the question,

$\frac{x + \frac{1}{x}}{2} = 2$

$\Rightarrow x + \frac{1}{x} = 4$

On cubing both the sides,

$x^3 + \frac{1}{x^3} + 3x \times \frac{1}{x}\left(x + \frac{1}{x}\right) = 64$

$\Rightarrow x^3 + \frac{1}{x^3} + 3 \times 4 = 64$

$\Rightarrow x^3 + \frac{1}{x^3} = 52$

Hence, required average $= \frac{52}{2} = 26$

67. *(a)* $3\frac{4}{7} - \left[16\frac{1}{2} \div \left\{6^2 - \left(7 - 2\frac{1}{2}\right)\right\}\right]$

$= \frac{25}{7} - \left[\frac{33}{2} \div \left\{36 - \left(7 - \frac{5}{2}\right)\right\}\right]$

$= \frac{25}{7} - \left[\frac{33}{2} \div \left\{36 - \frac{9}{2}\right\}\right]$

$= \frac{25}{7} - \left[\frac{33}{2} \div \frac{63}{2}\right]$

$= \frac{25}{7} - \left[\frac{33}{2} \times \frac{2}{63}\right]$

$= \frac{25}{7} - \frac{11}{21}$

$= \frac{75 - 11}{21} = \frac{64}{21}$

68. *(b)* According to the question,

Required reduction percentage

$= \frac{(145 - 100)}{145} \times 100$

$= \frac{4500}{145} = 31.03\% \approx 31\%$

69. *(b)* Let required number of workers $= x$

According to the question,

$12 \times 8 = 8 \times 2 + (8 + x)\, 2$

$\Rightarrow 96 = 16 + 16 + 2x$

$\Rightarrow 96 - 32 = 2x$

$\Rightarrow x = \frac{64}{2} = 32$

70. *(d)* The years 2006, 2007, 2008 and 2009 were the imports more than the exports of Company N.

71. *(b)* Let the cost price of an article $= ₹\,100$

Marked price of an article $= ₹\,125$

$\therefore$ Selling price of an article

$= 125 \times \frac{60}{100} = ₹\,75$

Hence, the loss per cent

$= \frac{(100 - 75)}{100} \times 100 = 25\%$

72. *(c)* Given, the diameter of circle $= 26$ cm

Radius $(OB) = 13$ cm

Distance between the chords $= h$ cm

Length of chords $= 10$ cm

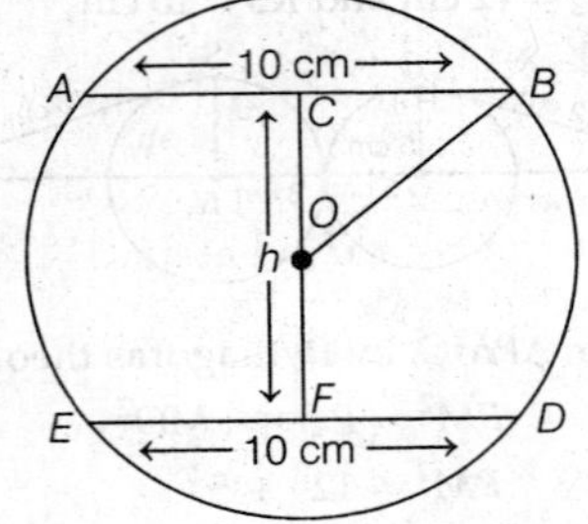

In ΔOCB, by Pythagoras theorem,

$OB^2 = OC^2 + BC^2$

$13^2 = OC^2 + 5^2$

$\Rightarrow OC^2 = 169 - 25$

$\Rightarrow OC = \sqrt{144}$

$\therefore OC = 12$ cm

Hence, $h = OC + OF = 12 + 12$ $[\because OC = OF]$

$= 24$ cm

73. *(a)* Let the present age of father $= x$ yr

and the present age of son $= y$ yr

According to the question,

$(x + 10) = 2(y + 10)$

$\Rightarrow x + 10 = 2y + 20$

$\Rightarrow x - 2y = 10$ ...(i)

and $(x - 10) = 6(y - 10)$

$\Rightarrow x - 10 = 6y - 60$

$\Rightarrow x - 6y = -50$ ...(ii)

From Eqs. (i) and (ii),

$x - 2y = 10$

$x - 6y = -50$

$(-)\ (+)\ (+)$

$4y = 60$

$\Rightarrow y = \frac{60}{4} = 15 \Rightarrow x = 40$

$\therefore \frac{40 + a}{15 + a} = \frac{3}{2}$

$\Rightarrow 80 + 2a = 45 + 3a$

$\Rightarrow 80 - 45 = 3a - 2a$

$\therefore a = 35$ yr

74. *(b)* Difference between the production by Companies X and Z.

In year 2016 = 141 − 128 = 13

In year 2017 = 192 − 110 = 82

In year 2018 = 145 − 102 = 43

In year 2019 = 130 − 80 = 50

In year 2020 = 122 − 109 = 13

In year 2021 = 170 − 161 = 9

Hence, in year 2017 the difference between the production by Companies X and Z is the maximum.

75. *(a)* Given, cost price of scooty $= ₹\,40000$

Cash down payment $= ₹\,25000$,

Left amount $= 40000 - 25000 = ₹\,15000$

Total interest $= 4 \times 4000 - 15000$

$= ₹\,1000$

According to the question,

$1000 = \frac{15000 \times R \times 1}{12 \times 100} + \frac{11000 \times R \times 1}{12 \times 100} + \frac{7000 \times R \times 1}{12 \times 100} + \frac{3000 \times R \times 1}{12 \times 100}$

$\Rightarrow 1000 = \frac{R}{12 \times 100}[36000]$

$\Rightarrow R = \frac{1000 \times 12 \times 100}{36000}$

$\therefore R = 33.33\% \approx 33\%$

76. *(d)* The 5th edition of the Khelo India Youth Games 2023 was hosted in January-February, 2023 by Madhya Pradesh.

- While all the sports events were organised in Madhya Pradesh, one game (cycling) was organised in Delhi.
- Nisith Pramanik (Union Minister of State for Youth Affairs and Sports) was present as a special guest at the opening event.

77. *(a)* Page setup dialog box

78. *(a)* Protoderm is a part of apical meristem found in roots.
Apical meristems may differentiate into three kinds of primary meristem:
- **Protoderm** It lies around the outside of the stem and develops into the epidermis.
- **Procambium** It lies just inside of the protoderm and developed into primary xylem and primary phloem.
- **Ground Meristem** These systems produce hypodermis, cortex, endodermis pericycle, pith and medullary rays.

79. *(c)* The institute established by Kaka Hathrasi in 1932 is Sangeet Karyalaya.
- It is a publishing house for the books on Indian classical music and dance.
- It started publishing a monthly magazine 'Sangeet' in 1935.
- Kaka Hathrasi was awarded Padma Shri by the Government of India in 1985.
- Kaka Hathrasi Award is annual award for outstanding contribution in the literary field.

80. *(b)* In an electric circuit, the ammeter reading decrease to one-half when the length of the wire is doubled.

Since, current $I = \dfrac{V}{R}$

and Resistance $R = \dfrac{\rho l}{A}$

So, $I = \dfrac{VA}{\rho l}$

According to the question,

$$I' = \frac{VA}{\rho(2l)} = \frac{I}{2}$$

81. *(b)* Select cell → Right click → Format cell. Steps is used to format a cell in an MS-Excel spreadsheet.

82. *(c)* The correct matching is A-4, B-2, C-1 and D-3.
- Mormugao Port is one of the India's oldest ports. This port is located on the Western coast of India, in the coastal state of Goa.
- Paradip Port is the only major port in the state of Odisha. Late Biju Patnaik is the founding Father of Paradip Port.
- Haldia Port is an industrial port situated in West Bengal.
- Tuticorin Port is also called VO Chidambaranar port. It is located in Tamiln Nadu.

83. *(a)* Kerala is the first state to receive rain from the monsoon in India.
- Rainfall received from the South-West monsoons is seasonal, which occurs between June and September.

Additional
- The North-East monsoon occurs between October-November.

84. *(b)* The Asian Wrestling Championship 2023 was held in Astana.
- It was the 19th edition of Asian Wrestling Championship of combined events.
- It is organised by (AAWC) Asian Associated Wrestling Committee.
- The women's tournament was first staged in 1996.
- The Asian Wrestling Championship 2024 was held in Bishek, Kyrgyzstan from 11th to 16th April.

85. *(d)* Federalism in the Indian constitutional context means the existence of more than one level of government in the country.
- It is a system of government in which the power is divided between a central authority and various constituent units of the country.

Additional
- India is considered a quasi-federal or semi-federal form of government.

86. *(a)* The scheme related to minimising the use of chemical fertilisers in the Union Budget 2023-24 is PM-PRANAM.
- PM-PRANAM aims to reduce the use of chemical fertilizers in agriculture and shift to bio-fertilisers.
- The Finance Minister Nirmala Sitaraman announced this scheme to 'incentivise' States and Union Territories.

87. *(b)* Jagoi and Cholom are two divisions in the Indian classical dance form of Manipuri.
- Jagoi predominant in Ras Leela, this steam represents the Lasya element described in Bharata's 'Natya Shastra'.
- Cholom represents the Tandava form of classical dance.
- Manipuri is an ancient classical dance form that originated in the North-Eastern state of Manipur in India.

88. *(d)* All rounder is not any position in the Basketball sport.
- Point guard also called the one or the point, is one of the five positions in a regulation basketball game.
- Shooting guard is typically played by a player in Basketball who is adept at shooting from the perimeter and creating their own shot.
- Small forward, also known as the three, is one of the five positions in a regulation Basketball game.

89. *(a)* As of August 2023, Madhya Pradesh has India's first fully functionally literate district.
The Mandla region of MP has become the first fully functionally literate district in the country.

90. *(b)* Thaawar Chand Gehlot was appointed by the President of India as the Governor of Karnataka in July 2021.
- He was appointed the 13th Governor of Karnataka.
- Article 53 provides the executive power to the President to appoint Governor, CAG, CJI, AGI etc.

91. *(c)* There are 10 thaats in the origins of Ragas in Hindustani classical music.
- Thaats are a way to classify various Ragas into groups based on which Swaras are used in a specific Raag.
- The ten thaats are Bitwal, Kalyan, Khamaj, Bhairav, Poorvi, Marwa, Kafi, Asavari, Bhairavi and Todi.

92. *(a)* The Prarthana Samaj was established in Bombay by Dr. Atmaram Pandurang.
- It was established on 31st March, 1867.
- Prarthana Samaj played a very important role in the Maharashtra renaissance.
- The 'Subodh-Patrika' was run by the Prarthana Samaj.

93. *(c)* Jamnagar is the oldest centre of lace work located in Guajrat.
- Crotchet lace work is done by the women of the Vohra community.

- These women make several crotchet items for household use.
- These items are usually made in black, brown and white colours.

94. *(a)* The Chhau dancers of West Bengal organise a festival named Chhau-Jhumur Utsav, where an open stage is designed for the performance by Chhau groups.

- Chhau-Jhumur Utsav was launched in 2010, to celebrate the traditional and cultural folk art forms of Purulia.
- Chhau dance was inscribed in the UNESCO representative list of Intangible Cultural Heritage of Humanity in 2010.

95. *(a)* The 'Aatmanirbhar Bharat Rojgar Yojana' was launched by the Government of India in 2020.

- It was was launched to boost employment in formal sector.
- And to incentivise creation of new employment opportunities.

96. *(d)* The period of 1966-1969 was considered plan holidays in Independent India.

- Plan holiday is the gap of three years.
- That was introduced in the Indian economy after the failure of the Third Economic Plan.
- This plan established to amend the economic gaps and has a significant role in the economic development of India.

97. *(a)* Fiscal deficit is defined as excess of total expenditure over total receipts excluding borrowings during a fiscal year.

- Income deficit is the difference between a single person or family's income and its poverty threshold or poverty line, when the former is exceeded by the latter.
- Structural deficit is when a country posts a deficit even though its economy is operating at its full potential.
- Gross Primary deficit refers to the difference between the current year's fiscal deficit and interest payments made on the previous year's borrwings.

98. *(b)* Part IV A of the Indian Constitution is related to Fundamental Duties.

- Fundamental Duties prescribe the fundamental obligations of the states to its citizens and the duties and the rights of the citizens to the state.
- It was added in Constitution of India by 42nd Amendment Act of 1976.
- Later 86th Amendment Act 2002 added the 11th Fundamental Duty to the list which was previously 10 Fundamental Duties.

99. *(b)* The planet Saturn is a gas giant made up mostly of hydrogen and helium and the density is less than than of water.

- Mars planet has its surface reddish in colour.
- Uranus was the seventh planet discovered in the solar system.
- Jupiter and Saturn has the cloud like outer regions consist of methane in the gaseous form and the ammonia in crystalline form.

100. *(a)* Prithviraj Chauhan defeated Mohammad Ghori in the First Battle of Tarain fought in 1191.

Prithviraj Chauhan or Rai Pithora was a king from the Chauhan (Chahamana) dynasty.

Set 16 04 July, 2024 (Shift IV)

SSC CHSL Tier-I SOLVED PAPER

Instructions

1. This paper contains 100 questions.
2. It has 4 Parts, **Part I** General English, **Part II** General Intelligence & Reasoning, **Part III** Quantitative Aptitude and **Part IV** General Awareness.
3. Each question carries **2 marks**.

Part I

General English

1. The following sentence has been divided into four segments. Identify the segment that contains a grammatical error.

She was singing / beautifully in / the concert hall / last night.

(a) the concert hall
(b) last night
(c) She was singing
(d) beautifully in

2. Identify the error in the following sentence and select the option with the correct use of the phrasal verb.

The police inspector was trying to give out the contradicting stories in the scene of the accident.

(a) The police inspector was trying to sign up the contradicting stories in the scene of the accident.
(b) The police inspector was trying to rush out the contradicting stories in the scene of the accident.
(c) The police inspector was trying to sort out the contradicting stories in the scene of the accident.
(d) The police inspector was trying to lighten up the contradicting stories in the scene of the accident.

3. Parts of the following sentence have been given as options. Select the option that contains an error.

I will be study around 7 o'clock.

(a) around 7 o'clock
(b) be study
(c) will
(d) I

4. The given sentence is divided into four segments. Select the option that has the segment with the grammatical error.

My daughter participate / in the dance competition / that is organised every year / by the Lion's Club.

(a) in the dance competition
(b) that is organised every year
(c) My daughter participate
(d) by the Lion's Club

Directions (Q. Nos. 5-9) *In the following passage, some words have been deleted. Read the passage carefully and select the most appropriate option to fill in each blank.*

Nutrition experts have researched the bad effects of junk food and have come to the (1)......... that junk food manufacturing companies are fooling the people by (2)......... deceptive advertisements that show junk food as healthy. We must substitute junk food with (3)......... food like fruits and vegetables.

So, the next time you think of (4)......... that burger, hotdog, pizza, samosa, kachori or even ice cream in a restaurant, eating joint or a party, stop your instincts and look for some healthier food (5)......... instead.

5. Select the most appropriate option to fill in blank number 1.

(a) conclusion (b) derivation
(c) solution (d) assumption

6. Select the most appropriate option to fill in blank number 2.

(a) observing (b) showing
(c) blowing (d) assuming

7. Select the most appropriate option to fill in blank number 3.

(a) powerful (b) expensive
(c) healthier (d) cleaner

8. Select the most appropriate option to fill in blank number 4.

(a) skipping (b) grabbing
(c) building (d) turning

9. Select the most appropriate option to fill in blank number 5.

(a) comparisons (b) chances
(c) additions (d) options

10. Select the most appropriate synonym of the given word.

Desire

(a) Loathing
(b) Aversion
(c) Disgust
(d) Longing

11. Select the most appropriate option that can substitute the underlined segment in the given sentence.

He <u>takes his always dog for a walk</u> in the park.

(a) takes his dog for always a walk
(b) takes his dog for an always walk
(c) always takes his dog for a walk
(d) his dog for a walk always

12. Select the most appropriate option that can substitute the underlined segment in the given sentence. If there is no need to substitute it, select 'No substitution required'.

She was thinking <u>at</u> the fun they had.

(a) beside
(b) by
(c) No substitution required
(d) about

13. Select the most appropriate antonym of the given word.

Vehement

(a) Reliable (b) Smashed
(c) Passionate (d) Mild

14. Select the most appropriate option of the given word to fill in the blank.

The new construction sites have ……… attack by the environmentalists.

(a) come off (b) come upon
(c) come under (d) come out

15. Select the most appropriate antonym of the underlined word.

The growth of the cell wall is very rarely <u>uniform</u>.

(a) paired (b) balanced
(c) fixed (d) variegated

16. Identify the most appropriate antonym of the underlined word in the following sentence.

There is no <u>transparency</u> in the procedure followed by the company.

(a) coherence (b) reliability
(c) clarity (d) opacity

17. Select the incorrectly spelt word in the given sentence.

Shreya prefers wearing green coloured saree on marriage funcktions.

(a) prefers (b) wearing
(c) funcktions (d) marriage

18. Select the most appropriate antonym of the given word.

Noble

(a) Grand
(b) Indescribable
(c) Common
(d) Magical

19. Select the most appropriate antonym of the underlined word in the given sentence.

The performance of the team in the lost match was <u>dismal.</u>

(a) luminous (b) sadden
(c) cheap (d) dainty

20. Select the most appropriate meaning of the given idiom.

A bolt from the blue

(a) A sudden and unexpected event
(b) Thunder and rain in a strom
(c) Raining heavily
(d) A spontaneous but expected event

21. Select the most appropriate antonym of the given word.

Benevolent

(a) Cruel (b) Happy
(c) Patient (d) Harmless

22. Select the most appropriate option that can substitute the underlined word in the given sentence.

A newer, more effective computer system was installed in place of the <u>obsolete</u> one.

(a) outdated (b) current
(c) modern (d) advanced

23. Select the most appropriate option that can substitute the underlined segment in the given sentence. If there is no need to substitute it, select 'No substitution required'.

I had to write a letter of <u>mistake</u> to my father for the blunder I made.

(a) apology
(b) No substitution required
(c) gratitude
(d) circumstance

24. Select the incorrectly spelt word.

(a) Physiologist (b) Contagious
(c) Gracious (d) Couragious

25. Select the most appropriate meaning of the given idiom.

Walk a tightrope

(a) To walk on a narrow road
(b) To act carefully in a difficult situation
(c) To be tensed about something
(d) To try and balance yourself

Part II
General Intelligence

26. Select the set in which the numbers are related in the same way as are the numbers of the following sets.

(**Note** Operations should be performed on the whole numbers, without breaking down the numbers into its constituent digits. E.g. 13 – Operations on 13 such as adding / subtracting/multiplying etc. to 13 can be performed. Breaking down 13 into 1 and 3 and then performing mathematical operations on 1 and 3 is not allowed.)

(35, 5, 7)
(108, 12, 9)

(a) (118, 15, 9) (b) (91, 13, 7)
(c) (254, 17, 7) (d) (114, 14, 8)

27. What would be the symbol on the opposite side of '*', if the given sheet is folded to form a cube?

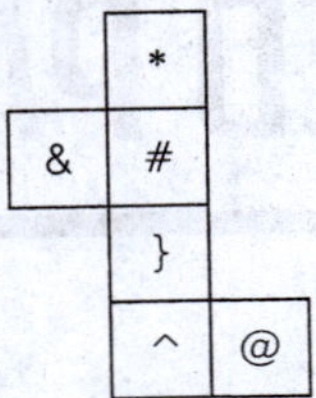

(a) & (b) }
(c) @ (d) ^

28. The position of how many, letters will remain unchanged, if each of the letters in the word 'COUNTED' is arranged in English alphabetical order?

(a) None
(b) Two
(c) More than three
(d) Three

29. In a certain code language, 'now or never' is coded as 'ak bj ut' and 'never be late' is coded as 'bj tl cv'. How is 'never' coded in that language?

(a) cv (b) bj (c) ak (d) tl

30. Select the correct mirror image of the given figure, when the mirror is placed at MN, as shown.

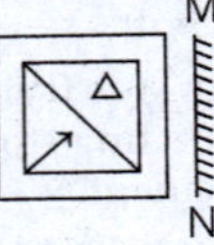

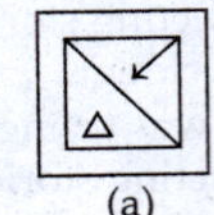
(a)
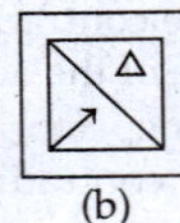
(b)
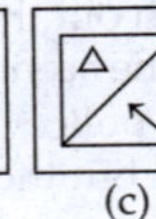
(c)
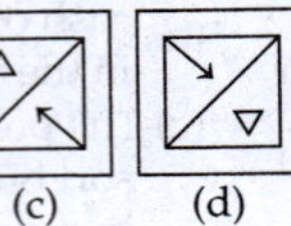
(d)

31. What would be the Roman numeral on the opposite side of 'VI', if the given sheet is folded to form a cube?

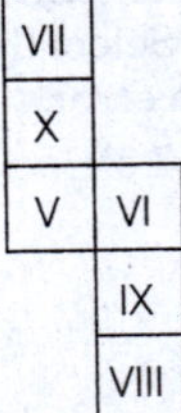

(a) VII (b) VIII
(c) V (d) X

32. What should come in place of question mark (?) in the given series?

119, 128, 137, 146, 155, ?

(a) 164 (b) 163 (c) 161 (d) 162

33. If 'A' stands for '÷', 'B' stands for '×', 'C' stands for '+' and 'D' stands for '–', then the resultant of which of the following will be 652?

(a) 109 B 6 A 16 D 2 C 6
(b) 109 B 6 D 16 A 2 C 6
(c) 109 C 6 D 16 A 2 B 6
(d) 109 A 6 D 16 B 2 C 6

34. Which of the following letter-clusters will replace the question mark (?) in the given series to make it logically complete?

LPT, ?, BBF, JUL, RNR

(a) COD
(b) TIZ
(c) FIZ
(d) UTL

35. A square sheet of paper is folded along the dotted line successively along the directions shown and is then punched in the last. How would the paper look when unfolded?

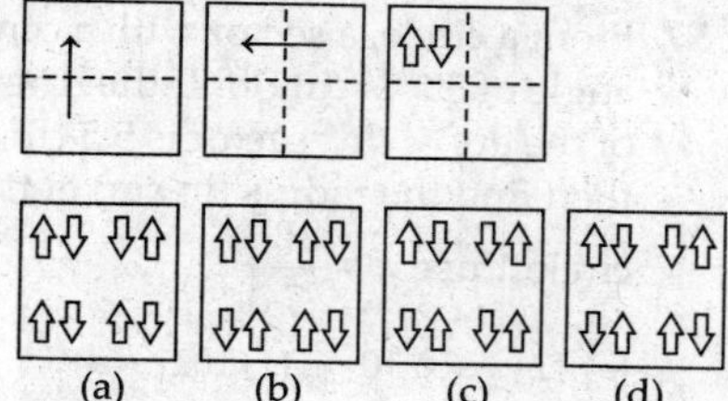

36. The position of how many letters will remain unchanged, if each of the letters in the word 'POWDERS' is arranged in English alphabetical order?

(a) More than three
(b) Three
(c) None
(d) One

37. Select the word-pair that best represents a similar relationship to the one expressed in the pair of words given below.

(The words must be considered as meaningful English words and must not be related to each other based on the number of letters/number of consonants/vowels in the word)

Dog-Barking

(a) Snake-Roar (b) Cows-Squeal
(c) Donkey-Bray (d) Cats-Hissing

38. Select the combination of letters that when sequentially placed in the blanks of the given series will complete the series.

PQRSO_TT_UV_MW_V

(a) TSUX (b) NTUY
(c) SNUX (d) XTUS

39. Identify the figure given in the options, which when put in place of the question mark (?) will logically complete the series?

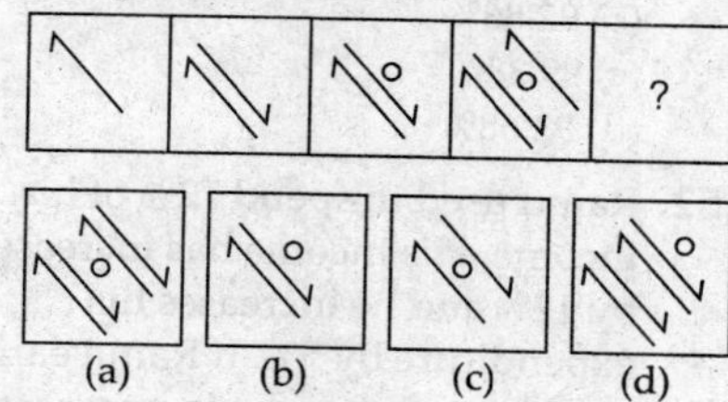

40. Choose the alternative, which closely resembles the mirror image of the given combination.

A
ABUSE
B

(a) E Ƨ ∩ B A
(b) Ǝ Ƨ U B A
(c) E Ƨ U B A
(d) E Ƨ U B A

41. Select the word-pair that best represents a similar relationship to the one expressed in the pair of words given below.

(The words must be considered as meaningful English words and must not be related to each other based on the number of letters/number of consonants/vowels in the word)

Pleasure : Pain

(a) Fast : Quick
(b) Gentle : Brutal
(c) Smart : Intelligent
(d) Angry : Furious

42. Four letter-clusters have been given, out of which three are alike in some manner and one is different. Select the letter-cluster that is different.

(**Note** The odd one out is not based on the number of consonants/vowels or their position in the letter-cluster)

(a) CWSR
(b) MGCA
(c) KEAY
(d) SMIG

43. In a certain code language,
'P + Q' means 'P is the wife of Q'.
'P – Q' means 'P is the brother of Q'.
'P / Q' means 'P is the son of Q'.
'P × Q' means 'P is the father of Q'.
If 'V / K × T + M × O', then how is K related to O?

(a) Mother's father
(b) Mother
(c) Father's mother
(d) Father

44. If 'T' stands for '+', 'P' stands for '÷', 'Q' stands for '×' and 'R' stands for '–', what will come in place of the question mark (?) in the following equation?

24 T 36 P 48 Q 32 R 40 T 53 = ?

(a) 61 (b) 73
(c) 31 (d) 48

45. If 'A' stands for '÷', 'B' stands for '×', 'C' stands for '+' and 'D' stands for '–', what will come in place of the question mark (?) in the following equation?

26 B 3 C 5 D 120 A 4 = ?

(a) 53
(b) 57
(c) 51
(d) 55

46. How many rectangles are there in the given figure?

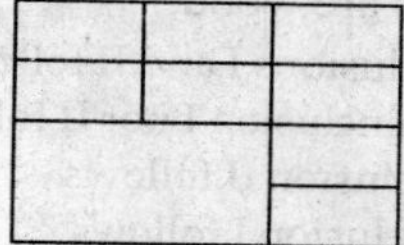

(a) 31 (b) 33 (c) 34 (d) 32

47. What should come in place of the question mark (?) in the given series?

512, 1000, 1728, 2744, 4096, 5832, ?

(a) 4000
(b) 8000
(c) 9261
(d) 6000

48. In a certain language, 'How are you' is written as 'Co De Ki' and 'You look happy' is written as 'Th De Mo'. How is 'you' written in the given language?
(a) Ki
(b) Co
(c) De
(d) Mo

49. 17 is related to 136 following a certain logic. Following the same logic, 23 is related to 184. To which of the following is 29 related following the same logic?
(**Note** Operations should be performed on the whole numbers, without breaking down the numbers into its constituent digits. E.g. 13 – Operations on 13 such as adding/subtracting/multiplying etc. to 13 can be performed. Breaking down 13 into 1 and 3 and then performing mathematical operations on 1 and 3 is not allowed.)
(a) 228 (b) 234 (c) 232 (d) 230

50. Three statements are followed by conclusions numbered I, II. You have to consider these statements to be true, even if they seem to be at variance with commonly known facts. Decide which of the given conclusions logically follow(s) from the given statements.
Statements
Some bags are paper.
All wood are paper.
Some bags are dolls.
Conclusions
I. All dolls are paper.
II. Some bags are wood.
(a) Both Conclusions I and II follow
(b) Neither Conclusion I nor II follows
(c) Only Conclusion II follows
(d) Only Conclusion I follows

Part III
Quantitative Aptitude

51. Study the given graph and answer the question that follows.
The graph shows the marks obtained by Riya and Rida in six subjects in the CBSE 12th exam. The maximum marks in Maths, Physics and Chemistry are 140 and that in English, IP, Biology are 180.

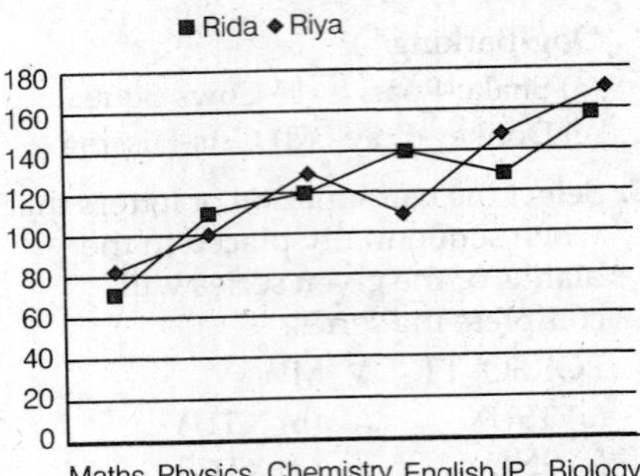

What is the percentage of marks obtained by Riya in Chemistry?
(a) 95.87%
(b) 92.86%
(c) 99.38%
(d) 92.68%

52. Ramu used to spend 72% of his income. His income has increased by 12% and he increases his expenditure by 5%. If Ramu earlier saved y and after the increases, now he saves x, then what is the value of $\left(\frac{x-y}{y}\times 100\right)$%?
(a) 25%
(b) 22%
(c) 27%
(d) 30%

53. The ratio of the lateral surface area to the total surface area of a cylinder with base diameter 60 cm and height 10 cm is
(a) 1:9 (b) 1:7 (c) 1:4 (d) 1:3

54. If $\cot\theta = \frac{3}{4}$, θ is an acute angle, then $(\sin\theta + \cos\theta - \tan\theta)$ is equal to
(a) $\frac{1}{11}$ (b) $\frac{1}{15}$
(c) $\frac{1}{13}$ (d) $\frac{1}{18}$

55. A man bought 4 books for ₹ 50 each, 5 books for ₹ 60 each and 6 books for ₹ 70 each. The average cost of a book for the man is (round up to two decimal places)
(a) ₹ 36.33
(b) ₹ 50.33
(c) ₹ 61.33
(d) ₹ 60.33

56. A student has 5 subjects in an examination. The distribution of hard work of 16 h per day over 5 subjects and marks obtained 400 out of 500 are shown in the charts.

Hard Work in time

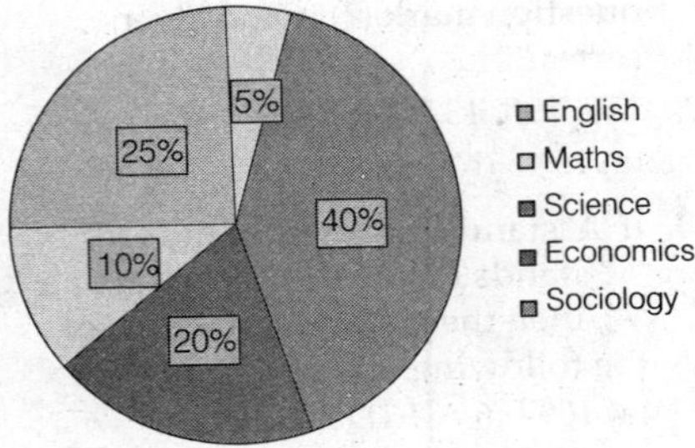

Marks Obtained

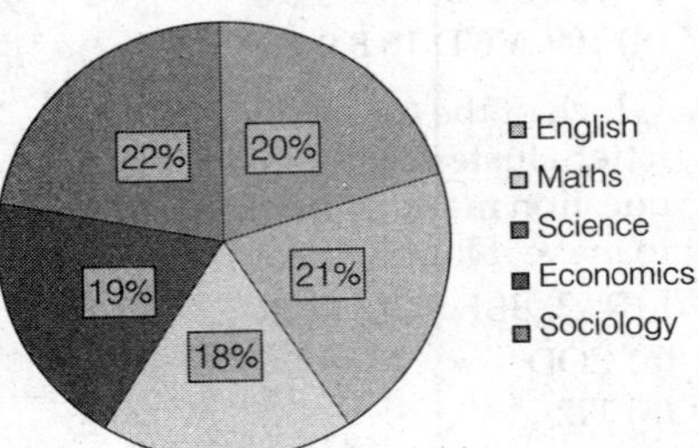

How much time did the student spend on Maths and how much marks were obtained in Maths?
(a) 9.6 h and 84 marks
(b) 6.4 h and 84 marks
(c) 40 h and 21 marks
(d) 6.4 h and 90 marks

57. From a circle, a sector with a central angle of 30° is cut off. If the length of the arc of this sector is 5.5 cm, then find the radius (in cm) of the circle. $\left[\text{use } \pi = \frac{22}{7}\right]$
(a) 12 (b) 10 (c) 10.5 (d) 11

58. The following table shows the production of food grains in a country over the five years.

Years	Production (in ten lakh tonnes)			
	Wheat	Rice	Maize	Other grains
2016-17	650	250	200	450
2017-18	800	440	240	400
2018-19	680	390	220	500
2019-20	700	400	260	480
2020-21	640	440	300	520

The difference between the average production (in ten lakh tonnes) of wheat and maize over the years is
(a) 140 (b) 310 (c) 450 (d) 224

59. For what positive values of k do the following pair of linear equations have infinitely many solutions?
$kx + 3y - (k-3) = 0$
$12x + ky - k = 0$
(a) 6 (b) 2 (c) 12 (d) 4

60. The following bar-graph represents the production of three types of buses by a company over the years (in thousands).

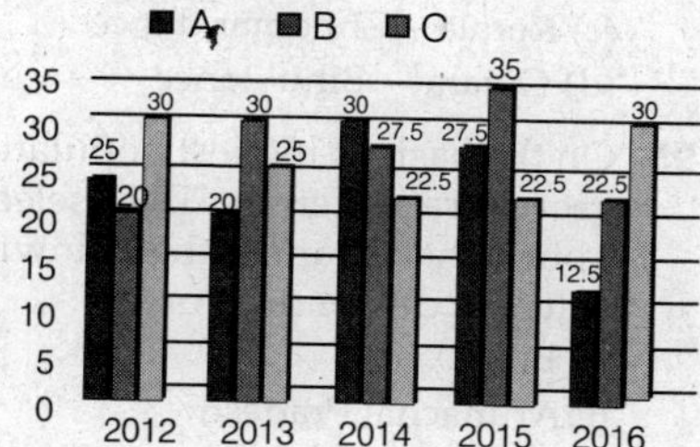

In which of the following years was the percentage production of B type buses to C type buses, the maximum?

(a) 2015 (b) 2013
(c) 2016 (d) 2014

61. If the price of tea is increased by 40%, by what percentage must the consumption of tea be decreased, so as not to increase the expenditure?

(a) $15\frac{2}{9}\%$ (b) $31\frac{3}{5}\%$
(c) $35\frac{9}{2}\%$ (d) $28\frac{4}{7}\%$

62. If the height of a solid right circular cylinder is 27 cm and diameter of its base is 30 cm, the total surface area (in cm^2) of the right circular cylinder is $\left(\text{Take } \pi = \frac{22}{7}\right)$

(a) 3976 (b) 3964
(c) 3978 (d) 3960

63. Akhil can complete a piece of work in 24 days. Shyam can complete the same piece of work in 12 days. If both of them work together, in how many days can they complete the same piece of work?

(a) 12 days (b) 6 days
(c) 10 days (d) 8 days

64. An amount of ₹ 8000 was invested for 2 yr, partly in scheme 1 at the rate of 5% simple interest per annum and the rest in scheme 2 at the rate of 4% simple interest per annum. The total interest received at the end was ₹ 720. The amount of money invested in scheme 1 is

(a) ₹ 3640
(b) ₹ 7200
(c) ₹ 4400
(d) ₹ 4000

65. In a circle, O is the centre and AOB is the diameter. AT is a tangent to the circle. Line TB intersects the circle at Q. Given that $\angle AOQ = 94°$, find $\angle ATQ$.

(a) 86° (b) 43° (c) 47° (d) 133°

66. In a 100 m race, A beats B by 20 m and B beats C by 5 m. In the same race, find the distance by which A beats C.

(a) 22 m (b) 24 m (c) 26 m (d) 25 m

67. A shopkeeper buys 1800 kg wheat for ₹ 32400. If 20% of this wheat is spoiled due to rain, at what rate (₹/kg) should he sell the rest to earn 20%?

(a) 29 (b) 26
(c) 25 (d) 27

68. Simplify the given expression.

$$\left[3 \times 6 - 3\left\{2\left(2 \div \frac{1}{2} - 2\right) + 2 \div \frac{1}{2}\right\} - 18\right]$$

(a) 24 (b) 18
(c) –24 (d) –18

69. A 35% profit is made, when a discount of 35% is given on the marked price of an item. When the discount is 45%, then the profit percentage will be

(a) $17\frac{1}{13}\%$ (b) $11\frac{3}{13}\%$
(c) $14\frac{3}{13}\%$ (d) $13\frac{3}{17}\%$

70. Two parallel chords of length 5 units and 8 units are on opposite sides of the centre of a circle of radius 7 units. What is the distance between the chords? (round your answer to two decimal places)

(a) 11.82 units (b) 12.28 units
(c) 11.28 units (d) 12.82 units

71. In a triangle ABC, $AB = AC$. BC is extended to D such that $CD = AB$ and the angle ADC is 30°. What are the angles of triangle ABC?

(a) 30°, 60°, 90°
(b) 50°, 60°, 70°
(c) 60°, 60°, 60°
(d) 45°, 60°, 75°

72. If the income of Neha is 5% more than that of Monica, then the income of Monica is what percentage less than that of Neha?

(a) $4\frac{5}{21}\%$ (b) $4\frac{13}{21}\%$
(c) $4\frac{11}{21}\%$ (d) $4\frac{16}{21}\%$

73. A mixture contains alcohol and water in the ratio of 12 : 5. On adding 14 L of water, the ratio of alcohol to water becomes 4 : 3. The quantity of alcohol in mixture is

(a) 18 L (b) 28 L
(c) 30 L (d) 42 L

74. What is the smallest number that must be added to 19487161, so that it is divisible by 11?

(a) 11 (b) 5 (c) 16 (d) 10

75. 3 solid spheres of diameters 6 cm, 8 cm and 10 cm are melted together to form a single solid sphere. Find its radius.

(a) 12 cm
(b) 9 cm
(c) 3 cm
(d) 6 cm

Part III

General Awareness

76. Which part of the Constitution of India deals with 'Citizenship'?

(a) Part I
(b) Part III
(c) Part IV
(d) Part II

77. In a symport

(a) a molecule moves across a membrane independent of other molecules
(b) both molecules cross the membrane in the same direction
(c) both molecules cross the membrane in the opposite direction
(d) a molecule moves across a membrane dependent of other molecules

78. The Braj festival in .... is held every year for two days in the Shukla Paksha of the Phalgun month, a few days before Holi.

(a) Rajasthan
(b) Himachal Pradesh
(c) Madhya Pradesh
(d) Haryana

79. The Kailasha temple at Ellora near Aurangabad in Maharashtra was built by a king from the .... dynasty.

(a) Rashtrakuta
(b) Pratihara
(c) Gurjara Pratihara
(d) Chandella

80. Where and when was India's first Senior National Archery Championship held?
(a) Delhi, 1973 (b) Chennai, 1973
(c) Chennai, 1975 (d) Delhi, 1975

81. Which of the following persons was sworn in as chief of the Central Information Commission of India in November 2023?
(a) Bimal Julka
(b) Yashovardhan Azad
(c) Divya Prakash Sinha
(d) Heeralal Samariya

82. Which of the following committees had recommended the inclusion of a chapter on the Fundamental Duties in the Constitution of India and stressed that the citizens should become conscious that, in addition to the enjoyment of rights, they also have certain duties to perform?
(a) Balwant Rai Mehta Committee (1976)
(b) JR Varma Committee (1996)
(c) Ashok Mehta Committee (1977)
(d) Swaran Singh Committee (1976)

83. Which of the following is not an alignment option for text in a cell?
(a) Center (b) Right
(c) Justified (d) Left

84. The Thomas Cup is associated with which of the following sports?
(a) Badminton female
(b) Tennis female
(c) Tennis male
(d) Badminton male

85. Which of the following is the most dominant species of the Tropical Deciduous Forests?
(a) Mulberry (b) Rubber
(c) Coconut (d) Teak

86. Which of the following songs did AR Rahman record with Michael Jackson?
(a) Ekam Satyam
(b) You are My Destiny
(c) The Oracle
(d) Infinity Love

87. .... is one of the well-known schemes sponsored by the Union Government of India. It was launched in November 2015 with the aim of rescuing the country's ailing electricity distribution companies.
(a) Integrated Power Development Scheme (IPDS)
(b) One Nation, One Grid
(c) Deendayal Upadhyaya Gram Jyoti Yojana
(d) Ujwal DISCOM Assurance Yojana

88. Which of the following statements is/are False about the Special Economic Zones (SEZs) of India?
1. One of the main objectives of the Zones Act was promotion of exports of goods and services.
2. The Government of India announced the Special Economic Zones (SEZs) Policy in the year 2011.
3. The SEZ Rules provided for different minimum land requirement for different classes of SEZs.

Codes
(a) Only 2 (b) 1 and 2
(c) 2 and 3 (d) Only 3

89. Which of the following tribes does not live in India?
(a) Maasai
(b) Tharu
(c) Gond
(d) Santhal

90. How can we add text to a slide in MS PowerPoint?
(a) Note box (b) Dialogue box
(c) Notes page (d) Textbox

91. Who was the first to use the term 'horsepower' that refers to the power produced by an engine?
(a) John Dalton
(b) Amedeo Avogadro
(c) Albert Einstein
(d) James Watt

92. Which of the following is not a Moon of Jupiter?
(a) Triton
(b) Callisto
(c) Europa
(d) Ganymede

93. Under the discretionary power of which Article of the Indian Constitution did the SC of India recognise sex work as a profession?
(a) Article 142
(b) Article 143
(c) Article 141
(d) Article 140

94. Which of the following pairs of state and folk dance is correctly paired?
(a) Punjab – Bhangra dance
(b) Haryana – Garia or Goria dance
(c) Kerala – Ghoomar dance
(d) Gujarat – Bihu dance

95. On the basis of highest population growth rate (Census 2011), select the option that arranges the following states in descending order.
A. Bihar
B. Arunachal Pradesh
C. Meghalaya

Codes
(a) C, B, A (b) A, B, C
(c) C, A, B (d) B, C, A

96. Former Union Minister .... from Manipur was awarded Padma Shri in 2023 by the Union Government for his contribution in public affairs in the last four decades.
(a) Thokchom Radheshyam Singh
(b) Thounaojam Chaoba
(c) Yumnam Joykumar
(d) Okram Ibobi Singh

97. National income at constant prices means
(a) income estimated for next year prices
(b) income estimated at base year prices
(c) income estimated at current year prices
(d) income estimated at any year prices

98. Who composed the music of the patriotic song 'Maa Tujhe Salaam'?
(a) Anu Malik
(b) Shankar Mahadevan
(c) Himesh Reshammiya
(d) AR Rahman

99. Where did the indigenous sport 'Gatka' originate from?
(a) Rajasthan
(b) Manipur
(c) Punjab
(d) Jammu and Kashmir

100. The birthday of .... is celebrated as the International Day of Non-Violence.
(a) Bhimrao Ambedkar
(b) Mahatma Gandhi
(c) Sardar Vallabhbhai Patel
(d) Rabindranath Tagore

Answers

1. (c)	2. (c)	3. (b)	4. (c)
5. (a)	6. (b)	7. (c)	8. (b)
9. (d)	10. (c)	11. (c)	12. (d)
13. (d)	14 (c)	15. (d)	16. (d)
17. (c)	18. (c)	19. (a)	20. (a)
21. (a)	22. (a)	23. (a)	24. (d)
25. (b)	26. (b)	27. (b)	28. (b)
29. (b)	30. (c)	31. (b)	32. (a)
33. (b)	34. (b)	35. (d)	36. (c)
37. (c)	38. (c)	39. (a)	40. (b)
41. (b)	42. (a)	43. (a)	44. (a)
45. (a)	46. (a)	47. (b)	48. (c)
49. (c)	50. (b)	51. (b)	52. (d)
53. (c)	54. (b)	55. (c)	56. (b)
57. (c)	58. (c)	59. (a)	60. (a)
61. (d)	62. (d)	63. (d)	64. (d)
65. (b)	66. (b)	67. (d)	68. (c)
69. (c)	70. (b)	71. (c)	72. (d)
73. (d)	74. (d)	75. (d)	76. (d)
77. (b)	78. (a)	79. (a)	80. (a)
81. (d)	82. (d)	83. (c)	84. (d)
85. (d)	86. (a)	87. (d)	88. (a)
89. (a)	90. (d)	91. (d)	92. (a)
93. (a)	94. (a)	95. (a)	96. (b)
97. (b)	98. (d)	99. (c)	100. (b)

Explanations

1. *(c)* Part 'She was singing' contains an error. As the sentence presents a time expression of the past, simple past tense should be used. Hence, use 'sang' in place of 'was singing' to correct the sentence.

2. *(c)* The phrasal verb 'give out, in the given sentence is incorrect as it means to distribute.
The correct phrasal verb for the sentence would be 'sort out' which means categorise.

3. *(b)* Part 'be study' contains an error. Use 'studying' to correct the sentence.

4. *(c)* Part 'My daughter participate' contains an error.

Use 'participates' to correct the sentence. As the subject of the sentence is singular, singular verb should be used.

5. *(a)* The correct filler for the given blank is 'conclusion'.

6. *(b)* The correct filler for the given blank is 'showing'.

7. *(c)* The correct filler for the given blank is 'healthier'.

8. *(b)* The correct filler for the given blank is 'grabbing'.

9. *(d)* The correct filler for the given blank is 'options'.

10. *(c)* The word 'Desire' means 'a longing or want of something'. 'Loathing' and 'Aversion' means dislike and disgust.

11. *(c)* The underlined part of the given sentence contains an error.

Use 'always takes his dog for a walk' to correct the sentence.

12. *(d)* The underlined part of the given sentence contains an error. Use 'about' to correct the sentence.

13. *(d)* 'Vehement' means showing strong feeling; forceful, passionate, or intense. Hence, its antonym is 'mild'.
- 'Reliable' means dependable.
- 'Smashed' means broken.
- 'Passionate' means having, showing, or caused by strong feelings or beliefs.

14. *(c)* The correct filler for the given blank is 'come under'.
- 'Come off' means to appear or sound like something.
- 'Come upon' means to meet someone unexpectedly.
- 'Come out' means to become public.

15. *(d)* 'Uniform' means same for all. Hence, its antonym is 'Variegated' means various or different.

16. *(d)* 'Transparency' means the quality of allowing light to pass through so that objects behind can be distinctly seen. Hence, its antonym is 'Opacity' which means the quality of being difficult to understand or know about, especially because things have been intentionally kept secret or made complicated.
- 'Coherence' means unity.
- 'Reliability' means dependable.
- 'Clarity' means the quality of being clear and easy to understand, see, or hear.

17. *(c)* The incorrectly spelt word is 'funcktions'. The correct spelling is 'functions'.

18. *(c)* 'Noble' means someone with high or elevated character, or who is impressive in appearance.

Hence, its antonym is 'common'.

19. *(a)* 'Dismal' means causing a mood of gloom or depression. Hence, its antonym is 'luminous' which means well-lit. 'Dainty' means delicate.

20. *(a)* If a piece of news comes like a bolt from the blue, it is completely unexpected and very surprising.

21. *(a)* 'Benevolent' means kind and noble. Hence, its antonym is 'Cruel'.

22. *(a)* Obsolete means old and out-dated.

23. *(a)* The underlined part of the given sentence contains an error. Use 'apology' to correct the sentence.

24. *(d)* The incorrectly spelt word is 'couragious'. The correct spelling is 'courageous'.

25. *(b)* Walk a tightrope means to act carefully in a difficult situation.

26. *(b)* As,

$$(35, 5, 7) \rightarrow 35 = 5 \times 7$$

and $$(108, 12, 9) \rightarrow 108 = 12 \times 9$$

Similarly,

$$(91, 13, 7) \rightarrow 91 = 13 \times 7$$

27. *(b)* According to the question,

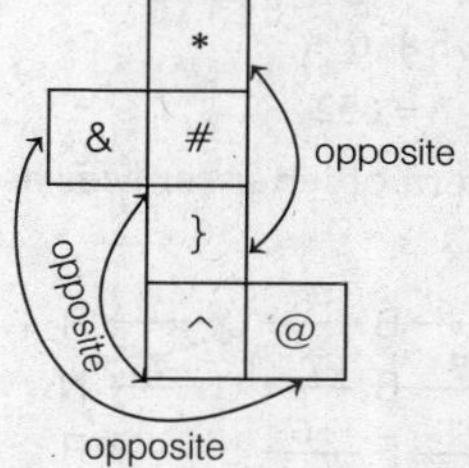

∴ '}' will be opposite to '*'.

28. *(b)* According to the question,

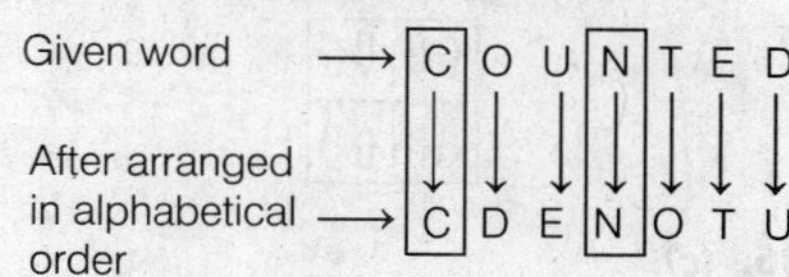

Hence, positions of two letters C and N will remain unchanged.

29. *(b)* According to the question,

now or never → ak bj ut

never be late → bj tl cv

∴ Code for 'never' will be 'bj'.

30. *(c)* The correct mirror image of given question figure is as shown below.

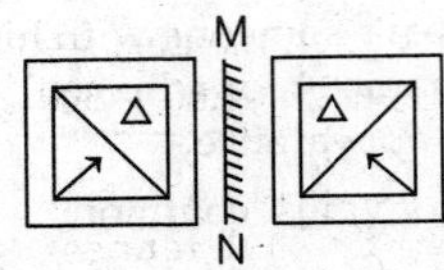

31. *(b)* According to the question,

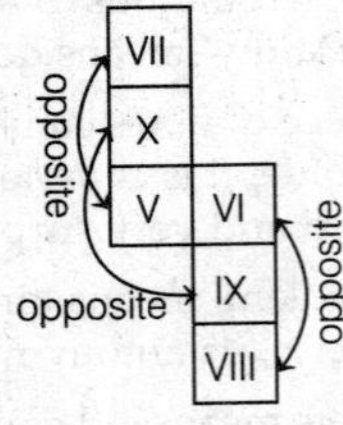

∴ Roman numeral 'VIII' will opposite to roman numeral 'VI'.

32. *(a)* The pattern of the series is as follows,

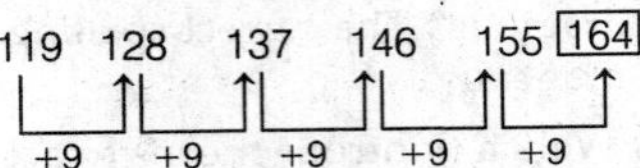

33. *(b)* According to the question,

A → ÷, B → ×, C → +, D → −

From option (b),

109 B 6 D 16 A 2 C 6

Putting the signs in place of letters, we get

$109 \times 6 - 16 \div 2 + 6$

$= 654 - 8 + 6$

$= 660 - 8 = 652$

34. *(b)* The pattern of letter series is as follows,

L $\xrightarrow{+8}$ T $\xrightarrow{+8}$ B $\xrightarrow{+8}$ J $\xrightarrow{+8}$ R

P $\xrightarrow{-7}$ I $\xrightarrow{-7}$ B $\xrightarrow{-7}$ U $\xrightarrow{-7}$ N

T $\xrightarrow{+6}$ Z $\xrightarrow{+6}$ F $\xrightarrow{+6}$ L $\xrightarrow{+6}$ R

35. *(d)* When the paper will unfolded, it will look like option (d).

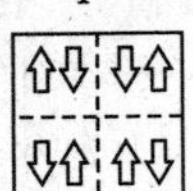

36. *(c)*

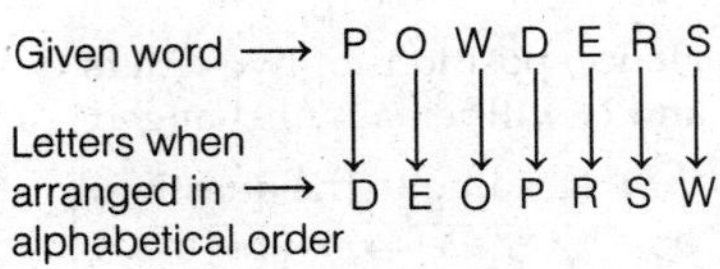

∴ None of the letters will remain unchanged.

37. *(c)* As, 'Bark' is a sound produced by 'Dog'.

Similarly, 'Bray' is the sound produced by 'Donkey'.

38. *(c)* The pattern of series is as follows,

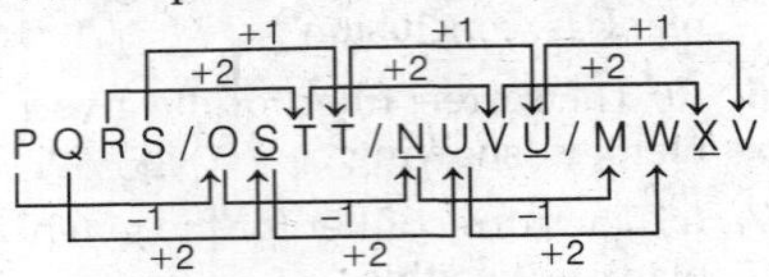

∴ Required combination = SNUX

39. *(a)* In series, 1 arrow and 1 circle is adding on right side of figure alternatively in each next step.

40. *(b)* The mirror image of given combination is given below,

41. *(b)* As, the 'Pleasure' and 'Pain' are antonyms of each other.

Similarly, 'Gentle' and 'Brutal' are antonyms of each other.

42. *(a)* As,

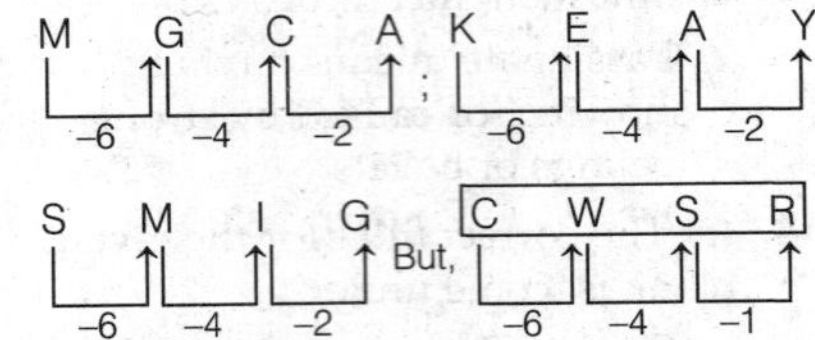

Hence, 'CWSR' is odd one out.

43. *(a)* Given expression,

V / K × T + M × O

According to the question,

K(+) —Son→ V(+); V(+) ←Sibling— T(−) ←Wife— M(+); M(+) —Father→ O(+/−)

+ → Male
− → Female

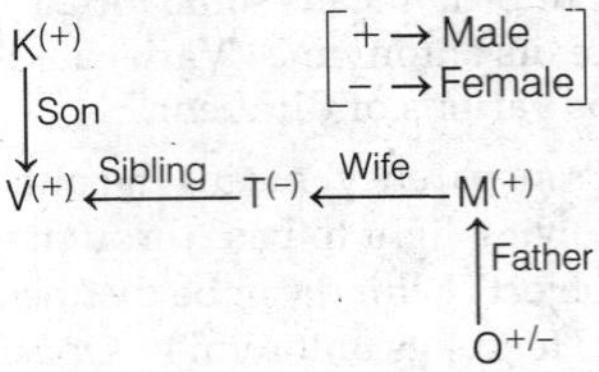

Hence, K is 'mother's father' of O.

44. *(a)* According to the question,

T → +, P → ÷, Q → ×, R → −

Given equation,

24 T 36 P 48 Q 32 R 40 T 53 = ?

Replacing the letters with symbols, we get

$24 + 36 \div 48 \times 32 - 40 + 53 = ?$

$\Rightarrow \quad 24 + 24 - 40 + 53 = ?$

$\Rightarrow \quad 48 - 40 + 53 = ? \Rightarrow 8 + 53 = ?$

$\therefore \quad ? = 61$

45. *(a)* According to the question,

A → ÷, B → ×, C → +, D → −

Given equation,

26 B 3 C 5 D 120 A 4 = ?

Replacing the letters with symbols, we get

$26 \times 3 + 5 - 120 \div 4 = ?$

$\Rightarrow \quad 78 + 5 - 30 = ?$

$\Rightarrow \quad 83 - 30 = ?$

$\therefore \quad ? = 53$

46. *(a)* Numbering the figure,

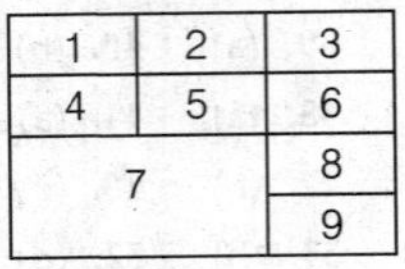

1	2	3
4	5	6
7		8
		9

Rectangles can be represent as

(1), (2), (3), (4), (5), (6), (7), (8), (9), (1, 2), (2, 3), (1, 2, 3), (4, 5), (5, 6), (1, 4), (2, 5), (3, 6), (4, 5, 6), (8, 9), (6, 8), (4, 5, 7), (3, 6, 8), (6, 8, 9), (7, 8, 9), (3, 6, 8, 9), (1, 2, 4, 5), (1, 2, 3, 4, 5, 6), (4, 5, 6, 7, 8, 9), (1, 2, 4, 5, 7), (2, 5, 6, 3), (1, 2, 3, 4, 5, 6, 7, 8, 9)

∴ Total 31 rectangles are present in the given figure.

47. *(b)* The pattern of the given series is as follows,

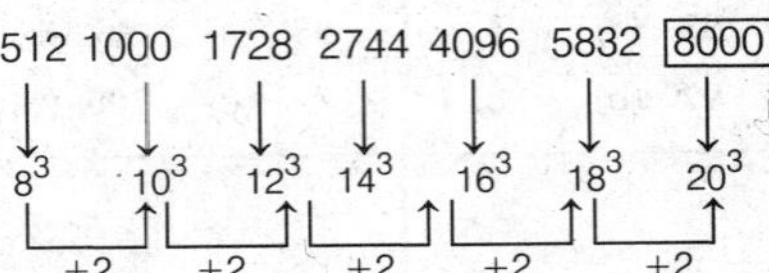

48. *(c)* According to the question,

How are you ⟶ Co De Ki

You look happy ⟶ Th De Mo

Hence, the code for 'you' is 'De'.

49. *(c)* As, 17 $\xrightarrow{\times 8}$ 136

and 23 $\xrightarrow{\times 8}$ 184

Similarly, 29 $\xrightarrow{\times 8}$ 232

50. *(b)* According to the statements,

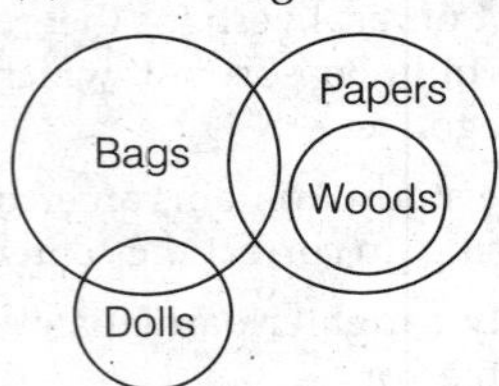

Conclusions I. (✗)

II. (✗)

Hence, neither Conclusion I nor II follows.

51. *(b)* Marks obtained by Riya in Chemistry = 130

Maximum marks in Chemistry = 140

$\therefore$ Required percentage $= \frac{130}{140} \times 100$

$= 92.857 \sim 92.86\%$

52. *(d)* Let the income and expenditure of Ramu be $100k$ and $72k$, respectively.

$\therefore$ Savings = Income – Expenditure

$= 100k - 72k = ₹28k$

$\therefore \quad y = 28k$

New income $= 100 \times \frac{112}{100} = ₹112k$

New expenditure $= 72 \times \frac{105}{100} = ₹75.6k$

$\therefore$ New savings $= 112k - 75.6k = ₹36.4k$

$\therefore x = 36.4k$

Now, putting the $y = 28k$ and $x = 36.4k$ in given equation, we get

$$\left[\frac{x-y}{y} \times 100\right]\%$$

$$= \left[\frac{36.4k - 28k}{28k} \times 100\right]\%$$

$$= \frac{8.4k}{28k} \times 100 = 30\%$$

53. *(c)* Given, diameter $(d) = 60$ cm,

Height $(h) = 10$ cm

According to the question,

$$\frac{2\pi rh}{2\pi r(h+r)} = \frac{h}{h+r}$$

$$= \frac{10}{10 + \frac{60}{2}} \qquad \left[\because r = \frac{d}{2}\right]$$

$$= \frac{10}{10+30} = \frac{10}{40}$$

$\therefore$ Required ratio = 10 : 40 = 1 : 4

54. *(b)* Given, $\cot\theta = \frac{3}{4} = \frac{AB}{AC}$

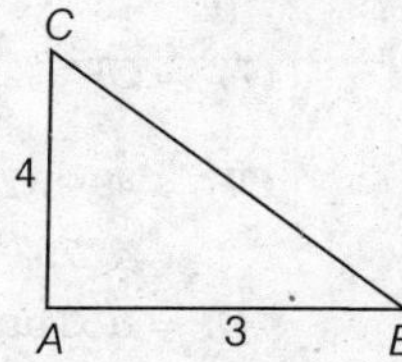

Now in ΔABC, using Pythagoras theorem,

$$BC^2 = AC^2 + AB^2$$

$$\Rightarrow \quad BC^2 = (3)^2 + (4)^2$$

$$\Rightarrow BC^2 = 9 + 16 = 25$$

$$\therefore \quad BC = 5$$

So, $\sin\theta = \frac{AC}{BC} = \frac{4}{5}$, $\cos\theta = \frac{AB}{BC} = \frac{3}{5}$

and $\tan\theta = \frac{AC}{AB} = \frac{4}{3}$

Now,

$$\sin\theta + \cos\theta - \tan\theta = \frac{4}{5} + \frac{3}{5} - \frac{4}{3}$$

$$= \frac{7}{5} - \frac{4}{3}$$

$$= \frac{21-20}{15} = \frac{1}{15}$$

55. *(c)* Average cost

$$= \left[\frac{4 \times 50 + 5 \times 60 + 6 \times 70}{4 + 5 + 6}\right]$$

$$= \left[\frac{200 + 300 + 420}{15}\right]$$

$$= \frac{920}{15}$$

$= ₹\,61.33$

56. *(b)* Given, total hard work = 16 h per day

Total marks obtained = 400 out of 500

From pie-chart,

Time spend on Maths

$$= \frac{40}{100} \times 16 = 6.4 \text{ h}$$

Marks obtained in Maths

$$= \frac{21}{100} \times 400$$

= 84 marks

$\therefore$ Total time and marks obtained in Maths are 6.4 h and 84 marks, respectively.

57. *(c)* Given, central angle = 30°,

Length of the arc = 5.5 cm

We know that,

$$\text{Length of arc} = 2\pi r \times \frac{\theta}{360°}$$

$$5.5 = 2 \times \frac{22}{7} \times r \times \frac{30°}{360°}$$

$$\Rightarrow \quad 5.5 = 2 \times \frac{22}{7} \times r \times \frac{1}{12}$$

$$\Rightarrow \quad r = \frac{5.5 \times 7 \times 12}{2 \times 22}$$

$$\therefore \quad r = 10.5 \text{ cm}$$

Hence, the radius of circle is 10.5 cm.

58. *(c)* Average production of wheat

$$= \frac{650 + 800 + 680 + 700 + 640}{5}$$

$$= \frac{3470}{5} = 694 \text{ (ten lakh tonnes)}$$

Average production of maize

$$= \frac{200 + 240 + 220 + 260 + 300}{5}$$

$$= \frac{1220}{5} = 244 \text{ (ten lakh tonnes)}$$

$\therefore$ Required difference

$= 694 - 244$

$= 450$ (ten lakh tonnes)

59. *(a)* Given, $Kx + 3y - (K-3) = 0$

($Kx \to a_1$, $3y \to b_1$, $(K-3) \to c_1$)

and $12x + Ky - K = 0$

($12x \to a_2$, $Ky \to b_2$, $K \to c_2$)

For infinitely many solutions,

$$\frac{a_1}{a_2} = \frac{b_1}{b_2} = \frac{c_1}{c_2}$$

Condition 1,

$$\frac{a_1}{a_2} = \frac{b_1}{b_2} \Rightarrow \frac{K}{12} = \frac{3}{K}$$

$$\Rightarrow \quad K^2 = 12 \times 3 \Rightarrow \quad K = \pm 6$$

Condition 2,

$$\frac{b_1}{b_2} = \frac{c_1}{c_2} \Rightarrow \frac{3}{K} = \frac{-(K-3)}{-K}$$

$$\Rightarrow \quad 3K = K^2 - 3K$$

$$\Rightarrow K^2 - 6K = 0$$

$$\Rightarrow K(K-6) = 0 \Rightarrow K = 0, K = 6$$

From both Conditions 1 and Condition 2,

$$K = 6$$

Hence, when $K = 6$, then following pair of linear equations has infinitely solutions.

60. *(a)* From options,

Production of type B buses to type C buses in year 2015

$$= \frac{35}{22.5} \times 100 = 155.56\%$$

Production of type B buses to type C buses in year 2013 $= \frac{30}{25} \times 100 = 120\%$

Production of type B buses to type C buses in year 2016 $= \frac{22.5}{30} \times 100 = 75\%$

Production of type B buses to type C buses in year 2014 $= \frac{27.5}{22.5} \times 100$

$= 122.23\%$

$\therefore$ Production in year 2015 was maximum.

61. (*d*) Let the original price of tea is ₹ 100.

Then, increased price $= 100 \times \frac{140}{100}$

$= ₹ 140$

∴ Reduction in consumption

$= \left[\frac{140-100}{140} \times 100\right]$

$= \left[\frac{40}{140} \times 100\right]$

$= \frac{200}{7}\%$

$= 28\frac{4}{7}\%$

62. (*d*) Given, height of cylinder (h) = 27 cm

Diameter (d) of cylinder = 30 cm

∴ Radius $(r) = \frac{d}{2} = \frac{30}{2} = 15$ cm

Total surface area $= 2\pi r(h + r)$

$= 2 \times \frac{22}{7} \times 15[27 + 15]$

$= 2 \times \frac{22}{7} \times 15 \times 42$

$= 3960 \text{ cm}^2$

63. (*d*) Akhil's 1 day's work $= \frac{1}{24}$

Shyam's 1 day's work $= \frac{1}{12}$

(Akhil + Shyam)'s 1 day's work

$= \frac{1}{24} + \frac{1}{12}$

$= \frac{1+2}{24} = \frac{3}{24}$

$= \frac{1}{8}$

∴ Akhil and Shyam complete the work together in 8 days.

64. (*d*) Let the amount invested at rate of 5% is x and amount invested at 4% is $(8000 - x)$.

According to the question,

$\frac{x \times 5 \times 2}{100} + \frac{(8000-x) \times 4 \times 2}{100} = 720$

$\Rightarrow \frac{x \times 10}{100} + 640 - \frac{x \times 8}{100} = 720$

$\Rightarrow \frac{x \times 10}{100} - \frac{x \times 8}{100} = 720 - 640$

$\Rightarrow \frac{x \times 2}{100} = 80$

$\Rightarrow x = 4000$

∴ Amount invested at Scheme 1
= Amount invested at 5% per annum
= ₹ 4000

65. (*b*) According to the question,

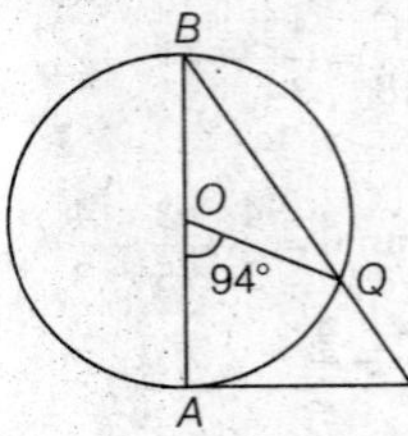

As, AT is a tangent, therefore $\angle BAT = 90°$

Now, $\angle ABQ = \frac{1}{2}\angle AOQ$

$= \frac{1}{2} \times 94° = 47°$

In ΔABT,

$\angle BAT + \angle ABT + \angle ATB = 180°$

$\Rightarrow 90° + 47° + \angle ATQ = 180°$

$[\because \angle ATB = \angle ATQ]$

$\Rightarrow \angle ATQ = 180° - 137°$

$\therefore \angle ATQ = 43°$

66. (*b*) According to the question,

When A covers 100 m, B covers (100 – 20) m = 80 m

∴ $A:B = 100:80 = 5:4$

When B covers 100 m, C covers (100 – 5) m = 95 m

∴ $B:C = 100:95 = 20:19$

Now, $A:B$ and $B:C$

5 : 4   20 : 19

$A:B:C = 25:20:19$

= 100 : 80 : 76 [multiply with 4]

So, A beats C by (100 – 76) m = 24 m

67. (*d*) Given, total quantity of wheat = 1800 kg

Total cost price = ₹ 32400

If 20% wheat was spoiled, remaining wheat $= 1800 \times \frac{80}{100} = 1440$ kg

Cost price of 1 kg of wheat $= \left[\frac{32400}{1440}\right]$

= ₹ 22.5

∴ Selling price $= \left[22.5 \times \frac{120}{100}\right]$

= ₹ 27

68. (*c*) Given expression,

$\left[3 \times 6 - 3\left\{2\left(2 \div \frac{1}{2} - 2\right) + 2 \div \frac{1}{2}\right\} - 18\right]$

$= [18 - 3\{2(4-2) + 4\} - 18]$

$= [18 - 3\{4 + 4\} - 18]$

$= [18 - 24 - 18]$

$= -24$

69. (*c*) Let the marked price = ₹ 100

∴ Selling price $= \left[100 \times \frac{65}{100}\right]$

= ₹ 65

Cost price $= \left[65 \times \frac{100}{135}\right] = ₹\ \frac{1300}{27}$

$\left[\because \text{CP} = \frac{\text{SP} \times 100}{100 + \text{Profit}\%}\right]$

When 45% discount is given on marked price.

∴ New selling price $= \left[100 \times \frac{55}{100}\right]$

= ₹ 55

∴ Required profit $= \frac{55 - \frac{1300}{27}}{\frac{1300}{27}} \times 100$

$= \frac{1485 - 1300}{1300} \times 100$

$= \frac{185}{13}$

$= 14\frac{3}{13}\%$

70. (*b*) According to the question,

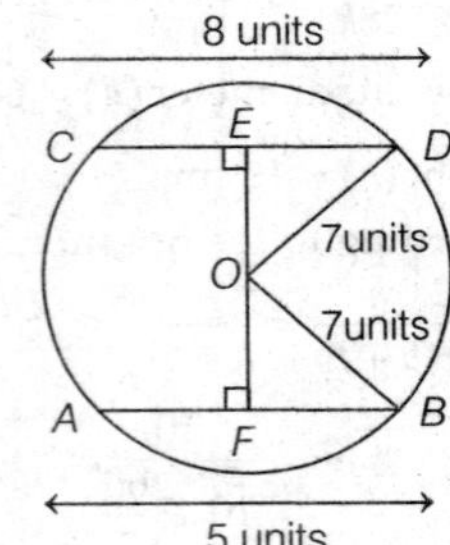

In ΔFOB, $OB^2 = OF^2 + FB^2$

$\Rightarrow OB^2 = OF^2 + \left(\frac{AB}{2}\right)^2$

[∵ Perpendicular from centre to chord bisect the chord]

$(7)^2 = OF^2 + \left(\frac{5}{2}\right)^2$

$\Rightarrow OF^2 = 49 - 6.25$

$= 42.75$

$\Rightarrow OF = 6.53$ units

In ΔEOD,

$OD^2 = OE^2 + ED^2$

$\Rightarrow OD^2 = OE^2 + \left(\frac{CD}{2}\right)^2$

$\Rightarrow 7^2 = OE^2 + \left(\frac{8}{2}\right)^2$

$\Rightarrow OE^2 = 49 - 16 = 33$

$\therefore OE = 5.74$ units

Distance between the chords
$= OF + OE$
$= 6.53 + 5.74$
$= 12.27 \sim 12.28$ units

71. *(c)* According to the question,

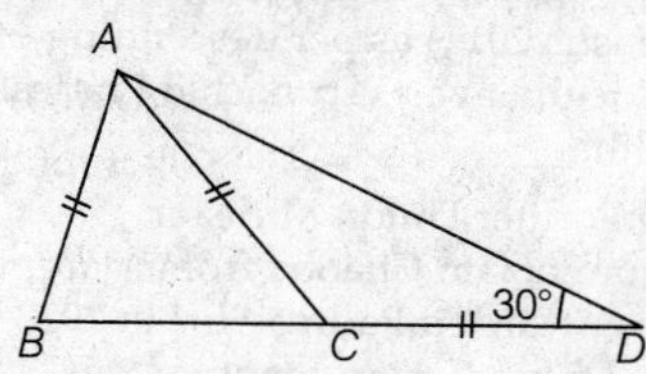

Here, $\angle ADC = \angle DAC = 30°$ $[\because AC = AB = CD]$

$\therefore \quad \angle ACD = 180° - (\angle ADC + \angle DAC)$

$\Rightarrow \quad \angle ACD = 180° - (30° + 30°)$

$\therefore \quad \angle ACD = 120°$

Now,

$\angle ACB = 180° - \angle ACD = 180° - 120°$
$= 60°$

$\therefore \quad \angle ACB = \angle ABC = 60°$ $[\because AB = AC]$

Now, $\angle BAC = 180° - (\angle ACB + \angle ABC)$
$= 180° - (60 + 60)°$

$\angle BAC = 60°$ [$\because$ Angles sum property]

Hence, all angles of triangle are $\angle ACB$, $\angle ABC$ and $\angle BAC = 60°, 60°$ and $60°$.

72. *(d)* Let the income of Monica is ₹ $100x$.

$\therefore$ Income of Neha $= \left[100x \times \frac{105}{100}\right]$
$= ₹105x$

$\therefore$ Required percentage

$= \left[\frac{105x - 100x}{105x} \times 100\right]$

$= \left[\frac{5x}{105x} \times 100\right]$

$= \left[\frac{100}{21}\right]\%$

$= 4\frac{16}{21}\%$

73. *(d)* Let the amount of alcohol be $12x$. and amount of water be $5x$.

According to the question,

$\frac{12x}{5x + 14} = \frac{4}{3}$

$\Rightarrow \quad 36x = 20x + 56$

$\Rightarrow 36x - 20x = 56$

$\Rightarrow \quad 16x = 56$

$x = \frac{56}{16} = 3.5$ L

$\therefore$ Quantity of alcohol
$= 12 \times 3.5$
$= 42$ L

74. *(d)* Given number, 19487161

Sum of numbers at odd place
$= 1 + 4 + 7 + 6 = 18$

Sum of numbers at even place
$= 9 + 8 + 1 + 1 = 19$

Thus, difference $= 19 - 18 = 1$

We add 10 i.e.$1 + 10 = 11$ to make it divisible by 11.

75. *(d)* Given, diameter$_1$ $(d_1) = 6$ cm

Diameter$_2$ $(d_2) = 8$ cm

Diameter$_3$ $(d_3) = 10$ cm

$\therefore$ Radius$_1$ $(r_1) = \frac{d_1}{2} = \frac{6}{2} = 3$ cm

Radius$_2$ $(r_2) = \frac{d_2}{2} = \frac{8}{2} = 4$ cm

Radius$_3$ $(r_3) = \frac{d_3}{2} = \frac{10}{2} = 5$ cm

Let the radius of single sphere $= R$

According to the question,

$\frac{4}{3}\pi r_1^3 + \frac{4}{3}\pi r_2^3 + \frac{4}{3}\pi r_3^3 = \frac{4}{3}\pi R^3$

$\Rightarrow \frac{4}{3}\pi(3)^3 + \frac{4}{3}\pi(4)^3 + \frac{4}{3}\pi(5)^3 = \frac{4}{3}\pi R^3$

$\Rightarrow \frac{4}{3}\pi[27 + 64 + 125] = \frac{4}{3}\pi R^3$

$\Rightarrow \quad \frac{4}{3}\pi[216] = \frac{4}{3}\pi R^3$

$\Rightarrow \quad R^3 = \frac{\frac{4}{3}\pi \times 216}{\frac{4}{3}\pi}$

$\Rightarrow \quad R^3 = 216$

$\therefore \quad R = 6$ cm

Hence, the radius of single solid sphere is 6 cm.

76. *(d)* Part II of the Constitution of India deals with 'Citizenship'.

- Citizenship of India is governed by Articles 5-11 (Part II) of the Constitution.
- The Citizenship Act, 1955 is the legislation dealing with Citizenship.

1. Citizenship at the commencement of the Constitution
2. Citizenship by birth
3. Citizenship by descent
4. Citizenship by registration
5. Citizenship by naturalisation
6. By incorporation of territory (by GOI).

77. *(b)* In a symport, both molecules cross the membrane in the same direction.

- Symport is a type of cotransport, which is when two molecules move together across a membrane using a carrier protein.
- In symport, the molecules move in the same direction relative to each other.
- This is different from antiport, where the molecules move in opposite directions.

78. *(a)* The Braj festival in Rajasthan is held every year for two days in the Shukla Paksh of Phalgun month.

- A few day prior holi.
- This festival is dedicated to Lord Krishna. The one who is believed to have spent a considerable amount of time in a region called Braj in Rajasthan.

79. *(a)* Kailasha temple at Ellora near Aurangabad in Maharashtra was built by a king from the Rashtrakuta dynasty.

- Dantivarman or Dantidurga (735-756) was the founder of the Rashtrakuta dynasty.
- Dantidurga occupied all territories between the Godavari and Vima.
- He is said to have conquered Kalinga, Kosala, Kanchi, Srisril, Malava, Lata etc.

80. *(a)* The India's first Senior National Archery Championship held in Delhi 1973.

- 50 participants participated in first Senior National Archery Championship.
- They used Bamboo Bow and Arrows made in Meghalaya and West Bengal.
- Ist NTPC National Ranking Archery Tournament took place at Nehru Stadium in Guwahati, Assam from 10th-19th August, 2024.

81. *(d)* Heeralal Samariya was sworn in as Chief of the Central Information Commission of India in November 2023.

- The Central Information Commission (CIC) is a statutory body in India.
- It was established under the provisions of the Right to Information Act (2005).
- The CIC is appointed by President of India.

82. *(d)* The Swaran Singh Committee (1976) had recommended the inclusion of a chapter on the Fundamental Duties in the constitution of Indian and stressed that the citizens should become conscious that, in addition to the enjoyment of rights, they also have certain duties to perform.

These duties are set out in Part IV A of the Indian Constitution.

83. *(c)* Justified is not an alignment option for text in a cell.

84. *(d)* The Thomas Cup is associated with Badminton male sport.

The Thomas Cup signifying world supremacy in the sport of Badminton.

- The cup was donated in 1939 by Sir George Thomas.
- It is managed by the IBF (International Badminton Federation)

85. *(d)* Teak is the most dominant species of the Tropical Deciduous Forests.

- These forests occur in regions with heavy rainfall for part of the year followed by a marked dry season.
- These forest formations are dense and lush during the wet summers, but become a dry landscape during the dry winters when most trees shed their leaves.
- Some examples are Teak, Sal, Bamboo etc.

86. *(a)* AR Rahman recorded the 'Ekam Satyam' song with Michael Jackson.

- 'You Are My Destiny' is a song written and performed by Paul Anka.
- 'The Oracle' is sung by AR Rahman.
- 'Infinity Love' is also composed by AR Rahman.

87. *(d)* Ujwal DISCOM Assurance Yojana is one of the well-known schemes sponsored by the Union Government of India.

- It was launched in November 2015, with the aim of rescuing the country's ailing electricity distribution companies.
- The scheme acts as a debt restructuring plan to uplift DISCOMS from their distressed state.

88. *(a)* Only Statement (2) is false.

- The Government of India announced the Special Economic Zones (SEZs) Policy in the April 2000.
- The main objectives of the Zones Act was promotion of exports of goods and services.
- The SEZ Rules provided for different minimum land requirement for different classes of SEZs.

89. *(a)* Maasai tribe does not live in India.

Tharu people are an ethnic group live foremost in Uttarkhand, Uttar Pradesh and Bihar.

- Gond is a Scheduled Tribe, lives in the state of Madhya Pradesh, Maharashtra, Telangana etc.
- The Santhal are from Munda ethnic group/tribe of Odisha, Bihar, Assam and Tripura.

90. *(d)* From Textbox, we can add text to a slide in MS PowerPoint.

91. *(d)* James Watt was the first to use the term 'horse power' that refers to the power produce by an engine.
We can define the power as the rate of doing work and the SI unit of power is watt, and 1 horse power = 746 watt.

92. *(a)* Triton is not a Moon of Jupiter.

- Jupter has 95 Moons.
- That have been officially recognised by the International Astronomical Union.
- Callisto, Europa and Ganymede are the Moons of Jupiter.

93. *(a)* Under the Article 142, the discretionary power of Supreme Court of India recognised sex work as a profession.

- And it observed that its practitioners are entitled to dignity and equal protection under law.
- It is necessary to ensure 'Complete Justice' in any case before it.

94. *(a)* Bhangra dance is folk dance of Punjab.

- Garia or Goria dance is performed by the Tripuri and Jamatia tribes of Tripura.
- Ghoomar dance is a tradition folk dance of Rajasthan.
- Bihu dance is an indigenous folk dance from the Indian state of Assam.

95. *(a)* The descending order of the states is C, B, A.

The highest population growth rate (census 2011) as per descending order is Meghalaya > Arunachal Pradesh > Bihar

96. *(b)* Former Union Minister Thounaojam Chaoba from Manipur was awarded Padma Shri in 2023 by the Union Government for this contribution in public affairs in the last four decades.

He is popularly known as Utlou Chaoba.

97. *(b)* National income at constant prices means income estimated as base year prices.

- It means the money value of the finished goods and services that normal country residents produce in a year when calculated at base year.
- A base year is a regular year that is free from price.

98. *(d)* AR Rahman composed the music of the patriotic song 'Maa Tujhe Salaam'.

- AR Rahman received the Padma Bhushan Award in 1954 and 2010.
- He also received the Padma Shri Award in 2000.

99. *(c)* Gatka is originated from Punjab.

- It is a form of martial arts performed by the Sikhs of Punjab.
- It is a style of fighting which uses wooden sticks.
- It originated in the 15th century and is now usually performed as a sword-dance at various Sikh festival.

100. *(b)* The birthday of Mahatma Gandhi 2nd October is celebrated as the International Day of Non-Violence.

- International Day of Non-Violence means. protest and persuasions, from marches to vigils.
- The non-violence actions are Non-cooperation ; and non-violent, intervention, such as blockades and occupations.

Set 17 05 July, 2024 (Shift I)

SSC CHSL Tier-I SOLVED PAPER

Instructions

1. This paper contains 100 questions.
2. It has 4 Parts, **Part I** General English, **Part II** General Intelligence & Reasoning, **Part III** Quantitative Aptitude and **Part IV** General Awareness.
3. Each question carries **2 marks**.

Part I
General English

1. The following sentence has been divided into four parts. Identify the part that contains an error.

This is / a doll / and there is / a umbrella.

(a) This is (b) a doll
(c) and there is (d) a umbrella

2. The following sentence has been divided into parts. One of them may contain an error. Select the part that contains the error from the given options. If you don't find any error, mark 'No error' as your answer.

The aeroplane took down / without the passengers after / making a sudden announcement.

(a) making a sudden announcement
(b) No error
(c) without the passengers after
(d) The aeroplane took down

3. The following sentence has been split into four segments. Identify the segment that contains an error.

She shall being / travelling / by this time / tomorrow.

(a) travelling
(b) She shall being
(c) by this time
(d) tomorrow

4. Parts of the following sentence have been given as options. Select the option that contains an error.

Emily is a American living in Paris for her work.

(a) a American
(b) living in Paris
(c) Emily is
(d) for her work

Directions (Q. Nos. 5-9) *In the following passage, some words have been deleted. Read the passage carefully and select the most appropriate option to fill in each blank.*

The Sun is about 1.4 million kilometres (1) .... diameter, while the Earth is about 13,000 kilometres wide. This indicates that the Sun's width would need to be filled by more than one hundred Earths. Sunspots are dreary (2) .... on the Sun's surface that are two thousand degrees celsius cooler than the rest of the surface. The coolest piece of the sunspot is the dim focus called the umbra. The penumbra surrounds it. On the Sun's surface, some sunspots are just specks. Additionally, they appear in groups up to ten times larger than Earth. They can sometimes reach 2,00,000 miles in length. As the Sun rotates, these groups (3) .... to travel across the Sun over two weeks. Every 11 years, the number of sunspots reaches its maximum. The solar or sunspot cycle (4) .... to this. The Earth's weather may become more extreme and warm during the peak of sunspot activity. According to the (5) .... made by satellites like Nimbus 7, when sunspots are at their largest, less heat reaches Earth.

5. Select the most appropriate option to fill in blank number (1).

(a) in (b) of (c) on (d) at

6. Select the most appropriate option to fill in blank number (2).

(a) regions (b) section
(c) belt (d) province

7. Select the most appropriate option to fill in blank number (3).

(a) act
(b) show
(c) shape
(d) appear

8. Select the most appropriate option to fill in blank number (4).

(a) refers (b) pass
(c) cite (d) entrust

9. Select the most appropriate option to fill in blank number (5).

(a) perceptions (b) inspections
(c) observations (d) invalidations

10. Select the most appropriate option that can substitute the underlined word segment in the following sentence.

They are leaving <u>there coats there</u>.

(a) their coats there
(b) they're coats there
(c) there coats their
(d) their coats their

11. Select the most appropriate synonym of the word 'Swap' from the given sentence.

The original buyer attempted to resell the tickets online because there was no option to exchange them for a new date.

(a) Resell (b) Exchange
(c) Original (d) Option

12. Select the most appropriate antonym for the underlined word in the given sentence.

He feels that wealthy people view him with <u>contempt</u> because he is poor.

(a) derision
(b) admiration
(c) scorn
(d) obscurity

13. Select the most appropriate option to fill in the blank.

She went on a shopping spree with her friend and made him .... the fat bill.

(a) paid (b) do
(c) pay (d) give

14. Identify the incorrectly spelt word and select its correct spelling.

You shall recieve proper pay for your work.

(a) resieve (b) propper
(c) receive (d) propeer

15. Select the most appropriate antonym of the given word.

Transient

(a) Permanent
(b) Transparent
(c) Transitory
(d) Irregular

16. Select the most appropriate antonym of the given word.

Innocent

(a) Guilty (b) Mischievous
(c) Unfair (d) Righteous

17. Select the correct spelling of the underlined word.

He is one of the most <u>underated</u> players in the team.

(a) undereted (b) underatted
(c) underrated (d) underreted

18. Select the most appropriate meaning of the given idiom.

To be at daggers drawn

(a) To be about to collapse
(b) Ready to fight
(c) Under suspicion
(d) To be under control

19. The following sentence has been split into four segments. Identify the segment that contains a grammatical error.

The hotel room, / which we / booked, / isn't enough big.

(a) isn't enough big
(b) The hotel room
(c) which we
(d) booked,

20. Select the most appropriate synonym of the given word.

Appalled

(a) Applied (b) Clap
(c) Disgusted (d) Allied

21. Select the most appropriate antonym of the given word.

Cramped

(a) Filthy
(b) Spacious
(c) Tight
(d) Crammed

22. Select the most appropriate option that can substitute the underlined word in the given sentence.

Even in cold weather, the <u>reliable</u> car always started on the first try.

(a) dependable (b) inaccurate
(c) erratic (d) flaky

23. Select the most appropriate meaning of the given idiom.

To cost an arm and a leg

(a) Someone is badly hurt
(b) Something is very expensive
(c) Someone does not have money to buy something
(d) Someone has borne losses

24. Select the most appropriate antonym of the underlined word.

The news gave him inexpressible <u>ecstasy</u>.

(a) delight (b) passion
(c) depression (d) disappointment

25. Select the most appropriate option that can substitute the underlined segment in the given sentence.

Mrs. Lakshmi's <u>purchases add around to</u> ₹ 2,650.

(a) purchases add out to
(b) purchases add from to
(c) purchases add up to
(d) purchases add for to

Part II
General Intelligence

26. Select the correct mirror image of the given figure, when the mirror is placed at MN as shown below.

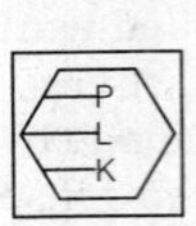

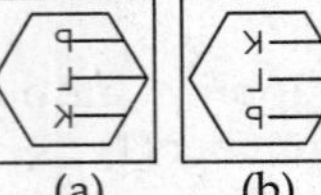
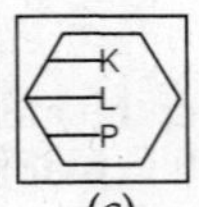
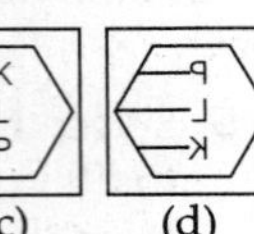

(a) (b) (c) (d)

27. Select the set in which the numbers are related in the same way as are the numbers of the following sets.

(**Note** Operations should be performed on the whole numbers, without breaking down the numbers into its constituent digits. E.g. 13 – Operations on 13 such as adding /subtracting /multiplying etc., to 13 can be performed. Breaking down 13 into 1 and 3 and then performing mathematical operations on 1 and 3 is not allowed.)

(11, 8, 352)
(15, 6, 360)

(a) (11, 7, 231) (b) (8, 9, 352)
(c) (16, 5, 320) (d) (17, 6, 102)

28. Which two numbers should be interchanged to make the given equation correct ?

$(99 - 42 + 11) + (36 \div 6) \times 7 - 50 = 73$

(**Note** Numbers must be interchanged and not the constituent digits e.g., if 2 and 3 are to be interchanged in the equation $43 \times 3 + 4 \div 2$, then interchanged equation is $43 \times 2 + 4 \div 3$)

(a) 50 and 99
(b) 50 and 11
(c) 7 and 11
(d) 42 and 36

29. Select the correct mirror image of the given combination, when the mirror is placed at MN as shown below.

M

Vb72mR

N

(a) ꓤmS7dV (b) ꓤmS7dV
(c) 2mRꓶdV (d) ꓤmS7dV

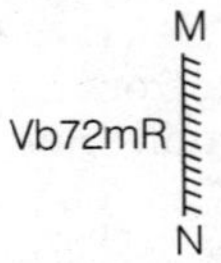

30. Select the correct mirror image of the given figure, when the mirror is placed at MN.

M

R 4 b m L 2

N

(a) S ⅃ m q 4 ꓤ (b) 2 ⅃ m b 4 ꓤ
(c) S ⅃ m d 4 ꓤ (d) S ⅂ ɯ d 4 ꓤ

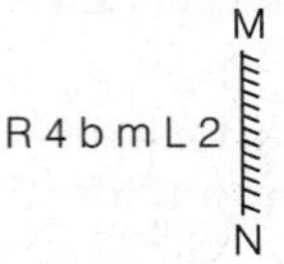

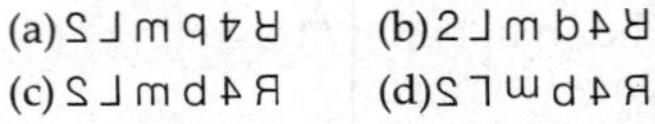

31. If 4th December, 2014 was Thursday, then what was the day of the week on 10th December, 2018 ?

(a) Wednesday (b) Tuesday
(c) Monday (d) Friday

32. If 18th August, 2000 was Friday, then what was the day of the week on 21st August, 2005?

(a) Friday
(b) Wednesday
(c) Monday
(d) Sunday

33. Select the option in which the given figure is embedded. (rotation is not allowed.)

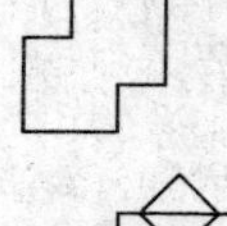

(a) 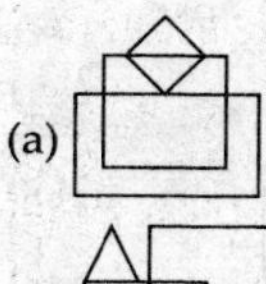 (b) 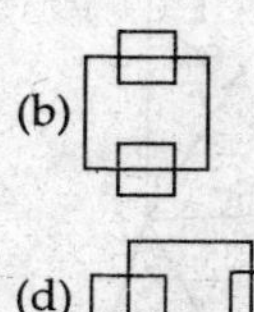

(c) (d)

34. What should come in place of question mark (?) in the given series based on the English alphabetical order?

OWL, QAQ, ?, UIA, WMF

(a) XMB
(b) SEV
(c) LQJ
(d) PNL

35. In a certain code language, 'BAKE' is coded as '2496' and 'CAKE' is coded as '4369'. How is 'B' coded in that language?

(a) 6 (b) 2
(c) 4 (d) 9

36. LJNR is related to IGLP in a certain way based on the English alphabetical order. In the same way, FDHL is related to CAFJ.

To which of the following is HFJN related, following the same logic?

(a) EDHL
(b) EDGL
(c) EBIL
(d) ECHL

37. If 'A' stands for '÷', 'B' stands for '×', 'C' stands for '+' and 'D' stands for '–', then the resultant of which of the following will be 1049?

(a) 94 D 11 B 180 A 4 C 60
(b) 94 A 11 D 180 B 4 C 60
(c) 94 C 11 D 180 A 4 B 60
(d) 94 B 11 D 180 A 4 C 60

38. What should come in place of the question mark (?) in the given series?

32, 61, 90, 119, ?, 177

(a) 148
(b) 147
(c) 149
(d) 146

39. If 'A' stands for '÷', 'B' stands for '×', 'C' stands for '+' and 'D' stands for '–' what will come in place of the question mark (?) in the following equation?

35 B 7 D 120 A 12 C 38 = ?

(a) 173 (b) 473
(c) 373 (d) 273

40. NGPZ is related to JCLV in a certain way based on the English alphabetical order. In the same way, XDLM is related to TZHI. To which of the following is RUKV related, following the same logic?

(a) NQRG (b) NGRQ
(c) NQGR (d) NGQR

41. Select the combination of letters that, when sequentially placed in the blanks of the given series will complete the series.

xy_z_xxy_zbx_yx_bx_y_z_x

(a) xbxyzxxb (b) xyxxzxxb
(c) xzxxyyzx (d) xbxxzxxb

42. How many triangles are there in the given figure?

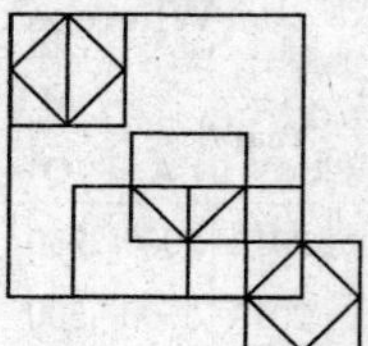

(a) 17 (b) 18
(c) 16 (d) 15

43. In a certain code language,

A + B means 'A is the brother of B'
A – B means 'A is the father of B'
A × B means 'A is the wife of B'
A ÷ B means 'A is the mother of B'

Based on the above, how is P related to T, if 'P ÷ Q × R – S + T'?

(a) Father's mother
(b) Father's sister
(c) Mother's sister
(d) Mother's mother

44. 161 is related to 23 following a certain logic. Following the same logic, 301 is related to 43. To which of the following is 427 related following the same logic?

(**Note** Operations should be performed on the whole numbers, without breaking down the numbers into its constituent digits. e.g. 13 – Operations on 13 such as adding /deleting /multiplying etc., to 13 can be performed. Breaking down 13 into 1 and 3 and then performing mathematical operations on 1 and 3 is not allowed.)

(a) 63 (b) 59 (c) 57 (d) 61

45. Which two numbers should be interchanged to make the given equation correct?

$69 + 15 - (14 \times 4) \div 2 + (48 \div 3) = 58$

(**Note** Numbers must be interchanged and not the constituent digits E.g., if 2 and 3 are to be interchanged in the equation $43 \times 3 + 4 \div 2$, then interchanged equation is $43 \times 2 + 4 \div 3$)

(a) 69 and 48 (b) 4 and 2
(c) 3 and 4 (d) 48 and 15

46. A paper is folded and cut as shown below. How will it appear when unfolded?

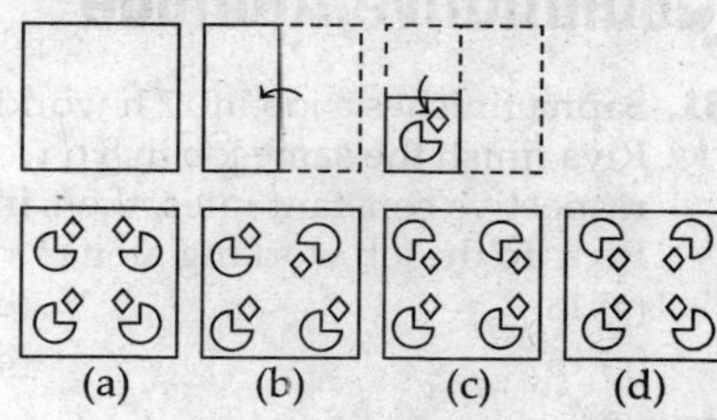

47. In a certain code language, 'CODE' is coded as '1573' and 'DICE' is coded as '7185'. How is 'O' coded in the given language?

(a) 8 (b) 7 (c) 5 (d) 3

48. In this question, three statements are given, followed by three conclusions numbered I, II and III. Assuming the statements to be true, even if they seem to be at variance with commonly known facts, decide which of the conclusion(s) logically follows/follow from the statements.

Statements

Some strawberries are oranges.
Some oranges are kiwis.
All kiwis are melons.

Conclusions

I. No strawberry is a melon.
II. All strawberries are melons.
III. Some strawberries are kiwis.

(a) Both Conclusions II and III follow
(b) All Conclusions I, II and III follow

(c) Neither Conclusion I, II nor III follows
(d) Both Conclusions I and II follow

49. Identify the figure given in the options, which when put in place of the question mark (?) will logically complete the series?

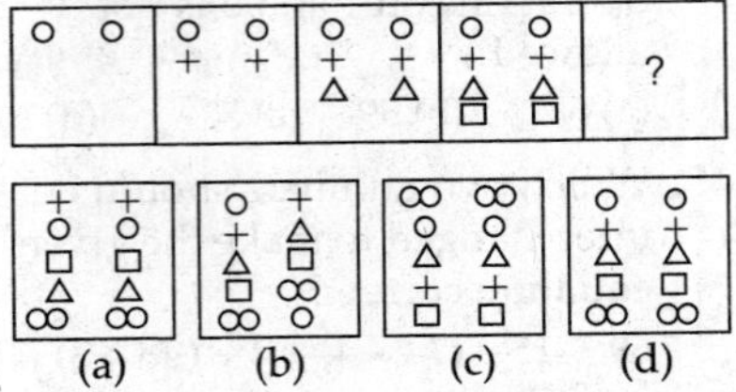

50. Three of the following four are alike in a certain way and thus form a group. Which is the one that does not belong to that group?
(**Note** The odd one out is not based on the number of consonants/vowels or their position in the letter-cluster.)

(a) DGL (b) QTY
(c) MPU (d) FIM

Part III
Quantitative Aptitude

51. Sapna finishes a job in 12 h working alone. If Sapna and Riya finish the same job in 8 h working together at their respective constant rates, then, in how many hours can Riya do the job working alone?

(a) 18 (b) 24
(c) 16 (d) 20

52. If $\tan A = a \tan B$ and $\sin A = b \sin B$, then the value of $\cos^2 A$ is

(a) $\frac{b^2 - 1}{a^2 - 1}$ (b) $\frac{a^2 - 1}{b^2 - 1}$ (c) $\frac{b^2 + 1}{a^2 + 1}$ (d) $\frac{a^2 + 1}{b^2 + 1}$

53. The distance between the centres of two circles of radii 7 cm and 5 cm is 15 cm. Find the length of the transverse common tangent to these circles.

(a) 7 cm (b) 13 cm
(c) 11 cm (d) 9 cm

54. A coffee maker with marked price ₹ 4000 is available on successive discounts of 15%, 10% and 5%. Find the selling price of the coffee maker.

(a) ₹ 2900 (b) ₹ 2903
(c) ₹ 2905 (d) ₹ 2907

55. A girl walking at a speed of 9 km/h crosses a bridge in 45 min. Find the length of the bridge in metres.

(a) 6349 (b) 6398
(c) 6750 (d) 7532

56. Rajesh is playing with a football having diameter of 28 cm. He wants to get a photo of his favourite player painted on the entire ball. The painter charges ₹ 2/cm^2. What will be the cost (in ₹) of painting the ball $\left(\text{take } \pi = \frac{22}{7}\right)$?

(a) 4928 (b) 4828
(c) 2414 (d) 2464

57. Study the given pie-chart and answer the question that follow. The given pie-chart represents the percentage of valid votes obtained by five candidates in a university election.

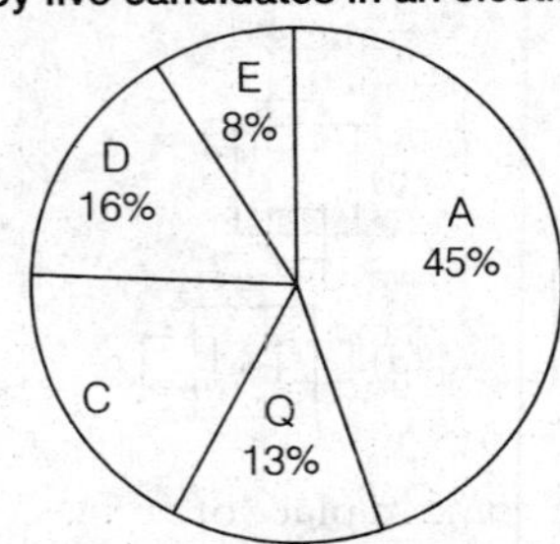

If candidate C has obtained 270 valid votes, then which are the two candidates for whom the difference in valid votes obtained is 45 ?

(a) D and Q (b) Q and C
(c) C and D (d) A and Q

58. Study the given table and answer the question that follow. The table represents the number of candidates appeared, qualified and selected in national level examination from four different schools M, N, O and P over the years 2012 to 2017.
Where A : Appeared; Q: Qualified; S : Selected

Year	M			N			O			P		
	A	Q	S	A	Q	S	A	Q	S	A	Q	S
2012	7000	750	84	3000	400	34	2000	250	27	1500	160	23
2013	5500	500	55	3500	420	56	2500	340	36	2500	290	56
2014	6500	455	42	3800	460	66	3500	380	48	2700	480	67
2015	8500	854	89	4500	485	72	4500	560	57	3400	540	87
2016	9000	922	92	4690	678	86	5670	660	68	3700	650	89
2017	9200	942	94	6700	700	92	6780	680	89	4500	670	93

For which school is the average number of candidates selected over the years the maximum?

(a) O (b) M
(c) N (d) P

59. Monthly salary of Jitvik in the month of December 2020 was ₹ 24800. Every year his salary increases by 5% from the month of January. What was his salary (in ₹) in the month of February 2022?

(a) 27342 (b) 26485
(c) 27486 (d) 27180

60. The population of a town first decreased by 16% due to migration to a big city for better job opportunities. The next year, the population of the town increased by 21% as there were better facilities for jobs. What is the net percentage change (correct to 2 decimal places) in the population?

(a) Decrease by 2.54%
(b) Increase by 2.54%
(c) Increase by 1.64%
(d) Decrease by 1.64%

61. Simplify the following expression.
$99-[169\div(13\times13)-(-4)-\{3-17+10\}]$
(a) 80 (b) 87 (c) 107 (d) 90

62. If 3c2933k is divisible by both 5 and 11, where c and k are single digit natural numbers, then $c+k=$ ....
(a) 7 (b) 8 (c) 6 (d) 5

63. Raju has ₹ 11000 and starts saving ₹ 5000 each week towards buying a new laptop. At the same time, Ramesh has ₹ 60000 and begins spending ₹ 2000 per week on supplies for his art class. Will there be a week, when they have the same amount of money?
(a) Yes, after 7 weeks
(b) Yes, after 6 weeks
(c) No, they will never have the same amount
(d) Yes, after 5 weeks

64. The following line graph shows the ratio of imports to exports of two companies over the years.
Study the graph carefully and answer the question that follow.

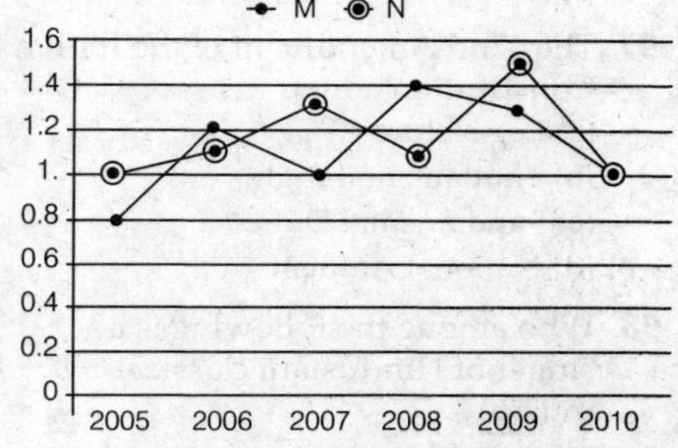

If the exports of Company M in 2008 were ₹ 210 crores, what were the imports of the company in the same year?
(a) ₹ 186 crores (b) ₹ 294 crores
(c) ₹ 150 crores (d) ₹ 268 crores

65. A cylindrical oil tank has a radius of 5 m and a total surface area of 628 m^2, what would be its curved surface area? (round off to the second decimal place)
(a) 371.83 m^2 (b) 401.43 m^2
(c) 470.8 m^2 (d) 481.43 m^2

66. The length, breadth and height of a cuboid are in ratio of 3 : 4 : 5. If the volume of the cuboid is 1620 m^3, find the total surface area of the cuboid.
(a) 646 m^2 (b) 846 m^2
(c) 423 m^2 (d) 712 m^2

67. The difference between 31% and 26% of votes for the same party at different places is 2350. What is 7% of those votes?
(a) 2270 (b) 3090
(c) 4090 (d) 3290

68. Ravath had to sell vegetables worth ₹ 4960 for ₹ 4712 due to weather conditions. What is the loss percentage that he has incurred?
(a) 20% (b) 10%
(c) 5% (d) 15%

69. ΔABC is similar to ΔDEF and the ratio of the area of triangle ABC to triangle DEF is 25 : 144. If $AB=p$ cm, $AC=q$ cm and $BC=r$ cm, then $DE=$?
(a) $\frac{5}{12}q$ (b) $\frac{12}{5}q$ (c) $\frac{5}{12}p$ (d) $\frac{12}{5}p$

70. A sum of ₹ 18000 gives a simple interest of ₹ 3240 in 2 yr and 3 months. The rate of interest per annum is
(a) 10% (b) 12%
(c) 8% (d) 7%

71. Abhishek's marks in Mathematics were incorrectly entered as 93 instead of 63. Due to this, the average marks of the class in Mathematics got increased by 0.5. How many students were there in class?
(a) 45 (b) 55
(c) 60 (d) 50

72. AB is parallel to DC in a trapezium $ABCD$. It is given that $AB>DC$ and the diagonals AC and BD intersect at O. If $AO=3x-15$, $OB=x+9$, $OC=x-5$ and $OD=5$ and x has two values x_1 and x_2, then the value of $(x_1^2+x_2^2)$ is
(a) 45 (b) 61 (c) 73 (d) 56

73. The given chart represents the sales of automobiles in India (by type, in million units) from the year 2011 to 2014. Study the chart and answer the question that follow.

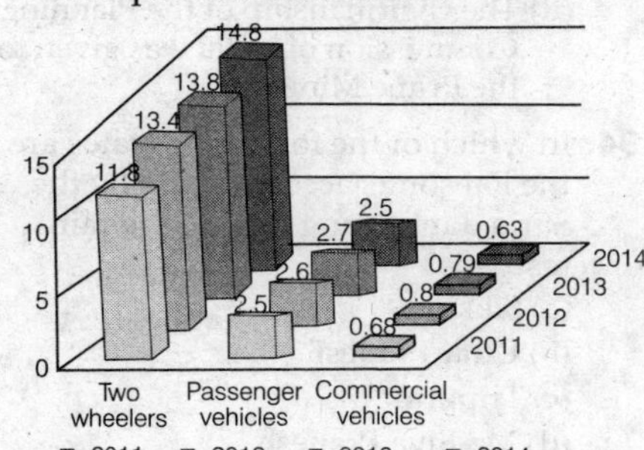

If the same percentage increase in the number of two wheelers as in 2014 over 2013 is expected in 2015, approximately how many two wheelers will be sold in 2015?
(a) 15.8 millions (b) 16.8 millions
(c) 17.8 millions (d) 14.8 millions

74. In triangles XYZ, $XY=YZ$ and $m\angle X=78°$. Find the value of $m\angle Y$.
(a) 28° (b) 24°
(c) 34° (d) 39°

75. If $a:b=3:4$, $b:c=2:3$ and $c:d=5:6$, then $a:b:c:d$ is
(a) 15 : 25 : 30 : 36 (b) 15 : 20 : 30 : 36
(c) 15 : 20 : 35 : 36 (d) 10 : 20 : 30 : 36

Part IV
General Awareness

76. Brihadiswara Temple, which exhibits Dravidian temple architecture, is located in ....
(a) Thanjavur
(b) Dharmapuri
(c) Madurai
(d) Thiruvananthapuram

77. In cricket, ... is called by the umpire when the bowler doesn't deliver the ball within reach of the batter.
(a) wide (b) dead ball
(c) no ball (d) yorker

78. Which of the following rocky planets is the fastest planet in our solar system – travelling through space at about 29 miles (47 kilometres) per second?
(a) Earth (b) Venus
(c) Mars (d) Mercury

79. Who among the following rulers was a part of the Tripartite Struggle for the possession of Kannauj?
(a) Dharmapala (b) Yashovarman
(c) Mahendrapal (d) Prithvi Raj III

80. Bankim Chandra Chatterjee wrote a novel 'Anand Math' based on which of the following rebellions/revolts?
(a) Mappila Rebellion
(b) Paika Rebellion
(c) Sanyasi Rebellion
(d) Kuki Revolt

81. Which of the following statements is/are incorrect *vis-à-vis* Fundamental Duties?
1. They are obligatory in nature.

2. Fundamental Rights and Fundamental Duties are complementary to each other.
3. The introduction of Article 51A created strong base for a concrete national character and strong harmony.
4. Eleventh Fundamental Duty was added by 78th Constitutional Amendment Act.

Codes
(a) 1 and 2 (b) 2 and 3
(c) Only 3 (d) Only 4

82. The phenomenon of the interaction between nonallelic genes at two or more loci resulting in one gene masking the phenotypic expression of another gene, is known as
(a) linkage
(b) complete inheritance
(c) epistasis
(d) incomplete inheritance

83. Sanjukta Panigrahi, a legendary dancer, is associated with which of the following dance forms?
(a) Bihu (b) Laho
(c) Kuchipudi (d) Odissi

84. .... was appointed British High Commissioner to India in April 2024.
(a) Nicholas Fenn
(b) Philip Barton
(c) Lindy Cameron
(d) Dominic Asquith

85. Pinjore Heritage Festival is organised by the state of ....
(a) Jharkhand (b) Uttarakhand
(c) Sikkim (d) Haryana

86. In Microsoft Word, which option allows you to exclude specific sections or types of text from the spelling and grammar check?
(a) Spell check
(b) AutoCorrect
(c) Exclusion Dictionary
(d) Thesaurus

87. As per Census of India 2011, which of the following groups of states recorded the lowest literacy rate?
(a) Rajasthan and Assam
(b) Bihar and Arunachal Pradesh
(c) Rajasthan and Jharkhand
(d) Bihar and Madhya Pradesh

88. The Maritime Anti-Piracy Act, 2022 was enacted to give effect to which of the following?
(a) United Nations Convention on the Law of the Sea relating to repression of piracy on high seas
(b) United Nations Convention on Oceans and Seas relating to repression of piracy on high seas
(c) United Nations Regional Seas Convention relating to repression of piracy on high seas
(d) United Nations Treaty on Oceans relating to repression of piracy on high seas

89. With which of the following sports is Lovlina Borgohain associated?
(a) Hockey
(b) Cricket
(c) Basketball
(d) Boxing

90. Which of the following states has mangrove forests?
(a) Telangana
(b) Andhra Pradesh
(c) Rajasthan
(d) Manipur

91. Which state hosts the Nehru trophy boat race?
(a) Karnataka (b) Tamil Nadu
(c) Kerala (d) Goa

92. Which of the following devices is used to accelerate charged particles to high velocities?
(a) Cryotron
(b) Copatron
(c) Cosmotron
(d) Cyclotron

93. Which of the following options is incorrect?
(a) Distinguished economists from India and abroad were invited to advise on India's economic development during the First Five-Year Plan Period.
(b) India borrowed the idea of Five-Year Plans from the former Soviet Union.
(c) The Planning Commission of India was set up in 1950.
(d) The chairmanship of the Planning Commission of India was given to the Prime Minister.

94. In which of the following states are the Pai songs accompanied by the Saria dance sung during the rain festivals?
(a) Sikkim
(b) Uttar Pradesh
(c) Tripura
(d) Madhya Pradesh

95. The relationship between which of the following is correct?
(a) NDP at market price = GDP at market price + depreciation
(b) Domestic income = NDP at market price + net indirect taxes
(c) GDP at market price = price + quantity of final goods and services
(d) National income = NDP at factor cost + net factor income from abroad

96. Match the states in List I to their ports in List II.

List I (States)	List II (Ports)
A. Goa	1. Mormugao Port
B. West Bengal	2. Kandla Port
C. Tamil Nadu	3. Tuticorin Port
D. Gujarat	4. Haldia Port

Codes

	A	B	C	D		A	B	C	D
(a)	1	4	3	2	(b)	1	4	2	3
(c)	4	1	3	2	(d)	1	3	4	2

97. The 42nd Amendment of the Indian Constitution added ....
(a) Legislature
(b) Fundamental Rights
(c) Fundamental Duties
(d) National Anthem

98. Who among the following is a singer of Hindustani classical music?
(a) Aruna Sairam
(b) Sudha Ragunathan
(c) S. Sowmya
(d) Shubha Mudgal

99. Which organisation, in collaboration with the Central Board of Secondary Education (CBSE), and the Ministry of Education, announced the launch of the 'AI For All' initiative with the purpose of creating a basic understanding of artificial intelligence for everyone in India?
(a) Intel (b) Infosys
(c) TCS (d) IBM

100. Rows in MS-Excel are identified by
(a) letters
(b) numbers with letters
(c) numbers
(d) timings

Answers

1. (d)	2. (d)	3. (b)	4. (a)
5. (a)	6. (a)	7. (d)	8. (a)
9. (c)	10. (a)	11. (b)	12. (b)
13. (c)	14 (c)	15. (a)	16. (a)
17. (c)	18. (b)	19. (a)	20. (c)
21. (b)	22. (a)	23. (c)	24. (c)
25. (c)	26. (a)	27. (c)	28. (d)
29. (d)	30. (c)	31. (c)	32. (d)
33. (c)	34. (b)	35. (b)	36. (d)
37. (d)	38. (a)	39. (d)	40. (c)
41. (d)	42. (c)	43. (d)	44. (d)
45. (a)	46. (d)	47. (d)	48. (c)
49. (d)	50. (d)	51. (b)	52. (a)
53. (d)	54. (d)	55. (c)	56. (a)
57. (a)	58. (b)	59. (a)	60. (c)
61. (d)	62. (c)	63. (b)	64. (b)
65. (c)	66. (b)	67. (d)	68. (c)
69. (d)	70. (c)	71. (c)	72. (b)
73. (a)	74. (b)	75. (b)	76. (a)
77. (a)	78. (d)	79. (a)	80. (c)
81. (d)	82. (c)	83. (d)	84. (c)
85. (d)	86. (c)	87. (b)	88. (a)
89. (d)	90. (b)	91. (c)	92. (d)
93. (a)	94. (d)	95. (d)	96. (a)
97. (c)	98. (d)	99. (a)	100. (c)

Explanations

1. *(d)* Part 'a umbrella' contains an error. Use 'an' as the word 'umbrella' starts with a vowel sound.

2. *(d)* Part 'The aeroplane took down' contains an error. The use of 'took down' meaning to defeat is incorrect in the sentence. Use 'off' making 'took off' to correct the sentence.

3. *(b)* Part 'She shall being' contains an error. Use 'will be' to correct the sentence.

4. *(a)* Part 'a American' contains an error. Use 'an', as the word 'American' starts with a vowel sound, to correct the sentence.

5. *(a)* The correct filler for the given blank is 'in'.

6. *(a)* The correct filler for the given blank is 'regions'.

7. *(d)* The correct filler for the given blank is 'appear'.

8. *(a)* The correct filler for the given blank is 'refers'.

9. *(c)* The correct filler for the given blank is 'observations'.

10. *(a)* The underlined part of the given sentence contains an error. Use 'their coats there' to correct the sentence.

11. *(b)* The word 'swap' means 'to exchange'.

12. *(b)* 'Contempt' means dislike or hate. Hence, its antonym is 'admiration'.

- 'Derision' means ridicule or mockery.
- 'Scorn' means a feeling and expression of contempt or disdain for someone or something.
- 'Obscurity' means the state of being unknown or unimportant.

13. *(c)* The correct filler for the given blank is 'pay'.

14. *(c)* The incorrectly spelt word is 'recieve'. The correct spelling is 'receive'.

15. *(a)* 'Transient' means temporary. Hence, its antonym is 'permanent'.

- 'Transparent' means allowing light to pass through so that objects behind can be distinctly seen.
- 'Transitory' means momentary.

16. *(a)* The antonym of 'innocent' is 'guilty'.

17. *(c)* The correct spelling is 'underrated'.

18. *(b)* 'To be at daggers drawn' means to be ready to fight.

19. *(a)* Part 'isn't enough big' contains an error. The word 'enough' should be placed after 'big' to correct the sentence.

20. *(c)* 'Appalled' means greatly dismayed, disgusted or horrified.

21. *(b)* 'Cramped' means uncomfortably small or restricted. Hence, its antonym is 'spacious'.

- 'Filthy' means dirty.
- 'Crammed' means completely fill (a place or container) to the point of overflowing.

22. *(a)* 'Reliable' means dependable.

- 'Erratic' means no ever or regular.
- 'Flaky' means unreliable.

23. *(c)* 'To cost an arm and a leg' means that something is very expensive.

24. *(c)* 'Ecstasy' means happiness and joy. Hence, its antonym is 'depression'.

25. *(c)* The underlined part of the given sentence contains an error. Use 'purchases add up to' to correct the sentence.

26. *(a)* The correct mirror image of given figure as shown below,

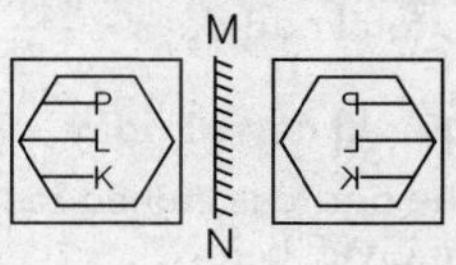

27. *(c)* As, $(11, 8, 352) \rightarrow (11 \times 8) \times 4 = 352$

and $(15, 6, 360) \rightarrow (15 \times 6) \times 4 = 360$

Similarly,

$(16, 5, 320) \rightarrow (16 \times 5) \times 4 = \boxed{320}$

28. *(d)* Given equation,

$(99 - 42 + 11) + (36 \div 6) \times 7 - 50 = 73$

From option (d), interchanging 42 and 36, we get

$(99 - 36 + 11) + (42 \div 6) \times 7 - 50 = 73$

$\Rightarrow 74 + 7 \times 7 - 50 = 73$

$\Rightarrow 74 + 49 - 50 = 73$

$\Rightarrow 123 - 50 = 73 \Rightarrow 73 = 73$

29. *(d)* The correct mirror image of given question figure is as shown below,

M

Vb72mR | ЯmS7dV

N

30. *(c)* The correct mirror image of given question figure is as shown below,

M

R 4 b m L 2 | 2 ⅃ m d 4 Я

N

31. *(c)* Given,

4th December, 2014 $\rightarrow$ Thursday

Number of odd days between 4th December, 2014 to 4th December, 2018

Year $\Rightarrow$ 2015 + 2016 + 2017 + 2018

Days $\Rightarrow 1 + 2 + 1 + 1 = 5$ odd days

Number of odd days between 4th December, 2018 to 10th December, 2018 = 6 odd days

$\therefore$ Total odd days $= \frac{5 + 6}{7} = \frac{11}{7} = 4$

Required day

= Thursday + 4 = Monday

32. *(d)* Given, 18th August, 2000 $\rightarrow$ Friday

Number of odd days between 18th August, 2000 to 18th August, 2005

$= 2001 + 2002 + 2003 + 2004 + 2005$

$= 1 + 1 + 1 + 2 + 1 = 6$ odd days

Number of odd days between 18th August, 2005 to 21th August, 2005 $= 3$ odd days

Now, total odd days $= \frac{6+3}{7} = \frac{9}{7} = 2$

$\therefore$ Required day = Friday + 2 = Sunday

33. *(c)* The figure is embedded in option figure given below,

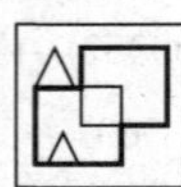

34. *(b)* The pattern of given series is as follows,

O $\xrightarrow{+2}$ Q $\xrightarrow{+2}$ S $\xrightarrow{+2}$ U $\xrightarrow{+2}$ W

W $\xrightarrow{+4}$ A $\xrightarrow{+4}$ E $\xrightarrow{+4}$ I $\xrightarrow{+4}$ M

L $\xrightarrow{+5}$ Q $\xrightarrow{+5}$ V $\xrightarrow{+5}$ A $\xrightarrow{+5}$ F

$\therefore$? = SEV

35. *(b)* According to the question,

B A K E → 2 4 9 6

C A K E → 4 3 6 9

$\therefore$ Code for B is 2.

36. *(d)* As, and

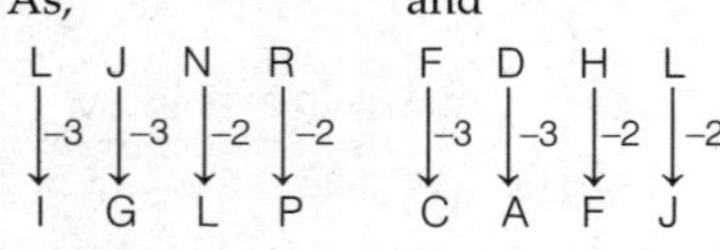

Similarly, H F J N

−3 −3 −2 −2

E C H L

37. *(d)* According to the question,

A → ÷, B → ×, C → +, D → −

From option (d),

94 B 11 D 180 A 4 C 60

Substituting the letters with respective symbols, we get

$= 94 \times 11 - 180 \div 4 + 60$

$= 1034 - 45 + 60$

$= 1094 - 45 = 1049$

38. *(a)* The pattern of the series is as follows,

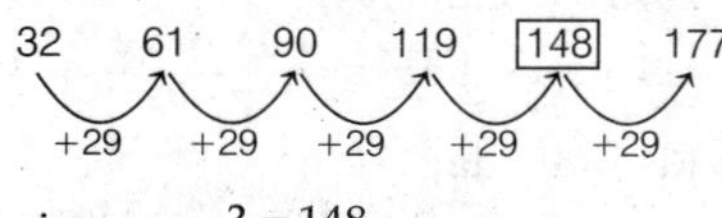

$\therefore$? = 148

39. *(d)* According to the question,

A → ÷, B → ×, C → +, D → −

Given equation,

35 B 7 D 120 A 12 C 38 = ?

Substituting the letters with their respective symbols, we get

$35 \times 7 - 120 \div 12 + 38 = ?$

$\Rightarrow 245 - 10 + 38 = ?$

$\Rightarrow 283 - 10 = ?$

$\Rightarrow ? = 273$

40. *(c)* As, and

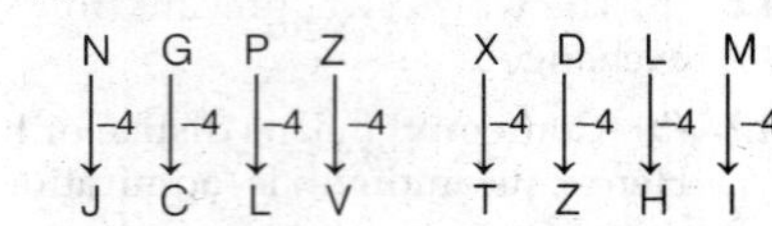

Similarly, R U K V

−4 −4 −4 −4

N Q G R

41. *(d)* The correct pattern of series is as follows,

x y x z b x / x y x z b x / x y x z b x / x y x z b x

$\therefore$ Required combination = xbxxzxxb

42. *(c)* Naming of the figure,

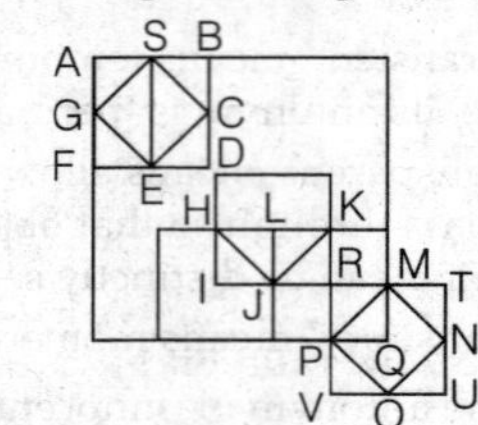

There are total 16 triangles

ΔASG, ΔSBC, ΔEDC, ΔGFE, ΔHIJ, ΔLKJ, ΔHKJ, ΔHLJ, ΔKRJ, ΔPRM, ΔMTN, ΔMQP, ΔNUO, ΔPVO, ΔGSE and ΔSCE.

43. *(d)* Given, P ÷ Q × R − S + T

According to the question,

P(−) ↑ Mother — Q(−) ←Wife— R(+) ↑ Father — S(+) ←Brother— T

[+ → Male, − → Female]

Hence, P is T's mother's mother.

44. *(d)* As, $\frac{161}{7} = 23$

and $\frac{301}{7} = 43$

Similarly, $\frac{427}{7} = 61$

45. *(a)* Given equation,

$69 + 15 - (14 \times 4) \div 2 \times (48 \div 3) = 58$

From option (a), interchanging 69 and 48, we get

$48 + 15 - (14 \times 4) \div 2 + (69 \div 3) = 58$

$\Rightarrow 63 - 56 \div 2 + 23 = 58$

$\Rightarrow 63 - 28 + 23 = 58$

$\Rightarrow 35 + 23 = 58$

$\therefore 58 = 58$

46. *(d)* When the paper is unfolded, it will look like option figure (d).

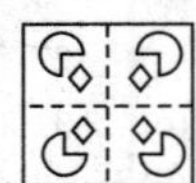

47. *(d)* According to the question,

C △ D E → 1 5 7 3

D I C E → 7 1 8 5

$\therefore$ Code for O is 3.

48. *(c)* According to the statements,

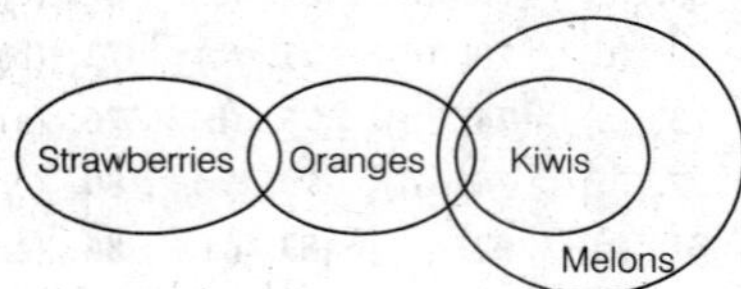

Conclusions

I. (✗) II. (✗) III. (✗)

Hence, neither Conclusion I, II nor III follows.

49. *(d)* Two new symbols are adding in bottom of previous symbols in each next step.

50. *(d)* Here,

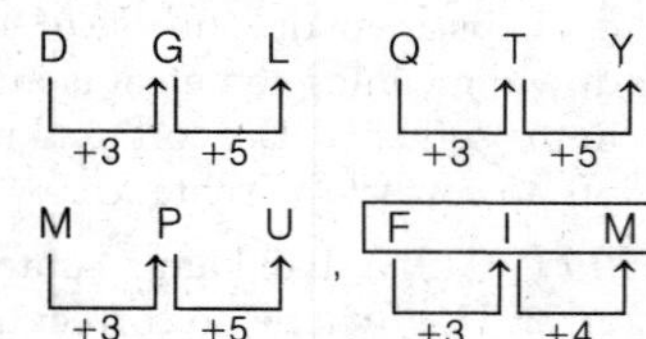

Hence, FIM is different among all.

51. *(b)* 1 h work of Sapna $= \frac{1}{12}$

1 h work of Sapna and Riya $= \frac{1}{8}$

1 h work of Riya $= \left(\frac{1}{8} - \frac{1}{12}\right)$

$= \frac{3-2}{24} = \frac{1}{24}$

$\therefore$ Riya can do the job working alone in 24 h.

52. *(a)* Given, $\tan A = a \tan B$

$$\tan B = \frac{1}{a}\tan A$$

$$\therefore \quad \cot B = \frac{a}{\tan A}$$

Also, $\sin A = b\sin B$

$$\sin B = \frac{1}{b}\sin A$$

$$\therefore \quad \text{cosec } B = \frac{b}{\sin A}$$

Putting the values in

$\text{cosec}^2 B - \cot^2 B = 1$, we get

$$\Rightarrow \frac{b^2}{\sin^2 A} - \frac{a^2}{\tan^2 A} = 1$$

$$\Rightarrow \frac{b^2}{\sin^2 A} - \frac{a^2\cos^2 A}{\sin^2 A} = 1$$

$$\Rightarrow \frac{b^2 - a^2\cos^2 A}{\sin^2 A} = 1$$

$$\Rightarrow b^2 - a^2\cos^2 A = \sin^2 A$$

$$\Rightarrow b^2 - a^2\cos^2 A = 1 - \cos^2 A$$

$$\Rightarrow b^2 - 1 = a^2\cos^2 A - \cos^2 A$$

$$\Rightarrow b^2 - 1 = (a^2 - 1)\cos^2 A$$

$$\Rightarrow \frac{b^2 - 1}{a^2 - 1} = \cos^2 A$$

53. *(d)* Given, $\text{radius}_1 (r_1) = 7$ cm,

$\text{radius}_2 (r_2) = 5$ cm

distance $(d) = 15$ cm

We know that,

Length of transverse common tangent

$$= \sqrt{d^2 - (r_1 + r_2)^2}$$

$$= \sqrt{(15)^2 - (7+5)^2}$$

$$= \sqrt{225 - 144}$$

$$= \sqrt{81} = 9 \text{ cm}$$

54. *(d)* Given, marked price = ₹ 4000

Successive discounts = 15%, 10% and 5%

∴ Selling price

$$= \left[4000 \times \frac{100-15}{100} \times \frac{100-10}{100} \times \frac{100-5}{100}\right]$$

$$= \left[4000 \times \frac{85}{100} \times \frac{90}{100} \times \frac{95}{100}\right]$$

= ₹ 2907

55. *(c)* Speed of girl = 9 km/h

Time to cross a bridge = 45 min

Length of the bridge = Speed × Time

$$= 9 \times \frac{45}{60} \times 1000 \text{ m} \quad [\because 1 \text{ km} = 1000 \text{ m}]$$

= 6750 m

56. *(a)* Given, diameter (d) of ball = 28 cm

$$\therefore \text{Radius } (r) \text{ of ball} = \frac{d}{2} = \frac{28}{2} = 14 \text{ cm}$$

We know that,

Total surface area of ball $= 4\pi r^2$

$$= 4 \times \frac{22}{7} \times 14 \times 14$$

$$= 2464 \text{ cm}^2$$

∴ Cost of painting a ball

= 2464 × 2 = ₹ 4928

57. *(a)* Percentage of valid votes obtained by C

= [100 − (45 + 13 + 16 + 8)]%

= (100 − 82)% = 18%

According to the question,

18% = 270

$$100\% = \frac{270}{18} \times 100$$

= 1500 votes

From option (a),

Total valid votes obtained by D

$$= \frac{16}{100} \times 1500 = 240$$

Total valid votes obtained by Q

$$= \frac{13}{100} \times 1500 = 195$$

∴ Required difference = 240 − 195 = 45

58. *(b)* Average number of candidates selected from School M

$$= \frac{84 + 55 + 42 + 89 + 92 + 94}{6}$$

$$= \frac{456}{6} = 76$$

Average number of candidates selected from School N

$$= \frac{34 + 56 + 66 + 72 + 86 + 92}{6}$$

$$= \frac{406}{6} = 67.66 \sim 68$$

Average number of candidates selected from School O

$$= \frac{27 + 36 + 48 + 57 + 68 + 89}{6}$$

$$= \frac{325}{6} = 54.16 \sim 52$$

Average number of candidates selected from School P

$$= \frac{23 + 56 + 67 + 87 + 89 + 93}{6}$$

$$= \frac{415}{6} = 69.16 \sim 70$$

∴ Average number of candidates selected over the years is maximum in school 'M'.

59. *(a)* Jitvik's salary in month of December 2020 = ₹ 24800

Increament in salary every year = 5%

Jitvik's salary in month of February 2022

$$= \left[24800 \times \frac{105}{100} \times \frac{105}{100}\right]$$

= ₹ 27342

60. *(c)* Let $a = -16$, $b = 21$

Net percentage change

$$= \left[(a + b) + \frac{a \times b}{100}\right]\%$$

$$= \left[(-16 + 21) - \frac{16 \times 21}{100}\right]\%$$

= [5 − 3.36]%

= 1.64% increment

61. *(d)* Given expression,

99 − [169 ÷ (13 × 13) − (− 4) − {3 − 17 + 10}]

= 99 − [169 ÷ 169 + 4 − {− 4}]

= 99 − (1 + 4 + 4) = 90

62. *(c)* If number 3C2933*K* is divisible by 5, where C and *K* are single digit natural number.

Then, *K* must be 5.

The number becomes = 3C29335

Now, to check the divisiblity with 11 difference between sum of odd place digits and sum of even place digit must be 11 or 0.

∴ (3 + 2 + 3 + 5) − (C + 9 + 3) = 11 or 0

⇒ 13 − (12 + C) = 11 or 0

⇒ C = 1

Now, C + K = 1 + 5 = 6

63. *(b)* The amount of Raju has per week are ₹ 16000, ₹ 21000 ...., respectively.

The amount of Ramesh has per week are ₹ 58000, ₹ 56000 ..., respectively.

∴ This is an arithmetic series, therefore their last term will be equal.

$$\therefore \quad 16000 + (n - 1) \times 5000 = 58000 - (n - 1) \times 2000$$

$$\Rightarrow (n - 1) \times 7000 = 42000$$

$$\Rightarrow (n - 1) = 6$$

$$\Rightarrow n = 7$$

∴ In the beginning of 7th week or after 6 weeks both the amount will be equal.

64. *(b)* Ratio of imports to export of Company M in year 2008.

$$\frac{\text{Import}}{\text{Export}} = 1.4 = \frac{14}{10} = \frac{7}{5}$$

According to the question,
Total imports in year 2008

$= \left[\frac{7}{5} \times 210\right]$ crores

= 294 crores

65. *(c)* Given, radius $(r) = 5$ m

Total surface area = 628 m^2
Let height = h m
We know that,
Total surface area $= 2\pi r(h + r)$

$$2 \times \frac{22}{7} \times 5(h + 5) = 628$$

$$h + 5 = \frac{628 \times 7}{2 \times 22 \times 5}$$

$$h + 5 = 19.98$$

$$h = 1998 - 5 = 14.98 \text{ m}$$

Now, curved surface area $= 2\pi rh$

$$= \left[2 \times \frac{22}{7} \times 5 \times 14.98\right]$$

$$= 470.8 \text{ m}^2$$

66. *(b)* Let length (l), breadth (b) and height (h) of cuboid be $3x : 4x : 5x$.
According to the question,

$$3x \times 4x \times 5x = 1620$$

$$60x^3 = 1620$$

$$x^3 = \frac{1620}{60} = 27$$

$$x = 3 \text{ m}$$

$\therefore$ Length $(l) = 3x = 3(3) = 9$ m
Breadth $(b) = 4x = 4(3) = 12$ m
Height $(h) = 5x = 5(3) = 15$ m
Now, total surface area of cuboid

$$= 2(lb + bh + hl)$$
$$= 2(9 \times 12 + 12 \times 15 + 15 \times 9)$$
$$= 2(108 + 180 + 135)$$
$$= 2 \times 423 = 846 \text{ m}^2$$

67. *(d)* According to the question,

$$31\% - 26\% = 2350$$
$$5\% = 2350$$
$$\therefore \quad 7\% = \frac{2350}{5} \times 7 = 3290$$

68. *(c)* Loss per cent $= \left[\frac{4960 - 4712}{4960} \times 100\right]$

$$= \left[\frac{248}{4960} \times 100\right] = 5\%$$

69. *(d)* Given, $\Delta ABC \sim \Delta DEF$,

So, $\frac{\text{Area of } \Delta ABC}{\text{Area of } \Delta DEF} = \left(\frac{AB}{DE}\right)^2$

$$\Rightarrow \quad \frac{25}{144} = \frac{P^2}{DE^2}$$

$$\Rightarrow \quad DE^2 = \frac{144}{25} P^2$$

$$\Rightarrow \quad DE = \sqrt{\frac{144}{25} P^2}$$

$$\Rightarrow \quad DE = \frac{12}{5} P$$

70. *(c)* Given, Principal $(P) =$ ₹ 18000
Simple interest (SI) = ₹ 3240,
Time $(T) = 2$ yr 3 months

$$= 2\frac{3}{12} = \frac{9}{4} \text{ months}$$

We know that,
$\therefore$ Simple interest

$$= \frac{\text{Principal } (P) \times \text{Rate } (R) \times \text{Time } (T)}{100}$$

$$\Rightarrow \quad 3240 = \frac{18000 \times \text{Rate} \times 9}{100 \times 4}$$

$$\Rightarrow \quad \text{Rate} = \left[\frac{3240 \times 100 \times 4}{18000 \times 9}\right]$$

$\therefore$ Rate = 8%

71. *(c)* Increment in marks due to mistake $(x) = 93 - 63 = 30$
Increase in average $(a) = 0.5$

$\therefore$ Total students in class $= \frac{x}{a} = \frac{30}{0.5} = 60$

72. *(b)* According to the question,

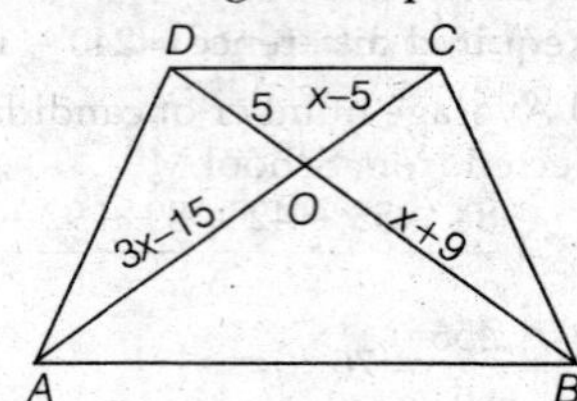

In ΔAOB and ΔDOC,
$\angle DOC = \angle AOB$
[$\because$ Vertically opposite angle]
$\angle ODC = \angle OBA$ [$\because$ Alternate angle]
$\therefore \quad \Delta DOC \sim \Delta BOA$

$$\therefore \quad \frac{DO}{BO} = \frac{OC}{OA}$$

$$\frac{5}{x + 9} = \frac{x - 5}{3x - 15}$$

$$5(3x - 15) = (x - 5)(x + 9)$$
$$15x - 75 = x^2 - 5x + 9x - 45$$
$$\Rightarrow \quad x^2 - 11x + 30 = 0$$
$$\Rightarrow \quad x^2 - 6x - 5x + 30 = 0$$
$$\Rightarrow \quad x(x - 6) - 5(x - 6) = 0$$
$$\Rightarrow \quad (x - 6)(x - 5) = 0$$
$$\Rightarrow \quad x = 6, 5$$
$$\therefore \quad x_1 = 6, x_2 = 5$$

Now, $x_1^2 + x_2^2 = 6^2 + 5^2 = 36 + 25 = 61$

73. *(a)* Percentage increase in two wheelers in 2014 over 2013

$$= \frac{14.8 - 13.8}{13.8} \times 100$$

$$= \frac{100}{13.8} = 7.2\%$$

$\therefore$ Percentage increase in two wheelers in year 2015

$$= \frac{14.8 \times 107.2}{100}$$

= 15.8 millions

74. *(b)* According to the question,

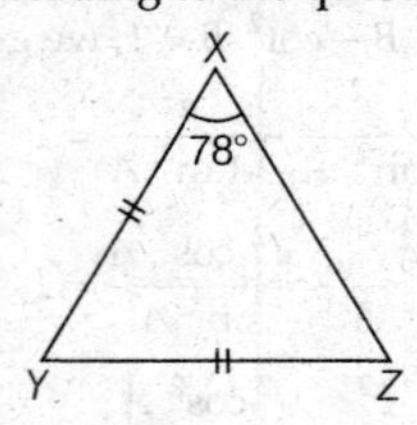

As, $XY = YZ$, therefore,

$$\angle X = \angle Z = 78°$$
$$\therefore \quad \angle Y = [180° - (78 + 78)°]$$
$$\angle Y = (180° - 156°)$$
$$\therefore \quad \angle Y = 24°$$

75. *(b)* Given,

$$a : b = (3 : 4) \times 5 = (15 : 20)$$
$$b : c = (2 : 3) \times 10 = (20 : 30)$$
$$c : d = (5 : 6) \times 6 = (30 : 36)$$
$$\therefore \quad a : b : c : d = 15 : 20 : 30 : 36$$

76. *(a)* Brihadiswara Temple, which exhibits Dravidian temple architecture, is located in Thanjavur.

- It was built by Raja Raja Chola I between 1003 and 1010 AD.
- It is also called as Dakshina Meru which simplifies 'Meru of South'.
- It is a Hindu temple dedicated to Lord Shiva and it is also in the list of UNESCO Word Heritage site.

77. *(a)* In cricket, wide is called by the umpire when the bowler doesn't deliver the ball within reach of the batter.

- **Dead Ball** A dead ball is a ball that is out of play, batters are not allowed to score runs.
- **No Ball** The umpire shall call and signal 'No ball' for any delivery which, after pitching, passes or would have passed over head height of the striker standing upright at the crease.
- **Yorker** A yorker is a ball bowled which hits the cricket pitch around the batsman's feet or toe.

78. *(d)* Mercury is the fastest planet in our solar system, zipping around the Sun every 88 Earth days.
- Mercury spins slowly on its axis and complete one rotation every 59 Earth days, when it moves fastest in its elliptical orbit around the Sun, each rotation is not accompanied by sunrise and sunset like it is on most other planets.
- Its axis of rotation is titled just 2 degrees with respect to the plane of its orbit around the Sun.

79. *(a)* Dharmapala was a part of the Tripartite Struggle for the possession of Kannauj.
- The Tripartite Struggle or the Kannauj Triangle Wars occured between Polas, the Gurjara-Pratiharas and the Rashtrakutas.
- Both Dharmapala (the Pala king) and Vatsraja (Pratihara king) clashed against each other for Kannauj.
- This struggle continued for almost two hundred years and it's resulted finally ended in favour of the Gurjara-Pratihara ruler Nagbhatta II.

80. *(c)* Banking Chandra Chatterjee wrote a novel 'Anandmath' on Sanyasi Rebellion.
- It was a rebellion by displaced peasants and demobilised soldiers led by religious monk.
- This revolt was crushed under the leadership of Warren Hastings.
- 'Vande Mataram' is a part of 'Anandmath'.

81. *(d)* Only Statement (4) is incorrect regarding Fundamental Duties because there are only 11 Fundamental Duties, and they were introduced by the 42nd Constitutional Amendment Act (1976), not the 78th Constitutional Amendment Act.
- Fundamental Duties come under Part IVA and Article 51A.
- These duties are statutory and are not enforceable by law but are taken into account by the courts while adjudicating any matter.

82. *(c)* The phenomenon of the interaction between the non-allelic genes at two or more loci resulting in one gene masking the phenotypic expression of another gene, is known as epistasis.

Epistasis is a phenomenon in genetics in which the effect of a gene mutation is dependent on the presence or absence of mutations in one or more other genes, respectively, termed modifier genes.

83. *(d)* Sanjukta Panigrahi (1944-1997) was a renowned Indian dancer who was closely associated with the Odissi dance form.
- Panigrahi was known for her technical mastery, graceful movements and expressive Abhinaya (facial expressions).
- She was being honoured with the Padma Shri (1975) and Sangeet Natak Akademi Award in 1976.

84. *(c)* Lindy Cameron was appointed as the British High Commissioner to India in April 2024. She is the first woman to hold this position.

Cameron previously served as the CEO of the UK's National Cyber Security Centre (2020-2024) and as Director-General in the Northern Ireland Office (2019-2020).

85. *(d)* The Pinjore Heritage Festival is organised by the state of Haryana, specifically in the Pinjore Gardens located in Pinjore, Panchkula district, Haryana.
- The most popular fairs celebrated in Haryana are - the Surajkund Fair, the Mango Mela, the Baisakhi Mela.
- The celebrations of the Pinjore Festival started in 2006.

86. *(c)* In Microsoft Word, Exclusion Dictionary allows you to exclude specific sections or types of text from the spelling and grammar check.

87. *(b)* According to 2011 census, the states of Bihar and Arunachal Pradesh recorded the lowest literacy rate following by Rajasthan, Jharkhand and Andhra Pradesh.
- The literacy rates of Bihar, Arunachal Pradesh, Rajasthan, Jharkhand and Andhra Pradesh were 63.8, 67.0, 67.1, 67.6 and 67.7 respectively.
- Kerala has the highest total literacy rate and female literacy rate whereas Lakshadweep had the highest male literacy rate.
- The literacy rate in the country is 74.04 per cent, 82.14 for males and 65.46 for females.

88. *(a)* The Maritime Anti-Piracy Act, 2022 was enacted to give effect to the United Nations Convention on the Law of the Sea (UNCLOS), which relates to the repression of piracy on high seas.
- UNCLOS is an international treaty that sets out the legal framework for the use of the world's oceans and seas, including provisions related to piracy.
- It is an act to give effect to the United Nations Convention on the Law of the Sea relating to repression of piracy on high seas and for matters connected therewith or incidental thereto.

89. *(d)* Lovlina Borgohain is an Indian professional boxer who has won numerous international medals. Lovlina Borgohain's achievements in boxing include
- Olympic bronze medal (2020)
- World Championship bronze medal (2018, 2019)
- Asian Championship gold medal (2020)
- Summer Olympics (Tokyo) bronze medal (2020)

90. *(b)* Andhra Pradesh is one of the states in India where mangrove forests can be found. The state's coastal regions, particularly around the Krishna and Godavari deltas, have extensive mangrove forests.
- These forests provide a habitat for a diverse range of flora and fauna and play a crucial role in protecting the coastline from erosion and cyclone.
- Other Indian states with significant mangrove forests include West Bengal (Sundarbans), Odisha, Tamil Nadu, Kerala, Gujarat, Maharashtra and Goa.

91. *(c)* The Nehru trophy boat race is held in the state of Kerala, India.
- It is an annual event that happens on the second Saturday of August, and it's a major tourist attraction in Kerala.
- The race features traditional Kerala boats, known as 'snake boats' or 'Chundan Vallams', which are long, narrow boats that are decorated with colourful umbrellas and paddled by skilled oarsmen.
- The event was first held in 1952, when Jawaharlal Nehru visited Kerala and was impressed by the traditional boat races in the region.

92. *(d)* Cyclotron is a device which is used to accelerate charged particles to high velocities. It works on the principle that a charged particle moving normal to a magnetic field experiences the magnetic Lorentz force due to which the particle moves in a circular path.

93. *(a)* Statement (a) is incorrect because the First Five-Year Plan (1951-1956) was prepared without much input from external economists. Instead, it was largely influenced by the Bombay Plan (1944) and the Gandhian approach to economic development.

- India did borrow the idea of Five-Year Plans from the former Soviet Union.
- The Planning Commission of India was indeed set up in 1950, with the aim of promoting economic development and social justice.
- The Planning Commission was replaced by the National Institution for Transforming India (NITI Aayog) in 2015.

94. *(d)* In Madhya Pradesh, the Pai songs accompanied by the Saria dance sung during the rain festivals.

- This song is sung in the rainy season to pray for a good monsoon and a good harvest. Saria dance is also performed with this song.
- Young boys and girls participate in this dance with sticks in their hands. Krishna Leela is the major theme of these dances.
- Major Instruments are Dholak, Timki, Manjira, Mridang, Flute.

95. *(d)* This equation represents the correct relationship between National Income (NI) and Net Domestic Product (NDP).

NI = NDP at factor cost + Net Factor Income from Abroad

- National Income (NI) is the total income earned by citizens of a country.
- Net Domestic Product (NDP) at factor cost is the total value of goods and services produced within the country, minus depreciation, and valued at factor cost (i.e., without indirect taxes).
- Net Factor Income from Abroad (NFIA) is the income earned by citizens of the country from foreign sources, minus income earned by foreigners within the country.

96. *(a)* The correct matching is A-1, B-4, C-3, D-2.

- Mormugao Port is a port on the western coast of India, in the coastal state of Goa. Commissioned in 1885 on the site of a natural harbour, it is one of India's oldest ports.
- Haldia Port is an industrial port city in Purba Medinipur district in the Indian state of West Bengal.
- Tuticorin Port is one of the 12 major ports of India. It was declared to be a major port on 11th July, 1974. It is located in the state of Tamil Nadu.
- Kandla Port, also known as the Deendayal Port, is a seaport in Kutch District of Gujarat State.

97. *(c)* The 42nd Amendment added a new section 'Fundamental Duties' in the Constitution.

- The new section required citizens "to promote harmony and the spirit of common brotherhood among all the people of India, transcending religious, linguistic and regional or sectional diversities."
- The 42nd Amendment Act was enacted by Indian National Congress headed by Indira Gandhi. Words 'Socialist', 'Secular' and 'Integrity' were added in Preamble.

98. *(d)* Shubha Mudgal is a renowned Indian singer of Hindustani classical music. She is known for her powerful and soulful voice, and has performed extensively in India and abroad.

- Aruna Sairam, Sudha Ragunathan and S. Sowmya are Carnatic classical music singer.
- Hindustani and Carnatic are two distinct styles of Indian classical music, with different traditions and approaches.

99. *(a)* Intel is the organisation that collaborated with the Central Board of Secondary Education (CBSE) and the Ministry of Education to launch the 'AI for All' initiative. This initiative aims to create a basic understanding of artificial intelligence for everyone in India.

100. *(c)* Rows in MS Excel are identified by numbers.

Set 18 05 July, 2024 (Shift II)

SSC CHSL Tier-I SOLVED PAPER

Instructions

1. This paper contains 100 questions.
2. It has 4 Parts, **Part I** General English, **Part II** General Intelligence & Reasoning, **Part III** Quantitative Aptitude and **Part IV** General Awareness.
3. Each question carries **2 marks**.

Part I General English

1. Select the option that corrects the following sentence.

All tickets of the FIFA World Cup have been sold away.

(a) All tickets of the FIFA World Cup have been sold into.
(b) All tickets of the FIFA World Cup have been sold across.
(c) All tickets of the FIFA World Cup have been sold out.
(d) All tickets of the FIFA World Cup have been sold among.

2. The following sentence has been split into four segments. Identify the segment that contains a grammatical error.

The soldiers / were selected / on the section / of 'gallantry of spirits'.

(a) were selected
(b) The soldiers
(c) on the section
(d) of 'gallantry of spirits'

3. The following sentence has been split into four segments. Identify the segment that contains a grammatical error.

We has travelled / to many states / of India to get / an essence of its diversity.

(a) to many states
(b) of India to get
(c) an essence of its diversity
(d) We has travelled

4. Select the most appropriate option to fill in the blank.

The captain dropped the trophy while he .... the victory with his teammates.

(a) celebrated (b) celebrates
(c) is celebrating (d) was celebrating

Directions (Q.Nos. 5-9) *In the following passage, some words have been deleted. Read the passage carefully and select the most appropriate option to fill in each blank.*

For decades, humans have tried to theorise the origin and evolution of the universe. Many theories have been proposed and rejected. However, the Big Bang theory has been the most (1) .... accepted. According to this theory, the universe began as a single point, or singularity, around 13.8 billion years ago. This singularity contained all the matter and energy that would eventually (2)......... the stars, galaxies and other structures that make up our universe today. The Big Bang theory is supported by a (3)......... of observational evidence, including the cosmic microwave background radiation, the (4)......... of light elements in the universe and the large-scale structure of the cosmos. Despite its success, the Big Bang theory is still an active area of research, with scientists seeking to better understand the earliest moments of the universe and the (5).........of dark matter and energy.

5. Select the most appropriate option to fill in blank number (1).

(a) widely (b) vastly
(c) largely (d) loosely

6. Select the most appropriate option to fill in blank number (2).

(a) form (b) design
(c) prepare (d) destroy

7. Select the most appropriate option to fill in blank number (3).

(a) rich (b) wealth
(c) debt (d) store

8. Select the most appropriate option to fill in blank number (4).

(a) abundance (b) plenty
(c) fortune (d) success

9. Select the most appropriate option to fill in blank number (5).

(a) nature (b) environment
(c) capture (d) brand

10. Select the most appropriate option that can substitute the underlined word segment in the following sentence.

The girl <u>which is wearing a blue shirt is</u> my sister.

(a) which is wearing the blue shirt
(b) who is wearing a blue shirt
(c) which wear a blue shirt
(d) who wear a blue shirt

11. Select the most appropriate meaning of the underlined idiom.

The United Nations is working to eliminate <u>the vicious cycle</u> of poverty.

(a) The barrier of poverty
(b) One problem causes other
(c) Loophole of something
(d) Strength of something

12. Select the incorrectly spelt word.

(a) Innoculate
(b) Irreverent
(c) Immense
(d) Immaculate

13. Identify the most appropriate antonym of the underlined word in the given sentence.

The vendor said that the apples were of <u>superior</u> quality.

(a) Excellent (b) Distasteful
(c) Small (d) Inferior

14. Select the most appropriate synonym of the given word.

Permit

(a) Disgrace
(b) Flout
(c) Approve
(d) Abandon

15. Select the most appropriate meaning of the given idiom.
Bag and baggage
(a) At the service
(b) By force
(c) With all goods
(d) Fair and honest

16. Select the most appropriate homophone to fill in the blank.
Arun knows perfectly well how to mix the food items with ....
(a) sauce (b) saws
(c) sause (d) source

17. Select the most appropriate antonym of the underlined word.
No one trusts her as her reasons are always explicit .
(a) Precise (b) Ambiguous
(c) Exact (d) Distant

18. Read the sentence carefully and select the most appropriate option to substitute the underlined part.
The clamour distracted the priest and made him angry.
(a) loud and confused noise
(b) narrow-mindedness
(c) introduction of new things
(d) humorous deception

19. Select the most appropriate antonym of the underlined word in the given sentence.
Essays must be concise.
(a) Excise (b) Lengthy
(c) Precise (d) Total

20. Select the most appropriate option to fill in the blank.
Which .... do you usually take to reach your office?
(a) rude (b) route (c) root (d) rout

21. Select the correct collocation to complete the following sentence.
He made .... use of the opportunity to travel.
(a) full
(b) total
(c) entire
(d) whole

22. The following sentence has been split into four segments. Identify the segment that contains a spelling error.
The make-up room was filled / with incadescent lights / which added to the misery / of those subjected to make-up.
(a) which added to the misery
(b) with incadescent lights
(c) of those subjected to make-up
(d) The make-up room was filled

23. Select the most appropriate synonym of the given word.
Tedious
(a) Exciting (b) Boring
(c) Working (d) Happening

24. Select the most appropriate option that can substitute the underlined segment in the given sentence.
Employers in many developing countries report that a lack of skilled workers is a major and increasing bottleneck for their operations, affected their capacity to innovate.
(a) affect their capacity
(b) effecting their capacity
(c) effect their capacity
(d) affecting their capacity

25. Select the most appropriate option that can substitute the underlined word in the given sentence.
The dedicated teacher laboured assiduously to aid her pupils in achieving success.
(a) un-biased (b) committed
(c) uninvolved (d) apathetic

Part II
General Intelligence

26. TMBF is related to ATIM in a certain way based on the English alphabetical order. In the same way, CLGP is related to JSNW. To which of the following is QEAD related, following the same logic?
(a) XKHL (b) XLKH
(c) XLHK (d) XHKL

27. What should come in place of question mark (?) in the given series based on the English alphabetical order?
TUV, RXR, ?, NDJ, LGF
(a) PAN (b) VOI
(c) NAP (d) CAL

28. Which figure should replace the question mark (?) if the following figure series were to be continued?

Q □ 3	I 5 △	△ I 5	Q 9 3	
△	Q	3	△	?
I 5 G	G □ 3	Q 9 G	G I 5	

(a)	(b)	(c)	(d)
3 Q 9	3 Q 9	3 Q 9	3 Q 9
E	I	5	5
5 G I	5 △ G	△ E G	△ G E

29. Select the correct option that when filled in the blanks in the same sequence will make the series logically complete.
GH_ST_HO_RGHOSPG_OS_
(a) GORNH (b) ORHSN
(c) OGSHN (d) GOHNP

30. 12 is related to 72 following a certain logic. Following the same logic, 19 is related to 114. To which of the following is 29 related following the same logic?
(**Note** Operations should be performed on the whole numbers, without breaking down the numbers into its constituent digits. E.g. 13 – Operations on 13 such as adding /subtracting /multiplying etc. to 13 can be performed. Breaking down 13 into 1 and 3 and then performing mathematical operations on 1 and 3 is not allowed.)
(a) 171 (b) 174 (c) 170 (d) 173

31. If 19th July, 2012 is Thursday, then what will be the day of the week on 11th January, 2018?
(a) Monday (b) Saturday
(c) Thursday (d) Wednesday

32. Four letter-clusters have been given, out of which three are alike in some manner and one is different. Select the one that is different. (**Note** The odd one out is not based on the number of consonants/vowels or their position in the letter-cluster.)
(a) OMJ (b) PNK
(c) RTQ (d) BZW

33. The position of how many letters will remain unchanged, if all the letters in the word DIALECT are arranged in alphabetical order?
(a) Two (b) Four
(c) One (d) Three

34. What should come in place of the question mark (?) in the given series?
63, 64, 66, 69, 73, ?
(a) 78
(b) 80
(c) 79
(d) 77

35. In a certain code language,
A + B means 'A is the daughter of B'
A – B means 'A is the wife of B'
A × B means 'A is the brother of B'
A ÷ B means 'A is the father of B'
Based on the above, if 'P + Q × R – S ÷ T', which of the following is true?
(a) T is S's son
(b) Q is the brother of S
(c) P is the sister of T
(d) P is the daughter of T's mother's brother

36. Select the correct mirror image of the given combination when the mirror is placed at MN as shown below.

M
Pam@43k
N

(a) ʞƐ4@ɯɐd
(b) ʞƐ4@ɯɒq
(c) ʞƐ4@ɯɐq
(d) ʞ43@ɯɒq

37. Which of the following numbers will replace the question mark (?) in the given series?
11, 4, 22, 20, 44, 100, 88, 500, ?
(a) 176 (b) 182 (c) 160 (d) 154

38. A square sheet of paper is folded along the dotted line successively along the directions shown and is then punched in the last. How would the paper look when unfolded?

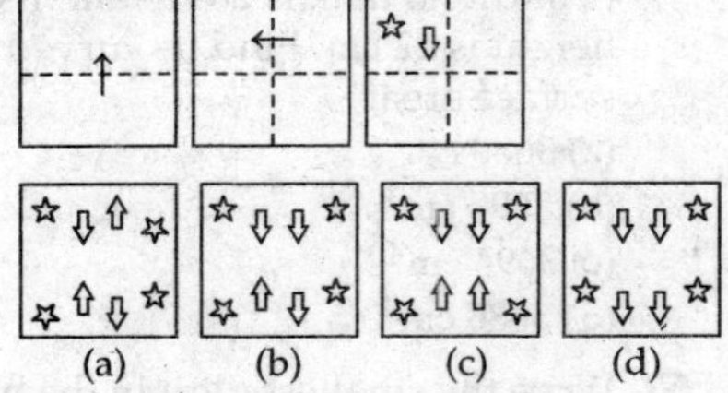

39. What will come in place of question mark (?) in the following equation, if '+' and '–' are interchanged and '×' and '÷' are interchanged?
$15 + 2 - 13 \times 13 \div 3 = ?$
(a) 23 (b) 24 (c) 18 (d) 16

40. If 'A' stands for '÷', 'B' stands for '×', 'C' stands for '+' and 'D' stands for '–', what will come in place of the question mark (?) in the following equation?
17 C 69 A 3 D 22 B 1 = ?
(a) 18 (b) 16 (c) 12 (d) 14

41. How many triangles are there in the given figure?

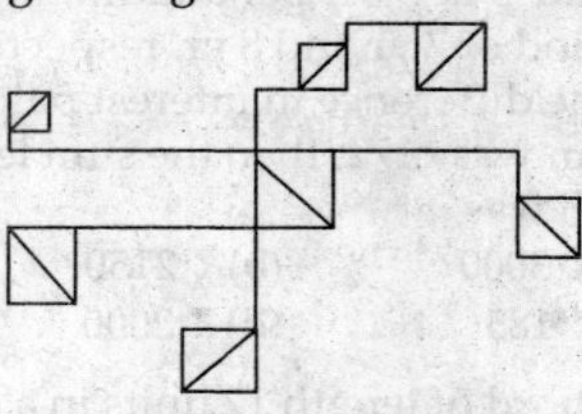

(a) 15 (b) 13 (c) 14 (d) 12

42. Select the option in which the given figure is embedded. (rotation is not allowed.)

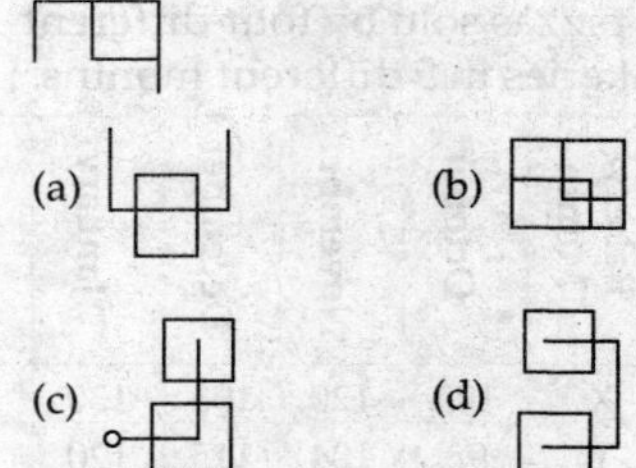

43. In a certain code language, 'SOAP' is coded as '4629' and 'SPOT' is coded as '9824'. How is 'A' coded in the given language?
(a) 4 (b) 2
(c) 8 (d) 6

44. Select the set in which the numbers are related in the same way as are the numbers of the following sets.
(**Note** Operations should be performed on the whole numbers, without breaking down the numbers into its constituent digits. E.g. 13 – Operations on 13 such as adding /subtracting /multiplying etc., to 13 can be performed. Breaking down 13 into 1 and 3 and then performing mathematical operations on 1 and 3 is not allowed.)
(13, 234, 9)
(15, 180, 6)
(a) (17, 340, 5) (b) (16, 240, 5)
(c) (14, 196, 7) (d) (12, 108, 9)

45. What would be the number on the opposite side of '8', if the given sheet is folded to form a cube?

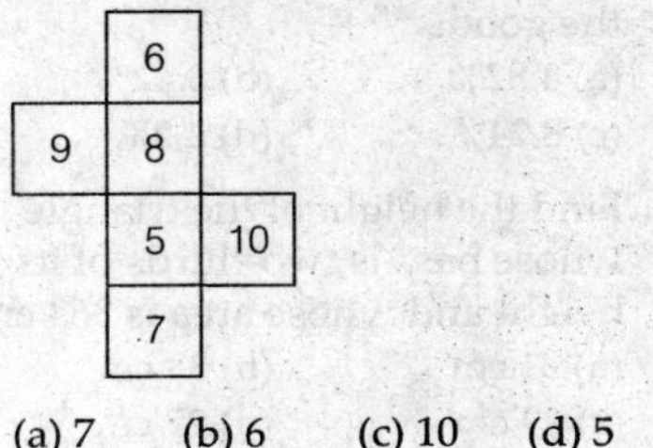

(a) 7 (b) 6 (c) 10 (d) 5

46. Select the correct mirror image of the given figure when the mirror is placed at MN as shown below.

M
Wph4y
N

(a) y4dqW
(b) ʎ4dqW
(c) y4hqW
(d) yph4W

47. Three statements are followed by conclusions numbered I and II. You have to consider these statements to be true, even if they seem to be at variance with commonly known facts. Decide which of the given conclusions logically follow(s) from the given statements.

Statements
All jams are butter.
Some nibs are ink.
Some nibs are butter.

Conclusions
I. Some ink are butter.
II. All jams are nibs.
(a) Only Conclusion II follows
(b) Only Conclusion I follows
(c) Neither Conclusion I nor II follows
(d) Both Conclusions I and II follow

48. What will come in the place of question mark (?) in the following equation, if '+' and '×' are interchanged and '–' and '÷' are interchanged?
$21 - 7 \times 26 + 46 \div 36 = ?$
(a) 1163
(b) 8667
(c) 760
(d) 908

49. In a certain code language, 'pleased to meet' is written as 'bj sc vw' and 'meet and greet' is written as 'ih bj tf'. How is 'meet' written in the given language?
(a) vw (b) tf (c) bj (d) ih

50. RTVX is related to SUWY in a certain way based on the English alphabetical order. In the same way, KMOQ is related to LNPR. To which of the following is FHJL related, following the same logic?
(a) GIKM
(b) GHJK
(c) GIJK
(d) GIKN

Part III

Quantitative Aptitude

51. To reach at a destination, D takes 45 min, if he drives at a speed of 60 km/h. Due to some urgency, he is to reach the destination in 30 min. What should be his speed in km/h?

(a) 90 (b) 60
(c) 80 (d) 75

52. Study the given graph and answer the question that follows.

The graph shows the exports from three companies (A, B and C) over the years (in ₹ crore).

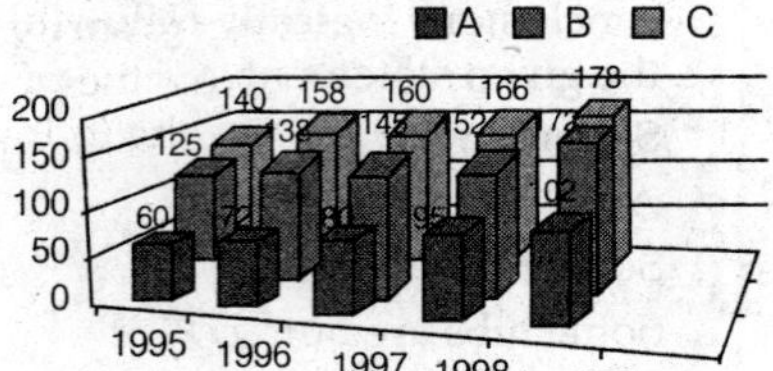

In how many given years, were the exports from company C less than the average annual exports over the given years?

(a) 5 (b) 3
(c) 2 (d) 4

53. If $\frac{1}{M}:\frac{1}{N}:\frac{1}{O}=3:4:5$, then $M:N:O$ is equal to

(a) 12 : 15 : 20
(b) 15 : 20 : 12
(c) 20 : 12 : 15
(d) 20 : 15 : 12

54. Study the given pie-chart and answer the question that follows.

The pie-chart shows the marks obtained by a student in an examination. The total marks he scored is 450.

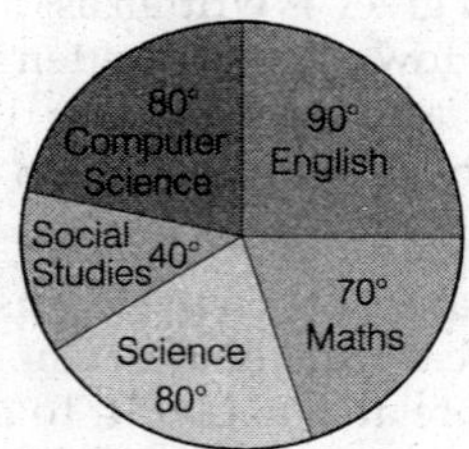

The difference between the marks obtained in (English + Maths) and (Computer Science + Science) is

(a) 10 (b) 30
(c) 0 (d) 20

55. An equal sum of money was lent to P and Q at 8.6% per annum for a period of 7 yr and 8 yr, respectively. If the difference in interest paid by them was ₹172, then the sum lent to each was

(a) ₹ 3000 (b) ₹ 2150
(c) ₹ 185 (d) ₹ 2000

56. A chord of length 12 units in a circle of radius 10 units is .... units away from its centre.

(a) 8 (b) 9 (c) 10 (d) 6

57. The given table shows the number of pizzas sold by four different bakeries in 5 different months.

Bakery/ Month	October	November	December	January	February
X	102	120	105	130	140
Y	98	104	115	120	136
Z	89	106	112	118	126
W	96	105	97	110	122

What is the respective ratio of the total number of pizzas sold by bakeries Y and Z together in November to the total number of pizzas sold by bakeries X and W together in the same month?

(a) 34 : 37 (b) 42 : 45
(c) 32 : 45 (d) 42 : 49

58. Raju spends 80% of his income. His income increased by 20%, while his spending rise by 10%. The percentage of increase in his savings is

(a) 48% (b) 40%
(c) 60% (d) 30%

59. The sum of two-digit number and the number obtained by interchanging the digit is 77. If the difference of digits is 1, then the number is

(a) 67 (b) 45 (c) 34 (d) 12

60. A shopkeeper marks up his goods 32% above the cost price and gives a discount of 21% on the marked price. Find his gain percentage on the goods.

(a) 4.82% (b) 8.42%
(c) 8.24% (d) 4.28%

61. Find the height of the triangle whose base is two-thirds of its height and whose area is 363 cm^2.

(a) 31 cm (b) 33 cm
(c) 29 cm (d) 27 cm

62. A solid copper sphere of radius 9 cm is drawn into a wire of radius 4 mm. Find the length of the wire.

(a) 60.75 m
(b) 70.25 m
(c) 65.25 m
(d) 20.75 m

63. The radii of two concentric circles are 35 cm and 21 cm. If the chord of the greater circle is a tangent to the smaller circle, then the length of that chord is

(a) 70 cm (b) 42 cm
(c) 56 cm (d) 28 cm

64. Shobhita can complete a painting work in 20 h while Saroj can complete the same work in 15 h. In how much time (in hours) can the entire work of painting be completed, if both Shobhita and Saroj work simultaneously?

(a) 7 (b) $8\frac{4}{7}$
(c) $7\frac{4}{7}$ (d) 8

65. If $\sin(X-Y)=\sin X\cos Y-\cos X\sin Y$, then the value of $\frac{\sin(A-B)}{\cos A\cos B}+\frac{\sin(B-C)}{\cos B\cos C}$ is

(a) $\frac{\sin(C-A)}{\cos A\cos C}$ (b) $\frac{\sin(A-C)}{\cos A\cos C}$
(c) $\frac{\cos(A+C)}{\cos A\cos C}$ (d) $\frac{\cos(A+C)}{\sin A\sin C}$

66. The diameter of the base of a cylindrical tank is 28 cm and its height is 42 cm. Find its curved surface area.

(a) 3680 cm^2
(b) 3690 cm^2
(c) 3696 cm^2
(d) 3686 cm^2

67. Write the smallest digit in the blank space of a number 7... 7624, so that the number formed is divisible by 3.

(a) 1 (b) 2
(c) 0 (d) 3

68. A number is first increased by 44% and then decreased by 30%. The net percentage change (rounded off to the nearest integer) in the original number is

(a) increase by 1%
(b) decrease by 4%
(c) increase by 4%
(d) decrease by 1%

69. The given graph shows the higher secondary result of a particular school, from 2019 to 2021. Study the graph and answer the question that follows.

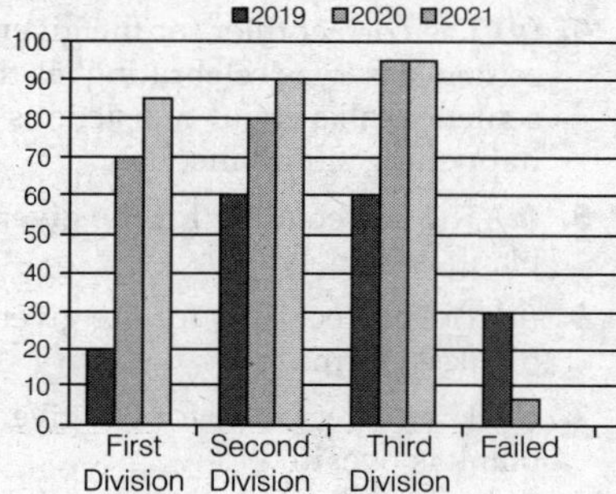

The percentage of students who passed in the year 2020 is
(a) 98% (b) 28% (c) 30% (d) 70%

70. Simplify

$$\frac{\frac{1}{2} \div \frac{3}{4} \text{ of } \frac{5}{6}}{\frac{1}{2} \div \frac{3}{4} \times \frac{5}{6}} + \frac{2+2\times 2}{2\div 2\times 2}$$

(a) $\frac{121}{25}$ (b) 4 (c) $\frac{111}{25}$ (d) $\frac{75}{36}$

71. PQ is a chord of a circle. The tangent XR at point X on the circle intersects the extension of PQ at point R. Given that $XR = 12$ cm, $PQ = x$ cm, and $QR = (x-2)$ cm, find the value of x.
(a) 11 cm (b) 9 cm
(c) 8 cm (d) 10 cm

72. Ramendra purchased some watermelons for ₹ 1500. He sold one-fourth of them at a loss of 12%. At what gain percentage should the remaining watermelons be sold so as to gain 25% on the whole transaction (correct to two decimal places)?
(a) 37.33% (b) 33.73%
(c) 37.65% (d) 33.43%

73. ΔABC and ΔDEF are similar and their areas are respectively 0.64 m^2 and 0.0121 m^2. If $EF = 0.154$ m, then BC is
(a) 1.15 m (b) 11.2 m
(c) 1.12 m (d) 2.12 m

74. In an election between two candidates, one candidate gets 72% of the total votes cast. If the total votes are 1000, by how many votes does the winner win the election?
(a) 360 (b) 250 (c) 720 (d) 440

75. The average age of 24 workers and their supervisor is 41 yr. If the supervisor's age is excluded, the average reduces by 0.75 yr. The age of the supervisor is
(a) 59 yr
(b) 41 yr 9 months
(c) 40 yr 9 months
(d) 49 yr

Part III
General Awareness

76. Who is the author of the Indian national anthem?
(a) Bankim Chandra Chattopadhyay
(b) Ishwar Chandra Vidyasagar
(c) Kazi Nazrul Islam
(d) Rabindranath Tagore

77. Which MS Excel function can be used to sum up the numbers entered in a group of cells?
(a) COUNT (b) AVERAGE
(c) MAX (d) SUM

78. Which of the Mendel's laws states that a diploid organism passes a randomly selected allele for a trait to its offspring, such that the offspring inherit one allele from each parent?
(a) Law of dominance
(b) Law of paired factor
(c) Law of independent assortment
(d) Law of segregation

79. In 2026, which country will host Asian Games?
(a) India (b) China (c) Japan (d) Nepal

80. Which directive principle has been implemented in establishing Handloom and Handicrafts Boards?
(a) Promote cottage industries on cooperative basis.
(b) Provision for just and humane condition of work.
(c) Participation of workers in management of Industries.
(d) Protection and improvement of environment.

81. Give Plastic and Take Gold scheme was launched in the village of which State/UT in year 2023?
(a) Gujarat
(b) Lakshadweep
(c) Jammu and Kashmir
(d) Assam

82. Marathi language is in the .... language family.
(a) Austro (b) Sino-India
(c) Austric (d) Indo Aryan

83. The music of traditional .... consists of Thumri and other lyrical song forms.
(a) Kuchipudi
(b) Kathak
(c) Kathakali
(d) Sattriya

84. Gandhi Jayanti marks the birthday of the father of the nation Mahatma Gandhi, who was born at ....
(a) Ahmedabad (b) Vadodara
(c) Porbandar (d) Gandhinagar

85. Ohira folk music is primarily associated with one of the popular festivals of which of the following states?
(a) Kerala
(b) Assam
(c) Jharkhand
(d) Karnataka

86. Which of the following planets' atmosphere is made up of thick white and yellowish clouds of sulphuric acid?
(a) Venus (b) Neptune
(c) Mars (d) Jupiter

87. Which of the following is a public sector owned and operated entity?
(a) Bajaj Auto Ltd
(b) Oil India Ltd.
(c) BHEL
(d) Tata Steel Ltd

88. According to Census of India 2011, which district in India has the lowest literacy rate in India?
(a) Rampur
(b) Madhubani
(c) Alirajpur
(d) Aizwal

89. The Tokyo Paralympics 2020 gold medal winner Krishna Nagar is associated with ....
(a) shooting (b) wrestling
(c) table tennis (d) badminton

90. Which is the standard meridian of India?
(a) 84°40′ E
(b) 82°30′ E
(c) 81°30′ E
(d) 83°30′ E

91. Who is Chairman of the Union Public Service Commission as on 31st March, 2024?
(a) Mrs. Preeti Sudan
(b) Shri Manoj Soni
(c) Shri BN Jha
(d) Ms. Smita Nagaraj

92. The process of merging data from a data source into a main document in a word-processing application is called
(a) data concatenation
(b) mail merge
(c) data accumulation
(d) data integration

93. In 1960, which isotope was used to define the standard measure of length?
(a) Krypton-86 (b) Krypton-88
(c) Krypton-83 (d) Krypton-90

94. Who is the Union Minister of Civil Aviation in Government of India? (As of March, 2024).
(a) G Kishan Reddy
(b) Kiren Rijiju
(c) Raj Kumar Singh
(d) Jyotiraditya M. Scindia

95. Which of the following is not a feature of a monopoly?
(a) No close substitutes
(b) Full control over the price by the seller
(c) One buyer and many sellers
(d) One seller and many buyers

96. There is a cable manufacturing facility at HCL in Rupnarainpur. It is belong to which state?
(a) Assam (b) Haryana
(c) Andhra Pradesh
(d) West Bengal

97. Due to the efforts of whom among the following social reformers was the first Hindu Widow Remarriage Act introduced and passed in 1856?
(a) Radhakant Deb
(b) Atmaram Pandurang
(c) Ishwar Chandra Vidyasagar
(d) Raja Ram Mohan Roy

98. Who among the following was the first Sultan of Delhi to style himself as 'Zil-i-Ilahi'?.
(a) Qutbuddin Aibak
(b) Feroz Shah
(c) Balban (d) Iltutmish

99. The Constitution of India was adopted on ....
(a) 26th, November, 1949
(b) 24th, November, 1947
(c) 26th, January, 1949
(d) 26th, January, 1950

100. Who was the first Indian wrestler to win Gold at the World Championships in 2010?
(a) Alka Tomar (b) Sushil Kumar
(c) Bajrang Punia (d) Geeta Phogat

Answers

1. (c)	2. (c)	3. (d)	4. (d)
5. (a)	6. (a)	7. (b)	8. (a)
9. (a)	10. (b)	11. (b)	12. (a)
13. (d)	14 (b)	15. (c)	16. (a)
17. (b)	18. (a)	19. (b)	20. (b)
21. (a)	22. (b)	23. (b)	24. (d)
25. (b)	26. (c)	27. (a)	28. (c)
29. (c)	30. (b)	31. (c)	32. (c)
33. (c)	34. (a)	35. (d)	36. (b)
37. (a)	38. (c)	39. (d)	40. (a)
41. (c)	42. (b)	43. (d)	44. (c)
45. (a)	46. (a)	47. (c)	48. (a)
49. (c)	50. (a)	51. (a)	52. (b)
53. (d)	54. (c)	55. (d)	56. (a)
57. (b)	58. (c)	59. (c)	60. (d)
61. (b)	62. (a)	63. (c)	64. (b)
65. (b)	66. (c)	67. (a)	68. (a)
69. (a)	70. (c)	71. (d)	72. (a)
73. (c)	74. (d)	75. (a)	76. (d)
77. (b)	78. (d)	79. (c)	80. (a)
81. (c)	82. (d)	83. (b)	84. (c)
85. (c)	86. (a)	87. (c)	88. (c)
89. (d)	90. (b)	91. (b)	92. (b)
93. (a)	94. (d)	95. (c)	96. (d)
97. (c)	98. (c)	99. (a)	100. (b)

Explanations

1. *(c)* The given sentence contains an error. The phrasal verb 'sold away' is incorrect. The correct phrasal verb that should be used is 'sold out'.

2. *(c)* Part (c) 'on the section' contains an error. Use 'on the basis' to correct the sentence.

3. *(d)* Part (d) 'We has travelled' contains an error. Use 'have' to correct the sentence. As the subject of the subject is plural, plural verbs should be used.

4. *(d)* The correct filler for the given sentence is 'was celebrating' as the sentence talks about two actions happening simultaneously.

5. *(a)* The correct filler for the given blank is 'widely'.

6. *(a)* The correct filler for the given blank is 'form'.

7. *(b)* The correct filler for the given blank is 'wealth'.

8. *(a)* The correct filler for the given blank is 'abundance'.

9. *(a)* The correct filler for the given blank is 'nature'.

10. *(b)* The underlined part of the given sentence contains an error.
Use 'who is wearing a blue shirt' to correct the sentence as relative pronoun 'who' is used for people.

11. *(b)* Vicious cycle refers to a sequence of reciprocal cause and effect in which two or more elements intensify and aggravate each other, leading inexorably to a worsening of the situation.

12. *(a)* The incorrectly spelt word is 'innoculate'. The correct spelling is 'inoculate'.

13. *(d)* The antonym of 'superior' is inferior.

14. *(b)* The word 'permit' means to allow someone to do something.
'Flout' means to break a rule or law.

15. *(c)* Bag and baggage means with all goods.

16. *(a)* The correct filler for the given blank is 'sauce'.

17. *(b)* Explicit means clear and direct. Hence, its antonym is 'ambiguous' which means confusing.
'Precise' means exact.

18. *(a)* The word 'clamour' means a loud and confused noise, especially that of people shouting.

19. *(b)* 'Concise' means short and brief. Hence, its antonym is 'Lengthy'.
'Excise' means tax.

20. *(b)* The correct filler for the given blank is 'route'.

21. *(a)* The correct filler for the given blank is 'full'.

22. *(b)* Part (b) 'with incadescent lights' contains a spelling error.
The correct spelling is 'incandescent' which means emitting light as a result of being heated.

23. *(b)* Tedious mean boring.

24. *(d)* The underlined part of the given sentence contains an error. Use 'affecting their capacity' to correct the sentence.

25. *(b)* The word 'dedicated' means 'committed'.

The other options are

- 'Un-biased' means fair or impartial.
- 'Apathetic' means not caring.

26. *(c)* As, T M B F → (+7, +7, +7, +7) → A T I M

and

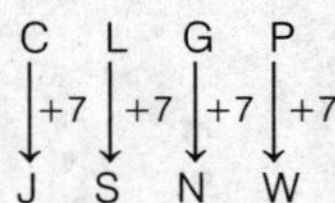

Similarly, Q E A D → (+7, +7, +7, +7) → X L H K

27. *(a)* The pattern of the series is as follows,

T $\xrightarrow{-2}$ R $\xrightarrow{-2}$ P $\xrightarrow{-2}$ N $\xrightarrow{-2}$ L

U $\xrightarrow{+3}$ X $\xrightarrow{+3}$ A $\xrightarrow{+3}$ D $\xrightarrow{+3}$ G

V $\xrightarrow{-4}$ R $\xrightarrow{-4}$ N $\xrightarrow{-4}$ J $\xrightarrow{-4}$ F

28. *(c)* Here, the series follows the two alternative pattern.

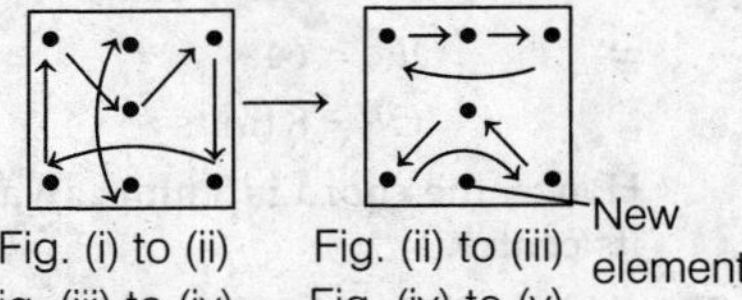

Hence, option (c) completes the given figure series.

29. *(c)* The correct pattern of the sequence is as follows,

G H O S T/G H O S R/G H O S P/G H O S N (−2, −2, −2)

∴ Required combination = OGSHN

30. *(b)* As, 12 $\xrightarrow{\times 6}$ 72

and 19 $\xrightarrow{\times 6}$ 114

Similarly, 29 $\xrightarrow{\times 6}$ 174

31. *(c)* Given, 19th July, 2012 → Thursday

Number of odd days from 19th July, 2012 to 19th July, 2017

Year →
2013 + 2014 + 2015 + 2016 + 2017

Odd days → 1 + 1 + 1 + 2 + 1
= 6 days

Number of odd days from 19th July, 2017 to 11th January, 2018

Months → July + August + September + October + November + December + January

Odd days →
12 + 31 + 30 + 31 + 30 + 31 + 11

$= \frac{176}{7}$

= 25 week and 1 odd day

∴ Required day = Thursday + 6 + 1
= Thursday + 7 = Thursday

32. *(c)*

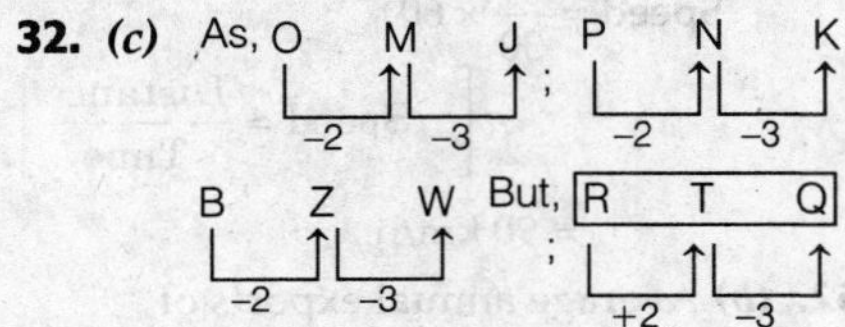

Hence, 'RTQ' is different among all.

33. *(c)*

Given word → D I A L E C T

Arranging the word in alphabetical order → A C D E I L T

∴ Only 'T' will remain unchanged.

34. *(a)* The pattern of the series is as follows,

63 (+1) 64 (+2) 66 (+3) 69 (+4) 73 (+5) 78

35. *(d)* Given expression, P + Q × R − S ÷ T

According to the question,

[+ → Male, − → Female]

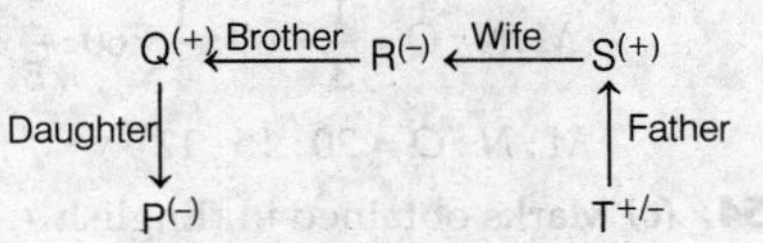

Q(+) —Brother— R(−) —Wife— S(+); Q —Daughter— P(−); S —Father— T(+/−)

Hence, from option (d) "P is the daughter of T's mother's brother" is true.

36. *(b)* The figure given in option (b) is the correct mirror image of the given figure.

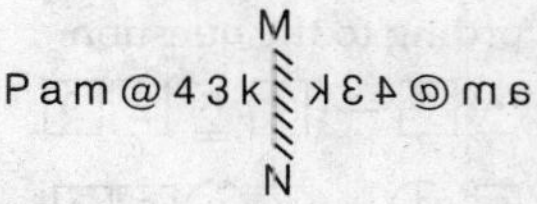

Pam@43k | M N | (mirror image)

37. *(a)* The pattern of series is as follows,

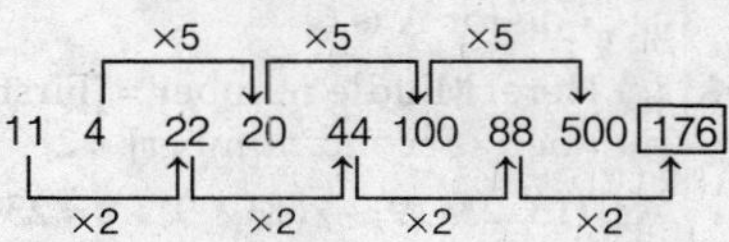

38. *(c)* When piece of paper is unfolded, it will look like option figure (c).

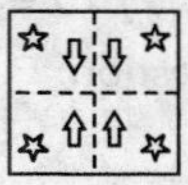

39. *(d)* Given equation,

15 + 2 − 13 × 13 ÷ 3 = ?

Interchanging + and −, × and ÷, we get

⇒ 15 − 2 + 13 ÷ 13 × 3 = ?

⇒ 13 + 1 × 3 = ?

⇒ ? = 13 + 3

∴ ? = 16

40. *(a)* Given expression,

17 C 69 A 3 D 22 B 1 = ?

Substituting the letters with symbols, we get

A → ÷	B → ×
C → +	D → −

17 + 69 ÷ 3 − 22 × 1 = ?

⇒ 17 + 23 − 22 = ? ⇒ 17 + 1 = ?

∴ ? = 18

41. *(c)* Naming the figure,

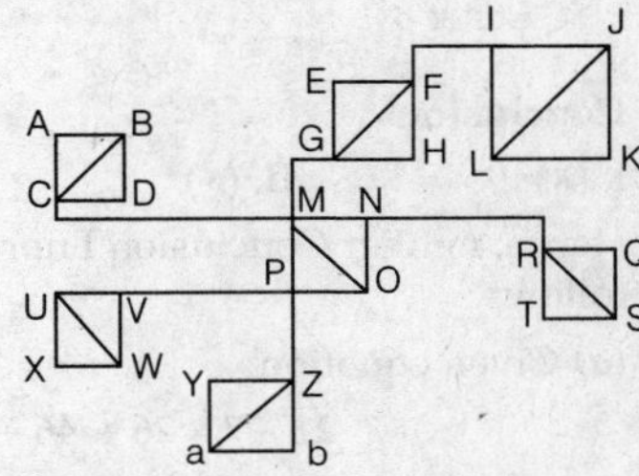

ΔABC, ΔBDC, ΔEFG, ΔFHG, ΔIJL, ΔJKL, ΔMNO, ΔMOP, ΔRQS, ΔRST, ΔUVW, ΔUWX, ΔYZa and ΔZba

Hence, there are 14 triangles in the given figure.

42. *(b)* The given question figure is embedded in option figure(b).

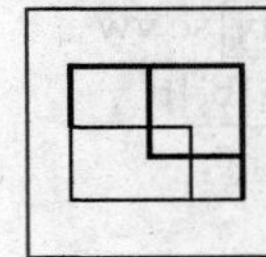

43. *(d)* According to the question,

S O A P → 4 6 2 9

S P O T → 9 8 2 4

∴ Code for A is 6.

44. *(c)* Here, Middle number = [First number × Second number] × 2

As, (13, 234, 9) → (13 × 9) × 2 = 234

and (15, 180, 6) → (15 × 6) × 2 = 180

Similarly, (14, 196, 7) → (14 × 7) × 2 = 196

45. *(a)* According to the question,

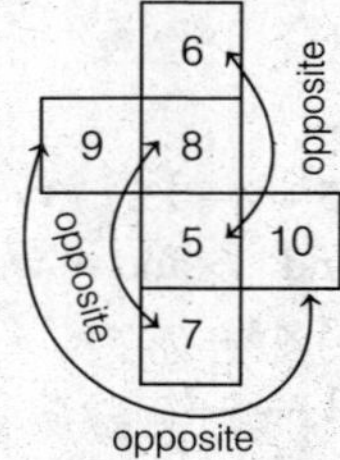

∴ '7' would be opposite to '8'.

46. *(a)* The figure given in option (a) is the correct mirror image of given figure

M

Wph4y | yA dqW

N

47. *(c)* According to the statements,

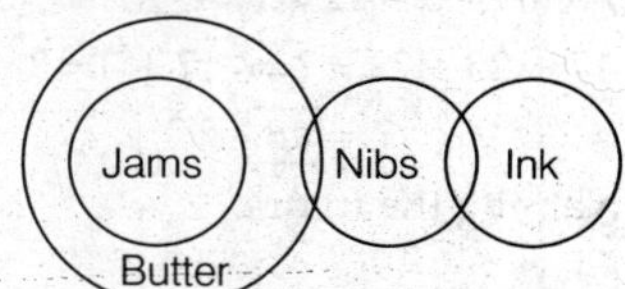

Conclusions

I. (✗) II. (✗)

Hence, neither Conclusion I nor II follows.

48. *(a)* Given equation,

$$21 - 7 \times 26 + 46 \div 36 = ?$$

Interchanging '+' and '×', '−' and '÷', we get,

$$21 \div 7 + 26 \times 46 - 36 = ?$$

$\Rightarrow$ $3 + 1196 - 36 = ?$

$\Rightarrow$ $1199 - 36 = ?$

$\therefore$ $? = \boxed{1163}$

49. *(c)* According to the question,

pleased to meet → bj sc vw

meet and greet → ih bj tf

∴ Code for 'meet' is 'bj'.

50. *(a)* As, R T V X

+1 +1 +1 +1

S U W Y

and K M O Q

+1 +1 +1 +1

L N P R

Similarly, F H J L

+1 +1 +1 +1

G I K M

51. *(a)* Given, Time = 45 min,

Speed = 60 km/h

We know that,

$$\text{Distance} = \text{Speed} \times \text{Time} = 60 \times \frac{45}{60}$$

$= 45$ km

To reach destination in 30 min,

$$\text{Speed} = \frac{45}{30} \times 60 \quad \left[\because \text{Speed} = \frac{\text{Distance}}{\text{Time}}\right]$$

$= 90$ km/h

52. *(b)* Average annual exports of company C

$$= \frac{140 + 158 + 160 + 166 + 178}{5}$$

$$= \frac{802}{5} = 160.4 \text{ crore}$$

From bar-graph,

1. In year, 1995 i.e. export of 140 crores
2. In year, 1996 i.e export of 158 crores and
3. In year 1997 i.e. export of 160 crores are less than average annual exports of company C.

∴ Required number of years = 3

53. *(d)* Given, $\frac{1}{M} : \frac{1}{N} : \frac{1}{O} = 3 : 4 : 5$

$$M : N : O = \frac{1}{3} : \frac{1}{4} : \frac{1}{5} \quad [\text{LCM} = 60]$$

$$M : N : O = \frac{1}{3} \times 60 : \frac{1}{4} \times 60 : \frac{1}{5} \times 60$$

$$M : N : O = 20 : 15 : 12$$

54. *(c)* Marks obtained in (English + Maths)

$$= \frac{(90 + 70)^\circ}{360^\circ} \times 450$$

$$= \frac{160^\circ}{360^\circ} \times 450 = 199.99 \sim 200$$

Marks obtained in (Computer Science + Science)

$$= \frac{(80 + 80)^\circ}{360} \times 450$$

$$= \frac{160^\circ}{360^\circ} \times 450$$

$= 199.99 \sim 200$

∴ Required difference = 200 − 200 = 0

55. *(d)* Let the money lent was P.

According to the question,

$$\frac{P \times 8.6 \times 8}{100} - \frac{P \times 8.6 \times 7}{100} = ₹\, 172$$

$\Rightarrow P \times 8.6 = ₹\, 172 \times 100$

$\Rightarrow$ $P = ₹\, \frac{172 \times 100}{8.6}$

$\therefore$ $P = ₹\, 2000$

Hence, the sum lent to each was ₹ 2000.

56. *(a)* According to the question,

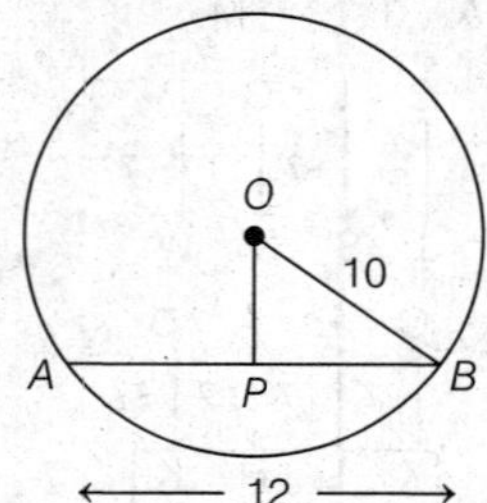

We know that, in a circle a perpendicular divides a chord into 2 equal side.

So, $AP = PB = \frac{AB}{2} = \frac{12}{2} = 6$ units

In ΔPOB, $OP^2 = OB^2 - PB^2$

$OP^2 = (10)^2 - (6)^2$

$\Rightarrow$ $OP^2 = 100 - 36$

$\Rightarrow$ $OP^2 = 64$

$\therefore$ $OP = 8$ units

Hence, the chord is 8 units away from its centre.

57. *(b)* Total number of pizzas sold by bakeries Y and Z together in month of November = 104 + 106 = 210

Total number of pizzas sold by bakeries X and W together in month of November = 120 + 105 = 225

∴ Required ratio = 210 : 225

= 42 : 45

58. *(c)* Let the income of Raju be $100x$.

$$\text{Expenditure} = \left[100x \times \frac{80}{100}\right] = 80x$$

$\therefore$ Savings $= \left[\dfrac{100x - 80x}{100} \times 100\right] = 20x$

New income $= \left[100x \times \dfrac{120}{100}\right] = 120x$

New expenditure $= \left(80x \times \dfrac{110}{100}\right) = 88x$

$\therefore$ New savings $= 120x - 88x$

$= 32x$

Percentage increase in savings

$= \left[\dfrac{32x - 20x}{20x} \times 100\right]\%$

$= \left[\dfrac{12x}{20x} \times 100\right]\%$

$= 60\%$

59. *(c)* Let the ten's digit of number be y and unit digit of number be x, then number is $10y + x$.

According to the question,

$10y + x + 10x + y = 77$

$\Rightarrow \quad 11x + 11y = 77$

$\Rightarrow \quad 11(x + y) = 77$

$\Rightarrow \quad x + y = 7 \quad$ ...(i)

Also, given $x - y = 1 \quad$ ...(ii)

Solving Eqs. (i) and (ii), we get

$x = 4, y = 3$

$\therefore$ Required number $= 10y + x$

$= 10(3) + 4$

$= 34$

60. *(d)* Given, Marked Price (MP) = 32%

Cost price (CP) = 21%

Percentage gain

$= \left[\text{MP} - \text{CP} - \dfrac{\text{MP} \times \text{CP}}{100}\right]\%$

$= \left[32 - 21 - \dfrac{32 \times 21}{100}\right]\%$

$= [11 - 6.72]\ \%$

$= 4.28\%$

61. *(b)* Given,

Base $= \dfrac{2}{3}$ Height

$\dfrac{\text{Base}}{\text{Height}} = \dfrac{2}{3} = \dfrac{2x}{3x}$

Area of triangle $= \dfrac{1}{2} \times$ Base $\times$ Height

$\dfrac{1}{2} \times 2x \times 3x = 363$

$\Rightarrow \quad x^2 = \dfrac{363}{3} = 121$

$\therefore \quad x = 11$ cm

$\therefore$ Height of triangle $= 3x$

$= 3 \times 11$

$= 33$ cm

62. *(a)* Given, radius of sphere $(r_1) = 9$ cm

Radius of wire $(r_2) = 4$ mm

According to the question,

Volume of sphere = Volume of wire

$\dfrac{4}{3}\pi \times \dfrac{9}{100} \times \dfrac{9}{100} \times \dfrac{9}{100}$

$= \pi \times \dfrac{4}{1000} \times \dfrac{4}{1000} \times h$

$\Rightarrow \quad h = \dfrac{4 \times \pi \times 9 \times 9 \times 9}{\pi \times 3 \times 4 \times 4}$

$h = 60.75$ m

63. *(c)* According to the question,

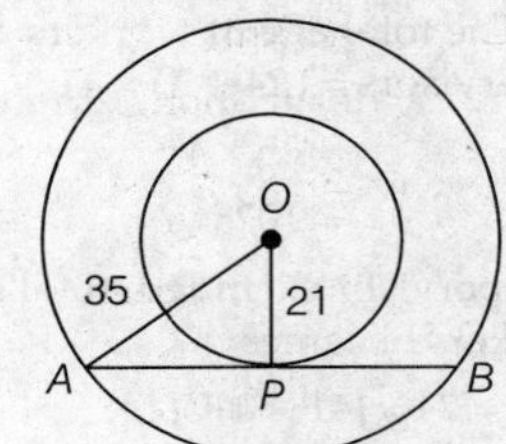

In ΔAOP, $\quad AO^2 = AP^2 + PO^2$

$35^2 = AP^2 + 21^2$

$\Rightarrow \quad AP^2 = 35^2 - 21^2$

$\Rightarrow \quad AP^2 = 1225 - 441$

$\Rightarrow \quad AP^2 = 784$

$\therefore \quad AP = 28$ cm

Length of chord $= 28 \times 2$

$= 56$ cm

64. *(b)* Given, Shobita's 1 h work $= \dfrac{1}{20}$

Saroj's 1 h work $= \dfrac{1}{15}$

(Shobita's + Saroj's) 1 h work

$= \dfrac{1}{20} + \dfrac{1}{15}$

$= \dfrac{3 + 4}{60} = \dfrac{7}{60}$

Both can complete the entire work in

$= \dfrac{60}{7} = 8\dfrac{4}{7}$ h

65. *(b)* $\dfrac{\sin(A - B)}{\cos A \cos B} + \dfrac{\sin(B - C)}{\cos B \cos C}$

$= \dfrac{\sin A \cos B - \cos A \sin B}{\cos A \cos B} + \dfrac{\sin B \cos C - \cos B \sin C}{\cos B \cdot \cos C}$

$= \dfrac{\cos C[\sin A \cdot \cos B - \cos A \cdot \sin B] + \cos A[\sin B \cdot \cos C - \cos B \sin C]}{\cos A \cdot \cos B \cdot \cos C}$

$= \dfrac{\sin A \cdot \cos B \cdot \cos C - \cos A \sin B \cos C + \sin B \cdot \cos C \cdot \cos A - \cos A \cdot \cos B \cdot \sin C}{\cos A \cdot \cos B \cdot \cos C}$

$= \dfrac{\sin(A - C)}{\cos A \cdot \cos C}$

66. *(c)* Given, diameter = 28 cm,

height = 42 cm

We know,

Curved surface area $= 2\pi rh$

$= 2 \times \dfrac{22}{7} \times \dfrac{28}{2} \times 42$

$= 3696 \text{ cm}^2$

67. *(a)* Let the number at blank space be x.

$\therefore 7x7624$ must be divisible by 3.

To check divisibility by 3, sum of digits of number must be divisible by 3.

$\therefore 7 + x + 7 + 6 + 2 + 4 = x + 26$

The least greatest number which is divisible by 3 is 27

$\therefore x + 26 = 27$

$x = 27 - 26 = 1$

68. *(a)* Net percentage change

$= 44 - 30 - \dfrac{44 \times 30}{100}$

$= 14 - 13.2$

$= 0.8\% \sim 1\%$ increase

69. *(a)* Percentage of students passed in year 2020

$= \dfrac{\text{Total number of passed students}}{\text{Total students}} \times 100$

$= \left[\dfrac{70 + 80 + 95}{70 + 80 + 95 + 5} \times 100\right]\%$

$= \left[\dfrac{245}{250} \times 100\right]\%$

$= 98\%$

70. *(c)* Given,

$= \dfrac{\dfrac{1}{2} \div \dfrac{3}{4} \text{ of } \dfrac{5}{6}}{\dfrac{1}{2} \div \dfrac{3}{4} \times \dfrac{5}{6}} + \dfrac{2 + 2 \times 2}{2 \div 2 \times 2}$

$$= \frac{\frac{1}{2} \div \frac{5}{8}}{\frac{1}{2} \times \frac{4}{3} \times \frac{5}{6}} + \frac{6}{2}$$

$$= \frac{\frac{1}{2} \times \frac{8}{5}}{\frac{5}{9}} + 3$$

$$= \frac{4}{5} \times \frac{9}{5} + 3 = \frac{36}{25} + 3$$

$$= \frac{36 + 75}{25} = \frac{111}{25}$$

71. *(d)* According to the question,

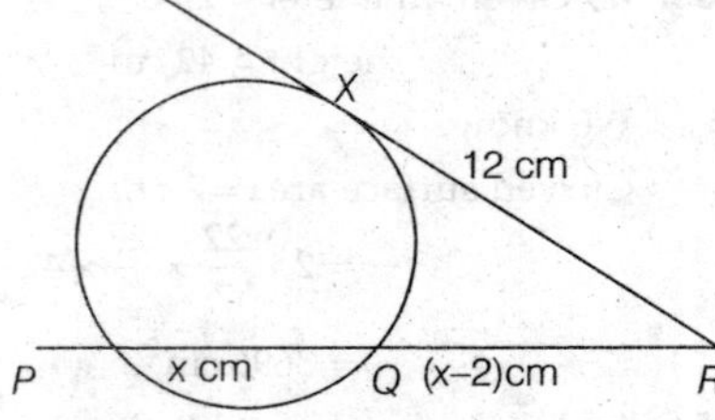

Now, when RX is a tangent and PQ is a chord in circle.

So, $RX^2 = QR \times PR$

$(12)^2 = (x - 2) \times (x + x - 2)$

$\Rightarrow \quad 144 = (x - 2)(2x - 2)$

$\Rightarrow \quad 144 = 2x^2 - 2x - 4x + 4$

$\Rightarrow \quad 2x^2 - 6x - 140 = 0$

$\Rightarrow \quad x^2 - 3x - 70 = 0$

$\Rightarrow x^2 + 7x - 10x - 70 = 0$

$\Rightarrow \quad (x - 10)(x + 7) = 0$

$\Rightarrow \quad x = -7, 10$

Hence, $x = 10$ cm

72. *(a)* Given, total CP = ₹ 1500

$\therefore \quad$ Total SP $= 1500 \times \frac{125}{100} =$ ₹ 1875

He sold one-fourth at 12% loss.

$\therefore \quad$ SP $= \frac{1500}{4} \times \frac{88}{100} =$ ₹ 330

Remaining SP = ₹ [1875 – 330]

= ₹ 1545

Remaining CP = ₹ $1500 \times \frac{3}{4}$

= ₹ 1125

Required profit $= \frac{1545 - 1125}{1125} \times 100$

$= \frac{420}{1125} \times 100$

= 37.33%

73. *(c)* Given, $\Delta ABC \sim \Delta DEF$

So, $\frac{\text{Area of } \Delta ABC}{\text{Area of } \Delta DEF} = \frac{BC^2}{EF^2}$

$$\frac{0.64}{0.121} = \frac{BC^2}{0.154^2}$$

$$\Rightarrow \quad BC = \frac{0.8 \times 0.154}{0.11}$$

$$\therefore \quad BC = 1.12 \text{ m}$$

74. *(d)* Let total votes are 100%.

Given, one candidate gets = 72% of total votes

$\therefore$ Other person gets

= [100 – 72]%

= 28%

$\therefore$ Required difference

$= \frac{72 - 28}{100} \times 1000$

$= \frac{44}{100} \times 1000 = 440$

Hence, the winner won by 440 votes.

75. *(a)* The total age of workers and supervisors = (24 + 1) × 41

= 25 × 41

= 1025 yr

If supervisor excluded, total age of workers becomes

= 24 × [41 – 0.75]

= 24 × 40.25 = 966 yr

$\therefore$ Age of supervisor

= [1025 – 966] yr

= 59 yr

76. *(d)* The author of the Indian national anthem, 'Jana Gana Mana', is Rabindranath Tagore.He wrote the song in Bengali in 1911, and it was later adopted as the national anthem of India in 1950.

- Rabindranath Tagore was a renowned Bengali poet, philosopher and playwright who was awarded the Nobel Prize in Literature in 1913.
- The song was first sung at the Calcutta session of the Indian National Congress in 1911, and it was later adopted as the National Anthem of India by the Constituent Assembly on 24th January, 1950,

77. *(b)* AVERAGE MS Excel function can be used to sum up the numbers entered in a group of cells.

78. *(d)* The law of segregation, also known as Mendel's second law, states that a diploid organism passes a randomly selected allele for a trait to its offspring, such that the offspring inherit one allele from each parent.

- When gametes are formed, each allele from one parent segregates randomly into the gametes.
- This means that half of the parent's gametes carry each allele.

79. *(c)* The 2026 Asian Games will be co-hosted by the Aichi Prefecture and the city of Nagoya in Japan.

- It will mark the third time the Asian Games has been held in Japan, following Tokyo in 1958 and Hiroshima in 1994.
- The Olympic Council of Asia (0CA) is a governing body of sports in Asia with its headquarter at Kuwait City, Kuwait.
- Raja Randhir Singh is currently serving as the President of OCA.

80. *(a)* The establishment of Handloom and Handicrafts Boards is an implementation of the directive principle to 'Promote cottage industries on cooperative basis' (Article 43 of the Indian Constitution). The other options are

- Provision for just and humane conditions of work (Article 42) is related to labour rights and working conditions.
- Participation of workers in management of industries (Article 43A) is related to industrial democracy and worker participation.
- Protection and improvement of environment (Article 48A) is related to environmental conservation and protection.

81. *(c)* The Give Plastic and Take Gold scheme was launched in the village of Jammu and Kashmir in 2023.

- The scheme was launched by the village head of Sadiwara, Farooq Ahmad Ganai.Under the scheme, if someone gives 20 quintals of plastic waste, then the Panchayat will give him a gold.
- The objective of the scheme is to save the environment by collecting plastic waste and coin promoting cleanliness in the village.

82. *(d)* Marathi language belongs to the Indo-Aryan branch of the Indo-European language family.

- It is a descendant of the ancient Indian language of Sanskrit and is closely related to other Indo-Aryan languages such as Hindi, Gujarati and Punjabi.

- Marathi is the official language of the Indian state of Maharashtra and is spoken by around 83 million people worldwide.

83. *(b)* The music of traditional Kathak consists of Thumri and other lyrical song forms.

- Thumri is North India's most popular light-classical song form, developed during the 19th century at the court of Lucknow's ruler Wajid Ali Shah.
- A Thumri is usually performed as the last item of a Khayal concert.Three main Gharanas of Thumri are Benaras, Lucknow and Patiala.
- Begum Akhtar is one of the most popular singers of Thumri style.

84. *(c)* Mahatma Gandhi was born on 2nd October, 1869, in Porbandar, marks this day as Gandhi Jayanti. The United Nations celebrates the day as International Day of Non-Violence.

- Mahatma Gandhi is known as the Father of the Nation because of the Tireless efforts he put in to free the country from the British Raj.
- His non-violent resistance helped end British rule in India and has influenced modern Civil Disobedience Movements across the globe.
- 30th January is recognised nationally as Martyrs' Day in India, to mark the assassination of Mahatma Gandhi in 1948.

85. *(c)* Ohira is a popular folk music style in Jharkhand, particularly among the tribal communities.

- It is characterised by its unique rhythms, melodies and lyrics, which often reflect the region's cultural heritage and everyday life.
- Ohira is primarily practiced by the tribal communities of Jharkhand, including the Santhals, Mundas and Ho tribes.
- Ohira music has been recognised by UNESCO as an intangible cultural heritage of humanity, highlighting its importance and value.

86. *(a)* Venus planet's atmosphere is made up of thick white and yellowish clouds of sulphuric acid.

87. *(c)* BHEL (Bharat Heavy Electricals Limited) is a public sector company that specialises in manufacturing electrical equipment.

- Bajaj Auto is a private sector company that specialises in manufacturing two wheelers and three wheelers.
- OIL India limited is a government of India enterprises, under the administrative control of Ministry of Petroleum and Natural Gas.
- Tata Steel was established in India as Asia's first Integrated private steel company at Jamshedpur.

88. *(c)* According to the Census of India 2011, Alirajpur district in Madhya Pradesh has the lowest literacy rate in India, with a literacy rate of 37.22%.

Alirajpur is a tribal-dominated district, and the low literacy rate is due to various factors such as lack of access to education poverty and socio-economic backwardness.

- Rampur is a district in Uttar Pradesh, and its literacy rate is around 55%.
- Madhubani is a district in Bihar, and its literacy rate is around 60%.
- Aizawl is the capital of Mizoram, and the state has a high literacy rate of over 90%.

89. *(d)* Krishna Nagar is an Indian para-badminton player from Rajasthan. He had been ranked world number 2 in para-badminton men's singles SH6.

- He won a gold medal at the 2020 Summer Paralympics.
- In the 2018 Asian Para Games in Indonesia, Krishna Nagar won a bronze medal in the singles event.
- In the 2019 BWF Para-Badminton World Championships in Basel, Switzerland. Krishna Nagar won the silver medal in the men's doubles event alongside compatriot Raja Magotra. He also won a bronze in the singles event.

90. *(b)* The standard meridian of India is 82°30'E.

- A standard meridian was adopted among many meridians for the country to bring about uniformity in time across the country.
- It passes through Mirzapur (Uttar Pradesh). The time of this meridian is taken as the standard time for the whole country.

91. *(b)* Shri Manoj Soni is appointed as the Chairman of Union Public Service Commission (UPSC) as on 31st March, 2024.

- The UPSC is a constitutional body in India that conducts direct recruitment of officers to the All India Services and the Central Civil Services (Groups A and B) through examinations.
- The agency's charter is granted by Part XIV of the Constitution of India, titled as Services Under the Union and the States.

92. *(b)* The process of merging data from a data source into main document in a word - processing application is called mail merge.

93. *(a)* In 1960, Krypton - 86 was used to define the standard measure of length. A distance of 1 metre is equal to 1650763.73 wavelength of orange - red light of Kr - 86.

94. *(d)* Jyotiraditya M. Scindia is the Union Minister of Civil Aviation in Government of India.

- He has been given the charge of the Ministry of Communications and the Ministry of Development of the North Eastern Region.
- The Ministry of Civil Aviation in India is the nodal ministry responsible for the formulation of national policies and programmes for the development and regulation of civil aviation.

95. *(c)* 'One buyer and many sellers' is not a feature of a monopoly.

- In monopoly market form, there is only one seller (single producer of a commodity) and large number of buyers.
  This situation gives the seller full control over the market and price of the commodity.
- A monopoly must have barriers to entry or else there will be new entrants trying to earn some of the positive economic profit the monopolist currently enjoys.
- Key features of a monopoly include sole selling, price-setting authority, barriers to entry for others, control over supply, and an absence of competition.

96. *(d)* The cable manufacturing facility at HCL (Hindustan Copper Limited) in Rupnarainpur is indeed located in West Bengal.

- Hindustan Copper Limited (HCL) is a public sector undertaking under the Ministry of Mines, Goverment of India.

- The company's head office is located in Noida. HCL was established in 1976 as one of India's IT start-ups.

97. *(c)* Ishwar Chandra Vidyasagar was a prominent social reformer in India, and his efforts led to the introduction and passage of the Hindu Widow Remarriage Act in 1856.

- The greatest contribution of Ishwar Chandra Vidyasagar can be for his fervent push for the introduction of widow remarriage and girl's education in Indian society.
- Sanskrit College, Calcutta gave him the title Vidyasagar, due to his excellent performance in Sanskrit studies and philosophy.

98. *(c)* Balban was the first Sultan of Delhi to style himself as 'Zil-i-Ilahi', which means 'Shadow of God' or 'Representative of God'.

- Balban was a slave-soldier who rose to become the Sultan of Delhi in 1266 and ruled until 1287. He is known for his authoritarian and centralised style of governance, and his efforts to establish a strong and stable monarchy.
- The title 'Zil-i-Ilahi' was later adopted by other Sultans of Delhi, including the Mughal emperors, to emphasise their divine right to rule.

99. *(a)* The Constitution of India was adopted on 26th November, 1949.

- It came into effect on 26th January 1950. 26th January is celebrated as Republic Day in India to commemorate this historic event.
- The Constitution replaced the Government of India Act (1935) as the governing document of India, marking the country's transition to a republic.

100. *(b)* The first Indian wrestler to win gold at the World Championships in 2010 was Sushil Kumar.

- He won the gold medal in the 66 kg freestyle category at the 2010 World Championships in Moscow, Russia.
- In July 2009, he received the Major Dhyan Chand Khel Ratna, Padma Shri in 2011 and Arjuna Award in 2005.

Set 19 05 July, 2024 (Shift III)

SSC CHSL Tier-I SOLVED PAPER

Instructions

1. This paper contains 100 questions.
2. It has 4 Parts, **Part I** General English, **Part II** General Intelligence & Reasoning, **Part III** Quantitative Aptitude and **Part IV** General Awareness.
3. Each question carries **2 marks**.

Part I General English

1. The following sentence has been split into four segments. Identify the segment that contains a grammatical error.

With hard work, commitment / and proper guidance, / Sivaram has become / a IPS officer.

(a) With hard work, commitment
(b) and proper guidance,
(c) a IPS officer
(d) Sivaram has become

2. Parts of the following sentence have been given as options. Select the option that contains an error.

A owl is a bird which has wide eyes, asymmetrical ears and is found mostly in forests.

(a) and is found mostly in forests
(b) asymmetrical ears
(c) A owl is a bird
(d) which has wide eyes,

3. The following sentence has been split into four segments. Identify the segment that contains a grammatical error.

The teacher will never / give you punishment / if you will / come on time.

(a) give you punishment
(b) if you will
(c) come on time
(d) The teacher will never

4. The following sentence has been split into four segments. Identify the segment that contains an error.

If she exercises daily, / she would / remain energetic / and fit forever.

(a) remain energetic
(b) If she exercises daily
(c) and fit forever
(d) she would

Directions (Q. Nos. 5-9) *In the following passage, some words have been deleted. Read the passage carefully and select the most appropriate option to fill in each blank.*

Romantic poetry is a literary movement that emerged in the late 18th century and continued through the mid-19th century. It is (1)......... by an emphasis on emotion, imagination and individualism. Romantic poets sought to express their innermost thoughts and feelings through their poetry, often exploring (2)......... such as love, beauty and mortality. One of the defining features of Romantic poetry is its use of language and imagery to evoke powerful emotions in the reader. Many Romantic poets, such as William Wordsworth and Samuel Taylor Coleridge (3)......... that poetry should be written in the language of common people, rather than in the lofty, formal language of the past. They also incorporated vivid descriptions of nature and the natural world into their poetry, using it as a source of inspiration and spiritual renewal. (4)......... important aspect of Romantic poetry is its focus on the individual and the subjective experience. Romantic poets believed that each persons experience of the world was unique and valuable, and sought to capture this individuality in their writing. This led to a greater emphasis on personal expression and introspection in poetry, (5)......... a rejection of the traditional poetic forms and structures of the past.

5. Select the most appropriate option to fill in blank number 1.

(a) characterises (b) characteristic
(c) characterised (d) characterising

6. Select the most appropriate option to fill in blank number 2.

(a) concerns (b) arguments
(c) problems (d) themes

7. Select the most appropriate option to fill in blank number 3.

(a) could believe (b) will believe
(c) believes (d) believed

8. Select the most appropriate option to fill in blank number 4.

(a) Mostly (b) Additional
(c) Another (d) Farther

9. Select the most appropriate option to fill in blank number 5.

(a) whereas (b) therefore
(c) as well as (d) but

10. Select the most appropriate antonym for the underlined word in the given sentence.

As a punishment for his <u>betrayal</u> to his country, the spy who sold secrets was sent to prison.

(a) infidelity (b) loyalty
(c) perilous (d) nasty

11. Select the most appropriate antonym of the given word.

Skeptic

(a) Believer (b) Atheist
(c) Careful (d) Infidel

12. Select the most appropriate option that can substitute the underlined segment in the given sentence. If there is no need to substitute it, select 'No substitution required'.

He asked his father when <u>would come the next letter.</u>

(a) No substitution required
(b) the next letter would come
(c) would the next letter come
(d) come the next letter

13. Select the most appropriate idiomatic expression that can substitute the underlined segment in the given sentence.

Last year art critics praised Animesh as if he were a master, but he turned out to be <u>a pleasure for a short time.</u>

(a) a nine days' wonder
(b) a dish fit for Gods
(c) a house of cards
(d) a bull in a China shop

14. Select the most appropriate option that can substitute the underlined word in the given sentence.
The professor did an <u>objective</u> evaluation.
(a) unfair (b) prejudiced
(c) unbiased (d) unjust

15. Select the most appropriate antonym of the given word.
Comical
(a) Tragic (b) Remedial
(c) Farcical (d) Rebellious

16. Select the most appropriate option to fill in the blank.
The bride had a big villa in comparison to the bridegroom's .... house.
(a) large (b) small
(c) distinct (d) different

17. Select the incorrectly spelt word.
(a) Aquarium (b) Mantain
(c) Accurate (d) Excellence

18. Select the most appropriate meaning of the given idiom.
Bread and butter
(a) An activity you do to get help others
(b) An activity you do with determination
(c) An activity you do to improve your culinary skills
(d) An activity you do to get money for basic needs

19. Select the most appropriate option that can substitute the underlined words in the following sentence.
If you do hard work, you will have the <u>expected results.</u>
(a) good results (b) required results
(c) desired results (d) bad results

20. Select the most appropriate option that can substitute the underlined words in the given sentence.
Although I have a lot of work to do, I am determined to finish it all by the end of the day so that I can enjoy my weekend <u>not having any imminent due dates.</u>
(a) without any looming deadlines
(b) not with any pressure of due date
(c) with no pending reservations
(d) not leaving any work incomplete

21. Select the most appropriate antonym of the word given in bracket to fill in the blank.
Her voice, soft and ...., (shrill) flowed effortlessly through the room.
(a) mellow (b) nasal
(c) croaky (d) piercing

22. Identify the incorrectly spelt word and select its correct spelling.
It is his previlage to present all the candidates for ordination to the bishop of the diocese.
(a) deocease
(b) privilege
(c) prevalage
(d) odination

23. Select the most appropriate option that can substitute the underlined segment in the given sentence.
Planets in our solar system <u>close and big</u> for them to twinkle.
(a) is close and big
(b) are quite close and big
(c) are too close and big
(d) very close and big

24. Which of the following sentences contains the antonym of the word 'ignore'?
(a) Avoid foods which make you sick.
(b) He did not succeed in gaining custody of his daughter.
(c) Ritika recognised Kavita in the gathering.
(d) To keep a tidy kitchen, do not neglect washing your dishes.

25. Select the most appropriate connotation to fill in the blank.
Raju is such a .... always prying into other people's business!
(a) cheeky (b) stingy
(c) nosy (d) perky

Part II
General Intelligence

26. If 'A' stands for '÷', 'B' stands for '×', 'C' stands for '+' and 'D' stands for '−', what will come in place of the question mark (?) in the following equation?
28 B 7 D 176 A 8 C 13 = ?
(a) 185 (b) 184 (c) 187 (d) 186

27. How many triangles are there in the given figure?

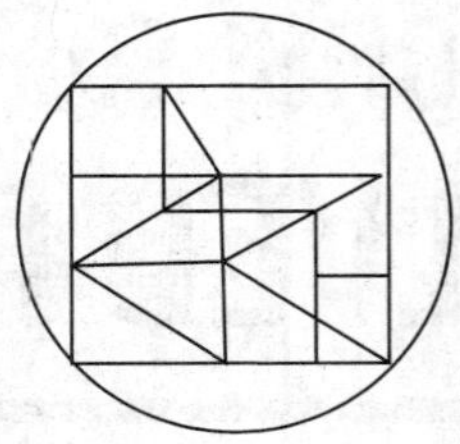

(a) 14 (b) 16
(c) 15 (d) 13

28. What would be the word on the opposite side of 'Kiwi', if the given sheet is folded to form a cube?

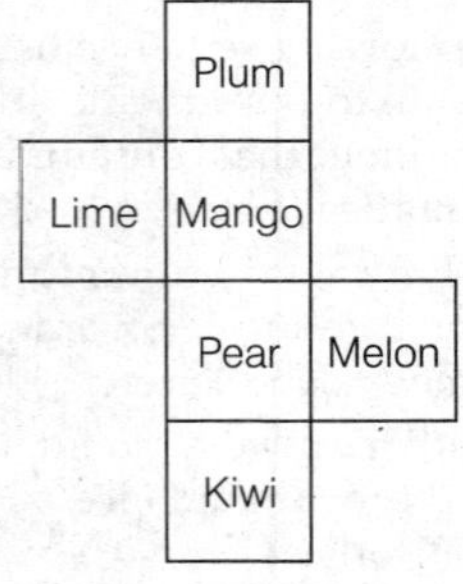

(a) Melon (b) Plum
(c) Lime (d) Mango

29. What should come in place of question mark (?) in the given series based on the English alphabetical order?
TMF, UNE, VOD, ?, XQB
(a) KOT (b) WPC
(c) ACE (d) WPI

30. What should come in place of the question mark (?) in the given series based on the English alphabetical order?
CPW, HRA, MTE, RVI, ?
(a) VXN (b) VYN
(c) XXM (d) WXM

31. Select the correct mirror image of the given figure, when the mirror is placed at MN.

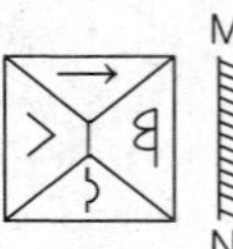

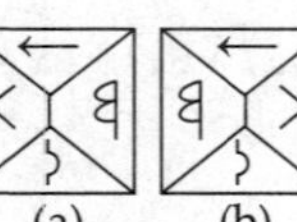 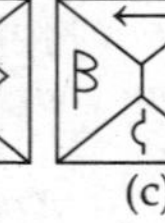 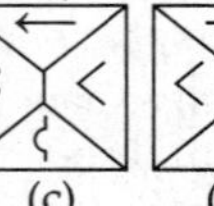 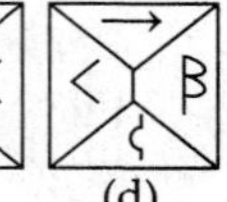

(a) (b) (c) (d)

32. ZBRL is related to UWMG in a certain way based on the English alphabetical order. In the same way, IDSQ is related to DYNL. To which of the following is EVNA related, following the same logic?
(a) ZIVQ (b) ZIQV
(c) ZQVI (d) ZQIV

33. If 15th August, 2006 is a Tuesday, then what will the day of the week on 7th September, 2017?
(a) Thursday (b) Wednesday
(c) Monday (d) Sunday

34. What should come in place of the question mark (?) in the given series?
23, 27, 35, 47, 63, ?
(a) 83 (b) 84
(c) 85 (d) 82

35. In a certain code language, 'RUIN' is coded as '3098' and 'TURN' is coded as '9630'. How is 'I' coded in the given language?
(a) 6 (b) 3 (c) 8 (d) 9

36. YZWT is related to DEAX in a certain way based on the English alphabetical order. In the same way, QROL is related to VWSP. To which of the following is RSPM related, following the same logic?
(a) WXTQ (b) WXUQ
(c) WYUQ (d) WTXQ

37. What will come in the place of the question mark (?) in the following equation, if '+' and '÷' are interchanged and '×' and '–' are interchanged?
$39 + 13 \times 12 \div 5 - 4 = ?$
(a) 13 (b) 11
(c) 9 (d) 7

38. Three of the following four are alike in a certain way and thus form a group. Which is the one that does not belong to that group?
(**Note** The odd one out is not based on the number of consonants/vowels or their position in the letter-cluster)
(a) PSU (b) HKN
(c) TWZ (d) DGJ

39. Which two numbers should be interchanged to make the given equation correct?
$136 - (176 \div 11) \times 8 + 22 \times 3 = 105$
(**Note** Numbers must be interchanged and not the constituent digits e.g, if 2 and 3 are to be interchanged in the equation $43 \times 3 + 4 \div 2$, then interchanged equation is $43 \times 2 + 4 \div 3$)
(a) 11 and 22 (b) 8 and 3
(c) 22 and 176 (d) 8 and 11

40. Select the correct mirror image of the given figure, when the mirror is placed at MN as shown below.

M
Lj3r4pa
N

(a) paᔭɿƐį⅃
(b) ɒdᔭɿƐį⅃
(c) ɒqᔭɿƐį⅃
(d) ɒqᔨɿƐį⅃

41. Select the word-pair that best represents a similar relationship to the one expressed in the pair of words given below.
(The words must be considered as meaningful English words and must not be related to each other based on the number of letters/number of consonants/vowels in the word)
Light : Blind
(a) Voice : Vibration
(b) Tongue : Sound
(c) Language : Deaf
(d) Speech : Dumb

42. What would be the word on the opposite side of 'Feb', if the given sheet is folded to form a cube?

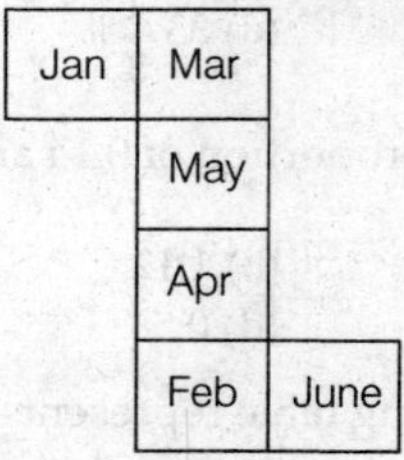

(a) June (b) Jan
(c) May (d) Mar

43. In a certain code language, 'AUDIO' is coded as '59416' and 'BEND' is coded as '6238'. How is 'D' coded in that language?
(a) 6 (b) 4
(c) 2 (d) 1

44. Select the set in which the numbers are related in the same way as are the numbers of the following sets.
(**Note** Operations should be performed on the whole numbers, without breaking down the numbers into its constituent digits. E.g. 13 – Operations on 13 such as adding/subtracting/multiplying etc. to 13 can be performed. Breaking down 13 into 1 and 3 and then performing mathematical operations on 1 and 3 is not allowed)
(12, 132, 11)
(13, 104, 8)
(a) (9, 128, 14)
(b) (16, 146, 9)
(c) (7, 105, 15)
(d) (18, 132, 7)

45. 14 is related to 126 following a certain logic. Following the same logic, 21 is related to 189. To which of the following is 32 related following the same logic?
(**Note** Operations should be performed on the whole numbers, without breaking down the numbers into its constituent digits. E.g. 13 – Operations on 13 such as adding /deleting /multiplying etc., to 13 can be performed. Breaking down 13 into 1 and 3 and then performing mathematical operations on 1 and 3 is not allowed)
(a) 288 (b) 320
(c) 286 (d) 318

46. Identify the figure given in the options that, when put in place of the question mark (?) will logically complete the series.

☆ F / △ / 0 3	3 0 / ☆ / F △	0 △ / B / 3 F	F 3 / 0 / △ B	?

(a)	(b)	(c)	(d)
B △ / 9 / 3 F	B △ / 3 / 0 F	△ F / 9 / B 3	3 B / 9 / F △

47. 'A ÷ B' means 'A is B's son'.
'A × B' means 'A is B's sister'.
'A + B' means 'A is B's brother'.
'A – B' means 'A is B's mother'.
Using the mathematical operators meaning the same as given above, which of the following means that 'S is T's husband'?
(a) T × R – V + S
(b) T – R ÷ V × S
(c) T – R + V ÷ S
(d) T ÷ R × V ÷ S

48. What will come in the place of the question mark (?) in the following equation, if '+' and '−' are interchanged and '×' and '÷' are interchanged?

$13 \div 3 + 2 \times 2 - 11 = ?$

(a) 59 (b) 39
(c) 29 (d) 49

49. A square sheet of paper is folded along the dotted line successively along the directions shown and is then punched in the last. How would the paper look when unfolded?

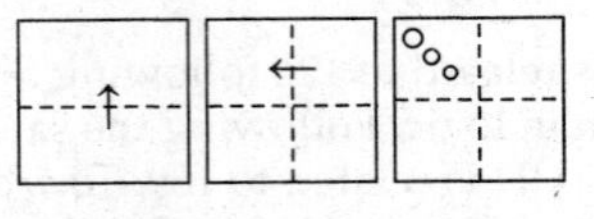

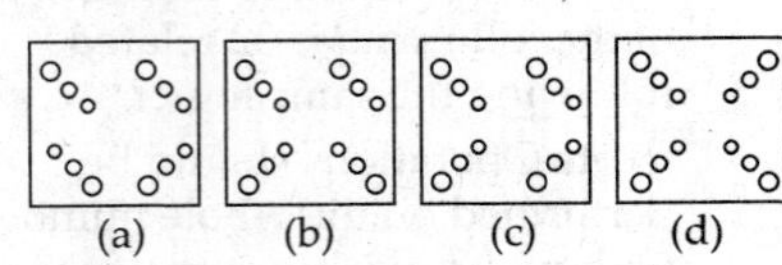

50. In this question, three statements are given, followed by three conclusions numbered I, II and III. Assuming the statements to be true, even if they seem to be at variance with commonly known facts, decide which of the conclusion(s) logically follows/follow from the statements.

Statements

Some lions are panthers.
No panther is a tiger.
Some lions are cats.

Conclusions

I. No tiger is a cat.
II. Some lions are tiger.
III. No cat is a panther.

(a) Only Conclusion I follow
(b) Neither Conclusion I, II nor III follows
(c) Both Conclusions II and III follow
(d) Both Conclusions I and II follow

Part III
Quantitative Aptitude

51. If the length, breadth and total surface area of a cuboid are 30 cm, 20 cm and 2600 cm^2, respectively, then find its height.

(a) 30 cm (b) 15 cm
(c) 50 cm (d) 14 cm

52. A train 550 m long is running at a speed of 78 km/h. How many seconds will it take to cross a 350 m long train running in the opposite direction at a speed of 30 km/h?

(a) 40 sec (b) 20 sec
(c) 50 sec (d) 30 sec

53. Evaluate the given expression.

$$\left[\frac{7 + 9 - 2\left\{\left(3 \div \frac{1}{3}\right) - 3\right\} + 27 \div 3 +}{(27 \div 9 + 3) - 6}\right] + 2$$

(a) 15 (b) 19
(c) 22 (d) 20

54. What is the area (in cm^2) of an equilateral triangle, whose perimeter is 24 cm? (Round off to the nearest two decimal places)

(a) 28.14 (b) 27.71
(c) 13.86 (d) 27.14

55. R gives $\frac{3}{8}$ of the toffees, he has with him to S. If now R has k% of the toffies with S, then find the value of k.

(a) $\frac{200}{3}$ (b) 200
(c) $\frac{500}{3}$ (d) 140

56. A retailer gets a discount of 40% on the printed price of an article. If the retailer sells it at the printed price, then his gain percentage is

(a) $66\frac{1}{3}$% (b) $66\frac{2}{3}$%
(c) $37\frac{2}{3}$% (d) $33\frac{1}{3}$%

57. The mean proportion of 0.14 and 2.24 is

(a) 1.02 (b) 1.12
(c) −2.39 (d) 0.56

58. The following table represents the number of computers (in thousands) manufactured by four companies during the period from 2010 to 2014

Years	A	B	C	D
2010	240	120	270	280
2011	300	530	490	650
2012	1250	650	430	710
2013	470	320	1180	890
2014	320	1070	550	480

What is the difference (in thousands) between the number of computers manufactured by company A and C during the period from 2010 to 2014?

(a) 230 (b) 430 (c) 320 (d) 340

59. If the ratio of principal and simple interest for 5 yr is 10 : 7, then the rate of interest per annum is

(a) 10% (b) 15% (c) 14% (d) 11%

60. A mobile phone dealer buys a phone for ₹ 10000 and sells it for ₹ 12000. Later, he realizes that he could have sold it for ₹ 13000. What is the percentage loss that he incurs?

(a) 10% (b) 20% (c) 15% (d) 25%

61. A quantity $\frac{4}{5}$ is changed to $\frac{5}{6}$. How much percentage change is given to the quantity?

(a) 4.71% (b) 4.73%
(c) 4.17% (d) 4.37%

62. In an assembly election, a candidate got 60% of the total valid votes. 3% of the total votes were declared invalid. If the total number of voters is 240000, then find the number of valid votes polled in favour of the candidate.

(a) 193680 (b) 139680
(c) 139860 (d) 139608

63. The perpendicular length from the origin to the line $6x + 8y - 48 = 0$ is

(a) 2.6 units (b) 4.8 units
(c) 8.3 units (d) 5.2 units

64. A work can be done by a man and a woman in 12 days and 8 days, respectively. In how many days will the work be done by 6 men and 4 women?

(a) 1 (b) $\frac{1}{2}$
(c) 2 (d) $\frac{3}{4}$

65. A motorcyclist rides his motorcycle at a speed of 90 km/h in the first one hour and the next two hours at a speed of 120 km/h. Find the average speed of the rider.

(a) 110 km/h (b) 120 km/h
(c) 105 km/h (d) 115 km/h

66. After the division of a number successively by 2,3 and 5, the remainders are 1,2 and 3, respectively. What will be the remainder, if 13 divides the same number (if the last quotient is 1)?

(a) 1 (b) 2
(c) 0 (d) 3

67. Study the given table and answer that question that follows.

The given table shows the loan disbursed by five banks (in crores) over four years.

Banks \ Years	2016	2017	2018	2019
A	15	20	10	12
B	15	20	15	20
C	20	25	15	20
D	15	20	35	10
E	10	20	25	30

Which two banks have disbursed the same sum of loan over all four years?

(a) A and B (b) B and C
(c) C and D (d) B and D

68. If the angle of the sector with radius 7 cm is 120°, then find the length of the sector (in cm). $\left(\text{Use } \pi = \frac{22}{7}\right)$

(a) $\frac{67}{3}$ (b) $\frac{22}{3}$
(c) $\frac{47}{3}$ (d) $\frac{44}{3}$

69. In a triangle ABC, BD is perpendicular to AC. E is a point on BC such that angle $BEA = x°$. If angle $EAC = 38°$ and angle $EBD = 40°$, then the value of x is

(a) 82 (b) 88
(c) 96 (d) 48

70. Find the percentage increase in surface area of a cube by triple each side.

(a) 800% (b) 650%
(c) 700% (d) 500%

71. If θ be an acute angle and $\cos\theta = \frac{24}{25}$, then the value of $\cot(90° - \theta)$ is equal to

(a) $\frac{5}{24}$ (b) $\frac{7}{24}$
(c) $\frac{7}{25}$ (d) $\frac{6}{25}$

72. Two parallel chords are drawn in a circle of radius 25 cm. The distance between the two chords is 27 cm. If the length of one chord is 48 cm, then length of the other chord is equal to

(a) 42 cm (b) 36 cm
(c) 48 cm (d) 30 cm

73. Study the given graph and answer the question that follows.

The graph shows the number of projects completed by five companies.

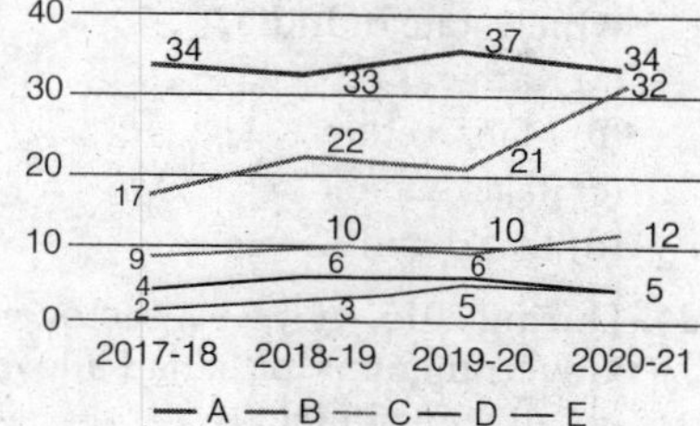

Which company has the highest growth in percentage in completed projects from 2017-18 to 2020-21?

(a) C (b) A (c) B (d) D

74. If three spheres of radius 75 cm, 60 cm and 45 cm are melted into one big sphere, then the radius of the big sphere is

(a) 90 cm (b) 85 cm
(c) 95 cm (d) 80 cm

75. Following pie-chart presents monthly expenditure by Sushma and Preeti in different heads. Sushma and Preeti make equal expenditure every month.

Sushma's Expenditure (in ₹)

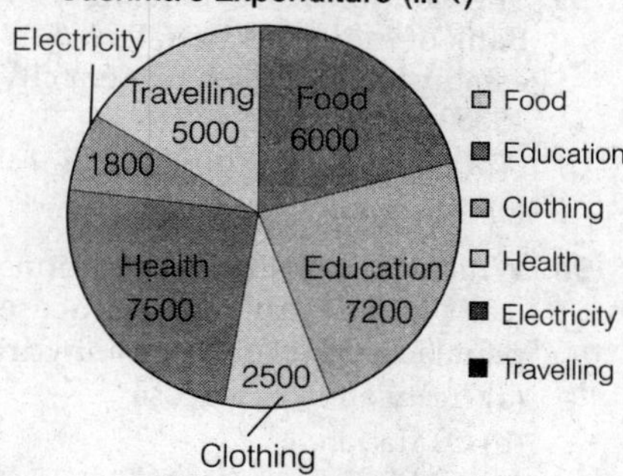

Preeti's Expenditure (in %)

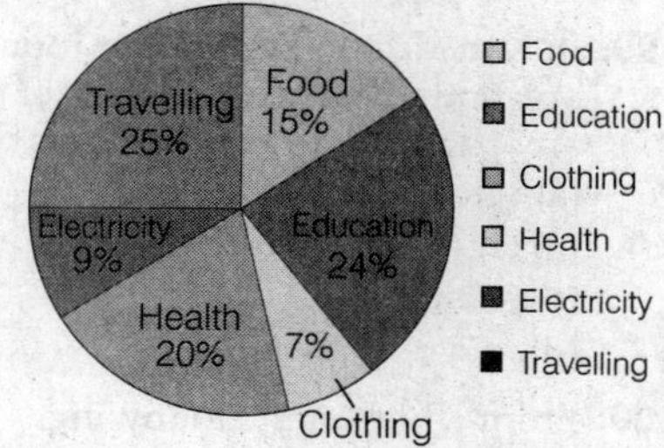

What is the difference between the central angle corresponding to the expenditure incurred on Health by Sushma and Preeti?

(a) 102° (b) 18° (c) 12° (d) 112°

Part IV

General Awareness

76. Which of the following represents the Two-Factor Authentication (2FA)?

(a) A technique for organising files and folders on a PC
(b) A tool for optimising system resources
(c) The use of two different credentials to verify identity
(d) A security measure to prevent physical damage to a PC

77. Former Karnataka CM .... received the Padma Vibhushan at Rashtrapati Bhavan in New Delhi for his contribution in the field of Public Affairs in 2023.

(a) D. Devaraj Urs
(b) HD Deve Gowda
(c) S. Nijalingappa
(d) SM Krishna

78. According to the Census of India 2011, which state has the lowest sex ratio?

(a) Maharashtra (b) Haryana
(c) Rajasthan (d) Bihar

79. Which view in MS PowerPoint is useful for editing or formatting a single slide at a time?

(a) Reading view
(b) Slide Sorter view
(c) Outline view
(d) Normal view

80. Which of the following articles in the Constitution of India provides protection to President and Governors and Rajpramukhs?

(a) Article 361 (b) Article 352
(c) Article 370 (d) Article 356

81. As on 31st March, 2024, apart from the Ministry of Home Affairs, which of the following ministries is headed by Shri Amit Shah?

(a) Ministry of Cooperation
(b) Ministry of Minority Affairs
(c) Ministry of Coal
(d) Ministry of Corporate Affairs

82. Which was the first dynasty of the Delhi Sultanate?

(a) Tughlaq dynasty
(b) Khilji dynasty
(c) Mamluk dynasty
(d) Lodi dynasty

83. When was air transport nationalised in India?
(a) 1950 (b) 1951
(c) 1952 (d) 1953

84. Which of the following is one of the largest spiral galaxies?
(a) NGC 6872 (b) Milky Way
(c) Cygnus A (d) Maffei 1

85. Which device is used to measure the current flow using needle deflection caused by a magnetic field force acting upon a current-carrying wire?
(a) Galvanometer (b) Psophometer
(c) Potentiometer (d) Ammeter

86. The Ayush Ministry has collaborated with the UK's London School of Hygiene and Tropical Medicine (LSHTM) to conduct a study on .... for promoting recovery from COVID-19.
(a) Gotu Kola (b) Boswellia
(c) Ashwagandha (d) Brahmi

87. Sangeeta Shankar was awarded Sangeet Natak Akademi Award 2021 for her contribution in playing which musical instrument?
(a) Santoor (b) Veena
(c) Violin (d) Flute

88. Of which of the following states/UTs is Rauf a folk dance?
(a) Lakshadweep
(b) Jammu and Kashmir
(c) Kerala
(d) Karnataka

89. 'Ujjwala', a ...., was the official mascot of Khelo India – Para Games 2023.
(a) goose (b) sparrow
(c) duck (d) hen

90. Which of the following exchange rates is determined by the market forces of demand and supply?
(a) Soft pegged exchange rate
(b) Floating exchange rate
(c) Fixed exchange rate
(d) Hard pegged exchange rate

91. With which of the following communities is the word 'Langar' (community kitchen) mainly associated?
(a) Jainism (b) Buddhism
(c) Hinduism (d) Sikhism

92. Which city hosted the Asian Champions Trophy hockey tournament in 2023?
(a) Delhi (b) Surat
(c) Chennai (d) Ahmedabad

93. The district of Shivamogga that is famous for its Iron-Ore and Manganese mineral is located in which state of India?
(a) Karnataka
(b) Maharashtra
(c) Rajasthan
(d) Jharkhand

94. During 2015, in .... sector, Government of India had allowed about 49% of FDI.
(a) education
(b) defence
(c) manufacture of medical devices
(d) food products

95. Community tradition is related to which of the following music streams?
(a) Karnataka Lokgeet
(b) Hindustani classical music
(c) Hindustani Lokgeet
(d) Karnataka classical music

96. As per the Census of India 2011, the density of population per km^2 was .... persons.
(a) 320 (b) 382 (c) 345 (d) 394

97. The Central Office of the Reserve Bank of India was initially established in which present city in 1935?
(a) Delhi (b) Mumbai
(c) Kolkata (d) Chennai

98. Which of the following reactions leads to the formation of glucose pentaacetate from acetic anhydride?
(a) Acetylation of glucose
(b) Oxidation
(c) Addition of ketone
(d) Reduction

99. In Kabaddi, when a raider touches any body part of any defender or any part of their clothing, it is called
(a) catch
(b) tag
(c) pursuit
(d) raid

100. From which of the following Constitutions has the Indian Constitution adopted the system of 'First Past the Post'?
(a) Irish Constitution
(b) United States Constitution
(c) French Constitution
(d) British Constitution

Answers

1. (c)	2. (c)	3. (b)	4. (d)
5. (c)	6. (d)	7. (d)	8. (c)
9. (c)	10. (b)	11. (a)	12. (b)
13. (a)	14 (c)	15. (a)	16. (b)
17. (b)	18. (d)	19. (c)	20. (a)
21. (a)	22. (b)	23. (c)	24. (c)
25. (c)	26. (c)	27. (c)	28. (d)
29. (b)	30. (d)	31. (c)	32. (d)
33. (a)	34. (a)	35. (c)	36. (a)
37. (b)	38. (a)	39. (a)	40. (c)
41. (d)	42. (c)	43. (a)	44. (c)
45. (a)	46. (d)	47. (c)	48. (d)
49. (d)	50. (b)	51. (d)	52. (d)
53. (a)	54. (b)	55. (c)	56. (b)
57. (d)	58. (d)	59. (c)	60. (a)
61. (c)	62. (b)	63. (b)	64. (a)
65. (a)	66. (a)	67. (c)	68. (d)
69. (b)	70. (a)	71. (b)	72. (d)
73. (b)	74. (a)	75. (b)	76. (c)
77. (d)	78. (b)	79. (d)	80. (a)
81. (a)	82. (c)	83. (d)	84. (a)
85. (a)	86. (c)	87. (c)	88. (b)
89. (b)	90. (b)	91. (d)	92. (c)
93. (a)	94. (b)	95. (b)	96. (b)
97. (c)	98. (a)	99. (b)	100. (d)

Explanations

1. *(c)* Part 'a IPS officer' contains an error. Use 'an' before the abbreviation to correct the sentence.

2. *(c)* Part 'A owl is a bird' contains an error. Use 'an' to correct the sentence.

3. *(b)* Part 'if you will' contains an error. Remove 'will' to correct the sentence. The given sentence is future conditional, the 'if' clause should be in present tense.

4. *(d)*. Part 'she would' contains an error. Use 'will' to correct the sentence.

5. *(c)* The correct filler for the given blank is 'characterised'.

6. *(d)* The correct filler for the given blank is 'themes'.

7. *(d)* The correct filler for the given blank is 'believed'.

8. *(c)* The correct filler for the given blank is 'Another'.

9. *(c)* The correct filler for the given blank is 'as well as'.

10. *(b)* 'Betrayal' means an act of deliberate disloyalty. Hence, its antonym is 'loyalty'.
- 'Infidelity' means disloyalty.
- 'Perilous' means dangerous.

11. *(a)* 'Skeptic' is a person inclined to question or doubt accepted opinions. Hence, its antonym is 'believer'.
- 'Atheist' means someone who does not believe in God.
- 'Infidel' means a person who has no religion or whose religion is not that of the majority.

12. *(b)* The underlined part of the given sentence contains an error. Use 'the next letter would come' to correct the sentence.

13. *(a)* The most appropriate substitution will be 'a nine days' wonder'. It means something that attracts great interest for a short while but is then forgotten.
- 'A dish fit for gods' means a high quality meal.
- 'A house of cards' means a plan or system that is most likely to fail.
- 'A bull in a China shop' means careless.

14. *(c)* The word 'objective' means not influenced by personal feelings or opinions in considering and representing facts. Hence, its synonym is 'unbiased'.

15. *(a)* The antonym of 'comical' is 'tragic'.
- 'Remedial' means giving or intended as a remedy or cure.
- 'Farcical' means having absurd or ridiculous aspects.
- 'Rebellious' means showing a desire to resist authority, control, or convention.

16. *(b)* The correct filler for the given blank is 'small'.

17. *(b)* The incorrectly spelt word is 'Mantain'. The correct spelling is 'Maintain'.

18. *(d)* 'Bread and butter' means an activity you do to get money for basic needs.

19. *(c)* The underlined segment 'expected results' means 'desired results'.

20. *(a)* The most appropriate substitution will be 'without any looming deadlines'. It means not having any imminent due dates.

21. *(a)* 'Shrill' means (of a voice or sound) high-pitched and piercing. Hence, its antonym is 'mellow' which means (especially of a sound, flavour, or colour) pleasantly smooth or soft; free from harshness.

The other options are
- 'Nasal' means relating to nose.
- 'Croaky' means (of a person's voice) deep and hoarse.
- **'Piercing'** means having or showing shrewdness or keen intelligence.

22. *(b)* The incorrectly spelt word is 'previlage'. The correct spelling is 'privilege'.

23. *(c)* 'Close and big' means are too close and big.

24. *(c)* 'Ignore' means refuse to take notice of or acknowledge; disregard intentionally. The antonym is 'recognised'. Its sentence with the antonym is- Ritika recognised Kavita in the gathering.

25. *(c)* The correct filler for the given blank is 'nosy'.

26. *(c)* Given equation,

28 B 7 D 176 A 8 C 13 = ?

Substituting the letters with symbols, we get

$A \rightarrow \div, B \rightarrow \times, C \rightarrow +, D \rightarrow -$

$28 \times 7 - 176 \div 8 + 13 = ?$

$\Rightarrow \quad 196 - 22 + 13 = ?$

$\Rightarrow \quad 209 - 22 = ?$

$\Rightarrow \quad ? = 187$

27. *(c)* Naming the figure,

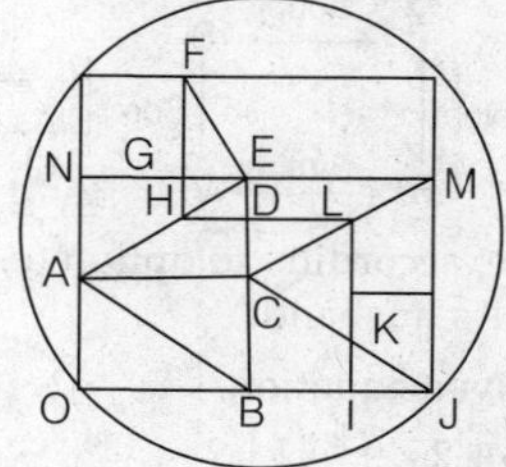

Triangles can be represented as,

ΔABC, ΔACD, ΔABD, ΔGHE, ΔGEF, ΔHEF, ΔHDE, ΔAOB, ΔANE, ΔCDL, ΔCEM, ΔIKJ, ΔBCJ, ΔKCL, ΔJCM

So, there are total 15 triangles present in given figure.

28. *(d)* According to question,

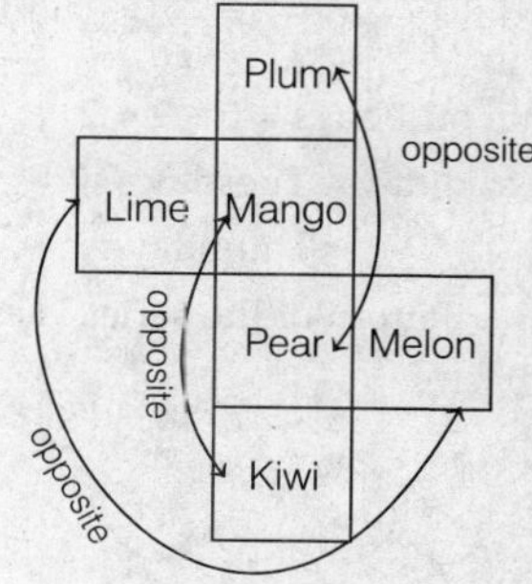

∴

Hence, 'Mango' will be opposite to 'Kiwi'.

29. *(b)* The pattern of the series is as follows,

$T \xrightarrow{+1} U \xrightarrow{+1} V \xrightarrow{+1} \boxed{W} \xrightarrow{+1} X$

$M \xrightarrow{+1} N \xrightarrow{+1} O \xrightarrow{+1} \boxed{P} \xrightarrow{+1} Q$

$F \xrightarrow{-1} E \xrightarrow{-1} D \xrightarrow{-1} \boxed{C} \xrightarrow{-1} B$

30. *(d)* The pattern of the series is as follows,

$C \xrightarrow{+5} H \xrightarrow{+5} M \xrightarrow{+5} R \xrightarrow{+5} \boxed{W}$

$P \xrightarrow{+2} R \xrightarrow{+2} T \xrightarrow{+2} V \xrightarrow{+2} \boxed{X}$

$W \xrightarrow{+4} A \xrightarrow{+4} E \xrightarrow{+4} I \xrightarrow{+4} \boxed{M}$

31. *(c)* The correct mirror image of the given figure as given below,

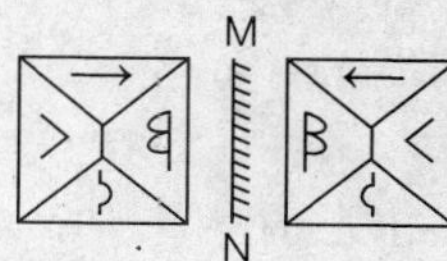

32. *(d)* As,

Z	B	R	L
↓ −5	↓ −5	↓ −5	↓ −5
U	W	M	G

and

I	D	S	Q
↓ −5	↓ −5	↓ −5	↓ −5
D	Y	N	L

Similarly,

E	V	N	A
↓ −5	↓ −5	↓ −5	↓ −5
Z	Q	I	V

33. *(a)* Given, 15th August, 2006 → Tuesday

Number of odd days from 15th August, 2006 to 15th August, 2017

Years →

2007 + 2008 + 2009 + 2010 + 2011 + 2012 + 2013 + 2014 + 2015 + 2016 + 2017

Odd days →

$1 + 2 + 1 + 1 + 1 + 2 + 1 + 1 + 1 + 2 + 1$

$= \frac{14}{7} = 0$ odd days

Now, number of odd days from 15th August, 2017 to 7th September, 2017

Months $\rightarrow$ August + September

Odd days $\rightarrow 16 + 7 = \frac{23}{7} = 2$ odd days

$\therefore$ Total odd days = 0 + 2 = 2

Required day = Tuesday + 2

= Thursday

34. *(a)* The pattern of the series is as follows,

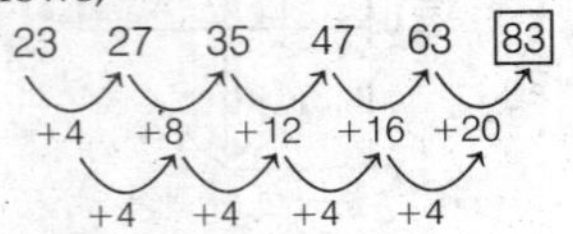

35. *(c)* According to the question,

R U I N $\longrightarrow$ 3 0 9 8

T U R N $\longrightarrow$ 9 6 3 0

$\therefore$ The code for 'I' is '8'.

36. *(a)* As, Y Z W T $\xrightarrow{+5,\ +5,\ +4,\ +4}$ D E A X and Q R O L $\xrightarrow{+5,\ +5,\ +4,\ +4}$ V W S P

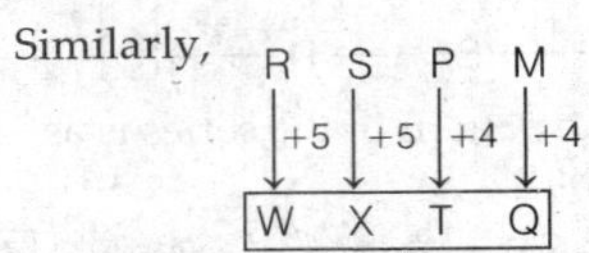

37. *(b)* Given equation,

$39 + 13 \times 12 \div 5 - 4 = ?$

After interchanging '+' and '÷', '×' and '–', we get

$39 \div 13 - 12 + 5 \times 4 = ?$

$\Rightarrow \quad 3 - 12 + 20 = ?$

$\Rightarrow \quad 23 - 12 = ? \Rightarrow ? = \boxed{11}$

38. *(a)* H K N (+3, +3) ; T W Z (+3, +3)

D G J (+3, +3) But, P S U (+3, +2)

39. *(a)* Given equation,

$136 - (176 \div 11) \times 8 + 22 \times 3 = 105$

From option (a), interchanging 11 and 22, we get

$136 - (176 \div 22) \times 8 + 11 \times 3 = 105$

$\Rightarrow \quad 136 - 8 \times 8 + 33 = 105$

$\Rightarrow \quad 136 - 64 + 33 = 105$

$\Rightarrow \quad 169 - 64 = 105$

$\Rightarrow \quad 105 = 105$

40. *(c)* The correct mirror image of given figure is as shown below,

M

Lj3r4pa | ɐd4ɹ3[˩

N

41. *(d)* As, a 'Blind' person cannot see in 'Light'. Similarly, a 'Dumb' person cannot give 'Speech'.

42. *(c)* According to the question,

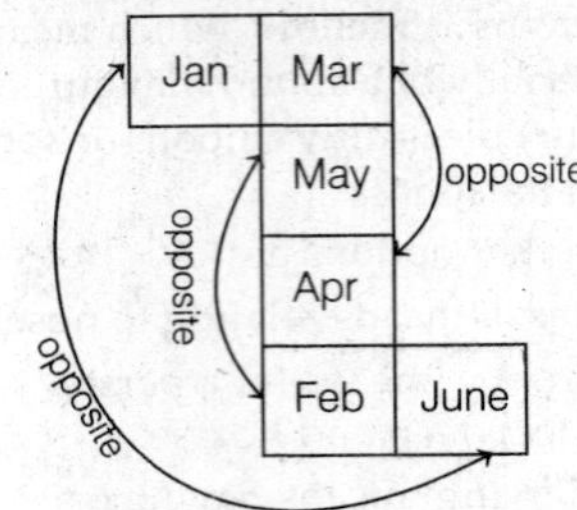

$\therefore$ 'May' is opposite to 'Feb'.

43. *(a)* According to the question,

A U D I O $\longrightarrow$ 5 9 4 1 6

B E N D $\longrightarrow$ 6 2 3 8

$\therefore$ Code for 'D' is '6'.

44. *(c)* First number × Third number = Second number

As, (12, 132, 11) $\rightarrow 12 \times 11 = 132$

and (13, 104, 8) $\rightarrow 13 \times 8 = 104$

Similarly, (7, 105, 15) $\rightarrow 7 \times 15 = 105$

45. *(a)* As, $14 \xrightarrow{\times 9} 126$

and $21 \xrightarrow{\times 9} 189$

Similarly, $32 \xrightarrow{\times 9} \boxed{288}$

46. *(d)* The pattern of elements in figure series is as follows,

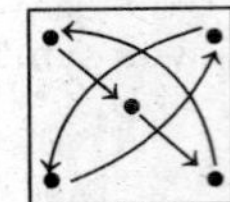

From figure 1 to 2
Figure 3 to 4

New Element

From figure 2 to 3
Figure 4 to 5

Hence, option figure (d) will replace the question mark.

47. *(c)* From option (c),

T(–) ← Couple → S(+); Mother: R+ → T; Son: S → V+; Brother: V+ → R+

[+ → Male, – → Female]

Hence, according to option (c), "S is T's husband".

48. *(d)* Given equation,

$13 \div 3 + 2 \times 2 - 11 = ?$

Interchanging '+' and '–', '×' and '÷', we get

$13 \times 3 - 2 \div 2 + 11 = ?$

$\Rightarrow \quad 39 - 1 + 11 = ?$

$\Rightarrow \quad 50 - 1 = ?$

$\Rightarrow \quad ? = 49$

49. *(d)* When paper is unfolded along reverse the dotted line, it will look like option figure (d).

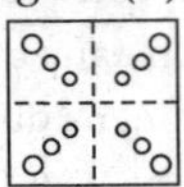

50. *(b)* According to the statements,

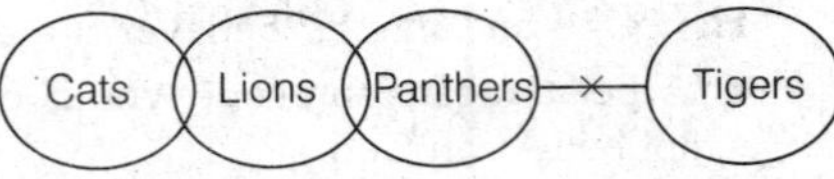

Conclusions

I. (✗) II. (✗) III. (✗)

Hence, neither Conclusion I, II nor III follows.

51. *(d)* Given, length = 30 cm

Breadth = 20 cm

Total surface area = 2600 cm^2

Let height of cuboid be 'h' cm.

According to the question,

$2(lb + bh + hl) = 2600$

$2(30 \times 20 + 20 \times h + h \times 30) = 2600$

$\Rightarrow 600 + 20h + 30h = 1300$

$\Rightarrow \quad 50h = 700 \Rightarrow h = 14$ cm

52. *(d)* According to the question,

Total length of two trains = 550 + 350 = 900 m

Relative speeds of two trains = 78 + 30 = 108 km/h

$= 108 \times \frac{5}{18}$ m/sec = 30 m/sec

[$\because$ Trains are moving in the opposite direction, relative speeds will be sum of speed of both trains]

$\therefore$ Required time $= \frac{900}{30} = 30$ sec

53. *(a)* Given expression,

$$\left[\frac{7 + 9 - 2\left\{\left(3 \div \frac{1}{3}\right) - 3\right\} + 27 \div 3 +}{(27 \div 9 + 3) - 6}\right] + 2$$

(using BODMAS rule)

$= [7 + 9 - 2\{9 - 3\} + 9 + (3 + 3) - 6] + 2$

$= [16 - 12 + 9 + 6 - 6] + 2$

$= 13 + 2 = 15$

54. *(b)* Let the side of an equilateral triangle be 'a' cm.

Given,

Perimeter of triangle = 24 cm

$a + a + a = 24 \Rightarrow 3a = 24$

$\Rightarrow \quad a = 8$ cm

$\therefore$ Area of equilateral triangle

$= \frac{\sqrt{3}}{4}(8)^2 = \frac{\sqrt{3}}{4} \times 64 = 16\sqrt{3}$

$= 16 \times 1.732 = 27.71 \; cm^2$

55. *(c)* Let R has 8 toffees initially.

R gives $\frac{3}{8}$ of toffees with him to S.

$\therefore$ Number of toffees with $S = \frac{3}{8} \times 8 = 3$

$\therefore$ Number of toffees left with R

$= 8 - 3 = 5$

Toffees with $R = K\%$ toffees with S

$\Rightarrow \quad 5 = \frac{K}{100} \times (3) \Rightarrow \frac{500}{3} = K$

56. *(b)* Let the printed price be ₹ $100x$.

Cost price to retailer

$= 100x - \frac{40}{100} \times 100x$

$=$ ₹ $60x$

Retailer sells an article at printed price = ₹ $100x$

$\therefore$ Required gain percentage

$= \frac{100x - 60x}{60x} \times 100$

$= \frac{40x}{60x} \times 100 = \frac{200}{3}\% = 66\frac{2}{3}\%$

57. *(d)* We know, mean proportion of a and $b = \sqrt{ab}$

$\therefore$ Mean proportion of 0.14 and 2.24

$= \sqrt{0.14 \times 2.24} = \sqrt{0.3136} = 0.56$

58. *(d)* From 2010 to 2014,

Total number of computers manufactured by company A

$= 240 + 300 + 1250 + 470 + 320 = 2580$

Total number of computers manufactured by company C

$= 270 + 490 + 430 + 1180 + 550$

$= 2920$

$\therefore$ Required difference $= 2920 - 2580$

$= 340$

59. *(c)* Given,

$\frac{\text{Principal } (P)}{\text{SI}} = \frac{10}{7}$

$\frac{P \times 100}{P \times R \times T} = \frac{10}{7} \quad \left[\because \text{SI} = \frac{P \times R \times T}{100}\right]$

$\frac{100}{5 \times R} = \frac{10}{7}$

$\Rightarrow \quad \frac{2}{R} = \frac{1}{7}$

$\Rightarrow \quad R = 14\%$

60. *(a)* CP of phone = ₹ 10000

Original SP of phone = ₹ 12000

New SP of phone = ₹ 13000

$\therefore$ Difference between original and new SP = 13000 − 12000 = ₹ 1000

$\therefore$ Required loss per cent

$= \frac{1000}{10000} \times 100 = 10\%$

61. *(c)* We know,

Percentage change

$= \frac{\text{New quantity} - \text{Old quantity}}{\text{Old quantity}} \times 100$

$\therefore$ Required percentage change

$= \frac{\frac{5}{6} - \frac{4}{5}}{\frac{4}{5}} \times 100 = \frac{25 - 24}{30} \times \frac{5}{4} \times 100$

$= \frac{1}{30} \times \frac{5}{4} \times 100 = \frac{100}{24} = \frac{25}{6} = 4.17\%$

62. *(b)* Given,

Total number of votes = 240000

According to the question,

Total number of valid votes

$= 240000 - \frac{3}{100} \times 240000 = 232800$

$\therefore$ Total number of votes polled in favour of candidate

$= \frac{60}{100} \times 232800 = 139680$

63. *(b)* Given, Point $P(0, 0)$

Line : $6x + 8y - 48 = 0$

We know,

Distance of a point from a line (D)

$= \left| \frac{ax_1 + by_1 + c}{\sqrt{a^2 + b^2}} \right|$

Here, $a = 6, b = 8, c = -48$,

$x = 0, y = 0$

$\therefore D = \left| \frac{6(0) + 8(0) - 48}{\sqrt{(6)^2 + (8)^2}} \right|$

$D = \left| \frac{-48}{10} \right| = 4.8$ units

64. *(a)* Let men and women be denoted by M and W.

According to the question,

$1M \times 12 = 1W \times 8$

$\frac{M}{W} = \frac{8}{12} = \frac{2}{3}$

Let $M = 2K$, $W = 3K$

$\therefore$ Total work $= 2K \times 12 = 24K$ units

$\therefore$ Required time to complete the work by 6 men and 4 women

$= \frac{24K}{6 \times 2K + 4 \times 3K}$

$= \frac{24K}{12K + 12K} = \frac{24K}{24K} = 1$ day

65. *(a)* We know,

Distance = Speed × Time

$\therefore$ Distance covered in first hour

$= 90 \times 1 = 90$ km

Distance covered in next two hour

$= 120 \times 2 = 240$ km

We know,

Average speed

$= \frac{\text{Total distance covered}}{\text{Total time taken}}$

$= \frac{240 + 90}{2 + 1} = \frac{330}{3} = 110$ km/h

66. *(a)* Let the original number be n.

We know, by Division Algorithm,

Dividend = Divisor × Quotient + Remainder

When divided by 5

$n = 5q + 3$

When further divided by 3

$\therefore \quad n = 3(5q + 3) + 2$

$n = 15q + 9 + 2 = 15q + 11$

When further divided by 2

$\therefore \quad n = 2(15q + 11) + 1$

$= 30q + 22 + 1 = 30q + 23$

If Quotient $(q) = 1$

$\therefore \; n = 30(1) + 23 = 53$

$\therefore$ When divided by 13, remainder = 1

67. *(c)*

Banks	Years				Total amount disbursed
	2016	2017	2018	2019	
A	15	20	10	12	57
B	15	20	15	20	70
C	20	25	15	20	80
D	15	20	35	10	80
E	10	20	25	30	85

$\therefore$ Two banks which disbursed the same sum are C and D.

68. *(d)* Given, radius of sector = 7 cm

Angle of sector = 120°

We know,

Length of an arc $= \frac{\theta}{360^\circ} \times 2\pi r$

$= \frac{120^\circ}{360^\circ} \times 2 \times \frac{22}{7} \times 7$

$= \frac{1}{3} \times 2 \times 22 = \frac{44}{3}$ cm

69. *(b)*

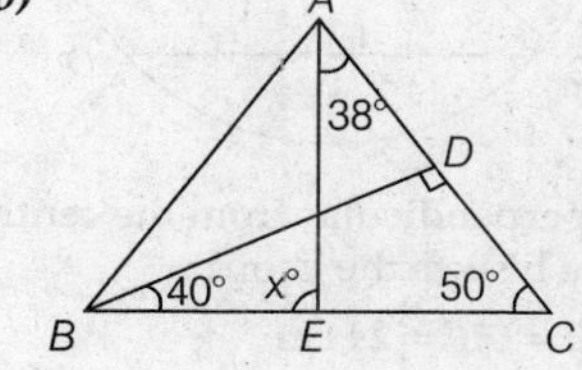

Given,

$\angle BEA = x°$,

$\angle EAC = 38°$

$\angle EBD = 40°$ and $\angle BDC = 90°$

In ΔBDC,

$\angle BCD = 180° - \angle BDC - \angle CBD$

[∵ Sum of all the interior angles of a triangle is 180°]

$\angle BCD = 180° - 90° - 40° = 50°$

As, $\angle BEA$ is an exterior angle of ΔAEC.

$\therefore \angle BEA = \angle EAC + \angle ECA$

$x° = 38° + 50° = 88°$

70. *(a)* Let the original side of cube be a cm.

∵ Original surface area $= 6a^2$

New side of cube $= 3a$ cm

∴ New surface area $= 6(3a)^2$

$= 54a^2$

∴ Required percentage increase

$$= \frac{54a^2 - 6a^2}{6a^2} \times 100$$

$$= \frac{48}{6} \times 100 = 800\%$$

71. *(b)* Given, $\cos\theta = \frac{24}{25}$

As, $\sin\theta = \sqrt{1-\cos^2\theta} = \sqrt{1-\left(\frac{24}{25}\right)^2}$

$$= \sqrt{1-\frac{576}{625}} = \sqrt{\frac{49}{625}} = \frac{7}{25}$$

As, $\cot(90° - \theta)$

$$= \tan\theta = \frac{\sin\theta}{\cos\theta} = \frac{\frac{7}{25}}{\frac{24}{25}} = \frac{7}{24}$$

72. *(d)* Given,

$OE = OC = 25$ cm,

$AB = 27$ cm

$EF = 48$ cm

Let $AO = x$ cm

∴ $OB = (27 - x)$ cm

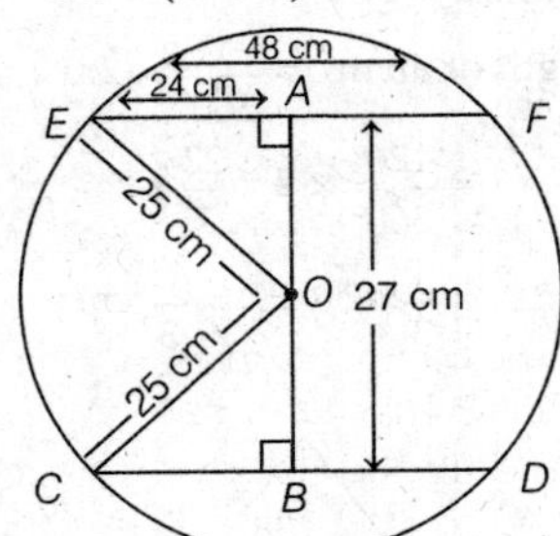

As, perpendicular from the centre of a circle bisects the chord.

∴ $AE = AF = 24$ cm

In ΔAOE,

$EO^2 = AO^2 + AE^2$

$(25)^2 = (x)^2 + (24)^2$

$\Rightarrow x^2 = 625 - 576 = 49$

$\Rightarrow x = 7$ cm

∴ $OB = 27 - 7 = 20$ cm

In ΔOBC,

$BC^2 = OC^2 - OB^2$

$= (25)^2 - (20)^2 = 625 - 400 = 225$

∴ $BC = 15$ cm

∴ $CD = 2BC = 2(15) = 30$ cm

73. *(b)* According to the question,

Percentage growth are as follows,

$$E = \frac{34-34}{34} \times 100 = 0\%$$

$$D = \frac{32-17}{17} \times 100 = \frac{1500}{17} = 88.23\%$$

$$C = \frac{12-9}{9} \times 100 = 33.33\%$$

$$B = \frac{5-4}{4} \times 100 = 25\%$$

$$A = \frac{5-2}{2} \times 100 = \frac{3}{2} \times 100 = 150\%$$

∴ Company A has the highest growth in percentage in completed projects.

74. *(a)* Let the radius of big sphere be 'R' cm.

Also, let the radii of three new circles be r_1, r_2 and r_3 cm.

We know, volume of sphere $= \frac{4}{3}\pi r^3$

According to the question,

$$\frac{4}{3}\pi[r_1^3 + r_2^3 + r_3^3] = \frac{4}{3}\pi R^3$$

$(75)^3 + (60)^3 + (45)^3 = R^3$

$\Rightarrow R^3 = (15)^3[(5)^3 + (4)^3 + (3)^3]$

$R^3 = (15)^3[125 + 64 + 27]$

$R^3 = (15)^3(216)$

$\Rightarrow R = \sqrt[3]{(15)^3 \times 216}$

$= 15 \times 6 = 90$ cm

75. *(b)* Total expenditure of Sushma

$= 1800 + 5000 + 6000 + 7200 + 2500 + 7500 = ₹ 30000$

As,

Expenditure of Sushma = Expenditure of Preeti = ₹ 30000

Central angle of Sushma corresponding to Health

$$= \frac{7500}{30000} \times 360° = 90°$$

Central angle of Preeti corresponding to Health

$$= \frac{20}{100} \times 360° = 72°$$

∴ Required difference $= 90° - 72° = 18°$

76. *(c)* The use of two different credentials to verify identity represents the Tow Factor Authentication (2FA).

77. *(d)* Former Karnataka CM SM Krishna received the Padma Vibhushan at Rashtrapati Bhavan in New Delhi for his contribution in the field of Public Affairs in 2023.

- He was awarded along with Kumar Mangalam Birla.
- Ms. Vyjayanthimala Bali, Shri M. Venkaiah Naidu, Shri Konidela Chiranjeevi, Shri Bindeshwar Pathak (Posthumous), Ms. Padma Subrahmanyam were conferred Padma Vibhushan for 2024.

78. *(b)* According to Census 2011, Haryana has lowest sex ratio.

- Kerala has highest sex ratio of 1084.
- In union territory of Daman and Diu has lowest sex ratio.
- Sex ratio of India is 943.

79. *(d)* Normal view in MS PowerPoint is useful for editing or formating a single slide at a time.

80. *(a)* Article 361 provides protection to President and Governor and Rajpramukhs.

- Article 361 comes under Part XIX of the Indian Constitution.
- Article 352 gives the right to the President to declare National Emergency.
- Article 356 gives the right to President to impose President rule in state.

81. *(a)* As on 31th March, 2024, apart from the Ministry of Home Affairs, Ministry of Cooperation is headed by Shri Amit Shah.

- Shri Kiren Rijiju is the Hon'ble Union Cabinet Minister for Minority Affairs.
- Shri G. Kishan Reddy is presently Minister of Coal.
- Sitharaman is presently heading the Ministry of Corporate Affairs.

82. *(c)* Mamluk dynasty is the first dynasty of Delhi Sultanate.

- It is also called Slave dynasty. It ruled from 1206-1290 CE.
- It was founded by Qutub-ud-din Aibak, slave of Muhammad Ghori.

83. *(d)* Air transport was nationalised in 1953.
- Two corporations were created -first for domestic service called Indian Airlines Corporation and second for international service, Air-India International Corporation.
- The latter's name was abbreviated to Air-India in 1962.
- Transportation in India is categorised as air, water and land.

84. *(a)* NGC 6872 is one of the largest spiral galaxies.
- The Milky Way is a huge collection of stars, dust and gas.
- Cygnus A is an elliptical galaxy, with billions of stars in its featureless oval.
- Maffei 1 is a slightly flattened core type elliptical galaxy.

85. *(a)* A galvanometer is an electrical measuring instrument used to measure the flow of electric current. It works on the principle that a magnetic field is generated around a current carrying wire, causing a needle to deflect. The other options are
- 'Psophometer' measures sound levels.
- 'Potentiometer' measures voltage or potential difference.
- 'Ammeter' measures current but typically uses a shunt resistor and does not rely on needle deflection.

86. *(c)* The Ayush Ministry has collaborated with the UK's London School of Hygiene and Tropical Medicine (LSHTM) to conduct a study on Ashwagandha for promoting recovery from COVID-19.
- Gotu Kola is a traditional Chinese and Ayurvedic medicine.
- Boswellia helps to reduce inflammation in people with conditions such as arthritis and asthma.
- Brahmi enhances brain function and reduces stress levels.

87. *(c)* Sangeeta Shankar was awarded Sangeet Natak Akademi Award 2021 for her contribution in playing violin.
- She was born on 12th August, 1965 in Banaras.
- She is an Indian classical violinist who performs Hindustani classical music and fusion music.
- She is the daughter and disciple of the famed violinist N. Rajam.

88. *(b)* Rauf is a folk dance of Jammu and Kashmir Island.
- Kolkali dance is the traditional folk dance of the people of Lakshadweep.
- Mohiniyattam is a traditional dance form of Kerala.
- Yakshagana is a traditional dance of Karnataka.

89. *(b)* 'Ujjwala', a sparrow, was the official mascot of Khelo-India Para Games 2023.
- A total of seven sports were included.
- It was organised in New Delhi.
- Haryana won the inaugural title by securing 105 medals.

90. *(b)* Managed floating exchange rate is determined by the market forces of demand and supply.
- It is also called 'dirty floating'.
- It is a hybrid of fixed exchange rate and flexible exchange rate.
- Its aim is to keep the exchange rate close to desired target value.

91. *(d)* The word 'Langar' (community kitchen) is mainly associated Sikhism.
- Langar is the community kitchen of a Gurdwara, which serves meals to all, free of charge, regardless of religion, caste, gender.
- It was started by Guru Nanak, the founder and the first Guru of Sikhism.

92. *(c)* Asian Champions Trophy hockey tournament for 2023 was hosted by Chennai.
- India was at first position for fourth time.
- Malaysia secured the second position.
- Best Player of the Tournament was conferred to Mandeep Singh (India).

93. *(a)* The district of Shivamogga that is famous for its iron-Ore and Manganese mineral is located in Karnataka.
- Important iron ore producing states are Odisha, Chhattisgarh, Goa and Jharkhand.
- Important manganese ore producing states are Madhya Pradesh, Odisha, Rajasthan etc.

94. *(b)* During 2015, in defence sector, the Government of India had allowed about 49% of FDI.
- In 2023, FDI in banking is upto 49% automatic and above 49% is government.
- 100% FDI is on food products retail trading.
- FDI in mining and mineral is upto 100%.

95. *(b)* Community tradition is related to Hindustani classical music.
- Indian classical music has 2 major traditions : Hindustani music and Carnatic music.
- Hindustani music is popular in northern region.
- Carnatic music is popular in southern region.

96. *(b)* According to Census 2011, the density of population per km^2 was 382.
- The motto of Census 2011 is 'Our Census, Our Future'.
- The most densely populated state is Bihar.
- Least densely populated state is Arunachal Pradesh.

97. *(c)* The Centrel Office of the Reserve Bank of India in 1935 was established in Kolkata.
- Presently, it is situated in Mumbai.
- It is owned by Union Ministry of Finance.
- It regulates Indian banking system and acts as 'Banker of the Banks'.

98. *(a)* Acetylation of glucose reaction leads to the formation of glucose pentaacetate from acetic anhydride. This reaction is used to confirm the presence of five hydroxyl (OH) groups in the glucose structure.

99. *(b)* In Kabaddi, when a raider touches any body part of any defender or any part of their clothing, is called 'tag'.
- The words specially used in the game of Kabbadi are raider, anti raider, tag, mid line, lona, raid.
- In Kabaddi, each team has 12 players, but only 7 players are allowed in court at a time.

100. *(d)* 'First Past the Post' has been taken from British Constitution.
- It means the candidate with most votes, is declared winner.
- Directive Principles of State Policy is taken from Irish Constitution.
- Concurrent List is taken from Australian Constitution.

Set 20 05 July, 2024 (Shift IV)

SSC CHSL Tier-I
SOLVED PAPER

Instructions

1. This paper contains 100 questions.
2. It has 4 Parts, **Part I** General English, **Part II** General Intelligence & Reasoning, **Part III** Quantitative Aptitude and **Part IV** General Awareness.
3. Each question carries **2 marks.**

Part I
General English

1. Select the most appropriate option to fill in the blank.

He ………the truth.

(a) spoken
(b) speaking
(c) spoke
(d) speak

2. The following sentence has been divided into four segments. Identify the segment in which the article has been used incorrectly.

Ms. Rose is a / sweetest of / all the girls / in the class.

(a) sweetest of
(b) all the girls
(c) in the class
(d) Ms. Rose is a

3. The following sentence has been divided into four segments. Identify the segment that contains a grammatical error.

The shop / usually opened / ten minutes / late.

(a) usually opened
(b) late
(c) The shop
(d) ten minutes

4. The following sentence has been split into four segments. Identify the segment that contains a grammatical error.

I am going / to buy a red car / with a leather seats / and a sunroof.

(a) I am going
(b) and a sunroof
(c) to buy a red car
(d) with a leather seats

Directions (Q.Nos. 5-9) *In the following passage, some words have been deleted. Read the passage carefully and select the most appropriate option to fill in each blank.*

Today, lets explore the significant role of human beings in shaping the world as we know it. Can you (1)……… a world without human beings? Who would have (2)……… the resources and created social and cultural environment? The people are (3)……… to develop the economy and the society. The people make and use resources and are themselves resources with (4)……… quality. Coal is but a piece of rock, until people were able to (5)……… technology to obtain it and make it a 'resource'.

5. Select the most appropriate option to fill in blank number (1).

(a) ignore (b) fabricate
(c) neglect (d) imagine

6. Select the most appropriate option to fill in blank number (2).

(a) broken
(b) destroyed
(c) crippled
(d) utilised

7. Select the most appropriate option to fill in blank number (3).

(a) crucial (b) frantic
(c) hopeful (d) hasty

8. Select the most appropriate option to fill in blank number (4).

(a) deviating (b) alternating
(c) inconstant (d) varying

9. Select the most appropriate option to fill in blank number (5).

(a) fashion (b) mint
(c) invent (d) open

10. Identify the most appropriate antonym of the underlined word in the given sentence.

His <u>jovial</u> nature has won him many friends.

(a) Shrewd (b) Miserable
(c) Dumb (d) Cunning

11. Select the most appropriate antonym of the given word.

Lazy

(a) Barren (b) Helpful
(c) Diligent (d) Genuine

12. Select the most appropriate meaning of the given idiom.

Spill the beans

(a) To help someone extraordinarily
(b) To leak a secret
(c) The act of loving beans
(d) Cook the beans carefully

13. Identify the most appropriate meaning of the given word.

Accept

(a) Agree (b) Refuse
(c) Present (d) Regret

14. Select the most appropriate antonym of the word 'Plausible' from the given sentence.

The trend of improvement is unlikely to continue for the foreseeable future.

(a) unlikely
(b) trend
(c) foreseeable
(d) future

15. Select the most appropriate option to fill in the blank.

The grass on my lawn is glistening with the morning ……… .

(a) duo (b) due
(c) dew (d) do

16. Select the most appropriate option that can substitute the underlined segment in the given sentence.
Vihaan is clumsy at dancing.
(a) all thumbs (b) easy handed
(c) master skill (d) heavy duty

17. Select the option to fill in the blank with the most appropriate collocation.
In boarding schools, students need to .... by themselves.
(a) wash the bed (b) turn the bed
(c) make the bed (d) run the bed

18. Select the incorrectly spelt word.
(a) Scatered (b) Brazen
(c) Crowded (d) Imprudent

19. Select the most appropriate option that can substitute the underlined segment in the following sentence.
Play cards is not allowed here.
(a) Play card (b) Played cards
(c) Playing cards (d) Playing card

20. Identify the correct spelling of the underlined word.
The police issued a varant to the criminals.
(a) Warant (b) Varrant
(c) Warent (d) Warrant

21. Select the most appropriate synonym of the given word.
Change
(a) Resolute (b) Renew
(c) Adjust (d) Alter

22. Select the most appropriate option to substitute the underlined segment in the following sentence.
There was a noise that was wake me up.
(a) woken me up (b) has woke me up
(c) woke me up (d) wakes me up

23. Select the most appropriate antonym of the given word.
Absurd
(a) Reasonable (b) Foolish
(c) Nonsensical (d) Insane

24. Read the sentence carefully and select the most appropriate option to substitute the underlined part.
The crux of the study has been delineated by the researcher.
(a) relevant part
(b) fixed limitation
(c) collected data
(d) central point

25. Select the most appropriate meaning of the underlined idiom in the given sentence.
When I got an opportunity to start a new business, Ravikanth queered my pitch.
(a) Supported me with money
(b) Helped me by standing beside me
(c) Ruined my plan
(d) Advised me

Part II
General Intelligence

26. In a certain code language, 'sanitiser saves us' is written as 'ra kl mq' and 'let us go' is written as 'kl mt ax'. How is 'us' written in the given language?
(a) mt (b) ra
(c) kl (d) mq

27. Select the option in which the given figure is embedded (rotation is not allowed).

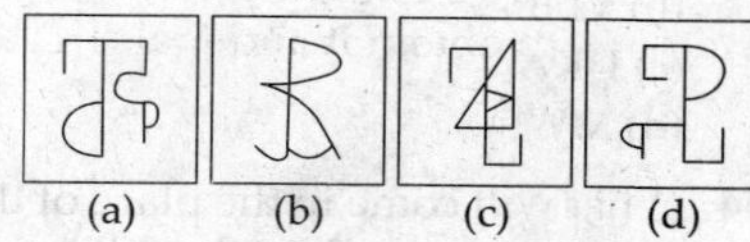

(a) (b) (c) (d)

28. The position of how many letters will remain unchanged, if all the letters in the word HARMONY are arranged in alphabetical order?
(a) Four (b) Three
(c) Two (d) One

29. CKMZ is related to VDFS in a certain way based on the English alphabetical order. In the same way, LPBV is related to EIUO. To which of the following is UXBN related, following the same logic?
(a) NGUQ
(b) NGQU
(c) NQUG
(d) NQGU

30. Read the given statements and conclusions carefully. Assuming that the information given in the statements is true, even if it appears to be at variance with commonly known facts, decide which of the given conclusions logically follow(s) from the statements.

Statements
Some movies are videos.
No video is audio.
All audios are songs.
Conclusions
I. All movies can never be audios.
II. No video is a song.
(a) None of the conclusions follow
(b) Only Conclusion II follows
(c) Only Conclusion I follows
(d) Both Conclusions I and II follow

31. In a certain code language, 'WILT' is coded as '6194' and 'SLIT' is coded as '9413'. What is the code for 'S' in the given code language?
(a) 4
(b) 9
(c) 1
(d) 3

32. How many triangles are there in the given figure?

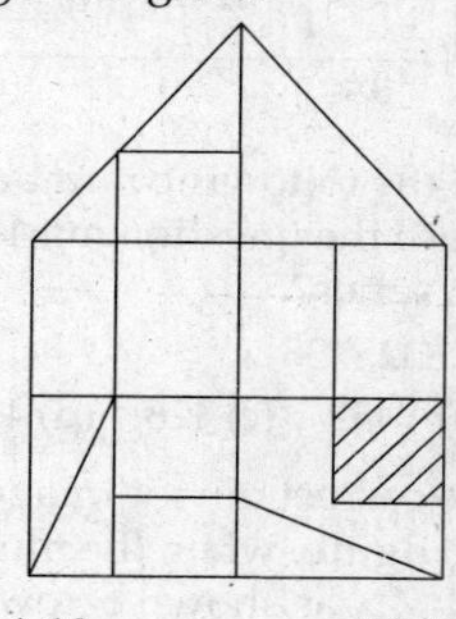

(a) 18 (b) 15
(c) 17 (d) 16

33. What should come in place of question mark (?) in the given series?
251, 268, 285, 302, 319, ?
(a) 306
(b) 315
(c) 326
(d) 336

34. Which letter-cluster will replace the question mark (?) to complete the given series?
GLYC, FNVG, ?, DRPO, CTMS
(a) EQRK
(b) EPSK
(c) EPRJ
(d) EQSJ

35. 84 is related to 21 following a certain logic. Following the same logic, 180 is related to 45. To which of the following is 252 related following the same logic?

(**Note** Operations should be performed on the whole numbers, without breaking down the numbers into its constituent digits. E.g. 13 – Operations on 13 such as adding /deleting/multiplying etc., to 13 can be performed. Breaking down 13 into 1 and 3 and then performing mathematical operations on 1 and 3 is not allowed.)

(a) 63 (b) 67
(c) 61 (d) 65

36. Select the option in which the given figure X is embedded (rotation is not allowed).

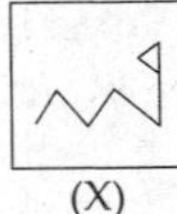

(X)

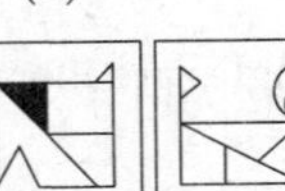
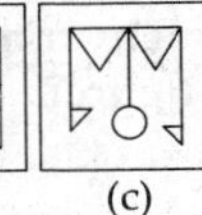
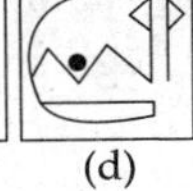

(a) (b) (c) (d)

37. Which of the following numbers will replace the question mark (?) in the given series?

876, 865, 832, 733, ?

(a) 446 (b) 453 (c) 426 (d) 436

38. Select the correct mirror image of the given figure, when the mirror is placed at MN as shown below.

M
D7WOO3
N

(a) ƐOOW7ᗡ (b) D7MOO3
(c) D7WOO3 (d) ƐOOM7ᗡ

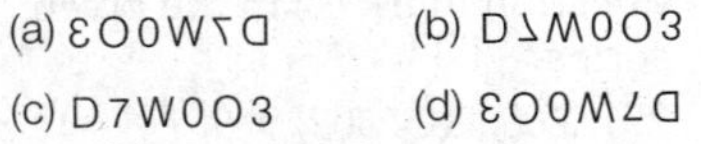

39. Select the set in which the numbers are related in the same way as are the numbers of the following sets.

(**Note** Operations should be performed on the whole numbers, without breaking down the numbers into their constituent digits. E.g. 13 – Operations on 13 such as adding/subtracting/ multiplying etc. to 13 can be performed. Breaking down 13 into 1 and 3 and then performing mathematical operations on 1 and 3 is not allowed.)

(4, 16, 32)
(6, 36, 72)

(a) (9, 81, 164) (b) (9, 27, 162)
(c) (9, 81, 162) (d) (9, 81, 160)

40. What will be the day on 31st December, 2006, if 1st January, 2006 is a Wednesday?

(a) Thursday (b) Monday
(c) Wednesday (d) Friday

41. Select the correct mirror image of the given figure, when the mirror is placed at MN as shown below.

M
hRk72a
N

(a) ɒS7ʞЯʜ (b) hRk72a
(c) ɒS7ʞRh (d) ɒ27ʞЯh

42. If 'A' stands for '÷', 'B' stands for '×', 'C' stands for '+' and 'D' stands for '–', what will come in place of the question mark (?) in the following equation?

321 A 3 C 11 B 10 D 19 = ?

(a) 198 (b) 188 (c) 168 (d) 178

43. What should come in place of question mark (?) in the given series based on the English alphabetical order?

EMU, GQA, IUG, KYM, ?

(a) MCS
(b) VLB
(c) UKA
(d) MWD

44. What will come in the place of the question mark (?) in the following equation, if '+' and '×' are interchanged and '–' and '÷' are interchanged?

$39 \div 6 - 3 \times 9 + 4 = ?$

(a) 56 (b) 83
(c) 73 (d) 81

45. Identify the figure in the options that, when put in place of the question mark (?) will logically complete the series?

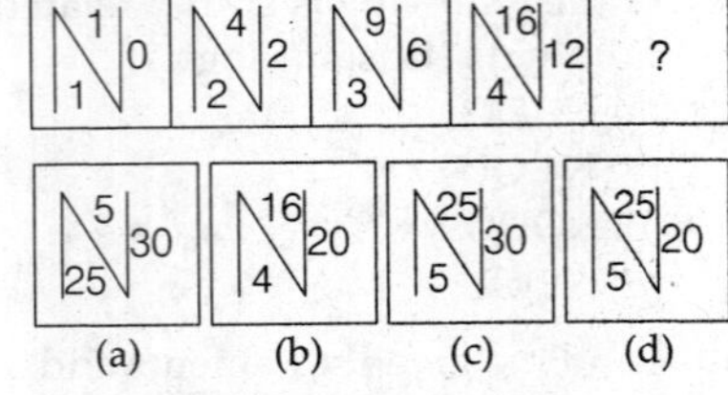

(a) (b) (c) (d)

46. S % T = S is the father of T.
X – W = X is the mother of W.
U * V = U is the sister of V.
Z + Y = Z is the husband of Y.
If A + J – B * V% G, find the relation between A and G.

(a) Father
(b) Paternal grandfather
(c) Maternal grandfather
(d) Mother

47. In a certain code language,
'A + B' means 'A is the mother of B',
'A × B' means 'A is the husband of B',
'A ÷ B' means 'A is the daughter of B'.
Based on the above, how is Q related to T, if 'P ÷ Q ÷ R × S + T'?

(a) Father's sister (b) Mother
(c) Sister (d) Daughter

48. What will come in the place of question mark (?) in the following equation, if '+' and '–' are interchanged and '×' and '÷' are interchanged?

$32 \times 8 \div 4 - 6 + 15 = ?$

(a) 7 (b) 15
(c) 5 (d) 13

49. BHJL is related to FLNP in a certain way based on the English alphabetical order. In the same way, HNPR is related to LRTV.
To which of the following is JPRT related, following the same logic?

(a) NUVX (b) NTVX
(c) NTYX (d) NUWX

50. A paper is folded and cut as shown below . How will it appear, when unfolded?

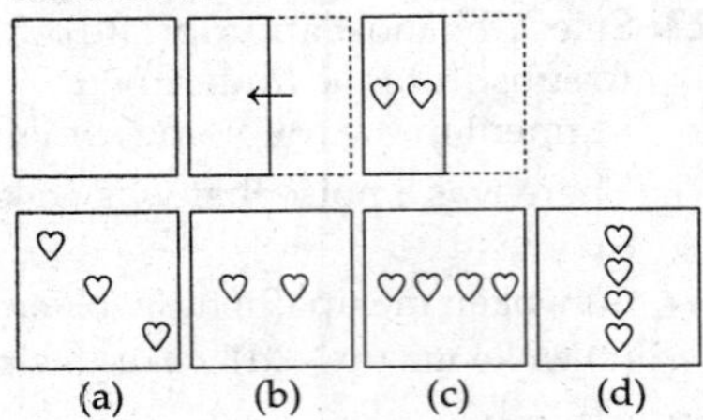

(a) (b) (c) (d)

Part III
Quantitative Aptitude

51. A shopkeeper cheats 25% in weight, while buying rice and cheats 25% while selling it. If he sells the rice at $12\frac{1}{2}\%$ profit, then find his net profit percentage.

(a) 82.5%
(b) 62.5%
(c) 87.5%
(d) 92.5%

52. The following graph shows the data of the production of clothes (in lakh tonnes) by three different companies A, B and C over the years.

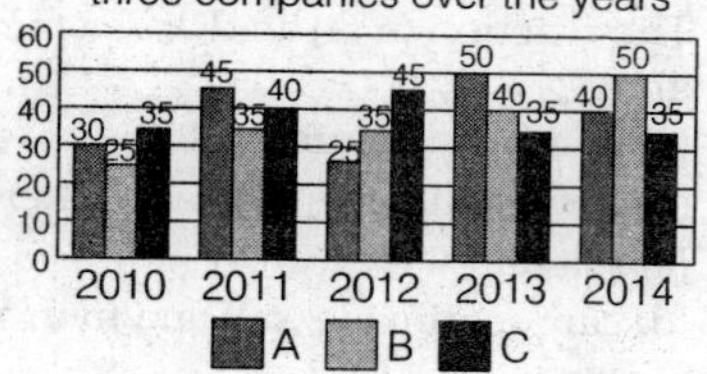

What is the ratio of the average production of Company A in the period 2012-2014 to the average production of Company B in the same period?

(a) 25 : 23 (b) 5 : 3
(c) 23 : 25 (d) 3 : 5

53. A person travels from one place to another at 60 km/h and returns at 75 km/h. If the total time taken is 6 h, then find the total distance travelled.

(a) 400 km (b) 250 km
(c) 240 km (d) 300 km

54. Find the fourth proportion to 1.25, 5.75 and 3.5.

(a) 4.5 (b) 16.1
(c) 6.5 (d) 12.5

55. $\left[\frac{\text{cosec } 31° - \sec 59°}{\sin 18° \div \cos 72°} \times \frac{\tan 26°}{\cot 26°}\right] + \left[\frac{\tan 30° + \tan 15°}{1 - \tan 30° \tan 15°}\right] = \ldots\ldots\ldots$

(a) 0 (b) –1
(c) 1 (d) 2

56. Two similar triangles have area 490 sq cm. and 640 sq cm. If the length of the one side of the first triangle is 21 cm, then what is the length of the corresponding side of the second triangle?

(a) 24 cm (b) 21 cm
(c) 16 cm (d) 14 cm

57. K being any odd number greater than 1, $k^{33} - k$ is always divisible by

(a) 24 (b) 13
(c) 5 (d) 15

58. Find the amount to be paid at the end if ₹ 4500 is invested for a period of 4 yr at the rate of 8% simple interest per annum.

(a) ₹ 5490 (b) ₹ 6080
(c) ₹ 5940 (d) ₹ 6300

59. If the graph of the equation $20x + 21y = 420$ cuts the co-ordinate axis at P and Q, then what is the measure of the length (in units) of PQ?

(a) 25 (b) 29
(c) 40 (d) 35

60. Let ABC be a triangle such that $\angle ABC = 70°$ and $\angle ACB = 50°$. Let O be the incentre of the triangle. Find $\angle BOC$.

(a) 120° (b) 100°
(c) 60° (d) 130°

61. Study the given bar-graph carefully and answer the questions that follow.

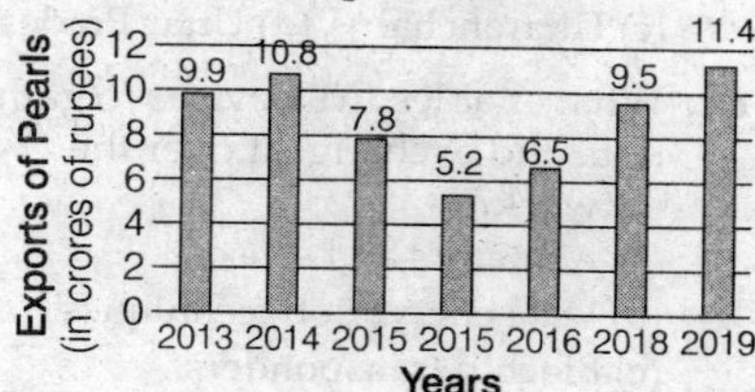

For how many years was the export above-average for the period, 2013-2019?

(a) 1 (b) 4
(c) 3 (d) 2

62. How many factors of 14400 are divisible by 18 but not by 36?

(a) 5 (b) 2 (c) 4 (d) 3

63. A person divides his total route of journey into three equal parts and decides to travel the three parts at the speeds of 80 km/h, 60 km/h and 30 km/h, respectively. What is the average speed during the journey?

(a) 45 km/h (b) 40 km/h
(c) 49 km/h (d) 48 km/h

64. Let ABC be a right-angled triangle such that $\angle C = 90°$. Let D be a point on AB such that CD is perpendicular to AB. If $AC = 5$ cm and $BC = 12$ cm, find the length of CD (in cm).

(a) $\frac{60}{13}$ (b) $\frac{40}{13}$
(c) $\frac{40}{23}$ (d) $\frac{50}{23}$

65. The diameter of a roller is 35 cm and its length is 100 cm. It takes 200 complete revolutions to level a playground. Find the area of the playground (in m^2).

(a) 110000
(b) 110
(c) 22000000
(d) 220

66. In an election, a voter has choices to vote for one candidate out of three candidates. There is also an option 'None Of The Above' (NOTA) to reject all candidates. The three candidates get votes that are 6 times NOTA. The winner gets votes that are twice the second runner-up's votes. The first runner-up gets 900 votes more than NOTA and defeats the second runner-up by 150 votes. What is the total number of votes polled?

(a) 17715 (b) 15177
(c) 11025 (d) 11577

67. The number of subjects in which the students of a class have failed is given in the following table.

Number of subjects in which students have failed	0	1	2	3	4	5
Number of students	10	18	5	6	7	4

Find the total number of students, who have failed in more than 3 subjects.

(a) 11 (b) 10 (c) 17 (d) 12

68. In ΔABC, O is the point of intersection of the bisectors of $\angle B$ and angle $\angle A$. If the $\angle BOC = 108°$, then $\angle BAO$ is

(a) 26° (b) 16°
(c) 22° (d) 18°

69. The difference (in ₹) between a discount of 37% on ₹ 2635 and two successive discounts of 23% and 7% on the same amount is (rounded off to 2 decimal places)

(a) 248.36 (b) 226.87
(c) 235.65 (d) 242.25

70. The following pie-chart represents the percentage domestic expenditure of Raman over his family. Study the pie-chart carefully and answer the question given below.

Raman's total monthly income = ₹ 45000

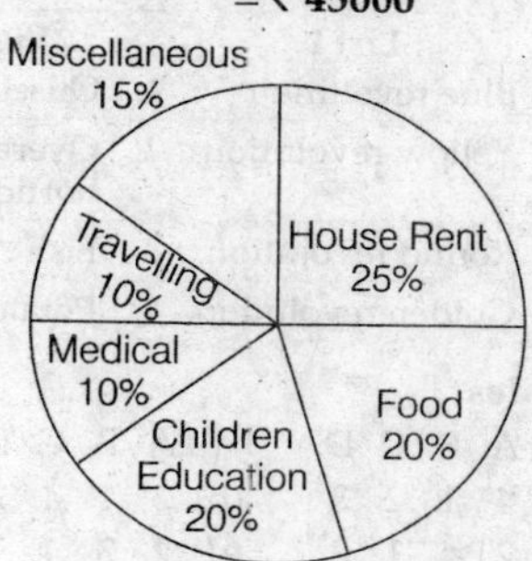

After paying the House Rent and expending over Food and Children's Education, what is Raman's remaining monthly income (in ₹) ?
(a) 12750 (b) 20250
(c) 15750 (d) 29250

71. The price of a motorcycle was $750 last year. The price increased by 20% this year. What is the price of the motorcycle this year?
(a) $ 750 (b) $ 900 (c) $ 600 (d) $ 790

72. The altitude of an equilateral triangle is $3\sqrt{3}$ cm. Find its area.
(a) 9 sq cm (b) 27 sq cm
(c) $9\sqrt{3}$ sq cm (d) $3\sqrt{3}$ sq cm

73. X and Y can do a job in 18 days. Y and Z can do the same in 24 days. If all the three can finish the job in 12 days, in how many days can X and Z can complete the job?
(a) 5 days (b) $12\frac{3}{5}$ days
(c) 7 days (d) $14\frac{2}{5}$ days

74. The whole surface area of a cube is 294 cm^2. The volume of the cube is
(a) 243 cm^3 (b) 343 cm^3
(c) 512 cm^3 (d) 216 cm^3

75. A person spends 60% of his salary on family expenses, 10% on medical expenses, 5% on charity and saves the remaining amount. If the amount on savings is ₹ 4000, find his monthly salary.
(a) ₹ 16000 (b) ₹ 12000
(c) ₹ 14000 (d) ₹ 15000

Part IV
General Awareness

76. Where is the Narora Nuclear Power plant located?
(a) Uttar Pradesh (b) Tamil Nadu
(c) Maharashtra (d) Karnataka

77. Match the items in List-I with those in List-II.

List I	List II
A. Blue revolution	1. Oilseeds
B. Yellow revolution	2. Overall horticulture
C. Round revolution	3. Fish
D. Golden revolution	4. Potato

Codes

	A	B	C	D		A	B	C	D
(a)	4	1	2	3	(b)	3	1	4	2
(c)	2	4	1	3	(d)	2	3	4	1

78. Sardar Vallabhbhai Patel, who was the first Home Minister of India, is known by which sobriquet?
(a) Grand Old Man of India
(b) Iron Man of India
(c) Morning Star of Indian Renaissance
(d) Father of Indian Unrest

79. What is the wavelength range of visible light?
(a) 0.2 to 0.3 μm (b) 0.7 to 0.9 μm
(c) 0.4 to 0.7 μm (d) 1 to 2 μm

80. Terah taali dance belongs to which of the following states?
(a) Kerala (b) Rajasthan
(c) Uttaranchal (d) Uttar Pradesh

81. What enables IoT devices to gather data and exchange it over the network?
(a) Actuators and sensors
(b) Data encryption techniques
(c) Biochip transponders
(d) Human interaction

82. As of January 2023, who among the following is the Chief Minister of Puducherry?
(a) Shri V. Narayanasamy
(b) Shri N. Rangaswamy
(c) Shri V. Vaithilingam
(d) Shri P. Shanmugam

83. In which year did the Indian Constitution declare Hindi in Devanagari script to be the official language of the Union?
(a) 1951 (b) 1952
(c) 1949 (d) 1955

84. As per the Economic Survey of India 2022-23, unemployment rates fell from 5.8% in 2018-19 to ....in 2020-21.
(a) 3.8% (b) 4.7%
(c) 4.2% (d) 3.4%

85. Who has written the patriotic song 'Sandese Aate Hai'?
(a) Irshad Kamil (b) Samir Anjan
(c) Javed Akhtar (d) Gulzar

86. The 'Western disturbances' originates from the ....
(a) East China Sea
(b) Mediterranean Sea
(c) Arabian Sea
(d) Red Sea

87. Bails are used in which of the following games/sports?
(a) Cricket (b) Badminton
(c) Football (d) Hockey

88. In Gujarat, the festival Makar Sankranti is celebrated as:
(a) Paschimayan
(b) Purbayan
(c) Dakshinayan
(d) Uttarayan

89. The reaction of an acid and a metal gives
(a) hydrogen gas and salt
(b) carbon dioxide, salt and water
(c) salt and water
(d) carbon dioxide, salt and hydrogen gas

90. The length of a day on .... is approximately 16 hours.
(a) Mercury (b) Mars
(c) Venus (d) Neptune

91. After being passed by both the Lok Sabha and Rajya Sabha, the Competition (Amendment) Bill, 2023 received the President's assent on .... to become the Competition (Amendment) Act, 202(c)
(a) 21st April, 2023
(b) 11th April, 2023
(c) 1st April, 2023 (d) 14th April, 2023

92. Which among the following Chola emperors defeated the Pandya king Maravarman Rajsimha II in the battle of Vellore?
(a) Rajendra I
(b) Vijayalaya
(c) Parantaka I
(d) Rajaraja I

93. What is the standard size of basketball for men?
(a) 06 (b) 07
(c) 08 (d) 05

94. As of 1st January, 2023, who is the chairman of UPSC?
(a) Dr. Manoj Soni
(b) Shri Rajeev Nayan Choubey
(c) Dr. TCA Anant
(d) Mrs. Preeti Sudan

95. Which of the following extensions is used to save MS-PowerPoint applications?
(a) .docx (b) .txt
(c) .doc (d) .ppt

96. In India, statutory liquidity ratio is fixed by ....
(a) India Brand Equity Foundation
(b) State government
(c) Commercial banks
(d) Reserve Bank of India

97. Which folk music is a mix of Indian and western music and is popular in Goa?
(a) Mando (b) Maand
(c) Pai songs (d) Pawada

98. Pusarla Venkata Sindhu won silver medal in badminton in which Olympics Games?
(a) London 2012 (b) Beijing 2008
(c) Tokyo 2020 (d) Rio 2016

99. Which committee is related to fundamental duties?
(a) Verma Committee
(b) LM Singhvi Committee
(c) Vasantrao Naik Committee
(d) Rajmannar Committee

100. A .... is issued to prevent an inferior court or tribunal from exceeding its jurisdiction, which is not legally vested, or acting without jurisdiction or acting against the principles of natural justice.
(a) writ of mandamus
(b) writ of habeas corpus
(c) writ of prohibition
(d) writ of quo-warranto

Answers

1. (c)	2. (d)	3. (a)	4. (d)
5. (d)	6. (d)	7. (a)	8. (d)
9. (c)	10. (b)	11. (b)	12. (b)
13. (a)	14 (a)	15. (c)	16. (a)
17. (c)	18. (a)	19. (c)	20. (d)
21. (b)	22. (c)	23. (a)	24. (d)
25. (c)	26. (c)	27. (d)	28. (c)
29. (c)	30. (c)	31. (d)	32. (d)
33. (d)	34. (b)	35. (a)	36. (d)
37. (d)	38. (a)	39. (c)	40. (c)
41. (b)	42. (a)	43. (a)	44. (c)
45. (d)	46. (b)	47. (c)	48. (a)
49. (b)	50. (c)	51. (c)	52. (c)
53. (a)	54. (b)	55. (c)	56. (a)
57. (a)	58. (c)	59. (b)	60. (a)
61. (b)	62. (d)	63. (d)	64. (a)
65. (d)	66. (c)	67. (a)	68. (d)
69. (b)	70. (c)	71. (b)	72. (c)
73. (d)	74. (b)	75. (a)	76. (a)
77. (b)	78. (b)	79. (c)	80. (b)
81. (a)	82. (b)	83. (c)	84. (c)
85. (c)	86. (b)	87. (a)	88. (d)
89. (a)	90. (d)	91. (b)	92. (c)
93. (b)	94. (a)	95. (d)	96. (d)
97. (a)	98. (d)	99. (a)	100. (c)

Explanations

1. *(c)* The correct filler for the given blank is 'spoke'.

2. *(d)* Part (d) 'Ms. Rose is a' contains an error. Use 'the' to correct the sentence as definite article is used before superlative degree of adjective.

3. *(a)* Part (a) 'usually opened' contains an error. Use 'opens' to correct the sentence. The given sentence presents a habitual action, so simple present tense should be used.

4. *(d)* Part (d) 'with a leather seats' contains an error. Remove 'a' to correct the sentence.

5. *(d)* The correct filler for the given blank is 'imagine'.

6. *(d)* The correct filler for the given blank is 'utilised'.

7. *(a)* The correct filler for the given blank is 'crucial'.

8. *(d)* The correct filler for the given blank is 'varying'.

9. *(c)* The correct filler for the given blank is 'invent'.

10. *(b)* Jovial means happy. Hence, its antonym is 'miserable' which means unhappy.
- 'Shrewd' means evil.
- 'Cunning' means clever.

11. *(b)*The antonym of 'lazy' is 'diligent' which means hard working.
- 'Barren' means unproductive.
- 'Genuine' means true.

12. *(b)* Spill the beans means to reveal a secret unknowingly.

13. *(a)* The word 'accept' means 'to agree'.

14. *(a)* 'Plausible' means (of an argument or statement) seeming reasonable or probable. Hence, its antonym is 'unlikely'.

15. *(c)* The correct filler for the given blank is 'dew' which refers to tiny drops of water that form on cool surfaces at night, when atmospheric vapour condenses.

16. *(a)* The most appropriate substitution will be- all thumbs. It means not graceful and clumsy.

17. *(c)* The correct filler for the given blank is 'make the bed'.

18. *(a)* The incorrectly spelt word is 'scatered'. The correct spelling is 'scattered'.

19. *(c)* The underlined part of the given sentence contains an error. Use 'playing cards' to correct the sentence.

20. *(d)* The correct spelling is 'warrant'.

21. *(b)* Alter means to change.
- 'Resolute' means determined.
- 'Renew' means to take a service again.
- 'Adjust' means to modify slightly.

22. *(c)* The underlined part of the given sentence contains an error. Use 'woke me up' to correct the sentence.

23. *(a)* 'Absurd' means strange. Hence, its antonym is 'unreasonable'.

24. *(d)* The 'crux' means central point.

25. *(c)* 'Queered my pitch' means ruined my plan.

26. *(c)* According to the code question,

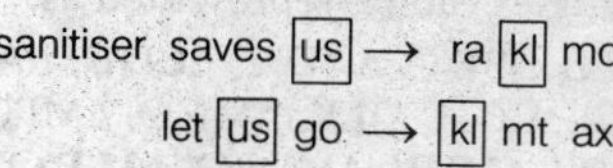

∴ Code for 'us' is 'kl'.

27. *(d)* Given figure is embedded in option figure (d).

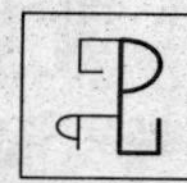

28. *(c)* According to the question,

Original positions of letters in word	H	A	R	M	O	N	Y
Letters after arranging in alphabetical order	A	H	M	N	O	R	Y

Thus, positions of 2 letters 'O' and 'Y' will remain unchanged.

29. *(c)* As, C K M Z → (−7 each) → V D F S

and L P B V → (−7 each) → E I U O

Similarly,

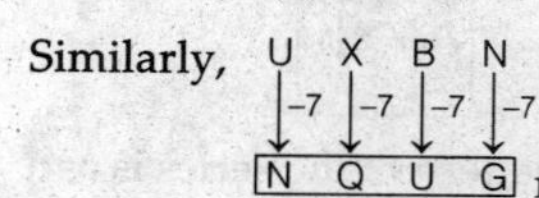

30. *(c)* According to the statements,

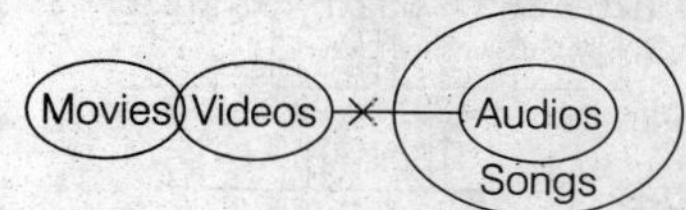

Conclusions I. (✓) II. (✗)

Hence, only Conclusion I follows.

31. *(d)* According to the question,

W I L T → 6 1 9 4

S L I T → 9 4 1 3

∴ Code for 'S' is '3'.

32. *(d)* Naming the figure,

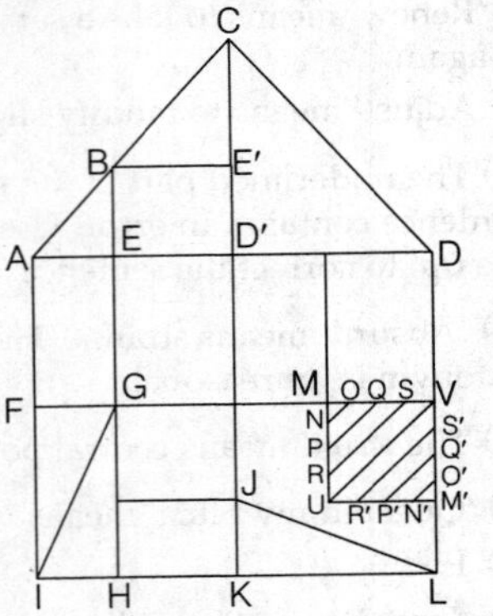

Triangles can be represented as,
ΔAEB, ΔBE'C, ΔAD'C, ΔCD'D, ΔACD, ΔFGI, ΔIGH, ΔJLK, ΔMNO, ΔMPQ, ΔMRS, ΔMUV, ΔM'N'O', ΔM'P'Q', ΔM'R'S', ΔM'UV.
Hence, total 16 triangles present in given figure.

33. *(d)* The pattern of the series is as follows,

251 → 268 → 285 → 302 → 319 → 336

+17, +17, +17, +17, +17

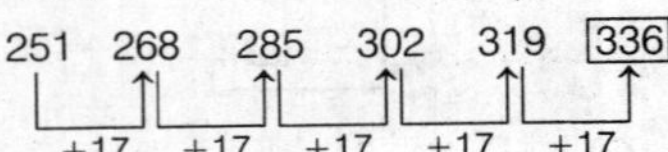

34. *(b)* The pattern of the series is as follows,

G $\xrightarrow{-1}$ F $\xrightarrow{-1}$ E $\xrightarrow{-1}$ D $\xrightarrow{-1}$ C

L $\xrightarrow{+2}$ N $\xrightarrow{+2}$ P $\xrightarrow{+2}$ R $\xrightarrow{+2}$ T

Y $\xrightarrow{-3}$ V $\xrightarrow{-3}$ S $\xrightarrow{-3}$ P $\xrightarrow{-3}$ M

C $\xrightarrow{+4}$ G $\xrightarrow{+4}$ K $\xrightarrow{+4}$ O $\xrightarrow{+4}$ S

35. *(a)* As, $84 \xrightarrow{\div 4} 21$

and $180 \xrightarrow{\div 4} 45$

Similarly, $252 \xrightarrow{\div 4} 63$

36. *(d)* The given figure is embedded in option figure (d).

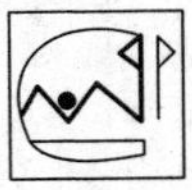

37. *(d)* The pattern of the series is as follows,

876 → 865 → 832 → 733 → 436

−11, −33, −99, −297

×3, ×3, ×3

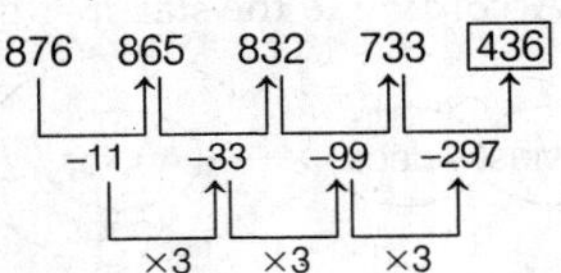

38. *(a)* The correct mirror image of given figure shown below,

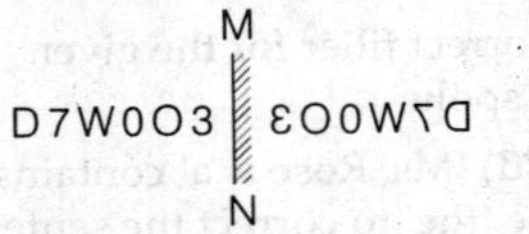

39. *(c)* $[\text{First number}]^2$ = Second number × 2 → Third number

As, (4, 16, 32) → $(4)^2 = 16 \times 2 \rightarrow 32$

(6, 36, 72) → $(6)^2 = 36 \times 2 \rightarrow 72$

Similarly,

(9, 81, 162) → $(9)^2 = 81 \times 2 \rightarrow 162$

40. *(c)* Given, 1st December, 2006 → Wednesday

In a non-leap year, (here 2006) the first day and the last day of the year always same. Therefore, 31st December, 2006 will also be Wednesday.

41. *(b)* The mirror image of given figure is as follows,

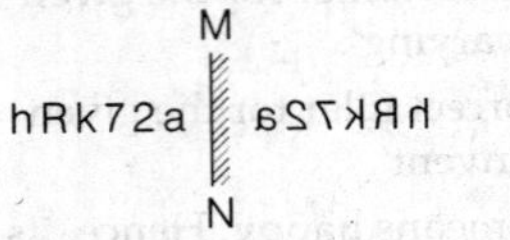

42. *(a)* According to the question,

A → ÷, B → ×, C → +, D → −

Given equation,

321 A 3 C 11 B 10 D 19 = ?

Substituting the letters with symbols, we get

$321 \div 3 + 11 \times 10 - 19 = ?$

$\Rightarrow 107 + 110 - 19 = ?$

$\Rightarrow 217 - 19 = ?$

$\Rightarrow ? = 198$

43. *(a)* The pattern of the series is as follows,

E $\xrightarrow{+2}$ G $\xrightarrow{+2}$ I $\xrightarrow{+2}$ K $\xrightarrow{+2}$ M

M $\xrightarrow{+4}$ Q $\xrightarrow{+4}$ U $\xrightarrow{+4}$ Y $\xrightarrow{+4}$ C

U $\xrightarrow{+6}$ A $\xrightarrow{+6}$ G $\xrightarrow{+6}$ M $\xrightarrow{+6}$ S

44. *(c)* Given equation,

$39 \div 6 - 3 \times 9 + 4 = ?$

Interchanging '+' and '×', '−' and ÷, we get

$39 - 6 \div 3 + 9 \times 4 = ?$

$\Rightarrow 39 - 2 + 36 = ?$

$\Rightarrow 75 - 2 = ?$

$\therefore ? = 73$

45. *(d)* The pattern of the series is given below.

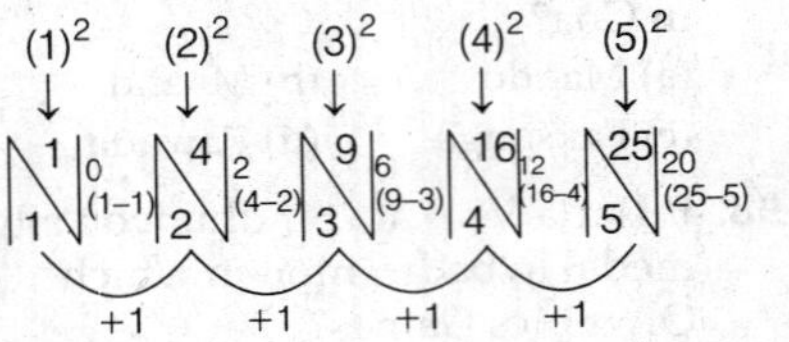

∴ ? =

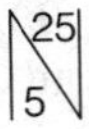

46. *(b)* Given expression,

A + J − B * V % G

According to the question,

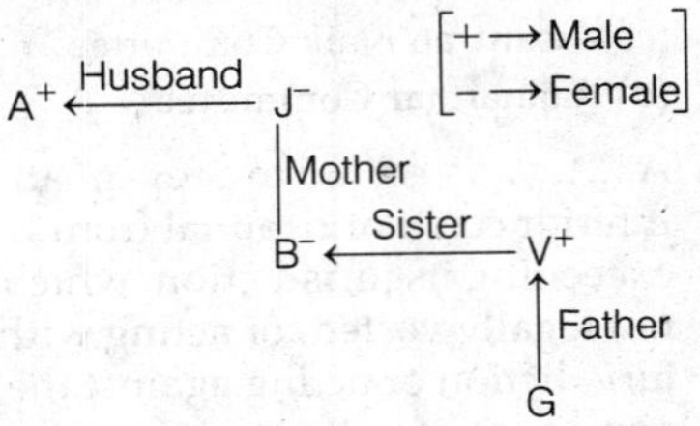

Hence, A is the paternal grandfather of G.

47. *(c)* Given expression,

$P \div Q \div R \times S + T$

According to the question,

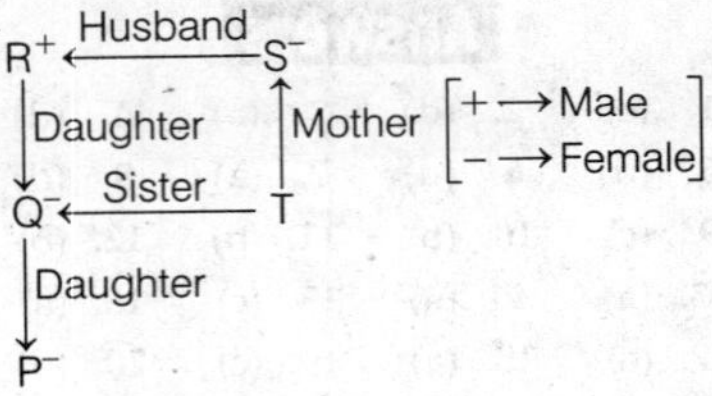

Hence, Q is sister of T.

48. (a) Given equation,

$32 \times 8 \div 4 - 6 + 15 = ?$

Interchanging + and −, × and ÷, we get

$32 \div 8 \times 4 + 6 - 15 = ?$

$\Rightarrow 4 \times 4 + 6 - 15 = ?$

$\Rightarrow 16 + 6 - 15 = ?$

$\Rightarrow 22 - 15 = ?$

$\therefore ? = 7$

49. *(b)* As, B H J L → (+4 each) → F L N P

and H N P R → (+4 each) → L R T V

Similarly, J P R T → (+4 each) → N T V X

50. *(c)* When the paper is unfolded, it will look like option figure (c).

51. *(c)* Let cost price of 1000 gm = ₹ $1000x$

Quantity of rice bought by shopkeeper

$$= 1000 \times \left(1 + \frac{25}{100}\right) = 1250 \text{ gm}$$

$\therefore$ Actual price of 1000 gm

$$= \frac{1000x}{1250} \times 1000 = ₹\ 800x$$

Quantity of rice sold by shopkeeper

$$= 1000 \times \left(1 - \frac{25}{100}\right)$$

$$= 750 \text{ gm}$$

$$= 1000x \times \left(1 + \frac{12.5}{100}\right) = ₹\ 1125x$$

$\therefore$ Actual price for 1000 gm

$$= \frac{1125x}{750} \times 1000$$

$$= ₹\ 1500x$$

$$\therefore \text{Net profit \%} = \frac{1500x - 800x}{800x} \times 100$$

$$= 87.5\%$$

52. *(c)* Average production of Company A in the period 2012-2014

$$= \frac{25 + 50 + 40}{3}$$

$$= \frac{115}{3} \text{ lakh tonnes}$$

Average production of Company B in the period 2012-2014

$$= \frac{35 + 40 + 50}{3}$$

$$= \frac{125}{5} \text{ lakh tonnes}$$

$$\therefore \text{Required ratio} = \frac{115}{3} : \frac{125}{5}$$

$$= 23 : 25$$

53. *(a)* Given, first speed (x) = 60 km/h and second speed (y) = 75 km/h and time = 6 h

We know that,

$$\therefore \text{Average speed} = \frac{2xy}{x + y}$$

$$= \frac{2 \times 60 \times 75}{60 + 75} = 66\frac{2}{3} \text{ km/h}$$

$\therefore$ Total distance = Average speed × Total time

$$= 66\frac{2}{3} \times 6 = 400 \text{ km}$$

54. *(b)* Let x be the fourth proportion.

We can write

$1.25 : 5.75 :: 3.5 : x$

Here, $1.25 \times x = 5.75 \times 3.5$

$x = 16.1$

55. *(c)* Given expression,

$$\left[\frac{\text{cosec } 31° - \sec 59°}{(\sin 18° \div \cos 72°)} \times \frac{\tan 26°}{\cot 64°}\right] + \left[\frac{\tan 30° + \tan 15°}{1 - \tan 30° \cdot \tan 15°}\right]$$

$$= \left[\frac{\sec (90 - 31)° - \sec 59°}{\cos (90 - 18)° \div \cos 72°} \times \frac{\cot(90 - 26)°}{\cot 64°}\right] + \left[\frac{\tan 30° + \tan 15°}{1 - \tan 30° \cdot \tan 15°}\right]$$

$$= \left[\frac{\sec 59° - \sec 59°}{\cos 72° \div \cos 72°} \times \frac{\cot 64°}{\cot 64°}\right] + \frac{\tan 30° + \tan 15°}{1 - \tan 15° \cdot \tan 30°}$$

$$\left[\because \text{cosec } (90 - \theta) = \sec \theta,\ \sin(90 - \theta) = \cos\theta,\ \tan(90 - \theta) = \cot\theta\right]$$

$$= 0 + \tan(15° + 30°)$$

$$\left[\because \tan(A + B) = \frac{\tan A + \tan B}{1 - \tan A \cdot \tan B}\right]$$

$$= 0 + \tan 45° = 1 \quad (\because \tan 45° = 1)$$

56. *(a)* Given, area of first triangle = 490 sq cm

Area of other triangle = 640 sq cm

Length of side of first triangle = 21 cm

In similar triangle,

We know that,

$$\frac{\text{Area of first triangle}}{\text{Area of other triangle}} = \left(\frac{\text{Side of first triangle}}{\text{Side of other triangle}}\right)^2$$

$$\frac{490}{640} = \frac{(21)^2}{(\text{Side of other triangle})^2}$$

$$\Rightarrow \frac{\text{Side of other triangle}}{21} = \frac{8}{7}$$

Side of other triangle = 24 cm

57. *(a)* Given number,

$$k^{33} - k = k(k^{32} - 1)$$

We know that,

$x^n - a^n$ is always divisible by $(x - a)$.

$\therefore$ $k(k^{32} - 1)^{32}$ is always divisible by $(k - 1)$.

Here, k = odd number

$\therefore$ $k - 1$ = even number

$\therefore$ $k^{32} - 1$ is always divisible by even number. i.e., 24 only.

58. *(c)* Principal = ₹ 4500

Time = 4 yr

Rate = 8%

We know that,

Amount

$$= \text{Principal} + \frac{\text{Principal} \times \text{Time} \times \text{Rate}}{100}$$

$$= 4500 + \frac{4500 \times 4 \times 8}{100}$$

$$= 4500 + 1440 = ₹\ 5940$$

59. *(b)* Given, $20x + 21y = 420$ ...(i)

At P, $y = 0$ put in Eq. (i),

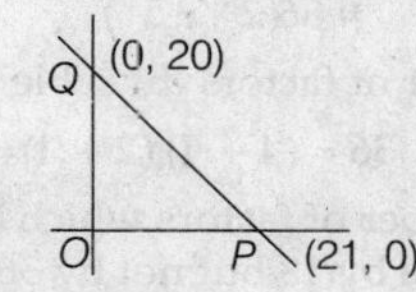

$20x = 420$

$x = 21$

$\therefore$ Coordinate at $P = (21, 0)$

At Q, $x = 0$ put in Eq. (i)

$21y = 420$

$y = 20$

$\therefore$ Coordinate at $Q = (0, 20)$

$\therefore$ Length of

$$PQ = \sqrt{(y_2 - y_1)^2 + (x_2 - x_1)^2}$$

$$= \sqrt{(0 - 20)^2 + (21 - 0)^2}$$

$$= \sqrt{400 + 441}$$

$$= \sqrt{841}$$

PQ = 29 units

60. *(a)* Given, $\angle ABC = 70°$

and $\angle ACB = 50°$

Incentre of triangle,

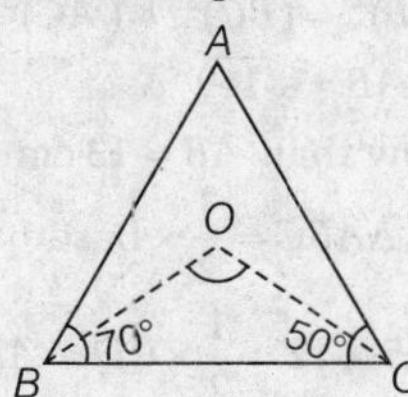

We know that,

$$\angle BOC = 180° - \left(\frac{\angle B + \angle C}{2}\right)$$

$$= 180° - \frac{(50° + 70°)}{2}$$

$$\angle BOC = 180° - 60°$$

$$\angle BOC = 120°$$

61. *(b)* Average of export for 2013-2019

$$= \frac{9.9 + 10.8 + 7.8 + 5.2 + 6.5 + 9.5 + 11.4}{7}$$

$$= \frac{61.1}{7} = 8.728$$

Number of years when export is above average = 4 (2013, 2014, 2018, 2019)

62. *(d)* $14400 = 2^6 \times 3^2 \times 5^2$

Now, $14400 = 2^1 \times 3^2 \times (2^5 \times 5^2)$
$= 18 \times (2^5 \times 5^2)$

Number of factors divisible by
$18 = (5+1)(2+1) = 18$

and $14400 = 2^2 \times 3^2\ (2^4 \times 5^2)$
$= 36(2^4 \times 5^2)$

Number of factors divisible by
$36 = (4+1)(2+1) = 15$

$\therefore$ Number of factors which are divisible by 18 but not by 36 is $18 - 15 = 3$

63. *(d)* Let the distance of equal past = 1 unit

$$\text{Average speed} = \frac{\text{Total distance}}{\text{Total time}}$$

$$= \frac{1+1+1}{\frac{1}{80}+\frac{1}{60}+\frac{1}{30}} = \frac{240 \times 3}{15}$$

$= 16 \times 3 = 48$ km/h

64. *(a)* Given, $BC = 12$ cm, $AC = 5$ cm

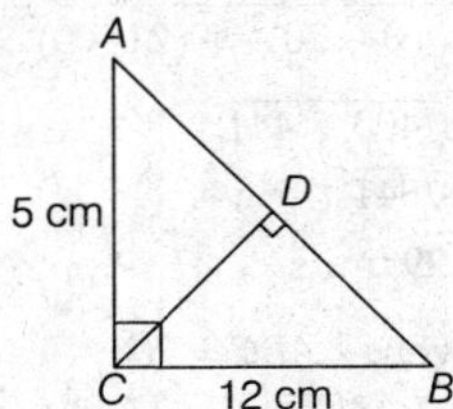

By Pythagoras theorem

$(AB)^2 = (BC)^2 + (AC)^2 = 25 + 144$

$AB = \sqrt{169}$

We know that, $AB = 13$ cm

Area of $\Delta ABC = \frac{1}{2} \times \text{Base} \times \text{height}$

$\frac{1}{2} \times 5 \times 12 = \frac{1}{2} \times CD \times AB$

$\frac{1}{2} \times 5 \times 12 = \frac{1}{2} \times CD \times 13$

$\therefore \quad CD = \frac{60}{13}$ cm

65. *(d)* Given, diameter $(d) = 35$ cm

$\therefore$ Radius $(r) = \frac{35}{2}$ cm $= \frac{35}{200}$ m

Length $(h) = 100$ cm $= 1$ m

Revolution = 200

Surface area of roller $= 2\pi rh$

$= 2 \times \frac{22}{7} \times \frac{35}{200} \times 1 = 1.1\ \text{m}^2$

$\therefore$ Area of playground

= Surface area × Number of revolutions

$= 1.1 \times 200$

$= 220\ \text{m}^2$

66. *(c)* Let NOTA got x votes.

$\therefore$ First runner up got votes $= x + 900$

$\therefore$ Second runner up got votes
$= x + 900 - 150$
$= x + 750$

$\therefore$ Winner got votes $= 2(x + 750)$
$= 2x + 1500$

According to the question,

The three candidates got votes that are 6 times NOTA.

$\therefore x + 900 + x + 750 + 2x + 1500 = 6x$

$\Rightarrow \quad 2x = 3150$

$\Rightarrow \quad x = \frac{3150}{2} = 1575$

$\therefore$ Total votes polled $= x + 6x$
$= 7x = 7 \times 1575$
$= 11025$

67. *(a)* Number of students who have failed in more than 3 subjects
$= 7 + 4$
$= 11$

68. *(d)* We know that, $\angle BOC = 108°$

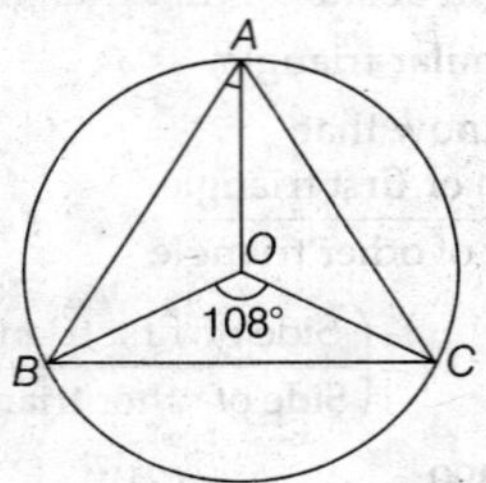

$$\angle BOC = 90° + \frac{\angle A}{2}$$

$\Rightarrow \quad 108° = 90° + \frac{\angle A}{2}$

$\Rightarrow \quad \angle A = 36°$

$\therefore \quad \angle BAO = \frac{\angle A}{2} = 18°$

69. *(b)* **Case I**, Price = ₹ 2635

Discount % = 37%

$\therefore \quad \text{Discount} = \text{Price} \times \frac{\text{Discount\%}}{100}$

$= 2635 \times \frac{37}{100}$

= ₹ 974.95

Case II, Price = ₹ 2635

Discount% = 23% and 7%

$\therefore$ Effective discount% $= a + b + \frac{ab}{100}$

$= -23 - 7 + \frac{(-23) \times (-7)}{100}$

$= -30 + 1.61 = -28.39\%$

$\therefore \text{Discount} = \text{Price} \times \frac{\text{Discount\%}}{100}$

$= 2635 \times \frac{28.39}{100} = 748.0765$

$\therefore$ Required difference
$= 974.95 - 748.0765$
$=$ ₹ $226.885 \approx$ ₹ 226.87

70. *(c)* Spending on house rent, food and children's education

$= 45000\left(\frac{25}{100} + \frac{20}{100} + \frac{20}{100}\right)$

= ₹ 29250

$\therefore$ Remaining monthly salary of Raman
$= 45000 - 29250$
= ₹ 15750

71. *(b)* Given, price = \$ 750

Rate of increase = 20%

We know that,

$\text{Final price} = \text{Price} \times \left(1 + \frac{\text{Rate}}{100}\right)$

$\text{Final price} = 750\left(1 + \frac{20}{100}\right) = \$\ 900$

72. *(c)* Given, altitude $= 3\sqrt{3}$ cm

We know that,

Altitude of equilateral triangle

$= \frac{\sqrt{3}}{2} \times \text{Side}$

$\therefore \quad 3\sqrt{3} = \frac{\sqrt{3}}{2} \times \text{side}$

Side = 6 cm

$\therefore \quad \text{Area} = \frac{\sqrt{3}}{4} \times (\text{side})^2 = \frac{\sqrt{3}}{4} \times (6)^2$

$= 9\sqrt{3}$ sq cm

73. *(d)* Given, X and Y can do a job in 18 days and Y and Z can do a job in 24 days.

All three can finish the job in 12 days.

Let total work $= 72x$ units

$\therefore$ X and Y's efficiency

$= X + Y = \frac{72x}{18} = 4x \quad \ldots\text{(i)}$

Y and Z's efficiency

$= Y + Z = \frac{72x}{24} = 3x \quad \ldots\text{(ii)}$

All three's efficiency $= X + Y + Z$

$= \frac{72x}{12} = 6x \quad ...(iii)$

On solving Eqs. 2 (iii) – [(i) + (ii)]

$2(X + Y + Z) - (X + Y + Y + Z)$

$= 2 \times 6x - (3x + 4x)$

$\Rightarrow 2X + 2Y + 2Z - X - 2Y - Z$

$= 12x - 7x$

$\Rightarrow \quad X + Z = 5x$

$\therefore$ X and Z can do a job in $\frac{72x}{5x}$

$= 14\frac{2}{5}$ days.

74. *(b)* Total surface area $= 294\text{ cm}^2$

We know that,

Total surface area $= 6a^2$,

where a = side

$\Rightarrow \quad 294 = 6a^2$

$\Rightarrow \quad 49 = a^2$

$a = 7$ cm

$\therefore$ Volume of cube $= a^3$

$= 7 \times 7 \times 7$

$= 343\text{ cm}^3$

75. *(a)* Let monthly income be ₹ $100x$.

$\therefore$ 60% on family expenses

$= 100x \times \frac{60}{100} =$ ₹ $60x$

10% on medical expenses

$= 100x \times \frac{10}{100} =$ ₹ $10x$

5% on charity $= 100x \times \frac{5}{100} =$ ₹ $5x$

$\therefore$ Remaining salary

$= 100x - (60x + 10x + 5x)$

$=$ ₹ $25x$

According to the question,

Remaining salary = 4000

$\Rightarrow \quad 25x = 4000 \Rightarrow x =$ ₹ 160

$\therefore$ Monthly salary $= 100 \times 160 =$ ₹ 16000

76. *(a)* Narora Nuclear Plant is situated in Uttar Pradesh.

- Kudankulam Nuclear Power Plant is in Tamil Nadu.
- Tarapur Atomic Power Station is in Maharashtra.
- Kaiga Nuclear Power Plant is in Karnataka.

77. *(b)* The correct matching is A-3, B-1, C-4, D-2.

- Blue revolution deals with fish production.
- Yellow revolution deals with oilseeds.
- Round revolution deals with potato.
- Golden revolution deals with horticulture.

78. *(b)* Sardar Vallabhbhai Patel is referred as Iron Man of India.

- Dadabhai Naoroji is called as Grand Old Man of India.
- Bal Gangadhar Tilak is referred as Father of Indian Unrest.
- Raja Ram Mohan Roy is known as the 'Morning Star of the Indian Renaissance'.

79. *(c)* Wavelength range of visible light is approximately between 0.4 to 0.7 μm.

- These waves lie between inferred rays and UV rays in electromagnetic spectrum.
- Visible light waves are the only wavelength that humans can see.

80. *(b)* Terah taali dance belongs to Rajasthan.

- Mohiniattam dance belongs to Kerala.
- Kalbelia dance belongs to Rajasthan.
- Kathak dance belongs to Uttar Pradesh.

81. *(a)* Actuators and sensors enable IoT devices to gather data and exchange it over the network.

82. *(b)* As of January 2023, Shri N Rangaswamy was the CM of Puducherry.

- Velu Narayanasamy is an Indian politician who served as the 10th Chief Minister of Puducherry from 2016 to 2021.
- V. Vaithilingam held the position as 11th Chief Minister of Puducherry from 1991 to 1996 and 16th Chief Minister of Puducherry again from 2008 to 2011.
- P Shanmugam served from 22th March, 2000 to 27th October, 2001.

83. *(c)* In 1949, Indian Constitution declare Hindi in Devanagari script to be the official language of the union.

- The Official Languages Act of 1967 states that English will not be discontinued until all states that have not adopted Hindi as their official language.
- The Act also requires the use of both Hindi and English for official work.

84. *(c)*. As per the Economic Survey of India 2022-23, unemployment rates fell from 5.8% in 2018-19 to 4.2% in 2020-21.

The Economic Survey 2022-23's Social Infrastructure and Employment section highlights that the unemployment rate in India was 76% in 2022-23.

85. *(c)* 'Sandeshe Ate Hai' song was written by Javed Akhtar.

- Irshad Kamil is lyricist of Indian film industry.
- Samir Anjan is also an Indian lyricist.
- Gulzar is an Indian Urdu poet, lyricist, author, screenwriter in Indian film industry.

86. *(b)* The 'Western disturbances' originates from Mediterranean sea.

- It specifically the ones in winter, bring moderate to heavy rain in low-lying areas and heavy snow to mountainous areas of the Indian Subcontinent.
- They are the cause of most winter and post-monsoon season rainfall across Pakistan and North-West India.

87. *(a)* Bails are used in cricket.

Important terminology used in cricket are:

- Powerplay - The initial overs in limited-overs formats where fielding restrictions apply.
- Declaration - The act of a team captain ending their team's innings voluntarily.
- Follow-on - When a team enforces the opponent to bat again without having to bat themselves in the second innings.

88. *(d)* In Gujarat, the Makar Sankranti festival is called Uttarayan.

- The term Uttarayana is derived from two different Sanskrit words-'uttaram' and 'ayanam' -thus indicating the northward movement of the Sun.
- Other Important festival of Gujrat are Rann utsav, Tarnetar, Modhera.

89. *(a)* The reaction of an acid and a metal gives hydrogen gas and salt.

The general word equation for this reaction is metal + acid $\rightarrow$ salt + hydrogen

90. *(d)* The length of a day on Neptune is approximately 16 hours.

- It is the eighth and most distant planet in our Solar System.
- It is dark, cold and has a presence of supersonic winds.

91. *(b)* After being passed by both the Lok Sabha and Rajya Sabha, the Competition (Amendment) Bill, 2023 received the President's assent on 11th April, 2023 to become the Competition (Amendment) Act, 2023.

- It seeks to revise India's current competition law in response to instances of anti-competitive conduct by major corporations.
- The provision for 'settlement and commitment' has been modified.
- The Bill extends the Director General's powers to investigate defilements under the Act.

92. *(c)* Parantaka I defeated the Pandya king Maravarman Rajsimha II in the battle of Vellore.

- Koranganath temple was constructed by the Parantaka I of Medieval Cholas and is dedicated to the god Ranganatha.
- He conquered Madurai from the Pandyas and gave himself the title of 'Maduraikonda', which literally means the captor of Madurai.

93. *(b)* The standard size for a men's basketball is 7 with a circumstance of 29.5 inches (75 cm).

- This is the official size used in NBA, NCAA and other men's professional leagues.
- Basketball is a team sport played between two teams of five players each.

94. *(a)* As of 1st January, 2023, Dr. Manoj Soni is the Chairman of UPSC, his tenure will finish on 15th May, 2029.

- Union Public Service Commission (UPSC) is a constitutional body in India that conducts direct recruitment of officers to the All India Services and the Central Civil Services through examinations.
- The term of office for members of the Union Public Service Commission (UPSC) is six years or until they reach the age of 65, whichever comes first.
- Rose Millian Bathew Kharbuli was the first Indian women Chairman of the UPSC.

95. *(d)* .ppt is used to save MS PowerPoint application.

96. *(d)* The Reserve Bank of India (RBI) sets the Statutory Liquidity Ratio (SLR) for banks in India.

- The SLR is the minimum percentage of deposits that banks must keep in liquid cash, gold or other securities before lending to customers.
- The SLR is calculated as the ratio of a bank's liquid assets to its Net Demand and Time Liabilities (NDTL).
- The Reserve Bank of India was established on 1st April, 1935.
- Its headquarter is located in Mumbai.

97. *(a)* Mando is folk music which is mix of Indian and western Music popular in Goa.

- Maand is a folk singing in Rajasthan that is similar to the Thumri and Ghazal of North Indian music.
- Pai song is from Madhya Pradesh sung in the rainy season to pray for a good monsoon and a good harvest.
- Pawada is a traditional dance form that has its roots in the state of Maharashtra.

98. *(d)* Pusarla Venkata Sindhu won silver medal in badminton in Rio 2016.

- Its motto was 'A New World'.
- Total 207 nations took part.

99. *(a)* Verma committee is related to fundamental duties.

- LM Singhvi Committee was set up for revitalisation of Panchayati Raj.
- Rajamannar Committee was set up examine all aspects of Centre-State relations.

100. *(c)* A writ of prohibition is issued to prevent an inferior court or tribunal from exceeding its jurisdiction, which is not legally vested, or acting without jurisdiction or acting against the principles of natural justice.

Mandamus a judicial writ issued as a command to an inferior court or ordering a person to perform a public or statutory duty.

Set 21 08 July, 2024 (Shift I)

SSC CHSL Tier-I SOLVED PAPER

Instructions

1. This paper contains 100 questions.
2. It has 4 Parts, **Part I** General English, **Part II** General Intelligence & Reasoning, **Part III** Quantitative Aptitude and **Part IV** General Awareness.
3. Each question carries **2 marks.**

Part I
General English

1. The following sentence has been divided into three segments. One of them may contain an adverbial usage error. Select the option that has the segment with the error. If you don't find any error, select 'No error' as your answer.

Mrs. Arunima / speaks / Telugu well.

(a) speaks (b) Mrs. Arunima
(c) Telugu well (d) No error

2. Parts of the following sentence have been given as options. Select the option that contains an error.

According to the encyclopaedia, a oasis is an area which is made fertile by a source of freshwater.

(a) a source of freshwater
(b) a oasis is an area
(c) According to the encyclopaedia,
(d) which is made fertile by

3. The following sentence has been divided into four segments. Identify the segment that contains a grammatical error.

He have / workers from / Ireland and France / in his factory.

(a) in his factory
(b) workers from
(c) Ireland and France
(d) He have

4. Select the most appropriate option that can substitute the underlined segment in the given sentence.

Sarita speaks French <u>best.</u>

(a) worst (b) better
(c) good (d) well

Directions (Q. Nos. 5-9) *In the following passage, some words have been deleted. Read the passage carefully and select the most appropriate option to fill in each blank.*

Family plays a vital role in our lives, serving as a source of love, support and stability. It is (1)……… the family unit that we develop lasting bonds, learn essential values, and find comfort during (2) ……… times. Families provide a nurturing environment for personal growth and emotional well-being. They (3) ……… guidance, share experiences, and create cherished memories. The strength and (4) ……….. of a family contribute to individual happiness, societal harmony, and the (5) ……… of a strong community.

5. Select the most appropriate option to fill in blank (1).

(a) within (b) among
(c) beyond (d) between

6. Select the most appropriate option to fill in blank (2).

(a) joyful (b) challenging
(c) initial (d) wasteful

7. Select the most appropriate option to fill in blank (3).

(a) deliver (b) offer
(c) contribute (d) propose

8. Select the most appropriate option to fill in blank (4).

(a) intrusion (b) cohesion
(c) disruption (d) commotion

9. Select the most appropriate option to fill in blank (5).

(a) foundation
(b) undermining
(c) collision
(d) erosion

10. Select the most appropriate antonym of the given word.

Forbidden

(a) Protected (b) Prevented
(c) Banned (d) Allowed

11. Identify the most appropriate Antonym of the underlined word based on the context of the sentence.

He gave a <u>haughty</u> consent without honouring him with a single word.

(a) proud (b) happy
(c) modest (d) indifferent

12. Select the most appropriate option that can substitute the underlined segment in the given sentence.

We have carried out <u>an successful raid</u> on a fraudulent minister.

(a) the successful raid
(b) successful raid
(c) these successful raid
(d) a successful raid

13. Select the incorrectly spelt word from the given sentence.

They were good-hearted girls, unclean, clothed in rags and profiundly ignorant.

(a) Hearted (b) Profiundly
(c) Unclean (d) Clothed

14. Select the most appropriate homophone to fill in the blank.

The hospital is ……… the river.

(a) buy (b) by (c) bye (d) bi

15. Select the most appropriate synonym of the given word.

Erudite

(a) Humble
(b) Honest
(c) Strong
(d) Educated

16. Select the most appropriate meaning of the given idiom.

Fish out of water

(a) To be out of place
(b) No knowledge of marine life
(c) To die soon
(d) Not good at swimming

17. Select the Incorrectly spelt word.

(a) Comendation (b) Reimbursement
(c) Competition (d) Intertwined

18. Select the most appropriate option to fill in the blank.

The .... today will be cloudy and humid.

(a) wither (b) waiter
(c) weather (d) whether

19. Select the most appropriate option that can substitute the underlined segment in the given sentence.

Yoga may manage pain and <u>helping reduce</u> stress.

(a) help reduction for
(b) helped reduce
(c) help reduced
(d) help in reducing

20. Select the most appropriate option that can substitute the underlined segment in the given sentence.

I like <u>played</u> cricket after school.

(a) playing (b) play
(c) played (d) having to play

21. Select the most appropriate meaning of the given idiom.

Bells and whistles

(a) To take on a difficult task
(b) An innovative development
(c) At a serious disadvantage
(d) Attractive but unnecessary features added to products

22. Select the option that will improve the underlined part of the given sentence. In case no improvement is needed, select 'No improvement'.

Since my friend was not feeling well, she asked me to come over and take care of her.

(a) No improvement
(b) come across
(c) come into
(d) come through

23. Select the most appropriate synonym of the given word.

Injustice

(a) Discrimination (b) Equality
(c) Complacency (d) Demand

24. Select the most appropriate antonym of the given word.

Generous

(a) Needy (b) Mean
(c) Considerate (d) Clever

25. Select the most appropriate option to fill in the blank.

After finishing all my pending assignments, I plan to .... in Goa.

(a) land a meal
(b) forgive a debt
(c) take a holiday
(d) go bankrupt

Part II

General Intelligence

26. What should come in place of the question mark (?) in the given series based on the English alphabetical order?

DFA, HJE, LNI, PRM, ?

(a) UWR (b) TVO
(c) UVP (d) TVQ

27. How many triangles are there in the given figure?

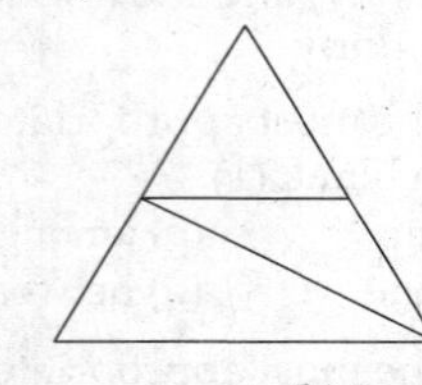

(a) 6 (b) 3
(c) 5 (d) 4

28. In this question, three statements are given, followed by three conclusions numbered I, II and III. Assuming the statements to be true, even if they seem to be at variance with commonly known facts, decide which of the conclusion(s) logically follow(s) from the statements.

Statements

No copper is silver.
All gold is copper.
All aluminium is gold.

Conclusions

I. No aluminium is silver.
II. Some gold is silvers.
III. All aluminium is copper.

(a) Both Conclusions I and II follow
(b) Only Conclusion II follows
(c) Only Conclusion I follows
(d) Both Conclusions I and III follow

29. In a certain code language, 'watch is disturb' is written as 'xr pa qm' and 'don't watch him' is written as 'tu bg pa'. How is 'watch' written in the given language?

(a) pa (b) bg
(c) tu (d) xr

30. Which figure should replace the question mark (?) if the following figure series were to be continued?

Q S B = T	T = Q S B	= Q S T F	F T = Q S	?

Q F T = 3	T = F S Q	T = Q F 3	= S Q F T
(a)	(b)	(c)	(d)

31. In a certain code language,
'A + B' means 'A is the mother of B',
'A − B' means 'A is the daughter of B',
'A × B' means 'A is the husband of B',
'A ÷ B' means 'A is the sister of B'.

Based on the above, how is M related to Q if 'M ÷ N − O × P + Q'?

(a) Mother (b) Daughter
(c) Sister (d) Father's sister

32. What will come in the place of the question mark (?) in the following equation, if '+' and '÷' are interchanged and '−' and '×' are interchanged?

$44 \div 78 + 6 - 3 \times 19 = ?$

(a) 68 (b) 64
(c) 74 (d) 78

33. Choose the alternative which closely resembles the mirror image of the given combination.

A
CAREOF |
B

(a) ꟻOƎЯAↃ (b) FOƎЯAC
(c) ꟻ EOЯAↃ (d) ꟻOƎЯAC

34. What would be the symbol on the opposite side of '@' if the given sheet is folded to form a cube?

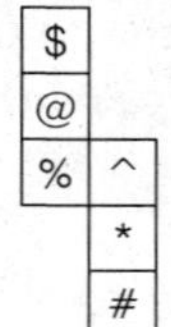

(a) * (b) %
(c) ^ (d) #

35. In a certain code language, 'call on him' is coded as 'ol ni vc' and 'awaiting your call' is coded as 'ni dx sb'. How is 'call' coded in that language?
(a) dx (b) ni (c) sb (d) vc

36. Select the word-pair that best represents a similar relationship to the one expressed in the pair of words given below.
(The words must be considered as meaningful English words and must not be related to each other based on the number of letters/number of consonants/vowels in the word.)
Withdraw : Extract
(a) Exploit : Utilise
(b) Rent : Contrive
(c) Explore : Ignore
(d) Expend : Relish

37. Which of the following numbers will replace the question mark (?) in the given series?
56, ?, 38, 29, 20
(a) 47 (b) 46
(c) 42 (d) 48

38. Each of the letters in the word MUSICAL is arranged in alphabetical order. How many letters are there in the English alphabetical series between the letter which is fourth from the left and the one which is second from the right in the new letter cluster thus formed?
(a) Seven (b) Six
(c) Eight (d) Five

39. Three of the following four are alike in a certain way and thus form a group. Which is the one that does not belong to that group?
(**Note** The odd one out is not based on the number of consonants/ vowels or their position in the letter cluster.)
(a) CEH (b) TVY
(c) PQT (d) LNQ

40. WVSO is related to XXUP in a certain way based on the English alphabetical order. In the same way, ONKG is related to PPMH. To which of the following is VURN related, following the same logic?
(a) WWTO
(b) XXTP
(c) XWSP
(d) XXSP

41. Select the set in which the numbers are related in the same way as are the numbers of the given sets.
(**Note** Operations should be performed on the whole numbers, without breaking down the numbers into its constituent digits. E.g. 13 – Operations on 13 such as adding/subtracting/multiplying etc. to 13 can be performed. Breaking down 13 into 1 and 3 and then performing mathematical operations on 1 and 3 is not allowed.)
(9, 21, 193)
(12, 15, 184)
(a) (29, 6, 170) (b) (24, 8, 192)
(c) (8, 17, 140) (d) (18, 8, 140)

42. If 'A' stands for '÷', 'B' stands for '×', 'C' stands for '+' and 'D' stands for '–', what will come in place of the question mark (?) in the following equation?
88 B 3 D 12 A 4 C 6 = ?
(a) 265 (b) 264
(c) 267 (d) 268

43. If 19th November, 2003 is Wednesday, then what will be the day of the week on 25th March, 2011?
(a) Thursday
(b) Friday
(c) Sunday
(d) Tuesday

44. 4 is related to 64 following a certain logic. Following the same logic, 9 is related to 729. To which of the following is 12 related following the same logic?
(**Note** Operations should be performed on the whole numbers, without breaking down the numbers into its constituent digits. E.g. 13 – Operations on 13 such as adding /deleting /multiplying etc. to 13 can be performed. Breaking down 13 into 1 and 3 and then performing mathematical operations on 1 and 3 is not allowed.)
(a) 1420 (b) 1728
(c) 1788 (d) 1808

45. A square sheet of paper is folded along the dotted line successively along the directions shown and is then punched in the end. How would the paper look when unfolded?

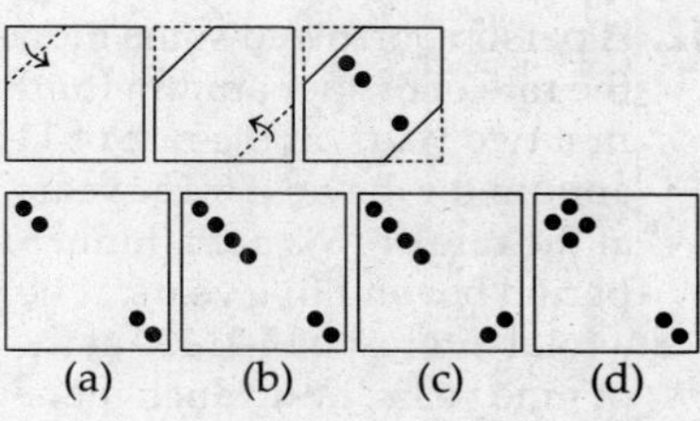

46. A paper is folded and cut as shown below. How will it appear when unfolded?

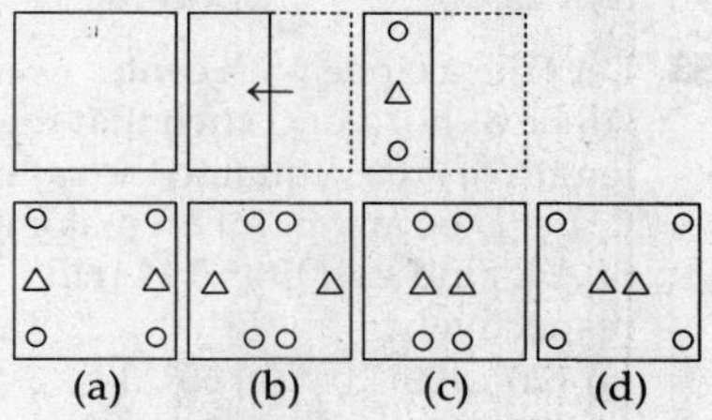

47. What should come in place of the question mark (?) in the given series based on the English alphabetical order?
GEB, JHE, MKH, PNK, ?
(a) SNQ (b) SQN (c) NQS (d) NSQ

48. What should come in place of the question mark (?) in the given series?
56, 53, 50, 47, 44, ?
(a) 41 (b) 43 (c) 42 (d) 40

49. Select the correct mirror image of the given figure when the mirror is placed at MN as shown below.

(a) IRNUƎƆ (b) IRUИƎƆ
(c) IЯИUCE (d) IЯUИƎƆ

50. What will come in the place of '?' in the following equation if '+' and '–' are interchanged and '×' and '÷' are interchanged?
18 ÷ 9 + 24 × 3 – 16 = ?
(a) 450 (b) 170 (c) 678 (d) 980

Part III
Quantitative Aptitude

51. The list price of a hand mixer at a showroom is ₹ 2000 and it is being sold at successive discounts of 15% and 10%. What is its net selling price in rupees?
(a) 1600 (b) 1530 (c) 1560 (d) 1440

52. A person borrowed some money at the rate of 8% per annum for the first two years, at the rate of 11% per annum for the next three years, and at the rate of 16% per annum for the period beyond five years. If he pays a total interest of ₹ 21400 at the end of nine years, how much money did he borrow (round to the nearest unit)?

(a) ₹ 11938 (b) ₹ 18738
(c) ₹ 15938 (d) ₹ 18938

53. Let C be a circle with center O and AB be a chord of C such that the length of AB is equal to the radius of C. Let D be any point on major arc of AB. Find $\angle AOB$ and $\angle ADB$, respectively.

(a) 120°; 100° (b) 60°; 30°
(c) 100°; 80° (d) 90°; 60°

54. A's marks in Mathematics are directly proportional to practice time. In 6 h of practice, A gets 70 marks. What should be the practice time (approximately) to get 90 marks?

(a) 8 h (b) 8.3 h
(c) 7 h (d) 7.7 h

55. Two circles of radii 16 cm and 4 cm, respectively, touch each other externally at point A. PQ is the direct common tangent of these circles with centres C_1 and C_2, respectively. What is the length of PQ?

(a) 15 cm (b) 20 cm
(c) 16 cm (d) 18 cm

56. Study the given graph carefully and answer the question that follows. The graph shows the demand and production of different companies.

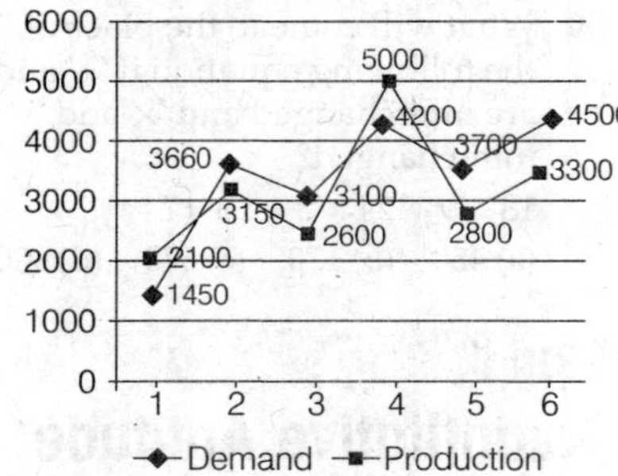

The ratio between the companies having more production than demand and more demand than the production is

(a) 2 : 1 (b) 1 : 4
(c) 4 : 1 (d) 1 : 2

57. An interval of 2 h 25 min is wrongly estimated by 2 h 30.5 min. The error percentage is

(a) $3\frac{23}{29}\%$ (b) $2\frac{27}{29}\%$
(c) $3\frac{19}{29}\%$ (d) $2\frac{21}{29}\%$

58. How many numbers between 10 and 65 are divisible by 2, 3 and 4?

(a) 3 (b) 7
(c) 9 (d) 5

59. A shopkeeper charges his customer 14% more than the cost price. If a customer paid ₹ 18240 for a mobile phone, then the cost price of the mobile phone was

(a) ₹ 20793.60
(b) ₹ 15686.40
(c) ₹ 16600
(d) ₹ 16000

60. The given pie-diagram shows the expenditure incurred on the preparation of a book by a publisher, under various heads. Study the pie-diagram and answer the question that follows.

Various Expenditures (in percentage) incurred in Publishing a Book

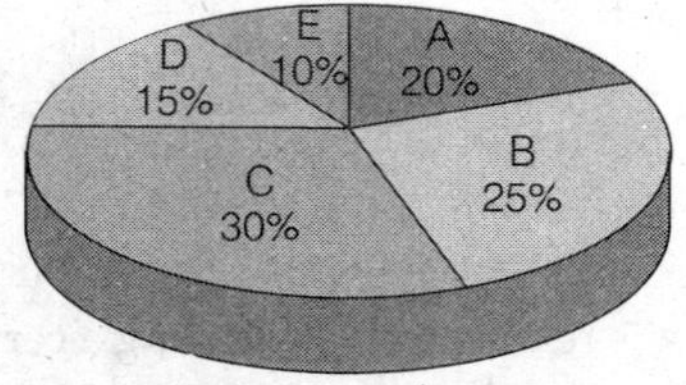

The marked price of a book is 20% more than the CP. If the marked price of the book is ₹ 30, then what is the cost of paper used in a single copy of the book?

(a) ₹ 5 (b) ₹ 4.50
(c) ₹ 6.50 (d) ₹ 6

61. A father is presently 3 times his daughter's age. After 10 yr, he will be twice as old as her. Find the daughter's present age.

(a) 5 yr (b) 10 yr (c) 20 yr (d) 15 yr

62. The weights of the five friends are 67 kg, 85 kg, 70 kg, 90 kg and 103 kg. Find the average of their weights in kg.

(a) 83 (b) 87 (c) 80 (d) 90

63. In a triangle ABC, D and E are two points on sides AB and AC, respectively, such that DE is parallel to BC and $AD : DB = 3 : 5$. If $AC = 5.6$ cm, then find the value (in cm) of AE.

(a) 2.3 (b) 2.1
(c) 1.9 (d) 2.5

64. If $\cot A = \frac{5}{12}$, then find the value of $\frac{\sqrt{\sec A - \operatorname{cosec} A}}{\sqrt{\sec A + \operatorname{cosec} A}} - \sqrt{\frac{17}{7}}$.

(a) $\frac{24}{\sqrt{119}}$ (b) 0
(c) $-\frac{10}{\sqrt{119}}$ (d) $\frac{10}{\sqrt{119}}$

65. The given table shows the number of entertainment shows (in hundreds) held in various cities. Study the table and answer the question that follows.

City	Entertainment Shows (in hundreds)				
	A	B	C	D	E
M	15	21	24	0.8	0.9
N	12.4	13	26	2	0.5
O	5.7	8	12	0.3	0.2
P	11.3	6	18	1	1.5
Q	17	12.4	11	3	0.4
R	14	10.5	9.8	0.7	0.1

What is the average number of entertainment shows held in city P?

(a) 766 (b) 756
(c) 750 (d) 700

66. A solid sphere of radius 8 cm is melted and then recast into small spherical balls each of diameter 4 cm. Find the number of balls thus obtained $\left(\text{use } \pi = \frac{22}{7}\right)$.

(a) 48 (b) 64
(c) 24 (d) 32

67. Antony and Julie can simultaneously complete a work of floor decoration in 15 days and Julie alone in 20 days. In how many days can Antony alone complete the work of floor decoration?

(a) 55 (b) 45
(c) 50 (d) 60

68. If the radius of a sphere is increased by 5%, then by what percentage will the surface area of the sphere increase?

(a) 13.25% (b) 11.25%
(c) 10.25% (d) 15.25%

69. Simplify the following expression.
$4 \times 7 - 3\{7 \times 4 \div (6 \times 2)\}$
(a) 21 (b) 4 (c) 19 (d) 12

70. The price of a car is decreased by 15% and 20% in two successive years respectively. What percentage of the price of the car is decreased after two years?
(a) 32% (b) 25%
(c) 46% (d) 15%

71. A policeman is chasing a thief at a speed of 12 km/h, and the thief is running at a speed of 8 km/h. If the policeman started 30 min late, find the time taken by the policeman to catch the thief.
(a) 120 min (b) 60 min
(c) 90 min (d) 100 min

72. The average of the areas of two similar triangles is 706.5 m^2 whose perimeters are in the ratio of 6 : 11. What is 20% of the difference (in m^2) in areas of both triangles?
(a) 157 (b) 149
(c) 153 (d) 164

73. The perimeter of a rectangle is 70 cm and its diagonal is 25 cm. The area of the rectangle is
(a) 425 cm^2 (b) 300 cm^2
(c) 625 cm^2 (d) 420 cm^2

74. If the price of rice is reduced by 24%, it enables Alok to buy 10 kg more rice for ₹ 2500. The reduced rate of rice per kg is
(a) ₹ 25 (b) ₹ 50
(c) ₹ 60 (d) ₹ 75

75. Study the given pie-charts and answer the question that follows. The pie-charts show the characteristics of foreign tourists visiting India during a given year.

Countrywise distribution

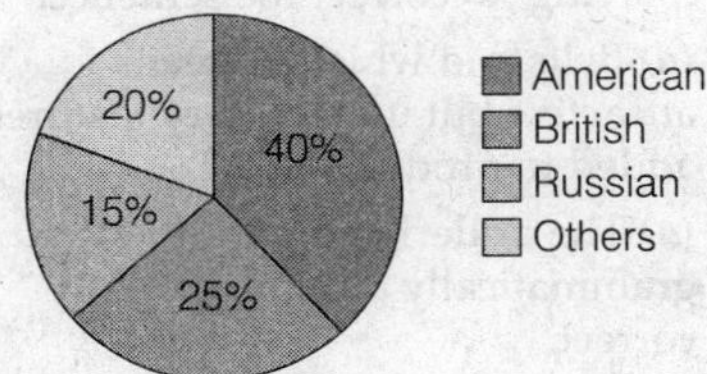

Agewise Distribution

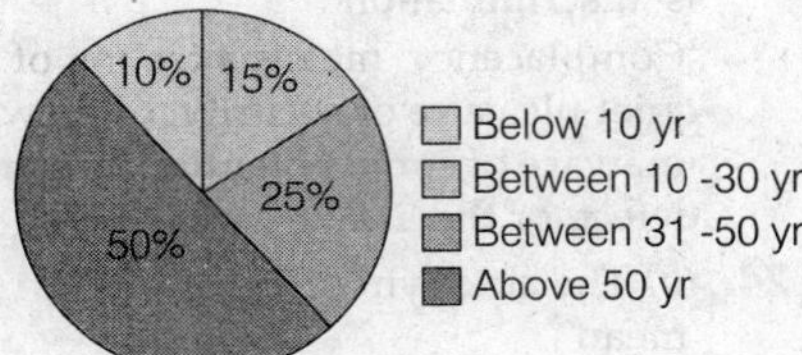

If in a given year, 250000 tourists visited India and the agewise distribution of data applies to all the countries, then the number of Russian tourists who visited India during the year and were in the age group above 50 yr is
(a) 3850 (b) 385
(c) 375 (d) 3750

Part IV
General Awareness

76. According to the Census of India 2011, which state has the lowest population growth rate?
(a) Jharkhand (b) Punjab
(c) Uttar Pradesh (d) Nagaland

77. In 2023, Praveen Chithravel won the men's triple jump event at the 'Prueba de Confrontacion' athletics meet held in ....
(a) Canada (b) Cuba
(c) Brazil (d) Portugal

78. Which is the waterbody that separates Andaman Islands and Nicobar Islands?
(a) Eight Degree Channel
(b) Nine Degree Channel
(c) Ten Degree Channel
(d) Eleven Degree Channel

79. According to the Census 2011 of India, which metropolitan has the second highest population?
(a) Kolkata (b) Mumbai
(c) Chennai (d) Delhi

80. Which article provides that all minorities have the right to establish and administer educational institutions of their choice?
(a) Article 26 (b) Article 24
(c) Article 32 (d) Article 30

81. What is the IUPAC name of the compound CH_3NH_2?
(a) Propan-1-amine
(b) Methanamine
(c) 2-Methyl propan-1-amine
(d) Ethanamine

82. As of March 2024, who is the minister of the Ministry of Cooperation, Government of India?
(a) Smriti Zubin Irani
(b) Amit Shah
(c) Dharmendra Pradhan
(d) Nitin Gadkari

83. Which amongst the following statements is correct about Mughal emperor Akbar?
(a) He was declared emperor in 1602.
(b) He founded a new religion called 'Din-e Ilahi'.
(c) He was highly educated and knew many languages.
(d) He fought and won the Third Battle of Panipat against the Hindu king Hemu.

84. Which of the following is an example of system software?
(a) Windows operating system
(b) Adobe Photoshop
(c) Microsoft Word
(d) Google Chrome

85. What is the duration of single round in free style wrestling?
(a) 2 min (b) 3.5 min
(c) 3 min (d) 2.5 min

86. Which of the following teams won the 9th Pro Kabaddi League 2022?
(a) Puneri Paltan
(b) Jaipur Pink Panthers
(c) Bengaluru Bulls
(d) UP Yoddhas

87. Name the web portal launched by the Department of Telecommunication sharing information on mobile towers and EMF Emission Compliances.
(a) Bharat Net
(b) National Optical Fibre Network
(c) Tarang Sanchar
(d) Bharat Sanchar

88. Which South-Eastern Dravidian language has been approved by Odisha state to be included in the Eighth Schedule of the Constitution of India on 10th July, 2023?
(a) Tulu (b) Kodagu
(c) Kui (d) Malto

89. Who was the first to develop a mathematical predictive heliocentric model of the solar system?
(a) Pierre-Simon Laplace
(b) Immanuel Kant
(c) Galileo Galilei
(d) Nicolaus Copernicus

90. Brahmo Samaj was earlier known as
(a) Veda Samaj
(b) Prarthana Samaj
(c) Arya Samaj
(d) Bramho Sabha

91. Which of the following committees recommended the inclusion of Fundamental Duties in the Constitution of India?
(a) Balwant Rai Mehta Committee
(b) Sarkaria Committee
(c) Swaran Singh Committee
(d) Raja Mannar Committee

92. What happens in case of market equilibrium?
1. Market demand = Market supply
2. There is no excess supply in the market.

Codes
(a) Neither (1) nor (2)
(b) Only (1)
(c) Both (1) and (2)
(d) Only (2)

93. Bhavai is a dance form that belongs to which of the following states?
(a) Rajasthan (b) Odisha
(c) Madhya Pradesh
(d) Bihar

94. Mahavir Jayanti celebrates the birthday of Lord Mahavira who is the .... Tirthankara of Jainism.
(a) 25th (b) 26th (c) 23rd (d) 24th

95. Which of the following causes enlargement and extension growth of cells?
(a) Imbibition
(b) Pressure potential
(c) Osmotic pressure
(d) Turgor pressure

96. In July 2021, which of the following persons declared herself/himself brand ambassador of 'Khadi Prakritik Paint', made from cow dung by the Khadi and Village Industries Commission?
(a) Nitin Gadkari
(b) Nirmala Sitharaman
(c) Narendra Singh Tomar
(d) Rajnath Singh

97. In which year was the Marris College of Music established in India?
(a) 1919 (b) 1901 (c) 1926 (d) 1922

98. In MS Word, which option allows you to insert a new column in a table while simultaneously shifting the existing columns to the right?
(a) Insert Column to the Right
(b) Insert Columns
(c) Insert Table
(d) Insert Column to the Left

99. Which of the following is not a part of Carnatic music?
(a) Varnam (b) Dhrupad
(c) Pallavi (d) Charana

100. According to the Department of Industrial Policy and Promotion, which of the following is not a major industry?
(a) Electricity (b) Jute
(c) Fertiliser (d) Crude oil

Answers

1. (d)	2. (b)	3. (d)	4. (d)
5. (a)	6. (b)	7. (b)	8. (b)
9. (a)	10. (d)	11. (c)	12. (d)
13. (b)	14 (b)	15. (d)	16. (a)
17. (a)	18. (c)	19. (d)	20. (a)
21. (d)	22. (a)	23. (a)	24. (b)
25. (c)	26. (d)	27. (c)	28. (d)
29. (a)	30. (c)	31. (c)	32. (b)
33. (a)	34. (a)	35. (b)	36. (a)
37. (a)	38. (b)	39. (c)	40. (a)
41. (c)	42. (c)	43. (b)	44. (b)
45. (b)	46. (c)	47. (b)	48. (a)
49. (d)	50. (b)	51. (b)	52. (d)
53. (b)	54. (d)	55. (c)	56. (d)
57. (a)	58. (d)	59. (d)	60. (a)
61. (b)	62. (a)	63. (b)	64. (c)
65. (b)	66. (b)	67. (d)	68. (c)
69. (a)	70. (a)	71. (b)	72. (c)
73. (b)	74. (c)	75. (d)	76. (d)
77. (b)	78. (c)	79. (d)	80. (d)
81. (b)	82. (b)	83. (b)	84. (a)
85. (c)	86. (b)	87. (c)	88. (c)
89. (d)	90. (d)	91. (c)	92. (c)
93. (a)	94. (d)	95. (d)	96. (a)
97. (c)	98. (a)	99. (b)	100. (b)

Explanations

1. *(d)* The given sentence is grammatically correct and contextually meaningful.

2. *(b)* Part (b) 'a oasis is an area' contains an error. Use 'an' to correct the sentence.

3. *(d)* Part (d) 'He have' contains an error. Use 'has' to correct the sentence. The subject of the given sentence is singular, the singular verb should be used.

4. *(d)* The underlined part of the given sentence contains an error. Use 'well' to correct the sentence as the sentence needs an adverb and not an adjective.

5. *(a)* The correct filler for the given blank is 'within'.

6. *(b)* The correct filler for the given blank is 'challenging'.

7. *(b)* The correct filler for the given blank is 'offer'.

8. *(b)* The correct filler for the given blank is 'cohesion'.

9. *(a)* The correct filler for the given blank is 'foundation'.

10. *(d)* Forbidden means not allowed to do something. Hence, its antonym is 'allowed'.

11. *(c)* 'Haughty' means arrogant. Hence, its antonym is 'modest' which means 'kind and polite'.

12. *(d)* The underlined part of the given sentence contains an error. Use 'a successful raid' to correct the sentence.

13. *(b)* The incorrectly spelt word is 'profiundly'. The correct spelling is 'profoundly'.

14. *(b)* The correct filler for the given blank 'by'.

15. *(d)* The word 'erudite' means 'educated'.

16. *(a)* Fish out of water means to be out of place.

17. *(a)* The incorrectly spelt word is 'comendation'. The correct spelling is 'commendation'.

18. *(c)* The correct filler for the given blank is 'weather'.

19. *(d)* The underlined part of the given sentence contains an error. Use 'help in reducing' to correct the sentence.

20. *(a)* The underlined part of the given sentence contains an error. Use 'playing' to correct the sentence.

21. *(d)* Bells and whistles means attractive but unnecessary features added to products.

22. *(a)* The underlined part is grammatically and contextually correct.

23. *(a)* The nearest synonym of 'injustice' is 'discrimination'.
'Complacency' means a feeling of quiet pleasure or security, often while unaware of some potential danger, defect, or the like.

24. *(b)* The antonym of 'generous' is 'mean'.

25. *(c)* The correct filler for the given blank is 'take a holiday'.

26. *(d)* The pattern of the series is as shown below,

D $\xrightarrow{+4}$ H $\xrightarrow{+4}$ L $\xrightarrow{+4}$ P $\xrightarrow{+4}$ [T]

F $\xrightarrow{+4}$ J $\xrightarrow{+4}$ N $\xrightarrow{+4}$ R $\xrightarrow{+4}$ [V]

A $\xrightarrow{+4}$ E $\xrightarrow{+4}$ I $\xrightarrow{+4}$ M $\xrightarrow{+4}$ [Q]

∴ ? = TVQ

27. *(c)* Naming of the figure,

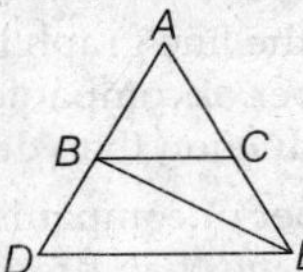

There are total 5 triangles,

ΔABC, ΔBCE, ΔBDE, ΔABE and ΔADE.

28. *(d)* According to the statements,

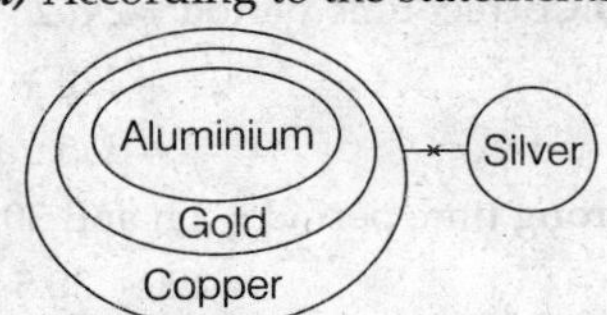

Conclusions

I. (✓) II. (✗) III. (✓)

Hence, both Conclusions I and III follow.

29. *(a)* According to the question,

[watch] is disturb → xr [pa] qm

don't [watch] him → tu bg [pa]

Hence, 'watch' is coded as 'pa'.

30. *(c)* The pattern of the series is as shown below,

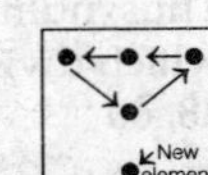

From fig. (1) to (2) and fig. (3) to (4)

From fig. (2) to (3) and fig. (4) to (5)

According to this option figure (c) is the correct answer.

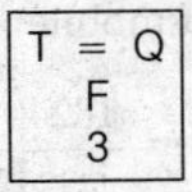

T = Q
F
3

31. *(c)* Given expression,

M ÷ N – O × P + Q

According to the question,

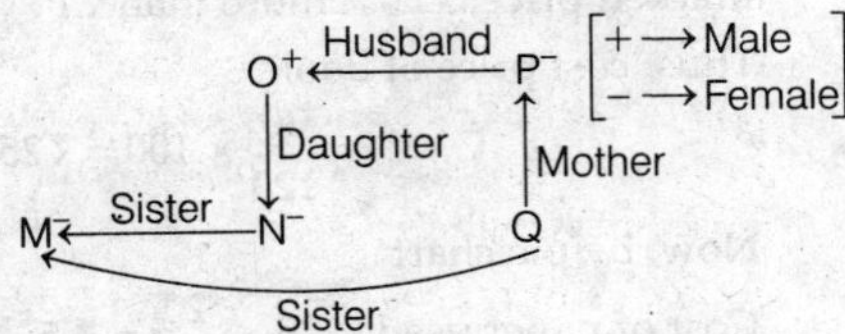

Hence, 'M' is the sister of 'Q'.

32. *(b)* Given expression,

44 ÷ 78 + 6 – 3 × 19 = ?

After interchanging + and ÷ , – and × we get,

⇒ 44 + 78 ÷ 6 × 3 – 19 = ?

⇒ 44 + 13 × 3 – 19 = ?

⇒ 44 + 39 – 19 = ?

⇒ 44 + 20 = ?

∴ ? = 64

33. *(a)* The mirror image of given question figure is as shown below,

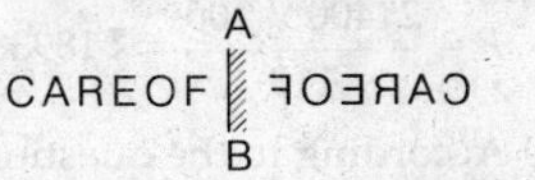

A

CAREOF | FOERAC (mirror)

B

34. *(a)* According to the question,

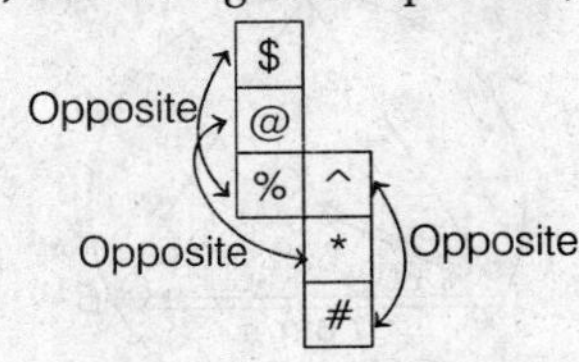

∴ '*' would be opposite side of '@'.

35. *(b)* According to the question,

(call) on him —— ol (ni) vc

awaiting your (call) —— (ni) dx sb

Hence, 'call' is coded as 'ni'.

36. *(a)* As, 'withdraw' and 'extract' are synonyms of each other.

Similarly, 'exploit' and 'utiise' are synonyms of each other.

37. *(a)* The pattern of the series is as follows,

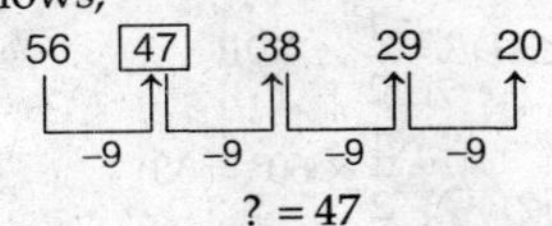

∴ ? = 47

38. *(b)* Given word → MUSICAL

Arranging the letters of word according to English alphabetical series, it becomes

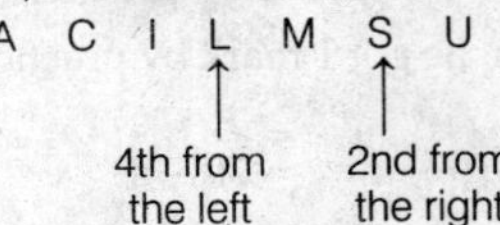

∴ Required number of letters

= S – L – 1

= 19 – 12 – 1 = 6

39. *(c)* As,

C E H (+2, +3) T V Y (+2, +3)

[P Q T] (+1, +3) L N Q (+2, +3)

Hence, PQT is not belong to the group.

40. *(a)* As,

W V S O (+1, +2, +2, +1) → X X U P

and

O N K G (+1, +2, +2, +1) → P P M H

Similarly,

V U R N (+1, +2, +2, +1) → [W W T O]

41. *(c)* Logic here is,

[First number × Second number] + 4 = Third number

As, (9, 21, 193)

→ [9 × 21] + 4 = 189 + 4 = 193

and, (12, 15, 184)

→ [12 × 15] + 4 = 180 + 4 = 184

Similarly,

(8, 17, 140)

→ [8 × 17] + 4 = 136 + 4 = 140

42. *(c)* Given equation,

88 B 3 D 12 A 4 C 6 = ?

After substituting the letters with symbols respectively, we get

88 × 3 – 12 ÷ 4 + 6 = ?

⇒ 264 – 3 + 6 = ?

⇒ 270 – 3 = ?

∴ ? = 267

43. *(b)* Given, 19th November, 2003 → Wednesday

25th March, 2011 → ?

The number of odd days from 19th November, 2003 to 19th November, 2010

Years → 2004 + 2005 + 2006 + 2007 + 2008 + 2009 + 2010

Odd days → 2 + 1 + 1 + 1 + 2 + 1 + 1

$= \frac{9}{7} = 2$ odd days

Now, the number of odd days from 19th November, 2010 to 25th March, 2011

Months → November + December + January + February + March

Odd days → 11 + 31 + 31 + 28 + 25

$= \frac{126}{7} = 0$ odd days

∴ Required day = Wednesday + 2

= Friday

44. *(b)* As, $(4)^3 = 64$

and $(9)^3 = 729$

Similarly, $(12)^3 = 1728$

45. *(b)* When the paper is unfolded, it would look like option figure (b).

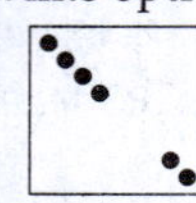

46. *(c)* When the paper is unfolded, it would look like option figure (c).

○ ○
△ △
○ ○

47. *(b)* The pattern of the series is as follows,

G $\xrightarrow{+3}$ J $\xrightarrow{+3}$ M $\xrightarrow{+3}$ P $\xrightarrow{+3}$ S

E $\xrightarrow{+3}$ H $\xrightarrow{+3}$ K $\xrightarrow{+3}$ N $\xrightarrow{+3}$ Q

B $\xrightarrow{+3}$ E $\xrightarrow{+3}$ H $\xrightarrow{+3}$ K $\xrightarrow{+3}$ N

$\therefore$? = SQN

48. *(a)* The pattern of the series is as follows,

56 53 50 47 44 41

−3 −3 −3 −3 −3

$\therefore$? = 41

49. *(d)* The correct mirror image of given question figure is as shown below,

M
CEUNRI | IRNUEC
N

50. *(b)* Given equation,

$18 \div 9 + 24 \times 3 - 16 = ?$

After interchanging + and −, × and ÷ we get,

$\Rightarrow 18 \times 9 - 24 \div 3 + 16 = ?$

$\Rightarrow 162 - 8 + 16 = ?$

$\Rightarrow 154 + 16 = ?$

$\therefore ? = 170$

51. *(b)* Given, list price = ₹2000

Successive discounts = 15% and 10%

$\therefore$ Net effective discount

$= \left(-a - b + \frac{ab}{100}\right)\%$

$= \left(-15 - 10 + \frac{150}{100}\right)\%$

$= (-25 + 1.5)\%$

$= -23.5\%$

= 23.5% discount

$\therefore$ Net selling price $= 2000 \times \frac{76.5}{100}$

= ₹1530

52. *(d)* Let the money initially borrowed be ₹P.

We know that, $SI = \frac{P \times R \times T}{100}$

According to the question,

$$21400 = \frac{P \times 8 \times 2}{100} + \frac{P \times 11 \times 3}{100} + \frac{P \times 16 \times 4}{100}$$

$\Rightarrow 16P + 33P + 64P = 21400 \times 100$

$\Rightarrow 113P = 21400 \times 100$

$\therefore P = \frac{21400 \times 100}{113} =$ ₹18938

53. *(b)* According to the question,

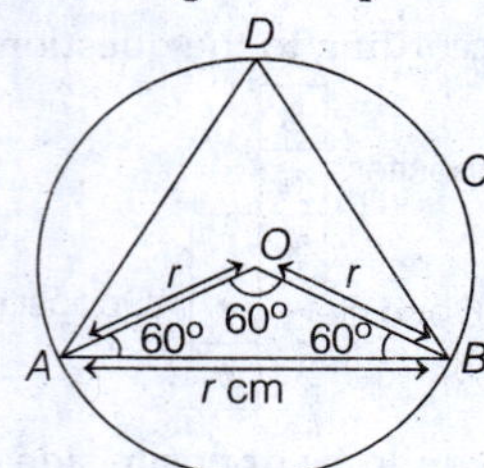

Given,

Chord $AB = OA = OB$

$\therefore \Delta OAB$ is an equilateral triangle.

$\therefore \angle OAB = \angle OBA = \angle AOB = 60°$

We know that,

angle subtended at the centre is twice the angle subtended by the same arc at any other remaining part of the circle.

$\therefore \angle AOB = 2\angle ADB$

$\therefore \angle ADB = \frac{1}{2}\angle AOB$

$= \frac{1}{2} \times 60° = 30°$

Hence, the angles are 60° and 30° respectively.

54. *(d)* Marks ∝ Practice time

He got 70 marks by practicing 6 h.

Then, he got 1 mark by practicing

$= \frac{6}{70}$ h

Then, he got 90 marks by practicing

$= \frac{6}{70} \times 90 = \frac{54}{7} = 7.7$ h

55. *(c)* Radii of circles are 16 cm and 4 cm.

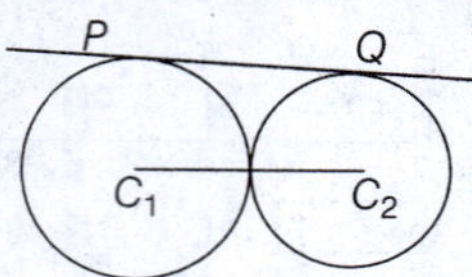

Distance between C_1 and C_2

$= 16 + 4 = 20$ cm

Length of common tangent

$= \sqrt{d^2 - (r_2 - r_1)^2}$

$= \sqrt{(20)^2 - (16 - 4)^2}$

$= \sqrt{(20)^2 - (12)^2}$

$= \sqrt{400 - 144}$

$= \sqrt{256} = 16$ cm

$\therefore$ Hence, required length of common tangent is 16 cm.

56. *(d)* From the line graph it is observed that number of companies having more production than demand = 2

and number of companies having more demand than production = 4

Thus, required ratio = 2 : 4

= 1 : 2

57. *(a)* Correct time period = 2 h 25 min

= 120 + 25

= 145 min

Wrong time period = 2 h and 30.5 min

= 120 + 30.5

= 150.5

Hence, error percentage

$= \frac{150.5 - 145}{145} \times 100$

$= \frac{5.5}{145} \times 100$

$= \frac{550}{145} = \frac{110}{29}$

$= 3\frac{23}{29}\%$

58. *(d)* LCM of 2, 3 and 4 = 12

Thus, numbers between 10 and 65 which divisible by 12 are 12, 24, 36, 48, 60

Thus, there are total 5 numbers.

59. *(d)* Customer paid for mobile

= ₹18240

According to the question,

Cost price of mobile $\times \frac{114}{100} =$ ₹18240

CP of mobile $= \frac{18240 \times 100}{114}$

$\therefore$ CP of mobile = ₹16000

60. *(a)* Marked price of the book = ₹30

Marked price is 20% more than CP.

Thus, cost price of book

$= \frac{30}{120} \times 100 =$ ₹25

Now, by pie chart

Cost of paper used $= 25 \times \frac{20}{100} =$ ₹5

61. (b) Let the daughter's age be x yr at present, then, father's age be $(3x)$ yr.

After 10 yr,

$\Rightarrow \quad (3x + 10) = 2(x + 10)$

$\Rightarrow \quad 3x + 10 = 2x + 20$

$\therefore \quad x = 10$ yr

Thus, present age of daughter is 10 yr.

62. (a) Sum of weight of all the five friends

$= (67 + 85 + 70 + 90 + 103)$

$= 415$ kg

$\therefore$ Average of their weight

$= \frac{415}{5} = 83$ kg

63. (b) Here, ABC is a triangle.

$DE \parallel BC$ and $AD : DB = 3 : 5$ and $AC = 5.6$ cm,

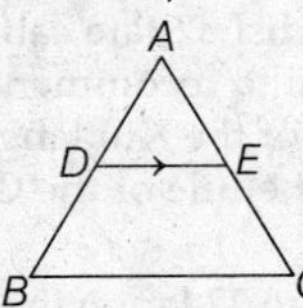

As we know,

ΔADE is similar to ΔABC.

Thus, by BPT theorem

$$\frac{AD}{AB} = \frac{3}{3+5} = \frac{3}{8} = \frac{AE}{AC}$$

Here, $AC = 5.6$ cm

$\Rightarrow \quad \frac{AE}{AC} = \frac{3}{8}$

$\Rightarrow \quad \frac{AE}{5.6} = \frac{3}{8}$

$\Rightarrow \quad AE = \frac{5.6 \times 3}{8}$

$\Rightarrow \quad AE = 0.7 \times 3 = 2.1$ cm

64. (c) Given, $\cot A = \frac{5}{12}$

$$\frac{\sqrt{\sec A - \operatorname{cosec} A}}{\sqrt{\sec A + \operatorname{cosec} A}} - \sqrt{\frac{17}{7}}$$

On dividing by $\sec A$ in first term, we get

$$= \sqrt{\frac{1 - \cot A}{1 + \cot A}} - \sqrt{\frac{17}{7}}$$

$$= \sqrt{\frac{1 - \frac{5}{12}}{1 + \frac{5}{12}}} - \sqrt{\frac{17}{7}}$$

$$= \sqrt{\frac{7}{17}} - \sqrt{\frac{17}{7}}$$

$$= \frac{7 - 17}{\sqrt{119}}$$

$$= \frac{-10}{\sqrt{119}}$$

65. (b) Average number of entertainment shows held in city P

$$= \frac{11.3 + 6 + 18 + 1 + 1.5}{5}$$

$$= 7.56 = 7.56 \times 100 = 756$$

66. (b) Given, radius of larger sphere $(R) = 8$ cm

Radius of smaller sphere $(r) = \frac{4}{2}$ cm

$= 2$ cm

We know that,

Volume of sphere $= \frac{4}{3}\pi$ (radius)^3

$\therefore$ Number of balls

$$= \frac{\text{Volume of larger sphere}}{\text{Volume of smaller sphere}}$$

$$= \frac{\frac{4}{3}\pi R^3}{\frac{4}{3}\pi r^3}$$

$$= \frac{R^3}{r^3} = \frac{(8)^3}{(2)^3} = 64$$

67. (d) Antony and Julie's one day work

$$= \frac{1}{15}$$

Julie's one day work $= \frac{1}{20}$

$\therefore$ Antony's one day work

$$= \frac{1}{15} - \frac{1}{20} = \frac{1}{60}$$

$\therefore$ Antony complete the work in 60 days.

68. (c) Given,

percentage increase = 5%

Effective percentage increase in surface area $= \left(a + b + \frac{ab}{100}\right)\%$

$$= \left(5 + 5 + \frac{5 \times 5}{100}\right)\%$$

$= 10.25\%$

69. (a) $4 \times 7 - 3 \{7 \times 4 \div (6 \times 2)\}$

By using BODMAS rule,

$= 28 - 3 \{7 \times 4 \div 12\}$

$= 28 - 3\left(\frac{7}{3}\right)$

$= 28 - 7$

$= 21$

70. (a) $x = -15\%$

$y = -20\%$

Total (Net) percentage decrease after two years $= x + y + \frac{xy}{100}$

$$= -15 - 20 + \frac{(-15) \times (-20)}{100}$$

$$= -35 + \frac{300}{100} = -35 + 3 = -32\%$$

$\therefore$ Required percentage decrease in price of car is 32%.

71. (b) Let the distance be D km.

According to the question,

$$\frac{D}{8} - \frac{D}{12} = \frac{30}{60} \Rightarrow \frac{D}{24} = \frac{1}{2}$$

$\therefore \quad D = 12$ km

Time taken by police $= \frac{\text{Distance}}{\text{Speed}} = \frac{12}{12}$

$= 1$ h $= 60$ min

72. (c) Given,

Average of the areas of two similar triangle $= 706.5$ m^2

Perimeter ratio = 6 : 11

In two similar triangle,

We know that,

$$\frac{\text{Area of first triangle}}{\text{Area of second triangle}} = \left(\frac{\text{Perimeter of first triangle}}{\text{Perimeter of second triangle}}\right)^2$$

$$\frac{\text{Area of first triangle}}{\text{Area of second triangle}} = \left(\frac{6}{11}\right)^2 = \frac{36}{121}$$

Let area of first triangle $= 36x$ m^2 and area of second triangle $= 121x$ m^2

We have,

average of area = 706.5

$\Rightarrow \quad \frac{121x + 36x}{2} = 706.5$

$\Rightarrow \quad 157x = 706.5 \times 2$

$\therefore \quad x = 9$

$\therefore$ Difference of area $= 121x - 36x$

$= 85x = 85 \times 9 = 765$ m^2

$\therefore$ 20% of difference $= \frac{20}{100} \times 765$

$= 153$ m^2

73. (b) Let length be l and breadth be b.

We know that,

Diagonal $= \sqrt{l^2 + b^2}$

$\Rightarrow \quad (25)^2 = l^2 + b^2$

$\Rightarrow \quad l^2 + b^2 = 625 \quad \ldots$(i)

We know that,

Perimeter of rectangle = 70 cm

$\Rightarrow \quad 2(l + b) = 70$

$\Rightarrow \quad l + b = 35 \quad \ldots$(ii)

We know that,

$(l - b)^2 + (l + b)^2 = 2(l^2 + b^2)$

Put the value from Eqs. (i) and (ii),

$(l-b)^2 + (35)^2 = 2(625)$

$\Rightarrow \quad (l-b)^2 = 25$

$\Rightarrow \quad l - b = 5 \quad \ldots(iii)$

On solving Eqs. (ii) and (iii),

$l = 20$ and $b = 15$

We know that,

Area of triangle $= l \times b$

$= 20 \times 15 = 300 \text{ cm}^2$

74. *(c)* We have,

New price of Rice $= \frac{2500}{10} \times 24\%$

$= \frac{2500}{10} \times \frac{24}{100}$

$= \frac{5}{2} \times 24 =$ ₹ 60

75. *(d)* Number of Russians who visited India

$= 250000 \times \frac{15}{100} = 37500$

Russians who visited India during the year and were in the age group above 50 yr

$= \frac{37500 \times 10}{100} = 3750$

76. *(d)* According to the Census of India 2011, Nagaland has the lowest population growth rate.

- Nagaland was the only Indian state which had negative growth rate of – 0.58% in Census 2011.
- Meghalaya has registered the highest decadal growth rate during 2001-11 (27.80%).
- India's decadal growth rate was 17.70%.

77. *(b)* In 2023, Praveen Chithravel won the men's triple jump event at the 'Prueba de Confrontacion' athletics meet held in Cuba.

- He surpassed the previous men's triple jump national record of 17.30 m by touching the mark of 17.37 m.
- He also beat the Asian Games 2023 qualifying standard of 16.60 m set by Athletic Federation of India.

78. *(c)* The Ten Degree Channel separates Andaman Islands and Nicobar Islands.

- It is 150 km wide from North to South with minimum depth of 7.3 m.
- Eight Degree Channel is between India and Maldives.
- Nine Degree Channel separates Minicoy Island from the main Lakshadweep archipelago.

79. *(d)* Acording to Census 2011 of India, Delhi is the second most populated metropolitan.

- Mumbai is the most populated metropolitan and Kolkata is the third most populated metropolitan in India.
- Delhi is the capital of India while Mumbai is the financial capital of India.

80. *(d)* Article 30 provides that all minorities have right to establish and administer educational institutions of their choice.

- Article 30 is the part of the Fundamental Rights.
- The Fundamental Rights are in Part III (Articles 12 to 35) of the Constitution of India.

81. *(b)* The IUPAC name of the compound CH_3NH_2 is methanamine.

82. *(b)* As of March 2024, Amit Shah was the minister of the Ministry of Cooperation, Government of India.

- After the general election 2024, Shri Amit Shah again made the minister of Ministry of Cooperation.
- Ministry of Cooperation was formed in 2021.

83. *(b)* Statment (b) is correct regarding Mughal emperor Akbar because he founded a new religious called 'Din-e-Ilahi'.

- Akbar was declared Emperor in year 1556.
- Akbar was not educated, he was not formally literate.
- Akbar fought Second Battle of Panipat in which he defeated Hindu king Hemu.

84. *(a)* Windows operating system is an example of system software. Adobe Photoshop, Microsoft Word and Google Chrome are application software.

85. *(c)* The duration of the single round in free style is 3 minutes.

- A free style wrestling bout is divided into two periods of three minutes each with a 30-second break in between.
- Antim Pangal, Vinesh Phogat, Anshu Malik, Nisha Dahiya and Ritika Hooda are the five female Indian wrestlers in the 2024 Olympic, while among males only Aman Sehrawat is contender.

86. *(b)* Jaipur Pink Panthers won the 9th Pro Kabaddi League 2022.

- Kabaddi is basically played with seven players each side, for a period of 40 minutes with 5 minutes break.
- In Pro kabaddi League, there are 12 teams.
- Puneri Paltan won the Pro Kabaddi League 2024.

87. *(c)* The name of the web portal is Tarang Sanchar.

- The portal will help users to view mobile towers in any locality.
- The user can also seek information on the EMF (Electro-Magnetic Frequency) emission at location by paying online fee of ₹ 4000.

88. *(c)* The Odisha State cabinet approved a proposal to recommend the inclusion of the Kui language in the Eighth Schedule of the Constitution of India.

- There are 22 languages in the eight Schedule of Indian Constitution.
- All the classical language are listed in Eighth Schedule.
- There is no fixed criteria for any language to be considered for inclusion in the Eighth Schedule.

89. *(d)* The Nicolaus Copernicus was the first to develop a mathematical predictive heliocentric model of the solar system.

- The heliocentric model of the solar system places Sun at the centre of the solar system.
- It also says that the Earth revolves around the Sun.

90. *(d)* Brahmo Samaj was earlier known as Brahmo Sabha.

- The Brahmo Samaj was formed in 1828.
- It was founded by Raja Ram Mohan Roy in Calcutta.
- It prohibited all forms of idolatry and sacrifice.
- It supported monotheism.

91. *(c)* Swaran Singh Committee recommended the inclusion of Fundamental Duties in the Constitution of India.

- It recommended addition of eight Fundamental Duties however later on ten duties were added.
- The 11th Fundamental Duty was added by 86th Constitutional Amendment Act, 2002.

- The Fundamental Duties are listed in Part IV A of the Constitution.

92. *(c)* Both (1) and (2) are the correct in case of market equilibrium.

- In a market equilibrium market demand exactly equals market supply. There is no excessive supply in the market.
- The market equilibrium leads to price stabilisation.

93. *(a)* Bhavai is a dance form that belongs to state of Rajasthan.

- Bhavai is an exciting pot balancing dance of snake charmer tribe.
- Bhavai theatre belongs to Gujarat but Bhavai dance is popular in Rajasthan.
- Kalbelia is another folk dance of Rajasthan performed by Kalbelia community.

94. *(d)* Mahavir Jayanti celebrates the birthday of Lord Mahavira who is the 24th Tirthankara of Jainism.

- Mahavir Jayanti celebrated in the month of Chaitra.
- On this occasion, statue of the lord given a ceremonial bath called Abhisheka.
- Among the teachings of Jainism, the Brahmacharya (celibacy) was added by the Mahavira.

95. *(d)* Turgor pressure is the driving force behind the enlargement and extension of cells.

- Turgor pressure is the pressure on the cell wall caused by the osmotic movement of water.
- Turgor pressure causes the expansion of cells and the extension of apical cells, pollen tubes and other plant structures such as root tips.

96. *(a)* Nitin Gadkari declared himself brand ambassador of 'Khadi Prakritik Paint'.

- Khadi Prakritik Paint is the India's first and only paint made from cow dung.
- It is developed by khadi and Village Industries Commission (KVIC).
- The paint is anti-fungal and anti-bacterial.

97. *(c)* The Marris College of Music established in year 1926.

- It was established in Lucknow and also known as the All India College of Hindustani Music.
- Marris College of Music renamed as Bhatkhande Music Institute.
- The founder of this college was Pt. Vishnu Narayan Bhatkhande.

98. *(a)* Insert Column to the Right allows you to insert a new column in a table while simultaneously shifting the existing columns to the right.

99. *(b)* Dhrupad is not a part of Carnatic music.

- Dhrupad is the oldest surviving classical Hindustani (North India) vocal music.
- The key components of Carnatic music are Pallavi, Anu Pallavi and Charana/Charanam.
- The Carnatic composition is mainly in Telugu, Tamil, Kannada, Sanskrit and Malayalam.

100. *(b)* The jute industry is not a major industry according to the Department of Industrial Policy and Promotion.

- The eight core industries of India are cement, coal, crude oil, electricity, fertilisers, natural gas, refinery products and steel industry.
- The jute industry mainly depends on West Bengal because of higher concentration of mills.
- The major producers of jute are West Bengal, Assam, Bihar, Odisha and Andhra Pradesh.

Set 22 08 July, 2024 (Shift II)

SSC CHSL Tier-I
SOLVED PAPER

Instructions

1. This paper contains 100 questions.
2. It has 4 Parts, **Part I** General English, **Part II** General Intelligence & Reasoning, **Part III** Quantitative Aptitude and **Part IV** General Awareness.
3. Each question carries **2 marks**.

Part I
General English

1. Parts of the following sentence have been given as options. Select the option that contains an error.

During winters, most of the trains are not running on time in North India.

(a) During winters
(b) on time in North India
(c) are not running
(d) most of the trains

2. The sentence below contains errors. Select the option with the correct use of tenses.

I will revised my course at least three times before my final examination.

(a) I would revised my course at least three times before my final examination.
(b) I will be revised my course at least three times since my final examination.
(c) I will have revised my course at least three times before my final examination.
(d) I must revised my course at least three times before my final examination.

3. Select the most appropriate adverb to fill in the blank.

He comes here ....

(a) quickly
(b) formerly
(c) daily
(d) lately

4. Parts of the following sentence have been given as options. Select the option that contains an error.

That day we reached late for the competition and even though the competition went on smooth, I felt bad about Shivani losing it.

(a) I felt bad
(b) losing it
(c) the competition went on smooth
(d) we reached late

Directions (Q.Nos. 5-9) *In the following passage, some words have been deleted. Fill in the blanks with the help of the alternatives given. Select the most appropriate option for each blank.*

Hierarchy is key in ensuring normal functioning of our increasingly (1)......... society. In the US, there is an enormous variety of industries, professional branches, specialisations, as well as a great (2)......... of other domains of human activity or interests. So, competence here is valued and opinion influencers have an important role to play. In fact, leadership evolves as a necessity almost in any realm of human activity/ thinking, (3)......... where more people are involved.

Thus, it isn't hard (4)......... why even in academic institutions throughout the US and worldwide, students are given leadership essay assignments. Most students will take on leadership roles with various degrees of responsibility and impact in their lives, hence, becoming (5)......... with typical challenges, solutions, or skills required is essential.

5. Select the most appropriate option to fill in blank (1).

(a) systematic
(b) complex
(c) easy
(d) fine

6. Select the most appropriate option to fill in blank (2).

(a) worry (b) difficulty
(c) uniformity (d) diversity

7. Select the most appropriate option to fill in blank (3).

(a) especially (b) only
(c) easily (d) tactfully

8. Select the most appropriate option to fill in blank (4).

(a) focusing (b) rejecting
(c) polishing (d) accepting

9. Select the most appropriate option to fill in blank (5).

(a) familiar (b) unusual
(c) unequal (d) strange

10. The following sentence has been split into four segments. Identify the segment that contains a grammatical error.

Are today / a working day / or a / holiday?

(a) Are today (b) holiday
(c) a working day (d) or a

11. Select the most appropriate option that can substitute the underlined segment in the given sentence. If there is no need to substitute it, select 'No substitution required'.

They appointed him as the manager, as he was due for <u>an</u> promotion.

(a) next (b) it's
(c) No substitution required
(d) a

12. Choose an appropriate word that can substitute the bracketed word and complete the sentence meaningfully.

What is the time (in) your watch?

(a) by (b) with (c) into (d) on

13. Select the most appropriate antonym of the underlined word in the given sentence.
His grandfather was quite <u>grumpy</u> .
(a) possible (b) tenable
(c) edible (d) amiable

14. Select the most appropriate antonym of the underlined word.
It's very cheap to display wealth by donning <u>gaudy</u> dresses.
(a) scanty (b) ornate
(c) cheap (d) sober

15. Select the incorrectly spelt word.
(a) Timorous (b) Amalgamate
(c) Unintended (d) Apropriate

16. Select the most appropriate antonym of the given word.
Morose
(a) Jovial (b) Practical
(c) Dramatic (d) Hurried

17. Select the most appropriate antonym of the given word.
Despondency
(a) Hopelessness (b) Satisfaction
(c) Cheerfulness (d) Dejection

18. Select the most appropriate antonym of the underlined word in the given sentence.
The <u>humble</u> pupil sat on the floor with respect.
(a) capitalist (b) corrupt
(c) sturdy (d) proud

19. Select the most appropriate meaning of the given idiom.
Sell like hot cakes
(a) Extremely hot and humid
(b) Not bothering about money
(c) Selling out quickly
(d) Become very famous

20. Select the most appropriate option to fill in the blank.
He hasn't .... any attention to my miserable state.
(a) made (b) had
(c) gave (d) paid

21. Select the most appropriate option that can substitute the underlined segment in the given sentence. If there is no need to substitute it, select 'No substitution required'.
She <u>developing</u> a remarkable resistance to cold and altitude.
(a) developed
(b) has develop
(c) No substitution required
(d) has been developing

22. Which of the following idioms means 'going to sleep'?
(a) Keep an ear to the ground
(b) Run around in circles
(c) Break new grounds
(d) Hit the sack

23. Select the incorrectly spelt word.
(a) Creator
(b) Skewed
(c) Agressive
(d) Apparent

24. Select the most appropriate synonym of the bracketed word in the following sentence to fill in the blank.
The setting Sun turned the .... (calm) ocean into a sea of gold.
(a) volatile
(b) placid
(c) furtive
(d) scattered

25. Select the most appropriate synonym of the underlined word in the given sentence.
He is just <u>jealous</u> that he didn't get picked for the job.
(a) envious (b) spiteful
(c) greedy (d) suspicious

Part II
General Intelligence

26. What will come in the place of the question mark (?) in the following equation, if '+' and '×' are interchanged and '−' and '÷' are interchanged?
$55 \times 84 - 12 + 9 \div 26 = ?$
(a) 90 (b) 95
(c) 92 (d) 96

27. Select the correct mirror image of the given figure, when the mirror is placed at MN as shown below.

SLq2bV5 (mirror MN)

(a) ƧVdƧp⅃Ƨ (b) 5VdƧpLƧ
(c) ƧΛdƧp⅃Ƨ (d) 5VbƧp⅃Ƨ

28. After 36 days, it will be a Sunday. What day is it today?
(a) Friday (b) Monday
(c) Sunday (d) Saturday

29. If 'A' stands for '÷', 'B' stands for '×', 'C' stands for '+' and 'D' stands for '−', then the resultant of which of the following will be 338?
(a) 32 A 11 D 80 B 4 C 6
(b) 32 D 11 B 80 A 4 C 6
(c) 32 C 11 D 80 A 4 B 6
(d) 32 B 11 D 80 A 4 C 6

30. In a certain code language,
M & N means 'M is the son of N',
M @ N means 'M is the brother of N',
M \$ N means 'M is the father of N',
M # N means ' M is the mother of N'.
Based on this, how is E related to A, if 'A # B \$ C @ D & E'?
(a) Daughter's husband
(b) Son's wife
(c) Son
(d) Daughter

31. Which of the following letter-clusters can replace the question mark (?) in the given series to make it logically complete?
IPX, ? , OTZ, RVA, UXB
(a) LOM (b) LRY
(c) YHR (d) COP

32. What would be the letter on the opposite side of 'N', if the given sheet is folded to form a cube?

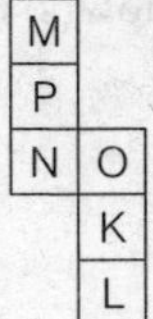

(a) O (b) L (c) M (d) K

33. This question consists of a pair of words, which have a certain relationship to each other. Select the pair, which does not have the same relationship.
Demolish : Repair
1. Condemn : Approve
2. Consequence : Outcome
3. Bind : Release
4. Adamant : Flexible
(a) 3 (b) 4 (c) 2 (d) 1

34. Select the option in which the given figure is embedded (rotation is not allowed).

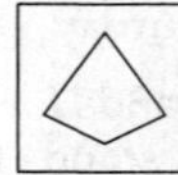

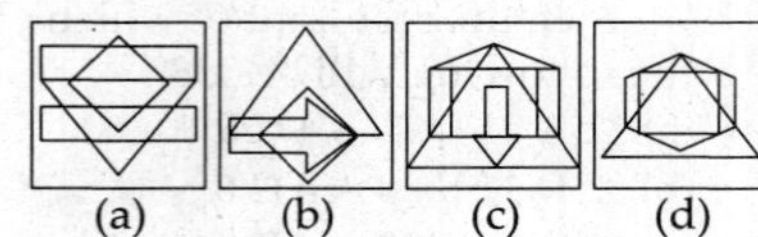

(a) (b) (c) (d)

35. Select the correct mirror image of the given figure, when the mirror is placed at MN as shown below.

WHPRZY | M N

(a) YZЯꟼWH (b) YZЯꟼHW
(c) YИЯꟼHW (d) YZЯHPW

36. Four letter-clusters have been given, out of which three are alike in some manner and one is different. Select the letter-cluster that is different.

(**Note** The odd one out is not based on the number of consonants/vowels or their position in the letter-cluster)

(a) FUHS (b) YCAZ
(c) AZCX (d) MNOL

37. Three statements are followed by two conclusions numbered I, II. You have to consider these statements to be true, even if they seem to be at variance with commonly known facts. Decide which of the given conclusions logically follow(s) from the given statements.

Statements

Some roses are flowers.

All buds are roses.

All lilies are flowers.

Conclusions

I. Some buds are lilies.

II. All flowers are buds.

(a) Both Conclusions I and II follow
(b) Only Conclusion I follows
(c) Only Conclusion II follows
(d) Neither Conclusion I nor II follows

38. 27 is related to 3 following a certain logic. Following the same logic, 343 is related to 7. To which of the following is 1331 related following the same logic?

(**Note** Operations should be performed on the whole numbers, without breaking down the numbers into its constituent digits. E.g. 13 – Operations on 13 such as adding /deleting/multiplying etc., to 13 can be performed. Breaking down 13 into 1 and 3 and then performing mathematical operations on 1 and 3 is not allowed)

(a) 11 (b) 13
(c) 17 (d) 9

39. Identify the figure given in the options, which when put in place of question mark (?) will logically complete the series.

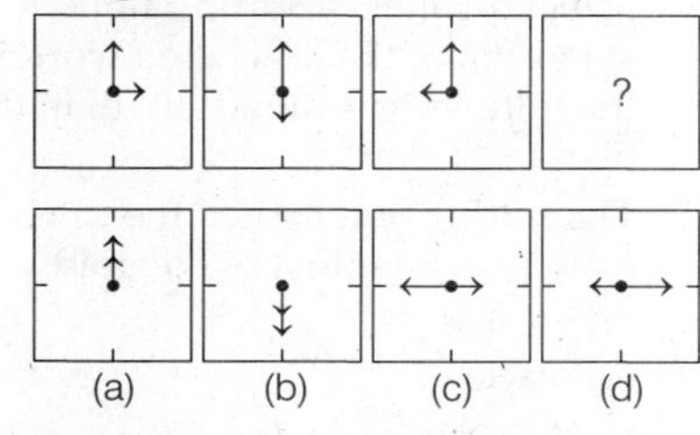

40. If 11th November, 2009 was Wednesday, then what was the day of the week on 17th November, 2013?

(a) Friday (b) Sunday
(c) Saturday (d) Thursday

41. What should come in place of the question mark (?) in the given series based on the English alphabetical order?

XVS, AYV, DBY, GEB, ?

(a) EJH (b) JEH
(c) EHJ (d) JHE

42. What should come in place of the question mark (?) in the given series?

77, 144, 278, 546, ?

(a) 1082 (b) 1028
(c) 1208 (d) 1802

43. Which of the following numbers will replace the question mark (?) in the given series?

106, 106, 108, 36 ,40 ,8, ?

(a) 14 (b) 10
(c) 28 (d) 22

44. Select the set in which the numbers are related in the same way as are the numbers of the following sets.

(59, 246, 23)

(68, 300, 32)

(**Note** Operations should be performed on the whole numbers, without breaking down the numbers into its constituent digits. E.g. 13 – Operations on 13 such as adding /subtracting /multiplying etc., to 13 can be performed. Breaking down 13 into 1 and 3 and then performing mathematical operations on 1 and 3 is not allowed)

(a) (32, 188, 71) (b) (42, 213, 29)
(c) (31, 169, 53) (d) (47, 248, 15)

45. In a certain code language, 'FORK' is coded as '6851' and 'FROG' is coded as '5981'. How is 'K' coded in the given language?

(a) 1 (b) 5 (c) 9 (d) 6

46. If 'A' stands for '÷', 'B' stands for '×', 'C' stands for '+' and 'D' stands for '–', what will come in place of the question mark (?) in the following equation?

91 B 2 D 22 A 11 C 8 = ?

(a) 188 (b) 128
(c) 148 (d) 168

47. KLOQ is related to NORT in a certain way based on the English alphabetical order. In the same way, HILN is related to KLOQ. To which of the following is PQTV related, following the same logic?

(a) STWY (b) SWTY
(c) SUVY (d) STUY

48. Select the option figure in which the given figure is embedded as its part (rotation is not allowed).

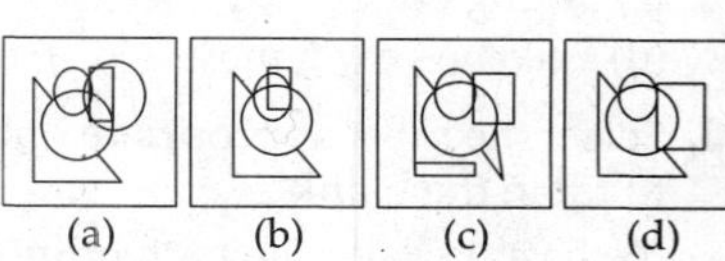

(a) (b) (c) (d)

49. How many triangles are there in the given figure?

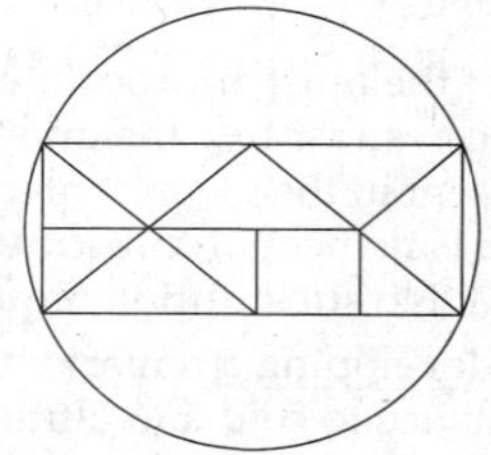

(a) 10 (b) 8 (c) 14 (d) 11

50. What should come in place of question mark (?) in the given series?

281, 392, 503, 614, 725 ?

(a) 846 (b) 856
(c) 866 (d) 836

Part III
Quantitative Aptitude

51. The given table represents the percentage marks of three students in three subjects. Study the table and answer the question.

Subjects / Students	Geography	History	Economics
Rohan	78	77	74
Sohan	84	80	82
Mohan	87	83	86

The average marks obtain by Sohan in all three subjects is equal to

(a) 78 (b) 80
(c) 82 (d) 84

52. Two circles have radii of 27 cm and 36 cm. The distance between their centres is 45 cm. What is the length (in cm) of their common chord?

(a) 37.2 cm (b) 40.5 cm
(c) 43.2 cm (d) 47.5 cm

53. When the integer n is divided by 5, the remainder is 3. What is the remainder, if $6n$ is divided by 5?

(a) 2 (b) 1
(c) 3 (d) 0

54. Study the given pie-chart and answer the question that follows.
The pie-chart represents the total number of valid votes obtained by four students, who contested for school leadership. The total number of valid votes polled was 720.

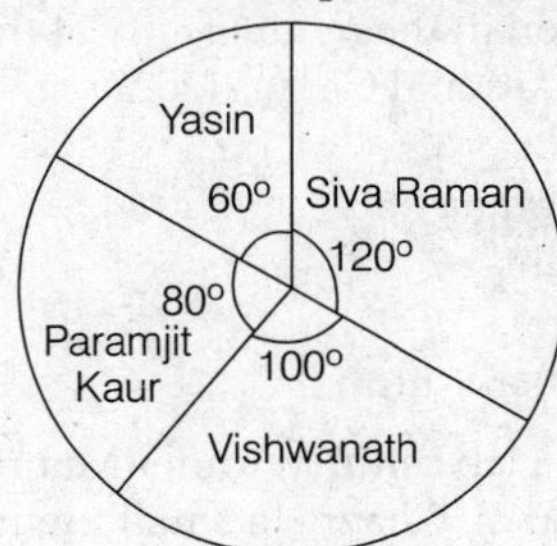

Who won the election?

(a) Yasin (b) Vishwanath
(c) Siva Raman (d) Paramjit Kaur

55. The profit obtained by selling an article for ₹ 86 is twice the loss obtained by selling the same article for ₹ 53. Find the cost price.

(a) ₹ 33 (b) ₹ 22
(c) ₹ 64 (d) ₹ 75

56. Study the given graph and answer the question that follows. The graph represents the depreciation of a car from 2001 to 2007.

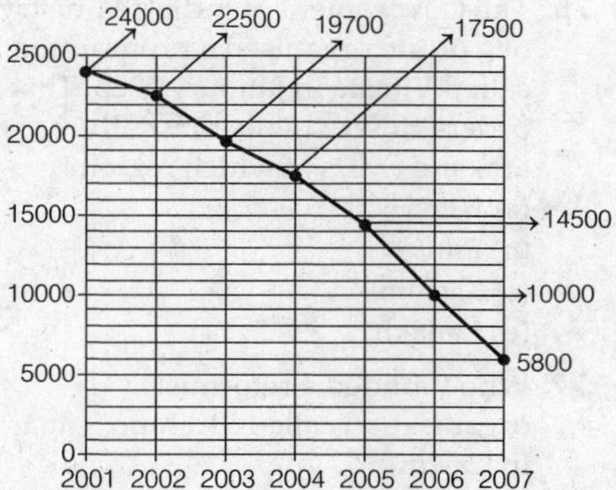

What is the depreciation of the car from 2001 to 2007 in percentage?

(a) 62% (b) 81.32%
(c) 75.83% (d) 58%

57. The average of the first 10 natural numbers is

(a) 5.5 (b) 6.5
(c) 5 (d) 6

58. A metallic solid cuboid of dimensions 36 cm × 22 cm × 12 cm is melted and recast in the form of cubes of side 6 cm. Find the number of the cubes so formed.

(a) 46 (b) 43 (c) 45 (d) 44

59. To clear the old stock, Arshad offers a discount scheme to his customers - on buying 24 glass tumblers get 12 glass tumblers free. What is the effective percentage discount given by Arshad to his customers?

(a) $30\frac{1}{3}\%$ (b) $32\frac{2}{3}\%$
(c) $33\frac{1}{3}\%$ (d) $34\frac{2}{3}\%$

60. Suresh studies the pattern of daily sale of a shop. He finds that on Monday, the sale was decreased by 10% in comparison to the sale on Sunday. On Tuesday, the sale was increased by 10% in comparison to the sale of Monday. If the sale on Tuesday was of ₹ 1485, how much was the sale on Sunday?

(a) ₹ 1495 (b) ₹ 1475
(c) ₹ 1485 (d) ₹ 1500

61. Identify a single-digit number other than 1, which may exactly divide the number $17^3 + 18^3 - 16^3 - 15^3$.

(a) 2 (b) 3
(c) 5 (d) 7

62. If $\tan(t) = \frac{3}{7}$, t is an acute angle, then what is the value of cosec (t)?

(a) $\frac{\sqrt{53}}{7}$ (b) $\frac{\sqrt{53}}{3}$
(c) $\frac{\sqrt{58}}{3}$ (d) $\frac{\sqrt{58}}{7}$

63. Pranav gave 30% of the money, he had to his wife and 86% of the remaining to his two children. Half of the amount left was spent on other things and the remaining amount of ₹ 98000 was deposited in the bank. How much money did he have initially?

(a) ₹ 2000000 (b) ₹ 4000000
(c) ₹ 1000000 (d) ₹ 3000000

64. What will be the amount due on ₹ 12000 in 2 yr, when the rate of simple interest on successive years is 9% and 10%, respectively?

(a) ₹ 14250 (b) ₹ 14280
(c) ₹ 14350 (d) ₹ 14150

65. If the radius of a sphere is increased by 3.5 cm, its surface area increases by 550 cm^2. What was the original radius of the sphere? $\left(\text{use } \pi = \frac{22}{7}\right)$

(a) 4.5 cm (b) 3.5 cm
(c) 4 cm (d) 6 cm

66. ABC is a right-angled triangle, at A in such a way that $AB = AC$ and the bisector of angle B intersects the side AC at D. DM is perpendicular to BC, intersecting BC at M. If $AB = 12$ cm and $BC = 12\sqrt{2}$ cm, then find the length of side AD.

(a) $12(\sqrt{2}+2)$ cm (b) $12(\sqrt{2}-2)$ cm
(c) $12(\sqrt{2}-1)$ cm (d) $12(\sqrt{2}+1)$ cm

67. Rohan takes 10 h to mow a large lawn. Rohan and Mohan together can mow it in 4 h. How long will Mohan take to mow the lawn, if he works alone?

(a) $\frac{16}{3}$ h (b) $\frac{20}{3}$ h
(c) $\frac{40}{3}$ h (d) $\frac{10}{3}$ h

68. Two numbers are in the ratio 2 : 3. Their sum is 135. Find the numbers.

(a) 50,85 (b) 60, 75
(c) 54, 81 (d) 45,90

69. *A*'s income is equal to 125% of the income of *B*, while *B*'s savings are 120% of the savings of A. If the expenditure of B is 75% of the expenditure of *A*, then how much are *B*'s savings as a percentage of her expenditure?

(a) 20% (b) $22\frac{1}{2}\%$
(c) $18\frac{3}{4}\%$ (d) $16\frac{2}{3}\%$

70. The ratio of the speeds of a boat, while going upstream and going downstream is 2 : 3 and the sum of these two speeds is 15 km/h. What is the speed of the stream?

(a) 3.5 km/h (b) 1.5 km/h
(c) 3 km/h (d) 2.5 km/h

71. The following line graph shows the ratio of imports to exports of two companies over the years. Study the graph carefully and answer the question that follows.

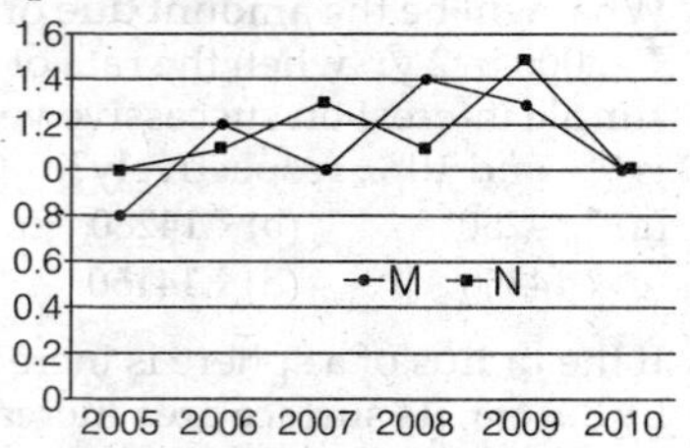

The exports of Company M with relation to imports was the maximum, in which of the following years?

(a) 2005 (b) 2009 (c) 2008 (d) 2006

72. The two-digits number is 12 more than five times the sum of its digits. The number formed by reversing the digits is 9 less than the original number. The number is

(a) 96 (b) 78 (c) 69 (d) 87

73. The length of a common external tangent to two circles of an equal radius of 5 units is equal to the diameter of the circle.
Which of the following can be the distance between the centres of the circles in units?

(a) 10 (b) 12 (c) 9 (d) 8

74. *X* and *Y* are two points on the circumference of a circle having diameter 20 cm. The length of the line segment *XY* is 16 cm. Find the distance (in cm) of the line segment *XY* from the centre of the circle.

(a) 6 (b) 3 (c) 5 (d) 4

75. The perimeter of a square, whose area is the same as the area of a semi-circle of radius $2\sqrt{2}$ cm is

(a) $4\sqrt{\pi}$ cm (b) $16\sqrt{\pi}$ cm
(c) $8\sqrt{2\pi}$ cm (d) $8\sqrt{\pi}$ cm

Part IV
General Awareness

76. The Government of India's Ministry of Culture organised a programme called Vitasta in January 2023. This programme exhibits rich culture, arts and crafts of which region?

(a) Himachal
(b) Punjab
(c) Kashmir
(d) Ladakh

77. Who founded a reformist organisation called 'Brahmo Samaj' in Calcutta?

(a) Vinoba Bhave
(b) Raja Ram Mohan Roy
(c) Ishwar Chandra Vidyasagar
(d) Jyotiba Phule

78. Which state organises the Lokrang festival?

(a) Arunachal Pradesh
(b) Uttar Pradesh
(c) Himachal Pradesh
(d) Madhya Pradesh

79. 'Pankhida' songs are sung by peasants of .... while working on the fields.

(a) Odisha (b) Bihar
(c) Rajasthan (d) Uttar Pradesh

80. Which cost is considered for calculating the National Income in India?

(a) Factor cost (b) Product cost
(c) Market cost (d) Sunk cost

81. Which of the following organisation's initiative is 'India Justice Report'?

(a) Tata Trusts
(b) Azim Premji Foundation
(c) Infosys Foundation
(d) HCL Foundation

82. Which of the following is an input device?

(a) Speaker
(b) Monitor
(c) Printer
(d) Keyboard

83. Western disturbances are responsible for

(a) extremely chilled weather of North-East India
(b) dusty storms in Eastern costal area of India
(c) rainfall during winters in North-western part of India
(d) hot winds during summers in northern India

84. Which type of electromagnetic radiation was discovered by Johann Wilhelm Ritter in 1801?

(a) X-rays (b) Ultraviolet rays
(c) Infrared rays (d) Gamma rays

85. Indian Railway was introduced in the year ....

(a) 1852 (b) 1851
(c) 1853 (d) 1850

86. Which of the following statements is/are true with respect to MRTP Act?

1. The Monopolies and Restrictive Trade Practices Act (MRTP Act) was repealed and replaced by the Competition Act, 2002.
2. The asset limit for MRTP companies was fixed at ₹ 25 crores by the first/original Monopolies and Restrictive Trade Practices Act (MRTP Act).
3. The Monopolies and Restrictive Trade Practices Act (MRTP Act) was first passed in 1969.

Codes

(a) 1 and 3 (b) 2 and 3
(c) Only 3 (d) 1 and 2

87. .... is a musical composition that expresses devotion through Madhura Bhakti.

(a) Tillana (b) Padam
(c) Gita (d) Kriti

88. Which state secured over-all third position in the medals tally at the 36th National Games (2022) of India?

(a) Haryana
(b) Delhi
(c) Kerala
(d) Maharashtra

89. In the 11th century, under Mahmud of Ghazni, Ghazni, a small town in ...., became the capital of the vast empire of the Ghaznavids.

(a) Turkey (b) Egypt
(c) Persia (d) Afghanistan

90. Which set of articles in the Constitution of India is known as 'Cultural and Educational Rights'?
(a) Articles 19-20 (b) Articles 29-30
(c) Articles 14-15 (d) Articles 23-24

91. In which of the following regions of India is the Mundari language spoken?
(a) Malwa plateau
(b) Thar desert
(c) Chota Nagpur plateau
(d) Baghelkhand

92. Pandit Birju Maharaj was related to
(a) Ozele (b) Kathak
(c) Odissi (d) Tapu

93. A school teacher asks students to stand up every time National Anthem is sung. Which article enshrines this Fundamental Duty?
(a) Article 51 (d) (b) Article 51 (c)
(c) Article 51 (b) (d) Article 51A (a)

94. In which year did the Indian football team go on its first known official international tour?
(a) 1947 (b) 1914 (c) 1950 (d) 1924

95. Why is the six membered cyclic structure of glucose called a pyranose structure?
(a) Pyran is a non-cyclic organic compound, with one oxygen atom and five carbon atoms in the ring.
(b) Pyran is a cyclic organic compound, with one oxygen atom and five carbon atoms in the ring.
(c) Furan is a five membered non-cyclic compound, with one oxygen and four carbon atoms.
(d) Furan is a five membered cyclic compound, with one oxygen and four carbon atoms.

96. When a new text document is created in MS-Office 2016, the default text size of the document is ....
(a) 10 points (b) 14 points
(c) 12 points (d) 11 points

97. Recently, a bill on Uniform Civil Code (UCC) was introduced. Consider the following statements about UCC and identify the correct statement(s) from them.
1. The Uniform Civil Code in India Bill, 2020, was introduced in the Lok Sabha as a private member bill.
2. UCC refers to the same set of civil laws applicable to all the citizens of India in all the personal matters.
3. The provision for UCC in the Constitution of India is mentioned under Article 44.

Codes
(a) Only 1 (b) 1 and 3
(c) 2 and 3 (d) Only 3

98. According to the National Multidimensional Poverty Index 2021, which of the following states has the lowest percentage of population being multidimensional poor?
(a) Maharashtra (b) Punjab
(c) Sikkim (d) Bihar

99. India is home to the second oldest cricket club in the world. Where is it situated?
(a) Kolkata (b) Chennai
(c) Mumbai (d) Hyderabad

100. Which of the following types of crops are sown at the beginning of the monsoon season?
(a) Zaid crops (b) Rabi crops
(c) Vital crops (d) Kharif crops

Answers

1. (c)	2. (c)	3. (c)	4. (c)
5. (b)	6. (d)	7. (a)	8. (d)
9. (a)	10. (a)	11. (d)	12. (a)
13. (d)	14 (d)	15. (d)	16. (a)
17. (c)	18. (d)	19. (c)	20. (d)
21. (a)	22. (d)	23. (c)	24. (b)
25. (a)	26. (c)	27. (a)	28. (d)
29. (d)	30. (b)	31. (b)	32. (c)
33. (c)	34. (d)	35. (b)	36. (b)
37. (d)	38. (a)	39. (a)	40. (b)
41. (d)	42. (a)	43. (a)	44. (b)
45. (d)	46. (a)	47. (a)	48. (d)
49. (c)	50. (d)	51. (c)	52. (c)
53. (c)	54. (c)	55. (c)	56. (c)
57. (a)	58. (d)	59. (c)	60. (d)
61. (a)	62. (c)	63. (a)	64. (b)
65. (a)	66. (c)	67. (b)	68. (c)
69. (a)	70. (b)	71. (a)	72. (d)
73. (a)	74. (a)	75. (d)	76. (c)
77. (b)	78. (d)	79. (c)	80. (a)
81. (a)	82. (d)	83. (c)	84. (b)
85. (c)	86. (a)	87. (b)	88. (a)
89. (d)	90. (b)	91. (c)	92. (b)
93. (d)	94. (d)	95. (b)	96. (d)
97. (c)	98. (c)	99. (a)	100. (d)

Explanations

1. *(c)* Part (c) 'are not running' contains an error. Use 'do not run' to correct the sentence. As the sentence presents a general statement, Simple Present tense should be used.

2. *(c)* The given sentence contains an error of tense. Future Perfect Tense should be used in the sentence. Hence, the correct sentence is- I will have revised my course at least three times before my final examination.

3. *(c)* The correct filler for the given blank is 'daily'.

4. *(c)* Part (c) 'the competition went on smooth' contains an error. Use 'smoothly' to correct the sentence.

5. *(b)* The correct filler for the given blank is 'complex'.

6. *(d)* The correct filler for the given blank is 'diversity'.

7. *(a)* The correct filler for the given blank is 'especially'.

8. *(d)* The correct filler for the given blank is 'accepting'.

9. *(a)* The correct filler for the given blank is 'familiar'.

10. *(a)* Part (a) 'Are today' contains an error. Use 'is today' to correct the sentence.

11. *(d)* The underlined part of the given sentence contains an error. Use 'a' to correct the sentence.

12. *(a)* The bracketed part of the given sentence contains an error. Use 'by' to correct the sentence.

13. *(d)* 'Grumpy' means irritated or angry. Hence, its antonym is 'Amiable' which means warm and friendly.
The other option one, 'Tenable' means capable of being held, maintained, or defended.
'Edible' means something that can be eaten.

14. *(d)* 'Gaudy' means extravagantly bright or showy, typically so as to be tasteless. Hence, its antonym is 'Sober' which means graceful.
- 'Scanty' means in less quantity.
- 'Ornate' means decorated.

15. *(d)* The incorrectly spelt word is 'apropriate'. The correct spelling is 'appropriate'.

16. *(a)* 'Morose' means sad and gloomy. Hence, its antonym is 'Jovial' which means happy.

17. *(c)* 'Despondency' means sad. Hence, its antonym is 'Cheerfulness'.

18. *(d)* 'Humble' means polite. Hence, its antonym is 'proud'.
- 'Capitalist' means someone who uses their wealth to invest in trade and industry.
- 'Corrupt' means dishonest.
- 'Sturdy' means strong.

19. *(c)* 'Sell like hot cakes' means selling very quickly.

20. *(d)* The correct filler for the given blank is 'paid'.

21. *(a)* The underlined part of the given sentence contains an error. Use 'developed' to correct the sentence.

22. *(d)* The idiom 'Hit the sack' means to go to sleep.
- 'Keep an ear to the ground' means to be well informed.
- 'Run aroundin circles' mean a purposeless action.
- 'Break new grounds' means to do something for the first time.

23. *(c)* The incorrectly spelt word is 'agressive'. The correct spelling is 'aggressive'.

24. *(b)* The word 'placid' means 'calm'.
- 'Volatile' means liable to change rapidly and unpredictably, especially for the worse.
- 'Furtive' means attempting to avoid notice or attention, typically because of guilt or a belief that discovery would lead to trouble; secretive.

25. *(a)* The word 'envious' means 'jealous'. 'Spiteful' means angry.

26. *(c)* Given expression,

$55 \times 84 - 12 + 9 \div 26 = ?$

After interchanging symbols,

$55 + 84 \div 12 \times 9 - 26$

$= 55 + 7 \times 9 - 26$

$= 55 + 63 - 26$

$= 118 - 26 = 92$

27. *(a)* The figure given in option (a) is the correct mirror image of the given question figure.

M

SLq2bV5 ‖ ƧVdƧp⅃Ƨ

N

28. *(d)* Everyday of the week is repeated after 7 days. After 36 days it will be a Sunday.

Then, $\frac{36}{7} = 1$ odd day

Then, Today

$=$ Sunday $- 1$

$=$ Saturday

29. *(d)* From option (d), we get

32 B 11 D 80 A 4 C 6

After substituting the symbols with signs, we get

$32 \times 11 - 80 \div 4 + 6$

$= 32 \times 11 - 20 + 6$

$= 352 - 20 + 6$

$= 358 - 20 = 338$

30. *(b)* Given expression,

A # B $ C @ D & E

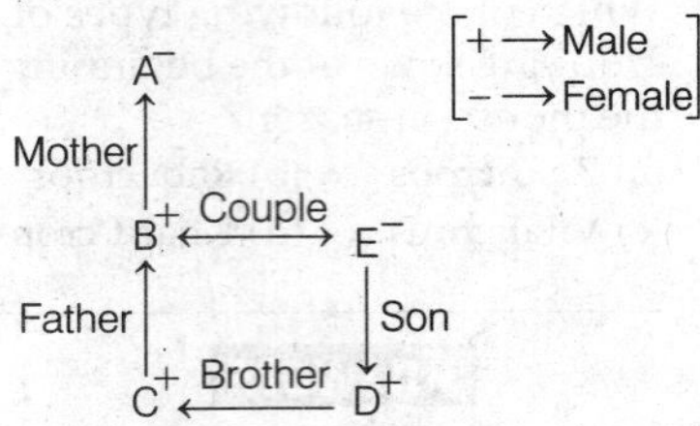

∴ 'E' is son's wife of 'A'.

31. *(b)* The pattern of the series is as follows,

$I \xrightarrow{+3} L \xrightarrow{+3} O \xrightarrow{+3} R \xrightarrow{+3} U$

$P \xrightarrow{+2} R \xrightarrow{+2} T \xrightarrow{+2} V \xrightarrow{+2} X$

$X \xrightarrow{+1} Y \xrightarrow{+1} Z \xrightarrow{+1} A \xrightarrow{+1} B$

32. *(c)* According to the question,

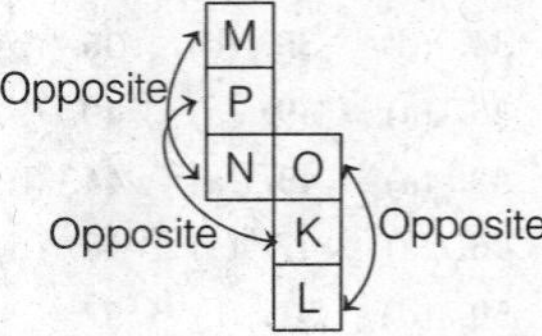

So, after folded the letter on the opposite side of 'N' is 'M'.

33. *(c)* As, every pair of words are synonym and antonym of each other except option (c) i.e.

Consequence : Outcome, they are synonym of each other.

34. *(d)* The given question figure is embedded in the given option (d) figure.

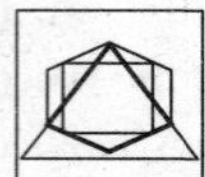

35. *(b)* The figure given in option (b) is the correct mirror image.

M

WHPRZY ‖ YZЯPHW

N

36. *(b)* In the given options, option (b) is odd from rest.As, in all the options , first letter is opposite to second letter and third letter is opposite to fourth letter. But in option (b) i.e.YCAZ is not happening.

37. *(d)* According to the statements,

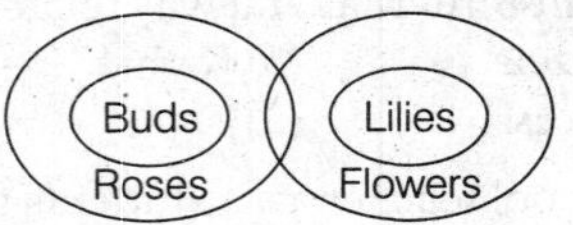

Conclusions I. (✗) II. (✗)

So, neither Conclusion I nor II follows.

38. *(a)* As, $\sqrt[3]{27} = 3$

and $\sqrt[3]{343} = 7$

Similarly, $\sqrt[3]{1331} = \boxed{11}$

So, option (a) is correct answer.

39. *(a)* In the given figure series, the small arrow is moving 90° in clockwise direction in successive figure.

Hence, option figure (a) will replace the question mark.

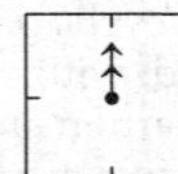

40. *(b)* Given, 11th November, 2009 was Wednesday.

Number of odd days left in 2009

$= 19 + 31 = \frac{50}{7} = 1$ odd day

As we know,

Number of odd days in ordinary year $= 1$

Number of odd days in leap year $= 2$

So, total number of odd days from 11th November, 2009 to 11th November, 2013

$= 1 + 1 + 2 + 1 = 5$ odd days

Day between 12th November, 2013 to 17th November, 2013 = 6 odd days

$= \frac{5+6}{7} = \frac{11}{7} = 4$ odd days

So, Wednesday + 4 = Sunday

So, the days of week on 17th November, 2013 = Sunday

41. *(d)* The pattern of the series is as follows,

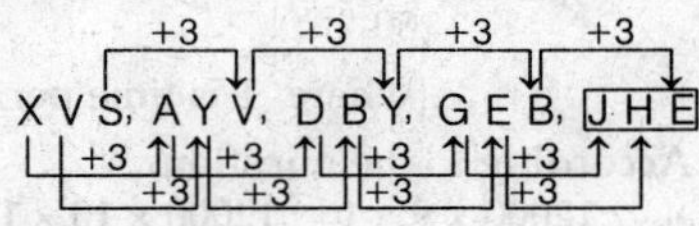

42. *(a)* The pattern of the series is as follows,

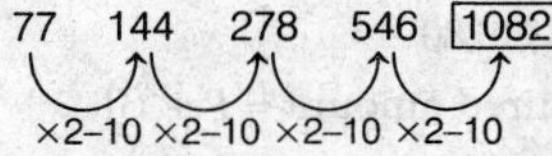

43. *(a)* The pattern of the series is as follows,

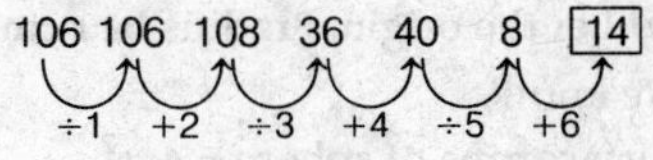

44. *(b)* As, $(59, 246, 23) = (59 + 23) \times 3$

$= 82 \times 3 = 246$

and $(68, 300, 32) = (68 + 32) \times 3$

$= 100 \times 3 = 300$

Similarly, $(42, 213, 29) = (42 + 29) \times 3$

$= 71 \times 3 = 213$

45. *(d)* According to the question,

FORK = 6851

FROG = 5981

Hence, the code for K is 6.

46. *(a)* Given equation,

91 B 2 D 22 A 11 C 8 = ?

After substituting the symbols, we get

A → ÷	B → ×
C → +	D → –

$91 \times 2 - 22 \div 11 + 8$

$= 91 \times 2 - 2 + 8$

$= 182 - 2 + 8$

$= 190 - 2 = \boxed{188}$

47. *(a)* As, K L O Q (+3 +3 +3 +3) → N O R T

and H I L N (+3 +3 +3 +3) → K L O Q

Similarly, P Q T V (+3 +3 +3 +3) → S T W Y

48. *(d)* The given figure is embedded in the option figure (d).

49. *(c)* Naming the figure,

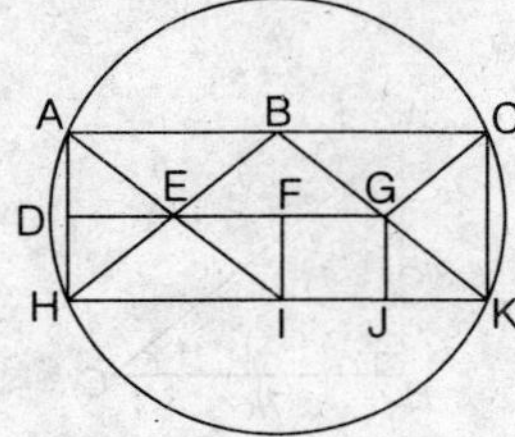

Number of triangles in given figure are

ΔADE, ΔAEB, ΔEBG, ΔBGC, ΔCGK, ΔDHE, ΔEIF, ΔJGK, ΔAEH, ΔAHI, ΔBKC, ΔHBK, ΔAHB and ΔEHI.

∴ Total = 14 triangles.

50. *(d)* The pattern of the series is as follows,

281 392 503 614 725 836

+111 +111 +111 +111 +111

51. *(c)* We know,

$$\text{Average} = \frac{\text{Sum of all the observations}}{\text{Total number of observations}}$$

∴ Required average

$$= \frac{84 + 80 + 82}{3} = \frac{246}{3} = 82$$

52. *(c)* Given, radii of circles are 27 cm and 36 cm.

Distance between centres = 45 cm

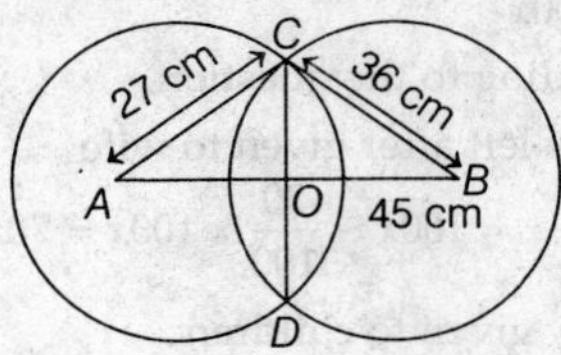

In ΔABC

Semi-perimeter,

$$s = \frac{27 + 36 + 45}{2} = \frac{108}{2} = 54$$

$\therefore \text{ar}(\Delta ABC)$

$= \sqrt{54(54 - 27)(54 - 36)(54 - 45)}$

$= \sqrt{27 \times 2 \times 27 \times 9 \times 2 \times 9}$

$= 9 \times 2 \times 27$

Also, $\text{ar}(\Delta ABC) = \frac{1}{2} \times AB \times OC$

$= \frac{1}{2} \times 45 \times OC$

$\therefore \frac{1}{2} \times 45 \times OC = 9 \times 2 \times 27$

$\Rightarrow OC = \frac{108}{5} = 21.6$

$\therefore CD = 2 \times OC = 2 \times 21.6 = 43.2$ cm

53. *(c)* As, integer n is divided by 5, remainder is 3.

By Division Algorithm,

$a = bq + r$

where, a = Dividend

q = Quotient

r = Remainder

$\therefore n = 5q + 3$

When $6n$ is divided by 5, then

$6n = 6(5q + 3)$

$= 30q + 18$

$= (30q + 15) + 3$

$= 5(6q + 3) + 3$

$6n = 5k + 3$ [Here, $k = 6q + 3$]

∴ Required remainder = 3

54. *(c)* Given,

Total number of votes polled = 720

We know,

Value of each sector

$= \frac{\theta}{360^\circ} \times$ Total number of votes polled

∴ The number of valid votes obtained by four students are as follows,

Yasin $= \frac{60^\circ}{360^\circ} \times 720 = 120$

Paramjit $= \frac{80^\circ}{360^\circ} \times 720 = 160$

Vishwanath $= \frac{100^\circ}{360^\circ} \times 720 = 200$

Siva Raman $= \frac{120^\circ}{360^\circ} \times 720 = 240$

∴ Siva Raman won the election.

55. *(c)* Let the CP of an article be ₹ x.

According to the question,

Profit obtained after selling an article for ₹ 86 = 2 (loss incurred by selling the same article for ₹ 53)

$\therefore (86 - x) = 2(x - 53)$

$\Rightarrow 86 - x = 2x - 106$

$\Rightarrow 86 + 106 = 3x$

$\Rightarrow 3x = 192$

$\Rightarrow x = 64$

Hence, the cost price of the article is ₹ 64.

56. *(c)* According to the question,

Value of cars in 2001 = ₹24000

Value of cars in 2007 = ₹5800

∴ Required depreciation percentage

$$= \frac{24000 - 5800}{24000} \times 100$$

$= 75.83\%$

57. (*a*) We know,

First 10 natural numbers are

1, 2, 3, 4, ..., 10

As, Average

$= \frac{\text{Sum of all the observations}}{\text{Total number of observations}}$

$\therefore$ Required average

$= \frac{1+2+3+4+5+6+7+8+9+10}{10}$

$= \frac{55}{10} = 5.5$

58. (*d*) Let the required number of cubes be n.

Given, dimensions of cuboid

= 36 cm × 22 cm × 12 cm

Dimension of cube = 6 cm

According to the question,

$n \times$ Volume of cube

= Volume of cuboid

$\therefore \quad n \times (6)^3 = 36 \times 22 \times 12$

$\Rightarrow n = 44$

59. (*c*) Required effective percentage discount

$= \frac{\text{Number of free items}}{\text{Total number of items}} \times 100$

$= \frac{12}{36} \times 100 = 33\frac{1}{3}\%$

60. (*d*) According to the question,

Sale of Tuesday = ₹1485

As, sale increased on Tuesday by 10%.

$\therefore$ Sale on Monday

$= 1485 \times \frac{100}{110}$

= ₹1350

As, sale decreased on Monday by 10%.

$\therefore$ Sale on Sunday

$= 1350 \times \frac{100}{90} =$ ₹1500

61. (*a*) According to the question,

Units digit of

$(17)^3 = (7)^3 = 3$

$(18)^3 = (8)^3 = 2$

$(16)^3 = (6)^3 = 6$

$(15)^3 = (5)^3 = 5$

$\therefore$ Unit digit of all the expression,

$(17)^3 + (18)^3 - (16)^3 - (15)^3$

$3 + 2 - 6 - 5$ (last digits)

$= 5 - 6 - 5$ (last digits)

$= -1 - 5$ (last digits)

$= 6$

We know, number whose last digit is 0, 2, 4, 6, 8 are divisible by 2.

62. (*c*) Given, $\tan(t) = \frac{3}{7}$, t is an acute angle.

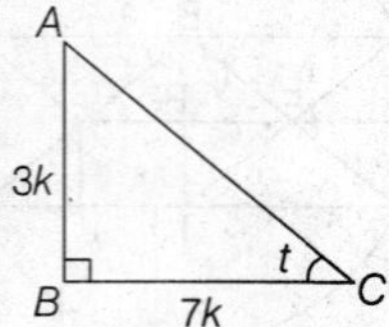

We know,

$\tan\theta = \frac{\text{Perpendicular } (P)}{\text{Base } (B)}$

$\therefore \quad \tan t = \frac{3}{7} = \frac{P}{B}$

Let $P = 3k$

$B = 7k$

In ΔABC,

$(AC)^2 = AB^2 + BC^2$

$\Rightarrow AC^2 = (3k)^2 + (7k^2)$

$= 9k^2 + 49k^2 = 58k^2$

As,

$AC = \sqrt{58}\,k$

$\therefore \operatorname{cosec}(t) = \frac{\text{Hypotenuse}}{\text{Perpendicular}}$

$= \frac{\sqrt{58}\,k}{3k}$

$= \frac{\sqrt{58}}{3}$

63. (*a*) Let money initially Pranav had be ₹100x.

According to the question,

Money left after given to wife

$= 100x - \frac{30}{100} \times 100x = 70x$

Money given to children

$= \frac{86}{100} \times 70x = 60.2x$

Money spent on other things

$= \frac{1}{2}(70x - 60.2x) = 4.9x$

$\therefore$ Remaining money

$= 9.8x - 4.9x$

$= 4.9x = 98000$

$\Rightarrow \quad x = \frac{98000 \times 10}{49} = 20000$

$\therefore$ Money initially Pranav had

$= 100 \times 20000$

= ₹2000000

64. (*b*) Given,

Principal (P) = ₹12000

Rate of interest for first year = 9%

Rate of interest for second year = 10%

We know,

$SI = \frac{P \times R \times T}{100}$

[where, T is time period]

According to the question,

$SI = \frac{12000 \times 9 \times 1}{100} + \frac{12000 \times 10 \times 1}{100}$

$= 1080 + 1200$

$\therefore$ SI = ₹2280

$\therefore$ Required amount = P + SI

= 12000 + 2280

= ₹14280

65. (*a*) Let the original radius be r cm.

We know,

Surface area of sphere $= 4\pi r^2$

According to the question,

$4\pi(r + 3.5)^2 = 4\pi r^2 + 550$

$\Rightarrow 4\pi(r^2 + 12.25 + 7r) = 4\pi r^2 + 550$

$\Rightarrow 4\pi r^2 + 49\pi + 28\pi r = 4\pi r^2 + 550$

$\Rightarrow \quad 7\pi(7 + 4r) = 550$

$\Rightarrow \quad 7 \times \frac{22}{7}(7 + 4r) = 550$

$\Rightarrow \quad 22 \times 7 + 88r = 550$

$\Rightarrow \quad 88r = 550 - 154 = 396$

$\Rightarrow \quad r = \frac{396}{88} = 4.5$ cm

66. (*c*) Let $AD = x$

$\therefore \quad CD = (12 - x)$ cm

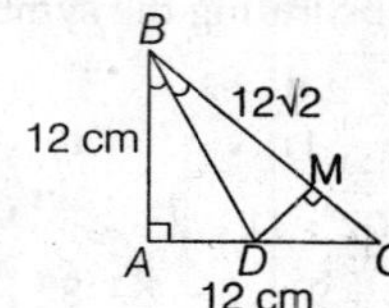

We know,

By Angle Bisector theorem,

$\frac{AB}{AC} = \frac{AD}{CD}$

$\frac{12}{12\sqrt{2}} = \frac{x}{12 - x}$

$\Rightarrow \quad \frac{1}{\sqrt{2}} = \frac{x}{12 - x}$

$\Rightarrow \quad 12 - x = x\sqrt{2}$

$\Rightarrow x(\sqrt{2} + 1) = 12$

$\Rightarrow \quad x = \frac{12}{\sqrt{2} + 1} \times \frac{\sqrt{2} - 1}{\sqrt{2} - 1}$

$\therefore \quad x = 12(\sqrt{2} - 1)$

67. (*b*) Given,

Rohan's 1 hour's work $= \frac{1}{10}$

(Rohan + Mohan)'s 1 hour's work $= \frac{1}{4}$

According to the question,

Mohan's 1 hour's work $= \frac{1}{4} - \frac{1}{10}$

$= \frac{5-2}{20} = \frac{3}{20}$

∴ Mohan can complete the work

$= \frac{20}{3}$ h

68. *(c)* Let the two numbers be $2x$ and $3x$, respectively.

According to the question,

$2x + 3x = 135 \Rightarrow 5x = 135$

$\Rightarrow x = \frac{135}{5} = 27$

∴ Required numbers are (2×27), (3×27)

$= 54, 81$

69. *(a)* Let income of B be ₹$100x$.

∴ Income of A = ₹$125x$

Also, assume savings of A = ₹$100s$

∴ Savings of B = ₹$120s$

∴ Expenditure of $A = 125x - 100s$

Expenditure of $B = 100x - 120s$

According to the question,

$\frac{75}{100}(125x - 100s) = 100x - 120s$

$\Rightarrow 9375x - 7500s = 10000x - 12000s$

$\Rightarrow 4500s = 625x$

$\Rightarrow x = \frac{4500s}{625} = 7.2s$

$\therefore \frac{x}{s} = \frac{72}{10}$

$\Rightarrow x = 72k, s = 10k$ (Assume)

∴ Income of A and B

$= (125 \times 72k), (100 \times 72k)$

$= 9000k, 7200k$

∴ Savings of $B = (120 \times 10k) = 1200k$

∴ Expenditure of $B = 7200k - 1200k$

$= 6000k$

∴ Required percentage

$= \frac{1200k}{6000k} \times 100$

$= 20\%$

70. *(b)* Let the upstream and downstream speeds be $2x$ and $3x$, respectively.

According to the question,

$2x + 3x = 15$

$\Rightarrow 5x = 15$

$\Rightarrow x = 3$

∴ Upstream speed $= 2 \times 3 = 6$ km/h

Downstream speed $= 3 \times 3 = 9$ km/h

∴ Required speed of streams

$= \frac{1}{2}$ (Downstream speed − Upstream speed)

$= \frac{1}{2}(9 - 6) = \frac{1}{2} \times 3 = 1.5$ **km/h**

71. *(a)* For company M,

In 2005,

Ratio of Import to Export

$= 0.8 = \frac{8}{10}$

Import = 8 units and Export = 10 units

In 2006,

Ratio of Import to Export

$= 1.2 = \frac{12}{10}$

Import = 12 units and Export = 10 units

In 2007,

Ratio of Import to Export $= 1 = \frac{10}{10}$

∴ Import = Export

= 1 unit or 10 units

In 2008,

Ratio of Import to Export $= 1.4 = \frac{14}{10}$

∴ Import = 14 units, Export = 10 units

Similar can be observed for 2009 and 2010 as in 2006, 2007, 2008 in which Imports are more than Exports.

∴ Required year = 2005

72. *(d)* Let ten's place digit and unit place digit be x and y, respectively.

∴ Original number $= 10x + y$

Number when digits are reversed

$= 10y + x$

According to the question,

$10x + y = 5(x + y) + 12$

$\Rightarrow 10x + y = 5x + 5y + 12$

$\Rightarrow 5x - 4y = 12$ ...(i)

Also, $10y + x + 9 = 10x + y$

$\Rightarrow 9x - 9y = 9$

$\Rightarrow x - y = 1$

$\Rightarrow x = 1 + y$ ...(ii)

From Eqs.(i) and (ii),

$5(1 + y) - 4y = 12$

$\Rightarrow 5 + 5y - 4y = 12$

$\Rightarrow y = 7$

$\therefore x = 1 + 7 = 8$

∴ Required original number

$= 10 \times 8 + 7 = 87$

73. *(a)* According to question,

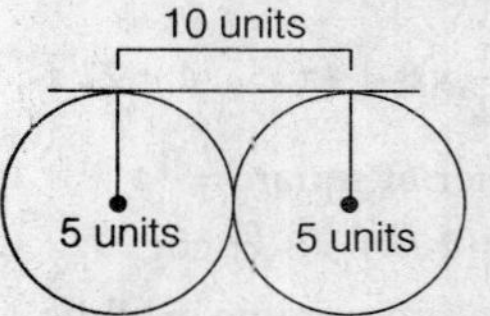

Given, length of direct common tangent = 10 units

Radius of both circles = 5 units

We know,

Length of direct common tangent

$= \sqrt{d^2 - (r_1 - r_2)^2}$

[where, d is distance between centres of two circles and r_1, r_2 be radius of two circles]

$10 = \sqrt{d^2 - (5-5)^2}$

Squaring of both sides, we get

$100 = d^2$

$\Rightarrow d = 10$ units

74. *(a)* Let OP be the perpendicular distance between chord and diameter.

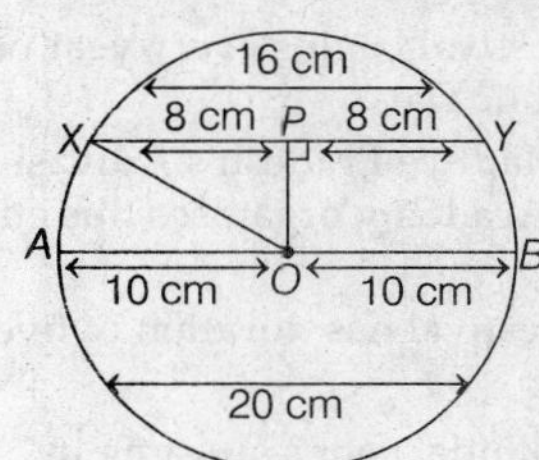

Given, $XY = 16$ cm

Diameter, $AB = 20$ cm

We know,

Perpendicular from the centre of circle to a chord bisects the chord.

Also, we know,

OX is radius of circle.

$\therefore OX = 10$ cm

In ΔOPX,

$OP^2 = OX^2 - (XP)^2$

$= (10)^2 - (8)^2$

$= 100 - 64 = 36$

$\therefore OP = 6$ units

75. *(d)* Given,

Radius of semi-circle $(r) = 2\sqrt{2}$ cm

Also, assume the side of square be a cm.

According to the question,

Area of square = Area of semi-circle

$a^2 = \frac{1}{2}\pi r^2$

$$\Rightarrow a^2 = \frac{1}{2} \times \pi \times (2\sqrt{2})^2$$

$$a^2 = \frac{\pi}{2} \times 8 = 4\pi \Rightarrow \quad a = 2\sqrt{\pi}$$

$\therefore$ Perimeter of square $= 4a$

$$= 4(2\sqrt{\pi}) = 8\sqrt{\pi} \text{ cm}$$

76. *(c)* Vitasta programme exhibits rich culture, arts and crafts of Kashmir.

- This programme started from Chennai and ended in Srinagar.
- In this programme, events like workshops, art installation camps, seminars, craft exhibitions were organised.

77. *(b)* Raja Ram Mohan Roy founded a reformist organisation called 'Brahmo Samaj' in Calcutta.

- It was founded in year 1828.
- It was earlier known as Brahmo Sabha.
- It prohibited all form of idolatry and sacrifice.

78. *(d)* Madhya Pradesh organises the Lokrang festival in Bhopal.

- The festival begins every year on Republic Day.
- The Madhya Pradesh's Adivasi Lok Kala Academy organises this ethnic show.
- This festival has duration of five days.

79. *(c)* 'Pankhida' songs are sung by peasants of Rajasthan.

- The meaning of 'Pankhida' is 'lover'.
- They play Algoza and Manjira while singing this song.
- It is folk song sung by peasants while working in field.

80. *(a)* The factor cost is considered for calculating the National Income in India.

- National Income is total value of final output of all goods and services produced in a country within a year.
- Factor cost is the actual cost incurred on goods and services production.

81. *(a)* 'India Justice Report' is an initiative of Tata Trusts.

- This report ranks the states in justice delivery system.
- It was first published in 2019.
- The India Justice Report 2022 was topped by Karnataka among the 18 states.

82. *(d)* Keyboard is an input device. Speaker, moniter and printer are output devices.

83. *(c)* Western disturbances are responsible for rainfall during winters in the North-western part of India.

- The low pressure system that develops over the Mediterranean sea are known as Western disturbances.
- These wind systems provide winter rains for the growth development of Rabi crops.
- This downpour known as Mahawat locally.

84. *(b)* Ultraviolet rays were discovered by Johann Wilhelm Ritter in 1801.

The Sun is an important source of these waves and these frequency ranges lie between 10^{14} Hz to 10^{17} Hz.

85. *(c)* Indian Railway was introduced in year 1853.

- The first passenger train ran between Bori Bunder (Bombay) to Thane.
- India's first passenger train was operated by Great Indian Peninsula Railway.
- It was for distance of 34 km.

86. *(a)* Statements (1) and (3) are true with respect to MRTP Act.

- The Monopolies and Restrictive Trade Practices Act (MRTP Act) of 1969 was replaced by the Competition Act of 2002 on 1st September, 2009.
- The Monopolies and Restrictive Trade Practices Act (MRTP Act) of 1969 was created to prevent the concentration of economic power, control monopolies, and prohibit monopolistic and restrictive trade practices.
- Statement (2) is incorrect because the asset limit for MRTP companies was fixed at ₹ 20 crores not at ₹ 25 crores by the first/original Monopolies Restrictive Trade Practices Act.

87. *(b)* Padam is a musical composition that expresses devotion through Madhura Bhakti.

- Madhura Bhakti was discovered, developed and dragged to climax by the devotees only and not by God.
- It is the main theme of the scripture 'Bhagavatam'.
- Scripture 'Bhagavatam' (Bhagavata Purana) is a central text in Vaishnavism.

88. *(a)* Haryana secured over-all third position in the medal tally at the 36th National Games of India.

- Gujarat hosted 36th National Games.
- Services Sports Control Board tops the medal tally at National Games 2022 followed by Maharashtra.
- 38th National Games 2024 will be hosted by Uttarakhand.

89. *(d)* In the 11th century, under Mahmud of Ghazni, a small town in Afghanistan became the capital of the vast empire of the Ghaznavids.

- Sultan Mahmud of Ghazni was the son of Sabuktigin, the founder of the Ghaznavid dynasty.
- Mahmud Ghazni attacked India 17 times between the years 1000 to 1027 AD, his famous attack was Somnath temple.
- He ruled regions in Iran, Central Asia and North-western parts of the Indian subcontinent.

90. *(b)* The set of Articles 29-30 in the Constitution of India is known as 'Cultural and Educational Rights'.

Article 29

- It provides that any section of the citizens residing in any part of India having a distinct language, script or culture of its own, shall have the right to conserve the same.
- It grants protection to both religious minorities as well as linguistic minorities.

Article 30

- All minorities shall have the right to establish and administer educational institutions of their choice.

91. *(c)* Mundari language is spoken in the Chota Nagpur plateau region of India.

- Mundari is an Austroasiatic language spoken by the Munda people in eastern India and Bangladesh.
- Chotanagpur plateau region consists of Jharkhand, Odisha and West Bengal, some parts of Madhya Pradesh.

92. *(b)* Pandit Birju Maharaj was related to Kathak.

- Pandit Birju Maharaj was an Indian dancer, composer and singer.

- He was the exponent of the Lucknow 'Kalka Bindadin' Gharana of Kathak dance in India.
- Kathak is a classical dance form that originated in Uttar Pradesh.
- Kathak is one of the nine major forms of Indian classical dance.

93. *(d)* Art 51A (a) says to abide by the Constitution and respect its ideals and institutions, the National Flag and the National Anthem.

- Article 51A of the Constitution of India lists 11 Fundamental Duties for citizens.
- Fundamental Duties are a set of responsibilities that Indian citizens have to fulfill, as outlined in the Indian Constitution.
- The 42nd Amendment of the Constitution of India in 1976 added Fundamental Duties to the Constitution, based on the recommendations of the Swaran Singh Committee.

94. *(d)* In 1924, the Indian football team went on its first known official international tour.

- In 1924, the Indian team which consisted of both Indian and British players. It was led by the legendary Indian footballer Gostha Pal made a trip to Sri Lanka.
- The All India Football Federation (AIFF) was formed in 1937.

95. *(b)* The six-membered cyclic structure of glucose called a pyranose structure because pyran is a cyclic organic compound, with one oxygen atom and five carbon atoms in the ring.

96. *(d)* When a new text document is created in MS Office 2016, the default text size of the document is 11 points.

97. *(c)* Statements (2) and (3) are correct regarding a bill on Uniform Civil Code (UCC).

- UCC (Uniform Civil Code), a proposal in India, to create a single set of personal laws that apply equally to all citizens, regardless of religion.
- The Uniform Civil Code (UCC) is a set of laws that are part of the Indian Constitution's Directive Principles of State Policy, as defined in Article 44.
- Statement (1) is incorrect because UCC Bill was proposed in March 2020 but was withdrawn without introduction in the Parliament.

98. *(c)* According to the National Multidimensional Poverty Index 2021, Sikkim has the lowest percentage of population being multidimensional poor in given options.

- The National Multidimensional Poverty measures simultaneous deprivations across three equally weighted dimensions of Health, Education and Standard of Living.
- NITI Aayog released National Multidimensional Poverty Index (MPI).
- As per NITI Aayog's 2023 MPI, Kerala tops the list followed by Goa and Tamil Nadu simultaneously.

99. *(a)* India is home to the second oldest cricket club in the world. It is situated in Kolkata.

- The Calcutta Cricket Club is second oldest cricket club in the world established in 1792.
- The oldest cricket club is the Marylebone Cricket Club (MCC), founded in 1787 in London.
- The Calcutta Cricket Club is now known as the Calcutta Cricket and Football Club.

100. *(d)* Kharif crops are sown at the beginning of the monsoon season.

- Kharif crops are also known as monsoon crops, they are sown in June or July and harvested in September to October.
  Examples Rice, Maize, Cotton etc.
- Zaid crops are seasonal fruits and vegetables grown in the Indian subcontinent during the summer months.
  Examples Cucumber, Pumpkin, Tomato, Bitter gourd etc.
- Rabi Crops, also known as winter crops, are typically sown between October and December and harvested between April and June.
  Examples Wheat, Barley, Oats, Bajra etc.

Set 23 08 July, 2024 (Shift III)

SSC CHSL Tier-I SOLVED PAPER

Instructions

1. This paper contains 100 questions.
2. It has 4 Parts, **Part I** General English, **Part II** General Intelligence & Reasoning, **Part III** Quantitative Aptitude and **Part IV** General Awareness.
3. Each question carries **2 marks**.

Part I
General English

1. The following sentence has been split into four segments. Identify the segment that contains an error.

In this cold weather, / there's nothing / like good / cup of coffee.

(a) In this cold weather
(b) like good
(c) cup of coffee
(d) there's nothing

2. The given sentence is divided into four segments. Select the option that has the segment with a grammatical error.

The general's address / was applauds / by all sections / of society.

(a) by all sections
(b) was applauds
(c) of society
(d) the general's address

3. Parts of the following sentence have been given as options. Select the option that contains an error.

There's an quiet street down the left that you can use for your dance practice.

(a) down the left
(b) that you can use
(c) There's an quiet street
(d) for your dance practice

4. The given sentence is divided into four segments. Select the option that has the segment with a grammatical error.

A part / of an / apple is / rotten.

(a) apple is (b) of an
(c) A part (d) rotten

Directions (Q. Nos. 5-9) *In the following passage, some words have been deleted. Read the passage carefully and select the most appropriate option to fill in each blank.*

Trees provide so many benefits (1)........ our everyday lives. They filter clean air, provide fresh drinking water, help (2)............ climate change and create homes for thousands of species of plants and animals. (3).......... a billion trees can help save the Earth from climate change and biodiversity loss. When we restore and (4).......... critical forests, we remove carbon and support biodiversity. A billion is a big number, but we know we can do it together. (5).......... the planet by planting your tree today. This can protect and restore forests for future.

5. Select the most appropriate option to fill in blank number (1).

(a) in (b) to
(c) for (d) with

6. Select the most appropriate option to fill in blank number (2).

(a) crib (b) cut
(c) curb (d) crust

7. Select the most appropriate option to fill in blank number (3).

(a) In planting
(b) With planting
(c) By planting
(d) Planting

8. Select the most appropriate option to fill in blank number (4).

(a) sabotage (b) conserve
(c) observe (d) curtail

9. Select the most appropriate option to fill in blank number (5).

(a) Denigrate (b) Complement
(c) Sustain (d) Supplement

10. Select the most appropriate option that can substitute the underlined segment in the given sentence.

He has grown <u>into a beautiful youth.</u>

(a) in a beautiful youth
(b) a beautiful youth
(c) in a handsome youth
(d) into a handsome youth

11. Select the most appropriate synonym of the given word.

Venom

(a) Poison (b) Butter
(c) Fruit juice (d) Honey

12. Select the most appropriate option that can substitute the underlined segment in the given sentence. If there is no need to substitute it, select 'No substitution required'.

The inspector <u>smile</u> after he was finished and patted Margie's head.

(a) No substitution required
(b) smiled
(c) was smiled
(d) has smiled

13. Select the most appropriate option to substitute the underlined segment in the following sentence.

<u>Rohit is write</u> to them three times.

(a) Rohit was beings written
(b) Rohit was write
(c) Rohit had write
(d) Rohit has written

14. Select the most appropriate meaning of the given idiom.

Where the shoe pinches

(a) Unknown paths
(b) Difficult roads
(c) Where the difficulty lies
(d) Where the shoe hurts

15. Select the most appropriate synonym of the given word.
Callous
(a) Cruel (b) Generous
(c) Affectionate (d) Exhausting

16. Select the most appropriate antonym of the underlined word in the given sentence.
The CEO called for <u>compulsory</u> participation from each employee.
(a) voluntary (b) compliantly
(c) obligatory (d) overtly

17. Select the most appropriate synonym of the given word.
Baffle
(a) Explicate (b) Confuse
(c) Barbarous (d) Equalise

18. Select the most appropriate antonym of the given word.
Logical
(a) Subtle (b) Random
(c) Reasonable (d) Illogical

19. Select the most appropriate option to fill in the blank.
The company's .... commitment to sustainability is admirable.
(a) shakeable (b) resolute
(c) wavering (d) strong

20. The given sentence is divided into four segments. Identify the segment that contains a spelling error.
To submit a report / on the recent fire accident, / a high level commitee / has been formed.
(a) To submit a report
(b) has been formed
(c) on the recent fire accident
(d) a high level commitee

21. Select the most appropriate idiom to fill in the blank.
Mala .... by cheating on the exam to win her bet with Priya.
(a) get the sack
(b) look down upon
(c) hit below the belt
(d) fell out

22. Identify the incorrectly spelt word in the following sentence and select the option with the correct spelling.
Stomach sleepers were rated as being more gregairious and uncomfortable with criticism.
(a) gregarious (b) criticicm
(c) ratedd (d) stomac

23. Select the most appropriate option to substitute the underlined segment in the following sentence.
<u>We are decorate</u> the living-room at the moment.
(a) We are being decorating
(b) We are being decorate
(c) We are decorates
(d) We are decorating

24. Select the most appropriate option to fill in the blank.
The perfume she uses has a strong ....
(a) sent (b) scent
(c) cent (d) send

25. Select the most appropriate option to fill in the blank.
Rosy and Nicky couldn't provide any evidence to support .... arguments.
(a) there (b) theirs
(c) their (d) they're

Part II
General Intelligence

26. Select the correct mirror image of the given figure, when the mirror is placed at MN.

Pb5dra | M N

(a) ɒɿbƨdq (b) ɐɹpϛqd
(c) ɒɿbƨdd (d) aɿb5dq

27. 'A × B' means 'A is B's mother'.
'A ÷ B' means 'A is B's son'.
'A + B' means 'A is B's husband'.
'A – B' means 'A is B's sister'.
Using the same meaning of the mathematical operators as given above, in 'D + E × F – G' what is the relation of F with D?
(a) Sister's daughter
(b) Mother
(c) Son
(d) Daughter

28. What will come in the place of the question mark (?) in the following equation, if '+' and '–' are interchanged and '×' and '÷' are interchanged?
61 + 80 – 48 × 3 ÷ 5 = ?
(a) 60 (b) 63 (c) 62 (d) 61

29. TOWB is related to CVDU in a certain way based on the English alphabetical order. In the same way, VKFA is related to BRMW. To which of the following is CMZU related, following the same logic?
(a) VGTD
(b) VGDT
(c) VTGD
(d) VTDG

30. Which of the following numbers will replace the question mark (?) in the given series?
454 , 515, 426, 481, 398, 447, 370, 413, ?
(a) 313 (b) 326
(c) 342 (d) 354

31. What should come in place of the question mark (?) in the given series?
12, 16, 25, 41, 66, ?
(a) 104 (b) 101
(c) 103 (d) 102

32. Select the combination of letters that when sequentially placed in the blanks of the given series will complete the series.
ZY_WZTX_Z_XU_JXT
(a) ZYOX (b) YVOZ
(c) XOVZ (d) XVOZ

33. Select the correct mirror image of the given figure, when the mirror is placed at MN as shown below.

QZGSIN | M N

(a) ИIGSZQ (b) ИIƧӘZQ
(c) ИIƧGZQ (d) ИIƧӘQZ

34. In a certain code language, 'WYNK' is coded as '9243' and 'YAWN' is coded as '3941'. How is 'A' coded in the given language?
(a) 2 (b) 9
(c) 3 (d) 1

35. Select the correct mirror image of the given figure, when the mirror is placed at MN as shown below.

jRp34da | M N

(a) ɒbᔭ3dЯį (b) abᔭƐqЯį
(c) ɒbᔭƐqЯį (d) ɘpᔭƐdЯ¡

36. Three statements are followed by conclusions numbered I, II. You have to consider these statements to be true, even if they seem to be at variance with commonly known facts. Decide which of the given conclusions logically follow(s) from the given statements.

Statements

Some rivers are huts.

All streams are grass.

Some grass are rivers.

Conclusions

I. All grass are streams.

II. Some grass are huts.

(a) Only Conclusion I follows
(b) Only Conclusion II follows
(c) Neither Conclusion I nor II follows
(d) Both Conclusions I and II follow

37. Which letter-cluster will replace the question mark (?) to complete the given series?

KLHO, LKIN, ?, QFNI, UBRE

(a) OJKL (b) NIKL
(c) NJKM (d) OIKM

38. If 5th August, 2005 is Friday, then what will be the day of the week on 17th April, 2011?

(a) Saturday (b) Wednesday
(c) Sunday (d) Monday

39. 13 is related to 39 following a certain logic. Following the same logic, 25 is related to 75. To which of the following is 42 related following the same logic?

(**Note** Operations should be performed on the whole numbers, without breaking down the numbers into its constituent digits. E.g. 13 – Operations on 13 such as adding /subtracting /multiplying etc., to 13 can be performed. Breaking down 13 into 1 and 3 and then performing mathematical operations on 1 and 3 is not allowed.)

(a) 128 (b) 126 (c) 118 (d) 120

40. Identify the figure in the options that when put in place of the question mark (?) will logically complete the series?

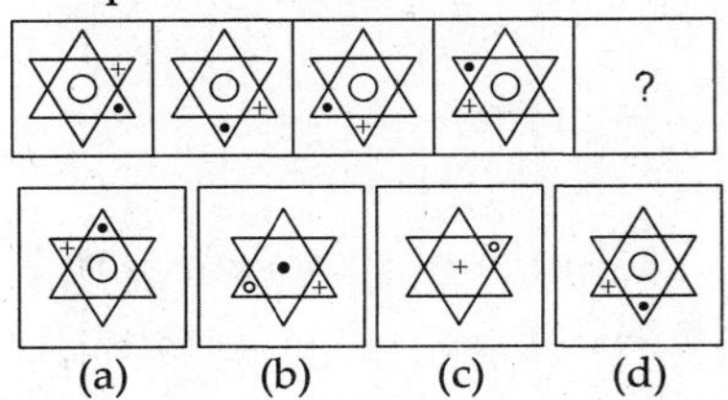

41. Each of the letters in the word TRAMPOLINE are arranged from left to right in alphabetical order to form a new word. How many letters are there in the English alphabetical series between the alphabet, which is fourth from the left and the one, which is first from the right in the newly formed word?

(a) Five
(b) Four
(c) Six
(d) Seven

42. How many triangles are there in the given figure?

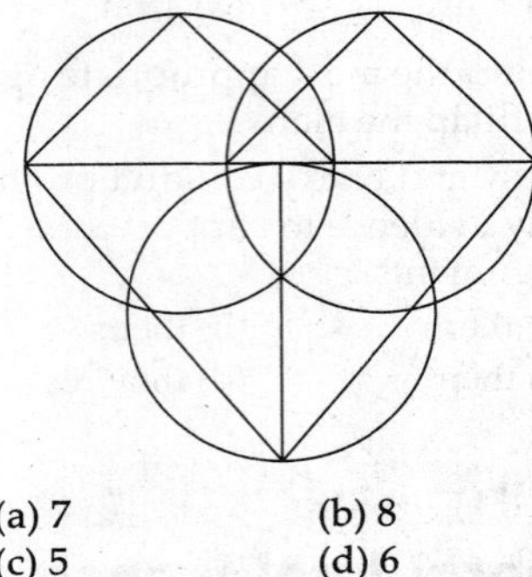

(a) 7 (b) 8
(c) 5 (d) 6

43. What will come in the place of the question mark (?) in the following equation, if '+' and '×' are interchanged and '–' and '÷' are interchanged?

$35 \times 16 + 3 \div 156 - 12 = ?$

(a) 70 (b) 63
(c) 64 (d) 72

44. 'YPCLY' is related to 'RIVER' in a certain way based on the English alphabetical order. In the same way, 'ZWHJL' is related to 'SPACE'. To which of the following is 'TVJRALZA' related, following the same logic?

(a) MOXKTEST
(b) MOOKTEST
(c) MOCTTEST
(d) MOCKTEST

45. Select the option figure in which the given figure (X) is embedded as its part (rotation is not allowed).

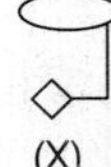

(X)

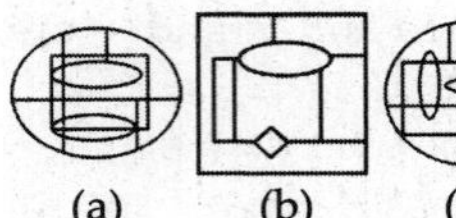

(a) (b) (c) (d)

46. Select the option in which the given figure (X) is embedded (i.e. contains figure (X) in the same form).

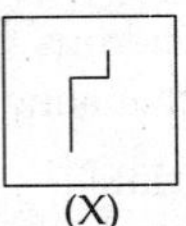

(X)

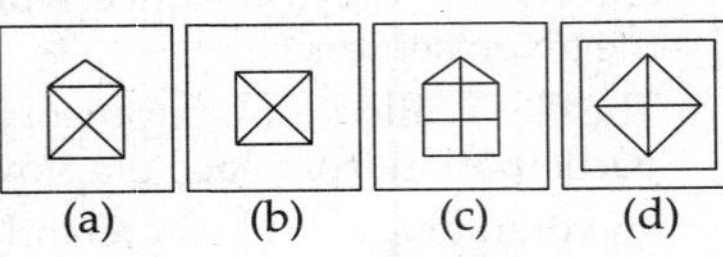

(a) (b) (c) (d)

47. While introducing Madhav, Jihaan said, "I am the only son of one of the sons of his mother."
How is Madhav related to Jihaan?

(a) Father or paternal uncle
(b) Son or brother
(c) Cousin
(d) Maternal nephew or paternal nephew

48. If 'A' stands for '÷', 'B' stands for '×', 'C' stands for '+', and 'D' stands for '–', what will come in place of the question mark (?) in the following equation?

45 B 6 D 78 A 3 C 15 = ?

(a) 256
(b) 257
(c) 259
(d) 258

49. In a certain code language, 'power' is coded as '45978' and 'rain' is coded as '7312'. How is 'r' coded in that language?

(a) 1 (b) 7
(c) 3 (d) 5

50. Select the set in which the numbers are related in the same way as are the numbers of the following sets.

(**Note** Operations should be performed on the whole numbers, without breaking down the numbers into its constituent digits. E.g. 13 – Operations on 13 such as adding/subtracting/multiplying etc. to 13 can be performed. Breaking down 13 into 1 and 3 and then performing mathematical operations on 1 and 3 is not allowed.)

(75, 89, 103)
(98, 112, 126)

(a) (95, 109, 118)
(b) (87, 101, 125)
(c) (82, 96, 110)
(d) (72, 91, 105)

Part III

Quantitative Aptitude

51. Study the given graph carefully and answer the question that follows.

The graph shows the demand and production of different companies.

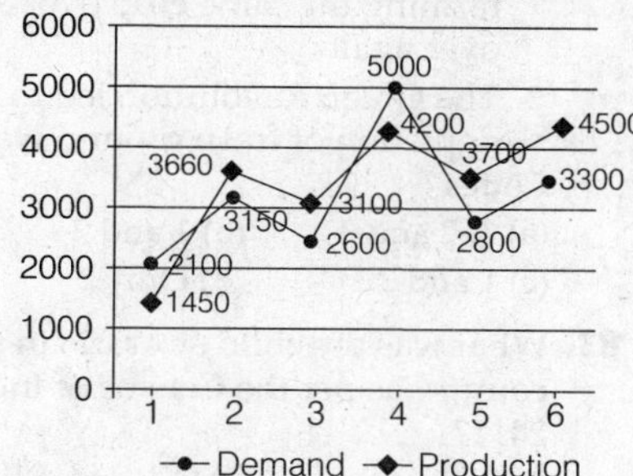

Lowest production is what percentage of the highest demand?

(a) 71% (b) 70% (c) 29% (d) 30%

52. Pradeep sells two fans at ₹ 480 each and by doing so he gains 20% on one fan and loses 20% on the other. His loss on the whole (in ₹) is

(a) 30 (b) 10
(c) 20 (d) 40

53. The area of an isosceles right-angled triangle is 16 m². Its hypotenuse is

(a) 0.8 m (b) 4 m (c) 8 cm (d) 8 m

54. 8 apples and 10 oranges weigh 5 kg. 12 apples and 20 oranges weigh 9 kg. What is the weight (in kg, rounded off to the nearest integer) of 15 apples and 24 oranges?

(a) 13 (b) 10
(c) 16 (d) 11

55. Simplify

$$4\frac{1}{4}\times 4\frac{1}{4} - 2\times 4\frac{1}{4}\times\frac{1}{4} + \frac{1}{4}\times\frac{1}{4}$$

(a) 64 (b) 32
(c) 4 (d) 16

56. Study the given bar-graph and answer the question that follows.

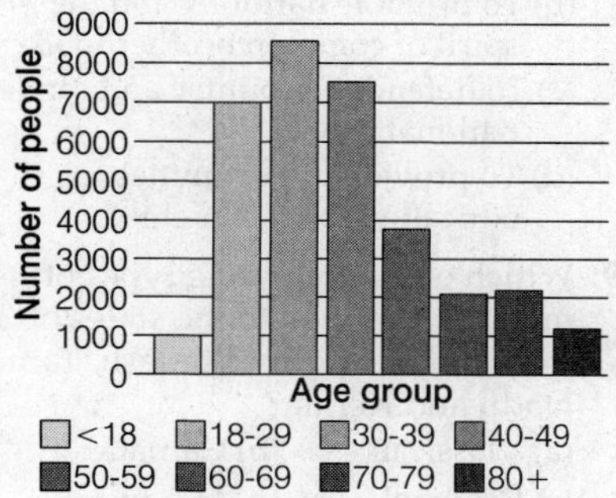

Which age group has the least number of people?

(a) 30-39 (b) 80+
(c) <18 (d) 50-59

57. The centres of two circles are 84 cm apart. If the radii of these two circles are 38 cm and 26 cm, respectively, then which of the following options gives the length (in cm) of a direct common tangent of these two circles?

(a) $36\sqrt{3}$ (b) $48\sqrt{3}$
(c) $42\sqrt{3}$ (d) $54\sqrt{3}$

58. If $\sin\theta = \frac{11}{12}$, then what will be the value of $(\tan\theta + \sec\theta)$?

(a) $\sqrt{23}$ (b) $\frac{11}{\sqrt{23}}$ (c) $\frac{12}{\sqrt{23}}$ (d) 23

59. At an election involving two candidates, 68 votes are declared invalid. The winning candidate gets 52% of the valid votes and wins by 98 votes. The total number of votes polled is

(a) 2475 (b) 2518
(c) 2500 (d) 2250

60. R can finish a work in 6 days if he works 10 h a day. S can finish it in 5 days, if he works 8 h a day. If both start a work and work daily for 6 h, the work will be finished in ..... days.

(a) 3 (b) 4 (c) 5 (d) 6

61. Find the mean proportional between 25 and 81.

(a) 36 (b) 12
(c) 45 (d) 81

62. R and S can finish a work in 10 days, S and T can finish it in 12 days and T and R can finish in 8 days. In how many days will the work be finished, if they all work simultaneously?

(a) $\frac{240}{31}$ (b) $\frac{240}{37}$ (c) $\frac{240}{39}$ (d) $\frac{240}{33}$

63. A solid metallic cylinder of base radius 6 cm and height 10 cm is melted to form small cylinders, each of height 2.5 cm and base radius 2 cm. Find the number of small cylinders.

(a) 32 (b) 36
(c) 80 (d) 360

64. From a circular sheet of circumference 264 cm, two equal maximum-sized circular plates are cut off. What will be the circumference of each plate? $\left(\text{use } \pi = \frac{22}{7}\right)$

(a) 264 cm (b) 135 cm
(c) 176 cm (d) 132 cm

65. The marked price of a battery-operated rickshaw is ₹ 90000. It is available for sale at two successive discounts of 10% and 5%. What is the selling price (in ₹) of the battery-operated rickshaw?

(a) 78950 (b) 76950
(c) 75850 (d) 77850

66. In a triangle ABC, P and Q are two points on AB and AC, respectively, such that PQ parallel to BC. If $AC = 5QC$, then the ratio $PQ : BC$ is equal to

(a) 3 : 4 (b) 5 : 4 (c) 4 : 5 (d) 4 : 3

67. Ramesh's pocket money was reduced by 25% and then the reduced pocket money was increased by 20%. Find the net increase or decrease percentage in his original pocket money.

(a) Decrease 12% (b) Increase 12%
(c) Increase 10% (d) Decrease 10%

68. Find the altitude (in cm) of side MT of triangle MNT with side $MN = 36$ cm, $MT = 36$ cm and $NT = 48$ cm.

(a) $16\sqrt{5}$ (b) $18\sqrt{3}$
(c) $12\sqrt{5}$ (d) $24\sqrt{3}$

69. Study the given graph carefully and answer the question that follows.

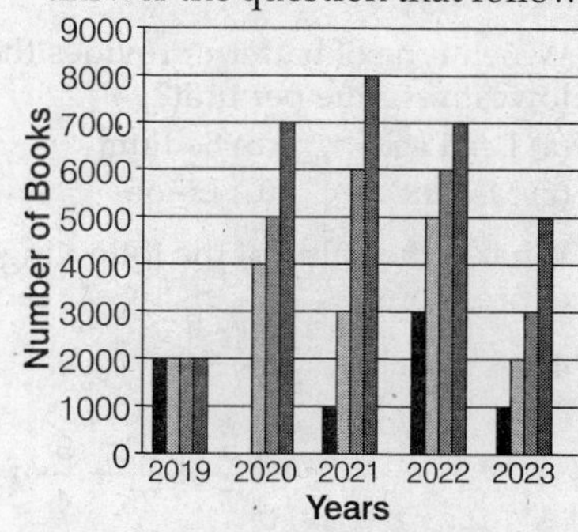

Number of Books in a School library

On the basis of this multiple bar graph, what is the change in the number of Literature books from the year 2020 to the year 2023.

(a) 1000 more (b) 2000 less
(c) No change (d) 2000 more

70. A sum of money becomes five times its original value in 15 yr, when invested at a certain simple interest rate. If the sum was invested twice the time at the same rate of interest, what would be the final amount?
(a) The money becomes 7 times its original value
(b) The money becomes 9 times its original value
(c) The money becomes 6 times its original value
(d) The money becomes 8 times its original value

71. A battery manufacturer manufactures five different types of batteries. The total revenue for the year 2020 is ₹ 2500000 and 20000 units were exported in 2020. The distribution of revenue and units for the five different types of batteries is shown in the charts.

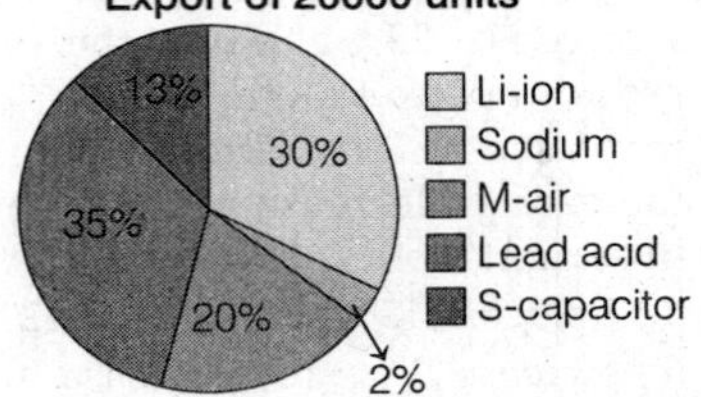

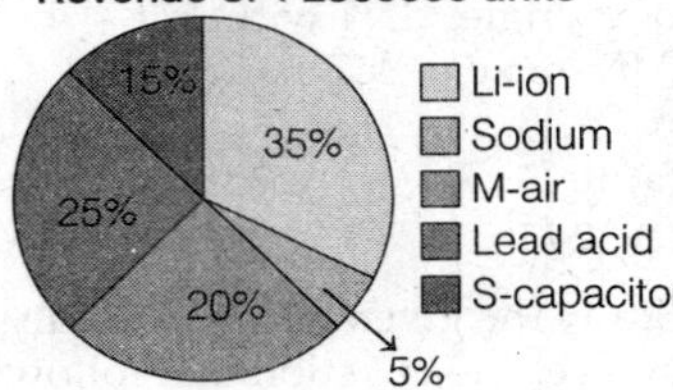

Which type of battery provides the lowest revenue per unit?
(a) Lead acid (b) Sodium
(c) M-Air (d) Li-ion

72. What is the value of the following expression?

$$420 \div \left[\frac{4}{9} \times \left(1 + \frac{4}{5}\right) \times 5\right] + \left[\frac{5}{7} \text{ of } \frac{21}{25} \div \frac{3}{4} \text{ of } \frac{2}{5}\right]$$

(a) 127 (b) 139 (c) 107 (d) 89

73. The speed of a boat in still water is 12 km/h and the speed of the stream is 3 km/h. A man goes to a place by boat, 45 km and comes back to the starting point. Find the total time taken by him.
(a) 9 h (b) 6 h
(c) 8 h (d) 7 h

74. In an election a candidate secured 47% of the votes and lost to his only opponent by 276 votes. Find the total number of votes polled.
(a) 4000 (b) 4200
(c) 4600 (d) 3800

75. Ramu mixes 2 L of water at 100°C and 18 L of water at 32° C. What temperature will the water have after mixing?
(a) 66°C (b) 20°C
(c) 38.8°C (d) 40°C

Part III
General Awareness

76. The parliamentary standing committees have a tenure of .... year(s).
(a) one (b) four
(c) three (d) two

77. Which military officer led the British forces in the Battle of Chinhat fought in 1857?
(a) Robert Maclagan
(b) Henry Lawrence
(c) James George Smith
(d) Charles Ellice

78. Citizens are not discriminated against on the basis of religion, caste or sex because of
(a) Right to Equality
(b) Right against Exploitation
(c) Right to Freedom
(d) Right to Freedom of Religion

79. Which is the nearest planet to the Sun?
(a) Uranus (b) Jupiter
(c) Mercury (d) Saturn

80. Name the Chola inscription that provided details of the way in which the Sabha was organised in the local administration in the Chola empire.
(a) Thiruvalangadu inscription
(b) Thirunanthikarai inscription
(c) Darsanam Koppu inscription
(d) Uttaramerur inscription

81. Since 1994, Winter Olympics traditionally take place .... after the Summer Olympics.
(a) 4 years
(b) 3 months
(c) 6 months
(d) 2 years

82. Which of the following statements about the Green Revolution is/are correct?
1. India became self-sufficient with the introduction of the Green Revolution.
2. The Green Revolution led to loss of nutrients in the soil from farming the same crop over and over again.
3. The Green Revolution led to depletion of fresh ground water.

Codes
(a) 1, 2 and 3 (b) 1 and 3
(c) 1 and 2 (d) Only 2

83. What was the child sex ratio in the country as per the Census of India 2011?
(a) 189 (b) 911 (c) 981 (d) 919

84. As per Census of India 2011, in which of the following states was the total population less than 10 lakh?
(a) Telangana (b) Sikkim
(c) Goa (d) Tripura

85. In MS-Word, a document may be printed using ....
(a) Ctrl+X (b) Ctrl+C
(c) Ctrl+P (d) Ctrl+V

86. Which of the following articles was amended in the Constitution (Fifth Amendment Act), 1955?
(a) Article 4 (b) Article 3
(c) Article 34 (d) Article 17

87. Which of the following is a string instrument commonly featured in the folk music of Gujarat?
(a) Turi (b) Bungal (c) Jantar (d) Pava

88. A housemaid gets her 12-year-old daughter to help in her work as a house cleaner at a residential colony instead of sending her to school. Which Fundamental Duty is violated by the housemaid?
(a) To safeguard public property and to abjure violence
(b) To promote harmony and the spirit of common brotherhood
(c) To defend the country and render national service
(d) To provide opportunities for education to his/her child

89. Which of the following types of music is confined to the states of Karnataka, Andhra Pradesh, Tamil Nadu and Kerala?
(a) Classical (b) Carnatic
(c) Regional (d) Hindustan

90. How can you access the Step by Step Mail Merge Wizard in Microsoft Word?
(a) Clicking on the File menu
(b) Pressing Ctrl + M
(c) Clicking on the Mailings tab
(d) Pressing F12

91. Which of the following is a medium-sized globular protein that acts as a pancreatic serine protease found in the digestive system of many vertebrates?
(a) Amylase (b) Lipase
(c) Trypsin (d) Pepsin

92. Buddh International Circuit is located at
(a) Chennai (b) Noida
(c) Mumbai (d) Delhi

93. The Supreme Court, in May 2023, observed that it can give divorce on the ground of irretrievable breakdown of marriage by exercising its discretionary power under ....
(a) Article 136 of the Constitution of India
(b) Article 32 of the Constitution of India
(c) Article 142 of the Constitution of India
(d) Article 143 of the Constitution of India.

94. What is known to be 'Ekaharya', where one dancer takes on many roles in a single performance?
(a) Bharatanatyam
(b) Kathak
(c) Kuchipudi
(d) Kathakali

95. Match the railway zones in column A with their headquarters in column B.

Column A (Railway zones)	Column B (Headquarters)
A. Central	1. New Delhi
B. Northern	2. Mumbai CST
C. Eastern	3. Chennai
D. Southern	4. Kolkata

Codes
(a) A-2, B-1, C-4, D-3
(b) A-2, B-4, C-1, D-3
(c) A-1, B-2, C-4, D-3
(d) A-2, B-1, C-3, D-4

96. The central stretch of the Western coastal plains of India is known as the
(a) Konkan coast
(b) Coromandel coast
(c) Malabar coast
(d) Kannad plains

97. The Kutch festival is held at ....
(a) Surat (b) Rajkot
(c) Bhuj (d) Ahmedabad

98. What is the use of Net National Product (NNP)?
(a) To calculate per capita income
(b) To calculate exports
(c) To calculate balance of payments
(d) To calculate imports

99. In which year did Galileo describe the regular, swinging motion of a pendulum by the action of gravity and acquired momentum?
(a) 1605 (b) 1600
(c) 1599 (d) 1602

100. In which year was the first Arjuna Award given to a woman hockey player?
(a) 1964 (b) 1963
(c) 1962 (d) 1961

Answers

1. (b)	2. (b)	3. (c)	4. (b)
5. (a)	6. (c)	7. (d)	8. (b)
9. (c)	10. (d)	11. (a)	12. (b)
13. (d)	14 (c)	15. (a)	16. (a)
17. (b)	18. (d)	19. (d)	20. (d)
21. (c)	22. (a)	23. (d)	24. (b)
25. (c)	26. (a)	27. (d)	28. (d)
29. (c)	30. (c)	31. (d)	32. (d)
33. (b)	34. (d)	35. (c)	36. (c)
37. (b)	38. (c)	39. (b)	40. (a)
41. (d)	42. (d)	43. (a)	44. (d)
45. (b)	46. (c)	47. (a)	48. (c)
49. (b)	50. (c)	51. (c)	52. (d)
53. (d)	54. (d)	55. (d)	56. (c)
57. (b)	58. (a)	59. (b)	60. (b)
61. (c)	62. (b)	63. (b)	64. (d)
65. (b)	66. (c)	67. (d)	68. (a)
69. (b)	70. (b)	71. (a)	72. (c)
73. (c)	74. (c)	75. (c)	76. (a)
77. (b)	78. (a)	79. (c)	80. (d)
81. (d)	82. (a)	83. (d)	84. (b)
85. (c)	86. (b)	87. (c)	88. (d)
89. (b)	90. (c)	91. (c)	92. (b)
93. (c)	94. (a)	95. (a)	96. (d)
97. (c)	98. (a)	99. (d)	100. (d)

Explanations

1. *(b)* Part 'like good' contains an error. Add 'a' after 'like' to correct the sentence.

2. *(b)* Part 'was applauds' contains an error. Use 'applauded' to correct the sentence.

3. *(c)* Part 'There's an quiet street' contains an error. Use 'a' in the place of 'an' to correct the sentence.

4. *(b)* Part 'of an' contains an error. Use 'the' to correct the sentence.

5. *(a)* The correct filler for the given blank is 'in'.

6. *(c)* The correct filler for the given blank is 'curb'.

7. *(d)* The correct filler for the given blank is 'Planting'.

8. *(b)* The correct filler for the given blank is 'conserve'.

9. *(c)* The correct filler for the given blank is 'Sustain'.

10. *(d)* The underlined part of the given sentence contains an error. Use 'into a handsome youth' to correct the sentence.

11. *(a)* The word 'venom' means 'poison'.

12. *(b)* The underlined part of the given sentence contains an error. Use 'smiled' to correct the sentence as the given sentence is in past tense.

13. *(d)* The underlined part of the given sentence contains an error. Use 'Rohit has written' to correct the sentence.

14. *(c)* 'Where the shoe pinches' refers to the place where difficulty lies.

15. *(a)* 'Callous' means evil and cruel. 'Exhausting' means tiring.

16. *(a)* 'Compulsory' means necessary to do. Hence, its antonym is 'voluntary' which means willingly.
- 'Compliantly' means in a way that shows that you are willing to do what other people want you to do.
- 'Obligatory' means required by a legal, moral, or other rule; compulsory.
- 'Overtly' means without concealment or secrecy; openly.

17. *(b)* 'Baffle' means to be confused.
- 'Explicate' means to analyse and develop (an idea or principle) in detail.
- 'Barbarous' means extremely brutal.
- 'Equalise' means to make things equal.

18. *(d)* The antonym of 'Logical' is 'Illogical'.

19. *(d)* The correct filler for the given blank is 'strong'.

20. *(d)* Part 'a high level commitee' contains an error. The correct spelling is 'committee'.

21. *(c)* The correct idiom for the given blank is 'hit below the belt'. It means to say something that is often too personal, usually irrelevant, and always unfair:

- 'Get the sack' means to be fired or removed from the job.
- 'Look down upon' means to think or treat someone or something as unimportant.
- 'Fell out' means to have a disagreement.

22. *(a)* The incorrectly spelt word is 'gregairious'. The correct spelling is 'gregarious'.

23. *(d)* The underlined part of the given sentence contains an error. Use 'We are decorating' to correct the sentence.

24. *(b)* The correct filler for the given blank is 'scent'.

25. *(c)* The correct filler for the given blank is 'their'.

26. *(a)* The figure given in option (a) is the correct mirror image of the given question figure.

M
Pb5dra
N

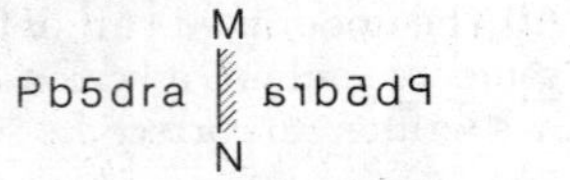

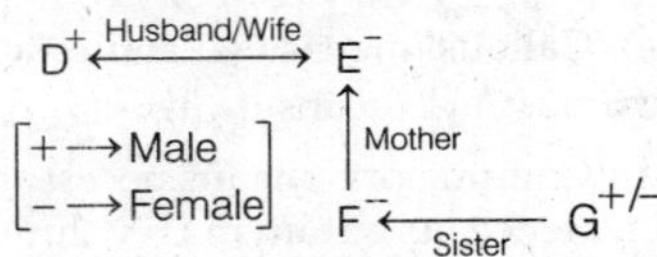

27. *(d)* Given expression, D + E × F − G

Husband/Wife
Mother
Sister
+ ⟶ Male
− ⟶ Female

Clearly, 'F' is daughter of 'D'.

28. *(d)* Given expression,

$$61 + 80 - 48 \times 3 \div 5 = ?$$

After interchanging the signs, we get

$61 - 80 + 48 \div 3 \times 5 = ?$

$? = 61 - 80 + 16 \times 5$

$= 61 - 80 + 80$

$= 141 - 80 = 61$

29. *(c)* As,

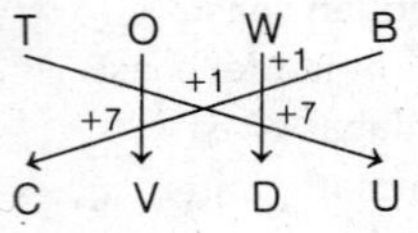

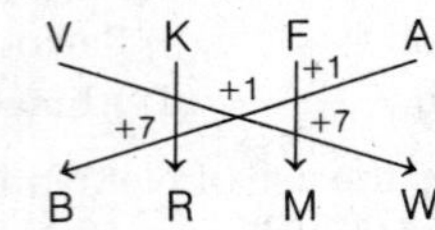

T O W B
+1 +1
+7 +7
C V D U

and

V K F A
+1 +1
+7 +7
B R M W

Similarly,

C M Z U
+1 +1
+7 +7
V T G D

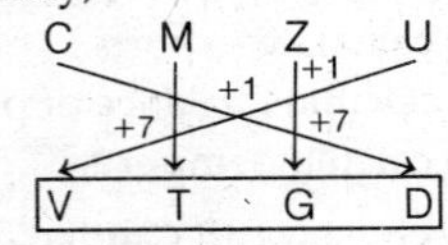

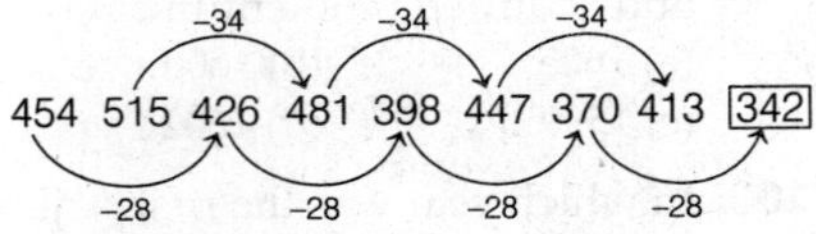

30. *(c)* The pattern of the series is as follows,

−34 −34 −34
454 515 426 481 398 447 370 413 342
−28 −28 −28 −28

31. *(d)* The pattern of the series is as follows,

12 16 25 41 66 102
+2² +3² +4² +5² +6²

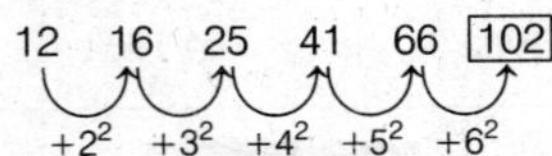

32. *(d)* The pattern of given series is as follows,

−5 −5 −5
ZYXW/ZTXV/ZOXU/ZJXT
−1 −1 −1

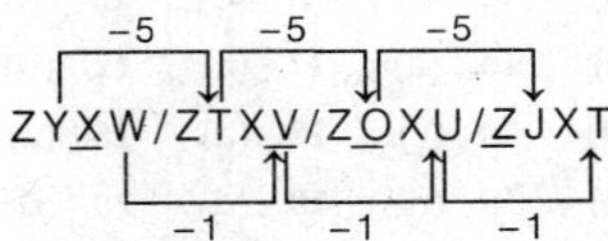

⇒ XVOZ

33. *(b)* The correct mirror image along MN is

M
QZGSIN
N

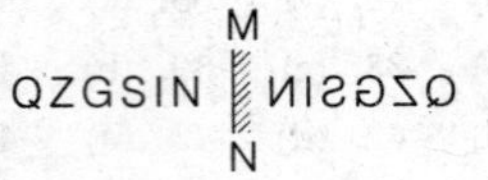

34. *(d)* According to the question,

W Y N K ⟶ 9 2 4 3

Y A W N ⟶ 3 9 4 1

So, the code for 'A' is '1'.

35. *(c)* The correct mirror image along MN is as follows,

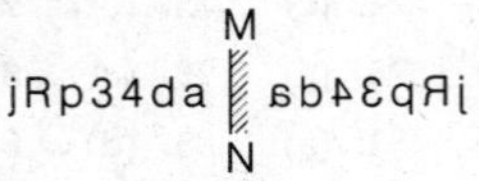

M
jRp34da
N

36. *(c)* According to the given statements,

Streams
Grass
Rivers
Huts

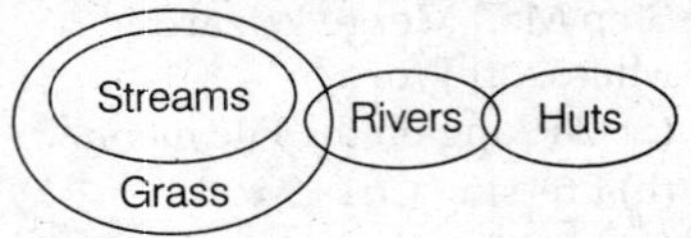

Conclusions I. (✗) II. (✗)

∴ Neither Conclusion I nor II follows.

37. *(b)* The pattern of series is as follows,

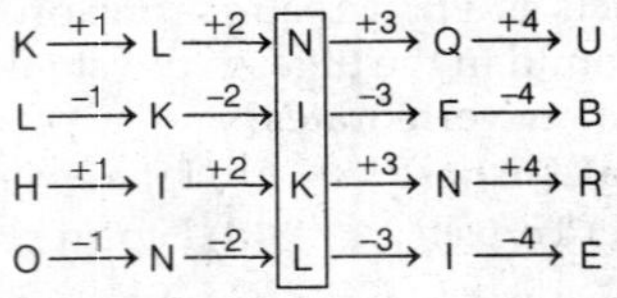

K +1 L +2 N +3 Q +4 U
L −1 K −2 I −3 F −4 B
H +1 I +2 K +3 N +4 R
O −1 N −2 L −3 I −4 E

38. *(c)* Given,

5th August, 2005 = Friday

Number of odd days left in 2005

$= 5 + 2 + 3 + 2 + 3 = 15$

As we know,

Number of odd days in ordinary year = 1

Number of odd days in leap year = 2

∴ Number of odd days up to 17th April, 2011

$= 15 + 1 + 1 + 2 + 1 + 1 + 3 + 0 + 3 + 17$

$= \frac{44}{7} \Rightarrow 2$ odd days

∴ Day of week on 17th April, 2011

= Friday + 2 = Sunday

39. *(b)* As, $13 \times 3 = 39$

and $25 \times 3 = 75$

Similarly, $42 \times 3 = 126$

40. *(a)* In the given figure, the plus sign and shaded dot is moving one place in the clockwise direction in successive figures. So, the option figure (a) is the correct figure.

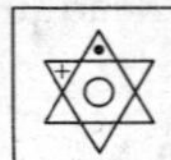

41. *(d)* The given word = TRAMPOLINE

After rearrangement in alphabetical order

AEILMNOPRT

4th alphabet from left end = L

and 1st alphabet from right end = T

∴ Number of letters between L and T = 7

42. *(d)* Naming the figure,

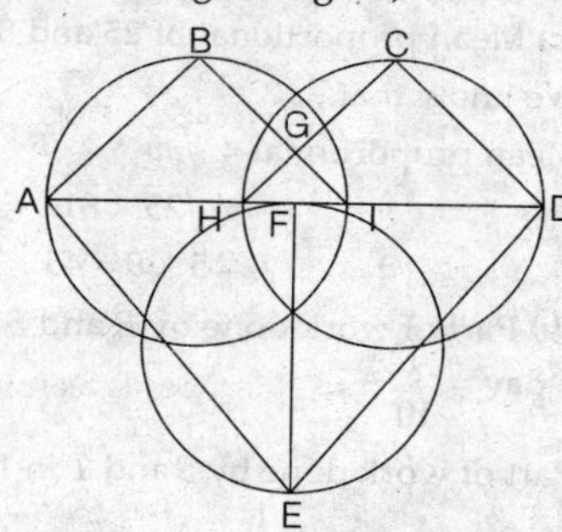

Triangles are ΔABI, ΔHCD, ΔGHI, ΔAED, ΔAFE and ΔFED

∴ Total '6' triangles are there in figure.

43. *(a)* Given equation,

$$35 \times 16 + 3 \div 156 - 12 = ?$$

After interchanging the signs, we get

$$35 + 16 \times 3 - 156 \div 12 = ?$$

$$? = 35 + 16 \times 3 - 13$$

$$= 35 + 48 - 13$$

$$= 83 - 13 = 70$$

44. *(d)* As,

Y P C L Y
−7 −7 −7 −7 −7
R I V E R

and

Z W H J L
−7 −7 −7 −7 −7
S P A C E

Similarly,

T V J R A L Z A
−7 −7 −7 −7 −7 −7 −7 −7
M O C K T E S T

45. *(b)* The given figure (X) is embedded in the figure (b).

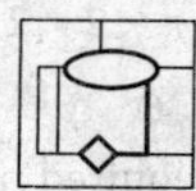

46. *(c)* The given figure (X) is embedded in the figure (c).

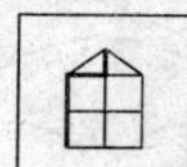

47. *(a)* According to the question,

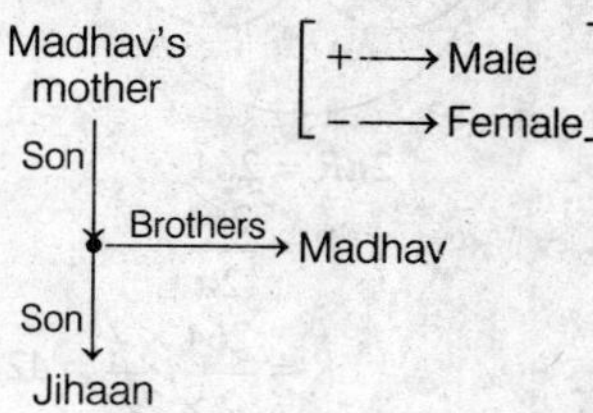

Or

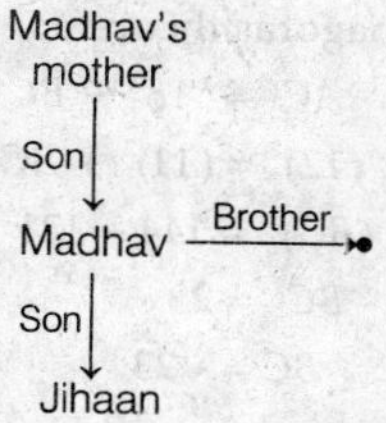

Madhav's mother
↓ Son
Madhav —Brother→
↓ Son
Jihaan

From the family tree, we derived that Madhav is either father or paternal uncle of 'Jihaan'.

48. *(c)* The given equation,

45 B 6 D 78 A 3 C 15 = ?

After substituting letters with symbols, we get

$$? = 45 \times 6 - 78 \div 3 + 15$$

$$= 45 \times 6 - 26 + 15$$

$$= 270 - 26 + 15$$

$$= 285 - 26$$

$$= 259$$

49. *(b)* The given code,

p o w e [r] → 4 5 9 [7] 8

[r] a i n → [7] 3 1 2

So, the code for r = 7

50. *(c)* As, (75, 89, 103)

$$= \frac{75 + 103}{2}$$

$$= \frac{178}{2} = 89$$

and (98, 112, 126)

$$= \frac{98 + 126}{2}$$

$$= \frac{224}{2} = 112$$

Similarly, (82, 96, 110)

$$= \frac{82 + 110}{2}$$

$$= \frac{192}{2} = 96$$

51. *(c)* According to given graph,

Lowest production of the companies

$$= 1450$$

and highest demand of the company

$$= 5000$$

Hence, required percentage

$$= \frac{1450}{5000} \times 100$$

$$= \frac{1450}{50}$$

$$= 29\%$$

52. *(d)* Given, selling price of each fan is ₹ 480.

∴ Cost price of first fan

$$= 480 \times \frac{100}{120} = ₹\ 400$$

and cost price of second fan

$$= 480 \times \frac{100}{80} = ₹\ 600$$

∴ Total cost price of the fans

$$= 600 + 400 = ₹\ 1000$$

Total selling price of the fans

$$= 480 + 480 = 960$$

∴ Loss = CP − SP

$$= 1000 - 960$$

$$= ₹\ 40$$

53. *(d)* Suppose, ΔABC is an isosceles triangle.

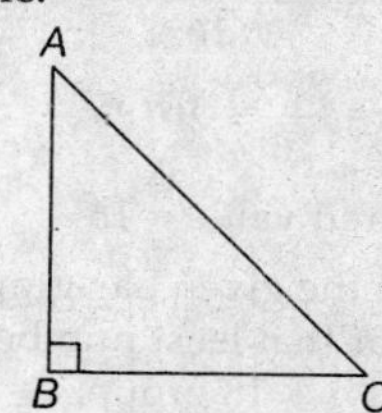

and let $BC = AB = x$ m

Then, by Pythagoras theorem,

$$AB^2 + BC^2 = AC^2$$

$$\Rightarrow \quad x^2 + x^2 = AC^2$$

$$\Rightarrow \quad 2x^2 = AC^2$$

$$\Rightarrow \quad AC = \sqrt{2}x \text{ m}$$

∴ Area of $\Delta ABC = \frac{1}{2} \times \text{Base} \times \text{Height}$

$$16 = \frac{1}{2} \times x \times x$$

$$\Rightarrow \quad 32 = x^2 \Rightarrow x = 4\sqrt{2} \text{ m}$$

Hence, hypotenuse of ΔABC

$$= \sqrt{2}x = \sqrt{2} \times 4\sqrt{2}$$

$$= 8 \text{ m}$$

54. *(d)* Let the weight of each apple be x kg and weight of each orange be y kg.

According to the question,

$$8x + 10y = 5 \text{ kg} \quad \ldots(i)$$

and $$12x + 20y = 9 \text{ kg} \quad \ldots(ii)$$

Multiplying Eq. (i) by 2 and subtract from Eq. (ii),

$$4x = 1 \Rightarrow x = \frac{1}{4}$$

Now, put in Eq. (i)

$$8 \times \frac{1}{4} + 10y = 5$$

$\Rightarrow \quad 2 + 10y = 5$

$\Rightarrow \quad y = \frac{3}{10}$

Hence, required weight of 15 apples and 24 oranges

$= 15x + 24y$

$= 15 \times \frac{1}{4} + 24 \times \frac{3}{10}$

$= \frac{15}{4} + \frac{72}{10} = 10.95$ kg

≈ 11 kg

55. *(d)* $4\frac{1}{4} \times 4\frac{1}{4} - 2 \times 4\frac{1}{4} \times \frac{1}{4} + \frac{1}{4} \times \frac{1}{4}$

$= \frac{17}{4} \times \frac{17}{4} - 2 \times \frac{17}{4} \times \frac{1}{4} + \frac{1}{16}$

$= \frac{289}{16} - \frac{34}{16} + \frac{1}{16}$

$= \frac{289 - 34 + 1}{16}$

$= \frac{256}{16} = 16$

$\therefore$ Required value = 16

56. *(c)* From the given bar-graph, it is very clear that least number of people occurred in < 18 group.

i.e., Number of people in (< 18) group is 1000, which is least among all group.

57. *(b)* Distance between centres = 84 cm

Radius of first circle, $R_2 = 38$ cm

Radius of second circle, $R_1 = 26$ cm

Then, length of direct common tangent

$= \sqrt{(\text{Distance between centres})^2 - (R_2 - R_1)^2}$

$= \sqrt{(84)^2 - (38 - 26)^2}$

$= \sqrt{84^2 - 12^2}$

$= \sqrt{96 \times 72}$

$= \sqrt{24 \times 4 \times 24 \times 3} = 48\sqrt{3}$ cm

Hence, required length of common tangent is $48\sqrt{3}$.

58. *(a)* $\sin\theta = \frac{11}{12}$

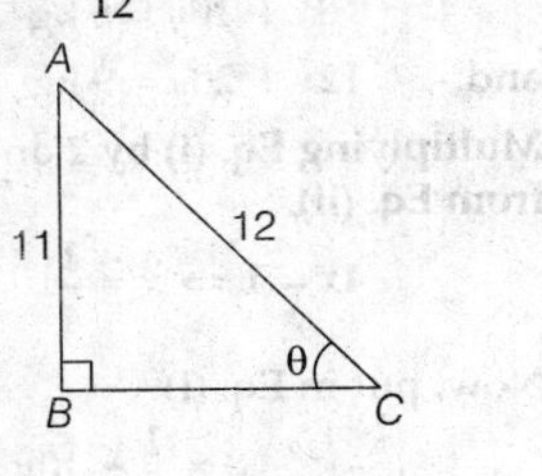

i.e. $AB = 11$

$AC = 12$

By Pythagoras theorem,

$AC^2 = AB^2 + BC^2$

$(12)^2 = (11)^2 + BC^2$

$\Rightarrow \quad (BC)^2 = 144 - 121$

$\Rightarrow \quad BC^2 = 23$

$\Rightarrow \quad BC = \sqrt{23}$

$\therefore \tan\theta + \sec\theta = \frac{AB}{BC} + \frac{AC}{BC}$

$= \frac{11}{\sqrt{23}} + \frac{12}{\sqrt{23}}$

$= \frac{23}{\sqrt{23}}$

$= \sqrt{23}$

$[\because 23 = \sqrt{23} \times \sqrt{23}]$

59. *(b)* Let total number of polled votes be $100x$.

But, 68 votes are invalid.

$\therefore$ Valid votes $= (100x - 68)$

According to question,

$(100x - 68) \times \frac{52}{100} - (100x - 68) \times \frac{48}{100} = 98$

$\Rightarrow \quad (100x - 68)\left[\frac{52}{100} - \frac{48}{100}\right] = 98$

$\Rightarrow \quad (100x - 68) \times \left[\frac{4}{100}\right] = 98$

$\Rightarrow \quad (100x - 68) \times \frac{1}{25} = 98$

$\Rightarrow \quad 100x - 68 = 2450$

$\Rightarrow \quad 100x = 2450 + 68$

$\Rightarrow \quad 100x = 2518$

Hence, total number of polled votes

$= 100x = 2518$

60. *(b)* R can complete the work

$= 6 \times 10 = 60$ h

S can complete the work

$= 5 \times 8 = 40$ h

R's 1 h work $= \frac{1}{60}$

S's 1 h work $= \frac{1}{40}$

$\therefore (R + S)$'s 1 h work $= \frac{1}{40} + \frac{1}{60} = \frac{5}{120}$

$\therefore$ Both can finish the work in $\frac{120}{5}$ h.

Both work for 6h daily i.e.,

Work will be finished in

$= \frac{120}{5} \times \frac{1}{6}$ days

$\therefore$ The work will be finished in 4 days.

61. *(c)* Mean proportional of 25 and 81

We know that,

Mean proportional $= \sqrt{ab}$

$= \sqrt{25 \times 81}$

$= 5 \times 9 = 45$

62. *(b)* Part of work done by R and S in 1 day $= \frac{1}{10}$

Part of work done by S and T in 1 day

$= \frac{1}{12}$

Part of work done by T and R in 1 day

$= \frac{1}{8}$

Part of work done by $2S$, $2T$ and $2R$ in 1 day $= \frac{1}{10} + \frac{1}{12} + \frac{1}{8}$

$= \frac{12 + 10 + 15}{120} = \frac{37}{120}$

Part of work done by S, R and T in 1 day $= \frac{37}{120} \times \frac{1}{2} = \frac{37}{240}$

$\therefore$ Required days when work done by all simultaneously

$= \frac{240}{37}$ days

63. *(b)* Let the number of small cylinder be n.

According to the question,

Volume of bigger cylinder

$= n \times$ Volume of smaller cylinder

$\pi \times R^2 H = n \times \pi r^2 h$

$\Rightarrow \pi \times 6 \times 6 \times 10 = n \times \pi \times 2 \times 2 \times 2.5$

$n = \frac{\pi \times 6 \times 6 \times 10}{\pi \times 2 \times 2 \times 2.5}$

$\therefore \quad n = 36$

Hence, the required number of smaller cylinder = 36

64. *(d)* Circumference of bigger circle

= 264 cm

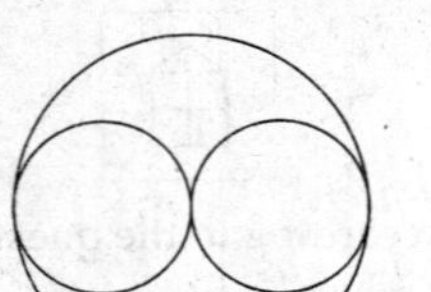

$2\pi R = 264$

$\Rightarrow \quad R = \frac{264}{2\pi}$

$\Rightarrow \quad R = \frac{264 \times 7}{2 \times 22} = 42$ cm

Then, radius of each smaller circular plates $= \frac{42}{2} = 21$ cm

Then, circumference of each small plates $= 2 \times \pi \times r$

$= 2 \times \frac{22}{7} \times 21 = 132$ cm

65. *(b)* Marked price of battery-operated rickshaw is ₹ 90000.

Successive discounts = 10% and 5%

Thus, selling price of battery-rickshaw after two successive discounts

$= 90000 \times \frac{(100-10)}{100} \times \frac{(100-5)}{100}$

$= 90000 \times \frac{90}{100} \times \frac{95}{100}$

$= 9 \times 90 \times 95 =$ ₹ 76950

∴ Required selling price = ₹ 76950

66. *(c)* In ΔABC,

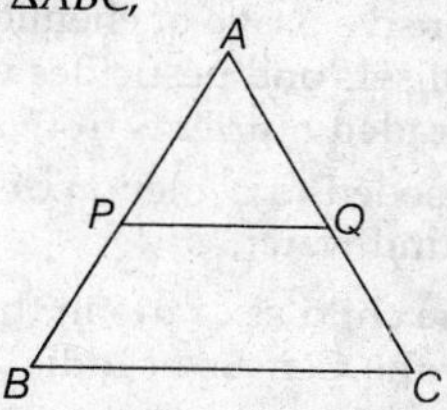

$PQ \parallel BC$ and $AC = 5\,QC$

∴ $\frac{AC}{QC} = \frac{5}{1}$

Then, ratio of $\frac{AQ}{AC} = \frac{(5-1)}{5} = \frac{4}{5}$

As we know,

ΔAPQ and ΔABC are similar because all angles are equal.

Then, ratio of all sides of triangles are equal.

Hence, $\frac{PQ}{BC} = \frac{4}{5}$

67. *(d)* Let Ramesh pocket money was ₹ $100x$.

Then, pocket money after decrease by 25%

$= 100x \times \frac{75}{100} = 75x$

Again, pocket money after increase of 20%

$= 75x \times \frac{(100+20)}{100}$

$= 75x \times \frac{120}{100} = 90x$

Thus, net decrease percentage

$= \frac{100x - 90x}{100x} \times 100$

$= \frac{10x}{100x} \times 100 = 10\%$

68. *(a)* In ΔMNT,

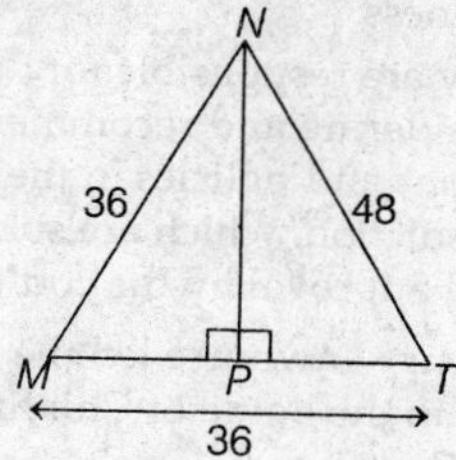

$MN = 36$ cm

$MT = 36$ cm

and $NT = 48$ cm

$s = \frac{a+b+c}{2} = \frac{36+36+48}{2}$

$= 60$

Area of ΔMNT

$= \sqrt{s(s-a)(s-b)(s-c)}$

$= \sqrt{60 \times 24 \times 24 \times 12}$

$= \sqrt{12 \times 5 \times 24 \times 24 \times 12}$

$= 12 \times 24 \times \sqrt{5}$ cm^2

Again, area of ΔMNT having MT as base.

Then,

$\frac{1}{2} \times MT \times NP = 12 \times 24 \times \sqrt{5}$

$\Rightarrow \frac{1}{2} \times 36 \times NP = 12 \times 24 \times \sqrt{5}$

∴ $NP = 16\sqrt{5}$ cm

69. *(b)* Number of Literature books in 2020

= 5000

Number of Literature books in 2023

= 3000

∴ Change in number of books

= 5000 − 3000

= 2000 less

70. *(b)* Let the principal sum be ₹ P.

It becomes $5P$ in 15 yr at certain rate.

$SI = \frac{P \times R \times T}{100}$

$5P - P = \frac{P \times R \times 15}{100}$

$\Rightarrow 4P = \frac{P \times R \times 15}{100}$

∴ $R = \frac{80}{3}\%$

Again, if time period be double, then time = 30 yr

∴ $SI = \frac{P \times R \times T}{100}$

$= P \times \frac{80}{3} \times \frac{30}{100}$

SI = ₹ $8P$

∴ Amount = SI + Principal

$= 8P + P =$ ₹ $9P$

Thus, final amount become 9 times its original value.

71. *(a)* Number of units of Li-ion

$= 20000 \times \frac{30}{100} = 6000$

Number of units of Sodium

$= 20000 \times \frac{2}{100} = 400$

Number of units of M-air

$= 20000 \times \frac{20}{100} = 4000$

Number of units of Lead-acid

$= 20000 \times \frac{35}{100} = 7000$

Number of units of S-capacitor

$= 20000 \times \frac{13}{100} = 2600$

Now, revenue of Li-ion

$= 2500000 \times \frac{35}{100} =$ ₹ 875000

Revenue of Li-ion per unit

$= \frac{875000}{6000} =$ ₹ 145.83

Revenue of Sodium

$= 2500000 \times \frac{5}{100} =$ ₹ 125000

Revenue of Sodium per unit = ₹ 312.5

Revenue of M-air

$= 2500000 \times \frac{20}{100} =$ ₹ 500000

Revenue of M-air per unit

$= \frac{500000}{4000} =$ ₹ 125

Revenue of lead acid

$= 2500000 \times \frac{25}{100} =$ ₹ 625000

Revenue of lead acid per unit

$= \frac{625000}{7000} =$ ₹ 89.28

Revenue of S-capacitor

$= 2500000 \times = \frac{15}{100} =$ ₹ 375000

Revenue of S-capacitor per unit

$= \frac{375000}{2600} =$ ₹ 144.23

Now, it is very clear that revenue of lead acid per unit is the lowest.

72. *(c)* $420 \div \left[\frac{4}{9} \times \left(1 + \frac{4}{5}\right) \times 5\right]$

$+ \left[\frac{5}{7} \text{ of } \frac{21}{25} \div \frac{3}{4} \text{ of } \frac{2}{5}\right]$

$= 420 \div \left[\frac{4}{9} \times \frac{9}{5} \times 5\right] + \left[\frac{5}{7} \times \frac{21}{25} \div \frac{3}{4} \times \frac{2}{5}\right]$

$= 420 \div [4] + \left[\frac{3}{5} \div \frac{3}{10}\right]$

$= 420 \div 4 + \left[\frac{3}{5} \times \frac{10}{3}\right]$

$= 420 \div 4 + 2$

$= 105 + 2 = 107$

73. *(c)* Speed of boat in still water is 12 km/h.

Speed of stream is 3 km/h.

Speed of boat in downstream

$= (12 + 3) = 15$ km/h

Speed of boat in upstream

$= (12 - 3) = 9$ km/h

According to the question,

Required time to travel 45 km

$= \frac{45}{15} + \frac{45}{9} = 3 + 5 = 8$ h

$\therefore$ Required time taken = 8 h

74. *(c)* Let total number of votes polled be $100x$.

One candidate got 47% of votes

$= 100x \times \frac{47}{100} = 47x$

and winner got 53% of votes

$= 100x \times \frac{53}{100} = 53x$

According to the question,

$53x - 47x = 276$

$\Rightarrow 6x = 276$

$\therefore x = 46$

Thus, total votes polled

$= 100x = 46 \times 100 = 4600$

75. *(c)* According to the question,

Let x be temperature after mixing both type of water

$2 \times 100 + 18 \times 32 = (2 + 18) \times x$

$\Rightarrow 200 + 576 = 20 \times x$

$\Rightarrow 776 = 20 \times x$

$\Rightarrow x = \frac{776}{20} = 38.8$

Hence, required temperature = 38.8°C

76. *(a)* The parliamentary standing committees have a tenure of one year.

- Parliamentary standing committees are permanent committees made up of Members of Parliament (MPs).
- It is constituted from time to time according to the provisions of an Act of Parliament or Rules of Procedure and Conduct of Business.
- They are responsible for considering and recommending actions and policies in their areas of jurisdiction, which are subject to final approval by the council.

77. *(b)* Henry Lawrence led the British forces in the Battle of Chinhat fought in 1857.

- The Battle of Chinhat was fought on the morning of 30th June, 1857 between British forces and Indian rebels at Ismailganj, near Chinhat, Awadh.
- The insurgents were led by Barkat Ahmad.

78. *(a)* Citizens are not discriminated against on the basis of religion, caste or sex because of Right to Equality.

- The Right to Equality is the idea that all people should be treated equally and without discrimination.
- In India, Right to Equality is a Fundamental Right.

Right to Equality	Article 14 to Article 18
Right against Exploitation	Article 23 and Article 24
Right to Freedom	Article 19 to Article 22
Right to Freedom of Religion	Article 26 to Article 28

79. *(c)* Mercury is the nearest planet to the Sun.

- Order of planets distance from the Sun is Mercury, Venus, Earth, Mars, Jupiter, Saturn, Uranus and Neptune.
- Our solar system is a collection of objects that orbit the Sun, 8 planets, Moons, asteroids, comets, dust and gas.

80. *(d)* Uttaramerur inscription provided detail about the local administration in Chola empire.

- These inscriptions tell that there were two village assemblies : Sabha and Ur.
- The Sabha included only Brahmin (priestly class).
- The Ur constituted people belonging to all the classes.

81. *(d)* Since 1994, Winter Olympics traditionally take place 2 years after the Summer Olympics.

- The Summer Olympic Games, also known as the Games of the Olympiad, is a major international multi-sport event normally held once every four years.
- The Winter Olympic Games is a major international multi-sport event held once every four years for sports practiced on snow and ice.
- 2024 Summer Olympics was hosted by Paris, France.
- 2026 Winter Olympics will be hosted by Italy.

82. *(a)* All three statements (1), (2) and (3) about Green Revolution are correct.

- The Green Revolution in India began in the late 1960s, with the introduction of modern technologies and methods and it made India self-sufficient.
- Green Revolution involved extensive usage of chemical fertilisers and pesticides which degraded nutrients from soil.
- It also led to depletion of fresh ground water.

83. *(d)* The child sex ratio in the country as per the Census of India 2011 is 919.

- The child sex ratio is defined as the number of females per 1000 males in the age group 0-6 years.
- As per the Census 2011, Arunachal Pradesh has the highest child sex ratio among the Indian states i.e. 972, Haryana has the lowest child sex ratio i.e., 834 per thousand males.
- Andaman and Nicobar Islands has the highest child sex ratio in union territory

84. *(b)* As per the Census of 2011, Sikkim has a population of 6.71 lakhs.

- As per Census of 2011, Sikkim is the least populated state in India, followed by Mizoram.
- Uttar Pradesh is the most populated state in India followed by Maharashtra.
- Kerala has the highest literacy rate and Bihar has the lowest literacy among the Indian states.

85. *(c)* In MS Word, a document may be printed using Ctrl + P.

86. *(b)* Article 3 was amended in the Constitution (Fifth Amendment Act), 1955.

- Article 3 of the Indian Constitution has been amended twice, in 1954 and 1955.
- Fifth Amendment states that a bill cannot be introduced in either House of Parliament unless the following conditions are met
  1. The President recommends it.
  2. The President has referred the bill to the Legislature of any state affected by the proposal.
  3. The Legislature has expressed its views within the specified period.
  4. The President allows a further period.
  5. The specified or allowed period has expired.

87. *(c)* Jantar is a string instrument commonly featured in the folk music of Gujarat.

- Jantar is a variety of fretted Veena.
- In structure, it is a contemporary of Rudra Veena and the Saraswati Veena.
- It has two resonators of gourd or wood. The resonator at the lower end of the Jantar is made of specially grown pumpkin.

88. *(d)* The housemaid by sending her child to work and not to school is violating Article 51A of Constitution of India, which deals with Fundamental Duties.

- It states that parent and guardians should provide opportunities for education to their children between ages of six to fourteen.
- Fundamental Duties were added in 1976 on recommendation of Swaran Singh Committee.

89. *(b)* Carnatic music is confined mainly in South India to the state of Tamil Nadu, Kerala, Karnataka and Andhra Pradesh.

- Indian music has mainly two forms: Hindustani and Carnatic.
- Hindustani music is confined in North India in the states of Uttar Pradesh, Madhya Pradesh and Rajasthan etc.

90. *(c)* Clicking on the Mailing tab you can access the Step by Step Mail Merge Wizard in Microsoft Word.

91. *(c)* Trypsin is a medium-sized globular protein that acts as a pancreatic serine protease found in the digestive system of many vertebrates.
Trypsin acts on complex protein molecules and converts those into smaller peptides.

92. *(b)* Buddh International Circuit is located in Noida, UP.

- It was inaugurated on 18th October 2011.
- It is built buy Jaypee Group in Jaypee Sports city.

93. *(c)* The Supreme Court can divorce on the ground of irretrievable break down of marriage by exercising its discretionary power under Article 142.
Article 142 gives the Supreme Court the power to pass any order or decree to achieve complete justice in any case or matter before it.

94. *(a)* 'Ekaharya' is used in Bharatanatyam where one single player plays multiple roles in single performance.

- Bharatanatyam is Indian classical dance from Tamil Nadu.
- This dance involves transitional movement of hips, legs and arms as well as eyes and hand gestures.

95. *(a)* The headquarter of Central Railway is located in Mumbai.

- The headquarter of Northern Railway is located at New Delhi.
- The headquarter of Eastern Railway is situated at Kolkata.
- The headquarter of South Railway is situated at Chennai.

96. *(d)* The central stretch of Western coastal plains is called as Kannad Plain or Karavali.

- The northernmost part of Western coastal plain is Konkan coast.
- The southernmost part of Western coastal plain is Malabar coast.

97. *(c)* The Kutch festival is held at Bhuj, Gujarat.

- Kutch festival or Rann festival is 3-month long festival of music, dance, nature of beauty. The Kutch festival dates from October till third week of February each year.

98. *(a)* Net National Product (NNP) is used to calculate per capita income.

- NNP provides indication for overall economic growth and marked thealth of country.
- NNP is obtained by subtracting depreciation from Gross National Product (GNP).

99. *(d)* Galileo Galilei, an italian physicists, astronomer and mathematician, described the regular, swinging motion of a pendulum due to gravity and acquired momentum in 1602. This discovery led to understanding of simple harmonic motion.

100. *(d)* In 1961, first Arjuna Award was given to women hockey player.

- Kumari Anne Lumsden was awarded first Arjuna Award in 1961 for hockey.
- KM Meena Shah, received second Arjuna Award in 1962. She was associated with badminton.

Set 24 08 July, 2024 (Shift IV)

SSC CHSL Tier-I SOLVED PAPER

Instructions

1. This paper contains 100 questions.
2. It has 4 Parts, **Part I** General English, **Part II** General Intelligence & Reasoning, **Part III** Quantitative Aptitude and **Part IV** General Awareness.
3. Each questions carries **2 mark**.

Part I General English

1. The given sentence is divided into four segments. Select the option that has the segment with a grammatical error.

The sun rises / in an east / and sets / in the west.

(a) in the west (b) and sets
(c) the sun rises (d) in an east

2. The given sentence is divided into three segments. Select the option that has the segment with a grammatical error. If there is no error, select 'No error'.

The judges eliminated the / classical singer, as she dropped of / in the middle of the competition.

(a) in the middle of the competition
(b) The judges eliminated the
(c) classical singer, as she dropped of
(d) No error

3. The following sentence has been divided into four segments. Identify the segment that contains an error.

How long are you working / for your current employer / and why don't you / look for better opportunities?

(a) look for better opportunities
(b) and why don't you
(c) How long are you working
(d) for your current employer

4. Select the most appropriate option to fill in the blank.

All the players from this athletic club participated in the tournament and ……… one of them got a medal.

(a) none (b) each
(c) they (d) all

Directions (Q.Nos. 5-9) *In the following passage, some words have been deleted. Read the passage carefully and select the most appropriate option to fill in each blank.*

A few months after Conrads death, the nobles met at Aix-la-Chapelle and elected Henry to be their king. At this time, it was the (1)............... in Europe to hunt various birds, such as the wild duck and partridge, with falcons. The falcons were long-winged birds of prey, (2)............... hawks. They were trained to (3)............... on their masters wrist and wait patiently until they were told to fly. Then they would swiftly (4) .... at their prey and bear it to the ground. Henry was very fond of falconry and hence was known as Henry the Fowler, or Falconer. As soon as the other dukes had elected him king, a messenger was sent to Saxony to (5)............... him of the honour done for him. After a search of some days, he was at last found, far up in the Hartz Mountains, hunting with his falcons.

5. Select the most appropriate option to fill in blank number (1).

(a) custom (b) ritualistic
(c) motive (d) conventions

6. Select the most appropriate option to fill in blank number (2).

(a) subjugating (b) echoing
(c) favouring (d) resembling

7. Select the most appropriate option to fill in blank number (3).

(a) lurch (b) chirp
(c) sitting (d) perch

8. Select the most appropriate option to fill in blank number (4).

(a) leapt (b) flight
(c) dart (d) dashed

9. Select the most appropriate option to fill in blank number (5).

(a) inform (b) nullify
(c) communicate (d) convey

10. Select the most appropriate option that can substitute the underlined segment in the given sentence.

The player was declared <u>fit and in excellent health</u> to play the final matches.

(a) right as rain
(b) left out in cold
(c) on cloud nine
(d) up in the arms

11. Select the most appropriate homonym to fill in the blank.

The prince is the ……… to the throne.

(a) air (b) heir
(c) err (d) ere

12. Select the most appropriate option that can replace the bracketed word segment in the following sentence.

Men (allowed) for Olympic artistic swimming for the first time at the 2024 Paris Games, the IOC confirmed on Thursday.

(a) are likely (b) have permitted
(c) will approve (d) are eligible

13. Select the most appropriate antonym of the given word.

Terminate

(a) Mark (b) Die
(c) Conclude (d) Begin

14. Select the most appropriate option to fill in the blank.

The .... purpose of the coaching was to identify the talented players.

(a) mane (b) mine
(c) mean (d) main

15. Select the most appropriate option that can substitute the underlined segment in the given sentence.

As there was no one to look thorough the orphan, he had to take refuge in the orphanage.

(a) look down upon
(b) look after
(c) look upon
(d) look through

16. Select the most appropriate pair of words to fill in the blanks.

Shyam has reserved a .... in the train for his wife as she will be giving .... to his child soon.

(a) birth; birth (b) berth; birth
(c) berth; berth (d) birth; berth

17. Select the most appropriate option that can substitute the underlined word in the given sentence.

Loud noise effects our ability to concentrate.

(a) affects (b) bestows
(c) results (d) intensifies

18. There is a spelling error in the given sentence. Select the option that contains the incorrectly spelt word.

They adressed the special gathering perfectly.

(a) addressed (b) special
(c) gathering (d) perfectly

19. Select the most appropriate homophone to fill in the blank.

These people are artists. .... skills are extraordinary.

(a) They or (b) There
(c) They're (d) Their

20. Select the incorrectly spelt word.

(a) Conscience (b) Consciencious
(c) Conspicuous (d) Conscious

21. Select the most appropriate meaning of the given idiom.

To read between the lines

(a) To grasp the hidden meaning
(b) To read without concentration
(c) To read aloud
(d) To whisper

22. Select the most appropriate antonym of the given word.

Peace

(a) Harmony
(b) Strange
(c) Turmoil
(d) Refusal

23. Select the most appropriate antonym of the underlined word in the given sentence.

His industrious attitude was the reason for his promotion.

(a) Efficient (b) Hazy
(c) Lazy (d) Pricey

24. Select the most appropriate option that can substitute the underlined words in the following sentence.

I cannot go out tonight because I will preparing of my interview tomorrow.

(a) I have to prepare for
(b) I will have prepare for
(c) I have been prepare to
(d) I had to prepare to

25. Complete the following sentence.

He .... to the manager about the terrible food in the hostel.

(a) made a complaint
(b) terribly complained
(c) said a complaint
(d) said a big complaint

Part II
General Intelligence

26. This question consists of a pair of words which have a certain relationship to each other. Select the pair which does not have the same relationship.

Adhere : Comply

(1) Accord : Harmony
(2) Busy : Engaged
(3) Eager : Keen
(4) Jubilant : Depressed

(a) 1 (b) 4 (c) 3 (d) 2

27. The position of how many letters will remain unchanged, if each of the letters in the word PRAISE is arranged in the alphabetical order?

(a) None (b) Two
(c) Three (d) One

28. What would be the roman numeral on the opposite side of 'IX', if the given sheet is folded to form a cube?

	X	
IX	VII	
	VI	
	V	VIII

(a) VI (b) X
(c) V (d) VIII

29. Select the correct mirror image of the given figure, when the mirror is placed at MN as shown below.

GFXD39ZL

M——N

(a) ɘꟻXᗡ3ɘZᒣ (b) ⅃Ƨ9ƐᗡX꟞Ɑ
(c) ɘꟻXD3ɘƧΓ (d) ɘ꟞XDƐɘƧΓ

30. Identify the figure given in the options that when put in place of the question mark (?) will logically complete the series.

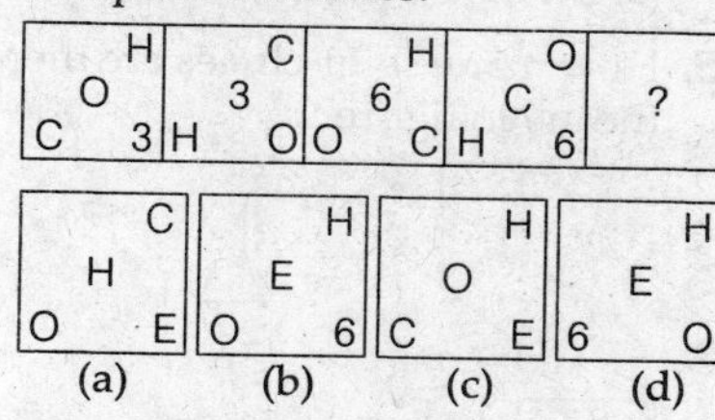

31. Which two numbers should be interchanged to make the given equation correct?

$(86 \div 43) + (66 \div 33) \times 2 + 72 - 6 \times 4 = 177$

(**Note** Numbers must be interchanged and not the constituent digits e.g. if 2 and 3 are to be interchanged in the equation $43 \times 3 + 4 \div 2$, then interchanged equation is $43 \times 2 + 4 \div 3$)

(a) 43 and 2 (b) 2 and 6
(c) 2 and 4 (d) 2 and 72

32. Four letter-clusters have been given, out of which three are alike in some manner and one is different. Select the letter-cluster that is different.

(**Note** The odd one out is not based on the number of consonants/ vowels or their position in the letter-cluster.)

(a) ZABX (b) NMNM
(c) TGHS (d) KPQJ

33. Select the set in which the numbers are related in the same way as are the numbers of the following sets.

(**Note** Operations should be performed on the whole numbers, without breaking down the numbers into its constituent digits. E.g. 13 – Operations on 13 such as adding /deleting /multiplying etc. to 13 can be performed. Breaking down 13 into 1 and 3 and then performing mathematical operations on 1 and 3 is not allowed.)

(60, 15, 5)
(96, 24, 8)

(a) (159, 39, 13)
(b) (150, 36, 13)
(c) (156, 39, 11)
(d) (156, 39, 13)

34. What should come in place of the question mark (?) in the given series based on the English alphabetical order?
FHB, KMG, PRL, UWQ, ?
(a) ZVB (b) ZDV
(c) ZCV (d) ZBV

35. How many semi-circles are there in the given figure?

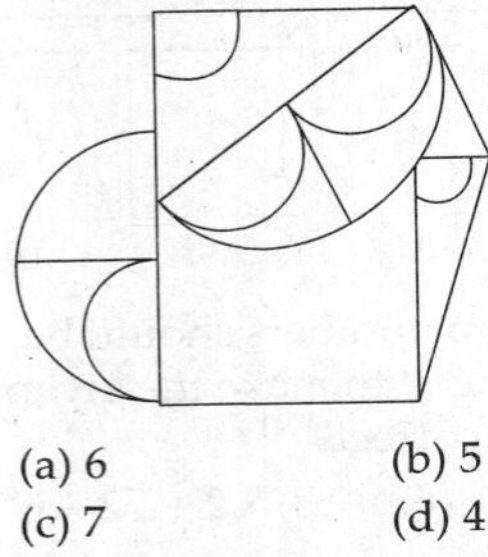

(a) 6 (b) 5
(c) 7 (d) 4

36. Select the option in which the given figure is embedded. (rotation is not allowed)

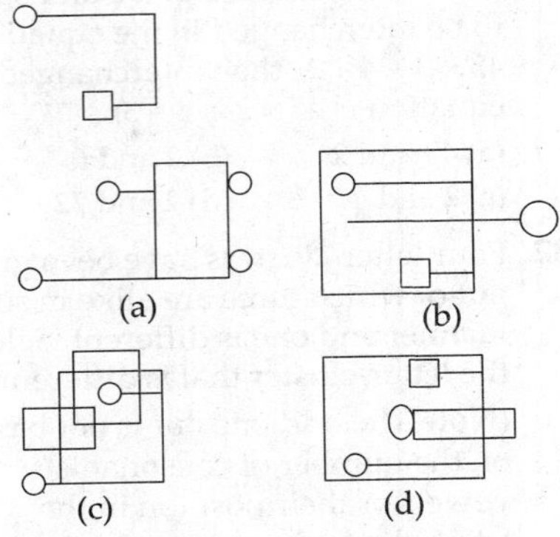

37. 21 is related to 59 by certain logic following the same logic, 32 is related to 81. To which of the following is 29 related, following the same logic?
(**Note** Operations should be performed on the whole numbers, without breaking down the numbers into its constituent digits. E.g. 13 – Operations on 13 such as adding/subtracting/multiplying etc. to 13 can be performed. Breaking down 13 into 1 and 3 and then performing mathematical operations on 1 and 3 is not allowed.)
(a) 58 (b) 75
(c) 60 (d) 62

38. In a certain code language, 'LDWR' is coded as 'NGUQ' and 'BFKZ' is coded as 'DIIY'. What is the code for 'YTGX' in the given code language?
(a) AWEW (b) ZVFV
(c) YWFV (d) BWFV

39. What would be the letter on the opposite side of 'S', if the given sheet is folded to form a cube?

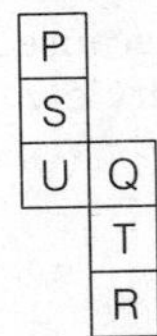

(a) Q (b) T (c) P (d) R

40. 'STAUNCH' is related to 'WXEYRGL' in a certain way based on the English alphabetical order. In the same way, 'BLISS' is related to 'FPMWW'. To which of the following is 'COWARD' related, following the same logic?
(a) GTAEVH (b) GSAEVH
(c) GSAFVH (d) GSZEVH

41. What should come in place of the question mark (?) in the given series?
138, 137, 140, 139, 142, ?
(a) 143 (b) 141 (c) 140 (d) 142

42. Select the correct mirror image of the given figure when the mirror is placed at MN as shown below.

M
Fd295ea
N

(a) ɒɘƨ9Ƨbꟻ (b) ɒeƨɘƧbꟻ
(c) ɒɘƨɘƧpꟻ (d) ɒɘƨɘƧbꟻ

43. What will come in the place of the question mark (?) in the following equation, if '+' and '–' are interchanged and '×' and '÷' are interchanged?
$34 + 56 \times 8 \div 2 - 16 = ?$
(a) 36 (b) 23
(c) 38 (d) 30

44. If 'A' stands for '÷', 'B' stands for '×', 'C' stands for '+' and 'D' stands for '–', what will come in place of the question mark (?) in the following equation?
404 B 2 D 101 A 101 C 6 = ?
(a) 831 (b) 830 (c) 813 (d) 803

45. The position of how many letters will remain unchanged if each of the letters in the word CHEMISTRY is arranged in alphabetical order?
(a) Three (b) Four
(c) One (d) Two

46. In a certain code language, 'DEAL' is coded as '0368' and 'DEAF' is coded as '2630'. What is the code for 'F' in that language?
(a) 3 (b) 2
(c) 0 (d) 8

47. Three statements are followed by conclusions numbered I, II. You have to consider these statements to be true, even if they seem to be at variance with commonly known facts. Decide which of the given conclusions logically follow(s) from the given statements.

Statements
All shoes are ties.
Some ties are pants.
All pants are buttons.

Conclusions
I. Some buttons are shoes.
II. No ties are buttons.
(a) Both Conclusions I and II follow
(b) Only Conclusion II follows
(c) Neither Conclusion I nor II follows
(d) Only Conclusion I follows

48. In a certain language,
A # B means A is the sister of B,
A @ B means A is the son of B,
A & B means A is the wife of B and
A % B means A is the father of B.
E & P @ D % K # L
Based on the above, how is E related to K?
(a) Sister
(b) Brother's wife
(c) Mother
(d) Mother's mother

49. What should come in place of the question mark (?) to complete the following letter-cluster series?
YBP, WDS, TGQ, OLT, ?
(a) HSR (b) HSP
(c) LSR (d) HTR

50. Which two numbers should be interchanged to make the given equation correct?
$79 - 43 + (23 + 75) \times 3 - (30 \div 15) \times 4 = 175$

(**Note** Numbers must be interchanged and not the constituent digits e.g. if 2 and 3 are to be interchanged in the equation $43 \times 3 + 4 \div 2$, then interchanged equation is $43 \times 2 + 4 \div 3$)

(a) 3 and 4 (b) 75 and 79
(c) 75 and 30 (d) 23 and 43

Part III

Quantitative Aptitude

51. The following table shows admitted students in an institute during the academic year 2015 to 2020 in different courses.

Academic year	Engineering	Science	Arts	Management
2015	1200	850	450	240
2016	1362	821	525	275
2017	1351	870	624	286
2018	1409	921	615	293
2019	1421	931	795	300
2020	1400	950	750	320

Which of the following course had either a consistent growth or a consistent decline in the admissions from 2015 to 2020?

(a) Management (b) Engineering
(c) Arts (d) Science

52. In an election contested by two candidates, one candidate got 42% of the total votes and still lost by 800 votes. Find the total number of votes that were cast.

(a) 7000 (b) 2000
(c) 8000 (d) 5000

53. Study the given three- dimensional chart and answer the question that follows.

The chart details the sale of fruits in different months.

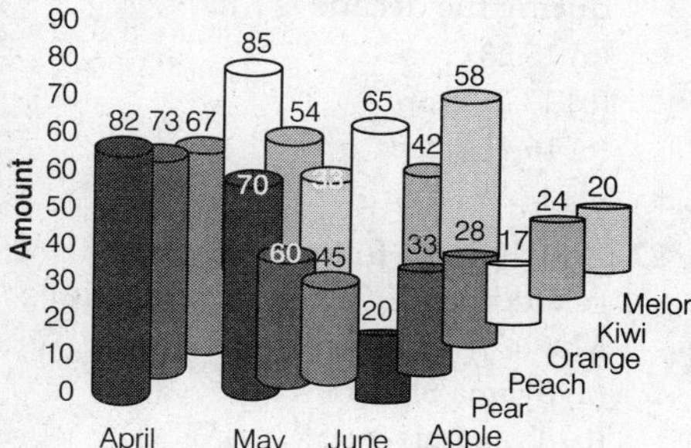

Which fruit was the most sold in the month of May and how much more than the lowest-sold fruit in that month?

(a) Kiwi, 23 (b) Apple, 28
(c) Orange, 23 (d) Kiwi, 22

54. Find the cost of painting a ball that is in the shape of a sphere with a radius of 14 cm. The painting cost of the ball is ₹ 5 per square centimetre $\left(\text{take } \pi = \frac{22}{7}\right)$.

(a) ₹ 12320 (b) ₹ 13220
(c) ₹ 13022 (d) ₹ 12230

55. The distance between the centres of two circles is 81 cm, and their radii are 42 cm and 51 cm. What is the length (in cm) of the direct common tangent to the circles?

(a) $51\sqrt{6}$ (b) $36\sqrt{5}$
(c) $31\sqrt{3}$ (d) $40\sqrt{2}$

56. The given graph shows the higher secondary result of a particular school, from 2019 to 2021. Study the graph and answer the question that follows:

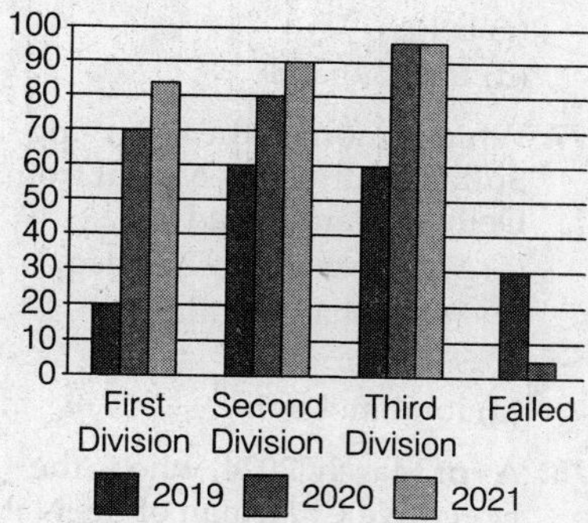

The ratio of the number of students who passed with first division in all the three years to the total number of students in 2020 is

(a) 7 : 10 (b) 7 : 13
(c) 7 : 15 (d) 17 : 10

57. Ram is 20 yr older than Rahul. 'n' yr ago, Ram was thrice as old as Rahul. '$2n$' yr from now the ratio of the ages of Ram and Rahul will be 15 : 11. What is the value of 'n'?

(a) 15 (b) 10
(c) 30 (d) 20

58. Which of the following statements is incorrect about the circle?

(a) The area of a sector $= \frac{1}{2}(\text{arc length} \times R)$

(b) The length of an arc $= \frac{\text{Central angle made by the arc}}{360°} \times \pi r^2$.

(c) The radius of an incircle of an equilateral triangle of side 's' is $\frac{s}{2\sqrt{3}}$

(d) Circles are congruent if they have same radii while similar circles may have different radii

59. The inner and outer radii of a hemispherical wooden bowl are 6 cm and 8 cm, respectively. Its entire surface has to be polished and the cost of polishing π cm^2 is ₹ 50. How much will it cost to polish the bowl?

(a) ₹ 12000 (b) ₹ 10000
(c) ₹ 11600 (d) ₹ 11400

60. A man can row a boat at speed 8 km/h in still water. It takes thrice as long to row upstream as it does to row downstream. Find the speed of the stream (in km/h).

(a) 5 (b) 4
(c) 6 (d) 3

61. The value of a machine depreciates every year by 5%. If the present value of the machine is ₹ 80000, what will be its value after 2 yr?

(a) ₹ 72200 (b) ₹ 74400
(c) ₹ 74000 (d) ₹ 72000

62. Simplify the expression :

$720 + 48 \div 8 \times 5 - 6 \times 3$

(a) $\frac{112}{5}$ (b) 732
(c) 161 (d) 242

63. If $A : B = 2 : 3$ and $B : C = 7 : 8$, find $A : C$.

(a) 12 : 7 (b) 7 : 12
(c) 4: 7 (d) 7 : 2

64. If $\cos^4\theta - \sin^4\theta = \frac{4}{5}$, then find the value of $\sin 4\theta$.

(a) $\frac{24}{25}$ (b) $\frac{21}{25}$
(c) $\frac{16}{25}$ (d) $\frac{18}{25}$

65. Two triangles ABC and DEF are similar. The smallest side of ABC is equal to 15 units. If the sides of ABC are in the ratio 3 : 4 : 5, and the area of DEF is half of the area of ABC, then what is the largest side of DEF (in units)?

(a) $25\sqrt{2}$ (b) $25\sqrt{3}$
(c) $\frac{25}{\sqrt{3}}$ (d) $\frac{25}{\sqrt{2}}$

66. Tanvi can do a work in 25 days, and Tai can complete the same work in 30 days. They started the work together for 5 days. How much work is left?

(a) $\frac{11}{30}$ (b) $\frac{19}{30}$ (c) $\frac{11}{12}$ (d) $\frac{1}{12}$

67. Two cubes, each of edge 5 cm, are joined face to face. Find the surface area of the cuboid thus formed.

(a) 300 cm^2 (b) 125 cm^2
(c) 200 cm^2 (d) 250 cm^2

68. Ram invested a certain sum of money at simple interest. It amounted to $\frac{5}{4}$ of itself in 3 yr. What will be its rate per cent per annum?

(a) 9.12 % (b) 8.33%
(c) 8.20% (d) 7.25%

69. *A* sells an object to *B* at 10% profit, *B* sells it to *C* at 60% profit and *C* sells it to *D* at $12\frac{1}{2}$% profit. If *D* paid ₹ 59.40, then at what price did *A* buy it?

(a) ₹ 30 (b) ₹ 32
(c) ₹ 28 (d) ₹ 34

70. Solve $\frac{2\times 2+2}{2\div 2\times 2}\div\frac{\frac{1}{2}\div\frac{1}{2}\text{ of }\frac{1}{2}}{\frac{1}{2}+\frac{1}{2}\text{ of }\frac{1}{2}}$.

(a) $4\frac{1}{8}$ (b) $3\frac{1}{8}$ (c) $2\frac{1}{8}$ (d) $1\frac{1}{8}$

71. On buying 24 bangles Meena gets 6 bangles free of cost. By what percentage does Meena get a discount?

(a) 20% (b) 5% (c) 15% (d) 10%

72. Study the given histogram and answer the question that follows.

The histogram shows the distribution of marks obtained by 115 students in a college.

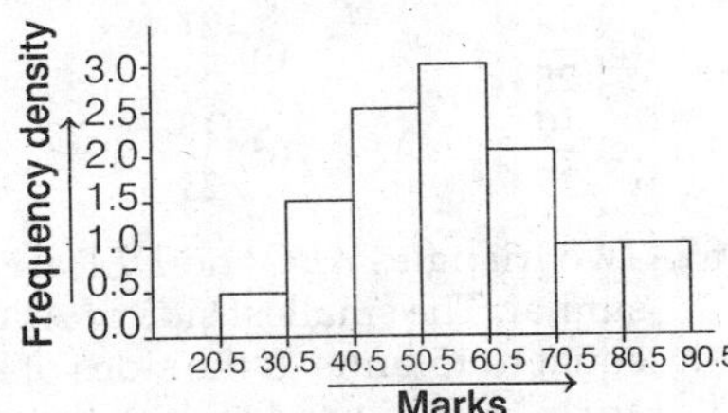

A student is marked as qualified if he/she obtains marks above 40.5. Here, the ratio of the number of qualified students to that of students who are not qualified is

(a) 9 : 2 (b) 5 : 1 (c) 19 : 4 (d) 17 : 4

73. The average weight of 35 students in a class is 40 kg. Five of the students of this class whose average weight is 42 kg left the class. Find the average weight of the remaining 30 students.

(a) $39\frac{2}{3}$ kg (b) $19\frac{2}{3}$ kg
(c) $49\frac{2}{3}$ kg (d) $29\frac{2}{3}$ kg

74. Side *BC* of a ΔABC is extended upto *D* such that $CD = AC$. If $\angle BAD = 118°$ and $\angle ACB = 80°$, then the value of $\angle ABC$ is equal to

(a) 36° (b) 32°
(c) 22° (d) 27°

75. 5% of 2% of 3 is equal to

(a) 0.3 (b) 3
(c) 0.003 (d) 0.03

Part IV
General Awareness

76. Khelo India Winter Games 2023 was held at ....

(a) Himachal Pradesh
(b) Jammu and Kashmir
(c) Leh
(d) Uttarakhand

77. Which amongst the following Sultans shifted his capital from Delhi to Daulatabad?

(a) Muhammad Bin Tughlaq
(b) Feroz Shah Tughlaq
(c) Sikandar Lodhi
(d) Ibrahim Lodhi

78. As of March, 2024, who is the Executive Chairman of the National Legal Services Authority of India?

(a) Justice UU Lalit
(b) Justice Sanjiv Khanna
(c) Justice Ranjan Gogoi
(d) Justice Sharad Bobde

79. .... of the Constitution of India has provisions for legal enforcement of the Fundamental rights.

(a) Article 28 (b) Article 19
(c) Article 32 (d) Article 29

80. Which statement about Classical Carnatic Music is correct?

(a) The compositions are either in Malayalam, Marathi, Tamil or Bengali.
(b) The compositions are either in Telugu, Kannada, Tamil or Sanskrit.
(c) The compositions are either in Telugu, Malayalam, Hindi or Sanskrit.
(d) The compositions are either in Marathi, Odia, Konkani or Bengali.

81. Which of the following is not compulsory equipment for a football referee?

(a) Red and yellow cards
(b) White flag
(c) Whistle(s)
(d) Watch(es)

82. To create a new MS Word document, which of the following steps is correct?

(a) File Tab → Open
(b) File Tab → Start
(c) File Tab → New
(d) File Tab → Recent

83. Lal Thanhawla holds the record for the longest-serving Chief Minister of ...., occupying the position for five terms.

(a) Sikkim
(b) Manipur
(c) Mizoram
(d) Meghalaya

84. Which of the following dances is listed in the UNESCO List of Intangible Cultural Heritage of India since 2010?

(a) Kalbelia (b) Garba
(c) Ghumar (d) Matki

85. The Assam government observed the birthday of .... on 31st March 2023, as Students Day in the state.

(a) Bodofa Upendra Nath Brahma
(b) Biraj Kumar Sarma
(c) Prafulla Kumar Mahanta
(d) Bhrigu Kumar Phukan

86. As per the Census 2011, the total absolute increase in population during the decade is ....

(a) 15.23 crore
(b) 17.21 crore
(c) 16.41 crore
(d) 18.19 crore

87. Which of the following is Not related to the 'Trinity of Carnatic Music'?

(a) Syama Shastri
(b) Tyagaraja
(c) Muthuswami Dikshitar
(d) Purandara Das

88. According to Koeppen's Scheme of classification of climate, which of the following characteristics is associated with 'Group E'?
(a) The average temperature of the coldest month is –3°C or below.
(b) The average temperature of the coldest month is higher than –3°C but below 18°C.
(c) The average temperature of the coldest month is 18°C or higher.
(d) The average temperature for all months is below 10°C.

89. Doljatra is a festival of which state from followings?
(a) Rajasthan (b) Assam
(c) Haryana (d) Uttar Pradesh

90. Price control and rationing are direct control measures to check ....
(a) disinflation (b) deflation
(c) inflation (d) reflation

91. Application software includes a variety of programs that are designed to meet the information processing needs of ....
(a) programmers (b) team leaders
(c) customers (d) end users

92. Which sport is not played in mixed doubles?
(a) Handball (b) Badminton
(c) Tennis (d) Table tennis

93. How many Fundamental Rights were initially provided in the Constitution of India?
(a) Six (b) Nine
(c) Seven (d) Eight

94. Which of the following is the correct relationship?
(a) $F = a/m$ (b) $F = m/a$
(c) $F = m^2a$ (d) $F = ma$

95. As of March 2020, which of the following solar power plants is the biggest plant in the world, with total installed capacity of 2,245 MW?
(a) Kamuthi Solar Power Project
(b) Sakri Photovoltaic Solar Energy Project
(c) Dhirubhai Ambani Solar Park
(d) Bhadla Solar park

96. Select the olfactory indicator from among the given options.
(a) Petunia (b) Clove oil
(c) Turmeric (d) Cabbage juice

97. Which of the following committees was associated with Industrial Licensing Policy Inquiry?
(a) Gadgil Committee
(b) Hazari Committee
(c) Sen Committee
(d) Dutt Committe

98. Which of the following is NOT one of the classical languages of India?
(a) Magahi (b) Malayalam
(c) Kannada (d) Odiya

99. Select the natural habitat of the Asiatic Lion from the following.
(a) Gir forest
(b) Sundarbans
(c) Kanha National Park
(d) Saranda forest

100. At which place did Raja Ram Mohan Roy form a reform association called Brahmo Sabha in the year 1828?
(a) Calcutta (b) Bombay
(c) Pune (d) Madras

Answers

1. (d)	2. (c)	3. (c)	4. (b)
5. (a)	6. (d)	7. (d)	8. (c)
9. (a)	10. (d)	11. (b)	12. (d)
13. (d)	14 (d)	15. (b)	16. (b)
17. (a)	18. (a)	19. (d)	20. (b)
21. (a)	22. (c)	23. (c)	24. (a)
25. (a)	26. (b)	27. (a)	28. (d)
29. (c)	30. (d)	31. (a)	32. (a)
33. (d)	34. (d)	35. (b)	36. (b)
37. (b)	38. (a)	39. (b)	40. (b)
41. (b)	42. (d)	43. (a)	44. (c)
45. (d)	46. (b)	47. (c)	48. (b)
49. (a)	50. (c)	51. (a)	52. (d)
53. (b)	54. (a)	55. (b)	56. (a)
57. (a)	58. (b)	59. (d)	60. (b)
61. (a)	62. (b)	63. (b)	64. (a)
65. (d)	66. (b)	67. (d)	68. (b)
69. (a)	70. (d)	71. (a)	72. (c)
73. (a)	74. (c)	75. (c)	76. (b)
77. (a)	78. (b)	79. (c)	80. (b)
81. (b)	82. (c)	83. (c)	84. (a)
85. (a)	86. (d)	87. (d)	88. (d)
89. (b)	90. (c)	91. (d)	92. (a)
93. (c)	94. (d)	95. (d)	96. (b)
97. (d)	98. (a)	99. (a)	100. (a)

Explanations

1. *(d)* Part (d) 'in an East' contains an error. Use 'the' to correct the sentence.

2. *(c)* Part 'classical singer, as she dropped of' contains an error. Use 'off' to correct the sentence.

3. *(c)* Part (c) 'How long are you working' contains an error. Use 'have you been working' to correct the sentence.

4. *(b)* The correct filler for the given blank is 'each'.

5. *(a)* The correct filler for the given blank is 'custom'.

6. *(d)* The correct filler for the given blank is 'resembling'.

7. *(d)* The correct filler for the given blank is 'perch'.

8. *(c)* The correct filler for the given blank is 'dart'.

9. *(a)* The correct filler for the given blank is 'inform'.

10. *(d)* The most appropriate substitute for the word is 'right as rain'. It means to be fit and in excellent health.
- 'Left out in old' means to be ignored or forgotten.
- 'On cloud nine' means to be very happy.
- 'Up in the arms' means to be protesting against something.

11. *(b)* The correct filler for the given blank is 'heir'.

12. *(d)* The bracketed part of the given sentence contains an error. Use 'are eligible' to correct the sentence.

13. *(d)* 'Terminate' means to end. Hence, its antonym is to 'Begin'.

14. *(d)* The correct filler for the given blank is 'main'.

15. *(b)* The underlined part of the given sentence contains an error. The use of 'look thorough' is incorrect. Use 'look after' to correct the sentence.

16. *(b)* The correct fillers for the given blanks are 'berth' and 'birth'. Berth means a fixed bunk on a ship, train, or other means of transport. Birth means to produce or create something.

17. *(a)* The underlined part of the given sentence contains an error. Use 'affects' to correct the sentence.

18. *(a)* The incorrectly spelt word is 'adressed'. The correct spelling is 'addressed'.

19. *(d)* The correct filler for the given blank is 'their'.

20. *(b)* The incorrectly spelt word is 'consciencious'. The correct spelling is 'conscientious'.

21. *(a)* To read between the lines means to grasp the hidden meaning of something.

22. *(c)* The antonym of 'peace' is 'turmoil' which means chaos and confusion.

23. *(c)* Industrious means hard working and diligent. Hence, its antonym is 'lazy'.

24. *(a)* The underlined part of the given sentence contains an error. Use 'I have to prepare for' to correct the sentence.

25. *(a)* The correct filler for the given blank is 'made a complaint'.

26. *(b)* As, adhere is synonyms of comply. Similarly, all the options are synonyms of each other except option (d) i.e., jubilant and depressed, are antonyms of each other. So, it is odd from rest.

27. *(a)* Given, Word → P R A I S E

After arranging alphabetically

→ A E I P R S

Clearly, none will remain unchanged after arranging alphabetically.

28. *(d)* According to the question,

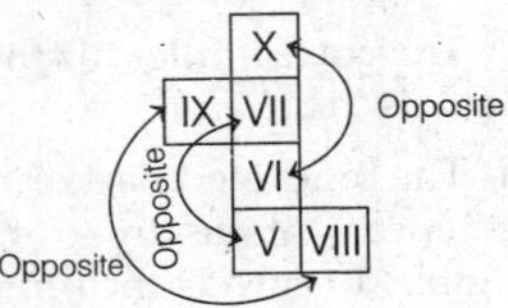

In the folded form of cube 'VIII' is opposite to 'IX'.

29. *(c)* The mirror image along MN is

GFXD39ZL

M ——————— N

ᘜℲXDƐ6ZΓ

30. *(d)* The following pattern is follows,

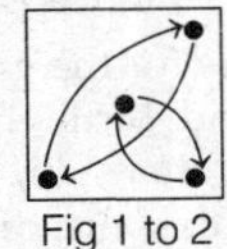

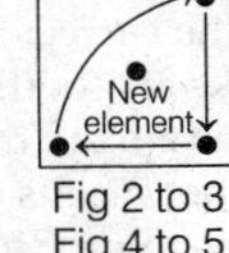

So, the answer figure is

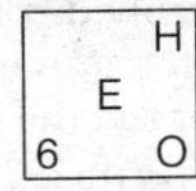

31. *(a)* Given equation,

$(86 \div 43) + (66 \div 33) \times 2 + 72 - 6 \times 4 = 177$

From option (a),

Interchanging 43 and 2, we get

$(86 \div 2) + (66 \div 33) \times 43 + 72 - 6 \times 4 = 177$

$\Rightarrow \quad 43 + 2 \times 43 + 72 - 6 \times 4 = 177$

$\Rightarrow \quad 43 + 86 + 72 - 24 = 177$

$\Rightarrow \quad 201 - 24 = 177$

$\Rightarrow \quad 177 = 177$

$\therefore \quad$ LHS = RHS

32. *(a)*

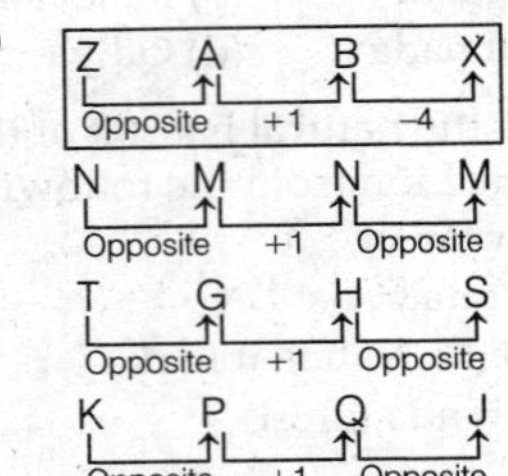

'Z' is opposite to 'A', but 'B' is not opposite to 'X'.

So, it is odd from rest.

33. *(d)* As, (60, 15, 5)

$= 5 \times 3 = 15 \times 4 = 60$

and (96, 24, 8)

$= 8 \times 3 = 24 \times 4 = 96$

Similarly,

(156, 39, 13)

$= 13 \times 3 = 39 \times 4 = 156$

34. *(d)* The pattern of the series is as follows,

F $\xrightarrow{+5}$ K $\xrightarrow{+5}$ P $\xrightarrow{+5}$ U $\xrightarrow{+5}$ Z

H $\xrightarrow{+5}$ M $\xrightarrow{+5}$ R $\xrightarrow{+5}$ W $\xrightarrow{+5}$ B

B $\xrightarrow{+5}$ G $\xrightarrow{+5}$ L $\xrightarrow{+5}$ Q $\xrightarrow{+5}$ V

35. *(b)* Naming the figure,

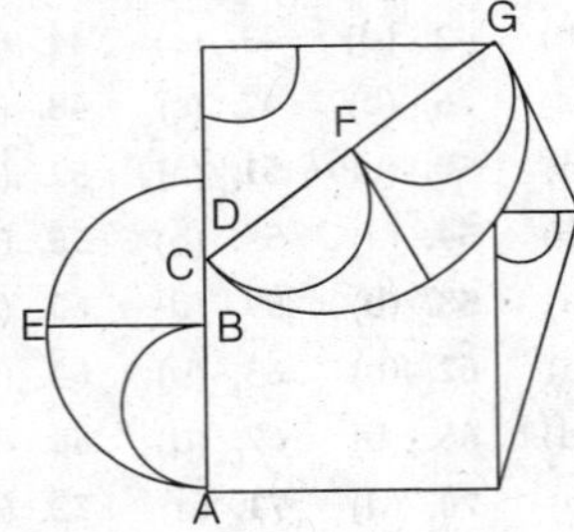

The number of semi-circles are along AB, AD, CF, FG and CG.

$\therefore$ Total number of semi-circle = 5

36. *(b)* The question figure embedded in the given figure (b),

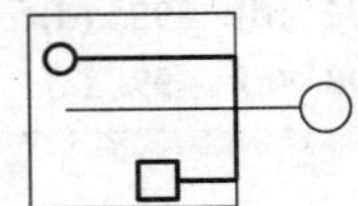

37. *(b)* As,

$21 \times 2 + 17 = 42 + 17 = 59$

and

$32 \times 2 + 17 = 64 + 17 = 81$

Similarly,

$29 \times 2 + 17 = 58 + 17 = \boxed{75}$

38. *(a)* As,

L D W R
+2 +3 −2 −1
N G U Q

and

B F K Z
+2 +3 −2 −1
D I I Y

Similarly,

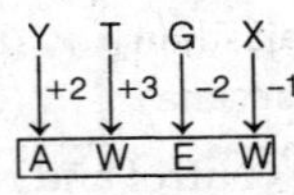

39. *(b)* According to the question,

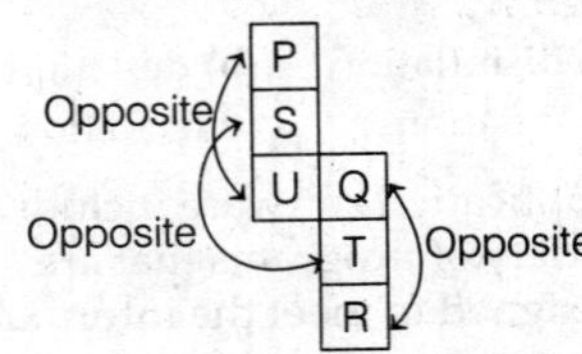

After folding the cube, we get 'T' opposite to 'S'.

40. *(b)* As,

S T A U N C H
+4 +4 +4 +4 +4 +4 +4
W X E Y R G L

and

B L I S S
+4 +4 +4 +4 +4
F P M W W

Similarly,

C O W A R D
+4 +4 +4 +4 +4 +4
G S A E V H

41. *(b)* The pattern of series is as follows,

138 137 140 139 142 $\boxed{141}$

−1 +3 −1 +3 −1

42. *(d)* The mirror image along MN is as shown below,

M

Fd295ea | ɘɒɘ592bꟻ

N

43. *(a)* Given equation,

$34 + 56 \times 8 \div 2 - 16 = ?$

After interchanging the symbols, we get

$34 - 56 \div 8 \times 2 + 16$

$= 34 - 7 \times 2 + 16$

$= 34 - 14 + 16$

$= 50 - 14 = 36$

44. *(c)* Given equation,

404 B 2 D 101 A 101 C 6 = ?

After substituting letters with symbols, we get

$$404 \times 2 - 101 \div 101 + 6$$
$$= 404 \times 2 - 1 + 6$$
$$= 808 - 1 + 6$$
$$= 814 - 1 = 813$$

45. *(d)*

Given word → [C] H E M I S T R [Y]

After arranging alphabetically → [C] E H I M R S T [Y]

∴ After arranging alphabetically 'Two' letters 'C and Y' are remain unchanged.

46. *(b)* According to the question,

[D E A] L = [0 3 6] 8

[D E A] F = 2 [6 3 0]

From the above, it is clear that code for 'F' is '2'.

47. *(c)* According to the statements,

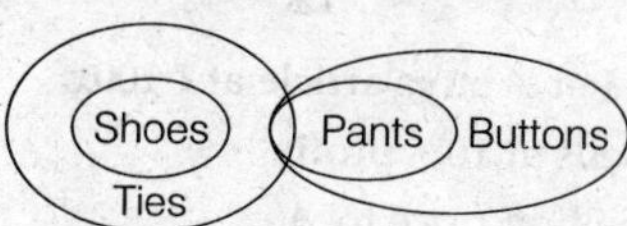

Conclusions

I. (✗) II. (✗)

Hence, neither Conclusion I nor II follows.

48. *(b)* Given equation,

E & P @ D % K # L

D^+ — Father — Married couple: $E^- \longleftrightarrow P^+ \xleftrightarrow{\text{Siblings}} K \xleftarrow{\text{Sister}} L^-$

[+ → Male, − → Female]

From the given family tree, we derived 'E' is brother's wife of 'K'.

49. *(a)* The pattern of the series is as follows,

$Y \xrightarrow{-2} W \xrightarrow{-3} T \xrightarrow{-5} O \xrightarrow{-7}$ [H]

$B \xrightarrow{+2} D \xrightarrow{+3} G \xrightarrow{+5} L \xrightarrow{+7}$ [S]

$P \xrightarrow{+3} S \xrightarrow{-2} Q \xrightarrow{+3} T \xrightarrow{-2}$ [R]

∴ ? = HSR

50. *(c)* The given equation,

$$79 - 43 + (23 + 75) \times 3 - (30 \div 15) \times 4 = 175$$

From option (c), after interchanging 75 and 30, we get

$$79 - 43 + (23 + 30) \times 3 - (75 \div 15) \times 4 = 175$$
$$\Rightarrow 79 - 43 + 159 - 20 = 175$$
$$\Rightarrow 238 - 63 = 175$$
$$\Rightarrow 175 = 175$$

51. *(a)* By observing the data in the table, we see that there is consistent growth in management course because admitted students are continuously increasing from 2015 to 2020.

52. *(d)* Let total votes = $100x$

One candidate got 42% of total votes

$$= 100x \times \frac{42}{100} = 42x$$

Other candidate got votes

$$= 100x - 42x = 58x$$

Given,

lost by 800 votes i.e.,

$$58x - 42x = 800$$
$$\Rightarrow 16x = 800$$
$$\therefore x = 50$$

∴ Total vote casted

$$= 100x = 100 \times 50$$
$$= 5000$$

53. *(b)* Most sold fruit in the month of May = Apple (70)

Lowest sold fruit in the month of May = 42

∴ Required difference

$$= 70 - 42 = 28$$

54. *(a)* Given,

Radius (r) = 14 cm

and cost of painting = ₹ 5/cm^2

We know that,

Surface area of sphere = $4\pi r^2$

$$= 4 \times \frac{22}{7} \times 14 \times 14$$
$$= 2464 \text{ cm}^2$$

∴ Total cost of painting

= Surface area of sphere × Cost

= 2464 × 5

= ₹ 12320

55. *(b)* Given,

Radius of one circle (r_1) = 42 cm

Radius of other circle (r_2) = 51 cm

Distance between centres = 81 cm

We know that,

Length of direct common tangent

$$= \sqrt{\{(\text{Distance between centres})^2 - (\text{Difference between radius of circles})^2\}}$$
$$= \sqrt{(81)^2 - (51 - 42)^2}$$
$$= \sqrt{(81)^2 - (9)^2}$$
$$= \sqrt{(81 + 9)(81 - 9)}$$
$$= \sqrt{72 \times 90}$$
$$= 9 \times 4\sqrt{5}$$
$$= 36\sqrt{5} \text{ cm}$$

56. *(a)* Students passed with first division in all the 3 yr

$$= 20 + 70 + 85 = 175$$

Total number of students in 2020

$$= 70 + 80 + 95 + 5$$
$$= 250$$

∴ Required ratio = 175 : 250

= 7 : 10

57. *(a)* Let the age of Rahul be x yr.

∴ Ram's age = $(x + 20)$ yr

According to the question,

$$(x + 20) - n = 3(x - n)$$
$$\Rightarrow x + 20 - n = 3x - 3n$$
$$\Rightarrow x - n = 10 \quad \text{...(i)}$$

Again,

$$\frac{(x + 20) + 2n}{x + 2n} = \frac{15}{11}$$
$$\Rightarrow 11x + 220 + 22n = 15x + 30n$$
$$\Rightarrow x + 2n = 55 \quad \text{...(ii)}$$

On solving Eqs. (i) and (ii),

$$\Rightarrow 3n = 45$$
$$\therefore n = 15$$

58. *(b)* Incorrect option about the circle is Option (b),

The length of an arc

$$= \frac{\text{Central angle made by arc}}{360°} \times \pi r^2$$

59. *(d)* Given,

Inner radius (r_1) = 6 cm

Outer radius (r_2) = 8 cm

Cost of polishing = ₹ 50/π cm^2

We know that,

Total surface area of a hemisphere

$$= \pi(r_2^2 - r_1^2) + 2\pi(r_1^2 + r_2^2)$$
$$= \pi(8^2 - 6^2) + 2\pi(8^2 + 6^2)$$
$$= 28\pi + 200\pi$$
$$= 228\pi$$

∴ Total cost of polishing

$$= 228\pi \times \frac{50}{\pi}$$

= ₹ 11400

60. *(b)* Given,

Speed of boat in still water = 8 km/h

Let the speed of stream be x km/h.

According to the question,

$$\frac{\text{Distance}}{8-x} = 3\left(\frac{\text{Distance}}{8+x}\right)$$

$$\frac{1}{8-x} = \frac{3}{8+x}$$

$\Rightarrow$ $8 + x = 24 - 3x$

$\Rightarrow$ $4x = 16$

$\therefore$ $x = 4$ km/h

61. *(a)* Given,

Present value of the machine

= ₹ 80000

Depreciation rate = 5% per yr

Time = 2 yr

We know that,

The value of machine after n yr

= Present value of machine $\times\left(1 \pm \frac{\text{Rate}}{100}\right)^n$

$\therefore$ The value of machine after n yr

$= 80000\left(1 - \frac{5}{100}\right)^2$

$= 80000 \times \frac{19}{20} \times \frac{19}{20}$

= ₹ 72200

62. *(b)* Given expression,

$720 + 48 \div 8 \times 5 - 6 \times 3$

(using BODMAS rule,)

$= 720 + 6 \times 5 - 6 \times 3$

$= 720 + 30 - 18 = 732$

63. *(b)* Given,

$A : B = 2 : 3$ and $B : C = 7 : 8$

Now,

A : B : C

2 : 3 3

→

7 7 : 8

←

14 : 21 : 24

$\therefore$ $A : C = 14 : 24 = 7 : 12$

64. *(a)* Given,

$\cos^4\theta - \sin^4\theta = \frac{4}{5}$

$\Rightarrow (\cos^2\theta - \sin^2\theta)(\cos^2\theta + \sin^2\theta) = \frac{4}{5}$

$[\because a^4 - b^4 = (a^2 + b^2)(a^2 - b^2)]$

$\Rightarrow$ $\cos^2\theta - \sin^2\theta = \frac{4}{5}$

$\Rightarrow$ $\cos 2\theta = \frac{4}{5}$

$[\because \cos 2\theta = \cos^2\theta - \sin^2\theta]$

We know that,

$\cos 4\theta = 2\cos^2 2\theta - 1$

$[\because \cos 2\theta = 2\cos^2\theta - 1]$

$= 2 \times \frac{16}{25} - 1 = \frac{7}{25}$

$\sin 4\theta = \sqrt{1 - \cos^2 4\theta}$

$[\because \sin\theta = \sqrt{1 - \cos^2\theta}]$

$= \sqrt{1 - \frac{49}{625}}$

$= \sqrt{\frac{576}{625}}$

$\therefore$ $\sin 4\theta = \frac{24}{25}$

65. *(d)* Given,

$\Delta ABC \sim \Delta DEF$

Ratio of sides of $\Delta ABC = 3 : 4 : 5$

Smaller side of ΔABC = 15 units

$\therefore$ Larger side $= \frac{15}{3} \times 5 = 25$ units

We know that,

$$\frac{(\text{Larger side of }\Delta ABC)^2}{(\text{Larger side of }\Delta DEF)^2} = \frac{\text{Area of }\Delta ABC}{\text{Area of }\Delta DEF}$$

$$\Rightarrow \frac{(25)^2}{(\text{Larger side of }\Delta DEF)^2} = \frac{\text{Area of }\Delta ABC}{\frac{1}{2}(\text{Area of }\Delta ABC)}$$

$$\Rightarrow \frac{(25)^2}{(\text{Larger side of }\Delta DEF)^2} = 2$$

$\therefore$ Larger side of $\Delta DEF = \frac{25}{\sqrt{2}}$

66. *(b)* Let the total work be 1 unit.

$\therefore$ Tanvi's one day work $= \frac{1}{25}$

Tai's one day work $= \frac{1}{30}$

$\therefore$ Work done in 5 days by both of them

$= 5 \times \left(\frac{1}{25} + \frac{1}{30}\right)$

$= 5 \times \frac{11}{150} = \frac{55}{150}$

$\therefore$ Left work $= 1 - \frac{55}{150}$

$= \frac{95}{150} = \frac{19}{30}$

67. *(d)* $\because$ Both cube joined,

$\therefore$ One of the sides = 5 + 5 = 10 cm

and remaining sides will be same.

$\therefore$ Side of cuboid

= 5 cm, 5 cm and 10 cm.

We know that,

Total surface area of cuboid

= 2 (length × breadth + breadth × height + height × length)

$= 2(5 \times 5 + 5 \times 10 + 5 \times 10)$

$= 2(25 + 50 + 50)$

$= 2 \times 125 = 250\text{ cm}^2$

68. *(b)* Given,

Amount $= \frac{5}{4}$ principal

Time = 3 yr

We know that,

Simple interest

$= \frac{\text{Principal} \times \text{Rate} \times \text{Time}}{100}$

$\Rightarrow \frac{5}{4}\text{Principal} - \text{Principal}$

$= \frac{\text{Principal} \times 3 \times \text{Rate}}{100}$

$\Rightarrow \frac{1}{4}\text{Principal} = \frac{\text{Principal} \times 3 \times \text{Rate}}{100}$

$\therefore$ Rate $= \frac{100}{12} = 8.33\%$

69. *(a)* Let A buys article at ₹ $100x$.

A sells at 10% profit

$\therefore$ Selling price to A

$= 100x \times \frac{110}{100}$ = ₹ $110x$

Now, cost price to B = ₹ $110x$

$\therefore$ Selling price to B

$= 110x \times \frac{160}{100}$ = ₹ $176x$

Now, cost price to C = ₹ $176x$

$\therefore$ Selling price to C

$= 176x \times \frac{112.5}{100}$ = ₹ $198x$

Now, cost price to D = ₹ $198x$

According to the question,

D paid $\Rightarrow$ ₹ 59.4 = $198x$

$\Rightarrow$ $x = 0.3$

$\therefore$ A buys article = ₹ $100x$

$= 100 \times 0.3$ = ₹ 30

70. *(d)* Given expression,

$$\frac{2 \times 2 + 2}{2 \div 2 \times 2} \div \frac{\frac{1}{2} \div \frac{1}{2}\text{ of }\frac{1}{2}}{\frac{1}{2} + \frac{1}{2}\text{ of }\frac{1}{2}}$$

(By using BODMAS rule)

$$= \frac{4 + 2}{1 \times 2} \div \frac{\frac{1}{2} \div \frac{1}{4}}{\frac{1}{2} + \frac{1}{4}}$$

$$= \frac{6}{2} \div \frac{\frac{2}{3}}{4}$$

$$= \frac{6}{2} \times \frac{8}{3} = \frac{9}{8} = 1\frac{1}{8}$$

71. *(a)* Meena gets 6 bangles free of cost on buying 24 bangles.

We know that,

Discount percentage

$$= \frac{\text{Number of free items}}{\text{Total number of items}} \times 100$$

$$= \frac{6}{24+6} \times 100 = 20\%$$

72. *(c)* Qualified students who got above 40.5 marks = 2.5 + 3 + 2 + 1 + 1 = 9.5

Not qualified students who got below 40.5 or 40.5 marks = 0.5 + 1.5 = 2

$\therefore$ Required ratio = 9.5 : 2

= 95 : 20 = 19 : 4

73. *(a)* Given,

Average weight of 35 students = 40 kg

Five students left whose average weight = 42 kg

We know that,

$\because$ Average weight

$$= \frac{\text{Total weight}}{\text{Total number of students}}$$

$\therefore$ Average weight of remaining

$$30 \text{ students} = \frac{35 \times 40 - 42 \times 5}{35 - 5}$$

$$= \frac{1400 - 210}{30}$$

$$= \frac{1190}{30} = 39\frac{2}{3} \text{ kg}$$

74. *(c)*

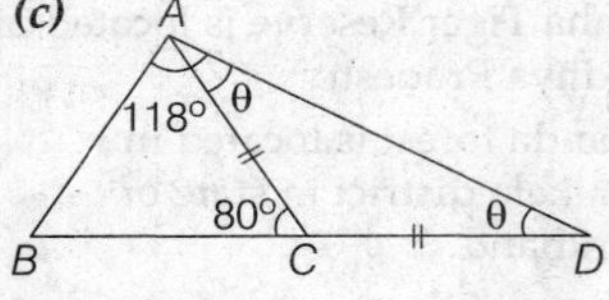

In ΔACD,

$\because \quad AC = CD$

$\therefore \quad \angle ADC = \angle CAD$

Let $\quad \angle ADC = \theta$

$\therefore \quad \angle CAD = \theta$

We know that,

An exterior angle of a triangle is equal to the sum of the two interior opposite angles.

In ΔACD,

$\angle\theta + \angle\theta = 80°$

$\Rightarrow \quad 2\angle\theta = 80°$

$\Rightarrow \quad \angle\theta = 40°$

$\therefore \quad \angle BAC = \angle BAD - \angle CAD$

$= 118° - \angle\theta$

$= 118° - 40° = 78°$

In ΔABC,

Sum of interior angle of a triangle = 180°

$\angle CBA + \angle BAC + \angle ACB = 180°$

$\Rightarrow \quad \angle ABC = 180° - (78° + 80°)$

$\therefore \quad \angle ABC = 22°$

75. *(c)* 5% of 2% of 3

$$= \frac{5}{100} \times \frac{2}{100} \times 3 = 0.003$$

76. *(b)* Khelo India Winter Games 2023 was held at Jammu and Kashmir.

- Khelo India Winter Games are the national level multidisciplinary grassroot winter games of India.
- The first Khelo India Winter Games were held in two legs at two different venues.
  1. Khelo India Ladakh Winter Games – Leh
  2. Khelo India Jammu and Kashmir Winter Games – Gulmarg

77. *(a)* Muhammad Bin Tughlaq shifted his capital from Delhi to Daulatabad.

- He was also name as Jauna Khan as Crown Prince.
- He was the eighteenth Sultan of Delhi.
- He reigned from February 1325 until his death in 1351.

78. *(b)* As of March, 2024, Justice Sanjiv Khanna is the Executive Chairman of the National Legal Services Authority of India.

- The National Legal Services Authority (NALSA) is a statutory body.
- It was established on 9th November, 1995.
- The prime objective of NALSA is speedy disposal of cases and reducing the burden of judiciary.

79. *(c)* Article 32 of the Constitution of India has provisions for legal enforcement of the Fundamental Rights.

- Article 32 (Right to Constitutional Remedies) which states that individuals have the right to approach the Supreme Court (SC).
- The Supreme Court is designated as the protector of these rights and issue writs to enforce them.
- Article 226 empowers the High Courts to issue writs and direction primarily within their territorial jurisdiction.

80. *(b)* The compositions of classical Carnatic music are either in Telugu, Kannada, Tamil or Sanskrit.

- Purandar Das a Saint from Karnataka, is known as the Father of Carnatic music.
- Carnatic music is associated with South India.
- There are 72 Nelokarta or parent or janak ragas in Carnatic music.

81. *(b)* White flag is not compulsory equipment for a football referee.

- Red and yellow cards used by referee to accomplish that task and keep the peace in soccer.
- White flag is used for fair calls in both field events and races.
- Whistle(s) used by referees and coaches for soccer, football, basketball and hockey.
- Sport watches are used in sport event because they can record less time.

82. *(c)* To create a new MS Word document 'File Tab $\rightarrow$ New' step is correct.

83. *(c)* Lal Thanhawla hold the record for the longest-serving Chief Minister of Mizoram, occupying the position for five terms.

- He occupied the CM position since 1984-2018.
- He received the Lifetime Achievement Award in 2014.
- He was a member of Indian National Congress.

84. *(a)* Kalbelia dance is listed in the UNESCO List of Intangible cultural Heritage of India since 2010.

- Kalbelia dance form belongs to the Kalbeliya tribe in Rajasthan.
- The dance involves women in black skirts in swirling, graceful movements that replicate the movements of a serpent.
- Other list of Dance in Intangible Cultural Heritage of India 2010 are Chhau dance, Sankirtana, Garba dance.

85. *(a)* On 31st March, 2023, the Assam Government observed the birthday of Bodofa Upendra Nath Brahma Students Day in the state.

- Bodofa (Guardian of Bodos) the title was given to Brahma on 8th May, 1990. In recognition of his vision and leadership.
- His life is celebrated each year on the anniversary of his death, which is now called Bodofa Day.

86. *(d)* As per the Census 2011, the total absolute increase in population during the decade is 18.19 crore.

- Percentage growth in 2001-2011 is 17.64. Males 17.19% and females 18.12%.
- Uttar Pradesh (199.5 million) is the most populous state in the country followed by Maharashtra with 112 million.

87. *(d)* Purandara Das is not related to the 'Trinity of Carnatic Music'.

- The Trinity of Carnatic music, also known as the Three Jewels of Carnatic Music.
- It refers to the outstanding trio of composer-musicians of Carnatic music.
- In the 18th century these person were Tyagaraja, Muthuswami Dikshitar and Syama Sastri.

88. *(d)* According to Koeppean's scheme, the average temperature for all month is below 10°C in Group E.

- Group E climates are regulated by the polar and arctic air masses of high latitudes which lie above 60° North and South latitudes.
- Two minor climate types exist
  1. ET or polar tundra.
  2. ET or polar ice caps.

89. *(b)* Doljatra is a festival of Assam, West Bengal, Odisha.

- Adjatra festival of colours is known as Holi in rest of India.
- It was introduced by Sankaradeva.
- Dol Jatra or Dol Purnima is celebrated on a full moon day and dedicated to Lord Krishna.

90. *(c)* Price control and rationing are direct control measures to check inflation.

- Price control means fixing an upper limit for the prices of essential consumer goods.
- They are the maximum prices fixed by law and anybody charging more than these prices is punished by law.

91. *(d)* Application software included a variety of programs that are designed to meet the information processing needs of end users.

92. *(a)* Handball is not played in mixed doubles.

- Mixed doubles or mixed pairs is a form of mixed-gender sports.
- That consists of teams of one man and one woman.
- Some mixed double games are Tennis, Badminton, Table Tennis, Curling.

93. *(c)* There were seven Fundamental Rights were initially provided in the Constitution of India.

- Right to Property were given in Fundamental Rights under Article-31.
- Right to property was removed as a Fundamental Rights through 44th Constitutional Amendment in 1978.
- A new provision, Article 300-A was added to the Constitution, which provided that "no person shall be deprived of his property save by authority of law".

94. *(d)* The correct relationship is $F = ma$.

The force (F) applied on a body is equal to the product of mass (m) of the body and the acceleration (a) produced in it.

95. *(d)* As of March 2020, Bhadla Solar Parker Plant is the biggest plant in the world.

- Bhadla solar park is with total installed capacity of 2245 MW.
- It is located in the Thar Desert of Rajasthan, India.
- It is one of the projects of India's National Solar Mission, which aims to install 100 Gigawatts (GW) of solar power by 2022.

96. *(b)* Clove oil is the olfactory indicator.

- An olfactory indicator is defined as a substance whose smell varies when it is mixed with an acidic or basic solution.
- Such substances can be used in the laboratory to test whether solution is a base or an acid and this process is called olfactory titration.

97. *(d)* Dutt Committee was associated with Industrial Licensing Policy Inquiry.

- According to the committee companies with assets, more than 35 crore was defined under large business houses.
- Hazari Committee was associated with Industrial Policy.
- Gadgil Committee is related to the Protection of Western Ghats.
- Sen Committee is related to review the legal and regulatory framework of ARCs.

98. *(a)* Magahi is not one of the classical languages of India.

- Magahi is a Indo-Aryan language spoken in Bihar, Jharkhand and West Bengal states of Eastern India and in the Terai of Nepal.
- Tamil, Telugu, Sanskrit, Kannada, Malayalam and Odia have been given the states of classical language.
- The first language to be accorded classical status is Tamil in 2004.

99. *(a)* At present Gir National Wildlife Sanctuary is the only abode of the Asiatic lion.

- Gir National Park is also known as Sasan Gir.
- It is located in Talala Gir in Gujarat, India.
- Sundarbans National Park is situated in West Bengal.
- Kanha Tiger Reserve is located in Madhya Pradesh.
- Saranda forest is located in Saraikela district in state of Jharkhand.

100. *(a)* At Calcutta, Raja Ram Mohan Roy form a reform association called Brahmo Sabha in (1828).

- The Brahmo Samaj/Sabha was a monotheistic sect of Hinduism.
- The Brahmo Sabha does not accept the control of the avatars, the Vedas and does not believe in Samsara or Karma.
- It focused on prayers, meditation and reading of the scriptures.

Set 25 09 July, 2024 (Shift I)

SSC CHSL Tier-I SOLVED PAPER

Instructions

1. This paper contains 100 questions.
2. It has 4 Parts, **Part I** General English, **Part II** General Intelligence & Reasoning, **Part III** Quantitative Aptitude and **Part IV** General Awareness.
3. Each question carries **2 marks.**

Part I
General English

1. The following sentence has been split into four segments. Identify the segment that contains a grammatical error.

In geography class, / the teacher told the students, / "Switzerland lies / inside Germany, France, Austria, and Italy."

(a) inside Germany, France, Austria, and Italy
(b) In geography class,
(c) Switzerland lies
(d) the teacher told the students,

2. Parts of the following sentence have been given as options. Select the option that contains an error.

There are eight planets in our solar system and a Earth is the third planet from the Sun.

(a) planet from the Sun
(b) in our solar system
(c) and a Earth is the third
(d) There are eight planets

3. The following sentence has been split into four segments. Identify the segment that contains a grammatical error.

You expressed your opinion/ very clearly /but I am sorry/ I cannot agree to you.

(a) You expressed your opinion
(b) very clearly
(c) I cannot agree to you
(d) but I am sorry

4. Select the most appropriate option to fill in the blank.

Serena .... from fever since the 5th of this month.

(a) is suffering (b) has been suffering
(c) suffers (d) suffered

Directions (Q. Nos. 5-9) *In the following passage, some words have been deleted. Read the passage carefully and select the most appropriate option to fill in each blank.*

The disclaimer read that no animals were harmed (1)............ the filming of that scene. However, they forgot that the brand of lipstick that was applied (2)............ the heroines lips for that scene was manufactured from crushed cochineal bugs, which release a pigment commonly used in red lipstick. The other items in the film studio (3)............ used animal fats during their manufacturing. The actors who (4)............ that they are vegan in past interviews are unaware of their indirect involvement in such acts of cruelty against animals. The indirect cruelty against animals does not stop here. For example, the extensive disposal of plastic waste in oceans has made plastic a part of the animal food chain, which is detrimental (5) .... our entire ecosystem.

5. Select the most appropriate option to fill in blank number (1).

(a) during (b) around
(c) from (d) for

6. Select the most appropriate option to fill in blank number (2).

(a) on (b) to
(c) over (d) upon

7. Select the most appropriate option to fill in blank number (3).

(a) long (b) also (c) least (d) too

8. Select the most appropriate option to fill in blank number (4).

(a) were confessing
(b) had confessed
(c) confessed
(d) are confessing

9. Select the most appropriate option to fill in blank number (5).

(a) to (b) on (c) in (d) for

10. Select the most appropriate antonym of the underlined word in the sentence.

She was asked by the elders to wear a skirt <u>covering</u> her knees.

(a) exposing (b) expanding
(c) expecting (d) expounding

11. Select the most appropriate antonym of the underlined word in the given sentence.

The company has to be able to <u>compete</u> globally.

(a) support (b) attack
(c) pervert (d) impede

12. Select the incorrectly spelt word.

(a) Dissociation
(b) Clandestine
(c) Pronounciation
(d) Denunciation

13. Select the most appropriate option that can substitute the underlined word in the given sentence.

There was enough room in the <u>spacious</u> flat for all of our furniture.

(a) tiny (b) cozy
(c) roomy (d) cramped

14. Select the most appropriate antonym of the underlined word.

The army <u>advanced</u> into enemy territory.

(a) protruded (b) retreated
(c) arose (d) commuted

15. Which of the following sentences contains the antonym of the word 'important'?

(a) You always make me do all the trivial stuff.
(b) Choose the right colour to make your bike stand out!
(c) Namita also makes some very salient points in her newly revised preface.
(d) I have some urgent questions for you.

16. Select the most appropriate option that can substitute the underlined word in the following sentence.
If it is sunny tomorrow, we go for a picnic.
(a) will going (b) will went
(c) will go (d) goes

17. Select the correct spelling of the underlined word in the following sentence.
I am in a hurry so I will see you tomorow.
(a) tomoorow (b) tomorrow
(c) toomorow (d) tomoorrow

18. Read the given sentence carefully. Change the meaning of the sentence by replacing the underlined word with its antonym from the following options.
William Shakespeare is considered to be the most celebrated dramatist in the world of literature.
(a) laureate
(b) acclaimed
(c) inglorious
(d) illustrious

19. Select the option that will improve the underlined part of the given sentence.
It is my custom to get up early in the morning.
(a) addiction (b) perfection
(c) oddity (d) habit

20. Select the most appropriate option to fill in the blank.
The teacher asked the students to .... attention towards the instructions given for the project.
(a) make (b) keen
(c) had (d) pay

21. Select the most appropriate option to substitute the underlined segment in the following sentence.
A gift from my teacher on the eve of the new year was a complete surprise.
(a) like a cat on hot bricks
(b) a bolt from the blue
(c) like striking one's colours
(d) spilling of beans

22. Select the appropriate option that can substitute the underlined phrase in the following sentence.
Even though she's a celebrity, she doesn't draw any attention towards herself.
(a) is hard to come by
(b) keeps a low profile
(c) keeps hot under the collar
(d) keeps up with the Joneses

23. Select the most appropriate option that can substitute the underlined segment in the given sentence. If there is no need to substitute it, select 'No substitution required'.
There is an old rivalry between the three families for ages.
(a) of the three families
(b) No substitution required
(c) among the three families
(d) in the three families

24. Select the most appropriate antonym of the given word.
Abundance
(a) Fortune (b) Excitement
(c) Scarcity (d) Prosperity

25. Identify the most appropriate synonym of the following word.
Sceptical
(a) Incredulous (b) Stoic
(c) Garrulous (d) Insensitive

Part II
General Intelligence

26. How many rectangles are there in the given figure?

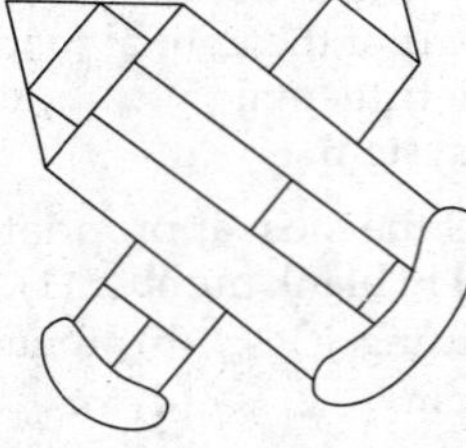

(a) 5 (b) 7 (c) 8 (d) 6

27. JNLO is related to ILIK in a certain way based on the English alphabetical order. In the same way, NRPS is related to MPMO. To which of the following is LPNQ related, following the same logic?
(a) KMKN (b) KNKM
(c) KOKM (d) KMKO

28. Select the option in which the given figure (X) is embedded. (rotation is not allowed).

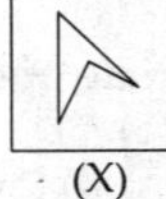

(X)

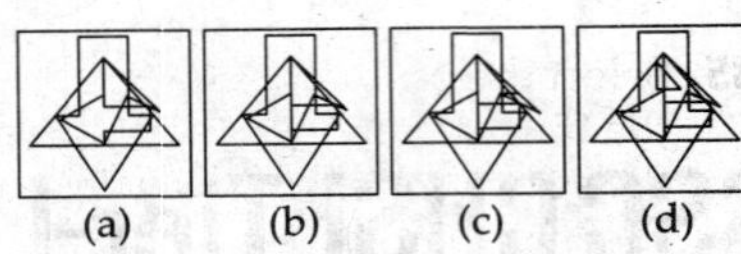

(a) (b) (c) (d)

29. What will come in the place of (?) in the following equation, if '+' and '–' are interchanged?
$47 + 10 \times 3 - 32 \div 8 = ?$
(a) 19 (b) 27 (c) 31 (d) 21

30. Select the set in which the numbers are related in the same way as are the numbers of the following sets.
(**Note** Operations should be performed on the whole numbers, without breaking down the numbers into its constituent digits. E.g. 13 – Operations on 13 such as adding/subtracting/multiplying etc. to 13 can be performed. Breaking down 13 into 1 and 3 and then performing mathematical operations on 1 and 3 is not allowed.)
(2, 3, 36)
(1, 7, 49)
(a) (4, 4, 252) (b) (3, 5, 225)
(c) (5, 4, 260) (d) (1, 9, 59)

31. Identify the figure given in the options that, when put in place of the question mark (?) will logically complete the series.

B 6 ↑ V O N	V ↑ 6 B N O	N 3 V ↑ 6 B	↑ V 3 N B 6	?

(a)	(b)	(c)	(d)
B 6 ↑ V 3 N	6 V B ↑ 3 T	3 T B V ↑ N	B T ↑ V 3 N

32. What should come in place of the question mark (?) in the given series based on the English alphabetical order?
GDJ, KHN, OLR, SPV, ?
(a) WUZ (b) VSX
(c) VTY (d) WTZ

33. In a certain code language, 'BILLION' is coded as '3264581' and 'MILLION' is coded as '3249581'. What is the code for 'M' in that language?
(a) 6 (b) 9 (c) 3 (d) 5

34. What should come in place of the question mark (?) in the given series?
69, 78, 103, 152, ?
(a) 323 (b) 332 (c) 231 (d) 233

35. Select the option that is related to the third number in the same way as the second number is related to the first number.

10 : 26 :: 50 : ?

(a) 344 (b) 343 (c) 342 (d) 341

36. Based on the alphabetical order, three of the following four letter-clusters are alike in a certain way and thus form a group. Which letter-cluster does not belong to that group?

(**Note** The odd one out is not based on the number of consonants/ vowels or their position in the letter-cluster.)

(a) PMO (b) EBD
(c) ROS (d) LIK

37. What should come in place of the question mark (?) in the given series?

24, 40, 56, 72, ?, 104

(a) 86 (b) 87
(c) 88 (d) 89

38. In a certain code language,

'A + B' means 'A is the sister of B',
'A – B' means 'A is the brother of B',
'A × B' means 'A is the father of B',
'A ÷ B' means 'A is the wife of B'.

Based on the above, how is P related to T, if 'P + Q ÷ R × S – T' ?

(a) Father's sister (b) Mother's sister
(c) Mother (d) Sister

39. If 'Y' stands for '÷', 'N' stands for '×', 'M' stands for '+' and 'G' stands for '–', what will come in place of the question mark (?) in the following equation?

100 N 80 G 40 Y 20 M 10 = ?

(a) 8008 (b) 5776
(c) 8976 (d) 987

40. If 19th February, 2004 was a Thursday, then what was the day of the week on 2nd March, 2019 ?

(a) Friday (b) Thursday
(c) Saturday (d) Monday

41. What would be the number on the opposite side of '16', if the given sheet is folded to form a cube?

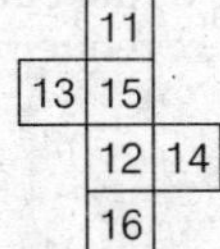

(a) 15 (b) 14 (c) 13 (d) 11

42. Select the combination of letters that, when sequentially placed in the blanks of the given series will complete the series.

ABC_C_CC_DCBG_CA

(a) DCEE (b) DCED
(c) EDCE (d) ECDC

43. Select the correct mirror image of the given figure, when the mirror is placed at MN as shown below.

(a)  (b) 

(c)  (d) 

44. Six letters E, J, K, L, M and P are written on different faces of a dice. Two positions of this dice are shown in the figure. Which is the letter on the face opposite to the face containing M?

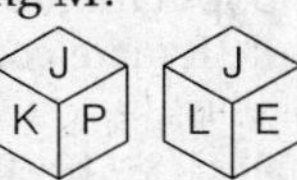

(a) P (b) K (c) J (d) E

45. Select the option in which the given figure (X) is embedded. (Rotation is not allowed.)

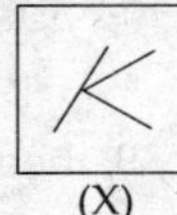
(X)

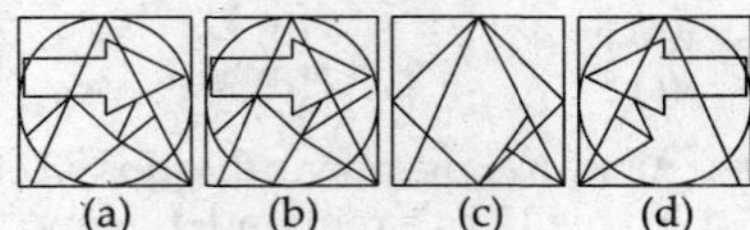

46. Select the word-pair that best represent a similar relationship to the one expressed in the pair of words given below.

(The words must be considered as meaningful English words and must not be related to each other based on the number of letters/number of consonants/vowels in the word)

Engage : Involve

(a) Secure : Vulnerable
(b) Entirety : Fragment
(c) Shrink : Grow
(d) Diverse : Varied

47. Which of the following numbers will replace the question mark (?) in the given series?

41, 49, 65, 89, 121, 161, ?

(a) 209 (b) 189 (c) 195 (d) 215

48. The position of how many letters will remain unchanged, if each of the letters in the word ENGLISH is arranged in alphabetical order?

(a) Two (b) Four (c) Three (d) One

49. Read the given statements and conclusions carefully. Assuming that the information given in the statements is true, even if it appears to be at variance with commonly known facts, decide which of the given conclusions logically follow(s) from the statements.

Statements

All papers are charts.
Some charts are notebooks.
Some notebooks are files.

Conclusions

I. Some charts are files.
II. All papers being notebooks is a possibility.

(a) Only Conclusion II follows
(b) Only Conclusion I follows
(c) None of the conclusions follow
(d) Both Conclusions I and II follow

50. What will come in the place of the question mark (?) in the following equation, if '+' and '–' are interchanged and '×' and '÷' are interchanged?

20 – 80 × 16 ÷ 5 + 15 = ?

(a) 35 (b) 32 (c) 36 (d) 30

Part III

Quantitative Aptitude

51. The following graph shows the demand and production of buses of five companies in 2022 (in thousands). Study the given graph carefully and answer the question that follows.

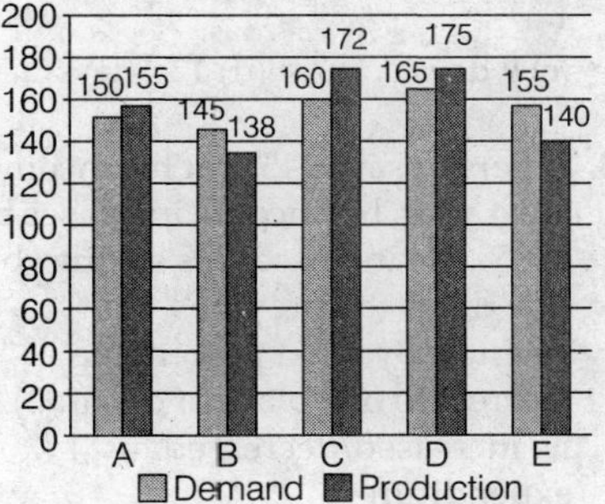

The number of companies, whose production of buses is equal to or more than the average demand of buses of all five companies is

(a) 3 (b) 1
(c) 4 (d) 2

52. The length of a rectangular shaped park exceeds its breadth by 15 m. If the perimeter of the park is 110 m, find the length of the park (in m).

(a) 20 (b) 35
(c) 25 (d) 40

53. The marked price of an item is 1.4 times the cost price. In order to earn 23.2% profit, what per cent discount can a shopkeeper allow?

(a) 13% (b) 17% (c) 15% (d) 12%

54. The hypotenuse of a right triangle is 6m more than twice the shortest side. If the third side is 2 m less than the hypotenuse, find the area (in m^2) of the triangle.

(a) 130 (b) 100 (c) 120 (d) 110

55. In a 2 km linear race, if P completes the race in 200 sec and Q in 220 sec, then the distance by which P beats Q is

(a) $167\frac{6}{11}$ m (b) $173\frac{7}{11}$ m
(c) $191\frac{7}{11}$ m (d) $181\frac{9}{11}$ m

56. A trader buys 500 kg cotton for ₹ 8000. If 10% of this cotton is spoiled due to rain, at what rate (₹/kg) should he sells the rest to earn a 20% profit?

(a) $21\frac{1}{3}$ (b) $22\frac{1}{3}$
(c) $25\frac{1}{3}$ (d) $23\frac{1}{3}$

57. Rohan can alone finish a work in 12 days and Hari can alone in 16 days. They both work for 3 days and then Rohan left. After that only Hari works and finishes the work. The total work will be completed in

(a) 12 days (b) $12\frac{2}{3}$ days
(c) 9 days (d) $12\frac{1}{3}$ days

58. A person saves 45% of his income. Next year, his income increases by 200%. He increases his savings by five times the previous year's savings. By what percentage (correct to one place of decimal) has he increased/decreased his expenditure?

(a) Decreased, 63.4%
(b) Decreased, 36.4%
(c) Increased, 63.4%
(d) Increased, 36.4%

59. In what proportion must tea worth ₹ 27 and ₹ 31 per kg be mixed, so as to gain 25% by selling the mixture at ₹ 36 per kg?

(a) 3 : 7 (b) 2 : 11
(c) 11 : 9 (d) 9 : 11

60. In a circle, the chords AB and CD intersect each other at point L (internally). If $AL = 9$ cm, $LB = 7$ cm and $LD = 3$ cm, then find CL (in cm).

(a) 20 (b) 21 (c) 18 (d) 19

61. The table shows the percentage distribution of the population (only male and female) according to Gender and Literacy.

States	Percentage literate	Gender	
		Literate	Illiterate
		M : F	M : F
A	55	5 : 6	4 : 5
B	72	1 : 1	3 : 2
C	78	4 : 3	3 : 2

The total population in state C, if the illiterate female count in state C is 440000, is

(a) 3600000 (b) 5000000
(c) 6000000 (d) 4600000

62. In how much time (in years) will ₹ 7200 amount to ₹ 8928 at simple interest at the rate of 8% per annum?

(a) 3 (b) 2
(c) 5 (d) 4

63. If 6428A83 is divisible by 9, then the value of A is equal to

(a) 6 (b) 7
(c) 5 (d) 3

64. A natural number n divides 732 and leaves 12 as a remainder. How many values of n are possible?

(a) 18 (b) 20
(c) 16 (d) 22

65. If lateral surface area of a cube is 144 cm^2, then find its volume.

(a) 216 cm^3 (b) 117.58 cm^3
(c) 1728 cm^3 (d) 864 cm^3

66. If $\cot\alpha = \frac{P}{Q}$, then find the value of

$$\frac{P\cos\alpha - Q\sin\alpha}{P\cos\alpha + Q\sin\alpha} - \frac{P^2 - Q^2}{P^2 + Q^2} + 3.$$

(a) $\frac{P}{P^2 + Q^2}$ (b) $\frac{P}{Q}$
(c) 0 (d) 3

67. A cylinder has a curved surface area equal to 350% of the curved surface area of another cylinder. If their radii are in the ratio 3 : 1, then the volume of the smaller cylinder is approximately .... % of the larger cylinder (the smaller cylinder has its radius and height smaller, when compared to the larger).

(a) 9.52 (b) 8.86
(c) 7.28 (d) 10.16

68. Find the length of the sides of a triangle, if its angles are in the ratio 2 : 4 : 6 and its circumradius is 12 cm.

(a) 5 cm, 6 cm, 10 cm
(b) 15 cm, $15\sqrt{3}$ cm, 30 cm
(c) 12 cm, $12\sqrt{3}$ cm, 24 cm
(d) 6 cm, $6\sqrt{3}$ cm, 12 cm

69. A bigger circle centre at O and a smaller circle centre at P touch each other externally such that the length of their common tangent LM is 12 cm. If the radius of the bigger circle is 18 cm, then what will be the radius (in cm) of the smaller circle ?

(a) 4 (b) 3
(c) 2 (d) 1

70. A battery manufacturer manufactures five different types of batteries. The total revenue for the year 2020 is ₹ 2500000 and 20000 units were exported in 2020. The distribution of revenue and units for the five different types of batteries is shown in the chats.

Export of 20000 units

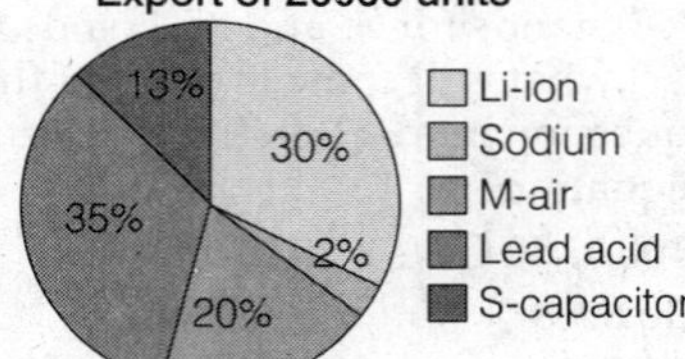

Revenue of 2500000 units

15%
35%
25%
5%
20%
Li-ion
Sodium
M-air
Lead acid
S-capacitor

Which type of the battery provides the highest revenue per unit of export?

(a) M-Air
(b) Li-ion
(c) Sodium
(d) Lead acid

71. In an election between two candidates, 10% of the voters did not cast their votes and 5% of the votes polled were found invalid. The successful candidate got 52.5% of the valid votes and won by a majority of 1710 votes. The number of voters enrolled on the voters list was
(a) 36000 (b) 40000
(c) 42000 (d) 48000

72. A covered wooden box has the inner measures as 128 cm, 90 cm, 25 cm and the thickness of wood is 5.5 cm. Find the volume of the wood.
(a) 329431 cm^3 (b) 217404 cm^3
(c) 819832 cm^3 (d) 192392 cm^3

73. Two numbers are, respectively, 30% and 60% more than a third number. The ratio of the two numbers is
(a) 13 : 17 (b) 12 : 13
(c) 11 : 15 (d) 13 : 16

74. If the areas of three adjacent faces of a cuboid are 5 cm^2, 15 cm^2 and 27 cm^2, respectively, the surface area of the cuboid is
(a) 45 cm^2 (b) 75 cm^2
(c) 47 cm^2 (d) 94 cm^2

75. Answer the following question on the basis of the bar-graph given.
Revenue obtained by publisher on the journals, magazines and books

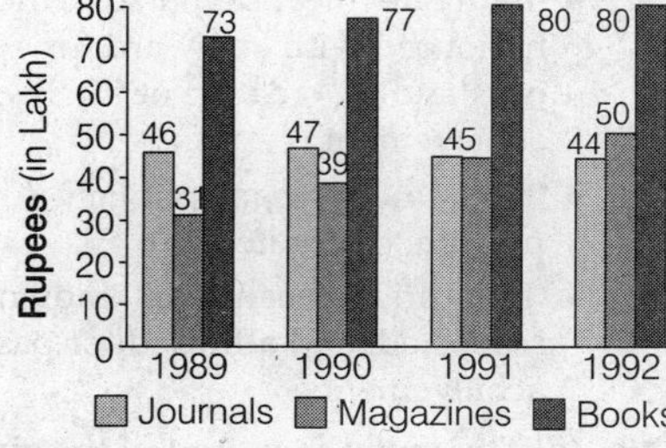

The number of years in which there was an increase in the revenue from atleast two categories is
(a) 1 (b) 3
(c) 4 (d) 2

Part IV
General Awareness

76. According to the Census of India 2011, what is the sex ratio (females per 1000 males) of India?
(a) 933 (b) 927
(c) 943 (d) 934

77. Who calculated the approximate location of the planet Neptune by studying gravity-induced disturbances in the motion of Uranus?
(a) John Couch Adams
(b) Johann Gottfried Galle
(c) Urbain-Jean-Joseph Le Verrier
(d) Percival Lowell

78. In which year was MS Dhoni awarded Padma Shri Award?
(a) 2010 (b) 2012 (c) 2007 (d) 2009

79. What was India's population growth rate (in percentage) during 2001-2011?
(a) 23.87% (b) 17.64%
(c) 24.66% (d) 21.54%

80. Where can you find the options 'From Beginning' and 'From Current Slide' to run a slide show in MS PowerPoint?
(a) Home tab
(b) Slide Show tab
(c) Slide Sorter tab
(d) View tab

81. Which of the following refers to the purchase and sale of government securities?
(a) Bank rate
(b) Open market operations
(c) Reserve ratio
(d) High powered money

82. Which act opposed by Mahatma Gandhi in 1919 was a direct attack on the civil liberties and democratic rights of the Indian people?
(a) Criminal Tribes Act
(b) Defence of India Act
(c) Pitt's India Act
(d) Rowlatt Act

83. Which of the following organisations said that India cannot have a parallel judicial system - one for the rich and the other for the poor?
(a) Supreme Court
(b) Himachal High Court
(c) Gujarat High Court
(d) Kerala High Court

84. Oil India Limited (OIL) is under the administrative structure of
(a) Ministry of Petroleum and Natural Gas
(b) Ministry of Power
(c) Ministry of Commerce and Industry
(d) Ministry of New and Renewable Energy

85. The number of white pawns in chess is ....
(a) 10 (b) 12
(c) 8 (d) 14

86. On the 74th Republic Day of India, President of Egypt, ..., was the Chief Guest at the Republic Day parade.
(a) Gamal Abdel Nasser Husain
(b) Abdel Fattah El-Sisi
(c) Muhammad Hosni El Sayed Mubarak
(d) Adly Mahmoud Mansour

87. Who is known as the Father of Modern Dance in India?
(a) Kelucharan Mohapatra
(b) Uday Shankar
(c) Pandit Birju Maharaj
(d) Atombapu Sharma

88. Which of the following is called the cyclic arrangement of time units in Hindustani classical music?
(a) Alap (b) Raga
(c) Tala (d) Jati

89. In honey bees, ...
(a) males are triploid and females are tetraploid
(b) males are haploid and females are diploid
(c) males are diploid and females are haploid
(d) males are tetraploid and females are triploid

90. Identify the Incorrect pair regarding the material media and their refractive index?
(a) Sapphire – 1.77
(b) Kerosene – 1.44
(c) Ruby – 1.71
(d) Benzene – 2.42

91. The Preamble of the Constitution describes India as
(a) a unitary state
(b) a federal state
(c) an atheist state
(d) a secular state

92. Which of the following is a style of Carnatic music?
(a) Svarajati (b) Chaturang
(c) Dhamar (d) Dhrupad

93. Which of the following rivers is called 'Singi Khamban' in Tibet?
(a) Brahmaputra
(b) Sutlej
(c) Kosi
(d) Indus

94. Judicial Review, a salient feature of the Constitution of India, has been borrowed from which of the following countries?
(a) South Africa (b) Canada
(c) Ireland (d) The US

95. Which of the following statements are true about the positive impact of the Green Revolution (GR) on yield levels in India?
1. During the post GR period, the yield of rice grew at a much faster rate than that of wheat.
2. GR technology had penetrated more in wheat crop than in the rice crop.
3. During post GR period, the area under rice achieved a relatively slow growth when compared to the area under wheat.

Codes
(a) 2 and 3 (b) 1, 2, and 3
(c) 1 and 2 (d) 1 and 3

96. In which year was the All India Football Federation (AIFF) formed?
(a) 1947 (b) 1967 (c) 1957 (d) 1937

97. The Press and Periodicals Registration Bill, 2023 replaced which act with a simplified law that decriminalises various provisions and brings digital media under its ambit?
(a) Censorship of Press Act, 1799
(b) Newspaper (Incitement to Offences) Act, 1908
(c) Press (Objectionable Matters) Act, 1951
(d) Press and Registration of Books Act, 1867

98. The founder of the Pallava dynasty was
(a) Singhamvishnu (b) Simhavishnu
(c) Simharaj (d) Balasimha

99. In November 2022, the Supreme Court upheld the 10% reservation of EWS quota. This EWS reservation was granted on the basis of recommendations from which of the following commissions?
(a) Sarkaria Commission
(b) Kelkar Commission
(c) Mandal Commission
(d) Sinho Commission

100. What should you click to choose the date for sorting in Gmail?
(a) The calendar icon
(b) The '1 Day' drop down menu
(c) The 'Date within' field
(d) The filter icon

Answers

1. (a)	2. (c)	3. (c)	4. (b)
5. (a)	6. (b)	7. (b)	8. (c)
9. (a)	10. (a)	11. (a)	12. (c)
13. (c)	14 (b)	15. (a)	16. (c)
17. (b)	18. (c)	19. (d)	20. (d)
21. (b)	22. (b)	23. (c)	24. (c)
25. (a)	26. (d)	27. (b)	28. (b)
29. (d)	30. (b)	31. (d)	32. (d)
33. (b)	34. (d)	35. (c)	36. (c)
37. (c)	38. (b)	39. (a)	40. (a)
41. (a)	42. (a)	43. (a)	44. (c)
45. (b)	46. (d)	47. (a)	48. (d)
49. (a)	50. (d)	51. (a)	52. (b)
53. (d)	54. (c)	55. (d)	56. (a)
57. (a)	58. (d)	59. (c)	60. (b)
61. (b)	62. (a)	63. (c)	64. (b)
65. (a)	66. (d)	67. (a)	68. (c)
69. (c)	70. (c)	71. (b)	72. (b)
73. (d)	74. (d)	75. (d)	76. (c)
77. (c)	78. (d)	79. (b)	80. (c)
81. (b)	82. (d)	83. (a)	84. (a)
85. (c)	86. (b)	87. (b)	88. (c)
89. (b)	90. (d)	91. (d)	92. (a)
93. (d)	94. (d)	95. (a)	96. (d)
97. (d)	98. (b)	99. (d)	100. (c)

Explanations

1. *(a)* Part 'inside Germany, France, Austria, and Italy' contains an error. Use 'surrounded by' in place of 'inside' to correct the sentence.

2. *(c)* Part 'and a Earth is the third' contains an error. Use 'the' in place of 'a' to correct the sentence.

3. *(c)* Part 'I cannot agree to you' contains an error. Use 'with' in place of 'to' to correct the sentence.

4. *(b)* The correct filler for the given blank is 'has been suffering'.

5. *(a)* The correct filler for the given blank is 'during'.

6. *(b)* The correct filler for the given blank is 'to'.

7. *(b)* The correct filler for the given blank is 'also'.

8. *(c)* The correct filler for the given blank is 'confessed'.

9. *(a)* The correct filler for the given blank is 'to'.

10. *(a)* The antonym of 'covering' is 'exposing'.

11. *(a)* The antonym of 'compete' is 'support'.

12. *(c)* The incorrectly spelt word is 'Pronounciation'. The correct spelling is 'Pronunciation'.

13. *(c)* The word 'spacious' means 'roomy'.

14. *(b)* 'Advanced' means to move forward. Hence, its antonym is 'retreated' means to go back.
- 'Protruded' means to stick out from or through something.
- 'Commuted' means to make the same journey regularly between work and home.

15. *(a)* The antonym of 'important' is 'trivial' which means insignificant. Hence, the correct sentence is–You always make me do all the trivial stuff.

16. *(c)* The underlined part of the given sentence contains an error. Use 'will go' to correct the sentence.

17. *(b)* The correct spelling is 'tomorrow'.

18. *(c)* The antonym of 'celebrated' is 'inglorious' which means (of an action or situation) causing shame or a loss of honour.
- 'Laureate' means a person who is honoured with an award for outstanding creative or intellectual achievement.
- 'Acclaimed' means publicly praised; celebrated.
- 'Illustrious' means well known, respected, and admired for past achievements.

19. *(d)* The underlined part of the given sentence contains an error. Use 'habit' to correct the sentence.

20. *(d)* The correct filler for the given blank is 'pay' as it is used with 'attention'.

21. *(b)* The most appropriate substitute for the given blank is 'a bolt from the blue'. It means a sudden and unexpected surprise.
- 'Like a cat on hot bricks' means nervous.
- 'Like striking one's colours' means to surrender.
- 'Spilling of beans' means to reveal a secret.

22. *(b)* The most appropriate substitute for the given blank is 'keeps a low profile'. It means that it doesn't draw any attention towards herself.

- 'Is hard to come by' means hard to find or get.
- 'Keep hot under the collar' means to get annoyed or angry.
- 'Keep up with the Joneses' means to own the same things as other people.

23. *(c)* The underlined part of the given sentence contains an error. Use 'among' to correct the sentence as we are referring to more than two beings.

24. *(c)* 'Abundance' means in large quantity. Hence, its antonym is 'scarcity' means 'in less quantity'.

25. *(a)* 'Sceptical' means doubtful. Hence, its synonym is 'incredulous' which means (of a person or their manner) unwilling or unable to believe something.

- 'Stoic' means a person who can endure pain or hardship without showing their feelings or complaining.
- 'Garrulous' means talkative.

26. *(d)* Naming the figure,

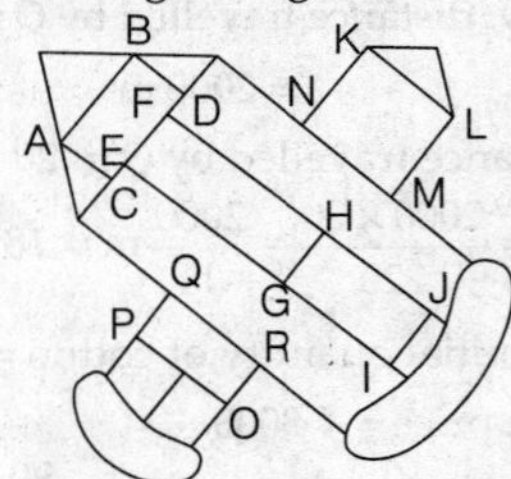

Rectangles are EFHG, GHJI, ABDC, NKLM, PORQ and EIJF.

∴ Total '6' rectangles are there in the given figure.

27. *(b)* As,

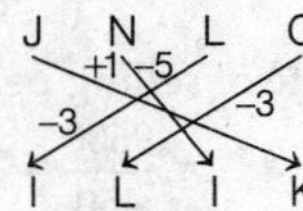

and

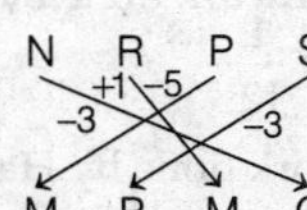

Similarly,

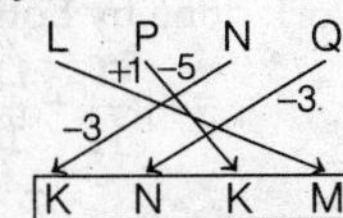

28. *(b)* The figure is embedded in the below figure.

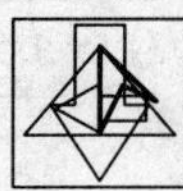

29. *(d)* $47 + 10 \times 3 - 32 \div 8 = ?$

When, '+' and '−' are interchanged, the equation become

$47 - 10 \times 3 + 32 \div 8$

$= 47 - 10 \times 3 + 4$

$= 47 - 30 + 4$

$= 51 - 30 = 21$

30. *(b)* As, (2, 3, 36)

$= 2 \times 3 = 6^2 = 36$

and (1, 7, 49)

$= 1 \times 7 = 7^2 = 49$

Similarly, (3, 5, 225)

$= 3 \times 5 = 15^2 = 225$

31. *(d)* As,

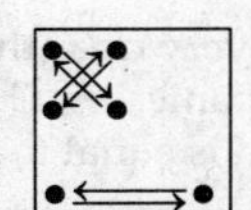

From fig. (1) to fig. (2) and fig. (3) to fig. (4)

and

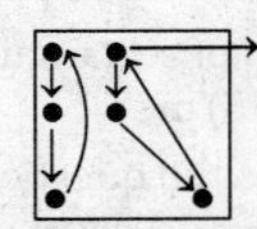

From fig. (2) to fig. (3) and fig. (4) to fig. (5)

32. *(d)* The given series follows the pattern below,

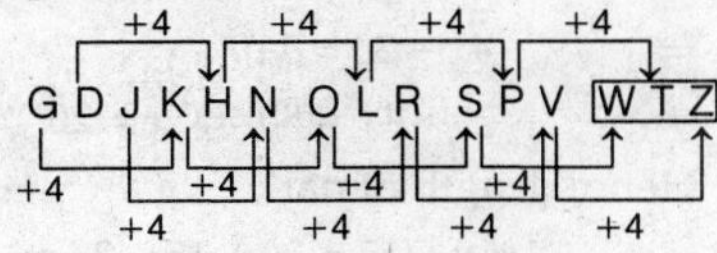

33. *(b)* B I L L I O N ⟶ 3 2 6 4 5 8 1

and M I L L I O N ⟶ 3 2 4 9 5 8 1

From the given we derived that the code for M = 9

34. *(d)* The given series follows the pattern,

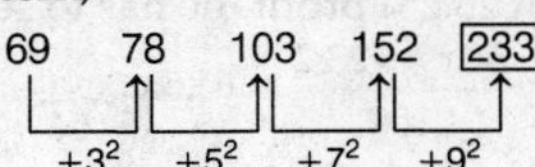

35. *(c)* As, Similarly,

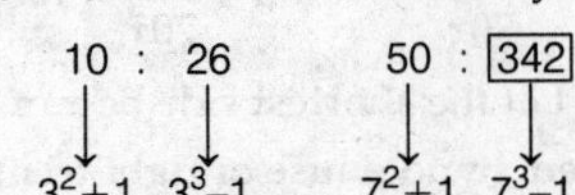

36. *(c)*

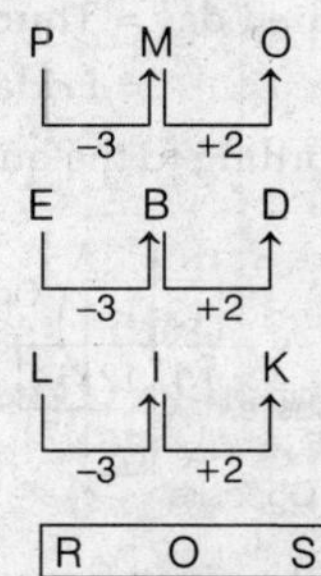

But,

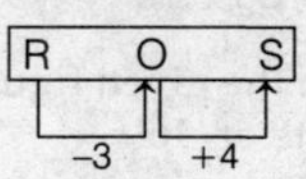

So, ROS is odd from rest.

37. *(c)* The given series follows the pattern,

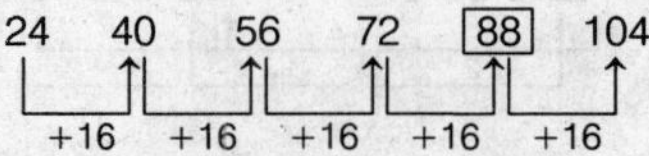

38. *(b)* The given relation,

P+ Q÷ R× S − T

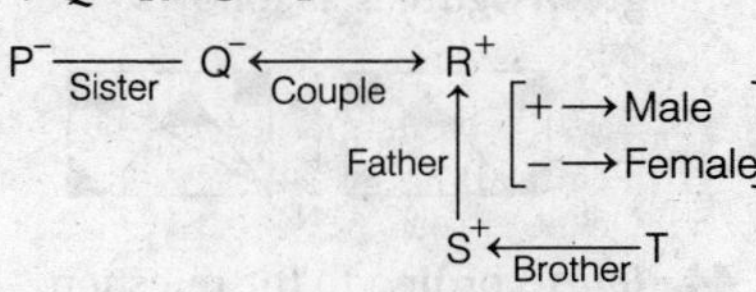

Here, P is mother's sister of T.

39. *(a)* The given equation,

100 N 80 G 40 Y 20 M 10 = ?

After substituting the symbol,

$100 \times 80 - 40 \div 20 + 10$

$= 100 \times 80 - 2 + 10$

$= 8000 - 2 + 10$

$= 8010 - 2$

$= 8008$

40. *(b)* Given, 19th February 2004 → Thursday

Number of odd days from 19th February 2004 to 19th February, 2019

Years → 2005 + 2006 + 2007 + 2008 + 2009 + 2010 + 2011 + 2012 + 2013 +2014 + 2015 + 2016 + 2017 + 2018 + 2019

Odd days → $2 + 1 + 1 + 1 + 2 + 1 + 1 + 1 + 2 + 1 + 1 + 1 + 2 + 1 + 1 = \frac{19}{7} = 5$ odd days

Now, number of odd days from 19th February, 2019 to 2nd March, 2019.

Months → February + March

Odd days → $8 + 2 = \frac{10}{7} = 3$ odd days

∴ Total odd days $= \frac{5 + 3}{7} = \frac{8}{7} \Rightarrow 1$

$\therefore$ Required day = Thursday + 1
= Friday

41. *(a)* According to the question,

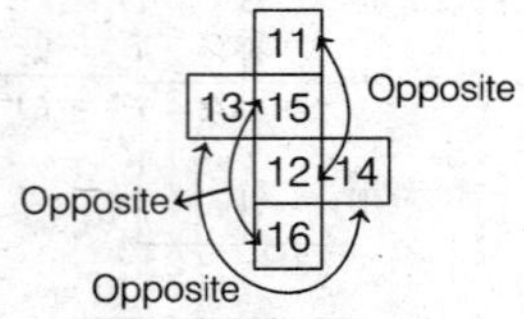

$\therefore$ From the given figure '15' is opposite of '16'.

42. *(a)* The given series is as follows,

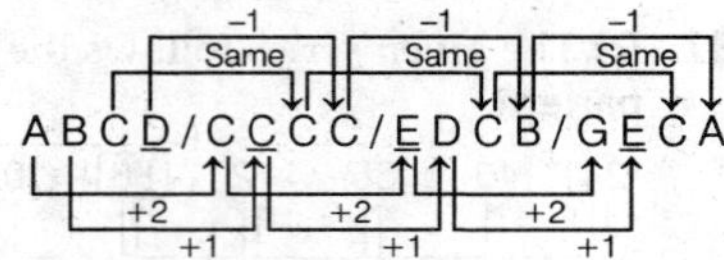

$\therefore$ Required combination 'DCEE'.

43. *(a)* The correct mirror image of the given figure is as follows

44. *(c)* According to the question,

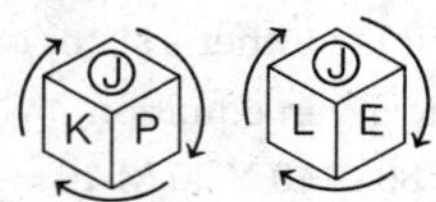

Here, J is common, so dice is rotated in clockwise direction from common face.

J	P	K
J	E	L

Here, 'P' is opposite to 'E' and 'K' is opposite to 'L'. Similarly, 'M' is opposite to 'J'.

45. *(b)* The given figure is embedded in option figure (b).

46. *(d)* As, engage is synonym of involve. Similarly, diverse is synonym of varied.

47. *(a)* The given series follows the pattern,

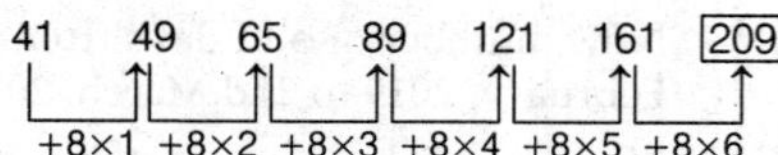

48. *(d)* The given word ENGLISH
In alphabetical order EGHILNS
$\therefore$ Only one remain unchanged after rearrangement, i.e., E.

49. *(a)* According to the question,

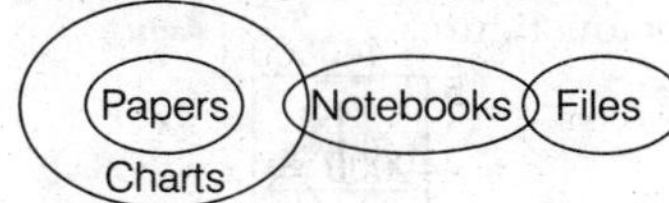

Conclusions
I. (✗) II. (✓)
Hence, only Conclusion II follows.

50. *(d)* The given equation,
$$20 - 80 \times 16 \div 5 + 15 = ?$$
After interchanging the symbols, we get
$$20 + 80 \div 16 \times 5 - 15$$
$$= 20 + 5 \times 5 - 15$$
$$= 20 + 25 - 15 = 45 - 15 = 30$$

51. *(a)* According to the question,
Average of demand of all companies buses
$$= \frac{150 + 145 + 160 + 165 + 155}{5}$$
$$= \frac{775}{5} = 155$$
Now, it is very clear that there are three companies, A, C and D, whose production is equal to 155 or greater than 155.
Thus, option (c) is correct.

52. *(b)* Let the breadth of park be x m.
Then, length of rectangular shaped park = $(x + 15)$ m
According to the question,
Perimeter of rectangular park = 110
$$2(l + b) = 110$$
$$\Rightarrow 2(x + 15 + x) = 110$$
$$\Rightarrow 2(2x + 15) = 110$$
$$\Rightarrow 4x + 30 = 110$$
$$\Rightarrow 4x = 80 \Rightarrow x = 20$$
Hence, length of park
$$= x + 15 = 20 + 15 = 35 \text{ m}$$

53. *(d)* Ratio of marked price and cost price $= \frac{14}{10}$
$$\frac{MP}{CP} = \frac{7}{5}$$
Let MP be ₹ $70x$ and CP be ₹ $50x$ to gain 23.2% profit, he has to sell item at $= \frac{50x \times 123.2}{100} = 61.6x$
Hence, required discount
$$= \frac{70x - 61.6x}{70x} \times 100 = \frac{8.4x}{70x} \times 100 = 12\ \%$$

54. *(c)* Let the shortest side be x m.
Then, hypotenuse of right triangle is $(2x + 6)$ m and third side $= 2x + 6 - 2 = (2x + 4)$ m

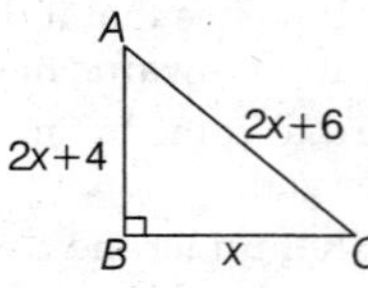

By Pythagoras theorem,
$$(2x + 6)^2 = (2x + 4)^2 + x^2$$
$$4x^2 + 36 + 24x = 4x^2 + 16 + 16x + x^2$$
$$x^2 - 8x - 20 = 0$$
$$\Rightarrow x^2 - 10x + 2x - 20 = 0$$
$$\Rightarrow x(x - 10) + 2(x - 10) = 0$$
$$\Rightarrow (x - 10)(x + 2) = 0$$
$$x = 10, -2$$
Thus, $BC = 10$ m
and $AB = 2x + 4 = 20 + 4 = 24$
$$\therefore \text{Area of triangle } ABC = \frac{1}{2} \times BC \times AB$$
$$= \frac{1}{2} \times 10 \times 24 = 120 \text{ m}^2$$

55. *(d)* According to the question,
Time taken by P = 200 sec
Time taken by Q = 220 sec
P defeat Q by 20 sec.
Now, distance travelled by Q in 220 sec
= 2000 m
Distance travelled by Q in 20 sec
$$= \frac{2000 \times 20}{220} = \frac{2000}{11} \text{ m} = 181\frac{9}{11} \text{ m}$$

56. *(a)* Initial quantity of cotton = 500 kg
Cost price = ₹ 8000
Remaining cotton $= 500 \times \frac{90}{100} = 450$ kg
Buyer went to gain 20%.
Thus, selling price of 450 kg cotton
$$= 8000 \times \frac{120}{100} = ₹9600$$
Hence, rate of selling per kg
$$= \frac{9600}{450} = ₹\ 21.3 = 21\frac{1}{3} \text{ kg}$$

57. *(a)* Part of work done by Rohan in one day $= \frac{1}{12}$
Part of work done by Hari in one day
$$= \frac{1}{16}$$
Part of work done by both in 3 days
$$= 3\left(\frac{1}{12} + \frac{1}{16}\right) = \frac{7}{16}$$
Remaining work $= 1 - \frac{7}{16} = \frac{9}{16}$

Remaining work done by Hari only

$= \frac{9}{16} \times 16 = 9$ days

Thus, total time to complete work

$= 9 + 3 = 12$ days

58. *(d)* Let his total income be ₹$100x$.

Then, initial saving

$= 100x \times 45\% =$ ₹ $45x$

and initial expenditure

$= 100x - 45x =$ ₹ $55x$

Now, new income

$= 100x \times \frac{300}{100} =$ ₹ $300x$

His new saving $= 45x \times 5 =$ ₹ $225x$

New expenditure of person

$= 300x - 225x =$ ₹ $75x$

Increase percentage in expenditure

$= \frac{75x - 55x}{55x} \times 100 = \frac{20x}{55x} \times 100$

$= 36.36 \sim 36.40\%$

59. *(c)* Rate of first type of tea = ₹27/kg

Rate of second type of tea = ₹ 31/kg

Cost price of mixture $= 36 \times \frac{100}{125}$

= ₹28.8/kg

Thus, by Alligation method,

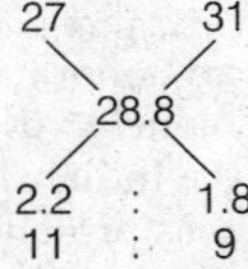

$\therefore$ Required ratio = 11 : 9

60. *(b)* *AB* and *CD* are two chords of circle, which intersect at Point *L*.

As, we know that,

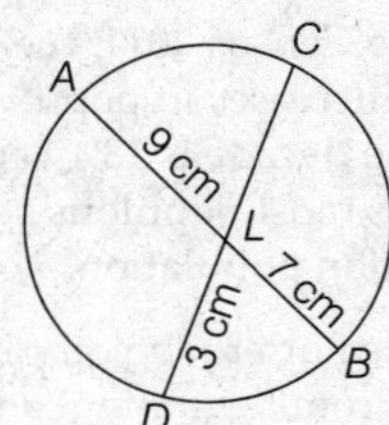

$AL \times LB = LC \times LD$

$9 \times 7 = LC \times 3$

$LC = 21$ cm

61. *(b)* Let total population of state C is $100x$.

Then, illiterate population

$= 100x \times \frac{22}{100} = 22x$

According to the question,

$22x \times \frac{2}{5} = 440000$

$\frac{44x}{5} = 440000 \Rightarrow x = 50000$

Thus, total population = 5000000

62. *(a)* Here,

Principal $(P) =$ ₹7200

Amount $(A) =$ ₹8928

SI = 8928 − 7200 = ₹1728

and rate interest $(R) = 8\%$

Let time = t yr

Then, SI $= \frac{P \times R \times T}{100}$

$\Rightarrow \quad 1728 = \frac{7200 \times 8 \times t}{100} \Rightarrow t = 3$ yr

Required time = 3 yr

63. *(c)* 6428 A83 is divisible by 9.

By divisibility rule of 9, the sum of digits of number must be divisible by 9.

Then,

$\frac{6+4+2+8+A+8+3}{9} = \frac{31+A}{9}$

To make divisible $(31 + A)$, we have to put $A = 5$

Thus, $\frac{31+5}{9} = 4$ (divisible)

Thus, value of *A* is 5.

64. *(b)* According to the question,

732 − 12 = 720

2	720
2	360
2	180
2	90
3	45
3	15
5	5
	1

$720 = 2 \times 2 \times 2 \times 2 \times 3 \times 3 \times 5$

$= 2^4 \times 5^1 \times 3^2$

Total factors $= (4+1) \times (2+1) \times (1+1)$

$= 5 \times 3 \times 2 = 30$

Now, factors of 720 till = 12

1, 2, 3, 4, 5, 6, 8, 9, 10 and 12

Then, total factors upto 12 = 10

Required number $(n) = 30 - 10 = 20$

65. *(a)* Lateral surface area of cube $= 144$ cm^2

$4a^2 = 144 \Rightarrow a^2 = 36 \Rightarrow a = 6$ cm

Thus, side of cube is 6 cm.

Then, volume of cube

$= a^3 = (6)^3 = 216$ cm^3

66. *(d)* $\cot\alpha = \frac{P}{Q}$

$\therefore \quad \tan\alpha = \frac{Q}{P}$

Thus, $\frac{P\cos\alpha - Q\sin\alpha}{P\cos\alpha - Q\sin\alpha} - \frac{P^2 - Q^2}{P^2 + Q^2} + 3$

$= \frac{P\cos\alpha}{P\cos\alpha}\left[\frac{1 - \frac{Q}{P}\tan\alpha}{1 + \frac{Q}{P}\tan\alpha}\right] - \left(\frac{P^2 - Q^2}{P^2 + Q^2}\right) + 3$

$= \frac{\left(1 - \frac{Q}{P} \times \frac{Q}{P}\right)}{\left(1 + \frac{Q}{P} \times \frac{Q}{P}\right)} - \left(\frac{P^2 - Q^2}{P^2 + Q^2}\right) + 3$

$= \frac{P^2 - Q^2}{P^2} \times \frac{P^2}{(P^2 + Q^2)} - \left(\frac{P^2 - Q^2}{(P^2 + Q^2)}\right) + 3$

$= 3$

67. *(a)* Let for cylinder *A*, radius *R* and height *H* and for cylinder *B*, radius *r* and height = *h*

According to the question,

$2\pi RH = 2\pi r \times h \times \frac{350}{100}$

$RH = rh \times \frac{7}{2}$ ...(i)

and $R : r = 3 : 1$

Let radii are $3x$ and x.

Thus,

$\frac{H}{h} = \frac{r}{R} \times \frac{7}{2} \Rightarrow \frac{H}{h} = \frac{1}{3} \times \frac{7}{2} = \frac{7}{6}$

Now, volume of cylinder *A* and cylinder *B*

$= \pi R^2 H : \pi r^2 h$

$= \pi \times 3^2 \times 7 : \pi \times 1^2 \times 6 = 63 : 6$

$\therefore$ Required percentage $= \frac{6}{63} \times 100$

$= 9.52\%$

68. *(c)* Let the angles of triangle are $2x$, $4x$ and $6x$.

$2x + 4x + 6x = 180°$

$12x = 180°$

$x = 15°$

Then, angles are $2x = 30°$

$4x = 60°$

$6x = 90°$

Circumradius of circle = 12 cm

As, we know in right-angled triangle.

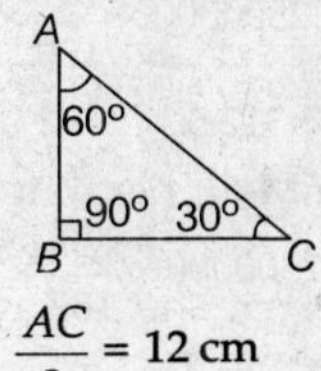

$\frac{AC}{2} = 12$ cm

$AC = 24$ cm

Then, $\sin 30° = \frac{AB}{AC}$ and $\cos 30° = \frac{BC}{AC}$

$\frac{1}{2} = \frac{AB}{AC}$ $\frac{\sqrt{3}}{2} = \frac{BC}{24}$

$\frac{1}{2} = \frac{AB}{24}$ $BC = 12\sqrt{3}$

$AB = 12$ cm

Hence, all sides are 12 cm, $12\sqrt{3}$ cm and 24 cm.

69. *(c)* According to the question,

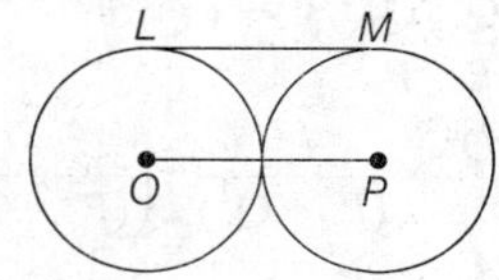

$r_1 = 18$ cm, $r_2 = ?$

$LM = 12$ cm

As, we know

Length of common tangent $= 2\sqrt{r_1 r_2}$

$12 = 2\sqrt{18 \times r_2}$

$\Rightarrow \sqrt{18 \times r_2} = 6$

$\Rightarrow 18 \times r_2 = 6^2 = 36$

$\Rightarrow r_2 = 2$ cm

Thus, radius of smaller circle = 2 cm

70. *(c)* Number of Lion units

$= 20000 \times \frac{30}{100} = 6000$

Number of sodium units

$= 20000 \times \frac{2}{100} = 400$

Number of M-air units

$= 20000 \times \frac{20}{100} = 4000$

Number of lead acid units

$= 20000 \times \frac{35}{100} = 7000$

Number of S-capacitor units

$= 20000 \times \frac{13}{100} = 2600$

Revenue of lion per unit

$= 2500000 \times \frac{35}{100} \times \frac{1}{6000}$

$= ₹\ 145.83$

Revenue of sodium per unit

$= 2500000 \times \frac{5}{100} \times \frac{1}{400}$

$= ₹\ 312.5$

Revenue of M-air per unit

$= 2500000 \times \frac{20}{100} \times \frac{1}{4000}$

$= ₹\ 125$

Revenue of lead acid per unit

$= 2500000 \times \frac{25}{100} \times \frac{1}{7000} = ₹\ 89.285$

Revenue of S-capacitor per unit

$= 2500000 \times \frac{15}{100} \times \frac{1}{2600} = ₹\ 144.45$

Thus, highest revenue per unit is of Sodium battery.

71. *(b)* Let total voters be $100x$.

Number of casted votes

$= 100x \times \frac{90}{100} = 90x$

Invalid votes = 5%

Number of valid votes $= 90x \times \frac{95}{100}$

$= 85.5x$

Number of votes got by winner

$= 85.5x \times 52.5\%$

Votes got by looser $= 85.5x \times 47.5\%$

According to the question,

$85.5x \times 52.5\% - 85.5x \times 47.5\% = 1710$

$85.5x(52.5 - 47.5)\% = 1710$

$85.5x \times 5\% = 1710$

$\Rightarrow x = \frac{1710 \times 100}{85.5 \times 5}$

$100x = \frac{1710 \times 100 \times 100}{85.5 \times 5} = 40000$

$\therefore$ Total votes = 40000

72. *(b)* Volume of box with wood

$= (128 + 11) \times (90 + 11) \times (25 + 11)$

$= 139 \times 101 \times 36$

$= 505404\ \text{cm}^3$

Volume of wooden box without word

$= 128 \times 90 \times 25 = 288000\ \text{cm}^3$

Thus, volume of wood

$= 505404 - 288000$

$= 217404\ \text{cm}^3$

73. *(d)* Let the third number be $100x$.

First number $= 100x \times \frac{130}{100} = 130x$

and second number $= 100x \times \frac{160}{100}$

$= 160x$

Thus, ratio of first number and second number $= 130x : 160x$

$= 13 : 16$

74. *(d)* Area of adjacent faces are $5\ \text{cm}^2$, $15\ \text{cm}^2$ and $27\ \text{cm}^2$.

Surface area of cuboid $= 2(lb + bh + hl)$

$= 2(5 + 15 + 27)$

$= 2 \times 47 = 94$

Surface area of cuboid $= 94\ \text{cm}^2$

75. *(d)* It is very clear from graph that there is increment atleast of two in year 1990 and 1991.

Thus, option (d) is correct.

76. *(c)* According to the Census of India 2011, the sex ratio (number of females per 1000 males) at all India level was 943 and the same for rural and urban areas are 949 and 929.

77. *(c)* Urbain-Jean-Joseph-Le Verrier calculated the appropriate location of the planet Neptune by studying gravity induced disturbance in the motion of Uranus.

- In 1845, astronomers Urbain Le Verrier in Paris and John Couch Adams in Cambridge separately began calculations to determine the nature and position of such a planet.
- The discovery of Neptune led to the discovery of its Moon, Triton, by William Lassell just seventeen days later.

78. *(d)* In 2009, MS Dhoni awarded Padma Shri Award.

- In 2008, Dhoni was awarded India's highest sport honour Major Dhyan Chand Khel Ratna Award.
- In 2018, he received the third highest civilian award Padma Bhushan.

Additional

Dhoni holds an honorary rank of Lieutenant Colonel in the Parachute Regiment of the Indian Territorial Army which was presented to him by the Indian Army in 2011.

79. *(b)* India's population growth rate during 2001-2011 is 17.64%. Percentage growth of males are 17.19 and females are 18.12.

As per the Census 2011, the total absolute increases in population during the decade is 18.19 crore. Uttar Pradesh is most populous state with 199.5 million population.

80. *(c)* In slide Sorter tab you can find the options 'From Beginning' and 'From Current Slide' to run a slide show in MS PowerPoint.

81. *(b)* OMO (Open Market Operations) refers to the purchase and sale of government securities.

- **Bank Rate** It is rate of which the Reserve Bank of India (RBI) provides the loan to commercial banks without keeping any security.

- **Reserve Ratio** It is the percentage of a commercial bank's deposits that it must keep in cash as a reserve.
- **High Powered Money** refers to the aggregate of the total currency (coins and notes) that are held by the public and the reserves of commercial banks.

82. *(d)* Rowlatt Act opposed by Mahatma Gandhi in 1919 was a direct attack on the civil liberties and democratic rights of the Indian people.
- Rowlatt Act was passed by the British Government to increase their grip on power over the common folk.
- It gave them the power to arrest any person without any trial.

83. *(a)* Supreme Court said that India cannot have a parallel judicial system-one for the rich and the other for the poor.
It means when a rich person has not been punished for something that a poor person would be punished for justice and fairness.

84. *(a)* Oil India Limited is under the administrative structure of Ministry of Petroleum and Natural Gas.
- Oil is a central public sector undertaking engaged in the business of exploration.
- Development and production of crude oil and natural gas.
- Transportation of crude oil and production of liquid petroleum gas.

85. *(c)* The number of white pawns in chess is 8.
- Chess sets contain sixteen total pawns.
- Each player begins the game with eight pawns.

86. *(b)* On the 74th Republic Day of India, President of Egypt Abdel Fattah El-Sisi was the Chief Guest at the Republic Day parade.
- Every year on Republic Day, we witness an important, foreign public figure or a politician as the Chief Guest.
- In the year 2024, the President of France, Emmanuel Macron, was the chief guest of 75th Republic Day parade.

87. *(b)* Uday Shankar is known as the 'Father of Modern Dance in India'.
Uday Shankar (1900-77), the elder brother of the musician Ravi Shankar belongs to a Rajasthani family with origin in what is now Bangladesh.

88. *(c)* Tala is called the cyclic arrangement of time units in Hindustani classical music.
A metric cycle with a specific number of beats- from 3 to 128, that recur in the same pattern throughout a musical performance.

89. *(b)* In honey bees, males are haploid and females are diploid. This is called haplodiploidy.
- The queen and worker bees are females and are diploid in nature that develop from fetilised eggs.
- Drones (Males) are haploid that produce sperm cells which contain the entire genome.

90. *(d)* Pair (d) is incorrect regarding the material media and their refractive index because the refractive index value in Benzene is 1.33.

91. *(d)* The Preamble of the Constitution describes India as a secular state.
- It declares India to be a sovereign, socialist, secular, democratic, republic committed to Justice, Equality and Liberty for the people.
- The Preamble has been amended only once so far, in 1976, by the 42nd Constitutional Amendment Act 1976.

92. *(a)* Svarajati is a style of Carnatic music.
- It consists of three sections, called Pallavi, Anupallavi and Charanam.
- The theme is either devotional, heroic or amorous.

93. *(d)* Indus river is called 'Singi Khamban' in Tibet.
- The Indus also known as the Sindhu.
- It originates from a glacier near Bokhar Chu (31°15'N latitude and 81°40'E longitude) in the Tibetan region at an altitude of 4.164 m in the Kailash Mountain range.
- In Tibet, it is known as 'Singi Khamban' or 'Lion's Mouth'.

94. *(d)* Judicial Review has been borrowed from the US.
- Article 226 of the Indian Consitution provides the High Courts with the power of judicial review.
- Judicial review, power of the courts of a country to examine the actions of the legislative, executive and administrative arms of the government.

95. *(a)* Statements (2) and (3) are correct.
- **Increase in crop production** During the post GR period, the High Yield Varieties of wheat and rice grew considerably making India one of the world's biggest agricultural producers.
- During post GR period, the area under rice achieved a relatively slow growth when compared to the area under wheat.

96. *(d)* In 1937, the All India Football Federation (AIFF) formed.
- It is the governing body of football, futsal and beach soccer in India.
- It is a member of FIFA and is affiliated with the Asian Football Confederation and South Asian Football Federation.
- It is affiliated with the Ministry of Youth Affairs and Sports.

97. *(d)* The Presss and Periodicals Registration Bill 2023 replaced the Press and Registration of Books Act, 1867 with a simplified law that decriminalises various provisions and brings digital media under its ambit.
- It provides for the registration of periodicals, which includes any publication containing public news or comments on public news.
- It does not include books or scientific and academic jounals.

98. *(b)* Simhavishnu was the founder of the Pallava dynasty.
- He was the first Pallava monarch whose domain extended beyond Kanchipuram in the South.
- He is also known as Avanisimha, son of Simhavarman III.

99. *(d)* In November 2022, the Supreme Court upheld the 10% reservation of EWS quota. This EWS reservation was granted on the basis of Sinho Commission recommendations.
- Sarkaria Commission suggested the empowerment of All-India Services.
- Kelkar Commission set up to study and evaluate the extend Public-Private Partnership (PPP) model in India.
- Mandal Commission was set up in 1979 by Morarji Desai Government to identify the socially or educationally backward classes to seat reservations.

100. *(c)* To sort emails by date in gmail, you can use the 'Date within' field in the advanced search options.

Set 26 09 July, 2024 (Shift II)

SSC CHSL Tier-I
SOLVED PAPER

Instructions

1. This paper contains 100 questions.
2. It has 4 Parts, **Part I** General English, **Part II** General Intelligence & Reasoning, **Part III** Quantitative Aptitude and **Part IV** General Awareness.
3. Each question carries **2 marks**.

Part I
General English

1. Identify the error in the given sentence and select the correct sentence from the given options.

This is the story of eight round planets, the few rocks in between, and some comets.

(a) This is story of eight round planets, few rocks in between, and some comets.
(b) This is a story of eight round planets, few rocks in between, and some comets.
(c) This is the story of eight round planets, few rocks in between, and some comets.
(d) This is the story of eight round planets, a few rocks in between, and some comets.

2. The following sentence has been split into four segments. Identify the segment that contains a grammatical error.

Everyone have/ to join health orientation/ classes before/ going for trekking.

(a) to join health orientation
(b) Everyone have
(c) going for trekking
(d) classes before

3. The following sentence has been split into four segments. Identify the segment that contains a grammatical error.

Our plane / arrived at / the Mumbai airport / at the right time.

(a) arrived at
(b) Our plane
(c) at the right time
(d) the Mumbai airport

4. The following sentence has been split into four segments. Identify the segment that contains a grammatical error.

It was noticed / that he truthful / answered the questions / raised by the Headmistress.

(a) that he truthful
(b) It was noticed
(c) raised by the Headmistress
(d) answered the questions

Directions (Q. Nos. 5-9) *In the following passage, some words have been deleted. Select the most appropriate option to fill in the blanks.*

Our country, India, is one of the 12 mega bio-diversity countries of the world. With about 47,000 plant species, India (1)......... tenth place in the world and fourth in Asia in plant diversity. There are (2)......... 15,000 flowering plants in India, which account for 6 per cent of the world's (3)......... number of flowering plants. The country has many non-flowering plants, (4)......... as ferns, algae and fungi. India also has approximately 90,000 (5)......... of animals, as well as a rich variety of fish in its fresh and marine waters.

5. Select the most appropriate option to fill in blank number (1).

(a) have (b) occupies
(c) had (d) occupy

6. Select the most appropriate option to fill in blank number (2).

(a) a (b) many
(c) of (d) about

7. Select the most appropriate option to fill in blank number (3).

(a) exact
(b) nearly
(c) exactly
(d) total

8. Select the most appropriate option to fill in blank number (4).

(a) as (b) such
(c) in (d) for

9. Select the most appropriate option to fill in blank number (5).

(a) specie (b) species
(c) kind (d) type

10. Select the most appropriate option that can substitute the underlined segment in the given sentence.

She finished her quickly breakfast and rushed to school.

(a) finished her breakfast quickly
(b) quickly her breakfast finished
(c) her breakfast finished quickly
(d) finished breakfast hers quickly

11. Select the most appropriate antonym of the bracketed word in the following sentence to fill in the blank.

Lewis was aggressive, ... (normal), moody, and brilliantly clever.

(a) feeble (b) eccentric
(c) dogmatic (d) selfish

12. Select the most appropriate option to fill in the blank.

I am scared of snakes; likewise, you are .... of lizards.

(a) passionate (b) critical
(c) fond (d) fearful

13. Select the option that can substitute the bracketed word segment meaningfully.

Writing can instil a number of emotions (as in a reader).

(a) until a reader
(b) among a reader
(c) within a reader
(d) instead a reader

14. Select the sentence which gives the most appropriate meaning of the given idiom.

A piece of cake

(a) Despite the heavy rain, they managed to have a successful outdoor event.
(b) The restaurant was crowded, but they found a table without any difficulty.
(c) The puzzle was so challenging that it took hours for Sam to solve it.
(d) After months of practice, Emily performed her piano piece flawlessly during the concert.

15. Select the most appropriate synonym of the given word.

Attire

(a) Park (b) Dress
(c) Theatre (d) Hote

16. Select the most appropriate antonym of the underlined word in the given sentence.

The dog was <u>agitated</u> and bit the child.

(a) steady (b) nerveless
(c) quiescent (d) serene

17. There is a spelling error in the given sentence. Select the option that contains the incorrectly spelt word.

He was thrilled when he heard about there journey to wonderland.

(a) journey
(b) thrilled
(c) there
(d) heard

18. Select the most appropriate option to fill in the blank.

I have observed that there is proper natural .... even at 6 o'clock on summer mornings.

(a) light (b) sparkle
(c) lucent (d) gleam

19. Select the most appropriate synonym of the given word.

Hypocrisy

(a) Harm (b) Sincerity
(c) Deceit (d) Truth

20. Select the most appropriate synonym of the given word.

Bliss

(a) Consecration
(b) Pleasure
(c) Genesis
(d) Avail

21. Select the most appropriate option that can substitute the underlined words in the following sentence.

I consider that every matter must be considered <u>in every point</u> of view.

(a) of every point
(b) from every point
(c) at every point
(d) on every point

22. Select the incorrectly spelt word.

(a) Condimnation
(b) Intermingled
(c) Imprisonment
(d) Conglomerate

23. Select the most appropriate synonym of the underlined word.

The sun was shining bright and <u>intense</u> in the sky.

(a) mild (b) strong
(c) subtle (d) weak

24. the most appropriate meaning of the given idiom.

Under the weather

(a) To feel secure
(b) To enjoy the weather
(c) To feel unwell
(d) To work against the weather

25. Select the most appropriate option that can substitute the underlined segment in the given sentence.

Once bitten, <u>thrice shy</u>.

(a) always shy (b) never shy
(c) once shy (d) twice shy

Part II
General Intelligence

26. What should come in place of the question mark (?) in the given series?

58, 73, 90, 109, ?

(a) 103 (b) 310
(c) 301 (d) 130

27. Based on the alphabetical order, three of the following four letter-clusters are alike in a certain way and thus form a group.

Which letter-cluster does not belong to that group?

(**Note** The odd one out is not based on the number of consonants/ vowels or their position in the letter-cluster.)

(a) ILO (b) NQU (c) DGK (d) JMQ

28. A paper is folded and cut as shown below. How will it appear when unfolded?

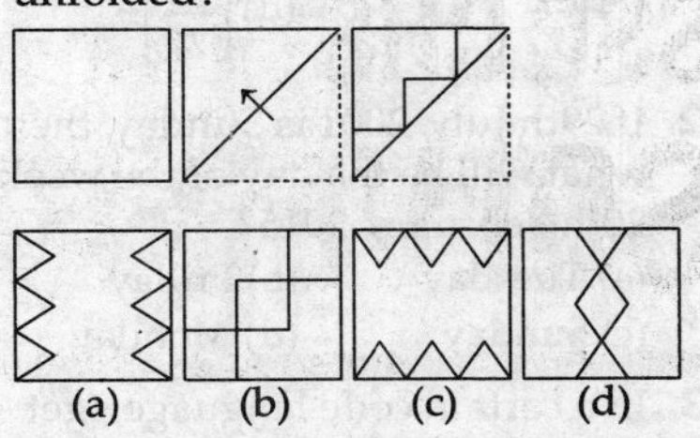

29. Three statements are followed by conclusions numbered I, II. You have to consider these statements to be true, even if they seem to be at variance with commonly known facts. Decide which of the given conclusions logically follow(s) from the given statements.

Statements

All dresses are clouds.
Some clouds are tables.
Some tables are stones.

Conclusions

I. All stones are dresses.
II. Some dresses are tables.

(a) Neither Conclusion I nor II follows
(b) Only Conclusion I follows
(c) Only Conclusion II follows
(d) Both Conclusions I and II follow

30. What should come in place of the question mark (?) in the given series based on the English alphabetical order?

ACW, FHB, KMG, PRL, ?

(a) UQW (b) UWQ
(c) VQW (d) VWQ

31. $\left[\frac{17}{41}\right]$ is related to $\left[\frac{34}{41}\right]$ following a certain logic. Following the same logic, $\left[\frac{11}{85}\right]$ is related to $\left[\frac{22}{85}\right]$.

To which of the following is $\left[\frac{13}{77}\right]$ related, following the same logic?

(**Note** Operations should be performed on the whole numbers, without breaking down the numbers into its constituent digits. E.g. 13 – Operations on 13 such as adding/subtracting/multiplying etc. to 13 can be performed. Breaking down 13 into 1 and 3 and then performing mathematical operations on 1 and 3 is not allowed.)

(a) $\begin{bmatrix}24\\75\end{bmatrix}$ (b) $\begin{bmatrix}29\\77\end{bmatrix}$

(c) $\begin{bmatrix}23\\77\end{bmatrix}$ (d) $\begin{bmatrix}26\\77\end{bmatrix}$

32. If 29th July, 2001 is Sunday, then what will be the day of the week on 20th February, 2015?

(a) Tuesday (b) Friday
(c) Sunday (d) Monday

33. In a certain code language, 'get enough sleep' is coded as 'ab de jf' and 'go get it' is coded as 'jk ab gh'. How is 'get' coded in that language?

(a) jk (b) de
(c) ab (d) jf

34. 'STEM' is related to 'HGVN' in a certain way based on the English alphabetical order. In the same way, 'QUIT' is related to 'JFRG'. To which of the following is 'ACCOUNTABLE' related, following the same logic?

(a) ZXXLFMGZYOV
(b) ZXXLFMGZYOU
(c) ZXXLFMZGYOV
(d) ZXXFLMGZYOV

35. What should come in place of the question mark (?) to complete the following letter-cluster series?

UME, OPG, ISJ, EVN, ?

(a) AYR (b) BYS
(c) AYS (d) AXS

36. Which of the following numbers will replace the question mark (?) in the given series?

$\begin{bmatrix}37\\5\end{bmatrix}, \begin{bmatrix}32\\5\end{bmatrix}, \begin{bmatrix}27\\5\end{bmatrix}, \begin{bmatrix}22\\5\end{bmatrix}, \begin{bmatrix}17\\5\end{bmatrix}, ?$

(a) $\begin{bmatrix}12\\5\end{bmatrix}$ (b) $\begin{bmatrix}9\\5\end{bmatrix}$

(c) $\begin{bmatrix}16\\5\end{bmatrix}$ (d) $\begin{bmatrix}14\\5\end{bmatrix}$

37. What will come in the place of the question mark (?) in the following equation, if '+' and '–' are interchanged and '×' and '÷' are interchanged?

$216 \times 9 + 52 - 7 \div 7 = ?$

(a) 20 (b) 22
(c) 21 (d) 19

38. Select the set in which the numbers are related in the same way as are the numbers of the given sets.

(**Note** Operations should be performed on the whole numbers, without breaking down the numbers into its constituent digits. E.g. 13 – Operations on 13 such as adding/subtracting/multiplying etc. to 13 can be performed. Breaking down 13 into 1 and 3 and then performing mathematical operations on 1 and 3 is not allowed.)

(180, 45, 90)

(128, 32, 64)

(a) (248, 60, 124) (b) (170, 43, 85)
(c) (224, 56, 112) (d) (186, 46, 93)

39. Select the correct mirror image of the given figure, when the mirror is placed at MN.

tgPL82 M N

(a) Ƨ8⅂Ԁgɟ (b) ꙅ8⅂ԀgƚI
(c) Ƨ8⅃ꟼgt (d) ꙅ8⅃ꟼgƚ

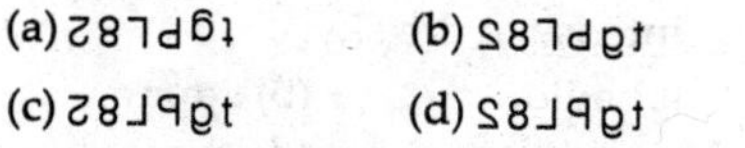

40. Which of the following numbers will replace the question mark (?) in the given series?

7, 13, 39, 46, 138, 146, 438, 447, ?

(a) 1247 (b) 1146
(c) 1138 (d) 1341

41. Select the correct mirror image of the given figure, when the mirror is placed at MN as shown below.

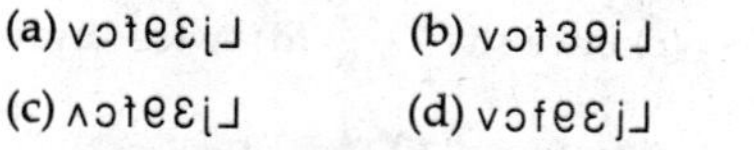

Lj39fcv M N

(a) vɔɟeƐį⅃ (b) vɔɟ39į⅃
(c) ʌɔɟeƐį⅃ (d) vɔfeƐj⅃

42. How many triangles are there in the given figure?

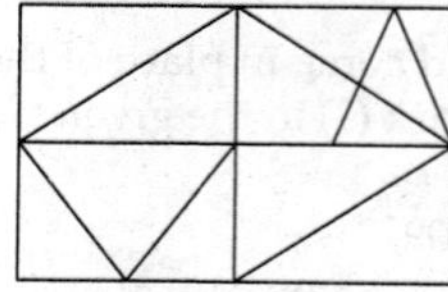

(a) 17 (b) 11
(c) 10 (d) 12

43. If 25th October, 2004 was Monday, then what was the day of the week on 2nd November, 2007?

(a) Friday (b) Saturday
(c) Thursday (d) Wednesday

44. In a certain code language,

A + B means 'A is the mother of B'
A – B means 'A is the brother of B'
A × B means 'A is the wife of B'
A ÷ B means 'A is the father of B'

Based on the above, how is G related to K, if 'G + J ÷ H × I – K'?

(a) Brother's wife's sister
(b) Brother's wife's mother
(c) Brother's wife's father's mother
(d) Brother's wife's father's sister

45. Select the word-pair that best represents a similar relationship to the one expressed in the pair of words given below.

(The words must be considered as meaningful English words and must not be related to each other based on the number of letters/number of consonants/vowels in the word.)

Trim : Hair

(a) Prune : Hedge (b) Pluck : Flower
(c) Clip : Clothes (d) Harvest : Corn

46. If 'A' stands for '÷', 'B' stands for '×', 'C' stands for '+' and 'D' stands for '–', then the resultant of which of the following will be 428?

(a) 113 A 4 D 62 B 2 C 7
(b) 113 B 4 D 62 A 2 C 7
(c) 113 B 4 A 62 D 2 C 7
(d) 113 B 4 C 62 A 2 D 7

47. What will come in the place of the question mark (?) in the following equation, if '+' and '×' are interchanged and '–' and '÷' are interchanged?

$98 - 14 \times 11 + 6 \div 23 = ?$

(a) 50 (b) 55
(c) 52 (d) 56

48. Select the correct mirror image of the given figure, when the mirror is placed at MN.

kL5Gre M N

(a) ɘɿↃƧ⅃k (b) ɘɿↃƧLʞ
(c) ɘɿↃƧ⅃ʞ (d) ɘɹↃƧ⅃ʞ

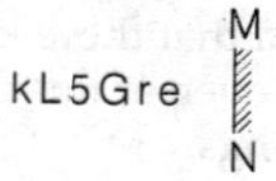

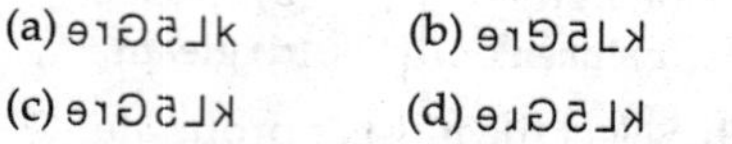

49. Identify the figure given in the options, which when put in place of question mark (?) will logically complete the series.

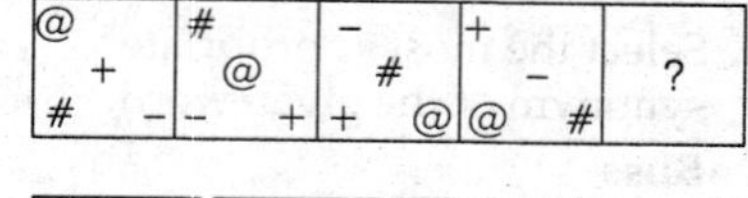

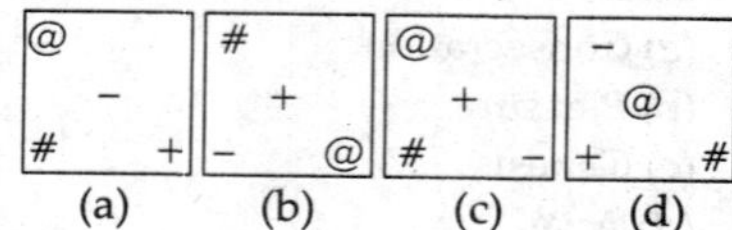

(a) (b) (c) (d)

50. Select the option figure in which the given figure (X) is embedded as its part (rotation is not allowed).

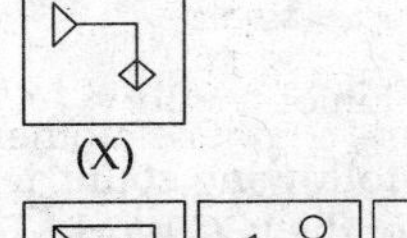

(X)

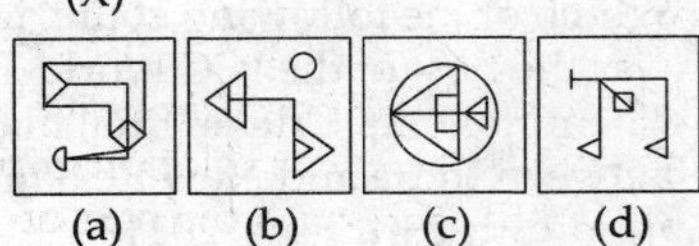

(a) (b) (c) (d)

Part III
Quantitative Aptitude

51. If the intersection point of the equations $3p - 2q + 23 = 0$ and $-2p + q - 13 = 0$ on the graph is (p, q), then the value of $(3p + q)$ is equal to

(a) 2 (b) 1
(c) −2 (d) −1

52. The age of a tree depends on the number of rings in the trunk. The value of a such tree is proportional to its age. If a tree with 40 rings and 50 yrs of age has a value of ₹ 50000, then a tree with 30 rings is ......yr of age and its value is ₹ ....

(a) 37.5, 57500 (b) 37.5, 37500
(c) 57.5, 57500 (d) 57.5, 37500

53. Simplify the following expression.

$$469 \div \left[270 \div \left(\frac{3}{7} \times 35\right) + (19 \times 3) - \left(\frac{21}{2} - \frac{5}{2}\right)\right]$$

(a) 7 (b) 13 (c) 11 (d) 9

54. How many cubes of edge 15 cm can be put in a cubical box of 3 m edge?

(a) 9000 (b) 1050
(c) 8000 (d) 2000

55. If a sum of ₹ 3260 on simple interest amounts to ₹ 5420 in 6 yr, then what will this sum amount to in 4 yr at the same rate of interest?

(a) ₹ 4700 (b) ₹ 3700
(c) ₹ 3900 (d) ₹ 4500

56. If $\tan\theta = \frac{7}{4}$, then the value of $\frac{4\sin\theta - 3\cos\theta}{4\sin\theta + 3\cos\theta}$ is equal to

(a) $\frac{2}{5}$ (b) $\frac{1}{3}$
(c) $\frac{4}{5}$ (d) $\frac{3}{5}$

57. A closed cylindrical tank of radius 1.5 m and height 3 m is made from a sheet of metal, how much sheet of metal is required to do it?

(a) 42.24 m^2 (b) 22.42 m^2
(c) 42.42 m^2 (d) 24.24 m^2

58. The total income of three families is ₹ 72000. Their expenditures are 80%, 85% and 75%, respectively. If the savings are in the ratio 8 : 9 : 20, then the income of the second family is

(a) ₹ 32000 (b) ₹ 16000
(c) ₹ 40000 (d) ₹ 24000

59. ΔXYZ is similar to ΔPQR. If the ratio of the perimeter of ΔXYZ to the perimeter of ΔPQR is 16 : 9 and $PQ = 3.6$ cm, then what is the length (in cm) of XY?

(a) $2\frac{3}{5}$ (b) $4\frac{3}{5}$ (c) $6\frac{2}{5}$ (d) $3\frac{4}{5}$

60. Two cubes have their volumes in the ratio 1 : 125. Find the ratio of their surface areas.

(a) 1 : 125 (b) 1 : 25
(c) 25 : 1 (d) 1 : 5

61. A dishonest dealer professes to sell his goods at the cost price, but he uses a false weight of 850 gm per 1 kg weight. Find the percentage of his gain. (Correct up to two decimal places)

(a) 17.65% (b) 17.45%
(c) 17.54% (d) 17.56%

62. What is the value of the following expression?

$$\left(24 \div 3 \text{ of } \frac{1}{6}\right) \times \left(\frac{4}{5} \div \frac{9}{8} \times \frac{3}{5}\right) \div \left(\frac{4}{7} \div \frac{3}{14} \text{ of } \frac{3}{14}\right)$$

(a) $\frac{579}{459}$ (b) $\frac{288}{175}$
(c) $\frac{379}{179}$ (d) $\frac{363}{553}$

63. Study the given bar-graph and answer the question that follows.

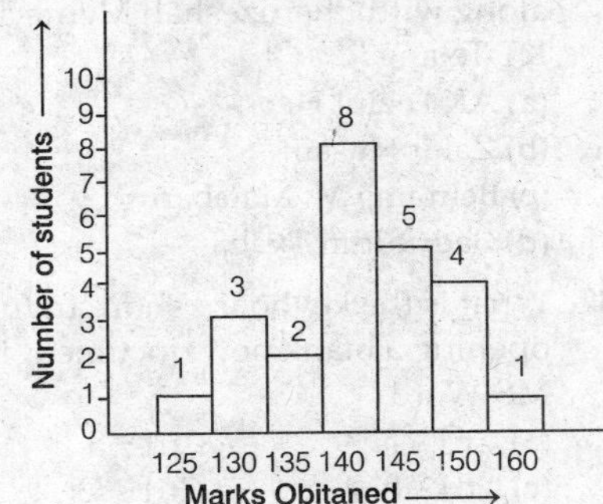

How many students obtained more than 135 marks?

(a) 17 (b) 19
(c) 13 (d) 18

64. If Ramu's salary is 30% less than Somu's salary, then by how much per cent is Somu's salary more than Ramu's salary?

(a) 42.67% (b) 42.86%
(c) 45.47% (d) 34.56%

65. A shopkeeper allows a discount of 22% to his customers and still gains 36%. Find the marked price (in ₹) of an article, which costs ₹ 1092 to the shopkeeper.

(a) 1792 (b) 2024
(c) 1872 (d) 1904

66. PQ and RS are two chords of a circle such that $PQ = 12$ cm and $RS = 20$ cm and PQ is parallel to RS. If the distance between PQ and RS is 4 cm, find the diameter of the circle.

(a) $2\sqrt{34}$ cm
(b) $3\sqrt{34}$ cm
(c) $6\sqrt{34}$ cm
(d) $4\sqrt{34}$ cm

67. The following table shows the number of employees working in four organisations during six years. Answer the question that follows.

Organisation	Years					
	2010	2011	2012	2013	2014	2015
X	52	82	62	34	68	76
Y	105	80	120	160	95	100
Z	103	86	88	212	180	129
T	153	221	128	126	97	106

What is the average number of employees in organisations Y, Z and T in 2013?

(a) 166 (b) 168
(c) 170 (d) 172

68. 30 men working 5 h a day can do work in 18 days. In how many days will 20 men working 7 h a day do the same work?

(a) $11\frac{3}{7}$ (b) $16\frac{5}{7}$
(c) $19\frac{2}{7}$ (d) $13\frac{1}{7}$

69. Study the given bar-graph and answer the question that follows. The bar-graph represents the number of boys and girls in different sections of Class XII.

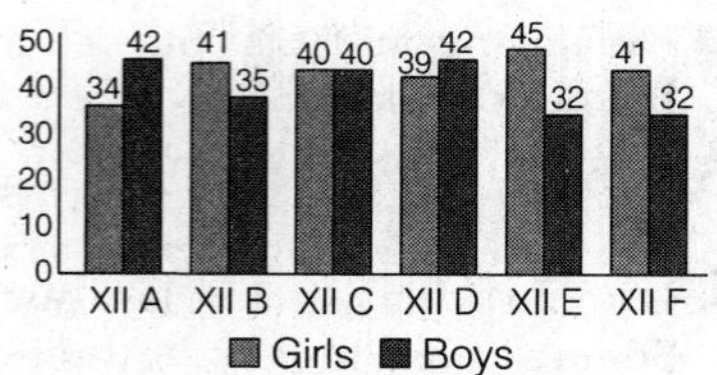

The average number of girls in each section is

(a) 42 (b) 43
(c) 37 (d) 40

70. The average salary of a group of 12 employees in an institution is ₹ 3950 per month and that of another group of employees is ₹ 1850. If the average salary of all employees is ₹ 2150, then the total number of employees is

(a) 100 (b) 88
(c) 84 (d) 72

71. A part of the journey is covered in 22.5 min at a speed of 68 km/h and the remaining part in 12 min at a speed of 72 km/h. The total distance of the journey is (to the nearest integer)

(a) 40 km (b) 38 km
(c) 42 km (d) 35 km

72. The pie-chart below depicts the percentage distribution of the costs associated with publishing a book.

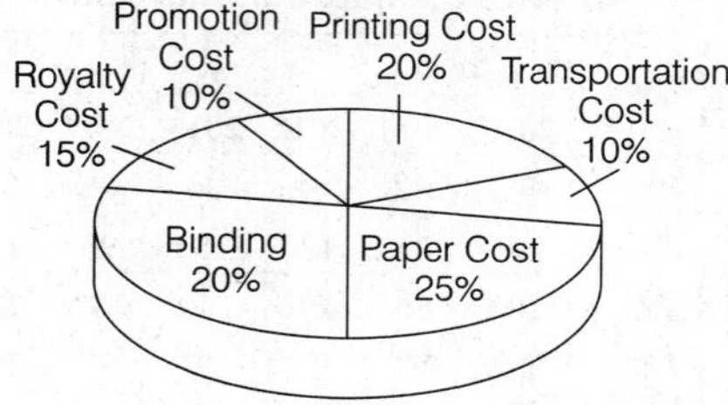

What will be the royalty rate for these books, if the publisher is required to pay ₹ 30600 in printing costs for a specific number of volumes?

(a) ₹ 21200 (b) ₹ 26150
(c) ₹ 19450 (d) ₹ 22950

73. PQ is the diameter of a circle with centre O. PT is a tangent touching the circle at P. The secant QT intersects the circle at S. O and S are joined. If $\angle SOP = 104°$, what is the measure (in degrees) of $\angle PTQ$?

(a) 45 (b) 62
(c) 76 (d) 38

74. A number is first decreased by 18% and the resulting number is then increased by 25%. What is the overall percentage change in the original number?

(a) Decrease by 2.5%
(b) Increase by 3.5%
(c) Increase by 2.5%
(d) Decrease by 3.5%

75. Consider AD is a tangent to a circle of radius 6 cm. AC is a secant meeting the circle at B and CD is a diameter. If AB is 7 cm, then the value of AC (in cm) is

(a) 9 (b) 18
(c) 20 (d) 16

Part IV
General Awareness

76. In which year was the 15th National Census Survey of India conducted?

(a) 1991 (b) 2011
(c) 2021 (d) 2001

77. Which of the following is a cyclic arrangement of time units in Hindustani classical music?

(a) Tala (b) Nyasa
(c) Jati (d) Raga

78. The Bhotia dance form is a folk-dance from which of the following Indian states?

(a) Goa (b) Tamil Nadu
(c) Odisha (d) Uttarakhand

79. What is the penalty for a wide ball in cricket?

(a) One run (b) Six runs
(c) Four runs (d) A free hit

80. The point in the orbit of an object (such as a satellite) orbiting the Earth that is at the greatest distance from the centre of the Earth is known as

(a) aphelion (b) perigee
(c) apogee (d) perihelion

81. Who founded the Bombay Presidency Association in 1885 along with Pherozeshah Mehta and KT Telang?

(a) AK Fazlul Haq
(b) Zakir Husain
(c) Behramji M. Malabari
(d) Badruddin Tyabji

82. What is the keyboard shortcut for opening a blank new document in MS-Word?

(a) Ctrl + N (b) Ctrl + S
(c) Ctrl + B (d) Ctrl + C

83. Which of the following is not a way to acquire citizenship in India?

(a) Renunciation
(b) Registration
(c) Birth
(d) Incorporation of territory

84. Which of the following countries was the host of the ICC World Test Championship Cricket final played between India and New Zealand from 18th-23rd June, 2021?

(a) South Africa (b) Australia
(c) India (d) England

85. Which city will host 2028 Olympics games?

(a) New York, USA
(b) Los Angeles, USA
(c) Boston, USA
(d) San Diego, USA

86. BVR Subrahmanyan was appointed as the……, in February, 2023.

(a) CEO of NITI Aayog
(b) CEO of IBRD
(c) Chairman of UPSC
(d) Chairman of NITI Aayog

87. Select the musical instrument which is not played by way of percussion or not played by way of striking any object?

(a) Shehnai (b) Tabla
(c) Pakhawaj (d) Drum

88. With reference to the Directive Principles of State policy contained in the Constitution of India, which of the following statements is/are correct?

1. Article 37 of the Constitution of India provides that the Directive Principles of State Policy are enforceable in the High Courts only.
2. Article 38 provides that the State shall strive to minimise the inequalities in income amongst individuals and groups of people.
3. Article 39 provides that the State shall direct its policy towards securing that there is equal pay for equal work for both men and women.

Codes

(a) Only 1 and 3 (b) Only 2
(c) Only 1 (d) Only 2 and 3

89. The Mundra Thermal Power Plant is located in which district of Gujarat?

(a) Gandhinagar (b) Kheda
(c) Kutch (d) Jamnagar

90. How many languages are included in the Eighth Schedule of the Constitution of India as scheduled languages?
(a) 23 (b) 21
(c) 22 (d) 24

91. Match the items in List I with List II.

List I	List II
A. Garibi Hatao	1. Fifth Five-Year Plan
B. LPG policies	2. Ninth Five-Year Plan
C. Rolling Plan	3. 1978-80
D. Growth with justice and equality	4. Eighth Five-Year Plan

Codes

	A	B	C	D		A	B	C	D
(a)	1	4	3	2	(b)	3	2	4	1
(c)	3	4	1	2	(d)	2	3	4	1

92. Which keyboard key is used to jump the cursor to the next cell of the table in MS Word?
(a) Shift (b) Tab
(c) Home (d) Ctrl

93. Which of the following is not a mutation-based disease?
(a) Sickle cell anaemia
(b) Malaria
(c) Phenylketonuria
(d) Down syndrome

94. In March 2023, Rashmi Shukla was appointed as the Director General of which organisation?
(a) Border Security Force
(b) Central Reserve Police Force
(c) Shashastra Seema Bal
(d) Indo-Tibetan Border Police

95. Which of the following statements is/are correct?
I. Maximum National Parks in India are located in the state of Madhya Pradesh.
II. Mudumalai National Park is located in Kerala.
III. The Salim Ali Centre for Ornithology and Natural History is located in Tamil Nadu.
Codes
(a) Both I and II are correct
(b) Only I is correct.
(c) Both I and III are correct
(d) Only III is correct

96. Easter is a religious festival of
(a) Christians (b) Hindus
(c) Buddhists (d) Sikhs

97. India's first indigenous Aircraft Carrier, ..., conducted its maiden sea travel in August, 2021 marking a significant step towards making military equipment in India.
(a) INS Vikrant (b) INS Swades
(c) INS Kranti (d) INS Vayudoot

98. Who was the founder of the Bahmani Sultanate?
(a) Alauddin Hasan Bahman Shah
(b) Muhammad Shah
(c) Feroz Shah Bahmani
(d) Muhammad Bin Tughlaq

99. Rotating Savings and Credit Association (ROSCA) was introduced by Shirley Ardener in the year ....
(a) 1970 (b) 1964 (c) 1963 (d) 1955

100. If an object of mass 2 kg is dropped from a height of 10 metres, what will be the ratio of its potential energy and kinetic energy at the height of 5 metres (g = m/sec^2)
(a) 1:1 (b) 4:1 (c) 1:4 (d) 1:2

Answers

1. (d)	2. (b)	3. (d)	4. (a)
5. (b)	6. (d)	7. (d)	8. (b)
9. (b)	10. (a)	11. (b)	12. (d)
13. (c)	14 (b)	15. (b)	16. (d)
17. (c)	18. (a)	19. (c)	20. (b)
21. (b)	22. (a)	23. (c)	24. (c)
25. (d)	26. (d)	27. (a)	28. (b)
29. (a)	30. (b)	31. (d)	32. (b)
33. (c)	34. (a)	35. (c)	36. (a)
37. (c)	38. (c)	39. (d)	40. (d)
41. (a)	42. (a)	43. (a)	44. (c)
45. (a)	46. (b)	47. (a)	48. (c)
49. (c)	50. (a)	51. (c)	52. (b)
53. (a)	54. (c)	55. (a)	56. (a)
57. (c)	58. (d)	59. (c)	60. (b)
61. (a)	62. (b)	63. (d)	64. (b)
65. (d)	66. (d)	67. (a)	68. (c)
69. (d)	70. (c)	71. (a)	72. (d)
73. (d)	74. (c)	75. (d)	76. (b)
77. (a)	78. (d)	79. (a)	80. (c)
81. (d)	82. (a)	83. (a)	84. (d)
85. (b)	86. (a)	87. (a)	88. (d)
89. (c)	90. (c)	91. (a)	92. (b)
93. (b)	94. (c)	95. (c)	96. (a)
97. (a)	98. (a)	99. (b)	100. (a)

Explanations

1. *(d)* The given sentence contains an error of articles. The correct sentence is- This is the story of eight round planets, a few rocks in between, and some comets.

2. *(b)* Part (b) 'Everyone have' contains an error. Use 'has' to correct the sentence. The word 'everyone' is a singular subject which will take a singular verb.

3. *(d)* Part (d) 'the Mumbai airport' contains an error. Remove 'the' to correct the sentence.

4. *(a)* Part (a) 'that he truthful' contains an error. Use 'truthfully' to correct the sentence.

5. *(b)* The correct filler for the given blank is 'occupies'.

6. *(d)* The correct filler for the given blank is 'about'.

7. *(d)* The correct filler for the given blank is 'total'.

8. *(b)* The correct filler for the given blank is 'such'.

9. *(b)* The correct filler for the given blank is 'species'.

10. *(a)* The underlined part of the given sentence contains an error. Use 'finished her breakfast quickly' to correct the sentence.

11. *(b)* The antonym of normal is eccentric which means strange.
- 'Feeble' means weak.
- 'Dogmatic' means inclined to lay down principles as undeniably true.

12. *(d)* The correct word to fill in the blank is 'fearful'.

13. *(c)* The bracketed part of the given sentence contains an error. Use 'within a reader' to correct the sentence.

14. *(b)* A piece of cake means a very easy task to do. Hence, the sentence that uses the idiom correctly is- The restaurant was crowded, but they found a table without any difficulty.

15. *(b)* The word 'attire' refers to the dress or clothes one wears.

16. *(d)* Agitated means angry and irritated. Hence, its antonym is 'serene' which means peaceful.
- 'Steady' means firmly fixed, supported, or balanced; not shaking or moving.

- 'Nerveless' means lacking vigour or feeling.
- 'Quiescent' means in a state or period of inactivity or dormancy.

17. *(c)* The incorrectly spelt word in the context of the sentence is 'there'. The correct spelling is 'their'.

18. *(a)* The correct filler for the given blank is 'light'.

19. *(c)* The word 'Hypocrisy' means the practice of claiming to have higher standards or more noble beliefs than is the case. Hence, its nearest synonym is 'deceit'.

20. *(b)* The word 'Bliss' means 'happiness and pleasure'.

- 'Consecration' means the action of making or declaring something, typically a church, sacred.
- 'Genesis' means the origin or beginning of something.
- 'Avail' means to get.

21. *(b)* The underlined part of the given sentence contains an error. Use 'from every point' to correct the sentence.

22. *(a)* The incorrectly spelt word is 'Condimnation'. The correct spelling is 'Condemnation'.

23. *(c)* The word 'intense' means of extreme force, degree, or strength. Hence, its synonym is 'strong'.

24. *(c)* 'Under the weather' means to be ill.

25. *(d)* The underlined part of the given sentence contains an error. Use 'twice shy' to correct the sentence.

26. *(d)* The pattern of the series is as follows,

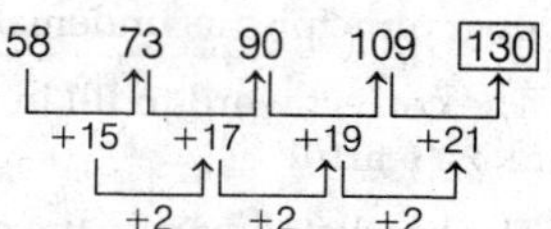

27. *(a)* As,

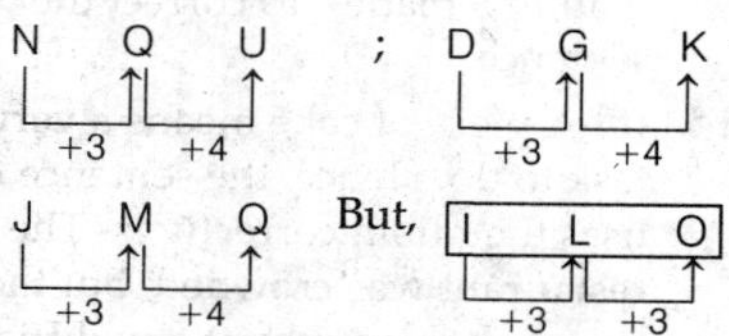

So, ILO is odd from the rest.

28. *(b)* After cutting the paper, when unfolded the following pattern appears.

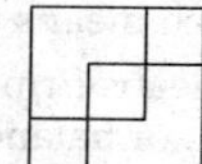

29. *(a)* From the statements,

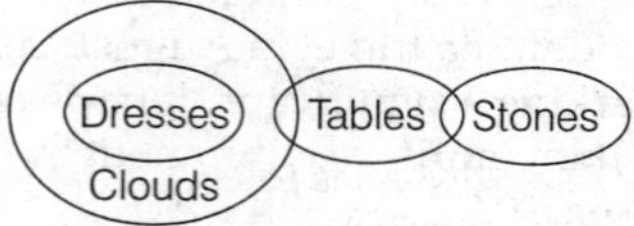

Conclusions I. (✗) II. (✗)

∴ Neither Conclusion I nor II follows.

30. *(b)* The pattern of the series is as follows,

A $\xrightarrow{+5}$ F $\xrightarrow{+5}$ K $\xrightarrow{+5}$ P $\xrightarrow{+5}$ U

C $\xrightarrow{+5}$ H $\xrightarrow{+5}$ M $\xrightarrow{+5}$ R $\xrightarrow{+5}$ W

W $\xrightarrow{+5}$ B $\xrightarrow{+5}$ G $\xrightarrow{+5}$ L $\xrightarrow{+5}$ Q

31. *(d)* As, $\left[\frac{17}{41}\right]=\left[\frac{17\times 2}{41}\right]=\left[\frac{34}{41}\right]$

and $\left[\frac{11}{85}\right]=\left[\frac{11\times 2}{85}\right]=\left[\frac{22}{85}\right]$

Similarly, $\left[\frac{13}{77}\right]=\left[\frac{13\times 2}{77}\right]=\left[\frac{26}{77}\right]$

32. *(b)* Given, 29th July, 2001 → Sunday

Remaining days in 2001 → 155

∴ Odd days in 2001 = 1

As we know,

Odd days in normal year = 1

Odd days in leap year = 2

Total odd days from 1st January, 2002 to 1st January, 2015.

$= 1 + 1 + 1 + 2 + 1 + 1 + 1 + 2 + 1 + 1 + 1 + 2 + 1 + 1$

$= \frac{17}{7} =$ 2 weeks and 3 odd days.

Number of odd days from 2nd January, 2002 to 20th February, 2015

= 30 + 20

$= \frac{50}{7} =$ 7 weeks and 1 odd day

So, total number of odd days

= 1 + 3 + 1 = 5 odd days

∴ Day of the week on 20th February, 2015 = Sunday + 5 = Friday

33. *(c)* According to the question,

[get] enough sleep = [ab] de jf

go [get] it = jk [ab] gh

∴ Code for 'get' is 'ab'.

34. *(a)* As,

S T E M → opposite alphabet
H G V N

and

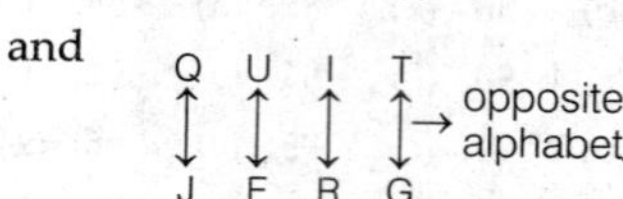

Similarly,

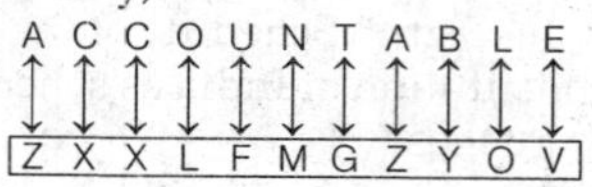

35. *(c)* The pattern of the series is as follows,

U $\xrightarrow{\text{Previous vowels}}$ O $\xrightarrow{\text{Previous vowels}}$ I $\xrightarrow{\text{Previous vowels}}$ E $\xrightarrow{\text{Previous vowels}}$ A

M $\xrightarrow{+3}$ P $\xrightarrow{+3}$ S $\xrightarrow{+3}$ V $\xrightarrow{+3}$ Y

E $\xrightarrow{+2}$ G $\xrightarrow{+3}$ J $\xrightarrow{+4}$ N $\xrightarrow{+5}$ S

36. *(a)* The pattern of given series is as follows,

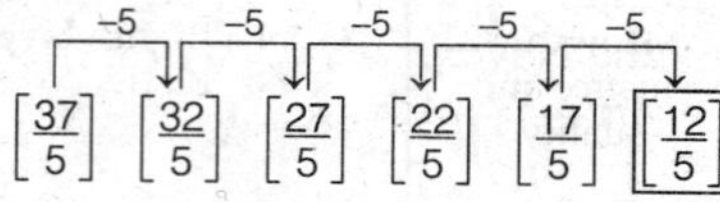

37. *(c)* The given equation,

$216 \times 9 + 52 - 7 \div 7 = ?$

After interchanging signs, '+' and '–' and '×' and '÷', we get

$216 \div 9 - 52 + 7 \times 7$

$= 24 - 52 + 7 \times 7 = 24 - 52 + 49$

$= 73 - 52 = 21$

38. *(c)* As, (180, 45, 90)

$\Rightarrow \frac{180}{4} = 45 \times 2 = 90$

and (128, 32, 64) $\Rightarrow \frac{128}{4} = 32 \times 2 = 64$

Similarly, (224, 56, 112)

$\Rightarrow \frac{224}{4} = 56 \times 2 = 112$

39. *(d)* The figure given in option (d) is the correct mirror image of the given question figure.

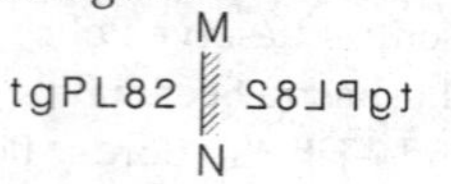

M
tgPL82 | 28LPgt
N

40. *(d)* The pattern of the series is as follows,

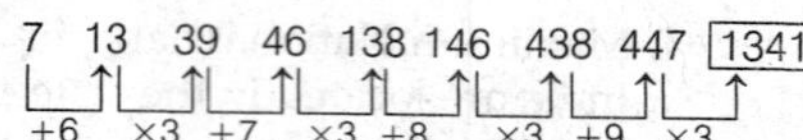

41. *(a)* The figure given in option (a) is the mirror image of the given figure.

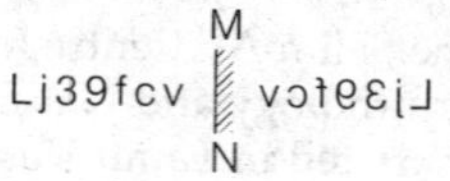

M
Lj39fcv | vcf93jL
N

42. *(a)* Naming the figure,

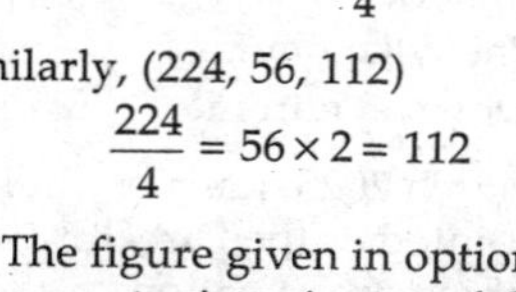

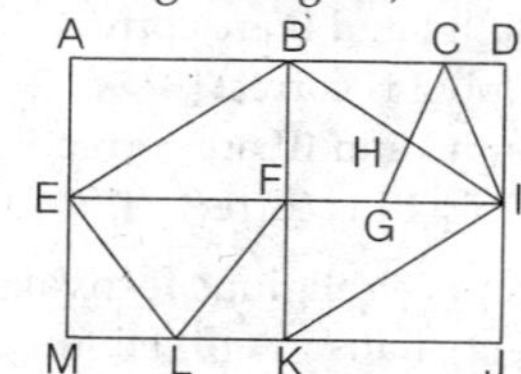

Triangles are

$\Delta ABE, \Delta EFB, \Delta BFI, \Delta CGI, \Delta CHI, \Delta BHC, \Delta CID, \Delta EML, \Delta ELF, \Delta LKF, \Delta FKI, \Delta KIJ, \Delta BID, \Delta EBI, \Delta BKI, \Delta GHI$ and ΔBIC

$\therefore$ Total triangles = 17

43. *(a)* Given, 25th October, 2004 $\rightarrow$ Monday

$\therefore$ Number of odd days in 2004 = 4

Number of odd days in 2005 = 1

Number of odd days in 2006 = 1

Number of odd days in 2007 upto 2nd November = 5

$\therefore$ Total number of odd days

$$= \frac{4+1+1+5}{7} = \frac{11}{7} \Rightarrow 4 \text{ odd days}$$

Monday + 4 = Friday.

$\therefore$ Day of week on 2nd November, 2007 is Friday.

44. *(c)* Given expression, $G + J \div H \times I - K$

According to the question,

G⁻ ↑ Mother J⁺ ↑ Father H⁻ ←Wife I⁺ ←Brother K

[+ ⇒ Male, − ⇒ Female]

$\therefore$ G is brother's wife's father's mother to K.

45. *(a)* Hair is trimmed in order to make it shorter. Similarly, hedge is pruned in order to make it shorter.

46. *(b)* After substituting letters with signs, we get

A → ÷	B → ×
C → +	D → −

From option (b),

$$113 \times 4 - 62 \div 2 + 7$$
$$= 452 - 31 + 7$$
$$= 459 - 31 = 428$$

47. *(a)* The given equation,

$98 - 14 \times 11 + 6 \div 23 = ?$

After interchanging the signs '+' and '×', '−' and '÷', we get

$$98 \div 14 + 11 \times 6 - 23$$
$$= 7 + 11 \times 6 - 23$$
$$= 7 + 66 - 23$$
$$= 73 - 23 = 50$$

48. *(c)* The figure given in option (c) is the correct mirror image of the given question figure.

M

kL5Gre

N

49. *(c)* Here, the series follows the pattern which is as follows

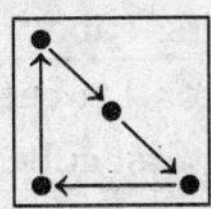

So, the answer figure (c) will replace the question mark.

50. *(a)* The given figure (X) is embedded in the option figure (a).

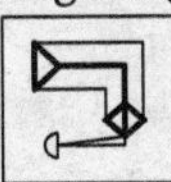

51. *(c)* Given equations,

$$3p - 2q + 23 = 0 \quad \ldots(i)$$
$$-2p + q - 13 = 0 \quad \ldots(ii)$$

On solving Eqs. (i) and (ii),

2 × Eq.(ii) + Eq. (i)

$$3p - 2q + 23 = 0$$
$$\underline{-4p + 2q - 26 = 0}$$
$$-p - 3 = 0$$
$$\therefore \quad p = -3$$

Put $p = -3$ in Eq. (ii), we get

$$-2 \times (-3) + q - 13 = 0$$
$$\Rightarrow \quad +6 + q - 13 = 0$$
$$\therefore \quad q = 7$$
$$\therefore \quad (p, q) = (-3, 7)$$

The value of $(3p + q) = 3 \times (-3) + 7 = -2$

52. *(b)* According to the question,

Age of tree $\propto$ Number of rings

$\therefore$ Let age of tree = x yr

$$\therefore \quad \frac{x}{50} = \frac{30}{40}$$
$$x = 37.5 \text{ yr}$$

$\therefore$ Age of tree having 30 rings = 37.5 yr

Now, value $\propto$ age

Let age of tree having 30 rings = ₹ y

$$\therefore \quad \frac{y}{50000} = \frac{37.5}{50}$$
$$y = ₹\ 37500$$

$\therefore$ Value of tree having 30 rings = ₹ 37500

53. *(a)* $469 \div \left[270 \div \left(\frac{3}{7} \times 35\right) + (19 \times 3) - \left(\frac{21}{2} - \frac{5}{2}\right)\right]$

By using BODMAS rule,

$$469 \div [270 \div 15 + 57 - 8]$$
$$= 469 \div [18 + 57 - 8]$$
$$= 469 \div 67 = 7$$

54. *(c)* Given,

Edge of cubical box = 3 m = 300 cm

Edge of cube = 15 cm

We know that,

Volume of cubical box = $(\text{Side})^3 = (300)^3$

and volume of cube = $(\text{Side})^3 = (15)^3$

$$\therefore \text{Number of cube} = \frac{(300)^3}{(15)^3} = 8000$$

55. *(a)* Given,

Principal = ₹ 3260

Amount = ₹ 5420

Time = 6 yr

We know that,

Amount

$$= \text{Principal} + \frac{\text{Principal} \times \text{Rate} \times \text{Time}}{100}$$
$$5420 = 3260 + \frac{3260 \times 6 \times \text{Rate}}{100}$$
$$\Rightarrow 2160 = \frac{3260 \times 6 \times \text{Rate}}{100}$$
$$\Rightarrow \text{Rate} = \frac{2160 \times 100}{3260 \times 6}$$

When, time = 4 yr

$\therefore$ Amount

$$= \text{Principal} + \frac{\text{Principal} \times \text{Rate} \times \text{Time}}{100}$$
$$= 3260 + \frac{3260 \times \frac{2160 \times 100}{3260 \times 6} \times 4}{100}$$
$$= 3260 + 1440 = ₹\ 4700$$

56. *(a)* Given,

$$\tan\theta = \frac{7}{4} \quad \ldots(i)$$

$$\frac{4\sin\theta - 3\cos\theta}{4\sin\theta + 3\cos\theta} = \frac{4\frac{\sin\theta}{\cos\theta} - 3}{4\frac{\sin\theta}{\cos\theta} + 3} = \frac{4\tan\theta - 3}{4\tan\theta + 3}$$

[From Eq. (i)]

$$= \frac{4 \times \frac{7}{4} - 3}{4 \times \frac{7}{4} + 3} = \frac{7-3}{7+3} = \frac{4}{10} = \frac{2}{5}$$

57. *(c)* Given, $r = 1.5$ m

$h = 3$ m

Total sheet required

= Total surface area

We know that,

Total surface area of cylinder

$= 2\pi r^2 + 2\pi rh$

$= 2\pi r(r + h)$

$= 2 \times \frac{22}{7} \times 1.5\,(1.5 + 3)$

$= 2 \times \frac{22}{7} \times 1.5 \times 4.5 = 42.42\text{ m}^2$

Hence, sheet of metal required

$= 42.42\text{ m}^2$

58. *(d)* Given,

Total income of three family = ₹ 72000

Their expenditure are 80%, 85%, 75%.

Savings ratio are 8 : 9 : 20.

Let first family savings = ₹ $8x$

Second family savings = ₹ $9x$

and third family savings = ₹ $20x$

∴ First family savings = 20% of income

⇒ $8x$ = 20% of income

Income of first family = ₹ $40x$

Similarly, second family savings

= 15% of income

⇒ $9x$ = 15% of income

Income of second family = ₹ $60x$

Similarly, third family savings

= 25% of income

⇒ $20x$ = 25% of income

Income of third family = ₹ $80x$

∴ Total income = $80x + 60x + 40x$

$180x$ = ₹72000

x = ₹ 400

∴ Income of second family = $60x$

$= 60 \times 400$

= ₹ 24000

59. *(c)* Given,

$\Delta XYZ \sim \Delta PQR$

$$\frac{\text{Perimeter of } \Delta XYZ}{\text{Perimeter of } \Delta PQR} = \frac{16}{9}$$

$PQ = 3.6$ cm

If $\Delta XYZ \sim \Delta PQR$

Then, $\frac{\text{Perimeter of } \Delta XYZ}{\text{Perimeter of } \Delta PQR} = \frac{XY}{PQ}$

⇒ $\frac{16}{9} = \frac{XY}{3.6}$

∴ $XY = 6\frac{2}{5}$ cm

60. *(b)* Given,

$$\frac{\text{Volume of first cube}}{\text{Volume of second cube}} = \frac{1}{125}$$

We know that,

Volume of cube = $(\text{side})^3$

$$\therefore \frac{(\text{Side of first cube})^3}{(\text{Side of second cube})^3} = \frac{1}{125}$$

$$\frac{\text{Side of first cube}}{\text{Side of second cube}} = \frac{1}{5} \quad \ldots(i)$$

We know that,

Surface area of cube = $6\,(\text{side})^2$

$$\therefore \frac{\text{Surface area of first cube}}{\text{Surface area of second cube}} = \frac{6\,(\text{Side of first cube})^2}{6\,(\text{Side of second cube})^2}$$

$$= \left(\frac{1}{5}\right)^2 \quad \text{[From Eq. (i)]}$$

$$= \frac{1}{25}$$

61. *(a)* Given,

True weight = 1 kg = 1000 gm

False weight = 850 gm

Percentage of gain

$$= \left[\frac{\text{True weight} - \text{False weight}}{\text{False weight}}\right] \times 100$$

∴ Percentage gain

$$= \left(\frac{1000 - 850}{850}\right) \times 100$$

$$= \frac{150}{850} \times 100$$

$= 17.65\%$

62. *(b)* The given expression,

$$\left(24 \div 3 \text{ of } \frac{1}{6}\right) \times \left(\frac{4}{5} \div \frac{9}{8} \times \frac{3}{5}\right) \div \left(\frac{4}{7} \div \frac{3}{14} \text{ of } \frac{3}{14}\right)$$

By using BODMAS rule,

$$\left(24 \div \frac{1}{2}\right) \times \left(\frac{4}{5} \times \frac{8}{9} \times \frac{3}{5}\right) \div \left(\frac{4}{7} \div \frac{9}{196}\right)$$

$$= 48 \times \frac{32}{75} \div \frac{112}{9}$$

$$= 48 \times \frac{32}{75} \times \frac{9}{112}$$

$$= \frac{288}{175}$$

63. *(d)* Student got more than 135 marks

$= 8 + 5 + 4 + 1 = 18$

64. *(b)* Let Somu's salary be ₹ $100x$.

∴ Ramu's salary = $100x \times \left(\frac{100 - 30}{100}\right)$

= ₹ $70x$

∴ Required percentage

$$= \frac{\text{Somu's salary} - \text{Ramu's salary}}{\text{Ramu's salary}} \times 100$$

$$= \frac{100x - 70x}{70x} \times 100$$

$$= \frac{30x}{70x} \times 100 = 42.86\%$$

65. *(d)* Given,

Discount% = 22%

Gain% = 36%

CP (Cost Price) = ₹ 1092

We know that,

Marked price $\times \left(\frac{100 - \text{Discount\%}}{100}\right)$

= Selling price

Selling price

$= \text{Cost price} \times \left(\frac{100 + \text{Profit\%}}{100}\right)$

∴ Marked price $\times \left(\frac{100 - \text{Discount\%}}{100}\right)$

$= \text{Cost price} \times \left(\frac{100 + \text{Profit\%}}{100}\right)$

Marked price $\times \left(\frac{100 - 22}{100}\right)$

$= 1092 \times \left(\frac{100 + 36}{100}\right)$

∴ Marked price = ₹ 1904

66. *(d)* Given, $PQ = 12$ cm

$RS = 20$ cm

$TU = 4$ cm

Let $OT = x$ cm

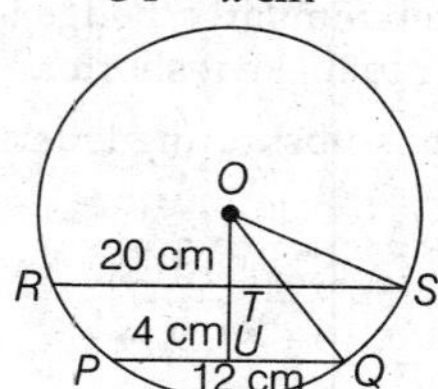

In ΔOQU,

By using Pythagoras theorem,

$OU^2 + UQ^2 = OQ^2 = (\text{Radius})^2 \quad \ldots(i)$

In ΔOST,

By using Pythagoras theorem,

$OT^2 + TS^2 = OS^2 = (\text{Radius})^2 \quad \ldots(ii)$

Equating both equations,

$OU^2 + UQ^2 = OT^2 + TS^2$

⇒ $(x + 4)^2 + (6)^2 = x^2 + (10)^2$

⇒ $8x + 52 = 100 \Rightarrow 8x = 48$

∴ $x = 6$ cm

∴ Radius $= \sqrt{x^2 + (10)^2}$

$= \sqrt{36 + 100}$ [from Eq. (ii)]

$= 2\sqrt{34}$

$\therefore$ Diameter $= 2 \times 2\sqrt{34} = 4\sqrt{34}$ cm

67. *(a)* Average number of employees in organisations *Y*, *Z* and *T* in 2013

$$= \frac{160 + 212 + 126}{3} = 166$$

68. *(c)* Given,

$M_1 = 30$ men, $M_2 = 20$ men

$H_1 = 5$ h, $H_2 = 7$ h

$D_1 = 18$ days, $D_2 = ?$

$W_1 = W_2$

We know that,

$$\frac{M_1D_1H_1}{W_1} = \frac{M_2D_2H_2}{W_2}$$

$$\Rightarrow \frac{30 \times 5 \times 18}{W_1} = \frac{20 \times 7 \times D_2}{W_1}$$

$$\therefore D_2 = 19\frac{2}{7} \text{ days}$$

69. *(d)* The average number of girls

$$= \frac{34 + 41 + 40 + 39 + 45 + 41}{6}$$

$$= \frac{240}{6} = 40$$

70. *(c)* Average salary of 12 employees group = ₹ 3950

Average salary of another group = ₹ 1850

Average salary of all employees = ₹ 2150

Let number of employees in another group $= x$

We know that,

Average salary $= \dfrac{\text{Total salary}}{\text{Number of employees}}$

$$2150 = \frac{3950 \times 12 + x \times 1850}{(12 + x)}$$

$$\Rightarrow 25800 + 2150x = 47400 + 1850x$$

$$\Rightarrow 21600 = 300x$$

$$x = 72$$

$\therefore$ Total number of employees $= x + 12$

$= 72 + 12 = 84$

71. *(a)* Given,

Speed $(s_1) = 68$ km/h

Time $(t_1) = 22.5$ min $= 0.375$ h

Speed $(s_2) = 72$ km/h

Time $(t_2) = 12$ min $= 0.2$ h

We know that,

Distance = Speed × Time

$\therefore$ Distance $= s_1t_1 + s_2t_2$

$= 68 \times 0.375 + 72 \times 0.2$

$= 25.5 + 14.4 = 39.9$ km

≈ 40 km

72. *(d)* Let the total cost be ₹ $100x$.

$\therefore$ Printing cost $= 100x \times \dfrac{20}{100} =$ ₹ $20x$

According to the question,

$20x = 30600$

$\therefore$ $x =$ ₹ 1530

$\therefore$ Royality rate $= 100x \times \dfrac{15}{100} = 15x$

$= 15 \times 1530 =$ ₹ 22950

73. *(d)* According to the question,

$OQ = OS = r$

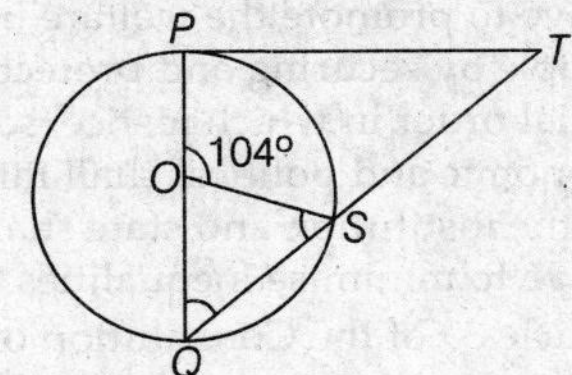

Let $\angle OSQ = \angle OQS = x$

(Angle opposite to equal sides are equal)

$\therefore x + x = 104°$ (Exterior angle theorem)

$x = 52°$

Now, in ΔPQT,

$\angle QPT = 90°$

(Angle made on tangent)

$\therefore \angle QPT + \angle PTQ + \angle PQT = 180°$

$90° + \angle PTQ + 52° = 180°$

$\angle PTQ = 180° - (142°)$

$\angle PTQ = 38°$

74. *(c)* Let the number be $100x$.

According to the question,

$$100x \times \left(\frac{100 - 18}{100}\right) \times \left(\frac{100 + 25}{100}\right) = 102.5x$$

$\therefore$ Overall percentage change

$$= \frac{102.5x - 100x}{100x} \times 100$$

$= 2.5\%$

$\therefore$ Increases by 2.5%.

75. *(d)* According to the question,

$r = 6$ cm, $AB = 7$ cm

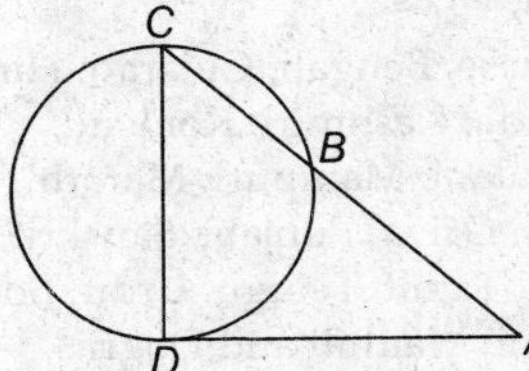

Let us assume $BC = x$ cm

$\therefore AD^2 = AC^2 - CD^2 = AB \times AC$

$= (7 + x)^2 - (12)^2 = 7(7 + x)$

$= 49 + x^2 + 14x - 144 = 49 + 7x$

$= x^2 + 7x - 144 = 0$

$= (x + 16)(x - 9) = 0$

$\therefore x = 9$

$\therefore AC = x + 7 = 9 + 7 = 16$ cm

76. *(b)* The 15th National Census Survey was conducted by the Census Organisation of India in the year 2011.

- It was conducted by the Registrar General and Census Commissioner of India after every 10 years Ministry of Home Affairs, Government of India.
- All the censuses since 1951 were conducted under the 1948 Census of India Act, which predates the Constitution of India.

77. *(a)* In Hindustani classical music, a Tala (or Tal) is a cyclic arrangement of time units, which is used to measure the rhythmic cycle of a composition.

- Tala is an ancient music concept traceable to Vedic era texts of Hinduism, such as the Samaveda and methods for singing the Vedic hymns.
- The basic units of time division are Laghu, Guru, and Pluta.

78. *(d)* The Bhotia dance form is a folk dance of Uttarakhand.

- The Bhotiyas are an ancient tribe of Uttarakhand, and the namesake dance is performed by them is closely linked to their death rituals.
- They were an occupational caste of shepherds who traded wool and salt between Tibet and India.

79. *(a)* The penalty for a wide ball in cricket is one run.

- A wide is a type of illegal delivery to a batter (the other type being a no-ball) that is judged by the umpire to be too wide or (in international cricket) too high to be hit by the batsman.
- Wide balls are covered by Law 22 of the Laws of Cricket.

80. *(c)* The point in the orbit of an object (such as a satellite) orbiting the Earth that is at the greatest distance from the centre of Earth is known as apogee.

At apogee, the object moves at its slowest speed in its orbit.

81. *(d)* Bombay Presidency Association was established by Phirozshah Mehta, KT Telang and Badruddin Tyabji.

- It was founded in 1885.
- The reactionary policies of Lytton and the Ilbert Bill controversy led to the formation of The Bombay Presidency Association.
- Badruddin Tyabji, Pherozeshah Mehta, and Kashinath Telang were known as 'The Triumvirate' or 'The Three Stars' of Bombay's public life.

82. *(a)* In MS-Word, pressing Ctrl+N simultaneously opens a blank new document. The other options is
- Ctrl + S → Save
- Ctrl + B → Bold
- Ctrl + C → Copy

83. *(a)* Renunciation is not a way to acquire citizenship of India, it is a process of giving up Indian citizenship by a person who already possesses it.
- A person can renounce their Indian citizenship if they are acquiring citizenship of another country or if they no longer wish to be an Indian citizen.
- The different ways to acquire citizenship in India are by Birth, Registration, Acquisition, Naturalisation and Descent.

84. *(d)* The final of the 2019-2021 ICC World Test Championship was played from 18th to 23rd June, 2021 at the Rose Bowl, Southampton, England, between India and New Zealand.

New Zealand won the match by eight wickets to be crowned as the winners of the inaugural ICC World Test Championship.

85. *(b)* Los Angeles, USA will host the 2028 Olympics Games.

Los Angeles was previously chosen to host the Summer Olympics in 1984, as well as 1932.

86. *(a)* BVR Subrahmanyam was appointed as the CEO of NITI Aayog in February, 2023.
- The Government has replaced Planning Commission with a new institution named NITI Aayog (National Institution for Transforming India) on 1st January, 2015.
- Sindhushree Khullar was the first CEO of NITI Aayog.

87. *(a)* The Shehnai is a woodwind instrument, played by blowing air reed, not played by way through a double of percussion or not played by way of striking any object.
- Tabla is a percussion instrument, played by striking the fingers on the drumheads.
- Pakhawaj is a percussion instrument, played by striking the fingers on the drumheads.
- Drum is a percussion instrument, played by striking the drumhead with sticks or hands.

88. *(d)* Statements (2 and 3) are correct.
- Article 38 of the Constitution of India provides the state shall give strive to promote the welfare of the people by securing and protecting a social order in which justice, social, economic and political shall inform all the institution and state shall strive to minimise inequalities.
- Article 39 of the Constitution of India provides that the state shall direct its policy towards securing that there is equal pay for equal work for both men and women and citizens are not forced by economic necessity to enter avocations unsuited to their age or strength.
- Statement (1) is incorrect because Article 37 of the Consitution of India states that the Directive Principles of State Policy are not enforceable in any court but are fundamental to the governance of the country.

89. *(c)* Mundra Thermal Power Station is located at Mundra in Kutch district in the Indian state of Gujarat.
- The Source of water for the power plant is sea water from the Gulf of Kutch.
- It is the world's 11th largest single location coal-based thermal power plant as well as India's second largest operational power plant after NTPC Vindhyanchal.

90. *(c)* The Eighth Schedule to the Constitution consists of the following 22 languages:

Assamese, Bengali, Gujarati, Hindi, Kannada, Kashmiri, Konkani, Malayalam, Manipuri, Marathi, Nepali, Oriya, Punjabi, Sanskrit, Sindhi, Tamil, Telugu, Urdu, Bodo, Santhali, Maithili and Dogri.
- Sindhi language was added by the 21st Amendment Act of 1967.
- Konkani, Manipuri, and Nepali were included by the 71st Amendment Act of 1992.
- Bodo, Dogri, Maithili, and Santhali were added by the 92nd Amendment Act of 2003 which came into force in 2004.

91. *(a)* The correct matching is A-1, B-4, C-3, D-2.
- Garibi Hatao' was the slogan given by Indira Gandhi at the time of the Fifth Five-Year Plan (1974-1979).
- Eighth Plan of 1992 to 1997 is also known as the liberalisation of the economy. It was also considered as the beginning of Liberalisation, Privatisation and Globalisation (LPG) in India.
- Rolling Plan was the sixth Five-Year Plan introduced by the Janata Government for the time period 1978-83.
- The Ninth Five-Year Plan (1997 to 2002) was started with an objective of 'Growth with Social Justice and Equality'.

92. *(b)* Tab keyboard key is used to jumb the cursor to the next cell of the table in MS Word.

93. *(b)* Malaria is not a mutation based disease. Malaria is caused by a parasite called *plasmodium*, which is spread to humans by the bite of an infected female *Anopheles* mosquito.
- Phenylketonuria (PKU) is an autosomal recessive disorder, caused by mutations in both alleles of the gene for phenylalanine hydroxylase found in chromosome 12.
- Sickle cell anemia is an autosomal recessive disease caused by a point mutation in the hemoglobin beta gene (HBB) found in chromosome 11p15.5.
- Down syndrome is a genetic condition caused by an extra copy of chromosome 21.

94. *(c)* Rashmi Shukla was appointed as the Director General of Shashastra Seema Bal (SSB) in March, 2023.
- She is the first woman Director General of Police of Maharashtra.
- She was heading the State Intelligence Department in Maharashtra Police when the phones of Shiv Sena leader Sanjay Raut and Nationalist Congress

Party leader Eknath Khadse were allegedly tapped in 2019.

95. *(c)* Both Statements (I) and (III) are correct.

- Madhya Pradesh has the maximum number of National Parks in India, with a total of 9 national parks.
- The Salim Ali Centre for Ornithology and Natural History (SACON) is located in Coimbatore, Tamil Nadu.
- Statement II is incorrect because Mudumalai National Park is located in Tamil Nadu, not Kerala.

96. *(a)* Easter is a religious festival celebrated by Christians around the world to commemorate the resurrection of Jesus Christ from the dead.

- Easter actually originated as an ancient pagan celebration of the spring equinox.
- Easter falls on the first Sunday following the Full Moon after the spring equinox. This day marks the Resurrection of Jesus Christ on the third day after his Crucifixion.

97. *(a)* INS Vikrant is India's first indigenous Aircraft Carrier, built by the Cochin Shipyard Limited (CsL) in Kerala. It conducted its maiden sea trial on 4th August, 2021 marking a significant step towards India's self-reliance in building military equipment.

- It is the first ever indigenously designed and constructed aircraft carrier which will strengthen the country's stand as a 'Blue Water Navy'.
- The ship has been designed in-house by the Indian Navy's Warship Design Bureau and constructed by M/s Cochin Shipyard Limited.

98. *(a)* Bahmani kingdom was a Muslim state of the Deccan in Southern India and was founded by Alauddin Hasan Bahaman Shah in 1347.

- It was the first Independent Islamic Kingdom in South India.
- The Bahmani capital was Ahsanabad (Gulbarga) between 1347 and 1425 when it was moved to Muhammadabad (Bidar).
- The last Bahmani ruler was Sultan Khalimullah Shah. After his death, the kingdom disintegrated.

99. *(b)* Shirley Ardener introduced the concept of Rotating Savings and Credit Association (ROSCA) in 1964.

- ROSCA is a informal financial organisation where members contribute a fixed amount of money at regular intervals, and the total amount is given to one member in each.
- ROSCAS are also known as 'Chit Funds' in India, 'Sus'u in West Arica, and 'Tandas' in Latin America, and are a common form of informal savings and credit association in many developing countries.

100. *(a)* Initial potential energy (PE) at 10 m,

$$PE = mgh$$
$$= 2\text{ kg} \times 9.8\text{ m/s}^2 \times 10 = 196\text{ J}$$

As the object falls to 5 m,

Remaining potential energy

$$(PE) = mgh$$
$$= 2 \times 9.8 \times 5 = 98\text{ J}$$

Kinetic energy (KE)

$$= \text{Initial PE} - \text{Remaining PE}$$
$$= 196 - 98 = 98\text{ J}$$

Ratio of PE to KE at 5 m;

$$PE : KE = 98\text{ J} : 98\text{J}$$
$$= 1 : 1$$

At the mid-point (5 m), the object's potential energy equals its kinetic energy.

Set 27 09 July, 2024 (Shift III)

SSC CHSL Tier-I SOLVED PAPER

Instructions

1. This paper contains 100 questions.
2. It has 4 Parts, **Part I** General English, **Part II** General Intelligence & Reasoning, **Part III** Quantitative Aptitude and **Part IV** General Awareness.
3. Each question carries **2 marks**.

Part I

General English

1. The following sentence has been split into four segments. Identify the segment that contains a grammatical error.

The workers called out / the strike because / the management acceded to / all their demands.

(a) the strike because
(b) all their demands
(c) the management acceded to
(d) The workers called out

2. The following sentence has been divided into four segments. Identify the segment that contains a grammatical error.

She / did not watched / Frankenstein / last night.

(a) did not watched
(b) Frankenstein
(c) She
(d) last night

3. The given sentence is divided into four segments. Identify the segment that contains a grammatical error.

A company can / make money by / obtain resources / more affordably.

(a) A company can
(b) make money by
(c) obtain resources
(d) more affordably

4. Select the most appropriate option that can substitute the underlined segment in the given sentence.

Mahima is as smarter as Shilpi.

(a) as smart as
(b) more smart as
(c) most smart as
(d) smartest than

Directions (Q. Nos. 5-9) *In the following passage, some words have been deleted. Read the passage carefully and select the most appropriate option to fill in each blank.*

Conversation is indeed the (1)......... teachable of all arts. All you need to do in order to become a good conversationalist is to find a (2) .... that interests you and your listeners. But the important thing is that you must talk about the other (3)......... hobby rather than your own. Therein lies the secret of your (4)......... . Talk to your friends about the things that interest them, and you will get a reputation for good fellowship, charming wit, and a brilliant mind. There is nothing that (5) .... people so much as your interest in their interest.

5. Select the most appropriate option to fill in blank number (1).

(a) more easily
(b) more likely
(c) most easily
(d) most occasionally

6. Select the most appropriate option to fill in blank number (2).

(a) credit (b) subject
(c) luxury (d) result

7. Select the most appropriate option to fill in blank number (3).

(a) worker's (b) self's
(c) victim's (d) fellow's

8. Select the most appropriate option to fill in blank number (4).

(a) popularity (b) audacity
(c) irrationality (d) capacity

9. Select the most appropriate option to fill in blank number (5).

(a) accompanies (b) admits
(c) pleases (d) advances

10. Select the most appropriate synonym of the underlined word.

The girl tried to alleviate her brother's problem.

(a) increase (b) soar
(c) reduce (d) worsen

11. Select the most appropriate antonym of the underlined word.

The encounter made the audience squirm.

(a) speak (b) relax
(c) chat (d) pray

12. Select the most appropriate option that can substitute the underlined segment in the given sentence. If there is no need to substitute it, select 'No substitution required'.

The small size of his store makes it impossible for him to stock all the items.

(a) made them impossible
(b) making it impossible
(c) is made it impossible
(d) No substitution required

13. Select the most appropriate option to fill in the blank.

I would like to reach the .... of the Everest.

(a) peek (b) pick
(c) pike (d) peak

14. Select the most appropriate synonym of the underlined word.

John is very generous; he regularly gives alms to the poor.

(a) popular (b) great
(c) kind (d) shrewd

15. Select the most appropriate option that can substitute the underlined segment in the given sentence.

Bill Gates' fortune was bequeathed for the old age home.

(a) into the old age home
(b) to the old age home
(c) by the old age home
(d) with the old age home

16. Select the most appropriate antonym of the underlined word in the given sentence.
The coach was optimistic that Ronald will play the quarter final.
(a) tasteful (b) cheerful
(c) doubtful (d) helpful

17. Select the most appropriate option to correct the sentence by using the proper meaning of the underlined word.
He scores good marks in exams as he is quite meticulous.
(a) selective (b) careful
(c) intelligent (d) lazy

18. Choose an appropriate word that can substitute the bracketed word and complete the sentence meaningfully.
He never (talks) the truth.
(a) speaks
(b) declares
(c) narrates
(d) utters

19. Select the most appropriate option that can substitute the underlined segment in the given sentence.
Professor Singh is not in the office today. I ask you try call him tomorrow.
(a) suggest you try calling
(b) am suggesting you calling
(c) ask you to try called
(d) asked you to call

20. The given sentence is divided into four segments. Identify the segment that contains a spelling error.
When the famous businessman / faced a huge loss / in his business, / no one expressed simpathy.
(a) in his business
(b) When the famous businessman
(c) no one expressed simpathy
(d) faced a huge loss

21. Select the most appropriate meaning of the given idiom.
A wild goose chase
(a) Ideal seeking
(b) Fruitless search
(c) Fruitful search
(d) On a hunt

22. Select the incorrectly spelt word in the given sentence.
The ministir ordered the engineers to build roads through high mountains and bridges across deep ravines in a week.
(a) ravines
(b) engineers
(c) ministir
(d) bridges

23. Select the most appropriate synonym of the bracketed word in the following sentence to fill in the blank.
The meeting was brought to a .... (rapid) conclusion.
(a) stubborn
(b) pervious
(c) grim
(d) hasty

24. Select the most appropriate meaning of the given idiom.
An old head on young shoulders
(a) A young person who looks old
(b) A young person who is lazy
(c) A person who is slow at understanding things
(d) A young person who acts or speaks like an older person

25. Select the most appropriate antonym of the underlined word.
The poet was lost in a reverie.
(a) reality
(b) fantasy
(c) daydream
(d) trance

Part II
General Intelligence

26. Four letter-clusters have been given, out of which three are alike in some manner and one is different. Select the letter-cluster that is different.
(**Note** The odd one out is not based on the number of consonants/ vowels or their position in the letter-cluster)
(a) DEWV (b) QRJI
(c) OPMK (d) JKQP

27. What would be the word on the opposite side of 'Green', if the given sheet is folded to form a cube?

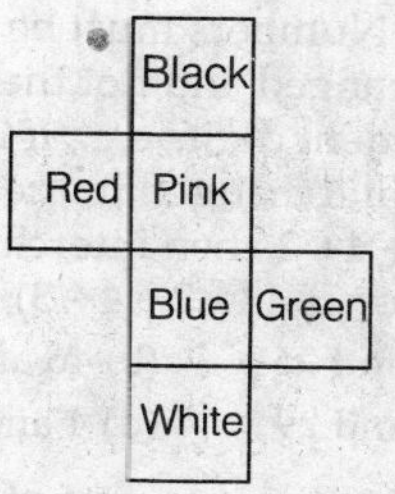

(a) Red (b) Black
(c) Pink (d) White

28. Identify the figure given in the options, which when put in place of question mark (?) will logically complete the series.

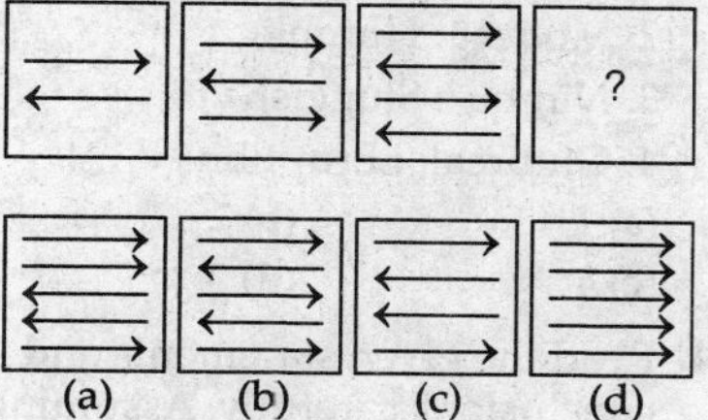

29. If 22nd March, 2000 is a Wednesday, then what will the day of the week on 16th January, 2010?
(a) Wednesday (b) Tuesday
(c) Sunday (d) Saturday

30. Select the set in which the numbers are related in the same way as are the numbers of the following sets.
(**Note** Operations should be performed on the whole numbers, without breaking down the numbers into its constituent digits. E.g. 13 – Operations on 13 such as adding/subtracting/multiplying etc. to 13 can be performed. Breaking down 13 into 1 and 3 and then performing mathematical operations on 1 and 3 is not allowed.)
(120, 8, 15)
(144, 24, 6)
(a) (134, 22,6) (b) (115, 23, 5)
(c) (106, 4, 26) (d) (124, 6, 21)

31. What should come in place of question mark (?) in the given series?
126, 1236, 12336, 123336, 1233336, ?
(a) 12333336 (b) 12333366
(c) 1233633 (d) 12333363

32. Which two numbers should be interchanged to make the given equation correct?
$29 + 46 - (48 \div 4) + (7 \times 3) - 26 = 61$

(**Note** Numbers must be interchanged and not the constituent digits e.g., if 2 and 3 are to be interchanged in the equation $43 \times 3 + 4 \div 2$, then interchanged equation is $43 \times 2 + 4 \div 3$)

(a) 46 and 26 (b) 46 and 48
(c) 26 and 29 (d) 4 and 3

33. This question consists of a pair of words, which have a certain relationship to each other. Select the pair, which does not have the same relationship.

Smart : Intelligent

1. Liable : Accountable
2. Modest : Humble
3. Nimble : Sluggish
4. Outbreak : Eruption

(a) 1 (b) 2
(c) 4 (d) 3

34. Read the given statements and conclusions carefully. Assuming that the information given in the statements is true, even if it appears to be at variance with commonly known facts, decide which of the given conclusions logically follow(s) from the statements.

Statements

No cloud is a mountain.
All mountains are rivers.
All rivers are oceans.

Conclusions

I. All rivers can never be clouds.
II. All mountains are oceans.

(a) None of the conclusions follow
(b) Only Conclusion I follows
(c) Only Conclusion II follows
(d) Both Conclusions I and II follow

35. If 19th February, 2014 was Wednesday, then what was the day of the week on 19th February, 2022?

(a) Thursday (b) Tuesday
(c) Wednesday (d) Saturday

36. How many triangles are there in the following figure ?

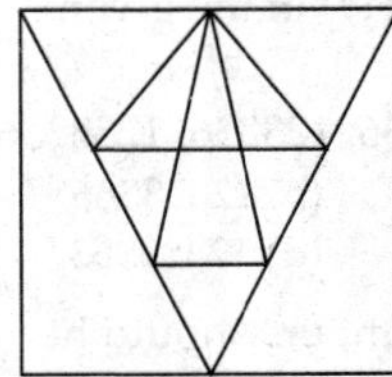

(a) 21 (b) 20
(c) 19 (d) 18

37. What should come in place of the question mark (?) in the given series based on the English alphabetical order ?

AEO, XAM, UWK, RSI, ?

(a) NMF (b) LMH
(c) OOG (d) MNH

38. In a certain code language,
'A @ B' means 'A is the husband of B',
'A # B' means 'A is the mother of B',
'A & B' means 'A is the daughter of B',
'A $ B' means 'A is the brother of B'.
Based on the above, how is P related to M, if 'M & N @ O # P $ Q'?

(a) Brother
(b) Son
(c) Father
(d) Father's brother

39. What will come in the place of question mark (?) in the following equation if '+' and '÷' are interchanged and '×' and '–' are interchanged?

$36 - 42 \div 26 + 13 \times 14 = ?$

(a) 3467 (b) 1324
(c) 1200 (d) 1500

40. EHJL is related to FJMP in a certain way based on the English alphabetical order. In the same way, BEGI is related to CGJM. To which of the following is DGIK related, following the same logic?

(a) EIJO (b) EILO
(c) ELIO (d) EJIO

41. In a certain code language, 'if you are' is coded as 'go so lu' ans 'where are you' is coded as 'so lu ga'. What is the code for 'where' in that language?

(a) lu (b) ga
(c) so (d) go

42. 242 is related to 22 following a certain logic. Following the same logic, 385 is related to 35. To which of the following is 572 related following the same logic?

(**Note** Operations should be performed on the whole numbers, without breaking down the numbers into its constituent digits. E.g. 13 – Operations on 13 such as adding/deleting /multiplying etc. to 13 can be performed. Breaking down 13 into 1 and 3 and then performing mathematical operations on 1 and 3 is not allowed.)

(a) 56 (b) 54 (c) 50 (d) 52

43. Select the option in which the given figure is embedded (Rotation is not allowed).

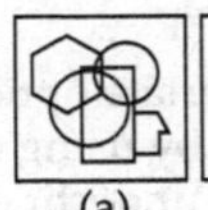  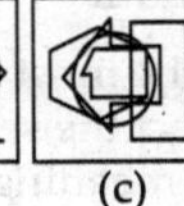 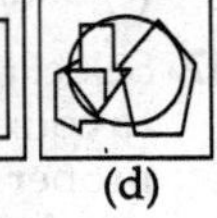

(a) (b) (c) (d)

44. Select the option in which the given figure is embedded (Rotation is not allowed).

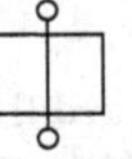

(a) 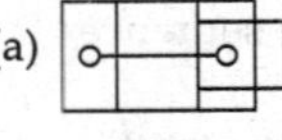

(b) 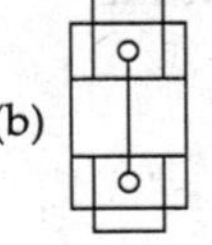

(c) 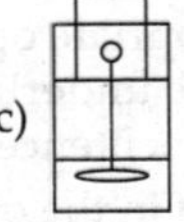

(d) 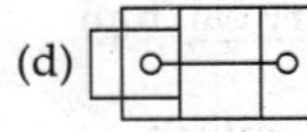

45. Which of the following number will replace the question mark (?) in the given series ?

86, 129, 105, 118, 124, 107, 143, 96, ?

(a) 149 (b) 138
(c) 162 (d) 153

46. Select the term from among the given options that can replace that question mark (?) in the following series based on the English alphabetical order.

JKL, LHP, NET, ?, RYB, TVF

(a) RAL (b) PBX
(c) POF (d) COL

47. In a certain code language, 'future is bright' is coded as 'pl mk ni' and 'bright shooting star' is coded as 'dg rz pl'. How is 'bright' coded in that language?

(a) dg (b) pl (c) mk (d) ni

48. A paper is folded and cut as shown below. How will it appear when unfolded ?

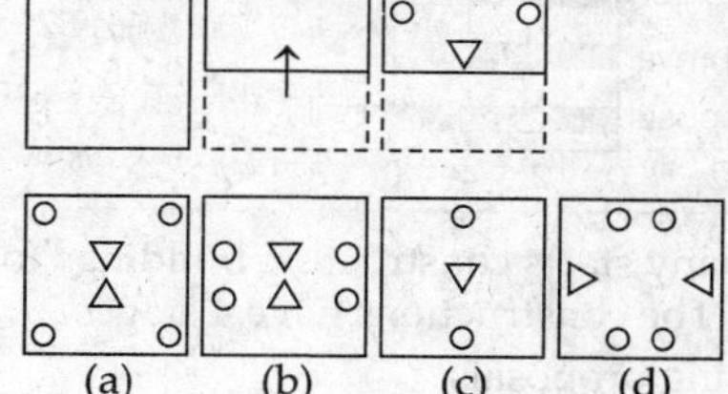

49. Select the correct mirror image of the given figure, when the mirror is placed at MN.

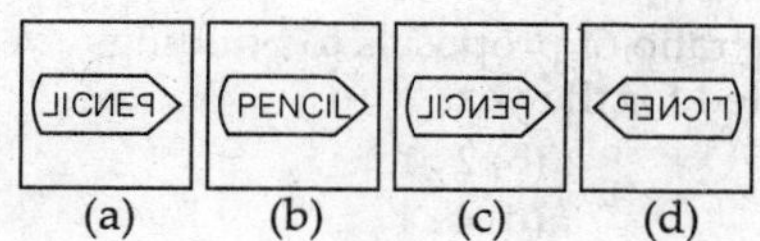

50. If 'A' stands for '÷' 'B' stands for '×', 'C' stands for '+' and 'D' stands for '–', what will come in place of the question mark (?) in the following equation?

222 A 2 C 7 B 3 D 11 = ?

(a) 141 (b) 131
(c) 121 (d) 111

Part III
Quantitative Aptitude

51. Study the following bar chart, which represents the income and expenditure of a company.

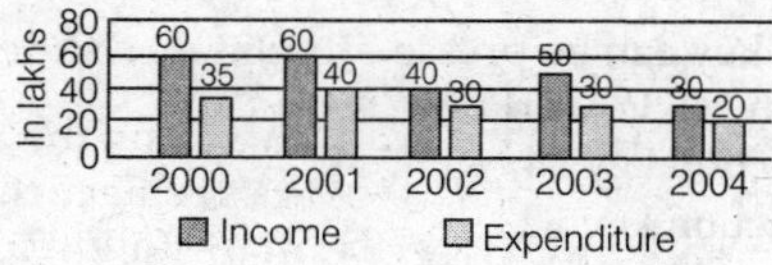

In how many years is the income of company less than the average income ?

(a) 5 (b) 4
(c) 2 (d) 3

52. Ramesh sells an article for ₹ 34440, after allowing an 18% discount on the marked price and still manages to gain 40 % profit. If Ramesh sold the article at a 12 % discount on the marked price, then what will be his profit, correct to two places of decimals ?

(a) 50.42% (b) 48.24 %
(c) 50.24% (d) 48.42%

53. A tangent is drawn from a point that is at a distance of 37 cm from centre of the circle *O*, and diameter is 24 cm. The length (in cm) of the tangent is

(a) 30 (b) 35
(c) 28.16 (d) 37

54. If $\sin\theta = \frac{7}{25}$, then $\cos\theta$ and $\tan\theta$ are respectively .... (where, θ is in the first quadrant)

(a) $\frac{25}{24}$ and $\frac{24}{7}$ (b) $\frac{25}{7}$ and $\frac{7}{24}$
(c) $\frac{24}{25}$ and $\frac{24}{7}$ (d) $\frac{24}{25}$ and $\frac{7}{24}$

55. The average marks scored by the students of a class is 75. If the average marks scored by the girls in the same class is 90 and that of boys is 70, what is the percentage of boys in the class?

(a) 60% (b) 65%
(c) 70% (d) 75%

56. By selling 60 pens, a man gains an amount equal to the selling price of 12 pens. What is his gain percentage?

(a) 20 % (b) 22%
(c) 25% (d) 27%

57. The lines $x + y = 10$ and $-3x + y = 2$ have a unique solution. What is the distance (in units) between the unique solution and the point of intersection of the line $x + y = 10$ and the *X*-axis?

(a) $8\sqrt{2}$ (b) 8
(c) 10 (d) $10\sqrt{2}$

58. Evaluate the given expression.

$(45 + 9) \div 2 - 7 \times 33 \div 7 + \{(7 + 18) \times 6\} + 9 \times 8 - 89$

(a) 112 (b) 118
(c) 125 (d) 127

59. An amount invested fetched a total simple interest of ₹ 4050 at the rate of 9% per annum in 5 yr. What is the amount invested (in ₹)?

(a) 9000 (b) 8300
(c) 7500 (d) 9050

60. If 6 engineers can complete a work in 5 days and 5 skilled workers can complete the same work in 7 days, then the time taken (in days) to complete the same work by 7 engineers and 4 skilled workers will be

(a) $2\frac{64}{70}$ (b) $3\frac{64}{73}$
(c) $2\frac{64}{73}$ (d) $2\frac{65}{73}$

61. The given bar-graph shows the percentage of production of three companies C_1, C_2 and C_3 over five years. Study the bar-graph and answer the question that follows.

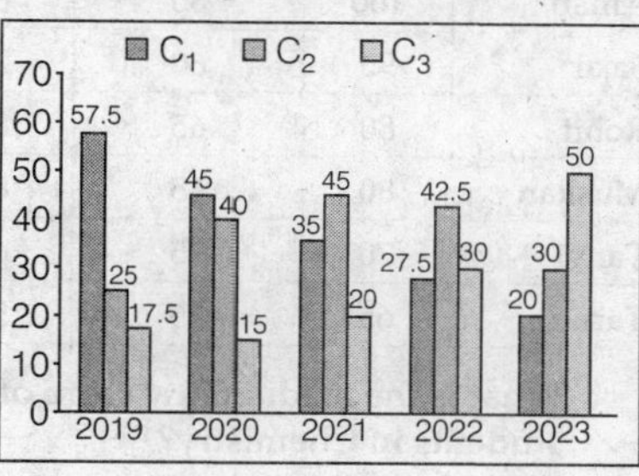

If the ratio of the total production in the year 2019 and 2022 is 3 : 5 and the total production in C_1 in 2022 is 4125, then the total production of C_3 in the year 2019 is

(a) 5175 (b) 9000
(c) 2250 (d) 1575

62. If Tanya walks at the speed of 6 km/h, she misses a train by 2 min. However, if she walks at the speed of 8 km/h, she reaches the station 3 min before the arrival of the train. The distance covered by Tanya to reach the station is

(a) 3 km (b) 2.5 km
(c) 2.75 km (d) 2 km

63. Find the equation of the sphere having centre (–1, 2, –3) and the radius of 3 units.

(a) $x^2 + y^2 + z^2 - 2x + 4y - 6z + 5 = 0$
(b) $x^2 + y^2 + z^2 + x - 2y + 3z + 5 = 0$
(c) $x^2 + y^2 + z^2 + 2x^2 - 4y + 6z + 5 = 0$
(d) $x^2 + y^2 + z^2 - x + 2y - 3z + 5 = 0$

64. A tangent is drawn from a point at a distance of 25cm from the centre of a circle $C(0, r)$ of radius 7cm. The length of the tangent is

(a) 24 cm (b) 20 cm
(c) 8 cm (d) 16 cm

65. If a person's salary increases from ₹ 200 per day to ₹ 234 per day, then the percentage increase in the person's salary is

(a) 17% (b) 14%
(c) 15% (d) 16%

66. Read the given informatin and answer the question that follows.
The following table give s the percentage of marks obtained by seven students in six different subjects in an examination.
The number in the brackets gives the maximum marks in each subject.

Students	Subjects (Max. Marks)					
	Maths	Chemistry	Physics	Geography	History	Computer Science
	(150)	(130)	(120)	(100)	(60)	(40)
Ayush	90	50	90	60	70	80
Aman	100	80	80	40	80	70
Sajal	90	60	70	70	90	70
Rohit	80	65	80	80	60	60
Muskan	80	65	85	95	50	90
Tanvi	70	75	65	85	40	60
Tarun	65	35	50	77	80	80

What is the median raw score of the marks obtained by the seven students in Chemistry?
(a) 65 (b) 81.25
(c) 84.5 (d) 62.5

67. The value of $\dfrac{5+7\times5\div8 \text{ of } 5+3\div3\times5}{6\div6 \text{ of } 4+9\times9\div3\times2\times2}$ is
(a) $\dfrac{77}{861}$ (b) $\dfrac{97}{881}$
(c) $\dfrac{67}{859}$ (d) $\dfrac{87}{866}$

68. A car is sold for ₹ 500000, which is 20% less than its original price. What was the original price of the car ?
(a) ₹ 625000 (b) ₹ 650000
(c) ₹ 675000 (d) ₹ 600000

69. The area of three adjacent faces of a cuboidal box is 120 cm^2, 72 cm^2 and 60 cm^2, respectively. Find the volume (in cm^3) of the box.
(a) 425 (b) 650
(c) 720 (d) 864

70. If the radius of the base and slant height of the cone is 6 cm and 10 cm, respectively, then the volume of the cone is equal to
(a) $98\pi\, cm^3$ (b) $106\pi\, cm^3$
(c) $96\pi\, cm^3$ (d) $108\pi\, cm^3$

71. If $A:B=5:8$ and $B:C=7:8$, then find $A:C$.
(a) 35 : 64 (b) 55 : 30
(c) 34 : 64 (d) 35 : 56

72. In an election, there were only two candidates. One of the candidates secured 35% of votes and is defeated by the other candidate by 381 votes. The total number of votes polled is
(a) 635 (b) 1028
(c) 1270 (d) 514

73. In a right-angled triangle with sides 12 cm and 16 cm and hypotenuse 20 cm, the length of altitude drawn on the hypotenuse from the opposite vertex is K. Find the value of K.
(a) 6.9 cm (b) 9.6 cm
(c) 6.8 cm (d) 8.6 cm

74.

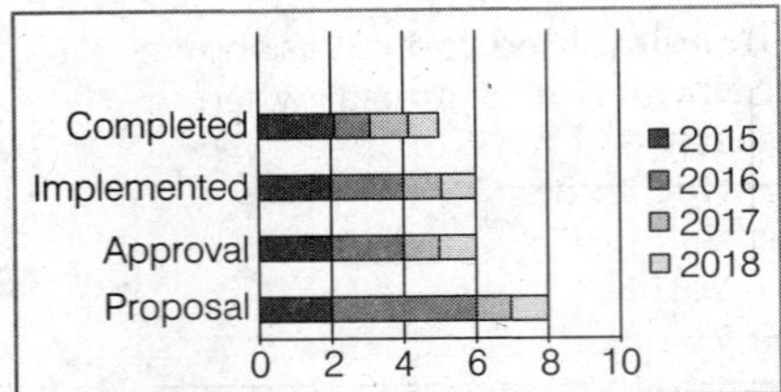

A company starts constructing buildings for a college. The constructions have 4 stages.
1. building proposals
2. proposals approval
3. constructions implemented
4. buildings completed
The above 3D-bar graph indicates the status of constructions for 4 yr 2015 to 2018.
The X-axis scale 0,2,4,6,8,10 indicates 0,20%,40%,60%, 80%, 100%.
Study the bar-graph carefully and answer the following question.
Find the ratio of proposals to buildings completed for the year 2016.
(a) 2 : 3 (b) 2 : 1
(c) 3 : 1 (d) 4 : 1

75. The sides ST and TR and the median SU of the ΔSTR are equal to the sides MN and NJ and the median MV of the ΔMNJ respectively.
If $\angle TSU = 46°$, $\angle NMJ = 79°$ and $\angle MVN = 88°$, what is the degree measure of $\frac{7}{11}\angle SRT$?
(a) 35° (b) 55°
(c) 56° (d) 47°

Part IV
General Awareness

76. Which of the following is a food-borne disease caused by the consumption of contaminated food or beverages?
(a) Malaria (b) Tuberculosis
(c) Chicken pox (d) Cholera

77. Which key can be pressed to initiate a slide show in MS PowerPoint?
(a) Function key F4
(b) Function key F2
(c) Function key F8
(d) Function key F5

78. Which of the following Fundamental Rights has been deleted from the original list of Fundamental Rights provided in the Constitution of India?
(a) Right to Freedom of Religion
(b) Cultural and Educational Rights
(c) Right to Constitutional Remedies
(d) Right to Property

79. The approach driven by seven engines, which is powered by Clean Energy and 'Sabka Prayas' is related to which scheme?
(a) Aatmanirbhar Bharat Rojgar Yojana
(b) Pradhan Mantri Mudra Yojana
(c) Garib Kalyan Rojgar Abhiyan
(d) PM Gati Shakti Master Plan

80. Bilhana was a court poet in which of the following kingdoms?
(a) Vikramaditya VI
(b) Rajaraja II
(c) Vijayaditya VII
(d) Kulottunga I

81. Manipur's .... tribe celebrates the 'Gaan-Ngai' festival, which is a post-harvest festival of the tribe living in the regions of Manipur.
(a) Zeliangrong (b) Chothe
(c) Gangte (d) Inpui

82. Who among the following confirmed Maxwell's theories with the discovery of radio waves and also became the first person to transmit and receive controlled radio waves in 1886?
(a) Guglielmo Marconi
(b) William Hopkins
(c) Michael Faraday
(d) Heinrich Hertz

83. Who was the first Indian wrestler to win a world championship medal?
(a) Udey Chand (b) Dara Singh
(c) Malwa Singh (d) KD Jadhav

84. Calcualte personal income (in ₹ crore) from the given data.

Particlular	₹ (in crore)
Private income	1800
Net retained earning of private enterprises	500
Corporation tax	250

(a) 950 (b) 1100
(c) 2050 (d) 1000

85. Match the pairs correctly.

	National Waterways		Stretch
A.	NW-1	1.	Kakinada - Puducherry
B.	NW-2	2.	Kottapuram -Kallam
C.	NW-3	3.	Allahabad -Haldia
D.	NW-5	4.	Sadiya-Dhubri
		5.	Talchar- Dhamra

Codes

	A	B	C	D
(a)	3	4	2	5
(b)	1	2	4	5
(c)	4	3	5	1
(d)	2	5	3	1

86. The Wild Life (Protection) Amendment Act, 2022 received the assent of the President on ....
(a) 19th December, 2022
(b) 14th December, 2022
(c) 17th December, 2022
(d) 10th December, 2022

87. Which Excel feature allows you to simultaneously edit the same cell or range of cells with multiple users in real-time?
(a) Co-authoring
(b) Data Validation
(c) Conditional Formatting
(d) Track Changes

88. Which statement about Syama Sastri is correct?
(a) His signature name was Guruguha.
(b) His famous composition is 'Pancharatna Kritis'.
(c) He is one among the trinity of Carnatic music.
(d) A crater on planet Mercury is named after him.

89. Article 15 of the Constitution of India entails
(a) cultural and educational rights
(b) equality of opportunity for all citizens in matters relating to employment or appointment
(c) freedom of speech and expression
(d) prohibition of discrimination against any citizen on grounds only of religion, race, caste, sex or place of birth

90. What was the name of the campaign led by the Ali brothers and Maulana Abul Kalam Azad to save the Ottoman Caliphate as a symbol of unity among the Muslim community?
(a) Wahabi Movement
(b) Khilafat Movement
(c) Ahmadiya Movement
(d) Faraizi Movement

91. Which of the following food grains highly benefitted from the Green Revolution?
(a) Millet (b) Barley
(c) Maize (d) Wheat

92. What is 'Padam' in Carnatic music?
(a) A patriotic poem
(b) A poem about courage
(c) A love poem
(d) A lullaby

93. Which of the following airports is being built as India's first 'carbon-neutral airport'?
(a) Jammu airport
(b) Kangra airport
(c) Srinagar airport
(d) Leh airport

94. In which country do Kachin, Karen, Karenni, Chin and Mon ethnic groups belong?
(a) Myanmar
(b) Afghanistan
(c) Sri Lanka
(d) Nepal

95. In the year 2021, which of the following ministries published the amended rules related to Corporate Social Responsibility (CSR)?
(a) Ministry of Science and Technology
(b) Ministry of Corporate Affairs
(b) Ministry of New and Renewable Energy
(b) Ministry of Home Affairs

96. A flat ring of small, icy bodies that revolve around the Sun beyond the orbit of the planet Neptune is called
(a) Asteroid Belt
(b) Bow Shock
(c) Kuiper Belt
(d) Oort Cloud

97. In cricket, the bowler does not get credit for ....
(a) bowled (b) LBW
(c) run out (d) catch

98. The Chilika Lake is located to the South of the .... delta.
(a) Narmada (b) Kaveri
(c) Mahanadi (d) Godavari

99. Mohiniyattam is a classical dance form of
(a) Tripura
(b) Kerala
(c) Assam
(d) Tamil Nadu

100. In which year was the Board of Control for Cricket in India (BCCI) formed ?
(a) 1914 (b) 1931 (c) 1947 (d) 1928

Answers

1. (d)	2. (a)	3. (c)	4. (a)
5. (c)	6. (b)	7. (d)	8. (a)
9. (c)	10. (c)	11. (b)	12. (d)
13. (d)	14 (c)	15. (b)	16. (c)
17. (b)	18. (a)	19. (a)	20. (c)
21. (b)	22. (c)	23. (d)	24. (d)
25. (a)	26. (c)	27. (a)	28. (b)
29. (d)	30. (b)	31. (a)	32. (d)
33. (d)	34. (d)	35. (d)	36. (b)
37. (c)	38. (a)	39. (d)	40. (b)
41. (b)	42. (d)	43. (b)	44. (b)
45. (c)	46. (b)	47. (b)	48. (a)
49. (c)	50. (c)	51. (c)	52. (c)
53. (b)	54. (d)	55. (d)	56. (c)
57. (a)	58. (d)	59. (a)	60. (c)
61. (d)	62. (d)	63. (c)	64. (a)
65. (a)	66. (c)	67. (d)	68. (a)
69. (c)	70. (c)	71. (a)	72. (c)
73. (b)	74. (d)	75. (a)	76. (d)
77. (d)	78. (d)	79. (d)	80. (a)
81. (a)	82. (d)	83. (a)	84. (c)
85. (a)	86. (a)	87. (a)	88. (c)
89. (d)	90. (b)	91. (d)	92. (c)
93. (d)	94. (a)	95. (b)	96. (c)
97. (c)	98. (c)	99. (b)	100. (d)

Explanations

1. *(d)* Part (d) 'the workers called out' contains an error. The use of 'called out' which means 'to rebuke or humiliate' is incorrect in the sentence. Use 'called off' which means 'to end' to correct the sentence.

2. *(a)* Part (a) 'did not watched' contains an error. Use 'watch' to correct the sentence. The verb 'did/do/does' takes the base form of the verb.

3. *(c)* Part (c) 'obtain resources' contains an error. Use 'obtaining' to correct the sentence.

4. *(a)* The underlined part of the given sentence contains an error. Use 'as smart as' to correct the sentence. The as....as expression takes the positive degree of adjective.

5. *(c)* The correct filler for the given blank is 'most easily'.

6. *(b)* The correct filler for the given blank is 'subject'.

7. *(d)* The correct filler for the given blank is 'fellow's'.

8. *(a)* The correct filler for the given blank is 'popularity'.

9. *(c)* The correct filler for the given blank is 'pleases'.

10. *(c)* The word 'alleviate' means 'to reduce'.

11. *(b)* 'Squirm' means to be nervous. Hence, its antonym is 'relax'.

12. *(d)* The underlined part is grammatically and contextually correct.

13. *(d)* The correct filler for the given blank is 'peak' which indicates the top of the Everest.

14. *(c)* The word 'generous' means 'kind'.

15. *(b)* The underlined part of the given sentence contains an error. Use 'to the old age home' to correct the sentence.

16. *(c)* The word 'optimistic' means positive and sure about something. Hence, its antonym is 'doutbful'.

17. *(b)* The word 'meticulous' means 'be very careful and perfect'.

18. *(a)* The bracketed word of the given sentence contains an error. Use 'speaks' to correct the sentence.

19. *(a)* The underlined part of the given sentence contains an error. Use 'suggest you try calling' to correct the sentence.

20. *(c)* Part (c) 'no one expressed simpathy' contains the spelling error. The correct spelling is 'sympathy'.

21. *(b)* A wild goose chase is a fruitless activity or search.

22. *(c)* The incorrectly spelt word is 'ministir'. The correct spelling is 'minister'.

23. *(d)* The word 'rapid' means quick. Hence, its synonym is 'hasty' which means the same and is the correct filler for the given blank.

24. *(d)* 'An old head on young shoulders' means being a young person who acts or speaks like an older person.

25. *(a)* The underlined word 'reverie' means a state of being pleasantly lost in one's thoughts; a daydream. Hence, its antonym is 'reality'.

26. *(c)* From options,

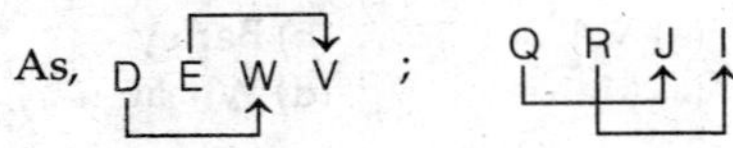

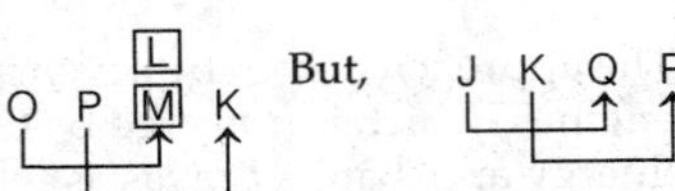

Here, in all the options first two letters are opposite alphabets of last two letters. But in option (c), this logic is not followed.

27. *(a)* We know that, cube is paired as

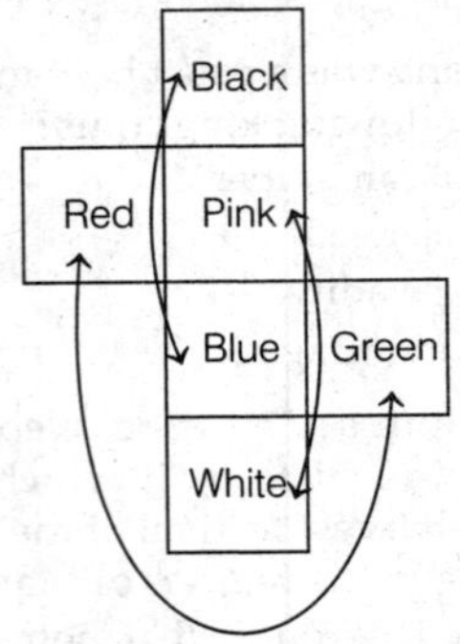

In the given figure, 'Red' is opposite of green.

28. *(b)* The given series is as follows,

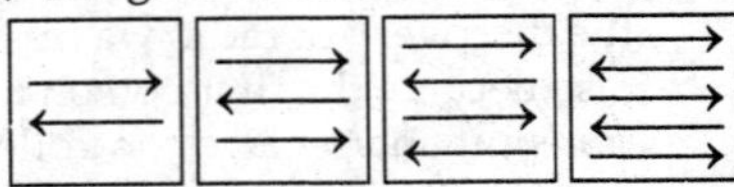

One arrow is increasing in successive figure. In the alternate figure face of arrow is interchange.

29. *(d)* Given, 22nd March, 2000 is Wednesday.

Number of odd days in 2000 from 22nd March

March + April + May + June + July + August + September + October + November + December

$$= \frac{9 + 30 + 31 + 30 + 31 + 31 + 30 + 31 + 30 + 31}{7}$$

$$= \frac{284}{7} = 4 \text{ odd days.}$$

Number of odd days from 2001 to 16th January, 2010

2001 + 2002 + 2003 + 2004 + 2005 + 2006 + 2007 + 2008 + 2009 + upto 16th January, 2010

$= 1 + 1 + 1 + 2 + 1 + 1 + 1 + 2 + 1 + 16$

[∴ Odd days in ordinary year = 1;
Odd days in leap year = 2]

$$= \frac{27}{7} = 6 \text{ odd days}$$

$$\therefore \text{Total odd days} = \frac{4 + 6}{7} = 3 \text{ odd days}$$

∴ Required day = Wednesday + 3 = Saturday

30. *(b)* As, (120, 8, 15) ⇒ (15 × 8 = 120)
and (144, 24, 6) ⇒ (24 × 6 = 144)
Similarly,
(115, 23, 5) ⇒ (5 × 23 = 115)

31. *(a)* The given pattern is as follows,
126, 1236, 12336, 123336, 1233336, 12333336
One 3 is added before the unit digit in successive number.

32. *(d)* The given equation,
29 + 46 − (48 ÷ 4) + (7 × 3) − 26 = 61
After interchanging '4' and '3', we get
29 + 46 − (48 ÷ 3) + (7 × 4) − 26 = 61
⇒ 29 + 46 − 16 + 28 − 26 = 61
⇒ 103 − 42 = 61 ⇒ 61 = 61

33. *(d)* As, Smart is synonym of intelligent. Similarly, all the options are synonyms to each other, but option (c) i.e., Nimble : Sluggish is antonyms of each other.

34. *(d)* According to the statements,

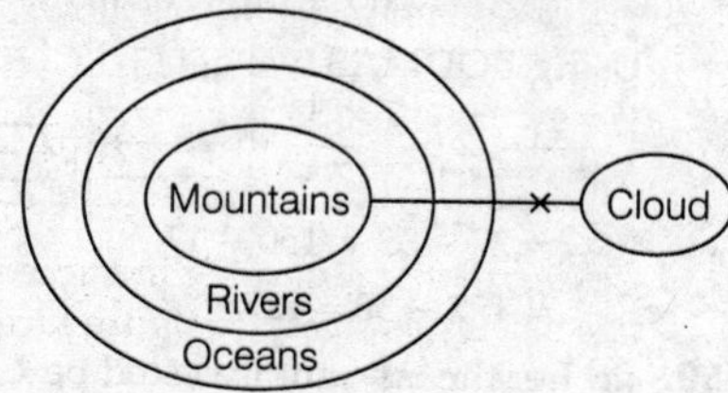

Conclusions I. (✓) II. (✓)
∴ Both Conclusions I and II follow.

35. *(d)* Given,
19th February, 2014 = Wednesday
Number of odd days in 2014 from 19th February
February + March + April + May + June + July + August + September + October + November + December

$$= \frac{9 + 31 + 30 + 31 + 30 + 31 + 31 + 30 + 31 + 30 + 31}{7}$$

$$= \frac{315}{7} = 0 \text{ odd days}$$

Number of odd days from 2015 to 19th February, 2022
= 2015 + 2016 + 2017 + 2018 + 2019 + 2020 + 2021 + upto 19th February 2022

$$= \frac{1 + 2 + 1 + 1 + 1 + 2 + 1 + 50}{7}$$

$$= \frac{59}{7} = 3 \text{ odd days}$$

$$\therefore \text{Total odd days} = \frac{0 + 3}{7} = 3 \text{ odd days}$$

∴ Required day = Wednesday + 3
= Saturday

36. *(b)* Naming the figure,

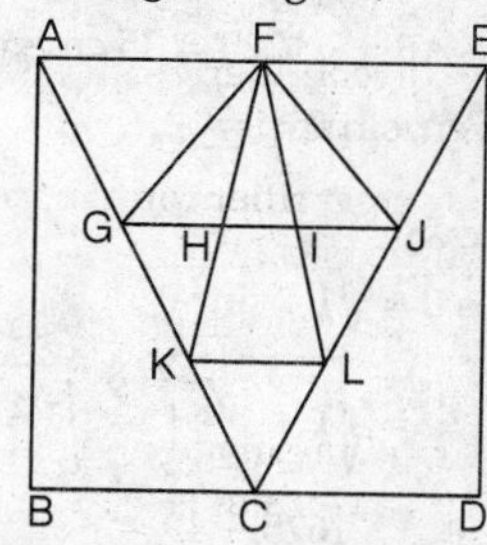

ΔABC, ΔCDE, ΔAGF, ΔFJE, ΔGFH, ΔFHI, ΔFIJ, ΔGFI, ΔFHJ, ΔGFJ, ΔFKL, ΔGKH, ΔILJ, ΔACE, ΔKLC, ΔAKF, ΔLFJ, ΔGKF, ΔFLE and ΔGJC.
Total number of triangles = 20

37. *(c)* The given pattern is as follows,

A →(−3) X →(−3) U →(−3) R →(−3) O
E →(−4) A →(−4) W →(−4) S →(−4) O
O →(−2) M →(−2) K →(−2) I →(−2) G

∴ ? = OOG

38. *(a)* Given, 'M & N @ O # P $ Q'

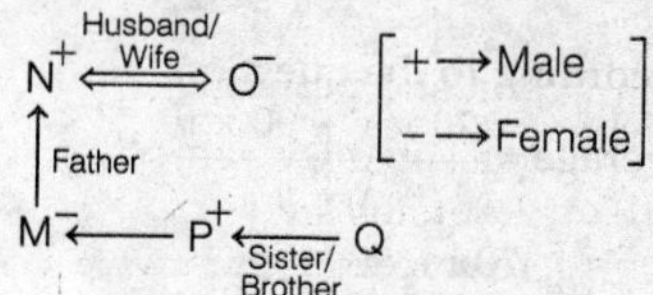

Here, 'P' is brother of 'M'.

39. *(d)* Given equation,
36 − 42 ÷ 26 + 13 × 14 = ?
After interchanging the sign, we get
36 × 42 + 26 ÷ 13 − 14
= 36 × 42 + 2 − 14
= 1512 + 2 − 14
= 1514 − 14 = 1500

40. *(b)* As,
E →(+1) F, H →(+2) J, J →(+3) M, L →(+4) P
and
B →(+1) C, E →(+2) G, G →(+3) J, I →(+4) M
Similarly,
D →(+1) E, G →(+2) I, I →(+3) L, K →(+4) O

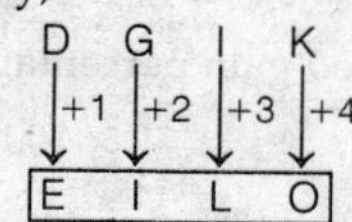

41. *(b)* According to the question,

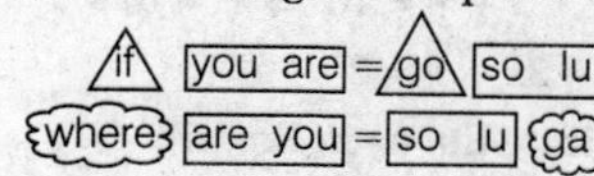

∴ Code for 'where' is 'ga'.

42. *(d)* As, 242 ÷ 11 = 22
and 385 ÷ 11 = 35
Similarly, 572 ÷ 11 = 52

43. *(b)* The question figure is embedded in the given option figure.

44. *(b)* The question figure is embedded in the given option figure.

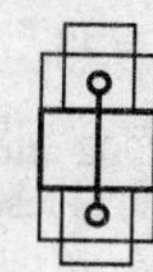

45. *(c)* The series follows the given pattern,

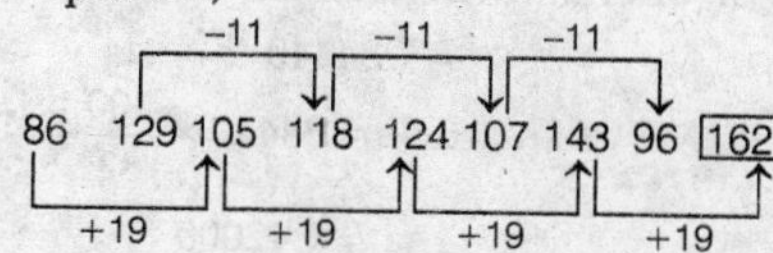

46. *(b)* The series follows the given pattern,

J →(+2) L →(+2) N →(+2) P →(+2) R →(+2) T
K →(−3) H →(−3) E →(−3) B →(−3) Y →(−3) V
L →(+4) P →(+4) T →(+4) X →(+4) B →(+4) F

47. *(b)* According to the question,

Future is bright = pl mk ni
bright shooting star = dg rz pl

∴ The code for 'bright' is 'pl'.

48. *(a)* After cutting and unfolding the paper, the below pattern appears,

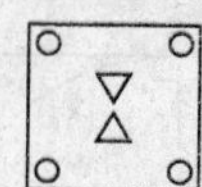

49. *(c)* The mirror image of the given question figure is as shown below,

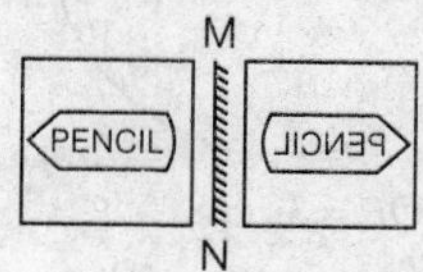

50. *(c)* The given equation,
222 A 2 C 7 B 3 D 11 = ?
After substituting the letters with symbols, we get
222 ÷ 2 + 7 × 3 − 11
= 111 + 7 × 3 − 11
= 111 + 21 − 11
= 132 − 11 = 121

51. *(c)* According to the question,

Years	2000	2001	2002	2003	2004
Incomes	60	60	40	50	30

We know,

Average

$$= \frac{\text{Sum of all the observations}}{\text{Total number of observations}}$$

∴ Required average

$$= \frac{60 + 60 + 40 + 50 + 30}{5}$$

$$= \frac{240}{5} = 48$$

∴ In 2 yr i.e., 2002 and 2004, income of the company, is less than the average income.

52. *(c)* Given,

SP after allowing discount of 18%

$= ₹\ 34440$

∴ MP of an article $= 34440 \times \frac{100}{82}$

$= ₹\ 42000$

As, Ramesh manages to earn a gain of 40%.

∴ CP of an article $= 34440 \times \frac{100}{140}$

$= ₹\ 24600$

Now, if discount of 12% is allowed on the marked price, then

SP of an article $= 42000 - \frac{12}{100} \times 42000$

$= ₹\ 36960$

∴ Actual profit % $= \frac{12360}{24600} \times 100$

$= 50.24\%$

53. *(b)*

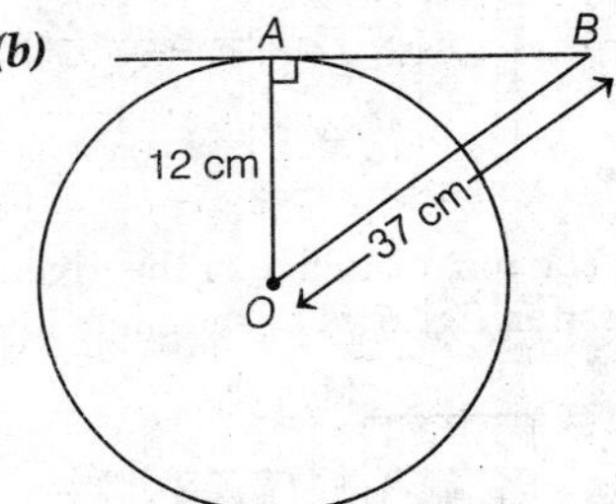

Given, $OB = 37$ cm

Diameter = 24 cm

∴ Radius $(OA) = 12$ cm

As we know,

Radius of circle is always perpendicular to the tangent.

∴ ΔOAB is a right-angled triangle.

In ΔOAB,

$$(AB)^2 = (OB)^2 - (OA)^2$$

$$= (37)^2 - (12)^2$$

$$= 1369 - 144 = 1225$$

∴ $AB = \sqrt{1225} = 35$ cm

54. *(d)* Given, $\sin\theta = \frac{7}{25}$

We know,

$$\cos\theta = \sqrt{1 - \sin^2\theta}$$

$$= \sqrt{1 - \left(\frac{7}{25}\right)^2} = \sqrt{1 - \frac{49}{625}}$$

$$= \sqrt{\frac{625 - 49}{625}}$$

$$\cos\theta = \sqrt{\frac{576}{625}} = \frac{24}{25}$$

As, $\tan\theta = \frac{\sin\theta}{\cos\theta} = \frac{\frac{7}{25}}{\frac{24}{25}} = \frac{7}{24}$

55. *(d)* Let the number of boys and girls be x and y, respectively.

We know,

Combined/weighted average

$$= \frac{n_1 a_1 + n_2 a_2}{n_1 + n_2}$$

According to the question,

Average $= \frac{70 \times x + 90 \times y}{x + y}$

$$\frac{70x + 90y}{x + y} = 75$$

$\Rightarrow$ $70x + 90y = 75x + 75y$

$\Rightarrow$ $5x = 15y$

$\Rightarrow$ $x = 3y$

∴ Required percentage

$$= \frac{x}{x + y} \times 100$$

$$= \frac{3y}{3y + y} \times 100$$

$$= \frac{3y}{4y} \times 100 = 75\%$$

56. *(c)* Let the selling price of 60 pens be ₹ $60x$.

∴ SP of 12 pens = ₹ $12x$ = Gain amount

∴ CP of 60 pens = SP – Profit

$= 60x - 12x = ₹\ 48x$

∴ Required gain percentage

$$= \frac{12x}{48x} \times 100 = 25\%$$

57. *(a)* Given equations,

$x + y = 10 \Rightarrow y = 10 - x$ ...(i)

$-3x + y = 2$ ...(ii)

Substitute Eq. (i) in Eq. (ii),

$-3x + (10 - x) = 2$

$\Rightarrow$ $-3x + 10 - x = 2$

$\Rightarrow$ $-4x + 10 = 2$

$\Rightarrow$ $4x = 8$

$\Rightarrow$ $x = 2$

From Eq. (i),

$y = 10 - 2 = 8$

Now, point of intersection of the line $x + y = 10$ and X-axis i.e., $(x, 0)$

∴ $x + 0 = 10$

$\Rightarrow$ $x = 10$

∴ Point of intersection = (10, 0)

Required distance between (2, 8) and (10, 0)

$$= \sqrt{(10 - 2)^2 + (0 - 8)^2}$$

$$= \sqrt{(8)^2 + (8)^2} = \sqrt{64 + 64}$$

$$= \sqrt{64 \times 2} = 8\sqrt{2}$$

58. *(d)* Given expression,

$(45 + 9) \div 2 - 7 \times 33 \div 7 + \{(7 + 18) \times 6\} + 9 \times 8 - 89$

Using BODMAS, we get

$$54 \div 2 - \frac{7 \times 33}{7} + \{25 \times 6\} + 72 - 89$$

$$= 27 - 33 + 150 - 17$$

$$= 177 - 50 = 127$$

59. *(a)* Let the amount invested be ₹ P.

Given, SI = ₹ 4050

Rate of interest $(R) = 9\%$

Time $(T) = 5$ yr

We know,

$$SI = \frac{P \times R \times T}{100}$$

$$4050 = \frac{P \times 9 \times 5}{100}$$

$\Rightarrow$ $P = \frac{4050 \times 100}{45}$

$= ₹\ 9000$

60. *(c)* Let engineers and skilled workers be denoted by E and W, respectively.

According to the question,

$$6E \times 5 = 5W \times 7$$

$\Rightarrow$ $\frac{E}{W} = \frac{7}{6}$

Let $E = 7k$, $W = 6k$

∴ Total work $= 6(7k) \times 5 = 210k$ units.

∴ Time taken by 7 engineers and 4 skilled workers

$$= \frac{210k}{7(7k) + 4(6k)}$$

$$= \frac{210k}{73k} = 2\frac{64}{73} \text{ days}$$

61. *(d)* Let total production in 2022 be x.
Given, total production in C_1 in 2022 $= 4125$

$\therefore$ 27.5% of $x = 4125$

$\Rightarrow x = 4125 \times \frac{100}{27.5} = 15000$

Let total production in 2019 and 2022 be $3k$ and $5k$, respectively.

$\therefore 5k = 15000$

$\Rightarrow k = 3000$

$\therefore$ Production in 2019

$= 3(3000) = 9000$

$\therefore$ Production of C_3 in 2019

$= \frac{17.5}{100} \times 9000 = 1575$

62. *(d)* Let the total distance be x km and time taken to cover this distance be t h.

According to the question,

Case I

Tanya's speed = 6 km/h

$\therefore t + \frac{2}{60} = \frac{x}{6}$

$\Rightarrow t = \frac{x}{6} - \frac{2}{60}$ ...(i)

Case II

Tanya's speed = 8 km/h

$t - \frac{3}{60} = \frac{x}{8}$

$\Rightarrow t = \frac{x}{8} + \frac{3}{60}$ ...(ii)

From Eqs. (i) and (ii),

$\frac{x}{6} - \frac{2}{60} = \frac{x}{8} + \frac{3}{60}$

$\Rightarrow \frac{x}{6} - \frac{x}{8} = \frac{5}{60}$

$\Rightarrow \frac{4x - 3x}{24} = \frac{5}{60}$

$\Rightarrow \frac{x}{24} = \frac{5}{60}$

$\therefore x = 2$ km

63. *(c)* Given,

Centre point = (– 1, 2, – 3)

Radius = 3 units

We know,

General form of equation of sphere is

$(x - a)^2 + (y - b)^2 + (z - c)^2 = (r)^2$

Here, $a = -1, b = 2, c = -3, r = 3$

$\therefore$ Required equation of sphere is

$[x - (-1)]^2 + (y - 2)^2 + [z - (-3)]^2 = (3)^2$

$\Rightarrow (x + 1)^2 + (y - 2)^2 + (z + 3)^2 = 9$

$\Rightarrow x^2 + 1 + 2x + y^2 + 4 - 4y + z^2 + 9 + 6z = 9$

$\Rightarrow x^2 + y^2 + z^2 + 2x - 4y + 6z + 14 - 9 = 0$

$\Rightarrow x^2 + y^2 + z^2 + 2x - 4y + 6z + 5 = 0$

64. *(a)*

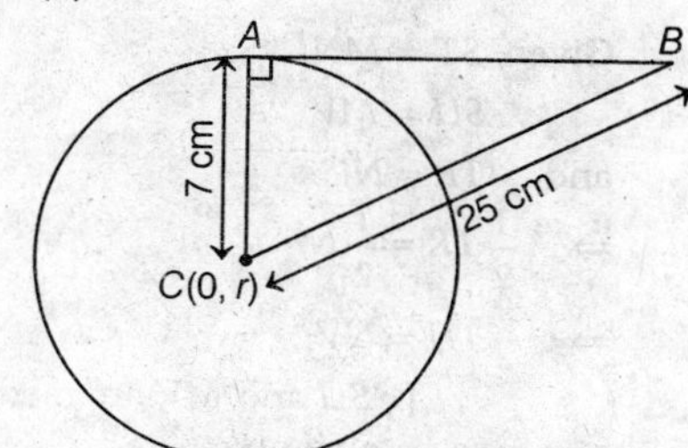

Let AB represents the tangent of a circle.

Given,

Radius (AC) = 7 cm

and BC = 25 cm

We know,

Radius of circle is perpendicular to the tangent of circle.

$\therefore \Delta ABC$ is a right-angled triangle.

In ΔABC,

$(AB)^2 = (BC)^2 - (AC)^2$

$= (25)^2 - (7)^2$

$= 625 - 49 = 576$

$\therefore AB = 24$ cm

65. *(a)* Given,

Initial salary = ₹ 200/day

New salary = ₹ 234/day

We know,

Percentage increase

$= \frac{\text{New salary} - \text{Initial salary}}{\text{Initial salary}} \times 100$

$= \frac{234 - 200}{200} \times 100 = 17\%$

66. *(c)* According to the question,

Arranging the percentage marks of Chemistry of all the students in ascending order, we get

35, 50, 60, 65, 65, 75, 80

As,

Number of observations = 7

$\therefore$ Median $= \left(\frac{n+1}{2}\right)$ th term

$= \left(\frac{7+1}{2}\right)$ th term

$= \left(\frac{8}{2}\right)$ th term

= 4 th term

$\therefore$ Required median $= \frac{65}{100} \times 130$

= 84.5 marks

67. *(d)* Given expression,

$\frac{5 + 7 \times 5 \div 8 \text{ of } 5 + 3 \div 3 \times 5}{6 \div 6 \text{ of } 4 + 9 \times 9 \div 3 \times 2 \times 2}$

$= \frac{5 + 7 \times 5 \div 40 + 3 \div 3 \times 5}{6 \div 24 + 9 \times 9 \div 3 \times 2 \times 2}$

$= \frac{5 + 7 \times \frac{5}{40} + \frac{3}{3} \times 5}{\frac{6}{24} + 9 \times \frac{9}{3} \times 2 \times 2}$

$= \frac{5 + \frac{7}{8} + 5}{\frac{1}{4} + 9 \times 3 \times 4}$

$= \frac{\frac{40 + 7 + 40}{8}}{\frac{433}{4}} = \frac{87 \times 4}{8(433)} = \frac{87}{866}$

68. *(a)* Given,

SP of car = ₹ 500000

As, car is sold at 20% less than its original price.

$\therefore$ Required CP of car

$= 500000 \times \frac{100}{80} =$ ₹ 625000

69. *(c)* Given,

Area of first face $(lb) = 120 \text{ cm}^2$ ...(i)

Area of second face $(bh) = 72 \text{ cm}^2$ ...(ii)

Area of third face $(hl) = 60 \text{ cm}^2$ ...(iii)

From Eqs. (i), (ii) and (iii), we get

$(lb)(bh)(hl) = 120 \times 72 \times 60$

$\therefore (lbh)^2 = 120 \times 72 \times 60$

$\Rightarrow lbh = \sqrt{120 \times 72 \times 60}$

$= \sqrt{518400}$

$\therefore$ Volume of cuboid = 720 cm^3

70. *(c)* Given,

Radius (r) of cone = 6 cm

Slant height (l) = 10 cm

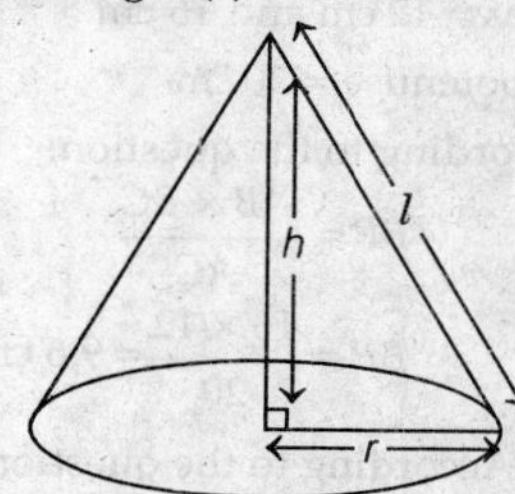

We know,

$\therefore$ Height $(h) = \sqrt{l^2 - r^2}$

$= \sqrt{(10)^2 - (6)^2}$

$= \sqrt{100 - 36} = \sqrt{64}$

$h = 8$ cm

As, volume of cone

$= \frac{1}{3}\pi r^2 h = \frac{1}{3} \times \pi \times (6)^2 \times 8$

$= 96\pi$ cm^3

71. *(a)* Given, $A : B = 5 : 8$

$B : C = 7 : 8$

According to the question,

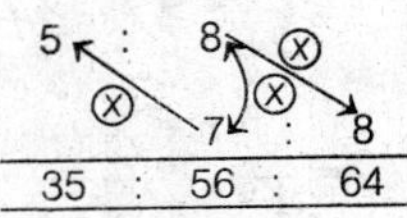

[**Note** Here, X denotes multiplication]

$\therefore$ Required ratio i.e., $A : C = 35 : 64$

72. *(c)* Let total number of votes polled be $100x$.

$\therefore$ Total number of votes that one of the candidates got

$= \frac{35}{100} \times 100x = 35x$

$\therefore$ Total number of votes that the other candidate got $= 100x - 35x = 65x$

According to the question,

$65x - 35x = 381$

$\Rightarrow \quad 30x = 381$

$\Rightarrow \quad 100x = \frac{381}{30} \times 100 = 1270$

73. *(b)*

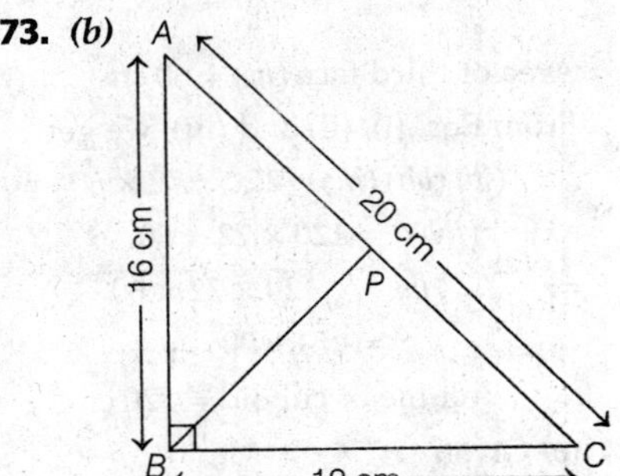

Given,

Sides = 12 cm and 16 cm

Hypotenuse = 20 cm

According to the question,

$BP = \frac{AB \times BC}{AC}$

$BP = \frac{16 \times 12}{20} = 9.6$ cm

74. *(d)* According to the question,

In 2016,

Proposals = 40%

Completed = 10%

$\therefore$ Required ratio = 40% : 10% = 4 : 1

75. *(a)*

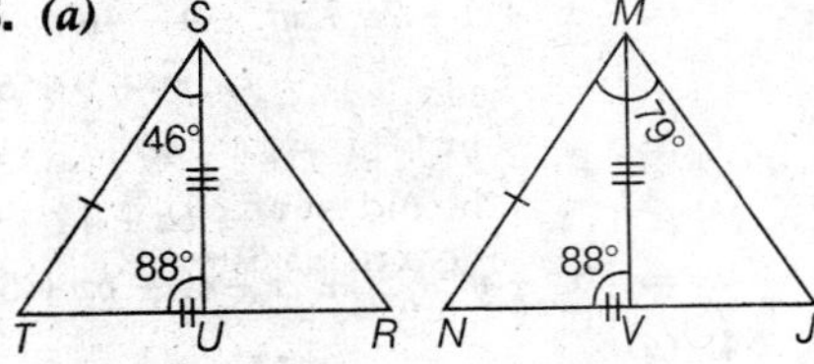

Given, $ST = MN$

$SU = MV$

and $TR = NJ$

$\Rightarrow \quad \frac{1}{2}TR = \frac{1}{2}NJ$

$\Rightarrow \quad TU = NV$

[$\because$ SU and MV are medians]

In ΔSUT and ΔMVN,

$ST = MN$ (Given)

$SU = MV$ (Given)

$TU = NV$ (Proved above)

$\therefore$ $\Delta SUT \cong \Delta MVN$ (SSS)

$\Rightarrow \quad \angle SUT = \angle MVN = 88°$

and $\angle VMJ = \angle USR = 33°$

[$\because \angle USR = 79° - 46° = 33°$]

$\therefore \quad \angle SUT = \angle USR + \angle SRU$

[Exterior angle property]

$\therefore \quad \angle SRU = \angle SRT$

$= 88° - 33° = 55°$

$\therefore$ Required value $= \frac{7}{11} \times 55° = 35°$

76. *(d)* Cholera is a food-borne disease caused by consuming contaminated food or water.

- Cholera is caused by the bacterium *vibrio cholerae.*
- Symptoms include abdominal pain, vomiting and watery diarrhea, which can lead to dehydration and death.

77. *(d)* Function key F5 can be pressed to initiate a slide show in MS PowerPoint.

78. *(d)* The Fundamental Right to Property has been deleted from original list of Fundamental Rights provided in the Constitution of India.

- The right to property was been removed from the list of Fundamental Rights in the Indian Constitution in 1978 by the 44th Amendment.
- The right to property was then converted into a legal right under Article 300A states that no person shall be deprived of his property save by authority of law.

Right to Freedom of Religion	Articles 25-28
Cultural and Educational Rights	Articles 29-30
Right to Constitutional Remedies	Article 32

79. *(d)* The approach driven by seven engines, which is powered by Clean Energy and 'Sabka Prayas' is related to PM Gati Shakti Master Plan.

- PM Gati Shakti Master Plan was presented in the Union Budget 2022-23 in Parliament. It is a revolutionary strategy for sustainable development and economic prosperity.
- The seven engines are roads, railways, airports, ports, mass transit, waterways and logistics infrastructure-power the strategy.

80. *(a)* Bilhana was a court poet of Vikramaditya VI.

- Kavi Bilhana was an 11th century Kashmiri poet, is known for his love poem, the 'Chaurisurata Panchashik'.
- Bilhan wrote a famous book called 'Vikramank Dev-Charit', in this book he wrote about the life and achievements of this famous king Vikramaditya VI.
- Vikramaditya VI is the greatest monarch of the Kalyani Chalukya dynasty.

81. *(a)* Manipur's Zeliangrong tribe celebrates the 'Gaan-Ngai' festival, which is a post-harvest festival of the tribe living in the regions of Manipur.

- Zeliangrong people are one of the major indigenous Naga communities living in the tri-junction of Assam, Manipur and Nagaland in India.
- The Zeliangrong celebrates the festival of Gaan-Ngai, to pay tribute to those who passed away.
- During the festival, people decorate the graves of the deceased with flowers, dance, and offer a feast to the dead.

82. *(d)* Heinrich Hertz, a German Physicist, confirmed James Clerk Maxwell's theories by discovering radio waves in 1887 and transmitting and receiving controlled radio waves in 1886.

Hertz's experiments marked the beginning of radio communication technology.

83. *(a)* Udey Chand was the first indian wrestler to win a world championship medal.

- He bagged a bronze in the men's freestyle 67 kg category at the 1961 world championships held in Yokohama, Japan.
- Sushil Kumar became India's first wrestling world champion in 2010
- Bajrang Punia has won the most medals (4) for the country in wrestling world champion.

84. *(c)* The personal income of the given data is 2050.

- Personal income is the total income received by individuals or households in a country during a financial year.
- Personal Income = National Income + transfer payment – Corporate tax

PI = 1800 + 500 – 250
= 2300 – 250 = 2050

85. *(a)* The correct matching is A-3, B-4, C-2, D-5.

NW-1	Allahabad-Haldia
NW-2	Sadiya-Dhubri
NW-3	Kottapuram-Kallam
NW-5	Talchar-Dhamra

- In 1986, the Government of India created the Inland Waterways Authority of India (WAI) for regulation and development of Inland Waterways for navigation and shipping.
- Its headquarters is in Noida, Uttar Pradesh.
- Kakinada-Puducherry is National Waterway (NW)-4.

86. *(a)* The Wild Life (Protection) Amendment Act, 2022 received the assent of the President on 19th December, 2022.

- The Wild Life (Protection) Amendment Act, 2022 amended the Wild Life Protection Act of 1972.
- The act seeks to increase the species protected under the law, and implement the Convention on International Trade in Endangered Species of Wild Fauna and Flora (CITES).

87. *(a)* Co-authoring excel feature allows you to simultaneously edit the same cell or range of cells with multiple users in real-time.

Co-authoring enhanced collaboration, reduce conflicts and improved productivity.

88. *(c)* Statement (c) is correct regarding Syama Sastri.

- Syama Sastri was a musician and composer of Carnatic music.
- He was the oldest among the trinity of Carnatic music, also known as the Three Jewels of Carnatic Music.
- It refers to the outstanding trio of composer-musicians of Carnatic music in the 18th century Tyagaraja, Muthuswami Dikshitar and Syama Sastri.

89. *(d)* Article 15 of the Constitution of India entails prohibition of discrimination against any citizen on grounds only of religion, race, caste, sex or place of birth.

- The Constitution of India was adopted by the Constituent Assembly on 26th November, 1949 and came into force on 26th January, 1950.
- The Constitution provides for a Parliamentary form of government which is federal in structure with certain unitary features.

Cultural and educational rights	Article 29 and Article 30
Equality of opportunity for all citizens in matters relating to employment or appointment	Article 16
Freedom of speech and expression	Article 19 (1)(a)

90. *(b)* Khilafat Movement was the campaign led by the Ali brothers and Maulana Abul Kalam Azad to save the Ottoman Caliphate as a symbol of unity among the Muslim community.

- It aimed to protest against British policies towards Turkey and the dismantling of the Ottoman empire after World War.
- The Khilafat Movement was supported by the Non-Cooperation Movement.
- The movement sought to address the grievances of Turkey and promote Hindu Muslim unity.

91. *(d)* Wheat was highly benefitted from Green Revolution.

- The Green Revolution was a period that began in the 1960's during which agriculture in India was converted into a modern industrial system by the adoption of technology.
- The use of High Yielding Variety (HYV) seeds, mechanised farm tools, irrigation facilities, pesticides and fertilisers were introduced.
- Dr. MS Swaminathan is known as the father of the Indian Green Revolution.

92. *(c)* 'Padam' is a love poem in Carnatic music.

- A 'Padam' is slow in tempo and grave in import, and it is usually treated as allegorical.
- The best-regarded Padams were written in Sanskrit and Telugu by Jayadeva (12th century) and Kshetrayya (17th century).
- Padams are also an important part of a Bharatanatyam.

93. *(d)* Leh airport is India's first carbon-neutral airport.

- It is located in the Leh district of Ladakh.
- The airport is Kushok Bakula Rimpochee Airport after the 13th Dalai Lama.
- It is one of the highest airports in the world at an elevation of 3,256 m (10,682 ft) above mean sea level.

94. *(a)* Kachin, Karen, Karenni, Chin and Mon ethnic groups belong to Myanmar. Kachin, Karen, Karenni, Chin and Mon are five of the seven ethnic minority groups in Myanmar.

- **Kachin** Known for their independence, craftsmanship, herbal healing, and complex clan relations. Most Kachin are Christian.
- **Karen** One of the five largest ethnic groups in Myanmar. During World War II, the Karen fought alongside the British and were promised an independent state in return.
- **Karenni** The most important celebration for Karenni people is Kay Htoe Bo, a festival that reflects the story of how the Earth came into being. During the festival, Karenni people dance around a pole to maintain good health.
- **Chin** Sino-Tibetan origin and live in the southernmost part of the mountain ranges separating Myanmar from India.
- **Mon** They are one of the oldest ethnic groups in Myanmar and South-East Asia, and are considered to have influenced the region's culture, language, architecture and religion.

95. *(b)* In the year 2021, under the Ministry of Corporate Affairs, amended rules related to Corporate Social Responsibility (CSR) were published.

- These rules provide amendments to the Companies (Corporate Social Responsibility Policy) Rules, 2014.
- The objective of amending the rules was to improve disclosures and simplify compliance, and to strengthen the CSR ecosystem.

96. *(c)* A flat ring of small, icy bodies that revolve around the Sun beyond the orbit of the planet Neptune is called Kuiper Belt.

- The Kuiper Belt is a doughnut-shaped region.
- Asteroid Belt is a torus-shaped region of space in our solar system that contains millions of asteroids orbiting the Sun between the orbits of Mars and Jupiter.
- Bow Shock is a curved shock wave that forms when a supersonic object causes material in a medium to compress, heat up and pile up.
- Oort Cloud is a theoretical spherical shell of icy objects that surrounds our solar system, extending far beyond Pluto and the Kuiper Belt.

97. *(c)* The bowler does not get credit for run out.

- In run out, the credit is given to the 'primary' fielder who gathers the ball and either puts down the wicket or makes the ball available for another player to do so.
- **Bowled** A batter is out bowled if his or her wicket is put down by a ball delivered by the bowler.
- **LBW** stands for 'Leg Before Wicket'. The umpire may rule a batter out LBW if the ball would have hit the wicket but was instead blocked by any part of the batsman's body, except their hands.
- **Catch** A batsman is out caught if the batsman hits the ball, from a legitimate delivery, with the bat, and the ball is caught by the bowler or a fielder before it hits the ground.

98. *(c)* Chilika Lake is located to the South of the Mahanadi delta in the state of Odisha, India.

- The lake is situated at the mouth of the Daya river, a tributary of the Mahanadi.
- Chilika Lake is Asia's largest lagoon.
- It is India's largest saltwater lake and brackish water coastal lake.

99. *(b)* Mohiniyattam is a classical dance form of Kerala.

- This dance is based on the Hindu myth of Mohini, the female avatar of Vishnu, and often reflects themes of love and devotion.
- Mohiniyattam is known for its graceful movements, expressive facial expressions, and elaborate costumes.
- It's one of the eight classical dances of India recognised by the Sangeet Natak Akademi.

100. *(d)* The Board of Control for Cricket in India (BCCI) was set-up on 4th December, 1928 at Madras.

- The Board of Control for Cricket in India (BCCI) is the principal national governing body of cricket in India.
- Its headquarters is situated in Mumbai.
- The BCCI is involved in talent development through grassroots programs and cricket academies.
- As of July 2024, Roger Binny is the President of BCCI.

Set 28 09 July, 2024 (Shift IV)

SSC CHSL Tier-I
SOLVED PAPER

Instructions

1. This paper contains 100 questions.
2. It has 4 Parts, **Part I** General English, **Part II** General Intelligence & Reasoning, **Part III** Quantitative Aptitude and **Part IV** General Awareness.
3. Each question carries **2 marks.**

Part I
General English

1. The given sentence is divided into four segments. Identify the segment that contains a grammatical error.

A great / culture of hospitality of / the Spanish / is well-known.

(a) the Spanish
(b) culture of hospitality of
(c) A great
(d) is well-known

2. The following sentence has been split into four segments. Identify the segment that contains a grammatical error.

After a while, / she look up / and saw that / it was getting dark.

(a) and saw that
(b) it was getting dark
(c) she look up
(d) After a while

3. Parts of the following sentence have been given as options. Select the option that contains an error.

There was an gang of thieves spotted at our local bank, make sure to be careful.

(a) at our local bank
(b) make sure to be careful
(c) There was an gang
(d) of thieves spotted

4. Select the option that will improve the given sentence by using the most appropriate verb.

Alexa have being working as a teacher for five years now.

(a) Alexa has been working as a teacher for five years now.
(b) Alexa has being working as a teacher for five years now.
(c) Alexa is being working as a teacher for five years now.
(d) Alexa was been working as a teacher for five years now.

Directions (Q. Nos. 5-9) *In the following passage, some words have been deleted. Read the passage carefully and select the most appropriate option to fill in each blank.*

How does a camel survive in the desert? Many people think that the camel stores water in its hump, but the hump is really made up of fats. When a camel (1) .... find water, it passes less urine to conserve (2) .... small amount of water it has in its body. Furthermore, the camel has a higher body temperature than (3) .... of most mammals. This means that it starts to sweat (4) .... a higher temperature than that which human beings, for example, (5) .... to perspire. This also helps it to keep water loss through sweating to a minimal.

5. Select the most appropriate option to fill in blank number (1).

(a) do not (b) cannot
(c) hasn't (d) can

6. Select the most appropriate option to fill in blank number (2).

(a) the (b) which
(c) a (d) very

7. Select the most appropriate option to fill in blank number (3).

(a) some (b) the
(c) that (d) all

8. Select the most appropriate option to fill in blank number (4).

(a) in (b) with
(c) at (d) for

9. Select the most appropriate option to fill in blank number (5).

(a) started (b) start
(c) starting (d) starts

10. Select the most appropriate option to substitute the underlined segment in the given sentence.

Shantanu always <u>buries his head in the sand</u> whenever he explains his professional failures to his father.

(a) hides from the truth
(b) shows a blind eye against social issues
(c) escapes from all the difficulties
(d) blames the others for his mistakes

11. Select the most appropriate option to fill in the blank.

The cat's entry into the store room was ....

(a) quite (b) quiet
(c) cute (d) quit

12. Select the most appropriate option to fill in the blank.

The .... of the whale is 2 tonnes.

(a) wait (b) weight
(c) vet (d) wet

13. Select the most appropriate option that can substitute the underlined segment in the given sentence.

Grasslands should not be <u>foraged and some places are to be</u> closed for grazing.

(a) over-grazed and some areas should be
(b) cut and few areas
(c) grazed and some places is
(d) planted or

14. Select the most appropriate option that can substitute the underlined segment in the given sentence.

Things that do not come from the ground <u>not safe</u> to compost.

(a) has not been safe
(b) are not safe
(c) is not safe
(d) be not safe

15. Select the most appropriate meaning of the underlined idiom in the given sentence.

He got medals <u>time after time</u> by following the instructions of his mentor.

(a) Repeatedly (b) Twice
(c) Rarely (d) Once

16. Select the most appropriate option that can substitute the underlined segment in the given sentence. If there is no need to substitute it, select 'No substitution required'.

I quietly went out <u>at</u> the door into the veranda.

(a) No substitution required
(b) by
(c) through
(d) from

17. Select the option with the correct spelling to replace the underlined word in the given sentence.

A natural <u>clamity</u> causing huge destruction and loss of life and property.

(a) calamity (b) clamanity
(c) calamitey (d) climanity

18. Select the most appropriate antonym of the underlined word.

We should not run after <u>transient</u> pleasures of the world.

(a) unnatural (b) sinful
(c) permanent (d) joyful

19. Select the most appropriate synonym of the given word.

Luminous

(a) Radiant (b) Laborious
(c) Luxurious (d) Amiable

20. Select the most appropriate option that can substitute the underlined word in the given sentence.

Modest stores and welcoming residents populated the <u>charming</u> tiny town.

(a) delightful (b) unpleasant
(c) hideous (d) nasty

21. Select the incorrectly spelt word in the given sentence.

King Zheng is known to lead an army of a million armoured soldiers, a thousand chariots and ten thousand horses in his misssion to conquer the neighbouring kingdoms.

(a) Misssion (b) Kingdoms
(c) Chariots (d) Thousand

22. Fill in the blank with the most appropriate antonym of the underlined word.

In spring the leaves are <u>bright</u> green, whereas they appear .... in autumn.

(a) gleaming (b) luminous
(c) dazzling (d) dull

23. Select the most appropriate option to fill in the blank.

It is the .... to reach Delhi.

(a) lowest route
(b) strongest route
(c) quickest route
(d) fastest route

24. Identify the most appropriate antonym of the underlined word in the following sentence.

Harry's behaviour was very <u>blunt</u> during his school days.

(a) excited (b) polite
(c) dull (d) curious

25. Select the most appropriate synonym of the given word.

Rectify

(a) Connect (b) Consider
(c) Correct (d) Count

Part II

General Intelligence

26. What will come in the place of the question mark (?) in the following equation, if '+' and '−' are interchanged and '×' and '÷' are interchanged?

$16 \div 5 - 24 \times 6 + 3 = ?$

(a) 82 (b) 85
(c) 80 (d) 81

27. How many rectangles are there in the given figure?

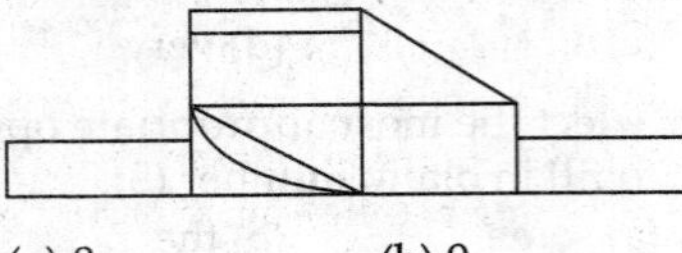

(a) 8 (b) 9
(c) 10 (d) 11

28. What will come in the place of the question mark (?) in the following equation, if '+' and '−' are interchanged and '×' and '÷' are interchanged?

$14 - 15 \div 2 + 56 \times 14 = ?$

(a) 40 (b) 35
(c) 45 (d) 30

29. What should come in place of the question mark (?) in the given series based on the English alphabetical order?

CEG, FHJ, IKM, LNP, ?

(a) OQS (b) QTV
(c) OQR (d) QRS

30. What should come in place of the question mark (?) in the given series based on the English alphabetical order?

RPM, USP, XVS, AYV, ?

(a) BDY (b) DYB
(c) BYD (d) DBY

31. In a certain code language, 'BACK' is coded as '4162' and 'CAB' is coded as '214'. What is the code for 'K' in that language?

(a) 2 (b) 1
(c) 4 (d) 6

32. Six letters A, R, T, W, Y and Z are written on different faces of a dice. Two positions of this dice are shown in the figure. Which is the letter on the face opposite to the face containing A?

(a) Z (b) W
(c) Y (d) R

33. If 10 days before was a Sunday and 6 days after would be a Tuesday, then what day is it today?

(a) Wednesday
(b) Monday
(c) Friday
(d) Tuesday

34. The position of how many letters will remain unchanged if each of the letters in the word WANDERLUST is arranged from left to right in alphabetical order?

(a) Three (b) One
(c) None (d) Two

35. Select the correct mirror image of the given figure when the mirror is placed at MN as shown below.

M WPQJK2GE N

(a) ʍbꝊ٦KƧGE
(b) ʍdꝊ ٦ꓘ ƧGE
(c) ʍbꝊſK2GE
(d) ƎƏƧꓘႱꝹꟼW

36. In a certain code language, 'time and again' is coded as 'zx df mo' and 'value your time' is coded as 'df pn tv'. How is 'time' coded in the given language?
(a) mo
(b) df
(c) tv
(d) zx

37. What will come in the place of the question mark (?) in the following equation, if '+' and '–' are interchanged and '×' and '÷' are interchanged?
$15 \div 4 - 128 + 123 \times 3 = ?$
(a) 187
(b) 147
(c) 167
(d) 127

38. Read the given statements and conclusions carefully. Assuming that the information given in the statements is true, even if it appears to be at variance with commonly known facts, decide which of the given conclusions logically follow(s) from the statements.

Statements
Some sweaters are jackets.
Some jackets are pullovers.
No pullover is a glove.

Conclusions
I. No jacket is a glove.
II. Some sweaters are pullovers.
(a) Only Conclusion I follows
(b) Only Conclusion II follows
(c) None of the conclusions follow
(d) Both Conclusions I and II follow

39. Select the word-pair that best represents a similar relationship to the one expressed in the pair of words given below.
(The words must be considered as meaningful English words and must not be related to each other based on the number of letters/number of consonants/vowels in the word.)
Referee : Field
(a) Arbitrator : Deadlock
(b) Judge : Courtroom
(c) Experimenter : Result
(d) Gladiator : Ring

40. Select the option figure in which the given figure (X) is embedded as its part (rotation is not allowed).

(X)

(a) 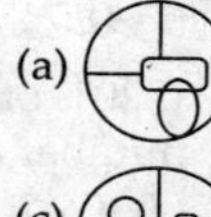 (b) 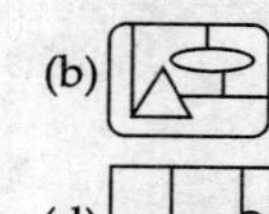

(c) (d)

41. 33 is related to 726 by certain logic. Following the same logic, 43 is related to 946. To which of the following is 53 related, following the same logic?
(**Note** Operations should be performed on the whole numbers, without breaking down the numbers into its constituent digits. E.g. 13 – Operations on 13 such as adding/subtracting/multiplying etc. to 13 can be performed. Breaking down 13 into 1 and 3 and then performing mathematical operations on 1 and 3 is not allowed.)
(a) 846 (b) 980
(c) 1060 (d) 1166

42. Select the correct mirror image of the given combination when the mirror is placed at MN as shown below.

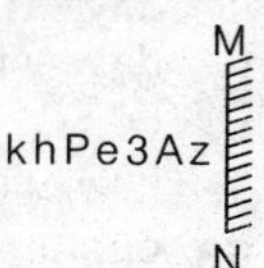

(a) zAƐeꟼhꓘ (b) ꓘhꟼeƐAz
(c) zƐAePhꓘ (d) zAƐeꟼdk

43. Select the set in which the numbers are related in the same way as are the numbers of the following sets.
(**Note** Operations should be performed on the whole numbers, without breaking down the numbers into its constituent digits. E.g. 13 – Operations on 13 such as adding/deleting/ multiplying etc. to 13 can be performed. Breaking down 13 into 1 and 3 and then performing mathematical operations on 1 and 3 is not allowed.)
(6, 12, 72)
(8, 16, 96)
(a) (7, 28, 144) (b) (12, 24, 140)
(c) (12, 24, 144) (d) (11, 24, 144)

44. 'T + W' means 'T is the father of W'
'T – W' means 'T is the wife of W'
'T × W' means 'T is the brother of W'
'T ÷ W' means 'T is the daughter of W'.
What does 'S + T ÷ U' mean?
(a) S is the husband of U
(b) S is the uncle of U
(c) S is the son of U
(d) S is the brother of U

45. Which of the following numbers will replace the question mark (?) in the given series?
112, 113, 122, 147, 196, ?
(a) 282 (b) 277
(c) 294 (d) 253

46. What should come in place of the question mark (?) in the given series?
3, 7, 15, 31, 63, ?
(a) 125 (b) 126
(c) 127 (d) 128

47. Select the option figure in which the given figure (X) is embedded as its part (rotation is not allowed).

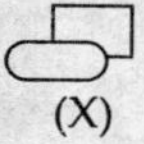
(X)

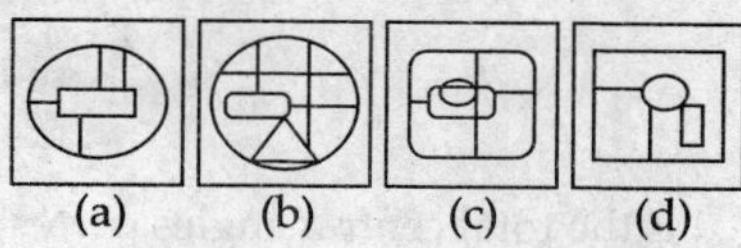
(a) (b) (c) (d)

48. Based on the alphabetical order, three of the following four letter-clusters are alike in a certain way and thus form a group. Which letter-cluster does not belong to that group?
(**Note** The odd one out is not based on the number of consonants/ vowels or their position in the letter cluster.)
(a) PRT (b) TVY (c) RTV (d) HJL

49. DFIK is related to EGJL in a certain way based on the English alphabetical order. In the same way, GILN is related to HJMO. To which of the following is MORT related to, following the same logic?
(a) NQSU
(b) NPSV
(c) NPVS
(d) NPSU

50. Identify the figure in the options that when put in place of the question mark (?) will logically complete the series?

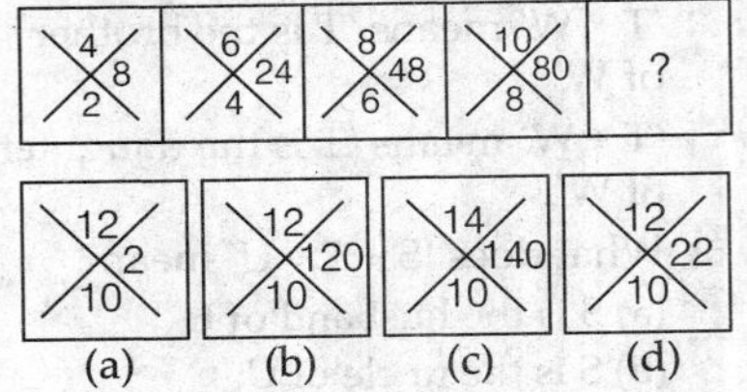

Part III

Quantitative Aptitude

51. Find the number of paper balls, each 2 cm in diameter, that can be made from a sphere of diameter 18 cm.
(a) 1020 (b) 625 (c) 729 (d) 484

52. A shopkeeper sells an item at 20% discount on the marked price and earns a profit of 90%. If he sells the same item at 40% discount, then his new profit percentage will be
(a) 48.2% (b) 45.8% (c) 41.8% (d) 42.5%

53. Study the following pie-chart carefully and answer the given question. The pie-chart represents the marks obtained by Sanya in different subjects in class 12. Total marks scored by her in class 12 was 450.

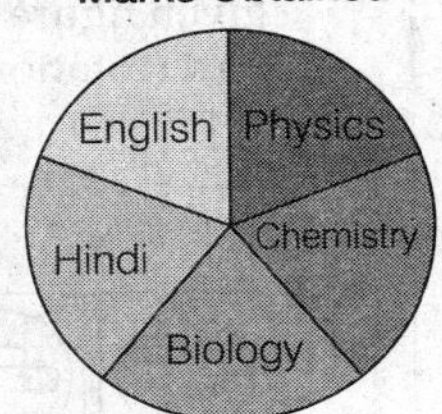

If the total central angles corresponding to the pair of subjects (Physics and Hindi), (Chemistry and Physics) and (Hindi and Chemistry) were 156°, 144° and 140°, respectively, then find the total marks obtained by her in (English and Biology).
(a) 175 (b) 160 (c) 180 (d) 190

54. Study the given pie-charts and answer the question that follows.

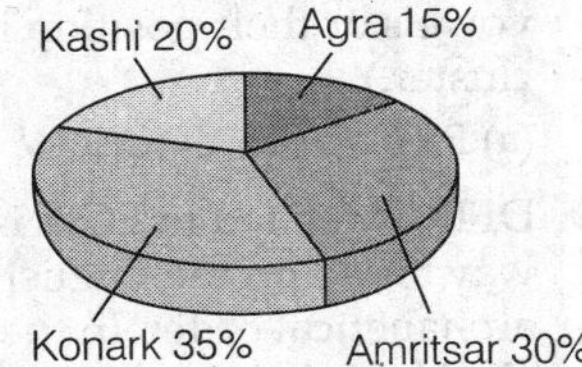

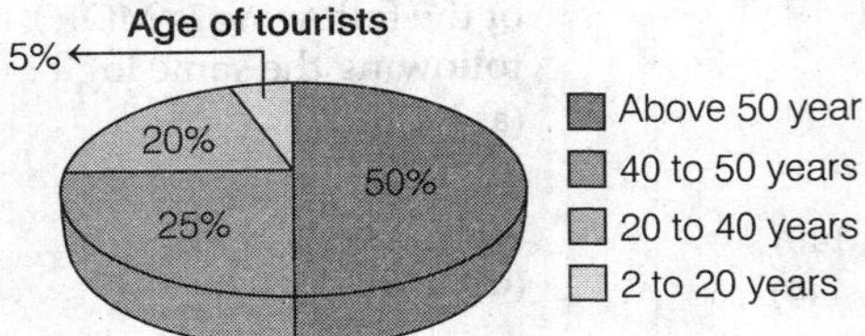

If A = Percentage of tourists who went to Agra, Amritsar and Kashi, and B = percentage of tourists whose age lies between 2 yr to 50 yr, then what is $A : B$?
(a) 10:7 (b) 10:13 (c) 13:10 (d) 11:13

55. If 20% of 35% of a number is 240.8, then 18% of that number (rounded off to 1 decimal place) is
(a) 619.2 (b) 618.2
(c) 621.2 (d) 623.2

56. The following bar graph represents the percentage marks obtained in grade 9, 10, 11 and 12 students in Economics, English and History. Study the given bar graph carefully and answer the question that follows.

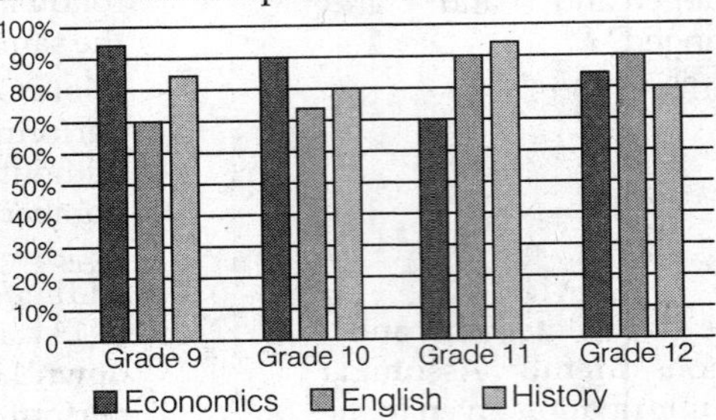

If the full marks in Economics is 100, English is 80 and History is 50, then find the total marks obtained by grade 10 students.
(a) 190 (b) 220
(c) 200 (d) 245

57. A can finish a piece of work by working alone in 4 days. B, while working alone, can finish the same work in 12 days. If both of them work together, then in how many days will the work be completed?
(a) 8 (b) 6
(c) 3 (d) 4

58. Simplify the following expression.
$11\frac{1}{4} \div 3\frac{3}{5} \times 6\frac{2}{3} + \frac{1}{6} = \ldots\ldots\ldots$
(a) 23 (b) 21
(c) 25 (d) 19

59. In a circle with center O, the diameter AB extended to the point C, outside the circle. CD is a tangent at the point D on the circle. If the radius of circle is 6 cm and $\angle DBC = 120°$, then the length of CD is equal to
(a) $5\sqrt{3}$ cm (b) $3\sqrt{3}$ cm
(c) $6\sqrt{3}$ cm (d) $4\sqrt{3}$ cm

60. In a class with a certain number of students, if one student weighing 30 kg is added, then the average weight of the class increases by 1 kg. If one more student weighing 30 kg is added, then the average weight of the class increases by 1.5 kg over the original average. What is the original average weight (in kg) of the class?
(a) 27 (b) 26.5
(c) 25.5 (d) 24

61. What is the maximum value of $7\cos A + 24\sin A + 32$?
(a) 57 (b) 32
(c) 25 (d) 39

62. The given table shows the percentage of marks obtained by 5 students in different subjects. Study the table and answer the question that follows. (Maximum marks are given beside subject).

Subjects →	Physics	Maths	Music	Hindi	Botany
Students ↓	300	300	100	100	200
Ram	60	80	90	60	95
Shyam	90	70	80	70	40
Sohan	70	90	95	80	75
Mohan	80	60	70	95	80
Karn	90	50	85	85	80

The marks obtained by Ram in Botany are less/more than Karn's marks in Botany by how much?

(a) 25 less (b) 30 more (c) 25 more (d) 30 less

63. The speed of a thief is $\frac{4}{5}$ times the speed of a policeman. The thief covers a distance of 6 km before he was caught by the policeman in 30 min. Initially, what was the distance between the policeman and the thief (in km)?

(a) 0.8 (b) 1.0 (c) 1.5 (d) 1.2

64. After decreasing 30%, an article costs ₹ 3500. Find its actual cost.

(a) ₹ 4500 (b) ₹ 6500 (c) ₹ 5000 (d) ₹ 5500

65. A metallic sphere of volume 3136π cm^3 is melted and then, recast into smaller cones, each of radius 3.5 cm and height 4 cm. How many cones are obtained?

(a) 148 (b) 192 (c) 196 (d) 172

66. In the diagram, if $\overline{AB} \parallel \overline{CE}$, $AG = GD = DH = HB$, then which of the following is correct?

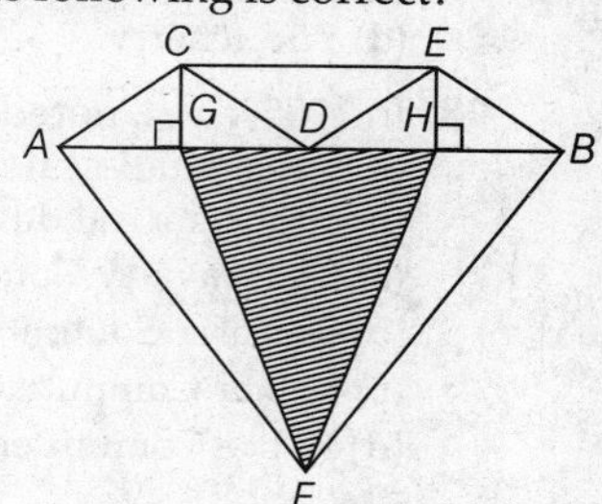

I. $\Delta ACG \cong \Delta BEH$

II. $\Delta CDE \cong \Delta DEB \cong \Delta DCA$

III. $\Delta HFB \cong \Delta AFG$

(a) I and III (b) I and II (c) I, II and III (d) Only I

67. Simplify

$$\left[6-2\left\{3-4\left(4\div\frac{1}{4}-1\right)+2\div\frac{1}{3}\right\}-3\times 2\right]$$

(a) 102 (b) 98 (c) 96 (d) 92

68. If three sides of a triangle are 6 cm, 8 cm and 10 cm, then the area of the triangle is

(a) 30 cm^2 (b) $12\sqrt{3}$ cm^2 (c) 24 cm^2 (d) $24\sqrt{3}$ cm^2

69. Study the given pie-chart and answer the question that follows.

The pie-chart shows the monthly expenditure incurred by a family on various items and their savings.

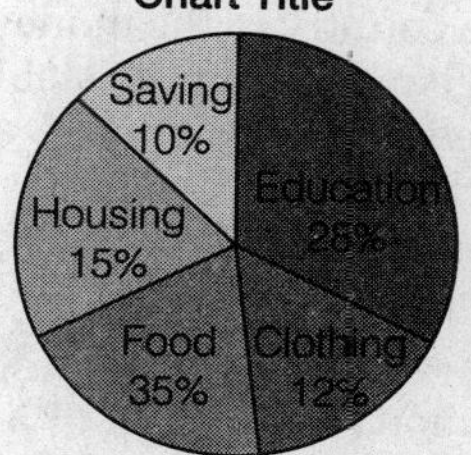

If the total expenditure on education is ₹23520, then what is the expenditure on clothing (in ₹)?

(a) 10000 (b) 10080
(c) 12300 (d) 11000

70. By selling 22 items, Rohit gains the selling price of 6 items. His gain per cent is

(a) $37\frac{1}{2}\%$ (b) $37\frac{1}{3}\%$
(c) $33\frac{1}{2}\%$ (d) $33\frac{1}{3}\%$

71. The price of an electronic watch is first reduced by 25% and then increased by 50%. If the resulting price of the electronic watch is ₹ 7650, then what was its original price (in ₹)?

(a) 6900 (b) 6500
(c) 6600 (d) 6800

72. By decreasing 17° from each angle of a triangle, the ratio of their angles is 3 : 4 : 7. The radian measure of the greatest angle is

(a) $\frac{153\pi}{360}$ (b) $\frac{167\pi}{180}$
(c) $\frac{163\pi}{360}$ (d) $\frac{163\pi}{180}$

73. The lengths of the three sides of a triangle are 19 cm, 25 cm and y cm. Which of the following options most accurately gives the possible values of 'y'?

(a) $6 \le y < 44$ (b) $6 < y < 44$
(c) $6 \le y \le 44$ (d) $6 < y \le 44$

74. The strength of a school is 640, with the number of boys being 400. Find the ratio of girls to boys.

(a) 8 : 5 (b) 5 : 6
(c) 4 : 5 (d) 3 : 5

75. What will be the amount due on ₹ 36000 in 2 yr when the rate of simple interest for successive years is 8% and 6%, respectively?

(a) ₹ 38880
(b) ₹ 40320
(c) ₹ 41760
(d) ₹ 41040

Part IV

General Awareness

76. Intervention by the monetary authority of a country in the money market to keep money supply stable against exogenous or sometimes external shocks is called ....
(a) Sterilisation
(b) Capitalisation
(c) Conservation
(d) Neutralisation

77. In PPT, what method can be used to move among slides if your hands are already on the keyboard?
(a) Pressing the Esc key to exit the presentation
(b) Using the keyboard directional keys
(c) Scrolling with the mouse wheel
(d) Clicking on the slide thumbnail in the Slides tab

78. What was the name of the person who has been elected as the Chair of the 62nd session of the United Nations Commission for Social Development?
(a) Ruchira Kamboj
(b) Satinder Kumar Lambah
(c) BM Vinod Kumar
(d) Nirupama Menon Rao

79. Which of the following is not an Olympics sport? (As of March, 2023)
(a) Cricket
(b) Rowing
(c) Sailing
(d) 3 × 3 Basketball

80. According to Census 2011, India's population accounts .... of the world's population.
(a) 20% (b) 15% (c) 10% (d) 17.5%

81. Jharkhand and Chhattisgarh states are rich with .... material deposits.
(a) gold (b) silicon
(c) petroleum (d) coal

82. Fundamental Duties were introduced in Part IVA of the Constitution by the
(a) Forty-third Amendment Act, 1977
(b) Forty-first Amendment Act, 1976
(c) Forty-second Amendment Act, 1976
(d) Forty-fourth Amendment Act, 1978

83. How does the CPU distinguish between each memory cell?
(a) By its address (b) By its data item
(c) By its capacity (d) By its byte size

84. The Big Dipper is an asterism formed by the seven brightest stars in the constellation
(a) Ursa Major (b) Orion
(c) Cassiopeia (d) Leo Major

85. Aajeevika - National Rural Livelihoods Mission (NRLM) - was launched by the Ministry of Rural Development (MoRD), Government of India, in the year ....
(a) 2013 (b) 2010 (c) 2012 (d) 2011

86. Baiga is a folk music of Baiga tribe from which of the following states?
(a) Uttarakhand
(b) Assam
(c) Bihar
(d) Madhya Pradesh

87. The cell wall of bacteria is made up of
(a) peptidoglycan (b) cellulose
(c) glycogen (d) peptone

88. Which of the following articles of the Indian Constitution are related to Fundamental Rights?
(a) 14-32 (b) 32-51
(c) 12-35 (d) 12-36

89. According to rules laid down by the International Football Association Board (IFAB), what can be the maximum length of a goal line in football?
(a) 90 m (b) 100 m (c) 40 m (d) 50 m

90. What kind of a satellite is CMS-01, that was launched by ISRO in December, 2020?
(a) Navigation
(b) Resource management
(c) Tsunami observation
(d) Communication

91. Shattantri Veena, meaning a Veena with hundred strings, is the ancient Sanskrit name of which instrument?
(a) Tambura/Tanpura (b) Sarangi
(c) Sarod (d) Santoor

92. Which party won the Jalandhar (a city in Punjab) Lok Sabha by poll election held in May, 2023?
(a) Indian National Congress
(b) Akali Dal
(c) Aam Aadmi Party
(d) Bharatiya Janata Party

93. Which of the following dates is observed as a National Festival?
(a) 24th October (b) 25th October
(c) 2nd October (d) 10th October

94. Milk of magnesia is a suspension of .... in water.
(a) magnesium oxalate
(b) magnesium hydroxide
(c) magnesium chlorate
(d) magnesium bromide

95. Warren Hastings became the Governor-General of Bengal from Governor of Bengal after the passing of which of the following acts?
(a) Indian Council Act of 1861
(b) Pitt's India Act, 1784
(c) Regulating Act, 1773
(d) Charter Act, 1813

96. In a test match, the captain of the fielding side may demand a new ball after ....
(a) 85 overs (b) 80 overs
(c) 70 overs (d) 75 overs

97. Rouf is the traditional dance of ...., which is practiced on the festive occasions of Eid and during Ramzan days.
(a) Jammu and Kashmir
(b) Chandigarh
(c) Leh
(d) Puducherry

98. In 1955, ... noted the possibility of using small-scale industries for promoting rural development.
(a) Chakravarty Committee
(b) Sarkaria Committee
(c) Kelkar Committee
(d) Karve Committee

99. The Union Cabinet, in August 2022, approved the enhancement in the limit of Emergency Credit Line Guarantee Scheme (ECLGS) by .... , with the additional amount being earmarked exclusively for enterprises in hospitality and related sectors.
(a) ₹10,000 crore (b) ₹50,000 crore
(c) ₹60,000 crore (d) ₹30,000 crore

100. Who amongst the following Mughal emperors got classical Hindu mythological texts 'Ramayana' and 'Mahabharata' translated into Persian?
(a) Jahangir (b) Aurangzeb
(c) Akbar (d) Shahjahan

Answers

1. (c)	2. (c)	3. (c)	4. (a)
5. (b)	6. (a)	7. (c)	8. (c)
9. (b)	10. (a)	11. (b)	12. (b)
13. (a)	14 (b)	15. (a)	16. (c)
17. (a)	18. (c)	19. (a)	20. (a)
21. (a)	22. (d)	23. (d)	24. (b)
25. (c)	26. (d)	27. (c)	28. (a)
29. (a)	30. (d)	31. (d)	32. (c)
33. (a)	34. (b)	35. (a)	36. (b)
37. (b)	38. (c)	39. (b)	40. (d)
41. (d)	42. (a)	43. (c)	44. (a)
45. (b)	46. (c)	47. (b)	48. (b)
49. (d)	50. (b)	51. (c)	52. (d)
53. (a)	54. (c)	55. (a)	56. (a)
57. (c)	58. (b)	59. (c)	60. (a)
61. (a)	62. (b)	63. (c)	64. (c)
65. (b)	66. (b)	67. (a)	68. (c)
69. (b)	70. (a)	71. (d)	72. (c)
73. (b)	74. (d)	75. (d)	76. (a)
77. (b)	78. (a)	79. (a)	80. (d)
81. (d)	82. (c)	83. (a)	84. (a)
85. (d)	86. (d)	87. (a)	88. (c)
89. (a)	90. (d)	91. (d)	92. (c)
93. (c)	94. (b)	95. (c)	96. (b)
97. (a)	98. (d)	99. (b)	100. (c)

Explanations

1. *(c)* Part (c) 'A great' contains an error. Use 'the' correct the sentence.

2. *(c)* Part (c) 'she look up' contains an error. Use 'looked' to correct the sentence as the sentence is in past tense.

3. *(c)* Part (c) 'There was an gang' contains an error. Use 'a' to correct the sentence.

4. *(a)* The given sentence has an error of subject verb agreement. As singular subject takes a singular verb, the correct sentence would be- Alexa has been working as a teacher for five years now.

5. *(b)* The correct filler for the given blank is 'cannot'.

6. *(a)* The correct filler for the given blank is 'the'.

7. *(c)* The correct filler for the given blank is 'that'.

8. *(c)* The correct filler for the given blank is 'at'.

9. *(b)* The correct filler for the given blank is 'start'.

10. *(a)* Buries his head in the sand means hides from the truth.

11. *(b)* The correct filler for the given blank is 'quiet'.

12. *(b)* The correct filler for the given blank is 'weight'.

13. *(a)* The underlined part of the given sentence contains an error. Use 'over-grazed and some areas should be' to correct the sentence.

14. *(b)* The underlined part of the given sentence contains an error. Use 'are not safe" to correct the sentence.

15. *(a)* The underlined part of the given sentence contains an error. Use 'repeatedly' to correct the sentence.

16. *(c)* The underlined part of the given sentence contains an error. Use 'through' to correct the sentence.

17. *(a)* The correct spelling is 'calamity'.

18. *(c)* 'Transient' means temporary. Hence, its antonym is 'permanent'.

19. *(a)* The word 'Luminous' means giving off light; bright or shining. Hence, its synonym is 'Radiant'.

- 'Laborious' means requiring hard work.
- 'Luxurious' means rich and wealthy.
- 'Amiable' means friendly.

20. *(a)* The word 'charming' means 'attractive, pleasant and delightful'.

21. *(a)* The incorrectly spelt word is 'Misssion'. The correct spelling is 'Mission'.

22. *(d)* The correct filler for the given blank is 'dull'.

23. *(d)* The correct filler for the given blank is 'fastest route'.

24. *(b)* 'Blunt' means rude. Hence, its antonym is 'polite'.

25. *(c)* The word 'rectify' means 'to correct a mistake'.

26. *(d)* Given expression,

$16 \div 5 - 24 \times 6 + 3 = ?$

After interchanging + and –, × and ÷, we get

$\Rightarrow \quad 16 \times 5 + 24 \div 6 - 3 = ?$

$\Rightarrow \quad 80 + 4 - 3 = ?$

$\therefore \quad ? = 81$

27. *(c)* Naming the figure,

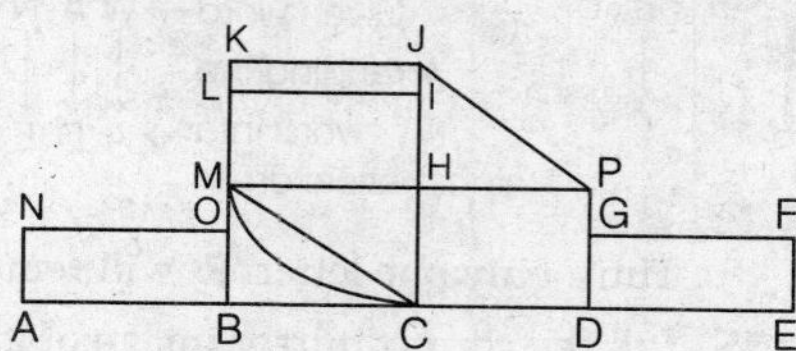

Rectangles can be represented as, ANOB, BMHC, CHPD, DGFE, MLIH, LKJI, MKJH, BLIC, BKJC, BMPD

Hence, total 10 rectangles are present in given figure.

28. *(a)* Given equation,

$14 - 15 \div 2 + 56 \times 14 = ?$

After interchanging + and –, × and ÷, we get

$\Rightarrow \quad 14 + 15 \times 2 - 56 \div 14 = ?$

$\Rightarrow \quad 14 + 30 - 4 = ?$

$\Rightarrow \quad 44 - 4 = ?$

$\therefore \quad ? = 40$

29. *(a)* The pattern of the series is as follows,

C →(+3) F →(+3) I →(+3) L →(+3) O

E →(+3) H →(+3) K →(+3) N →(+3) Q

G →(+3) J →(+3) M →(+3) P →(+3) S

$\therefore \quad ? = $ OQS

30. *(d)* The pattern of the series is as follows,

R →(+3) U →(+3) X →(+3) A →(+3) D

P →(+3) S →(+3) V →(+3) Y →(+3) B

M →(+3) P →(+3) S →(+3) V →(+3) Y

$\therefore$? = DBY

31. *(d)* According to the question,

B A C (K) → 4 1 (6) 2

C A B → 2 1 4

∴ Code for 'K' is '6'.

32. *(c)* From positions I and II, common letter is Z, so

Z ↑ Common Z; A ↑ Opposite Y; R ↑ Opposite T

∴ Y is opposite to letter A.

33. *(a)* Let today is x.

According to the question,

$x - 10 =$ Sunday

$x =$ Sunday + 10 = Sunday + 3

$\therefore \quad x =$ Wednesday

Thus, today is Wednesday.

34. *(b)*

Given word → W A N D E R L U S T

Arranging the word into alphabetical order → A D E L N R S T U W

Thus, only one letter 'R' will remain unchanged.

35. *(a)* The correct mirror image of given figure is as shown below,

M WPQJK2GE N

36. *(b)* According to the question,

time and again — zx df mo

value your time — df pn tv

∴ Code for 'time' is 'df'.

37. *(b)* Given expression,

$15 \div 4 - 128 + 123 \times 3 = ?$

After interchanging + and –, × and ÷, we get

$\Rightarrow \quad 15 \times 4 + 128 - 123 \div 3 = ?$

$\Rightarrow \quad 60 + 128 - 41 = ?$

$\Rightarrow \quad 188 - 41 = ?$

$\therefore \quad ? = 147$

38. *(c)* According to the statements,

Conclusions I. (✗) II. (✗)

Hence, none of the conclusion follows.

39. *(b)* As, 'Referee' making decision about the game on 'Field'. Similarly, 'Judge' making decision about the legal cases in 'Courtroom'.

40. *(d)* The given figure (X) is embedded in option figure (d).

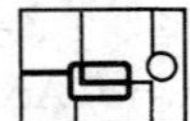

41. *(d)* As, $33 \xrightarrow{\times 22} 726$

and $43 \xrightarrow{\times 22} 946$

Similarly, $53 \xrightarrow{\times 22} \boxed{1166}$

42. *(a)* The correct mirror image of given combination is shown below,

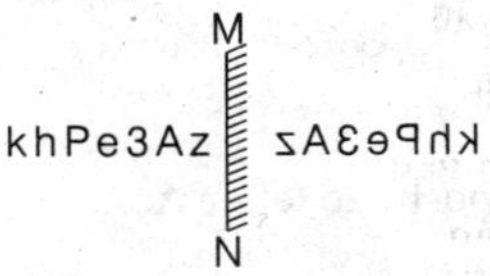

khPe3Az | M/N mirror

43. *(c)* As, $(6, 12, 72) \Rightarrow 6 \xrightarrow{\times 2} 12 \xrightarrow{\times 6} 72$

and $(8, 16, 96) \Rightarrow 8 \xrightarrow{\times 2} 16 \xrightarrow{\times 6} 96$

Similarly,

$(12, 24, 144) \Rightarrow 12 \xrightarrow{\times 2} 24 \xrightarrow{\times 6} 144$

44. *(a)* Given expression, S + T ÷ U

According to the question,

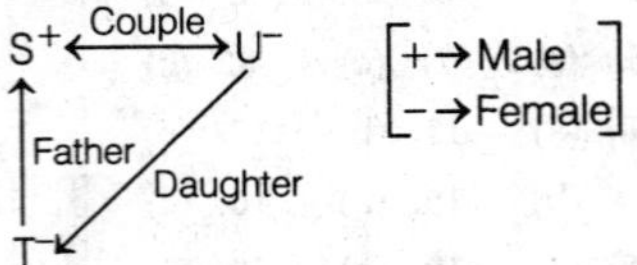

Hence, S is the husband of U.

45. *(b)* The pattern of the series is as follows,

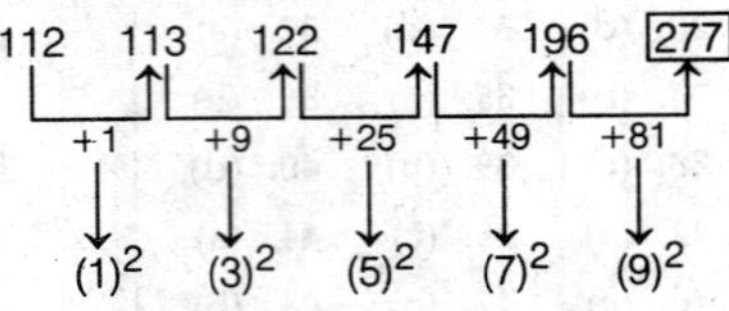

46. *(c)* The pattern of the series is as follows,

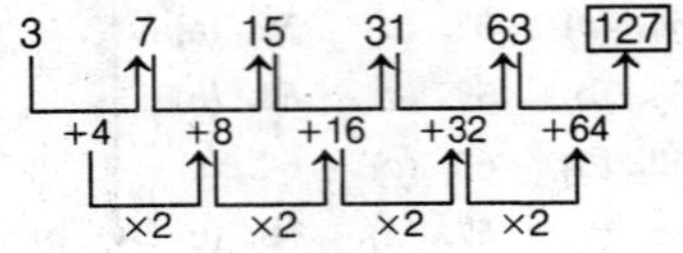

∴ ? = 127

47. *(b)* The given figure (X) is embedded in option figure (b).

48. *(b)* As, P →(+2) R →(+2) T, R →(+2) T →(+2) V

H →(+2) J →(+2) L But, T →(+2) V →(+3) Y

Hence, 'TVY'is different among all.

49. *(d)* As, D F I K and G I L N

D →(+1) E, F →(+1) G, I →(+1) J, K →(+1) L; G →(+1) H, I →(+1) J, L →(+1) M, N →(+1) O

Similarly, M O R T

M →(+1) N, O →(+1) P, R →(+1) S, T →(+1) U

50. *(b)* The pattern of the given series as follows,

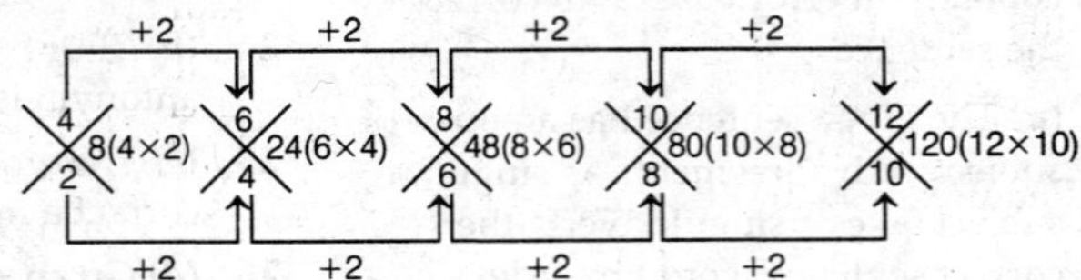

51. *(c)* Let the number of paper balls be *n*.

Given, diameter of original sphere

= 18 cm

∴ Radius of original sphere

$(R) = \frac{18}{2} = 9 \text{ cm}$

Also, diameter of paper ball = 2 cm

$\therefore$ Radius of paper ball $(r) = \frac{2}{2} = 1$ cm

According to the question,

$$n \times \frac{4}{3}\pi r^3 = \frac{4}{3}\pi R^3$$

$$\Rightarrow \quad n(1)^3 = (9)^3$$

$$\therefore \quad n = 729$$

52. *(d)* Let the marked price of an item be ₹ 100 x.

$\therefore$ SP of an item after 20% discount

$= 100x - 20x = 80x$

As, shopkeeper earns a profit of 90%,

$\therefore$ CP of an item $= 80x \times \frac{100}{190} = 42.10x$

If discount is 40%, then

SP of an item $= 100x - 40x = 60x$

$\therefore$ Required profit percentage

$= \frac{60x - 42.10x}{42.10x} \times 100$

$= 42.5\%$

53. *(a)* Given, total marks = 450

According to the question,

2 (Physics + Hindi + Chemistry)

$= 156° + 144° + 140°$

$\therefore$ Physics + Hindi + Chemistry

$= \frac{440°}{2} = 220°$

$\therefore$ English and Biology

$= 360° - 220° = 140°$

$\therefore$ Total marks obtained by Sanya in English and Biology $= \frac{140°}{360°} \times 450$

$= 175$

54. *(c)* Required ratio $= \frac{15 + 30 + 20}{5 + 20 + 25}$

$= \frac{65}{50} = \frac{13}{10}$

$\therefore$ Required ratio = 13 : 10

55. *(a)* Let the number be x.

$\therefore \frac{20}{100} \times \frac{35}{100} \times x = 240.8$

$\Rightarrow x = \frac{240.8 \times 100 \times 100}{20 \times 35} = 3440$

$\therefore$ Required 18% of the number

$= 3440 \times \frac{18}{100}$

$= 619.2$

56. *(a)* According to the question,

Marks obtained in Economics

$= \frac{90}{100} \times 100 = 90$

Marks obtained in English

$= \frac{75}{100} \times 80 = 60$

Marks obtained in History

$= \frac{80}{100} \times 50 = 40$

$\therefore$ Total marks obtained

$= 90 + 60 + 40 = 190$

57. *(c)* A's 1 day's work $= \frac{1}{4}$

B's 1 day's work $= \frac{1}{12}$

$\therefore (A + B)$'s 1 day's work

$= \frac{1}{4} + \frac{1}{12} = \frac{3+1}{12} = \frac{4}{12} = \frac{1}{3}$

$\therefore$ A and B can complete the work in

= 3 days

58. *(b)* Given expression,

$11\frac{1}{4} \div 3\frac{3}{5} \times 6\frac{2}{3} + \frac{1}{6}$

$= \frac{45}{4} \div \frac{18}{5} \times \frac{20}{3} + \frac{1}{6}$

[using BODMAS]

$= \frac{45}{4} \times \frac{5}{18} \times \frac{20}{3} + \frac{1}{6}$

$= \frac{25}{8} \times \frac{20}{3} + \frac{1}{6}$

$= \frac{500}{24} + \frac{1}{6} = \frac{504}{24} = 21$

59. *(c)*

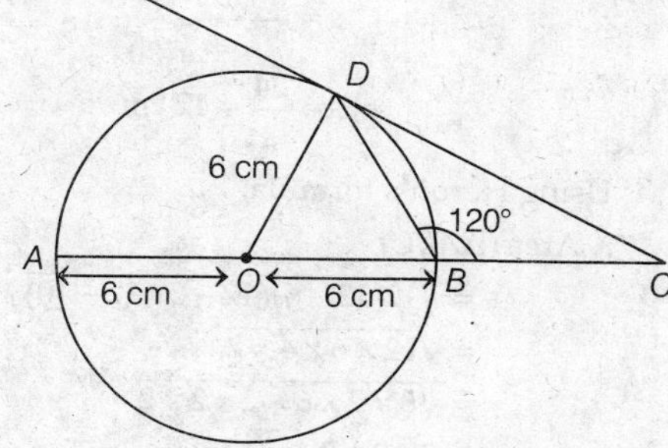

Given, $OA = OB = OD = 6$ cm

As, we know,

radius of a circle is always perpendicular to the tangent of a circle.

$\therefore \quad \angle ODC = 90°$

Also, given, $\angle DBC = 120°$

$\therefore \angle DBO = 180° - 120° = 60°$

[Linear pair]

$\Rightarrow \quad \angle ODB = \angle DBO = 60°$

$\therefore \quad \angle BOD = 180° - \angle ODB - \angle DBO$

$= 180° - 60° - 60°$

$= 60°$

$\therefore \Delta OBD$ is an equilateral triangle.

$\therefore \quad \angle BDC = 90° - 60° = 30°$

$\Rightarrow \quad \angle BCD = 180° - 120° - 30° = 30°$

$\therefore \Delta BCD$ is an isosceles triangle

$\therefore \quad CB = DB = 6$ cm

In ΔOCD

$CD^2 = OC^2 - OD^2 = (6+6)^2 - (6)^2$

$= 144 - 36 = 108$

$\therefore \quad CD = 6\sqrt{3}$ cm

60. *(a)* Let the weight of n number of students having an average weight (A) be $w_1, w_2, w_3 \ldots w_n$.

$\therefore$ Average (A)

$= \frac{w_1 + w_2 + w_3 + \ldots + w_n}{n}$

$\Rightarrow \quad w_1 + w_2 + w_3 + \ldots + w_n = nA \quad \ldots$(i)

If one student having 30 kg weight is added, then

$A + 1 = \frac{w_1 + w_2 + \ldots + w_n + 30}{n+1}$

$\Rightarrow \quad nA + n + A + 1$

$= w_1 + w_2 + \ldots + w_n + 30$

$\Rightarrow \quad nA + n + 1 + A = nA + 30$

[from (i)]

$\Rightarrow \quad n + A = 29$

$\Rightarrow \quad n = 29 - A \quad \ldots$(ii)

Now, if one more student of 30 kg is added, then

$A + 1.5 = \frac{w_1 + w_2 + \ldots + w_n + 30 + 30}{n + 2}$

$\Rightarrow \quad (A + 1.5)(n + 2) = nA + 60$

[$\because$ from (i)]

$\Rightarrow \quad nA + 2A + 1.5n + 3 = nA + 60$

$\Rightarrow \quad 2A + 1.5(29 - A) + 3 = 60$

[$\because$ from Eq. (ii)]

$\Rightarrow \quad 0.5A + 46.5 = 60$

$\Rightarrow \quad 0.5A = 13.5$

$\therefore \quad A = 27$

61. *(a)* We know, maximum value of $m\cos\theta + n\sin\theta \le \sqrt{m^2 + n^2}$

$\therefore \quad 7\cos A + 24\sin A \le \sqrt{(7)^2 + (24)^2}$

$= \sqrt{49 + 576} = \sqrt{625}$

$= 25$

$\therefore$ Maximum value of

$7\cos A + 24\sin A + 32$

$= 25 + 32 = 57$

62. *(b)* According to the question,

Ram's marks in Botany more than Karn's marks by $(95 - 80) = 15\%$

$\therefore$ Required marks $= \frac{15}{100} \times 200 = 30$

63. *(c)* Let the speed of policeman be $5x$ km/h.

$\therefore$ Speed of thief $= \frac{4}{5}(5x) = 4x$ km/h

According to the question,

Thief covers 6 km in 30 min i.e. $\left(\frac{1}{2}\right)$h.

$\therefore$ Distance covered by thief in 1 h $= 12$ km

$\therefore$ Actual speed of thief $= 12$ km/h

$\therefore$ Actual speed of policeman $= 12 \times \frac{5}{4} = 15$ km/h

$\therefore$ Distance between policeman and thief

$= \frac{1}{2}(15 - 12)$

$= \frac{1}{2} \times 3 = 1.5$ km

[$\because$ 30 min = 1/2 h]

64. *(c)* According to the question,

Actual cost of an article $= 3500 \times \frac{100}{70}$

$= ₹\,5000$

65. *(b)* Let the required number of cones be n.

According to the question,

$n \times$ Volume of smaller cone = Volume of sphere

$\Rightarrow \quad n \times \frac{1}{3}\pi(3.5)^2 \times (4) = 3136\pi$

$\Rightarrow \quad n = \frac{3136 \times 3}{49} = 192$

66. *(b)*

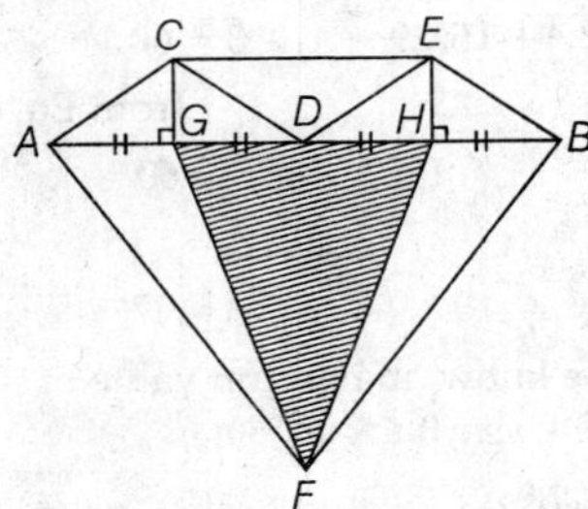

Given, $AB \parallel CE$,

$AG = GD = DH = HB$

In ΔACG and ΔBEH,

$AG = BH$ (Given)

$\angle AGC = \angle BHE$ (Each 90°)

$CG = EH$

(Distance between parallel sides)

$\therefore \quad \Delta ACG \cong \Delta BEH$ (SAS)

In ΔCDE and ΔDEB,

$DE = DE$ (common)

$\angle CED = \angle BDE$

(Alternate Interior Angles as $AB \parallel CE$)

$CE = BD$ [$\because CE = GH \Rightarrow CE = BD$]

$\therefore \Delta CDE \cong \Delta DEB$ (SAS)

Similarly, $\Delta CDE \cong \Delta ACD$

$\therefore \quad \Delta CDE \cong \Delta DEB \cong \Delta ACD$

67. *(a)* Given expression,

$$\left[6 - 2\left\{3 - 4\left(4 \div \frac{1}{4} - 1\right) + 2 \div \frac{1}{3}\right\} - 3 \times 2\right]$$

Using BODMAS,

$$= \left[6 - 2\left\{3 - 4\left(4 \times \frac{4}{1} - 1\right) + 2 \times \frac{3}{1}\right\} - 3 \times 2\right]$$

$= [6 - 2\{3 - 60 + 6\} - 6]$

$= [6 + 102 - 6]$

$= 102$

68. *(c)* Given, sides of triangle are 6 cm, 8 cm and 10 cm.

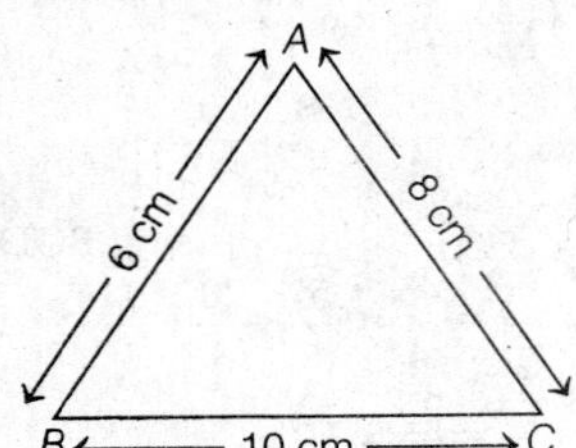

We know,

Semi-perimeter $(s) = \frac{a + b + c}{2}$

$\therefore \quad s = \frac{6 + 8 + 10}{2}$

$s = \frac{24}{2} = 12$ cm

Using Heron's formula,

$\therefore$ Area (ΔABC)

$= \sqrt{12(12-6)(12-8)(12-10)}$

$= \sqrt{12 \times 6 \times 4 \times 2}$

$= \sqrt{6 \times 2 \times 6 \times 2 \times 2 \times 2}$

$= 6 \times 2 \times 2 = 24\text{ cm}^2$

69. *(b)* Given,

Total expenditure on education $= ₹\,23520$

According to the question,

Total expenditure $= 23520 \times \frac{100}{28}$

$= 84000$

$\therefore$ Expenditure on clothing

$= 84000 \times \frac{12}{100} = ₹\,10080$

70. *(a)* Let selling price of 22 items be $₹\,22x$.

$\therefore$ Profit = Selling price of 6 items $= 6x$

$\therefore$ CP of 22 items $= 22x - 6x = 16x$

$\therefore$ Required gain per cent $= \frac{6x}{16x} \times 100$

$= 37\frac{1}{2}\%$

71. *(d)* According to the question,

Net percentage change

$= \left(a - b - \frac{ab}{100}\right)\%$

$= \left(-25 + 50 - \frac{25 \times 50}{100}\right)\%$

$= (-25 + 50 - 12.50)\%$

$= (25 - 12.50)\% = 12.50\%$

As, resultant price $= ₹\,7650$

$\therefore \quad$ Original price $= 7650 \times \frac{100}{112.5}$

$= ₹\,6800$

72. *(c)* Let the angles after decrement be $3x$, $4x$ and $7x$, respectively.

According to the question,

$(3x + 17°) + (4x + 17°) + (7x + 17°) = 180°$

$\therefore \quad 14x + 51 = 180°$

$\Rightarrow \quad 14x = 129$

$\Rightarrow \quad x = \frac{129}{14}$

$\therefore \quad$ Greatest angle $= 7 \times \frac{129}{14} + 17$

$= \frac{129°}{2} + 17 = \frac{163°}{2}$

$\therefore$ Required radian measure

$= \frac{163}{2} \times \frac{\pi}{180} = \frac{163\pi}{360}$

73. *(b)* We know that,

If a, b and c are the sides of triangle where $(a > b)$

$(a - b) < c < (a + b)$

Here, $a = 25$, $b = 19$, $c = y$

$\therefore \quad (25 - 19) < y < (25 + 19)$

$\Rightarrow \quad 6 < y < 44$

74. *(d)* Total strength of school = 640

Number of boys = 400

$\therefore$ Number of girls $= 640 - 400 = 240$

$\therefore$ Required ratio $= 240 : 400 = 3 : 5$

75. *(d)* Given, $P = 36000$, $t = 2$ yr,

$R_1 = 8\%$ and $R_2 = 6\%$

We know that,

$$\text{SI} = \frac{P \times R \times T}{100}$$

SI in two years

$= \frac{36000 \times 1 \times 8}{100} + \frac{36000 \times 1 \times 6}{100}$

$= 2880 + 2160 = 5040$

$\therefore$ Amount due after 2 yr

$= 36000 + 5040 = 41040$

76. *(a)* Intervention by the monetary authority of a country in the money market to keep money supply stable against exogenous or sometimes external shocks is called Sterilisation.

- Neutralisation refers to measures taken to counter balance or offset the effects of certain actions, ensuring that the overall impact remains neutral or balanced.
- Capitalisation the total value of a company's outstanding shares of stock.
- Conservation generally refers to the sustainable management and use of natural resources to ensure their availability for future generations.

77. *(b)* In PPT, using the keyboard directional keys can be used to move among slides if your hands are already on the keyboard.

78. *(a)* Ruchira Kamboj is elected as the Chair for the 62nd Session of the United Nations Commission for Social Development.

- Satinder Kumar Lambah was an Indian civil servant of 1964 batch of Indian Foreign Service cadre who served as the Prime Minister of India's special envoy for Afghanistan and Pakistan between 2005 and 2014.
- Nirupama Menon Rao is a retired civil servant of 1973 batch of Indian Foreign Service cadre who served as India's Foreign Secretary from 2009 to 2011.

79. *(a)* Cricket is not an Olympics sport.

- Rowing, sailingand 3×3 basketball are Olympics sports.
- Olympics sports are contested as the Summer Olympic Games and Winter Olympic Games.
- Swimming, diving water polo are summer games while ice hockey, ice skating are winter games.

80. *(d)* According to Census 2011, India's population accounts 17.5% of the world's population.

- Total population of India is 1,21,05,69,573 (68.8% urban and 31.2% rural) and density of population is 382 persons/km^2.
- The Decadal population growth from 2001 to 2011 is 17.64%.
- Literacy rate is 74.04% of total population.
- India's population is now bigger than the combined population of USA, Indonesia, Brazil, Pakistan and Bangladesh.

81. *(d)* Jharkhand and Chhattisgarh states are rich with coal material deposits.

- The main coal belts of Chhattisgarh are in Chirimiri, Jhagrakhand, Churcha, Katkona, Pandavpara and Sonhat.
- The main coal belts of Jharkhand are Jharia, Bokaro, Karanpura, Hutur, Auranga, Daltonganj, Deoghar, Rajmahal Coal Fields.
- Dhanbad city in the state of Jharkhand is known as the Coal Capital of India.

82. *(c)* Fundamental Duties were introduced in Part IVA of the Constitution by the Forty-second Amendment Act, 1976.

- It is also known as Mini-Constitution, the 42nd Amendment Act 1976.
- The description of India changed from a 'sovereign democratic republic' to a 'sovereign, socialist, secular, democratic, republic'.
- The 'Unity of the Nation' was transformed into 'Unity and Integrity of the Nation'.

83. *(a)* By its address the CPU distinguises between each memory cell.

84. *(a)* The Big Dipper is an asterism formed by the seven brightest stars in the constellation Ursa Major.

- Ursa Major, also known as the Great Bear, is the third-largest constellation in the sky and the largest constellation in the Northern Hemisphere.
- There are 12 major constellations that line up along the Sun's path along the sky.
- Important ones are Aries, Taurus, Gemini, Crab/Cancer, Leo, Virgo, Libra, Scorpion, Saggitarius, Capricorn, Aquarius, Pisces.

85. *(d)* Aajeevika National Rural Livelihoods Mission (NRLM) - was launched by the Ministry of Rural Development (MoRD), Government of India, in the year 2011.

- The initiative to move towards a demand-driven strategy enabling the states to formulate their own livelihoods-based poverty reduction action plan is at the core of the mission.
- The scheme is an improved version of the earlier Swarnjayanti Gram Swarozgar Yojana (SGSY).
- The programme is supported partially by the World Bank.

86. *(d)* Baiga is a folk music of Baiga tribe from Madhya Pradesh.

- Kachari music is performed by the Kachari tribe of Nagaland.
- Kalbelia music and dance are performed by the Kalbelia community of Rajasthan.
- The Baul songs performed by Baul tribe of West Bengal.

87. *(a)* The cell wall of bacteria is made up of peptidoglycan.

Peptidoglycan is a mesh like polymer made of long chains of N-acetylmuramic acid and N-acetylglucosamine, cross linked by short peptides.

88. *(c)* Articles 12-35 of the Indian Constitution are related to Fundamental Rights.

There are 6 Fundamenal Rights mentioned below

- Right to Equality (Articles 14-18)
- Right to Freedom (Articles 19-22)
- Right against Exploitation (Articles 23-24)
- Right to Freedom of Religion (Articles 25-28)
- Cultural and Educational Rights (Articles 29-30)
- Right to Constitutional Remedies (Article 32)

89. *(a)* According to rules laid down by the International Football Association Board (IFAB), maximum length of a goal line in football is 90 m.

- The International Football Association Board is an international self-regulatory body of association football that is known for determining the laws of the game, the regulations for the gameplay of football.
- It was founded on 2nd June, 1886, headquarters at Zurich, Switzerland.

90. *(d)* CMS-01 is a communication Satellite that was launched by ISRO in December, 2020.

- In mid-2024, the Indian Space Research Organisation (ISRO) launched the Gaganyaan mission, which aims to send astronauts into space.

- In 17th January, 2020, ISRO launched GSAT-30 which is communication satellite that supports telecommunication and satellite-based communication services.
- In 27th November, 2019 ISRO launched Cartosat-3 which is an advanced Earth observation satellite with high-resolution imaging capabilities.

91. *(d)* Shattantri Veena, meaning a Veena with hundred strings, is the ancient Sanskrit name of Santoor.

In the 'Natya Shastra' musical instruments have been divided into four main categories.

- The Tata Vadya or Chordophones are stringed instruments.
- The Sushira Vadya or Aerophones are wind instruments.
- The Avanaddha Vadya or Membranophones are percussion instruments.
- The Ghana Vadya or Idiophones solid instruments which do not require tuning categories on the basis of how sound is produced.

92. *(c)* Aam Aadmi Party won the Jalandhar (a city in Punjab) Lok Sabha by poll election held in May, 2023.

- Aam Aadmi Party candidate Sushil Kumar Rinku won by defeating Congress candidate Karamjit Kaur Chaudhary.
- Aam Aadmi Party was founded on 2nd October, 2012 by Arvind Kejriwal.

93. *(c)* 2nd October is observed as a National Festival.

- Gandhi Jayanti is an event celebrated in India to mark the birthday of Mahatma Gandhi on 2nd October.
- International Artist's Day is celebrated on 26th October.
- United Nations Day originated on 24th October.
- World Mental Health Day is observed on 10th October.

94. *(b)* Milk of magnesia is a suspension of magnesium hydroxide in water. Its chemical formula is mg $(OH)_2$. Milk of magnesia is slightly basic with a pH of 10.08.

95. *(c)* Warren Hastings became the Governor-General of Bengal from Governor of Bengal after the passing of Regulating Act, 1773.

Important provisions of Regulating Act, 1773 are

- It prohibited the servants of company from engaging in any private trade or accepting presents or bribes from the 'natives'.
- The act made Governor of Bengal, Warren Hastings, to Governor-General of Bengal and subsumed the presidencies of Madras and Bombay under Bengal's control.

96. *(b)* In a Test match, the captain of fielding side may demand a new ball after 80 overs.

Important cricket terminologies are

- **Drive** A powerful shot played with the full face of the bat, usually along the ground.
- **Cut** A shot played with a horizontal bat, typically aimed at a ball delivered short outside off-stump.
- **Pull** A shot played to a short-pitched ball by hitting it to the leg side.

97. *(a)* Rouf is the traditional dance of Jammu and Kashmir, which is practiced on the festive occasions of Eid and during Ramzan days.

- Kathak is traditional dance of Uttar Padesh.
- Kuchipudi is traditional dance of Andhra Padesh.
- Kathakali is traditional dance of Kerala.

98. *(d)* In 1955, Karve Committee noted the possibility of using small scale industries for promoting rural development.

- Sarkaria Committee was set-up to review the of centre-state relations.
- Kelkar Committee was set-up to study and evaluate the Public-Private Partnership (PPP) model in India.
- Chakravarty Committee was set-up to review the working of monetary system.

99. *(b)* The Union Cabinet, in August 2022, approved the enhancement in the limit of Emergency Credit Line Guarantee Scheme (ECLGS) by ₹ 50,000 crore with the additional amount being earmarked exclusively for enterprises in hospitality and related sectors.

- Total 27 sectors have been identified by the Kamath Committee for one time debt restructuring.
- The tenor has been upgraded to 5 years with a 1-year moratorium on repayment of principal.

100. *(c)* The Mughal emperor Akbar got 'Ramayana' and 'Mahabharata' translated into Persian.

- He abolished Jaziya Tax in 1564.
- He transferred its capital from Agra to Fatehpur Sikri in 1571.
- He opened Ibadat Khana (House of Worship) for all religion in 1578.

Set 29 10 July, 2024 (Shift I)

SSC CHSL Tier-I SOLVED PAPER

Instructions

1. This paper contains 100 questions.
2. It has 4 Parts, **Part I** General English, **Part II** General Intelligence & Reasoning, **Part III** Quantitative Aptitude and **Part IV** General Awareness.
3. Each question carries **2 marks**.

Part I

General English

1. The given sentence is divided into three segments. Select the option that has the segment with a grammatical error. If there is no error, select 'No error'.

The volunteer gave on to / the food packets to the/children of the orphanage.

(a) The volunteer gave on to
(b) the food packets to the
(c) No error
(d) children of the orphanage

2. The given sentence is divided into four segments. Select the option that has the segment with a grammatical error.

It was my niece / who was leaving college / last year, and / not my son.

(a) last year, and
(b) not my son
(c) It was my niece
(d) who was leaving college

3. Parts of the given sentence have been underlined. One of them contains an error. The underlined parts are given as options with some changes. Select the option that correctly rectifies the error.

<u>Raveena's daughter</u> Kavya is <u>most intelligent</u> student and <u>she consistently</u> achieves <u>top grades</u>.

(a) Raveenas' daughter
(b) she has consistently
(c) an intelligent
(d) topper grades

4. Select the most appropriate option that can substitute the underlined segment in the given sentence.

UNICEF builds partnerships across the <u>global community on accelerate</u> gender equality.

(a) global community with accelerate
(b) global community till accelerate
(c) global community to accelerate
(d) global community in accelerate

Directions (Q. Nos. 5-9) *In the following passage, some words have been deleted. Select the most appropriate option for each blank.*

I was reading a book two days back. It was titled Charlie and the Chocolate Factory by Roland Dahl. It was fantastic. It has now become my favourite (1) .... It is about a boy named Charlie who is (2) .... poor. He wins a golden ticket that (3) .... him to enter the most famous chocolate factory in the world. He (4) .... it with his grandfather. But the other kids who accompany him are nasty. They are all spoilt. But you have to read the book to (5) .... out more about them. The amazing part of the book is that it is like a dream come true.

5. Select the most appropriate option to fill in blank no. (1).

(a) text (b) guide
(c) book (d) manual

6. Select the most appropriate option to fill in blank no. (2).

(a) very (b) nicely
(c) properly (d) finally

7. Select the most appropriate option to fill in blank no. (3).

(a) bears (b) gets
(c) suffers (d) allows

8. Select the most appropriate option to fill in blank no. (4).

(a) examines (b) explores
(c) visits (d) inspects

9. Select the most appropriate option to fill in blank no. (5).

(a) find (b) unlearn
(c) spot (d) locate

10. Select the most appropriate antonym of the given word.

Sluggish

(a) Hassled
(b) Lethargic
(c) Leisurely
(d) Rapid

11. Select the most appropriate antonym of the given word.

Timid

(a) Resolute
(b) Blunt
(c) Audacious
(d) Assertive

12. Select the most appropriate synonym of the given word.

Retract

(a) Disturb (b) Please
(c) Implement (d) Revoke

13. Select the option that will improve the underlined part of the given sentence.

<u>Allusive handwriting</u> creates a poor impression.

(a) Legal handwriting
(b) Eligible handwriting
(c) Descriptive handwriting
(d) Illegible handwriting

14. Select the option that rectifies the spelling of the underlined word in the given sentence.

It was a <u>privvilege</u> to receive the award from the President.

(a) privilegge
(b) privileege
(c) privilege
(d) privillege

15. Select the sentence that brings out the most appropriate meaning of the idiom 'Dog in the manger'.
(a) Mohit was so loyal and committed to his company that he rejected lucrative offers from different companies.
(b) To prove this is not a trap, I want to check the credibility of your plan.
(c) Rachit had some important work and so he cancelled the show tickets for everyone.
(d) You are here just because you have recognised your hidden potential.

16. Select the most appropriate synonym of the given word.
Alert
(a) Inactive (b) Dull
(c) Smart (d) Vigilant

17. Select the most appropriate option to fill in the blank.
I find that students nowadays are not interested in .... letters by hand.
(a) rioting (b) rating
(c) writing (d) righting

18. Select the most appropriate synonym of the underlined word.
For Rana, unable to see a thing, the <u>parade</u> seemed to last forever.
(a) hiding (b) darkness
(c) concealment (d) procession

19. Select the most appropriate antonym of the given word.
Enormous
(a) Minute (b) Strong
(c) Monstrous (d) Tremendous

20. Select the most appropriate option to correct the sentence by using the denotation of the underlined word.
Mr. Sen is <u>clever</u> enough to handle his professional hazards.
(a) Foolish (b) Callous
(c) Intelligent (d) Bold

21. Select the option that will improve the underlined part of the given sentence. In case no improvement is needed, select 'No improvement required'.
Although uncountable files stack up on the tables of government officials, they prefer doing their work <u>at a more leisure pace</u>.
(a) at a more leisurely pace
(b) at a more leisure paced
(c) No improvement needed
(d) at a more leisurely paced

22. Select the most appropriate meaning of the underlined idiom.
The technicians who were repairing the broken elevator <u>called it a day</u>.
(a) Felt unhappy
(b) Shouted with anger
(c) Stopped to take a short break
(d) Stopped work for the day

23. Select the incorrectly spelt word in the given sentence.
The Chinese are believed to have a longer history than that of any other civilisation in the wolrd.
(a) Wolrd (b) Civilisation
(c) Believed (d) Chinese

24. Select the most appropriate option that can replace the bracketed word segment in the following sentence.
Classical buildings in ancient Greek and Roman times were (characteristically built) from marble or some other attractive, durable stone.
(a) typically built
(b) fascinating to build
(c) strange build
(d) mainly having been built

25. Select the most appropriate option that can substitute the underlined segment in the given sentence.
The housing loan taken <u>by Ramesh effected</u> his daily expenses adversely.
(a) by Ramesh affected
(b) for Ramesh effected
(c) from Ramesh effected
(d) of Ramesh effected

Part II
General Intelligence

26. What should come in place of question mark (?) in the given series based on the English alphabetical order?
BJR, ?, RTH, MYC, HDX
(a) MOW (b) OMW
(c) WOM (d) OWM

27. The position of how many letters will remain unchanged, if each of the letters in the word DOCUMENTARY is arranged from left to right in alphabetical order?
(a) Two (b) Three
(c) None (d) One

28. In a certain code language,
A + B means 'A is the mother of B'
A – B means 'A is the brother of B'
A × B means 'A is the husband of B'
A ÷ B means 'A is the father of B'
Based on the above, how is K related to L, if 'K × Q + R – S ÷ L'?
(a) Father's father
(b) Father's mother's father
(c) Father's brother
(d) Father's father's brother

29. Select the set in which the numbers are related in the same way as are the numbers of the following sets.
(**Note** Operations should be performed on the whole numbers, without breaking down the numbers into its constituent digits. E.g. 13 – Operations on 13 such as adding/ subtracting/multiplying etc. to 13 can be performed. Breaking down 13 into 1 and 3 and then performing mathematical operations on 1 and 3 is not allowed.)
(5, 4, 41)
(7, 2, 53)
(a) (9, 3, 90)
(b) (10, 5, 130)
(c) (13, 6, 208)
(d) (11, 9, 204)

30. Select the correct mirror image of the given figure, when the mirror is placed at MN as shown below.

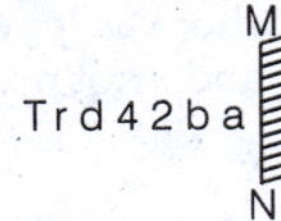

(a) ɒ d ꙅ 4 p r T
(b) ɒ d ꙅ 4 b ɿ T
(c) ɒ d 2 4 p ɿ T
(d) ɒ b ꙅ 4 b ɿ T

31. How many quadrilaterals are there in the given figure?

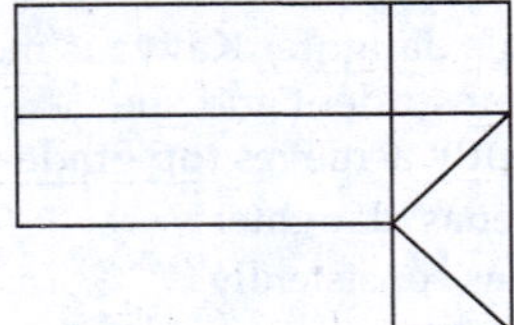

(a) 11
(b) 10
(c) 12
(d) 7

32. Select the correct mirror image of the given figure, when the mirror is placed at MN as shown below.

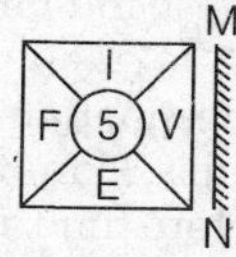

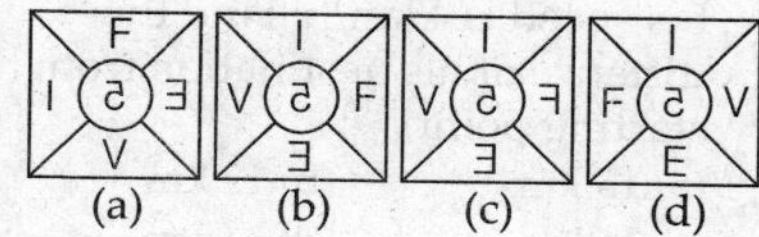

33. Select the word-pair that best represents a similar relationship to the one expressed in the pair of words given below.

(The words must be considered as meaningful English words and must not be related to each other based on the number of letters/number of consonants/vowels in the word)

Flower-Petal

(a) Clarify - Explain
(b) Fruit - Seed
(c) Horse - Mare
(d) Tiny - Large

34. Three statements are followed by conclusions numbered I, II. You have to consider these statements to be true, even if they seem to be at variance with commonly known facts. Decide which of the given conclusions logically follow(s) from the given statements.

Statements

All houses are trees.
All trees are stones.
All stones are rocks.

Conclusions

I. Some stones are trees.
II. All houses are rocks.

(a) Neither Conclusion I nor II follows
(b) Only Conclusion I follows
(c) Both Conclusions I and II follow
(d) Only Conclusion II follows

35. If 23rd June, 2008 was Monday, then what was the day of the week on 23rd June, 2020?

(a) Wednesday (b) Saturday
(c) Sunday (d) Tuesday

36. Select the letter-cluster pair that best represents a similar relationship to the one expressed in the pairs of letter-clusters given below.

VPN : ZTR
SMK : WQO

(a) HDB : MIG (b) KFD : OJK
(c) PMK : TOL (d) LFD : PJH

37. Select the correct mirror image of the given figure, when the mirror is placed at MN as shown below.

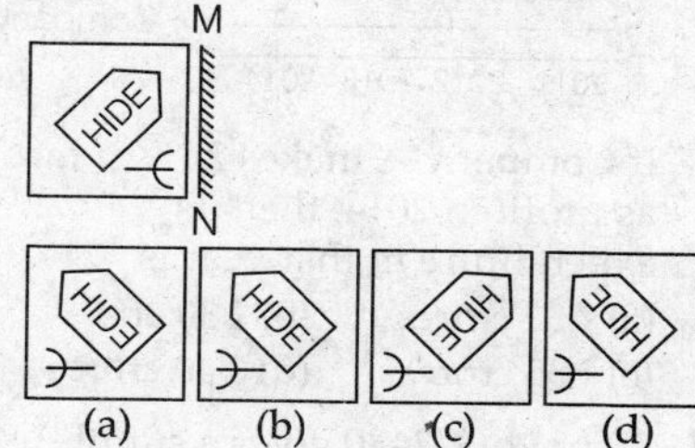

38. Which of the following numbers will replace the question mark (?) in the given series?

612, 571, 535, 504, 478, ?

(a) 444 (b) 435
(c) 457 (d) 468

39. Three of the following four letter-clusters are alike in a certain way and thus form a group. Which is the one that does not belong to that group?

(**Note** The odd one out is not based on the number of consonants/vowels or their position in the letter-cluster.)

1. EFINU 2. BCFKR
3. JKNSZ 4. HIMQX

(a) EFINU (b) HIMQX
(c) JKNSZ (d) BCFKR

40. If 'A' stands for '÷', 'B' stands for '×', 'C' stands for '+' and 'D' stands for '–', then the resultant of which of the following will be 218?

(a) 32 A 8 D 160 B 2 C 42
(b) 32 B 8 D 160 C 2 A 42
(c) 32 B 8 D 160 A 2 C 42
(d) 32 C 8 D 160 A 2 B 42

41. Select the correct mirror image of the given figure, when the mirror is placed at MN as shown below.

(a) TJZHBD
(b) TZLBHD
(c) TZLHBD
(d) TZLHBD

42. Which two numbers should be interchanged to make the given equation correct?

$15\times5-75+(300\div6)+3\times19=115$

(**Note** Numbers must be interchanged and not the constituent digits e.g., if 2 and 3 are to be interchanged in the equation $43\times3+4\div2$, then interchanged equation is $43\times2+4\div3$)

(a) 15 and 6 (b) 15 and 19
(c) 6 and 5 (d) 6 and 3

43. If 'A' stands for '÷', 'B' stands for '×', 'C' stands for '+' and 'D' stands for '–', what will come in place of the question mark (?) in the following equation?

14 B 11 D 22 C 328 A 8 = ?

(a) 153 (b) 173
(c) 133 (d) 163

44. In a certain code language, 'DIVERT' is coded as '36' and 'DOLDRUMS' is coded as '64'. What is the code for 'DOGMA' in the given code language?

(a) 36 (b) 25
(c) 49 (d) 64

45. What should come in place of question mark (?) in the given series?

155, 146, 137, 128, 119, ?

(a) 133 (b) 110
(c) 122 (d) 111

46. Which of the following letter-clusters can replace the question mark (?) in the given series to make it logically complete?

AFK, ? , IXM, MTN, QPO

(a) FAE (b) EBC
(c) FAL (d) EBL

47. Identify the figure given in the options that when put in place of the question mark (?) will logically complete the series.

T = 9 R O S ♡	O S T = ♡ R 9	T O S V 9 ♡ R	9 ♡ T O R V S	?

(a)	(b)	(c)	(d)
T 9 ♡ 2 S R V	♡ T 9 2 S R V	R V 9 2 S ♡ T	T 9 ♡ 2 V S R

48. A square sheet of paper is folded along the dotted line successively along the directions shown and is then punched in the last. How would the paper look when unfolded?

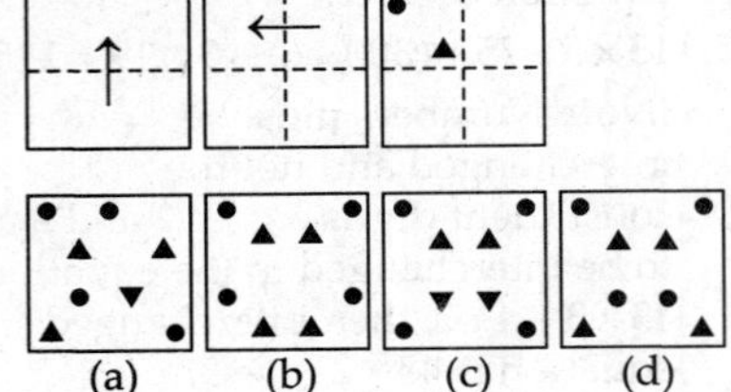

49. In a certain code language, 'strength to innovate' is coded as '426432' and 'strength to create' is coded as '324224'. What is the code for 'create' in that language?
(a) 32 (b) 42
(c) 24 (d) 64

50. 92 is related to 23 following a certain logic. Following the same logic, 136 is related to 34. To which of the following is 224 related, following the same logic?
(**Note** Operations should be performed on the whole numbers, without breaking down the numbers into its constituent digits. E.g. 13 – Operations on 13 such as adding /deleting /multiplying etc. to 13 can be performed. Breaking down 13 into 1 and 3 and then performing mathematical operations on 1 and 3 is not allowed)
(a) 54 (b) 58
(c) 52 (d) 56

Part III
Quantitative Aptitude

51. 55 workers can finish a work in 16 days. For finishing the same work in 10 days, how many more workers are required?
(a) 68 (b) 33
(c) 88 (d) 31

52. The radii of the two circles are 7 cm and 4 cm. If the distance between their centres is 25 cm, then the length of the transverse common tangent is equal to
(a) $6\sqrt{12}$ cm (b) $6\sqrt{11}$ cm
(c) $6\sqrt{14}$ cm (d) $6\sqrt{13}$ cm

53. If the radius of a circle is 48 cm and the length of the arc is 15 cm, then the area of the sector corresponding to that arc is
(a) 360 m^2 (b) 360 cm^2
(c) 720 cm^2 (d) 7200 m^2

54. Read the given information and answer the question that follows.

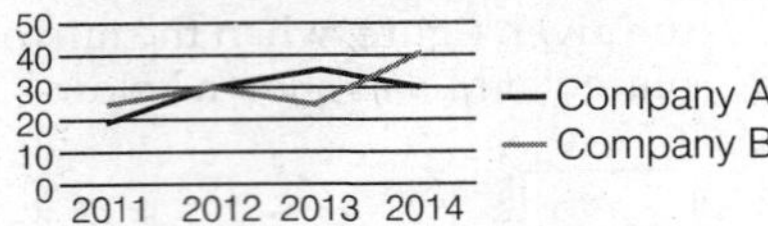

If Company A makes 25% of income as profit in 2014, then its expenditure in that year is
(a) ₹ 32 crores (b) ₹ 30 crores
(c) ₹ 35 crores (d) ₹ 40 crores

55. A sum of ₹ 2430 gives a simple interest of ₹ 1093.50 in 3 yr. The rate of interest per annum is
(a) 20% (b) 10% (c) 15% (d) 25%

56. Raju and Ramu have more land than Sonu by 15% and 25%, respectively. What is the ratio of land owned by Raju and Ramu?
(a) 23 : 25
(b) 25 : 23
(c) 21 : 23
(d) 15 : 25

57. A mirror is placed on the ground facing upwards. A man sees the top of a tower in the mirror, which is at a distance of 105 m from the mirror. The man is 0.5 m away from the mirror and his height is 1.5 m. Find the height of the tower (in metres).
(a) 315 (b) 115
(c) 210 (d) 280

58. A cyclist rides 10 km at an average speed of 15 km/h and then the next 15 km at an average speed of 10 km/h. The average speed of the entire ride is
(a) 20 km/h (b) 12.5 km/h
(c) 10 km/h (d) 11.54 km/h

59. The total number of students in different subjects of a college and percentage of girls and boys are shown in the below table.
Girls students and boys students are not having multiple subjects.

Subjects	Number of Students	Girls %	Boys %
Mathematics	840	40	60
Chemistry	220	70	30
Physics	450	30	70
Biology	200	80	20

What is the percentage of girl students in the college?
(a) 45.2 (b) 46.9
(c) 45.9 (d) 42.9

60. A person reaches his destination 30 min late, if his speed is 3 km/h, and reaches 30 min before time, if his speed is 4 km/h. Find the distance of his destination from his starting point.
(a) 13 km (b) 12 km
(c) 14 km (d) 11 km

61. To finish a work, *P* takes half of the number of days required by *Q* to finish it. If they together can finish the work in 36 days, then in how many days *Q* alone can finish the work?
(a) 108 (b) 84
(c) 60 (d) 24

62. A patient in a hospital is given tea daily in a cylindrical cup of diameter 7 cm. If the cup is filled with tea to a height of 4 cm, how much tea the hospital has to prepare daily to serve 180 patients? $\left(\text{Use } \pi = \frac{22}{7}\right)$
(a) 22.27 L (b) 22.77 L
(c) 27.27 L (d) 27.72 L

63. Simplify the following.
$12 \div 4$ of $3 \times 6 + 8 \div 16$ of $4 \times 8 - 4 \div 6 \times 9$
(a) 13 (b) −1
(c) 1 (d) $6\frac{1}{4}$

64. In an election between two candidates, *A* gets 63% of the total valid votes. If the total votes polled were 8750, what is the number of valid votes that the other candidate *B* gets, if 20% of the total votes were declared invalid?
(a) 2590 (b) 3560
(c) 4410 (d) 6450

65. If $\tan A = \sqrt{2} - 1$, then find the value of $\sin A \cos A + \tan A$.
(a) $\frac{24\sqrt{2}+15}{4}$ (b) $\frac{5\sqrt{2}-4}{4}$
(c) $\frac{24\sqrt{2}-15}{4}$ (d) $\frac{5\sqrt{2}+4}{4}$

66. The sum of the digits of a two-digit number is 9. If the digits are reversed, then the number is increased by 27. Find the number.
(a) 36 (b) 63 (c) 54 (d) 45

67. A rectangle with the largest area is cut out of a circle with radius 5 units. What is the area of the remaining portion?
(a) $25(2\pi - 3)$ (b) $25(\pi - 2)$
(c) $25(2\pi - 5)$ (d) $25(\pi - 3)$

68. A vendor sells his goods using weights 19% less than true weights and makes a profit of 35%. His net gain percentage (rounded off to 2 decimal places) is
(a) 66.67% (b) 66.33%
(c) 81.33% (d) 81.67%

69. The savings and expenditure of a family in a month on different heads is shown in the given pie-chart. The family saves ₹ 8000 per months.

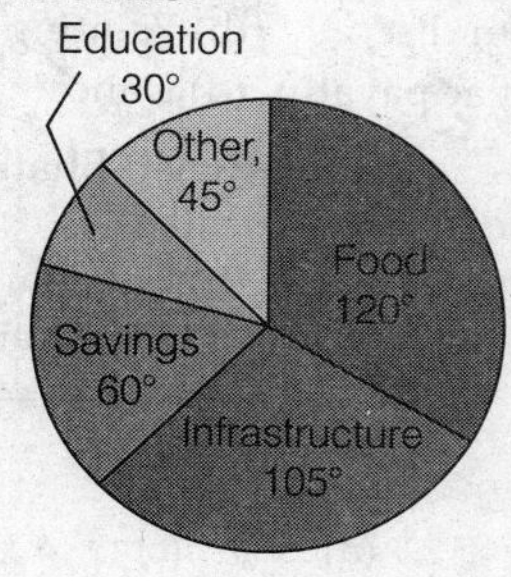

Find the ratio of the expenditure on food to that on savings.
(a) 3 : 1 (b) 5 : 1 (c) 4 : 1 (d) 2 : 1

70. Four years ago, Ravi was four times as old as Kavya. Seven years from now, Ravi will be three times as old as Kavya. Find the sum of their present ages.
(a) 118 yr (b) 122 yr
(c) 117 yr (d) 115 yr

71. Ram spends 30% of his salary on food, 10% on house rent, 7% on entertainment, and 6% on conveyance. If at the end of a month his savings are ₹ 1880, then his monthly salary is
(a) ₹ 4500 (b) ₹ 4000
(c) ₹ 5000 (d) ₹ 5500

72. Study the given pie-charts and answer the question that follows.

Distribution of Overseas Tourists

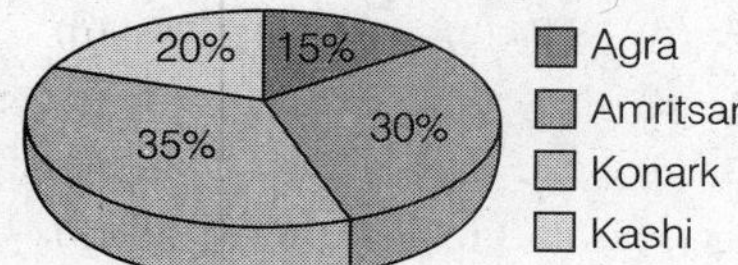

Age of Tourists

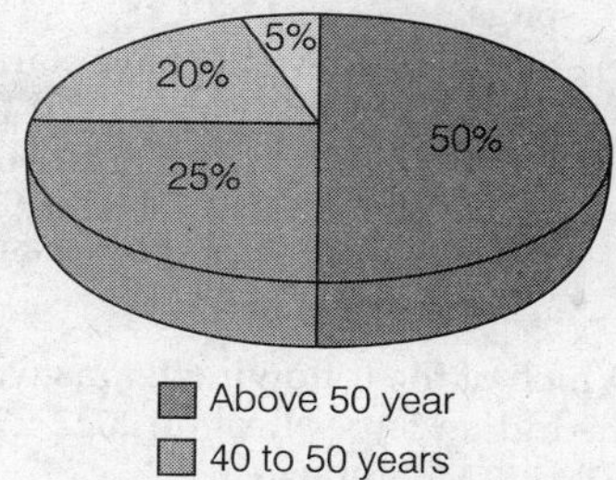

Above 50 year
40 to 50 years
20 to 40 years
2 to 20 years

What percentage of tourists went to Agra and Kashi?
(a) 20% (b) 17.5% (c) 35% (d) 15%

73. A cuboidal water purifier can carry 10 L of water. Its breadth is $\frac{1}{5}$ of its height and length is $\frac{1}{3}$ of the sum of the breadth and height. The height of the tank is
(a) 80 cm (b) 10 cm
(c) 20 cm (d) 50 cm

74. $(8^6 + 1)$ when divided by 7, would leave a remainder of
(a) 4 (b) 6 (c) 1 (d) 2

75. *R* wishes to use a stick of length 6 units as common internal tangent to two circles of radius two units and three units. What can be the maximum distance (in units) between the centres of the circle?
(a) $\sqrt{67}$ (b) $\sqrt{61}$ (c) $\sqrt{33}$ (d) $\sqrt{37}$

Part IV
General Awareness

76. National Sports Day is celebrated on the birthday of ....
(a) Roop Singh
(b) Kapil Dev
(c) MS Dhoni
(d) Major Dhyan Chand

77. What is the duration of International hockey match?
(a) 50 min (b) 55 min
(c) 70 min (d) 60 min

78. In which year was the National Human Rights Commission established in India?
(a) 2005 (b) 1993 (c) 1995 (d) 2003

79. In 1812, who described the hypothesis that equal volumes of different gases contain an equal number of molecules?
(a) Amedeo Avogadro
(b) James Watt
(c) John Dalton
(d) Albert Einstein

80. In which year did the Bhopal gas tragedy occur?
(a) 1988
(b) 1982
(c) 1985
(d) 1984

81. Which of the following Fundamental Rights is available for Indians as well as foreigners?
(a) Right of minorities to establish and administer educational institutions.
(b) Equality of opportunity in matters of public employment.
(c) Right to protection of language, script and culture of minorities.
(d) Right to elementary education.

82. In addition to using the arrow keys and mouse clicks, what other method can be used to move around a table in Microsoft Word?
(a) Right-clicking on the cell and selecting 'Move to Next Cell'.
(b) Pressing the 'Enter' key or using the scroll wheel.
(c) Using the Tab key or double-clicking on the cell.
(d) Pressing the 'Ctrl' key and clicking on the cell.

83. On 2nd March, 2023, the Supreme Court delivered an order on appointments to the Election Commission. According to this order, appointments will be done under the recommendation of a committee having which of the following members?
(a) Prime Minister, Chief Justice of India and Speaker of the Lok Sabha.
(b) Prime Minister, Leader of the opposition and Chairman of the Rajya Sabha.
(c) Prime Minister, Leader of the opposition and Speaker of the Lok Sabha.
(d) Prime Minister, Leader of the opposition and Chief Justice of India.

84. Which of the following persons was appointed Chairman of the Second National Judicial Pay Commission?
(a) Justice JS Verma
(b) Justice AS Anand
(c) Justice PV Reddi
(d) Justice R. Basant

85. Identify a carbohydrate but does not fit into the definition.
(a) Maltose (b) Sucrose
(c) Fructose (d) Rhamnose

86. A constellation of the Northern sky easily recognised by a group of five bright stars forming a slightly irregular 'W' is called
(a) Cygnus (b) Cassiopeia
(c) Ursa Major (d) Orion

87. Which revolutionary organisation was established at Feroz Shah Kotla in New Delhi in 1928?
(a) Indian Home Rule Society
(b) Bharat Naujawan Sabha
(c) Hindustan Socialist Republican Association
(d) Swadesh Bandhab Samiti

88. Which of the following is not a characteristics of the National Investment and Manufacturing Zones (NIMZs) of India?
(a) The State Government will provide power connectivity, water and other infra structural facilities.
(b) A special purpose vehicle will be constituted to take care of the functioning of NIMZs.
(c) It prescribes a minimum area of 10000 hectares for establishing NIMZs.
(d) At least 30% of the total land area proposed for the NIMZ is to be utilised for manufacturing units.

89. In MS Word, which icon from the icons below the Menu Bar is commonly used to save the current document?
(a) The envelope icon
(b) The floppy disk icon
(c) The printer icon
(d) The undo icon

90. Which of the following statements is incorrect about the Music of India?
(a) Tala is a cyclic arrangement of time units.
(b) The musical instrument Kamaicha is majorly used by the 'Manganiar' Community of Manipur as a popular accompaniment to their songs.
(c) A raga is believed to have started as a tribal or folk tune.
(d) The sruti is a unit of measure or small difference between the various consecutive pitches within a grama or a scale.

91. Which of the following teams won the Indian Super League 2022-23?
(a) AKT Mohun Bagan
(b) Hyderabad FC
(c) Bengaluru FC
(d) Mumbai City FC

92. Which of the following states is famous for celebrating the festival of Vijaya Dashami, which marks the end of Durga Puja?
(a) Telangana (b) West Bengal
(c) Rajasthan (d) Chhattisgarh

93. Which of the following is/are an example of public goods?
1. Defence
2. House
(a) Only 2 (b) Both 1 and 2
(c) Only 1 (d) Neither 1 nor 2

94. Consider the following
Which of the following reasons may be considered as India's pull factors for migration?
1. Labour demand
2. Natural disaster
3. Protection of human and civil rights
4. High consumption and living standards

Codes
(a) Only 2
(b) Both 1 and 4
(c) Only 2, 3 and 4
(d) Only 1, 3 and 4

95. In which of the following states is the Sanchi Stupa UNESCO world heritage site located?
(a) Punjab
(b) Bihar
(c) Rajasthan
(d) Madhya Pradesh

96. The Himalayas' outermost range is called ....
(a) Kanchenjunga (b) Dhaula Dhar
(c) Pir Panjal (d) Shivaliks

97. Which of the following statements about Akbar are true?
1. He introduced the Mansabdari system.
2. He defeated and merged the state of Bijapur in his empire.
3. He made Fatehpur Sikri his capital.
(a) Only 1 and 2 (b) All 1, 2, 3
(c) Only 2 and 3 (d) Only 1 and 3

98. Which of the following Amendment Acts led to the insertion of Article 21 A?
(a) Eighty-seventh Amendment Act, 2003
(b) Eighty-sixth Amendment Act, 2002
(c) Eighty-fourth Amendment Act, 2002
(d) Eighty-fifth Amendment Act, 2002

99. Rukmini Devi Arundale is associated with which art form?
(a) Mural (b) Painting
(c) Kalaripayattu (d) Dance

100. Where is the renowned Bhatkhande Music Institute located?
(a) Lucknow (b) Chennai
(c) Surat (d) Madurai

Answers

1. (a)	2. (d)	3. (c)	4. (c)
5. (c)	6. (a)	7. (d)	8. (c)
9. (a)	10. (d)	11. (c)	12. (d)
13. (d)	14 (c)	15. (c)	16. (d)
17. (c)	18. (d)	19. (a)	20. (c)
21. (a)	22. (d)	23. (a)	24. (a)
25. (a)	26. (c)	27. (a)	28. (a)
29. (a)	30. (b)	31. (a)	32. (c)
33. (b)	34. (c)	35. (d)	36. (d)
37. (d)	38. (c)	39. (b)	40. (c)
41. (c)	42. (b)	43. (b)	44. (b)
45. (b)	46. (d)	47. (a)	48. (c)
49. (c)	50. (d)	51. (b)	52. (c)
53. (b)	54. (b)	55. (c)	56. (a)
57. (a)	58. (d)	59. (c)	60. (b)
61. (a)	62. (d)	63. (c)	64. (a)
65. (b)	66. (a)	67. (b)	68. (a)
69. (d)	70. (a)	71. (b)	72. (c)
73. (d)	74. (d)	75. (b)	76. (d)
77. (d)	78. (b)	79. (a)	80. (d)
81. (d)	82. (b)	83. (d)	84. (c)
85. (d)	86. (b)	87. (c)	88. (c)
89. (b)	90. (b)	91. (a)	92. (b)
93. (c)	94. (d)	95. (d)	96. (d)
97. (d)	98. (b)	99. (d)	100. (a)

Explanations

1. *(a)* Part (a) 'The volunteer gave on to' contains an error. Use 'out' in place of 'on to' correct the sentence. Gave out means to distribute.
2. *(d)* Part (d) 'who was leaving college' contains an error. Use 'left' to correct the sentence as the sentence is in simple past tense.
3. *(c)* Part (c) 'most intelligent' contains an error. Use 'an intelligent' to correct the sentence.
4. *(c)* The underlined part of the given sentence contains an error. Use 'global community to accelerate' to correct the sentence.
5. *(c)* The correct filler for the given blank is 'book'.
6. *(a)* The correct filler for the given blank is 'very'.
7. *(d)* The correct filler for the given blank is 'allows'.
8. *(c)* The correct filler for the given blank is 'visits'.
9. *(a)* The correct filler for the given blank is 'find'.
10. *(d)* 'Sluggish' means slow and lazy. Hence, its antonym is 'Rapid' which means fast.
    - 'Hassled' means irritating inconvenience.
    - 'Lethargic' means lazy.
    - 'Leisurely' means in a slow manner.
11. *(c)* 'Timid' means fearful. Hence, its antonym is 'Audacious' which means bold and brave.
    - 'Resolute' means determined.
    - 'Blunt' means rude.
    - 'Assertive' means having or showing a confident and forceful personality.
12. *(d)* The word 'retract' means 'to take back'. Hence, its synonym is 'revoke'.
13. *(d)* Allusive handwriting means illegible handwriting.
14. *(c)* The correct spelling is 'privilege'.
15. *(c)* Dog in the manger is used for a person who has no need of, or ability to use, a possession that would be of use or value to others, but who prevents others from having it. The sentence that uses the idiom correctly is- Rachit had some important work and so he cancelled the show tickets for everyone.
16. *(d)* The word 'vigilant' means 'alert and careful'.
17. *(c)* The correct filler for the given blank is 'writing'.
18. *(d)* Parade refers to a public procession, especially one celebrating a special day or event.
19. *(a)* The word 'enormous' means huge. Hence, its antonym is 'minute' which means too small.
20. *(c)* The underlined word denotes that Mr. Sen is intelligent.
21. *(a)* The underlined part of the given sentence contains an error. Use 'at a more leisurely pace' to correct the sentence.
22. *(d)* The underlined idiom 'called it a day' means stopped work for the day.
23. *(a)* The incorrectly spelt word is 'wolrd'. The correct spelling is 'world'.
24. *(a)* The bracketed word the given sentence contains an error. Use 'typically built' to correct the sentence.
25. *(a)* The bracketed word of the given sentence contains an error. Use 'by Ramesh affected' to correct the sentence.
26. *(c)* The pattern of the series is as follows,

B —(−5)→ W —(−5)→ R —(−5)→ M —(−5)→ H
J —(+5)→ O —(+5)→ T —(+5)→ Y —(+5)→ D
R —(−5)→ M —(−5)→ H —(−5)→ C —(−5)→ X

27. *(a)*

Given word → D O C U M E N T A R Y
After arranging in alphabetical order → A C D E M N O R T U Y

Hence, two letters M and Y position remain unchanged.

28. *(a)* According to the question,

Given expression, $K \times Q + R - S \div L$

(+)K ←Husband— Q(−); Q —Mother→ R(+); (+)R ←Brother— S(+); S —Father→ L
[+ → Male, − → Female]

Hence, K is father's father to L.

29. *(a)* As, $(5, 4, 41) = (5^2 + 4^2)$
$= 25 + 16 = 41$
and $(7, 2, 53) = (7^2 + 2^2) = 49 + 4 = 53$
Similarly, $(9, 3, 90)$
$= (9^2 + 3^2) = 81 + 9 = 90$
30. *(b)* The figure given in option (b) is the correct mirror image of the given question figure.

M
Trd42ba | ɐdƧ4bɿT
N

31. *(a)* Naming the figure,

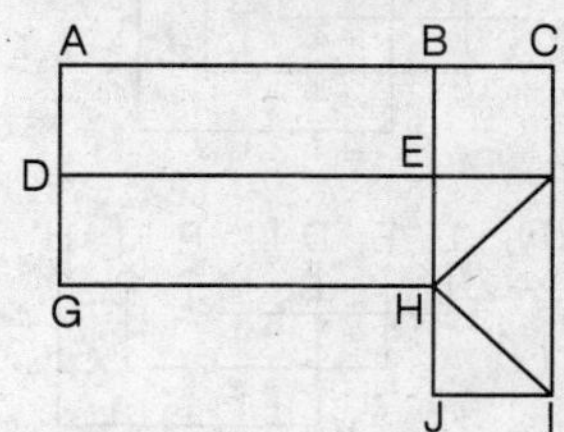

There are 11 quadrilaterals in the given figure,
ABED, DEHG, ABHG, BCFE, ACFD, EFIJ, BCIJ, DGHF, BCIH, EFIH and HJIF.

32. *(c)* The figure given in option (c) is the correct mirror image of the given figure.

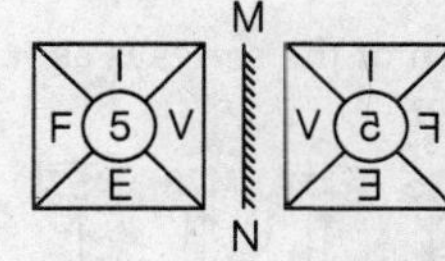

33. *(b)* As, petal is a part of flower. Similarly, seed is a part of fruit.
34. *(c)* According to the statements,

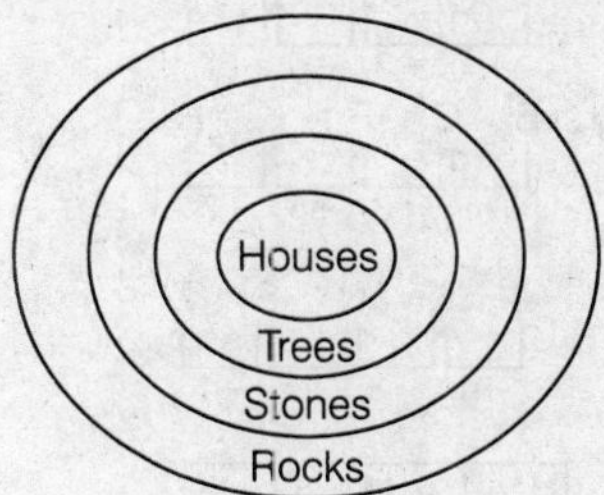

Conclusions I. (✓) II. (✓)

Hence, both Conclusions I and II follow.

35. *(d)* Odd days in ordinary year = 1

Odd days in leap year = 2

Day on 23rd June, 2008 = Monday

Number of odd days from 23rd June, 2008 to 23rd June, 2020

$= 1 + 1 + 1 + 2 + 1 + 1 + 1 + 2$
$+ 1 + 1 + 1 + 2$

$= \frac{15}{7} = 2$ weeks + 1 odd day

∴ The day of week on 23rd June, 2020

= Monday + 1 = Tuesday

36. *(d)* As,

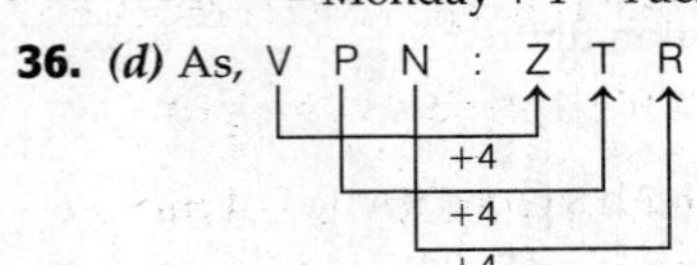

and

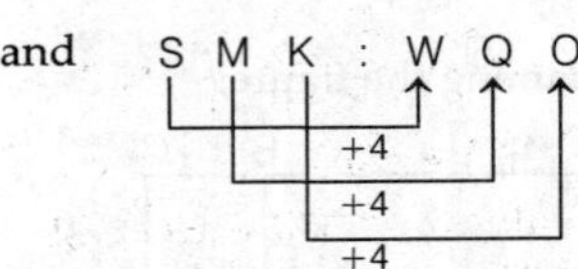

Similarly,

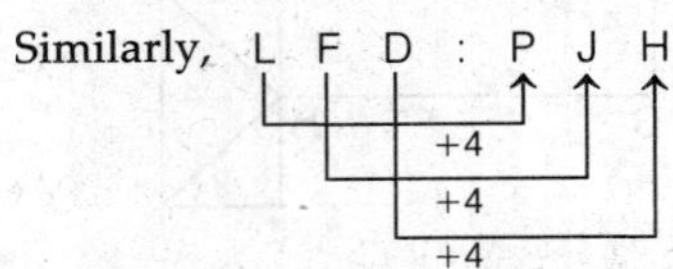

37. *(d)* The figure given in option (d) is the correct mirror image of the given figure.

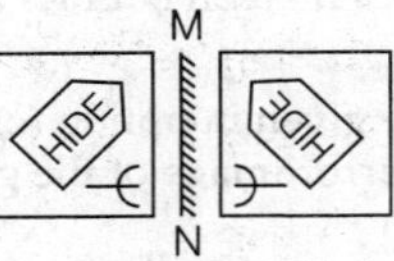

38. *(c)* The pattern of the series is as follows,

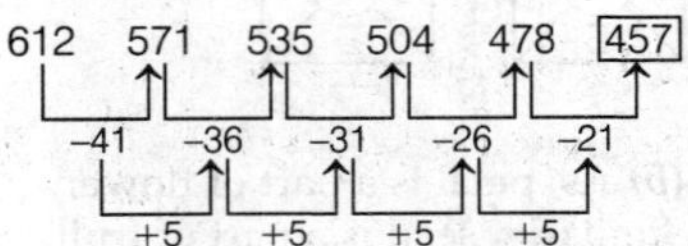

39. *(b)* As, E F I N U
+1 +3 +5 +7

B C F K R ;
+1 +3 +5 +7

J K N S Z
+1 +3 +5 +7

But,

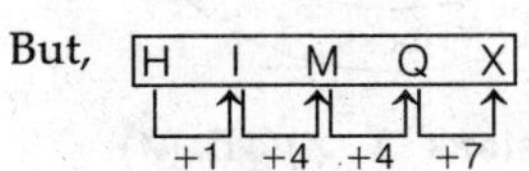

40. *(c)* According to the question,

A → ÷	B → ×
C → +	D → −

From option (c),

32 B 8 D 160 A 2 C 42

$= 32 \times 8 - 160 \div 2 + 42$

$= 256 - 80 + 42$

$= 298 - 80 = 218$

41. *(c)* The figure given in option (c) is the correct mirror image of the given figure.

M

DBHJZT | DBHJZT (mirrored)

N

42. *(b)* Given expression,

$15 \times 5 - 75 + (300 \div 6) + 3 \times 19 = 115$

From option (b),

After interchanging numbers 15 and 19, we get

$= 19 \times 5 - 75 + (300 \div 6) + 3 \times 15$

$= 95 - 75 + 50 + 45$

$= 190 - 75$

$= 115$

43. *(b)* Given expression,

14 B 11 D 22 C 328 A 8 = ?

After substituting letters with signs, we get

$= 14 \times 11 - 22 + 328 \div 8$

$= 154 - 22 + 41$

$= 195 - 22$

$= 173$

44. *(b)* As,

DIVERT → 36

[∵ (Number of letters in word)^2]

∴ $(6)^2 = 36$

and DOLDRUMS → 64

$(8)^2 = 64$

Similarly, DOGMA → 25

$(5)^2 = 25$

45. *(b)* The pattern of the given series is as follows,

155 146 137 128 119 110
−9 −9 −9 −9 −9

46. *(d)* The pattern of the given series is as follows,

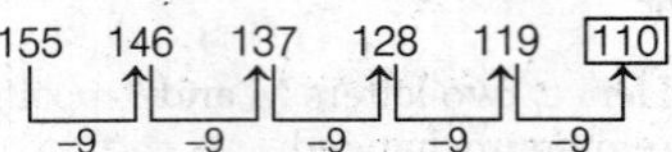

47. *(a)* There are two alternate series in the given question, which are as follows,

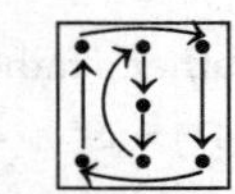

From figure 1 to 2
figure 3 to 4

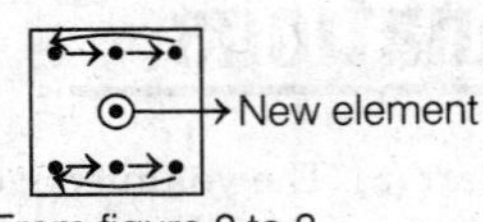

From figure 2 to 3
figure 4 to 5

Hence, option figure (a) will replace the question mark.

48. *(c)* When we unfolded the paper, then it will appear as the figure given in option (c).

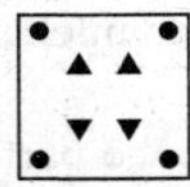

49. *(c)* According to the question,

Strength to innovate → 42 64 32

Strength to create → 32 42 24

Hence, the code for 'create' is '24'.

50. *(d)* As, $92 \div 4 = 23$

and $136 \div 4 = 34$

Similarly, $a \times 4 = 224$

$a = \frac{224}{4}$

$a = 56$

51. *(b)* Let x be more number of workers required to complete work in 10 days.

By MDH formula,

$M_1D_1 = M_2D_2$

$55 \times 16 = (55 + x) \times 10$

$\Rightarrow 11 \times 16 = (55 + x) \times 2$

$\Rightarrow 55 + x = 88$

$\Rightarrow x = 88 - 55 = 33$

$\Rightarrow x = 33$

Hence, 33 more workers required to complete work in 10 days.

52. *(c)* Radius of circle are 7 cm and 4 cm.

Distance between centres $(d) = 25$ cm

Thus, length of transverse common tangent

$= \sqrt{d^2 - (r_2 + r_1)^2}$

$= \sqrt{(25)^2 - (7+4)^2}$

$= \sqrt{625 - 121}$

$= \sqrt{504}$

$= 6\sqrt{14}$ cm

Hence, length of transverse common tangent $= 6\sqrt{14}$ cm.

53. *(b)* Radius of circle = 48 cm

Length of arc = 15 cm

Angle of sector $(\theta) = \frac{\text{Arc}}{\text{Radius}} = \frac{15}{48}$

$= \frac{5}{16}$ Radian

Now, area of sector $= \frac{\theta}{360^\circ} \times \pi r^2$

$\left[1R = \frac{180}{\pi} \text{ degree}\right]$

$= \frac{5}{16} \times \frac{180}{\pi} \times \frac{1}{360^\circ} \times \pi \times 48 \times 48$

$= 360 \text{ cm}^2$

54. *(b)* For company A,

25% of income = Profit

Income of company A in 2014

= 40 crores

Profit of company A in 2014

$= 40 \times 25\% = 10$ crores

Expenditure of company A in 2014

$= 40 - 10 =$ ₹ 30 crores

55. *(c)* Principal sum $(P) =$ ₹ 2430

Simple interest (SI) = ₹ 1093.50

Time $(T) = 3$ yr

Let rate = R

$\therefore \quad SI = \frac{P \times R \times T}{100}$

$\Rightarrow 1093.50 = \frac{2430 \times R \times 3}{100}$

$\Rightarrow \quad R = \frac{1093.5 \times 100}{2430 \times 3}$

$\Rightarrow \quad R = 15\%$

Hence, rate of interest = 15%

56. *(a)* Let Sonu has $100x$ land.

Then, Raju has $100x \times \frac{115}{100} = 115x$ land

and Ramu has $100x \times \frac{125}{100} = 125x$ land

$\therefore$ Required ratio of land by Raju and Ramu $= \frac{115x}{125x} = \frac{23}{25}$

Hence, required ratio = 23 : 25

57. *(a)*

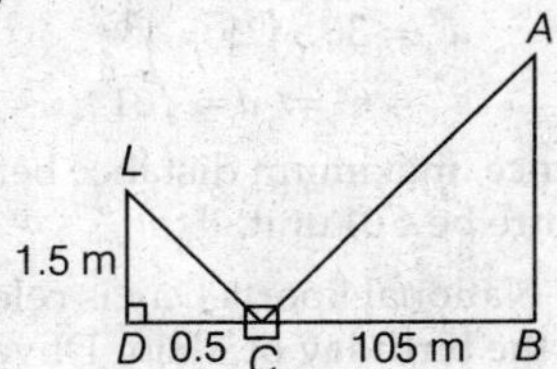

Let LD and AB be height of man and tower, respectively and Point C be the mirror and point of incidence of tower in the mirror.

In ΔLDC and ΔABC [$\angle B = \angle D = 90^\circ$

$\therefore \angle LDC = \angle ABC$]

Both triangles are similar.

Then, $\Delta LDC \sim \Delta ABC$

$\frac{AB}{LD} = \frac{CB}{DC}$

$\Rightarrow \quad \frac{AB}{1.5} = \frac{105}{0.5}$

$\Rightarrow \quad AB = 315$ m

$\therefore$ Length of tower is 315 m.

58. *(d)* Average speed of entire ride

$= \frac{\text{Total distance}}{\text{Total time}}$

$= \frac{10 + 15}{\frac{10}{15} + \frac{15}{10}}$

$= \frac{25}{\frac{2}{3} + \frac{3}{2}}$

$= \frac{25 \times 6}{13}$

$= 11.54$ km/h

59. *(c)* Number of girls in Mathematics

$= 840 \times \frac{40}{100} = 336$

Number of girls in Chemistry

$= 220 \times \frac{70}{100} = 154$

Number of girls in Physics

$= 450 \times \frac{30}{100} = 135$

Number of girls in Biology

$= 200 \times \frac{80}{100} = 160$

Now, total girls = 785

Total students = 1710

$\therefore$ Required percentage

$= \frac{785}{1710} \times 100 = 45.90\%$

60. *(b)* Let the distance be d km.

According to the question,

$\frac{d}{3} - \frac{d}{4} = 1\text{ h} \qquad \left(\frac{1}{2} + \frac{1}{2} = 1\right)$

$\Rightarrow \quad \frac{4d - 3d}{12} = 1$

$\therefore \quad d = 12$ km

Thus, required distance = 12 km

61. *(a)* Ratio of time taken by P and Q

$= P : Q$

Time ratio $= \frac{x}{2} : x$

$= 1 : 2$

Efficiency ratio = 2 : 1

Thus, total work done

$= (2 + 1) \times 36 = 108$ units

Time taken by Q alone to finish the work $= \frac{108}{1} = 108$ days

62. *(d)* Diameter of cylindrical cup = 7 cm

Radius of cylindrical cup $= \frac{7}{2}$ cm

Height of cylindrical cup = 4 cm

Volume of each cylindrical cup $= \pi r^2 h$

$= \frac{22}{7} \times \frac{7}{2} \times \frac{7}{2} \times 4$

$= 154 \text{ cm}^3$

Thus, volume of cylindrical cup 180 patients, $= 154 \times 180$

$= 27720 \text{ cm}^3$

$= 27.72$ L

$[\because 1 \text{ L} = 1000 \text{ cm}^3]$

63. *(c)* $12 \div 4$ of $3 \times 6 + 8 \div 16$ of $4 \times 8 - 4 \div 6 \times 9$

$= 12 \div 4 \times 3 \times 6 + 8 \div 16 \times 4 \times 8 - 4 \div 6 \times 9$

[Using BODMAS rule]

$= 12 \div 12 \times 6 + 8 \div 64 \times 8 - \frac{4}{6} \times 9$

$= 1 \times 6 + \frac{1}{8} \times 8 - \frac{2}{3} \times 9$

$= 6 + 1 - 6$

$= 1$

64. *(a)* Total votes are 8750.

Then, valid votes $= 8750 \times \frac{80}{100} = 7000$

According to the question,

Opponent votes

$= 7000 \times \frac{(100 - 63)}{100}$

$= 7000 \times \frac{37}{100}$

$= 2590$

Thus, opponent got 2590 votes.

65. *(b)* $\tan A = \frac{\sqrt{2} - 1}{1}$

Then,

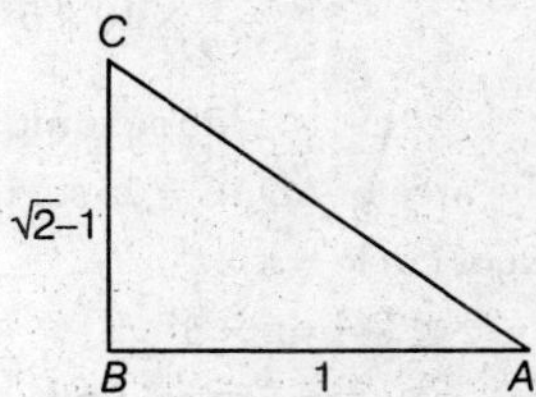

Thus, by Pythagoras theorem,

$AC^2 = BC^2 + BA^2$

$= (\sqrt{2} - 1)^2 + 1^2$

$= 2 + 1 - 2\sqrt{2} + 1$

$$AC^2 = 4 - 2\sqrt{2}$$
$$AC = \sqrt{4 - 2\sqrt{2}}$$

Thus, $\sin A \cdot \cos A + \tan A$

$$\frac{\sqrt{2}-1}{\sqrt{4-2\sqrt{2}}} \times \frac{1}{\sqrt{4-2\sqrt{2}}} + \frac{\sqrt{2}-1}{1}$$
$$= \frac{\sqrt{2}-1}{4-2\sqrt{2}} + \frac{\sqrt{2}-1}{1}$$
$$= \frac{2\sqrt{2}}{8} + \frac{\sqrt{2}-1}{1} = \frac{2\sqrt{2}+8\sqrt{2}-8}{8}$$
$$= \frac{10\sqrt{2}-8}{8} = \frac{5\sqrt{2}-4}{4}$$

66. *(a)* Let the two digits number be $10x + y$.

If digits are reverse $= 10y + x$

According to question,

$$10y + x - (10x + y) = 27$$
$$\Rightarrow \quad 10y + x - 10x - y = 27$$
$$\Rightarrow \quad 9y - 9x = 27$$
$$\Rightarrow \quad 9(y - x) = 27$$
$$\Rightarrow \quad y - x = 3 \quad \text{... (i)}$$

and $\quad x + y = 9 \quad$ [given] ... (ii)

Adding Eqs. (i) and (ii),

$$2y = 12$$
$$\Rightarrow \quad y = 6 \text{ and } x = 3$$

Thus, required number = 36

67. *(b)* Here, AC = diameter of circle

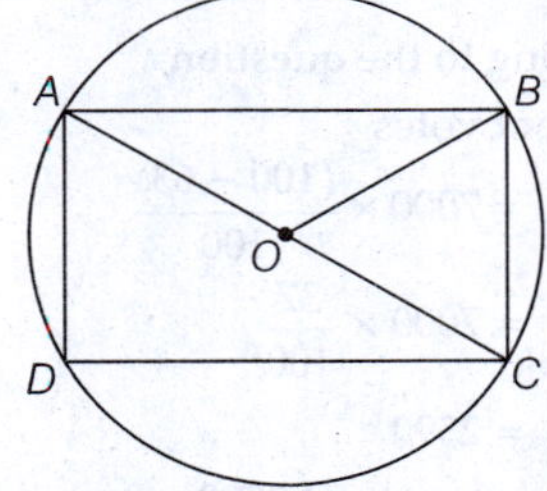

Radius of circle = 5 units

Thus, area of $\Delta ABC = \frac{1}{2} \times AC \times BO$

$$= \frac{1}{2} \times 10 \times 5$$
$$= 25 \text{ sq. unit}$$

Similarly, area of ΔDAC = 25 sq. unit

and area of circle $= \pi \times r^2$

$$= \pi \times 5^2$$
$$= 25\pi \text{ sq. unit}$$

Hence, area of remaining portion

$$= 25\pi - 50$$
$$= 25(\pi - 2) \text{ sq. unit}$$

68. *(a)* Let CP of 100 gm goods be ₹ 100.

But, he gave 19% less, while selling.

Thus, SP of 81 gm of goods

$$= 100 \times \frac{135}{100}$$

SP of 81 gm of goods = ₹ 135

Thus, actual SP of 100 gm of goods

$$= \frac{135}{81} \times 100 = ₹\ 166.67$$

Thus, net gain percentage

$$= \frac{166.67 - 100}{100} \times 100$$
$$= 66.67\%$$

69. *(d)* Central angle for food expenditure = 120°

Central angle for saving = 60°

Thus, ratio of expenditure on food and savings = 120 : 60 = 2 : 1

70. *(a)* Let four years ago age of Kavya be x yr.

Then, age of Ravi four years ago $= 4x$ yr

After seven years,

Kavya's age $= (x + 11)$ yr

Ravi's age $= (4x + 11)$ yr

According to the question,

$$(4x + 11) = 3(x + 11)$$
$$\Rightarrow \quad 4x + 11 = 3x + 33$$
$$\Rightarrow \quad x = 22$$

Age of Kavya at present,

$$= x + 4 = 22 + 4 = 26$$

Age of Ravi at present

$$= 4x + 4 = 22 \times 4 + 4 = 92$$

Thus, sum of ages of both

$$= 92 + 26 = 118 \text{ yr}$$

71. *(b)* Let Ram's monthly salary be $100x$.

Then, savings after deduction of all expenses

$$= 100x - (30x + 10x + 7x + 6x)$$
$$= 100x - (53x) = 47x$$

But, $47x = 1880$ (given)

$$x = 40$$

Hence, Ram's monthly salary

$$= 40 \times 100 = ₹\ 4000$$

72. *(c)* Percentage of tourist went to Agra = 15%

Percentage of tourist went to Kashi = 20%

Then, required percentage

$$= 20 + 15 = 35\%$$

73. *(d)* Let height of tank be x cm.

Then, breadth of tank $(b) = \frac{x}{5}$ cm

and length of tank $(l) = \frac{1}{3}\left(\frac{x}{5} + x\right)$

$$= \frac{1}{3} \times \frac{6x}{5} = \frac{2x}{5}$$

Then, volume of cuboidal tank

$$= l \times b \times h$$
$$10 \times 1000 = \frac{2x}{5} \times \frac{x}{5} \times x$$

[$\because$ 1 L = 1000 cm^3]

$$\Rightarrow \quad 10000 = \frac{2 \times x^3}{25}$$
$$\Rightarrow \quad x^3 = 5000 \times 25$$
$$\Rightarrow \quad x = 5 \times 10 \Rightarrow x = 50 \text{ cm}$$

Hence, height of tank is 50 cm.

74. *(d)* $8^6 + 1$ is divide by 7.

For remainder $= \frac{(8^6 + 1)}{7}$

When, 8^6 divide by 7, it gives 1 as remainder, then

$$= \frac{1^6 + 1}{7} \quad \left[\frac{8}{7} = 1 \text{ as remainder}\right]$$
$$= \frac{2}{7}$$

When 2 is divide by 7, it gives 2 as remainder.

75. *(b)* Here, length of common internal tangent = 6 units

Radius of circles are 2 units and 3 units.

For maximum distance between centre the tangent must be a transverse tangent.

For maximum length between centre

Length of tangent

$$= \sqrt{d^2 - (r_2 + r_1)^2}$$
$$6 = \sqrt{d^2 - (2 + 3)^2}$$
$$\Rightarrow \quad 36 = d^2 - 5^2$$
$$\Rightarrow \quad d^2 = 36 + 25$$
$$\Rightarrow \quad d^2 = 61 \Rightarrow d = \sqrt{61}$$

Hence, maximum distance between centre be $\sqrt{61}$ unit.

76. *(d)* National Sports Day is celebrated on the birthday of Major Dhyan Chand.

- It is celebrated on 29th August every year.
- The Rajiv Gandhi Khel Ratna award is renamed as Major Dhyan Chand Award.

- It comes with a cash prize of ₹ 25 lakh.

77. *(d)* The total duration of a hockey match as per the International Hockey Federation Rule is 60 minutes.
- A hockey team consists of 11 players per side.
- The important terms associated with hockey are kick shot, killing, line and major penalty.
- Hockey pitches are rectangular, with the longer edges measuring 91.4 m long and the shorter edges measuring 55 m wide.

78. *(b)* National Human Right Commission (NHRC) was established in the year 1993.
- It established under the provisions of the Protection of Human Rights Act.
- It is a statutory body in India.
- The headquarters of the NHRC is in New Delhi.

79. *(a)* In 1812, Amedeo Avogadro described the hypothesis that equal volumes of different gases contain an equal number of molecules.

80. *(d)* The Bhopal gas tragedy occur in 1984.
- It was a chemical accident on the night of 2rd to 3rd December, 1984 at the Union Carbide India Limited in Bhopal, Madhya Pradesh.
- It tragedy took place due release of Methyl Isocyanate gas.
- The plant was owned by a subsidiary of the US based Union Carbide Corporation.

81. *(d)* Right to elementary education is available to both Indians as well as foreigners. Hence Statement (4) is correct.
- Fundamental rights available only to Indian citizens are
  - Right to protection of language, script and culture of minorities.
  - Equality of opportunity in matters of public employment.
  - Right of minorities to establish and administer educational institutions.

82. *(b)* In addition to using the arrow keys and mouse clicks, pressing the 'Enter' key or using the scroll wheel can be used to move around a table in Microsoft Word.

83. *(d)* Since 2nd March, 2023, appointment to Election Commission will be done under the recommendation of a committee comprising of Prime Minister, Leader of opposition and Chief Justice of India.
- It is a permanent constitutional body.
- It was established in accordance with the Constitution on 25th January, 1950.

84. *(c)* Justice PV Reddi was appointed as Chairman of the National Judicial Pay Commission.
- It is a body established to review and recommend changes to the pay and allowances of judges in a particular country.
- Justice JS Verma was an Indian jurist who served as the 27th Chief Justice of India from 25th March, 1997 to 18th January, 1998.

85. *(d)* Rhamnose is a carbohydrate that doesn't fit into the general formula for carbohydrates, $C_x(H_2O)_y$.
Rhamnose has the chemical formula $C_6H_{12}O_5$.

86. *(b)* A constellation of the Northern sky recognised by a group of five bright stars forming a slightly irregular 'W' is called Cassiopeia.
- Cassiopeia is a constellation of the Northern sky easily recognised by a group of five bright stars forming a slightly irregular.
- Ursa Major is known as the Big Dipper in the United States and Canada, or the Plough in the UK and Ireland.
- Orion is one of the most prominent and easily recognisable constellations in the night sky.

87. *(c)* Hindustan Socialist Republican Association revolutionary organisation was established at Feroz Shah Kotla in New Delhi in 1928.
- It was founded by Chandrasekhar Azad, Bhagat Singh, and Sukhdev Thapa in 1928.
- Kakori Conspiracy was a train robbery done by HRSA.
- The killing of John Saunders to take revenge was conducted by HRSA.

88. *(c)* National Investment and Manufacturing Zones (NIMZs) of India prescribes a minimum area of 5000 hectares for establishing NIMZs. Hence Statement (3) is incorrect.
- The State Government will provide power connectivity, water and other infrastructural facilities. Hence Statement (1) is correct.
- A special purpose vehicle will be constituted to take care of the functioning of NIMZs. Hence Statement (2) is also correct.
- At least 30% of the total land area proposed for the NIMZ is to be utilised for manufacturing units. Hence, Statement (4) is also correct.

89. *(b)* In MS Word, the floppy disk icon from the icons below the Menu Bar is commonly used to save the current document.

90. *(b)* Statement (b) is incorrect because Kamaicha is a traditional stringed instrument used by the Manganier community of Rajasthan not Manipur. It is an important part of their folk music.
Statements (a, c and d) are correct.
- Tala indeed refers to a cyclic arrangement of time unit in Indian music.
- Ragas are believed to have originated from tribal or folk tunes.
- Sruti is a unit of measure or small differences between consecutive pitches within a grama or scale.

91. *(a)* AKT Mohun Bagan won the Indian Super League (ISL)2022-23.
- ISL was founded By All India Football Federation, IMG-Reliance, Star Sports.
- It was launched on 21st October, 2013.
- The total number of teams is Eleven.

92. *(b)* West Bengal is famous for celebrating the festival of Vijaya Dashmi.
- It celebrates the victory of Lord Rama over King Ravana. In Kerala, Vijayadashami is celebrated as Vidhyarambham day.
- In Karnataka, 'Dussehra Procession', known as Jambu savar.

93. *(c)* Defence is an example of public goods.
- A private good is a good that is purchased and used by one party and is not available to others. e.g. personal house, car.
- A public good is a good that is offered free to consumers e.g. national defence, government parks.

94. *(d)* Labour demand, Protection of human and civil rights and high consumption and living standard are considered as India's pull factor for migration.

- Push factors incorporate reasons people want to leave a region e.g. war, political instability, famine.
- Pull factors incorporate reasons people want to move into a certain region e.g. educational opportunities, higher living standards.

95. *(d)* Sanchi Stupa ,located in Madhya Pradesh, is a UNESCO world heritage site.

- It was built by Ashoka in 3rd century BCE.
- The original structure was made out of bricks. Later on, it was covered with stone, vedica, and the torana (gateway).
- The stupa contains and a (hemispherical dome), harmika(square railing) chhatra (top umbrella).

96. *(d)* Himalaya's outermost layer is called as Shivaliks.

- Dhauladhar range is part of lesser Himalayas.
- Pir Panjal is the largest range of the lower Himalayas.
- Kanchenjunga is the third-highest mountain in the world.

97. *(d)* Statements (1) and (3) are true.

- Akbar introduced Mansabdari system.
- He made Fatehpur his capital.
- Aurangzeb defeated and merged the state of Bijapur in his empire. Hence, Statement (2) is incorrect.

98. *(b)* 86th Amendment Act, 2002 led to the insertion of Article 21 A.

- The 86th Amendment Act added provisions regarding the Fundamental Right of a child to free and compulsory education.
- The 87th Amendment Act provided for the delimitation of constituencies on the basis of 2001 census.
- The 84th Amendment Act says that the constituency boundaries were frozen until the first census after 2026 or at least after 2031.
- The 85th Constitution amendment was made to provide consequential seniority in case of promotions of SC/ST employees.

99. *(d)* Rukmiani Devi Arundale is associated with dance.

- She is associated with Bharatanatyam dance.
- She is the first woman to be nominated as member of Rajya Sabha.
- Google featured her in its 2017 Google Doodle for International Women's Day.

100. *(a)* Bhatkhande Music Institute is located in Lucknow.

- It was established by Pt Vishnu Narayan Bhatkhande in 1926.
- Kanika Kapoor and Amit Prakash Mishra are former students of this institute.

Set 30 10 July, 2024 (Shift II)

SSC CHSL Tier-I
SOLVED PAPER

Instructions

1. This paper contains 100 questions.
2. It has 4 Parts, **Part I** General English, **Part II** General Intelligence & Reasoning, **Part III** Quantitative Aptitude and **Part IV** General Awareness.
3. Each question carries **2 marks.**

Part I
General English

1. The following sentence has been divided into four parts. Identify the part that contains an error.

(A) It is sad / (B) that you / (C) are believing / (D) in superstitious rituals.

(a) A (b) C
(c) B (d) D

2. The following sentence has been split into four segments. Identify the segment that contains a grammatical error.

Since childhood, Monty / ate his food / fast and he / will not change.

(a) fast and he
(b) ate his food
(c) Since childhood, Monty
(d) will not change

3. The following sentence has been divided into four segments. Identify the segment that contains a grammatical error.

After your insistence, / my sister / checked / a mailbox again.

(a) a mailbox again
(b) After your insistence,
(c) my sister
(d) checked

4. The following sentence has been split into four segments. Identify the segment that contains a grammatical error.

In order to connect / these themes to a wider / historical context, Rahul go / beyond aesthetic analysis.

(a) In order to connect
(b) beyond aesthetic analysis
(c) these themes to a wider
(d) historical context, Rahul go

Directions (Q. Nos. 5-9) *In the following passage, some words have been deleted. Read the passage carefully and select the most appropriate option to fill in each blank.*

There is nothing more (1) .... than when you sit down at your table to study with the most sincere of intentions and instead of being able to finish the task at hand you find your thoughts (2) .... However, there are certain techniques that you can use to (3) .... your concentration. To begin with, one should (4) .... to create the physical environment that is conducive to (5) .... thought.

5. Select the most appropriate option to fill in blank no. (1).

(a) frustrating (b) exciting
(c) interesting (d) surprising

6. Select the most appropriate option to fill in blank no. (2).

(a) wandering (b) interesting
(c) tiring (d) worrying

7. Select the most appropriate option to fill in blank no. (3).

(a) enhance (b) commit
(c) discover (d) convince

8. Select the most appropriate option to fill in blank no. (4).

(a) attempt (b) imagine
(c) announce (d) lead

9. Select the most appropriate option to fill in blank no. (5).

(a) focussed (b) joyful
(c) cautious (d) dazzling

10. Select the most appropriate meaning of the underlined idiom in the following sentence.

Manish told Rounak <u>time and again</u> of the ill consequences of his habit of being late to the college.

(a) Repeatedly (b) Hardly ever
(c) At intervals (d) Not often

11. Select the most appropriate option to fill in the blank.

Seema has a dominating nature, so she wants to .... of everything in her life.

(a) keep touch (b) keep calm
(c) keep record (d) keep control

12. Select the most appropriate option to fill in the blank.

I am doubtful about his story, though you seem to be ....

(a) regretting (b) uncertain
(c) pleasant (d) convinced

13. Select the most appropriate antonym of the given word.

Powerful

(a) Strong (b) Impotent
(c) Manly (d) Wild

14. Select the most appropriate antonym of the underlined word.

The government is planning to <u>abolish</u> child care leave for female employees.

(a) Ensure (b) Eradicate
(c) Encourage (d) Establish

15. Select the incorrectly spelt word.

(a) Appraisal (b) Definate
(c) Stretch (d) Genuine

16. Select the most appropriate synonym of the given word.

Estimate

(a) Evaluate (b) Appropriate
(c) Profit (d) Verify

17. Select the most appropriate option that can substitute the underlined segment in the given sentence.

We shall rehearse thrice before the final performance <u>at least we make errors</u> in the dialogues.

(a) for we make errors
(b) but we make errors
(c) can we make errors
(d) lest we make errors

18. Select the most appropriate antonym for the underlined word in the given sentence.

Because the politician made a <u>candid</u> speech, he earned the respect of the voters.

(a) reticent (b) prudent
(c) deceitful (d) reckless

19. Select the correct spelling of the underlined word in the given sentence.

She decided to file a complaint with HR after being <u>harrasad</u> by her supervisor for several weeks.

(a) harassed (b) harrassd
(c) harrased (d) harased

20. Select the most appropriate option that can substitute the underlined word in the following sentence.

They studied <u>during</u> three hours.

(a) by (b) for
(c) at (d) from

21. Select the most appropriate option that can substitute the underlined words in the given sentence.

This newly arisen evidence <u>could have proved</u> to finally put the culprit behind bars.

(a) is proof
(b) can proof
(c) can be proven
(d) could have been proven

22. Select the most appropriate antonym of the given word.

Innovate

(a) Solve (b) Finance
(c) Invent (d) Copy

23. Select the most appropriate idiom to fill the blank in the given situation.

They were waiting for their family members who were returning from a pilgrimage. Therefore, they were .... on the platform.

(a) running behind time
(b) playing a joke
(c) pacing up and down
(d) rolling up their sleeves

24. Select the most appropriate synonym of the underlined word.

The removal of <u>petty</u> restrictions has made life easier.

(a) big (b) consequential
(c) large (d) small

25. Select the most appropriate option that can substitute the underlined segment in the given sentence. If there is no need to substitute it, select 'No substitution required'.

If you <u>give away</u> smoking, your health will improve.

(a) No substitution required
(b) give up
(c) give off
(d) give out

Part II
General Intelligence

26. In a certain code language, 'cooler is hot' is written as 'tp rc dl' and 'hot weather comes' is written as 'rc dn nz'. How is 'hot' written in the given language?

(a) rc (b) nz (c) dn (d) dl

27. Choose the alternative which closely resembles the mirror image of the given combination.

nETFLIcKs (mirror AB)

(a) ƨꓘɔI⅃ꟻTƎn (b) ƨꓘɔI⅃Ʇ⊥Ǝn
(c) ƨꓘIc⅃ꟻTƎn (d) ƨꓘɔI⅃ꟻTEn

28. What will come in the place of the question mark (?) in the following equation, if '+' and '−' are interchanged and '×' and '÷' are interchanged?

$204 \times 4 - 9 \div 2 + 6 = ?$

(a) 64 (b) 63 (c) 61 (d) 62

29. Select the set in which the numbers are related in the same way as are the numbers of the following sets.

(**Note** Operations should be performed on the whole numbers, without breaking down the numbers into its constituent digits. E.g. 13 – Operations on 13 such as adding/deleting/multiplying etc. to 13 can be performed. Breaking down 13 into 1 and 3 and then performing mathematical operations on 1 and 3 is not allowed.)

(6, 12, 48),
(8, 16, 64)

(a) (12, 28, 112) (b) (14, 28, 110)
(c) (14, 24, 112) (d) (14, 28, 112)

30. If 'A' stands for '÷', 'B' stands for '×', 'C' stands for '+' and 'D' stands for '−', what will come in place of the question mark (?) in the following equation?

82 B 6 D 114 A 2 C 35 = ?

(a) 470 (b) 460
(c) 450 (d) 480

31. If 20th March, 2011 was Sunday, then what was the day of the week on 20th March, 2019?

(a) Monday (b) Wednesday
(c) Saturday (d) Friday

32. What should come in place of the question mark (?) in the given series?

13, 17, 26, ?, 67, 103, 152

(a) 59 (b) 47 (c) 33 (d) 42

33. Select the correct mirror image of the given combination when the mirror is placed at MN as shown below.

M2aPvd (mirror MN)

(a) bvꟼɒƧM (b) pʌꟼɒƧW
(c) bvꟼɒƧM (d) PvdɒƧM

34. What should come in place of the question mark (?) in the given series?

268, 259, 250, 241, 232, ?

(a) 221 (b) 224
(c) 223 (d) 220

35. In a certain code language,

'M & N' means 'M is the wife of N',
'M @ N' means 'M is the brother of N',
'M $ N' means 'M is the daughter of N',
'M # N' means 'M is the son of N'.

Based on the above, how is Q related to N, if 'N # M @ O $ P & Q'?

(a) Brother
(b) Father
(c) Mother's father
(d) Father's father

36. Select the word-pair that best represents a similar relationship to the one expressed in the pair of words given below.

(The words must be considered as meaningful English words and must not be related to each other based on the number of letters/number of consonants/vowels in the word).

Dawn - Sunrise

(a) Touch - Toes (b) Joy - Sad
(c) Easy - Simple (d) Old - New

37. Three statements are followed by conclusions numbered I, II. You have to consider these statements to be true, even if they seem to be at variance with commonly known facts. Decide which of the given conclusions logically follows from the given statement.

Statements

All water is earth.
All earth is fire.
Some fire is air.

Conclusions

I. Some air is earth.
II. Some fire is water.

(a) Both Conclusions I and II follow
(b) Only Conclusion II follows
(c) Only Conclusion I follows
(d) Neither Conclusion I nor II follows

38. Three of the following four letter-clusters are alike in a certain way and thus form a group. Select the letter-cluster that does not belong to that group.

(**Note** The odd one out is not based on the number of consonants/vowels or their position in the letter cluster)

(a) XBF (b) QUY
(c) LHJ (d) FJN

39. Select the correct mirror image of the given combination when the mirror is placed at MN as shown below.

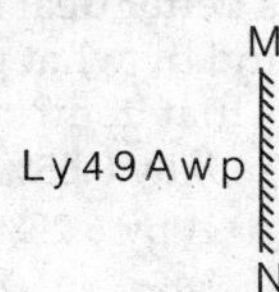

(a) dʍAɘ4ʎ⅃
(b) qwA6ϸʎL
(c) Awpɘ4ʎ⅃
(d) qwAɘ4ʎ⅃

40. What should come in place of question mark (?) in the given series based on the English alphabetical order?

JMP, UZE, FMT, QZI, ?

(a) BMX (b) LNP
(c) XHN (d) SLP

41. Six letters N, P, R, S, T and U are written on different faces of a dice. Two positions of this dice are shown in the figure. Which is the letter on the face opposite to the face containing U?

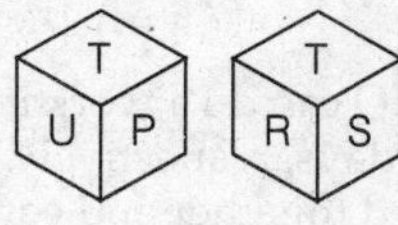

(a) P (b) S (c) N (d) R

42. How many rectangles are there in the given figure?

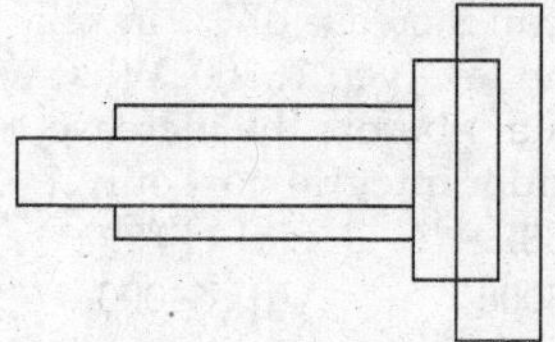

(a) 6 (b) 7 (c) 5 (d) 8

43. A paper is folded and cut as shown below. How will it appear when unfolded?

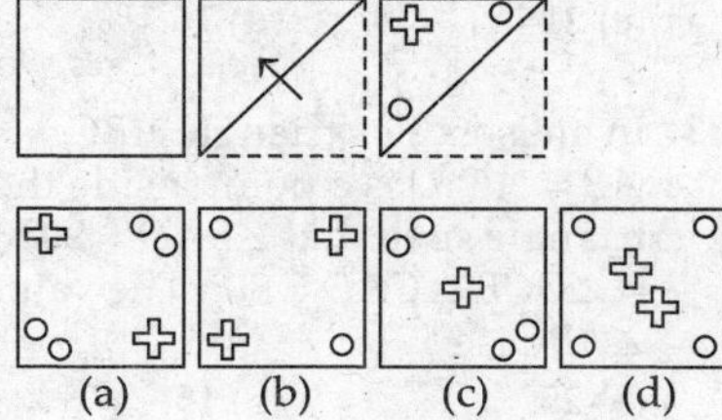

44. In a certain code language, 'PBI' is coded as '27' and 'ZEBRA' is coded as '125'. What is the code for 'BIRD' in the given code language?

(a) 49 (b) 64 (c) 37 (d) 25

45. Select the word-pair that best represents a similar relationship to the one expressed in the pair of words given below.

(The words must be considered as meaningful English words and must not be related to each other based on the number of letters/number of consonants/vowels in the word).

Strong : Robust

(a) Kind : Generous
(b) Knowledge : Ignorance
(c) Brave : Fearful
(d) Create : Destroy

46. The position of how many letters will remain unchanged if each of the letters in the word DETAIL is arranged in the alphabetical order?

(a) None (b) Three
(c) Two (d) One

47. Identify the figure given in the options that when put in place of the question mark (?) will logically complete the series.

I X ♡ B 7	B 7 X I ♡	I ♡ B X 7	X 7 ♡ I B	?

B ♡ I 7 X	I B X ♡ 7	B I X 7 ♡	I B 7 X ♡
(a)	(b)	(c)	(d)

48. 72 is related to 8 following a certain logic. Following the same logic, 198 is related to 22. To which of the following is 351 related following the same logic?

(**Note** Operations should be performed on the whole numbers, without breaking down the numbers into its constituent digits. E.g. 13 – Operations on 13 such as adding /deleting /multiplying etc. to 13 can be performed. Breaking down 13 into 1 and 3 and then performing mathematical operations on 1 and 3 is not allowed.)

(a) 41 (b) 43
(c) 39 (d) 37

49. What will come in the place of '?' in the following equation if '×' and '–' are interchanged and '+' and '÷' are interchanged?

$36 + 18 \times 9 \div 13 - 19 = ?$

(a) 234 (b) 246
(c) 280 (d) 240

50. Which of the following letter-clusters will replace the question mark (?) in the given series?

PAZ, REV, TIR, VOL, ?

(a) XUF (b) XVG
(c) XVF (d) XUE

Part III

Quantitative Aptitude

51. If $f(p) = \sin^{p+2} x + \cos^{p+2} x$, then the value of $6f(2) - 4f(4) + 10f(0)$ is

(a) 14 (b) 10
(c) 12 (d) 11

52. A policeman was asked to chase a thief. Before the policeman started the chase, he realised that the thief was 200 m ahead of him and was running at a speed of 16 km/h. The policeman started the chase at a

speed of 20 km/h. How far will the thief run before he is overtaken by the policeman?
(a) 1000 m (b) 700 m
(c) 800 m (d) 600 m

53. A certain sum of money is lent out at simple interest. If that money becomes ₹24000 in 2 yr and ₹32000 in 4 yr, the annual rate of interest is
(a) 30% (b) 16%
(c) 25% (d) 20%

54. The volume of the hemisphere (to the nearest integer) with a radius of 5.5 cm is (use $\pi = 3.14$)
(a) 378 cm^3 (b) 325 cm^3
(c) 348 cm^3 (d) 362 cm^3

55. If $x : y = 5 : 6$, then $2x + 3y : 3x + 5y$ is
(a) 28 : 48 (b) 28 : 45
(c) 18 : 45 (d) 18 : 35

56. The following table shows the production of food grains in a country over five years.

Year	Production (in ten lakh tonnes)			
	Wheat	Rice	Maize	Other grains
2016-17	650	250	200	450
2017-18	800	440	240	400
2018-19	680	390	220	500
2019-20	700	400	260	480
2020-21	640	440	300	520

What was the percentage increase in the production of rice in 2020-21 in comparison to the previous year?
(a) 10% (b) 25%
(c) 20% (d) 40%

57. If $A = \frac{9}{16} \div \frac{25}{36}, B = 9 \div [(16 \div 25) \div 36]$,
$C = [9 \div (16 \div 25)] \div 36$,
$D = (9 \div 16) \div (25 \div 36)$, then which of the following is true?
(a) B and D are equal
(b) C and D are equal
(c) A and B are equal
(d) A and D are equal

58. If $A = 60\left[\frac{6}{25} \div \left(\frac{16}{15} \text{ of } \frac{3}{8}\right) + 5 - \left(1 - 2\frac{1}{12}\right)\right]$, then the sum of the digits of A is
(a) 7 (b) 3 (c) 5 (d) 6

59. The ratio of the outer and the inner circumference of a circular path is 7:6. If the path is 45 m wide, then what is the radius (in m) of the inner circle?
(a) 240 (b) 120
(c) 150 (d) 270

60. P and Q can do a work in 12 days and 9 days, respectively. They both worked together and earned ₹63000. The share of P (in ₹) is
(a) 21000 (b) 36000
(c) 9000 (d) 27000

61. After an increase of 9% in salary, a person received ₹6300. What was his salary before the increase (consider integral part only)?
(a) ₹ 3879 (b) ₹ 5779
(c) ₹ 5000 (d) ₹ 4000

62. A vendor buys 20 dozen bananas for ₹1200 and sells 5 dozen for ₹ 350, then his gain percentage is
(a) $15\frac{1}{3}\%$ (b) $13\frac{2}{3}\%$
(c) $21\frac{1}{3}\%$ (d) $16\frac{2}{3}\%$

63. In an isosceles triangle ABC, $AB = AC$. D is a point inside the triangle such that $\angle BAD = 20° = \angle DCB$, $\angle CAD = 80°$. The value of $\angle ABC$ is
(a) 25° (b) 15°
(c) 20° (d) 40°

64. Study the given graph and answer the question that follows.
The graph shows the profit percentage earned by two companies A and B over a period of six years.

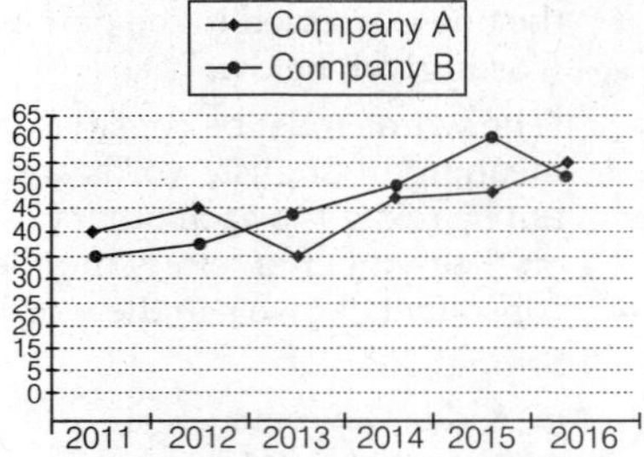

If the income of the company A in the year 2012 was ₹6.425 lakh, what was its expenditure in that year?
(a) ₹ 4.43 lakh
(b) ₹ 4.7 lakh
(c) ₹ 4.5 lakh
(d) ₹ 5.2 lakh

65. A line from point A is drawn that is tangent to the circle at point B. A secant is also drawn from point A to the circle intersecting it at points C and D. If $AB = 42$ cm and $AC = 21$ cm, then what is the ratio between AB and CD?
(a) 2 : 3 (b) 2 : 5
(c) 3 : 2 (d) 3 : 4

66. A cube of edge 4 cm is cut into cubes each of edge of 2 cm. The ratio of the total surface area of one of the small cubes to that of the large cube is equal to
(a) 1 : 64
(b) 1 : 16
(c) 1 : 4
(d) 1 : 8

67. The following pie-chart gives the distribution of constituents in the human body.

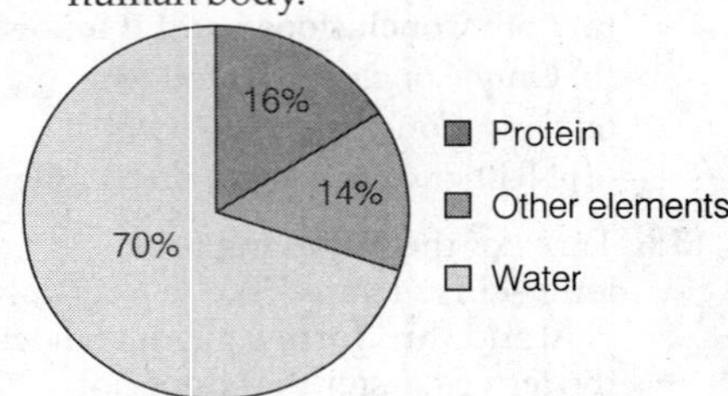

What is the central angle of the sector showing the distribution of protein and other constituents?
(a) 108° (b) 34°
(c) 120° (d) 45°

68. Shopkeeper A marks up his price for an item at 25% and offers a discount of 15%. The same item is marked up by at 20% by another shopkeeper B and sold at a discount of 12%. Who gets a better deal in terms of % profit and by what profit percentage he sells that item?
(a) B by 5.6% (b) B by 0.65%
(c) A by 0.55% (d) A by 6.25%

69. When 12 is subtracted from a number, it reduces to its 40%. Two-fifth of that number is
(a) 20 (b) 12
(c) 8 (d) 50

70. The length (in cm) of a direct common tangent to two circles of radii 14 cm and 5 cm whose centres are separated by a distance of 40 cm is
(a) 40 cm (b) 41 cm
(c) $\sqrt{1539}$ cm (d) $\sqrt{1519}$ cm

71. The given pie-chart shows the total number of passengers (in percentage) travelling from Ahmedabad junction to various districts. Study the pie-chart and answer the question that follows.

Total number of passengers travelling from Ahmedabad junction to various districts = 8000

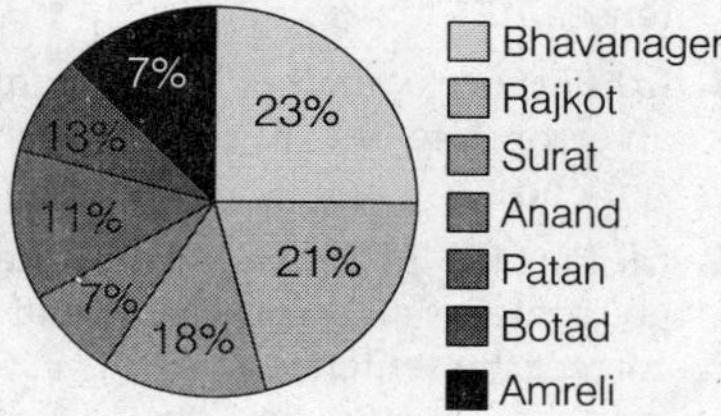

What is the average number of passengers travelling from Ahmedabad to Surat, Botad and Bhavanagar together?

(a) 1510 (b) 1360
(c) 1220 (d) 1440

72. The curved surface area of a right circular cone is 20π cm^2. If its radius is 4 cm, then find the volume of cone.

(a) 18π cm^3 (b) 21π cm^3
(c) 20π cm^3 (d) 16π cm^3

73. In an election there were three candidates. The first candidate got 40% votes and second candidate got 35% votes. If the total votes in the election are 50000, find the number of votes got by the third candidate.

(a) 12000 (b) 1250
(c) 12500 (d) 13500

74. *P* got married 15 ys ago. Today her age is $1\frac{3}{5}$ times her age at the time of her marriage. At present her son's age is $\frac{1}{5}$ of her age. What was her son's age 4 yr ago as a fraction of *P*'s age at that time?

(a) $\frac{1}{9}$ (b) $\frac{1}{8}$
(c) $\frac{5}{9}$ (d) $\frac{1}{10}$

75. Ratna buys 10 kg of rice for ₹88 per kg and another 20 kg of rice for ₹187 per kg. What is the per kg cost (in ₹) of the total mixture of rice for her?

(a) 148 (b) 150
(c) 158 (d) 154

Part IV
General Awareness

76. Which was the first socio-religious organisation established in Bombay in 1840 to work for the annihilation of caste?

(a) Satyashodhak Samaj
(b) Vishwa Jain Sangathan
(c) Paramhans Mandali
(d) Dharma Sabha

77. Which of the following is not applicable to force?

(a) Force may change the shape of an object.
(b) Force may change the direction of a moving object.
(c) Force may increase the mass of the object.
(d) Force may make an object move.

78. In the year 2021, the Department of Public Enterprises has now been made part of the .... Ministry, to speed up the privatisation process and exercise greater financial control over the state-run-enterprises.

(a) Micro, Small and Medium Enterprises
(b) Heavy Industries and Public Enterprises
(c) Finance
(d) Commerce and Industry

79. Competitive behaviour and competitive market structure are .... related.

(a) not (b) directly
(c) inversely (d) proportionately

80. How many basic talas are there in Indian Classical Carnatic music?

(a) 37 (b) 7 (c) 21 (d) 11

81. Which of the following is not a condition for acquiring the citizenship of India?

(a) Holding property
(b) Descent
(c) Registration
(d) Domicile

82. The catchphrase of which census is 'Our Census, Our Future'?

(a) 1981 (b) 2001 (c) 1991 (d) 2011

83. The Gulf of Khambhat, the Gulf of Kutch and Gangetic delta provide ideal conditions for utilising .... energy.

(a) solar (b) atomic
(c) geo thermal (d) tidal

84. How many times has India hosted the ICC Men's T-20 Cricket World Cup as of 2023?

(a) 3 (b) 4 (c) 2 (d) 1

85. 'Reservation in promotion' comes under which Article of the Constitution?

(a) Article 15 (3B)
(b) Article 19 (2)
(c) Article 14 (4A)
(d) Article 16 (4A)

86. Who took oath as the Chief Minister of Karnataka, in May 2023?

(a) Siddaramaiah
(b) Mallikarjun Kharge
(c) MK Stalin
(d) DK Sivakumar

87. Match the items in List I with those in List II.

List I	List II
A. Balanced Growth Theory	1. Rosenstein Rodan
B. Big Push Theory	2. Feldman-Mahalanobis
C. Secular Deterioration	3. Ragnar Nurkse
D. Capital Goods and Heavy Industry	4. Prebisch-Singer

Codes

	A	B	C	D		A	B	C	D
(a)	3	4	1	2	(b)	4	1	2	3
(c)	3	1	4	2	(d)	1	2	4	3

88. As of 2022, which among of the following is the leading tidal energy generation site of India?

(a) Sunderbans
(b) Seashore of Maharashtra
(c) Gulf of Kutch
(d) Gulf of Mannar

89. Which of the following is an example of multi-factor authentication for PC security?

(a) Antivirus software
(b) Fingerprint scan
(c) OS protection
(d) Firewall protection

90. Which of the following is a feature of Directive Principles of State Policy, and also distinguishes it from Fundamental Rights?

(a) It protects the interest of the individual.
(b) It is prohibitive in nature.
(c) It is non-justiciable.
(d) It is justiciable.

91. Which planet is the second largest planet in our solar system and also has the biggest and brightest rings around it?
(a) Saturn (b) Earth
(c) Uranus (d) Jupiter

92. Which of the following muscles regulates the exit of food from the stomach into the small intestine?
(a) Gastrocnemius
(b) Pectoralis
(c) Rectus
(d) Sphincter

93. Which of the following awards is presented for lifetime achievement in sports and games? It was instituted to honour those sports persons who have contributed to sports by their performance and continue to contribute to the promotion of sports even after their retirement from an active sporting career.
(a) Arjuna Award
(b) Dhyanchand Award
(c) Dronacharya Award
(d) Major Dhyan Chand Khel Ratna

94. What function does the public key serve in digital signature verification?
(a) To ensure confidentiality during transmission
(b) To encrypt the digital signature
(c) To decrypt the digital signature
(d) To calculate the hash value of the message or file content

95. Which of the following is the official language of Afghanistan?
(a) Uzbek
(b) Dhivehi
(c) Dari
(d) Turkmen

96. Bharatanatyam dance form is associated with
(a) Karnataka
(b) Tamil Nadu
(c) Himachal Pradesh
(d) Haryana

97. With which Gharana is the famous Tarana singer, Pandit Rattan Mohan Sharma associated?
(a) Talwandi Gharana
(b) Patiala Gharana
(c) Agra Gharana
(d) Mewati Gharana

98. What is the minimum number of football players required in a team for a match to start?
(a) 11 (b) 8
(c) 10 (d) 7

99. The founder of the Pala empire was
(a) Rayala
(b) Gopala
(c) Devapala
(d) Dharmapala

100. 'Tamu Lochar' is one of the traditional festivals of the .... of Sikkim. It is celebrated to mark the beginning of their new year, which falls on the 15th day of Pusa, according to the Hindu calendar Vikram Samvat and 30th December in the English calendar.
(a) Mangar community
(b) Bhutia community
(c) Lepcha community
(d) Gurung community

Answers

1. (b)	2. (b)	3. (a)	4. (d)
5. (a)	6. (a)	7. (a)	8. (a)
9. (a)	10. (a)	11. (d)	12. (d)
13. (b)	14 (d)	15. (b)	16. (a)
17. (d)	18. (c)	19. (a)	20. (b)
21. (a)	22. (d)	23. (c)	24. (d)
25. (b)	26. (a)	27. (a)	28. (b)
29. (d)	30. (a)	31. (b)	32. (d)
33. (c)	34. (c)	35. (d)	36. (c)
37. (b)	38. (c)	39. (d)	40. (a)
41. (d)	42. (b)	43. (a)	44. (b)
45. (a)	46. (a)	47. (b)	48. (c)
49. (d)	50. (a)	51. (c)	52. (c)
53. (c)	54. (c)	55. (b)	56. (a)
57. (d)	58. (c)	59. (d)	60. (d)
61. (b)	62. (d)	63. (d)	64. (a)
65. (a)	66. (c)	67. (a)	68. (d)
69. (c)	70. (d)	71. (d)	72. (d)
73. (c)	74. (a)	75. (d)	76. (c)
77. (c)	78. (c)	79. (c)	80. (b)
81. (a)	82. (d)	83. (d)	84. (d)
85. (d)	86. (a)	87. (c)	88. (c)
89. (b)	90. (c)	91. (a)	92. (d)
93. (b)	94. (c)	95. (c)	96. (b)
97. (d)	98. (d)	99. (b)	100. (d)

Explanations

1. *(b)* Part (c) 'are believing' contains an error. Use 'believe' to correct the sentence.

2. *(b)* Part (b) 'ate his food' contains an error. Use 'eats' to correct the sentence. The sentence presents a habit and would take simple present tense.

3. *(a)* Part (a) 'a mailbox again' contains an error. Use 'the' to correct the sentence.

4. *(d)* Part (d) 'historical context, Rahul go' contains an error. Use 'went' to correct the sentence.

5. *(a)* The correct filler for the given blank is 'frustrating'.

6. *(a)* The correct filler for the given blank is 'wandering'.

7. *(a)* The correct filler for the given blank is 'enhance'.

8. *(a)* The correct filler for the given blank is 'attempt'.

9. *(a)* The correct filler for the given blank is 'focussed'.

10. *(a)* The underlined idiom 'time and again' means repeatedly.

11. *(d)* The correct filler for the given blank is 'keep control'.

12. *(d)* The correct filler for the given blank is 'convinced'.

13. *(b)* The antonym of 'powerful' is impotent which means lacking power or strength.

14. *(d)* 'Abolish' means to end a rule or law. Hence, its antonym is 'establish'.

15. *(b)* The incorrectly spelt word is 'Definate'. The correct spelling is 'Definite'

16. *(a)* The word 'estimate' means to check or evaluate an approximate value of something.

17. *(d)* The underlined part of the given sentence contains an error. Use 'lest we make errors' to correct the sentence.

18. *(c)* The word 'candid' means truthful and honest. Hence, its antonym is 'deceitful'.
- 'Reticent' means not revealing one's thoughts or feelings readily.
- 'Prudent' means innocent.
- 'Reckless' means careless.

19. *(a)* The correct spelling is 'harassed'.

20. *(b)* The underlined part of the given sentence contains an error. Use 'for' to correct the sentence.

21. *(a)* The underlined part of the given sentence contains an error. Use 'is proof' to correct the sentence.

22. *(d)* 'Innovate' means to create something new. Hence, its antonym is to 'Copy'.

23. *(c)* The correct idiom for the given blank is 'pacing up and down'. It means to be nervous and anxious.

24. *(d)* The word 'petty' means 'small'.

25. *(b)* The underlined part of the given sentence contains an error. Use 'give up' to correct the sentence.

26. *(a)* According to the question,

cooler is hot → tp rc dl

hot weather comes → rc dn nz

Hence, the code for 'hot' is 'rc'.

27. *(a)* The figure given in option (a) is the correct mirror image of the given question figure.

A

nETFLIcKs | (mirror image)

B

28. *(b)* Given expression,

$204 \times 4 - 9 \div 2 + 6 = ?$

After interchanging '+' and '−' and '×' and '÷', we get

$? = 204 \div 4 + 9 \times 2 - 6$

$? = 51 + 18 - 6$

$? = 69 - 6 = 63$

29. *(d)* As, (6, 12, 48)

$\Rightarrow \quad 6 \times 2 = 12,\ 12 \times 4 = 48$

and (8, 16, 64) $\Rightarrow 8 \times 2 = 16,\ 16 \times 4 = 64$

Similarly, (14, 28, 112)

$\Rightarrow \quad 14 \times 2 = 28,\ 28 \times 4 = 112$

30. *(a)* Given expression,

82 B 6 D 114 A 2 C 35 = ?

After substituting letters with signs, we get

$= 82 \times 6 - 114 \div 2 + 35$

$= 492 - 57 + 35$

$= 527 - 57 = 470$

31. *(b)* Odd days in ordinary year = 1

Odd days in leap year = 2

Day on 20th March, 2011 = Sunday

Number of odd days from 20th March, 2011 to 20th March, 2019

$= 2 + 1 + 1 + 1 + 2 + 1 + 1 + 1$

$= \frac{10}{7} = 1$ week 3 odd days

∴ The day of week on 20th March, 2019 = Sunday + 3 = Wednesday

32. *(d)* The pattern of the given series is as follows,

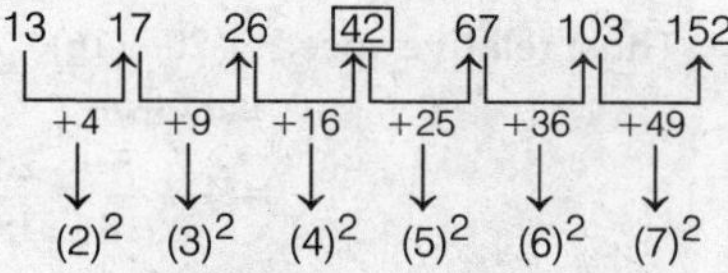

33. *(c)* The figure given in option (c) is the correct mirror image of the given figure.

M

M2aPvd | (mirror image)

N

34. *(c)* The pattern of the given series is as follows,

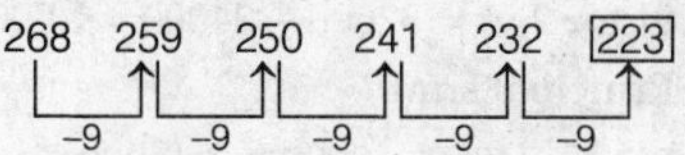

35. *(d)* Given expression,

N # M @ O $ P & Q

According to the question,

+ → Male
− → Female

(−)P ← Wife — Q(+)

P — Daughter → O(−)

(+)M ← Brother — O(−)

M — Son → (+)N

Hence, Q is father's father of N.

36. *(c)* As, dawn is synonym of sunrise. Similarly, easy is a synonym of simple.

37. *(b)* According to the question,

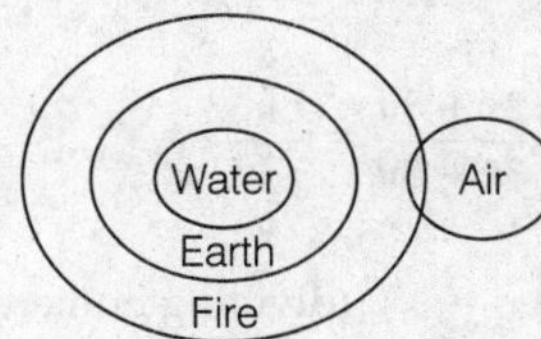

Conclusions

I. (✗) II. (✓)

Hence, only Conclusion II follows.

38. *(c)* As, X $\xrightarrow{+4}$ B $\xrightarrow{+4}$ F

Q $\xrightarrow{+4}$ U $\xrightarrow{+4}$ Y

F $\xrightarrow{+4}$ J $\xrightarrow{+4}$ N

But, L $\xrightarrow{-4}$ H $\xrightarrow{+2}$ J

39. *(d)* The option figure (d) is the correct mirror image of the given question figure.

M

Ly49Awp | (mirror image)

N

40. *(a)* The pattern of the given series is as follows,

J $\xrightarrow{+11}$ U $\xrightarrow{+11}$ F $\xrightarrow{+11}$ Q $\xrightarrow{+11}$ B

M $\xrightarrow{+13}$ Z $\xrightarrow{+13}$ M $\xrightarrow{+13}$ Z $\xrightarrow{+13}$ M

P $\xrightarrow{+15}$ E $\xrightarrow{+15}$ T $\xrightarrow{+15}$ I $\xrightarrow{+15}$ X

41. *(d)* In both the dices T is common.

So, moving in clockwise direction from T.

Figure I → T P U

Figure II → T S R

Hence, letter R is on the face opposite to the face containing letter U.

42. *(b)* Naming the figure,

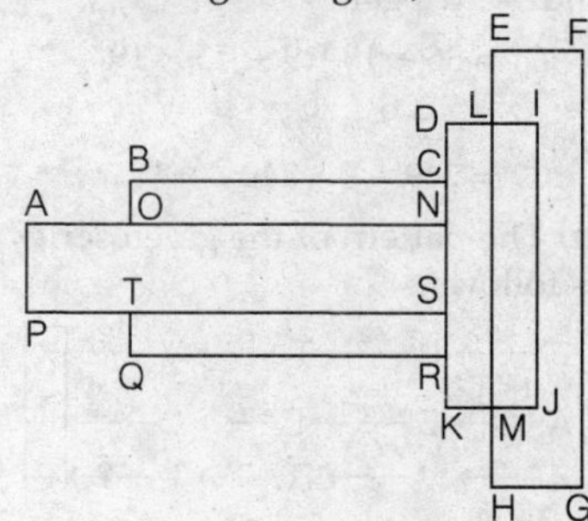

▭BCNO, ▭ANSP, ▭TSRQ, ▭DLMK, ▭LIJM, ▭DIJK and ▭EFGH.

Hence, there are 7 rectangles in the figure.

43. *(a)* The unfolded paper will appear as shown in the figure (a).

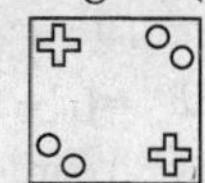

44. *(b)* As, PBI → 27

[∵ (Number of letters in word)^3]

$(3)^3 = 27$

and ZEBRA → 125

$(5)^3 = 125$

Similarly, BIRD → 64

$(4)^3 = 64$

45. *(a)* As, strong is a synonyms of robust. Similarly, kind is a synonyms of generous.

46. *(a)* Given word ⟶ D E T A I L

Arranged in alphabetical order ⟶ A D E I L T

Hence, none of the letter is there whose position remain unchanged.

47. *(b)* There are two alternate series, which follows the pattern,

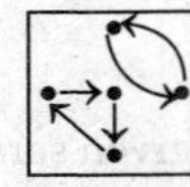 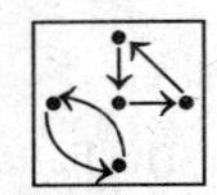

From figure 1 to 2 Figure 3 to 4 — From figure 2 to 3 Figure 4 to 5

Hence, option figure (b) will replace the question mark.

48. *(c)* As, $8 \times 9 = 72$

and $22 \times 9 = 198$

Similarly, $a \times 9 = 351$

$$a = \frac{351}{9} = 39$$

49. *(d)* Given expression,
$36 + 18 \times 9 \div 13 - 19$

After interchanging '×' and '–' and '+' and '÷', we get

$$? = 36 \div 18 - 9 + 13 \times 19$$
$$? = 2 - 9 + 247$$
$$= 249 - 9 = 240$$

50. *(a)* The pattern of the given series is as follows,

P $\xrightarrow{+2}$ R $\xrightarrow{+2}$ T $\xrightarrow{+2}$ V $\xrightarrow{+2}$ X

A $\xrightarrow{\text{Next vowel}}$ E $\xrightarrow{\text{Next vowel}}$ I $\xrightarrow{\text{Next vowel}}$ O $\xrightarrow{\text{Next vowel}}$ U

Z $\xrightarrow{-4}$ V $\xrightarrow{-4}$ R $\xrightarrow{-6}$ L $\xrightarrow{-6}$ F

51. *(c)* Given, $f(p) = \sin^{p+2} x + \cos^{p+2} x$

$$f(2) = \sin^4 x + \cos^4 x$$
$$= (\sin^2 x + \cos^2 x)^2 - 2\sin^2 x \cos^2 x \quad [\because \sin^2 x + \cos^2 x = 1]$$
$$= 1 - 2\sin^2 x \cos^2 x$$
$$f(4) = \sin^6 x + \cos^6 x$$
$$= (\sin^2 x)^3 + (\cos^2 x)^3$$
$$[\because a^3 + b^3 = (a+b)(a^2 - ab + b^2)]$$
$$= (\sin^2 x + \cos^2 x)(\sin^4 x - \sin^2 x \cos^2 x + \cos^4 x)$$
$$= (\sin^4 x + \cos^4 x - \sin^2 x \cos^2 x)$$
$$= (\sin^2 x + \cos^2 x)^2 - 2\sin^2 x \cos^2 x - \sin^2 x \cos^2 x$$
$$= 1 - 3\sin^2 x \cos^2 x$$
$$f(0) = \sin^2 x + \cos^2 x = 1$$

Now, $6f(2) - 4f(4) + 10f(0)$

$$= 6(1 - 2\sin^2 x \cos^2 x) - 4(1 - 3\sin^2 x \cos^2 x) + 10$$
$$= 6 - 12\sin^2 x \cos^2 x - 4 + 12\sin^2 x \cos^2 x + 10 = 12$$

52. *(c)* Given, speed of police = 20 km/h

Speed of thief = 16 km/h

Distance between thief and police = 200 m

Thus, relative speed = (20 – 16)

$$= 4 \text{ km/h}$$
$$= 4 \times \frac{5}{18} = \frac{20}{18} \text{ m/s}$$

According to the question,

$$\text{Time} = \frac{200}{\frac{20}{18}} = \frac{200 \times 18}{20} = 180 \text{ sec.}$$

Thus, police captured thief after 180 sec.

Distance travelled by thief

$$= 180 \times 16 \times \frac{5}{18} = 800 \text{ m}$$

53. *(c)* Given, Amount in 2 yr = ₹ 24000

Amount in 4 yr = ₹ 32000

SI for 2 yr = 32000 – 24000 = ₹ 8000

Principal sum

= 24000 – 8000 = ₹ 16000

$$\text{SI for 2 yr} = \frac{16000 \times R \times 2}{100}$$

(Here R = rate of interest p.a.)

$$\Rightarrow \quad 8000 = \frac{16000 \times R \times 2}{100}$$

$\therefore$ $R = 25\%$ p.a.

54. *(c)* Given, radius of hemisphere (r) = 5.5 cm

$$\therefore \text{Volume of hemisphere} = \frac{2}{3}\pi r^3$$
$$= \frac{2}{3}\pi \times (5.5)^3$$
$$= \frac{2}{3} \times 3.14 \times 5.5 \times 5.5 \times 5.5$$
$$= 348.27 \text{ cm}^3 \approx 348 \text{ cm}^3$$

55. *(b)* Given, $\frac{x}{y} = \frac{5}{6}$

$$\frac{2x + 3y}{3x + 5y} = \frac{2\frac{x}{y} + 3}{3\frac{x}{y} + 5}$$

(dividing numerator and denominator by y)

$$= \frac{2 \times \frac{5}{6} + 3}{3 \times \frac{5}{6} + 5} = \frac{\frac{5}{3} + 3}{\frac{5}{2} + 5}$$

$$= \frac{\left(\frac{14}{3}\right)}{\left(\frac{15}{2}\right)} = \frac{28}{45} = 28 : 45$$

56. *(a)* Production of Rice in 2019-20 = 400 tonnes

Production of Rice in 2020-21 = 440 tonnes

$\therefore$ Required percentage

$$= \frac{440 - 400}{400} \times 100$$
$$= \frac{40}{400} \times 100 = 10\%$$

57. *(d)* Given, $A = \frac{9}{16} \div \frac{25}{36}$

$$= \frac{9}{16} \times \frac{36}{25} = \frac{81}{100}$$

$$B = 9 \div [(16 \div 25) \div 36]$$
$$= 9 \div \left[\frac{16}{25} \times \frac{1}{36}\right]$$
$$= 9 \div \left[\frac{4}{25 \times 9}\right]$$
$$= \frac{9}{4} \times 25 \times 9 = \frac{2025}{4}$$

$$C = [9 \div (16 \div 25)] \div 36$$
$$= \left[9 \div \frac{16}{25}\right] \div 36$$
$$= \left(\frac{9}{16} \times 25\right) \div 36$$
$$= \frac{9}{16} \times 25 \times \frac{1}{36} = \frac{75}{12 \times 16} = \frac{25}{64}$$

$$D = (9 \div 16) \div (25 \div 36)$$
$$= \frac{9}{16} \div \left(\frac{25}{36}\right)$$
$$= \frac{9}{16} \times \frac{36}{25} = \frac{81}{100}$$

Thus, $A = D$

58. *(c)*

$$A = 60\left[\frac{6}{25} \div \left(\frac{16}{15} \text{ of } \frac{3}{8}\right) + 5 - \left(1 - 2\frac{1}{12}\right)\right]$$
$$= 60\left[\frac{6}{25} \div \left(\frac{16}{15} \times \frac{3}{8}\right) + 5 - \left(1 - \frac{25}{12}\right)\right]$$
$$= 60\left[\frac{6}{25} \div \frac{2}{5} + 5 + \frac{13}{12}\right]$$
$$= 60\left[\frac{6}{25} \times \frac{5}{2} + 5 + \frac{13}{12}\right]$$
$$= 60 \times \left[\frac{3}{5} + \frac{5}{1} + \frac{13}{12}\right]$$
$$= 60 \times \left[\frac{36 + 300 + 65}{60}\right]$$
$$= 60 \times \frac{401}{60} = 401$$

Thus, sum of digits = 4 + 0 + 1 = 5

59. *(d)* Let the radius of outer circle be R.
And radius of inner circle $= r$
According to the question,
$$(R - r) = 45 \quad \text{...(i)}$$
and $\frac{2\pi R}{2\pi r} = \frac{7}{6}$
$\therefore \quad R = \frac{7}{6} \times r$
Then, from Eq. (i),
$\frac{7}{6}r - r = 45 \Rightarrow \frac{r}{6} = 45$
$\therefore \quad r = 270$ m

60. *(d)* Total work = LCM of 12 and 9
= 72 unit
Efficiency of $P = \frac{72}{12} = 6$ unit/day
Efficiency of $Q = \frac{72}{9} = 8$ unit/day
The share of $P = \frac{6}{6+8} \times 63000$
$= \frac{6}{14} \times 63000 =$ ₹ 27000

61. *(b)* Let the salary be ₹ $100x$.
Salary after increment
$= 100x \times \frac{109}{100} =$ ₹ $109x$
Then, according to question,
$\Rightarrow \quad 109x = 6300$
$\Rightarrow \quad x = 57.79$
Thus, salary $= 100x = 57.79 \times 100$
= ₹ 5779

62. *(d)* Given, CP of 20 dozen Bananas
= ₹ 1200
and SP of 5 dozen Bananas = ₹ 350
∴ SP of 20 dozen Bananas = 350×4
= ₹ 1400
Thus, gain% $= \frac{1400 - 1200}{1200} \times 100$
$= \frac{200}{1200} \times 100 = 16\frac{2}{3}\%$

63. *(d)* In ΔABC,

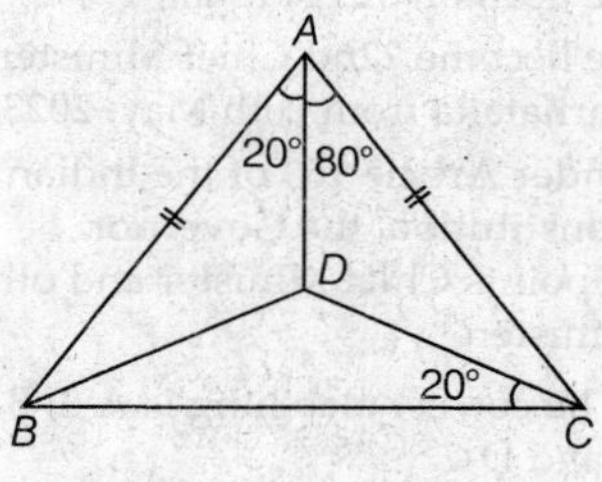

$AB = AC$
[∵ ΔABC is an isosceles triangle]
$\angle B = \angle C$
Thus, $\angle BAC = \angle BAD + \angle DAC$
$= 20 + 80 = 100°$
$\therefore \quad \angle ABC = \angle ACB = \frac{180° - 100°}{2}$
$= \frac{80°}{2} = 40° \quad [\because AB = AC]$

64. *(a)* According to the question,
Let expenditure be ₹ x.
$\therefore \quad x \times \frac{145}{100} = 6.425$ lakh
$\Rightarrow \quad x = \frac{6.425 \times 100}{145}$
= ₹ 4.43 lakh
∴ Thus, initial expenditure = ₹ 4.43 lakh

65. *(a)* Let AB = tangent and AD is secant, and $AC = 21$ cm.

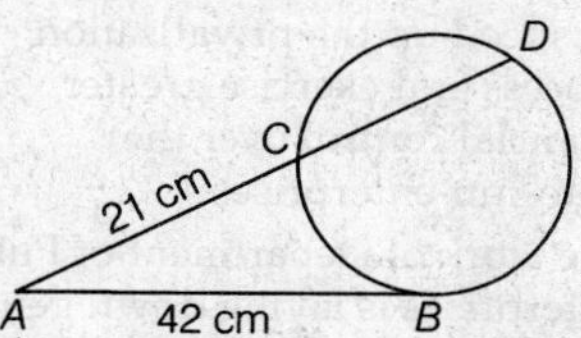

Thus, by tangent secant theorem,
$AB^2 = AC \times AD$
$\Rightarrow 42 \times 42 = 21 \times AD$
$\Rightarrow \quad AD = 84$ cm
Thus, $CD = AD - AC = 84 - 21 = 63$ cm
∴ Required ratio $= \left(\frac{AB}{CD}\right)$
$= \frac{42}{63} = \frac{2}{3} = 2:3$

66. *(c)* Given, side of bigger cube (a)
= 4 cm
and side of smaller cube $(b) = 2$ cm
Total surface area of bigger cube $= 6a^2$
$= 6 \times 4 \times 4 = 96 \text{ cm}^2$
Total surface area of smaller cube $= 6b^2$
$= 6 \times 2 \times 2 = 24 \text{ cm}^2$
∴ Required ratio $= \frac{24}{96} = \frac{1}{4}$

67. *(a)* Central angle of protein and other constituent $= \frac{(16 + 14)}{100} \times 360°$
$= \frac{30}{100} \times 360° = 108°$

68. *(d)* Let cost price of item be $100x$.
For shopkeeper A,
Selling price of item
$= 100x \times \frac{125}{100} \times \frac{85}{100}$
= ₹ $106.25x$
∴ Profit percentage $= \frac{6.25x}{100x} \times 100$
$= 6.25\%$
For shopkeeper B,
Selling price $= 100x \times \frac{120}{100} \times \frac{88}{100}$
Gain % = ₹ $105.6x$
$\therefore \quad$ Gain % $= \frac{5.6x}{100x} \times 100 = 5.6\%$
Hence, for shopkeeper A the deal is better and he gains 6.25% profit.

69. *(c)* Let the number be x.
Then, according to question,
$x - 12 = x \times \frac{40}{100}$
$\Rightarrow \quad x - 12 = \frac{2}{5} \times x$
$\Rightarrow \quad x - \frac{2}{5}x = 12$
$\Rightarrow \quad \frac{3x}{5} = 12$
$\Rightarrow \quad x = 20$
Thus, required number $= 20 \times \frac{2}{5} = 8$

70. *(d)* Given, radii of circle are 14 cm and 5 cm and distance between center = 40 cm
Direct common tangent
$= \sqrt{d^2 - (r_2 - r_1)^2}$
$= \sqrt{(40)^2 - (14 - 5)^2}$
$= \sqrt{1600 - 81}$
$= \sqrt{1519}$ cm

71. *(d)* Given, total passenger = 8000
Passenger travelling from Ahmedabad to Surat $= 8000 \times \frac{18}{100}$
= 1440
Passenger travelled to Botad
$= 8000 \times \frac{13}{100} = 1040$
Passenger travelled to Bhavanagar
$= \frac{23}{100} \times 8000 = 1840$
∴ Required average of passenger
$= \frac{1840 + 1040 + 1440}{3}$
= 1440

72. *(d)* Given, Curved surface area of cone $= 20\pi$
$\Rightarrow \quad \pi rl = 20\pi$
$\Rightarrow \quad rl = 20$
$\therefore \quad l = 5$ cm $\quad [\because r = 4]$

Thus, we know,

$l^2 = r^2 + h^2$

$\Rightarrow \quad 5^2 = 4^2 + h^2$

$\Rightarrow \quad h^2 = 5^2 - 4^2 = 3^2$

$\Rightarrow \quad h^2 = 3^2$

$\Rightarrow \quad h = 3$

$\therefore$ Volume of cone $= \frac{1}{3}\pi r^2 h$

$= \frac{1}{3} \times \pi \times 4 \times 4 \times 3$

$= 16\pi \text{ cm}^3$

73. *(c)* Total votes = 50000

First candidate got = 40%

Second candidate got = 35%

$\therefore$ Third candidate got

= 100 − 40 − 35 = 25%

Thus, third candidate got votes

= 25% of 50000 = 12500

74. *(a)* Let age of P at the time of marriage be x yr.

Thus, the present age of P

$\Rightarrow \quad x + 15 = x \times \frac{8}{5}$

$\Rightarrow \quad \frac{8}{5}x - x = 15$

$\Rightarrow \quad \frac{3x}{5} = 15$

$\Rightarrow \quad x = 25$ yr

$\therefore$ Present age of $P = x + 15 = 25 + 15$

= 40 yr

and age of son = $40 \times \frac{1}{5} = 8$ yr

$\therefore$ Required fraction

$= \frac{8-4}{(40-4)} = \frac{4}{36} = \frac{1}{9}$

75. *(d)* Cost of 1 kg of rice = ₹ 88

Cost of 10 kg of rice = ₹ 880

Cost of other type of rice for 1 kg = ₹ 187

Cost of other type of rice for 20 kg

= 20× 187

= ₹ 3740

Total cost of 30 kg rice = 3740 + 880

= ₹ 4620

Cost of rice per kg = $\frac{4620}{30}$ = ₹ 154

76. *(c)* Paramhans Mandali was the first socio-religious organisation established in Bombay in 1840.

- To work for the annihilation of caste.
- Paramhans Mandali was founded by Durgaram Mehtaji, Dadoba Pandurang and a group of his friends.
- Its founders believed in one God and were primarily interested in breaking caste rules.
- They also believed in education for women, widow remarriage.

77. *(c)* Force is push or pull which may change the shape and moving direction of the object but the mass of an object can't be changed by it.

Because mass is a property of an object which is constant everywhere.

78. *(c)* The Department of Public Enterprises has now been made part of the Finance Ministry in 2021.

- To speed up the privatisation process and exercise greater financial control over the state-run-enterprises.
- The work of Department of Public Enterprises is laying down general policies and guidelines for effective management, marketing, finance, series etc. of PSU and periodic review of their performance.

79. *(c)* Competitive behaviour and competitive market structure are inversely related.

The more competitive the market structure, less competitive is the behaviour of the firms.

80. *(b)* There are 7 talas in Indian Classical Carnatic music.

The seven talas structure are known as the Suladi Sapta talas which are

1. Dhruva
2. Matya
3. Jhampa
4. Ata
5. Rupaka
6. Eka
7. Triputa

81. *(a)* Holding property is not a condition for acquiring the citizenship of India.

The Citizenship Act, 1955

Citizenship of India can be acquired in the following ways

1. Citizenship at the commencement of the Constitution
2. Citizenship by birth
3. Citizenship by registration
4. Citizenship by naturalisation
5. Citizenship by descent

82. *(d)* In 2011 census, the catchphrase is 'Our Census, Our Future'.

- It emphasises the role of the census in directing future planning and resource allocation.
- The 2011 census was the 15th National Census of India since 1872.
- It conducted under the guidance of the Registrar-General and Census Commissioner, India in the Ministry of Home Affairs.

83. *(d)* The Gulf of Khambhat, the Gulf of Kutch and Gangetic delta provide ideal conditions for utilising tidal energy.

- The potential at the Gulf of Khambhat alone was found to be above 7000 MW.
- The potential at the Gulf of Kutch in Gujarat was found to be 1200 MW.

84. *(d)* Only 1 time India hosted the ICC Men's T-20 Cricket World Cup as of 2023.

- The England cricket team won the ICC T-20 World Cup 2023 by beating the Pakistan cricket team.
- In 2024, ICC T-20 World Cup, India National cricket team won by defeating the South Africa team.

85. *(d)* 'Reservation in promotion' comes under Article 16(4A) in our Indian Constitution.

- It states that nothing in this article shall prevent the state from making any provision for the reservation in matter of promotion or posts in favour of any backward class of citizens.
- This article allows the state to make provisions for reservations in promotions for scheduled castes and scheduled tribes in government services.

86. *(a)* Siddaramaiah took oath as the Chief Minister of Karnataka in May, 2023.

- He born on 3rd August, 1947.
- He become 22nd Chief Minister of Karnataka from 20th May, 2023.
- Under Article 163 of the Indian Constitution, the Governor appoints Chief Minister and other minister.

87. *(c)* The correct matching is A-3, B-1, C-4 and D-2.

- The Balanced Growth Theory is an economic theory pioneered by the economist Ragnar Nurkse (1907-1959).

- The Big Push Theory first put forward by PN Rosenstein Rodan.
- Prebisch Singer explained that the secular deterioration in terms of trade.
- Prasanta Chandra Mahalanobis emphasises the importance of heavy industries and capital goods.

88. *(c)* Gulf of Kutch is the leading tidal energy generation site of India as of 2022.

- The Gulf of Khambhat, the Gulf of Kutch are providing potential ideal condition for utilising tidal energy.
- The potential at the Gulf of Kutch in Gujarat found to be 1200 MW.

89. *(b)* Fingerprint scan is an example of multi-factor authentication for PC security.

90. *(c)* The non-justiciable nature of Directive Principles of State Policy (DPSP) distinguishes them from Fundamental Rights, which are enforceable in a court of law.

- The DPSP are guidelines for the government to follow while making laws and policies, enshrined in Part IV of the Constitution.
- Fundamental Rights can be enforced in a court of law, protect individual rights and freedoms and enshrined in Part III of the Constitution.

91. *(a)* Saturn is the second largest in our solar system and also has the biggest and brightest rings around it.

- Saturn is the sixth planet from the Sun.
- It is a gas giant with an average radius of about nine and a half times that of Earth.
- It has only one-eighth the average density of Earth, but is over 95 times more massive.

92. *(d)* The muscle that regulates the exit of food from the stomach into the small intestine is the pyloric sphincter.

This is a circular muscle located at the bottom of the stomach that acts as a value to control the movement of food into the small intestine.

93. *(b)* Major Dhyan Chand Award is presented for lifetime achievement in sports and games.

- It was instituted to honour those sports persons who have contributed to sports by their performance.
- And continue to contribute to the promotion of sports even after their retirement from an active sporting career.
- In 2021, the Rajiv Gandhi Khel Ratna Award renamed as Major Dhyan Chand Khel Ratna Award.

94. *(c)* In digital signature verification, the public key serves to :

- Verify the authenticity of the sender.
- Decrypt the digital signature.

95. *(c)* Dari is the official language of Afghanistan.

- Uzbek is predominantly spoken in the Republic of Uzbekistan.
- Dhivehi is an Indo-Aryan language and the official language of the Republic of the Maldives.
- Turkmen is the official language of Turkmenistan.

96. *(b)* Bharatanataym dance is associated with Tamil Nadu.

- Yakshagana is traditional dance form of Karnataka.
- Dangi and Nati Dances are widely performed in Himachal Pradesh.
- Phag dance is a devotional dance of Haryana.

97. *(d)* Pandit Rattan Mohan Sharma is associated with Mewati Gharana and he is famous of Tarana singer and Khyal.

He won several awards, these are

- Shankar Rao Vyas Award
- Title (Acharya Varishtha)
- Title (Sur Ratna)
- IWAF (Gharana Award)

98. *(d)* Minimum 7 number of football players required in a team for a match to start.

- Football, also called Association Football or Soccer.
- Football is a game involving two teams of 11 players who try to maneuver the ball into the other team's goal without using their hands or arms.

99. *(b)* Gopala was the founder of the Pala empire.

- Gopala also served as the kingdom's first emperor.
- He unified Bengal under his control, and even brought Magadha (Bihar) under his control.
- His successor was the Dharmapala.

100. *(d)* 'Tamu Lochar' is one of the traditional festival of the Gurung community of Sikkim.

It is celebrated to make the beginning of their new year, which falls on the 15th day of Pusa' according to the Hindu calender Vikram Samvat and 30th December in the English calender.

Set 31 10 July, 2024 (Shift III)

SSC CHSL Tier-I SOLVED PAPER

Instructions

1. This paper contains 100 questions.
2. It has 4 Parts, **Part I** General English, **Part II** General Intelligence & Reasoning, **Part III** Quantitative Aptitude and **Part IV** General Awareness.
3. Each question carries **2 marks**.

Part I

General English

1. The following sentence has been split into four segments. Identify the segment that contains a grammatical error.

I used to eat into / in the evening / when my parents / were on night shifts.

(a) I used to eat into
(b) when my parents
(c) in the evening
(d) were on night shifts

2. The following sentence has been split into four segments. Identify the segment that contains a grammatical error.

A. Ganga was
B. out shopping at the mall
C. and ran over
D. her schoolmate.

(a) D (b) A
(c) B (d) C

3. The following sentence has been split into four segments. Identify the segment that contains an error.

Shall have / you bring / your note-book / tomorrow?

(a) Shall have
(b) you bring
(c) tomorrow
(d) your note-book

4. Select the option with the correct use of future tense.

(a) If you worked hard in the same manner, you will soon achieve success.
(b) If you had work hard in the same manner, you will soon achieve success.
(c) If you have work hard in the same manner, you will soon achieve success.
(d) If you work hard in the same manner, you will soon achieve success.

Directions (Q. Nos. 5-9) *In the following passage, some words have been left out. Select the most appropriate option to fill in each blank.*

In todays fast-paced and technology-driven world, (1) .... is crucial to disconnect occasionally for the sake of our health. (2) .... exposure to screens and the demands of the digital era can lead to stress, anxiety and reduced well-being. Taking time to unplug and engage (3) .... activities that promote relaxation, such as spending time in nature, (4) .... hobbies or simply enjoying quality time with loved ones allows us to recharge, find balance and (5) .... our mental and physical health.

5. Select the most appropriate option to fill in blank no. (1).

(a) that (b) this
(c) these (d) it

6. Select the most appropriate option to fill in blank no. (2).

(a) Interrupted
(b) Sporadic
(c) Constant
(d) Redundant

7. Select the most appropriate option to fill in blank no. (3).

(a) in (b) into
(c) to (d) for

8. Select the most appropriate option to fill in blank no. (4).

(a) constructing (b) pursuing
(c) chasing (d) trailing

9. Select the most appropriate option to fill in blank no. (5).

(a) precede (b) focus
(c) prioritise (d) underscore

10. Select the most appropriate option to fill in the blank.

I don't like dirty cars, so you should keep it ....

(a) shabby (b) similar
(c) new (d) spotless

11. Select the most appropriate idiom to complete the given sentence.

With the increasing market prices and stagnant salaries, he is ....

(a) taking a break
(b) feeling the pinch
(c) beating the rap
(d) getting it off his chest

12. Select the most appropriate antonym of the given word.

Stoic

(a) Tolerant (b) Apathetic
(c) Fervent (d) Cooperative

13. Select the most appropriate antonym of the underlined word in the given sentence.

The stone was also said to have <u>occult</u> powers.

(a) latent
(b) intelligible
(c) ambiguous
(d) unfathomable

14. Select the incorrectly spelt word.

(a) Connoisseur
(b) Circumlocution
(c) Haphazard
(d) Disintigrate

15. Read the given sentence carefully. Change the meaning of the sentence by replacing the underlined word with its antonym from the following options.

His father warned him not to use vulgar language at home.

(a) decorous (b) ribald
(c) impervious (d) licentious

16. Select the option that will improve the underlined part of the given sentence.

She's under the allusion that she'll get the job.

(a) illusion (b) hallucination
(c) vision (d) unreality

17. Select the most appropriate option that can substitute the underlined segment in the given sentence.

The common masses have waited for three hours to meet the king in the royal court.

(a) has been waiting
(b) had waiting
(c) have been waiting
(d) will waiting

18. Complete the given sentence with an appropriate homophone from the given options.

There was no one .... a few of my friends.

(a) except (b) expect
(c) accept (d) excerpt

19. Choose an appropriate word that can substitute the bracketed word and complete the sentence meaningfully.

Shelley was very happy (while) I accepted her invitation to her birthday party.

(a) when (b) as
(c) after (d) before

20. There is a spelling error in the given sentence. Select the option that contains the incorrectly spelt word.

The choice of buying a yahct was poor.

(a) buying (b) yahct
(c) choice (d) poor

21. Select the most appropriate synonym of the given word.

Absurd

(a) Sudden (b) Arbitrary
(c) Irrational (d) Abstruse

22. Select the most appropriate option to substitute the underlined segment in the following sentence.

There was some drawing-pins in my desk.

(a) There is some
(b) There has some
(c) Theirs some
(d) There are some

23. Select the most appropriate antonym of the given word.

Calm

(a) Urban (b) Impressed
(c) Quiet (d) Upset

24. Select the most appropriate option to substitute the underlined part of the given sentence.

Mr. Sengupta's complaint to the higher authority was only a red herring.

(a) candid confession
(b) fortunate evidence
(c) clever bluff
(d) discouraging act

25. Select the most appropriate word to fill in the blank.

He has .... vision because of his illness.

(a) blurred (b) unfocused
(c) obscured (d) faded

Part II
General Intelligence

26. If 'A' stands for '÷', 'B' stands for '–', 'C' stands for '×' and 'D' stands for '+', what will come in place of the question mark (?) in the following equation?

36 B 8 A 56 C 49 D 53 = ?

(a) 53 (b) 82
(c) 46 (d) 30

27. The position of how many letters will change, if each of the letters in the word SKYLINE is arranged in alphabetical order?

(a) Seven (b) Six
(c) Five (d) Four

28. 'RENT' is related to 'IVMG' in a certain way based on the English alphabetical order. In the same way, 'PAYABLE' is related to 'KZBZYOV'. To which of the following is 'BARGUANDY' related, following the same logic?

(a) YZITFAMWB (b) YZITVZMWB
(c) YZITFZMWB (d) YZITFZMYB

29. How many triangles are there in the given figure?

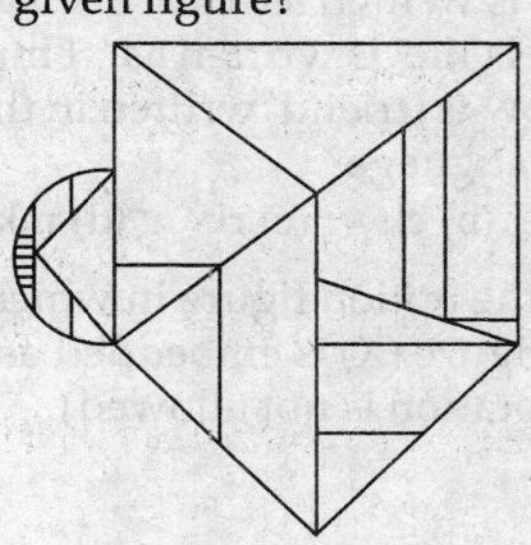

(a) 13 (b) 11
(c) 10 (d) 12

30. What will come in the place of question mark (?) in the following equation, if '×' and '÷' are interchanged?

$45 \times 9 + 23 - 16 \div 7 = ?$

(a) –84 (b) –79
(c) –64 (d) –76

31. 15 is related to 195 following a certain logic. Following the same logic, 19 is related to 247. To which of the following is 24 related following the same logic?

(**Note** Operations should be performed on the whole numbers, without breaking down the numbers into its constituent digits. E.g. 13 – Operations on 13 such as adding /subtracting /multiplying etc. to 13 can be performed. Breaking down 13 into 1 and 3 and then performing mathematical operations on 1 and 3 is not allowed)

(a) 322 (b) 332
(c) 300 (d) 312

32. What should come in place of the question mark (?) in the given series?

160, 187, 216, 247, ?

(a) 290 (b) 280 (c) 209 (d) 208

33. In a certain code language,

'A+ B' means 'A is the son of B',
'A – B' means 'A is the brother of B',
'A × B' means 'A is the wife of B',
'A ÷ B' means 'A is the daughter of B'.

Based on the above, how is L related to M, if 'L – N ÷ O × M +P'?

(a) Father's father
(b) Brother
(c) Son
(d) Father

34. In a certain code language, 'my best friend' is written as 'ck rl mk' and 'friend is life' is written as 'rt mp ck'. How is 'friend' written in the given language?
(a) rt (b) ck (c) rl (d) mk

35. Select the option figure in which the given figure (X) is embedded as its part (rotation is not allowed).

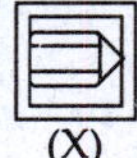
(X)

(a) 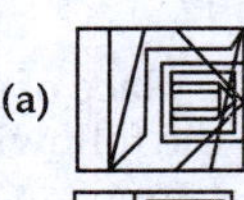 (b) 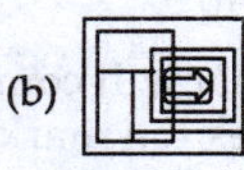

(c) 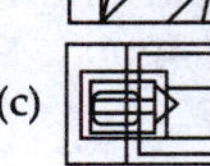 (d) 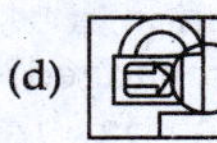

36. A paper is folded and cut as shown below. How will it appear when unfolded?

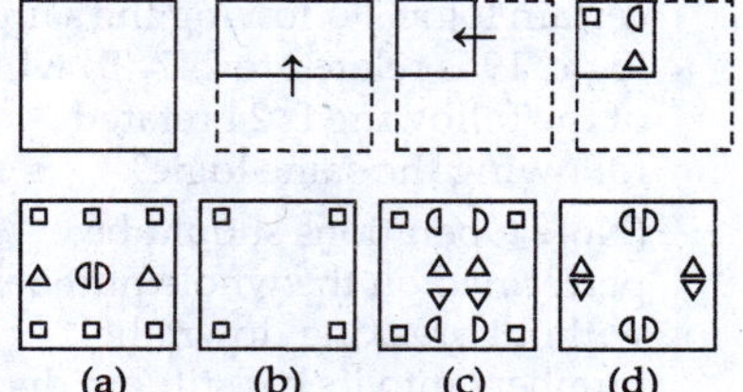

37. Identify the figure in the options that when put in place of the question mark (?) will logically complete the series?

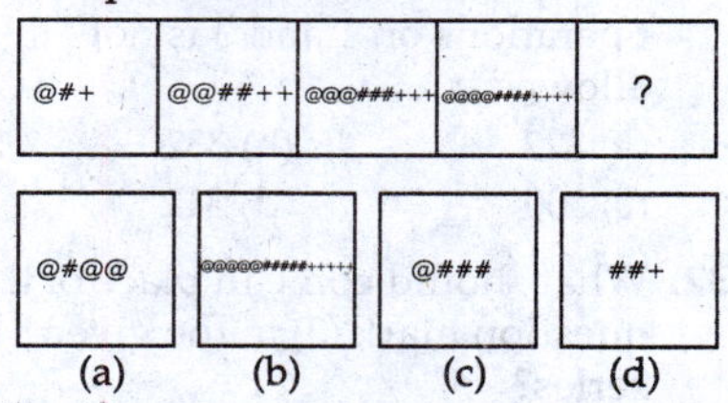

38. What should come in place of the question mark (?) in the given series?
23, 44, 65, 86, ?, 128
(a) 103 (b) 109
(c) 107 (d) 105

39. The position of how many letters will remain unchanged, if each of the letters in the word COMPLEXITY is arranged from left to right in alphabetical order?
(a) One
(b) Two
(c) None
(d) Three

40. Read the given statements and conclusions carefully. Assuming that the information given in the statements is true, even if it appears to be at variance with commonly known facts, decide which of the given conclusions logically follow(s) from the statements.

Statements

Some laptops are computers.

No computer is a robot.

Some robots are humans.

Conclusions

I. All humans can never be computers.

II. Some robots are laptops.

(a) Only Conclusion II follows
(b) Only Conclusion I follows
(c) Both Conclusions I and II follow
(d) None of the conclusions follow

41. What should come in place of the question mark (?) in the given series based on the English alphabetical order?
BRK, XUH, TXE, PAB, ?
(a) NCX (b) MDX
(c) LDY (d) MCZ

42. Select the word-pair that best represents a similar relationship to the one expressed in the pair of words given below.
(The words must be considered as meaningful English words and must not be related to each other based on the number of letters/number of consonants/vowels in the word)
Conquer : Surrender
(a) Lively : Vibrant (b) Rich : Affluent
(c) Unite : Divide (d) Gentle : Mild

43. 'A – B' means 'A is B's wife'.
'A + B' means 'A is B's brother'.
'A × B' means 'A is B's father'.
'A ÷ B' means 'A is B's sister'.
Using the same meaning of the mathematical operators as given above, in 'T × X ÷ Y + Z' what is T of Z's ?
(a) Brother (b) Son
(c) Mother (d) Father

44. What should come in place of question mark (?) in the given series based on the English alphabetical order?
VOH, YPN, BQT, ?, HSF
(a) MOJ (b) ERZ
(c) AXY (d) JHI

45. Select the set in which the numbers are related in the same way as are the numbers of the following sets.
(**Note** Operations should be performed on the whole numbers, without breaking down the numbers into its constituent digits. E.g. 13 – Operations on 13 such as adding/subtracting/multiplying etc. to 13 can be performed. Breaking down 13 into 1 and 3 and then performing mathematical operations on 1 and 3 is not allowed)
(84, 28, 7)
(144, 48, 12)
(a) (180, 50, 15)
(b) (180, 60, 10)
(c) (180, 60, 15)
(d) (160, 60, 15)

46. What will come in the place of the question mark (?) in the following equation, if '+' and '÷' are interchanged and '×' and '–' are interchanged?
$5 - 63 + 9 \div 10 \times 6 = ?$
(a) 39 (b) 33
(c) 36 (d) 30

47. Select the option in which the given figure is embedded (rotation is not allowed).

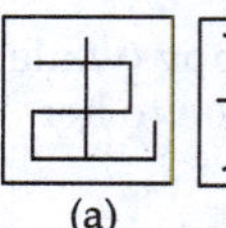 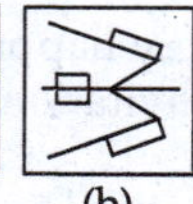 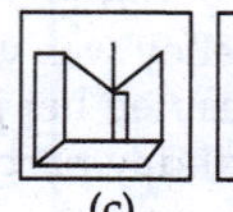 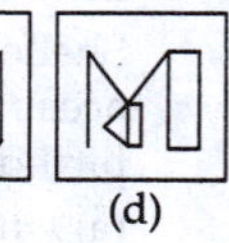
(a) (b) (c) (d)

48. Which of the following numbers will replace the question mark (?) in the given series?
165, 192, 227, 270, 321, ?
(a) 347 (b) 361
(c) 380 (d) 392

49. What would be the Roman numeral on the opposite side of 'VI', if the given sheet is folded to form a cube?

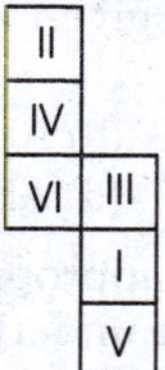

(a) V (b) III (c) I (d) II

50. Select the option figure in which the given figure is embedded as its part (rotation is not allowed).

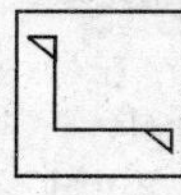

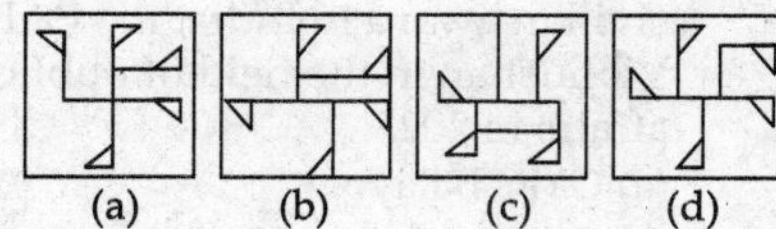

Part III
Quantitative Aptitude

51. A student has 5 subjects in an examination. The distribution of hard work of 16 h per day over 5 subjects and marks obtained 400 out of 500 are shown in the charts.

Hardwork in time

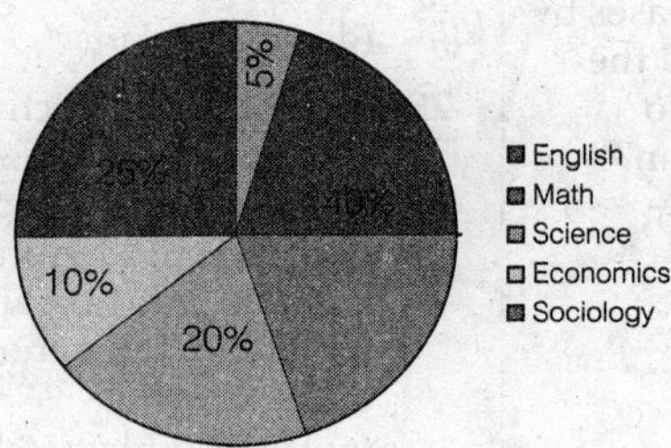

Marks obtained

22% 20% 19% 21% 18%

English
Math
Science
Economics
Sociology

In which subject did the student get the highest outcome of the hard work (ratio of marks to hard work is highest)?

(a) English (b) Math (c) Economics (d) Science

52. The bar-graph given below shows the sales of books (in thousands) from five branches of a publishing company during two consecutive years 2015 and 2016.

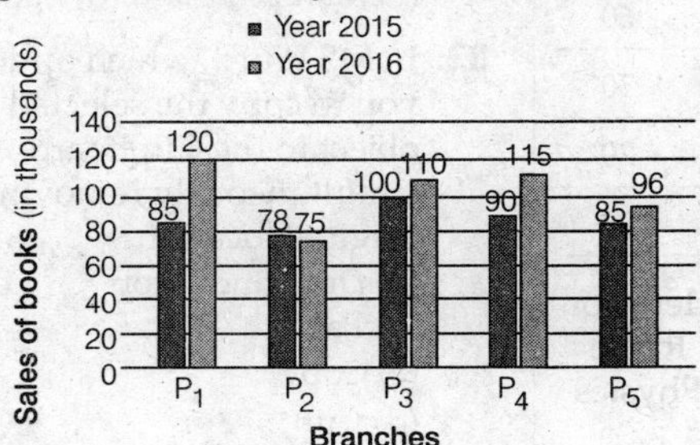

What percentage (round off to 2 decimal places) of the average sales of branches P_1, P_3 and P_5 in 2016 is the average sales of branches P_1, P_2, P_3 and P_4 in 2015?

(a) 88.15% (b) 76.53% (c) 81.21% (d) 80.12%

53. The value of $[3^3\{(40\times5)+(7\times6)\}\div11]\ +(2^3\times15\div24)$ is

(a) 959 (b) 595 (c) 599 (d) 559

54. A cuboid with dimensions 20 cm, 12 cm and 10 cm is cut into 8 identical pieces by 3 cuts. What will be the total surface area of all the pieces?

(a) 1680 cm^2 (b) 3360 cm^2 (c) 2240 cm^2 (d) 1220 cm^2

55. An article is of size 9 cm × 6 cm × 3 cm. The number of such articles that can be packed in a box measuring 63 cm × 42 cm × 21 cm is

(a) 343 (b) 243 (c) 49 (d) 196

56. Reena and Riya together can complete a piece of work in 36 days. Riya and Geeta together can complete it in 54 days. Reena and Geeta together can complete it in 81 days. In how many days can Reena alone complete the work?

(a) $82\frac{4}{7}$ days (b) $87\frac{4}{7}$ days (c) $97\frac{4}{7}$ days (d) $92\frac{4}{7}$ days

57. Which of the following ratios is greater?

(a) 7 : 4 (b) 2 : 3 (c) 8 : 3 (d) 1 : 5

58. Let $ABCD$ be a quadrilateral and AC, BD be diagonals. The length of $BD = 20$ cm and the heights of the triangles ABD and BCD are, 6 cm and 8 cm respectively. Find the area of the quadrilateral $ABCD$ (in cm^2).

(a) 140 (b) 120
(c) 148 (d) 1282

59. Chords AB and CD of a circle, when produced, meet at a point P outside the circle. If $AB = 6$ cm, $CD = 3$ cm and $PD = 5$ cm, then PB is equal to

(a) 9 cm (b) 8 cm (c) 4 cm (d) 6 cm

60. A certain sum of money amounts to ₹ 1860 in 2 yr and to ₹ 2130 in $3\frac{1}{2}$ yr at simple interest. Find the sum and the rate of interest, respectively.

(a) ₹ 1500, 12% (b) ₹ 1200, 10%
(c) ₹ 1500, 15% (d) ₹ 1200, 12%

61. The given chart represents the sales of automobiles in India (by type, in million units) from the year 2011 to 2014. Study the chart and answer the question that follows.

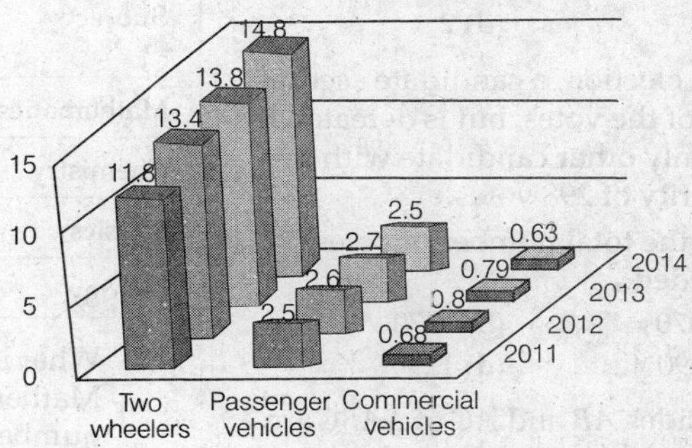

The number of commercial vehicles sold in 2012 was approximately, what percentage of the number of vehicles sold in 2011? (Correct to two decimal places)

(a) 6.12% (b) 5.34%
(c) 4.56% (d) 3.88%

62. With a uniform speed, a car covers a distance in 16 h. Had the speed been increased by 20 km/h, the same distance would have been covered in 12 h. The total distance covered by the car is
(a) 720 km (b) 1080 km
(c) 960 km (d) 480 km

63. The centres of two circles of radii 20 cm and 32 cm are 60 cm apart. What is the ratio of the length of the direct common tangent to the length of the transverse common tangent to these circles?
(a) $3\sqrt{3} : \sqrt{7}$ (b) $3\sqrt{2} : \sqrt{7}$
(c) $3\sqrt{7} : \sqrt{3}$ (d) $7\sqrt{3} : 3$

64. In a triangle *PQR*, *RS* intersects *PQ* at point *S*. The sides of the triangle $QR = 36$ cm, $SQ = 27$ cm, $RS = 18$ cm and $\angle QRS = \angle QPR$. What is the ratio of the perimeter ΔPRS to that of ΔQSR?
(a) $\frac{8}{6}$ (b) $\frac{9}{12}$
(c) $\frac{7}{9}$ (d) $\frac{5}{8}$

65. A merchant sells 195 kg of wheat for ₹ 10,260 at a profit of ₹ 4.50 per kg of wheat. What is the cost price (in ₹, to the nearest integer) of 15 kg of wheat?
(a) 722 (b) 682
(c) 595 (d) 750

66. A coat marked at ₹ 145 is offered at ₹ 127.6. The rate of retail discount offered is
(a) 11% (b) 12%
(c) 13% (d) 10%

67. If $42 \div 3 + k \times 3 - 22 \div 11 + 4 = 28$, then the value of *k* is
(a) 0 (b) 1
(c) 4 (d) 2

68. In an election, a candidate secures 40% of the votes, but is defeated by the only other candidate with a majority of 298 votes.
Find the total number of votes recorded.
(a) 1470 (b) 1270
(c) 1490 (d) 1290

69. The sides *AB* and *AC* of ΔABC are produced to points *D* and *E*, respectively. The bisectors of $\angle CBD$ and $\angle BCE$ meet at *P*. If $\angle A = 72°$, then the measure of $\angle P$ is
(a) 55° (b) 65°
(c) 54° (d) 35°

70. The cost of 21 pencils and 9 pens is ₹ 276 and the cost of 6 pencils and 3 pens is ₹ 84 The cost of 1 pencil and 1 pen is
(a) ₹ 20 (b) ₹ 10
(c) ₹ 40 (d) ₹ 30

71. If $4\sin^2\theta - 4\sqrt{3}\sin\theta + 3 = 0$, then find the value of θ. $(0 < \theta < 90°)$
(a) 30° (b) 75°
(c) 60° (d) 45°

72. A public library has an average attendance of 410 on Sundays and 230 for the remaining days. The average attendance per day of a month of 30 days beginning with Sunday would be
(a) 230 (b) 254 (c) 320 (d) 260

73. Due to decrease in manpower, the production in a factory decreases by 25%. By what per cent should the working hours be increased to restore the original production?
(a) 25%
(b) 50%
(c) $43\frac{6}{7}\%$
(d) $33\frac{1}{3}\%$

74. Two numbers are, respectively, 30% and 40% more than the third number. The ratio of the second number to the first number is
(a) 26:28 (b) 14:13
(c) 39:42 (d) 13:14

75. Total number of students in different subjects of a college and percentage of girls and boys are shown in the below table.
Girls students and boys students are not having multiple subjects.

Subjects	Number of Students	Girls %	Boys %
Mathematics	840	40	60
Chemistry	220	70	30
Physics	450	30	70
Biology	200	80	20

What is the ratio of girls students of Mathematics and Chemistry to the number of boys students of Physics and Biology?
(a) 49 : 39
(b) 36 : 49
(c) 61 : 98
(d) 98 : 71

Part IV
General Awareness

76. .... was posthumously conferred the second highest civilian award in India, the Padma Vibhushan in the field of public affairs in 2023.
(a) GMC Balayogi
(b) Dilip Mahalanabis
(c) Mulayam Singh Yadav
(d) Balkrishna Doshi

77. A proton bonds to the oxygen atom of a solvent water to give a .... hydronium ion.
(a) square pyramid
(b) trigonal pyramidal
(c) tetrahedral
(d) square planar

78. In July 2021, which State Government announced the creation of an independent department to protect and preserve the 'faith, culture and traditions of tribes and indigenous communities' of the state?
(a) Uttar Pradesh (b) Bihar
(c) Karnataka (d) Assam

79. Who among the following is a Choreographer in Indian film Industry?
(a) Anu Malik (b) Pritam
(c) Prabhu Deva (d) Arijit Singh

80. Which does social networking service place the biggest emphasis on professional networking?
(a) Facebook (b) Google+
(c) LinkedIn (d) Twitter

81. 'Lai Phi' and 'Chin Phi' are the cultural costumes of which state?
(a) Nagaland (b) Uttarakhand
(c) Manipur (d) Sikkim

82. In MS Word, which option allows you to copy the selected text or object to the Clipboard while simultaneously removing it from its original location?
(a) Drag-and-Drop
(b) Paste
(c) Copy
(d) Cut

83. The headquarters of the Indian Institute of Tourism and Travel Management are located at
(a) Bhuvneshwar (b) New Delhi
(c) Guwahati (d) Gwalior

84. In April 2022, Chief Justice of India NV Ramana recommended the creation of an 'independent umbrella institution', so as to bring various agencies under one roof". Which of the following agencies did he suggest be brought under this umbrella?
(a) ED, CBI and SFIO
(b) SFIO and CBI
(c) ED and NIA
(d) CBI, SFIO and NIA

85. Gurpurab is celebrated to commemorate the birthday of Guru Nank Dev Ji. He was the .... guru of Sikhs.
(a) second
(b) third
(c) first
(d) fourth

86. In which direction is the general elevation of the peninsular plateau of India?
(a) From North to South
(b) From West to East
(c) From South to North
(d) From East to West

87. All historical monuments have signages with instructions that public should not write on the walls.
To which Fundamental Duty does the given statement belong?
(a) To develop the scientific temper
(b) To defend the country and render national service
(c) To promote harmony and spirit of common brotherhood
(d) To safeguard public property and to abjure violence

88. Where is the largest football stadium in India located?
(a) Kolkata
(b) Goa
(c) Bengaluru
(d) New Delhi

89. In which of the following years was the National Anthem adopted in its Hindi version by the Constituent Assembly?
(a) 1947 (b) 1950
(c) 1942 (d) 1954

90. .... oblong orbit overlaps the orbit of Neptune.
(a) Mars' (b) Pluto's
(c) Jupiter's (d) Venus'

91. Match the following

	List I		List II
A.	National Manufacturing Policy	1.	2014
B.	Make in India initiative	2.	2016
C.	Startup India scheme	3.	2011
D.	Smart City Project	4.	2015

Codes

	A	B	C	D		A	B	C	D
(a)	4	3	1	2	(b)	1	2	3	4
(c)	3	1	2	4	(d)	1	2	4	3

92. Lakshmibai National College of Physical Education is located at ....
(a) Shahdara, Delhi
(b) Patiala, Punjab
(c) Gwalior, Madhya Pradesh
(d) Thiruvananthapuram, Kerala

93. What is the literacy rate of India as per the National Survey of India-2022?
(a) 78.3% (b) 74.2% (c) 72.1% (d) 77.7%

94. Which of the following word sequences is correct as per the Preamble to the Constitution?
(a) Sovereign, socialist, secular, democratic, republic
(b) Socialist, secular, democratic, republic, sovereign
(c) Secular, democratic, secular, socialist, sovereign
(d) Sovereign, secular, socialist, democratic, republic

95. Which non-essential amino acid is synthesised by the hydroxylation of phenylalanine in a reaction catalysed by phenylalanine hydroxylase?
(a) Glutamine (b) Tyrosine
(c) Cysteine (d) Glycine

96. Who invaded India during the rule of Tughlaq Dynasty?
(a) Timur
(b) Mahmud of Ghazni
(c) Chengiz Khan
(d) Muhammad Ghori

97. What is the impact of proportional taxes?
(a) Increases the marginal propensity to consume
(b) Reduces the autonomous expenditure multiplier
(c) Increases the induced expenditure multiplier
(d) Increases the autonomous expenditure multiplier

98. Annamacharya composed Sankirtans in praise of which God?
(a) Lord Rama
(b) Lord Krishna
(c) Lord Venkateshwara
(d) Lord Shiva

99. Which important event that started in 1930 played a significant role in motivating and mobilising Indians to join the Non-Violent Movement for independence?
(a) Swadeshi Movement
(b) Gadar Movement
(c) Quit India Movement
(d) Salt Satyagraha

100. What are the standard measurements of a cricket pitch?
(a) 20 yards by 12 ft
(b) 22 yards by 12 ft
(c) 20 yards by 10 ft
(d) 22 yards by 10 ft

Answers

1. (a)	2. (d)	3. (a)	4. (d)
5. (d)	6. (c)	7. (a)	8. (b)
9. (c)	10. (d)	11. (b)	12. (c)
13. (b)	14 (d)	15. (a)	16. (a)
17. (c)	18. (a)	19. (a)	20. (b)
21. (c)	22. (d)	23. (d)	24. (c)
25. (a)	26. (b)	27. (b)	28. (c)
29. (d)	30. (a)	31. (d)	32. (b)
33. (c)	34. (b)	35. (a)	36. (c)
37. (b)	38. (c)	39. (b)	40. (b)
41. (c)	42. (c)	43. (d)	44. (b)
45. (c)	46. (a)	47. (c)	48. (c)
49. (d)	50. (a)	51. (a)	52. (c)
53. (c)	54. (c)	55. (a)	56. (d)
57. (c)	58. (a)	59. (c)	60. (a)
61. (b)	62. (c)	63. (a)	64. (c)
65. (a)	66. (b)	67. (c)	68. (c)
69. (c)	70. (a)	71. (c)	72. (d)
73. (d)	74. (b)	75. (d)	76. (c)
77. (b)	78. (d)	79. (c)	80. (c)
81. (c)	82. (d)	83. (d)	84. (a)
85. (c)	86. (b)	87. (d)	88. (a)
89. (b)	90. (b)	91. (c)	92. (d)
93. (d)	94. (a)	95. (b)	96. (a)
97. (b)	98. (c)	99. (d)	100. (d)

Explanations

1. *(a)* Part (a) 'I used to eat into' contains an error. Use 'out' in place of 'into' to correct the sentence.
2. *(d)* Part (C) 'and ran over' contains an error. The use of 'ran over', which means to kill by car, is incorrect in the sentence. Use 'ran into', which means to meet suddenly, to correct the sentence.
3. *(a)* Part (a) 'Shall have' contains an error. Use 'will' to correct the sentence.
4. *(d)* The sentence in future tense is- If you work hard in the same manner, you will soon achieve success.
5. *(d)* The correct filler for the given blank is 'it'.
6. *(c)* The correct filler for the given blank is 'Constant'.
7. *(a)* The correct filler for the given blank is 'in'.
8. *(b)* The correct filler for the given blank is 'pursuing'.
9. *(c)* The correct filler for the given blank is 'prioritise'.
10. *(d)* The correct filler for the given blank is 'spotless'.
11. *(b)* The correct idiom for the given blank is 'feeling the pinch' means to have problems with money because you are earning less than before.
12. *(c)* 'Stoic' means a person who can endure pain or hardship without showing their feelings or complaining. Hence, the antonym is 'Fervent' which means having or displaying a passionate intensity. Apathetic means uncaring.
13. *(b)* Occult means mystical, supernatural, or magical powers, practices, or phenomena. Hence, its nearest antonym is 'intelligible'.
    - 'Latent' means existing but not yet developed or manifest; hidden or concealed.
    - 'Ambiguous' means confusing.
    - 'Unfathomable' means unimaginable.
14. *(d)* The incorrectly spelt word is 'Disintigrate'. The correct spelling is 'Disintegrate'.
15. *(a)* 'Vulgar' means lacking sophistication or good taste. Hence, its antonym is 'decorous' which means in keeping with good taste and propriety; polite and restrained.
    - 'Ribald' means referring to sexual matters in an amusingly coarse or irreverent way.
    - 'Impervious' means not allowing fluid to pass through.
    - 'Licentious' means that they are very immoral in their behaviour.
16. *(a)* The underlined part of the given sentence contains an error. Use 'illusion' to correct the sentence.
17. *(c)* The underlined part of the given sentence contains an error. Use 'have been waiting' to correct the sentence.
18. *(a)* The correct filler for the given blank is 'except'.
19. *(a)* The bracketed part of the given sentence contains an error. Use 'when' to correct the sentence.
20. *(b)* The incorrectly spelt word is 'yahct'. The correct spelling is 'yatch'.
21. *(c)* 'Absurd' means strange and irrational.
    - 'Arbitrary' means based on random choice or personal whim, rather than any reason or system.
    - 'Abstruse' means difficult to understand; obscure.
22. *(d)* The underlined part of the given sentence contains an error. Use 'There are some' to correct the sentence.
23. *(d)* The antonym of 'Calm' is 'Upset'.
24. *(c)* A red herring means an idea or a subject which takes people's attention away from what is really important or a clever bluff.
25. *(a)* The correct filler for the given blank is 'blurred'.
26. *(b)* Given expression,

    36 B 8 A 56 C 49 D 53 = ?

    After substituting letters with signs, we get

A → ÷	B → –
C → ×	D → +

$36 - 8 \div 56 \times 49 + 53$

$= 36 - 7 + 53$

$= 89 - 7 = 82$

27. *(b)* Given word ⟶ SKYLINE

    After arranging in alphabetical order ⟶ EIKLNSY

    Hence, position of six letters will change.
28. *(c)* As,

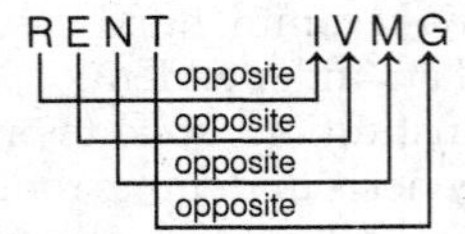

and

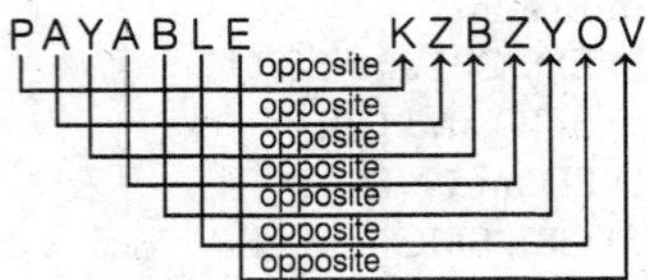

Similarly,

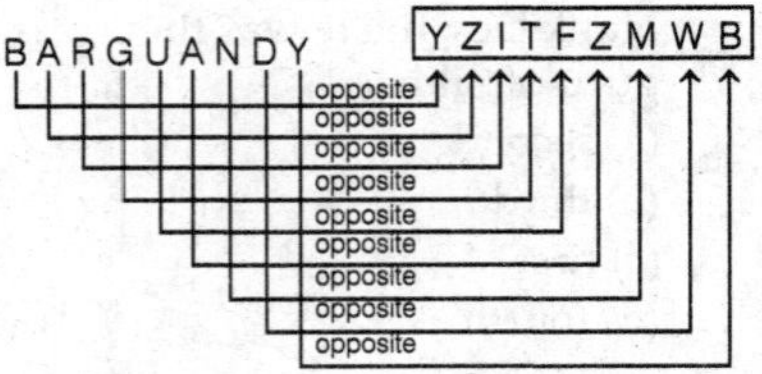

29. *(d)* Naming the figure,

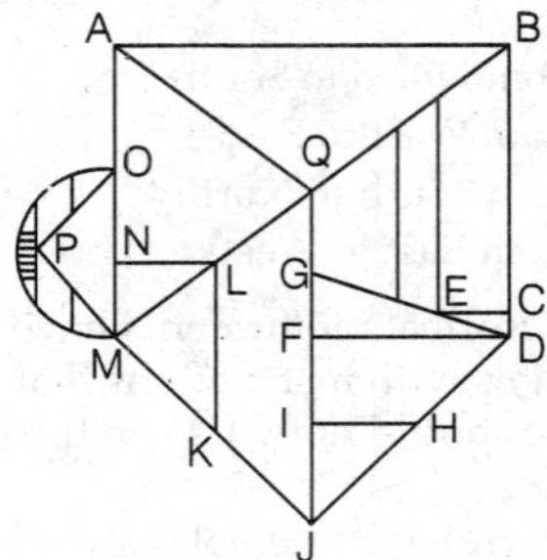

ΔABQ, ΔAQM, ΔNLM, ΔMLK, ΔOMP, ΔABM, ΔMQJ, ΔECD, ΔGDF, ΔIHJ, ΔGDJ and ΔFDJ.

Hence, there are 12 triangles in the figure.

30. *(a)* Given expression,

    $45 \times 9 + 23 - 16 \div 7 = ?$

    After interchanging '×' and '÷' signs, we get

    $= 45 \div 9 + 23 - 16 \times 7$

    $= 5 + 23 - 112$

    $= 28 - 112 = -84$
31. *(d)* As, $15 \times 13 = 195$

    and $19 \times 13 = 247$

    Similarly,

    $24 \times 13 = \boxed{312}$
32. *(b)* The pattern of the series is as follows,

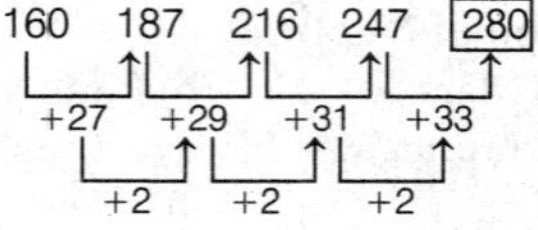

33. *(c)* According to the question,

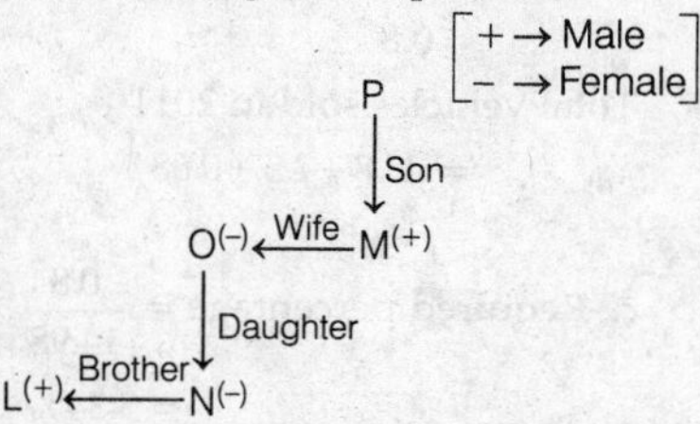

Hence, L is the son of M.

34. *(b)* According to the question,

my best friend → ck rl mk

friend is life → rt mp ck

Hence, the code for 'friend' is 'ck'.

35. *(a)* The given figure (X) is embedded in the option figure (a).

36. *(c)* The unfolded paper will appear as option figure (c).

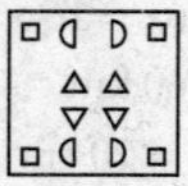

37. *(b)* In the given series, every symbol and signs is increasing by 1 in every next figure. Hence, option figure (b) will replace the question mark.

38. *(c)* The pattern of the series is as follows,

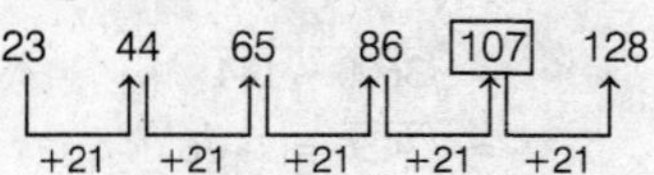

39. *(b)* According to the question,

Given word → C O M P L E X I T Y

After arranging in alphabetical order → C E I L M O P T X Y

Hence, the position of C and Y (two letters) will remain unchanged.

40. *(b)* According to the statements,

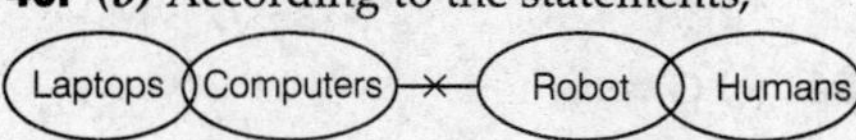

Conclusions I. (✓) II. (✗)

Hence, only Conclusion I follows.

41. *(c)* The pattern of the series is as follows,

B $\xrightarrow{-4}$ X $\xrightarrow{-4}$ T $\xrightarrow{-4}$ P $\xrightarrow{-4}$ L

R $\xrightarrow{+3}$ U $\xrightarrow{+3}$ X $\xrightarrow{+3}$ A $\xrightarrow{+3}$ D

K $\xrightarrow{-3}$ H $\xrightarrow{-3}$ E $\xrightarrow{-3}$ B $\xrightarrow{-3}$ Y

42. *(c)* As, Conquer is the antonym of surrender. Similarly, Unite is the antonym of divide.

43. *(d)* According to the question,

[+ → Male, – → Female]

T(+)

Father

X(–) ← Sister — Y(+) ← Brother — Z

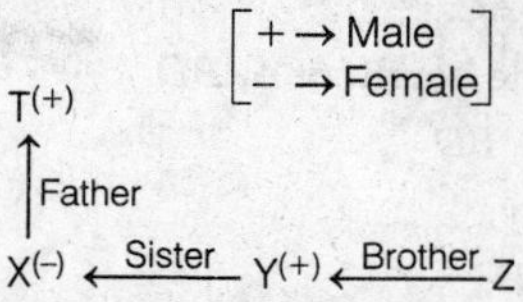

Hence, T is father of Z.

44. *(b)* The pattern of the series is as follows,

V $\xrightarrow{+3}$ Y $\xrightarrow{+3}$ B $\xrightarrow{+3}$ E $\xrightarrow{+3}$ H

O $\xrightarrow{+1}$ P $\xrightarrow{+1}$ Q $\xrightarrow{+1}$ R $\xrightarrow{+1}$ S

H $\xrightarrow{+6}$ N $\xrightarrow{+6}$ T $\xrightarrow{+6}$ Z $\xrightarrow{+6}$ F

45. *(c)* As,

$(84, 28, 7) = \frac{84}{3} = 28; \frac{28}{4} = 7$

and $(144, 48, 12) = \frac{144}{3} = 48; \frac{48}{4} = 12$

Similarly,

$(180, 60, 15) = \frac{180}{3} = 60$

$\frac{60}{4} = 15$

46. *(a)* Given expression,

$5 - 63 + 9 \div 10 \times 6 = ?$

After interchanging '+' and '÷' and '×' and '–', we get

$5 \times 63 \div 9 + 10 - 6$

$= 35 + 10 - 6$

$= 45 - 6$

$= 39$

47. *(c)* The given figure is embedded in the option figure (c).

48. *(c)* The pattern of the series is as follows,

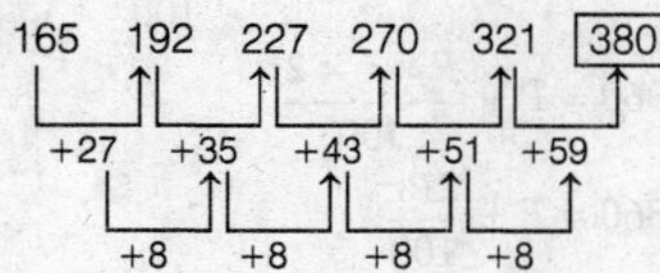

49. *(d)* According to the question,

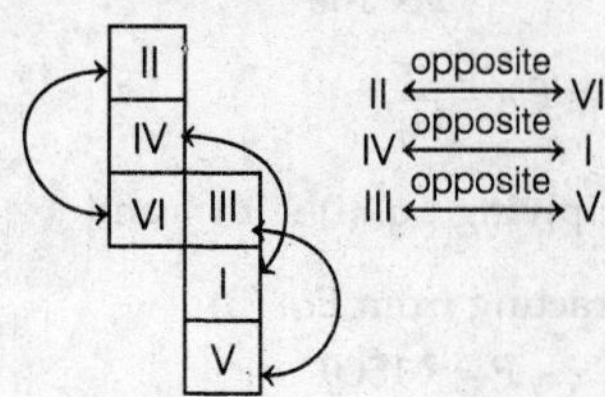

Hence, II is opposite side of VI.

50. *(a)* The given figure is embedded in the option figure (a).

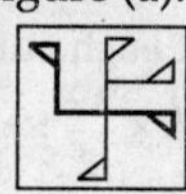

51. *(a)* Ratio of marks to the hardwork in Science

$= 400 \times \frac{18}{100} : 16 \times \frac{20}{100}$

$= 360 : 16 = 22.5$

Ratio of marks to the hardwork in Maths

$= 400 \times \frac{21}{100} : 16 \times \frac{40}{100}$

$= 210 : 16 = 13.125$

Ratio of marks to the hardwork in Economics

$= 400 \times \frac{19}{100} : 16 \times \frac{10}{100}$

$= 760 : 16 = 47.5$

Ratio of marks to the hardwork in English

$= 400 \times \frac{20}{100} : 16 \times \frac{5}{100}$

$= 100 : 1 = 100$

Hence, in English marks to the hardwork is highest.

52. *(c)* Average sales of branches P_1, P_3 and P_5 in 2016

$= \frac{120 + 110 + 96}{3} = 108.66$

Average sales of branches P_1, P_2, P_3 and P_4 in 2015

$= \frac{85 + 78 + 100 + 90}{4} = 88.25$

∴ Required percentage

$= \frac{88.25}{108.66} \times 100$

$= 81.21\%$

53. *(c)* $[3^3\{(40 \times 5) + (7 \times 6)\} \div 11] + (2^3 \times 15 \div 24)$

By using BODMAS rule,

$[3^3\{(200) + 42\} \div 11] + \left(\frac{8 \times 15}{24}\right)$

$= [3^3 \times 22] + \left(\frac{120}{24}\right)$

$= 594 + 5 = 599$

54. *(c)* Given,

Sides of cuboid = 20 cm, 12 cm and 10 cm

To divide a cuboid into 8 equal pieces, the cuboid must be cut through the middle of each surface.

$\therefore$ Sides of smaller cuboid $= \frac{20}{2}, \frac{12}{2}, \frac{10}{2}$

$\therefore$ Volume of each cuboid

$$= \frac{20}{2} \times \frac{12}{2} \times \frac{10}{2} \text{ cm}^3$$

Total surface area of 8 smaller cuboid

$$= 8 \times 2\,[10 \times 6 + 6 \times 5 + 5 \times 10]$$
$$= 16\,[60 + 30 + 50] = 2240 \text{ cm}^2$$

55. *(a)* Given,

Article dimensions = 9 cm, 6 cm, 3 cm

and box dimensions = 63 cm, 42 cm, 21 cm

We know that,

Volume = length × breadth × height

$\therefore$ Number of articles

$$= \frac{63 \times 42 \times 21}{9 \times 6 \times 3} = 7 \times 7 \times 7 = 343$$

56. *(d)* (Reena and Riya)'s one day's work

$$= \frac{1}{36}$$

(Riya and Geeta)'s one day's work $= \frac{1}{54}$

(Reena and Geeta)'s one day's work $= \frac{1}{81}$

$\therefore$ (Reena + Riya + Geeta)'s one day's work

$$= \frac{1}{2}\left(\frac{1}{36} + \frac{1}{54} + \frac{1}{81}\right)$$
$$= \frac{1}{2} \times \frac{19}{324} = \frac{19}{648}$$

$\therefore$ Reena's one day's work $= \frac{19}{648} - \frac{1}{54}$

$$= \frac{7}{648}$$

Hence, Reena alone can do complete the work in $\frac{648}{7} = 92\frac{4}{7}$ days

57. *(c)* Given,

$7 : 4 = 1.75$

$2 : 3 = 0.66$

$8 : 3 = 2.66$

$1 : 5 = 0.2$

Greater ratio = 2.66 = 8 : 3

58. *(a)* $ABCD$ is a quadrilateral.

AC and BD are diagonals.

$BD = 20$ cm

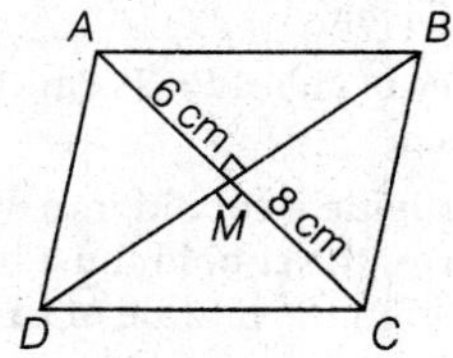

Let M be the intersecting point of BD and AC.

AM is the height of ΔABD.

$\therefore$ $AM \perp BD$

Similarly,

$CM \perp BD$

$\therefore$ □$ABCD$ is a rhombus.

Area of rhombus

$$= \frac{1}{2} \times d_1 \times d_2$$
$$= \frac{1}{2} \times BD \times AC$$
$$= \frac{1}{2} \times 20 \times (6 + 8) = 140 \text{ cm}^2$$

59. *(c)* Let $PB = x$ cm

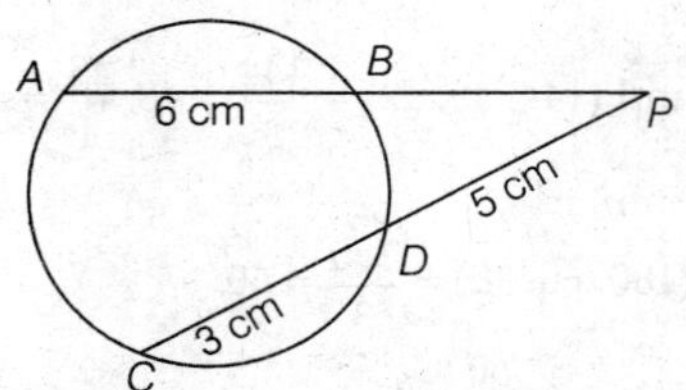

Using Intersecting Chords theorem,

$$AP \times BP = PD \times PC$$
$$(x + 6) \times x = 5 \times 8$$
$$x^2 + 6x = 40$$
$$x^2 + 6x - 40 = 0$$
$$x^2 + 10x - 4x - 40 = 0$$
$$(x + 10)(x - 4) = 0$$
$$\therefore \quad x = 4 \text{ cm}$$

60. *(a)* Time = 2 yr, Time = $3\frac{1}{2}$ yr

Amount = ₹1860, Amount = ₹2130

Let principal be ₹ P and rate be r%.

We know that,

Amount = Principal $+ \frac{\text{Principal} \times \text{Rate} \times \text{Time}}{100}$

$$1860 = P + \frac{P \times r \times 2}{100}$$
$$1860 = P + \frac{2Pr}{100} \quad \text{...(i)}$$
$$2130 = P + \frac{7 \times P \times r}{2 \times 100}$$
$$2130 = P + \frac{7Pr}{200} \quad \text{...(ii)}$$

Multiplying Eq. (i) with $\frac{7}{4}$ and subtracting from Eq. (ii)

$$P = ₹1500$$

Putting value of P in Eq. (i),

$$\therefore \quad r = 12\%$$

61. *(b)* Commercial vehicles sold in 2012

$$= 0.8$$

Total vehicles sold in 2011

$$= 11.8 + 2.5 + 0.68$$
$$= 14.98$$

$\therefore$ Required percentage $= \frac{0.8}{14.98} \times 100$

$$= 5.34\%$$

62. *(c)* Let the speed of car be x km/h.

We know that,

Distance = Speed × Time

$\therefore$ Distance = $16x$

New speed = $(x + 20)$ km/h

According to the question,

$$\frac{16x}{x + 20} = 12$$
$$16x = 12x + 240$$
$$\Rightarrow \quad x = 60 \text{ km/h}$$

Distance travelled by car

$$= 16x = 16 \times 60$$
$$= 960 \text{ km}$$

63. *(a)* Given, $r_1 = 20$ cm

$$r_2 = 32 \text{ cm}$$

Distance between centres (d) = 60 cm

Length of direct common tangent

$$= \sqrt{d^2 - (r_1 - r_2)^2}$$
$$= \sqrt{(60)^2 - (20 - 32)^2}$$
$$= \sqrt{3600 - 144}$$
$$= \sqrt{3456} = 24\sqrt{6}$$

Length of transversal common tangent

$$= \sqrt{d^2 - (r_1 + r_2)^2}$$
$$= \sqrt{(60)^2 - (20 + 32)^2}$$
$$= 8\sqrt{14}$$

$\therefore$ Required ratio $= 24\sqrt{6} : 8\sqrt{14}$

$$= 3\sqrt{3} : \sqrt{7}$$

64. *(c)* Given,

$QR = 36$ cm, $SQ = 27$ cm, $RS = 18$ cm

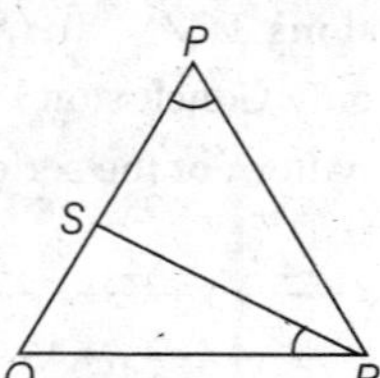

In ΔPQR and ΔRQS,

$\therefore$ $\angle RPQ = \angle SRQ$

$\Delta PQR \sim \Delta RQS$

$\frac{PQ}{RQ} = \frac{QR}{QS} = \frac{PR}{RS}$

$\frac{27 + PS}{36} = \frac{36}{27} = \frac{PR}{18}$

$\Rightarrow \frac{27 + PS}{36} = \frac{36}{27}$

$27 + PS = 48$

$\therefore PS = 21 \text{ cm}$

$\therefore PQ = PS + SQ$

$= 21 + 27 = 48 \text{ cm}$

Now, $\frac{PR}{18} = \frac{36}{27}$

$\therefore PR = 24 \text{ cm}$

Perimeter of ΔPRS

$= 24 + 18 + 21 = 63 \text{ cm}$

Perimeter of ΔQSR

$= 27 + 18 + 36 = 81 \text{ cm}$

$\therefore$ Required ratio = 63 : 81 = 7 : 9

65. (*a*) Given,

195 kg of wheat for ₹10260 at a profit of ₹4.5 per kg of wheat.

$\therefore$ Price for 1 kg of wheat $= \frac{10260}{195}$

$= ₹\frac{684}{13}$

Actual price for wheat

$= \frac{684}{13} - 4.5$

$= ₹\frac{1251}{26}$ per kg

$\therefore$ Cost price for 15 kg of wheat

$= \frac{1251}{26} \times 15 = ₹722$

66. (*b*) Given,

Marked Price (MP) = ₹145

Selling Price (SP) = ₹ 127.6

$\therefore$ Discount per cent

$= \left(\frac{\text{MP} - \text{SP}}{\text{MP}}\right) \times 100$

$= \frac{145 - 127.6}{145} \times 100 = 12\%$

67. (*c*) Given, expression,

$42 \div 3 + k \times 3 - 22 \div 11 + 4 = 28$

Using BODMAS rule,

$14 + 3k - 2 + 4 = 28$

$14 + 3k + 2 = 28$

$3k = 12$

$k = 4$

68. (*c*) Let total votes = $100x$

Loser got votes $= 100x \times \frac{40}{100} = 40x$

Winner got votes $= 100x \times \left(\frac{100 - 40}{100}\right)$

$= 60x$

$\therefore$ Difference of votes

$= 60x - 40x = 298$

$x = 14.9$

Hence, total votes $= 100 \times 14.9$

$= 1490$

69. (*c*) Given,

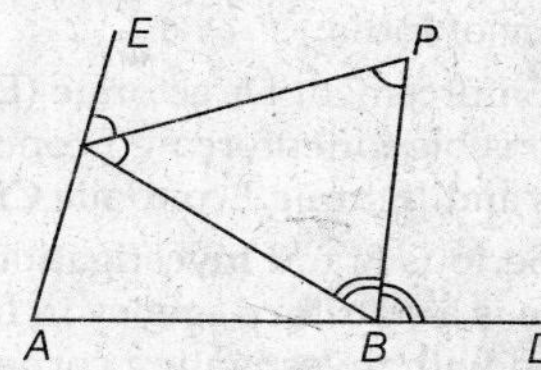

Using Angle Bisector theorem,

$\angle BPC = 90° - \frac{\angle A}{2}$

$= 90° - \frac{72°}{2} = 90° - 36° = 54°$

70. (*a*) Let the cost price of pencil = ₹x

and the cost price of pen = ₹y

According to the question,

$21x + 9y = ₹276$

$7x + 3y = ₹92$ ...(i)

$6x + 3y = ₹84$ ...(ii)

On solving Eq. (i) and Eq. (ii),

$x = ₹8$ and $y = ₹12$

$\therefore$ Cost of (1 pencil + 1 pen) $= x + y$

$= 8 + 12 = ₹20$

71. (*c*) $4\sin^2\theta - 4\sqrt{3}\sin\theta + 3 = 0$

$4\sin^2\theta - 2\sqrt{3}\sin\theta - 2\sqrt{3}\sin\theta + 3 = 0$

$2\sin\theta(2\sin\theta - \sqrt{3}) - \sqrt{3}$

$(2\sin\theta - \sqrt{3}) = 0$

$(2\sin\theta - \sqrt{3})(2\sin\theta - \sqrt{3}) = 0$

$\sin\theta = \frac{\sqrt{3}}{2}$

$\sin\theta = \sin 60°$

$\theta = 60°$

72. (*d*) Average attendance on Sunday $= 410$

Average attendance on remaining days = 230

5 Sunday in 30 days month

Remaining days = 30 − 5 = 25

$\therefore$ Required average

$= \frac{5 \times 410 + 25 \times 230}{30}$

$= \frac{7800}{30} = 260$

73. (*d*) Decrease in production = 25%

Effective increase in working hours for basic production

$= \frac{25}{(100 - 25)} \times 100$

$= \frac{25}{75} \times 100 = 33\frac{1}{3}\%$

74. (*b*) Let the third number be $100x$.

$\therefore$ Second number

$= 100x \times \left(\frac{40}{100} + 1\right)$

$= 140x$

and first number $= 100x \times \left(\frac{30}{100} + 1\right)$

$= 130x$

$\therefore \frac{\text{Second number}}{\text{First number}} = \frac{140x}{130x}$

$= 14 : 13$

75. (*d*) Number of girls students of Mathematics

$= 840 \times \frac{40}{100} = 336$

Number of girls students of Chemistry

$= 220 \times \frac{70}{100} = 154$

$\therefore$ Total girls = 336 + 154 = 490

Number of boys students of Physics

$= 450 \times \frac{70}{100} = 315$

Number of boys students of Biology

$= 200 \times \frac{20}{100} = 40$

$\therefore$ Total boys = 315 + 40 = 355

$\therefore$ Required ratio = 490 : 355

= 98 : 71

76. (*c*) Mulayam Singh Yadav was posthumously conferred the second highest civilian award in India, the Padma Vibhushan in the field of public affairs in 2023.

- GMC Balayogi was former Speaker of the Lok Sabha.
- Balkrishna Doshi designed the Life Insurance Corporation Housing in Ahmedabad (1973) and the Aranya Low Cost Housing in Indore (1989).
- Dilip Mahalanabis got nobel prize for oral rehydration theraphy.

77. (*b*) A proton bonds to the oxygen atom of a solvent water to give a trigonal pyramidal hydronium ion.

78. (*d*) In July 2021, Assam Government announced the creation of an independent department to protect and preserve the 'faith, culture and traditions of tribes and indigenous communities' of the state.

- Assam is home to many tribes, including the Bodos, Rabhas, Garos, and Moran.
- Important festival of Assam is Baishagu, a springtime festival that marks the new year celebrated in mid-April.

79. *(c)* Prabhu Deva is a Choreographer of Indian film industry.

- He is a film director, producer and actor who has worked predominantly in Tamil, Hindi, Telugu and Kannada language films.
- Anu Malik and Pritam are music director and composer in Indian film industry.
- Arijit singh is playback singer who belong to Indian film industry.

80. *(c)* LinkedIn is the biggest social networking service which places emphasis on professional networking.

- Ryan Roslansky is the CEO of LinkedIn, the world's largest and most powerful network of professionals.
- Facebook started by Mark Zuckerberg with four other Harvard College students and roommates Eduardo Saverin, Andrew McCollum.
- Twitter is one of the world's largest social media websites and the fifth-most visited website in the world presently ownwd by Elon Musk.

81. *(c)* 'Lai Phi' and 'Chin Phi' are the cultural costumes of Manipur.

- Lai Phi is a beautiful white piece of cloth bordered with yellow.
- Chin Phi is a blouse paired with an embroidered phanek.
- Other important dress of Manipur are Naphi, Phanek, Mayek, Naibi.

82. *(d)* In MS Word, cut option allows you to copy the selected text or object to the clipboard while simultaneously removing it from its original location.

83. *(d)* Headquarters of the Indian Institute of Tourism and Travel Management are located at Gwalior.

- Other important institutes are :
- Indian institute of ecology and environment is located in New Delhi.
- National institute of Ocean technology in Chennai.
- Indian Institute of Plantation Management in Bengaluru.

84. *(a)* In April 2022, Chief Justice of India NV Ramana recommended the creation of an 'independent umbrella institution', by integrating ED, CBI and SFIO.

- The Central Bureau of Investigation is the domestic crime investigating agency of India.
- The Enforcement Directorate (ED) is responsible for enforcing Economic Laws and fighting Economic Crime.
- The Serious Fraud Investigation Office is a statutory agency in India tasked with investigating corporate fraud.

85. *(c)* Guru Nanak Dev Ji was the first guru of Sikhs.

- Gurpurab is celebrated to commemorate the birthday of Guru Nank Dev ji.
- He started the institution of Guru Ka Langar which refers to common kitchen where food is served to everyone without any discrimination.
- He was the contemporary of Mughal emperor — Babur.

86. *(b)* The general elevation of the peninsular plateau of India is from West to East.

- It was produced by the breakup and drifting of the Gondwana continent, making it the oldest landmass.
- The plateau is characterised by vast and shallow valleys and rounded hills.
- The Central Highlands and the Deccan Plateau are the two major sections of this plateau.

87. *(d)* All historical monuments have signages with instructions that public should not write on the walls belong to Fundamental Duty that says to safeguard public property and to abjure violence.

- The Swaran Singh Committee in 1976 recommended Fundamental Duties.
- The 42nd Amendment Act of 1976 added 10 Fundamental Duties to the Indian Constitution.
- The 86th Amendment Act 2002 later added the 11th Fundamental Duty relating to Right of Children to Free and Compulsory Education (RTE).

88. *(a)* Largest football stadium of India is Vivekananda Yuba Bharati Krirangan (Salt Lake Stadium) in Kolkata.

- It's also the second-largest football stadium in the world.
- It has hosted major events like the 1987 South Asian Federation Games and the 2017 FIFA U-17 World Cup.

89. *(b)* In 1950, the National Anthem adopted its Hindi version by the Constituent Assembly.

- The National Anthem of India is titled "Jana Gana Mana".
- This song was originally composed in Bengali by India's first Nobel laureate Rabindranath Tagore on 11th December, 1911.
- The text was first published in 1905 in Tatwabodhini Patrika.

90. *(b)* Pluto's oblong orbit overlaps the orbit of Neptune.

- Pluto was reclassified as a dwarf planet in 2006 by the International Astronomical Union (IAU).
- Pluto orbit overlaps Neptune's orbit between 29.7 and 49.3 Astronomical Units (AU) from the sun.

91. *(c)* The correct matching is A-3, B-1, C-2, D-4.

- The National Manufacturing Policy (2011), aims at increasing the manufacturing sector's.
- The Make in India Initiative (2014) to make India a hub for manufacturing, design and innovation.
- Startup India (2016) intended to catalyse startup culture and build a strong and inclusive ecosystem for innovation and entrepreneurship in India.
- The Smart City Project (2015), with the key objective of improving cities' basic infrastructure.

92. *(d)* Lakshmibai National College of Physical Education is situated at Thiruvananthapuram, Kerala.

- It is the academic wing of the Sports Authority of India.
- Netaji Subhas National Institute of Sports, commonly known as

National Institute of Sports, is the academic wing of the Sports Authority of India and Asia's largest sports institute located in city of Patiala.

93. *(d)* Literacy rate of India as per the National Survey of India-2022 is 77.7%.

- Literacy rate is the percentage of a population that can read and write, usually adults aged 15 and older, who can understand a simple statement about their daily lives.
- The literacy rate also varies by gender, with literate males at 84.70% and literate females at 70.30%.
- Kerala is the most literate state in India.

94. *(a)* Sovereign, socialist, secular, democratic, republic is correct word sequences is as per the Preamble.

- The ideals behind the Preamble to India's Constitution were laid down by Jawaharlal Nehru's Objectives Resolution.
- It was adopted by the Constituent Assembly on 22nd January, 1947.

95. *(b)* Tyrosine is a non-essential amino acid and can be formed by the hydroxylation of phenylalanine in the liver when the intake of tyrosine in the diet is low.

In a diet low in tyrosine as much as half the ingested phenylalanine may be converted to tyrosine in the body.

96. *(a)* Timur invaded India during the rule of Tughlaq dynasty.

- Timur Lang invaded India in 1398, with an aim of destroying the Hindu kings and rulers.
- Timur felt that the Muslim sultans of Delhi were showing great tolerance to their Hindu subordinates.
- After crossing the Sindh river he started his journey from Samarkand and entered Punjab on 24th September, 1398.

97. *(b)* Proportional taxes reduces the autonomus expenditure multiplier.

- The proportional tax is in proportion to the amount subject to taxation.
- It is the same for low, middle, and high-income taxpayers.
- Income Tax, Luxury Sales Tax, Estate tax and surcharge are few examples of proportional tax.

98. *(c)* Annamacharya composed Sankirtans in praise of Lord Venkateshwara.

- He was a 15th-century Hindu saint and is the earliest known Indian musician to compose songs called sankirtanas.
- He was born in Kadapa district of Andhra Pradesh.
- He is remembered for his saintly life, and is honoured as a great devotee of Vishnu by devotees and saintly singers.

99. *(d)* Salt Satyagraha is important event that started in 1930 played a significant role in mobilising Indians to join the Non-Violent Movement for independence.

- It began with the iconic Dandi March on 12th March, 1930, where Gandhi and his followers walked 240 miles from Sabarmati Ashram to the coastal village of Dandi.
- On 6th April, Gandhi symbolically broke the British salt laws by making salt from seawater.

100. *(d)* 22 yards by 10 ft is the standard measurements of a cricket pitch.

The distance between two wickets is normally is 20.12 met.

Important terms related to cricket are

- **Belter** A pitch that provides little assistance to bowlers while significantly favouring hitters.
- Chest-on When a bowler delivers the ball with his chest facing the batsman, he is said to be side on.

Set 32 10 July, 2024 (Shift IV)

SSC CHSL Tier-I SOLVED PAPER

Instructions

1. This paper contains 100 questions.
2. It has 4 Parts, **Part I** General English, **Part II** General Intelligence & Reasoning, **Part III** Quantitative Aptitude and **Part IV** General Awareness.
3. Each question carries **2 marks.**

Part I
General English

1. Select the option with the correct use of article(s).
(a) William Wordsworth was a romantic poet. He did things in an unusual manner.
(b) William Wordsworth was romantic poet. He did things in an unusual manner.
(c) William Wordsworth was the romantic poet. He did things in a unusual manner.
(d) William Wordsworth was a romantic poet. He did things in a unusual manner.

2. The following sentence has been divided into four segments. Identify the segment that contains a grammatical error.
The manager noticed / that Pragya / was first to reach / the office on Saturday.
(a) that Pragya
(b) The manager noticed
(c) was first to reach
(d) the office on Saturday

3. Parts of the following sentence have been given as options. Select the option that contains an error.
The chief guest/gave out prizes/to the meritorious students/of the school.
(a) of the school
(b) gave out prizes
(c) to the meritorious students
(d) The chief guest

4. The following sentence has been split into four segments. Identify the segment that contains a grammatical error.
Mathematics help/ in developing/ the logical mindset /of students.
(a) in developing
(b) the logical mindset
(c) Mathematics help
(d) of students

Directions (Q. Nos. 5-9) *In the following passage, some words have been deleted. Read the passage carefully and select the most appropriate option to fill in each blank.*

Water is (1) ……… for life and for good health. Not only is it necessary for us to be able to meet our daily needs but safe drinking water can (2) ……… many water-related diseases. India has one of the largest number of cases of (3) ……… such as diarrhoea, dysentery, and cholera. Over 1,600 Indians, most of them children below the age of five, (4) ……… die every day because of waterrelated diseases. These deaths can be prevented if people have (5) ……… to safe drinking water.

5. Select the most appropriate option to fill in blank (1).
(a) primary (b) essential
(c) intrinsic (d) insistent

6. Select the most appropriate option to fill in blank (2).
(a) forbid (b) prevent
(c) restrain (d) hamper

7. Select the most appropriate option to fill in blank (3).
(a) diseases (b) distress
(c) laments (d) sufferings

8. Select the most appropriate option to fill in blank (4).
(a) distinctly
(b) assuredly
(c) reportedly
(d) ostensibly

9. Select the most appropriate option to fill in blank (5).
(a) entrance (b) access
(c) providence (d) accession

10. Select the most appropriate option that can substitute the underlined segment in the following sentence.
Had you been to Dubai, <u>I would also go</u> with you.
(a) I shall be gone
(b) I will have went
(c) I would has also gone
(d) I would have gone

11. Select the most appropriate meaning of the given idiom.
Costing an arm and a leg
(a) Very attractive and cheap
(b) Very rough and tough
(c) Very costly and luxurious
(d) Very entertaining and jovial

12. Select the most appropriate antonym of the word given in brackets to fill in the blank.
You can't stop the …………(outflow) of current.
(a) deluge (b) influx
(c) torrent (d) income

13. Select the most appropriate antonym of the given word.
Massive
(a) Tiny (b) Tall
(c) Formidable (d) Heavy

14. Select the most appropriate option that can substitute the underlined word in the given sentence.
She argued against the unnecessary <u>split</u> in the committee.
(a) division
(b) blend
(c) combination
(d) mix

15. Select the most appropriate option that can substitute the underlined segment in the following sentence.

This serum contains ingredients enabling the hair to grow.

(a) the enable grow hair
(b) for growth hair
(c) for growing many hair
(d) that enable the hair to grow

16. Select the incorrectly spelt word.

(a) Dilemma (b) Committee
(c) Warranty (d) Neice

17. Select the word segment from the options that can substitute the bracketed word segment meaningfully.

Telangana artists (are know for the amazing bronze castings).

(a) Are known for their amazing bronze castings
(b) Have been knew to the amazing bronze castings
(c) Is known to the amazing bronze castings
(d) Have to know the amazing bronze castings

18. Select the most appropriate option that can substitute the underlined segment in the given sentence. If there is no need to substitute it, select 'No substitution required'.

It has been found that the trees are being destroyed by a moth.

(a) have destroyed
(b) is being destroyed
(c) have been destroying
(d) No substitution required

19. Select the most appropriate option to fill in the blank.

Tom is trying to ....as soon as possible.

(a) receive a job
(b) experience a job
(c) get a job
(d) learn a job

20. Select the most appropriate meaning of the given idiom.

Going through a sticky patch

(a) To experience a bad period in life
(b) Try to paste something unsuccessfully
(c) To walk on a muddy road
(d) To feel sad

21. Select the most appropriate antonym of the underlined word in the given sentence.

His feeble opponent was no match to him and ultimately he won the challenge.

(a) Strong (b) Mystic
(c) Major (d) Intelligent

22. Select the most appropriate antonym of the given word.

Impulsive

(a) Passive (b) Aggressive
(c) Hasty (d) Cautious

23. Identify the incorrectly spelt word and select its correct spelling.

There are a number of artists currently creating unique, collectble teapots.

(a) currantly (b) collectable
(c) collectibile (d) currintly

24. Select the most appropriate antonym of the word 'Commence' from the given sentence.

Let's put an end to this discussion about voodoo and instead talk about something amusing.

(a) end (b) voodoo
(c) amusing (d) discussion

25. Select the most appropriate synonym of the given word.

Evasive

(a) Cohesive (b) Ambiguous
(c) Accessible (d) Abrasive

Part II

General Intelligence

26. How many rectangles are there in the following figure?

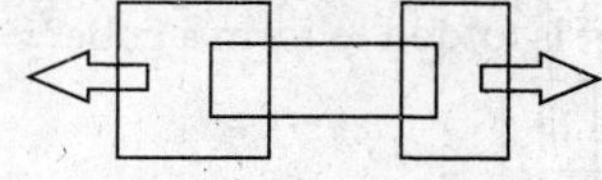

(a) 10 (b) 8 (c) 11 (d) 7

27. What should come in place of the question mark (?) in the given series based on the English alphabetical order?

DGB, GKG, JOL, MSQ, ?

(a) RXV (b) PWV
(c) QWU (d) PVT

28. What will come in the place of the question mark (?) in the following equation, if '+' and '×' are interchanged and '−' and '÷' are interchanged?

$123 - 41 \times 14 + 2 \div 7 = ?$

(a) 20 (b) 22 (c) 23 (d) 24

29. In a certain code language,
'M & N' means 'M is the wife of N',
'M @ N' means 'M is the son of N',
'M $ N' means 'M is the mother of N'.

Based on the above, how is R related to O, if 'N $ O @ P @ Q & R'?

(a) Father's father
(b) Mother's brother
(c) Father's brother
(d) Mother's father

30. Which two numbers should be interchanged to make the given equation correct?

$35 + (25 \times 3 - 45) \div 2 + (15 \times 4) = 125$

(**Note** Numbers must be interchanged and not the constituent digits e.g., if 2 and 3 are to be interchanged in the equation $43 \times 3 + 4 \div 2$, then interchanged equation is $43 \times 2 + 4 \div 3$)

(a) 2 and 15 (b) 25 and 35
(c) 15 and 25 (d) 35 and 45

31. In a certain code language, 'try something new' is coded as 'db kl jk' and 'something hurt him' is coded as 'db pt uk'. How is 'something' coded in that language?

(a) uk (b) jk
(c) db (d) kl

32. Which figure should replace the question mark (?), if the following figure series were to be continued?

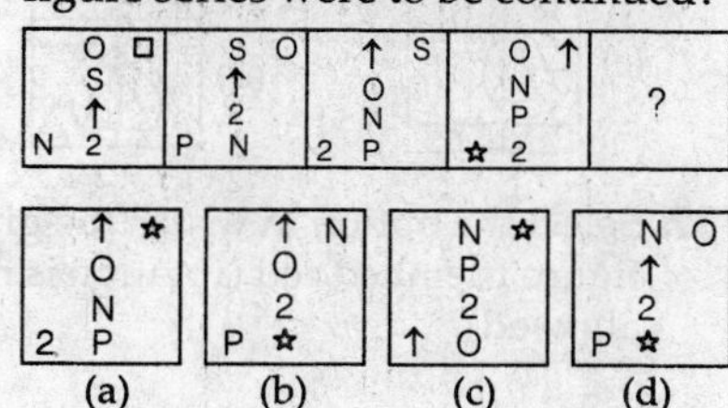

33. Select the set in which the numbers are related in the same way as are the numbers of the following sets.

(**Note** Operations should be performed on the whole numbers, without breaking down the numbers into its constituent digits. E.g. 13 – Operations on 13 such as adding /subtracting /multiplying etc. to 13 can be performed. Breaking down 13 into 1 and 3 and then performing mathematical operations on 1 and 3 is not allowed)

(32, 35, 201)
(26, 29, 165)

(a) (28, 31, 197) (b) (34, 37, 203)
(c) (39, 42, 256) (d) (23, 26, 147)

34. Select the word-pair that best represents a similar relationship to the one expressed in the pair of words given below.
(The words must be considered as meaningful English words and must not be related to each other based on the number of letters/number of consonants/vowels in the word)

Lend : Borrow
(a) Cold : Frigid
(b) Cruel : Kind
(c) Silent : Quiet
(d) Neat : Tidy

35. In a certain code language, 'RIVER' is coded as 'SJWFS' and 'SYSTEM' is coded as 'TZTUFN'. How is 'PACK' coded in that language?
(a) QCEL (b) RCEK
(c) QBDL (d) RBDL

36. Select the option figure in which the given figure (X) is embedded as its part (rotation is not allowed).

(X)

(a) 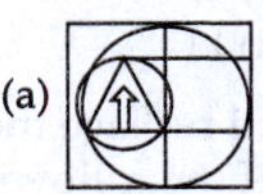 (b) 

(c) 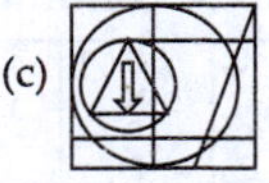 (d) 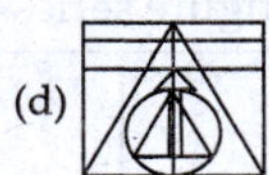

37. Select the option in which the given figure is embedded (rotation is not allowed).

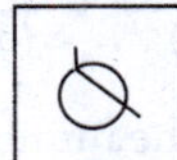

(a) 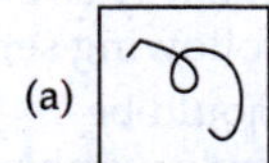 (b) 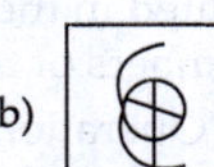

(c) 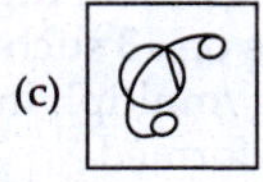 (d) 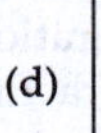 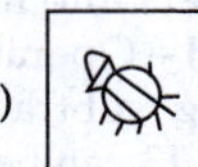

38. What should come in place of question mark (?) in the given series?
33, 32, 35, 34, 37, ?
(a) 38 (b) 37 (c) 36 (d) 40

39. Select the correct mirror image of the given figure, when the mirror is placed at MN as shown below.

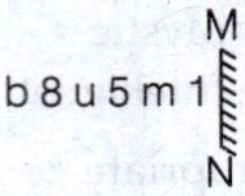

b8u5m1 (mirror MN below)

(a) p8nƨɯ⅂
(b) ɾmƨu8d
(c) b8u5m1
(d)  ⅂ɯƨn8q

40. 102 is related to 34 following a certain logic. Following the same logic, 171 is related to 57. To which of the following is 237 related following the same logic?
(**Note** Operations should be performed on the whole numbers, without breaking down the numbers into its constituent digits. E.g. 13 – Operations on 13 such as adding/deleting/multiplying etc., to 13 can be performed. Breaking down 13 into 1 and 3 and then performing mathematical operations on 1 and 3 is not allowed.)
(a) 73 (b) 79
(c) 71 (d) 77

41. What will come in the place of the question mark (?) in the following equation, if '+' and '–' are interchanged and '×' and '÷' are interchanged?
$24 \div 10 + 68 \times 2 - 16 = ?$
(a) 242 (b) 222
(c) 252 (d) 232

42. What would be the number on the opposite side of '7', if the given sheet is folded to form a cube?

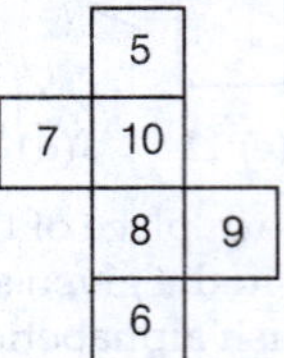

(a) 9 (b) 8
(c) 6 (d) 5

43. What will come in the place of the question mark (?) in the following equation, if '+' and '–' are interchanged and '×' and '÷' are interchanged?
$92 \times 2 - 13 + 2 \div 6 = ?$
(a) 48 (b) 47
(c) 46 (d) 49

44. If 17th December, 2012 was Monday, then what was the day of the week on 18th November, 2020?
(a) Tuesday (b) Sunday
(c) Thursday (d) Wednesday

45. QTWA is related to ZCFJ in a certain way based on the English alphabetical order. In the same way, MKBZ is related to VTKI. To which of the following is EYCM related, following the same logic?
(a) NLVH (b) NLHV
(c) NVHL (d) NHLV

46. Four letter-clusters have been given, out of which three are alike in some manner and one is different. Select the one that is different.
(**Note** The odd one out is not based on the number of consonants/vowels or their position in the letter-cluster)
(1) FGNOP (2) IJQRS
(3) OPWXY (4) RSXYZ
(a) OPWXY (b) IJQRS
(c) RSXYZ (d) FGNOP

47. If 27th September, 2001 was a Thursday, then what was the day of the week on 22nd October, 2009?
(a) Thursday (b) Wednesday
(c) Friday (d) Sunday

48. Three statements are followed by conclusions numbered I, II. You have to consider these statements to be true, even if they seem to be at variance with commonly known facts. Decide which of the given conclusions logically follow(s) from the given statements.

Statements
Some leaves are trees.
All stones are grain.
Some grains are leaves.

Conclusions
I. All grains are trees.
II. Some leaves are stones.
(a) Only Conclusion II follows
(b) Neither Conclusion I nor II follows
(c) Both Conclusions I and II follow
(d) Only Conclusion I follows

49. Select the term from among the given options that can replace the question mark (?) in the following series based on the English alphabetical order.
XYZ, YAC, ?, AEI, BGL, CIO
(a) ZCF (b) ZAB (c) YZL (d) MOP

50. A square sheet of paper is folded along the dotted line successively along the directions shown and is then punched in the last. How would the paper look when unfolded?

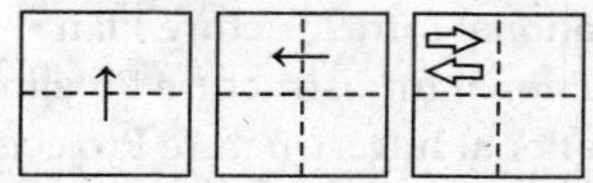

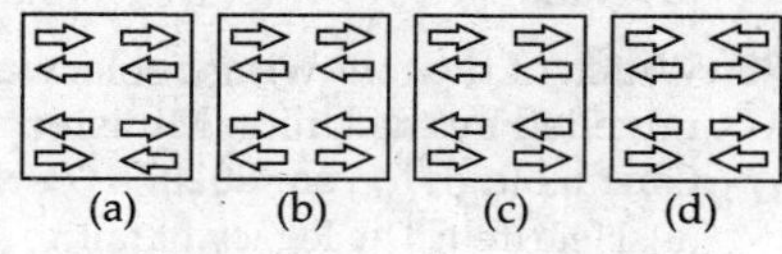

(a) (b) (c) (d)

Part III

Quantitative Aptitude

51. If the surface areas of two spheres are in the ratio of 49 : 81, then find the ratio of their volumes.

(a) 27 : 64 (b) 125 : 512 (c) 343 : 729 (d) 216 : 512

52. For what value of k ($k > 0$) will the lines $5x + ky - 2 = 0$ and $(k + 1)x + 4y + 7 = 0$ be parallel?

(a) 4 (b) 3 (c) 2 (d) 5

53. P completes a work in 12 days and Q in 24 days. In how many days P and Q working together can complete the same work?

(a) 12 days (b) 8 days (c) 6 days (d) 16 days

54. The details of books of 6 subjects on the first floor of the college library are given in the following table.

	English	French	Computers	Circuit Theory	Maths	Graph Theory
No. of books	7532	308	14308	9948	17462	642

The ratio of Maths and Computers to Circuit Theory and Graph Theory is:

(a) 1 : 3 (b) 2 : 1 (c) 3 : 1 (d) 2 : 3

55. The following table gives the percentage of marks obtained by six students in five different subjects in an examination.

The numbers in the brackets give the maximum marks in each subject.

Student's Name	Subjects (Maximum marks)				
	Maths (150)	English (130)	Hindi (120)	Physics (100)	Chemistry (60)
Aanya	90	100	90	90	80
Aarav	100	80	90	70	70
Lavi	90	90	80	60	50
Monika	80	70	100	50	100
Devyansh	50	60	100	100	90
Tanmay	60	80	70	70	80

What are the average marks obtained by all the six students in Hindi?

(a) 172 (b) 127 (c) 610 (d) 106

56. A solid metallic cube having surface area of 54 cm^2 is melted to form smaller cubes of surface area $\frac{8}{12}$ cm^2 each. Find the number of smaller cubes.

(a) 729 (b) 216 (c) 343 (d) 512

57. If the surface area of the sphere is 616 cm^2, then the radius of the sphere is equal to

(a) 18.0 cm (b) 14.0 cm (c) 7.0 cm (d) 3.5 cm

58. In an election between two candidates, 15% of the votes were invalid and one candidate got 52% of the total valid votes. If the total number of votes was 8000, what was the number of valid votes that the other candidate got?

(a) 3264 (b) 3536 (c) 3840 (d) 6800

59. When 2^{256} is divided by 17, the remainder would be

(a) 2 (b) 5 (c) 0 (d) 1

60. A number is divisible by 11, if and only if the difference of the sum of the digits in the even and odd positions in the number is

(a) 0 (b) 1
(c) 0 or multiple of 11 (d) 11

61. In ΔABC, if $AB = \sqrt{3}$ units, $BC = 1$ unit and $AC = 2$ units, then $\angle ACB$ is equal to

(a) 60° (b) 90° (c) 30° (d) 45°

62. Study the given pie-charts and answer the question that follows.

The pie-charts show the characteristics of foreign tourists visiting India during a given year.

Countrywise distribution

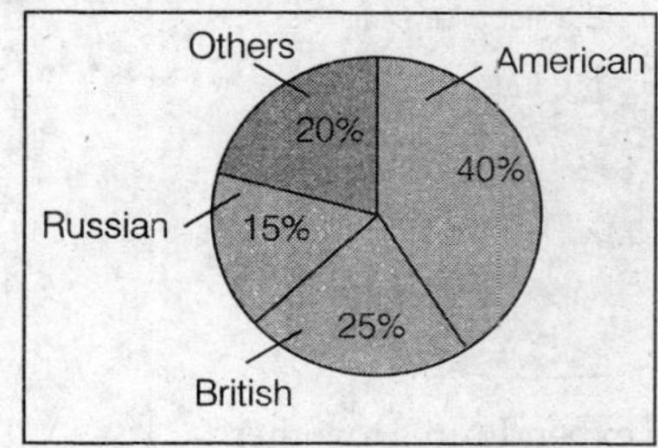

Agewise distribution

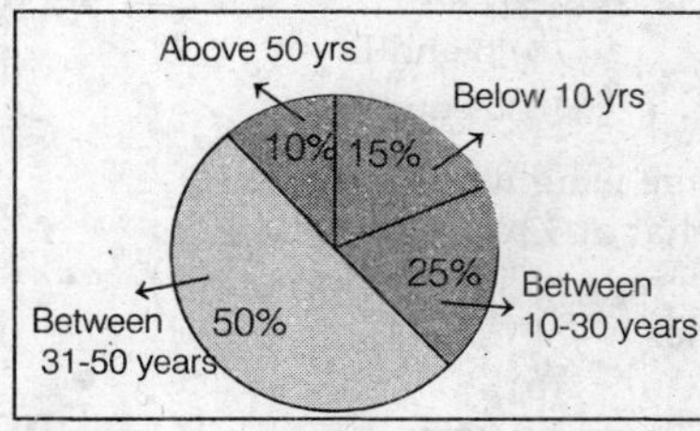

If in a given year, 250000 tourists visited India and the age wise distribution of data applies to all the countries, then what is the ratio of American tourists below 10 yr to the other tourists above 50 yr?

(a) 1 : 3 (b) 3 : 1 (c) 5 : 1 (d) 1 : 5

63. Two numbers are respectively 61% and 35% less than a third number. The first number is what percentage of the second number?

(a) 24% (b) 48% (c) 30% (d) 60%

64. Two chords AB and CD of a circle are produced to intersect each other at a point P outside the circle. If $AB = 7$ cm, $BP = 4.2$ cm and $PD = 2.8$ cm, then the length of CD is
(a) 11 cm (b) 18 cm
(c) 16 cm (d) 14 cm

65. A costs thrice as much as B. A is sold at a loss of 10% and B is sold at $\frac{5}{4}$ of its own price. If the selling price of A is ₹ 5800 more than the selling price of B, then the cost price of A is
(a) ₹ 4000 (b) ₹ 12000
(c) ₹ 15000 (d) ₹ 9600

66. If '÷' means '×', '×' means '÷', '+' means '–', '–' means '+', then $47 \div (10 \times 5) + (4 - 5) - 6$ is
(a) 91 (b) 59 (c) 79 (d) 100

67. The given pie-diagram shows the expenditure incurred on the preparation of a book by a publisher, under various heads. Study the pie-diagram and answer the question that follows.
Various Expenditures (in percentage) incurred in Publishing a Book
A. Paper B. Printing C. Binding
D. Royalty E. Miscellaneous

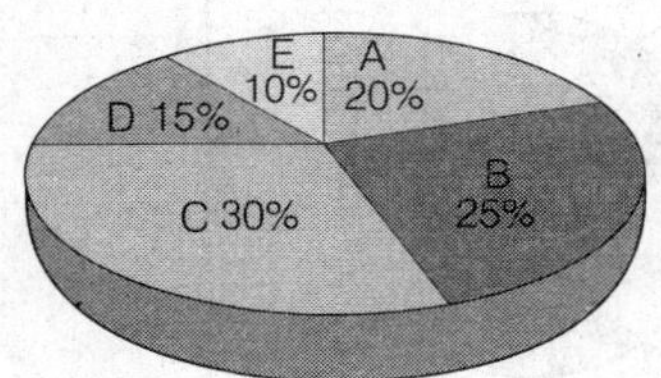

Which two expenditures together will form an angle of 108° at the centre of the pie-diagram?
(a) A and D (b) B and E
(c) D and E (d) A and E

68. If the average weight of 40 apples is 33 kg and that of 32 apples is 60 kg, then the average weight (in kg) of all the apples is
(a) 46.5 (b) 45
(c) 44 (d) 45.2

69. Evaluate $\frac{(9\sin\theta + 2\cos\theta)}{9\sin\theta - 2\cos\theta}$, if $3\tan\theta = 4$.
(a) $\frac{9}{7}$ (b) $\frac{5}{7}$
(c) $\frac{7}{5}$ (d) $\frac{6}{5}$

70. In an election between two candidates, Ananth and Aravind, Ananth got 55% of the total valid votes, and 20% of the votes were invalid. If the total number of votes was 30000, find the number of valid votes that Aravind got.
(a) 10800 (b) 1080
(c) 24000 (d) 13200

71. In an isosceles triangle, the vertex angle is four times the sum of the base angles. The measure of the square root of the vertex angle is
(a) 16° (b) 18° (c) 10° (d) 12°

72. A bucket contains a mixture of milk and water in the proportion of 7: 5. If 9 L of milk is replaced by water, then the ratio becomes 7 : 9. How much milk was there in the bucket initially?
(a) 36 L (b) 35 L
(c) 30 L (d) 25 L

73. Ramu invested some money at 8% simple interest per annum, and it was grown up to ₹ 820 in 8 yr. If the same sum was invested at 20% simple interest per annum for a period of 10 yr, find the amount.
(a) ₹ 1000 (b) ₹ 1200
(c) ₹ 1320 (d) ₹ 1500

74. A man walking at the speed of 4 km/h covers a certain distance in 6 h and 15 min. If he covers the same distance by cycle in 5 h and 10 min, then the speed of the cycle (in km/h) is
(a) $2\frac{9}{31}$ (b) $3\frac{11}{31}$
(c) $4\frac{26}{31}$ (d) $3\frac{21}{31}$

75. ΔABC and ΔPQR are similar. The areas of these two triangles are 289 sq.cm and 576 sq.cm, respectively. If $PR = 12$ cm, then $AC = ?$
(a) 7.25 cm (b) 8.5 cm
(c) 12 cm (d) 6 cm

Part IV
General Awareness

76. Folk music sung on the birth of a child in some Indian states like Bihar, Uttar Pradesh, etc. is called ……… .
(a) Gari (b) Banna
(c) Kohbar (d) Sohar

77. The country's infrastructure vision for FY-2025 and the first exercise to be conducted in India is named as ………… .
(a) National Infrastructure Plan
(b) National Infrastructure Pipeline
(c) National Infrastructure Projects
(d) National Infrastructure Planning

78. Which of the following books was unveiled by the Union Minister Giriraj Singh in year 2022?
(a) Heartfelt: The legacy of faith
(b) Agenda for Members of Panchayati Raj Institutions for Rural Development
(c) Modi @20: Dreams Meet Delivery
(d) Pandemic disruptions and Odisha's lessons in governance

79. 'The Life Divine', 'The Synthesis of Yoga' and 'Savitri' are the popular works of which of the following extremist freedom fighters of India?
(a) Lala Lajpat Rai
(b) Aurobindo Ghosh
(c) Bal Gangadhar Tilak
(d) Bipin Chandra Pal

80. Which of the following statements accurately describes application software?
(a) Application software is used only by software developers and does not impact regular users.
(b) Application software refers to the operating system that provides a user-friendly interface to interact with the computer.
(c) Application software is responsible for managing and controlling computer hardware components.
(d) Application software is designed to perform specific tasks or functions to meet the user's needs.

81. Which is the only surviving specimen of the ancient Sanskrit theatre recognised by UNESCO as a Masterpiece of the Oral and Intangible Heritage of Humanity?
(a) Kutiyattam (b) Kathakali
(c) Yakshagana (d) Bhavai

82. The velocity of circulation of money will be higher when the ……….. is less than the requirements of the economy.
(a) velocity of money
(b) elasticity of money
(c) demand for money
(d) supply of money

83. Suppose a mine worker asks his son, aged 9 years, to help him in his work instead of going to school. Which Article of the Constitution of India will be violated in this case?
(a) Article 18 (b) Article 24
(c) Article 20 (d) Article 29

84. In 1835, who developed the process of applying a thin layer of metallic silver to one side of a clear glass pane and created the first mirror?
(a) CV Raman
(b) Victor Francis Hess
(c) CH Townes
(d) Justus von Liebig

85. Where is the Kailasa temple built by Rashtrakutas located?
(a) Ellora (b) Amravati
(c) Kanchi (d) Hampi

86. The 10th Five-Year Plan aimed at reducing poverty by:
(a) 2% (b) 5%
(c) 8% (d) 9%

87. Which of the following is not mentioned in fundamental duties provided under Indian Constitution?
(a) To join defence forces
(b) To develop scientific temper
(c) To safeguard public property
(d) To respect the national flag

88. In MS Word, which option allows you to quickly remove all formatting from selected text while retaining the underlying text content?
(a) Clear Formatting
(b) Paste Special
(c) Cut
(d) Format Painter

89. Which of the following statements is correct?
(a) Mars is the warmest planet.
(b) The size of Jupiter and Mars is similar.
(c) The size of Earth and Venus is almost similar.
(d) The density of Saturn is similar to that of Earth.

90. Kalbelia dance, also known as the 'Sapera Dance', is the folk dance of ....
(a) Madhya Pradesh
(b) Rajasthan
(c) Gujarat
(d) Uttar Pradesh

91. In which of the following sports/games is the attacking player known as a 'raider'?
(a) Badminton (b) Kabaddi
(c) Tennis (d) Hockey

92. On 12th February, 2023 the President of India appointed the Governor of States. Which of the following is not correctly matched?
(a) Phagu Chauhan - Meghalaya
(b) Ramesh Baish - Maharashtra
(c) S Abdul Nazeer - Bihar
(d) Shiv Pratap Shukla-Himachal Pradesh

93. Where was the 36th National Games of India held in the year 2022?
(a) Kerala (b) Delhi
(c) Goa (d) Gujarat

94. International Kite Festival is a popular cultural festival of which state?
(a) Manipur (b) Gujarat
(c) Goa (d) Chhattisgarh

95. In March 2023, the Government of India announced the set up of how many PM MITRA (Pradhan Mantri Mega Integrated Textile Region and Apparel) parks for the textile industry?
(a) 9 (b) 5 (c) 2 (d) 7

96. The Salal Project, also called the Salal Hydroelectric Power Station, is on which river?
(a) Ganga (b) Ravi
(c) Krishna (d) Chenab

97. When is National Javelin Day celebrated in India?
(a) 7th August (b) 6th August
(c) 12th January (d) 29th August

98. In which of the following plants do roots arise from parts of a plant other than the radicle?
(a) Monstera
(b) Turnip
(c) Mustard plant
(d) Maize

99. What is Miyan ki Todi in Hindustani music?
(a) Chhand (b) Raag
(c) Kirtan (d) Tanam

100. What is the literacy rate of males in India as per the report published in the National Survey of India-2022?
(a) 83.4% (b) 86.3%
(c) 84.7% (d) 81.2%

Answers

1. (a)	2. (c)	3. (b)	4. (c)
5. (b)	6. (b)	7. (a)	8. (c)
9. (b)	10. (d)	11. (c)	12. (b)
13. (a)	14 (a)	15. (d)	16. (d)
17. (a)	18. (d)	19. (c)	20. (a)
21. (a)	22. (d)	23. (b)	24. (a)
25. (b)	26. (a)	27. (b)	28. (d)
29. (a)	30. (d)	31. (c)	32. (d)
33. (d)	34. (b)	35. (c)	36. (a)
37. (d)	38. (c)	39. (b)	40. (b)
41. (b)	42. (a)	43. (b)	44. (d)
45. (d)	46. (c)	47. (a)	48. (b)
49. (a)	50. (d)	51. (c)	52. (a)
53. (b)	54. (c)	55. (d)	56. (a)
57. (c)	58. (a)	59. (d)	60. (c)
61. (a)	62. (b)	63. (d)	64. (d)
65. (b)	66. (a)	67. (d)	68. (b)
69. (c)	70. (a)	71. (d)	72. (a)
73. (d)	74. (c)	75. (b)	76. (d)
77. (b)	78. (b)	79. (b)	80. (d)
81. (a)	82. (c)	83. (b)	84. (d)
85. (a)	86. (b)	87. (a)	88. (a)
89. (c)	90. (b)	91. (b)	92. (c)
93. (d)	94. (b)	95. (d)	96. (d)
97. (a)	98. (a)	99. (b)	100. (c)

Explanations

1. *(a)* The sentence which correctly uses articles is- William Wordsworth was a romantic poet. He did things in an unusual manner.

2. *(c)* Part (c) 'was first to reach' contains an error. Add 'the' before 'first' to correct the sentence.

3. *(b)* Part (b) 'gave out prizes' is incorrect. Gave out 'the' prizes will be used or 'gave away' the prizes can also be used.

4. *(c)* Part (c) 'Mathematics help' contains an error. Use 'helps' to correct the sentence. The names of subject form singular nouns and thus, would take singular verbs.

5. *(b)* The correct filler for the given blank is 'essential'.

6. *(b)* The correct filler for the given blank is 'prevent'.

7. *(a)* The correct filler for the given blank is 'diseases'.

8. *(c)* The correct filler for the given blank is 'reportedly'.

9. *(b)* The correct filler for the given blank is 'access'.

10. *(d)* The underlined part of the given sentence contains an error. Use 'I would have gone' to correct the sentence.

11. *(c)* Costing an arm and a leg means to be very expensive.

12. *(b)* Outflow means going outside. Hence, its antonym is 'influx' which means 'to come in'.
- 'Deluge' means a severe flood.
- 'Torrent' means a strong and fast-moving stream of water or other liquid.

13. *(a)* Massive means 'huge'. Hence, its antonym is 'Tiny'.

14. *(a)* The underlined part of the given sentence contains an error. Use 'division' to correct the sentence.

15. *(d)* The underlined part of the given sentence contains an error. Use 'that enable the hair to grow' to correct the sentence.

16. *(d)* The incorrectly spelt word is 'Neice'. The correct spelling is 'Niece'.

17. *(a)* The bracketed part of the given sentence contains an error. Use 'Are known for their amazing bronze castings' to correct the sentence.

18. *(d)* The underlined part is grammatically and contextually correct.

19. *(c)* The correct filler for the given blank is 'get a job'.

20. *(a)* Going through a sticky patch means to experience a bad period in life.

21. *(a)* Feeble means weak. Hence, its antonym is 'strong'.

22. *(d)* Impulsive means acting or done without forethought. Hence, the antonym is 'Cautious'.
- 'Aggressive' means angry.
- 'Hasty' means quick.

23. *(b)* The incorrectly spelt word is 'collectble'. The correct spelling is 'collectable'.

24. *(a)* Commence means to begin. Hence, its antonym is to 'End'.

25. *(b)* Evasive means tending to avoid commitment or self-revelation, especially by responding only indirectly. Hence, its antonym is 'Ambiguous' means confusing.

26. *(a)* Naming the figure,

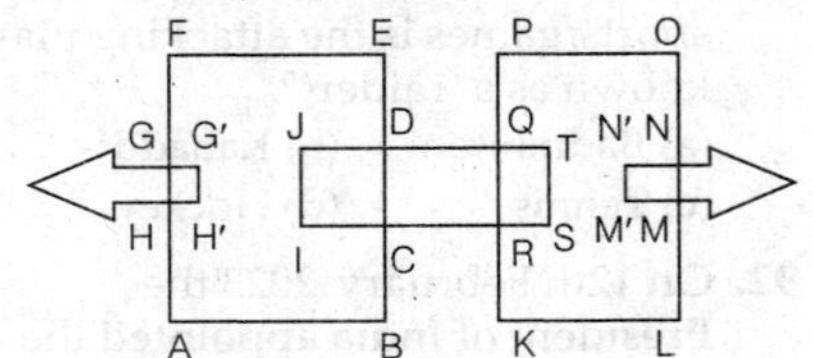

Rectangles can be represented as,
□ABEF, □GHH'G', □JDCI, □DQRC,
□KLOP, □RSTQ, □M'MNN',
□JIRQ, □DCST, □JIST

Thus, total 10 rectangles are present in given figure.

27. *(b)* The pattern of the series is as follows,

D →(+3) G →(+3) J →(+3) M →(+3) **P**
G →(+4) K →(+4) O →(+4) S →(+4) **W**
B →(+5) G →(+5) L →(+5) Q →(+5) **V**

28. *(d)* Given equation,

$$123 - 41 \times 14 + 2 \div 7 = ?$$

After interchanging + and ×, – and ÷, we get

$123 \div 41 + 14 \times 2 - 7 = ?$

$\Rightarrow \quad 3 + 28 - 7 = ?$

$\therefore \quad ? = 24$

29. *(a)* Given expression,
N $ O @ P @ Q & R

According to the question,

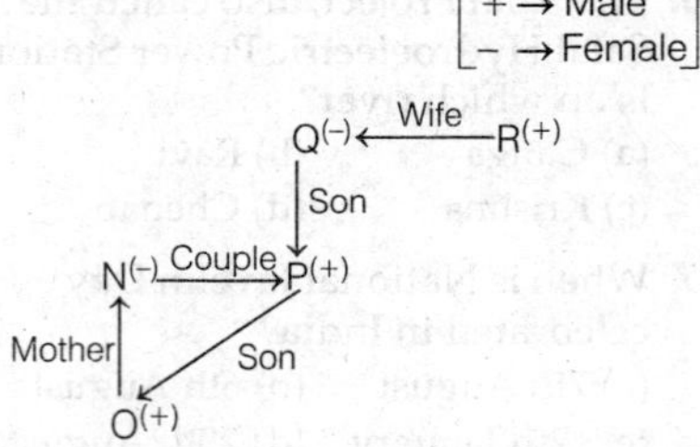

Hence, R is O's father's father.

30. *(d)* Given equation,

$35 + (25 \times 3 - 45) \div 2 + (15 \times 4) = 125$

From option (d), interchanging 35 and 45, we get

$45 + (25 \times 3 - 35) \div 2 + (15 \times 4) = 125$

$\Rightarrow \quad 45 + (75 - 35) \div 2 + 60 = 125$

$\Rightarrow \quad 45 + 40 \div 2 + 60 = 125$

$\Rightarrow \quad 45 + 20 + 60 = 125$

$\Rightarrow \quad 125 = 125$

31. *(c)* According to the question,

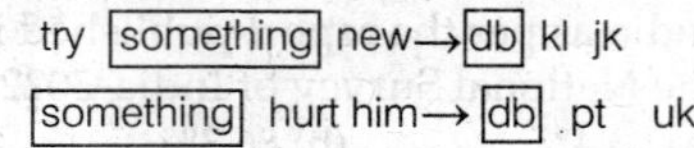

∴ Code for 'something' is 'db'.

32. *(d)* The pattern of the elements in figure series is as follows,

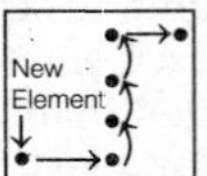

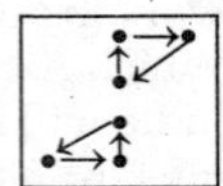

Figure 1 to Figure 2 Figure 2 to Figure 3
Figure 3 to Figure 4 Figure 4 to Figure 5

Thus, figure given in option (d) will replace the question mark.

33. *(d)* According to the question,

Logic [First number + second number] × 3 = Third number

As, (32, 35, 201) → [32 + 35] × 3 = 201

(26, 29, 165) → [26 + 29] × 3 = 165

Similarly,

(23, 26, 147) → [23 + 26] × 3 = 147

34. *(b)* As, 'Lend' and 'Borrow' are opposite to each other.

Similarly, 'Cruel' and 'Kind' are opposite to each other.

35. *(c)* As,

R I V E R
+1 +1 +1 +1 +1
S J W F S

and

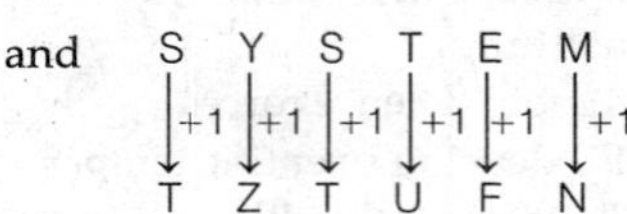

Similarly,

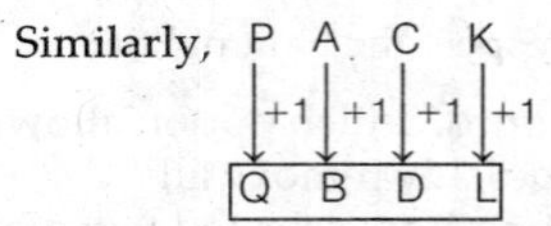

36. *(a)* The given figure (X) is embedded in option figure (a).

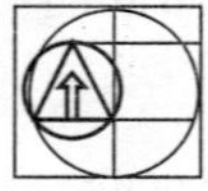

37. *(d)* The given figure is embedded in option figure (d).

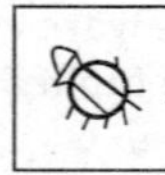

38. *(c)* The pattern of the series is as follows,

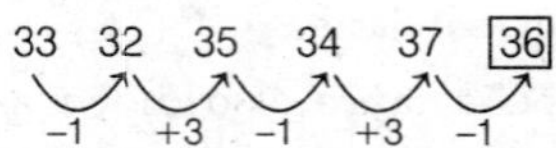

39. *(b)* The correct mirror image of given figure is as shown below,

M
b 8 u 5 m 1 | ɿ m ƨ u 8 d
N

40. *(b)* As, $102 \xrightarrow{\div 3} 34$

and $171 \xrightarrow{\div 3} 57$

Similarly, $237 \xrightarrow{\div 3} \boxed{79}$

41. *(b)* Given equation,

$24 \div 10 + 68 \times 2 - 16 = ?$

After interchanging + and −, × and ÷, we get

$24 \times 10 - 68 \div 2 + 16 = ?$

$\Rightarrow \quad 240 - 34 + 16 = ?$

$\Rightarrow \quad 256 - 34 = ?$

$\therefore \quad ? = \boxed{222}$

42. *(a)* According to the question,

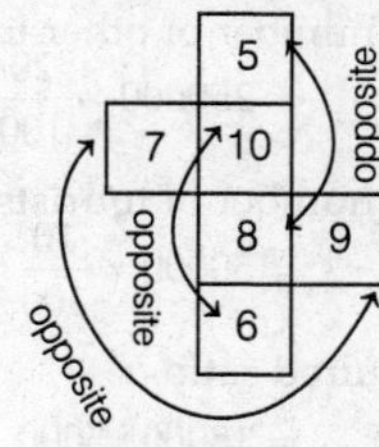

∴ Number '9' would be opposite to number '7'.

43. *(b)* Given equation,

$92 \times 2 - 13 + 2 \div 6 = ?$

After interchanging + and −, × and ÷, we get

$92 \div 2 + 13 - 2 \times 6 = ?$

$\Rightarrow 46 + 13 - 12 = ? \Rightarrow 59 - 12 = ?$

$\therefore \quad ? = 47$

44. *(d)* Given, 17th December, 2012 → Monday

Number of odd days from 17th December, 2012 to 17th December, 2019

Years → 2013 + 2014 + 2015 + 2016 + 2017 + 2018 + 2019

Odd days → 1 + 1 + 1 + 2 + 1 +1 + 1

$= \frac{8}{7} = 1$ odd day

Now, number of odd days from 17th December, 2019 to 18th November, 2020.

Months → December + January + February + March + April + May + June + July + August + September + October + November

Odd days → 14 + 31 + 29 + 31 + 30 + 31 + 30 + 31 + 31 + 30 + 31 + 18

$= \frac{337}{7} = 1$ odd day

∴ Required odd day

= Monday + 1 + 1 = Wednesday

45. *(d)* As,

Q T W A
+9 +9 +9 +9
Z C F J

and

M K B Z
+9 +9 +9 +9
V T K I

Similarly,

E Y C M
+9 +9 +9 +9
N H L V

46. *(c)* As,

F G N O P
+1 +7 +1 +1

I J Q R S
+1 +7 +1 +1

O P W X Y
+1 +7 +1 +1

But,

R S X Y Z
+1 +5 +1 +1

47. *(a)* Given, 27th September, 2001 → Thursday.

Number of odd days from 27th September, 2001 to 27th September, 2009.

Years → 2002 + 2003 + 2004 + 2005 + 2006 + 2007 + 2008 + 2009

Odd days → 1 + 1 + 2 + 1 + 1 + 1 + 2 + 1

$= \frac{10}{7} = 3$ odd days

Number of odd days from 27th September, 2009 to 22nd October, 2009.

Months → September + October

$3 + 22 = \frac{25}{7} = 4$ odd days.

Total odd days $= \frac{3+4}{7} = 0$ odd days.

∴ Required day

= Thursday + 0 = Thursday.

48. *(b)* According to the statements,

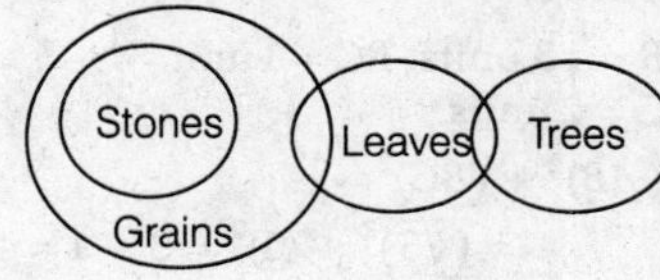

Conclusions I. (✗) II. (✗)

Hence, neither Conclusion I nor II follows.

49. *(a)* The pattern of the series is as follows,

X →(+1) Y →(+1) [Z] →(+1) A →(+1) B →(+1) C

Y →(+2) A →(+2) [C] →(+2) E →(+2) G →(+2) I

Z →(+3) C →(−3) [F] →(+3) I →(+3) L →(+3) O

50. *(d)* When the square sheet of paper is unfolded, it will look like option figure (d).

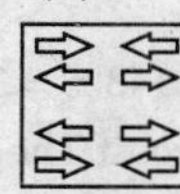

51. *(c)* Given, ratio of areas of two spheres = 49 : 81

We know, surface area of sphere $= 4\pi r^2$

Let radii of two spheres be r_1 and r_2.

According to the question,

$\frac{4\pi r_1^2}{4\pi r_2^2} = \frac{49}{81} \Rightarrow \left(\frac{r_1}{r_2}\right)^2 = \frac{49}{81}$

$\Rightarrow \quad \frac{r_1}{r_2} = \frac{7}{9}$

$\therefore \quad r_1 : r_2 = 7 : 9$

∴ Ratio of their volumes

$= \frac{\frac{4}{3}\pi r_1^3}{\frac{4}{3}\pi r_2^3} = \left(\frac{7}{9}\right)^3 = \frac{343}{729}$

52. *(a)* Given equations,

$5x + ky - 2 = 0$ and

$(k + 1)x + 4y + 7 = 0$

We know, condition for parallel lines is

$\frac{a_1}{a_2} = \frac{b_1}{b_2} = \frac{c_1}{c_2}$

Here, $a_1 = 5, b_1 = k, c_1 = -2$

$a_2 = (k+1), b_2 = 4, c_2 = 7$

$\therefore \quad \frac{5}{k+1} = \frac{k}{4} = \frac{-2}{7}$

$\Rightarrow \frac{5}{k+1} = \frac{k}{4} \Rightarrow k^2 + k = 20$

$\Rightarrow \quad k^2 + k - 20 = 0$

$\Rightarrow \quad k^2 + 5k - 4k - 20 = 0$

$\Rightarrow k(k+5) - 4(k+5) = 0$

$\Rightarrow \quad (k+5)(k-4) = 0$

$\Rightarrow \quad k = 4, -5$

As, $k > 0$

$\therefore \quad k = 4$

53. *(b)* P's 1 day's work $= \frac{1}{12}$

Q's 1 day's work $= \frac{1}{24}$

$\therefore$ $(P + Q)$'s 1 day's work

$$= \frac{1}{12} + \frac{1}{24} = \frac{2+1}{24}$$

$$= \frac{3}{24} = \frac{1}{8}$$

$\therefore$ $(P + Q)$ can complete the work in $= 8$ days

54. *(c)* Total number of Maths and Computer books

$$= 17462 + 14308 = 31770$$

Total number of Circuit Theory and Graph Theory books

$$= 9948 + 642 = 10590$$

$\therefore$ Required ratio

$$= 31770 : 10590 = 3 : 1$$

55. *(d)* According to the question,

Ananya's marks $= 120 \times \frac{90}{100} = 108$

Aarav's marks $= 120 \times \frac{90}{100} = 108$

Lavi's marks $= 120 \times \frac{80}{100} = 96$

Monika's marks $= 120 \times \frac{100}{100} = 120$

Devyanshi's marks $= 120 \times \frac{100}{100} = 120$

Tanmay's marks $= 120 \times \frac{70}{100} = 84$

$\therefore$ Required average

$$= \frac{108 + 108 + 96 + 120 + 120 + 84}{6}$$

$$= \frac{636}{6} = 106$$

56. *(a)* Let the number of smaller cubes be n.

Let the side of original and new cube be A cm and a cm, respectively.

As, surface area of original cube

$$= 54 \text{ cm}^2$$

$\Rightarrow$ $6A^2 = 54$

$\Rightarrow$ $A^2 = 9 \Rightarrow A = 3$ cm

Also, surface area of smaller cube

$$= \frac{8}{12} \text{ cm}^2$$

$\therefore$ $6a^2 = \frac{8}{12}$

$\Rightarrow a^2 = \frac{8}{72} = \frac{1}{9} \Rightarrow a = \frac{1}{3}$

According to the question,

$n \times$ Volume of new cube = Volume of original cube

$\therefore$ $n \times a^3 = A^3$

$\Rightarrow$ $n \times \frac{1}{27} = 27$

$\Rightarrow n = 27 \times 27 = 729$

57. *(c)* Given, surface area of sphere

$$= 616 \text{ cm}^2$$

$\therefore$ $4\pi r^2 = 616$

$\Rightarrow$ $r^2 = 616 \times \frac{7}{22} \times \frac{1}{4} = 49$

$\therefore$ $r = 7$ cm

58. *(a)* Given, total number of votes

$$= 8000$$

Total number of valid votes

$$= 8000 - \frac{15}{100} \times 8000$$

$$= 6800$$

$\therefore$ Total number of votes that one candidate got

$$= \frac{52}{100} \times 6800 = 3536$$

$\therefore$ Total number of valid votes that the other candidate got

$$= 6800 - 3536 = 3264$$

59. *(d)* We need to find the remainder when, 2^{256} is divided by 17.

$\therefore$ $\frac{2^{256}}{17} = \frac{(2^4)^{64}}{17} = \frac{(16)^{64}}{17}$

Now, when 16 is divided by 17, remainder is -1.

$\therefore$ $\frac{(16)^{64}}{17} = \frac{(-1)^{64}}{17} = \frac{1}{17}$

$\therefore$ Remainder = 1

60. *(c)* We know,

Divisibility rule of 11.

A number is divisible by 11 if and only if the difference of the sum of the digits in the even and odd positions in the number is 0 or multiple of 11.

61. *(a)* Given,

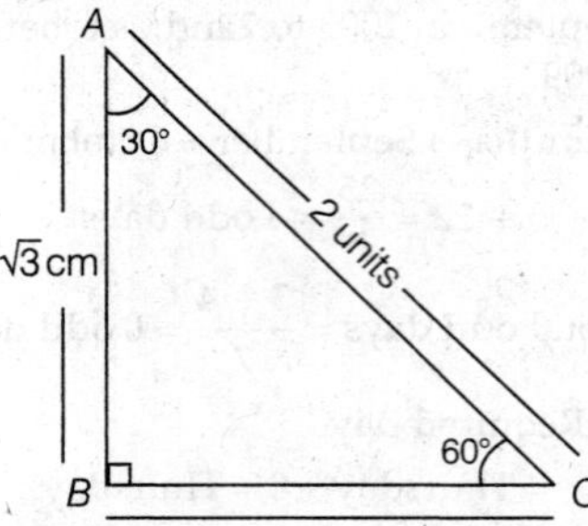

In ΔABC,

$AB = \sqrt{3}$ units, $BC = 1$ unit, $AC = 2$ units.

$\therefore$ $(AB)^2 + (BC)^2$

$$= (\sqrt{3})^2 + (1)^2 = 3 + 1 = 4$$

$$= (2)^2$$

$$= (AC)^2$$

$\therefore (AB)^2 + (BC)^2 = (AC)^2$

ΔABC is a right-angled triangle.

$\therefore$ Ratio of sides $= 1 : \sqrt{3} : 2$

$\therefore$ Using $30° - 60° - 90°$ theorem, angle opposite to the side $= \sqrt{3}$ will be $60°$.

$\therefore$ $\angle ACB = 60°$

62. *(b)* Given, total number of Tourists

$$= 250000$$

Total number of Americans

$$= \frac{40}{100} \times 250000$$

$$= 100000$$

Total number of Americans below 10 yr

$$= 15000$$

Total number of other tourists

$$= 250000 \times \frac{20}{100} = 50000$$

Total number of tourists above 50 yr

$$= 50000 \times \frac{10}{100} = 5000$$

$\therefore$ Required ratio

$$= 15000 : 5000$$

$$= 3 : 1$$

63. *(d)* Let the third number be $100x$.

$\therefore$ First number

$$= 100x - \frac{61}{100} \times 100x = 39x$$

Second number

$$= 100x - \frac{35}{100} \times 100x = 65x$$

$\therefore$ Required percentage

$$= \frac{39x}{65x} \times 100 = 60\%$$

64. *(d)* Given, $AB = 7$ cm, $BP = 4.2$ cm, $PD = 2.8$ cm.

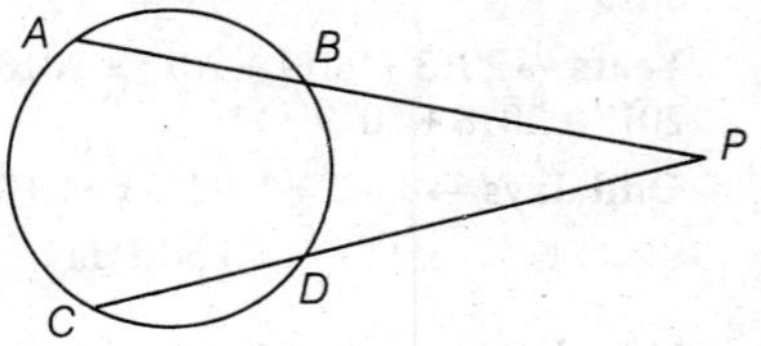

We know, when chords AB and CD are produced outside the circle and intersect at P, then

$BP \times AP = DP \times CP$

$4.2 \times 11.2 = 2.8 \times CP$

[$\because$ $AP = AB + BP = 7 + 4.2 = 11.2$ cm]

$\Rightarrow$ $CP = \frac{4.2 \times 11.2}{2.8} = 16.8$

$\therefore$ $CD = CP - DP$

$$= 16.8 - 2.8$$

$$= 14 \text{ cm}$$

65. *(b)* Let cost price of B be ₹ $100x$.

$\therefore$ Cost price of $A = 3(100x)$

$= ₹\ 300x$

SP of $A = 300x - \frac{10}{100} \times 300x$

$= 300x - 30x = 270x$

SP of $B = \frac{5}{4}(100x) = ₹125x$

According to the question,

$270x - 125x = 5800$

$\Rightarrow \quad 145x = 5800 \Rightarrow x = 40$

$\therefore$ Cost price of $A = 300(40) = ₹12000$

66. *(a)* Given, expression,

After interchanging the sign '+' and '−' and '÷' and '×', we get

$47 \div (10 \times 5) + (4 - 5) - 6$

$= 47 \times (10 \div 5) - (4 + 5) + 6$

Using BODMAS,

$= 47 \times (2) - 9 + 6$

$= 94 - 3$

$= 91$

67. *(d)* Given, angle formed by two expenditures = 108°

$\therefore$ Percentage of two expenditures

$= \frac{108}{360°} \times 100$

$= 30\%$

$\therefore$ Percentage of expenditure A = 20%

Percentage of expenditure E = 10%

$\therefore$ Combined percentage of A and E

$= (20 + 10)\%$

$= 30\%$

68. *(b)* We know, combined average

$= \frac{n_1a_1 + n_2a_2}{n_1 + n_2}$

$= \frac{40 \times 33 + 32 \times 60}{40 + 32}$

$= \frac{1320 + 1920}{72}$

$= \frac{3240}{72} = 45$

69. *(c)* Given, $3 \tan\theta = 4$

$\Rightarrow \quad \tan\theta = \frac{4}{3}$

$\frac{9\sin\theta + 2\cos\theta}{9\sin\theta - 2\cos\theta}$

Dividing numerator and denominator by $\cos\theta$, we get

$= \frac{9\frac{\sin\theta}{\cos\theta} + \frac{2\cos\theta}{\cos\theta}}{9\frac{\sin\theta}{\cos\theta} - \frac{2\cos\theta}{\cos\theta}} = \frac{9\tan\theta + 2}{9\tan\theta - 2}$

$= \frac{9\left(\frac{4}{3}\right) + 2}{9\left(\frac{4}{3}\right) - 2} = \frac{12 + 2}{12 - 2}$

$= \frac{14}{10} = \frac{7}{5}$

70. *(a)* Given, total number of votes

$= 30000$

Total number of valid votes

$= 30000 - 30000 \times \frac{20}{100}$

$= 30000 - 6000 = 24000$

Total number of valid votes that Ananth got

$= 24000 \times \frac{55}{100}$

$= 13200$

$\therefore$ Total number of valid votes that Aravind got

$= 24000 - 13200 = 10800$

71. *(d)* Let the base angle be x.

$\therefore$ Vertex angle $= 4(x + x) = 8x$

We know, sum of the interior angle of a triangle is 180°.

$\therefore \quad 8x + x + x = 180°$

$\Rightarrow \quad 10x = 180°$

$\Rightarrow \quad x = 18°$

$\therefore$ Vertex angle $= 8(18) = 144°$

$\therefore$ Required square root of vertex angle

$= \sqrt{144} = 12°$

72. *(a)* Let the milk and water in the bucket be $7x$ and $5x$ L.

According to the question,

$\frac{7x - 9}{5x + 9} = \frac{7}{9}$

$\Rightarrow \quad 63x - 81 = 35x + 63$

$\Rightarrow \quad 28x = 144$

$\Rightarrow \quad x = \frac{144}{28} = \frac{36}{7}$

$\therefore$ Original quantity of milk $= 7\left(\frac{36}{7}\right)$

$= 36$ L

73. *(d)* Let the sum initially invested be P.

We know, $\text{SI} = \frac{P \times R \times T}{100}$

According to the question,

$\text{Amount} = P + \frac{P \times 8 \times 8}{100}$

[$\because$ Amount = ₹820, R = 8%, T = 8 yr]

$\Rightarrow 820 = P + \frac{64P}{100}$

$\Rightarrow 820 = \frac{164P}{100}$

$\Rightarrow \quad P = 500$

If the same amount invested for 10 yr.

$\text{Amount} = P + \frac{P \times R \times T}{100}$

$= 500 + \frac{500 \times 20 \times 10}{100}$

$= 500 + 1000$

$= ₹\ 1500$

74. *(c)* Given, original speed (s) = 4 km/h

Original time taken (T) = 6 h 15 min

$= 6\frac{15}{60}$ h

$= 6\frac{1}{4}$ h $= \frac{25}{4}$ h

We know, distance (D)

$=$ speed (s) × time (T)

$= 4 \times \frac{25}{4} = 25$ km

Now, if a man takes 5 h 10 min for the same distance, then

$\therefore$ Required speed

$= \frac{25 \times 6}{31}$

[$\because$ Speed $= \frac{\text{Distance}}{\text{Time}}$]

and Time = 5 h 10 min $= 5\frac{1}{6} = \frac{31}{6}$ h]

$= \frac{150}{31}$

$= 4\frac{26}{31}$ km/h

75. *(b)* Given, $\Delta ABC \sim \Delta PQR$

$\therefore \quad \frac{\text{ar}(\Delta ABC)}{\text{ar}(\Delta PQR)} = \frac{AC^2}{PR^2}$

$\frac{289}{576} = \left(\frac{AC}{PR}\right)^2$

$\Rightarrow \quad \frac{17}{24} = \frac{AC}{12}$

$\Rightarrow \quad AC = \frac{17}{2}$

$= 8.5$ cm

76. *(d)* Folk music sung on the birth of a child in some Indian states like Bihar, Uttar Pradesh, is called Sohar.
- Kohbar is the most auspicious ritual painting made during a marriage ceremony in the Mithila region.
- Hori, Chaiti and Kajri are important folk songs of Bihar.

77. *(b)* The country's infrastructure vision for FY-2025 and the first exercise to be conducted in India is named as National Infrastructure Pipeline.
- The Central Government has constituted a task force to draw up a National Infrastructure Pipeline for each of the financial years from 2019-20 to 2024-25.
- The Task Force is chaired by the Secretary, Department of Economic Affairs, Ministry of Finance.

78. *(b)* Agenda for Members of Panchayati Raj Institutions for Rural Development was a book unveiled by the Union Minister Giriraj Singh in year 2022.
- Heartfelt : The Legacy of Faith is written by Rajiv Chandrashekhar.
- Modi@20 : Dreams Meet Delivery is written by S Jaishankar.
- Pandemic disruptions and Odisha's Lessons in Governance is written by Amar Patnaik.

79. *(b)* 'The Life Divine', 'The Synthesis of Yoga' and 'Savitri' are the popular works of Aurobindo Ghosh.
- He passed the Indian Civil Service Examination in 1890 but failed in the horsemanship test due to which he could not enter the service. He left his job at Baroda to join the Bengal National College.
- Prime Minister Narendra Modi participated in a programme commemorating Sri Aurobindo's 150th birth anniversary on 13th December, 2022.

80. *(d)* Application software is designed to perform specific tasks or functions to meet the user's needs.

81. *(a)* Kutiyattam is the only surviving specimen of the ancient Sanskrit theatre recognised by UNESCO as a Masterpiece of the Oral and Intangible Heritage of Humanity.
- Kathakali is a traditional Indian dance-drama form of Andhra Pradesh that combines dance, music, acting, and storytelling.
- Yakshagana is a traditional theatre form of Karnataka.
- Bhavai is a form of folk theatre with musical and dance elements of gujarat.

82. *(c)* The velocity of circulation of money will be higher when the demand for money is less than the requirements of the economy.
- Velocity of money is a measurement of the rate at which money is exchanged in an economy.
- Elasticity of money is a measure of the responsiveness of the demand for money to changes in interest rates.
- The money supply includes all cash in circulation and all bank deposits that the account holder can easily convert to cash.

83. *(b)* Article 24 prohibits the employment of children below the age of 14 years in any factory, mine, or hazardous occupation.
- Article 18 talks about the abolition of titles.
- Article 20 of the Constitution provides for the protection in respect of conviction for offences.
- Article 29 aims to protect the interests of religious, linguistic, and cultural minorities in India.

84. *(d)* In 1835, Justus von Liebig developed the process of applying a thin layer of metallic silver to one side of a clear glass pane and created the first mirror.
Mirror is a reflective surface that bounces off light, producing either a real image or a virtual image.

85. *(a)* Kailasa temple built by Rashtrakutas is located at Ellora.
- The Kailasa or Kailasanatha temple is the largest of the **rock-cut** Hindu temples at Ellora Caves in Maharashtra.
- The temple's construction began during the reign of Rashtrakuta king Dantidurga (735-757 AD).
- The Nandi mandap is linked to Gopuram by a bridge.

86. *(b)* The 10th Five-Year Plan aimed at reducing poverty by 5%.
- The plan also emphasised improving infrastructure, increasing private sector investment, and boosting economic reforms.
- The plan was led by former Prime Minister Atal Bihari Vajpayee and Manmohan Singh.
  It also focuses on reducing gender-based discrimination.

87. *(a)* To join Defence forces is not mentioned in fundamental duties provided under Constitution.
- Important Fundamental duties include:
- To develop scientific temper.
- To safeguard public property.
- To respect the national flag.

88. *(a)* In MS Word, clear formatting option allows you to quickly remove all formatting from selcted text while retaining the underlying text content.

89. *(c)* The correct statement is "The size of Earth and Venus is almost similar".
- Mars is the coolest planet.
- Jupiter's diameter is 22 times the diameter of Mars.

90. *(b)* Kalbelia dance, is also known as 'Sapera Dance' is the folk dance of Rajasthan.
- In 2010 UNESCO added the Kalbelia folk songs and dances to its Representative List of the Intangible Cultural Heritage of Humanity.
- Kathi is folk dance of Madhya Pradesh.
- Garba is a form of Gujarati dance which originates from the state of Gujarat, India.

91. *(b)* In kabaddi,the attacking player is known as "Raider".
- Some important terms associated with kabbaddi are:
- **All out** When all seven defenders are declared out
- **All in** When all seven defenders return to the court after an all out.
- **Center** The defender who stands in the middle of the defensive formation.

92. *(c)* The Statement (c) is incorrect because the Governor of Bihar since 2023 is Rajendra Arlekar not S. Abdul Nazeer.

- S Abdul Nazeer is the Governor of Andhra Pradesh.

93. *(d)* In 2022, 36th National Games of India were held in Gujarat.

- The National Games 2022 was held across six cities Gujarat, Ahmedabad, Gandhinagar, Surat, Vadodara, Rajkot and Bhavnagar.
- Raja Bhalindra Singh Trophy to the hybrid contingent of Services for the fourth time in succession.
- Maharashtra bagged the Indian Olympic Association's Best State trophy for finishing second in the medals tally with the most medals amongst States and UTs.

94. *(b)* International Kite Festival is celebrated in Gujarat.

- The festival is being organised by Gujarat Tourism on the G20 theme of One Earth, One Family, One Future.
- Ahmedabad first hosted the International Kite Festival on the occasion of Uttarayan in 1989.

95. *(d)* In March 2023,the Government of India announced the set up of 7 PM Mitra (Pradhanmantri mega integrated textile region and apparel) parks and textile.

- The Prime Minister of India has laid the foundation stone of 2 mega textile parks in Maharashtra and Gujarat under the PM Mega Integrated Textile Regions and Apparel (PM MITRA) scheme.
- The Ministry of Textiles will provide financial support in the form of Development Capital Support up to ₹ 500 crores per.

96. *(d)* The Salal project, also known Salal hydroelectric power station, is on Chenab river.

- Salal Dam is a run-of-the river hydropower project on the Chenab River in the Reasi district of the Jammu and Kashmir.
- It was the firsthydropower project built by India in Jammu and Kashmir uner Indus water treaty region.

97. *(a)* National Javelin Day is celebrated on 7th August.

- 6th August is celebrated as Hiroshima Day.
- 12th January is celebrated as National Youth Day.
- 29th August is celebrated as National Sports Day.

98. *(a)* Monstera plant roots arise from parts of a plant other than the radicle.

Roots that develop from parts of a plant other than the radicle are called adventitious roots, and 'Monstera' is a plant known to produce adventitious roots.

99. *(b)* Raag is Miyan ki Todi in Hindustani music.

- Chhand is a quatrain used in poetic traditions of North India and Pakistan.
- Kirtan, somtimes referred to as sankirtana (literally, 'collective performance') is a call-and-response chanting or musical conversation.
- Tanam consists of expanding the raga with syllables "a-nam-tam".

100. *(c)* 84.7% is the literacy rate of males in India as per report published in National survey of India 2022.

According to the National Survey of India (NSO), India's literacy rate in 2022 was 77.7%. In 2020, the literacy rate was 73.5% in rural areas and 87.7% in urban areas.

Set 33 11 July, 2024 (Shift I)

SSC CHSL Tier-I SOLVED PAPER

Instructions

1. This paper contains 100 questions.
2. It has 4 Parts, **Part I** General English, **Part II** General Intelligence & Reasoning, **Part III** Quantitative Aptitude and **Part IV** General Awareness.
3. Each question carries **2 marks.**

Part I

General English

1. Parts of the following sentence have been given as options. Select the option that contains an error.

She was fond of walking along the path besides the lake.

(a) besides the lake
(b) along the path
(c) She was
(d) fond of walking

2. Parts of the following sentence have been underlined and given as options. Select the option that contains an error.

Policeman came to my village and asked about a person who burgled a house last night.

(a) Policeman (b) a house
(c) my village (d) a person

3. Select the option that will improve the given sentence by using the most appropriate verb.

Soorya walking to college every day.

(a) Soorya is walking to college every day.
(b) Soorya walked to college every day.
(c) Soorya walk to college every day.
(d) Soorya have walked to college every day.

4. The following sentence has been divided into parts. One of them may contain an error. Select the part that contains the error from the given options. If you don't find any error mark 'No error' as your answer.

Father took the newspaper / in his hand to / go through it once again.

(a) in his hand to
(b) Father took the newspaper
(c) go through it once again
(d) No error

Directions (Q. Nos. 5-9) *In the following passage, some words have been deleted. Read the passage carefully and select the most appropriate option to fill in each blank.*

What is literacy? It is the golden key that (1)........... the gates to a whole new world. It heralds the dawn of a new (2)........... . But the media hype seems to give the impression that literacy simply means the ability to sign one's name, instead of putting thumb impression. Isn't that a very (3)..........., simplistic interpretation of the word?

Taking up this narrow meaning of the word, politicians proclaim that their states have achieved 80 or 90 per cent literacy or even (4)........... . But quite often, what happens is, once the training course is over, to produce (5)..........., the neo-literates soon lapse into illiteracy.

5. Select the most appropriate option to fill in blank no. (1).

(a) opens (b) closes
(c) controls (d) leads

6. Select the most appropriate option to fill in blank no. (2).

(a) year (b) day
(c) month (d) season

7. Select the most appropriate option to fill in blank no. (3).

(a) limited (b) daunted
(c) wide (d) small

8. Select the most appropriate option to fill in blank no. (4).

(a) better (b) higher
(c) lower (d) moderate

9. Select the most appropriate option to fill in blank no. (5).

(a) education (b) literates
(c) beginners (d) pupils

10. Select the most appropriate synonym of the given word.

Magnificent

(a) Modest (b) Regular
(c) Humble (d) Splendid

11. Select the most appropriate synonym of the given word.

Indigenous

(a) Aboriginal (b) Artificial
(c) Tangible (d) Literary

12. Select the most appropriate spelling of the underlined word in the given sentence.

He lost all senisation in his legs through a cramp.

(a) syansation (b) sensition
(c) sansation (d) sensation

13. The following sentence has been split into four segments. Identify the segment that contains a grammatical error.

When Serena / will arrive, / she will / call you.

(a) call you (b) will arrive
(c) she will (d) When Serena

14. Select the most appropriate meaning of the given idiom.

A sting in the tail

(a) An unexpected, typically unpleasant or problematic end to something
(b) Something which seems bad at first but contains a pleasant part at the end
(c) To initiate a situation that is very complicated or problematic
(d) A situation in which a large group has to do something to satisfy a small group

15. Identify the incorrectly spelt word in the following sentence.

To avoid indigetion, it is necessary to chew food properly.

(a) chew (b) necessary
(c) properly (d) indigetion

16. Select the most appropriate option that can substitute the underlined words in the following sentence.

The interdisciplinary approach utilised in this study <u>facilitates comprehensive understanding of the</u> complex phenomenon under investigation.

(a) facilitated a comprehensive understanding
(b) will have facilitated a comprehensive understanding
(c) utilises a comprehensive understanding
(d) is facilitates a comprehensive understanding

17. Select the most appropriate antonym of the given word.

Abandon

(a) Adopt (b) Randomise
(c) Destroy (d) Surrender

18. Select the most appropriate meaning of the given idiom.

Gift of the gab

(a) Witty
(b) Humorous
(c) Talent for speaking
(d) Talent for singing

19. Select the most appropriate collocation to fill in the blank.

Ujjwal was imprisoned for .... a crime.

(a) making (b) undertaking
(c) committing (d) involving

20. Identify the most appropriate antonym of the given word.

He worked alone as he did not want anyone to <u>hamper</u> his project.

(b) care (b) help
(c) impede (d) finish

21. Select the most appropriate antonym of the underlined word in the given sentence.

He is not <u>friendly</u> with him in the office.

(a) revel (b) hostile
(c) gregarious (d) intelligent

22. Select the most appropriate option that can substitute the underlined segment in the given sentence.

No sooner did we reach at the party <u>that it began to rain</u>.

(a) it began to rain
(b) before it began to rain
(c) than it began to rain
(d) as it began to rain

23. Select the most appropriate option that can substitute the underlined segment in the given sentence. If there is no need to substitute it, select 'No substitution required'.

I cannot use my office at the moment because <u>it being painted</u>.

(a) it is being painted
(b) it had been paint
(c) it has being painted
(d) No substitution required

24. Select the most appropriate synonym of 'amazement' to fill the blank.

Leena was filled with .... when she saw the diamond ring as her wedding gift.

(a) happiness (b) measurement
(c) haughtiness (d) astonishment

25. Select the most appropriate pair of words to fill in the blanks.

Yesterday, he .... pizza and .... burgers in one go.

(a) eight; ate (b) ate; ate
(c) eight; eight (d) ate; eight

Part II
General Intelligence

26. Select the correct mirror image of the given figure, when the mirror is placed at MN as shown below.

M
Dh57erk
N

(a) ꓘɹɘ7ƨʜᗡ (b) ꓘɿɘ7ƨʜᗡ
(c) kɿɘ7ƨhᗡ (d) ꓘɿɘ7ꙅʜᗡ

27. What will come in the place of the question mark (?) in the following equation, if '+' and '−' are interchanged and '×' and '÷' are interchanged ?

$204 \times 6 - 6 \div 4 + 7 = ?$

(a) 41 (b) 21
(c) 51 (d) 31

28. 14 is related to 43 by certain logic. Following the same logic, 17 is related to 52 To which of the following is 19 related, following the same logic?

(**Note** Operations should be performed on the whole numbers, without breaking down the numbers into its constituent digits. E.g. 13 – Operations on 13 such as adding/subtracting/ multiplying etc. to 13 can be performed. Breaking down 13 into 1 and 3 and then performing mathematical operations on 1 and 3 is not allowed.)

(a) 57 (b) 50 (c) 38 (d) 58

29. JHDC is related to KGEB in a certain way based on the English alphabetical order. In the same way, QOKJ is related to RNLI. To which of the following is USON related, following the same logic?

(a) VRPM (b) VSQM
(c) VRQM (d) VSPM

30. If 'A' stands for '÷', 'B' stands for '×', 'C' stands for '+' and 'D' stands for '−', then the resultant of which of the following will be 100?

(a) 15 C 9 D 810 A 9 B 55
(b) 15 D 9 B 810 A 9 C 55
(c) 15 B 9 D 810 A 9 C 55
(d) 15 A 9 D 810 B 9 C 55

31. Identify the figure given in the options, which when put in place of the question mark (?) will logically complete the series?

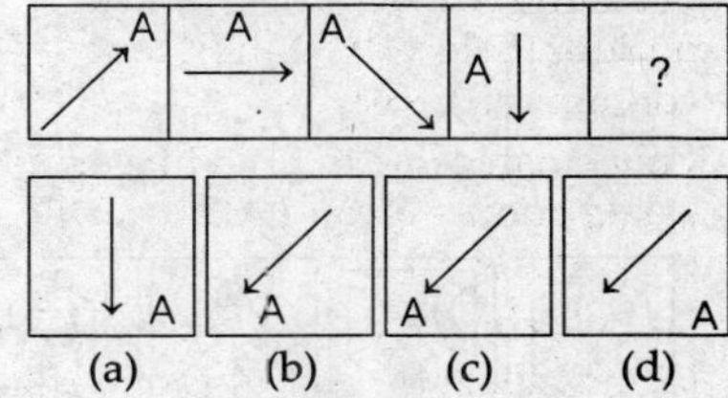

32. If 24th July, 1999 was Saturday, then what was the day of the week on 28th July, 2003?

(a) Monday
(b) Saturday
(c) Sunday
(d) Tuesday

33. Select the option figure in which the given figure is embedded as its part (rotation is not allowed).

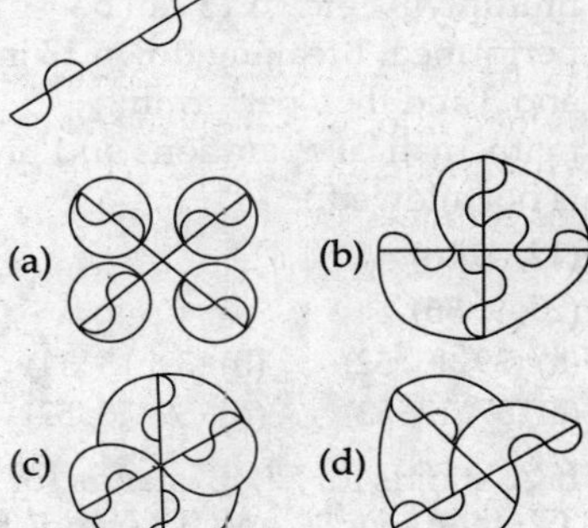

34. How many rectangles are there in the following figure?

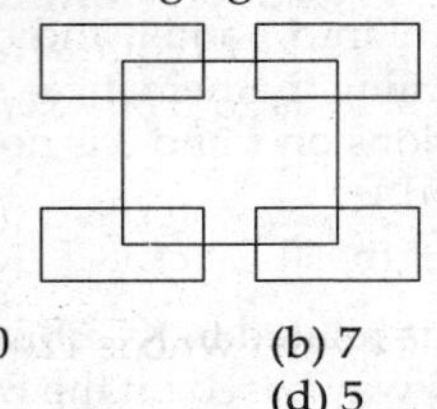

(a) 10 (b) 7
(c) 9 (d) 5

35. Which of the following numbers will replace the question mark (?) in the given series ?

214, 111, 179, 126, 144, 141, 109, 156, ?

(a) 96 (b) 89 (c) 61 (d) 74

36. What would be the number on the opposite side of '23' if the given sheet is folded to form a cube ?

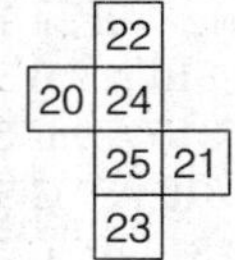

(a) 24 (b) 20 (c) 21 (d) 22

37. Select the option in which the given figure (X) is embedded (rotation is not allowed).

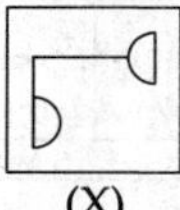

(X)

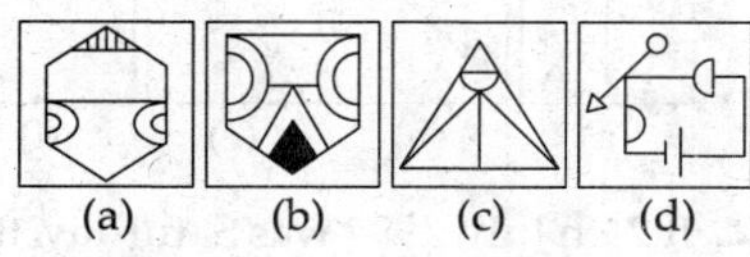

(a) (b) (c) (d)

38. Select the set in which the numbers are related in the same way as are the numbers of the following sets.

(**Note** Operations should be performed on the whole numbers, without breaking down the numbers into their constituent digits. E.g. 13 – Operations on 13 such as adding/subtracting/multiplying etc. to 13 can be performed. Breaking down 13 into 1 and 3 and then performing mathematical operations on 1 and 3 is not allowed.)

(12, 4, 16)

(27, 9, 36)

(a) (39, 15, 52) (b) (39, 13, 54)
(c) (37, 13, 52) (d) (39, 13, 52)

39. If 'A' stands for '÷', 'B' stands for '×', 'C' stands for '+' and 'D' stands for '–', what will come in place of the question mark (?) in the following equation ?

62 B 2 D 190 A 5 C 7 = ?

(a) 90 (b) 91 (c) 93 (d) 92

40. GJHK is related to IMKM in a certain way based on the English alphabetical order. In the same way, QTRU is related to SWUW. To which of the following is ILJM related, following the same logic?

(a) KOMO (b) KNMN
(c) KMON (d) KPNP

41. Select the word-pair that best represents a similar relationship to the one expressed in the pair of words given below.

(The words must be considered as meaningful English words and must not be related to each other based on the number of letters/number of consonants/vowels in the word.)

Leaf : Oak

(a) Berry : Fruit (b) Bulb : Tulip
(c) Needle : Pine (d) Tree : Forest

42. Select the correct option that when filled in the blanks in the same sequence will make the series logically complete.

QUAI_Q_YIL_U_ILQUU_L

(a) LWQUI (b) LIQAU
(c) LUQWI (d) LXIUQ

43. What should come in place of the question mark (?) in the given series?

66, 77, 99, 132, 176, ?

(a) 232 (b) 230 (c) 233 (d) 231

44. In a certain code language, 'BORN' is coded as '8234' and 'NORM' is coded as '6328'. How is 'M' coded in the given language ?

(a) 8 (b) 2 (c) 4 (d) 6

45. In this question, three statements are given, followed by three conclusions numbered I, II and III. Assuming the statements to be true, even if they seem to be at variance with commonly known facts, decide which of the conclusion(s) logically follow/follows from the statements.

Statements

All ladders are chairs.

All chairs are tables.

No table is a stair.

Conclusions

I. Some tables are ladders.
II. No chair is a stair.
III. Some ladders are stairs.

(a) Only Conclusion II follows
(b) Only Conclusion III follows
(c) Both Conclusions I and II follow
(d) Only Conclusion I follows

46. Four letter-clusters have been given, out of which three are alike in some manner and one is different. Select the letter-cluster that is different.

(**Note** The odd one out is not based on the number of consonants/vowels or their position in the letter-cluster)

(a) MNOL (b) AZCX
(c) PKRI (d) PLRI

47. In a certain language,

A & B means 'A is the wife of B',
A ÷ B means 'A is the daughter of B',
A × B means 'A is the son of B',
A + B means 'A is the sister of B' and
A @ B means 'A is the father of B'.

P & Q @ L + T & U @ V

Based on the above, how is Q related to V ?

(a) Sister
(b) Mother
(c) Father's mother
(d) Mother's father

48. What should come in place of the question mark (?) in the given series?

33, 61, 117, 229, ?

(a) 354 (b) 543
(c) 453 (d) 435

49. In a certain code language, 'DZLV' is coded as 'HDJT' and 'CQYH' is coded as 'GUWF'. What is the code for 'MTBE' in the given code language ?

(a) YAYB (b) QZYB
(c) QXZC (d) YZXB

50. A square sheet of paper is folded along the dotted line successively along the direction shown and is then punched in the end. How would the paper look when unfolded?

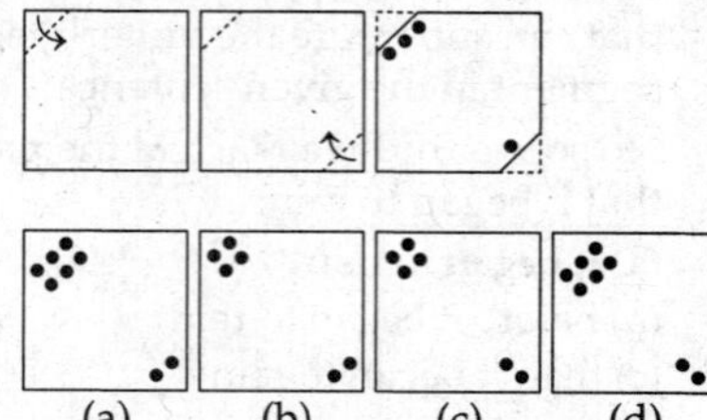

(a) (b) (c) (d)

Part III

Quantitative Aptitude

51. The sum of two numbers is 76. Three times the larger number is 46 more than four times the smaller one. Find the two numbers.
(a) 35 and 41 (b) 40 and 36
(c) 44 and 32 (d) 50 and 26

52. If the number $6p5157q$ is divisible by 88, then $p \times q = \ldots\ldots\ldots$, where p and q are single digit numbers.
(a) 15 (b) 18
(c) 20 (d) 12

53. A number increased by 20% gives 240. Find the number.
(a) 240 (b) 280
(c) 200 (d) 250

54. PBA and PDC are two secants. AD is the diameter of the circle with the centre at O. $\angle A = 30°, \angle P = 20°$. Find the measure of $\angle DBC$.

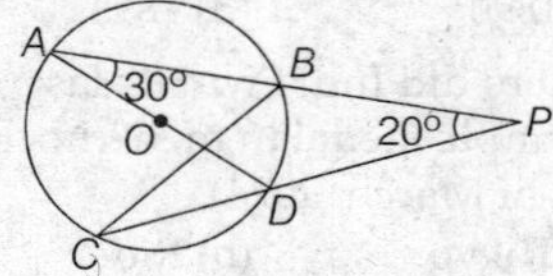

(a) 50° (b) 30°
(c) 45° (d) 40°

55. The value of

$$\left(\frac{\sin\theta}{1+\cos\theta}+\frac{1+\cos\theta}{\sin\theta}\right)\left(\frac{1}{\tan\theta+\cot\theta}\right)$$

is equal to
(a) $\tan\theta$ (b) 1
(c) $2\cos\theta$ (d) $2\sin\theta$

56. By selling an article for ₹ 2160, Prashant allows a 20 % discount and earns 28% profit. If the article is sold without any discount, the profit will be
(a) 55% (b) 60% (c) 65% (d) 50%

57. The ratio of red to green sweets in a bag is 3 : 4. How many red sweets are there in the bag, if the number of green sweets is 120?
(a) 100 (b) 80 (c) 70 (d) 90

58. A solid metallic sphere of radius 6 cm is melted and recast into spherical balls of radius 3 cm. The number of spherical balls thus obtained is
(a) 6 (b) 10 (c) 4 (d) 8

59. The following line graph shows the units manufactured by a company in some months. In which month did the company report the highest growth (in %) in production as compared with the respective previous month's production?

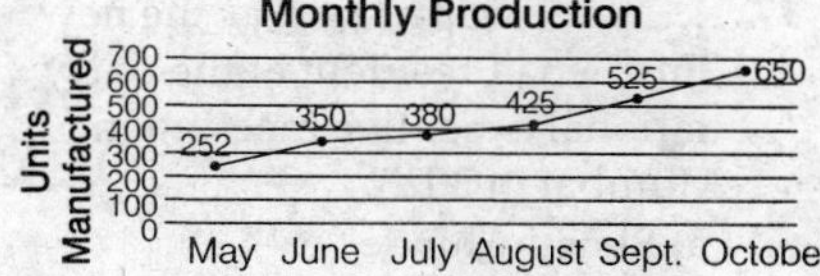

(a) July (b) October
(c) June (d) September

60. What is the value of

$$\frac{\left[\frac{1}{4}\div\frac{1}{4}\times\frac{1}{4}\right]\times\frac{1}{4}}{\left[\frac{1}{8}+\frac{1}{8}\times\frac{1}{8}\right]}+\left(1-\frac{4}{9}\right)?$$

(a) 2 (b) 0 (c) 3 (d) 1

61. PQR is a triangle. MN is a line segment intersecting PQ in M and PR in N such that $MN \parallel QR$ and divides ΔPQR into two parts, which are equal in area. What is the ratio of MQ to PQ?
(a) $\sqrt{2} : (\sqrt{2}-1)$ (b) $\sqrt{2} : 1$
(c) $(\sqrt{2}-1) : \sqrt{2}$ (d) $1 : \sqrt{2}$

62. Find the altitude (in cm) from the vertex Q to side PR of triangle PQR with side lengths $PQ = 40$ cm, $PR = 40$ cm and $QR = 60$ cm.
(a) $25\sqrt{7}$ (b) $15\sqrt{7}$
(c) $30\sqrt{7}$ (d) $20\sqrt{7}$

63. Study the given graph and answer the question that follows.
The graph shows the marks obtained by Riya and Rida in six subjects in the CBSE 12th exam. The maximum marks in Maths, Physics and Chemistry are 140 and that in English, IP and Biology are 180.

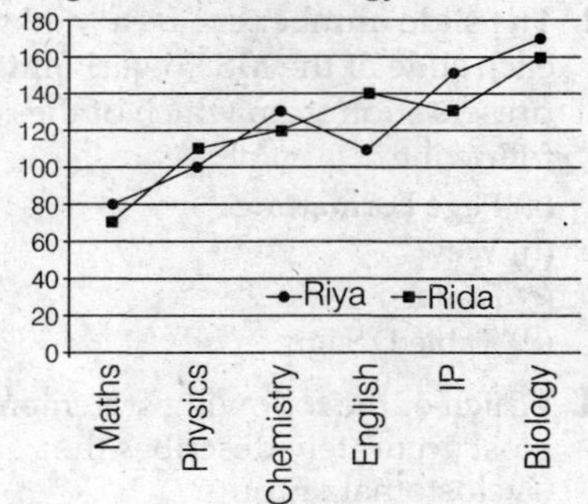

What is the difference between the percentage of marks obtained by Riya and Rida in IP ?
(a) 11.11% (b) 19%
(c) 20% (d) 31%

64. Nirmal completed the school project in 45 days. How many days will Amit take to complete the same work, if he is 25% more efficient than Nirmal?
(a) 36 (b) 25 (c) 38 (d) 30

65. A police travelling at 65 km/h is chasing a thief who is 1200 m away from him and is travelling at 41 km/h. Find the time taken by the policeman to catch the thief.
(a) 1 min (b) 3 min
(c) 2 min (d) 4 min

66. A shopkeeper sells goods at 40% loss on cost price but uses 25% less weight. What is his percentage profit or loss?
(a) Profit, 20% (b) Loss, 10%
(c) Loss, 20% (d) Profit, 10%

67. A laptop charger is sold for ₹ 2540 in cash or for a down payment of ₹ 1340 in cash together with ₹ 1205 to be paid after one month. Find the rate of interest charged in the instalment scheme.
(a) 20% p.a. (b) 10% p.a.
(c) 5% p.a. (d) 15% p.a.

68. What is the area of a quadrilateral $ABCD$, (shown below) in which sides AB and BC are equal sides AD and CD are of lengths 5 cm and 13 cm, respectively, and side AD is perpendicular to the diagonal AC?

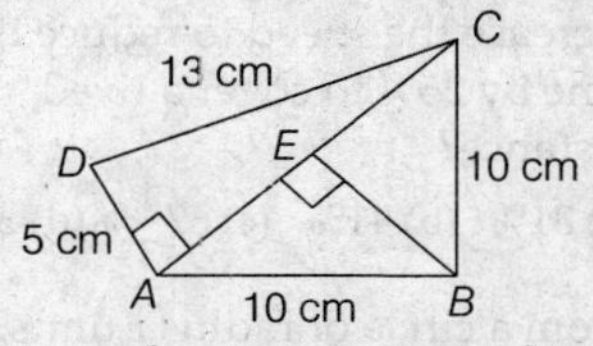

(a) 75 cm^2 (b) 78 cm^2
(c) 82 cm^2 (d) 80 cm^2

69. The given table represents the percentage marks of three students in three subjects. Study the table and answer the question.

Students \ Subject	Geography	History	Economics
Rohan	78	77	74
Sohan	84	80	82
Mohan	87	83	86

The average marks (to the nearest integer) obtained by the students in History and Economics (respectively) are
(a) 80 and 81 (b) 81 and 80
(c) 78 and 80 (d) 80 and 78

70. The following tables shows the loan disbursed by four banks (on Crores) over four years"

	Years			
Banks	**2016**	**2017**	**2018**	**2019**
A	10	15	20	22
B	5	10	15	18
C	20	25	15	20
D	5	10	25	20

In which year total disbursement of loans of banks A and B is exactly equal to the total disbursement of loans of banks C and D?
(a) 2017 (b) 2019 (c) 2016 (d) 2018

71. The population of a village was 400000. It increased by 20% in the first year and increased by 30% in the second year. Its population after two years is
(a) 625000 (b) 624000
(c) 540000 (d) 520000

72. Find the surface area (in cm^2) of a cardboard box in th shape of a cuboid, whose length is 60 cm, breadth is half its length and height is one-third of its breadth.
(a) 2700 (b) 5400 (c) 10800 (d) 8100

73. The average age of Ruby and Soni is 40 yrs. The ratio of their ages is 11:5 respectively. What is the age (in years) of Soni?
(a) 15 (b) 30 (c) 55 (d) 25

74. By what percentage should a racer increase the speed to reduce the time by 25% to cover a fixed distance?
(a) 31% (b) 41% (c) $37\frac{1}{3}$% (d) $33\frac{1}{3}$%

75. From a circle of radius r units, the largest equilateral triangle is cut out. What is the length (in units) of the side of the triangle?
(a) $\sqrt{2}r$ (b) $\frac{r}{\sqrt{3}}$ (c) $\sqrt{3}r$ (d) $\frac{r}{\sqrt{2}}$

Part IV
General Awareness

76. On 11th August 2021, the General Insurance Business (Nationalisation) Amendment Bill, 2021 was passed by the Parliament and it amended the ....
(a) Life Insurance (Nationalisation) Act, 1975
(b) General Business (Nationalisation) Act, 1970
(c) Motor Insurance (Nationalisation) Act, 1980
(d) General Insurance Business (Nationalisation) Act, 1972

77. .... was named as the new Shiv Sena President at the party national executive meeting in Mumbai in 2023.
(a) Eknath Shinde
(b) Narayan Rane
(c) Rahul Ramesh Shewale
(d) Aditya Uddhav Thackeray

78. The Parliament of India has passed the 86th Constitutional Amendment Act 2002, which establishes the basic rights of primary education for children between
(a) 7-16 Years (b) 5-11 years
(c) 6-14 Years (d) 6-17 Years

79. Which commission drew the boundary line between India and Pakistan?
(a) Radcliffe Boundary Commission
(b) Gandhi Irwin Pact
(c) Hilton Young Commission
(d) Bretton Woods Commission

80. In which Gharana do singers perform the Khandhar Vani and Gauhar Vani?
(a) Talwandi Gharana
(b) Darbhanga Gharana
(c) Dagari Gharana
(d) Bettiah Gharana

81. Delhi Ridge is the water divide between which of the following rivers?
(a) Ganges and Yamuna
(b) Indus and Mahi
(c) Ganges and Indus
(d) Ganges and Sind

82. The slide number can be added to each slide of the MS PowerPoint presentation from which of the following?
(a) Page Formatting
(b) View
(c) Footer
(d) Table Design

83. Which of the following statements most accurately describes the Cyclostomata group?
(a) They are ectothermic animals having mucus glands in the skin, and a three-chambered heart.
(b) They are warm-blooded, oviparous, bipedal, feathered, winged and toothless vertebrates.
(c) They are characterised by having an elongated eel-like body, circular mouth, slimy skin and are scaleless.
(d) Their skin is covered with scales/plates and their hearts have only two chambers.

84. What is/are the objective(s) of Fiscal Policy?
1. Boost growth
2. Control inflation

Codes
(a) Neither 1 nor 2 (b) Both 1 and 2
(c) Only 2 (d) Only 1

85. The Fundamental Duties of Citizens were introduced by the 42nd Amendment in the year:
(a) 1978 (b) 1980
(c) 1976 (d) 1988

86. In which year did Swami Vivekananda give his speech at the Chicago Parliament of Religions?
(a) 1892 (b) 1891
(c) 1890 (d) 1893

87. Where did India win its last Olympic medal in men's hockey? (As of March, 2024)
(a) Tokyo (b) Rio
(c) Munich (d) Mexico City

88. Which of the following statements is /are true with respect to Supreme Court Observation in AG Perarivalan v/s The State of Tamil Nadu State?
1. It highlighted that the Governor's powers are qualified by the constitutional mandate, chiefly requiring them to act in aid and advice of the Council of Ministers.
2. The bench headed by Justice L. Nageswara Rao ordered the freedom of one of the convicts in the Rajiv Gandhi assassination case.
3. The bench was of the opinion that there are three sources of power-Governor, Council of Ministers and the Constitution.

Codes
(a) Only 1 (b) 1 and 2
(c) Only 3 (d) 2 and 3

89. Which of the following is not the colour of a warning card in Kabaddi?
(a) Black (b) Red
(c) Green (d) Yellow

90. Articles 344 (1) and 351 of the Constitution of India are related to the
(a) Third Schedule
(b) Sixth Schedule
(c) Fifth Schedule
(d) Eighth Schedule

91. Which Mughal ruler was responsible for the execution of Guru Tegh Bahadur in the year 1675?
(a) Aurangzeb (b) Shahjahan
(c) Akbar (d) Jahangir

92. Match the states in column A with their official languages in column B.

Column A (State)		Column B (Official Language)	
A.	Andhra Pradesh	1.	Malayalam
B.	Kerala	2.	Telugu
C.	Karnataka	3.	Konkani
D.	Goa	4.	Kannada

Codes

	A	B	C	D		A	B	C	D
(a)	2	1	3	4	(b)	2	1	4	3
(c)	1	2	4	3	(d)	1	2	3	4

93. Which of the following isotopes is used as a fuel in nuclear power plants for generating electricity?
(a) Uranium- 235
(b) Arsenic-74
(c) Carbon-14
(d) Sodium-24

94. Most major sports awards are accompanied by a cash reward. Which of the following is the only national sports award that does not include a cash reward?
(a) Rashtriya Khel Protsahan Puruskar
(b) Major Dhyan Chand Khel Ratna
(c) Maulana Abul Kalam Azad Trophy
(d) Dronacharya Award

95. Which Indian festival is a festival of lights ?
(a) Holi (b) Onam
(c) Bihu (d) Diwali

96. The famous folk music of Rajasthan that was developed in royal courts is known as
(a) Dandiya (b) Sohar
(c) Lavani (d) Maand

97. The Howrah bridge was officially opened in the year ....
(a) 1943 (b) 1948
(c) 1930 (d) 1935

98. Which of the following statements about planet Saturn is true?
(a) Satellites like Enceladus and Titan of Saturn are home to internal oceans, could possibly support life.
(b) Saturn is the fourth planet from the Sun and the largest planet in our solar system.
(c) Saturn's environment is conducive to life.
(d) Saturn is a massive ball made up mostly of nitrogen.

99. The Lucknow Gharana of Kathak was founded by ...., a devotee of the Bhakti Movement who lived in Southeast Uttar Pradesh.
(a) Bhagwan Ram (b) Ishwari Prasad
(c) Shyam Kumar (d) Ram Kumar

100. In Microsoft Office, how is the font size determined?
(a) Pixels (b) Points
(c) Inches (d) Centimetres

Answers

1. (a)	2. (a)	3. (c)	4. (d)
5. (a)	6. (b)	7. (a)	8. (b)
9. (b)	10. (d)	11. (a)	12. (d)
13. (b)	14 (a)	15. (d)	16. (a)
17. (a)	18. (c)	19. (c)	20. (b)
21. (b)	22. (c)	23. (a)	24. (d)
25. (d)	26. (b)	27. (c)	28. (d)
29. (a)	30. (c)	31. (c)	32. (a)
33. (c)	34. (c)	35. (d)	36. (a)
37. (d)	38. (d)	39. (c)	40. (a)
41. (c)	42. (c)	43. (d)	44. (d)
45. (c)	46. (d)	47. (d)	48. (c)
49. (c)	50. (d)	51. (d)	52. (b)
53. (c)	54. (d)	55. (c)	56. (b)
57. (d)	58. (d)	59. (c)	60. (d)
61. (c)	62. (b)	63. (a)	64. (a)
65. (b)	66. (c)	67. (c)	68. (b)
69. (a)	70. (b)	71. (b)	72. (b)
73. (d)	74. (d)	75. (c)	76. (d)
77. (a)	78. (c)	79. (a)	80. (b)
81. (c)	82. (c)	83. (c)	84. (b)
85. (c)	86. (d)	87. (a)	88. (b)
89. (a)	90. (d)	91. (a)	92. (b)
93. (a)	94. (a)	95. (d)	96. (d)
97. (a)	98. (a)	99. (b)	100. (b)

Explanations

1. *(a)* Part (a) 'besides the lake' contains error. Change 'besides' to 'beside' as besides means in addition to and beside means at the side or adjacent.

2. *(a)* Part 'Policeman' contains an error. Add 'The' before 'policeman' to correct the sentence.

3. *(c)* The given sentence contains an error. As the sentence presents a habit, simple present tense should be used. Hence, the correct sentence is- Soorya walks to college every day.

4. *(d)* The given sentence is grammatically correct and contextually meaningful.

5. *(a)* The correct filler for the given blank is 'opens'.

6. *(b)* The correct filler for the given blank is 'day'.

7. *(a)* The correct filler for the given blank is 'limited'.

8. *(b)* The correct filler for the given blank is 'higher'.

9. *(b)* The correct filler for the given blank is 'literates'.

10. *(d)* The word 'Magnificent' means 'great and splendid'.
'Humble' and 'Modest' mean polite and kind.

11. *(a)* 'Indigenous' means originating or occurring naturally in a particular place; native. Hence, the synonym is 'Aboriginal' which means originating or occurring naturally in a particular place; native.

12. *(d)* The incorrectly spelt word is 'senisation'. The correct spelling is 'sensation'.

13. *(b)* Part (b) 'will arrive' contains an error. Use 'arrives' to correct the sentence. The given sentence is a future conditional in which one clause is in simple future and the other is in simple present.

14. *(a)* A sting in the tail means an unexpected, typically unpleasant or problematic end to something.

15. *(d)* The incorrectly spelt word is 'indigetion'. The correct spelling is 'indigestion'.

16. *(a)* The underlined part of the given sentence contains an error. Use 'facilitated a comprehensive understanding' to correct the sentence.

17. *(a)* 'Abandon' means to cease to support or look after (someone); desert. Hence, its antonym is to 'Adopt'.

'Randomise' means make (a set of items, people, etc.) unpredictable, unsystematic, or random in order or arrangement.

18. *(c)* Gift of the gab means talent for speaking.

19. *(c)* The correct filler for the given blank is 'committing'.

20. *(b)* 'Hamper' means to obstruct and impede. Hence, its antonym is 'Help'.

21. *(b)* The antonym of 'friendly' is 'hostile' which means 'not friendly'.

- 'Revel' means enjoy oneself in a lively and noisy way, especially with drinking and dancing.
- 'Gregarious' means (of a person) fond of company; sociable.

22. *(c)* The underlined part of the given sentence contains an error. Use 'than it began to rain' to correct the sentence.

23. *(a)* The underlined part of the given sentence contains an error. Use 'it is being painted' to correct the sentence.

24. *(d)* The synonym of 'astonishment' is amazement which is the correct filler for the given blank.

25. *(d)* The correct filler for the given blanks are 'ate' and 'eight'.

26. *(b)* The figure given in option (b) is the correct mirror image of the given question figure.

M

Dh57erk | Dh57erk (mirror image)

N

27. *(c)* Given equation,

$$204 \times 6 - 6 \div 4 + 7 = ?$$

Interchanging signs + and –, × and ÷, we get

$$204 \div 6 + 6 \times 4 - 7 = ?$$

$\Rightarrow \quad 34 + 24 - 7 = ?$

$\Rightarrow \quad 58 - 7 = ?$

$\therefore \quad ? = \boxed{51}$

28. *(d)* As, $14 \xrightarrow{\times 3 + 1} 43$

and $17 \xrightarrow{\times 3 + 1} 52$

Similarly, $19 \xrightarrow{\times 3 + 1} \boxed{58}$

29. *(a)* As,

J H D C → (+1, –1, +1, –1) → K G E B

and

Q O K J → (+1, –1, +1, –1) → R N L I

Similarly,

U S O N → (+1, –1, +1, –1) → V R P M

30. *(c)* According to the question,

A → ÷, B → ×, C → +, D → –

From option (c),

15 B 9 D 810 A 9 C 55

Substituting the letters with symbols, we get

$$15 \times 9 - 810 \div 9 + 55$$
$$= 135 - 90 + 55$$
$$= 190 - 90 = 100$$

31. *(c)* In given series, letter 'A' is moving half arm backward and arrow is moving 45° in clockwise direction in each next step.

Hence, figure in option (c) will replace the question mark in the series.

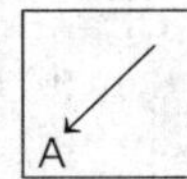

32. *(a)* Given, 24th July, 1999 → Saturday

Number of odd days from 24th July, 1999 to 24th July, 2003

Years → 2000 + 2001 + 2002 + 2003

Odd days → 2 + 1 + 1 + 1 = 5

Number of odd days from 24th July, 2003 to 28th July, 2003 = 4 days

$$\text{Total odd days} = \frac{5+4}{7}$$
$$= \frac{9}{7} = 2 \text{ odd days}$$

∴ Required day = Saturday + 2

= Monday

33. *(c)* The given figure is embedded in option figure (c).

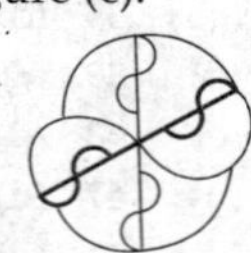

34. *(c)* Naming the figure,

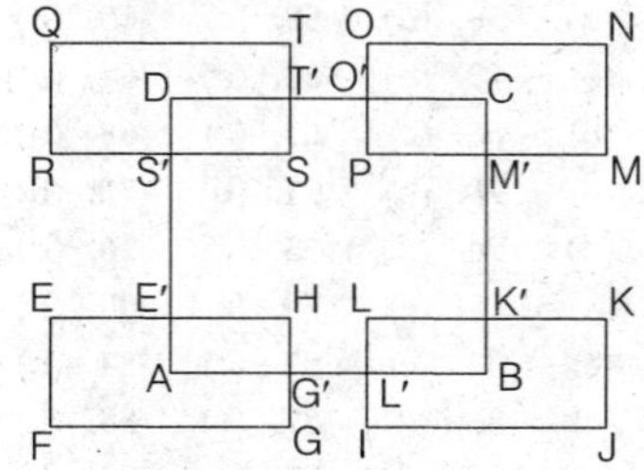

Rectangles can be represented as

□EFGH, □IJKL, □MNOP, □QRST, □DS'ST, □PM'CO', □E'AG'H, □LL'BK', □ABCD

Hence, there are total 9 rectangles in the given figure.

35. *(d)* The pattern of the series is as follows,

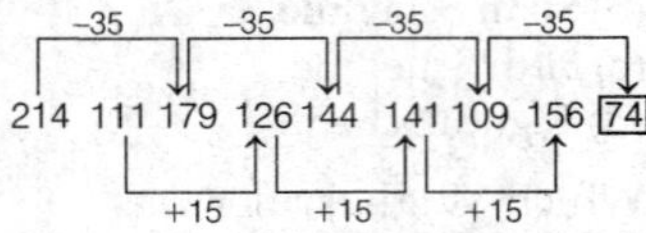

36. *(a)* According to the question,

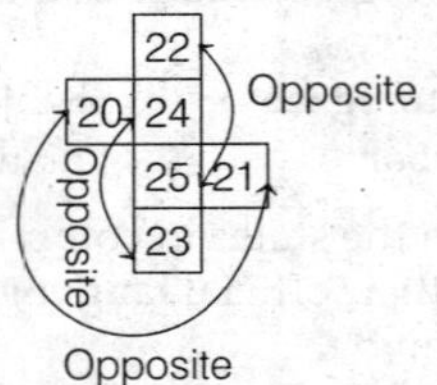

Hence, '24' would be opposite to '23'.

37. *(d)* The given figure (X) is embedded in option figure (d).

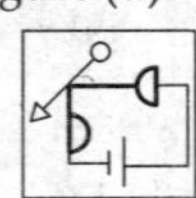

38. *(d)* As, $(12, 4, 16) \rightarrow \frac{12}{3} = 4 \times 4 = 16$

and $(27, 9, 36) \rightarrow \frac{27}{3} = 9 \times 4 = 36$

Similarly,

$(39, 13, 52) \rightarrow \frac{39}{3} = 13 \times 4 = 52$

39. *(c)* Given equation,

62 B 2 D 190 A 5 C 7 = ?

After substituting the letters with their respective symbols, we have

A → ÷, B → ×, C → +, D → –

$$62 \times 2 - 190 \div 5 + 7 = ?$$

$\Rightarrow \quad 124 - 38 + 7 = ?$

$\Rightarrow \quad 131 - 38 = ?$

$\therefore \quad ? = \boxed{93}$

40. *(a)* As,

G J H K → (+2, +3, +3, +2) → I M K M

and

Q T R U → (+2, +3, +3, +2) → S W U W

Similarly,

I L J M → (+2, +3, +3, +2) → K O M O

41. *(c)* As, 'Leaf' is a part of 'Oak' trees. Similarly, 'Needle' is a part of 'Pine' trees.

42. *(c)* The pattern of the series is as shown below,

QUAIL / QUYIL / QUWIL / QUUIL (–2, –2, –2)

∴ Required combination 'LUQWI'.

43. *(d)* The pattern of the series is as follows,

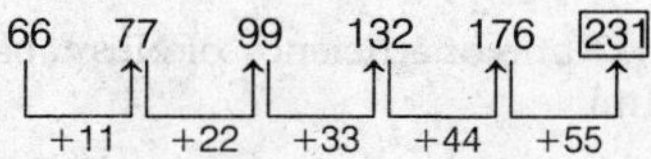

44. *(d)* According to the question,

B O R N ⟶ 8 2 3 4

N O R M ⟶ 6 3 2 8

Hence, 'M' is coded as '6'.

45. *(c)* According to the statements,

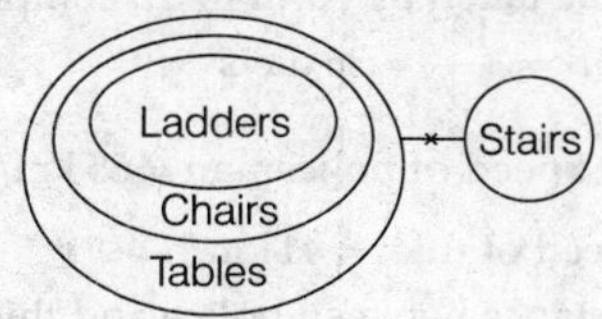

Conclusions

I. (✓) II. (✓) III. (✗)

Hence, both Conclusions I and II follow.

46. *(d)* As, M N — Opposite; O L — Opposite

A Z — Opposite; C X — Opposite

P K — Opposite; R I — Opposite

But, P L — −4; R I — Opposite

47. *(d)* According to the question,

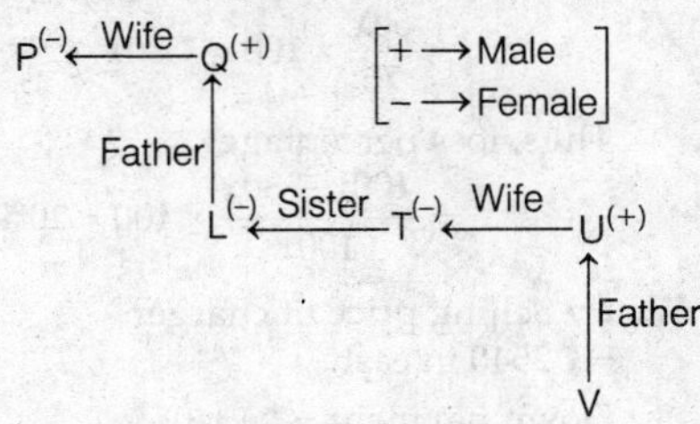

Hence, Q is V's mother's father.

48. *(c)* The pattern of the series is as follows,

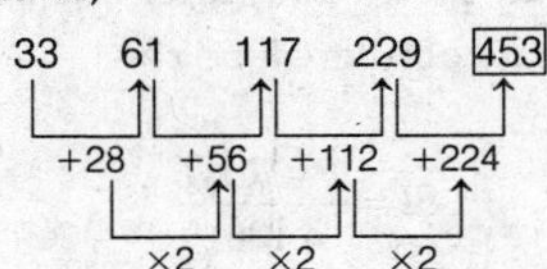

49. *(c)* As, D Z L V (+4, +4, −2, −2) → H D J T ; and C Q Y H (+4, +4, −2, −2) → G U W F

Similarly, M T B E (+4, +4, −2, −2) → Q X Z C

50. *(d)* When given sheet is unfolded, it will look like option figure (d).

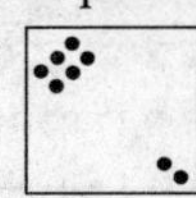

51. *(d)* Let the larger number be x.

Then, smaller number be $(76 - x)$.

According to the question,

$$3x - 4 \times (76 - x) = 46$$

$$\Rightarrow \quad 3x - 304 + 4x = 46$$

$$\Rightarrow \quad 7x = 46 + 304$$

$$\Rightarrow \quad 7x = 350$$

$$\therefore \quad x = 50$$

Then, other number = 76 − 50 = 26

Thus, both numbers are 50 and 26.

52. *(b)* Number $6p5157q$ is divisible by 88, it means number is divisible by 8 and 11.

By rule of divisibility of 8, if last three digits are divisible by 8, then whole number is divide by 8.

$57q$ is divisible by 8, when $q = 6$

and by rule of divisibility of 11.

"Difference of alternate digits of number is 0 or multiple of 11".

Thus, $6p5157q$

$$6 + 5 + 5 + 6 = 22 \qquad [\because q = 6]$$

$$p + 1 + 7 = 8 + p$$

$22 - (8 + p) = 0$ or multiple of 11

$14 - p = 0$ or multiple of 11

Thus, $p = 3$, then it become 11.

Then, required value of $p \times q$

$$= 3 \times 6 = 18$$

53. *(c)* Let the number be x.

According to the question,

$$x \times \frac{(100 + 20)}{100} = 240$$

$$\Rightarrow \quad x \times \frac{120}{100} = 240$$

$$x = 200$$

Hence, required number = 200

54. *(d)* Given,

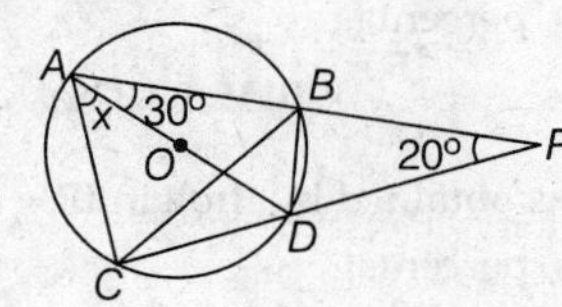

Joining A to C,

As, given AD is diameter.

Then, $\angle ACD = 90°$

[angle made in semi-circle is 90°]

Now, in ΔACP,

$$\angle PAC + \angle ACP + \angle CPA = 180°$$

$$\Rightarrow \quad 30 + x + 90° + 20° = 180°$$

$$x = 40°$$

Here, $\angle DAC = x = 40°$

$$\angle DAC = \angle DBC = 40°$$

[Angle in same segment are equal]

55. *(c)* Given,

$$\left(\frac{\sin\theta}{1+\cos\theta} + \frac{1+\cos\theta}{\sin\theta}\right)\left(\frac{1}{\tan\theta + \cot\theta}\right)$$

$$= \left(\frac{\sin^2\theta + 1 + \cos^2\theta + 2\cos\theta}{(1+\cos\theta)\sin\theta}\right)\left(\frac{1}{\dfrac{\sin\theta}{\cos\theta} + \dfrac{\cos\theta}{\sin\theta}}\right)$$

$$= \frac{2(1+\cos\theta)}{(1+\cos\theta)\sin\theta} \times \frac{\sin\theta \times \cos\theta}{(\sin^2\theta + \cos^2\theta)}$$

$$= \frac{2}{\sin\theta} \times \frac{\sin\theta \times \cos\theta}{1} \qquad [\because \sin^2\theta + \cos^2\theta = 1]$$

$$= 2\cos\theta$$

56. *(b)* Selling price of article = ₹ 2160

After allowing discount of 20%,

$$\text{Marked price} \times \frac{80}{100} = ₹\ 2160$$

Marked price of article

$$= \frac{2160 \times 100}{80}$$

$$= ₹\ 2700$$

and on selling at ₹ 2160, Prashant earn 28% profit.

Then, cost price of article

$$\times \frac{(100 + 28)}{100} = 2160$$

$$\text{CP of article} = \frac{2160 \times 100}{128}$$

$$= ₹\ 1687.5$$

If article is sold without discount, then,

MP = SP

Thus, profit percentage

$$= \frac{2700 - 1687.5}{1687.5} \times 100$$

$$= \frac{1012.5}{1687.5} \times 100 = 60\%$$

57. *(d)* Let the number of red and green sweets be $3x$ and $4x$.

According to the question,

$$4x = 120 \Rightarrow x = 30$$

Then, number of red sweets

$$= 3x = 3 \times 30 = 90$$

Hence, required number of red sweets $= 90$

58. *(d)* Let the number of small spherical balls be n.

Then, volume of bigger sphere = Volume of small sphere

$$\frac{4}{3}\pi R^3 = n \times \frac{4}{3}\pi r^3$$

$$\Rightarrow \frac{4}{3}\pi \times 6 \times 6 \times 6 = n \times \frac{4}{3} \times \pi \times 3 \times 3 \times 3$$

$$\Rightarrow n = \frac{\frac{4}{3} \times \pi \times 6 \times 6 \times 6}{\frac{4}{3}\pi \times 3 \times 3 \times 3}$$

$$\Rightarrow n = 2 \times 2 \times 2 = 8$$

$\therefore$ Required number of small sphere $= 8$

59. *(c)* Production growth in June as compared to previous one

$$= \frac{350 - 252}{252} \times 100 = 38.88\%$$

Production growth in October

$$= \frac{650 - 525}{525} \times 100 = \frac{125}{525} \times 100 = 23.80\%$$

Production growth in July

$$= \frac{380 - 350}{350} \times 100 = \frac{30}{350} \times 100 = 8.57\%$$

Production growth in September

$$= \frac{525 - 425}{425} \times 100 = 23.52\%$$

Thus, highest production occurred in June month.

60. *(d)* $\dfrac{\left[\frac{1}{4} \div \frac{1}{4} \times \frac{1}{4}\right] \times \frac{1}{4}}{\left[\frac{1}{8} + \frac{1}{8} \times \frac{1}{8}\right]} + \left(1 - \frac{4}{9}\right)$

$$= \frac{\left[\frac{1}{4} \times \frac{4}{1} \times \frac{1}{4}\right] \times \frac{1}{4}}{\frac{1}{8} + \frac{1}{64}} + \frac{5}{9}$$

$$= \frac{\frac{1}{4} \times \frac{1}{4}}{\frac{9}{64}} + \frac{5}{9} = \frac{1}{16} \times \frac{64}{9} + \frac{5}{9}$$

$$= \frac{4}{9} + \frac{5}{9} = \frac{9}{9} = 1$$

61. *(c)* $MN \parallel RQ$

and area of ΔPMN = area of $\square MNRQ$

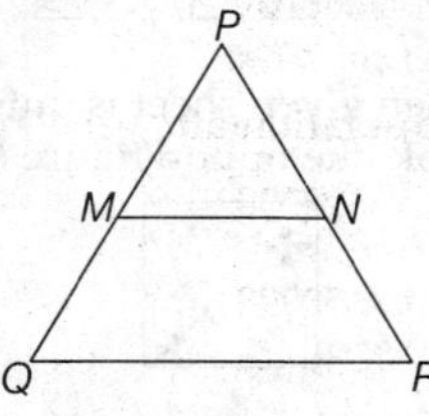

Area of both parts are equal.

Thus, $\dfrac{\text{area of } \Delta PMN}{\text{area of } \Delta PQR} = \dfrac{1}{2}$

$$= \frac{(\text{side of } \Delta PMN)^2}{(\text{side of } \Delta PQR)^2}$$

$$\left(\frac{PM}{PQ}\right)^2 = \frac{1}{2}$$

[$\because \Delta PMN$ is similar to ΔPQR]

$$\frac{PM}{PQ} = \frac{1}{\sqrt{2}}$$

Thus, $MQ = \sqrt{2} - 1$

and $PQ = \sqrt{2}$

$\therefore$ Required ratio $= \dfrac{MQ}{PQ} = \dfrac{\sqrt{2} - 1}{\sqrt{2}}$

62. *(b)* In ΔPQR,

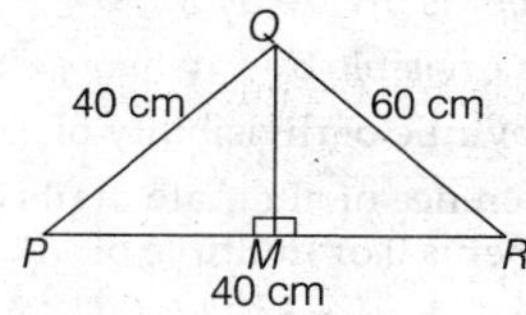

By Heron's formula,

$$s = \frac{a + b + c}{2} = \frac{40 + 40 + 60}{2} = 70 \text{ cm}$$

Area of $\Delta PQR = \sqrt{s(s-a)(s-b)(s-c)}$

$$= \sqrt{70 \times 30 \times 30 \times 10}$$

Area of $\Delta PQR = 30 \times 10 \times \sqrt{7} = 300\sqrt{7}$

Again,

Area of ΔPQR taking PR as base.

Then, $\dfrac{1}{2} \times PR \times QM = 300\sqrt{7}$

$$\Rightarrow \frac{1}{2} \times 40 \times QM = 300\sqrt{7}$$

$$\Rightarrow QM = \frac{300\sqrt{7}}{40} \times 2$$

$$\therefore QM = 15\sqrt{7} \text{ cm}$$

Hence, required altitude $= 15\sqrt{7}$ cm

63. *(a)* Marks obtained by Riya in IP $= 150$

Thus, percentage

$$= \frac{150}{180} \times 100 = 83.33\%$$

Marks obtained by Rida in IP $= 130$

Thus, percentage

$$= \frac{130}{180} \times 100 = 72.22\%$$

$\therefore$ Required difference of percentage

$$= (83.33 - 72.33)\% = 11.11\%$$

64. *(a)* Ratio of efficiency of Nirmal and Amit

$$N : A$$

$$100 : 100 \times \frac{125}{100}$$

Efficiency $= 4 : 5$

Thus, total work done by Nirmal

$$= 45 \text{ days} \times 4 = 180 \text{ units}$$

Time taken by Amit to do complete work $= \dfrac{180}{5} = 36$ days

65. *(b)* Speed of policeman $= 65$ km/h

Speed of thief $= 41$ km/h

Distance between police and thief

$$= 1200 \text{ m}$$

Relative speed of policeman and thief

$$= 65 - 41 = 24 \text{ km/h}$$

$\therefore$ Required time to catch thief by police

$$= \frac{12}{24} \quad [1200 \text{ m} = 1.2 \text{ km}]$$

$$= \frac{1}{20} \text{ h} = \frac{1}{20} \times 60 \text{ min} = 3 \text{ min}$$

66. *(c)* Let the cost price of 100 gm goods be ₹ $100x$.

But, he sold at 40% loss.

and he sales at $100x \times \dfrac{60}{100} =$ ₹ $60x$

and he uses 25% less weight.

Thus, selling price of 75 gm of goods = ₹ $60x$

Selling price of 100 gm of goods

$$= \frac{60x}{75} \times 100 = ₹\ 80x$$

Thus, loss percentage

$$= \frac{100x - 80x}{100x} \times 100 = 20\%$$

67. *(c)* Selling price of charger = ₹ 2540 in cash

Down payment = ₹ 1340

Amount after down payment

= 2540 − 1340 = ₹ 1200

But, he paid ₹ 1205 after one month.

Let rate of interest be $r\%$.

Then,

$$SI = \frac{P \times R \times T}{100}$$

$$1205 - 1200 = 1200 \times \frac{R \times 1}{12 \times 100}$$

$$\Rightarrow 5\% = R$$

Thus, rate of interest is 5%.

68. *(b)* Given,

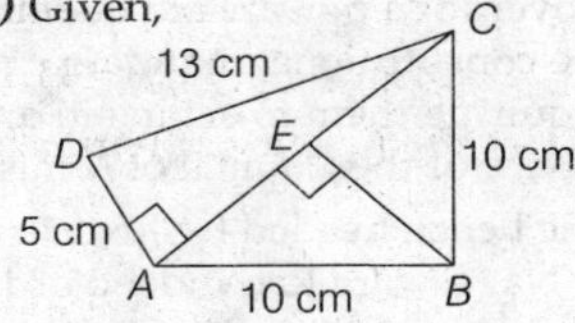

Here,

$AD = 5$ cm, $DC = 13$ cm

$AB = 10$ cm, $CB = 10$ cm

ΔADC is right-angled triangle

$AC^2 = 13^2 - 5^2$ [∵ By Pythagoras theorem]

$AC = 12$ cm

Now,

Area of $\Delta CAD = \frac{1}{2} \times \text{Base} \times \text{Altitude}$

$= \frac{1}{2} \times 5 \times 12$

$= 30 \text{ cm}^2$ ...(i)

Again in ΔABC,

Semi-perimeter of ΔABC

$s = \frac{10 + 10 + 12}{2} = 16$ cm

Area of ΔABC

$= \sqrt{s \times (s-a)(s-b)(s-c)}$

$= \sqrt{16 \times 6 \times 6 \times 4}$

$= 4 \times 6 \times 2$

$= 48 \text{ cm}^2$

Thus, total area of quadrilateral $ABCD$

$= 30 + 48 = 78 \text{ cm}^2$

69. *(a)* Marks obtained by Rohan, Sohan and Mohan in History are 77, 80 and 83, respectively.

Average marks of students in History

$= \frac{77 + 80 + 83}{3} = \frac{240}{3} = 80$

and marks obtained by Rohan, Sohan and Mohan in Economics are 74, 82 and 86, respectively.

Average marks of students in Economics

$= \frac{74 + 82 + 86}{3}$

$= \frac{242}{3} = 80.66 \approx 81$

Thus, average are 80 and 81 in History and Economics.

70. *(b)* In 2019,

Total disbursement of loans of Bank A and Bank B

$= 22 + 18 = 40$ cr

and total disbursement of loans of Bank C and Bank D $= 20 + 20 = 40$ cr

Thus, both are equal.

71. *(b)* Current population of the city was 400000.

First increased by 20% and then increased by 30%.

Thus, population after one yr

$= 400000 \times \frac{120}{100}$

$= 480000$

Again, population after 2 yr

$= 480000 \times \frac{130}{100} = 624000$

Hence, required population

$= 624000$

72. *(b)* Length of cuboid shaped cardboard = 60 cm

Breadth of cardboard $= \frac{60}{2} = 30$ cm

Height of cardboard $= 30 \times \frac{1}{3} = 10$ cm

Thus, surface area of cardboard

$= 2(lb + bh + hl)$

$= 2(60 \times 30 + 30 \times 10 + 10 \times 60)$

$= 2(1800 + 300 + 600)$

$= 2(2700) = 5400 \text{ cm}^2$

73. *(d)* Let the age of Rubi and Soni are $11x$ and $5x$.

According to the question,

$\frac{11x + 5x}{2} = 40$

$\Rightarrow \frac{16x}{2} = 40$

$\Rightarrow 8x = 40 \Rightarrow x = 5$

Thus, age of Soni $= 5x = 5 \times 5 = 25$ yr

74. *(d)* Let the distance be d km and speed be s km/h and time is 't' h.

Initial speed $= \frac{d}{t}$

$s = \frac{d}{t}$ km/h

Again, after time reduce by 25%.

New time $= t \times \frac{75}{100} = \frac{3}{4}t$

New speed $(s') = \frac{d}{\frac{3}{4}t} = \frac{4d}{3t}$

Required percentage increase in speed

$= \frac{\frac{4}{3}\frac{d}{t} - \frac{d}{t}}{\frac{d}{t}} \times 100$

$= \frac{\frac{1}{3}\frac{d}{t}}{\frac{d}{t}} \times 100$

$= \frac{1}{3} \times 100 = 33\frac{1}{3}\%$

75. *(c)* Let ΔABC be an equilateral triangle.

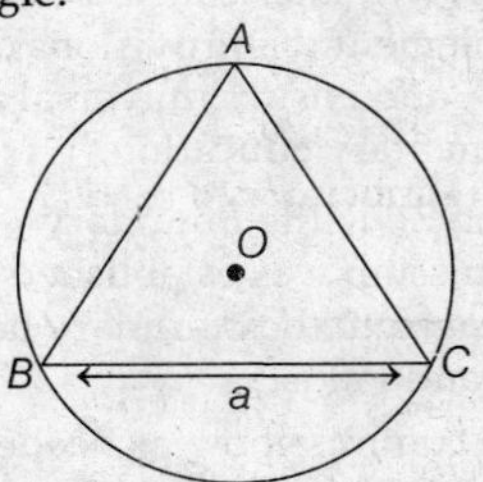

Let side of equilateral triangle be a m and radius of circle be r.

Then, we know that,

Radius of circle circumscribing an equilateral triangle,

$r = \frac{a}{\sqrt{3}}$

Thus, $a = \sqrt{3} \times \text{radius of circle}$

$a = \sqrt{3} \times r$

76. *(d)* On 11th August, 2021, the General Insurance Business (Nationalisation) Amendment Bill, 2021 was passed by the Parliament and it amended the General Insurance Business (Nationalisation) Act, 1972.

- The General Insurance Business (Nationalisation) Act, 1972, was enacted on 20th September, 1972.
- The 2021 Amendment Bill aimed to increase the maximum foreign investment allowed in Indian insurance companies from 49% to 74%.

77. *(a)* Eknath Shinde was named as the new Shiv Sena President at the party national executive meeting in Mumbai in 2023.

- Eknath Shinde is the current Chief Minister of Maharashtra, heading a coalition government with the Bharatiya Janata Party (BJP).
- The Shiv Sena Party was founded by Bal Thackeray in 1966, and Uddhav Thackeray took over as President after his father's death in 2012.

78. *(c)* The Parliament of India has passed the 86th Constitutional Amendment Act 2002, which establishes the basic rights of primary education for children between 6-14 years.

- Article 21 A states that "the state shall provide free and compulsory education to all children of the age of six to fourteen years in such manner as the state may, by law, determine".

- The Right to Education (RTE) Act, 2009, was later enacted to implement the provisions of Article 21 A and ensure universal access to elementary education.

79. *(a)* The Radcliffe Boundary Commission was established in 1947 to demarcate the boundary between India and Pakistan.

- The commission was headed by Sir Cyril Radcliffe, a British lawyer and judge. The commission's task was to divide the provinces of Punjab and Bengal between India and Pakistan, based on the principle of separating Muslim-majority areas from Hindu-majority areas.
- It was named after Sir Cyril Radcliffe, was announced on 17th August, 1947.

80. *(b)* In Darbhanga Gharana, they used to sing the Khandhar Vani and Gauhar Vani.

- They emphasise on the raga alap as well as composed songs over an improvised alap.
- Khandhar Vani and Gauhar Vani are styles of Dhrupad singing.
- Prominent singers of this Gharana are Kchitpal Mallick, Pt. Nehal Mallick (Veena), Pt. Rajitram Mallick, Pt. Vishnudev Pathak.

81. *(c)* Delhi ridge is the water divide between Ganges and Indus rivers.

- In Delhi, the spurs of the Aravallis are commonly called as the Delhi Ridge which is divided into the Northern, Central, South-Central and Southern Ridge.
- It is believed that the Aravallis are one of the oldest mountain ranges in India which evolved around 2.5 billion years ago in the Archaeozoic times.

82. *(c)* The slide number can be added to each slide of the MS PowerPoint presentation from Footer.

83. *(c)* Given option (c) most accurately describes the Cyclostomata group.

- All living members of Cyclostomata are ectoparasites on some fishes.
- They have an elongated body bearing 6-15 pairs of gill slits.
- They have a sucking and circular mouth without jaws.

84. *(b)* Both (1) and (2) are correct.

The objectives of Fiscal Policy are

- **Boost Economic Growth** Fiscal policy aims to stimulate economic activity during periods of slow growth or recession by increasing government spending or cutting taxes.
- **Control Inflation** Fiscal Policy also aims to control inflation by reducing government spending or increasing taxes to reduce aggregate demand and curb rising prices.

85. *(c)* The Fundamental Duties of citizens were added to the Constitution by the 42nd Amendment in 1976.

- The 42nd Amendment of Indian Constitution is also known as the Mini Constitution.
- It added 10 Fundamental Duties to the Indian Constitution.

86. *(d)* Swami Vivekananda (1863-1902) is best known in the United States for his groundbreaking speech to the 1893 World's Parliament of Religions.

- He introduced Hinduism to America and called for religious tolerance and an end to fanaticism.
- He was the chief disciple of the 19th-century mystic Ramakrishna Paramhans.
- On 1st May, 1897 in Calcutta, Vivekananda founded the Ramakrishna Mission for social service.

87. *(a)* India win its last Olympic medal in men's hockey at the 2020 Summer Olympics in Tokyo.

- The Indian men's hockey team won the bronze medal by defeating Germany (5-4).
- This was India's first Olympic medal in men's hockey since the 1980 Moscow Olympics, where they won the gold medal.
- India was the first non-European team to be a part of the International Hockey Federation.
- In 1928, the team won its first Olympic gold medal and until 1960, the Indian men's team remained unbeaten in the Olympics, winning six gold medals in a row.

88. *(b)* The statements (1) and (2) are true with respect to Supreme Court Observation in AG Perarivalan v/s The State of Tamil Nadu State.

- The Supreme Court's observation in AG Perarivalan v/s The State of Tamil Nadu (2021) states that the Governor's powers are qualified by the constitutional mandate, chiefly requiring them to act in aid and advice of the Council of Ministers.
- The bench headed by Justice L. Nageswara Rao indeed ordered the release of AG Perarivalan, one of the convicts in the Rajiv Gandhi assassination case, citing the Governor's delay in deciding on his pardon plea.
- Statement (3) is not true as the court did not explicitly state that there are three sources of power-Governor, Council of Ministers and the Constitution.

89. *(a)* Black is not the colour of warning card in Kabaddi.

- **Green Card** As an initial warning.
- **Yellow Card** Two minutes' suspension from the game along with one technical point to the opponent team.
- **Red Card** One technical point to the team along with the suspension from the match. The team who has lost the player has to continue the match with the remaining number.

90. *(d)* Articles 344(1) and 351 of the Constitution of India are related to the Eighth Schedule, which deals with the recognition of languages in the Constitution.

- Article 344(1) provides for the recognition of languages in the Eighth Schedule.
- Article 351 directs the Union to promote the spread of the Hindi language and secure its enrichment.
- The Eighth Schedule to the Constitution consists of the following 27 languages.
- Assamese, Bengali, Gujarati, Hindi, Kannada, Kashmiri, Konkani, Malayalam, Manipuri, Marathi, Nepali, Oriya, Punjabi, Sanskrit, Sindhi, Tamil, Telugu, Urdu, Bodo, Santhali, Maithili and Dogri.

91. *(a)* Aurangzeb (the sixth Mughal emperor) was responsible for the execution of Guru Tegh Bahadur, the ninth Sikh Guru, in 1675.

- Guru Tegh Bahadur was arrested and executed on 11th November, 1675, in Chandni Chowk, Delhi, on charges of blasphemy and refusal to convert to Islam.
- Guru Tegh Bahadur was the ninth Sikh Guru, often venerated as the

'Protector of Humanity' (Srisht-di-Chadar) by the Sikhs.

- The ninth of the 10 Gurus of the Sikh religion was Guru Tegh Bahadur, revered as the Ninth Nanak.

92. *(b)* The correct matching is A-2, B-1, C-4 and D-3.

- Telugu is the official language of the Indian states of Andhra Pradesh and Telangana.
- Malayalam is the official language of the state of Kerala and the union territory of Lakshadweep.
- Kannada has been declared as official language of the Karnataka State.
- The Goa, Daman and Diu Official Language Act, 1987 makes Konkani the sole official language of Goa.
- The 8th Schedule of the Indian Constitution deals with the official languages in India. 22 official languages have been mentioned in the Indian Constitution.

93. *(a)* Uranium - 235 is used as fuel in nuclear power plants for generating electricity because it can undergo induced fission, where its nucleus splits after absorbing a neutron, releasing a significant amount of energy (about 200 MeV) and generating more neutrons to continue the process.

94. *(a)* Rashtriya Khel Protsahan Puruskar does not include a cash reward. It is awarded annually by the Ministry of Youth Affairs and Sports.

- The Khel Ratna was established in 1991-92 as the Rajiv Gandhi Khel Ratna Award but later it was renamed to Major Dhyan Chand Khel Ratna Award in 2021. The award consists of a medallion, a certificate, and a cash prize of ₹ 25 lakh.
- The Maulana Abul Kalam Azad Trophy, abbreviated as MAKA Trophy, is a sports honour of the Republic of India. The award consists a rolling MAKA Trophy and a cash prize of ₹ 15 lakh.
- Dronacharya Award is given to coaches for producing medal winners at prestigious international events. The award comprises a bronze statuette of Dronacharya, a certificate, ceremonial dress and a cash prize of ₹ 15 lakh.

95. *(d)* Diwali is commonly known as the 'Festival of Lights'. The festival symbolises the triumph of light over darkness, good over evil and knowledge over ignorance.

- Holi is a festival of colours, celebrated with coloured powders and waters.
- Onam is a harvest festival celebrated in Kerala, marked by boat races, flower arrangements and traditional dances.
- Bihu is a harvest festival celebrated in Assam, marked by traditional dances, music and feasting.

96. *(d)* The famous folk music of Rajasthan that was developed in royal courts is known as Maand. Some examples of traditional folk music in Rajasthan are Panihaari, Pabuji Ki Panch among others.

- Dandiya Raas is the socio-religious folk dance originating from Indian state of Gujarat and popularly performed in the festival of Navaratri.
- Sohar is mainly a folk song of Uttar Pradesh and Bihar.
- Lavani dance originated from Maharashtra in the 18th and 19th century.

97. *(a)* The Howrah Bridge was officially inaugurated on 3rd February, 1943.

- Howrah Bridge was the third-longest cantilever bridge (now sixth) in the world.
- It is also known as Rabindra Setu, it connects Howrah and Kolkata.

98. *(a)* The Statement (a) is true about planet Saturn because satellite like Enceladus and Titan of Saturn are home to internal ocean and could possibly support life.

Saturn is a massive ball made up of hydrogen and helium.

99. *(b)* The Lucknow Gharana of Kathak dance was founded by Shri Ishwari Prasad. He was a devotee of the Bhakti Movement who lived in Prayagraj (Allahabad).

- Kathak is put under three Gharanas– Lucknow is one of the main Gharanas while the others are Varanasi, Jaipur and Raigarh.
- The Lucknow Gharana, also known as 'Purab Gharana' for tabla.

100. *(b)* In Microsoft Office, 'points' is the font size determined.

Set 34 11 July, 2024 (Shift II)

SSC CHSL Tier-I
SOLVED PAPER

Instructions

1. This paper contains 100 questions.
2. It has 4 Parts, **Part I** General English, **Part II** General Intelligence & Reasoning, **Part III** Quantitative Aptitude and **Part IV** General Awareness.
3. Each question carries **2 marks.**

Part I
General English

1. The following sentence has been split into four segments. Identify the segment that contains a grammatical error.

It is his job / to chase out / clients with / outstanding debts.

(a) clients with
(b) to chase out
(c) outstanding debts
(d) It is his job

2. Parts of the following sentence have been given as options. Select the option that contains an error.

Mumbai is the city of dreams but it is a expensive city too.

(a) a expensive city too
(b) but it is
(c) Mumbai is the
(d) city of dreams

3. Select the most appropriate option to fill in the blanks.

(ϕ = No article)

.... road to Taj Mahal passes through ...... forest.

(a) A; the
(b) ϕ; ϕ
(c) The; a
(d) A; a

4. The given sentence is divided into four segments. Select the option that has the segment with a grammatical error.

He do not / fear the / repercussions of / this decision.

(a) repercussions of
(b) this decision
(c) He do not
(d) fear the

Directions (Q. Nos. 5-9) *In the following passage, some words have been deleted. Read the passage carefully and select the most appropriate option to fill in each blank.*

When Prime Minister Narendra Modi announced that rupees with the denominations of 500/- and 1000/- would (1)........... to be the legal tender from the 9th of November, the whole country was stunned. This decision caused a sensation in the whole country. Social media was flooded with messages and information. People started counting the cash they had (2)........... for years legally or illegally. The main objective of this move was to curb black money, corruption and fake money menace. All the people but those who indulged in (3)........... welcomed the move. The whole opposition shook hands against this move under one pretence or the other.

They called this decision a (4)........... law and wanted the government to roll it back. Severe criticisms were made to target the decision. The government also carried out (5)............ attacks.

5. Select the most appropriate option to fill in blank no. (1).

(a) collaborate (b) seize
(c) cease (d) unify

6. Select the most appropriate option to fill in blank no. (2).

(a) dispersed
(b) distributed
(c) accumulated
(d) withdrawn

7. Select the most appropriate option to fill in blank no. (3).

(a) amalgamation
(b) indecision
(c) malpractices
(d) announcement

8. Select the most appropriate option to fill in blank no. (4).

(a) like (b) draconian
(c) comprehensive (d) fragile

9. Select the most appropriate option to fill in blank no. (5).

(a) ineffectual (b) revengeful
(c) case (d) example

10. Select the most appropriate idiom that can substitute the underlined word segment in the given sentence.

I know Covid has made you terribly ill, but <u>the good thing</u> is that you have developed immunity against it for further infections.

(a) the silver spoon
(b) the silver lining in the cloud
(c) being in the quicksilver
(d) crossing palms with silver

11. Select the incorrectly spelt word.

(a) Psychometric (b) Concentrate
(c) Vindication (d) Conglomirate

12. Select the most appropriate option that can substitute the underlined segment in the given sentence.

<u>At his wit's end</u>, he decided to return to his parents as he was unable to cope with the stress of adjusting at a new place.

(a) Not knowing what to do
(b) Taking all notes
(c) After thinking
(d) Deciding after contemplation

13. Select the most appropriate option that can substitute the underlined segment in the following sentence.

He passed away <u>in the year 1950 at 10 a.m. on 13 July</u>.

(a) in the year 1950 at 10 a.m. on 13 July
(b) at 10 a.m. on 13 July in the year 1950

(c) on 13 July at 10 a.m. in the year 1950
(d) in the year 1950 on 13 July at 10 a.m.

14. Select the most appropriate homophones to fill in the blanks.
Her father .... her to opt for a chemistry .... in her final year.
(a) aloud; course
(b) aloud; coarse
(c) allowed; coarse
(d) allowed; course

15. Select the most appropriate synonym of the given word.
Perilous
(a) Dangerous (b) Ugly
(c) Bad (d) Adverse

16. Select the most appropriate homonym to fill in the blank.
Please .... more sugar to the juice so that it becomes sweeter.
(a) ad (b) add (c) aide (d) aid

17. Select the most appropriate option that can substitute the underlined segment in the given sentence.
The meeting <u>closed</u> with a vote of thanks.
(a) completed (b) finished
(c) stopped (d) concluded

18. Select the most appropriate option that can substitute the underlined segment in the given sentence.
I was in Oman <u>around</u> two months.
(a) from (b) for
(c) into (d) since

19. Select the correct collocation to complete the following sentence.
She suppressed a .... urge to yawn.
(a) tough (b) stout
(c) hard (d) strong

20. Select the most appropriate antonym of the given word.
Precarious
(a) Luminous (b) Reliable
(c) Colossal (d) Doubtful

21. Select the most appropriate meaning of the given idiom.
Out of the frying pan and into the fire
(a) Things getting intense by the hour
(b) Being a horrible cook
(c) Being with someone through good times as well as bad times
(d) Things going from bad to worse

22. Select the most appropriate antonym of the underlined word in the given sentence.
The vendor said that the apples were of <u>superior</u> quality.
(a) excellent (b) inferior
(c) small (d) distasteful

23. Select the most appropriate synonym of the given word.
Advanced
(a) Foreign (b) Progressive
(c) Discarded (d) Elementary

24. Select the most appropriate synonym of the underlined word.
My grandmother is fond of giving <u>homilies</u> to all my friends who visit my place.
(a) suggestions (b) sermons
(c) alternatives (d) strictures

25. Select the correctly spelt word.
(a) Immediately (b) Immedeatly
(c) Imediately (d) Immidiately

Part II
General Intelligence

26. Select the letter-cluster from among the given options that can replace the question mark (?) in the following series.
EFG, KLM, QRS, ?
(a) WXZ (b) XYZ
(c) WXY (d) UVW

27. In a certain code language, '78623' is coded as 'TAKEN' and '32685' is coded as 'TOKEN'. What is the code for '5' in that language ?
(a) E (b) A (c) O (d) T

28. Three of the following four are alike in a certain way and thus form a group. Which is the one that does not belong to that group?
(**Note** The odd one out is not based on the number of consonants/vowels or their position in the letter cluster.)
(a) QSV (b) LNP
(c) BDG (d) FHK

29. Three statements are followed by conclusions numbered I and II. You have to consider these statements to be true, even if they seem to be at variance with commonly known facts. Decide which of the given conclusions logically follow(s) from the given statements.

Statements
Some tables are gates.
All mats are tables.
All plates are gates.
Conclusions
I. All gates are mats.
II. All tables are plates.
(a) Both Conclusions I and II follow
(b) Only Conclusion II follows
(c) Only Conclusion I follows
(d) Neither Conclusion I nor II follows.

30. Six numbers 1, 2, 4, 5, 7 and 9 are written on different faces of a dice. Two positions of this dice are shown in the figure. Which is the number on the face opposite to the face containing 9 ?

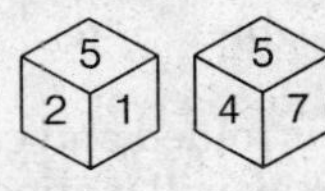

(a) 1 (b) 7
(c) 2 (d) 5

31. If 'A' stands for '÷', 'B' stands for '×', 'C' stands for '+' and 'D' stands for '–', what will come in place of the question mark (?) in the following equation ?
128 A 4 C 16 B 7 D 5 = ?
(a) 129 (b) 159
(c) 139 (d) 149

32. In a certain code language, 'YOUR' is coded as '5627' and 'CROY' is coded as '2769'. What is the code for 'C' in the given code language?
(a) 9 (b) 2
(c) 6 (d) 7

33. What will come in the place of the question mark (?) in the following equation, if '+' and '–' are interchanged and '×' and '÷' are interchanged ?
$10 - 12 \div 7 + 84 \times 21 = ?$
(a) 95 (b) 85
(c) 93 (d) 90

34. If 19th July, 2000 is Wednesday, then what will be the day of the week on 14th June, 2009?
(a) Friday (b) Sunday
(c) Tuesday (d) Thursday

35. Six letters D, H, K, L, R and Y are written on different faces of a dice. Two positions of this dice are shown in the figure. Which is the letter on the face opposite to the face containing H ?

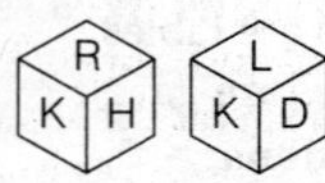

(a) K (b) L
(c) D (d) Y

36. The sequence of folding a piece of paper and the manner in which the folded paper is punched is shown in the following figures. How would this paper look when unfolded?

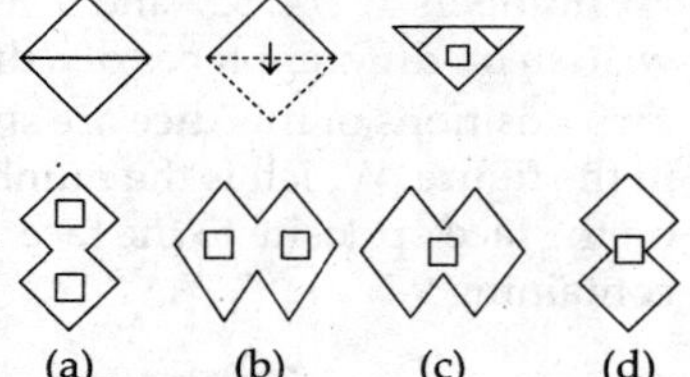

(a) (b) (c) (d)

37. A paper is folded and cut as shown below. How will it appear when unfolded?

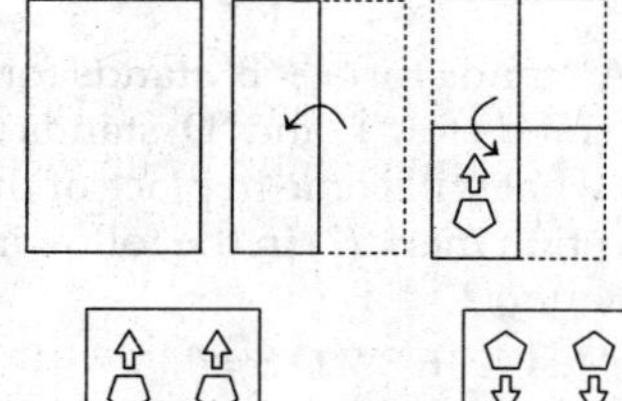

(a) 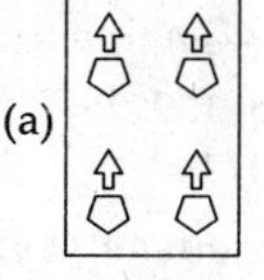 (b) 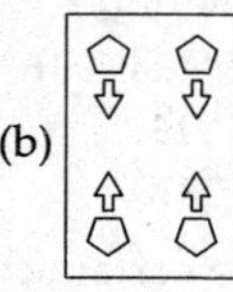

(c) 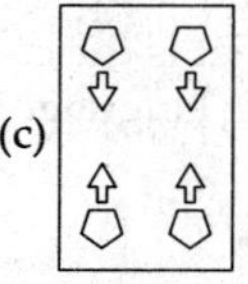 (d) 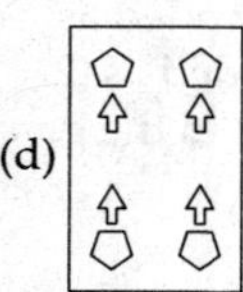

38. What should come in place of '?' in the given series based on the English alphabetical order ?
RKD, ?, ZUP, QMI, HEB
(a) ZYZ (b) ICW
(c) WCI (d) ABC

39. Select the set in which the numbers are related in the same way as are the numbers of the following sets.
(**Note** Operations should be performed on the whole numbers, without breaking down the numbers into its constituent digits. E.g. 13–Operations on 13 such as adding /subtracting/multiplying etc. to 13 can be performed. Breaking down 13 into 1 and 3 and then performing mathematical operations on 1 and 3 is not allowed)
(81, 53, 70)
(94, 66, 83)
(a) (68, 40, 67) (b) (77, 59, 76)
(c) (99, 71, 88) (d) (86, 58, 65)

40. Which of the following numbers will replace the question mark (?) in the given series?
19, ?, 43, 55, 67
(a) 33 (b) 34 (c) 31 (d) 41

41. What will come in the place of the question mark (?) in the following equation, if '+' and ÷' are interchanged and '−' and '×' are interchanged ?
$28 \div 90 + 6 - 5 \times 17 = ?$
(a) 84 (b) 82 (c) 80 (d) 86

42. What should come in place of '?' in the given series ?
131, 141, 161, 191, 231, ?
(a) 271 (b) 291
(c) 281 (d) 261

43. 38 is related to 80 following a certain logic. Following the same logic, 42 is related to 88. To which of the following is 29 related, following the same logic?
(a) 78 (b) 66
(c) 54 (d) 62

44. If 2nd August, 2016 is a Tuesday, then what will the day of the week on 19th October, 2020?
(a) Saturday (b) Wednesday
(c) Monday (d) Thursday

45. Select the option that is embedded in the given figure (rotation in not allowed).

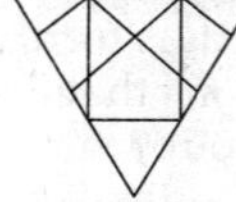

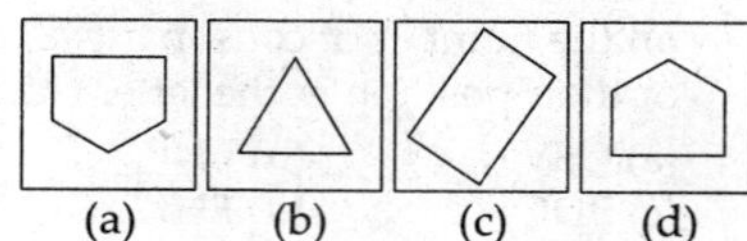

(a) (b) (c) (d)

46. In a certain code language,
'M & N' means 'M is the wife of N',
'M @ N' means 'M is the brother of N',
'M $ N' means 'M is the mother of N',
'M # N' means 'M is the sister of N'.
Based on this, how is Q related to U, if 'P & Q @ R $ T # U'?
(a) Mother's brother
(b) Father
(c) Brother
(d) Father's brother

47. Select the pair which follows the same pattern as that followed by the two set of pairs given below. Both pairs follow the same pattern.
FJM : UQN
DPQ : WKJ
(a) MNO : ONM
(b) IEB : ACK
(c) OVC : LEX
(d) LHE : VUT

48. MAZQ is related to GUTK in a certain way based on the English alphabetical order. In the same way, CPNR is related to WJHL. To which of the following is KOEV related, following the same logic?
(a) EYIP (b) EIYP
(c) EYPI (d) EIPY

49. What is the maximum number of rectangles in the given figure?

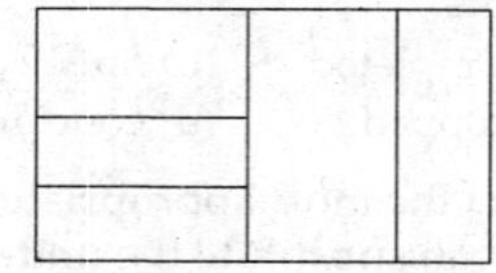

(a) 12 (b) 9
(c) 8 (d) 10

50. Which figure should replace the question mark (?), if the following figure series were to be continued ?

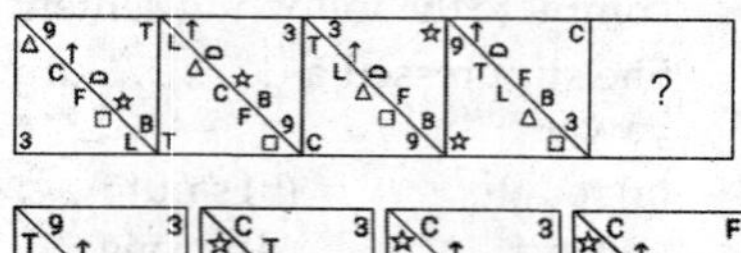

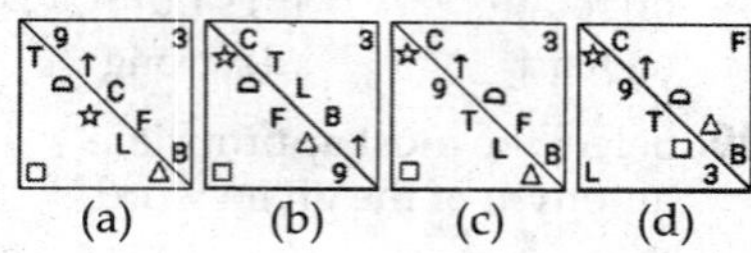

(a) (b) (c) (d)

Part III
Quantitative Aptitude

51. The measure of each side of an equilateral triangle is 16 cm. What is the ratio of its perimeter to the sum of its medians ?
(a) $\sqrt{3} : 2$ (b) $1 : 2\sqrt{3}$
(c) $2\sqrt{3} : 1$ (d) $2 : \sqrt{3}$

52. Study the given pie-chart and answer the question that follows.
The pie-chart represents the total number of valid votes obtained by four students who contested for school leadership. The total number of valid votes polled was 720.

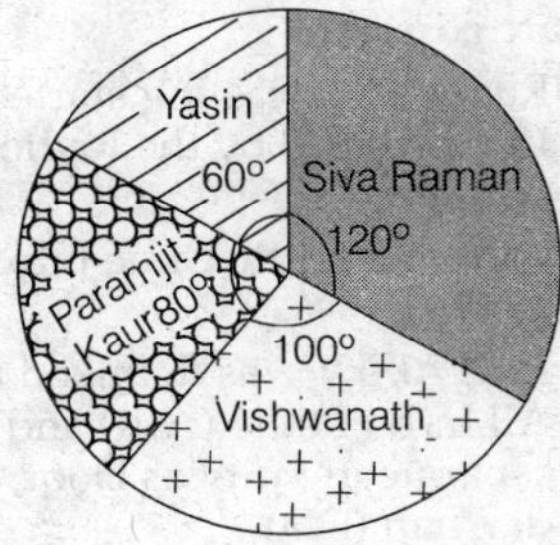

By how many votes did the winner defeat the nearest contestant?
(a) 30 (b) 40 (c) 20 (d) 10

53. In an election, there were only two candidates. One of the candidates secured 44% of the votes and is defeated by the other candidate by 1440 votes. If there were no invalid votes, then the total number of votes polled is
(a) 15000 (b) 12000 (c) 14000 (d) 13000

54. Pomegranate juice contains 10% sugar solution and orange juice contains 30% sugar solution. What is the percentage of sugar solution in a mixture of two litres of pomegranate juice and three litres of orange juice?
(a) 22% (b) 25% (c) 20% (d) 40%

55. Three cubes each of side 5 cm are joined end to end. The surface area of the resulting cuboid is
(a) 150 cm^2 (b) 175 cm^2
(c) 350 cm^2 (d) 75 cm^2

56. A vertical pole of length 6 m casts a 4 m long shadow on the ground. At the same time, a tower casts a 28 m long shadow. Find the height of the tower.
(a) 42 m (b) 32 m (c) 36 m (d) 48 m

57. The sum of the digits of a two-digit number is 9. The number obtained by interchanging its digits exceeds the given number by 45, then the original number is
(a) 18 (b) 27 (c) 36 (d) 54

58. In $\Delta DEW, AB \parallel EW$. If $AD = 4$ cm, $DE = 12$ cm and $DW = 24$ cm, then find the length of DB.
(a) 7 cm (b) 6 cm (c) 9 cm (d) 8 cm

59. What is the value of $\cos^{-1}\left(\frac{7}{25}\right) - \cos^{-1}\left(\frac{15}{17}\right)$?
(a) $\sin^{-1}\left(\frac{304}{425}\right)$ (b) $\cot^{-1}\left(\frac{297}{425}\right)$
(c) $\tan^{-1}\left(\frac{297}{425}\right)$ (d) $\cos^{-1}\left(\frac{304}{425}\right)$

60. A hemispherical bowl is made of silver and has an inner diameter of 4 cm, if the thickness of silver is 0.5 cm. Find the volume of silver used in making the bowl correct to two places of decimals (use $\pi = 3.14$)
(a) 15.96 cm^3 (b) 51.96 cm^3
(c) 15.69 cm^3 (d) 51.69 cm^3

61. In an election between two candidates, 30% voters did not cast their votes and 200 votes were declared invalid. The winner got 65% of the valid votes. If he won by 1200 votes, then find the total votes.
(a) 9000 (b) 6000 (c) 7000 (d) 8000

62. Which of the following is not true regarding a circle?
(a) The largest chord in a circle has a length twice its radius
(b) Given any three points in a plane, there is always a circle passing through these points
(c) The ratio of the perimeter and radius of a circle is always constant
(d) A triangle with vertices on a circle and one side as its diameter is a right-angled triangle

63. A and B are two stations 420 km apart. A train starts from A at 11 am and travels towards B at the speed of 70 km/h. Another train starts from B at 12 noon and travels towards A at the speed of 30 km/h. At what time do they meet?
(a) 2 pm (b) 1 : 30 pm
(c) 3 : 30 pm (d) 3 pm

64. Mira can complete a piece of work in 20 days, Nina in 30 days and Sima in 40 days. Mira and Sima worked together for 4 days and then Mira was replaced by Nina. In how many days, altogether, was the work completed?
(a) 14 (b) 18 (c) 16 (d) 20

65. Divide 25 into two parts such that 6 times of the larger part added to 4 times of the smaller part is equal to 130. Find the larger part.
(a) 20 (b) 14
(c) 13 (d) 15

66. Study the given table and answer the question that follows.
The table shows the results of half-yearly and annual examinations of three sections A, B, C of class X students in a school.

Result	Number of students		
	Section A	Section B	Section C
Students failed in both exams	39	20	12
Students failed in half-yearly but passed in annual exams	16	14	6
Students passed in half-yearly but failed in annual exams	10	12	8
Students passed in both exams	65	45	35

Find the pass percentage of section A in at least one of the two examinations.
(a) 80% (b) 65%
(c) 75% (d) 70%

67. On dividing a certain number by 459, we get 19 as remainder. What will be the remainder, when the same number is divided by 17?
(a) 13 (b) 2 (c) 11 (d) 1

68. What is the value of a so that the seven-digit number $4645a52$ is divisible by 72?
(a) 3 (b) 2 (c) 0 (d) 1

69. The following table shows the number of trees axed in 2016-2020. Study the given information carefully and answer the question that follows.

Year	Neem	Banyan	Teak
2016	15000	20000	25000
2017	18000	28000	28000
2018	22000	32000	32000
2019	25000	35000	35000
2020	28000	38000	38000

What was the percentage increase in the number of banyan trees axed in 2020 compared to the number of banyan trees axed in 2016?
(a) 60% (b) 90%
(c) 47.4% (d) 9%

70. Shyam's income is 20% less than Ram's. How much is Ram's income more than Shyam's in percentage terms?
(a) 80% (b) 30%
(c) 25% (d) 20%

71. A sum of ₹ 5000 was lent to two people, one at the rate of 16% and the other at the rate of 24%. If the simple interest after one year is ₹ 960, what is the sum lent at the higher rate ?
(a) ₹ 1500 (b) ₹ 3000
(c) ₹ 2500 (d) ₹ 2000

72. A shopkeeper sells his goods using weights 27% less than true weights and claims to sell his goods at the cost price. His gain per cent (rounded off to 1 decimal place) is
(a) 47.9% (b) 37.0%
(c) 39.8% (d) 40.0%

73. O is the centre of the circle. Its two chord AB and CD intersect each other at the point P (internally) within the circle. If $AB = 22$ cm, $PB = 14$ cm, $CP = 8$ cm, then find the value of PD.
(a) 14 cm (b) 11 cm (c) 22 cm (d) 12 cm

74. Study the given graph and answer the question that follows.
The graph shows the profit percentage earned by two companies - A and B over a period of six years.

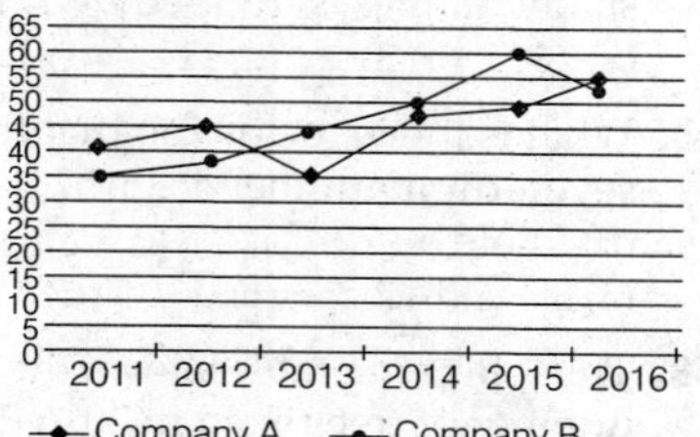

What is the percentage increase in profit percentage of company B in the year 2014 from the previous year ?
(a) 13.63% (b) 7.5%
(c) 5.75% (d) 6.55%

75. If the area of a rhombus is 70 m^2 and its height is 5 m, its perimeter is ....
(a) 56 m (b) 35 m (c) 64 m (d) 25 m

Part IV
General Awareness

76. To which Hindustani music Gharana are the Gundecha brothers related?
(a) Dagari Gharana
(b) Agra Gharana
(c) Patiala Gharana
(d) Indore Gharana

77. When and where did the first Asian Games take place?
(a) 1951, New Delhi
(b) 1982, Punjab
(c) 2014, Maharashtra
(d) 2010, New Delhi

78. The Battle of Khanwa was fought between Babur and ....
(a) Medini Rao
(b) Maharana Pratap
(c) Rana Ratna Singh
(d) Rana Sanga

79. Which of the following pairs of Indian rivers is West flowing?
(a) Mahanadi and Godavari
(b) Krishna and Kaveri
(c) Mahanadi and Krishna
(d) Narmada and Tapi

80. Any citizen of India can make a declaration renouncing his/her Indian citizenship under the ....
(a) Citizenship Act, 1975
(b) Citizenship Act, 1985
(c) Citizenship Act, 1955
(d) Citizenship Act, 1965

81. El Nino is a climate pattern that describes the unusual warming of surface waters in which ocean?
(a) Indian Ocean (b) Atlantic Ocean
(c) Arctic Ocean (d) Pacific Ocean

82. With reference to Chethiagiri Vihar festival, consider the following statements and select the correct option.
1. It is a Buddhist festival.
2. It is held at Sanchi, Madhya Pradesh.
3. Relics of Sari Putta and Maha Moggallana are worshiped.

Codes
(a) 1 and 3 (b) 2 and 3
(c) 1 and 2 (d) 1, 2 and 3

83. Formulas in MS-Excel always start with which of the following symbols?
(a) == (b) – (c) ! (d) =

84. In August 2021, the Administrator of Lakshadweep, Praful Khoda Patel, highlighted that .... style water villas, a project which is a first of its kind, will soon be set up in Lakshadweep, at a cost of ₹ 800 crores, in a bid to attract tourists to scenic beauty of the union territory.
(a) Mexico (b) Maldives
(c) Fiji (d) Malaysia

85. In which year did a trio of scientists, Avery, MacLeod and McCarty, prove that except viruses, all living organisms have DNA as their genetic material?
(a) 1918 (b) 1902 (c) 1944 (d) 1961

86. Which of the following statements is/are correct?
1. Radio broadcasting started in India in 1923 by the Radio Club of Bombay.
2. All India Radio came into being in 1936.
3. In 1976, TV was delinked from All India Radio (AIR) and got a separate identity as Door darshan (DD).

(a) 1, 2 and 3 are correct
(b) Both 1 and 2 are correct.
(c) Both 2 and 3 are correct.
(d) Only 3 is correct.

87. In which year was the Rajiv Gandhi Khel Ratna Award renamed as Major Dhyan Chand Khel Ratna Award, which is the highest sporting honour in the nation?
(a) 2014 (b) 2021
(c) 1991 (d) 2019

88. Which of these is not true for the second phase of the Green Revolution ?
(a) It was adopted by farmers living in dry and semi-arid regions of India.
(b) It covered the period of the 1980s.
(c) It covered the period of the 1960s and 1970s.
(d) It was launched in areas with a significant shift from dry to wet (irrigated) cultivation.

89. Where was the first Durand Cup, India's oldest football tournament, held?
(a) Madras (b) Shimla
(c) Calcutta (d) Delhi

90. The UIDAI is under the jurisdiction of which of the following ministries?
(a) Ministry of Finance
(b) Ministry of Electronics and Information Technology
(c) Ministry of Home Affairs
(d) Ministry of Education

91. In which year was Micro Units Development and Refinance Agency (MUDRA) introduced?
(a) 2017 (b) 2013
(c) 2009 (d) 2015

92. Which shortcut key is used to paste a slide in Microsoft PowerPoint?
(a) CTRL + C (b) CTRL + P
(c) CTRL + V (d) CTRL + X

93. In the Hindustani music system, the .... are allotted to different hours of the day and different seasons.
(a) Gita (b) Varnas
(c) Srutis (d) Ragas

94. Which organisation was started in the Pune district of Maharashtra in the 1870s with the aim of promoting education and social rights among the underprivileged group of the society?
(a) Satyashodhak Samaj
(b) Deepalaya Samaj
(c) Shoshit Seva Samaj
(d) Prarthana Samaj

95. Match the dances in column A with their states in column B.

	Column A (Dances)		Column B (States)
A.	Bharatanatyam	1.	Gujarat
B.	Mohiniyattam	2.	Tamil Nadu
C.	Garba	3.	Kerala
D.	Sattriya	4.	Assam

	A	B	C	D		A	B	C	D
(a)	3	2	1	4	(b)	1	3	2	4
(c)	2	3	4	1	(d)	2	3	1	4

96. Who proposed that 'Light is made up of waves propagating perpendicular to the direction of its movement'?
(a) Newton (b) Huygens
(c) Kepler (d) Pauli

97. Balasaraswati who was regarded as child prodigy by Vidhwans and Pandits played an important role in reviving the dance form ....
(a) Kuchipudi
(b) Mohiniyattam
(c) Bharatanatyam
(d) Kathak

98. Which of the following statements about the Mahila Samman Savings Certificate is incorrect as of 31 March 2024 ?
(a) The tenure of the scheme is 5 years.
(b) The scheme is validup to 31 March 2025.
(c) The scheme was announced in the 2023-24 budget.
(d) The maximum limit of deposit in the scheme is 2 lakhs per year.

99. As per the Economic Survey 2022-23, the Labour Force Participation Rate for males has gone up to .... in 2020-21.
(a) 55.1% (b) 59.3%
(c) 54.2% (d) 57.5%

100. The Indian Constitution borrowed the concept of concurrent list from ....
(a) Australia (b) Germany
(c) USSR (d) Japan

Answers

1. (b)	2. (a)	3. (c)	4. (c)
5. (c)	6. (c)	7. (c)	8. (b)
9. (d)	10. (b)	11. (d)	12. (a)
13. (b)	14 (d)	15. (a)	16. (b)
17. (d)	18. (b)	19. (d)	20. (b)
21. (d)	22. (b)	23. (b)	24. (b)
25. (a)	26. (c)	27. (c)	28. (b)
29. (d)	30. (d)	31. (c)	32. (a)
33. (d)	34. (b)	35. (c)	36. (a)
37. (b)	38. (b)	39. (c)	40. (c)
41. (d)	42. (c)	43. (d)	44. (c)
45. (d)	46. (a)	47. (c)	48. (b)
49. (d)	50. (d)	51. (d)	52. (b)
53. (b)	54. (a)	55. (c)	56. (a)
57. (b)	58. (d)	59. (a)	60. (a)
61. (b)	62. (b)	63. (c)	64. (c)
65. (d)	66. (d)	67. (b)	68. (d)
69. (b)	70. (c)	71. (d)	72. (b)
73. (a)	74. (a)	75. (a)	76. (a)
77. (a)	78. (d)	79. (d)	80. (c)
81. (d)	82. (d)	83. (d)	84. (b)
85. (c)	86. (a)	87. (b)	88. (c)
89. (b)	90. (b)	91. (d)	92. (c)
93. (d)	94. (a)	95. (d)	96. (b)
97. (c)	98. (a)	99. (d)	100. (a)

Explanations

1. *(b)* Part (b) 'to chase out' contains an error. The use of 'chase out' is incorrect in the sentence. Use 'look for' to correct the sentence.

2. *(a)* Part (a) 'a expensive city too' contains an error. Use 'an' to correct the sentence.

3. *(c)* The correct filler for the given blanks are 'the' and 'a'.

4. *(c)* Part (c) 'he do not' contains an error. Use 'does' to correct the sentence. As the subject of the sentence is singular, singular verb should be used.

5. *(c)* The correct filler for the given blank is 'cease'.

6. *(c)* The correct filler for the given blank is 'accumulated'.

7. *(c)* The correct filler for the given blank is 'malpractices'.

8. *(b)* The correct filler for the given blank is 'darconian' which means (of laws or their application) excessively harsh and severe.

9. *(d)* The correct filler for the given blank is 'example'.

10. *(b)* The most appropriate substitute for the underlined words is- the silver lining in the cloud. It means every sad or unpleasant situation has a positive side to it.

11. *(d)* The incorrectly spelt word is 'Conglomirate'. The correct spelling is 'Conglomerate'.

12. *(a)* At his wit's end means completely puzzled and perplexed, not knowing what to do.

13. *(b)* The underlined part of the given sentence contains an error. Use 'at 10 a.m. on 13 July in the year 1950' to correct the sentence.

14. *(d)* The correct filler for the given blanks are 'allowed' and 'course'.

15. *(a)* The underlined word 'Perilous' means 'Dangerous'.
'Adverse' means strict and severe.

16. *(b)* The correct filler for the given blank is 'add'.

17. *(d)* The words 'concluded' and 'closed' are synonymous.

18. *(b)* The underlined part of the given sentence contains an error. Use 'for' to correct the sentence.

19. *(d)* The correct filler for the given blank is 'strong'.

20. *(b)* 'Precarious' means not securely held or in position; dangerously likely to fall or collapse. Hence, its antonym is 'Reliable' which means dependable. 'Luminous' means giving off light; bright or shining.
'Colossal' means huge.

21. *(d)* Out of the frying pan and into the fire means from a bad situation to one that is worse.

22. *(b)* The antonym of 'superior' is 'inferior'.

23. *(b)* Advanced means modern and recently developed. Hence, its synonym is 'Progressive' which means moving forward or onward.

24. *(b)* The word 'homilies' means a religious discourse which is intended primarily for spiritual edification rather than doctrinal instruction. Hence, its synonym is 'sermon' which means the same.

25. *(a)* The correct spelling is 'immediately'.

26. *(c)* The pattern of the series is as follows,

$E \xrightarrow{+6} K \xrightarrow{+6} Q \xrightarrow{+6} \boxed{W}$

$F \xrightarrow{+6} L \xrightarrow{+6} R \xrightarrow{+6} \boxed{X}$

$G \xrightarrow{+6} M \xrightarrow{+6} S \xrightarrow{+6} \boxed{Y}$

27. *(c)* According to the question,

7 8 6 2 3 ⟶ T A K E N

3 2 6 8 5 ⟶ T O K E N

Hence, code for '5' is 'O'.

28. *(b)* As, Q S V (+2, +3) and B D G (+2, +3)

F H K (+2, +3) But, L N P (+2, +2)

29. *(d)* According to the statements,

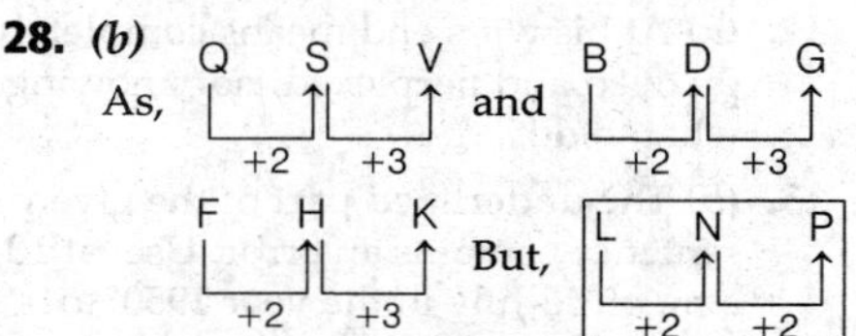

Conclusions I. (✗) II. (✗)

Hence, neither Conclusion I nor II follows.

30. *(d)* According to the question,

Here, common number is 5 in both the dice. So, moving in a clockwise direction from common number.

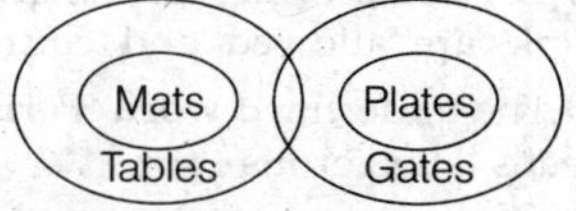

Hence, '5' will be opposite to '9'.

31. *(c)* Given equation,

128 A 4 C 16 B 7 D 5 = ?

After substituting the letters with their respective symbols, we get

A → ÷	B → ×
C → +	D → −

$\Rightarrow \quad 128 \div 4 + 16 \times 7 - 5 = ?$

$\Rightarrow \quad 32 + 112 - 5 = ? \Rightarrow 144 - 5 = ?$

$\therefore \quad ? = \boxed{139}$

32. *(a)* According to the code language,

Y O U R ⟶ 5 6 2 7

C R O Y ⟶ 2 7 6 9

∴ 'C' is coded as '9'.

33. *(d)* Given equation,

$10 - 12 \div 7 + 84 \times 21 = ?$

After interchanging the symbols, '+' and '−', '×' and '÷' we get,

$\Rightarrow 10 + 12 \times 7 - 84 \div 21 = ?$

$\Rightarrow \quad 10 + 84 - 4 = ?$

$\Rightarrow \quad 94 - 4 = ?$

$\therefore \quad ? = \boxed{90}$

34. *(b)* Given, 19th July, 2000 → Wednesday

Number of odd days from 19th July, 2000 to 19th July, 2008

Years → 2001 + 2002 + 2003 + 2004 + 2005 + 2006 + 2007 + 2008

Odd days → 1 + 1 + 1 + 2 + 1 + 1 + 1 + 2

$= \frac{10}{7} = 3$ odd days

Now, number of odd days from 19th July, 2008 to 14th June, 2009.

Months → July + August + September + October + November + December + January + February + March + April + May + June

Odd days → 12 + 31 + 30 + 31 + 30 + 31 + 31 + 28 + 31 + 30 + 31 + 14

$= \frac{330}{7} = 1$ odd day

Total odd days = 3 + 1 = 4

∴ Required day = Wednesday + 4 = Sunday

35. *(c)* In both dice, letter K is common so moving in a clockwise direction from common.

Dice I K R H

(Common, opposite, opposite)

Dice II K L D

Hence, 'D' is opposite to 'H'.

36. *(a)* When the piece of paper is unfolded, it would look like option (a).

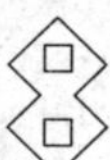

37. *(b)* When paper is unfolded, it will look like option figure (b).

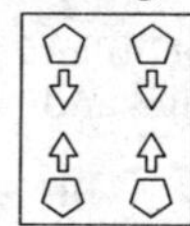

38. *(b)* The pattern of the series is as follows,

$R \xrightarrow{-9} \boxed{I} \xrightarrow{-9} Z \xrightarrow{-9} Q \xrightarrow{-9} H$

$K \xrightarrow{-8} \boxed{C} \xrightarrow{-8} U \xrightarrow{-8} M \xrightarrow{-8} E$

$D \xrightarrow{-7} \boxed{W} \xrightarrow{-7} P \xrightarrow{-7} I \xrightarrow{-7} B$

39. *(c)* As, (81, 53, 70)

$\Rightarrow \quad 81 \xrightarrow{-28} 53 \xrightarrow{+17} 70$

and (94, 66, 83) $\Rightarrow 94 \xrightarrow{-28} 66 \xrightarrow{+17} 83$

Similarly,

(99, 71, 88) $\Rightarrow 99 \xrightarrow{-28} 71 \xrightarrow{+17} 88$

40. *(c)* The pattern of the series is as follows,

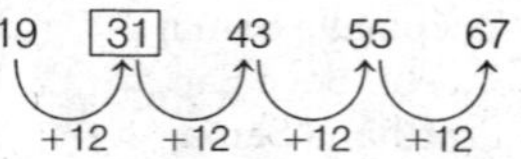

41. *(d)* Given equation,

$28 \div 90 + 6 - 5 \times 17 = ?$

After interchanging + and ÷, − and × signs we get,

$\Rightarrow 28 + 90 \div 6 \times 5 - 17 = ?$

$\Rightarrow \quad 28 + 15 \times 5 - 17 = ?$

$\Rightarrow \quad 28 + 75 - 17 = ?$

$\Rightarrow \quad 103 - 17 = ?$

$\therefore \quad ? = \boxed{86}$

42. *(c)* The pattern of the series is as follows,

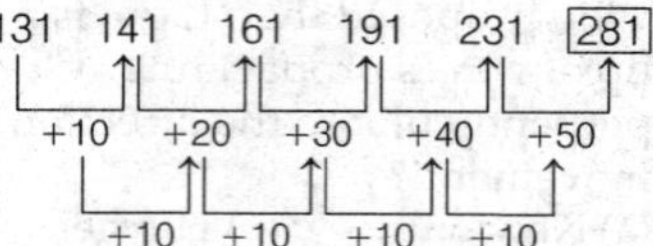

43. *(d)* As, $\underline{38} \times 2 + 4 = 80$

and $\underline{42} \times 2 + 4 = 88$

Similarly, $\underline{29} \times 2 + 4 = \boxed{62}$

44. *(c)* Given, 2nd August, 2016 → Tuesday

Number of odd days from 2nd August, 2016 to 2nd August, 2020

Years → 2017 + 2018 + 2019 + 2020

Odd days → 1 + 1 + 1 + 2 = 5 days

Number of odd days from 2nd August, 2020 to 19th October, 2020.

Months → August + September + October

Odd days → $29 + 30 + 19 = \frac{78}{7}$

= 1 odd day

Total odd days = 5 + 1 = 6

∴ Required day = Tuesday + 6 = Monday

45. *(d)* The option figure (d) is embedded in the given figure.

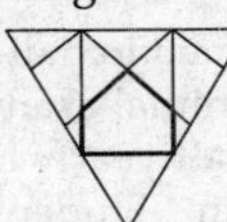

46. *(a)* Given expression,

P & Q @ R $ T # U

According to the question,

+ ⟶ Male
− ⟶ Female
P(−)
Wife
Q(+)
Brother
R(−)
Mother
T(−)
Sister
U

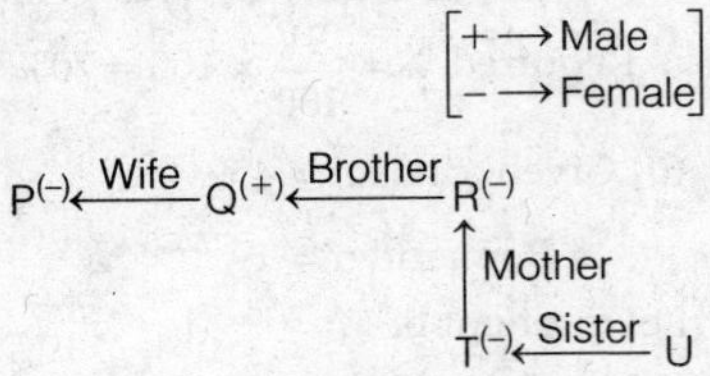

Hence, Q is U's mother's brother.

47. *(c)* As,

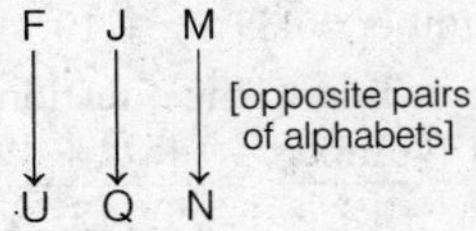

F J M
[opposite pairs of alphabets]
U Q N

and

D P Q
[opposite pairs of alphabets]
W K J

Similarly,

O V C
[opposite pairs of alphabets]
L E X

48. *(b)* As,

M A Z Q
−6 −6 −6 −6
G U T K

and

C P N R
−6 −6 −6 −6
W J H L

Similarly,

K O E V
−6 −6 −6 −6
E I Y P

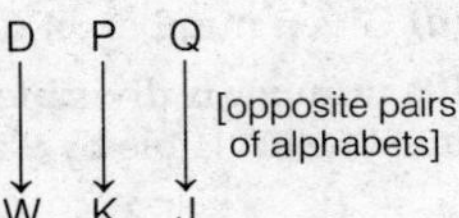

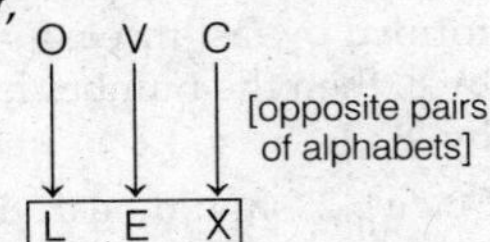

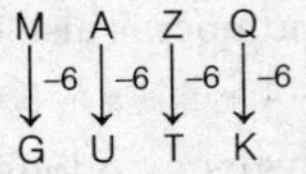

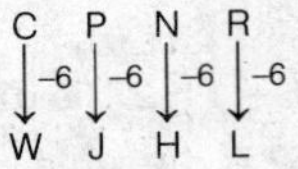

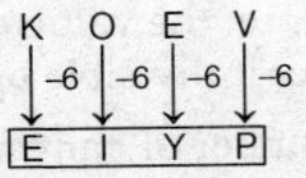

49. *(d)* Naming the figure,

H G F E
I L
J K
A B C D

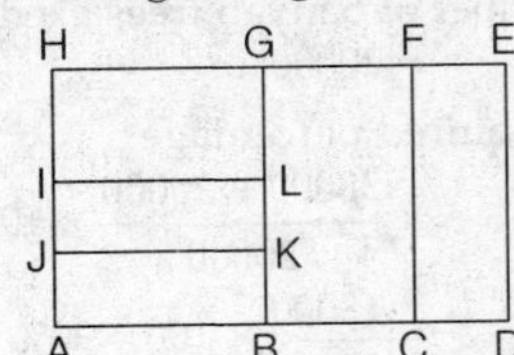

Rectangles can be represented as,

ABKJ, IJKL, HILG, HJKG, ABGH, BCFG, CDEF, BDEG, ACFH, ADEH

Hence, total 10 rectangles are present in the given figure.

50. *(d)* Here, the series follows the two alternative pattern which are as follows,

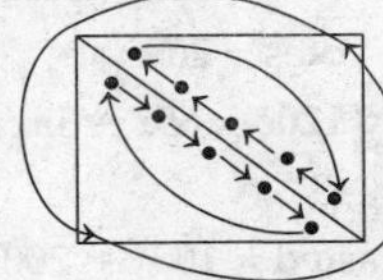

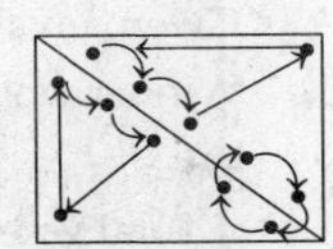

From figure 1 to 2
From figure 3 to 4

From figure 2 to 3
From figure 4 to 5

Hence, option figure (d) will replace the question mark.

51. *(d)* Given, side of equilateral triangle $(a) = 16$ cm

We know that,

Perimeter of equilateral triangle $= 3a = 3 \times 16 = 48$ cm

In equilateral triangle,

Height = Median

$\therefore$ Median $= \frac{\sqrt{3}}{2}a = \frac{\sqrt{3}}{2} \times 16 = 8\sqrt{3}$ cm

$\therefore$ Sum of median $= 3(8\sqrt{3}) = 24\sqrt{3}$ cm

$$\therefore \frac{\text{Perimeter of triangle}}{\text{Sum of its median}} = \frac{48}{24\sqrt{3}} = \frac{2}{\sqrt{3}} = 2 : \sqrt{3}$$

52. *(b)* Given, total votes = 720

Siva Raman got maximum vote and Vishwanath is the first runner up.

$\therefore$ Winner defeat the nearest contestant by

$$= \frac{120^\circ - 100^\circ}{360^\circ} \times 720 = 40$$

53. *(b)* Let total votes be $100x$.

One of the candidate got 44% of total votes $= 100x \times \frac{44}{100} = 44x$

Other candidate got votes $= 100x - 44x = 56x$

According to the question,

Vote difference between winner and loser = 1440

$\Rightarrow 56x - 44x = 1440$

$\Rightarrow 12x = 1440$

$x = 120$

$\therefore$ Total votes $= 100x = 12000$

54. *(a)* Given, sugar % in pomegranate juice = 10%

Sugar % in orange juice = 30%

Pomegranate juice = 2 L

and orange juice = 3 L

$\therefore$ Pomegranate juice to orange juice $= 2 : 3$

According to the rule of Alligation,

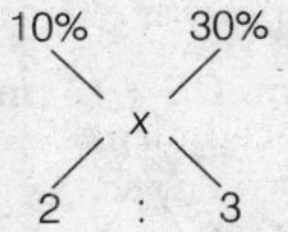

10%
30%
x
2 : 3

$$\therefore \frac{30 - x}{x - 10} = \frac{2}{3}$$

$\Rightarrow 90 - 3x = 2x - 20 \Rightarrow 5x = 110$

$\therefore x = 22\%$

55. *(c)* Given, cubes side are 5 cm.

When they joined end to end They become cuboid of side

$= (5 + 5 + 5), 5, 5 = 15, 5, 5$

$\therefore$ Length = 15 cm, breadth = 5 cm and height = 5 cm

Cuboid surface area = 2 (Length × Breadth + Breadth × Height + Height × Length)

$= 2(15 \times 5 + 5 \times 5 + 15 \times 5)$

$= 2(75 + 25 + 75) = 350 \text{ cm}^2$

56. *(a)*

A
6 m
θ
B
4 m
C
F
h
θ
E
28 m
D

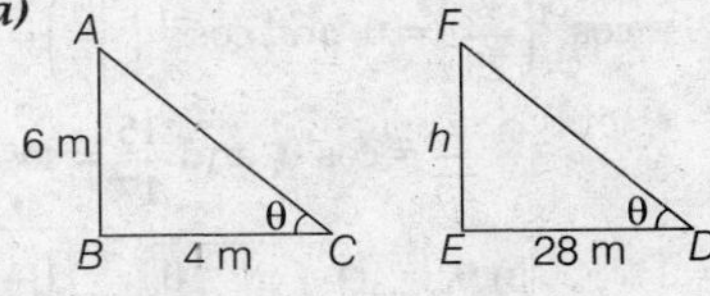

Let the height of tower be h cm.

In ΔABC,

$$\tan\theta = \frac{\text{Perpendicular}}{\text{Base}}$$

$$\tan\theta = \frac{6}{4} = \frac{3}{2} \quad \ldots\text{(i)}$$

In ΔDEF,

$$\tan\theta = \frac{\text{Perpendicular}}{\text{Base}}$$

$\Rightarrow \tan\theta = \frac{h}{28}$

$\Rightarrow \frac{3}{2} = \frac{h}{28}$ [$\because$ From Eq. (i)]

$\therefore h = 42$ m

57. *(b)* Let the number be $10x + y$ represented as xy.

Given, sum of digit = 9

$\therefore x + y = 9$ ...(i)

According to the question,

$(10y + x) - (10x + y) = 45$

$\Rightarrow 9y - 9x = 45$

$\Rightarrow y - x = 5$ ...(ii)

On solving Eqs. (i) and (ii),

$2y = 14$

$\therefore y = 7$ and $x = 2$

$\therefore$ Original number $= 10x + y = 20 + 7 = 27$

58. *(d)* Given,

$AD = 4$ cm, $DE = 12$ cm, $DW = 24$ cm

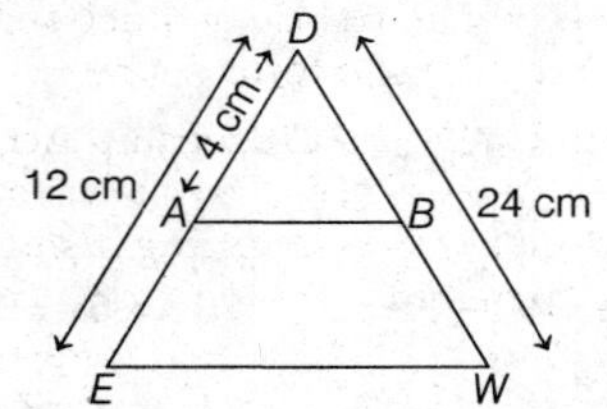

We know that,

Line drawn parallel to one side of a triangle, then

$$\frac{AD}{DE} = \frac{DB}{DW} \Rightarrow \frac{4}{12} = \frac{DB}{24}$$

$\therefore \quad DB = 8$ cm

59. *(a)* Let $\cos^{-1}\left(\frac{7}{25}\right) = \theta_1$

and $\cos^{-1}\left(\frac{15}{17}\right) = \theta_2$

$$\theta_1 - \theta_2 = \sin^{-1} x \quad \dots (i)$$

$$\cos^{-1}\left(\frac{7}{25}\right) = \theta_1 \text{ and } \cos^{-1}\left(\frac{15}{17}\right) = \theta_2$$

$$\frac{7}{25} = \cos\theta_1 \text{ and } \frac{15}{17} = \cos\theta_2$$

$$\therefore \quad \sin\theta_1 = \sqrt{1-\cos^2\theta_1} = \sqrt{1-\frac{49}{625}}$$

$$\sin\theta_1 = \sqrt{\frac{576}{625}} = \frac{24}{25}$$

and $\sin\theta_2 = \sqrt{1-\cos^2\theta_2} = \sqrt{1-\frac{225}{289}}$

$$\sin\theta_2 = \sqrt{\frac{64}{289}} = \frac{8}{17}$$

From Eq. (i), $(\theta_1 - \theta_2) = \sin^{-1} x$

$$\sin(\theta_1 - \theta_2) = x$$

$$x = \sin\theta_1\cos\theta_2 - \cos\theta_1\sin\theta_2$$

$[\because \sin(A-B) = \sin A\cdot\cos B - \cos A\cdot\sin B]$

$$= \frac{24}{25}\times\frac{15}{17} - \frac{7}{25}\times\frac{8}{17}$$

$$x = \frac{360}{425} - \frac{56}{425} = \frac{304}{425}$$

From Eq. (i),

$$\cos^{-1}\left(\frac{7}{25}\right) - \cos^{-1}\left(\frac{15}{17}\right) = \sin^{-1}\left(\frac{304}{425}\right)$$

60. *(a)* Given, diameter $(d) = 4$ cm

Inner radius $(r) = 2$ cm

Thickness = 0.5 cm

$\therefore$ Outer radius $(R) = 2.5$ cm

We know that,

Volume of silver used $= \frac{2}{3}\pi(R^3 - r^3)$

$$= \frac{2}{3} \times 3.14 \times 7.625$$

$$= 15.96 \text{ cm}^3$$

61. *(b)* Let valid votes be $100x$.

Winner got 65% of valid votes $= 65x$

and loser got 35% of valid votes $= 35x$

Given, invalid votes = 200

Winner won by $1200 = 65x - 35x$

$\Rightarrow \quad x = 40$

$\therefore$ Total votes casted $= 100x + 200$

$= 4000 + 200 = 4200$

70% are total casted votes = 4200

$\therefore$ Total votes $= \frac{4200}{70} \times 100 = 6000$

62. *(b)* Option (b) is false regarding a circle because three points can not always make a circle.

63. *(c)*

70km/h → ← 30km/h
420km
A 11 am ———— B 12 am

Let they meet after x h.

According to the question,

Distance = Speed × Time

$\Rightarrow 70 \times x + 30 \times (x-1) = 420$

$\Rightarrow \quad 70x + 30x - 30 = 420$

$\Rightarrow \quad 100x = 450$

$\therefore \quad x = 4.5$ h

$\therefore$ Meeting time = 11 am + 4.5 h

= 3 : 30 pm

64. *(c)* $\therefore$ Mira's one day work $= \frac{1}{20}$

Nina's one day work $= \frac{1}{30}$

and Sima's one day work $= \frac{1}{40}$

According to the question,

$$4\left(\frac{1}{20} + \frac{1}{40}\right) + x\left(\frac{1}{30} + \frac{1}{40}\right) = 1$$

$$\Rightarrow \quad \frac{12}{40} + x\left(\frac{7}{120}\right) = 1$$

$$\Rightarrow \quad \frac{7x}{120} = \frac{28}{40} \Rightarrow x = 4 \times 3$$

$\therefore \quad x = 12$ days

The work was completed in (12 + 4 =) 16 days in total.

65. *(d)* Let larger part be x.

$\therefore$ Smaller part $= 25 - x$

According to the question,

$6x + 4(25 - x) = 130$

$\Rightarrow \quad 6x + 100 - 4x = 130$

$\Rightarrow \quad 2x = 30$

$\therefore \quad x = 15$

Hence, larger part = 15

66. *(d)* At least pass in one exam from section A

Students failed in half-yearly but passed in annual exam + Students passed in half-yearly but failed in annual exam + Students passed in both exams

$= 16 + 10 + 65 = 91$

Total number of students in section A $= 39 + 16 + 10 + 65 = 130$

$\therefore$ Required % $= \frac{91}{130} \times 100 = 70\%$

67. *(b)* Given, divisor = 459

Remainder = 19

Let quotient be x.

$\therefore$ Number (Dividend)

= Divisor × Quotient + Remainder

Number $= 459 \times x + 19$

According to the question,

$$\therefore \quad \frac{\text{Number}}{17} \Rightarrow \frac{459x + 19}{17} \Rightarrow R = 2$$

68. *(d)* Given number : 4 6 4 5 a 5 2

If a number is divisible by 72 then, it must be divisible by 9 and 8.

as $\quad 72 = 9 \times 8$

Divisibility by 8 If the number formed by last three digits is divisible by 8, then the number is also divisible by '8'.

So, 'a 5 2' should be divisible by 8.

Divisibility by 9 If the sum of the digits of a number is divisible by 9, then the number is also divisible by 9.

$4 + 6 + 4 + 5 + a + 5 + 2 = 26 + a$

Out of the given options if we put $a = 1$, then,

26 + 1 = 27 (is divisible by 9)

and 152 is divisible by 8.

Therefore, the value of a should be '1' to make it divisible by 72.

69. *(b)* Number of banyan trees axed in 2020 = 38000

Number of banyan trees axed in 2016 = 20000

$\therefore$ Required percentage

$$= \frac{38000 - 20000}{20000} \times 100$$

$$= \frac{18000}{20000} \times 100 = 90\%$$

70. *(c)* Let Ram's salary $= 100x$

$\therefore$ Shyam's salary

$$= 100x \times \left(\frac{100 - 20}{100}\right) = 80x$$

Ram's salary more than Shyam's in terms of percentage

$$= \frac{100x - 80x}{80x} \times 100$$

$$= \frac{20x}{80x} \times 100 = 25\%$$

71. *(d)* Let one part be ₹ x.

∴ Other part be ₹ $(5000 - x)$.

We know that,

Simple interest

$$= \frac{\text{Rate} \times \text{Time} \times \text{Principle}}{100}$$

According to the question,

$$\frac{x \times 16 \times 1}{100} + \frac{(5000 - x) \times 24 \times 1}{100} = 960$$

$$\Rightarrow \quad 16x + 24 \times 5000 - 24x = 96000$$

$$\Rightarrow \quad 8x = 24000$$

$$\therefore \quad x = ₹\ 3000$$

Hence, sum lent at higher rate

$= 5000 - 3000$

$= ₹\ 2000$

72. *(b)* Let the cost price of 1000 gm be $100x$.

Weight less than 27%

$$= 1000 \times \left(\frac{100 - 27}{100}\right) = 730 \text{ gm}$$

∴ Cost price of 730 gm = $73x$

We know that,

Profit%

$$= \left(\frac{\text{CP} - \text{Original cost price}}{\text{Original cost price}}\right) \times 100$$

$$= \frac{100x - 73x}{73x} \times 100 = \frac{27x}{73x} \times 100$$

Profit % = 37%

73. *(a)* Given,

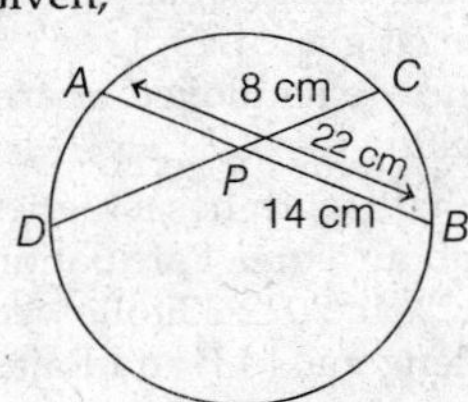

$AB = 22$ cm, $PB = 14$ cm, $CP = 8$ cm

Let the length of $PD = x$ cm

By intersecting theorem,

$$AP \times PB = DP \times PC$$

$$\Rightarrow \quad (AB - BP) \times BP = PD \times PC$$

$$\Rightarrow \quad (22 - 14) \times 14 = PD \times 8$$

$$\Rightarrow \quad 8 \times 14 = PD \times 8$$

$$\therefore \quad PD = 14 \text{ cm}$$

74. *(a)* Profit percentage of company B in the year 2014 = 50

and profit percentage of company B in the year 2013 = 44

$$\therefore \text{Required percentage} = \frac{50 - 44}{44} \times 100$$

$$= 13.63\%$$

75. *(a)* Given, area = 70 m^2

Height = 5 m

We know that,

Area of rhombus = Base × Height

$\Rightarrow \quad 70 = \text{Base} \times 5$

$\therefore \quad \text{Side} = \text{Base} = 14$ m

∴ Perimeter of rhombus = 4 × side

= 4 × 14 = 56 m

76. *(a)* The Gundecha brothers are related to Dagari Hindustani music Gharana.

- Gundecha brothers namely Umakant Gundecha and Ramakant Gundecha were awarded the Padma Shri for art for 2012.
- **Dagari Gharana** The Dagar family sings in the Dagar Vani.
- It is one of the oldest and grandest Dhrupad froms of Hindustani classical music.

77. *(a)* The first Asian Games took place in New Delhi in 1951.

- The game received names like First Asian and 1951 Asiad.
- The official logo of the first Asiad depicted a bright Sun in red with 16 rays and a white circle in the middle of the disc of the Sun.
- And eleven rings, representing each participating nation.
- On a white background, symbolising peace.

78. *(d)* The Battle of Khanwa was fought between Babur and Rana Sanga.

- The Battle of Khanwa happened in Agra on 16th March in 1527.
- Rana Sanga wanted to become the prime ruler of Indian nation.
- Mughal emperor Babur won the prestigious historical battle of Khanwa.

79. *(d)* Narmada and Tapi are West flowing rivers.

- Sabarmati, Mani, Bharathapuzha, Periyar Narmada and Tapi are all westward flowing rivers.
- The Narmada and Tapi rivers flow in the Rift valleys.

The reasons of westward flowing river are

- The slope of the Western Ghats is steep.
- And they do not have to travel much distance to drain into the sea.
- They do not carry much sediments required to form deltas.

80. *(c)* Under the Citizenship Act, 1955, any citizen of India can make a declaration renouncing his/her Indian citizenship.

- The Act 1955 provides for the acquistition of citizenship.
- After the commencement of the Constitution by birth, descent, registration, naturalisation.
- And incorporation of territory under certain circumstances.
- It also provides for the termination and deprivation of citizenship.

81. *(d)* El Nino, is a climate pattern of pacific Ocean that describes the unusual warming of surface water.

- In El Nino, the normally cool Eastern Pacific becomes warmer.
- It leads to increased rising motion over the Central or Easter Pacific and more convection and rainfall.
- It refers to the periodic cooling of ocean surface temperatures in the Central and East-Central Equatorial Pacific.
- La Nina typically occurs every 3 to 5 years.

82. *(d)* The Chethiagiri Vihar festival considers

- The Chethiagiri Vihar festival is Buddhist festival.
- During the event, the relics of Buddha are brought out and pilgrims from all across the country come to pay their respects.
- It is held in Sanchi in Raisen district, Madhya Pradesh.

83. *(d)* Formulas in MS Excel always start with (=) symbol.

84. *(b)* In August 2021, the Administrator of Lakshadweep, Praful Patel, highlighted the Maldives style water villas.

- It is a project which is a first of its kind.
- Project is at a cost of 800 crores.
- And it is in a bid to attract tourists to scenic beauty of the union territory.
- The project will come up at Kadmat, Minicoy and Suneli islands.

85. *(c)* Oswald Avery, Colin MacLeod and Maclyn McCarty proved that DNA is the genetic material of all living organisms (except viruses) in 1944.

Their research was based on the work of Frederick Griffith, who in 1928 discovered that bacteria could transfer a compound to other bacteria, changing their properties.

86. *(a)* Statements (1), (2) and (3) are correct.
- Radio broadcasting in India began with the setting of the Radio Club in Bombay in 1923.
- It was later acquired by the government and renamed All India Radio in 1936 and Akashwani in 1957.
- In 1976, TV was delinked from All India Radio (AIR) and got a separate identity as Door Darshan. (DD)

87. *(b)* In 2021, the Rajiv Gandhi Khel Ratna Award renamed as Major Dhyan Chand Khel Ratna Award.
- It is the highest sporting honour in the nation.
- It is awarded annually by the Ministry of Youth Affairs and Sports, Government of India.
- Recipients are selected by a committee for thier 'spectacular and most outstanding performance in the field of sports over a period of four years' at an international level.

88. *(c)* Statement (c) is not true.
- The second phase of green Revolution covered the period of the mid 1970s, to mid 1980s. Statements (a), (b) and (c) are true.
- The Green Revolution was covered by farmers living in dry and semi-arid region of India.
- It was launched in areas with a significant shift from dry to wet (irrigated) cultivation.
- It was characterised by introducing of High-Yield Variety seeds, increased use of fertilisers and improved irrigation facilities.

89. *(b)* The first Durand Cup held in Shimla in 1888. It was first (oldest) Indian football competition.
- Durand Cup is the original tournament trophy which became a rolling trophy since 1965.
- President Cup is a rolling trophy that replaced the Viceroy's Trophy post-independence by the President of India Dr. Rajendra Prasad.

90. *(b)* The UIDAI is under the jurisdiction of Ministry of Electronics and Information Technology.
- The UIDAI was established on 28th January, 2009 after the Planning Commission.
- Sh. Amit Agarwal is the Chief Executive Officer of the UIDAI.
- UIDAI is responsible for Aadhar enrolment and authentication.
- New Delhi is the headquarters of the UIDAI.

91. *(d)* In 2015, the Micro Units Development and Refinance Agency (MUDRA) introduced.
- Shri Vinay Hedaqo is the CEO of MUDRA Yojana.
- The purpose of MUDRA is to provide funding to the non-corporate small business sector through various Last Mile Financial institutions like Banks, NBFCS and MFIs.
- Generally loans upto ₹10 lakhs issued by banks under Micro Small Enterprises given without collaterals.

92. *(c)* Ctrl + V shortcut key is used to paste a slide in Microsoft PowerPoint.

93. *(d)* The Rogas are allotted to different hours of the day and different seasons in Hindustani Music System.

Ragas is a series of musical notes on which a melody in based and which expresses different moods for different times of the day.

94. *(a)* Satyashodhak Samaj was organised in the Pune district of Maharashtra in the 1870s.
- The aim of the Satyashodhak Samaj was to promote education and social rights among the underprivileged group of society.
- The Slogan 'Sarvasakhi Jagatpati, Tyalanak Madyashtee' was given by Satyashodhak Samaj.
- Krantijyoti Savitribai Phule led the women's division of Satyashodhak Samaj to support and uplift them.

95. *(d)* The correct matching is A-2, B-3, C-1, D-4.
- Bharatanatyam is the Classical dance of Tamil Nadu.
- Mohiniyattam is Classical dance from the Kerala in South India.
- Garba is a from of Gujarati dance which originates from the state of Gujarat.
- Sattriya is a dance form that is more than 500 year old and come from the Vaishnavite monasteries of Assam.

96. *(b)* According to the Huygen's wave theory of light, light is a form of energy which propagating perpendicular to the direction of its movement.
And the speed of light in a medium depends upon the nature of medium.

97. *(c)* Balasaraswati played an important role in reviving the dance form Bharatanatyam.

He was regarded as child prodigy by Vidhwas and pandits.
- She trained new dancers in the Bharatanatyam tradition.
- She established a dance school in association with the institution.

98. *(a)* Statement (1) is incorrect. The Mahila Samman Savings Certificate Scheme is
- This scheme is valid for a two-year tenure period upto 31st March, 2025.
- The Mahila Samman Savings Certificate Scheme was launched by Department of Economic Affairs, Ministry of Finance in 2023-24 Budget.
- The minimum of ₹1000 and any sum in multiple of 100 may be deposited within the maximum limit of ₹ 2,00,000.

99. *(d)* As per the Economic Survey 2022-23. The labour force participation rate for male has gone up to 27.5% in 2020-21.
- The labour force participation rate indicate the (%) percentage of working age people
Who are employed or are actively seeking work.
- Chhattisgarh has a highest LFPR (Labour Force Partipation Rate) of 70.2% in 2022-33 followed by Telengana, M.P and Rajasthan.

100. *(a)* The Indian Constitution borrowed the concept of Concurrent List from Australia.
- The Concurrent List consists of subjects of common interest to both the Union and the State.
- Concurrent list comes under (Seventh Schedule) of the Indian Constitution.
- The Concurrent List have 52 items.

Set 35 11 July, 2024 (Shift III)

SSC CHSL Tier-I SOLVED PAPER

Instructions

1. This paper contains 100 questions.
2. It has 4 Parts, **Part I General English**, **Part II** General Intelligence & Reasoning, **Part III** Quantitative Aptitude and **Part IV** General Awareness.
3. Each question carries **2 marks.**

Part I General English

1. Identify the error in the tense of the sentence and select the option that correctly rectifies the error.

Between two evils, I always picks the one I have never tried before.

(a) Between two evils, I always pick the one I have never tried before.
(b) Between two evils, I always is picking the one I have never tried before.
(c) Between two evils, I always picked the one I have never tried before.
(d) Between two evils, I always picking the one I have never tried before.

2. The following sentence has been split into four segments. Identify the segment that contains a grammatical error.

The teacher will / certainly help you / if you will / ask her.

(a) certainly help you
(b) The teacher will
(c) if you will
(d) ask her

3. The following sentence has been divided into three segments. Identify the segment that contains a grammatical error. If you don't find any error, select 'No error' as your answer.

It was possible to achieve anything, / if one has the grit and determination / to keep going.

(a) No error
(b) It was possible to achieve anything,
(c) if one has the grit and determination
(d) to keep going

4. The following sentence has been divided into four segments. Identify the segment that contains a grammatical error.

My Vice-Chancellor works / eighteen hours / a day, / seven days week.

(a) seven days week
(b) My Vice-Chancellor works
(c) eighteen hours
(d) a day,

Directions (Q. Nos. 5-9) *In the following passage, some words have been deleted. Read the passage carefully and select the most appropriate option to fill in each blank.*

Organic agriculture offers a means to substitute costlier agricultural inputs such as HYV seeds, chemical fertilisers and pesticides with locally produced organic inputs that are cheaper and thereby generate good returns on (1) .... Organic agriculture also generates income through exports as the demand for organically grown crops is on a (2) .... Studies across countries have shown that organically grown food has more nutritional value than chemical farming, thus providing us with healthy foods. Since organic farming requires more labour input than (3) .... farming, India will find organic farming an attractive (4) .... Finally, the produce is pesticide-free and produced in an environmentally (5) .... way.

5. Select the most appropriate option to fill in blank number (1).

(a) loss (b) profit
(c) expenditure (d) investment

6. Select the most appropriate option to fill in blank number (2).

(a) decline (b) rise
(c) growth (d) stagnation

7. Select the most appropriate option to fill in blank number (3).

(a) insipid (b) mechanical
(c) rigorous (d) conventional

8. Select the most appropriate option to fill in blank number (4).

(a) obstacle (b) proposition
(c) burden (d) challenge

9. Select the most appropriate option to fill in blank number (5).

(a) sustainable
(b) innovative
(c) destructive
(d) harmful

10. Select the option that will improve the underlined part of the given sentence.

Neither Janki <u>or</u> I am to receive the award.

(a) either (b) no
(c) nor (d) not

11. Select the most appropriate option that can substitute the underlined segment in the given sentence. If there is no need to substitute it, select 'No substitution required'.

The film was made in Botswana, whose wildlife parks <u>is larger to</u> those in Kenya.

(a) are larger than
(b) are large than
(c) No substitution required
(d) as large than

12. Select the most appropriate homophones to fill in the blanks.

It was against her .... to earn more .... than that decided by the Board of directors.

(a) principle, profit
(b) principal; profit
(c) principal; prophet
(d) principle; prophet

13. Select the most appropriate homophones to fill in the blanks.

I .... that he has been promoted to the post of .... officer.

(a) herd; sealing
(b) heard; sealing
(c) herd; ceiling
(d) heard; ceiling

14. Select the most appropriate meaning of the given idiom.

To throw dust in one's eyes

(a) To talk in an abusive language
(b) To mislead someone by tricks
(c) To make someone blind forever
(d) To hit someone with stone

15. Select the most appropriate antonym of the given word.

Queer

(a) Doubtful (b) Fantastic
(c) Eccentric (d) Ordinary

16. Select the correctly spelt word.

(a) Quintessential
(b) Quintessintial
(c) Quintesential
(d) Quientessential

17. Select the most appropriate option to fill in the blank and complete the sentence.

You just wait in the lobby. I will be back after ....

(a) a fast meal (b) a quick shower
(c) a fast shower (d) a quick food

18. Select the most appropriate synonym of the given word.

Anxiety

(a) Serenity (b) Distress
(c) Dilemma (d) Ease

19. Select the most appropriate antonym of the word 'contaminate' from the given sentence.

Crews were requested to purify the system since a brain-eating amoeba was discovered in the drinking water.

(a) requested (b) discovered
(c) purify (d) system

20. Select the most appropriate option to fill in the blank.

The guard did not want anything bad to happen, so he ordered the group to step back to avoid anything ....

(a) customary (b) terrible
(c) habitual (d) diplomatic

21. Rectify the sentence by selecting the correct spelling from the options.

Psycology developed as a significant discipline of study in the twentieth century.

(a) Pscycology (b) Psychology
(c) Pcychology (d) Psichology

22. Select the most appropriate meaning of the underlined idiom in the given sentence.

Every piece of furniture in her house is in <u>apple-pie order</u>.

(a) Very neatly arranged
(b) Painted in light colours
(c) Very delicately arranged
(d) Kept in a disorganised way

23. Select the most appropriate option that can substitute the underlined segment in the given sentence.

He has recovered now and is feeling <u>too strong to walk</u>.

(a) too weak to walk
(b) weak enough to walk
(c) strong to walk
(d) strong enough to walk

24. Select the most appropriate option that can substitute the underlined segment in the given sentence.

Peter was the last to know that she had been <u>cheating of him</u>.

(a) cheating up him
(b) cheating in him
(c) cheat of him
(d) cheating on him

25. Select the most appropriate antonym of the underlined word.

I left the job because of a <u>hostile</u> working environment.

(a) morose (b) friendly
(c) rustic (d) violent

Part II

General Intelligence

26. Select the word-pair that best represents a similar relationship to the one expressed in the pair of words given below.

(The words must be considered as meaningful English words and must not be related to each other based on the number of letters/number of consonants/vowels in the word)

Compress : Expand

(a) Hopeful : Optimistic
(b) Observe : Notice
(c) Limit : Boundless
(d) Defend : Protect

27. If 'A' stands for '÷', 'B' stands for '×', 'C' stands for '+' and 'D' stands for '–', what will come in place of the question mark(?) in the following equation?

5 B 5 C 216 A 9 D 3 = ?

(a) 64 (b) 46 (c) 23 (d) 32

28. Identify the figure in the options that when put in place of the question mark (?) will logically complete the series?

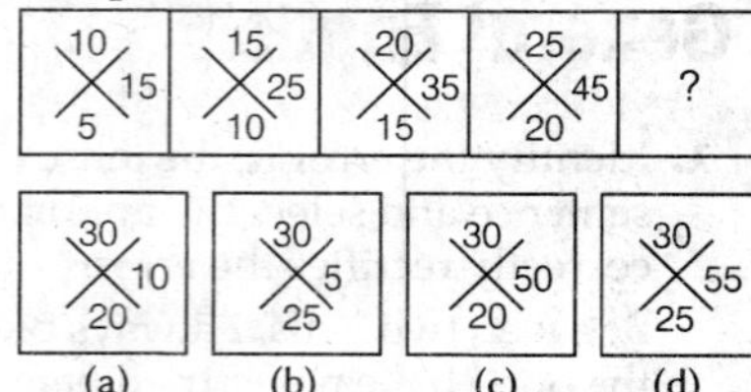

29. A square sheet of paper is folded along the dotted line successively along the directions shown and is then punched in the last. How would the paper look when unfolded?

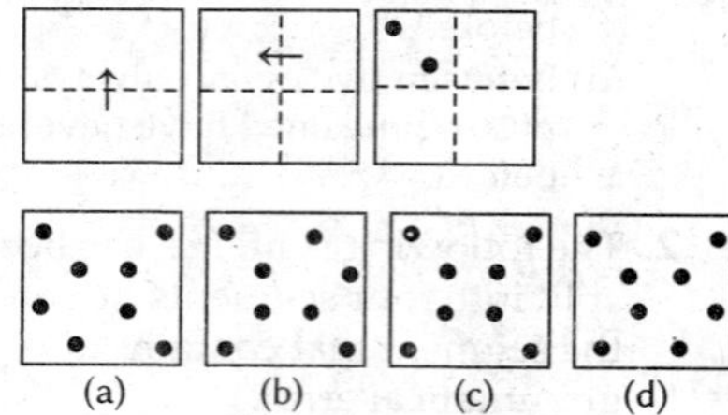

30. The position of how many letters will remain unchanged, if each of the letters in the word NUCLEAR is arranged in the alphabetical order?

(a) None (b) One
(c) Two (d) Three

31. Select the correct mirror image of the given figure, when the mirror is placed at MN as shown below.

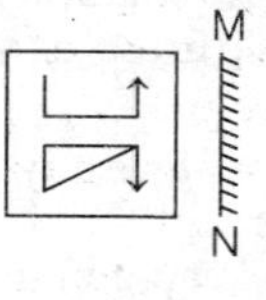

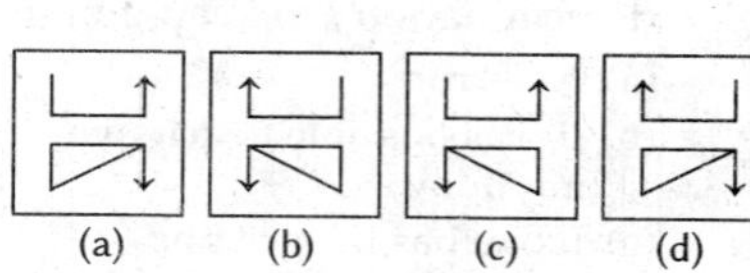

32. Select the combination of letters that when sequentially placed in the blanks of the given series will complete the series.

JIG_KG_U_EGZM_GE

(a) PGMC (b) NGCL
(c) NGMC (d) PGLC

33. Select the set in which the numbers are related in the same way as are the numbers of the following sets.
(**Note** Operations should be performed on the whole numbers, without breaking down the numbers into its constituent digits. E.g. 13 – Operations on 13 such as adding/subtracting/multiplying etc. to 13 can be performed. Breaking down 13 into 1 and 3 and then performing mathematical operations on 1 and 3 is not allowed)

(25, 8, 11)
(28, 8, 12)

(a) (22, 13, 19) (b) (17, 7, 8)
(c) (42, 6, 21) (d) (15, 5, 8)

34. What should come in place of the question mark (?) in the given series?

50, 51, 54, 55, 58, ?

(a) 62 (b) 64 (c) 59 (d) 60

35. Select the combination of letters that when sequentially placed in the blanks of the given series will complete the series.

a _ z b _ y c _ x _ a z _ b y c c _ a a _ b b _ c c x _ a z _ b y _ c x

(a) acbacxzyabc (b) bacazbxyacb
(c) bacabzxyabc (d) abcabxzyabc

36. What will come in the place of the question mark (?) in the following equation, if '+' and '–' are interchanged and '×' and '÷' are interchanged?

$24 \div 9 + 182 \times 13 - 2 = ?$

(a) 204 (b) 238 (c) 172 (d) 224

37. Select the option figure in which the given figure is embedded as its part (rotation is not allowed).

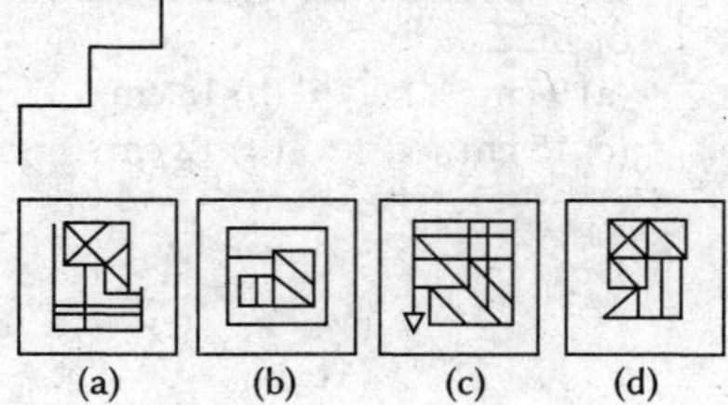

(a) (b) (c) (d)

38. CEHM is related to YADI in a certain way based on the English alphabetical order. In the same way, IKNS is related to EGJO. To which of the following is OQTY related, following the same logic?

(a) KOPU
(b) KNOU
(c) KMPU
(d) KNPU

39. 13 is related to 156 following a certain logic. Following the same logic, 22 is related to 264. To which of the following is 31 related following the same logic?
(**Note** Operations should be performed on the whole numbers, without breaking down the number into its constituent digits. E.g. 13 – Operations on 13 such as adding /subtracting /multiplying etc., to 13 can be performed. Breaking down 13 into 1 and 3 and then performing mathematical operations on 1 and 3 is not allowed)

(a) 376 (b) 370
(c) 374 (d) 372

40. Which of the following numbers will replace the question mark (?) in the given series?

800, 400, 480, 240, 320, ?

(a) 180 (b) 200
(c) 160 (d) 120

41. Three of the following four are alike in a certain way and thus form a group. Which is the one that does not belong to that group?
(**Note** The odd one out is not based on the number of consonants/vowels or their position in the letter-cluster.)

(a) RVX
(b) JNP
(c) CGI
(d) HKM

42. In a certain code language,
'A + B' means 'A is the sister of B',
'A – B' means 'A is the brother of B',
'A × B' means 'A is the father of B',
'A ÷ B' means 'A is the daughter of B'.

Based on the above, how is K related to P, if 'J ÷ K + L × O – P'?

(a) Mother
(b) Father's sister
(c) Mother's sister
(d) Sister

43. Select the correct mirror image of the given combination, when the mirror is placed at MN as shown below.

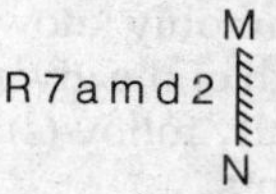

M
R 7 a m d 2
N

(a) Ƨ b a m Ꞁ Я
(b) d 2 m ɒ Ꞁ Я
(c) ᘔ p ɯ ɐ ㄥ ᴚ
(d) Ƨ b m ɒ Ꞁ Я

44. In a certain code language, 'DARK' is coded as '3975' and 'READ' is coded as '5873'. How is 'K' coded in the given language?

(a) 7 (b) 9
(c) 3 (d) 5

45. How many rectangles are there in the figure?

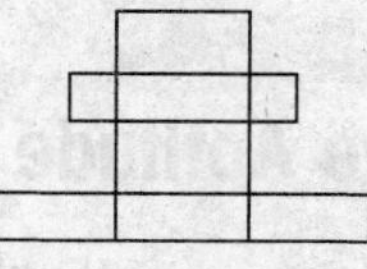

(a) 15 (b) 16
(c) 17 (d) More than 17

46. In a certain code language, 'TWIN' is coded as 2359 and 'WING' is coded as 5302. What is the code for 'T' in the given code language?

(a) 2 (b) 9 (c) 3 (d) 5

47. Select the correct mirror image of the given figure, when the mirror is placed at AB.

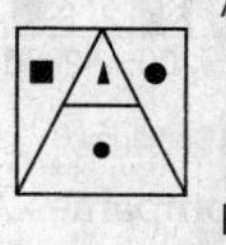

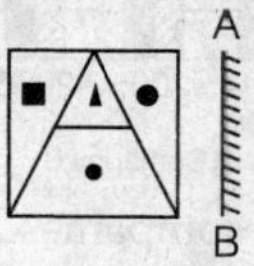

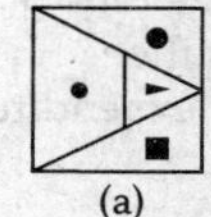
(a)

(b)

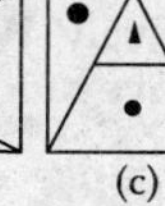
(c)

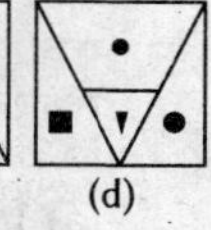
(d)

48. What will come in the place of the question mark (?) in the following equation, if '+' and '–' are interchanged and '×' and '÷' are interchanged?

$17 \div 4 - 28 + 125 \times 5 = ?$

(a) 71 (b) 74 (c) 73 (d) 72

49. If 18th January, 2013 was Friday, then what was the day of the week on 19th December, 2021?

(a) Sunday (b) Thursday
(c) Saturday (d) Wednesday

50. Three statements are followed by conclusions numbered I, II. You have to consider these statements to be true, even if they seem to be at variance with commonly known facts. Decide which of the given conclusions logically follow(s) from the given statements.

Statements

All ground is wind.

Some tables are ground.

All wind is earth.

Conclusions

I. No tables are earth.

II. All earth is ground.

(a) Only Conclusion I follows
(b) Neither Conclusion I nor II follows
(c) Only Conclusion II follows
(d) Both Conclusions I and II follow

Part III
Quantitative Aptitude

51. Study the following graph and answer the question that follows. The following bar-graph shows the percentage profit earned by two companies A and B over the given years.

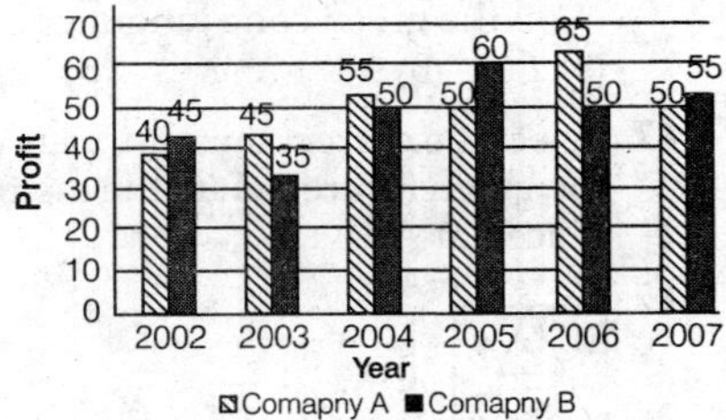

The incomes of two companies A and B in 2006 were in the ratio 3 : 4, respectively. What was the respective ratio of their expenditures in 2006?

(a) 14 : 19
(b) 7 : 22
(c) 27 : 35
(d) 15 : 22

52. Shantanu's income decreased from ₹42800 to ₹37236. Find the percentage decrease in his income.

(a) 12% (b) 11%
(c) 14% (d) 13%

53. The value of

$$1\frac{1}{3} \div \left[2\frac{1}{6} \div \left\{14\frac{1}{3} - \left(2\frac{1}{3} + 3\frac{1}{2}\right)\right\}\right] \text{ is}$$

(a) $3\frac{2}{13}$ (b) $5\frac{3}{13}$
(c) $4\frac{3}{17}$ (d) $3\frac{2}{17}$

54. The table shows the percentage distribution of the population (only male and female) according to Gender and Literacy.

State	Percentage literate	Gender	
		Literate	Illiterate
		M : F	M : F
A	55	5 : 6	4 : 5
B	72	1 : 1	3 : 2
C	78	4 : 3	3 : 2

If state B has 7 crore people, then the number of illiterate females in the state is

(a) 117.6 lakhs
(b) 78.4 lakhs
(c) 201.6 lakhs
(d) 130.67 lakhs

55. A shopkeeper sold an article at a 26% profit. On selling it for ₹2250 more, he would get a profit of 41%. If this article is sold at 12% profit, then the selling price would be

(a) ₹16800
(b) ₹15000
(c) ₹15800
(d) ₹16120

56. Study the given bar-graph and answer the question that follows. The bar-graph shows the production of refrigerators (in thousand) by five different companies A, B, C, D and E during 2004 to 2007.

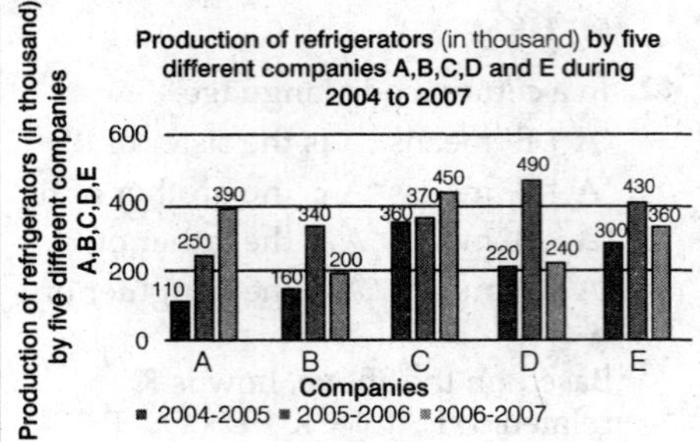

What is the difference between 60% of the average production of refrigerators by all the companies for the year 2005-2006 and 70% of the average of all the companies in 2006-2007?

(a) 4000 (b) 40 (c) 400 (d) 4

57. The following graph shows the wheat imports (in thousand tonnes) over the five years.

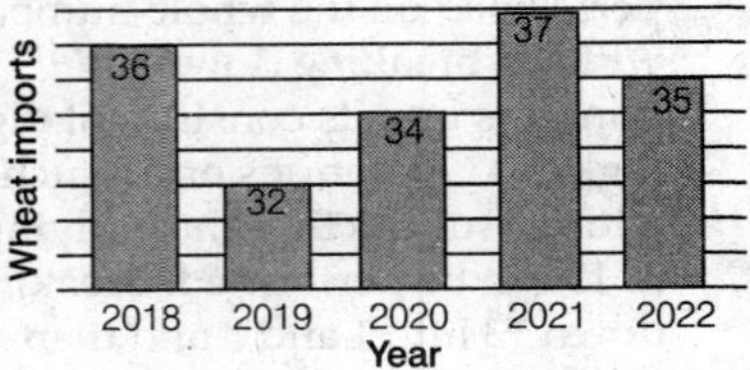

What is the ratio of the years, which have below average imports to those which have above average imports?

(a) 3 : 1 (b) 3 : 2
(c) 2 : 3 (d) 1 : 3

58. Out of a class of 200 people, 50 people's average marks is 40 and the remaining 150 people's average is 60. Find the people's weighted average.

(a) 50 (b) 55 (c) 150 (d) 200

59. In how many years will a sum of ₹4250 yield a simple interest of ₹510 at a rate of 6% per annum?

(a) $3\frac{1}{2}$ yr (b) $2\frac{1}{2}$ yr
(c) 3 yr (d) 2 yr

60. Teena does half of a task in 6 days. Later, with Shyam's help, she completes the remaining work in 4 days. Shyam alone can finish the entire work in

(a) 21 days
(b) 24 days
(c) 18 days
(d) 12 days

61. ΔABC and ΔDEF are similar triangles and their areas are 81 cm^2 and 144 cm^2, respectively. If $EF = 20$ cm, then what is the value of BC?

(a) 9 cm (b) 13 cm
(c) 15 cm (d) 12 cm

62. In two successive years, 75 and 50 employees of a company appeared at the departmental examination. Respectively, 84% and 52% of them passed. The average rate of pass percentage is
(a) $41\frac{1}{5}\%$ (b) 41%
(c) 71% (d) $71\frac{1}{5}\%$

63. Let C be a circle with centre O and PQ be the diameter of C. Let AB be a chord on C. If $\angle QOB = 40°$, $\angle AOP = 80°$, then find $\angle AOB$.
(a) 100° (b) 60°
(c) 90° (d) 70°

64. The sum of the present ages of a father and son is 50 yr. If after 5 yr, the father's age will be 5 times the age of the son, then what was the father's age 5 yr ago?
(a) 36 (b) 47
(c) 43 (d) 40

65. If $640 \div 8 + 930 \div 15 - k + 32 \times 5 = 1104 \div 16 \times 148 \div 37$, then the value of k is
(a) 276 (b) 26
(c) 35 (d) 302

66. Find the whole surface area of a cuboid having a length of 19 cm, breadth of 9 cm and height of 4.5 cm.
(a) 619 cm^2 (b) 497 cm^2
(c) 917 cm^2 (d) 594 cm^2

67. Simplify : $\frac{\sin 60° - \cos 60°}{\sin 60° + \cos 60°}$
(a) $2+\sqrt{3}$ (b) $\sqrt{3}-1$
(c) $2-\sqrt{3}$ (d) $\sqrt{3}-2$

68. $\Delta ABC \sim \Delta EDF$ and area (ΔABC) : area $(\Delta EDF) = 1 : 4$. If $AB = 7$ cm, $BC = 8$ cm and $CA = 9$ cm, then DF is equal to
(a) 16 cm (b) 18 cm
(c) 14 cm (d) 12 cm

69. Two circles of radii 3 units and r units, respectively, have 6 units distance between their centres. If the length of the direct common tangent is $\sqrt{35}$ units, then the value of r is .....units.
(a) 6 (b) 4
(c) 5 (d) 3

70. Find the mean proportion to 0.72 and 2.85 (round up to one decimal place).
(a) 0.4 (b) 2.8 (c) 0.7 (d) 1.4

71. There are two circles touching each other externally. The radius of the first circle with centre O is 12 cm. The radius of the second circle with centre A is 5 cm. Find the length of their common tangent touching the two circles at points P and Q.
(a) $4\sqrt{15}$ cm (b) $14\sqrt{5}$ cm
(c) $5\sqrt{41}$ cm (d) $5\sqrt{14}$ cm

72. The cost price of a fan is ₹ 4400. A merchant wants to make a 24% profit by selling it. At the time of sale, merchant declares a discount of 12% on the marked price. Find the marked price.
(a) ₹ 2600 (b) ₹ 2060
(c) ₹ 6200 (d) ₹ 6020

73. The price of a product increases by 10% in the first year and 20% in the second year. What is the overall percentage increase in the price of the product over the two years?
(a) 30% (b) 32%
(c) 28% (d) 36%

74. If the speed of a boat in still water is 3 km/h and if its speed upstream is 1 km/h, find the speed of the stream.
(a) 2 km/h (b) 1 km/h
(c) 0.25 km/h (d) 0.5 km/h

75. The surface area of a spherical ball is 1386 cm^2. What will be its volume?
(a) 4825 cm^3 (b) 5000 cm^3
(c) 4851 cm^3 (d) 4800 cm^3

Part IV
General Awareness

76. In badminton, 0 points is called ....
(a) in (b) love
(c) play (d) out

77. Which of the following statements is incorrect with respect to High Yielding Varieties (HYVs)?
(a) HYVs had a shorter period of maturity.
(b) The usage of HYVs was complemented with the attraction of more investment in farm machines.
(c) HYVs led to decrease in the cropping intensity.
(d) They made Green Revolution technology as land-saving technology.

78. The Sun Temple at Konark was built under the rule of which dynasty?
(a) Pallava dynasty
(b) Pandya dynasty
(c) Eastern Ganga dynasty
(d) Rashtrakuta dynasty

79. Who was the chief guest at the first Republic Day celebration of India in 1950?
(a) Sukarno
(b) Kwame Nkrumah
(c) Josip Broz Tito
(d) Gamal Abdel Nasser

80. From which of the following states was Vibrant Village programme launched, on 10th April, 2023?
(a) Sikkim
(b) Arunachal Pradesh
(c) Mizoram
(d) Nagaland

81. Which of the following planets does not have rings?
(a) Uranus (b) Venus
(c) Jupiter (d) Saturn

82. The Lucknow Gharana which came into existence in the time of Wajid Ali Shah was developed by who among the following?
(a) Ustad Bakhtawar Khan
(b) Pandit Kalka Prasad
(c) Pandit Thakur Prasad
(d) Pandit Bindawar Prasad

83. Which writ literally means 'what is your authority'?
(a) Habeas Corpus
(b) Mandamus
(c) Quo-Warranto
(d) Prohibition

84. As of 2022, which is the tallest hydroelectric power plant in India?
(a) Sardar Sarovar Hydropower Plant
(b) Nathpa Jhakri Power Plant
(c) Koyna Hydroelectric Power Plant
(d) Tehri Hydroelectric Power Plant

85. Which of the following types is not an element of classical Carnatic music?
(a) Kriti (b) Padam
(c) Sthayi (d) Thumri

86. Who was the Indian Buddhist monk who is credited with the development of many ancient martial art forms in the 5th century?
(a) Bodhidharma (b) Atisa
(c) Bodhiruchi (d) Paramartha

On rationalising the denominator

$$= \frac{\sqrt{3}-1}{\sqrt{3}+1} \times \frac{\sqrt{3}-1}{\sqrt{3}-1}$$

$$= \frac{(\sqrt{3}-1)^2}{(\sqrt{3})^2 - 1^2}$$

$$= \frac{3+1-2\sqrt{3}}{3-1}$$

$$= \frac{4-2\sqrt{3}}{2}$$

$$= 2-\sqrt{3}$$

68. *(a)* $\Delta ABC \sim \Delta EDF$

By Area Similarity theorem

$$\frac{\text{ar } \Delta ABC}{\text{ar } \Delta EDF} = \frac{BC^2}{DF^2}$$

$$\Rightarrow \frac{1}{4} = \frac{8^2}{DF^2}$$

$$\Rightarrow \frac{1}{4} = \frac{64}{DF^2} \Rightarrow DF = \sqrt{256}$$

$$\therefore DF = 16 \text{ cm}$$

69. *(b)* Length of direct common tangent

$$= \sqrt{(\text{Distance between centers})^2 - (\text{Difference between radius of two circles})^2}$$

$$\Rightarrow \sqrt{35} = \sqrt{6^2 - (r-3)^2}$$

$$\Rightarrow 35 = 6^2 - (r-3)^2$$

$$\Rightarrow 35 = 36 - (r-3)^2$$

$$\Rightarrow (r-3)^2 = 1$$

$$\Rightarrow r - 3 = 1$$

$$\therefore r = 4 \text{ units}$$

70. *(d)* Required mean proportion

$$= \sqrt{0.72 \times 2.85}$$

$$= \sqrt{2.052} = 1.4$$

(round upto one decimal place)

71. *(a)*

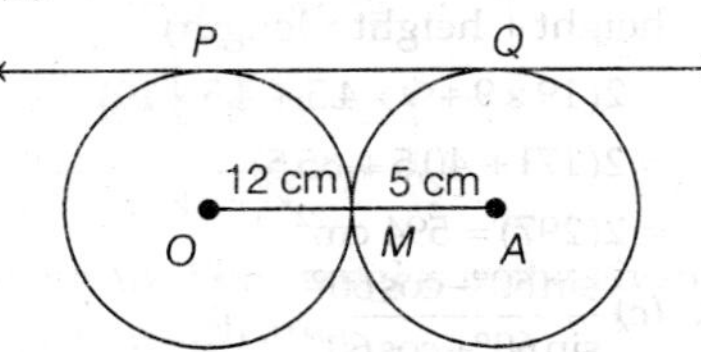

Length of common tangent

$$= \sqrt{(\text{Distance between centers})^2 - (\text{Difference between radius of two circles})^2}$$

$$PQ = \sqrt{(OA)^2 - (OM - AM)^2}$$

$$PQ = \sqrt{(17)^2 - (12-5)^2}$$

$$PQ = \sqrt{289 - 49}$$

$$PQ = \sqrt{240} \Rightarrow PQ = 4\sqrt{15} \text{ cm}$$

72. *(c)* Let the marked price of the article be ₹ x.

According to the question,

$$4400 \times \frac{124}{100} = x \times \left(\frac{100-12}{100}\right)$$

$$\Rightarrow 44 \times 124 = x \times \frac{88}{100}$$

$$\Rightarrow x = \frac{44 \times 124 \times 100}{88}$$

$$\therefore x = 6200$$

73. *(b)* Overall percentage increase in price of product over two years

$$= \left(10 + 20 + \frac{10 \times 20}{100}\right)$$

$$= (30 + 2)$$

$$= 32\%$$

74. *(a)* Speed of stream = Speed of boat in still water − Speed upstream

$$= 3 - 1$$

$$= 2 \text{ km/h}$$

75. *(c)* Let the radius of spherical ball be 'r' cm, then surface area of sphere

$$= 1386$$

$$\Rightarrow 4\pi r^2 = 1386$$

$$\Rightarrow r^2 = \frac{1386}{4 \times \frac{22}{7}}$$

$$\Rightarrow r^2 = 110.25$$

$$\therefore r = \sqrt{110.25}$$

$$= 10.5$$

Now,

$$\text{Volume of sphere} = \frac{4}{3}\pi r^3$$

$$= \frac{4}{3} \times \frac{22}{7} \times (10.5)^3$$

$$= 4851 \text{ cm}^3$$

76. *(b)* In badminton, 0 points is called love.

The word 'Love' (for zero score) comes from French word 'l'oeuf' which means 'egg' which is the shape of zero.

77. *(c)* Statement (c) is incorrect because HYVs led to increase in the cropping intensity.

Statements (a), (b) and (c) are correct.

- HYVs had a early maturation.
- The usage of HYVs was complemented with the attraction of more investment in farm machines.
- They made Green Revolution technology as land-saving technology.

78. *(c)* The Sun Temple at Konark was built under the rule of Eastern Ganga dynasty.

- The Konark Temple is located in Puri, Odisha.
- It was built by King Narasimha Deva I.
- The ruler of the Ganga dynasty during the 13th century.
- The temple is very famous for its intricate carving and motifs.

79. *(a)* Sukarno (President of Indonesia) was the chief guest at the first Republic Day celebration of India in 1950.

- The Republic Day celebrations are majorly divided into three parts i.e., the Republic Day Parade, the Beating Retreat and the Award Distributions.
- The President addresses the country on the eve of Republic Day.

80. *(b)* Arunachal Pradesh launched vibrant village programme, on 10th April, 2023.

- The objective of the programme is comprehensive development of these villages.
- To improve the quality of life of people and thereby reversing outmigration.
- The programme envisages focused area of interventions for creation of opportunities for livelihood generation.

81. *(b)* 'Venus' does not have a ring around it.

- The inner planets (Mercury, Venus, Earth, Mars) couldn't have likely that large rings.
- This is because the rings are made up of frozen icy dust. The inner planets are close to the Sun which is too hot for the rings to form.

82. *(c)* Pandit Thakur Prasad developed the Lucknow Gharana which came into existence in the time of Wajid Ali Shah.

- He blended the traditional Kathak style with elements of Persian and Urdu culture to create the Lucknow Gharana.
- Lucknow Gharana also known as 'Purab Gharana'.

83. *(c)* Quo-Warranto means 'what is your authority'.

- Habeas Corpus—You may have the body

- Mandamus—We command
- Certiorari—To be certified
- Prohibition—To forbid

84. *(d)* Tehri Hydroelectric Power Plant is the tallest power plant in India as of 2021.
- The Tehri dam is the tallest in India, a 575 m tall and 1128 m wide embankment with 52 square kilometres of surface area.
- Tehri hydroelectric complex consists of a 1000 MW.Tehri Pumped Storage Plant; 600 MW Tehri Dam.

85. *(d)* Thumri is a genre of classical music from the Hindustani tradition, not carnatic music.
- It originated in the courts of Lucknow and is characterised by its romantic and devotional lyrics.
- Few elements of classical carnatic music are

1. Raga 2. Kriti
3. Kirtanam 4. Taala
5. Pallavi 6. Swara
7. Jatisvaram

86. *(a)* Bodhidharma was the Indian Buddhist monk who is credited with the development of many ancient martial art forms in the 5th century.
- He developed Shaolin Kung Fu to help heal cramp from lengthy hours of meditation.
- He also developed it to protect himself from wild beats that crept close by the cave.

87. *(c)* Ctrl + M is the keyboard shortcut for inserting a new slide into an MS PowerPoint presentation.

88. *(a)* In Fencing, a defensive blade movement that blocks the opponent's offensive action is called parry.
- Reprise means to repeat the performance.
- Saber means a cavalry sword with a curved blade, thick back and guard.
- Redoublement means a new action made against an opponent who has parried without repositing or who has merely avoided the first action by retreating or displacing the target.

89. *(c)* Article 11 of the Constitution of India vests plenary powers in Parliament to legislate on the subject of citizenship.
- The Parliament has right to make any provision concerning the acquisition and termination of citizenship and any other matter relating to citizenship.
- **Article 8** Citizenship of certain migrants to Pakistan.
- **Article 5** Citizenship at the commencement of the Constitution.
- **Article 6** Citizenship of certain persons who have migrated from Pakistan.

90. *(a)* Tatipaka Refinery is located in the East Godavari district in Andhra Pradesh.
- Bina Refinery is an oil refinery located at Bina in the Sagar district of Madhya Pradesh.
- Koyali Refinery is located in Vadodara district of Gujarat.
- Numaligarh Refinery is located in Golaghat district of Assam.

91. *(c)* Khubakeshei is folk music of Manipur.

Khubakeshei is celebrated in rainy season with the temple, marking the chariot festival of the Lord.
- Ammanaivari are songs sung in praise of Chola monarch is from Tamil Nadu.
- Villu Pattu, also known as Villadichampaatu, is from Tamil Nadu, Kerala.
- Nattupura Pattu is a form of Tamil folk music and Tamil folk culture.

92. *(b)* Annie Besant was the famous British social reformer known for founding the Indian Home Rule league in 1916.
- This was first political party in India to have regime change as its main goal.
- She become the first female President of the Indian National Congress in 1917.

93. *(b)* The correct matching is A-3, B-1, C-2 and D-4.
- The official languages of Sri Lanka are Sinhala and Tamil.
- Mandarin is the official language of China.
- Burmese is the official language of Myanmar.
- Dzongkha is the official language of Bhutan.

94. *(c)* Albinism is a rare group of genetic disorders caused by mutations of certain genes affecting the colour (pigmentation) of the skin, hair and eyes.
- People with albinism are also sensitive to the effects of the Sun, so they're at higher risk of getting skin cancer.
- Although there is no cure for albinism, people with the disorder can take steps to protect their skin and eyes and get proper eye and skin care.

95. *(d)* In Microsoft Word, the Mail Merge Wizard is located under the Mailings tab.

96. *(b)* In 2021, the Juvenile Justice (Care and Protection of Children) Act, 2015 was amended.
- It replaced the Indian Juvenile Delinquency Law, 2000.
- It allows for juveniles in conflict with law in the age group of 16-18.
- It involved in heinous offences, to be tried as adults.

97. *(d)* The excess of expenditure over revenue, including interest payments on debt is a revenue deficit in the government budget.

Revenue deficit = Revenue expense – Revenue receipts

98. *(b)* The 'demographic dividend' results from an increase in the proportion of workers relative to non-workers in the population.
- India has one of the youngest population in an aging world.
- India's demographic dividend will peak around 2041, when the share of working-age, i.e. 20-59 years, population is expected to hit 59 %.

99. *(a)* The correct answer is option (a) for clarifying the mathematical relationship between electrical current, resistance and voltage. Georg Simon Ohm (1789-1854) a German physicist is best known for Ohm's Law i.e., $E = I \times R$.

100. *(c)* Section 375 of the Indian Penal Code deals with rape.
- It defines rape as 'sexual intercourse with a woman against her will without her consent, by coercion, misrepresentation or fraud or at a time when she has been intoxicated or duped".
- Or she is of unsound mental health and in any case if she is under 18 years of age.

Set 36 11 July, 2024 (Shift IV)

SSC CHSL Tier-I
SOLVED PAPER

Instructions

1. This paper contains 100 questions.
2. It has 4 Parts, **Part I** General English, **Part II** General Intelligence & Reasoning, **Part III** Quantitative Aptitude and **Part IV** General Awareness.
3. Each question carries **2 marks**.

Part I
General English

1. Parts of the following sentence have been given as options. Select the option that contains an error.
Geeta was working now but she can be seen swimming in the river every evening.
(a) swimming in the
(b) river every evening
(c) but she can be seen
(d) Geeta was working now

2. The following sentence has been split into four segments. Identify the segment that contains a grammatical error.
The manager asked / the cooking team, "Who / among you is to baked the / Christmas cake this year?"
(a) Christmas cake this year?"
(b) The manager asked
(c) among you is to baked the
(d) the cooking team, "Who

3. Select the grammatically incorrect sentence.
(a) They often meet each other.
(b) They always meet each other.
(c) They quite meet each other.
(d) They hardly meet each other.

4. The following sentence has been divided into four segments. Identify the segment that contains a grammatical error.
The new / secretary / does not likes / me.
(a) me
(b) secretary
(c) The new
(d) does not likes

Directions (Q. Nos. 5-9) *In the following passage, some words have been deleted. Read the passage carefully and select the most appropriate option to fill in each blank.*

Teachers (1) .... given continuous opportunities for self-improvement and to learn the latest innovations and advances in their professions. Each teacher (2) .... expected to participate in at least 50 hours of CPD opportunities every year for their own professional development, driven (3) .... their own interests. CPD opportunities will, in particular, (4) .... cover the latest pedagogies regarding foundational literacy and numeracy, formative and adaptive assessment of learning outcomes, competency based learning and related pedagogies, (5) .... experiential learning, arts-integrated, sports-integrated and storytelling-based approaches, etc.

5. Select the most appropriate option to fill in blank number (1).
(a) shall be (b) will be
(c) can be (d) would be

6. Select the most appropriate option to fill in blank number (2).
(a) shall be (b) would be
(c) can be (d) will be

7. Select the most appropriate option to fill in blank number (3).
(a) by (b) from
(c) at (d) for

8. Select the most appropriate option to fill in blank number (4).
(a) carelessly (b) systematically
(c) roughly (d) partially

9. Select the most appropriate option to fill in blank number (5).
(a) same as (b) such as
(c) from as (d) for as

10. Select the most appropriate antonym of the underlined word.
The waters of Germany are <u>abundant</u> in fish, but there are few genera and species in them.
(a) deficient (b) flourish
(c) allay (d) discord

11. Select the most appropriate synonym of the given word.
Revolution
(a) Stagnation (b) Gyration
(c) Harmony (d) Order

12. Select the most appropriate antonym for the given word.
Ghastly
(a) Agitated (b) Bitter
(c) Relaxing (d) Pleasant

13. Select the most appropriate option that can substitute the underlined segment in the given sentence. If there is no need to substitute it, select 'No substitution required'.
I opened the box beneath the table and <u>took of</u> a book, the 'Materia Medica'.
(a) took out
(b) take off
(c) took in
(d) No substitution required

14. Parts of the following sentence have been given as options. Select the option that contains a spelling error.
I was alarmed lest we should be wreked.
(a) I was (b) be wreked
(c) we should (d) alarmed lest

15. Based on the situation in the sentence, select the most appropriate idiom.
After many years of rivalry, the two schools decided to .... and

participate in a National Event together.
(a) bell the cat
(b) bury the hatchet
(c) go cold turkey
(d) be in the doldrums

16. Choose the option that best describes the meaning of the idioms and phrases underlined in the given sentence.
A jack of all trades cannot survive in the world of specialisation.
(a) A good communicator
(b) A person who can do many things but is not an expert in any
(c) An expert of many jobs
(d) A businessman

17. Select the most appropriate option that can substitute the underlined segment in the given sentence.
Do not later about the street.
(a) loiter around (b) litre about
(c) litter about (d) latter about

18. Select the most appropriate antonym of the given word.
Compulsory
(a) Optional (b) Reliable
(c) Factional (d) Full-fledged

19. Select the most appropriate option that can substitute the underlined segment in the given sentence.
Well, I prefer eating at home from eating out.
(a) and eating out
(b) than eating out
(c) while eating out
(d) to eating out

20. Rectify the sentence by selecting the correct spelling from the options.
The advertisement of vacencies in education sector has received huge response.
(a) vecencies
(b) vacansies
(c) vecancies
(d) vacancies

21. Select the most appropriate antonym of the underlined word in the given sentence.
The athlete looked unsettled before the race.
(a) confident
(b) reticent
(c) triumphant
(d) tangent

22. Select the most appropriate synonym of the given word.
Candid
(a) Cruel (b) Bright
(c) Top (d) Honest

23. Select the most appropriate option to fill in the blank.
The artist received a .... from the audience.
(a) handful of applause
(b) round of applause
(c) bunch of applause
(d) plenty of applause

24. Select the most appropriate option that can substitute the underlined word in the given sentence.
The experienced surgeon handled the delicate procedure with care and precision.
(a) seasoned (b) amateur
(c) untrained (d) unskilled

25. Select the most appropriate antonym of the underlined word in the following sentence.
I have left it to his discretion to accept or decline my offer.
(a) wisdom (b) calculation
(c) inattention (d) judgement

Part II
General Intelligence

26. Select the option figure in which the given figure (X) is embedded as its part (rotation is not allowed).

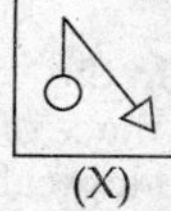
(X)

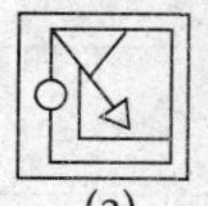
(a)

(b)

(c)

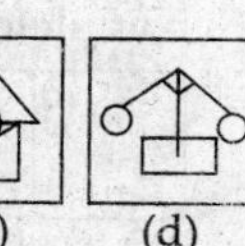
(d)

27. Each of the letters in the word FRANCHISE are arranged from left to right in alphabetical order to form a new word. How many letters are there in the English alphabetical series between the alphabet which is fifth from the left and the one which is third from the right in the newly formed word?
(a) Seven (b) Five
(c) Four (d) Six

28. CYRF is related to NJCQ in a certain way based on the English alphabetical order. In the same way, GBUM is related to RMFX. To which of the following is CZKP related, following the same logic?
(a) NKVA
(b) NAKV
(c) NKAV
(d) NAVK

29. If 'A' stands for '÷', 'B' stands for '×', 'C' stands for '+' and 'D' stands for '–', then the resultant of which of the following will be 421?
(a) 63 B 7 A 125 D 5 C 5
(b) 63 A 7 D 125 B 5 C 5
(c) 63 B 7 D 125 A 5 C 5
(d) 63 C 7 D 125 A 5 B 5

30. In this question, three statements are given, followed by three conclusions numbered I, II and III. Assuming the statements to be true, even if they seem to be at variance with commonly known facts, decide which of the conclusion(s) logically follow(s) from the statements.
Statements
No rose is an orchid.
All roses are lilies.
All lilies are lotuses.
Conclusions
I. Some lilies are orchids.
II. Some lotuses are orchids.
III. All lilies are orchids.
(a) Both Conclusions I and III follow
(b) Neither Conclusions I, II nor III follows
(c) Both Conclusions I and II follow
(d) Both Conclusions II and III follow

31. What would be the Roman numeral on the opposite side of 'V' if the given sheet is folded to form a cube?

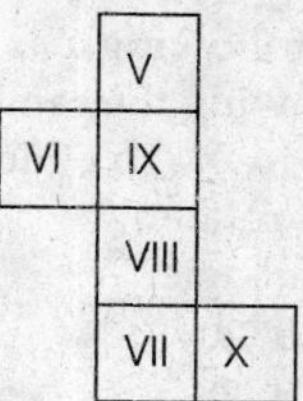

(a) VII
(b) X
(c) VIII
(d) VI

32. Select the correct mirror image of the given figure when the mirror is placed at AB as shown below.

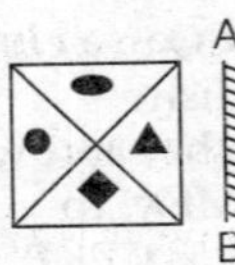

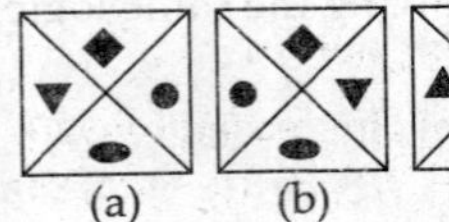
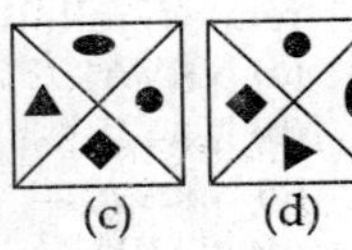

(a) (b) (c) (d)

33. What should come in place of '?' in the given series based on the English alphabetical order ?
QRS, MXB, IDK, EJT, ?
(a) PCA (b) CPA (c) APC (d) AAC

34. In a certain code language, 'mix jaggery well' is written as 'rb co ot' and 'well done boss' is written as 'cx rb op'. How is 'well' written in the given language?
(a) co (b) cx (c) ot (d) rb

35. Find the number of triangles in the given figure.

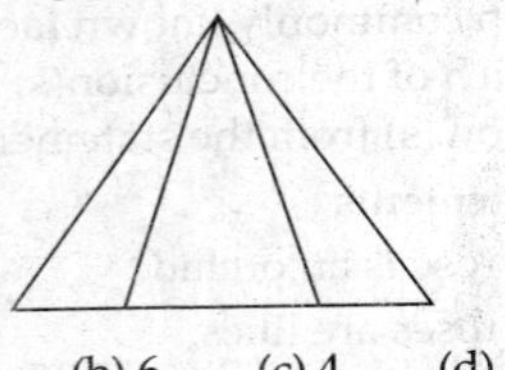

(a) 8 (b) 6 (c) 4 (d) 5

36. Which of the following letter-clusters can replace the question mark (?) in the given series to make it logically complete?
JMD, OHJ, ? , YXV, DSB
(a) RST (b) AOZ
(c) TCP (d) VCP

37. What should come in place of the question mark (?) in the given series?
86, 88, 90, 92, 94,?
(a) 99 (b) 96 (c) 97 (d) 98

38. 78 is related to 30 following a certain logic. Following the same logic, 67 is related to 26. To which of the following is 54 related, following the same logic?
(a) 18 (b) 20
(c) 16 (d) 28

39. What will come in the place of the question mark (?) in the following equation, if '+' and '–' are interchanged and '×' and '÷' are interchanged?
$125 \div 5 + 19 - 190 \times 19 = ?$
(a) 606 (b) 636 (c) 616 (d) 626

40. In a certain language, 'protect your health' is written as 'Df Bk Tu' and 'health is wealth' is written as 'Po Tu Le'. How is 'health' written in the given language?
(a) Df (b) Po (c) Bk (d) Tu

41. IJLO is related to GHJM in a certain way based on the English alphabetical order. In the same way, HIKN is related to FGIL. To which of the following is EFHK related, following the same logic?
(a) CEDI (b) CDFI
(c) CDEF (d) CEFI

42. Three of the following four are alike in a certain way and thus form a group. Which is the one that does not belong to that group?
(**Note** The odd one out is not based on the number of consonants/ vowels or their position in the letter cluster.)
(a) UXY (b) JMN
(c) DGH (d) ORT

43. What will come in the place of the question mark (?) in the following equation, if '+' and '–' are interchanged and '×' and '÷' are interchanged?
$87 \div 3 + 35 - 88 \times 11 = ?$
(a) 231 (b) 233 (c) 234 (d) 232

44. If 25th August, 2006 was Friday, then what was the day of the week on 25th August, 2018?
(a) Saturday
(b) Sunday
(c) Thursday
(d) Wednesday

45. Identify the figure given in the options that when put in place of the question mark (?) will logically complete the series.

0 B L T 4	T 4 B L C	L C 4 B ↑	B ↑ C 4 D	?

4 D ↑ B 8	4 D ↑ C 8	4 D 8 B ↑	4 D ↑ C B
(a)	(b)	(c)	(d)

46. Which of the following numbers will replace the question mark (?) in the given series?
$\left[\frac{5}{9}\right], \left[\frac{14}{9}\right], \left[\frac{23}{9}\right], \left[\frac{32}{9}\right], \left[\frac{41}{9}\right], ?$
(a) $\left[\frac{44}{9}\right]$ (b) $\left[\frac{51}{9}\right]$ (c) $\left[\frac{47}{9}\right]$ (d) $\left[\frac{50}{9}\right]$

47. A square sheet of paper is folded along the dotted line successively along the directions shown and is then punched in the last. How would the paper look when unfolded?

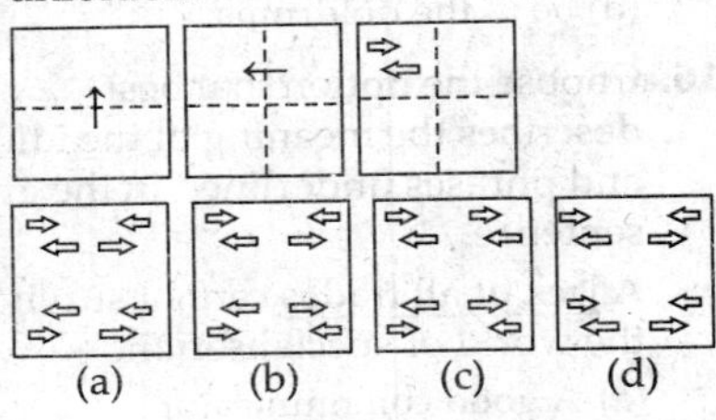

(a) (b) (c) (d)

48. Select the set in which the numbers are related in the same way as are the numbers of the following sets.
(**Note** Operations should be performed on the whole numbers, without breaking down the numbers into their constituent digits. E.g. 13– Operations on 13 such as adding/subtracting/ multiplying etc. to 13 can be performed. Breaking down 13 into 1 and 3 and then performing mathematical operations on 1 and 3 is not allowed.)
(4, 8, 32)
(7, 14, 56)
(a) (11, 22, 88) (b) (11, 33, 88)
(c) (11, 33, 77) (d) (11, 22, 77)

49. In a certain code language,
A % B means 'A is the mother of B'
A # B means 'A is the brother of B'
A @ B means 'A is the wife of B'
A & B means 'A is the father of B'
Based on the above, how is P related to T if 'P & Q % R # S @ T'?
(a) Wife's father
(b) Wife's mother's father
(c) Wife's mother's brother
(d) Wife's brother

50. What would be the letter on the opposite side of 'P', if the given sheet is folded to form a cube?

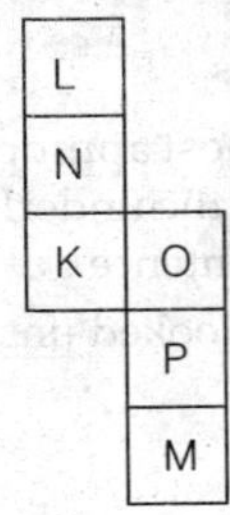

(a) L (b) N
(c) M (d) K

Part III

Quantitative Aptitude

51. The following bar graph represents the total number of students enrolled and the number of students who got campus placement in six different engineering colleges A, B, C, D, E, and F. Study the graph carefully and answer the question given below.

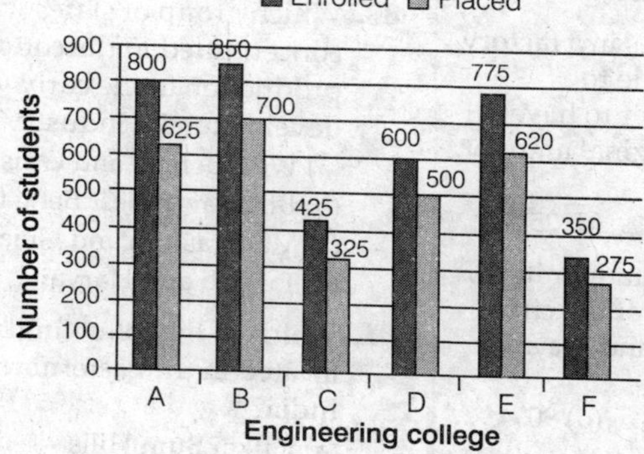

What per cent (correct up to two decimal places) of total enrolled students have got campus placements in colleges A, C and F?

(a) 86.67% (b) 77.78% (c) 82.78% (d) 79.67%

52. The following table gives the percentage of marks obtained by seven students in six different subjects in an examination. The numbers in the brackets give the maximum marks in each subject.

Student	Subject (Max. marks)					
	Maths	Chemistry	Physics	Geography	History	Computer Science
	(150)	(130)	(120)	(100)	(60)	(40)
Ayush	90	50	90	60	70	80
Aman	100	80	80	40	80	70
Sajal	90	60	70	70	90	70
Rohit	80	65	80	80	60	60
Muskan	80	65	85	95	50	90
Tanvi	70	75	65	85	40	60
Tarun	65	35	50	77	80	80

How many students secured a raw score of 135 in Maths?

(a) 0 (b) 2 (c) 1 (d) 3

53. If L is the mid-point of side BC of ΔABC and the area of ΔABL is 15 cm^2, then the area (in sq cm) of ΔABC is

(a) 32 (b) 30 (c) 27 (d) 25

54. In ΔABC, D and E are points on sides AB and AC, such that $DE \parallel BC$. If $AD = x$, $DB = x-3$, $AE = x+3$ and $EC = x-2$, then the value of x is

(a) 5.2 (b) 4.0 (c) 4.5 (d) 4.2

55. X, Y and Z can do a work in 24 days, 5 days and 12 days, respectively. In how many days can they do the same work, if they work together?

(a) 4 days (b) $3\frac{1}{13}$ days (c) $\frac{1}{24}$ days (d) $\frac{7}{24}$ days

56. If $\frac{15}{8}+\left[\left\{\frac{4}{5}\text{ of }\frac{5}{12}\div\left(1\frac{1}{15}\right)\right\}\times 1\frac{7}{12}\right]$ is expressed in the form of $\frac{a}{b}$, where a and b are integers and relatively prime to each other, the value $4b-a$ is

(a) 313 (b) 225
(c) 164 (d) 189

57. If the price of a commodity is increased by 36%, by what percentage (rounded off to 1 decimal place) should its consumption be decreased so that the expenditure of the commodity stays the same?

(a) 26.5% (b) 36%
(c) 29.5% (d) 32%

58. In an obtuse-angled triangle ABC, the length of its longest side AB is 50 cm and one of the other two sides is 42 cm. If the area of the triangle is 294 cm^2, what is the length (in cm) of its third side?

(a) $8\sqrt{35}$ (b) $15\sqrt{21}$
(c) $2\sqrt{58}$ (d) $12\sqrt{43}$

59. The given chart represents the sales of automobiles in India (by type, in million units) from the year 2011 to 2014. Study the chart and answer the question that follows.

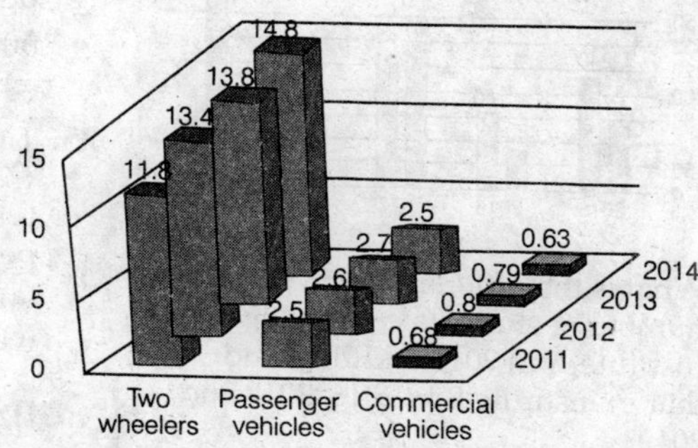

The percentage increase in the sales in 2013 over the previous year was the maximum for which of the categories of vehicles?

(a) Two wheelers
(b) Commercial vehicles
(c) Passenger vehicles
(d) Two wheelers and Passenger vehicles

60. Tom travelled 285 km in 6 h. In his total travelling, he travelled the first part by bus at 40 km/h and the remaining part by train at 55 km/h. How much distance has he travelled by train?

(a) 155 km (b) 120 km
(c) 165 km (d) 135 km

61. The average of 50 numbers is 23. If each number is multiplied by 13, then the new average is

(a) 219 (b) 299
(c) 650 (d) 88

62. What should be added to each term of the ratio 5 : 11 so that the ratio becomes 3 : 5 ?

(a) 6 (b) 4
(c) 2 (d) 5

63. A cylindrical candle, 14 cm in diameter and length 2 cm is melted to form a cuboid candle of dimensions 7 cm ×11 cm × 2 cm. How many cuboidal candles can be obtained?

(a) 4 (b) 5
(c) 2 (d) 3

64. A right angled triangle of area 600 m^2 is to be made such that the hypotenuse is double the base. For the triangle, the hypotenuse is .... more than the base.

(a) 20.36 m (b) 22.32 m
(c) 24.36 m (d) 26.32 m

65. How much simple interest will ₹5000 earn in 14 months at a 12% interest rate per annum?

(a) ₹ 600 (b) ₹ 800
(c) ₹ 700 (d) ₹ 500

66. Refer to the bar graph below and answer the question that follows.

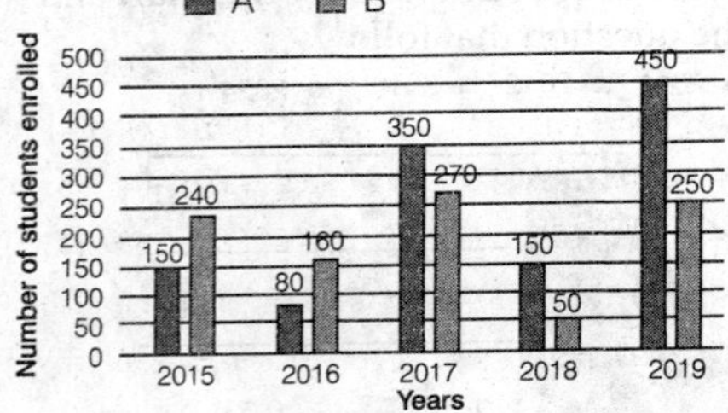

What is the difference between the number of students enrolled in Institute A in 2015 and 2017 and that in Institute B in 2016, 2018 and 2019?

(a) 40 (b) 150 (c) 75 (d) 100

67. If 10% of 24% of x is 240, then x = ?

(a) 100 (b) 1000
(c) 10000 (d) 100000

68. If $\tan A + \sin A = x, \tan A - \sin A = y$, what is the value of $x^2 - y^2$?

(a) $2\sqrt{\frac{x}{y}}$ (b) $4\sqrt{\frac{x}{y}}$
(c) $\sqrt{xy}$ (d) $4\sqrt{xy}$

69. The number 611611611611 is

1. divisible by both 6 and 11
2. neither divisible by 6 nor by 11
3. divisible by 6 only
4. divisible by 11 only

(a) (4) (b) (3) (c) (2) (d) (1)

70. My father is presently 25 yr older than me. The sum of our ages 5 yr ago was 39 yr. Find my present age.

(a) 13 yr (b) 12 yr (c) 15 yr (d) 20 yr

71. An election was held between two candidates. The winning candidate scored 54% of the valid votes and won by 88 votes. If 58 votes were declared invalid, then find the total number of votes polled in the election.

(a) 1850 (b) 1158
(c) 1156 (d) 2000

72. The salary of employees in a factory was reduced by 20% due to economic crisis. In order to have their salary back to original amount, it must be raised by

(a) 20% (b) 12.5% (c) 40% (d) 25%

73. What is the area (in square units) of the sector if the radius of the circle is given to be 24 units and the arc length is 7.5 units?

(a) 135 (b) 180 (c) 45 (d) 90

74. The volume of rectangular block is 12288 m^3. Its dimension are in the ratio of 4 : 3 : 2. If the entire surface is polished at the rate 2 paise per m^2, then find the total cost of polishing.

(a) ₹ 33.28 (b) ₹ 44.42
(c) ₹ 66.56 (d) ₹ 11.14

75. The marked price of a table lamp is ₹ 2165. During the festive season, it is sold for ₹ 1710.35. Find the percentage discount offered.

(a) 21% (b) 20.5%
(c) 18% (d) 22.5%

Part IV
General Awareness

76. Which of the following is the fastest way to open the Help window in Microsoft Word?

(a) Type 'help' in the search bar and then press Enter
(b) Click the Microsoft Office button and then, click Help
(c) Press F1
(d) Click the Help button on the ribbon

77. Which star is also known as the 'Pole Star'?

(a) The West star (b) The South star
(c) The North star (d) The East star

78. According to Census 2011, which union territory recorded the highest female literacy rate in India?

(a) Delhi (b) Lakshadweep
(c) Chandigarh (d) Puducherry

79. In Equestrian sports, ... occurs when a horse or rider lowers an element of a jump that establishes the height of an obstacle.

(a) canter
(b) curb
(c) clean round
(d) knockdown

80. Which group of states was concentrated in the cotton production in the early years to develop textile industry?

(a) West Bengal and Odisha
(b) Bihar and West Bengal
(c) Maharashtra and Gujarat
(d) Punjab and Haryana

81. Which of the following hills is located in the easternmost part of India?

(a) Patkai Bum Hills
(b) Jaintia Hills
(c) Khasi Hills
(d) Garo Hills

82. Who among the following is not associated with the Green Revolution?

(a) MS Swaminathan
(b) P. Chidambaram
(c) Norman Borlaug
(d) Chidambaram Subramaniam

83. Who among the following is related to Hindustani classical singing?

(a) Mallikarjun Mansur
(b) Srinavasa Iyer
(c) Aruna Sairam
(d) Ramanuj Iyengar

84. The original Constitution did not mention any Fundamental Duty because

(a) initially Fundamental Duties were not expected to be performed
(b) it was expected that the citizens of the country would perform their duties willingly
(c) it was expected that the citizens of the country would perform their duties forcefully
(d) initially Fundamental Duties were punishable as per the Constitution

85. Which of the following measures can be adopted by the government to reduce revenue deficit?

(a) Offering freebies
(b) Increasing subsidies
(c) Increasing money supply
(d) Tax reforms

86. Every year in the month of February, this camel festival is organised by Rajasthan Tourism Development Corporation in
(a) Barmer
(b) Bikaner
(c) Jaisalmer
(d) Jodhpur

87. MLAs in which of the following states/UTs received an increase of about 66% in salaries and allowances w.e.f. 14th February, 2023?
(a) Tamil Nadu
(b) Lakshadweep
(c) Delhi
(d) Bihar

88. From which book is the national song of India compiled?
(a) Anand Math
(b) Mandukya Upanishad
(c) Katha Upanishad
(d) Bharat Bharti

89. With reference to 'Saila dance' consider the following statements and select the correct code.
A. A group comprising of male performers.
B. The dance is performed with bamboo sticks.
C. It is performed after the cutting of crops.
Codes
(a) A, B and C
(b) B and C
(c) A and C
(d) A and B

90. Who was the first person to conduct a systematic study of chromosomes during division and called this process mitosis?
(a) Friedrich Miescher
(b) Thomas Hunt Morgan
(c) Antonie van Leeuwenhoek
(d) Walther Flemming

91. In cricket, a fast, head-high delivery of the ball is referred to as ....
(a) grubber (b) leg-bye
(c) duck (d) bouncer

92. According to the Census of India 2011, which of the following states has the largest Buddhist population?
(a) Uttar Pradesh
(b) Maharashtra
(c) Madhya Pradesh
(d) West Bengal

93. Who captained India to victory in the 2011 Cricket World cup final win over Sri Lanka?
(a) Sourav Ganguly
(b) Mahendra Singh Dhoni
(c) Sachin Tendulkar
(d) Rahul Dravid

94. Which function is used to calculate the maximum value in a selected column in MS Excel?
(a) Auto max
(b) High
(c) Max
(d) Auto high

95. Which British colonel is remembered as the Butcher of Amritsar for his role in the Jallianwala Bagh massacre in 1919?
(a) Reginald Dyer
(b) Robert Clive
(c) William Birdwood
(d) William Slim

96. The 42nd Constitutional Amendment Act of Indian Constitution was passed in the year ....
(a) 1976 (b) 1977
(c) 1978 (d) 1979

97. In which of the following liquids would anthracene dissolve easily?
(a) Benzene
(b) Sodium chloride
(c) Methane
(d) Water

98. In March 2023, the Uttarakhand government had approved how much horizontal reservation for statehood activists in state government jobs?
(a) 10%
(b) 15%
(c) 8%
(d) 5%

99. The Press and Registration of Books (PRB) Act was enacted in which year?
(a) 1887 (b) 1877
(c) 1867 (d) 1857

100. Who amongst the following Delhi Sultanate rulers sent his army under Malik Kafur's command to conquer South India?
(a) Ghiyas-ud-din Balban
(b) Iltutmish
(c) Alauddin Khilji
(d) Qutub-ud-din Aibak

Answers

1. (d)	2. (c)	3. (c)	4. (d)
5. (b)	6. (d)	7. (a)	8. (b)
9. (b)	10. (a)	11. (b)	12. (d)
13. (a)	14 (b)	15. (b)	16. (b)
17. (a)	18. (a)	19. (d)	20. (d)
21. (a)	22. (d)	23. (b)	24. (a)
25. (c)	26. (a)	27. (b)	28. (a)
29. (c)	30. (b)	31. (c)	32. (c)
33. (c)	34. (d)	35. (b)	36. (c)
37. (b)	38. (a)	39. (c)	40. (d)
41. (b)	42. (d)	43. (c)	44. (a)
45. (b)	46. (d)	47. (b)	48. (a)
49. (b)	50. (b)	51. (b)	52. (b)
53. (b)	54. (c)	55. (b)	56. (a)
57. (a)	58. (c)	59. (c)	60. (c)
61. (b)	62. (b)	63. (c)	64. (d)
65. (c)	66. (a)	67. (c)	68. (d)
69. (a)	70. (b)	71. (b)	72. (d)
73. (d)	74. (c)	75. (a)	76. (c)
77. (c)	78. (b)	79. (d)	80. (c)
81. (a)	82. (b)	83. (a)	84. (b)
85. (d)	86. (b)	87. (c)	88. (a)
89. (a)	90. (d)	91. (d)	92. (b)
93. (b)	94. (c)	95. (a)	96. (a)
97. (a)	98. (a)	99. (c)	100. (c)

Explanations

1. ***(d)*** Part 'Geeta was working now' contains an error. As the given sentence is in present tense, use 'is' to correct the sentence.

2. ***(c)*** Part 'among you is to baked the' contains an error. Use 'among you will bake the' to correct the sentence. The given sentence is a future conditional in which one clause is in simple future and the other is in simple present.

3. ***(c)*** The grammatically incorrect sentence is-They quite meet each other.
The correct sentence is-They frequently meet each other.

4. ***(d)*** Part 'does not likes' contains an error. Use 'does not like' to correct the sentence.

5. ***(b)*** The correct filler for the given blank is 'will be'.

6. *(d)* The correct filler for the given blank is 'will be'.

7. *(a)* The correct filler for the given blank is 'by'.

8. *(b)* The correct filler for the given blank is 'systematically'.

9. *(b)* The correct filler for the given blank is 'such as'.

10. *(a)* 'Abundant' means in large quantity. Hence, its antonym is 'deficient' which means in less quantity.

- 'Flourish' means to grow.
- 'Allay' means diminish or put at rest (fear, suspicion, or worry).
- 'Discord' means disagreement between people.

11. *(b)* The word 'revolution' means an instance of revolving. Hence, its synonym is 'gyration' which means a rapid movement in a circle or spiral; a whirling motion.

'Stagnation' means to be still.

12. *(d)* 'Ghastly' means causing great horror or fear. Hence, its antonym is 'Pleasant'.

13. *(a)* The underlined part of the given sentence contains an error. Use 'took out' to correct the sentence.

14. *(b)* Part (b) 'be wreked' contains an error. The correct spelling is 'wrecked'.

15. *(b)* The correct idiom for the given blank is 'bury the hatchet'. It means to end a quarrel or conflict and become friendly.

16. *(b)* A jack of all trades is someone who can do many things but is not an expert in any.

17. *(a)* The underlined part of the given sentence contains an error. Use 'loiter around' to correct the sentence.

18. *(a)* The antonym of 'compulsory' is 'optional'.

19. *(d)* The underlined part of the given sentence contains an error. Use 'to eating out' to correct the sentence.

20. *(d)* The incorrectly spelt word is 'vacencies'. The correct spelling is 'vacancies'.

21. *(a)* 'Unsettled' means nervous and anxious. Hence, its antonym is 'confident'.

- 'Reticent' means not revealing one's thoughts or feelings readily.
- 'Triumphant' means victorious.
- 'Tangent' means the straight line that just touches the curve at that point.

22. *(d)* The word 'candid' means 'honest'.

23. *(b)* The correct filler for the given blank is 'round of applause'.

24. *(a)* The word 'seasoned' means 'experienced' which is appropriate to fill in the blank.

25. *(c)* 'Discretion' means saying something or taking decision precisely or attentively. Hence, 'inattention' is its nearest antonym.

26. *(a)* Given figure (X) is embedded in figure of option (a).

27. *(b)* When each letter of FRANCHISE is arranged from left to right in alphabetical order. Then,

ACEFHINRS

Letter fifth from left = H

Letter third from right = N

Then, letters between H and N in English alphabetical series are I, J, K, L, M.

Hence, total number of letters between H and N = 5

28. *(a)* As, C Y R F → (+11, −15, −15, +11) → N J C Q

and G B U M → (+11, −15, −15, +11) → R M F X

Similarly,

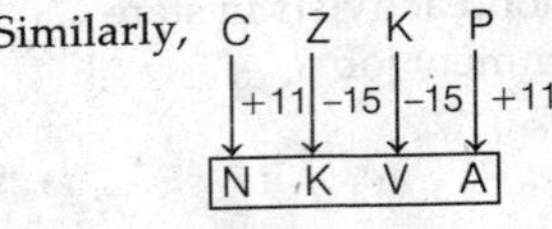

29. *(c)* Taking option (c) replacing the alphabets with numbers we get,

6 3 B 7 D 125 A 5 C 5

$= 63 \times 7 - 125 \div 5 + 5$

$= 441 - 25 + 5 = 446 - 25 = 421$

30. *(b)* According to the question,

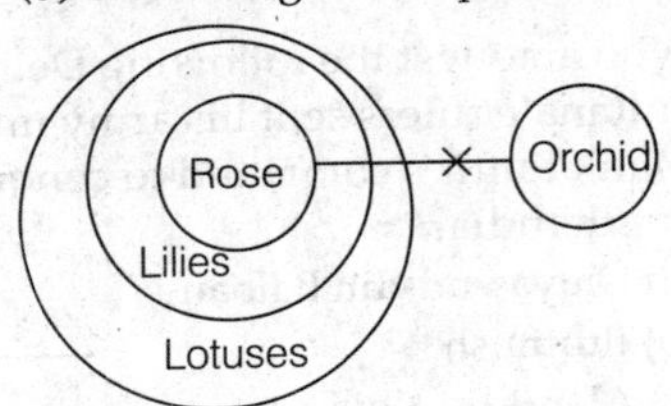

Conclusions I. (✗) II. (✗) III. (✗)

Hence, neither Conclusions I, II nor III follows.

Note One negative and one positive statement never gives +ve (positive) conclusion.

31. *(c)* According to the question,

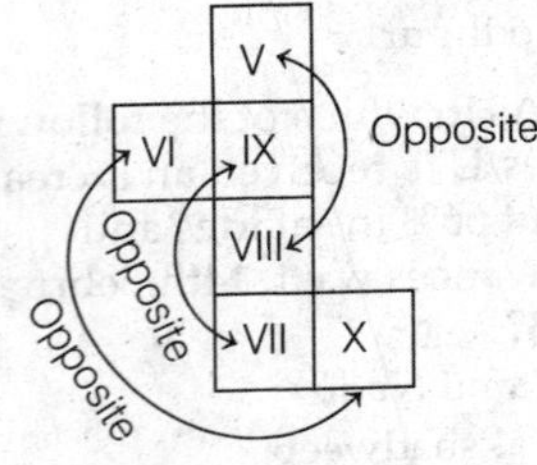

Hence, VIII is opposite of V.

32. *(c)* The correct mirror image of given figure is option (c).

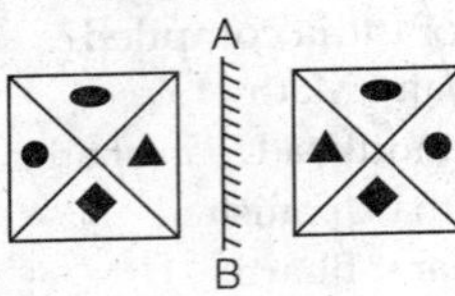

33. *(c)* The pattern of the given series is as follows,

Q →(−4) M →(−4) I →(−4) E →(−4) A

R →(+6) X →(+6) D →(+6) J →(+6) P

S →(+9) B →(+9) K →(+9) T →(+9) C

∴ ? = APC

34. *(d)* According to the question,

mix jaggery (well) → (rb) co ot

(well) done boss → cx (rb) op

Hence, 'well' is written as 'rb'.

35. *(b)* Naming the figure,

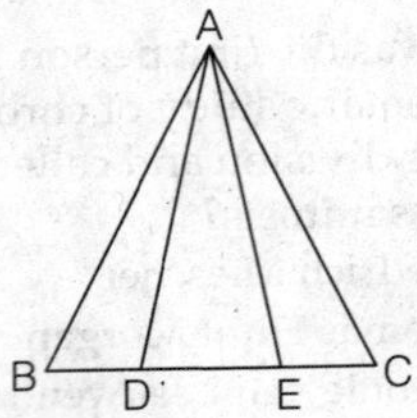

There are total six triangles in the given figure

ΔABD, ΔADE, ΔAEC, ΔABE, ΔADC, ΔABC

36. *(c)* The pattern of the series is as follows,

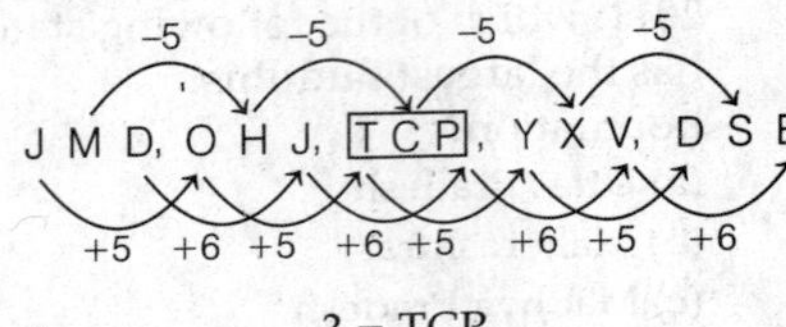

∴ ? = TCP

37. *(b)* The pattern of the series is as follows,

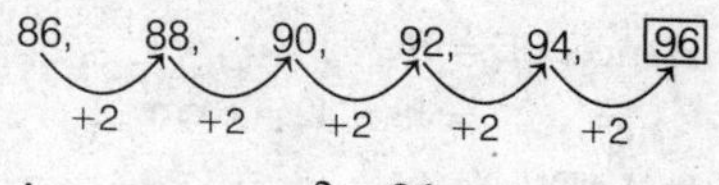

∴ $? = 96$

38. *(a)* According to the question,

Since, $78 \rightarrow 30$

$\Rightarrow \quad 7 + 8 = 15 \Rightarrow 15 \times 2 = 30$

and $67 \rightarrow 26$

$\Rightarrow \quad 6 + 7 = 13 \Rightarrow 13 \times 2 = 26$

Similarly, $54 \rightarrow 5 + 4 = 9 \Rightarrow 9 \times 2 = \boxed{18}$

39. *(c)* Given expression,

$125 \div 5 + 19 - 190 \times 19 = ?$

After interchanging + and − and × and ÷, we get

$125 \times 5 - 19 + 190 \div 19$

$= 625 - 19 + 10$

$= 635 - 19 = 616$

40. *(d)* According to the question,

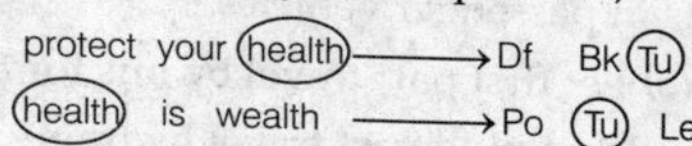

Hence, 'health' is written as 'Tu'.

41. *(b)* As, and

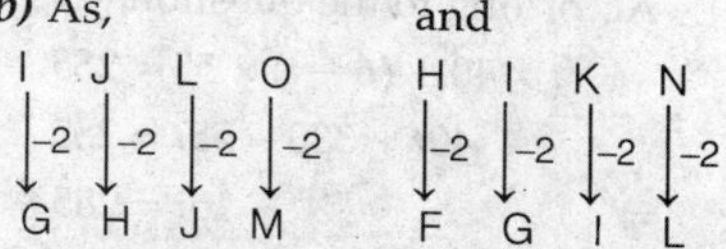

Similarly,

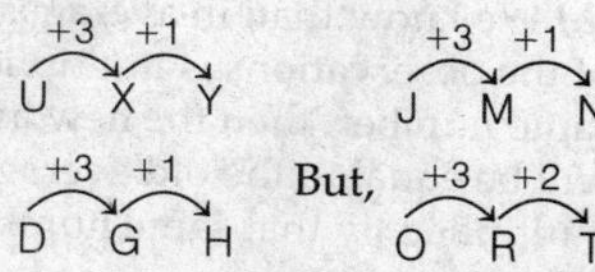

42. *(d)* As,

U X Y (+3, +1)   J M N (+3, +1)

D G H (+3, +1)   But, O R T (+3, +2)

Hence, ORT doesn't belong to the group.

43. *(c)* Given expression,

$87 \div 3 + 35 - 88 \times 11 = ?$

After interchanging + and −, and × and ÷, we get

$? = 87 \times 3 - 35 + 88 \div 11$

$= 261 - 35 + 8$

$= 269 - 35 = 234$

44. *(a)* Total years between 25th August, 2006 to 25th August, 2018

$= 2018 - 2006 = 12$ yr

Since, in ordinary year (+1) day is added and between 2006 to 2018, 2008, 2012, 2016 are leap years and in leap year extra (+1) day will be added.

Hence, total odd days between 25th August, 2006 to 25th August, 2018

$= 12 + 3 = 15$ days

∴ $\frac{15}{7} \Rightarrow 1$ odd day

Hence, required day = Friday + 1

= Saturday

45. *(b)* After observing the figures carefully we get option (b) is best following the series.

The pattern is as follows,

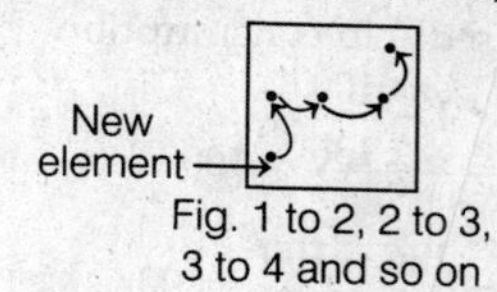

Fig. 1 to 2, 2 to 3, 3 to 4 and so on

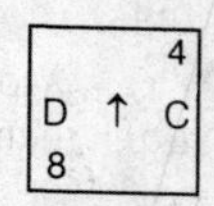

46. *(d)* The pattern of the given series is as follows,

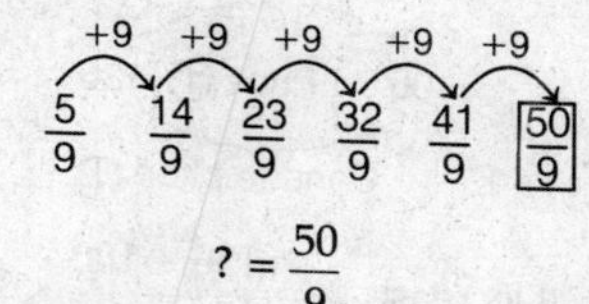

∴ $? = \frac{50}{9}$

47. *(b)* After unfolding the paper, we get option (b).

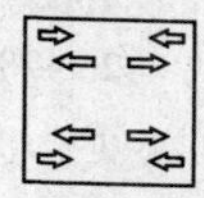

Note In each and every step during unfolding, we get mirror image of previous figure.

48. *(a)* As, and

4 → 8 → 32 (×2, ×4)   7 → 14 → 56 (×2, ×4)

Similarly, 11 → 22 → 88 (×2, ×4)

49. *(b)* Given expression,

P&Q%R#S@T

According to the question,

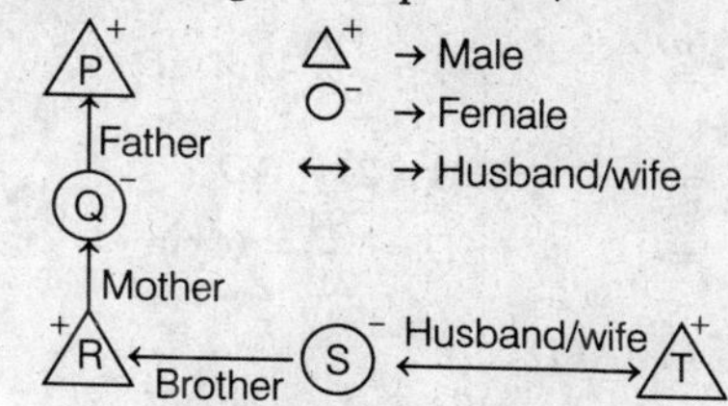

Hence, P is wife's mother's father of T.

50. *(b)* According to the question,

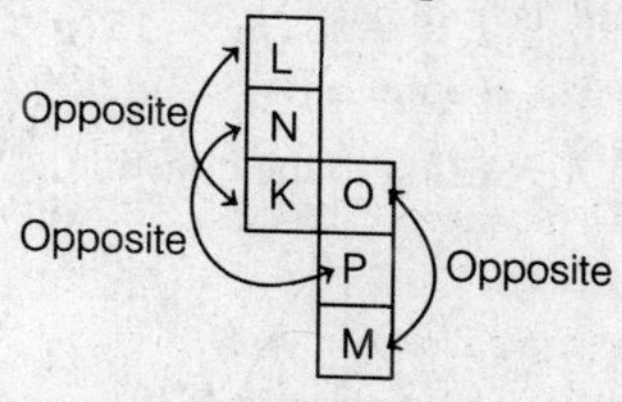

Hence, the letter on opposite side of P is 'N'.

51. *(b)* Total number of enrolled students in college A, C and F

$= 800 + 425 + 350 = 1575$

Total number of students who got campus placements in college A, C and F

$= 625 + 325 + 275 = 1225$

∴ Required percentage

$= \frac{1225}{1575} \times 100 = 77.78\%$

52. *(b)* Raw scores of different students in Maths is as follows,

Ayush $= 150 \times \frac{90}{100} = 135$

Aman $= 150 \times \frac{100}{100} = 150$

Sajal $= 150 \times \frac{90}{100} = 135$

Rohit $= 150 \times \frac{80}{100} = 120$

Muskan $= 150 \times \frac{80}{100} = 120$

Tanvi $= 150 \times \frac{70}{100} = 105$

Tarun $= 150 \times \frac{65}{100} = 97.5$

Hence, total number of students who got raw score 135 is two (Ayush, Sajal).

53. *(b)* According to the question,

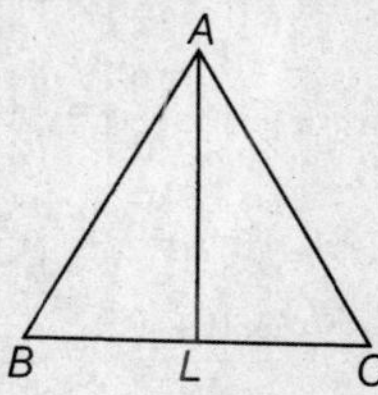

Since, L is mid-point of BC,

∴ AL is the median of ΔABC.

We know that median of a triangle divides it into two triangles of equal area.

$\Rightarrow$ ar (ΔABL) = ar (ΔACL)

∴ ar $(\Delta ACL) = 15$ cm^2

[∵ given ar $(\Delta ABL) = 15$ cm^2]

$\therefore$ ar (ΔABC) = ar (ΔABL) + ar (ΔACL)
$= 15 \text{ cm}^2 + 15 \text{ cm}^2$
$= 30 \text{ cm}^2$

54. *(c)* According to the question,

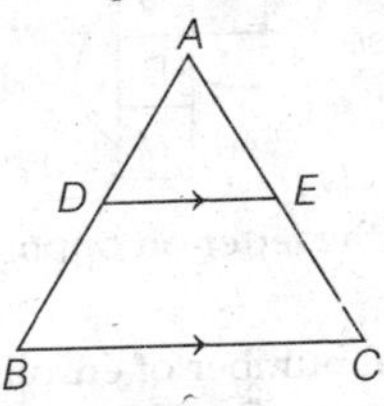

$\because$ $DE \parallel BC$

$\therefore \dfrac{AD}{BD} = \dfrac{AE}{EC}$ [Thales theorem]

$\Rightarrow \dfrac{x}{x-3} = \dfrac{x+3}{x-2}$

$\Rightarrow x(x-2) = (x-3)(x+3)$

$\Rightarrow x^2 - 2x = x^2 + 3x - 3x - 9$

$\Rightarrow -2x = -9$

$\therefore x = \dfrac{9}{2} = 4.5$

55. *(b)*

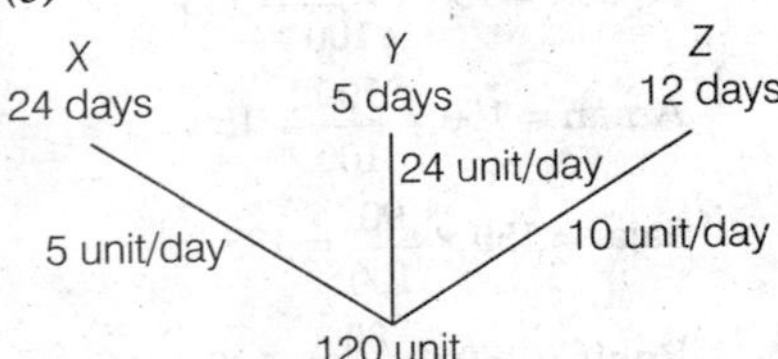

Total number of days if X, Y and Z work together

$= \dfrac{120}{(5 + 24 + 10)}$ unit/day

$= \dfrac{120}{39} = \dfrac{40}{13} = 3\dfrac{1}{13}$ days

56. *(a)* $\dfrac{15}{8} + \left[\left\{\dfrac{4}{5} \text{ of } \dfrac{5}{12} \div \left(1\dfrac{1}{15}\right)\right\} \times 1\dfrac{7}{12}\right] = \dfrac{a}{b}$

Applying VBODMAS,

$\dfrac{15}{8} + \left[\left\{\dfrac{1}{3} \times \dfrac{15}{16}\right\} \times \dfrac{19}{12}\right] = \dfrac{a}{b}$

$\Rightarrow \dfrac{15}{8} + \left[\dfrac{5}{16} \times \dfrac{19}{12}\right] = \dfrac{a}{b}$

$\Rightarrow \dfrac{15}{8} + \dfrac{95}{192} = \dfrac{a}{b}$

$\Rightarrow \dfrac{360 + 95}{192} = \dfrac{a}{b}$

$\Rightarrow \dfrac{455}{192} = \dfrac{a}{b}$

Hence, $a = 455$, $b = 192$

(Here a and b are coprime numbers)

$\therefore 4b - a = 4 \times 192 - 455$
$= 768 - 455$
$= 313$

57. *(a)* Let total consumption = 1kg and the price per kg = ₹ 100/kg

Hence, total expenditure

$= 1\text{kg} \times ₹100/\text{kg} = ₹ 100$

If price is increased by 36%.

So, new price $= 100 + 100 \times \dfrac{36}{100}$

$= ₹136/\text{kg}$

For making total expenditure same, then total consumption

$= \dfrac{₹ 100}{₹ 136/\text{kg}} = \dfrac{100}{136}$ kg

$\therefore$ Decreased% in consumption

$= \dfrac{1 - \dfrac{100}{136}}{1} \times 100$

$= \dfrac{136 - 100}{136} \times 100$

$= \dfrac{36}{136} \times 100 = 26.47\%$

$\approx 26.5\%$

Alternate Method

100 Price ⇧ 136
Consumption ⇩

$\therefore$ Decrease % $= \dfrac{136 - 100}{136} \times 100$

$= \dfrac{36}{136} \times 100$

$= 26.47\% \approx 26.5\%$

58. *(c)* According to the question,

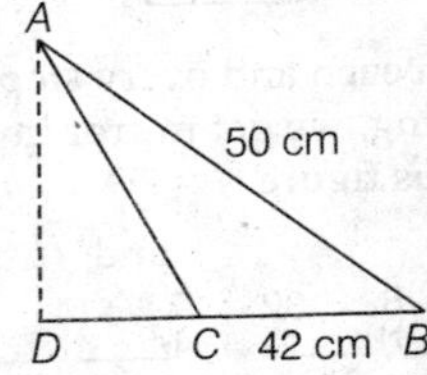

$AB = 50$ cm

$BC = 42$ cm

Draw AD perpendicular to extended part of BC.

Area of $\Delta ABC = \dfrac{1}{2} \times BC \times AD$

$\Rightarrow 294 = \dfrac{1}{2} \times 42 \times AD$

$\Rightarrow 294 = 21 \times AD$

$\Rightarrow AD = \dfrac{294}{21} = 14$ cm

In ΔABD,

$AB^2 = AD^2 + BD^2$

$\Rightarrow (50)^2 = (14)^2 + (BD)^2$

$\Rightarrow 2500 - 196 = (BD)^2$

$\therefore BD = \sqrt{2304} = 48$ cm

Hence, $CD = BD - BC$
$= 48 - 42 = 6$ cm

In ΔADC,

$AC^2 = (AD)^2 + (CD)^2$
$= (14)^2 + (6)^2 = 196 + 36 = 232$

$\therefore AC = \sqrt{232} = \sqrt{4 \times 58} = 2\sqrt{58}$

59. *(c)* Percentage increase in 2013 over 2012

In Two wheeler

$= \dfrac{13.8 - 13.4}{13.4} \times 100 = 2.98\%$

In Passenger vehicles

$= \dfrac{2.7 - 2.6}{2.6} \times 100 = 3.84\%$

In Commercial vehicles

$= \dfrac{0.79 - 0.80}{0.80} \times 100 = -12.5\%$

Hence, maximum percentage increase is in passenger vehicles.

60. *(c)* Let first part travel by bus for t h.

$\therefore$ Remaining part travel by train $= (6 - t)$ h

According to the question,

$t \times 40 + (6 - t) \times 55 = 285$

$40t + 330 - 55t = 285$

$\Rightarrow -15t = 285 - 330$

$\Rightarrow -15t = -45$

$\therefore t = \dfrac{45}{15} = 3$ h

Hence, distance travelled by train
$= 55 \text{ km/h} \times 3 = 165$ km

61. *(b)* We know that, in averages, if each of the observations is multiplied by same number, then the new average will be equal to the old average multiplied by that same number.

Hence, new average $= 23 \times 13 = 299$

62. *(b)* Let x is add in each term, then

$\dfrac{5 + x}{11 + x} = \dfrac{3}{5}$

$\Rightarrow 25 + 5x = 33 + 3x$

$\Rightarrow 2x = 33 - 25$

$\therefore x = 4$

63. *(c)* According to the question, in cylinder

Radius $(r) = \dfrac{\text{Diameter}}{2}$

$= \dfrac{14}{2} = 7$ cm

Length $(h) = 2$ cm

Cylinder is melted in cuboid hence volume will be same.

Volume of cylinder = $n \times$ volume of coboid [Here, n is the number of cuboidal candles]

$\Rightarrow \quad \pi \times r^2 \times h = n \times 7 \times 11 \times 2$

$\Rightarrow \quad \frac{22}{7} \times 7 \times 7 \times 2 = n \times 7 \times 11 \times 2$

$\Rightarrow \quad n = \frac{22 \times 7 \times 2}{7 \times 11 \times 2} = 2$

$\therefore$ Total two cuboidal candles will be formed.

64. *(d)* Let in right angled ΔABC, $BC = x$

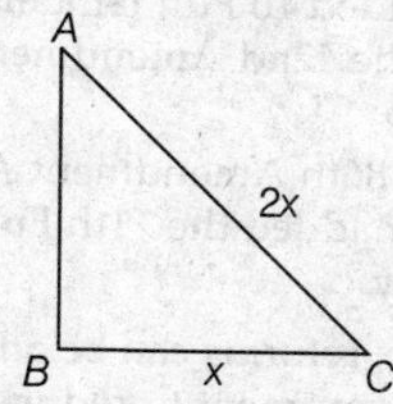

Then, $AC = 2x$

$\therefore \quad AC^2 = BC^2 + AB^2$

$\Rightarrow \quad (2x)^2 = x^2 + (AB)^2$

$\Rightarrow \quad AB^2 = 4x^2 - x^2 = 3x^2$

$\therefore \quad AB = \sqrt{3}x$

According to the question,

Area of $\Delta ABC = \frac{1}{2} \times AB \times BC$

$\Rightarrow \quad 600 = \frac{1}{2} \times \sqrt{3}x \times x$

$\Rightarrow \quad x^2 = \frac{1200}{\sqrt{3}} = \frac{400 \times 3}{\sqrt{3}}$

$\Rightarrow \quad x^2 = 400 \times \sqrt{3}$

$\Rightarrow \quad x = \sqrt{400 \times \sqrt{3}}$

$\Rightarrow \quad x = 20 \times (\sqrt{3})^{1/2}$

$\Rightarrow \quad x = 20 \times (3)^{1/4}$

$\therefore \quad x = 20 \times 1.31 = 26.32$ m

Hence, hypotenuse is 26.32 m greater than base.

65. *(c)* According to the question,

Principal (P) = ₹ 5000

Rate of interest (r) = 12%

Time (t) = 14 months

$\therefore$ Simple interest

$\text{SI} = \frac{P \times r \times t}{100}$

$= \frac{5000 \times 12 \times 14}{100 \times 12} =$ ₹ 700

66. *(a)* Total number of students enrolled in institute A in 2015 and 2017

$= 150 + 350 = 500$

And total number of students enrolled in institute B in 2016, 2018 and 2019

$= 160 + 50 + 250 = 460$

Hence, required difference

$= 500 - 460 = 40$

67. *(c)* According to the question,

10% of 24% of $x = 240$

$\Rightarrow x \times \frac{10}{100} \times \frac{24}{100} = 240$

$\Rightarrow \quad x = \frac{10000 \times 240}{240} = 10000$

68. *(d)* Given, if $\tan A + \sin A = x$ ...(i)

and $\tan A - \sin A = y$ ...(ii)

Hence, $x^2 - y^2 = (\tan A + \sin A)^2 - (\tan A - \sin A)^2$

$x^2 - y^2$

$= \tan^2 A + \sin^2 A + 2 \tan A \sin A - (\tan^2 A + \sin^2 A - 2 \sin A \tan A)$

$\Rightarrow x^2 - y^2 = \tan^2 A + \sin^2 A + 2 \tan A \sin A - \tan^2 A - \sin^2 A + 2 \tan A \cdot \sin A$

$\Rightarrow \quad x^2 - y^2 = 4 \tan A \cdot \sin A$ ... (iii)

Multiplying Eqs. (i) and (ii),

$(\tan A + \sin A)(\tan A - \sin A) = xy$

$\Rightarrow \quad \tan^2 A - \sin^2 A = xy$

$\Rightarrow \quad \frac{\sin^2 A}{\cos^2 A} - \sin^2 A = xy$

$\Rightarrow \sin^2 A \left(\frac{1 - \cos^2 A}{\cos^2 A}\right) = xy$

$\Rightarrow \quad \sin^2 A \times \tan^2 A = xy$

$\Rightarrow \quad \sin A \times \tan A = \sqrt{xy}$ ...(iv)

Now,

$\therefore \quad x^2 - y^2 = 4 \times \sin A \times \tan A$

$= 4\sqrt{xy}$ [$\because$ from Eq. (iv)]

69. *(a)* Given number, 611611611611

A number is divisible by 6 if it divisible by both 2 and 3. As, the number is odd, it cannot divisible by 2. So, it is also not divisible by 6.

The number is divisible by 11 only if the difference between 'sum of digits at even place' and 'sum of digits at odd place' must be either zero or divisible by 11.

Number is 611611611611

Sum of digits at odd places (A)

$= 6 + 1 + 1 + 6 + 1 + 1 = 16$

Sum of digits at even places (B)

$= 1 + 6 + 1 + 1 + 6 + 1 = 16$

$\because \quad A - B = 16 - 16 = 0$

$\therefore$ Number is divisible by only 11.

70. *(b)* Let my present age is x yr.

$\therefore$ My father's present age $= (x + 25)$ yr

According to the question,

$(x - 5) + (x + 25 - 5) = 39$

$\Rightarrow \quad x - 5 + x + 20 = 39$

$\Rightarrow \quad 2x = 39 - 15 = 24$

$\therefore \quad x = 12$ yr

71. *(b)* Let total number of votes $= x$

Total number of valid votes $= x - 58$

Number of votes got by winner

$= (x - 58)$ of 54%

Number of votes got by runner up.

$= (x - 58)$ of 46%

According to the question,

$(x - 58) \times \frac{54}{100} - (x - 58) \times \frac{46}{100} = 88$

$\Rightarrow \frac{(x - 58)}{100} \times (54 - 46) = 88$

$\Rightarrow (x - 58) = \frac{88 \times 100}{8} = 1100$

$\therefore \quad x = 1100 + 58 = 1158$

72. *(d)* Let actual salary = ₹ 100

After 20% reduction in salary, new salary

$= 100 - 100 \times \frac{20}{100}$

$= 100 - 20 =$ ₹ 80

In order to get original salary percentage increase $= \frac{100 - 80}{80} \times 100$

$= \frac{20}{80} \times 100 = 25\%$

73. *(d)* According to the question,

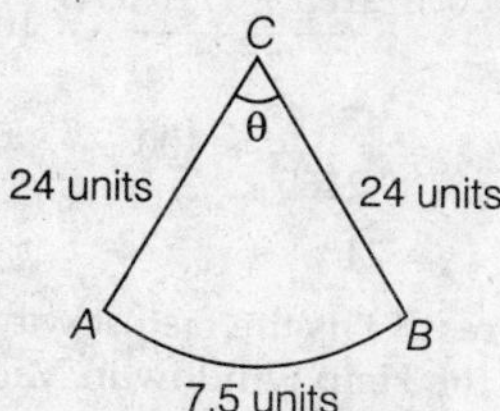

Radius of sector (r) = 24 units

Arc of sector (l) = 7.5 units

$\because \quad l = r \times \theta$

$\Rightarrow \quad 7.5 = 24 \times \theta$

$\Rightarrow \quad \theta = \left(\frac{7.5}{24}\right) = \left(\frac{180}{\pi} \times \frac{7.5}{24}\right)^\circ$

$\therefore$ Area of sector $= \frac{\theta}{360} \times \pi \times r^2$

$= \frac{\frac{180}{\pi} \times \frac{75}{240}}{360} \times \pi \times 24 \times 24$

$= \frac{180 \times 75}{360 \times 240 \times \pi} \times \pi \times 24 \times 24$

$= \frac{75}{10} \times 12 = 15 \times 6 = 90$ sq. units

74. *(c)* Given, dimensions are in the ratio of 4 : 3 : 2.

Let length be $4x$ m, height be $2x$ m and breadth be $3x$ m.

We know that,

Volume = Length × Breadth × Height

$\Rightarrow 12288 = 4x \times 3x \times 2x$

$\Rightarrow \quad 12288 = 24x^3$

$\Rightarrow \quad x^3 = 512$

$\therefore \quad x = 8$

$\therefore$ Length $= 4x = 4 \times 8 = 32$ m

Breadth $= 3x = 3 \times 8 = 24$ m

Height $= 2x = 2 \times 8 = 16$ m

We know that, total surface area = 2 (length × breadth + breadth × height + height × length)

$= 2(32 \times 24 + 24 \times 16 + 16 \times 32)$

Total surface area = 2 (1664)

$= 3328 \text{ m}^2$

Rate of polish = 2 paise per m^2

$\therefore$ Total cost of polishing

$= 2 \times 3328$ paise

$= 6656$ paise

$= ₹ 66.56$

75. *(a)* According to the question,

MP = ₹ 2165

SP = ₹ 1710.35

Percentage discount $= \frac{\text{MP} - \text{SP}}{\text{MP}} \times 100$

$= \frac{2165 - 1710.35}{2165} \times 100$

$= \frac{454.65}{2165} \times 100$

$= 21\%$

76. *(c)* 'Press F1' is the fastest way to open the Help window in Microsoft Word.

77. *(c)* The North star is also known as the 'Pole Star'.

- Pole Star is famous for holding nearly still in our sky while the entire nothern sky moved around it.
- Polaris/North star is visible in India becuase India's latitude range is from 8° to 30°.
- Polaris/North star can be located through the methods which involve drawing 'lines' from the Ursa Minor constellation.

78. *(b)* According to Census 2011, Lakshadweep recorded the highest female literacy rate (88.25%) as a union territory.

But as a state Kerala ranks the highest in terms of literacy rate with 91.98%.

79. *(d)* In Equestrian sports, knockdown occurs when a horse or rider lowers an element of a jump that established the additional height of an obstacle.

- Equestrian sports are certain riding events held at horse shows.
- Most specifically competitive horse and rider events held at the Summer Olympic games.
- The three events of Equestrian sports
  1. Show jumping
  2. Hunter trails
  3. Dressage

80. *(c)* Maharashtra and Gujarat states were concentrated in the cotton production in the early years to develop textile industry.

- It is because the moist climate of both the states strived for cotton cultivation.
- Gujarat and Maharashtra had ports which helped in the transportation of the finished goods to various locations.

81. *(a)* Patkai Bum Hills is located in the Easternmost part of India.

- The Patkai mountain range is located at the India's North-Eastern border with Burma.
- The Patkai ranges are a part of Arakan mountains.
- The popular Dehing Patkai Wildlife Sanctuary is located here.

82. *(b)* P. Chidambaram is not associated with Green Revolution.

- The father of the Green Revolution (India) was MS Swaminathan. It was stated in 1967.
- The Green Revolution changed the country's status from a food-deficient economy to one of the world's leading agricultural nations.

83. *(a)* Mallikarjun Mansur is Hindustani classical singer.

Pandit Mallikarjun Bheemaraayappa Mansur born on 31st December, 1910 and a Hindustani classical singer from Karnataka.

- He sang in the Khyal genre and belonged to the Jaipur-Atrauli gharana.
- He received all three National Padma Awards.
  - Padma Shri Award in 1970
  - Padma Bhushan Award in 1976
  - Padma Vibhushan in 1992.

84. *(b)* The original Constitution did not mention any Fundamental Duty because it was expected that citizens of the country would perform their duties willingly.

- Fundamental Duties are in Article 51A of the Indian Constitution.
- It was recommended by the Swaran Singh Committee in 1976, it added 10 Fundamental Duties by the 42nd Amendment Act 1976.
- The 86th Amendment Act, 2002 later added the 11th Fundamental Duty.

85. *(d)* Tax reforms can be adopted by the government to reduce revenue deficit.

- Disinvestment and selling off assets are another corrective measures to minimise a revenue deficit.
- It can be reduced by borrowing or raising money by cutting expenses.

86. *(b)* The camel festival is organised by Rajasthan Tourism Development corporation in Bikaner every year in the month of February.

- The camel festival is organised for 2 days.
- The celebration begins with a colourful procession of camels in the premises of Junagadh Fort.
- A variety of camel games and activities are also organised with great vigour.

87. *(c)* Delhi MLA's received an increase of about 66% in salaries and allowances.

- MLA's will now receive a total of ₹ 90,000 per month which earlier was ₹ 54,000.
- The salary of MLA in Delhi has increased after 12 years.

88. *(a)* From the book 'Anand Math', the national song of India was compiled.

- 'Vande Mataram' is a poem written in Sanskrit by Bankim Chandra Chatterjee in his Bengali novel 'Anand Math'.
- It later was made the national song of our country.

89. *(a)* Statements (A, B and C) are correct regarding 'Saila Dance'.

- The Saila dance is a folk dance which is performed during the post-harvest season.
- The dance is generally performed by the young boys with the help of bamboo sticks.
- This dance is basically performed in the month of Aghan.

90. *(d)* Walther Flemming was the first person to conduct a systematic study of chromosomes during division and called this process mitosis.

He is the pioneer of mitosis research and also the founder of cytogenetics.

91. *(d)* In cricket, a fast, head-high delivery of the ball is referred as bouncer.

- **Grubber** In cricket, when the ball is bowled (thrown to the batter) and does not move up as much as normal when it hits the ground.
- **Leg bye** It a type of extra, a run scored by the batting team without the batsman hitting the ball.
- **Duck** When a batter is dismissed without any run, but sometimes after the first ball.

92. *(b)* Maharashtra has the largest Buddhist population according to the Census of India 2011.

- 77.36% of total Buddhist population is present in Maharashtra.
- West Bengal, Madhya Pradesh and Uttar Pradesh were in row with 3.35%, 2.56% and 2.44% respectively in Buddhist population.

93. *(b)* Mahendra Singh Dhoni captained India to victory in the 2011 Cricket World Cup final win over Sri Lanka.

- In 2008, Dhoni was awarded Major Dhyan Chand Khel Ratna Award.
- MS Doni received Padma Shri in 2009.
- He also received Padma Bhushan Award in 2018.

94. *(c)* 'Max' function is used to calculate the maximum value in a selected column in MS Excel.

95. *(a)* Reginald Dyer is remembered as the Butcher of Amritsar for his role in the Jallianwala Bagh massacre in 1919.

- He was an officer of the Bengal army.
- He was responsible for the Jallianwala Bagh massacre on 13th April, 1919 in Amritsar because of his order of fire on a large gathering of people.

96. *(a)* The 42nd Constitutional Amendment Act of Indian Constitution was passed in the year 1976.

- The 42nd Amendment changed the description of India from a 'sovereign, democratic, republic' to a 'sovereign, socialist secular democratic republic'.
- It also changed the words 'unity of the nation' to 'unit and integrity of the nation'.
- The 42nd Amendment also known as Mini Constitution.

97. *(a)* Anthracene dissolves easily in benzene because of the 'like dissolves like' principle, which states that solutes dissolve in solvents with similar intermolecular interactions. Anthracence and benzene are both aromatic compounds, and anthracene is made up of three fused benzene rings.

98. *(a)* In March, 2023, the Uttarakhand Government has approved 10% horizontal reservation for statehood activities in State Government jobs.

99. *(c)* The Press and Registration of Books (PRB) Act was enacted in 1867 by the British Colonial Government in India.

- This act required printers and publishers to register their presses and provide copies of their publications to government.
- **1857** Indian Rebellion against British Rule.

100. *(c)* Alauddin Khilji was the ruler of Delhi Sultanate who sent his army under Malik Kafur's command to conquer South India.

- Malik Kafur invaded the Pandya Kingdom in present-day Tamil Nadu.
- He was unable to make the Pandya King a tributary.
- But he obtained huge quantities of plunder including elephants, horses, gold and precious stones.